THE LAWS OF ARMED CONFLICTS

THE LAWS OF ARMED CONFLICTS

A Collection of Conventions, Resolutions and Other Documents

Edited by

DIETRICH SCHINDLER

Professor Emeritus of International Law
University of Zurich
Honorary Member of the International Committee
of the Red Cross

and

JIRI TOMAN

Professor of Law
Santa Clara University

Fourth revised and completed edition

MARTINUS NIJHOFF PUBLISHERS
LEIDEN/BOSTON
2004

A C.I.P. Catalogue record for this book is available from the Library of Congress.

Printed on acid-free paper.

ISBN 90-04-13818-8

Brill Academic Publishers incorporates the imprint Martinus Nijhoff Publishers.
http://www.brill.nl

Printed and bound in The Netherlands

INTRODUCTION

THE DEVELOPMENT OF THE LAWS OF ARMED CONFLICTS

The present collection reproduces the texts of conventions, draft conventions and resolutions on the law of armed conflicts which have been adopted since the codification movement started in the nineteenth century. Its first edition appeared in 1973.[1] It was followed by two revised and completed editions in 1981 and 1988[2] and by a French edition in 1996.[3] With each edition, the number of texts has increased, due to the rapid development of this branch of international law. While the first edition contained 71. the second had 80, the third 87, the French edition has 107 and the present one 115. In order to give the reader access to all conventions and similar texts adopted since the nineteenth century, older conventions that in the course of time were replaced by newer ones (such as the Geneva Conventions adopted before 1949) have also been reproduced in all editions.

Developments up to World War I

Until the middle of the nineteenth century, only customary law regulated questions of warfare. Common traditions and practices of European states, military manuals of national armies and bilateral agreements concluded in wartime between belligerents (cartels, capitulations) contributed to the formation of customary rules. It was only in the second half of the nineteenth century that states started concluding mulilateral conventions. Several factors contributed to this development.

First, the introduction of compulsory military service changed the nature of warfare. Large national armies took the place of small professional forces which had been subject to rigid discipline. Wars therefore were fought on a different scale from before. In this situation, a growing need was felt for a binding and widely accessible codification of rules governing the conduct of war. The Institute of International Law, in the preface to its *Oxford Manual* of 1880 (*No. 3*), which served this purpose, called for a clear set of rules to end the "painful uncertainty" and the "endless accusations" experienced in recent wars. It emphasized that such rules must be made known among all people.

Second, the number of victims greatly increased due to the enlargement of armies and the improvement of arms technology. This was the decisive factor for the foundation of the Red Cross and the adoption of the Geneva Convention

[1] Schindler/Toman (eds.), *The Laws of Armed Conflicts: A Collection of Conventions, Resolutions and Other Documents,* Leiden, A.W. Sijthoff; Geneva, Henry Dunant Institute, 1973, 795 pp.

[2] Second revised and completed edition, Alphen aan den Rijn, Sijthoff & Noordhoff; Geneva, Henry Dunant Institute, 1981, 993 pp.; third revised and completed edition, Dordrecht, Martinus Nijhoff Publishers; Geneva, Henry Dunant Institute, 1988, 1033 pp.

[3] Schindler/Toman (eds.), *Droit des conflits armés. Recueil des conventions, résolutions et autres documents,* Geneva, Comité international de la Croix-Rouge/Institut Henry-Dunant, 1996, 1470 pp.

of 1864 (*No. 38*), which, in turn, gave the impetus to the conclusion of further conventions on the law of war.

Third, during the second half of the nineteenth century, a growing conviction spread over the Western world that civilization was rapidly advancing and that it was therefore imperative "to restrain the destructive force of war" (*Oxford Manual, No. 3,* preface). The Declaration of St. Petersburg of 1868 (*No. 9*) states "that the progress of civilization should have the effect of alleviating as much as possible the calamities of war". Similarly, the preamble to the Hague Conventions of 1899 and 1907 on the laws and customs of war on land (*Nos. 7 and 8*) speaks of the "ever increasing requirements of civilization".

Finally, the codification of the law of war was stimulated by the progress of the codification of private law on the European Continent in the same period.

The first steps taken in view of the codification of the laws of war were the Lieber Instructions of 1863 (*No. 1*) and the Geneva Convention of 1864 (*No. 38*). The codification movement reached its first and decisive peak at the two Hague Peace Conferences of 1899 and 1907. Never since that time has it been possible to adopt conventions on as many different aspects of the laws of war as at these conferences. The conventions adopted in the following decades were mainly intended to develop and refine rules embodied in earlier conventions and to adapt them to changed circumstances.

Among the basic principles to be found in all conventions, mention should first be made of the distinction between armed forces and civilians and between military objectives and civilian objects. This distinction is essential for both the question of who may take part in hostilities and the determination of the persons and objects against which acts of war may be directed or which are to be protected. The Declaration of St. Petersburg of 1868 (*No. 9*) states that "the only legitimate object which States should endeavour to accomplish during war is to weaken the military forces of the enemy". Persons who do not take part or who have ceased to take part in hostilities and civilian objects may not be attacked.

As to the means of warfare, the ruling principle remains "that the right of belligerents to adopt means of injuring the enemy is not unlimited"[4] and that it is forbidden "to employ arms, projectiles and material of a nature to cause unnecessary suffering".[5]

The period between the two world wars

After World War I, a period of neglect of the laws of war set in, although the war had given ample proof of the inadequacies of existing conventions. The prevailing opinion was that a revision of the laws of war would undermine confidence in the League of Nations and the new methods of preventing war. Only the Geneva Convention on wounded and sick was revised in 1929 (*No. 45*) and completed by a convention on prisoners of war (*No. 46*). Moreover, two rudimentary protocols on the prohibition of the use of poisonous gases (Geneva

4 Brussels Declaration of 1874 (*No. 2*), Article 12; *Oxford Manual* of 1880 (*No. 3*), Article 4; Hague Regulations of 1899 and 1907 (*Nos. 7–8,* Annex), Article 22; Resolution 2444 (XXIII) of the UN General Assembly of 19 December 1968 (*No. 33*), par. 1(a); Protocol I Additional to the Geneva Conventions, of 1977 (*No. 56*), Article 35(1).

5 St. Petersburg Declaration of 1868 (*No. 9*), Article 13(e), Preamble; Brussels Declaration of 1874 (*No. 2*), Article 13(e); *Oxford Manual* of 1880 (*No. 3*), Article 9(a); Hague Regulations of 1899 and 1907 (*Nos. 7-8,* Annex), Article 23(e); Protocol I Additional to the Geneva Conventions, of 1977 (*No. 56*), Article 35(2).

Protocol of 1925, *No. 13*) and on submarine warfare (London Protocol of 1936, *No. 87*) were adopted. Further attempts to regulate new problems, especially air warfare and the protection of civilians against modern means of warfare, remained unsuccessful (see *Nos. 27, 28, 47*). Thus, when World War II broke out, the laws of armed conflicts could not cope with the horrors of war which surpassed those of World War I.

Developments after World War II

World War II was followed by a similar period of neglect. When in 1949 the International Law Commission of the United Nations selected the topics for codification, the majority of the Commission declared itself opposed to the study of this subject. It was considered that if the Commission, at the very beginning of its work, were to undertake this study, public opinion might interpret its action as showing lack of confidence in the efficiency of the means at the disposal of the United Nations for maintaining peace.[6]

In the same year, however, on the initiative of the ICRC, the Geneva Conventions were revised and an additional convention on the protection of civilian persons in time of war was adopted (*Nos. 49–52*). Although the United Nations kept aloof from this enterprise, its efforts for an international guarantee of human rights, especially the Universal Declaration of Human Rights, adopted on 10 December 1948, left their imprint on the 1949 Conventions. They had the effect that the traditional law of war was gradually transformed into a human rights oriented law. The Conventions of 1949 speak of the "rights" of the protected persons instead of only imposing obligations on the belligerents. Moreover, the terms "law of war" and "law of armed conflicts" were slowly replaced by the new term "international humanitarian law".

The Hague Conventions of 1899 and 1907, dealing mainly with the conduct of hostilities, remained unchanged. This caused a growing discrepancy between the revised Geneva Conventions and the outdated Hague Conventions. However, on the initiative of UNESCO, a Hague Convention on the protection of cultural property in the event of armed conflict was adopted in 1954 (*No. 71*). In 1956, the ICRC, recognizing that the 1949 Conventions did not afford a sufficient protection to the civilian population against indiscriminate warfare, drafted "Rules for the limitation of the dangers incurred by the civilian population in time of war" (*No. 30*) with a view to having them adopted by an international conference. They were approved by the International Red Cross Conference of New Delhi in 1957, but remained virtually without any response from governments. This discouraged the ICRC from taking further steps until the United Nations gave a fresh impetus in 1968.

Between the 1960s and the 1980s

It was not until the mid-1960s that a new interest in the law of armed conflicts became apparent. It was brought about by the armed conflicts in Vietnam, the Middle East and Nigeria–Biafra and by the struggles of peoples against colonial and alien domination and racist regimes. Beginning in 1968, the UN General Assembly periodically adopted resolutions demanding that wars of

---

6 Report of the International Law Commission to the General Assembly on its First Session, *Yearbook of the International Law Commission,* 1949, p. 281, paragraph 18.

national liberation be regarded as international armed conflicts and freedom fighters treated as prisoners of war (see *No. 54*). Also in 1968, the International Conference on Human Rights in Teheran, convened by the United Nations, and the United Nations General Assembly adopted resolutions under the title "Respect for human rights in armed conflicts", requesting the Secretary-General to take steps (a) to secure the better application of existing humanitarian conventions, and (b) for the adoption of additional humanitarian international conventions to ensure the better protection of civilians, prisoners and combatants in all armed conflicts and the prohibition and limitation of the use of certain methods and means of warfare (*Nos. 32 and 33*). A remarkable aspect of these resolutions was that they linked the development of the law of armed conflicts with the international protection of human rights. In the following year, the International Red Cross Conference in Istanbul invited the ICRC to work out proposals for the completion of humanitarian conventions. The ICRC, in 1971 and 1972, convened two conferences of government experts and prepared two draft protocols additional to the Geneva Conventions of 1949. A Diplomatic Conference convened by the Swiss Federal Council held four sessions in Geneva between 1974 and 1977. On 8 June 1977, it adopted the two Protocols Additional to the Geneva Conventions (*Nos. 56 and 57*).

The two Protocols filled lacunae that had been strongly felt for years. In the first place, they contain provisions on the protection of the civilian population against effects of hostilities, provisions for which efforts had been undertaken in vain since the early 1920s. Secondly, the basic principles of the Hague Conventions of 1899 and 1907 on the conduct of hostilities were reaffirmed and developed, a fact particularly important in view of the considerable age of these conventions and the many new states that had no part in their elaboration. Thirdly, Protocol II brings more elaborate rules on non-international conflicts. The minimum rules embodied in Article 3 common to the Geneva Conventions of 1949 proved to be insufficient in view of the great number of internal conflicts and the magnitude of their humanitarian problems.

The Protocols of 1977 were supplemented by the United Nations Convention on prohibitions or restrictions on the use of certain conventional weapons, adopted in Geneva on 10 October 1980 (*No. 20*). In 1976, the UN General Assembly had already adopted a Convention on the prohibition of military or any hostile use of environmental modification techniques (*No. 18*).

Since the end of the Cold War

A new period in the development of international humanitarian law started with the end of the Cold War in 1989. It brought far-reaching innovations. Humanitarian issues and humanitarian law began to attract more international attention than in any earlier period. Most armed conflicts in this period have been internal conflicts. During the Cold War, the conflict between the superpowers had overshadowed all other conflicts. Internal divergencies, caused by ethnic, religious or political differences, could be held under control. When the Cold War ended, many regimes broke down and internal conflicts erupted. In several states rival groups, often driven by ethnic or religious fanaticism, became engaged in embittered fights. Internal conflicts began to cause even greater humanitarian problems than had occurred during the Cold War. Unlike international wars, these wars were not conducted by armed forces trained in the conduct of hostilities and familiar with the law of war, but by armed groups lacking a clear command structure, having no military discipline and unfamiliar with humanitarian principles. The conventions on humanitarian law, moreover, were inadequate insofar as they were primarily conceived for interstate wars, not for internal conflicts. Only Article 3, common to the four Geneva Conventions, and, in a more restricted way, Protocol II of 1977, are applicable in non-international conflicts.

Shocked by the systematic disregard of the most fundamental principles of human rights and humanitarian law, an International Conference for the Protection of Victims of War, convened in Geneva from 30 August to 1 September 1993, adopted a declaration urging all states to ensure respect for international humanitarian law and calling upon them to take certain measures to that effect (*No. 60*).

A most important development of the post-Cold War period was brought about by the Security Council, when it decided, for the first time in 1992, that large-scale violations of human right and humanitarian law and the ensuing magnitude of human suffering can constitute a threat to international peace and give rise to measures under Chapter VII of the Charter.[7] Based on this finding, the Security Council not only authorized the use of force in cases of humanitarian catastrophes, but also set up two international criminal tribunals, one for Yugoslavia in 1993, and one for Rwanda in 1994, to prosecute persons responsible for serious violations of international humanitarian law (*Nos. 109 and 110*). The Security Council, by these decisions, assumed the role of a supreme guardian of international humanitarian law.

The two Tribunals have greatly contributed to the clarification and development of humanitarian law. The Yugoslav Tribunal found that many rules originally applicable only in international armed conflicts have in the course of time become customary rules applicable also in non-international conflicts.[8] It enumerated a considerable number of such customary rules. Further, the Tribunal found that, as a consequence of this, the distinction between international and non-international conflicts has lost much of its importance. The law of internal armed conflicts, by way of custom, has been increasingly assimilated to the law of international armed conflicts. It is to be noticed in this connection also that most conventions on humanitarian law concluded in the past few years have been made applicable to both international and internal conflicts.[9]

The events that have occurred since the end of the Cold War have not only brought about important decisions of the Security Council and of the two international criminal tribunals but also induced governments to conclude a number of new treaties. The following treaties are to be mentioned: the Chemical Weapons Convention of 1993 (*No. 22*), the two new Protocols to the Weapons Convention of 1980, namely Protocol IV on blinding laser weapons and the amended Protocol II on mines, booby traps and similar devices (*No. 20*, annex), the Rome Statute of the International Criminal Tribunal of 1998 (*No. 111*), and

---

7 See especially resolutions 794 (1992) of 3 December 1992 (Somalia), 929 (1994) of 22 June 1994 (Rwanda), but also 770 (1992) of 13 August 1992 (Bosnia and Herzegovina) and 1244 (1999) of 10 June 1999 (Kosovo).

8 Decision of the Appeals Chamber of 2 October 1995 on the Tadic jurisdictional motion, paragraphs 96–137, in International Criminal Tribunal for the Former Yugoslavia, *Yearbook 1995*, pp. 54–110; and in International Criminal Tribunal for the Former Yugoslavia, *Reports 1994–1995*, I, pp. 461–501.

9 See the conventions listed in the following paragraph.

the Second Protocol to the Hague Convention for the protection of cultural property of 1999 (*No. 74*). The rules on "Observance by United Nations Forces of international humanitarian law", promulgated by the UN Secretary-General on 6 August 1999 (*No. 100*), also mark a significant development.

In fields where governments were not sufficiently ready to adopt new rules, private drafts have been elaborated that restate and develop existing law. The main examples are the San Remo Rules on non-international armed conflicts of 1990 (*No. 94*), the Turku Declaration on minumum humanitarian standards, also of 1990 (*No. 95*), the San Remo Manual on the law of armed conflicts at sea of 1994 (*No. 89*), the Helsinki Principles on the law of maritime neutrality of 1998 (*No. 115*), and the Resolution on the application of international humanitarian law and fundamental human rights in armed conflicts in which non-state entities are parties of 1999 (*No. 96*). These private drafts reinforce existing law and contribute to the formation of new rules.

In its Advisory Opinion on the legality of the threat or use of nuclear weapons of 8 July 1996, the International Court of Justice stated that the fundamental rules of humanitarian law "constitute intransgressible principles of international customary law".[10] By this pronouncement, the Court qualified the fundamental rules of humanitarian law as part of the most basic norms of the international community. In spite of this important statement, gross violations of human rights and humanitarian law are still being committed in many parts of the world. Obviously, a profound tension exists between what is recognized as an indispensable prerequisite of peaceful relations in the international community and the actual conduct of large parts of populations. Permanent and untiring efforts will be necessary to gradually improve the respect for humanitarian principles.

[10] *International Court of Justice, Reports 1996*, p. 257, paragraph 83.

EXPLANATORY NOTES

1. Selection of texts

The present collection contains texts on the law *of armed conflicts* (law of war, *ius in bello)* only. It excludes texts concerning:

- the limitation and prohibitions of force in international relations (*ius ad bellum);*
- the limitation of armaments, especially the prohibition on the manufacture or acquisition of certain arms, the testing of arms and trade in arms with exception of those which include also provisions on the use of arms;
- the neutralization, demilitarization and denuclearization of certain territories;
- human rights, with the exception of texts which are of direct concern to the situations of armed conflicts.

The collection reproduces all *multilateral conventions* on the law of armed conflicts:

- which are in force;
- which have not (or not yet) entered into force;
- which are no longer in force.

The following categories of *further texts* are reproduced:

- final acts and resolutions adopted by the intergovernmental conferences which drew up the conventions reproduced in this collection;
- resolutions of intergovernmental or non-governmental organizations in which rules of the law of armed conflicts are stated. No resolutions are, however, reproduced which contain only a recommendation to apply existing rules in a particular situation.

No national regulations or instructions are published, the only exception being the Lieber Instructions of 1863 (*No. 1* of this volume) which marked the beginning of the codification of the law of armed conflicts.

2. Order of the texts

The texts are grouped into chapters (see the table of contents). Minor overlappings between the chapters are inevitable, e.g. between Chapter III (Air Warfare) and Chapter IV (Protection of Populations against Effects of Hostilities).

Within the chapters the texts are reproduced in chronological order.

3. Types of print

The texts are printed in four different typefaces:

Normal type, large	used for	conventions in force
Normal type, small	used for	conventions which have not (or not yet) entered into force or which are no longer in force. Draft conventions and draft articles, including those adopted by non-governmental organizations
Italics, large	*used for*	*resolutions adopted by intergovernmental organizations. Final acts and resolutions adopted by intergovernmental conferences (except where small italics are applicable)*
Italics, small	*used for*	*resolutions adopted by non-governmental organizations. Final acts and resolutions adopted by intergovernmental conferences insofar as the conventions adopted by such conferences are no longer in force or have not entered into force*

4. Notes

The following editorial notes are made below the titles of the conventions, resolutions and other texts:

- introductory note: indications as to the events which led to the adoption of the texts and the bodies which adopted them;
- entry into force: only made if the text in question has entered into force;
- authentic text(s): authentic language(s) as well as the treaty collection or other publication from which the text has been reprinted;
- text published in: treaty collections and other publications in which the texts of the conventions or other documents are reprinted in English, French, Russian and Spanish;
- tables of contents of individual documents are furnished in the case of conventions which are divided into several parts or chapters.

5. Footnotes

Footnotes have no official character except where indicated.

6. Lists of signatures, ratifications, accessions, notifications of succession or continuity and reservations

The dates indicated under the heading "ratification, accession or notification of succession or continuity" refer to the day of the deposit of the instrument of ratification, accession or notification of continuity. In the case of notifications of succession or continuity, the conventions are effective for the respective states as from the date of their accession to independence.

The abbreviations "*Res.*" (reservation) and/or "*Dec.*" (declaration) are used under the heading "signature" when a reservation was made on signature. They are used under the heading "ratification, accession or notification of succession or continuity" when the reservation and/or declaration were made on ratification, accession or notification of succession or continuity.

All reservations are reproduced with their full text even when they have not been maintained or have subsequently been withdrawn.

Indications concerning signatures, ratifications, accessions, notifications of continuity and reservations are listed up to 15 October 2002 unless otherwise indicated.

TABLE OF CONTENTS

III. AIR WARFARE

IV. PROTECTION OF POPULATIONS AGAINST EFFECTS OF HOSTILITIES

See also Nos. 1–3, 7 and 8, 52, 56–60

V. VICTIMS OF WAR (WOUNDED, SICK, PRISONERS, CIVILIANS)

See also Nos. 7, 8, 20-36, 61–68

VI. PROTECTION OF HUMAN RIGHTS IN SITUATIONS OF ARMED CONFLICT

See also Nos. 33–36, 55–57, 95, 96

VII. PROTECTION OF CULTURAL PROPERTY

IX. CIVIL WAR

X. APPLICATION OF THE LAW OF ARMED CONFLICTS TO HOSTILITIES IN WHICH UNITED NATIONS FORCES ARE ENGAGED

XI. MERCENARIES

See also No. 56

XII. WAR CRIMES

XIII. NEUTRALITY

LIST OF REPRODUCED DOCUMENTS IN CHRONOLOGICAL ORDER

ABBREVIATIONS

AJIL	*The American Journal of International Law*
Arellano	Carlos Arellano Garcia, *Derecho Internacional Publico*, Mexico, Editorial Porrua, S.A., 1983, Vol. II
Bevans	*Treaties and other International Agreements of the USA, 1776–1949*, compiled under the direction of Charles I. Bevans, LL.B.; Department of State publication 8407, November 1968. Vol. I 1776–1917 Vol. II 1918–1930 Vol. III 1931–1945 Vol. IV 1946–1949
BFSP	*British and Foreign State Papers*, 1812–, published by His (or Her) Majesty's Stationery Office, London, from 1887
Blatova	N.T. Blatova (ed.), *Mezhdunarodnoe pravo v dokumentakh*, Moskva, Yuridicheskaya literatura, 1982, 856 pp.
Bluntschli-Komarovskii	J.C. Bluntschli, *Sovremennoe mezhdunarodnoe pravo tsivilizovannykh' gosuarstv' izlozhennoe v' vide Kodeska.* Perevod so vtorogo nemetskogo izdaniya V. Ul'yanitskogo i A. Lodyzhenskogo pod redaktsiei L. Kamarovskogo, Moskva, 1876
Briceño	Jose Enrique Briceño Berru, *Manual de derecho internacional maritimo*, Lima, Peru, 1976
Bustamante	Antonio S. Bustamante y Sirven, *La Segunda Conferencia de la Paz reunida en el Haya en 1907*, tomo segundo, Madrid, Libreria General de Victoriano Suarez, 1908
Ceppi	Guillermo Ceppi, *Normas de derecho maritimo de guerra*, Buenos Aires, Libreria de A. Garcia Santos, 1932
De Clercq	*Recueil des Traités de la France*, publié sous les auspices du Ministère des affaires étrangères par M. Jules de Clercq, Paris, A. Durand et Pedone-Lauriel, 1864–1907, 23 tomes
Conférence internationale de la Paix 1899	*Conférence internationale de la Paix* La Haye, 18 mai–29 juillet 1899, Ministère des Affaires étrangères, La Haye, Imprimerie Nationale, 1899
Conférence internationale de la Paix 1907	*Deuxième Conférence internationale de la Paix* La Haye 15 juin–18 octobre 1907; *Actes et documents* (tome premier: Séances plénières de la Conférence). Ministère des Affaires étrangères, La Haye, Imprimerie Nationale, 1907

CTS	*Consolidated Treaty Series*, edited and annotated by Clive Parry, Dobbs Ferry, New York, Oceana Publications, 1969–1981
Deltenre	*Receuil Général des lois et coutumes de la guerre terrestre, maritime, sous-marine et aérienne d'après les Actes élaborés par les Conférences internationales depuis 1856*, Documents recueillis et annotés par M. Marcel Deltenre, les Editions Fred. Wellens-Pay, Bruxelles, 1943
Derechos humanos	*Derechos humanos. Textos internacionales.* Edicion preparada por Luis Ignazio Sanchez Rodriguez y Javier Gonzalez Vega. Segunda edicion. Madrid, Editorial Tecnos, 1991
Deuxième Conference international de la Paix, 1907, Actes et documents	*Deuxieme Conference internationale de la paix. La Haye,* 15 juin–18 octobre 1907, *La Haye, Actes et documents.* Ministère des affaires étrangères. La Haye, Imprimerie Nationale, 1907
Droit des conflits armés	Schindler/Toman (eds.), *Droit des conflits armés. Recueil des conventions, résolutions et autres documents.* Genève, Comité international de la Croix-Rouge, Institut Henry Dunant, 1996, 1470 pp.
Fontes Historiae Iuris Gentium	*Fontes Historiae luris Gentium. Sourcess Relating to the History of the Law of Nations.* Edited by Wilhelm G. Grewe, in cooperation with the Institut für Internationales Recht an der Freien Universität Berlin. Volumes 2, 3/1.2; Berlin/New York, Walter de Gruyter, 1988–1992
Friedman	*The Law of War: A Documentary History*. Edited by Leon Friedman, New York, Random House, 1972, Vol. I
Genet	Raoul Genet, *Précis de droit maritime pour le temps de guerre*, Paris, 1907, Vol. II
GBTS	*Treaty Series No.* (year) Presented to both Houses of Parliament by Command of his (Her) Majesty, Stationery Office, 1892–.
Goldblat	Jozef Goldblat (ed.), *Arms Control: A Guide to Negotiations and Agreements*. Oslo/PRIO, London/SAGE Publications, 1996, 772 pp.
Handbook of the International Movement	*Handbook of the International Red Cross and Red Crescent Movement*, 13th ed., Geneva, ICRC, International Federation, 1994, 937 pp.
Handbook of the International Red Cross 1953	*Handbook of the International Red Cross*, 10th ed., Geneva, ICRC/LRCS, 1953
Heffter-Taube	A.G. Heffter, *Evropeiskoe mezhdunarodnoe pravo*, perevel' K. Taube, S. Peterburg', 1880, Prilozheniya

Higgins	*The Hague Peace Conferences and Other International Conferences Concerning the Laws and Usages of War*, texts of Conventions with commentaries, by A. Pearce Higgins, LL.D., Cambridge, at the University Press, 1909
Hudson	Manley O. Hudson, *International Legislation*, A collection of the texts of multipartite international instruments of general interest beginning with the Covenant of the League of Nations, Washington, Carnegie Endowment for International Peace, 1931–1950, 9 vols.
ICRC	International Committee of the Red Cross
International Red Cross Handbook, 1971	*International Red Cross Handbook*, 11th ed., Geneva, ICRC/LRCS, 1971
International Red Cross Handbook, 1983	*International Red Cross Handbook*, 12th ed., Geneva, ICRC/LRCS, 1983
IRRC	*International Review of the Red Cross*
Korovin	Prof. E.A. Korovin, *Mezhdunarodnye dogovory i akty novogo vremeni*, Moskva-Leningrad. Gosudarstvennoeizdatel'stvo, 1924
Les deux Conférences de la Paix	*Les deux Conférences de la Paix 1899 et 1907.* Recueil des textes arrêtés par ces Conférences et des différents documents complémentaires, avec un avant-propos de M. Louis Renault, 2ème édition, Paris, A. Rousseau, 1909, 225 pp.
Lillich	*International Human Rights Instruments: A Compilation of Treaties, Agreements and Declarations of Especial Interest to the United States.* Richard B. Lillich (ed.), Buffalo, New York, W. S. Hein Company, 1983
Liszt	Liszt F., *Mezhdunarodnoe pravo*, Jurjev, 1912
LNTS	*League of Nations Treaty Series*
Malloy	*Treaties, Conventions, International Acts, Protocols and Agreements between the United States of America and Other Powers* 1776–1909 (I, II) 1910–1923 (III) 1923–1937 (IV) compiled by William M. Malloy, Washington, Government Printing Office 1910–1938, 4 vols.
Manuel de la Cruz Roja	*Manual de la Cruz Roja internacional*, 10 edición, Ginebra, CICR/LSCR, 1953
Manuel de la Cruz Roja internacional, 1983	*Manual de la Cruz Roja internacional*, 12 edición, Ginebra, CICR/LSCR, 1983

Manual del Movimiento internacional	*Manual del Movimiento internacional de la Cruz Roja y de la Media Luna Roja*, 13 ed., Geneva, ICRC, Federacion internacional, 1994, 977 p.
Manuel de la Croix-Rouge internationale, 1953	*Manuel de la Croix-Rouge internationale*, 10ème édition, CICR/LSCR, Genève 1953
Manuel de la Croix-Rouge internationale, 1971	*Manuel de la Croix-Rouge internationale*, 11ème édition, CICR/LSCR, Genève, 1971
Manuel de la Croix-Rouge internationale, 1983	*Manuel de la Croix-Rouge internationale*, 12ème édition, CICR/LSCR, Genève, 1983
Manuel du Mouvement international	*Manuel du Mouvement international de la Croix-Rouge et du Croissant-Rouge*, 13 ed., Geneve, CICR, Federation international, 1994, 961 p.
Martens, *NRGT*	Georges Frederic de Martens, *Nouveau Recueil Général de Traités et autres actes relatifs aux rapports de droit international*, Gottingue (Leipzig, à partir du tome XXII, 1897), Dieterich. 1ère série, 1843–1875, 20 vols.; 2ème série 1876–1908, 35 vols.; 3ème série, 1915–1944, 41 vols.
Mezhdunarodnoe pravo	*Mezhdunarodnoe pravo v izbrannykh dokumentakh*, tom I–III, Moskva, Izdatelstvo IMO, 1957
Olivart	*Colleción de los tratados, convenios y documentos internacionales celebrados por nuestros gobernos con los estados extranjeros desde el reinado de Doña Isabel II hasta nuestros dias*, Marqués de Olivart, Madrid, 1890
Olivart, *Tratados*	*Tratados y documentos internacionales de España publicados oficilamente y collectionados en la Revista de derecho internacional y politica exterior*, Marqués de Olivart, tomo IV, 1908–1909, Madrid, 1912
The Proceedings of the Hague Peace Conferences, 1899	*The Proceedings of the Hague Peace Conferences.* Translation of the official texts. Prepared in the Division of International Law of the Carnegie Endowment for International Peace, under the supervision of James Brown Scott. *The Conference of 1899*, New York, Oxford University Press, 1920
The Proceedings of the Hague Peace Conferences, 1907	*The Proceedings of the Hague Peace Conferences.* Translation of the official texts. Prepared in the Division of International Law of the Carnegie Endowment for International Peace, under the supervision of James Brown Scott. *The Conference of 1907*, New York, Oxford University Press, 1920
RGDIP	*Revue génerale de droit international public*
RICR	*Revue internationale de la Croix-Rouge* (Genève)
RICR (Span.)	*Revista Internacional de la Cruz Roja* (Ginebra)

Roberts and Guelff	*Documents on the Laws of War.* Edited by Adam Roberts and Richard Guelff, 3rd ed., Oxford University Press, 2000
Sbornik dogovorov RSFSR	*Sbornik deistvuyushchikh dogovorov, soglashenii i Konventsii zaklyuchennykh RSFSR s inostrannymi gosudarstvami*, Petersburg, Gosudarstvennoe isdatelstvo, 1921–1923, 5 vols.
Sbornik dogovorov SSSR	*Sbornik deistvuyushchikh dogovorov, soglashenii i Konventsii zaklyuchennykh SSSR s inostrannymi gosudarstvami*, Moskva, NKID/MID, 1924–
Scott, *Hague Conventions*	*The Hague Conventions and Declarations of 1899 and 1907*, edited by James Brown Scott. 3rd edition, Carnegie Endowment for International Peace, New York, Oxford University Press, 1918
Scott, *Les Conventions de La Haye*	*Les Conventions et déclarations de La Haye de 1899 et 1907*, avec une introduction de James Brown Scott, Dotation Carnegie pour la Paix Internationale. New York, Oxford University Press, 1918
Scott, *Resolutions of the Institute of International Law*	*Resolutions of the Institute of International Law*, edited by James Brown Scott, New York, Carnegie Endowment for International Peace, 1916
Sobranie zakanov	*Sobranie zakonov i rasporiazhenii Rabochekrestianskogo Pravitelstva SSSR 1924–1938* (from 1938 to 1946 under the title *Sobranie postonovlenii i rasporiazhenii pravitelstva SSSR*)
TIAS	*Treaties and Other International Acts Series*, issued singly in pamphlets by the US Department of State
UNTS	*United Nations Treaty Series*
UST	*United States Treaties and Other International Agreements* (volumes published on a calendar year basis beginning as of 1 January 1950)
Wilson–Tucker	George G. Wilson, *International Law*, 9th ed. (edition 1901–1917 by G. G. Wilson and G. F. Tucker), New York, Silver, Burdett and Co., 1935

I

GENERAL RULES CONCERNING THE CONDUCT OF HOSTILITIES

No. 1

INSTRUCTIONS FOR THE GOVERNMENT OF ARMIES OF THE UNITED STATES IN THE FIELD

Prepared by Francis Lieber, promulgated as General Orders No. 100 by President Lincoln, 24 April 1863

INTRODUCTORY NOTE: The Lieber Instructions represent the first attempt to codify the laws of war. They were prepared during the American Civil War by Francis Lieber, then a professor at Columbia College in New York, revised by a board of officers and promulgated by President Lincoln. Although they were binding only on the forces of the United States, they correspond to a great extent to the laws and customs of war existing at that time. The Lieber Instructions strongly influenced the further codification of the laws of war and the adoption of similar regulations by other states. They formed the origin of the project of an international convention on the laws of war presented to the Brussels Conference in 1874 (*No. 2*) and stimulated the adoption of the Hague Conventions on land warfare of 1899 and 1907 (*Nos. 7 and 8*).

The text below is reprinted from the second edition of the United States Government Printing Office of 1898.

TEXT PUBLISHED IN: *Instructions for the Government of Armies of the United States in the Field*, prepared by Francis Lieber, LL.D., General Orders, No. 100, War Department, Adjutant General's Office, Washington, 24 April 1863, 26 pp. (Engl.); Francis Lieber, *Contributions to Political Science, Including Lectures on the Constitution of the United States and Other Papers,* Philadelphia, Lippincott, Miscellaneous Writings, Vol. II, 1881, p. 245 (Engl.); Wilson-Tucker, pp. VI–XXXVI (Engl.); Friedman, pp. 158–186 (Engl.); J. C. Bluntschli, *Le Droit international codifié*, 5th edn., Paris, 1895, appendix (French); *Les deux Conférences de la Paix*, pp. 195–214 (French); *Droit des conflits armés*, pp. 3–22 (French); *RICR*, 1953, pp. 401–409, 476–482, 635–645, 974–980 (French); Bluntschli-Komarovskii, pp. 513–544 (Russ.); Heffter-Taube, pp. 39–62 (Russ.); ICRC website: www.icrc.org/ihl.nsf.

TABLE OF CONTENTS

* * *

INSTRUCTIONS FOR THE GOVERNMENT OF ARMIES OF THE UNITED STATES IN THE FIELD

General Orders,
No. 100.

War Dept.,
Adjt. General's Office
Washington, April 24, 1863

The following "Instructions for the Government of Armies of the United States in the Field," prepared by Francis Lieber, LL.D., and revised by a board of officers, of which Maj. Gen. E. A. Hitchcock is president, having been approved by the President of the United States, he commands that they be published for the information of all concerned.

By order of the Secretary of War:

E. D. Townsend
Assistant Adjutant-General

Section I. Martial Law – Military jurisdiction – Military necessity – Retaliation

Article 1. A place, district, or country occupied by an enemy stands, in consequence of the occupation, under the Martial Law of the invading or occupying army, whether any proclamation declaring Martial Law, or any public warning to the inhabitants, has been issued or not. Martial Law is the immediate and direct effect and consequence of occupation or conquest.

The presence of a hostile army proclaims its Martial Law.

Art. 2. Martial Law does not cease during the hostile occupation, except by special proclamation, ordered by the commander in chief; or by special mention in the treaty of peace concluding the war, when the occupation of a place or territory continues beyond the conclusion of peace as one of the conditions of the same.

Art. 3. Martial Law in a hostile country consists in the suspension, by the occupying military authority, of the criminal and civil law, and of the domestic administration and government in the occupied place or territory, and in the substitution of military rule and force for the same, as well as in the dictation of general laws, as far as military necessity requires this suspension, substitution, or dictation.

The commander of the forces may proclaim that the administration of all civil and penal law shall continue either wholly or in part, as in times of peace, unless otherwise ordered by the military authority.

Art. 4. Martial Law is simply military authority exercised in accordance with the laws and usages of war. Military oppression is not Martial Law: it is the abuse of the power which that law confers. As Martial Law is executed by military force, it is incumbent upon those who administer it to be strictly guided by the principles of justice, honor, and humanity – virtues adorning a soldier even more than other men, for the very reason that he possesses the power of his arms against the unarmed.

Art. 5. Martial Law should be less stringent in places and countries fully occupied and fairly conquered. Much greater severity may be exercised in places or regions where actual hostilities exist, or are expected and must be prepared for. Its most complete sway is allowed – even in the commander's own country – when face to face with the enemy, because of the absolute necessities of the case, and of the paramount duty to defend the country against invasion.

To save the country is paramount to all other considerations.

Art. 6. All civil and penal law shall continue to take its usual course in the enemy's places and territories under Martial Law, unless interrupted or stopped by order of the occupying military power; but all the functions of the hostile government – legislative executive, or administrative – whether of a general, provincial, or local character, cease under Martial Law, or continue only with the sanction, or, if deemed necessary, the participation of the occupier or invader.

Art. 7. Martial Law extends to property, and to persons, whether they are subjects of the enemy or aliens to that government.

Art. 8. Consuls, among American and European nations, are not diplomatic agents. Nevertheless, their offices and persons will be subjected to Martial Law in cases of urgent necessity only: their property and businesses are not exempted. Any delinquency they commit against the established military rule may be punished as in the case of any other inhabitant, and such punishment furnishes no reasonable ground for international complaint.

Art. 9. The functions of Ambassadors, Ministers, or other diplomatic agents accredited by neutral powers to the hostile government, cease, so far as regards the displaced government; but the conquering or occupying power usually recognizes them as temporarily accredited to itself.

Art. 10. Martial Law affects chiefly the police and collection of public revenue and taxes, whether imposed by the expelled government or by the invader, and refers mainly to the support and efficiency of the army, its safety, and the safety of its operations.

Art. 11. The law of war does not only disclaim all cruelty and bad faith concerning engagements concluded with the enemy during the war, but also the breaking of stipulations solemnly contracted by the belligerents in time of peace, and avowedly intended to remain in force in case of war between the contracting powers.

It disclaims all extortions and other transactions for individual gain; all acts of private revenge, or connivance at such acts.

Offenses to the contrary shall be severely punished, and especially so if committed by officers.

Art. 12. Whenever feasible, Martial Law is carried out in cases of individual offenders by Military Courts, but sentences of death shall be executed only with the approval of the chief executive, provided the urgency of the case does not require a speedier execution, and then only with the approval of the chief commander.

Art. 13. Military jurisdiction is of two kinds: First, that which is conferred and defined by statute; second, that which is derived from the common law of war. Military offenses under the statute law must be tried in the manner therein directed; but military offenses which do not come within the statute must be tried and punished under the common law of war. The character of the courts which exercise these jurisdictions depends upon the local laws of each particular country.

In the armies of the United States the first is exercised by courts-martial, while cases which do not come within the "Rules and Articles of War," or the jurisdiction conferred by statute on courts-martial, are tried by military commissions.

Art. 14. Military necessity, as understood by modern civilized nations, consists in the necessity of those measures which are indispensable for securing the ends of the war, and which are lawful according to the modern law and usages of war.

Art. 15. Military necessity admits of all direct destruction of life or limb of *armed* enemies, and of other persons whose destruction is incidentally *unavoidable* in the armed contests of the war; it allows of the capturing of every armed enemy, and every enemy of importance to the hostile government, or of peculiar danger to the captor; it allows of all destruction of property, and obstruction of the ways and channels of traffic, travel, or communication, and of all withholding of sustenance or means of life from the enemy; of the appropriation of whatever an enemy's country affords necessary for the subsistence and safety of the army, and of such deception as does not involve the breaking of good faith either positively pledged, regarding agreements entered into during the war, or supposed by the modern law of war to exist. Men who take up arms against one another in public war do not cease on this account to be moral beings, responsible to one another and to God.

Art. 16. Military necessity does not admit of cruelty – that is, the infliction of suffering for the sake of suffering or for revenge, nor of maiming or wounding except in fight, nor of torture to extort confessions. It does not admit of the use of poison in any way, nor of the wanton devastation of a district. It admits of deception, but disclaims acts of perfidy; and, in general, military necessity does not include any act of hostility which makes the return to peace unnecessarily difficult.

Art. 17. War is not carried on by arms alone. It is lawful to starve the hostile belligerent, armed or unarmed, so that it leads to the speedier subjection of the enemy.

Art. 18. When a commander of a besieged place expels the noncombatants, in order to lessen the number of those who consume his stock of provisions, it is lawful, though an extreme measure, to drive them back, so as to hasten the surrender.

Art. 19. Commanders, whenever admissible, inform the enemy of their intention to bombard a place, so that the noncombatants, and especially the women and children, may be removed before the bombardment commences. But it is no infraction of the common law of war to omit thus to inform the enemy. Surprise may be a necessity.

Art. 20. Public war is a state of armed hostility between sovereign nations or governments. It is a law and requisite of civilized existence that men live in political, continuous societies, forming organized units, called states or nations, whose constituents bear, enjoy, suffer, advance and retrograde together, in peace and in war.

Art. 21. The citizen or native of a hostile country is thus an enemy, as one of the constituents of the hostile state or nation, and as such is subjected to the hardships of the war.

Art. 22. Nevertheless, as civilization has advanced during the last centuries, so has likewise steadily advanced, especially in war on land, the distinction between the private individual belonging to a hostile country and the hostile country itself, with its men in arms. The principle has been more and more acknowledged that the unarmed citizen is to be spared in person, property, and honor as much as the exigencies of war will admit.

Art. 23. Private citizens are no longer murdered, enslaved, or carried off to distant parts, and the inoffensive individual is as little disturbed in his private relations as the commander of the hostile troops can afford to grant in the overruling demands of a vigorous war.

Art. 24. The almost universal rule in remote times was, and continues to be with barbarous armies, that the private individual of the hostile country is destined to suffer every privation of liberty and protection, and every disruption of family ties. Protection was, and still is with uncivilized people, the exception.

Art. 25. In modern regular wars of the Europeans, and their descendants in other portions of the globe, protection of the inoffensive citizen of the hostile country is the rule; privation and disturbance of private relations are the exceptions.

Art. 26. Commanding generals may cause the magistrates and civil officers of the hostile country to take the oath of temporary allegiance or an oath of fidelity to their own victorious government or rulers, and they may expel everyone who declines to do so. But whether they do so or not, the people and the civil officers owe strict obedience to them as long as they hold sway over the district or country, at the peril of their lives.

Art. 27. The law of war can no more wholly dispense with retaliation than can the law of nations, of which it is a branch. Yet civilized nations acknowledge retaliation as the sternest feature of war. A reckless enemy often leaves to his opponent no other means of securing himself against the repetition of barbarous outrage.

Art. 28. Retaliation will, therefore, never be resorted to as a measure of mere revenge, but only as a means of protective retribution, and moreover, cautiously and unavoidably; that is to say, retaliation shall only be resorted to after careful enquiry into the real occurrence, and the character of the misdeeds that may demand retribution.

Unjust and inconsiderate retaliation removes the belligerents farther and farther from the mitigating rules of regular war, and by rapid steps leads them nearer to the internecine wars of savages.

Art. 29. Modern times are distinguished from earlier ages by the existence, at one and the same time, of many nations and great governments related to one another in close intercourse.

Peace is their normal condition, war is the exception. The ultimate object of all modern war is a renewed state of peace.

The more vigorously wars are pursued, the better it is for humanity. Sharp wars are brief.

Art. 30. Ever since the formation and coexistence of modern nations, and ever since wars have become great national wars, war has come to be acknowledged not to be its own end, but the means to obtain great ends of state, or to consist in defense against wrong; and no conventional restriction of the modes adopted to injure the enemy is any longer admitted; but the law of war imposes many limitations and restrictions on principles of justice, faith, and honor.

Section II. Public and private property of the enemy – Protection of persons, and especially of women, of religion, the arts and sciences – Punishment of crimes against the inhabitants of hostile countries

Art. 31. A victorious army appropriates all public money, seizes all public movable property until further direction by its government, and sequesters for its own benefit or of that of its government all the revenues of real property belonging to the hostile government or nation. The title to such real property remains in abeyance during military occupation, and until the conquest is made complete.

Art. 32. A victorious army, by the martial power inherent in the same, may suspend, change, or abolish, as far the martial power extends, the relations which arise from the services due, according to the existing laws of the invading country, from one citizen, subject, or native of the same to another.

The commander of the army must leave it to the ultimate treaty of peace to settle the permanency of this change.

Art. 33. It is no longer considered lawful – on the contrary, it is held to be a serious breach of the law of war – to force the subjects of the enemy into the service of the victorious government, except the latter should proclaim, after a fair and complete conquest of the hostile country or district, that it is resolved to keep the country, district, or place permanently as its own and make it a portion of its own country.

Art. 34. As a general rule, the property belonging to churches, to hospitals, or other establishments of an exclusively charitable character, to establishments of education, or foundations for the promotion of knowledge, whether public schools, universities, academies of learning or observatories, museums of the fine arts, or of a scientific character – such property is not to be considered public property in the sense of paragraph 31; but it may be taxed or used when the public service may require it.

Art. 35. Classical works of art, libraries, scientific collections, or precious instruments, such as astronomical telescopes, as well as hospitals, must be secured against all avoidable injury, even when they are contained in fortified places whilst besieged or bombarded.

Art. 36. If such works of art, libraries, collections, or instruments belonging to a hostile nation or government, can be removed without injury, the ruler of the conquering state or nation may order them to be seized and removed for the benefit of the said nation. The ultimate ownership is to be settled by the ensuing treaty of peace.

In no case shall they be sold or given away, if captured by the armies of the United States, nor shall they ever be privately appropriated, or wantonly destroyed or injured.

Art. 37. The United States acknowledge and protect, in hostile countries occupied by them, religion and morality; strictly private property; the persons of the inhabitants, especially those of women: and the sacredness of domestic relations. Offenses to the contrary shall be rigorously punished.

This rule does not interfere with the right of the victorious invader to tax the people or their property, to levy forced loans, to billet soldiers, or to appropriate property, especially houses, land, boats or ships, and churches, for temporary and military uses.

Art 38. Private property, unless forfeited by crimes or by offenses of the owner, can be seized only by way of military necessity, for the support or other benefit of the army or of the United States.

If the owner has not fled, the commanding officer will cause receipts to be given, which may serve the spoliated owner to obtain indemnity.

Art. 39. The salaries of civil officers of the hostile government who remain in the invaded territory, and continue the work of their office, and can continue it according to the circumstances arising out of the war – such as judges, administrative or police officers, officers of city or communal governments – are paid from the public revenue of the invaded territory, until the military government has reason wholly or partially to discontinue it. Salaries or incomes connected with purely honorary titles are always stopped.

Art. 40. There exists no law or body of authoritative rules of action between hostile armies, except that branch of the law of nature and nations which is called the law and usages of war on land.

Art. 41. All municipal law of the ground on which the armies stand, or of the countries to which they belong, is silent and of no effect between armies in the field.

Art. 42. Slavery, complicating and confounding the ideas of property (that is of a *thing*), and of personality (that is of *humanity*), exists according to municipal or local law only. The law of nature and nations has never acknowledged it. The digest of the Roman law enacts, the early dictum of the pagan jurist, that "so far as the law of nature is concerned, all men are equal." Fugitives escaping from a country in which they were slaves, villains, or serfs, into another country, have, for centuries past, been held free and acknowledged free by judicial decisions of European countries, even though the municipal law of the country in which the slave had taken refuge acknowledged slavery within its own dominions.

Art. 43. Therefore, in a war between the United States and a belligerent which admits of slavery, if a person held in bondage by that belligerent be captured by or come as a fugitive under the protection of the military forces of the United States, such person is immediately entitled to the rights and privileges of a freeman. To return such person into slavery would amount to enslaving a free person, and neither the United States nor any officer under their authority can enslave any human being. Moreover, a person so made free by the law of war is under the shield of the law of nations, and the former owner or State can have, by the law of postliminy, no belligerent lien or claim of service.

Art. 44. All wanton violence committed against persons in the invaded country, all destruction of property not commanded by the authorized officer, all robbery, all pillage or sacking, even after taking a place by main force, all rape, wounding, maiming, or killing of such inhabitants, are prohibited under the penalty of death, or such other severe punishment as may seem adequate for the gravity of the offense.

A soldier, officer or private, in the act of committing such violence, and disobeying a superior ordering him to abstain from it, may be lawfully killed on the spot by such superior.

Art. 45. All captures and booty belong, according to the modern law of war, primarily to the government of the captor.

Prize money, whether on sea or land, can now only be claimed under local law.

Art. 46. Neither officers nor soldiers are allowed to make use of their position or power in the hostile country for private gain, not even for commercial transactions otherwise legitimate. Offenses to the contrary committed by commissioned officers will be punished with cashiering or such other punishment as the nature of the offense may require; if by soldiers, they shall be punished according to the nature of the offense.

Art. 47. Crimes punishable by all penal codes, such as arson, murder, maiming, assaults, highway robbery, theft, burglary, fraud, forgery, and rape, if committed by an American soldier in a hostile country against its inhabitants, are not only punishable as at home, but in all cases in which death is not inflicted, the severe punishment shall be preferred.

Section III. Deserters – Prisoners of war – Hostages – Booty on the battlefield

Art. 48. Deserters from the American Army, having entered the service of the enemy, suffer death if they fall again into the hands of the United States, whether by capture, or being delivered up to the American Army; and if a deserter from the enemy, having taken service in the Army of the United States, is captured by the enemy, and punished by them with death or otherwise, it is not a breach against the law and usages of war, requiring redress or retaliation.

Art. 49. A prisoner of war is a public enemy armed or attached to the hostile army for active aid, who has fallen into the hands of the captor, either fighting or wounded, on the field or in the hospital, by individual surrender or by capitulation.

All soldiers, of whatever species of arms; all men who belong to the rising *en masse* of the hostile country; all those who are attached to the army for its efficiency and promote directly the object of the war, except such as are hereinafter provided for; all disabled men or officers on the field or elsewhere, if captured; all enemies who have thrown away their arms and ask for quarter, are prisoners of war, and as such exposed to the inconveniences as well as entitled to the privileges of a prisoner of war.

Art. 50. Moreover, citizens who accompany an army for whatever purpose, such as sutlers, editors, or reporters of journals, or contractors, if captured, may be made prisoners of war, and be detained as such.

The monarch and members of the hostile reigning family, male or female, the chief, and chief officers of the hostile government, its diplomatic agents, and all persons who are of particular and singular use and benefit to the hostile army or its government, are, if captured on belligerent ground, and if unprovided with a safe conduct granted by the captor's government, prisoners of war.

Art. 51. If the people of that portion of an invaded country which is not yet occupied by the enemy, or of the whole country, at the approach of a hostile army, rise, under a duly authorized levy *en masse* to resist the invader, they are now treated as public enemies, and, if captured, are prisoners of war.

Art. 52. No belligerent has the right to declare that he will treat every captured man in arms of a levy *en masse* as a brigand or bandit.

If, however, the people of a country, or any portion of the same, already occupied by an army, rise against it, they are violators of the laws of war, and are not entitled to their protection.

Art. 53. The enemy's chaplains, officers of the medical staff, apothecaries, hospital nurses and servants, if they fall into the hands of the American Army, are not prisoners of war, unless the commander has reasons to retain them. In this latter case, or if, at their own desire, they are allowed to remain with their captured companions, they are treated as prisoners of war, and may be exchanged if the commander sees fit.

Art. 54. A hostage is a person accepted as a pledge for the fulfillment of an agreement concluded between belligerents during the war, or in consequence of a war. Hostages are rare in the present age.

Art. 55. If a hostage is accepted, he is treated like a prisoner of war, according to rank and condition, as circumstances may admit.

Art. 56. A prisoner of war is subject to no punishment for being a public enemy, nor is any revenge wreaked upon him by the intentional infliction of any suffering, or disgrace, by cruel imprisonment, want of food, by mutilation, death, or any other barbarity.

Art. 57. So soon as a man is armed by a sovereign government and takes the soldier's oath of fidelity, he is a belligerent; his killing, wounding, or other warlike acts are not individual crimes or offenses. No belligerent has a right to declare that enemies of a certain class, color, or condition, when properly organized as soldiers, will not be treated by him as public enemies.

Art. 58. The law of nations knows of no distinction of color, and if an enemy of the United States should enslave and sell any captured persons of their army, it would be a case for the severest retaliation, if not redressed upon complaint.

The United States cannot retaliate by enslavement; therefore death must be the retaliation for this crime against the laws of nations.

Art. 59. A prisoner of war remains answerable for the crimes committed against the captor's army or people, committed before he was captured, and for which he has not been punished by his own authorities.

All prisoners of war are liable for the infliction of retaliatory measures.

Art. 60. It is against the usage of modern war to resolve, in hatred and revenge, to give no quarter. No body of troops has the right to declare that it will not give, and therefore will not expect, quarter, but a commander is permitted to direct his troops to give no quarter, in great straits, when his own salvation makes it *impossible* to cumber himself with prisoners.

Art. 61. Troops that give no quarter have no right to kill enemies already disabled on the ground, or prisoners captured by other troops.

Art. 62. All troops of the enemy known or discovered to give no quarter in general, or to any portion of the army, receive none.

Art. 63. Troops who fight in the uniform of their enemies, without any plain, striking, and uniform mark of distinction of the own, can expect no quarter.

Art. 64. If American troops capture a train containing uniforms of the enemy, and the commander considers it advisable to distribute them for use among his men, some striking mark or sign must be adopted to distinguish the American soldier from the enemy.

Art. 65. The use of the enemy's national standard, flag, or other emblem of nationality, for the purpose of deceiving the enemy in battle, is an act of perfidy by which they lose all claim to the protection of the laws of war.

Art. 66. Quarter having been given to an enemy by American troops, under a misapprehension of his true character, he may, nevertheless, be ordered to suffer death if, within three days after the battle, it be discovered that he belongs to a corps which gives no quarter.

Art. 67. The law of nations allows every sovereign government to make war upon another sovereign state, and, therefore, admits of no rules or laws different from those of regular warfare, regarding the treatment of prisoners of war, although they may belong to the army of a government which the captor may consider as a wanton and unjust assailant.

Art. 68. Modern wars are not internecine wars, in which the killing of the enemy is the object. The destruction of the enemy in modern war, and, indeed, modern war itself, are means to obtain that object of the belligerent which lies beyond the war.

Unnecessary or revengeful destruction of life is not lawful.

Art. 69. Outposts, sentinels, or pickets are not to be fired upon, except to drive them in, or when a positive order, special or general, has been issued to that effect.

Art. 70 The use of poison in any manner, be it to poison wells, or food, or arms, is wholly excluded from modern warfare. He that uses it puts himself out of the pale of the law and usages of war.

Art. 71. Whoever intentionally inflicts additional wounds on an enemy already wholly disabled, or kills such an enemy, or who orders or encourages soldiers to do so, shall suffer death, if duly convicted, whether he belongs to the Army of the United States, or is an enemy captured after having committed his misdeed.

Art. 72. Money and other valuables on the person of a prisoner, such as watches or jewelry, as well as extra clothing, are regarded by the American Army as the private property of the prisoner, and the appropriation of such valuables or money is considered dishonorable, and is prohibited.

Nevertheless, if *large* sums are found upon the persons of prisoners, or in their possession, they shall be taken from them, and the surplus, after providing for their own support, appropriated for the use of the army, under the direction of the commander, unless otherwise ordered by the government. Nor can prisoners claim, as private property, large sums found and captured in their train, although they have been placed in the private luggage of the prisoners.

Art. 73. All officers, when captured, must surrender their side arms to the captor. They may be restored to the prisoner in marked cases, by the commander, to signalize admiration of his distinguished bravery or approbation of his humane treatment of prisoners before his capture. The captured officer to whom they may be restored can not wear them during captivity.

Art. 74. A prisoner of war, being a public enemy, is the prisoner of the government, and not of the captor. No ransom can be paid by a prisoner of war to his individual captor or to any officer in command. The government alone releases captives, according to rules prescribed by itself.

Art. 75. Prisoners of war are subject to confinement or imprisonment such as may be deemed necessary on account of safety, but they are to be subjected to no other intentional suffering or indignity. The confinement and mode of treating a prisoner may be varied during his captivity according to the demands of safety.

Art. 76. Prisoners of war shall be fed upon plain and wholesome food, whenever practicable, and treated with humanity.

They may be required to work for the benefit of the captor's government, according to their rank and condition.

Art. 77. A prisoner of war who escapes may be shot or otherwise killed in his flight; but neither death nor any other punishment shall be inflicted upon him simply for his attempt to escape, which the law of war does not consider a crime. Stricter means of security shall be used after an unsuccessful attempt at escape.

If, however, a conspiracy is discovered, the purpose of which is a united or general escape, the conspirators may be rigorously punished, even with death; and capital punishment may also be inflicted on prisoners of war discovered to have plotted rebellion against the authorities of the captors, whether in union with fellow prisoners or other persons.

Art. 78. If prisoners of war, having given no pledge nor made any promise on their honor, forcibly or otherwise escape, and are captured again in battle after having rejoined their own army, they shall not be punished for their escape, but shall be treated as simple prisoners of war, although they will be subjected to stricter confinement.

Art. 79. Every captured wounded enemy shall be medically treated, according to the ability of the medical staff.

Art. 80. Honorable men, when captured, will abstain from giving to the enemy information concerning their own army, and the modern law of war permits no longer the use of any violence against prisoners in order to extort the desired information or to punish them for having given false information.

Section IV. Partisans – Armed enemies not belonging to the hostile army – Scouts – Armed prowlers – War-rebels

Art. 81. Partisans are soldiers armed and wearing the uniform of their army, but belonging to a corps which acts detached from the main body for the purpose of making inroads into the territory occupied by the enemy. If captured, they are entitled to all the privileges of the prisoner of war.

Art. 82. Men, or squads of men, who commit hostilities, whether by fighting, or inroads for destruction or plunder, or by raids of any kind, without commission, without being part and portion of the organized hostile army, and without sharing continuously in the war, but who do so with intermitting returns to their homes and avocations, or with the occasional assumption of the semblance of peaceful pursuits, divesting themselves of the character and appearance of soldiers – such men, or squads of men, are not public enemies, and, therefore, if captured, are not entitled to the privileges of prisoners of war, but shall be treated summarily as highway robbers or pirates.

Art. 83. Scouts, or single soldiers, if disguised in the dress of the country or in the uniform of the army hostile to their own, employed in obtaining information, if found within or lurking about the lines of the captor, are treated as spies, and suffer death.

Art. 84. Armed prowlers, by whatever names they may be called, or persons of the enemy's territory, who steal within the lines of the hostile army for the purpose of robbing, killing, or of destroying bridges, roads or canals, or of robbing or destroying the mail, or of cutting the telegraph wires, are not entitled to the privileges of the prisoner of war.

Art. 85. War-rebels are persons within an occupied territory who rise in arms against the occupying or conquering army, or against the authorities established by the same. If captured, they may suffer death, whether they rise singly, in small or large bands, and whether called upon to do so by their own, but expelled, government or not. They are not prisoners of war; nor are they if discovered and secured before their conspiracy has matured to an actual rising or armed violence.

Section V. Safe-conduct – Spies – War-traitors – Captured messengers

Art. 86. All intercourse between the territories occupied by belligerent armies, whether by traffic, by letter, by travel, or in any other way, ceases. This is the general rule, to be observed without special proclamation.

Exceptions to this rule, whether by safe-conduct, or permission to trade on a small or large scale, or by exchanging mails, or by travel from one territory into the other, can take place only according to agreement approved by the government, or by the highest military authority.

Contraventions of this rule are highly punishable.

Art. 87. Ambassadors, and all other diplomatic agents of neutral powers, accredited to the enemy, may receive safe-conducts through the territories occupied by the belligerents, unless there are military reasons to the contrary, and unless they may reach the place of their destination conveniently by another route. It implies no international affront if the safe-conduct is declined. Such passes are usually given by the supreme authority of the State, and not by subordinate officers.

Art. 88. A spy is a person who secretly, in disguise or under false pretense, seeks information with the intention of communicating it to the enemy.

The spy is punishable with death by hanging by the neck, whether or not he succeed in obtaining the information or in conveying it to the enemy.

Art. 89. If a citizen of the United States obtains information in a legitimate manner, and betrays it to the enemy, be he a military or civil officer, or a private citizen, he shall suffer death.

Art. 90. A traitor under the law of war, or a war-traitor, is a person in a place or district under Martial Law who, unauthorized by the military commander, gives information of any kind to the enemy, or holds intercourse with him.

Art. 91. The war-traitor is always severely punished. If his offense consists in betraying to the enemy anything concerning the condition, safety, operations, or plans of the troops holding or occupying the place or district, his punishment is death.

Art. 92. If the citizen or subject of a country or place invaded or conquered gives information to his own government, from which he is separated by the hostile army, or to the army of his government, he is a war-traitor, and death is the penalty of his offense.

Art. 93. All armies in the field stand in need of guides, and impress them if they cannot obtain them otherwise.

Art. 94. No person having been forced by the enemy to serve as guide is punishable for having done so.

Art. 95. If a citizen of a hostile and invaded district voluntarily serves as a guide to the enemy, or offers to do so, he is deemed a war-traitor, and shall suffer death.

Art. 96. A citizen serving voluntarily as a guide against his own country commits treason, and will be dealt with according to the law of his country.

Art. 97. Guides, when it is clearly proved that they have misled intentionally, may be put to death.

Art. 98. All unauthorized or secret communications with the enemy is considered treasonable by the law of war.

Foreign residents in an invaded or occupied territory, or foreign visitors in the same, can claim no immunity from this law. They may communicate with foreign parts, or with the inhabitants of the hostile country, so far as the military authority permits, but no further. Instant expulsion from the occupied territory would be the very least punishment for the infraction of this rule.

Art. 99. A messenger carrying written dispatches or verbal messages from one portion of the army, or from a besieged place, to another portion of the same army, or its government, if armed, and in the uniform of his army, and if captured, while doing so, in the territory occupied by the enemy, is treated by the captor as a prisoner of war. If not in uniform, nor a soldier, the circumstances connected with his capture must determine the disposition that shall be made of him.

Art. 100. A messenger or agent who attempts to steal through the territory occupied by the enemy, to further, in any manner, the interests of the enemy, if captured, is not entitled to the privileges of the prisoner of war, and may be dealt with according to the circumstances of the case.

Art. 101. While deception in war is admitted as a just and necessary means of hostility, and is consistent with honorable warfare, the common law of war allows even capital punishment for clandestine or treacherous attempts to injure an enemy, because they are so dangerous, and it is difficult to guard against them.

Art. 102. The law of war, like the criminal law regarding other offenses, makes no difference on account of the difference in sexes, concerning the spy, the war-traitor, or the war-rebel.

Art. 103. Spies, war-traitors, and war-rebels are not exchanged according to the common law of war. The exchange of such persons would require a special cartel, authorized by the government, or, at a great distance from it, by the chief commander of the army in the field.

Art. 104. A successful spy or war-traitor, safely returned to his own army, and afterwards captured as an enemy, is not subject to punishment for his acts as a spy or war-traitor, but he may be held in closer custody as a person individually dangerous.

Section VI. Exchange of prisoners – Flags of truce – Abuse of the flag of truce – Flags of protection

Art. 105. Exchanges of prisoners take place – number for number – rank for rank – wounded for wounded – with added condition for added condition – such, for instance, as not to serve for a certain period.

Art. 106. In exchanging prisoners of war, such numbers of persons of inferior rank may be submitted as an equivalent for one of superior rank as may be agreed upon by cartel, which requires the sanction of the government, or of the commander of the army in the field.

Art. 107. A prisoner of war is honor bound truly to state to the captor his rank; and he is not to assume a lower rank than belongs to him, in order to cause a more advantageous exchange, nor a higher rank, for the purpose of obtaining better treatment.

Offenses to the contrary have been justly punished by the commanders of released prisoners, and may be good cause for refusing to release such prisoners.

Art. 108. The surplus number of prisoners of war remaining after an exchange has taken place is sometimes released either by the payment of a stipulated sum of money, or, in urgent cases, of provision, clothing, or other necessities.

Such arrangement, however, requires the sanction of the highest authority.

Art. 109. The exchange of prisoners of war is an act of convenience to both belligerents. If no general cartel has been concluded, it cannot be demanded by either of them. No belligerent is obliged to exchange prisoners of war.

A cartel is voidable as soon as either party has violated it.

Art. 110. No exchange of prisoners shall be made except after complete capture, and after an accurate account of them, and a list of the captured officers, has been taken.

Art. 111. The bearer of a flag of truce cannot insist upon being admitted. He must always be admitted with great caution. Unnecessary frequency is carefully to be avoided.

Art. 112. If the bearer of a flag of truce offer himself during an engagement, he can be admitted as a very rare exception only. It is no breach of good faith to retain such flag of truce, if admitted during the engagement. Firing is not required to cease on the appearance of a flag of truce in battle.

Art. 113. If the bearer of a flag of truce, presenting himself during an engagement, is killed or wounded, it furnishes no ground of complaint whatever.

Art. 114. If it be discovered, and fairly proved, that a flag of truce has been abused for surreptitiously obtaining military knowledge, the bearer of the flag thus abusing his sacred character is deemed a spy.

So sacred is the character of a flag of truce, and so necessary is its sacredness, that while its abuse is an especially heinous offense, great caution is requisite, on the other hand, in convicting the bearer of a flag of truce as a spy.

Art. 115. It is customary to designate by certain flags (usually yellow) the hospitals in places which are shelled, so that the besieging enemy may avoid firing on them. The same has been done in battles, when hospitals are situated within the field of engagement.

Art. 116. Honorable belligerents often request that the hospitals within the territory of the enemy may be designated, so that they may be spared.

An honorable belligerent allows himself to be guided by flags or signals of protection as much as the contingencies and the necessities of the fight will permit.

Art. 117. It is justly considered an act of bad faith, of infamy or fiendishness, to deceive the enemy by flags of protection. Such act of bad faith may be good cause for refusing to respect such flags.

Art. 118. The besieging belligerent has sometimes requested the besieged to designate the buildings containing collections of works of art, scientific museums, astronomical observatories, or precious libraries, so that their destruction may be avoided as much as possible.

Section VII. Parole

Art. 119. Prisoners of war may be released from captivity by exchange, and, under certain circumstances, also by parole.

Art. 120. The term Parole designates the pledge of individual good faith and honor to do, or to omit doing, certain acts after he who gives his parole shall have been dismissed, wholly or partially, from the power of the captor.

Art. 121. The pledge of the parole is always an individual, but not a private act.

Art. 122. The parole applies chiefly to prisoners of war whom the captor allows to return to their country, or to live in greater freedom within the captor's country or territory, on conditions stated in the parole.

Art. 123. Release of prisoners of war by exchange is the general rule; release by parole is the exception.

Art. 124. Breaking the parole is punishable with death when the person breaking the parole is captured again.

Accurate lists, therefore, of the paroled persons must be kept by the belligerents.

Art. 125. When paroles are given and received there must be an exchange of two written documents, in which the name and rank of the paroled individuals are accurately and truthfully stated.

Art. 126. Commissioned officers only are allowed to give their parole, and they can give it only with the permission of their superior, as long as a superior in rank is within reach.

Art. 127. No noncommissioned officer or private can give his parole except through an officer. Individual paroles not given through an officer are not only void, but subject the individuals giving them to the punishment of death as deserters. The only admissible exception is where individuals, properly separated from their commands, have suffered long confinement without the possibility of being paroled through an officer.

Art. 128. No paroling on the battlefield; no paroling of entire bodies of troops after a battle; and no dismissal of large numbers of prisoners, with a general declaration that they are paroled, is permitted, or of any value.

Art. 129. In capitulations for the surrender of strong places or fortified camps the commanding officer, in cases of urgent necessity, may agree that the troops under his command shall not fight again during the war, unless exchanged.

Art. 130. The usual pledge given in the parole is not to serve during the existing war, unless exchanged.

This pledge refers only to the active service on the field, against the paroling belligerent or his allies actively engaged in the same war. These cases of breaking the parole are patent acts, and can be visited with the punishment of death; but the pledge does not refer to internal service, such as recruiting or drilling the recruits, fortifying places not besieged, quelling civil commotions, fighting against belligerents unconnected with the paroling belligerents, or to civil or diplomatic service for which the paroled officer may be employed.

Art. 131. If the government does not approve of the parole, the paroled officer must return into captivity, and should the enemy refuse to receive him, he is free of his parole.

Art. 132. A belligerent government may declare, by a general order, whether it will allow paroling, and on what conditions it will allow it. Such order is communicated to the enemy.

Art. 133. No prisoner of war can be forced by the hostile government to parole himself, and no government is obliged to parole prisoners of war, or to parole all captured officers, if it paroles any. As the pledging of the parole is an individual act, so is paroling, on the other hand, an act of choice on the part of the belligerent.

Art. 134. The commander of an occupying army may require of the civil officers of the enemy, and of its citizens, any pledge he may consider necessary for the safety or security of his army, and upon their failure to give it he may arrest, confine, or detain them.

Section VIII. Armistice – Capitulation

Art. 135. An armistice is the cessation of active hostilities for a period agreed between belligerents. It must be agreed upon in writing, and duly ratified by the highest authorities of the contending parties.

Art. 136. If an armistice be declared, without conditions, it extends no further than to require a total cessation of hostilities along the front of both belligerents.

If conditions be agreed upon, they shall be clearly expressed, and must be rigidly adhered to by both parties. If either party violates any express conditions, the armistice may be declared null and void by the other.

Art. 137. An armistice may be general, and valid for all points and lines of the belligerents; or special, that is, referring to certain troops or certain localities only.

An armistice may be concluded for a definite time; or for an indefinite time, during which either belligerent may resume hostilities on giving the notice agreed upon to the other.

Art. 138. The motives which induce the one or the other belligerent to conclude an armistice, whether it be expected to be preliminary to a treaty of peace, or to prepare during the armistice for a more vigorous prosecution of the war, does in no way affect the character of the armistice itself.

Art. 139. An armistice is binding upon the belligerents from the day of the agreed commencement; but the officers of the armies are responsible from the day only when they receive official information of its existence.

Art. 140. Commanding officers have the right to conclude armistices binding on the district over which their command extends, but such armistice is subject to the ratification of the superior authority, and ceases so soon as it is made known to the enemy that the armistice is not ratified, even if a certain time for the elapsing between giving notice of cessation and the resumption of hostilities should have been stipulated for.

Art. 141. It is incumbent upon the contracting parties of an armistice to stipulate what intercourse of persons or traffic between the inhabitants of the territories occupied by the hostile armies shall be allowed, if any.

If nothing is stipulated the intercourse remains suspended, as during actual hostilities.

Art. 142. An armistice is not a partial or a temporary peace; it is only the suspension of military operations to the extent agreed upon by the parties.

Art. 143. When an armistice is concluded between a fortified place and the army besieging it, it is agreed by all the authorities on this subject that the besieger must cease all extension, perfection, or advance of his attacking works as much so as from attacks by main force.

But as there is a difference of opinion among martial jurists, whether the besieged have the right to repair breaches or to erect new works of defense within the place during an armistice, this point shall be determined by express agreement between the parties.

Art. 144. So soon as a capitulation is signed, the capitulator has no right to demolish, destroy, or injure the works, arms, stores, or ammunition, in his possession, during the time which elapses between the signing and the execution of the capitulation, unless otherwise stipulated in the same.

Art. 145. When an armistice is clearly broken by one of the parties, the other party is released from all obligation to observe it.

Art. 146. Prisoners taken in the act of breaking an armistice must be treated as prisoners of war, the officer alone being responsible who gives the order for such a violation of an armistice. The highest authority of the belligerent aggrieved may demand redress for the infraction of an armistice.

Art. 147. Belligerents sometimes conclude an armistice while their plenipotentiaries are met to discuss the conditions of a treaty of peace; but plenipotentiaries may meet without a preliminary armistice; in the latter case, the war is carried on without any abatement.

Section IX. Assassination

Art. 148. The law of war does not allow proclaiming either an individual belonging to the hostile army, or a citizen, or a subject of the hostile government, an outlaw, who may be slain without trial by any captor, any more than the modern law of peace allows such intentional outlawry; on the contrary, it abhors such outrage. The sternest retaliation should follow the murder committed in consequence of such proclamation, made by whatever authority. Civilized nations look with horror upon offers of rewards for the assassination of enemies as relapses into barbarism.

Section X. Insurrection – Civil War – Rebellion

Art. 149. Insurrection is the rising of people in arms against their government, or a portion of it, or against one or more of its laws, or against an officer or officers of the government. It may be confined to mere armed resistance, or it may have greater ends in view.

Art. 150. Civil war is war between two or more portions of a country or state, each contending for the mastery of the whole, and each claiming to be the legitimate government. The term is also sometimes applied to war of rebellion, when the rebellious provinces or portions of the state are contiguous to those containing the seat of government.

Art. 151. The term rebellion is applied to an insurrection of large extent, and is usually a war between the legitimate government of a country and portions of provinces of the same who seek to throw off their allegiance to it and set up a government of their own.

Art. 152. When humanity induces the adoption of the rules of regular war toward rebels, whether the adoption is partial or entire, it does in no way whatever imply a partial or complete acknowledgement of their government, if they have set up one, or of them, as an independent and sovereign power. Neutrals have no right to make the adoption of the rules of war by the assailed government toward rebels the ground of their own acknowledgement of the revolted people as an independent power.

Art. 153. Treating captured rebels as prisoners of war, exchanging them, concluding of cartels, capitulations, or other warlike agreements with them; addressing officers of a rebel army by the rank they may have in the same; accepting flags of truce; or, on the other hand, proclaiming Martial Law in their territory, or levying war-taxes or forced loans, or doing any other act sanctioned or demanded by the law and usages of public war between sovereign belligerents, neither proves nor establishes an acknowledgement of the rebellious people, or of the government which they may have erected, as a public or sovereign power. Nor does the adoption of the rules of war toward rebels imply an engagement with them extending beyond the limits of these rules. It is victory in the field that ends the strife and settles the future relations between the contending parties.

Art. 154. Treating, in the field, the rebellious enemy according to the law and usages of war has never prevented the legitimate government from trying the leaders of the rebellion or chief rebels for high treason, and from treating them accordingly, unless they are included in a general amnesty.

Art. 155. All enemies in regular war are divided into two general classes – that is to say, into combatants and noncombatants, or unarmed citizens of the hostile government.

The military commander of the legitimate government, in a war of rebellion, distinguishes between the loyal citizen in the revolted portion of the country and the disloyal citizen. The disloyal citizens may further be classified into those citizens known to sympathize with the rebellion without positively aiding it, and those who, without taking up arms, give positive aid and comfort to the rebellious enemy without being bodily forced thereto.

Art. 156. Common justice and plain expediency require that the military commander protect the manifestly loyal citizens, in revolted territories, against the hardships of the war as much as the common misfortune of all war admits.

The commander will throw the burden of the war, as much as lies within his power, on the disloyal citizens, of the revolted portion or province, subjecting them to a stricter police than the noncombatant enemies have to suffer in regular war; and if he deems it appropriate, or if his government demands of him that every citizen shall, by an oath of allegiance, or by some other manifest act, declare his fidelity to the legitimate government, he may expel, transfer, imprison, or fine the revolted citizens who refuse to pledge themselves anew as citizens obedient to the law and loyal to the government.

Whether it is expedient to do so, and whether reliance can be placed upon such oaths, the commander or his government have the right to decide.

Art. 157. Armed or unarmed resistance by citizens of the United States against the lawful movements of their troops is levying war against the United States, and is therefore treason.

No. 2

BRUSSELS CONFERENCE OF 1874

I. FINAL PROTOCOL. Signed at Brussels, 27 August 1874
II. PROJECT OF AN INTERNATIONAL DECLARATION CONCERNING THE LAWS AND CUSTOMS OF WAR

INTRODUCTORY NOTE: On the initiative of Czar Alexander II of Russia the delegates of 15 European states met in Brussels on 27 July 1874 to examine the draft of an international agreement concerning the laws and customs of war submitted to them by the Russian government. The Conference adopted the draft with minor alterations. However, since not all the governments were willing to accept it as a binding convention it was not ratified. The project nevertheless formed an important step in the movement for the codification of the laws of war. In the year in which it was adopted, the Institute of International Law, at its session in Geneva, appointed a committee to study the Brussels Declaration and to submit to the Institute its opinion and supplementary proposals on the subject. The efforts of the Institute led to the adoption of the *Manual of the Laws and Customs of War* at Oxford in 1880 (*No. 3*). Both the Brussels Declaration and the *Oxford Manual* formed the basis of the two Hague Conventions on land warfare and the Regulations annexed to them, adopted in 1899 and 1907 (*Nos. 7 and 8*). Many of the provisions of the two Hague Conventions can easily be traced back to the Brussels Declaration and the *Oxford Manual.*

AUTHENTIC TEXT: French. The English translation of the Final Protocol is reprinted from Edward Hertslet, *Map of Europe by Treaties*, London, 1875, Vol. III, pp. 1974–1976. The English translation of the Declaration is reprinted from *The Proceedings of the Hague Peace Conferences, 1899*, pp. 564–578.

TEXT PUBLISHED IN:
Final Protocol and Declaration: Actes de la Conférence de Bruxelles (1874), Bruxelles, F. Hayez, 1874, pp. 297–308 (French); Martens, *NRGT*, 2ème série, Vol. IV, pp. 219–228 (French); Deltenre, pp. 575–595 (Engl., French, German, Dutch); *BFSP*, Vol. 65, 1873–1874, pp. 1005–1014, pp. 1110–1111 (French); *Droit des conflits armés*, pp. 23–32 (French).
Declaration only: Parliamentary Papers, 1875, LXXII, c. 1120 (Engl.); *The Proceedings of the Hague Peace Conferences, 1899*, pp. 564–578 (Engl.); *Conférence internationale de la Paix, 1899*, Deuxième Commission, pp. 133–146 (French); Friedman, pp. 194–203 (Engl.); *Les deux Conférences de la Paix*, pp. 215–221 (French); Heffter-Taube, pp. 73–83 (Russ.); ICRC website: www.icrc.org/ ihl.nsf.

TABLE OF CONTENTS

* * *

I. FINAL PROTOCOL

The Conference assembled at Brussels, on the invitation of the Government of His Majesty the Emperor of Russia, for the purpose of discussing a Project of International Rules on the Laws and Usages of War, has examined the Project submitted to it in a spirit in accordance with the elevated sentiment which had led to its being convoked, and which all the Governments represented had welcomed with sympathy.

This sentiment had already found expression in the Declaration exchanged between the Governments at St. Petersburg in 1868, with reference to the exclusion of explosive bullets.

It had been unanimously declared that the progress of civilization should have the effect of alleviating, as far as possible, the calamities of war; and that the only legitimate object which States should have in view during war is to weaken the enemy without inflicting upon him unnecessary suffering.

These principles met at that time with unanimous approval. At the present time the Conference, following the same path, participates in the conviction expressed by the Government of His Majesty the Emperor of Russia, that a further step may be taken by revising the laws and general usages of war, whether with the object of defining them with greater precision, or with the view of laying down, by a common agreement, certain limits which will restrain, as far as possible, the severities of war.

War being thus regulated would involve less suffering, would be less liable to those aggravations produced by uncertainty, unforeseen events, and the passions excited by the struggle; it would tend more surely to that which should be its final object, viz., the re-establishment of good relations, and a more solid and lasting peace between the belligerent States.

The Conference could respond to those ideas of humanity in no better way than by entering in the same spirit into the examination of the subject they were to discuss. The modifications which have been introduced into the Project, the comments, the reservations, and separate opinions which the Delegates have thought proper to insert in the Protocols, in accordance with instructions, and the particular views of their respective Governments, or their own private opinions, constitute the ensemble of their work. It is of opinion that it may be submitted to the respective Governments which it represents, as a conscientious inquiry of a nature to serve as a basis for an ulterior exchange of ideas, and for the development of the provisions of the Convention of Geneva of 1864 and of the Declaration of St. Petersburg of 1868. It will be their task to ascertain what portion of this work may become the object of an agreement, and what portion requires still further examination.

The Conference, in concluding its work, is of opinion that its debates will have in every case thrown light on those important questions, the regulations of which, should it result in a general agreement, would be a real progress of humanity.

Done at Brussels, 27 August 1874.

[Here follow signatures]

SIGNATURES

The Final Protocol was signed on 27 August 1874 by the representatives of the following states:

Austria-Hungary	Great Britain	Russia
Belgium	Greece	Spain
Denmark	Italy	Sweden and Norway
France	Netherlands	Switzerland
Germany	Portugal	Turkey

II. PROJECT OF AN INTERNATIONAL DECLARATION CONCERNING THE LAWS AND CUSTOMS OF WAR

On Military Authority over Hostile Territory

Article 1. Territory is considered occupied when it is actually placed under the authority of the hostile army.

The occupation extends only to the territory where such authority has been established and can be exercised.

Art. 2. The authority of the legitimate Power being suspended and having in fact passed into the hands of the occupant, the latter shall take all the measures in his power to restore and ensurc, as far as possible, public order and safety.

Art. 3. With this object he shall maintain the laws which were in force in the country in time of peace, and shall not modify, suspend or replace them unless necessary.

Art. 4. The functionaries and employees of every class who consent, on his invitation, to continue their functions, shall enjoy his protection. They shall not be dismissed or subjected to disciplinary punishment unless they fail in fulfilling the obligations undertaken by them, and they shall not be prosecuted unless they betray their trust.

Art. 5. The army of occupation shall only collect the taxes, dues, duties, and tolls imposed for the benefit of the State, or their equivalent, if it is impossible to collect them, and, as far as is possible, in accordance with the existing forms and practice. It shall devote them to defraying the expenses of the administration of the country to the same extent as the legitimate Government was so obligated.

Art. 6. An army of occupation can only take possession of cash, funds, and realizable securities which are strictly the property of the State, depots of arms, means of transport, stores and supplies, and generally, all movable property belonging to the State which may be used for the operations of the war.

Railway plant, land telegraphs, steamers and other ships, apart from cases governed by maritime law, as well as depots of arms and, generally, all kinds of war material, even if belonging to companies or to private persons, are likewise material which may serve for military operations and which cannot be left by the army of occupation at the disposal of the enemy. Railway plant, land telegraphs, as well as steamers and other ships abovementioned shall be restored and compensation fixed when peace is made.

Art. 7. The occupying State shall be regarded only as administrator and usufructuary of public buildings, real estate, forests, and agricultural estates belonging to the hostile

State, and situated in the occupied country. It must safeguard the capital of these properties, and administer them in accordance with the rules of usufruct.

Art. 8. The property of municipalities, that of institutions dedicated to religion, charity and education, the arts and sciences even when State property, shall be treated as private property. All seizure or destruction of, or wilful damage to, institutions of this character, historic monuments, works of art and science should be made the subject of legal proceedings by the competent authorities.

Who should be recognized as Belligerents: Combatants and Non-combatants

Art. 9. The laws, rights, and duties of war apply not only to armies, but also to militia and volunteer corps fulfilling the following conditions:
1. That they be commanded by a person responsible for his subordinates;
2. That they have a fixed distinctive emblem recognizable at a distance;
3. That they carry arms openly; and
4. That they conduct their operations in accordance with the laws and customs of war.

In countries where militia constitute the army, or form part of it, they are included under the denomination *army*.

Art. 10. The population of a territory which has not been occupied, who, on the approach of the enemy, spontaneously take up arms to resist the invading troops without having had time to organize themselves in accordance with Article 9, shall be regarded as belligerents if they respect the laws and customs of war.

Art 11. The armed forces of the belligerent parties may consist of combatants and non-combatants. In case of capture by the enemy, both shall enjoy the rights of prisoners of war.

Means of Injuring the Enemy

Art. 12. The laws of war do not recognize in belligerents an unlimited power in the adoption of means of injuring the enemy.

Art. 13. According to this principle are especially *forbidden*:
(a) Employment of poison or poisoned weapons;
(b) Murder by treachery of individuals belonging to the hostile nation or army;
(c) Murder of an enemy who, having laid down his arms or having no longer means of defense, has surrendered at discretion;
(d) The declaration that no quarter will be given;
(e) The employment of arms, projectiles or material calculated to cause unnecessary suffering, as well as the use of projectiles prohibited by the Declaration of St. Petersburg of 1868;
(f) Making improper use of a flag of truce, of the national flag or of the military insignia and uniform of the enemy, as well as the distinctive badges of the Geneva Convention;
(g) Any destruction or seizure of the enemy's property that is not imperatively demanded by the necessity of war.

Art. 14. Ruses of war and the employment of measures necessary for obtaining information about the enemy and the country (excepting the provisions of Article 36) are considered permissible.

Sieges and Bombardments

Art. 15. Fortified places are alone liable to be besieged. Open towns, agglomerations of dwellings, or villages which are not defended can neither be attacked nor bombarded.

Art. 16. But if a town or fortress, agglomeration of dwellings, or village, is defended, the officer in command of an attacking force must, before commencing a bombardment, except in assault, do all in his power to warn the authorities.

Art. 17. In such cases all necessary steps must be taken to spare, as far as possible, buildings dedicated to art, science, or charitable purposes, hospitals, and places where the sick and wounded are collected provided they are not being used at the time for military purposes. It is the duty of the besieged to indicate the presence of such buildings by distinctive and visible signs to be communicated to the enemy beforehand.

Art. 18. A town taken by assault ought not to be given over to pillage by the victorious troops.

Spies

Art. 19. A person can only be considered a spy when acting clandestinely or on false pretenses he obtains or endeavours to obtain information in the districts occupied by the enemy, with the intention of communicating it to the hostile party.

Art. 20. A spy taken in the act shall be tried and treated according to the laws in force in the army which captures him.

Art. 21. A spy who rejoins the army to which he belongs and who is subsequently captured by the enemy is treated as a prisoner of war and incurs no responsibility for his previous acts.

Art. 22. Soldiers not wearing a disguise who have penetrated into the zone of operations of the hostile army, for the purpose of obtaining information, are not considered spies.

Similarly, the following should not be considered spies, if they are captured by the enemy: soldiers (and also civilians, carrying out their mission openly) entrusted with the delivery of dispatches intended either for their own army or for the enemy's army.

To this class belong likewise, if they are captured, persons sent in balloons for the purpose of carrying dispatches and, generally, of maintaining communications between the different parts of an army or a territory.

Prisoners of War

Art. 23. Prisoners of war are lawful and disarmed enemies.

They are in the power of the hostile Government, but not in that of the individuals or corps who captured them.

They must be humanely treated.

Any act of insubordination justifies the adoption of such measures of severity as may be necessary.

All their personal belongings except arms shall remain their property.

Art. 24. Prisoners of war may be interned in a town, fortress, camp, or other place, under obligation not to go beyond certain fixed limits; but they can only be placed in confinement as an indispensable measure of safety.

Art. 25. Prisoners of war may be employed on certain public works which have no direct connection with the operations in the theatre of war and which are not excessive or humiliating to their military rank, if they belong to the army, or to their official or social position, if they do not belong to it.

They may also, subject to such regulations as may be drawn up by the military authorities, undertake private work.

Their wages shall go towards improving their position or shall be paid to them on their release. In this case the cost of maintenance may be deducted from said wages.

Art. 26. Prisoners of war cannot be compelled in any way to take any part whatever in carrying on the operations of the war.

Art. 27. The Government into whose hands prisoners of war have fallen charges itself with their maintenance.

The conditions of such maintenance may be settled by a reciprocal agreement between the belligerent parties.

In the absence of this agreement, and as a general principle, prisoners of war shall be treated as regards food and clothing, on the same footing as the troops of the Government which captured them.

Art. 28. Prisoners of war are subject to the laws and regulations in force in the army in whose power they are.

Arms may be used, after summoning, against a prisoner of war attempting to escape. If recaptured he is liable to disciplinary punishment or subject to a stricter surveillance.

If, after succeeding in escaping, he is again taken prisoner, he is not liable to punishment for his previous acts.

Art. 29. Every prisoner of war is bound to give, if questioned on the subject, his true name and rank, and if he infringes this rule, he is liable to a curtailment of the advantages accorded to the prisoners of war of his class.

Art. 30. The exchange of prisoners of war is regulated by a mutual understanding between the belligerent parties.

Art. 31. Prisoners of war may be set at liberty on parole if the laws of their country allow it, and, in such cases, they are bound, on their personal honour, scrupulously to fulfill, both towards their own Government and the Government by which they were made prisoners, the engagements they have contracted.

In such cases their own Government ought neither to require of nor accept from them any service incompatible with the parole given.

Art. 32. A prisoner of war cannot be compelled to accept his liberty on parole; similarly the hostile Government is not obliged to accede to the request of the prisoner to be set at liberty on parole.

Art. 33. Any prisoner of war liberated on parole and recaptured bearing arms against the Government to which he had pledged his honour may be deprived of the rights accorded to prisoners of war and brought before the courts.

Art. 34. Individuals in the vicinity of armies but not directly forming part of them, such as correspondents, newspaper reporters, sutlers, contractors, etc., can also be made prisoners. These prisoners should however be in possession of a permit issued by the competent authority and of a certificate of identity.

The Sick and Wounded

Art. 35. The obligations of belligerents with respect to the service of the sick and wounded are governed by the Geneva Convention of 22 August 1864, save such modifications as the latter may undergo.

On the Military Power with respect to Private Persons

Art. 36. The population of occupied territory cannot be forced to take part in military operations against its own country.

Art. 37. The population of occupied territory cannot be compelled to swear allegiance to the hostile Power.

Art. 38. Family honour and rights, and the lives and property of persons, as well as their religious convictions and their practice, must be respected. Private property cannot be confiscated.

Art. 39. Pillage is formally forbidden.

On Taxes and Requisitions

Art. 40. As private property should be respected, the enemy will demand from communes or inhabitants only such payments and services as are connected with the generally recognized necessities of war, in proportion to the resources of the country, and not implying, with regard to the inhabitants, the obligation of taking part in operations of war against their country.

Art. 41. The enemy in levying contributions, whether as an equivalent for taxes (see Article 5) or for payments that should be made in kind, or as fines, shall proceed, so far as possible, only in accordance with the rules for incidence and assessment in force in the territory occupied.

The civil authorities of the legitimate Government shall lend it their assistance if they have remained at their posts.

Contributions shall be imposed only on the order and on the responsibility of the commander in chief or the superior civil authority established by the enemy in the occupied territory.

For every contribution, a receipt shall be given to the person furnishing it.

Art. 42. Requisitions shall be made only with the authorization of the commander in the territory occupied.

For every requisition indemnity shall be granted or a receipt delivered.

On Parlementaires

Art. 43. A person is regarded as a parlementaire who has been authorized by one of the belligerents to enter into communication with the other, and who advances bearing a white flag, accompanied by a trumpeter (bugler or drummer) or also by a flag-bearer. He shall have aright to inviolability as well as the trumpeter (bugler or drummer) and the flag-bearer who accompany him.

Art. 44. The commander to whom a parlementaire is sent is not in all cases and under all conditions obliged to receive him.

It is lawful for him to take all the necessary steps to prevent the parlementaire taking advantage of his stay within the radius of the enemy's position to the prejudice of the latter, and if the parlementaire has rendered himself guilty of such an abuse of confidence, he has the right to detain him temporarily.

He may likewise declare beforehand that he will not receive parlementaires during a certain period. Parlementaires presenting themselves after such a notification, from the side to which it has been given, forfeit the right of inviolability.

Art. 45. The parlementaire loses his rights of inviolability if it is proved in a clear and incontestable manner that he has taken advantage of his privileged position to provoke or commit an act of treason.

Capitulations

Art. 46. The conditions of capitulations are discussed between the Contracting Parties.

They must not be contrary to military honour.

Once settled by a convention, they must be scrupulously observed by both parties.

Armistices

Art. 47. An armistice suspends military operations by mutual agreement, between the belligerent parties. If its duration is not defined, the belligerent parties may resume operations at any time, provided always that the enemy is warned within the time agreed upon, in accordance with the terms of the armistice.

Art. 48. The armistice may be general or local. The first suspends the military operations of the belligerent States everywhere; the second only between certain fractions of the belligerent armies and within a fixed radius.

Art. 49. An armistice must be officially and without delay notified to the competent authorities and to the troops. Hostilities are suspended immediately after the notification.

Art. 50. It rests with the Contracting Parties to settle, in the terms of the armistice, what communications may be held between the populations.

Art. 51. The violation of the armistice by one of the parties gives the other party the right of denouncing it.

Art. 52. A violation of the terms of the armistice by individuals acting on their own initiative only entitles the injured party to demand the punishment of the offenders or, if necessary, compensation for the losses sustained.

Interned Belligerents and Wounded Cared for by Neutrals

Art. 53. A neutral State which receives on its territory troops belonging to the belligerent armies shall intern them, as far as possible, at a distance from the theatre of war.

It may keep them in camps and even confine them in fortresses or in places set apart for this purpose.

It shall decide whether officers can be left at liberty on giving their parole not to leave the neutral territory without permission.

Art. 54. In the absence of a special convention, the neutral State shall supply the interned with the food, clothing and relief required by humanity.

At the conclusion of peace the expenses caused by the internment shall be made good.

Art. 55. A neutral State may authorize the passage through its territory of the wounded or sick belonging to the belligerent armies, on condition that the trains bringing them shall carry neither personnel nor material of war.

In such a case, the neutral State is bound to take whatever measures of safety and control are necessary for the purpose.

Art. 56. The Geneva Convention applies to sick and wounded interned in neutral territory.

No. 3

THE LAWS OF WAR ON LAND

Manual published by the Institute of International Law *(Oxford Manual)*
Adopted by the Institute of International Law at Oxford, 9 September 1880

INTRODUCTORY NOTE: The Institute of International Law, founded in 1873, is a scientific association composed of a fixed number of members and associates of different nations. Its objective is to aid the growth of international law by endeavouring to state the general principles of the science of international law and by giving assistance to the gradual and progressive codification of international law. The *Manual* reprinted below was drafted by Gustave Moynier and unanimously adopted by the Institute. Its purpose is stated in the preface. (See also the note on the Brussels Conference, *No. 2.*)

AUTHENTIC TEXT: French. The English translation below is reprinted from Scott, *Resolutions of the Institute of International Law*, pp. 26–42.

TEXT PUBLISHED IN: *Annuaire de l'Institut de Droit international*, Vol. V (1881–1882), pp. 156–174 (French); *Annuaire de l'Institut de Droit international,* édition abrégée, Vol. I, pp. 707–727 (French); Institut de Droit international, *Tableau général des résolutions (1873–1956),* publié par Hans Wehberg, Bâle, 1957, pp. 180–198 (French); Scott, *Resolutions of the Institute of International Law*, pp. 26–42 (Engl.); Deltenre, pp. 635–665 (Engl., French, German, Dutch); *Droit des conflits armés*, pp. 33–47 (French); ICRC website: www.icrc.org/ihl.nsf.

TABLE OF CONTENTS

* * *

PREFACE

War holds a great place in history, and it is not to be supposed that men will soon give it up – in spite of the protests which it arouses and the horror which it inspires – because it appears to be the only possible issue of disputes which threaten the existence of States, their liberty, their vital interests. But the gradual improvement in customs should be reflected in the method of conducting war. It is worthy of civilized nations to seek, as has been well said,[1] "to restrain the destructive force of war, while recognizing its inexorable necessities".

This problem is not easy of solution; however, some points have already been solved, and very recently the draft of Declaration of Brussels has been a solemn pronouncement of the good intentions of governments in this connection. It may be said that independently of the international laws existing on this subject, there are to-day certain principles of justice which guide the public conscience, which are manifested even by general customs, but which it would be well to fix and make obligatory. That is what the Conference of Brussels attempted, at the suggestion of His Majesty the Emperor of Russia, and it is what the Institute of International Law, in its turn, is trying to-day to contribute. The Institute attempts this although the governments have not ratified the draft issued by the Conference at Brussels, because since 1874 ideas, aided by reflection and experience, have had time to mature, and because it seems less difficult than it did then to trace rules which would be acceptable to all peoples.

The Institute, too, does not propose an international treaty, which might perhaps be premature or at least very difficult to obtain; but, being bound by its by-laws to work, among other things, for the observation of the laws of war, it believes it is fulfilling a duty in offering to the governments a *Manual* suitable as the basis for national legislation in each State, and in accord with both the progress of juridical science and the needs of civilized armies.

Rash and extreme rules will not, furthermore, be found therein. The Institute has not sought innovations in drawing up the *Manual*; it has contented itself with stating clearly and codifying the accepted ideas of our age so far as this has appeared allowable and practicable. By so doing, it believes it is rendering a service to military men themselves. In fact so long as the demands of opinion remain indeterminate, belligerents are exposed to painful uncertainty and to endless accusations. A positive set of rules, on the contrary, if they are judicious, serves the interests of belligerents and is far from hindering them, since by preventing the unchaining of passion and savage instincts – which battle always awakens, as much as it awakens courage and manly virtues, – it strengthens the discipline which is the strength of armies; it also ennobles their patriotic mission in the eyes of the soldiers by keeping them within the limits of respect due to the rights of humanity.

But in order to attain this end it is not sufficient for sovereigns to promulgate new laws. It is essential, too, that they make these laws known among all people, so that when a war is declared, the men called upon to take up arms to defend the causes of the

[1] Baron Jomini.

belligerent States, may be thoroughly impregnated with the special rights and duties attached to the execution of such a command.

The Institute, with a view to assisting the authorities in accomplishing this part of their task, has given its work a popular form, attaching thereto statements of the reasons therefor, from which the text of a law may be easily secured when desired.

PART I. GENERAL PRINCIPLES

Article 1. The state of war does not admit of acts of violence, save between the armed forces of belligerent States.

Persons not forming part of a belligerent armed force should abstain from such acts.

> This rule implies a distinction between the individuals who compose the "armed force" of a State and its other *ressortissants*. A definition of the term "armed force" is, therefore, necessary.

Art. 2. The armed force of a State includes:

1. The army properly so called, including the militia;
2. The national guards, landsturm, free corps, and other bodies which fulfil the three following conditions:
   (a) That they are under the direction of a responsible chief;
   (b) That they must have a uniform, or a fixed distinctive emblem recognizable at a distance, and worn by individuals composing such corps;
   (c) That they carry arms openly;
3. The crews of men-of-war and other military boats;
4. The inhabitants of non-occupied territory, who, on the approach of the enemy, take up arms spontaneously and openly to resist the invading troops, even if they have not had time to organize themselves.

Art. 3. Every belligerent armed force is bound to conform to the laws of war.

> The only legitimate end that States may have in war being to weaken the military strength of the enemy (*Declaration of St. Petersburg, 1868*),

Art. 4. The laws of war do not recognize in belligerents an unlimited liberty as to the means of injuring the enemy.

They are to abstain especially from all needless severity, as well as from all perfidious, unjust, or tyrannical acts.

Art. 5. Military conventions made between belligerents during the continuance of war, such as armistices and capitulations, must be scrupulously observed and respected.

Art. 6. No invaded territory is regarded as conquered until the end of the war; until that time the occupant exercises, in such territory, only a *de facto* power, essentially provisional in character.

PART II. APPLICATION OF GENERAL PRINCIPLES

I. Hostilities

A. Rules of Conduct with Regard to Individuals

(a) Inoffensive Populations

> The contest being carried on by "armed forces" only (Article 1),

Art. 7. It is forbidden to maltreat inoffensive populations.

(b) Means of Injuring the Enemy

As the struggle must be honourable (Article 4),

Art. 8. It is forbidden:
(a) To make use of poison, in any form whatever;
(b) To make treacherous attempts upon the life of an enemy; as, for example, by keeping assassins in pay or by feigning to surrender;
(c) To attack an enemy while concealing the distinctive signs of an armed force;
(d) To make improper use of the national flag, military insignia or uniform of the enemy, of the flag of truce and of the protective signs prescribed by the *Geneva Convention* (Articles 17 and 40).

As needless severity should be avoided (Article 4),

Art. 9. It is forbidden:
(a) To employ arms, projectiles, or materials of any kind calculated to cause superfluous suffering, or to aggravate wounds – notably projectiles of less weight than four hundred grams which are explosive or are charged with fulminating or inflammable substances (*Declaration of St. Petersburg*);
(b) To injure or kill an enemy who has surrendered at discretion or is disabled, and to declare in advance that quarter will not be given, even by those who do not ask it for themselves.

(c) The Sick and Wounded, and the Sanitary Service

The following provisions (Articles 10 to 18), drawn from the *Geneva Convention*, exempt the sick and wounded, and the personnel of the sanitary service, from many of the needless hardships to which they were formerly exposed:

Art. 10. Wounded or sick soldiers should be brought in and cared for, to whatever nation they belong.

Art. 11. Commanders in chief have power to deliver immediately to the enemy outposts hostile soldiers who have been wounded in an engagement, when circumstances permit and with the consent of both parties.

Art. 12. Evacuations, together with the persons under whose direction they take place, shall be protected by neutrality.

Art. 13. Persons employed in hospitals and ambulances – including the staff for superintendence, medical service, administration and transport of wounded, as well as the chaplains, and the members and agents of relief associations which are duly authorized to assist the regular sanitary staff – are considered as neutral while so employed, and so long as there remain any wounded to bring in or to succour.

Art. 14. The personnel designated in the preceding article should continue, after occupation by the enemy, to tend, according to their needs, the sick and wounded in the ambulance or hospital which it serves.

Art. 15. When such personnel requests to withdraw, the commander of the occupying troops sets the time of departure, which however he can only delay for a short time in case of military necessity.

Art. 16. Measures should be taken to assure, if possible, to neutralized persons who have fallen into the hands of the enemy, the enjoyment of fitting maintenance.

Art. 17. The neutralized sanitary staff should wear a white arm-badge with a red cross, but the delivery thereof belongs exclusively to the military authority.

Art. 18. The generals of the belligerent Powers should appeal to the humanity of the inhabitants, and should endeavour to induce them to assist the wounded by pointing out to them the advantages that will result to themselves from so doing (Articles 36 and 59). They should regard as inviolable those who respond to this appeal.

(d) The Dead

Art. 19. It is forbidden to rob or mutilate the dead lying on the field of battle.

Art. 20. The dead should never be buried until all articles on them which may serve to fix their identity, such as pocket-books, numbers, etc., shall have been collected. The articles thus collected from the dead of the enemy are transmitted to its army or government.

(e) Who May Be Made Prisoners of War

Art. 21. Individuals who form a part of the belligerent armed force, if they fall into the hands of the enemy, are to be treated as prisoners of war, in conformity with Articles 61 *et seq*. The same rule applies to messengers openly carrying official dispatches, and to civil aeronauts charged with observing the enemy, or with the maintenance of communications between the various parts of the army or territory.

Art. 22. Individuals who accompany an army, but who are not a part of the regular armed force of the State, such as correspondents, traders, sutlers, etc., and who fall into the hands of the enemy, may be detained for such length of time only as is warranted by strict military necessity.

(f) Spies

Art. 23. Individuals captured as spies cannot demand to be treated as prisoners of war.

But

Art. 24. Individuals may not be regarded as spies, who, belonging to the armed force of either belligerent, have penetrated, without disguise, into the zone of operations of the enemy, – nor bearers of official dispatches, carrying out their mission openly, nor aeronauts (Article 21).

In order to avoid the abuses to which accusations of espionage too often give rise in war it is important to assert emphatically that

Art. 25. No person charged with espionage shall be punished until the judicial authority shall have pronounced judgment.

Moreover, it is admitted that

Art. 26. A spy who succeeds in quitting the territory occupied by the enemy incurs no responsibility for his previous acts, should he afterwards fall into the hands of that enemy.

(g) Parlementaires

Art. 27. A person is regarded as a parlementaire and has a right to inviolability who has been authorized by one of the belligerents to enter into communication with the other, and who advances bearing a white flag.

Art. 28. He may be accompanied by a bugler or a drummer, by a colour-bearer, and, if need be, by a guide and interpreter, who also are entitled to inviolability.

> The necessity of this prerogative is evident. It is, moreover, frequently exercised in the interest of humanity.
>
> But it must not be injurious to the adverse party. This is why

Art. 29. The commander to whom a parlementaire is sent is not in all cases obliged to receive him.

> Besides,

Art. 30. The commander who receives a parlementaire has a right to take all the necessary steps to prevent the presence of the enemy within his lines from being prejudicial to him.

> The parlementaire and those who accompany him should behave fairly towards the enemy receiving them (Article 4).

Art. 31. If a parlementaire abuse the trust reposed in him he may be temporarily detained, and, if it be proved that he has taken advantage of his privileged position to abet a treasonable act, he forfeits his right to inviolability.

B. Rules of Conduct with Regard to Things

(a) Means of Injuring – Bombardment

> Certain precautions are made necessary by the rule that a belligerent must abstain from useless severity (Article 4). In accordance with this principle

Art. 32. It is forbidden:
(a) To pillage, even towns taken by assault;
(b) To destroy public or private property, if this destruction is not demanded by an imperative necessity of war;
(c) To attack and to bombard undefended places.

> If it is incontestable that belligerents have the right to resort to bombardment against fortresses and other places in which the enemy is intrenched, considerations of humanity require that this means of coercion be surrounded with certain modifying influences which will restrict as far as possible the effects to the hostile armed force and its means of defense. This is why

Art. 33. The commander of an attacking force, save in cases of open assault, shall, before undertaking a bombardment, make every due effort to give notice thereof to the local authorities.

Art. 34. In case of bombardment all necessary steps must be taken to spare, if it can be done, buildings dedicated to religion, art, science and charitable purposes, hospitals and places where the sick and wounded are gathered on the condition that they are not being utilized at the time, directly or indirectly, for defense. It is the duty of the besieged to indicate the presence of such buildings by visible signs notified to the assailant beforehand.

(b) Sanitary Material

The arrangements for the relief of the wounded, which are made the subject of Articles 10 *et seq.*, would be inadequate were not sanitary establishments also granted special protection. Hence, in accordance with the *Geneva Convention*,

Art. 35. Ambulances and hospitals for the use of armies are recognized as neutral and should, as such, be protected and respected by belligerents, so long as any sick or wounded are therein.

Art. 36. The same rule applies to private buildings, or parts of buildings, in which sick or wounded are gathered and cared for.

Nevertheless,

Art. 37. The neutrality of hospitals and ambulances ceases if they are guarded by a military force; this does not preclude the presence of police guard.

Art. 38. As the equipment of military hospitals remains subject to the laws of war, persons attached to such hospitals cannot, in withdrawing, carry away any articles but such as are their private property. Ambulances, on the contrary, retain all their equipment.

Art. 39. In the circumstances referred to in the above paragraph, the term "ambulance" is applied to field hospitals and other temporary establishments which follow the troops on the field of battle to receive the sick and wounded.

Art. 40. A distinctive and uniform flag is adopted for ambulances, hospitals, and evacuations. It bears a red cross on a white ground It must always be accompanied by the national flag.

II. Occupied Territory

A. Definition

Art. 41. Territory is regarded as occupied when, as the consequence of invasion by hostile forces, the State to which it belongs has ceased, in fact, to exercise its ordinary authority therein, and the invading State is alone in a position to maintain order there. The limits within which this state of affairs exists determine the extent and duration of the occupation.

B. Rules of Conduct with Respect to Persons

In consideration of the new relations which arise from the provisional change of government (Article 6),

Art. 42. It is the duty of the occupying military authority to inform the inhabitants at the earliest practicable moment, of the powers that it exercises, as well as of the local extent of the occupation.

Art. 43. The occupant should take all due and needful measures to restore and ensure public order and public safety.

To that end

Art. 44. The occupant should maintain the laws which were in force in the country in time of peace, and should not modify, suspend, or replace them, unless necessary.

Art. 45. The civil functionaries and employees of every class who consent to continue to perform their duties are under the protection of the occupant.

They may always be dismissed, and they always have the right to resign their places.

They should not be summarily punished unless they fail to fulfil obligations accepted by them, and should be handed over to justice only if they violate these obligations.

Art. 46. In case of urgency, the occupant may demand the cooperation of the inhabitants, in order to provide for the necessities of local administration.

As occupation does not entail upon the inhabitants a change of nationality,

Art. 47. The population of the invaded district cannot be compelled to swear allegiance to the hostile Power; but inhabitants who commit acts of hostility against the occupant are punishable (Article 1).

Art. 48. The inhabitants of an occupied territory who do not submit to the orders of the occupant may be compelled to do so. The occupant, however, cannot compel the inhabitants to assist him in his works of attack or defense, or to take part in military operations against their own country (Article 4).

Besides,

Art. 49. Family honour and rights, the lives of individuals, as well as their religious convictions and practice, must be respected (Article 4).

C. Rules of Conduct with Regard to Property

(a) Public Property

Although the occupant replaces the enemy State in the government of the invaded territory, his power is not absolute. So long as the fate of this territory remains in suspense – that is, until peace – the occupant is not free to dispose of what still belongs to the enemy and is not of use in military operation. Hence the following rules:

Art. 50. The occupant can only take possession of cash, funds and realizable or negotiable securities which are strictly the property of the State, depots of arms, supplies, and, in general, movable property of the State of such character as to be useful in military operations.

Art. 51. Means of transportation (railways, boats, etc.), as well as land telegraphs and landing-cables, can only be appropriated to the use of the occupant. Their destruction is forbidden, unless it be demanded by military necessity. They are restored when peace is made in the condition in which they then are.

Art. 52. The occupant can only act in the capacity of provisional administrator in respect to real property, such as buildings, forests, agricultural establishments, belonging to the enemy State (Article 6).

It must safeguard the capital of these properties and see to their maintenance.

Art. 53. The property of municipalities, and that of institutions devoted to religion, charity, education, art and science, cannot be seized.

All destruction or wilful damage to institutions of this character, historic monuments, archives, works of art, or science, is formally forbidden, save when urgently demanded by military necessity.

(b) Private Property

If the powers of the occupant are limited with respect to the property of the enemy State, with greater reason are they limited with respect to the property of individuals.

Art. 54. Private property, whether belonging to individuals or corporations, must be respected, and can be confiscated only under the limitations contained in the following articles.

Art. 55. Means of transportation (railways, boats, etc.), telegraphs, depots of arms and munitions of war, although belonging to companies or to individuals, may be seized by the occupant, but must be restored, if possible, and compensation fixed when peace is made.

Art. 56. Impositions in kind (requisitions) demanded from communes or inhabitants should be in proportion to the necessities of war as generally recognized, and in proportion to the resources of the country. Requisitions can only be made on the authority of the commander in the locality occupied.

Art. 57. The occupant may collect, in the way of dues and taxes, only those already established for the benefit of the State. He employs them to defray the expenses of administration of the country, to the extent in which the legitimate government was bound.

Art. 58. The occupant cannot collect extraordinary contributions of money, save as an equivalent for fines, or imposts not paid, or for payments not made in kind. Contributions in money can be imposed only on the order and responsibility of the general in chief, or of the superior civil authority established in the occupied territory, as far as possible, in accordance with the rules of assessment and incidence of the taxes in force.

Art. 59. In the apportionment of burdens relating to the quartering of troops and war contributions, account is taken of the charitable zeal displayed by the inhabitants in behalf of the wounded.

Art. 60. Requisitioned articles, when they are not paid for in cash, and war contributions are evidenced by receipts. Measures should be taken to assure the *bona fide* character and regularity of these receipts.

III. Prisoners of war

A. Rules for Captivity

The confinement of prisoners of war is not in the nature of a penalty for crime (Article 21): neither is it an act of vengeance. It is a temporary detention only, entirely without penal character.

In the following provisions, therefore, regard has been had to the consideration due them as prisoners, and to the necessity of their secure detention.

Art. 61. Prisoners of war are in the power of the hostile government, but not in that of the individuals or corps who captured them.

Art. 62. They are subject to the laws and regulations in force in the army of the enemy.

Art. 63. They must be humanely treated.

Art. 64. All their personal belongings, except arms, remain their property.

Art. 65. Every prisoner is bound to give, if questioned on the subject, his true name and rank. Should he fail to do so, he may be deprived of all, or a part, of the advantages accorded to prisoners of his class.

Art. 66. Prisoners may be interned in a town, a fortress, a camp, or other place, under obligation not to go beyond certain fixed limits; but they may only be placed in confinement as an indispensable measure of safety.

Art. 67. Any act of insubordination justifies the adoption towards them of such measure of severity as may be necessary.

Art. 68. Arms may be used, after summoning, against a prisoner attempting to escape.

If he is recaptured before being able to rejoin his own army or to quit the territory of his captor, he is only liable to disciplinary punishment, or subject to a stricter surveillance.

But if, after succeeding in escaping, he is again captured, he is not liable to punishment for his previous flight.

If, however, the fugitive so recaptured or retaken has given his parole not to escape, he may be deprived of the rights of a prisoner of war.

Art. 69. The government into whose hands prisoners have fallen is charged with their maintenance.

In the absence of an agreement on this point between the belligerent parties, prisoners are treated, as regards food and clothing, on the same peace footing as the troops of the government which captured them.

Art. 70. Prisoners cannot be compelled in any manner to take any part whatever in the operations of war, nor compelled to give information about their country or their army.

Art. 71. They may be employed on public works which have no direct connection with the operations in the theatre of war, which are not excessive and are not humiliating either to their military rank, if they belong to the army, or to their official or social position, if they do not form part thereof.

Art. 72. In case of their being authorized to engage in private industries, their pay for such services may be collected by the authority in charge of them. The sums so received may be employed in bettering their condition, or may be paid to them on their release, subject to deduction, if that course be deemed expedient, of the expense of their maintenance.

B. Termination of Captivity

The reasons justifying detention of the captured enemy exist only during the continuance of the war.

Art. 73. The captivity of prisoners of war ceases, as a matter of right, at the conclusion of peace; but their liberation is then regulated by agreement between the belligerents.

Before that time, and by virtue of the *Geneva Convention*,

Art. 74. It also ceases as of right for wounded or sick prisoners who, after being cured, are found to be unfit for further military service.

The captor should then send them back to their country.

During the war

Art. 75. Prisoners of war may be released in accordance with a cartel of exchange, agreed upon by the belligerent parties.

Even without exchange

Art. 76. Prisoners may be set at liberty on parole, if the laws of their country do not forbid it.

In this case they are bound, on their personal honour, scrupulously to fulfil the engagements which they have freely contracted, and which should be clearly specified. On its part, their own government should not demand or accept from them any service incompatible with the parole given.

Art. 77. A prisoner cannot be compelled to accept his liberty on parole. Similarly, the hostile government is not obliged to accede to the request of a prisoner to be set at liberty on parole.

Art. 78. Any prisoner liberated on parole and recaptured bearing arms against the government to which he had given such parole may be deprived of his rights as a prisoner of war, unless since his liberation he has been included in an unconditional exchange of prisoners.

IV. Persons Interned in Neutral Territory

It is universally admitted that a neutral State cannot, without compromising its neutrality, lend aid to either belligerent, or permit them to make use of its territory. On the other hand, considerations of humanity dictate that asylum should not be refused to individuals who take refuge in neutral territory to escape death or captivity. Hence the following provisions, calculated to reconcile the opposing interests involved.

Art. 79. A neutral State on whose territory troops or individuals belonging to the armed forces of the belligerents take refuge should intern them, as far as possible, at a distance from the theatre of war.

It should do the same towards those who make use of its territory for military operations or services.

Art. 80. The interned may be kept in camps or even confined in fortresses or other places.

The neutral State decides whether officers can be left at liberty on parole by taking an engagement not to leave the neutral territory without permission.

Art. 81. In the absence of a special convention concerning the maintenance of the interned, the neutral State supplies them with the food, clothing, and relief required by humanity.

It also takes care of the *matériel* brought in by the interned.

When peace has been concluded, or sooner if possible, the expenses caused by the internment are repaid to the neutral State by the belligerent State to which the interned belong.

Art. 82. The provisions of the *Geneva Convention* of 22 August 1864 (Articles 10–18, 35–40, 59 and 74 above given), are applicable to the sanitary staff, as well as to the sick and wounded, who take refuge in, or are conveyed to, neutral territory.

In particular,

Art. 83. Evacuations of wounded and sick not prisoners may pass through neutral territory, provided the personnel and material accompanying them are exclusively sanitary. The neutral State through whose territory these evacuations are made is bound to take whatever measures of safety and control are necessary to secure the strict observance of the above conditions.

PART III. PENAL SANCTION

If any of the foregoing rules be violated, the offending parties should be punished, after a judicial hearing, by the belligerent in whose hands they are. Therefore

Art. 84. Offenders against the laws of war are liable to the punishments specified in the penal law.

This mode of repression, however, is only applicable when the person of the offender can be secured. In the contrary case, the criminal law is powerless, and, if the injured party deem the misdeed so serious in character as to make it necessary to recall the enemy to a respect for law, no other recourse than a resort to reprisals remains.

Reprisals are an exception to the general rule of equity, that an innocent person ought not to suffer for the guilty. They are also at variance with the rule that each belligerent should conform to the rules of war, without reciprocity on the part of the enemy. This necessary rigour, however, is modified to some extent by the following restrictions:

Art. 85. Reprisals are formally prohibited in case the injury complained of has been repaired.

Art. 86. In grave cases in which reprisals appear to be absolutely necessary, their nature and scope shall never exceed the measure of the infraction of the laws of war committed by the enemy.

They can only be resorted to with the authorization of the commander in chief.

They must conform in all cases to the laws of humanity and morality.

No. 4

FINAL ACT OF THE INTERNATIONAL PEACE CONFERENCE

Signed at The Hague, 29 July 1899

INTRODUCTORY NOTE: The First Hague Peace Conference of 1899 was convened on the initiative of the Czar of Russia, Nicholas II, "with the object of seeking the most effective means of ensuring to all peoples the benefits of a real and lasting peace, and, above all, of limiting the progressive development of existing armaments" (Russian note of 30 December 1898/11 January 1899). The Conference, at which 26 governments were represented, assembled on 18 May 1899 and adjourned on 29 July 1899. It failed to reach agreement on the primary object for which it was called, namely the limitation or reduction of armaments, but adopted the three Conventions and the other acts mentioned in the Final Protocol. Provision was made for the convening of a second conference. Russia being at war with Japan in the following years, the President of the United States of America undertook the first steps with a view to convening this second conference. After the termination of the Russo-Japanese war the Czar of Russia resumed the initiative and proposed the holding of the Second International Peace Conference at The Hague. The programme was drafted by Russia. The Conference, at which 44 states were represented, lasted from 15 June until 18 October 1907. It revised the three Conventions of 1899 and adopted ten new Conventions as well as a number of other acts mentioned in the Final Act of 1907. It recommended the holding of a third international peace conference. Due to the outbreak of the First World War the third conference never took place.

The Final Acts constitute authoritative statements of the results achieved. They were signed by the delegates but not ratified by the participating states. They have no binding force.

AUTHENTIC TEXT: French. The English translation below is reprinted from Scott, *Hague Conventions*, pp. 1–31. It reproduces the translations of the United States Department of State.

TEXT PUBLISHED IN: *Conférence internationale de la Paix, 1899*, pp. 216–223 (French); *Les deux Conférences de la Paix*, pp. 5–11 (French); *Les Conférences de la Paix de La Haye de 1899 et 1907, Acte Final*, Paris, A. Pédone, 1927, pp. 3–7 (French); Scott, *Hague Conventions*, pp. 1–31, 39 (Engl.); Scott, *Les Conventions de La Haye*, pp. 1–31, 39 (French); Scott, *Les Conférences de La Haye*, pp. 3–7 (French); Martens, *NRGT*, 2ème série, Vol. XXVI, pp. 258–266 (French); Deltenre, pp. 146–151 (Engl., French, German, Dutch); Olivart, Vol. XII, pp. 549–566 (French); *BFSP*, Vol. 91, 1898–1899, pp. 963–970 (French); Higgins, pp. 60–71 (Engl., French); *AJIL*, Vol. 1, 1907, Suppl.. pp. 103–107 (Engl., French); De Clercq, Vol. XXI, pp. 745–754 (French); Bustamante, pp. 182–185 (Span.); *Droit des conflits armés*, pp. 49–52 (French); ICRC website: www.icrc.org/ihl.nsf.

* * *

The International Peace Conference, convoked in the best interests of humanity by His Majesty the Emperor of All the Russias, assembled, on the invitation of the Government of Her Majesty the Queen of the Netherlands, in the Royal House in the Wood at The Hague on 18 May 1899.

The Powers enumerated in the following list took part in the Conference, to which they appointed the delegates named below:

[Here follow the names of delegates]

In a series of meetings, between 18 May and 29 July 1899, in which the constant desire of the delegates above-mentioned has been to realize, in the fullest manner possible, the generous views of the august initiator of the Conference and the intentions of their Governments, the Conference has agreed, for submission for signature by the plenipotentiaries, on the text of the Convention and Declarations enumerated below and annexed to the present Act:

I. Convention for the peaceful adjustment of international differences.
II. Convention regarding the laws and customs of war on land.
III. Convention for the adaptation to maritime warfare of the principles of the Geneva Convention of 22 August 1864.
IV. Three Declarations:
   1. *To prohibit the launching of projectiles and explosives from balloons or by other similar new methods.*
   2. *To prohibit the use of projectiles, the only object of which is the diffusion of asphyxiating or deleterious gases.*
   3. *To prohibit the use of bullets which expand or flatten easily in the human body, such as bullets with a hard envelope, of which the envelope does not entirely cover the core or is pierced with incisions.*

These Conventions and Declarations shall form so many separate Acts. These Acts shall be dated this day, and may be signed up to 31 December 1899, by the Plenipotentiaries of the Powers represented at the International Peace Conference at The Hague.

Guided by the same sentiments, the Conference has adopted unanimously the following Resolution:

"The Conference is of opinion that the restriction of military charges, which are at present a heavy burden on the world, is extremely desirable for the increase of the material and moral welfare of mankind."

It has besides formulated the following Voeux*:*

1. *The Conference, taking into consideration the preliminary step taken by the Swiss Federal Government for the revision of the Geneva Convention, expresses the wish that steps may be shortly taken for the assembly of a special Conference having for its object the revision of that Convention.*

   This wish was voted unanimously.
2. *The Conference expresses the wish that the questions of the rights and duties of neutrals may be inserted in the program of a Conference in the near future.*
3. *The Conference expresses the wish that the questions with regard to rifles and naval guns, as considered by it, may be studied by the Governments with the object of coming to an agreement respecting the employment of new types and calibers.*

4. *The Conference expresses the wish that the Governments, taking into consideration the proposals made at the Conference, may examine the possibility of an agreement as to the limitation of armed forces by land and sea, and of war budgets.*
5. *The Conference expresses the wish that the proposal, which contemplates the declaration of the inviolability of private property in naval warfare, may be referred to a subsequent Conference for consideration.*
6. *The Conference expresses the wish that the proposal to settle the question of the bombardment of ports, towns, and villages by a naval force may be referred to a subsequent Conference for consideration.*

The last five wishes were voted unanimously, saving some abstentions.

In faith of which, the Plenipotentiaries have signed the present Act, and have affixed their seals thereto.

Done at The Hague, 29 July 1899, in one copy only, which shall be deposited in the Ministry for Foreign Affairs, and of which copies, duly certified, shall be delivered to all the Powers represented at the Conference.

[Here follow signatures]

SIGNATURES[1]

The Final Act was signed by the plenipotentiaries of all the powers represented at the Conference, to wit:

Austria-Hungary
Belgium
Bulgaria
China
Denmark
France
Germany
Great Britain
Greece
Italy
Japan
Luxemburg
Mexico
Montenegro
Netherlands
Persia
Portugal
Romania
Russia
Serbia
Siam
Spain
Sweden and Norway
Switzerland
Turkey
United States

[1] According to *Conférence internationale de la Paix, 1899*, pp. 216–223.

No. 5

FINAL ACT OF THE SECOND INTERNATIONAL PEACE CONFERENCE

Signed at The Hague, 18 October 1907

INTRODUCTORY NOTE: See note introducing the Final Act of the International Peace Conference of 1899 (*No. 4*).

AUTHENTIC TEXT: French. The English translation below is reprinted from Scott, *Hague Conventions*, pp. 1–31. It reproduces the translation of the United States Department of State.

TEXT PUBLISHED IN: *Conférence internationale de la Paix, 1907*, pp. 689–707 (French); *Les deux Conférences de la Paix*, pp. 61–71 (French); Scott, *Hague Conventions*, pp. 1–40 (Engl.); Scott, *Les Conventions de La Haye*, pp. 1–40 (French); Scott, *Les Conférences de La Haye*, pp. 29–41 (French); Martens, *NRGT*, 3ème série, Vol. III, pp. 323–359 (French, German); Deltenre, pp. 420–441 (Engl., French, German, Dutch); Higgins, pp. 60–71 (Engl., French); Malloy, Vol. II, pp. 2369–2385 (Engl.); *CTS*, Vol. 205, 1907, pp. 216–233 (French); *Droit des conflits armés*, pp. 53–57 (French); *AJIL*, Vol. 2, 1908, Suppl., pp. 1–43 (Engl., French); Briceño, pp. 202–205 (Span.); *Revista de Derecho Internacional y politica exterior*, Crónica, Año III, 1907, pp. 50–57 (Span.); Bustamante, pp. 235–250 (Span.); ICRC website: www.icrc.org/ihl.nsf.

* * *

The Second International Peace Conference, proposed in the first instance by the President of the United States of America, having been convoked, on the invitation of His Majesty the Emperor of All the Russias, by Her Majesty the Queen of the Netherlands, assembled on 15 June 1907, at The Hague, in the Hall of the Knights, for the purpose of giving a fresh development to the humanitarian principles which served as a basis for the work of the First Conference of 1899. The following Powers took part in the Conference, and appointed the delegates named below:

[Here follow the names of delegates]

At a series of meetings, held from 15 June to 18 October 1907, in which the above delegates were throughout animated by the desire to realize, in the fullest possible measure, the generous views of the august initiator of the Conference and the intentions of their Governments, the Conference drew up, for submission for signature by the plenipotentiaries, the text of the Conventions and of the Declaration enumerated below and annexed to the present Act.

I. *Convention for the pacific settlement of international disputes.*
II. *Convention respecting the limitation of the employment of force for the recovery of contract debts.*

III. Convention relative to the opening of hostilities.
IV. Convention respecting the laws and customs of war on land.
V. Convenion respecting the rights and duties of neutral powers and persons in case of war on land.
VI. Convention relative to the status of enemy merchant ships at the outbreak of hostilities.
VII. Convention relative to the conversion of merchant ships into warships.
VIII. Convention relative to the laying of automatic submarine contact mines.
IX. Convention respecting bombardment by naval forces in time of war.
X. Convention for the adaptation to naval war of the principles of the Geneva Convention.
XI. Convention relative to certain restrictions with regard to the exercise of the right of capture in naval war.
XII. Convention relative to the creation of an International Prize Court.
XIII. Convention concerning the rights and duties of neutral Powers in naval war.
XIV. Declaration prohibiting the discharge of projectiles and explosives from balloons.

These Conventions and Declarations shall form so many separate Acts. These Acts shall be dated this day, and may be signed up to 30 June 1908, at The Hague, by the Plenipotentiaries of the Powers represented at the Second Peace Conference.

The Conference, actuated by the spirit of mutual agreement and concession characterizing its deliberations, has agreed upon the following Declaration, which, while reserving to each of the Powers represented full liberty of action as regards voting, enables them to affirm the principles which they regard as unanimously admitted:

It is unanimous:

1. *In admitting the principle of compulsory arbitration.*
2. *In declaring that certain disputes, in particular those relating to the interpretation and application of the provisions of international agreements, may be submitted to compulsory arbitration without any restriction.*

Finally, it is unanimous in proclaiming that, although it has not yet been found feasible to conclude a Convention in this sense, nevertheless the divergences of opinion which have come to light have not exceeded the bounds of judicial controversy, and that, by working together here during the past four months, the collected Powers not only have learnt to understand one another and to draw closer together, but have succeeded in the course of this long collaboration in evolving a very lofty conception of the common welfare of humanity.

The Conference has further unanimously adopted the following Resolution:

"The Second Peace Conference confirms the Resolution adopted by the Conference of 1899 in regard to the limitation of military expenditure; and inasmuch as military expenditure has considerably increased in almost every country since that time, the Conference declares that it is eminently desirable that the Governments should resume the serious examination of this question."

It has besides expressed the following Voeux*:*

1.[1] *The Conference recommends to the Signatory Powers the adoption of the annexed draft Convention for the creation of a Judicial Arbitration Court,*[2] *and the bringing it into force as soon as an agreement has been reached respecting the selection of the judges and the constitution of the Court.*
2. *The Conference expresses the opinion that, in case of war, the responsible authorities, civil as well as military, should make it their special duty to ensure and safeguard the maintenance of pacific relations, more especially of the commercial and industrial relations between the inhabitants of the belligerent States and neutral countries.*
3. *The Conference expresses the opinion that the Powers should regulate, by special treaties, the position, as regards military charges, of foreigners residing within their territories.*
4. *The Conference expresses the opinion that the preparation of regulations relative to the laws and customs of naval war should figure in the programme of the next Conference, and that in any case the Powers may apply, as far as possible, to war by sea the principles of the Convention relative to the laws and customs of war on land.*

Finally, the Conference recommends to the Powers the assembly of a Third Peace Conference, which might be held within a period corresponding to that which has elapsed since the preceding Conference, at a date to be fixed by common agreement between the Powers, and it calls their attention to the necessity of preparing the programme of this Third Conference a sufficient time in advance to ensure its deliberations being conducted with the necessary authority and expedition.

In order to attain this object the Conference considers that it would be very desirable that, some two years before the probable date of the meeting, a preparatory committee should be charged by the Governments with the task of collecting the various proposals to be submitted to the Conference, of ascertaining what subjects are ripe for embodiment in an international regulation, and of preparing a programme which the Governments should decide upon in sufficient time to enable it to be carefully examined by the countries interested. This committee should further be entrusted with the task of proposing a system of organization and procedure for the Conference itself.

In faith whereof the Plenipotentiaries have signed the present Act and have affixed their seals thereto. Done at The Hague, 18 October 1907, in a single copy, which shall remain deposited in the archives of the Netherlands Government, and duly certified copies of which shall be sent to all the Powers represented at the Conference.

[Here follow signatures]

[1] For reservation in respect of *Voeu* No. 1 by Switzerland, see p. 48.
[2] Not reproduced in this volume.

SIGNATURES

The Final Act was signed by the representatives of the following states:

Argentine Republic
Austria-Hungary
Belgium
Bolivia
Brazil
Bulgaria
Chile
China
Columbia
Cuba
Denmark
Dominican Republic
Ecuador
El Salvador
France
Germany
Great Britain
Greece
Guatemala
Haiti
Italy
Japan
Luxemburg
Mexico
Montenegro
Netherlands
Nicaragua
Norway
Panama
Paraguay
Persia
Peru
Portugal
Romania
Russia
Serbia
Siam
Spain
Sweden
Switzerland *Res.*
Turkey
United States
Uruguay
Venezuela

RESERVATION

SWITZERLAND
Signed under reservation of *Voeu* No. 1, which the Swiss Federal Council does not accept.[3]

3 Declaration of Mr. Carlin, *The Proceedings of the Hague Peace Conferences, 1907*, Vol. I, pp. 327, 574; Scott, *Hague Conventions*, p. 40.

No. 6

CONVENTION (III) RELATIVE TO THE OPENING OF HOSTILITIES

Signed at The Hague, 18 October 1907

INTRODUCTORY NOTE: The war between Russia and Japan, which broke out in 1904 without a declaration of war, caused a movement for the adoption of some written rules on the commencement of war. The Institute of International Law adopted a resolution to that end in 1906 and the Second Hague Conference of 1907 produced the present Convention. Although this Convention concerns rather the *ius ad bellum* than the *ius in bello* it is reprinted in this collection in order to include all the Hague Conventions relating to the law of war.

ENTRY INTO FORCE: 26 January 1910.

AUTHENTIC TEXT: French. The English translation below is reprinted from Scott, *Hague Conventions*, pp. 96–98. It reproduces the translation by the United States Department of State. The marginal titles have no official character.

TEXT PUBLISHED IN: *Conférence internationale de la Paix, 1907*, pp. 623–625 (French); Scott, *Hague Conventions*, pp. 96–98 (Engl.); Scott, *Les Conventions de La Haye*, pp. 96–98 (French); Scott, *Les Conférences de La Haye*, pp. 56–57 (French); Martens, *NRGT*, 3ème série, Vol. III, pp. 437–460 (French, German); *CTS*, Vol. 205, 1907, pp. 264–276 (French); Deltenre, pp. 242–328 (French); *Fontes Historiae Juris Gentium*, Vol. III/1, pp. 607–609 (German, English, French – extract); *GBTS*, 1910, No. 9, Cd. 5029 (Engl., French); *US Statutes at Large*, Vol. 36, pp. 2259–2276 (Engl., French); Malloy, Vol. II, pp. 2259–2269 (Engl.); Bevans, Vol. I, pp. 619–630 (Engl.); *Droit des conflits armés*, pp. 59–64 (French); *AJIL*, Vol. 2, 1908, Suppl., pp. 85–90 (Engl.); *Revista de Derecho Internacional y politica exterior*, Crónica, Año III, 1907, pp. 73–75 (Span.), Bustamante, pp. 282–285 (Span.); Korovin, pp. 370–373 (Russ.); *Mezhdunarodnoe pravo*, Vol. III, p. 40 (Russ. – extract); Briceño, p. 207 (Span. – extract); Ceppi, p. 337 (Span. – extract); ICRC website: www.icrc.org/ihl.nsf.

TABLE OF CONTENTS

* * *

[List of contracting parties]

Purpose of Convention

Considering that it is important, in order to ensure the maintenance of pacific relations, that hostilities should not commence without previous warning;

That it is equally important that the existence of a state of war should be notified without delay to neutral Powers;

Being desirous of concluding a Convention to this effect, have appointed the following as their plenipotentiaries:

[Here follow the names of plenipotentiaries]

Plenipotentiaries

Who, after depositing their full powers, found in good and due form, have agreed upon the following provisions:

Notice of commencing hostilities

Article 1. The contracting Powers recognize that hostilities between themselves must not commence without previous and explicit warning, in the form either of a declaration of war, giving reasons, or of an ultimatum with conditional declaration of war.

Notice to neutral Powers

Art. 2. The existence of a state of war must be notified to the neutral Powers without delay, and shall not take effect in regard to them until after the receipt of a notification, which may, however, be given by telegraph. Neutral Powers, nevertheless, cannot rely on the absence of notification if it is clearly established that they were in fact aware of the existence of a state of war.

Effect on contracting Powers

Art. 3. Article 1 of the present Convention shall take effect in case of war between two or more of the contracting Powers.

Article 2 is binding as between a belligerent Power which is a party to the Convention and neutral Powers which are also parties to the Convention.

Ratification

Art. 4. The present Convention shall be ratified as soon as possible.

Deposit at The Hague

The ratifications shall be deposited at The Hague.

The first deposit of ratifications shall be recorded in a *procès-verbal* signed by the representatives of the Powers which take part therein and by the Netherland Minister for Foreign Affairs.

The subsequent deposits of ratifications shall be made by means of a written notification addressed to the Netherland Government and accompanied by the instrument of ratification.

Certified copies to Powers

A duly certified copy of the *procès-verbal* relative to the first deposit of ratifications, of the notifications mentioned in the preceding paragraph, as well as of the instruments of ratification, shall be at once sent by the Netherland Government through the diplomatic channel to the Powers invited to the Second Peace Conference, as well as to the other Powers which have adhered to the Convention. In the cases contemplated in the preceding paragraph, the said Government shall at the same time inform them of the date on which it received the notification.

Art. 5. Non-signatory Powers may adhere to the present Convention.

Non-signatory Powers may adhere

The Power which wishes to adhere notifies in writing its intention to the Netherland Government, forwarding to it the act of adhesion, which shall be deposited in the archives of the said Government.

Notification of Intent

The said Government shall at once forward to all the other Powers a duly certified copy of the notification as well as of the act of adhesion, stating the date on which it received the notification.

Communications to other Powers

Art. 6. The present Convention shall come into force, in the case of the Powers which were a party to the first deposit of ratifications, sixty days after the date of the *procès-verbal* of that deposit, and, in the case of the Powers which ratify subsequently or which adhere, sixty days after the notification of their ratification or of their adhesion has been received by the Netherland Government.

Effect of ratification

Art. 7. In the event of one of the high contracting Parties wishing to denounce the present Convention, the denunciation shall be notified in writing to the Netherland Government, which shall at once communicate a duly certified copy of the notification to all the other Powers, informing them of the date on which it was received.

Denunciation

The denunciation shall only have effect in regard to the notifying Power, and one year after the notification has reached the Netherland Government.

Notifying Power only affected

Art. 8. A register kept by the Netherland Ministry for Foreign Affairs shall give the date of the deposit of ratifications made in virtue of Article 4, paragraphs 3 and 4, as well as the date on which the notifications of adhesion (Article 5, paragraph 2) or of denunciation (Article 7, paragraph I) have been received.

Register of ratifications

Each contracting Power is entitled to have access to this register and to be supplied with duly certified extracts from it.

In faith whereof the plenipotentiaries have appended their signatures to the present Convention.

Signing

Done at The Hague, the 18th October, 1907, in a single copy, which shall remain deposited in the archives of the Netherland Government, and duly certified copies of which shall be sent, through the diplomatic channel, to the Powers which have been invited to the Second Peace Conference.

Deposit of original

[Here follow signatures]

SIGNATURES, RATIFICATIONS AND ACCESSIONS[1]

State	*Signature*	*Ratification* *Accession* *Notification of Continuity (C)*
Argentina	18 October 1907	–
Austria-Hungary	18 October 1907	27 November 1909
Belgium	18 October 1907	8 August 1910
Bolivia	18 October 1907	27 November 1909
Brazil	18 October 1907	5 January 1914
Bulgaria	18 October 1907	–
Chile	18 October 1907	–
China	–	15 January 1910
Colombia	18 October 1907	–
Cuba	18 October 1907	–
Denmark	18 October 1907	27 November 1909
Dominican Republic	–	18 October 1907
Ecuador	18 October 1907	–
El Salvador	18 October 1907	27 November 1909
Ethiopia	–	5 August 1935
Fiji[2]	–	2 April 1973
Finland[3]	–	30 December 1918
France	18 October 1907	7 October 1910
Germany[4]	18 October 1907	27 November 1909
Great Britain	18 October 1907	27 November 1909
Greece	18 October 1907	–
Guatemala	18 October 1907	15 March 1911
Haiti	18 October 1907	2 February 1910
Italy	18 October 1907	–
Japan	18 October 1907	13 December 1911
Liberia	–	4 February 1914
Luxembourg	18 October 1907	5 September 1912
Mexico	18 October 1907	27 November 1909
Montenegro	18 October 1907	–
Netherlands	18 October 1907	27 November 1909
Nicaragua	–	16 December 1909
Norway	18 October 1907	19 September 1910

[1] Based on a communication received from the Ministry of Foreign Affairs of the Netherlands of 12 December 2001. See also ICRC website: www.icrc.org/ihl.nsf.

[2] According to the communication of the depositary, Fiji and South Africa declared being bound by the Convention.

[3] By letter dated 12 May 1980, the Netherlands Ministry of Foreign Affairs stated (a) Finland's accession on 30 December 1918 to this and other 1907 Hague Conventions and to the 1907 Hague Declaration was initially regarded as provisional, pending the final resolution of Finland's international status; (b) after consultation with the other contracting powers, the depositary stated on 9 June 1922 that Finland's accession should be regarded as final and complete, and (c) the Conventions and the Declaration entered into force for Finland on 9 June 1922.

[4] By a letter received at the Ministry of Foreign Affairs of the Kingdom of the Netherlands on 9 February 1959, the Government of the German Democratic Republic has informed the Ministry that it reapplies the Convention. This declaration has lost its historical importance after the conclusion of the Treaty of 31 August 1990 (Unification Treaty) between the Federal Republic of Germany and German Democratic Republic. See note 3 of document *No. 18*, pp. 170–171 and note 35 of documents *Nos. 49–52*, pp. 639–640.

State	*Signature*	*Ratification* *Accession* *Notification of Continuity (C)*
Panama	18 October 1907	11 September 1911
Paraguay	18 October 1907	–
Persia	18 October 1907	–
Peru	18 October 1907	–
Poland	–	9 May 1925
Portugal	18 October 1907	13 April 1911
Romania	18 October 1907	1 March 1912
Russia[5]	18 October 1907	27 November 1909
Serbia	18 October 1907	–
Siam	18 October 1907	12 March 1910
South Africa[2]	–	10 March 1978
Spain	18 October 1907	18 March 1913
Sweden	18 October 1907	27 November 1909
Switzerland	18 October 1907	12 May 1910
Turkey	18 October 1907	–
United States of America	18 October 1907	27 November 1909
Uruguay	18 October 1907	–
Venezuela	18 October 1907	–

RESERVATIONS

None

By note of the Foreign Ministry of the USSR of 7 March 1955 "The Government of the USSR recognises the Conventions and Declarations of The Hague from 1899 and 1907, which were ratified by Russia to the extent that the Conventions and Declarations do not contradict the United Nations Charter and if they are not amended or replaced by ulterior international agreements to which the USSR is a Party, such as the 1925 Geneva Protocol for the Prohibition of Use of Asphyxiating, Poisonous and Other Gases and of Bacteriological Methods of Warfare and the 1949 Geneva Conventions for the Protection of Victims of War" (*Izvestiya*, 9 March 1955).

In January 1992, the Ministry of Foreign Affairs of the Russian Federation informed the heads of diplomatic missions in Moscow that the Russian Federation continues to be a party to all conventions which are in force for the Soviet Union. The Ministry of Foreign Affairs of the Kingdom of the Netherlands considers therefore that the Russian Federation is bound by the conventions to which the Soviet Union was party (communication of the depositary to the Henry Dunant Institute of 6 November 1992).

On 4 June 1962, the Byelorussian Soviet Socialist Republic made a declaration similar to that made by the USSR.

Nos. 7– 8

No. 7 CONVENTION (II) WITH RESPECT TO THE LAWS AND CUSTOMS OF WAR ON LAND

Signed at The Hague, 29 July 1899

No. 8 CONVENTION (IV) RESPECTING THE LAWS AND CUSTOMS OF WAR ON LAND

Signed at The Hague, 18 October 1907

INTRODUCTORY NOTE: One of the purposes for which the First Hague Peace Conference of 1899 was convened was "the revision of the declaration concerning the laws and customs of war elaborated in 1874 by the Conference of Brussels, and not yet ratified" (Russian circular note of 30 December 1898). The Conference of 1899 succeeded in adopting a Convention on land warfare to which Regulations are annexed. The Convention and the Regulations were revised at the Second International Peace Conference in 1907. As the two versions of the Convention and the Regulations differ only slightly from each other, they are printed side by side as in *The Hague Conventions and Declarations of 1899 and 1907*, by James Brown Scott, and in *The Hague Peace Conferences*, by A. Pearce Higgins. The differences between the two versions are indicated by italics. The marginal titles added to the Conventions have no official character. They are reproduced, with a few exceptions, from James Brown Scott's edition of the texts.

Eighteen of the states that ratified the 1899 Convention did not ratify the 1907 version (Argentina, Bulgaria, Chile, Colombia, Ecuador, Greece, Honduras, Italy, Korea, Montenegro, Paraguay, Persia, Peru, Serbia, Spain, Turkey, Uruguay, Venezuela). These states or their successor states remain formally bound by the 1899 Convention in their relations with the other parties thereto. As between the parties to the 1907 Convention, this Convention has replaced the 1899 Convention (see Article 4 of the 1907 Convention).

The provisions of the two Conventions on land warfare, like most of the substantive provisions of the Hague Conventions of 1899 and 1907, are considered as embodying rules of customary international law. As such they are also binding on states which are not formally parties to them. In 1946 the Nuremberg International Military Tribunal stated with regard to the Hague Convention on land warfare of 1907: "The rules of land warfare expressed in the Convention undoubtedly represented an advance over existing International Law at the time of their adoption ... but by 1939 these rules ... were recognized by all civilized nations, and were regarded as being declaratory of the laws and customs of war" (*Trial of the Major War Criminals before the International Military Tribunal, Nuremberg, 14 November 1945 – 1 October 1946*. Vol. I: *Official text in the English language.* Published at Nuremberg, Germany, 1947, pp. 253–254). The International Military Tribunal for the Far East expressed, in 1948, an identical view.

The rules embodied in the Regulations were partly reaffirmed and developed by Additional Protocol I to the Geneva Conventions of 1949, adopted in 1977 (*No. 56*).

ENTRY INTO FORCE: 4 September 1900 (Convention of 1899); 26 January 1910 (Convention of 1907).

AUTHENTIC TEXT: French. The English translation below is reprinted from Scott, *Hague Conventions*, pp. 100–132. It reproduces the translation of the United States Department of State.

TEXT PUBLISHED IN:
Convention of 1899: Conférence internationale de la Paix, 1899, pp. 239-249 (French); *Les deux Conférences de la Paix*, pp. 25–37 (French); Scott, *Hague Conventions*, pp. 100–130 (Engl.); Scott, *Les Conventions de La Haye*, pp. 100–130 (French); Scott, *Les Conférences de La Haye*, pp. 15–23 (French); Martens, *NRGT*, 2ème série, Vol. XXVI, pp. 949–979 (French, German); Olivart, Vol. XII, pp. 597–624 (French, Span.); Deltenre, pp. 94–123 (Engl., French, German, Dutch); *Fontes Historiae Juris Gentium*, Vol. III/1, pp. 576–599 (Engl., French, German); *BFSP*, Vol. 91, 1898–1899, pp. 988–1002 (French); *GBTS*, 1901, No. 11, Cd. 800 (Engl., French); *US. Statutes at Large*, Vol. 22, pp. 1803–1836, (Engl., French); Malloy, Vol. II, pp. 2042–2057 (Engl.); Bevans, Vol. I, pp. 247–262 (Engl.); *CTS*, Vol. 187, 1898–1899, pp. 429–443 (French); *AJIL*, Vol. 1, 1907, Suppl., pp. 129–153 (Engl.); Friedman, pp. 221–235 (Engl.); *Droit des conflits armés*, pp. 65–93 (French); Arellano, pp. 352–357 (Span.); Bustamante, pp. 209–229 (Span.); ICRC website: www.icrc.org/ihl.nsf.
Convention of 1907: Conférence internationale de la Paix, 1907, pp. 626–737 (French); *Les deux Conférences de la Paix*, pp. 103–116 (French); Scott, *Hague Conventions*, pp. 100–132 (Engl.); Scott, *Les Conventions de La Haye*, pp. 100–132 (French); Scott, *Les Conférences de la Haye*, pp. 58–66 (French); Martens, *NRGT*, 3ème série, Vol. III, pp. 461–503 (French, German); *CTS*, Vol. 205, 1907, pp. 227–298 (French); Deltenre, pp. 250–281 (Engl., French, German, Dutch); *Fontes Historiae Juris Gentium*, Vol. III/1, pp. 609–614 (Engl., French, German – extract); *International Red Cross Handbook*, 1983, pp. 322–332 (Engl.); *Manuel de la Croix-Rouge internationale*, 1983, pp. 334–344 (French); *Manual de la Cruz Roja internacionale*, 1983, pp. 326–336 (Span.); *Handbook of the International Movement*, pp. 299–309 (Engl.); *Manuel du Mouvement international*, pp. 311–321 (French); *Manual del Movimiento internacional*, pp. 303–313 (Span.); *BFSP*, Vol. 100, 1906–1907, pp. 338–359 (French); *GBTS*, 1910, No. 9, Cd. 5030 (Engl., French); *US. Statutes at Large*, Vol. 36, pp. 2227–2309 (Engl., French); Malloy, Vol. II, pp. 2269–2290 (Engl.); Bevans, Vol. I, pp. 631–653 (Engl.); *AJIL*, Vol. 2, 1908, Suppl., pp. 90–117 (Engl.); Friedman, pp. 308–323 (Engl.); Roberts and Guelff, pp. 67–84 (Engl.); *Droit des conflits armés*, pp. 65–93 (French); Arellano, pp. 362–369 (Span. – extracts); Briceño, pp. 207–217 (Span. – extracts); Bustamante, pp. 285–307 (Span.); Ceppi, pp. 339–352 (Span.); *Revista de Derecho Internacional y politica exterior*, Crónica, Año III, 1907, pp. 76–83 (Span.); Korovin, pp. 373–383 (Russ.); *Mezhdunarodnoe pravo*, Vol. III, pp. 41–53 (Russ. – extracts); ICRC website: www. icrc.org/ ihl.nsf.

TABLE OF CONTENTS

* * *

1899

CONVENTION (II) WITH RESPECT TO THE LAWS AND CUSTOMS OF WAR ON LAND AND ITS ANNEX: REGULATIONS RESPECTING THE LAWS AND CUSTOMS OF WAR ON LAND

Signed at The Hague, 29 July 1899

[List of Contracting Parties]

Purpose of Convention

Considering that, while seeking means to preserve peace and prevent armed conflicts among nations, it is likewise necessary to have regard to cases where an appeal to arms may be caused by events which their solicitude could not avert;

Animated by the desire to serve, even in this extreme hypothesis, the interests of humanity and the ever increasing requirements of civilization;

Thinking it important, with this object, to revise the laws and general customs of war, either with the view of defining them more precisely or of laying down certain limits for the purpose of modifying their severity as far as possible;

Inspired by these views which are enjoined at the present day, as they were twenty-five years ago at the time of the Brussels Conference in 1874, by a wise and generous foresight;

Have, in this spirit, adopted a great number of provisions, the object of which is to define and govern the usages of war on land.

In view of the High Contracting Parties, these provisions, the word-

1907

CONVENTION (IV) RESPECTING THE LAWS AND CUSTOMS OF WAR ON LAND AND ITS ANNEX: REGULATIONS RESPECTING THE LAWS AND CUSTOMS OF WAR ON LAND

Signed at The Hague, 18 October 1907[1]

[List of Contracting Parties]

Seeing that while seeking means to preserve peace and prevent armed conflicts between nations, it is likewise necessary to bear in mind the case where the appeal to arms has been brought about by events which their care was unable to avert;

Animated by the desire to serve, even in this extreme case, the interests of humanity and the ever progressive needs of civilization;

Thinking it important, with this object, to revise the general laws and customs of war, either with a view to defining them with greater precision or to confining them within such limits as would mitigate their severity as far as possible;

Have deemed it necessary to complete and explain in certain particulars the work of the First Peace Conference, which, following on the Brussels Conference of 1874, and inspired by the ideas dictated by a wise and generous forethought, adopted provisions intended to define and govern the usages of war on land.

According to the views of the High Contracting Parties, these

[1] Italics indicate differences between the Conventions of 1899 and 1907.

1899

ing of which has been inspired by the desire to diminish the evils of war so far as military necessities permit, are destined to serve as general rules of conduct for belligerents in their relations with each other and with populations.

It has not, however, been possible to agree forthwith on provisions embracing all the circumstances which occur in practice.

On the other hand, it could not be intended by the High Contracting Parties that the cases not provided for should, for want of a written provision, be left to the arbitrary judgment of the military commanders.

Until a more complete code of the laws of war is issued, the High Contracting Parties think it right to declare that in cases not included in the Regulations adopted by them, populations and belligerents remain under the protection and empire of the principles of international law, as they result from the usages established between civilized nations, from the laws of humanity, and the requirements of the public conscience;

They declare that it is in this sense especially that Articles 1 and 2 of the Regulations adopted must be understood;

The High Contracting Parties, desiring to conclude a Convention to this effect, have appointed as their Plenipotentiaries, to wit:

[Here follow the names of plenipotentiaries]

Who, after communication of their full powers, found in good

1907

provisions, the wording of which has been inspired by the desire to diminish the evils of war, as far as military requirements permit, are intended to serve as a general rule of conduct for the belligerents in their mutual relations and in their relations with the inhabitants.

It has not, however, been found possible at present to concert regulations covering all the circumstances which arise in practice;

On the other hand, the High Contracting Parties clearly do not intend that unforeseen cases should, in the absence of a written undertaking, be left to the arbitrary judgment of military commanders.

Until a more complete code of the laws of war has been issued, the High Contracting Parties deem it expedient to declare that, in cases not included in the Regulations adopted by them, the inhabitants and the belligerents remain under the protection and the rule of the principles of the law of nations, as they result from the usages established among civilized peoples, from the laws of humanity, and the dictates of the public conscience.

They declare that it is in this sense especially that Articles I and 2 of the Regulations adopted must be understood.

Plenipotentiaries

The High Contracting Parties, wishing to conclude a *fresh* Convention to this effect, have appointed the following as their Plenipotentiaries:

[Here follow the names of plenipotentiaries]

Who, after *having deposited* their full powers, found in good and

	1899	1907
	and due form, have agreed on the following:	due form, have agreed upon the following:
Instructions to armed land forces	*Article 1.* The High Contracting Parties shall issue instructions to their armed land forces, which shall be in conformity with the "Regulations respecting the laws and customs of war on land" annexed to the present Convention.	*Article 1.* The Contracting *Powers* shall issue instructions to their armed land forces which shall be in conformity with the Regulations respecting the laws and customs of war on land, annexed to the present Convention.
Powers bound	*Art. 2.* The provisions contained in the Regulations mentioned in Article I are only binding on the Contracting Powers, in case of war between two or more of them. These provisions shall cease to be binding from the time when, in a war between Contracting Powers, a non-Contracting Power joins one of the belligerents.	*Art. 2.* The provisions contained in the Regulations referred to in Article 1, *as well as in the present Convention, do not apply except between Contracting powers, and then only if all the belligerents are parties to the Convention.*
Penalty for violating regulations		*Art. 3.*[2] *A belligerent party which violates the provisions of the said Regulations shall, if the case demands, be liable to pay compensation. It shall be responsible for all acts committed by persons forming part of its armed forces.*
Prior Convention replaced		*Art. 4. The present Convention, duly ratified, shall as between the Contracting Powers, be substituted for the Convention of 29 July 1899, respecting the laws land customs of war on land.*
Continuance of former Convention		*The Convention of 1899 remains in force as between the Powers which signed it, and which do not also ratify the present Convention.*
Ratification	*Art. 3.* The present Convention shall be ratified as speedily as possible.	*Art. 5.* The present Convention shall be ratified as soon as possible.
Deposit at The Hague	The ratifications shall be deposited at The Hague.	The ratifications shall be deposited at The Hague.

2 For reservation in respect of this article by Turkey, see p. 87.

1899	1907	
	The first deposit of ratifications shall be recorded in a procès-verbal *signed by the Representatives of the Powers which take part therein and by the Netherlands Minister for Foreign Affairs.*	
	The subsequent deposits of ratifications shall be made by means of a written notification, addressed to the Netherlands Government and accompanied by the instrument of ratification.	
A *procès-verbal* shall be drawn up recording the receipt of each ratification, and a copy, duly certified, shall be sent through the diplomatic channel, to all the Contracting Powers.	*A duly certified copy of the procès-verbal relative to the first deposit of ratifications, of the notifications mentioned in the preceding paragraph, as well as of the instruments of ratification, shall be immediately sent by the Netherlands Government, through the diplomatic channel, to the powers invited to the Second Peace Conference, as well as to the other Powers which have adhered to the Convention. In the cases contemplated in the preceding paragraph the said Government shall at the same time inform them of the date on which it received the notification.*	Certified copies to Powers
Art. 4. Non-Signatory Powers are allowed to adhere to the present Convention.	*Art. 6.* Non-Signatory Powers may adhere to the present Convention.	Adherence of non-signatory Powers
For this purpose they must make their adhesion known to the Contracting Powers by means of a written notification, addressed to the Netherlands Government, and by it communicated to all the other Contracting Powers.	*The Power which desires to adhere notifies in writing its intention to the Netherlands Government, forwarding to it the act of adhesion, which shall be deposited in the archives of the said Government.*	Notification of intent
	This Government shall at once transmit to all the other Powers a duly certified copy of the notification as well as of the act of adhesion, mentioning the date on which it received the notification.	Communication to other Powers

	1899	1907
Effect of ratification		*Art. 7. The present Convention shall come into force, in the case of the Powers which were a party to the first deposit of ratifications, sixty days after the date of the procès-verbal of this deposit, and, in the case of the Powers which ratify subsequently or which adhere, sixty days after the notification of their ratification or of their adhesion has been received by the Netherlands Government.*
Denunciation	*Art. 5.* In the event of one of the High Contracting Parties denouncing the present Convention, such denunciation would not take effect until a year after the written notification made to the Netherlands Government, and by it at once communicated to all the other Contracting Powers.	*Art. 8.* In the event of one of the Contracting *Powers wishing to denounce* the present Convention, *the* denunciation *shall be notified in writing to the Netherlands Government, which shall at once communicate a duly certified copy of the notification to all the other Powers, informing them of the date on which it was received.*
Notifying Power only affected	This denunciation shall affect only the notifying Power	The denunciation shall only have effect in regard to the notifying Power, *and one year after the notification has reached the Netherlands Government.*
Register of ratifications		*Art. 9. A register kept by the Netherlands Ministry for Foreign Affairs shall give the date of the deposit of ratifications made in virtue of Article 5, paragraphs 3 and 4, as well as the date on which the notifications of adhesion (Article 6, paragraph 2), or of denunciation (Article 8, paragraph 1) were received.* *Each Contracting Power is entitled to have access to this register and to be supplied with duly certified extracts.*
Signing	In faith of which the Plenipotentiaries have signed the present Convention and affixed their seals thereto.	In faith whereof the Plenipotentiaries have *appended their signatures* to the present Convention.

1899

Done at The Hague 29 July 1899, in a single copy, which shall be kept in the archives of the Netherlands Government, and copies of which, duly certified, shall be delivered to the Contracting Powers through the diplomatic channel.

[Here follow signatures]

1907

Deposit of original

Done at The Hague *18 October 1907*, in a single copy, which shall remain deposited in the archives of the Netherlands Government, and duly certified copies of which shall be sent, through the diplomatic channel to the Powers *which have been invited to the Second Peace Conference*.

[Here follow signatures]

1899	1907
ANNEX TO THE CONVENTION	**ANNEX TO THE CONVENTION**
REGULATIONS RESPECTING THE LAWS AND CUSTOMS OF WAR ON LAND	REGULATIONS RESPECTING THE LAWS AND CUSTOMS OF WAR ON LAND
Section I. On Belligerents	**Section I. On Belligerents**
Chapter I. On the Qualifications of Belligerents	*Chapter I. The Qualifications of Belligerents*[3]

Application of laws of war to all forces

1899	1907
Article 1. The laws, rights, and duties of war apply not only to armies, but also to militia and volunteer corps fulfilling the following conditions: 1. To be commanded by a person responsible for his subordinates; 2. To have a fixed distinctive emblem recognizable at a distance; 3. To carry arms openly; and 4. To conduct their operations in accordance with the laws and customs of war. In countries where militia or volunteer corps constitute the army, or form part of it, they are included under the denomination "army."	*Article 1.* The laws, rights, and duties of war apply not only to armies, but also to militia and volunteer corps fulfilling the following conditions: 1. To be commanded by a person responsible for his subordinates; 2. To have a fixed distinctive emblem recognizable at a distance; 3. To carry arms openly; and 4. To conduct their operations in accordance with the laws and customs of war. In countries where militia or volunteer corps constitute the army, or form part of it, they are included under the denomination "army."

Levée en masse

1899	1907
Art. 2. The population of a territory which has not been occupied who, on the enemy's approach, spontaneously take up arms to resist the invading troops without having time to organize themselves in accordance with Article 1, shall be regarded as belligerent, if they respect the laws and customs of war.	*Art. 2.* The inhabitants of a territory which has not been occupied, who, on the approach of the enemy, spontaneously take up arms to resist the invading troops without having had time to organize themselves in accordance with Article 1, shall be regarded as belligerents *if they carry arms openly and* if they respect the laws and customs of war.

[3] For a more recent definition of the armed forces, see the Geneva Conventions of 1949; Convention I, Article 13 (*No. 49*), Convention II, Article 13 (*No. 50*), Convention III, Article 4 (*No. 51*) and Protocol I of 1977, Articles 43–47 (*No. 56*).

1899	1907	
Art. 3. The armed forces of the belligerent parties may consist of combatants and non-combatants. In case of capture by the enemy both have a right to be treated as prisoners of war.	*Art. 3.* The armed forces of the belligerent parties may consist of combatants and non-combatants. In the case of capture by the enemy, both have a right to be treated as prisoners of war.	Combatants and non-combatants
Chapter II. On Prisoners of War[4]	*Chapter II. Prisoners of War*[4]	
Art. 4. Prisoners of war are in the power of the hostile Government, but not in that of the individuals or corps who captured them.	*Art. 4.* Prisoners of war are in the power of the hostile Government, but not of the individuals or corps who capture them.	Responsibility of capturing government
They must be humanely treated.	They must be humanely treated.	Treatment
All their personal belongings, except arms, horses, and military papers remain their property.	All their personal belongings, except arms, horses, and military papers, remain their property.	Personal belongings
Art. 5. Prisoners of war may be interned in a town, fortress, camp, or any other locality, and bound not to go beyond certain fixed limits; but they can only be confined as an indispensable measure of safety.	*Art. 5.* Prisoners of war may be interned in a town, fortress, camp, or other place, and bound not to go beyond certain fixed limits; but they cannot be confined except as an indispensable measure of safety *and only while the circumstances which necessitate the measure continue to exist.*	Confinement
Art. 6. The State may utilize the labour of prisoners of war according to their rank and aptitude. Their tasks shall not be excessive, and shall have nothing to do with the military operations.	*Art. 6.* The State may utilize the labour of prisoners of war according to their rank and aptitude, *officers excepted.* The tasks shall not be excessive and shall have no connection with the operations of the war.	Employment at labour
Prisoners may be authorized to work for the public service, for private persons, or on their own account.	Prisoners may be authorized to work for the public service, for private persons, or on their own account.	
Work done for the State shall be paid for according to the tariffs in force for soldiers of the national army employed on similar tasks.	Work done for the State is paid for at the rates in force for work of a similar kind done by soldiers of the national army, *or, if there are*	Payment

4 For more recent provisions on prisoners of war, see the Geneva Conventions of 1929 and 1949 relative to the Treatment of Prisoners of War (*Nos. 46 and 51*) and Protocol I of 1977, Articles 43–47 (*No. 56*). Cf. Article 89 of the 1929 Convention and Article 135 of the 1949 Convention.

1899

When the work is for other branches of the public service or for private persons, the conditions shall be settled in agreement with the military authorities.

Use of wages

The wages of the prisoners shall go towards improving their position, and the balance shall be paid them at the time of their release, after deducting the cost of their maintenance.

Maintenance

Art. 7. The Government into whose hands prisoners of war have fallen is bound to maintain them.

General treatment

Failing a special agreement between the belligerents, prisoners of war shall be treated, as regards food, quarters, and clothing, on the same footing as the troops of the Government which has captured them.

Subject to military laws, etc.

Art. 8. Prisoners of war shall be subject to the laws, regulations, and orders in force in the army of the State into whose hands they have fallen.

Insubordination

Any act of insubordination warrants the adoption, as regards them, of such measures of severity as may be necessary.

Recaptured prisoners

Escaped prisoners, recaptured before they have succeeded in rejoining their army, or before quitting the territory occupied by the army that captured them, are liable to disciplinary punishment.

Prisoners who, after succeeding in escaping are again taken prisoners, are not liable to any punishment for the previous flight.

Restrictions for false statements

Art. 9. Every prisoner of war, if questioned, is bound to declare his true name and rank, and if he dis-

1907

none in force, at a rate according to the work executed.

When the work is for other branches of the public service or for private persons the conditions are settled in agreement with the military authorities.

The wages of the prisoners shall go towards improving their position, and the balance shall be paid them on their release, after deducting the cost of their maintenance.

Art. 7. The Government into whose hands prisoners of war have fallen is charged with their maintenance.

In the absence of a special agreement between the belligerents, prisoners of war shall be treated as regards board, lodging, and clothing on the same footing as the troops of the Government who captured them.

Art. 8. Prisoners of war shall be subject to the laws, regulations, and orders in force in the army of the State in whose power they are. Any act of insubordination justifies the adoption towards them of such measures of severity as may be considered necessary.

Escaped prisoners who are retaken before being able to rejoin their own army or before leaving the territory occupied by the army which captured them are liable to disciplinary punishment.

Prisoners who, after succeeding in escaping, are again taken prisoners, are not liable to any punishment on account of the previous flight.

Art. 9. Every prisoner of war is bound to give, if he is questioned on the subject, his true name and

1899	1907	
regards this rule, he is liable to a curtailment of the advantages accorded to the prisoners of war of his class.	rank, and if he infringes this rule, he is liable to have the advantages given to prisoners of his class curtailed.	
Art. 10. Prisoners of war may be set at liberty on parole if the laws of their country authorize it, and, in such a case, they are bound, on their personal honour, scrupulously to fulfil, both as regards their own Government and the Government by whom they were made prisoners, the engagements they have contracted. In such cases, their own Government shall not require of nor accept from them any service incompatible with the parole given.	*Art. 10.* Prisoners of war may be set at liberty on parole if the laws of their country allow, and, in such cases, they are bound, on their personal honour, scrupulously to fulfil, both towards their own Government and the Government by whom they were made prisoners, the engagements they have contracted. In such cases their own Government is bound neither to require of nor accept from them any service incompatible with the parole given.	Parole to be observed
Art. 11. A prisoner of war cannot be forced to accept his liberty on parole; similarly the hostile Government is not obliged to assent to the prisoner's request to be set at liberty on parole.	*Art. 11.* A prisoner of war cannot be compelled to accept his liberty on parole; similarly the hostile Government is not obliged to accede to the request of the prisoner to be set at liberty on parole.	Parole to be voluntary
Art. 12. Any prisoner of war, who is liberated on parole and recaptured, bearing arms against the Government to whom he had pledged his honour, or against the allies of that Government, forfeits his right to be treated as a prisoner of war, and can be brought before the courts.	*Art. 12.* Prisoners of war liberated on parole and recaptured bearing arms against the Government to whom they had pledged their honour, or against the allies of that Government, forfeit their right to be treated as prisoners of war, and can be brought before the courts.	Forfeiture of parole
Art. 13. Individuals who follow an army without directly belonging to it, such as newspaper correspondents and reporters, sutlers, contractors, who fall into the enemy's hands, and whom the latter think fit to detain, have a right to be treated as prisoners of war, provided they can produce a certificate from the mili-	*Art. 13.* Individuals who follow an army without directly belonging to it, such as newspaper correspondents and reporters, sutlers and contractors, who fall into the enemy's hands and whom the latter thinks expedient to detain, are entitled to be treated as prisoners of war, provided they are in possession of a certificate	Treatment of captured reporters, sutlers, etc.

	1899	1907
	tary authorities of the army they were accompanying.	from the military authorities of the army which they were accompanying.
Bureau of information to be established	*Art. 14.* A bureau for information relative to prisoners of war is instituted, on the commencement of hostilities, in each of the belligerent States, and, when necessary, in the neutral countries on whose territory belligerents have been received. This bureau is intended to answer all inquiries about prisoners of war, and is furnished by the various services concerned with all the necessary information to enable it to keep an individual return for each prisoner of war. It is kept informed of internments and changes, as well as of admissions into hospital and deaths.	*Art. 14.* An inquiry office for prisoners of war is instituted on the commencement of hostilities in each of the belligerent States, and, when necessary, in neutral countries which have received belligerents in their territory. It is the function of this office to reply to all inquiries about the prisoners. It receives from the various services concerned full information respecting internments arid transfers, *releases on parole, exchanges, escapes*, admissions into hospital, deaths, as well as other information necessary to enable it to make out *and keep up to date* an individual return for each prisoner of war. *The office must state in this return the regimental number, name and surname, age, place of origin, rank, unit, wounds, date and place of capture, internment, wounding, and death, as well as any observations of a special character. The individual return shall be sent to the Government of the other belligerent after the conclusion of peace.*
Receipt etc., of property	It is also the duty of the information bureau to receive and collect all objects of personal use, valuables, letters, etc., found on the battlefields or left by prisoners who have died in hospital or ambulance, and to transmit them to those interested.	It is likewise the function of the inquiry office to receive and collect all objects of personal use, valuables, letters, etc., found on the field of battle or left by prisoners who have *been released on parole, or exchanged, or who have escaped, or* died in hospitals or ambulances, and to forward them to those concerned.
Recognition of relief societies	*Art. 15.* Relief societies for prisoners of war, which are regularly	*Art. 15.* Relief societies for prisoners of war, which are properly

1899	1907	
constituted in accordance with the law of the country with the object of serving as the intermediary for charity, shall receive from the belligerents for themselves and their duly accredited agents every facility, within the bounds of military requirements and administrative regulations, for the effective accomplishment of their humane task. Delegates of these societies may be admitted to the places of internment for the distribution of relief, as also to the halting places of repatriated prisoners, if furnished with a personal permit by the military authorities, and on giving an engagement in writing to comply with all their regulations for order and police.	constituted in accordance with the laws of their country and with the object of serving as the channel for charitable effort shall receive from the belligerents, for themselves and their duly accredited agents every facility for the efficient performance of their humane task within the bounds imposed by military necessities and administrative regulations. Agents of these societies may be admitted to the places of internment for the purpose of distributing relief, as also to the halting places of repatriated prisoners, if furnished with a personal permit by the military authorities, and on giving an undertaking in writing to comply with all measures of order and police which the latter may issue.	
Art. 16. The information bureau shall have the privilege of free postage. Letters, money orders, and valuables, as well as postal parcels destined for the prisoners of war or dispatched by them, shall be free of all postal duties both in the countries of origin and destination, as well as in those they pass through. Gifts and relief in kind for prisoners of war shall be admitted free of all duties of entry and others, as well as of payments for carriage by the Government railways.	*Art. 16.* Inquiry offices enjoy the privilege of free postage. Letters, money orders, and valuables, as well as parcels by post, intended for prisoners of war, or dispatched by them, shall be exempt from all postal duties in the countries of origin and destination, as well as in the countries they pass through. Presents and relief in kind for prisoners of war shall be admitted free of all import or other duties, as well as of payments for carriage by the State railways.	Privileges allowed
Art. 17. Officers taken prisoners may receive, if necessary, the full pay allowed them in this position by their country's regulations, the amount to be repaid by their Government.	*Art. 17.* Officers taken prisoners shall receive *the same rate of pay as officers of corresponding rank in the country where they are detained*, the amount to be ultimately refunded by their own Government.	Pay to officers taken prisoner
Art. 18. Prisoners of war shall enjoy every latitude in the exer-	*Art. 18.* Prisoners of war shall enjoy complete liberty in the exer-	Religious liberty

	1899	1907
	cise of their religion, including attendance at their own church services, provided only they comply with the regulations for order and police issued by the military authorities.	cise of their religion, including attendance at the services of whatever church they may belong to, on the sole condition that they comply with the measures of order and police issued by the military authorities.
Wills	*Art. 19.* The wills of prisoners of war are received or drawn up on the same conditions as for soldiers of the national army.	*Art. 19.* The wills of prisoners of war are received or drawn up in the same way as for soldiers of the national army.
Burials, etc.	The same rules shall be observed regarding death certificates, as well as for the burial of prisoners of war, due regard being paid to their grade and rank.	The same rules shall be observed regarding death certificates as well as for the burial of prisoners of war, due regard being paid to their grade and rank.
Repatriation	*Art. 20.* After the conclusion of peace, the repatriation of prisoners of war shall take place as speedily as possible.	*Art. 20.* After the conclusion of peace, the repatriation of prisoners of war shall be carried out as quickly as possible.
	Chapter III. On the Sick and Wounded	*Chapter III. The Sick and Wounded*
Geneva Convention to govern	*Art. 21.* The obligations of belligerents with regard to the sick and wounded are governed by the Geneva Convention of 22 August 1864, subject to any modifications which may be introduced into it.	*Art. 21.* The obligations of belligerents with regard to the sick and wounded are governed by the Geneva Convention.
	Section II. On Hostilities[5]	**Section II. Hostilities**[5]
	Chapter I. On Means of Injuring the Enemy, Sieges, and Bombardments	*Chapter I. Means of Injuring the Enemy, Sieges, and Bombardments*
Restriction	*Art. 22.* The right of belligerents to adopt means of injuring the enemy is not unlimited.	*Art. 22.* The right of belligerents to adopt means of injuring the enemy is not unlimited.

[5] For more recent provisions concerning the subjects dealt with in this section, see the Geneva Convention IV of 1949 relative to the Protection of Civilian Persons in Time of War (*No. 52*), especially Article 154, as well as Protocol I of 1977, Parts III and IV (*No. 56*) and Protocol II, Part IV (*No. 57*).

1899	1907	
Art. 23. Besides the prohibitions provided by special Conventions, it is especially prohibited	*Art. 23.* In addition to the prohibitions provided by special Conventions, it is especially forbidden	Special prohibitions
(a) To employ poison or poisoned arms;	(a) To employ poison or poisoned weapons;	Poison
(b) To kill or wound treacherously individuals belonging to the hostile nation or army;	(b) To kill or wound treacherously individuals belonging to the hostile nation or army;	Treachery
(c) To kill or wound an enemy who, having laid down arms, or having no longer means of defence, has surrendered at discretion;	(c) To kill or wound an enemy who, having laid down his arms, or having no longer means of defence, has surrendered at discretion;	Killing those who have surrendered
(d) To declare that no quarter will be given;	(d) To declare that no quarter will be given;	Quarter
(e) To employ arms, projectiles, or material of a nature to cause superfluous injury;	(e) To employ arms, projectiles, or material calculated to cause unnecessary suffering;	Weapons causing unnecessary suffering
(f) To make improper use of a flag of truce, the national flag or military ensigns and uniform of the enemy, as well as the distinctive badges of the Geneva Convention;	(f) To make improper use of a flag of truce, of the national flag or of the military insignia and uniform of the enemy, as well as the distinctive badges of the Geneva Convention;	Abuse of flags and uniform
(g) To destroy or seize the enemy's property, unless such destruction or seizure be imperatively demanded by the necessities of war.	(g) To destroy or seize the enemy's property, unless such destruction or seizure be imperatively demanded by the necessities of war;	Unnecessary destruction or seizure of property
	(h) *To declare abolished, suspended, or inadmissible in a court of law the rights and actions of the nationals of the hostile party.*	Rights and actions
	A belligerent is likewise forbidden to compel the nationals of the hostile party to take part in the operations of war directed against their own country, even if they were in the belligerent's service before the commencement of the war.[6]	Forced service against one's own country
Art. 24. Ruses of war and the employment of methods necessary to obtain information about	*Art. 24.* Ruses of war and the employment of measures necessary for obtaining information	Obtaining information permitted

[6] Cf. Article 44 of the 1899 Convention, p. 78.

	1899	1907
	the enemy and the country, are considered allowable.	about the enemy and the country are considered permissible.
Assault on undefended towns, etc.	*Art. 25.* The attack or bombardment of towns, villages, habitations or buildings which are not defended, is prohibited.	*Art. 25.* The attack or bombardment, *by whatever means*, of towns, villages, dwellings, or buildings which are undefended is prohibited.
Warning of bombardments	*Art. 26.* The commander of an attacking force, before commencing a bombardment, except in the case of an assault, should do all he can to warn the authorities.	*Art. 26.* The officer in command of an attacking force must, before commencing a bombardment, except in cases of assault, do all in his power to warn the authorities.
Buildings etc. to be spared	*Art. 27.* In sieges and bombardments all necessary steps should be taken to spare as far as possible edifices devoted to religion, art, science, and charity, hospitals, and places where the sick and wounded are collected, provided they are not used at the same time for military purposes.	*Art. 27.* In sieges and bombardments all necessary steps must be taken to spare, as far as possible, buildings dedicated to religion, art, science, or charitable purposes, *historic monuments*, hospitals, and places where the sick and wounded are collected, provided they are not being used at the time for military purposes.
Notification of	The besieged should indicate these buildings or places by some particular and visible signs, which should previously be notified to the assailants.[7]	It is the duty of the besieged to indicate the presence of such buildings or places by distinctive and visible signs, which shall be notified to the enemy beforehand.[7]
Pillage prohibited	*Art. 28.* The pillage of a town or place, even when taken by assault, is prohibited.	*Art. 28.* The pillage of a town or place, even when taken by assault, is prohibited.
	Chapter II. On Spies	*Chapter II. Spies*
Definitions	*Art. 29.* An individual can only be considered a spy if, acting clandestinely, or on false pretences, he obtains, or seeks to obtain infor-	*Art. 29.* A person can only be considered a spy when, acting clandestinely or on false pretences, he obtains or endeavours to obtain

[7] In the relations between states which are bound by the Hague Convention for the Protection of Cultural Property in the Event of Armed Conflict of 14 May 1954 (*No. 71*) the latter Convention is supplementary to this Convention (see Article 36, paragraph 1, of the Convention of 1954). The emblem described in Article 16 of the Convention of 1954 is applicable.

1899	1907	
mation in the zone of operations of a belligerent, with the intention of communicating it to the hostile party.	information in the zone of operations of a belligerent, with the intention of communicating it to the hostile party.	
Thus, soldiers not in disguise who have penetrated into the zone of operations of a hostile army to obtain information are not considered spies. Similarly, the following are not considered spies: soldiers or civilians, carrying out their mission openly, charged with the delivery of despatches destined either for their own army or for that of the enemy. To this class belong likewise individuals sent in balloons to deliver despatches, and generally to maintain communication between the various parts of an army or a territory.	Thus, soldiers not wearing a disguise who have penetrated into the zone of operations of the hostile army, for the purpose of obtaining information, are not considered spies. Similarly, the following are not considered spies: Soldiers and civilians, carrying out their mission openly, entrusted with the delivery of despatches intended either for their own army or for the enemy's army. To this class belong likewise persons sent in balloons for the purpose of carrying despatches and, generally, of maintaining communications between the different parts of an army or a territory.	
Art. 30. A spy taken in the act cannot be punished without previous trial.	*Art. 30.* A spy taken in the act shall not be punished without previous trial.	Trial required
Art. 31. A spy who, after rejoining the army to which he belongs, is subsequently captured by the enemy, is treated as a prisoner of war, and incurs no responsibility for his previous acts of espionage.	*Art. 31.* A spy who, after rejoining the army to which he belongs, is subsequently captured by the enemy, is treated as a prisoner of war, and incurs no responsibility for his previous acts of espionage.	Subsequent capture
Chapter III. On Flags of Truce	*Chapter III. Flags of Truce*	
Art. 32. An individual is considered as a parlementaire who is authorized by one of the belligerents to enter into communication with the other, and who carries a white flag. He has a right to inviolability, as well as the trumpeter, bugler, or drummer, the flag-bearer and the interpreter who may accompany him.	*Art. 32.* A person is regarded as a parlementaire who has been authorized by one of the belligerents to enter into communication with the other, and who advances bearing a white flag. He has a right to inviolability, as well as the trumpeter, bugler or drummer, the flag-bearer and interpreter who may accompany him.	Inviolability of parlementaire

	1899	1907
Reception not compulsory	*Art. 33.* The chief to whom a parlementaire is sent is not obliged to receive him in all circumstances. He can take all steps necessary to prevent the parlementaire taking advantage of his mission to obtain information. In case of abuse, he has the right to detain the parlementaire temporarily.	*Art. 33.* The commander to whom a parlementaire is sent is not in all cases obliged to receive him. He may take all the necessary steps to prevent the parlementaire taking advantage of his mission to obtain information. In case of abuse, he has the right to detain the parlementaire temporarily.
Treason of parlementaire	*Art. 34.* The parlementaire loses his rights of inviolability if it is proved beyond doubt that he has taken advantage of his privileged position to provoke or commit an act of treason.	*Art. 34.* The parlementaire loses his rights of inviolability if it is proved in a clear and incontestable manner that he has taken advantage of his privileged position to provoke or commit an act of treason.
	Chapter IV. On Capitulations	*Chapter IV. Capitulations*
Military honour to be observed	*Art. 35.* Capitulations agreed on between the Contracting Parties must be in accordance with the rules of military honour. When once settled, they must be scrupulously observed by both the parties.	*Art. 35.* Capitulations agreed upon between the Contracting Parties must take into account the rules of military honour. Once settled, they must be scrupulously observed by both parties.
	Chapter V. On Armistices	*Chapter V. Armistices*
Effect	*Art. 36.* An armistice suspends military operations by mutual agreement between the belligerent parties. If its duration is not fixed, the belligerent parties can resume operations at any time, provided always the enemy is warned within the time agreed upon, in accordance with the terms of the armistice.	*Art. 36.* An armistice suspends military operations by mutual agreement between the belligerent parties. If its duration is not defined, the belligerent parties may resume operations at any time, provided always that the enemy is warned within the time agreed upon, in accordance with the terms of the armistice.
General or local	*Art. 37.* An armistice may be general or local. The first suspends all military operations of the belligerent States; the second, only	*Art. 37.* An armistice may be general or local. The first suspends the military operations of the belligerent States everywhere; the

1899	1907	
those between certain fractions of the belligerent armies and in a fixed radius.	second only between certain fractions of the belligerent armies and within a fixed radius.	
Art. 38. An armistice must be notified officially, and in good time, to the competent authorities and the troops. Hostilities are suspended immediately after the notification, or at a fixed date.	*Art. 38.* An armistice must be notified officially and in good time to the competent authorities and to the troops. Hostilities are suspended immediately after the notification, or on the date fixed.	Notification
Art. 39. It is for the Contracting Parties to settle, in the terms of the armistice, what communications may be held, on the theatre of war, with the population and with each other.	*Art. 39.* It rests with the Contracting Parties to settle, in the terms of the armistice, what communications may be held in the theatre of war with the inhabitants and between the inhabitants of one belligerent State and those of the other.	Communication allowed with inhabitants
Art. 40. Any serious violation of the armistice by one of the parties gives the other party the right to denounce it, and even, in case of urgency, to recommence hostilities at once.	*Art. 40.* Any serious violation of the armistice by one of the parties gives the other party the right of denouncing it, and even, in cases of urgency, of recommencing hostilities immediately.	Effect of violation by Powers
Art. 41. A violation of the terms of the armistice by private individuals acting on their own initiative, only confers the right of demanding the punishment of the offenders, and, if necessary, indemnity for the losses sustained.	*Art. 41.* A violation of the terms of the armistice by private persons acting on their own initiative only entitles the injured party to demand the punishment of the offenders or, if necessary, compensation for the losses sustained.	Violation by private persons
Section III. On Military Authority Over Hostile Territory[8]	**Section III. Military Authority Over The Territory Of The Hostile State**[8]	
Art. 42. Territory is considered occupied when it is actually placed under the authority of the hostile army.	*Art. 42.* Territory is considered occupied when it is actually placed under the authority of the hostile army.	Actual occupation

[8] For more recent provisions on occupied territories, see the Geneva Convention IV of 1949 relative to the Protection of Civilian Persons in Time of War (*No. 52*), especially Article 154, and Protocol I of 1977, Part IV (*No. 56*).

	1899	1907
Extent	The occupation applies only to the territory where such authority is established, and in a position to assert itself.	The occupation extends only to the territory where such authority has been established and can be exercised.
Preservation of order and safety	*Art. 43.* The authority of the legitimate power having actually passed into the hands of the occupant, the latter shall take all steps in his power to re-establish and insure, as far as possible, public order and safety, while respecting, unless absolutely prevented, the laws in force in the country.	*Art. 43.* The authority of the legitimate power having in fact passed into the hands of the occupant, the latter shall take all the measures in his power to restore, and ensure, as far as possible, public order and safety, while respecting, unless absolutely prevented, the laws in force in the country.
Forcing information from inhabitants forbidden	*Art. 44.*[9] Any compulsion of the population of occupied territory to take part in military operations against its own country is prohibited.	*Art. 44.*[10] A belligerent is forbidden to force the inhabitants of territory occupied by it to *furnish information about the army of the other belligerent, or about its means of defense.*
Requiring oath of allegiance forbidden	*Art. 45.* Any pressure on the population of occupied territory to take the oath to the hostile Power is prohibited.	*Art. 45.* It is forbidden to compel the inhabitants of occupied territory to swear allegiance to the hostile Power.
Rights and property to be respected	*Art. 46.* Family honours and rights, individual lives and private property, as well as religious convictions and liberty, must be respected.	*Art. 46.* Family honour and rights, the lives of persons, and private property, as well as religious convictions and practice, must be respected.
No confiscation	Private property cannot be confiscated.	Private property cannot be confiscated.
Pillage forbidden	*Art. 47.* Pillage is formally prohibited.	*Art. 47.* Pillage is formally forbidden.
Collection of taxes	*Art. 48.* If, in the territory occupied, the occupant collects the taxes, dues, and tolls imposed for the benefit of the State, he shall do it, as far as possible, in accordance with the rules in existence	*Art. 48.* If, in the territory occupied, the occupant collects the taxes, dues, and tolls imposed for the benefit of the State, he shall do so, as far as is possible, in accordance with the rules of

[9] Cf. the last paragraph of Article 23 of the 1907 Convention, p. 73.

[10] For reservations in respect of this article by Austria-Hungary, Germany, Japan, Montenegro and Russia, see pp. 86–87

1899	1907	
and the assessment in force, and will in consequence be bound to defray the expenses of the administration of the occupied territory on the same scale as that by which the legitimate Government was bound.	assessment and incidence in force, and shall in consequence be bound to defray the expenses of the administration of the occupied territory to the same extent as the legitimate Government was so bound.	
Art. 49. If, besides the taxes mentioned in the preceding Article, the occupant levies other money taxes in the occupied territory, this can only be for military necessities or the administration of such territory.	*Art. 49.* If, in addition to the taxes mentioned in the above article, the occupant levies other money contributions in the occupied territory, this shall only be for the needs of the army or of the administration of the territory in question.	Levies for military needs
Art. 50. No general penalty, pecuniary or otherwise, can be inflicted on the population on account of the acts of individuals for which it cannot be regarded as collectively responsible.	*Art. 50.* No general penalty, pecuniary or otherwise, shall be inflicted upon the population on account of the acts of individuals for which they cannot be regarded as jointly and severally responsible.	General penalty for acts of individuals forbidden
Art. 51. No tax shall be collected except under a written order and on the responsibility of a commander-in-chief. This collection shall only take place, as far as possible, in accordance with the rules in existence and the assessment of taxes in force. For every payment a receipt shall be given to the taxpayer.	*Art. 51.* No contribution shall be collected except under a written order, and on the responsibility of a commander-in-chief. The collection of the said contribution shall only be effected as far as possible in accordance with the rules of assessment and incidence of the taxes in force. For every contribution a receipt shall be given to the contributors.	Collection of contributions
Art. 52. Neither requisitions in kind nor services can be demanded from communes or inhabitants except for the necessities of the army of occupation. They must be in proportion to the resources of the country, and of such a nature as not to involve the population in the obligation of taking part in military operations against their country. These requisitions and services shall only be demanded on the	*Art. 52.* Requisitions in kind and services shall not be demanded from municipalities or inhabitants except for the needs of the army of occupation. They shall be in proportion to the resources of the country, and of such a nature as not to involve the inhabitants in the obligation of taking part in military operations against their own country. Such requisitions and services shall only be demanded on the	Requisitions for needs of army

	1899	1907
	authority of the commander in the locality occupied. The contributions in kind shall, as far as possible, be paid for in ready money; if not, their receipt shall be acknowledged.	authority of the commander in the locality occupied. Contributions in kind shall as far is possible be paid for in cash; if not, a receipt shall be given *and the payment of the amount due shall be made as soon as possible.*
Seizure of public cash, property etc. Telegraphs, transportation etc.	*Art. 53.* An army of occupation can only take possession of the cash, funds, and property liable to requisition belonging strictly to the State, depots arms, means of transport, stores and supplies, and, generally all movable property of the State which may be used for military operations. Railway plant, land telegraphs, telephones, steamers and other ships, apart from cases governed by maritime law, as well as depots of arms and, generally, all kinds of munitions of war, even though belonging to companies or to private persons, are likewise material which may serve for military operations, but they must be restored at the conclusion of peace, and indemnities paid for them.	*Art. 53.* An army of occupation can only take possession of cash, funds, and realizable securities which are strictly the property of the State, depots of arms, means of transport, stores and supplies, and, generally, all movable property belonging to the State which may be used for military operations. *All appliances, whether on land, at sea, or in the air, adapted for the transmission of news, or for the transport of persons or things*, exclusive of cases governed by naval law, depots of arms, and, generally, all kinds of munitions of war, *may be seized, even if they belong to private individuals*, but must be restored and compensation fixed when peace is made.
(1899) Plant of railways from neutral states (1907) Submarine cables to neutral territory	*Art. 54.*[11] The plant of railways coming from neutral States, whether the property of those States, or of companies, or of private persons, shall be sent back to them as soon as possible.	*Art. 54. Submarine cables connecting an occupied territory with a neutral territory shall not be seized or destroyed except in the case of absolute necessity. They must likewise be restored and compensation fixed when peace is made.*
Administration of public property in occupied territory	*Art. 55.* The occupying State shall only be regarded as administrator and usufructuary of the public buildings, real property, forests and agricultural works belonging to the hostile State, and situated in	*Art. 55.* The occupying State shall be regarded only as administrator and usufructuary of public buildings, real estate, forests, and agricultural estates belonging to the hostile State, and situated in the

[11] Cf. Article 19 of the Hague Convention (V) of 1907 respecting the Rights and Duties of Neutral Powers and Persons in Case of War on Land (*No. 112*).

1899	1907	
the occupied country. It must protect the capital of these properties, and administer it according to the rules of usufruct.	occupied country. It must safeguard the capital of these properties, and administer them in accordance with the rules of usufruct.	
Art. 56. The property of the communes, that of religious, charitable, and educational institutions, and those of arts and science, even when State property, shall be treated as private property.	*Art. 56.* The property of municipalities, that of institutions dedicated to religion, charity and education, the arts and sciences, even when State property, shall be treated as private property.	Municipal, religious etc. property
All seizure of and destruction, or intentional damage done to such institutions, to historical monuments, works of art or science, is prohibited, and should be made the subject of proceedings.	All seizure of, destruction or wilful damage done to institutions of this character, historic monuments, works of art and science, is forbidden, and should be made the subject of legal proceedings.	Legal proceedings for seizure etc.

Section IV. On the Internment of Belligerents and the Care of the Wounded in Neutral Countries[12]

Confinement of belligerents in neutral territory

Art. 57. A neutral State which receives in its territory troops belonging to the belligerent armies shall intern them, as far as possible, at a distance from the theatre of war.

It can keep them in camps, and even confine them in fortresses or locations assigned for this purpose.

It shall decide whether officers may be left at liberty on giving their parole that they will not leave the neutral territory without authorization.

Food, clothing etc.

Art. 58. Failing a special convention, the neutral State shall

[12] In 1907 the provisions on this subject, Articles 57, 58, 59 and 60 were transferred to the Hague Convention (V) respecting the Rights and Duties of Neutral Powers and Persons in Case of War on Land as Articles 11, 12, 14 and 15 thereof (*No. 112*). No change was made in their text except substitution of the word "Power" for the word "State" wherever the latter appears in these articles.

1899	1907

supply the interned with the food, clothing, and relief required by humanity.

Reimbursements

At the conclusion of peace, the expenses caused by the internment shall be made good.

Transit of wounded or sick through neutral territory

Art. 59. A neutral State may authorize the passage over its territory of wounded or sick belonging to the belligerent armies, on condition that the trains bringing them shall carry neither combatants nor war material. In such a case, the neutral State is bound to adopt such measures of safety and control as may be necessary for the purpose.

Neutral state must furnish guard

Wounded and sick brought under these conditions into neutral territory by one of the belligerents, and belonging to the hostile party, must be guarded by the neutral State, so as to insure their not taking part again in the military operations. The same duty shall devolve on the neutral State with regard to wounded or sick of the other army who may be committed to its care.

Geneva Convention applicable

Art. 60. The Geneva Convention applies to sick and wounded interned in neutral territory.

CONVENTION OF 1899

SIGNATURES, RATIFICATIONS, AND ACCESSIONS[1]

State	*Signature*	*Ratification, Accession, Notification of Continuity (C)*
Argentine Republic	–	17 June 1907
Austria-Hungary	29 July 1899	4 September 1900
Belarus	29 July 1899	4 September 1900
Belgium	29 July 1899	4 September 1900
Bolivia	–	7 February 1907
Brazil	–	25 February 1907
Bulgaria	29 July 1899	4 September 1900
Chile	–	19 June 1907
China	–	12 June 1907
Colombia	–	30 January 1907
Cuba	–	17 April 1907
Denmark	29 July 1899	4 September 1900
Dominican Republic	–	13 April 1907
Ecuador	–	31 July 1907
El Salvador	–	20 June 1902
Fiji	–	2 April 1973 (C)
France	29 July 1899	4 September 1900
Germany	29 July 1899	4 September 1900
Great Britain	29 July 1899	4 September 1900
Greece	29 July 1899	4 April 1901
Guatemala	–	2 May 1906
Haiti	–	24 May 1907
Honduras	–	21 August 1906
Italy	29 July 1899	4 September 1900
Japan	29 July 1899	6 October 1900
Korea	–	17 March 1903
Luxemburg	29 July 1899	12 July 1901
Mexico	29 July 1899	17 April 1901
Montenegro	29 July 1899	16 October 1900
Netherlands	29 July 1899	4 September 1900
Nicaragua	–	17 May 1907
Norway[2]	–	5 July 1907
Panama	–	20 July 1907
Paraguay	–	12 April 1907
Persia	29 July 1899	4 September 1900
Peru	–	24 November 1903
Portugal	29 July 1999	September 1900
Romania	9 July 1899	4 September 1900
Russia[3]	29 July 1899	4 September 1900

[1] Based on a communication received from the Ministry of Foreign Affairs of the Netherlands of 12 December 2001. See also ICRC website: www.icrc.org/ihl.nsf.

[2] Sweden and Norway constituted a Union until 1905. Action taken by them prior to that date was taken as a single power.

[3] By the note of the Foreign Ministry of the USSR of 7 March 1955 "The Government of the USSR recognises the Conventions and Declarations of The Hague from 1899 and 1907, which were ratified by Russia to the extent that the Conventions and Declarations do not

State	*Signature*	*Ratification, Accession, Notification of Continuity (C)*
Serbia[4]	29 July 1899	11 May 1901
Siam	1–9 July 1899	4 September 1900
South Africa	–	10 March 1978 (C)
Spain	29 July 1899	4 September 1900
Sweden[2]	29 July 1899	5 July 1907
Switzerland	–	20 June 1907
Turkey	29 July 1899	12 June 1907
United States of America	29 July 1899	9 April 1902
Uruguay	–	21 June 1906
Venezuela	–	I March 1907

RESERVATIONS

None

cont.
contradict the United Nations Charter and if they are not amended or replaced by ulterior international agreements to which the USSR is a Party, such as the 1925 Geneva Protocol for the Prohibition of Use of Asphyxiating, Poisonous and Other Gases and of Bacteriological Methods of Warfare and the 1949 Geneva Conventions for the Protection of Victims of War" (*Izvestiya*, 9 March 1955).

In January 1992, the Ministry of Foreign Affairs of the Russian Federation informed the heads of diplomatic missions in Moscow that the Russian Federation continues to be a party to all conventions which are in force for the Soviet Union. The Ministry of Foreign Affairs of the Kingdom of the Netherlands considers therefore that the Russian Federation is bound by the conventions to which the Soviet Union was party (Communication of the depositary to the Henry Dunant Institute of 6 November 1992).

On 4 June 1962, the Byelorussian Soviet Socialist Republic made a declaration similar to that made by the USSR.

4 The Government of the Socialist Federative Republic of Yugoslavia confirmed by its note of 27 March 1969, received by the Ministry of Foreign Affairs of the Netherlands on 8 April 1969, that it considers itself to be a Party to the Treaties and Declarations of The Hague of 29 July 1899, ratified by Serbia.

CONVENTION OF 1907

SIGNATURES, RATIFICATIONS AND ACCESSIONS[1]

State	*Signature*	*Ratification, Accession, Notification of Continuity (C)*
Argentine Republic	18 October 1907	
Austria-Hungary	18 October 1907 *Res.*	27 November 1909 *Res.*
Belgium	18 October 1907	8 August 1910
Bolivia	18 October 1907	27 November 1909
Brazil	18 October 1907	5 January 1914
Bulgaria	18 October 1907	
Chile	18 October 1907	
China	–	10 May 1917
Colombia	18 October 1907	
Cuba	18 October 1907	22 February 1912
Denmark	18 October 1907	27 November 1909
Dominican Republic	18 October 1907	16 May 1958
Ecuador	18 October 1907	
El Salvador	18 October 1907	27 November 1909
Ethiopia	–	5 August 1935
Fiji	–	2 April 1973 (C)
Finland[2]	–	10 April 1922
France	18 October 1907	7 October 1910
Germany[3]	18 October 1907 *Res.*	27 November 1909 *Res.*
Great Britain	18 October 1907	27 November 1909
Greece	18 October 1907	
Guatemala	18 October 1907	15 March 1911
Haiti	18 October 1907	2 February 1910
Italy	18 October 1907	
Japan	18 October 1907 *Res.*	13 December 1911 *Res.*
Liberia	–	4 February 1914
Luxemburg	18 October 1907	5 September 1912
Mexico	18 October 1907	27 November 1909
Montenegro	18 October 1907 *Res.*	
Netherlands	18 October 1907	27 November 1909
Nicaragua	–	16 December 1909
Norway	18 October 1907	19 September 1910

[1] Based on a communication received from the Ministry of Foreign Affairs of the Netherlands of 12 December 2001. See also ICRC website: www.icrc.org/ihl.nsf

[2] By letter dated 12 May 1980 the Netherlands Ministry of Foreign Affairs stated (a) Finland's accession on 30 December 1918 to this and other 1907 Hague Conventions and to the 1907 Hague Declaration was initially regarded as provisional, pending the final resolution of Finland's international status; (b) after consultation with the other contracting powers, the depositary stated on 9 June 1922 that Finland's accession should be regarded as final and complete; and (c) the Convention and the Declaration entered into force for Finland on 9 June 1922.

[3] By a letter received at the Ministry of Foreign Affairs of the Kingdom of the Netherlands on 9 February 1959, the Government of the German Democratic Republic has informed the Ministry that it reapplies the Convention. This declaration is only of historical importance after the conclusion of the Treaty of 31 August 1990 (Unification Treaty) between the Federal Republic of Germany and German Democratic Republic. See note 3 of the document *No. 18*, pp. 170–171 and note 35 of documents *Nos. 49-52*, pp. 639–640.

State	*Signature*	*Ratification, Accession, Notification of Continuity (C)*
Panama	18 October 1907	11 September 1911
Paraguay	18 October 1907	
Persia	18 October 1907	
Peru	18 October 1907	–
Poland	–	9 May 1925
Portugal	18 October 1907	13 April 1911
Romania	18 October 1907	1 March 1912
Russia[4]	18 October 1907 *Res.*	27 November 1909 *Res.*
Serbia	18 October 1907	
Slam	18 October 1907	12 March 1910
South Africa	–	10 March 1978 (C)
Sweden	18 October 1907	27 November 1909
Switzerland	18 October 1907	12 May 1910
Turkey	18 October 1907 *Res.*	
United States of America	18 October 1907	27 November 1909
Uruguay	18 October 1907	
Venezuela	18 October 1907	

RESERVATIONS

AUSTRIA-HUNGARY (*reservation made on signature and maintained in the* procès-verbal *of deposit of ratifications*)
Under reservation of the declaration made in the plenary session of the Conference of 17 August 1907.

Extract from the procès-verbal: The delegation of Austria-Hungary having accepted the new Article 22a,[5] on condition that Article 44 of the Convention now in force be maintained as it is, cannot consent to Article 44a, proposed by the Second Commission.[6]

GERMANY (*reservation made on signature and maintained in the act of ratification*)
Under reservation of Article 44 of the annexed Regulations.

---

4 By the note of the Foreign Ministry of the USSR of 7 March 1955 "The Government of the USSR recognises the Conventions and Declarations of The Hague from 1899 and 1907, which were ratified by Russia to the extent that the Conventions and Declarations do not contradict the United Nations Charter and if they are not amended or replaced by ulterior international agreements to which the USSR is a Party, such as the 1925 Geneva Protocol for the Prohibition of Use of Asphyxiating, Poisonous and Other Gases and of Bacteriological Methods of Warfare and the 1949 Geneva Conventions for the Protection of Victims of War" (*Izvestiya*, 9 March 1955).

In January 1992, the Ministry of Foreign Affairs of the Russian Federation informed the heads of diplomatic missions in Moscow, that the Russian Federation continues to be a party to all conventions which are in force for the Soviet Union. The Ministry of Foreign Affairs of the Kingdom of the Netherlands considers therefore that the Russian Federation is bound by the conventions to which the Soviet Union was party (communication of the depositary to the Henry Dunant Institute of 6 November 1992).

On 4 June 1962, the Byelorussian Soviet Socialist Republic made a declaration similar to that made by the USSR.

5 The proposed Article 22a became the last paragraph of Article 23.

6 Statement of Mr. Mérey von Kapos-Mère, *Deuxième Conférence internationale de la Paix, 1907*, Vol. I, p. 86; *The Proceedings of the Hague Peace Conferences, 1907*, Vol. I, p. 84. Article 44a became Article 44.

JAPAN (*reservation made on signature and maintained in the act of ratification*)
With reservation of Article 44.

MONTENEGRO (*reservation made on signature*)
Under the reservations formulated as to Article 44 of the Regulations annexed to the present Convention and contained in the minutes of the fourth plenary session of 17 August 1907.

Extract from the procès-verbal*:* The delegation of Montenegro has the honour to declare that having accepted the new Article 22a, proposed by the delegation of Germany, in the place of Article 44 of the existing Regulations of 1899, it makes reservations on the subject of the new wording of the said Article 44.[7]

RUSSIA (*reservation made on signature and maintained in the act of ratification*)
Under the reservations formulated as to Article 44 of the Regulations annexed to the present Convention and contained in the minutes of the fourth plenary session of 17 August 1907.

Extract from the procès-verbal*:* The delegation of Russia has the honour to declare that having accepted the new Article 22a, proposed by the delegation of Germany, in the place of Article 44 of the existing Regulations of 1899, it makes reservations on the subject of the new wording of the said Article 44a.[8]

TURKEY (*reservation made on signature*)
Under reservation of Article 3.

* * *

See also No. 56

7 Statement of Mr. Tcharykow, *Deuxième Conférence internationale de la Paix, 1907.* Vol. I, p. 86; *The Proceedings of the Hague Peace Conferences, 1907*, Vol. I, p. 84.

8 Statement of Mr. Martens, *Deuxième Conférence internationale de la Paix, 1907,* Vol. I, p. 86; *The Proceedings of the Hague Peace Conferences, 1907*, Vol. I, p. 84.

II

METHODS AND MEANS OF WARFARE

No. 9

DECLARATION RENOUNCING THE USE, IN TIME OF WAR, OF EXPLOSIVE PROJECTILES UNDER 400 GRAMMES WEIGHT

Signed at St. Petersburg, 29 November/11 December 1868

INTRODUCTORY NOTE: The Declaration of St. Petersburg is the first formal agreement prohibiting the use of certain weapons of war. It had its origin in the invention, in 1863, by Russian military authorities of a bullet which exploded on contact with a hard substance and whose primary object was to blow up ammunition wagons. In 1867 the projectile was so modified as to explode on contact with a soft substance. As such the bullet was considered an inhuman instrument of war. The Russian Government, unwilling to use the bullet itself or to allow another country to take advantage of it, suggested that the use of the bullet be prohibited by international agreement. The Declaration to that effect, adopted in 1868, which has the force of law, confirms the customary rule according to which the use of arms, projectiles and materials of a nature to cause unnecessary suffering is prohibited. This rule was later on laid down in Article 23(e) of the Hague Regulations on land warfare of 1899 and 1907. The Declaration of St. Petersburg prompted the adoption of further declarations of a similar nature at the two Hague Peace Conferences of 1899 and 1907. The Hague Declarations relating to the discharge of projectiles and explosives from balloons, the use of asphyxiating gases and the use of expanding bullets refer in their preambles to the Declaration of St. Petersburg.

ENTRY INTO FORCE: 29 November/11 December 1868.

AUTHENTIC TEXT: French. The English translation below is reprinted from *Parliamentary Papers*, 1869, LXIV, p. 659.

TEXT PUBLISHED IN: *Annuaire diplomatique de l'Empire de Russie pour l'année 1869*, St. Petersburg, 1869, Declaration and other related documents, pp. 245–286 (French); Martens, *NRGT*, 1ère série, Vol. XVIII, pp. 474–475 (French); Deltenre, pp. 48–51 (Engl., French, German, Dutch); *Fontes Historiae Juris Gentium*, Vol. III/1, pp. 556–557 (German, English, French); *International Red Cross Handbook*, 1983, pp. 319–320 (Engl.); *Manual de la Cruz Roja internacional*, 1983, pp. 323–324 (Span.); *Manuel de la Croix-Rouge internationale*, 1983, pp. 331–332 (French); *Handbook of the International Movement*, 1994, pp. 296–297 (Engl.); *Manuel du Mouvement international*, 1994, pp. 308–309 (French); *Manual del Movimiento internacional*, 1994, pp. 300–301 (Span.); *Parliamentary Papers*, 1869, LXIV, p. 659; BFSP, Vol. 58, 1867–1868, p. 16 (French); *Annuaire de l'Institut de droit international*, Vol. I, 1877, pp. 306–307 (French); *CTS*, Vol. 138, 1868–1869, pp. 297–299 (French); Higgins, pp. 5–7 (Engl.); *AJIL*, Vol. 1, 1907, Suppl., pp. 95–96 (Engl.); *IRRC*, No. 292, November–December 1993, pp. 515–516 (Engl.); *RICR*, No. 804, novembre–décembre 1993, pp. 543–544 (French); *Revista internacional de la Cruz Roja*, No. 120, noviembre–diciembre de 1993, pp. 543–544 (Span.); Friedman, pp. 192–193 (Engl.); Roberts and

Guelff, pp. 53–57 (Engl.); *Droit des conflits armés*, pp. 101–103 (French); De Clercq, Vol. 10, pp. 219–220 (French); *Les deux Conférences de la Paix*, p. 195 (French); Jules Basdevant, *Traités et Conventions en Vigueur entre la France et les Puissances Etrangères*, Vol. III, Paris, Imprimerie Nationale, 1920, pp. 750–751 (French); F. F. Martens, *Sobranie traktatov' i Konvencii, zaklyuchennykh' Rossieyu s' innostrannymi Derzhavami*, S. Peterburg', tome IV, No. 167, pp. 959–961 (Russ.); Heffter-Taube, pp. 96–97 (Russ.); Liszt, pp. LXXXV–LXXXVI (Russ.); *Mezhdunarodnoe pravo*, Vol. III, pp. 37–38 (Russ. – extract); Ceppi, p. 326 (Span. – extract); ICRC website: www. icrc.org/ihl.nsf.

* * *

On the proposition of the Imperial Cabinet of Russia, an International Military Commission having assembled at St. Petersburg in order to examine the expediency of forbidding the use of certain projectiles in time of war between civilized nations, and that Commission having by common agreement fixed the technical limits at which the necessities of war ought to yield to the requirements of humanity, the Undersigned are authorized by the orders of their Governments to declare as follows:

Considering:

That the progress of civilization should have the effect of alleviating as much as possible the calamities of war;

That the only legitimate object which States should endeavour to accomplish during war is to weaken the military forces of the enemy;

That for this purpose it is sufficient to disable the greatest possible number of men;

That this object would be exceeded by the employment of arms which uselessly aggravate the sufferings of disabled men, or render their death inevitable;

That the employment of such arms would, therefore, be contrary to the laws of humanity;

The Contracting Parties engage mutually to renounce, in case of war among themselves, the employment by their military or naval troops of any projectile of a weight below 400 grammes, which is either explosive or charged with fulminating or inflammable substances.

They will invite all the States which have not taken part in the deliberations of the International Military Commission assembled at St. Petersburg by sending Delegates thereto, to accede to the present engagement.

This engagement is compulsory only upon the Contracting or Acceding Parties thereto in case of war between two or more of themselves; it is not applicable to non-Contracting Parties, or Parties who shall not have acceded to it.

It will also cease to be compulsory from the moment when, in a war between Contracting or Acceding Parties, a non-Contracting Party or a non-Acceding Party shall join one of the belligerents.

The Contracting or Acceding Parties reserve to themselves to come hereafter to an understanding whenever a precise proposition shall be drawn up in view of future improvements which science may effect in the armament of troops, in order to maintain the principles which they have established, and to conciliate the necessities of war with the laws of humanity.

Done at St. Petersburg, 29 November [11 December] 1868.

[Here follow signatures]

SIGNATURES AND ACCESSIONS[1]

State	*Signature*	*Accession*[2]
Austria-Hungary	11 December 1868	–
Baden	–	11 January 1869
Bavaria	11 December 1868	–
Belgium	11 December 1868	–
Brazil	–	23 October 1869[3]
Denmark	11 December 1868	–
France	11 December 1868	–
Great Britain	11 December 1868	–
Greece	11 December 1868	–
Italy	11 December 1868	–
Netherlands	11 December 1868	–
Persia	11 December 1868	–
Portugal	11 December 1868	–
Prussia and the North German Confederation	11 December 1868	–
Russia	11 December 1868	–
Sweden and Norway	11 December 1868	–
Switzerland	11 December 1868	–
Turkey	11 December 1868	–
Wurtemberg	11 December 1868	–

RESERVATIONS

None

1 Information supplied in communications received from the Ministry of Foreign Affairs of the French Republic on 10 May 1995, the Foreign and Commonwealth Office of Great Britain of 29 June 1999 (www.fco.gov.uk/directory/treaty/asp), and the Ministry of Foreign Affairs of the USSR on 16 July 1991. See also ICRC wbsite: www. icrc.org/ihl.nsf. Neither the Declaration nor the minutes of the Commission's sessions have provisions concerning the depositary. According to the archives, Russia exercised *de facto* the functions of the depositary (certifying and distributing copies to the signatory states, taking statements of accession of other states, safeguarding of originals of the Declaration, the protocols of international commission and other related documents). The originals are held in the Archives of Foreign Policy of Russia, Historical-Diplomatic Office of the Ministry of Foreign Affairs of the Federation of Russia.

All dates in this table are according to the Western calendar, not the Julian one which was in use in Russia at that time.

2 The dates of accession of Baden and of Brazil were communicated to the Henry Dunant Institute by the Department of International Law of the Ministry of Foreign Affairs of the USSR on 16 July 1991. These indications are also given by Jules Basdevant, *Traités et Conventions en Vigueur entre la France et les Puissances Etrangères*, Vol. III, Paris, Imprimerie Nationale, 1920, pp. 750–751.

3 Based on a communication of the Government of the Federal Republic of Brazil, dated 8 July 1986.

No. 10

DECLARATION (IV, 2) CONCERNING ASPHYXIATING GASES

Signed at The Hague, 29 July 1899

INTRODUCTORY NOTE: This Declaration gives expression, with regard to a particular instrument of warfare, to the customary rules prohibiting the use of poison and of material causing unnecessary suffering. These general customary rules were formally enacted in Articles 23(a) and 23(e) of the Hague Regulations of 1899 and 1907. The prohibition of the use of poison is also mentioned in Article 70 of the Lieber Instructions (*No. 1*), Article 13(a) of the Brussels Declaration of 1874 (*No. 2*) and Article 8(a) of the *Oxford Manual* adopted by the Institute of International Law in 1880 (*No. 3*). For more recent conventions concerning the use of gases, see Treaty of Washington of 1922 (*No. 83*), the Geneva Protocol of 1925 (*No. 13*) and Resolution 2603 (XXIV) of 1969 of the United Nations General Assembly (*No. 15*). See also documents *No. 16* (Convention on the Prohibition of the Development, Production and Stockpiling of Bacteriological (Biological) and Toxin Weapons and on Their Destruction, of 1972) and *No. 22* (Convention on the Prohibition of the Development, Production, Stockpiling and Use of Chemical Weapons and on Their Destruction, of 1993).

ENTRY INTO FORCE: 4 September 1900.

AUTHENTIC TEXT: French. The English translation below is reprinted from Scott, *Hague Conventions*, pp. 225–226. It reproduces the translation of the United States Department of State.

TEXT PUBLISHED IN: *Conférence internationale de la Paix, 1899* pp. 250–251 (French); *Les deux Conférences de la Paix*, pp. 45–46 (French); Scott, *Hague Conventions*, pp. 225–226 (Engl.); Scott, *Les Conventions de La Haye*, pp. 225–226 (French); Scott, *Les Conférences de La Haye*, p. 27 (French); Martens, *NRGT*, 2ème série, Vol. XXVI, pp. 1002–1006 (French, German); Deltenre, pp. 142–145 (Engl., French, German, Dutch); Olivart, Vol. XII, pp. 647–650 (French, Span.); *GBTS*, 1907, No. 32 (Engl., French); *BFSP*, Vol. 91, 1898–1899, pp. 1017–1019 (French); *CTS*, Vol. 187, 1898–1899, pp. 453-455 (French); *AJIL*, Vol. 1, 1907, Suppl., pp. 155–157 (Engl., French); Friedman, pp. 249–250 (Engl.); Roberts and Guelff, pp. 59–61 (Engl.); *Droit des conflits armés*, pp. 105–108 (French); De Clercq, Vol. XXI, pp. 743–745 (French); Bustamante, pp. 231–232 (Span.); Korovin, pp. 367–368 (Russ.); *Mezhdunarodnoe pravo*, Vol. III, pp. 38–39 (Russ. – extract); ICRC website: www.icrc.org/ihl.nsf.

* * *

The undersigned, Plenipotentiaries of the Powers represented at the International Peace Conference at The Hague, duly authorized to that effect by their Governments, inspired by the sentiments which found expression in the Declaration of St. Petersburg of 29 November (11 December) 1868,

Declare as follows:

The Contracting Powers agree to abstain from the use of projectiles the sole object of which is the diffusion of asphyxiating or deleterious gases.

The present Declaration is only binding on the Contracting Powers in the case of a war between two or more of them.

It shall cease to be binding from the time when, in a war between the Contracting Powers, one of the belligerents shall be joined by a non-Contracting Power.

The present Declaration shall be ratified as soon as possible. The ratifications shall be deposited at The Hague.

A *procès-verbal* shall be drawn up on the receipt of each ratification, a copy of which, duly certified, shall be sent through the diplomatic channel to all the Contracting Powers.

The non-Signatory Powers can adhere to the present Declaration. For this purpose they must make their adhesion known to the Contracting Powers by means of a written notification addressed to the Netherlands Government, and by it communicated to all the other Contracting Powers.

In the event of one of the High Contracting Parties denouncing the present Declaration, such denunciation shall not take effect until a year after the notification made in writing to the Government of the Netherlands, and forthwith communicated by it to all the other Contracting Powers.

This denunciation shall only affect the notifying Power. In faith of which the Plenipotentiaries have signed the present Declaration, and affixed their seals thereto.

Done at The Hague, 29 July 1899, in a single copy, which shall be kept in the archives of the Netherlands Government, and copies of which, duly certified, shall be sent by the diplomatic channel to the Contracting Powers.

[Here follow signatures]

SIGNATURES, RATIFICATIONS AND ACCESSIONS[1]

State	*Signature*	*Ratification, Accession, Notification of Continuity (C)*
Austria-Hungary	29 July 1899	4 September 1900
Belgium	29 July 1899	4 September 1900
Bulgaria	29 July 1899	4 September 1900
China	29 July 1899	21 November 1904
Denmark	29 July 1899	4 September 1900
Ethiopia	–	9 August 1935
Fiji	–	2 April 1973
France	19 July 1899	4 September 1900
Germany	29 July 1899	4 September1900
Great Britain and Ireland	–	30 August 1907
Greece	29 July 1899	4 April 1901

1 Based on a communication received from the Ministry of Foreign Affairs of the Netherlands of 12 December 2001. See also ICRC website: www.icrc.org/ihl.nsf.

State	*Signature*	*Ratification, Accession, Notification of Continuity (C)*
Italy	29 July 1899	4 September 1900
Japan	29 July 1899	6 October 1900
Luxemburg	29 July 1899	12 July 1901
Mexico	29 July 1899	17 April 1901
Montenegro	29 July 1899	16 October 1900
Netherlands	29 July 1899	4 September 1900
Nicaragua	–	11 October 1907
Norway[2]	29 July 1899	4 September 1900
Persia	29 July 1899	4 September 1900
Portugal	29 July 1899	4 September 1900
Romania	29 July 1899	4 September 1900
Russia[3]	29 July 1899	4 September 1900
Serbia[4]	29 July 1899	11 May 1901
Siam	29 July 1899	4 September 1900
South Africa	–	10 March 1978
Spain	29 July 1899	4 September 1900
Sweden[2]	29 July 1899	4 September 1900
Switzerland	29 July 1899	29 December 1900
Turkey	29 July 1899	12 June 1907

RESERVATIONS

None

---

2 Sweden and Norway constituted a Union until 1905. Action taken by them prior to that date was taken as a single power.

3 By the note of the Foreign Ministry of the USSR of 7 March 1955 "The Government of the USSR recognises the Conventions and Declarations of The Hague from 1899 and 1907, which were ratified by Russia to the extent that the Conventions and Declarations do not contradict the United Nations Charter and if they are not amended or replaced by ulterior international agreements to which the USSR is a Party, such as the 1925 Geneva Protocol for the Prohibition of Use of Asphyxiating, Poisonous and Other Gases and of Bacteriological Methods of Warfare and the 1949 Geneva Conventions for the Protection of Victims of War" (*Izvestiya*, 9 March 1955).

In January 1992, the Ministry of Foreign Affairs of the Russian Federation informed the heads of diplomatic missions in Moscow, that the Russian Federation continues to be a party to all conventions which are in force for the Soviet Union. The Ministry of Foreign Affairs of the Kingdom of the Netherlands considers therefore that the Russian Federation is bound by the conventions to which the Soviet Union was party (communication of the depositary to the Henry Dunant Institute of 6 November 1992).

On 4 June 1962, the Byelorussian Soviet Socialist Republic made a declaration similar to that made by the USSR.

4 The Government of the Socialist Federative Republic of Yugoslavia confirmed by its note of 27 March 1969, received by the Ministry of Foreign Affairs of the Netherlands on 8 April 1969, that it considers itself to be a party to the Treaties and Declarations of The Hague of 29 July 1899, ratified by Serbia.

No. 11

DECLARATION (IV, 3) CONCERNING EXPANDING BULLETS

Signed at The Hague, 29 July 1899

INTRODUCTORY NOTE: Like the Declaration of St. Petersburg of 1868, the Hague Declaration (IV, 3) of 1899 gives expression, with regard to a particular bullet, to the customary rule prohibiting the use of weapons that cause superfluous injury or unnecessary suffering. The Declaration is aimed at the Dum-Dum bullet, which is so called after the arsenal near Calcutta where the bullet was first made.

ENTRY INTO FORCE: 4 September 1900.

AUTHENTIC TEXT: French. The English translation below is reprinted from Scott, *Hague Conventions*, pp. 227–228. It reproduces the translation of the United States Department of State.

TEXT PUBLISHED IN: *Conférence internationale de la Paix 1899*, pp. 254–255 (French); *Les deux Conférences de la Paix*, p. 44 (French); Scott, *Hague Conventions*, pp. 227–228 (Engl.); Scott, *Les Conventions de La Haye*, pp. 227–228 (French); Scott, *Les Conférences de La Haye*, p. 28 (French); Martens, *NRGT*, 2ème série, Vol. XXVI, pp. 998–1002 (French, German); Deltenre, pp. 138–141 (Engl., French, German, Dutch); Olivart, Vol. XII, pp. 643–646 (French, Span.); *International Red Cross Handbook*, 1983, p. 321 (Engl. – extract); *Manual de la Cruz Roja internacional*, 1983, p. 325 (Span. – extract); *Manuel de la Croix-Rouge internationale*, 1983, p. 333 (French – extract); *Handbook of the International Movement*, 1994, p. 298 (Engl.); *Manuel du Mouvement international*, 1994, p. 310 (French); *Manual del Movimiento internacional*, 1994, p. 302 (Span.); *GBTS*, 1907, No. 32 (Engl., French); *BFSP*, Vol. 91, 1898–1899, pp. 1014–1016 (French); *CTS*, Vol. 187, 1898–1899, pp. 459–461 (French); Higgins, pp. 491–492 (Engl., French); *AJIL*, Vol. 1, 1907, Suppl., pp. 157–159 (Engl., French); Friedman, pp. 247–248 (Engl.); Roberts and Guelff, pp. 63–66 (Engl.); *Droit des conflits armés*, pp. 109–112 (French); De Clercq, Vol. XXI, pp. 741–743 (French); Bustamante, pp. 232–234 (Span.); Korovin, p. 369 (Russ.); *Mezhdunarodnoe pravo*, Vol. III, p. 39 (Russ.); ICRC website: www.icrc.org/ihl.nsf.

* * *

The undersigned, Plenipotentiaries of the Powers represented at the International Peace Conference at The Hague, duly authorized to that effect by their Governments, inspired by the sentiments which found expression in the Declaration of St. Petersburg of 29 November [11 December] 1868,
Declare as follows:

The Contracting Parties agree to abstain from the use of bullets which expand or flatten easily in the human body, such as bullets with a hard envelope which does not entirely cover the core or is pierced with incisions.

The present Declaration is only binding for the Contracting Powers in the case of a war between two or more of them.

It shall cease to be binding from the time when, in a war between the Contracting Powers, one of the belligerents is joined by a non-Contracting Power.

The present Declaration shall be ratified as soon as possible.

The ratification shall be deposited at The Hague.

A *procès-verbal* shall be drawn up on the receipt of each ratification, a copy of which, duly certified, shall be sent through the diplomatic channel to all the Contracting Powers.

The non-Signatory Powers may adhere to the present Declaration. For this purpose they must make their adhesion known to the Contracting Powers by means of a written notification addressed to the Netherlands Government, and by it communicated to all the other Contracting Powers.

In the event of one of the High Contracting Parties denouncing the present Declaration, such denunciation shall not take effect until a year after the notification made in writing to the Netherlands Government, and forthwith communicated by it to all the other Contracting Powers.

This denunciation shall only affect the notifying Power.

In faith of which the Plenipotentiaries have signed the present Declaration, and have affixed their seals thereto.

Done at The Hague, 29 July 1899, in a single copy, which shall be kept in the archives of the Netherlands Government, and copies of which, duly certified, shall be sent through the diplomatic channel to the Contracting Powers.

[Here follow signatures]

SIGNATURES, RATIFICATIONS AND ACCESSIONS[1]

State	*Signature*	*Ratification, Accession, Notification of Continuity (C)*
Austria-Hungary	29 July 1899	4 September 1900
Belgium	29 July 1899	4 September 1900
Bulgaria	29 July 1899	4 September 1900
China	29 July 1899	21 November 1904
Denmark	29 July 1899	4 September 1900
Ethiopia	–	9 August 1935
Fiji	–	2 April 1973
France	29 July 1899	4 September 1900
Germany[2]	29 July 1899	4 September 1900

1 Based on a communication received from the Ministry of Foreign Affairs of the Netherlands of 12 December 2001. See also ICRC website: www.icrc.irg/ihl.nsf.

2 By a letter received at the Ministry of Foreign Affairs of the Kingdom of the Netherlands on 9 February 1959, the Government of the German Democratic Republic has informed the Ministry that it reapplies the Convention. This declaration has lost its importance after the

State	*Signature*	*Ratification, Accession, Notification of Continuity (C)*
Great Britain and Ireland	–	30 August 1907
Greece	29 July 1899	4 April 1901
Italy	29 July 1899	4 September 1900
Japan	29 July 1899	6 October 1900
Luxemburg	29 July 1899	12 July 1901
Mexico	29 July 1899	17 April 1901
Montenegro	29 July 1899	16 October 1900
Netherlands	29 July 1899	4 September 1900
Nicaragua	–	11 October 1907
Norway[3]	29 July 1899	4 September 1900
Persia	29 July 1899	4 September 1900
Portugal	–	29 August 1907
Romania	29 July 1899	4 September 1900
Russia[4]	29 July 1899	4 September 1900
Serbia[5]	29 July 1899	11 May 1901
Siam	29 July 1899	4 September 1900
South Africa	–	10 March 1978
Spain	29 July 1899	4 September 1900
Sweden[3]	29 July 1899	4 September 1900
Switzerland	29 July 1899	29 December 1900
Turkey	29 July 1899	12 June 1907

RESERVATIONS

None

cont.
conclusion of the Treaty of 31 August 1990 (Unification Treaty) between the Federal Republic of Germany and German Democratic Republic. See note 3 of document *No. 18*, pp. 170–171 and note 35 of documents Nos. *49-52* pp. 639–640.

3 Sweden and Norway constituted a Union until 1905. Action taken by them prior to that date was taken as a single power.

4 By the note of the Foreign Ministry of the USSR of 7 March 1955 "The Government of the USSR recognises the Conventions and Declarations of The Hague from 1899 and 1907, which were ratified by Russia to the extent that the Conventions and Declarations do not contradict the United Nations Charter and if they are not amended or replaced by ulterior international agreements to which the USSR is a Party, such as the 1925 Geneva Protocol for the Prohibition of Use of Asphyxiating, Poisonous and Other Gases and of Bacteriological Methods of Warfare and the 1949 Geneva Conventions for the Protection of Victims of War" (*Izvestiya*, 9 March 1955).

In January 1992, the Ministry of Foreign Affairs of the Russian Federation informed the heads of diplomatic missions in Moscow, that the Russian Federation continues to be a party to all conventions which are in force for the Soviet Union. The Ministry of Foreign Affairs of the Kingdom of the Netherlands considers therefore that the Russian Federation is bound by the conventions to which the Soviet Union was party (communication of the depositary to the Henry Dunant Institute of 6 November 1992).

On 4 June 1962, the Byelorussian Soviet Socialist Republic made a declaration similar to that made by the USSR.

5 The Government of the Socialist Federative Republic of Yugoslavia confirmed by its note of 27 March 1969, received by the Ministry of Foreign Affairs of the Netherlands on 8 April 1969, that it considers itself to be a party to the Treaties and Declarations of The Hague of 29 July 1899, ratified by Serbia.

No. 12

TREATY RELATING TO THE USE OF SUBMARINES AND NOXIOUS GASES IN WARFARE

Signed at Washington, 6 February 1922

INTRODUCTORY NOTE: Article 5 of this treaty relates to the use of noxious gases; the other provisions deal with submarine warfare. The treaty has not entered into force by reason of doubts concerning the provisions on submarine warfare. The wording of Article 5 dealing with gas warfare corresponds to that of the Geneva Protocol of 17 June 1925 (*No. 13*).

Text reprinted below *No. 85*, pp. 1139–1141.

No. 13

PROTOCOL FOR THE PROHIBITION OF THE USE IN WAR OF ASPHYXIATING, POISONOUS OR OTHER GASES, AND OF BACTERIOLOGICAL METHODS OF WARFARE

I. GENEVA PROTOCOL

Signed at Geneva on 17 June 1925

II. FINAL ACT OF THE CONFERENCE OF STATES PARTIES TO THE 1925 GENEVA PROTOCOL AND OTHER INTERESTED STATES ON THE PROHIBITION OF CHEMICAL WEAPONS

Paris, 7–11 January 1989

INTRODUCTORY NOTE: The Geneva Protocol of 1925 was drawn up and signed at the conference for the supervision of the international trade in arms and ammunition, which was held in Geneva under the auspices of the League of Nations from 4 May to 17 June 1925. The conference adopted a Convention for the supervision of the international trade in arms, munitions and implements of war, which has not entered into force and, as a separate document, the present Protocol on the use of gases. The earlier treaties prohibiting the use of gases to which the Protocol refers are in particular the Hague Declaration concerning asphyxiating gases of 29 July 1899 (*No. 10*) and the Treaty of Versailles of 28 June 1919 as well as the other peace treaties of 1919. Article 171 of the Treaty of Versailles provides: "The use of asphyxiating, poisonous or other gases and all analogous liquids, materials or devices being prohibited, their manufacture and importation are strictly forbidden in Germany." See also Article 5 of the Treaty of Washington of 6 February 1922 (*No. 83*) and the note introducing the Hague Declaration (IV, 2) of 1899 (*No. 10*).

The United Nations General Assembly has adopted several resolutions in which it calls for strict observance by all states of the principles and objectives of the Geneva Protocol of 1925, condemns all actions contrary to those objectives and invites all states to accede to the Protocol (resolutions 2162 B (XXI) of 5 December 1966, 2454 A (XXIIII) of 20 December, 1968, 2603 B (XXIV) of 16 December 1969, and 2662 (XXV) of 7 December, 1970). Resolution 2603 A (XXIV) of 16 December 1969 (*No. 15*) gives an interpretation of the Geneva Protocol of 1925.

We have also reproduced the Final Declaration of the Conference held in Paris in January 1989. The Secretary-General of the United Nations called the Declaration "a solemn proclamation that States refuse to use chemical weapons and deem it imperative to wipe them from the face of the earth; and a reminder of a legal, political and moral prohibition, an express and fervent determination to prohibit not only the use but also the production, stockpiling and transfer of such weapons". While the general debate proceeded, the Committee of the Whole of the Conference, chaired by Mr. Kalevi Sorsa, Foreign Minister of Finland, began to work on a draft final declaration. A group of "friends of the Chairman" from approximately 25 countries dealt with the most controversial questions, such as reservations to the 1925 Protocol, ways of giving greater impetus to the Geneva negotiations, the different aspects of non-proliferation, and the relationship between chemical disarmament and general disarmament. The draft text submitted by the Committee was adopted by the Conference by consensus as the Final Declaration of the Conference and was incorporated into the Final Act of the Paris Conference.

ENTRY INTO FORCE: According to paragraph 9, the Protocol comes into force for each signatory power as of the date of deposit of its ratification, and, from that moment, each power is bound as regards other powers that have already deposited their ratifications, according to paragraph 5 the accession will take effect on the date of the notification by the Government of the French Republic. The depositary indicates that the Protocol came into force on 8 February 1928.[1]

AUTHENTIC TEXTS: English, French. The text below is reprinted from *LNTS,* Vol. 94, 1929, p. 65.

TEXT PUBLISHED IN: *LNTS,* Vol. 94, 1929, p. 65 (Engl., French); *League of Nations Official Journal,* No. 8, 1925, pp. 1158–1167 (Engl., French); Martens, *NRGT*, 3ème série (1932–1933), Vol. XXVI, pp. 643–650 (Engl., French); Hudson, Vol. III, p. 1670 (Engl., French); Deltenre, pp. 442–443 (Engl., French, German, Dutch); *Fontes Historiae Juris Gentium*, Vol. III/2, pp. 1199-1200 (Engl., French – extracts); *International Red Cross Handbook*, 1983, p. 338 (Engl.); *Manuel de la Croix-Rouge internationale*, 1983, p. 350 (French); *Manual de la Cruz Roja internacional*, 1983, p. 342 (Span.); *Handbook of the International Movement*, 1994, p. 315 (Engl.); *Manuel du Mouvement international*, 1994, p. 327 (French); *Manual del Movimiento internacional*, 1994, p. 319 (Span.); *GBTS*, 1930, No. 24, Cmd. 3604 (Engl., French); *BFSP*, Vol. 126, 1927, pp. 324–325 (Engl.); *UST*, Vol. 26, Part 1, 1975, pp. 571–582 (Engl., French); *TIAS* 8061 (Engl., French); *Status of Multilateral Arms Regulation and Disarmament Agreements*, second edn., 1982, New York, United Nations, 1983 (E.83.IX.5), pp. 3–11 (Engl.); *Status of the Multilateral Arms Regulations and Disarmament Agreements*, fifth edn., 1996, New York, United Nations, 1997 (E.97.IX.3), pp. 5–21 (Engl.); *Etat des accords multilatéraux en matière de désarmement et de contrôle des armements*, troisième edn., 1996, New York, Nations Unies (F.97.IX.3), pp. 3–12 (French); *Situacion de los acuerdos multilaterales de regulacion de armamentos y de desarme*, tercera edicion, 1996, Nueva York, Naciones Unidas, 1997 (S.97.IX.3), pp. 3–12 (Span.); *AJIL,* Vol. 25, 1931, pp. 94–96 (Engl.); Friedman, pp. 454–456 (Engl.); Roberts and Guelff, pp. 137–145 (Engl.); *Droit des conflits armés*, pp. 115–136 (French); *Sbornik dogovorov, SSSR,* vyp. V, 1930, pp. 3–5 (Russ.); *Mezhdunarodnoe pravo,* Vol. III, p. 11 (Russ. – extracts); Blatova, pp. 675–676 (Russ. – extracts); United Nations website: http://disarmament.un.org/TreatyStatus.nsf; ICRC website: www.icrc.org/ihl.nsf.

* * *

[1] 8 February 1928 is the date of the second ratification by Venezuela. The first ratification, by France, took place on 10 May 1926.

I. GENEVA PROTOCOL OF 17 JUNE 1925

The undersigned Plenipotentiaries, in the name of their respective Governments:

[Here follow the names of plenipotentiaries]

Whereas the use in war of asphyxiating, poisonous or other gases, and of all analogous liquids materials or devices, has been, justly condemned by the general opinion of the civilized world; and

Whereas the prohibition of such use has been declared in Treaties to which the majority of Powers of the world are Parties; and

To the end that this prohibition shall be universally accepted as a part of International Law, binding alike the conscience and the practice of nations,

Declare:

That the High Contracting Parties, so far as they are not already Parties to Treaties prohibiting such use, accept this prohibition, agree to extend this prohibition to the use of bacteriological methods of warfare and agree to be bound as between themselves according to the terms of this declaration.

The High Contracting Parties will exert every effort to induce other States to accede to the present Protocol. Such accession will be notified to the Government of the French Republic, and by the latter to all Signatory and Acceding Powers, and will take effect on the date of the notification by the Government of the French Republic.

The present Protocol of which the French and English texts are both authentic, shall be ratified as soon as possible. It shall bear today's date.

The ratifications of the present Protocol shall be addressed to the Government of the French Republic, which will at once notify the deposit of such ratification to each of the Signatory and Acceding Powers.

The instruments of ratification and accession to the present Protocol will remain deposited in the archives of the Government of the French Republic.

The present Protocol will come into force for each Signatory Power as from the date of deposit of its ratification, and, from that moment, each Power will be bound as regards other Powers which have already deposited their ratifications.

In witness whereof the Plenipotentiaries have signed the present Protocol.

Done at Geneva in a single copy, the seventeenth day of June, One Thousand Nine Hundred and Twenty-Five.

[Here follow signatures]

SIGNATURES, RATIFICATIONS, ACCESSIONS AND NOTIFICATIONS OF CONTINUITY[1]

State	*Signature*	*Ratification, Accession, Notification of Succession (S) or Continuity (C)*[2]
Afghanistan (Democratic Republic of)	–	9 December 1986
Albania	–	20 December 1989
Algeria	–	27 January 1992 *Res.*
Angola	–	8 November 1990 *Res.*
Antigua and Barbuda	–	1 January 1989 (S)[3]
Argentina	–	12 May 1969
Australia	–	24 May 1930[4]
Austria	17 June 1925	9 May 1928
Bahrain	–	9 December 1988 *Res.*
Bangladesh	–	20 May 1989 *Res.*
Barbados[5]	–	16 July 1976 (S)
Belgium	17 June 1925	4 December 1928[5a]
Benin	–	9 December 1986
Bhutan	–	19 February 1979
Bolivia	–	13 August 1985
Brazil	17 June 1925	28 August 1970

[1] Information supplied by the French Ministry of Foreign Affairs on 4 February 2002 and completed by the United Nations website: http://disarmament.un.org/TreatyStatus.nsf; ICRC website: www. icrc.org/ihl.nsf.

[2] According to the information received from the depositary, the dates indicated in the table provide the following information: for the ratifications, the date indicated represents the date of deposit of the instruments of ratification, which coincides with the date of entry into force of the Protocol for the signatory Power that ratified the Protocol after its entry into force, i.e. after 8 February 1928. The dates of accession indicate the date of the entry into force, i.e. the date of the notification of the accession to the signatory and acceding Powers by the Government of the French Republic. For the succession, we have indicated the dates when the notifying power becomes party to the Protocol (i.e. the date of the accession to independence) and, in default of it, the date when the instrument (notification of succession or continuity) was transmitted to the French Government.

[3] In a note of 18 January 1989, received by the French Government on 1 February 1989, the Ministry of Foreign Affairs of Antigua and Barbuda, transmitted to the depositary the instrument of succession of 20 September 1988, according to which the Government of Antigua and Barbuda "declares that it considers itself a party to the Treaty by virtue of the ratification of the said Treaty by the Government of the United Kingdom of Great Britain and Northern Ireland and the application of the said Treaty to the territory of Antigua and Barbuda immediately prior to independence and by virtue of the exercise by the Government of Antigua and Barbuda of its right, pursuant to customary international law, to succeed to the rights and obligations arising under the said Treaty and undertakes faithfully to carry out the stipulations contained therein".

[4] The reservation of Australia made on accession was withdrawn as from 9 December 1986. See p. 116.

[5] In a note of 22 June 1976, addressed to and received by the French Government on 16 July 1976, the Government of Barbados declared that it considered the Protocol to be in force in respect of Barbados in virtue of its extension to Barbados by the United Kingdom. It further declared that it had withdrawn the reservation made on 9 April 1930 by the British Empire.

[5a] The reservation of Belgium made on ratification was withdrawn on 14 December 1997. See p. 116.

State	*Signature*	*Ratification,* *Accession,* *Notification of* *Succession (S)* *or Continuity (C)*
Bulgaria	17 June 192S	7 March 1934[6]
Burkina Faso	–	3 March 1971
Cambodia[7]	–	15 March 1983 *Res.*
Cameroon	–	20 July 1989
Canada	17 June 1925	6 May 1930 *Res.*[8]
Cape Verde	–	15 October 1991
Central African Republic	–	31 July 1970
Chile	17 June 1925	2 July 1935[9]
China[10]	–	24 August 1929 *Res.*
Côte d'Ivoire	–	27 July 1970
Cuba	–	24 June 1966
Cyprus[11]	–	12 December 1966 (S)[12]
[Czechoslovakia	17 June 1925	16 August 1938 *Res.*]
Czech Republic	17 June 1925	1 January 1993

6 The Ministry of Foreign Affairs of Bulgaria notified the depositary on 2 October 1991 that it withdrew the reservation made by Bulgaria on ratifying the Protocol. For the text of the reservation of Bulgaria, see p. 117.

7 By *note verbale*, dated 30 September 1993, the Ministry of Foreign Affairs and International Cooperation of Cambodia indicated that the Government of the Kingdom of Cambodia considered itself bound by the Protocol of 17 June 1925, to which the Coalition Government of Democratic Kampuchea has acceded on 15 March 1983. On 21 March 1983, the depositary informed the states parties to the Protocol that on 2 February 1983 it received a letter of 29 January 1983 concerning the accession by the Coalition Government of Democratic Kampuchea. This accession was considered null and void by the following thirteen states parties to the Protocol: Australia, Bulgaria, Cuba, Czechoslovakia, Ethiopia, France, German Democratic Republic, Hungary, Mauritius, Mongolia, Poland, USSR and Socialist Republic of Vietnam. The Kingdom of the Netherlands made a statement that the reception of the notifications does not represent in any case recognition of the Coalition Government of Democratic Kampuchea. By note of 15 September 1983, the Government of Niger informed the depositary that it considered the accession as valid.

8 The Government of Canada modified the reservations made by Canada upon ratification by withdrawing the reservations made to the Protocol with respect to bacteriological methods. (communication of Canada to the depositary government dated 20 August 1991, received on 20 August and notified on 6 September 1991). For the whole text of the reservation, see p. 117.

9 The Ministry for Foreign Affairs of Chile notified the depositary on 11 September 1991 that it withdrew the reservation made on ratification of the Protocol. For the text of the reservation of Chile, see p. 117.

10 Declaration of succession of the People's Republic of China, dated 13 July 1952, was received on 16 July 1952 by the Government of the French Republic. The notification was made on 25 July 1952, which is the date of the entry into force of the Protocol for the People's Republic of China. China acceded to the Protocol of 24 August 1929 (*LNTS*, Vol. 94, 1929, p. 70). For the reservation of the People's Republic of China, see pp. 117–118.

11 In a note of 21 November 1966, received by the depositary government on 29 November 1966 and notified on 12 December 1966, Cyprus declared itself to be bound by the Protocol which had been made applicable to it by the British Empire.

12 The Government of the Czech and Slovak Federal Republic withdrew the reservation upon ratification (decision of the President of the Republic of 25 September 1990, transmitted to the depositary on 22 October 1990 and notified on 8 November 1990). For the text of the reservation of Czechoslovakia of 16 August 1938 and the communication on withdrawal, see p. 118. After the dissolution of the Czech and Slovak Federal Republic effective on 1 January 1993, the Czech Republic and the Slovak Republic informed the depositaries that they

State	*Signature*	*Ratification, Accession, Notification of Succession (S) or Continuity (C)*
Denmark	17 June 1925	5 May 1930
Dominican Republic	–	8 December 1970
Ecuador	–	16 September 1970
Egypt	17 June 1925	6 December 1928
El Salvador	17 June 1925	–
Equatorial Guinea	–	20 May 1989
Estonia	17 June 1925	28 August 1931[12a]
Ethiopia	17 June 1925	7 October 1935[13]
Fiji	–	21 March 1973 (S) *Res.*[14]
Finland	17 June 1925	26 June 1929
France	17 June 1925	10 May 1926[15]
Gambia	–	5 November 1966 (C)[16]
Germany[17]	17 June 1925	25 April 1929
Ghana	-	3 May 1967
Greece	17 June 1925	30 May 1931

cont.
considered themselves bound, as of 1 January 1993, by multilateral international treaties to international treaties to which the Czech and Slovak Federal Republic was a party on that date including reservations and declarations to their provisions made earlier by the Czech and Slovak Federal Republic (see the declarations published in *Multilateral treaties deposited with the Secretary-General Status at 31 December 1994* (ST/LEG/ SER.E/13), New York, United Nations, 1995, pp. 8–9).

12a On 28 May 1999, the depositary government received a communication from Estonia withdrawing the reservation it had made upon ratification of the Protocol (notified by the depositary government on 29 July 1999. For the text of the reservation see p. 118.

13 The instrument deposited by Ethiopia, a signer of the Protocol, is registered as an accession. The date given is the date of notification by the French Government. The instrument of accession was deposited on 18 September 1935.

14 In a declaration of succession dated 26 January 1973, received by the depositary government on 21 March 1973, the Government of Fiji confirmed that the provisions of the Protocol were applicable to it by virtue of the ratification by the United Kingdom on 9 April 1930. The French Government notified this declaration to the contracting parties on 28 March 1973.

15 On 25 November 1996, France announced the withdrawal of its two reservations to the Protocol (notified by the depositary on 12 December 1996). See also Decree No. 07-760 of 11 July 1997, published in the *Journal Officiel* of 19 July 1997, p. 19859.

16 By declaration of 11 October 1966, received by the depositary government on 5 November 1966, Gambia confirmed its participation in the Protocol, which had been made applicable to it by Great Britain on 9 April 1930.

17 Through the accession of the German Democratic Republic to the Federal Republic of Germany with effect from 3 October 1990, the two German states have united to form one sovereign State (see note 3 in document *No. 18*, p. 170 and note 35 in document *Nos.49–52*, pp. 639–640. As regards treaties in respect of which formalities (i.e. signatures, ratifications, etc.) had been effected by both the Federal Republic of Germany and the former German Democratic Republic prior to unification, the entry in the status list indicates the type of formality effected by the Federal Republic of Germany, while the type of formality effected by the former German Democratic Republic appears in a footnote.

A document confirming the application of the Protocol by the German Democratic Republic was transmitted to the French Ministry of Foreign Affairs by the Embassy of Czechoslovakia on 2 March 1959 and again directly by the Embassy of the German Democratic Republic on 21 October 1974. On 5 January 1976, the Federal Republic of Germany transmitted to the depositary a declaration stating that the reapplication notified by GDR was not effective in the relations between the FRG and the GDR before 21 June 1973.

State	*Signature*	*Ratification, Accession, Notification of Succession (S) or Continuity (C)*
Grenada	–	3 January 1989 (S)[18]
Guatemala	–	3 May 1983
Guinea-Bissau	–	20 May 1989
Holy See	–	18 October 1966
Hungary	–	11 October 1952
Iceland	–	2 November 1967
India	17 June 1925	9 April 1930 *Res.*
Indonesia	–	21 January 1971 (S)[19]
Iran (Persia)	–	5 November 1929
Iraq	–	8 September 1931 *Res.*
Ireland	–	29 August 1930[20]
Israel	–	20 February 1969 *Res.*
Italy	17 June 1925	3 April 1928
Jamaica	–	28 July 1970 (S)[21]
Japan	17 June 1925	21 May 1970
Jordan	–	20 January 1977 *Res.*
Kampuchea Democratic (Coalition Government of) – see Cambodia		
Kenya	–	6 July 1970
Korea, Dem. People's Rep.	–	4 January 1989 *Res.*
Korea, Republic of	–	4 January 1989 *Res.*
Kuwait	–	15 December 1971 *Res.*
Laos	–	20 May 1989
Latvia	17 June 1925	3 June 1931
Lebanon	–	17 April 1969
Lesotho	–	10 March 1972 (S)[22]
Liberia	–	17 June 1927
Libyan Arab Jamahiriya	–	29 December 1971 *Res.*
Liechtenstein	–	6 September 1991
Lithuania	17 June 1925	15 June 1933
Luxembourg	17 June 1925	1 September 1936
Madagascar	–	2 August 1967
Malawi	–	14 September 1970

18 In a declaration of succession of 3 January 1989, Granada confirmed its participation in the Protocol which had been made applicable to it by Great Britain.

19 In a note of 13 January 1971, received by the depositary government on 21 January 1971, Indonesia confirmed its acceptance of the Protocol ratified in its name by the Kingdom of Netherlands on 31 October 1930.

20 The Government of Ireland in a note of 7 February 1972 notified the Government of France that it withdrew, with effect from 10 February 1972, the reservation made upon accession to the Protocol on 29 August 1930 (communication of the Government of Ireland of 10 February 1972, notified by the French Government on 25 May 1972). For the text of the reservation of Ireland, see pp. 118–119.

21 By declaration of 25 June 1970 received by the depositary government on 28 July 1970, and notified on 31 July 1970, Jamaica confirmed its participation in the Protocol which had been made applicable to it by virtue of its ratification by the United Kingdom (9 April 1930).

22 By declaration of succession dated 10 February 1972, received by the depositary government on 10 March 1972 and notified on 15 March 1972, Lesotho declared itself bound by the Protocol which had been made applicable to it by virtue of its ratification by the British Empire (9 April 1930).

State	*Signature*	*Ratification, Accession Notification of Succession (S) or Continuity (C)*
Malaysia	–	10 December 1970
Maldives Islands	–	27 December 1966 (S)[23]
Malta	–	21 September 1964 (S)[24]
Mauritius	–	12 March 1968 (S)[25]
Mexico	–	28 May 1932
Monaco	–	6 January 1967
Mongolia	–	6 December 1968[26]
Morocco	–	13 October 1970
Nepal	–	9 May 1969
Netherlands[27]	17 June 1925	31 October 1930[28]
New Zealand	–	24 May 1930[29]
Nicaragua	17 June 1925	5 October 1990
Niger	–	5 April 1967 (S)[30]
Nigeria	–	15 October 1968 Res.
Norway	17 June 1925	27 July 1932
Pakistan	–	15 April 1960 (S) *Res.*[31]
Panama	–	4 December 1970[32]

[23] By declaration of 19 December 1966, received by the depositary government on 27 December 1966, the Maldives Islands confirmed its adherence to the Protocol.

[24] By declaration of succession dated 25 September 1970, received by the depositary Government on 9 October 1970, and notified on 15 October 1970, the Government of Malta recognizes itself bound, with effect from the 21 September 1964, by the aforesaid Protocol, which was extended to Malta by the Government of the United Kingdom of Great Britain and Northern Ireland before the attainment of independence.

[25] By declaration of succession dated 27 November 1970, received by the depositary Government on 23 December 1970, the Government of Mauritius considers itself bound by the Protocol as from 12 March 1968, the date on which Mauritius became independent. This declaration was notified by the depositary on 8 January 1971.

[26] The Government of Mongolia notified the Government of France that it withdrew the reservation made upon accession to the Protocol on 18 November 1968 (communication of the Government of People's Republic of Mongolia of 15 May 1990, transmitted to the depositary on 25 June 1990 and notified by the French government on 18 July 1990). For the text of the reservation of Mongolia, see p. 120.

[27] Including the Netherlands Antilles, Surinam and Curaço. (On 17 August 1945 the Netherlands Indies became a sovereign state, as Indonesia, and on 25 November 1975 Suriname (formerly Surinam) became a sovereign state. Curaçao is now the Netherlands Antilles.)

[28] On 17 July 1995, the depositary government received a notification from the Government of the Netherlands that it was withdrawing the reservation that it had expressed upon ratification of the Protocol on 31 October 1930. The notification stated precisely that the withdrawal of reservation concerned the Kingdom in Europe, the Netherlands Antilles and Aruba (notified by the depositary government on 25 July 1995).

[29] The Government of New Zealand withdrew the two reservations made upon accession to the Protocol on 24 January 1930 (communication of the Government of New Zealand dated 6 January 1989, notified by the French Government on 20 May 1989). For the text of the reservation of New Zealand, see p. 121.

[30] By letter of 18 March 1967, received by the depositary government on 5 April 1967, Niger declared to be bound by the accession of France to the Protocol on 10 May 1926.

[31] In a note of 13 April 1960, received by the depositary government on 15 April 1960, the Government of Pakistan declared to be party to the Protocol by virtue of paragraph 4 of the Schedule to the Indian Independence (International Agreements) Order, 1947.

[32] Panama ratified its accession on 15 March 1971 (Communication from the depositary of 7 June 1991).

State	*Signature*	*Ratification, Accession, Notification of Succession (S) or Continuity (C)*[2]
Papua New Guinea	–	16 September 1975 (S) *Res.*[33]
Paraguay	–	22 October 1933[34]
Peru	–	13 August 1985
Philippines	–	8 June 1973
Poland	17 June 1925	4 February 1929
Portugal	17 June 1925	1 July 1930 *Res.*
Qatar	–	18 October 1976
Romania	17 June 1925	23 August 1929[35]
Russian Federation (formerly Union of Soviet Socialist Republics)[35a]	–	5 April 1928 *Res*
Rwanda	–	11 May 1964 (S)[36]
Saint Kitts and Nevis	–	27 April 1989 (S)[37]
Saint Lucia	–	22 February 1979 (S)[38]
Saint Vincent and the Grenadines	–	24 March 1999 (C)
Saudi Arabia	–	27 January 1971
Senegal	–	15 June 1977
Sierra Leone	–	20 March 1967
Slovakia	17 June 1925	1 January 1993 (S)[39]
Solomon Islands	–	1 June 1981 (S) *Res.*[40]

[33] In a note dated 2 September 1980, received by the depositary government on the same day, the Government of Papua New Guinea declared that it considers itself bound by the Protocol as from 16 September 1975, the date on which Papua New Guinea became independent and expressed its desire to be treated as a party to the Protocol in its own right. The Protocol was applied to Papua New Guinea by the accession of Australia on 22 January 1930.

[34] Date of the receipt of the instrument of accession, to be taken as effective date. Official notification to that effect was signed by the French Government on 13 January 1960.

[35] On 16 July 1991, the Government of Romania transmitted to the depositary an instrument of withdrawal of the reservation made upon ratification of the Protocol on 23 August 1929 (communication of the Government of Romania dated 16 July 1991, notified by the French Government on 23 July 1991). For the text of the reservation of Romania, see p. 122.

[35a] Membership of the Union of Soviet Socialist Republics (USSR) in the United Nations is continued as from 24 December 1991 by the Russian Federation. As from that date, the Russian Federation maintains full responsibility for all the rights and obligations of the USSR under the Charter of the United Nations. As from that date, the Russian Federation continues to exercise its rights and honour its commitments deriving from international treaties concluded by the USSR and performs the functions formerly performed by the Government of the USSR as depositary of international treaties.

[36] By declaration of 21 March 1964, received by the depositary government on 11 May 1964, Rwanda recognized to be bound by the Protocol, which had been made applicable to it by Belgium.

[37] In a declaration of succession dated 27 April 1989, received by the depositary on 26 October 1989, Saint Kitts and Nevis confirmed that it considers itself bound by the Protocol, which had been made applicable to it by the ratification by the United Kingdom. The declaration was notified by the depositary on 15 November 1989.

[38] In a declaration of succession of 8 November 1988, received by the French Government on 21 December 1988, Saint Lucia confirmed that it considers itself bound by the Protocol, which had been made applicable to it by the ratification by the United Kingdom on 9 April 1930 with the effect as from 22 February 1979, date of its accession to independence.

[39] See note 12 on pp. 109–110.

[40] In a declaration of succession dated 1 June 1981, received by the depositary on the same day, the Government of Solomon Islands confirmed that it considers itself bound by the Protocol,

State	*Signature*	*Ratification, Accession Notification of Succession (S) or Continuity (C)*[2]
South Africa	–	24 May 1930[41]
Spain	17 June 1925	22 August 1929[42]
Sri Lanka	–	20 January 1954
Sudan	–	17 December 1980
Swaziland	–	23 July 1991
Sweden	17 June 1925	25 April 1930
Switzerland	17 June 1925	12 July 1932
Syrian Arab Republic	–	17 December 1968 *Res.*
Tanzania, United Arab Rep.[43]	–	22 April 1963
Thailand (Siam)	17 June 1925	6 June 1931
Togo	–	5 April 1971
Tonga	–	19 July 1971 (S)[44]
Trinidad and Tobago	–	31 August 1962 (S)[45]
Tunisia	–	12 July 1967
Turkey	17 June 1925	5 October 1929

cont.
which had been made applicable to it by the ratification by the United Kingdom on 9 April 1930, with the effect as from 7 July 1978, date of its accession to independence.

41 On 20 October 1996, the depositary government informed all states parties that South Africa had withdrawn the reservation it had expressed at the time of succession to the Protocol.

42 By note of 25 November 1992, received by the depositary on 23 December and notified to the states parties to the Protocol on 28 December 1992, the Spanish Government informed the French Government that it had decided to withdraw the reservation entered on 17 June 1925. This withdrawal took effect on 28 December 1992. For the text of the reservation of Spain, see p. 122.

43 Accession, in the name of Tanganyika was made by declaration dated 28 February 1963, received by the depositary government on 26 March 1963 and notified by the depositary on 22 April 1963. In a note addressed to the Secretary-General of the United Nations on 6 May 1964, the Ministry of External Affairs of the United Republic of Tanzania informed him that, following the signature and ratification of the Articles of Union between the Republic of Tanganyika and the People's Republic of Zanzibar, the two countries had been united on 26 April 1964, as one sovereign state under the name of the United Republic of Tanganyika and Zanzibar. The Ministry further asked the Secretary-General "to note that the United Republic of Tanganyika and Zanzibar declares that ... all international treaties and agreements in force between the Republic of Tanganyika or the People's Republic of Zanzibar and other States or international organizations will, to the extent that there implementation is consistent with the constitutional position established by the Articles of the Union, remain in force within the regional limits prescribed on their conclusion and in accordance with the principles of international law." In a communication addressed to the Secretary-General on 2 November 1964, the Permanent Mission of the United Republic of Tanganyika and Zanzibar informed him that "the United Republic of Tanganyika and Zanzibar shall, with immediate effect, be known as the United Republic of Tanzania" (*Multilateral Treaties deposited with the Secretary-General, Status as at 31 December 1994*, New York, United Nations, 1995, United Nations Document ST/ALEG/ SER.E/13, p. 10, note 26).

44 By a declaration of 22 June 1971, received by the depositary government on 19 July 1971 and notified by it on 28 July 1971, the Government of Tonga "considers itself to be bound by virtue of the signature of the United Kingdom and pursuant to customary international law".

45 By a declaration of 9 October 1970, received by the depositary government on 24 November 1970 and notified by it on 30 November 1970, Trinidad and Tobago confirmed its participation in the Protocol, which had been made applicable to it before the date of independence, by the British Empire (9 April 1930). With effect of 31 August 1962 *(status of Multilateral Arms Regulation and Disarmament Agreements*, fifth edn., 1996, p. 20).

State	*Signature*	*Ratification, Accession, Notification of Succession (S) or Continuity (C)*[2]
Uganda	–	24 May 1965
[Union of Soviet Socialist Republics	–	5 April 1928 *Res.*[46]]
United Kingdom	17 June 1925	9 April 1930 *Res.*[47]
United States of America	17 June 1925	10 April 1975 *Res.*
Uruguay	17 June 1925	12 April 1977
Venezuela	17 June 1925	8 February 1928
Vietnam	–	15 December 1980 *Res.*
Yemen Arab Republic[48]	–	17 March 1971 *Res.*[49]
Yemen People's Democratic Republic[50]	–	9 December 1986 *Res.*
Yugoslavia (the Kingdom of the Serbs, Croats and Slovenes)[51]	17 June 1925	12 April 1929 *Res.*

[46] The USSR notified its accession on 5 April 1928 (communication of the depositary of 7 June 1991).

[47] Ratification was in the name of the British Empire and was not binding on India or any British Dominion, which was a separate member of the League of Nations.

The United Kingdom of Great Britain and Northern Ireland withdrew the part (2) of its reservation made upon ratification of the Protocol on 9 April 1930 (communication of the United Kingdom of Great Britain and Northern Ireland to the depositary of 7 November 1991 and notified by the French Government on 27 January 1992). See p. 123.

[48] On 22 May 1990, the People's Democratic Republic of Yemen and the Yemen Arab Republic merged to form a single state with the name "Republic of Yemen". Since that date they have been represented as one member in the United Nations. In a letter dated 19 May 1990, the Ministers of Foreign Affairs of the Yemen Arab Republic and the People's Democratic Republic of Yemen informed the Secretary-General that "all treaties and agreements concluded between either the Yemen Arab Republic or the People's Democratic Republic of Yemen and other States and international organizations in accordance with international law which are in force on 22 May 1990 will remain in effect, and international relations existing on 22 May 1990 between the People's Democratic Republic of Yemen and the Yemen Arab Republic and other States will continue" (*Status of Multilateral Arms Regulation and Disarmament Agreements*, fifth edn., 1996, p. 3).

[49] Reiterated on 16 September 1973.

[50] See note 48.

[51] Yugoslavia as from 1930.

RESERVATIONS[1]

ALGERIA (*reservation made on accession*)[2]
The Algerian Government will be bound by the Protocol only with regard to States that have ratified it or acceded to it and will cease to be bound by the said Protocol with regard to any State whose armed forces or whose allies' armed forces fail to comply with the provisions of the Protocol.

ANGOLA, PEOPLE'S REPUBLIC OF (*reservation made on accession*)[3]
In acceding to the Protocol of 17 June 1925, the People's Republic of Angola declares that it is bound by that Protocol only in relation to those States that have signed and ratified it or which have definitively acceded to it.

In acceding to the Protocol of 17 June 1925, the People's Republic of Angola declares that it shall cease to be bound by that Protocol in relation to any enemy State whose armed forces or whose *de jure* or *de facto* allies do not respect the prohibitions which are the object of the said Protocol.

AUSTRALIA (*reservation made on accession*)
Subject to the reservations that His Majesty is bound by the said Protocol only towards those Powers and States which have both signed and ratified the Protocol or have acceded thereto, and that His Majesty shall cease to be bound by the Protocol towards any Power at enmity with Him whose armed forces, or the armed forces of whose allies, do not respect the Protocol.
This reservation made on accession 24 May 1930 was withdrawn. Communication of the Australian Government to the depositary of 25 November 1986, notified by the French Government on 9 December 1986.

BAHRAIN (*reservation made on accession*)
(a) The said Protocol is only binding on the Government of the State of Bahrain as regards those States which have signed and ratified the Protocol or have acceded thereto;
(b) The said Protocol shall cease to be binding on the Government of the State of Bahrain in regard to any enemy State whose armed forces, or the armed forces of whose Allies, fail to respect the prohibitions laid down in the Protocol;
(c) The accession by the State of Bahrain to the said Protocol, signed on June 17, 1925, shall in no way constitute recognition of Israel or be a cause for the establishment of any relations of any kind therewith.

BANGLADESH, PEOPLE'S REPUBLIC OF (*reservation made on accession*)
1. The said Protocol is only binding on the Government of the People's Republic of Bangladesh as regards States which have signed and ratified it or which may accede to it;
2. The said Protocol shall *ipso facto* cease to be binding on the Government of the People's Republic of Bangladesh in regard to any enemy State whose armed forces or whose allies fail to respect the prohibitions laid down in the Protocol."

BELGIUM (*reservation made on ratification*)
1. The said Protocol is only binding on the Belgian Government as regards States which have signed or ratified it or which may accede to it.
2. The said Protocol shall *ipso facto* cease to be binding on the Belgian Government in regard to any enemy State whose armed forces or whose allies fail to respect the prohibitions laid down in the Protocol.

In a communication dated 14 February 1997, notified by the depositary government on 27 February 1997, Belgium withdrew the reservation made on ratification.

---

[1] When not otherwise indicated, the English text of the reservation was provided by the depositary.
[2] Translation by the editors.
[3] Instrument of accession of 2 March 1990. Original in Portuguese translated by the editors.

BULGARIA (*reservation made on ratification*)

1. The said Protocol is only binding on the Bulgarian Government as regards those States which have both signed and ratified the Protocol or have finally acceded thereto.
2. The said Protocol shall cease to be binding on the Bulgarian Government toward any Power at enmity with him whose armed forces, or the armed forces of whose allies, fail to respect the prohibitions which are the object of the Protocol.

In a communication to the depositary government dated 2 October 1991, notified by the depositary Government on 15 October 1991, the Ministry of Foreign Affairs of the Republic of Bulgaria stated that on 13 September 1991, the Great National Assembly adopted a law concerning the withdrawal of the reservation made by Bulgaria on ratification.

CAMBODIA (*reservation made on accession*)

The Coalition Government of Democratic Kampuchea (CGDK) reserves the right not to be bound by the aforesaid Protocol as regards any enemy whose armed forces or allies no longer respect the prohibitions contained in this Protocol.

The accession of the Coalition Government of Democratic Kampuchea is considered by the following thirteen states as being without effect: Australia, Bulgaria, Cuba, Czechoslovakia, Ethiopia, France, German Democratic Republic, Hungary, Mauritius, Mongolia, Poland, Union of Soviet Socialist Republics, Viet Nam.

CANADA (*reservation made on ratification*)

1. The said Protocol is only binding on His Britannic Majesty as regards those Powers and States which have both signed and ratified the Protocol or have finally acceded thereto.
2. The said Protocol shall cease to be binding on His Britannic Majesty toward any Power at enmity with him whose armed forces, or the armed forces of whose allies, fall to respect the prohibitions laid down in the Protocol.

In a note dated 20 August 1991 and notified on 6 September 1991, Canada modified the reservations made upon ratification by withdrawing the reservations made by Canada to the Protocol with respect to bacteriological methods.

CHILE (*reservation made on ratification*)

1. The said Protocol is only binding on the Government of Chile as regards those Powers and States which have both signed and ratified the Protocol or have finally acceded thereto.
2. The said Protocol shall cease to be binding on the Government of Chile toward any Power at enmity with it whose armed forces, or the armed forces of whose allies, fall to respect the prohibitions laid down in the Protocol.

In a communication to the depositary government dated 11 September 1991, notified by the depositary government on 15 October 1991, the Ministry of Foreign Affairs of Chile withdrew the reservation formulated on ratification.

CHINA, PEOPLE'S REPUBLIC OF (*reservation made in the declaration of succession*)[4]

By declaration of 13 July 1952, received by the depositary on 16 July 1952, the People's Republic of China recognized as binding upon it the accession to the Protocol made in the name of China in 1929:

The Central People's Government considers that the said Protocol is conductive to the strengthening of International Peace and Security and is in conformity with humanitarian principles, and therefore, has decided to recognize the accession to the Protocol. The Central People's Government shall undertake to implement strictly the provisions of the Protocol, provided that all the other contracting and acceding powers observe them reciprocally.

[4] English text of the communication of 13 July 1952 addressed to the depositary government.

CZECHOSLOVAKIA (*reservation made on ratification*)
The Czechoslovak Republic shall *ipso facto* cease to be bound by this Protocol towards any States whose armed forces or the armed forces of whose allies, fail to respect the prohibitions laid down in the Protocol.
The Government of the Czech and Slovak Republic withdrew the reservation upon ratification (decision of the President of the Republic of 25 September 1990, transmitted to the depositary on 22 October 1990 and notified by him on 8 November 1990).

DEMOCRATIC KAMPUCHEA (COALITION GOVERNMENT OF) *See Cambodia*

ESTONIA (*reservation made on ratification*)
1. The said Protocol is only binding on the Government of Estonia as regards those Powers and States which have both signed and ratified the Protocol or have finally acceded thereto.
2. The said Protocol shall cease to be binding on the Government of Estonia toward any Power at enmity with it whose armed forces, or the armed forces of whose allies, fail to respect the prohibitions laid down in the Protocol.

On 28 May 1999, the depositary government received a communication from Estonia withdrawing the reservation it had made upon ratification of the Protocol (notified by the depositary government on 29 July 1999).

FIJI (*reservation made on succession*)
1. The said Protocol is only binding on the Government of Fiji as regards those Powers and States which have both signed and ratified the Protocol or have finally acceded thereto, and
2. The said Protocol shall cease to be binding on the Government of Fiji towards any Power at enmity to it whose armed forces, or the armed forces of whose allies, fail to respect the prohibitions laid down in the Protocol.

FRANCE (*reservation made on ratification*)
1. The said Protocol is only binding on the Government of the French Republic as regards States which have signed or ratified it or which may accede to it.
2. The said Protocol shall ipso facto cease to be binding on the Government of the French Republic in regard to any enemy State whose armed forces or whose allies fall to respect the prohibitions laid down in the Protocol.

On 25 November 1996, France announced the withdrawal of its two reservations to the Protocol (notified by the depositary on 12 December 1996).

INDIA (*reservation made on ratification*)
1. The said Protocol is only binding on His Britannic Majesty as regards those Powers and States which have both signed and ratified the Protocol or have finally acceded thereto.
2. The said Protocol shall cease to be binding on His Britannic Majesty toward any Power at enmity with him whose armed forces, or the armed forces of whose allies, fail to respect the prohibitions laid down in the Protocol.

IRAQ (*reservation made on accession*)
Accession on condition that the Iraq Government shall be bound by the provisions of the Protocol only towards those States which have both signed and ratified it or have acceded thereto, and that they shall not be bound by the Protocol towards any State at enmity with them whose armed forces, or the armed forces of whose allies, do not respect the disposition of the Protocol.

IRELAND (*reservation made on accession*)
The Government of the Free State of Ireland does not by this adhesion assume any obligation but to the States which have signed and ratified the said Protocol or which have definitely acceded to it and

In the cases where armed forces of an enemy State or the ally of such a State should not respect the said Protocol, the Government of the Free State of Ireland should cease to be bound by the said Protocol towards that State.
The Government of Ireland notified the Government of France that it withdrew, with effect from 10 February 1972, the reservations that it made upon accession to the Protocol on 29 August 1930. Note of Ireland notified by depositary government on 25 May 1972.

ISRAEL (*reservation made on accession*)
The said Protocol is only binding on the State of Israel in relation to States which have signed and ratified it or have acceded thereto.

The said Protocol shall *ipso facto* cease to be binding on the State of Israel in regard to any enemy State whose armed forces, or regular or irregular forces or groups of individuals operating from its territory, or armed forces of whose Allies, fail to respect the prohibitions which are the object of this Protocol.
The state of Israel made a declaration concerning the reservations of Kuwait and Libyan Arab Jamahiriya, but not to the similar reservation of Jordan, Syria and Yemen. For the text of the declaration see the entry concerning Kuwait and Libyan Arab Jamahiriya.

JORDAN (*reservation made on accession*)
1. The Accession of the Hashemite Kingdom of Jordan to the aforesaid Protocol does not imply in any manner whatsoever the recognition of Israel.
2. The Accession of the Hashemite Kingdom of Jordan to the aforesaid Protocol does not obligate it to enter any arrangements specified in the Protocol vis-à-vis Israel.
3. The Government of the Hashemite Kingdom of Jordan undertakes to conform with, and abide by the obligations contained in the Protocol in respect of states that commit themselves likewise.
4. The Government of the Hashemite Kingdom of Jordan does not commit itself to states whose armed forces, regular or irregular, do not respect the provisions of the aforesaid Protocol.

KOREA, DEMOCRATIC PEOPLE'S REPUBLIC OF (*reservation made on accession*)
1. The Democratic People's Republic of Korea recognizes the 1925 Geneva Protocol as one of major elements for the promotion of disarmament and the maintenance of lasting peace and hereby expresses its conviction that the obligations of this Protocol will be faithfully carried out by all the Contracting Parties.
2. The Democratic People's Republic of Korea also states that it will not exclude the right to exercise its sovereignty *vis-a-vis* another Contracting Party which violates this Protocol in its implementation.

KOREA, REPUBLIC OF (*reservation made on accession*)
1. The said Protocol is only binding on the Government of the Republic of Korea as regards States which have signed and ratified it or which may accede to it;
2. The said Protocol shall *ipso facto* cease to be binding on the Government of the Republic of Korea in regard to any enemy State whose armed forces or whose allies fail to respect the prohibitions laid down in the Protocol.

KUWAIT (*reservation made on accession*)
1. The accession by the State of Kuwait to this Protocol does not in any case imply the recognition of Israel or the establishment of any relations with it;
2. In case of violation of the prohibition mentioned in this Protocol by any one of the Parties to it, the State of Kuwait shall not consider itself bound by the provisions of this Protocol.

Israel addressed the following note to the depositary on 25 January 1972, concerning the reservations of Kuwait:[5]

The Government of Israel has taken note of the political nature of the declaration made in the first sentence of the reservations formulated by the State of Kuwait and the Libyan Arab Republic. The Government of Israel feels that this Protocol cannot be used as a vehicle for political declarations of this nature. To the extent that the above-mentioned reservations are intended to rule out the Protocol's applicability to a conflict with the State of Israel, Article 19 of the 1969 Vienna Convention on the Law of Treaties applies as it stipulates that reservations are unacceptable if they are incompatible with the object and purpose of the treaty in connection with which they are formulated. The above-mentioned declarations therefore in no way affect the obligations by which the State of Kuwait and the Libyan Arab Republic are already bound under general international law. As regards the substance of the Protocol's provisions, the Government of Israel will be guided vis-à-vis the State of Kuwait and the Libyan Arab Republic by the principles enunciated in the reservation which accompanied the State of Israel's instrument of accession, done on 22 January 1969 in Jerusalem and deposited with the Ministry of Foreign Affairs of France on 20 February 1969.

As the depositary of the above-mentioned Protocol, the French government is asked kindly to take the measures required in the event of an objection to a reservation.

LIBYAN ARAB JAMAHARIYA (*reservation made on accession*)
The accession to this Protocol does not imply recognition of Israel or entry into any dealings with it whatsoever.

The Protocol is only binding on the Libyan Arab Republic in relation to States effectively bound by it, and ceases to bind the Libyan Arab Republic towards any States whose forces or the armed forces of whose allies fail to respect the prohibition laid down therein.

Israel addressed the following note to the depositary on 25 January 1972, concerning the reservations of Libyan Arab Republic:[6]
The Government of Israel has taken note of the political nature of the declaration made in the first sentence of the reservations formulated by the State of Kuwait and the Libyan Arab Republic. The Government of Israel feels that this Protocol cannot be used as a vehicle for political declarations of this nature. To the extent that the above-mentioned reservations are intended to rule out the Protocol's applicability to a conflict with the State of Israel, Article 19 of the 1969 Vienna Convention on the Law of Treaties applies as it stipulates that reservations are unacceptable if they are incompatible with the object and purpose of the treaty in connection with which they are formulated. The above-mentioned declarations therefore in no way affect the obligations by which the State of Kuwait and the Libyan Arab Republic are already bound under general international law. As regards the substance of the Protocol's provisions, the Government of Israel will be guided vis-à-vis the State of Kuwait and the Libyan Arab Republic by the principles enunciated in the reservation which accompanied the State of Israel's instrument of accession, done on 22 January 1969 in Jerusalem and deposited with the Ministry of Foreign Affairs of France on 20 February 1969.

As the depositary of the above-mentioned Protocol, the French government is asked kindly to take the measures required in the event of an objection to a reservation.

MONGOLIA, PEOPLE'S REPUBLIC OF (*reservation made on accession*)[7]
In case of violation of this prohibition by any State in relation to the People's Republic of Mongolia or its allies, the Government of the People's Republic of Mongolia shall not consider itself bound by the obligations of the Protocol towards this State.

---

5 Note of the Ministry of Foreign Affairs of Israel to the depositary (original: French; translated by the ICRC).

6 Note of the Ministry of Foreign Affairs of Israel to the depositary (original: French; translated by the ICRC).

7 Translation by the editors.

The Government of Mongolia notified the depositary government that it withdrew the reservation made upon accession to the Protocol on 18 November 1968. (communication of the Government of People's Republic of Mongolia of 15 May 1990, transmitted to the depositary on 25 June 1990 and notified by the French Government on 18 July 1990.)

NETHERLANDS (*reservation made on ratification*)
The said Protocol shall cease to be binding on the Royal Government of the Netherlands with respect to the use in war of asphyxiating, poisonous or other gases, and of analogous liquids, materials, or devices, with regard to an enemy State if such State or any of its allies fails to respect the prohibitions laid down in the Protocol.
On 17 July 1995, the depositary government received a notification from the Government of the Netherlands that it was withdrawing the reservation that it had expressed upon ratification of the Protocol on 31 October 1930. The notification stated precisely that the withdrawal of reservation concerned the Kingdom in Europe, the Netherlands Antilles and Aruba (notified by the depositary government on 25 July 1995).

NEW ZEALAND (*reservation made on accession*)
Subject to the reservations that His Majesty is bound by the said Protocol only towards those Powers and States which have both signed and ratified the Protocol or have acceded thereto, and that His Majesty shall cease to be bound by the Protocol towards any Power at enmity with him whose armed forces, or the armed forces of whose allies, do not respect the Protocol.
In a communication of 6 January, notified by the depositary government on 20 May 1989, New Zealand informed the depositary government of the decision of the Government of New Zealand to withdraw the reservations to the Protocol.

NIGERIA (*reservation made on accession*)
The Protocol is only binding on Nigeria in relation to States effectively bound by it and it ceases to bind Nigeria towards any States whose forces or the armed forces of whose allies fail to respect the prohibitions laid down therein.

PAKISTAN (*reservation made on succession*)
1. The said Protocol is only binding on His Britannic Majesty as regards those Powers and States which have both signed and ratified the Protocol or have finally acceded thereto.
2. The said Protocol shall cease to be binding on His Britannic Majesty toward any Power at enmity with him whose armed forces, or the armed forces of whose allies, fail to respect the prohibitions laid down in the Protocol.

PAPUA NEW GUINEA (*reservation made on succession*)
The Government of Papua New Guinea is bound by the said Protocol only towards those Powers and States which have both signed and ratified the Protocol or which have acceded thereto, and the Government of Papua New Guinea shall cease to be bound by the Protocol towards any Power at enmity with it whose armed forces or the armed forces of whose allies, do not respect the Protocol.

PORTUGAL (*reservation made on ratification*)
1. The said Protocol is only binding on the Government of Portugal as regards those Powers and States which have both signed and ratified the Protocol, or have finally acceded thereto.
2. The said Protocol shall cease to be binding on the Government of Portugal toward any Power at enmity with it whose armed forces, or the armed forces of whose allies, fail to respect the prohibitions laid down in the Protocol.

ROMANIA (*reservation made on ratification*)

1. The said Protocol only binds the Romanian Royal Government in relation to States which have signed and ratified or which have definitely acceded to the Protocol.
2. The said Protocol shall cease to be binding on the Romanian Royal Government in regard to all enemy States whose armed forces or whose allies de jure or in fact do not respect the restrictions, which are the object of this Protocol.

According to a communication of the Embassy of Romania in France dated 16 July 1991 and notified by the depositary on 23 July 1991, the Government of Romania withdrew the reservation made upon ratification (Act of the Romanian Parliament No. 39 of 1 June 1991).

RUSSIA *see Union of Soviet Socialist Republics*

SOLOMON ISLANDS (*reservation made on succession*)
The obligations stemming from the aforesaid Protocol shall be binding upon the Solomon Islands only in their relations with Sates which have ratified the Protocol or acceded to it and which respect its provisions.

SOUTH AFRICA (UNION OF) (*reservation made on accession*)
Subject to the reservations that His Majesty is bound by the said Protocol only towards those Powers and States which have both signed and ratified the Protocol or have acceded thereto, and that His Majesty shall cease to be bound by the Protocol towards any Power at enmity with him whose armed forces, or the armed forces of whose allies, do not respect the Protocol.
On 20 October 1996, the depositary government informed all states parties that South Africa had withdrawn the reservation it had expressed at the time of succession to the Protocol.

SPAIN (*reservation made on ratification*)
Declares as compulsory *ipso facto* and without special agreement in relation to any other Member or State accepting and executing the same obligation, that is to say, on condition of reciprocity, the Protocol for the prohibition of the Use in War of Asphyxiating, Poisonous or Other Gases and of Bacteriological Methods of Warfare, signed at Geneva, on June 17, 1925.
By a note of 25 November 1992, received by the depositary on 23 December and notified to the states parties to the Protocol on 28 December 1992, the Government of Spain informed the depositary government that it had decided to withdraw its reservation. The withdrawal took effect on 28 December 1992.

SYRIA (*reservation made on accession*)
The accession by the Syrian Arab Republic to this Protocol and the ratification of the Protocol by its Government does not in any case imply the recognition of Israel or lead to the establishment of relations with the latter concerning the provisions laid down in the Protocol.

UNION OF SOVIET SOCIALIST REPUBLICS (*reservation made on accession*)

1. The said Protocol is only binding on the Government of the Union of Soviet Socialist Republics in relation to the States which have signed and ratified or which have definitely acceded to the Protocol.
2. The said Protocol shall cease to be binding on the Government of the Union of Soviet Socialist Republics in regard to all enemy States whose armed forces or whose Allies *de jure* or in fact do not respect the restrictions, which are the object of this Protocol.

UNITED KINGDOM
Reservation made by the representative of the British Empire on signature
I declare that my signature does not bind India or any British Dominion which is a separate Member of the League of Nations and does not separately sign or adhere to the Protocol.

Reservation made on ratification
1. The said Protocol is only binding on His Britannic Majesty as regards those Powers and States which have both signed and ratified the Protocol or have finally acceded thereto.
2. The said Protocol shall cease to be binding on His Britannic Majesty toward any Power at enmity with him whose armed forces, or the armed forces of whose allies, fall to respect the prohibitions laid down in the Protocol.

In a communication dated 8 November 1991, and notified by the depositary government on 27 January 1992, the United Kingdom withdrew paragraph 2 of the reservation it had expressed during its ratification of the Protocol on 9 April 1930 in as far as it concerns resort to agents, toxins, arms, equipment and means of production specified in Article 1 of the Biological Weapons Convention.

UNITED STATES OF AMERICA (*reservation made on ratification*)
The Protocol shall cease to be binding on the government of the United States with respect to the use in war of asphyxiating, poisonous or other gases, and of all analogous liquids, materials, or devices, in regard to an enemy state if such state or any of its allies fails to respect the prohibitions laid down in the Protocol.

VIET NAM, SOCIALIST REPUBLIC OF (*reservation made on accession*)
The Socialist Republic of Viet Nam shall be bound by the aforesaid Protocol only in its relations with States which have signed and ratified it or which have acceded to it.
The Socialist Republic of Viet Nam shall not be bound by the aforesaid Protocol in its relations with enemy States whose armed forces or allies do not respect its provisions.

YEMEN, DEMOCRATIC AND PEOPLE'S REPUBLIC OF (*reservation formulated in the Act of accession of 16 July 1986*)
A. The accession by the Democratic and People's Republic of Yemen does not imply the recognition of any State or the establishment of relations with the State which is not recognized by the Democratic and People's Republic of Yemen or with which it has no relations.
B. In case that a State does not respect the prohibitions included in the Protocol, the Democratic People's Republic of Yemen shall not consider itself bound by the obligations of the Protocol towards this State.

YEMEN, ARAB REPUBLIC OF (*reservation made on 16 September 1973*)[8]
The Yemen Arab Republic's acceptance of this Protocol, which will be strictly complied with, in no way implies recognition of Israel or a willingness to enter into any dealings with Israel within the framework of the Protocol.

YUGOSLAVIA (*reservation made on ratification*)
The said Protocol shall cease to be binding on the Government of Serbs, Croats and Slovenes in regard to all enemy States whose armed forces or whose allies do not respect the restrictions which are object of this Protocol.

---

8 Note addressed to the depositary by the Government of the Arab Republic of Yemen on 16 September 1973 (translation from the Arabic by the ICRC).

II. FINAL ACT OF THE CONFERENCE OF STATES PARTIES TO THE 1925 GENEVA PROTOCOL AND OTHER INTERESTED STATES ON THE PROHIBITION OF CHEMICAL WEAPONS

Paris, 7–11 January 1989[1]

1. The Conference of States Parties to the 1925 Geneva Protocol and Other Interested States on the Prohibition of Chemical Weapons was held, at the invitation of the French Government, in Paris, January 7–11, 1989.
The following 149 States were represented at the Conference:

[Here follow the names of States participating at the Conference]

[2. –7. Provisions concerning the internal organization of the Conference]

8. The Secretary General of the United Nations, the Under Secretary General for Disarmament Affairs of the U.N. and the Secretary General of the Conference on Disarmament also attended. The Conference held nine plenary sessions, during which 109 delegations spoke, in the general debate. The Committee of the Whole held six sessions, during which it examined and finalized the draft declaration. The President of the Committee of the Whole reported to the Conference, and the Conference adopted the Final Declaration by consensus on January 11, 1989.

FINAL DECLARATION OF THE CONFERENCE OF STATES PARTIES TO THE 1925 GENEVA PROTOCOL AND OTHER INTERESTED STATES ON THE PROHIBITION OF CHEMICAL WEAPONS

The Representatives of States participating in the Conference an the Prohibition of Chemical weapons, bringing together States Parties to the Geneva Protocol of 1925 and other interested States in Paris from 7 to 11 January 1989, solemnly declare the following

1. The participating States are determined to promote international peace and security throughout the world in accordance with the Charter of the United Nations and to pursue effective disarmament measures. In this context, they are determined to prevent any recourse to chemical weapons by completely eliminating them. They solemnly affirm their commitments not to use chemical weapons and condemn such use. They recall their serious concern at recent violations as established and condemned by the competent organs of the United Nations. They support the humanitarian assistance given to the victims affected by chemical weapons.

[1] Reproduced from UN Document A/44/88 of 20 January 1989, Annex. The Final Declaration was transmitted by a letter, dated 19 January 1988, from the Permanent Representative of France to the United Nations addressed to the Secretary-General. The text was also reproduced in *ILM*, Vol. 28, 1989, pp. 1020–1022. For French text see *Droits des conflits armés*, pp. 134–136.

2. *The participating States recognize the importance and continuing validity of the Protocol for the prohibition of the use in war of asphyxiating, poisonous or other gases and bacteriological methods of warfare, signed on 17 June 1925 in Geneva. The States Parties to the Protocol solemnly reaffirm the prohibition as established in it. They call upon all States which have not yet done so to accede to the Protocol.*
3. *The participating States stress the necessity of concluding, at an early date, a Convention on the prohibition of the development, production, stockpiling and use of all chemical weapons, and on their destruction. This Convention shall be global and comprehensive and effectively verifiable. It should be of unlimited duration. To this end, they call on the Conference on Disarmament in Geneva to redouble its efforts, as a matter of urgency, to resolve expeditiously the remaining issues and to conclude the Convention at the earliest date. All States are requested to make, in an appropriate way, a significant contribution to the negotiations in Geneva by undertaking efforts in the relevant fields. The participating States therefore believe that any State wishing to contribute to these negotiations should be able to do so. In addition, in order to achieve as soon as possible the indispensable universal character of the Convention, they call upon all States to become parties thereto as soon as it is concluded.*
4. *The participating States are gravely concerned by the growing danger posed to international peace and security by the risk of the use of chemical weapons as long an such weapons remain and are spread. In this context, they stress the need for the early conclusion and entry into force of the Convention, which will be established on a non-discriminatory basis. They deem it necessary, in the meantime, for each State to exercise restraint and to act responsibly in accordance with the purpose of the present declaration.*
5. *The participating states confirm their full support for the United Nations in the discharge of its indispensable role, in conformity with its Charter. They affirm that the United Nations provide a framework and an instrument enabling the international community to exercise vigilance with respect to the prohibition of the use of chemical weapons. They confirm their support for appropriate and effective steps taken by the United Nations in this respect in conformity with its Charter. They further reaffirm their full support for the Secretary General in carrying out his responsibilities for investigations in the event of alleged violations of the Geneva Protocol. They express their wish for early completion of the work undertaken to strengthen the efficiency of existing procedures and call for the co-operation of all States, in order to facilitate the action of the Secretary-General.*
6. *The participating States, recalling the Final Document of the first Special Session of the United Nations General Assembly devoted to Disarmament in 1978, underline the need to pursue with determination their efforts to secure general and complete disarmament under effective international control, so as to ensure the right of all States to peace and security.*

[Signatures of the President and Secretary General of the Conference]

Paris, 11 January 1989

LIST OF STATES REPRESENTED AT THE PARIS CONFERENCE

The governments of the following 149 states were represented at the Conference:

Afghanistan, Albania, Algeria, Angola, Argentina, Australia, Austria, Bahrain, Bangladesh, Belgium, Belize, Benin, Bolivia, Brazil, Brunei, Bulgaria, Burkina Faso, Burma, Burundi, Cameroon, Canada, Cape Verde, Central African Republic, Chad, Chile, China, Colombia, Comoros, Congo, Cook Islands, Costa Rica, Cuba, Cyprus, Czechoslovakia, Democratic Kampuchea, Democratic People's Republic of Korea, Democratic Yemen, Denmark, Djibouti, Dominica, Dominican Republic, Ecuador, Egypt, El Salvador, Equatorial Guinea, Ethiopia, Finland, France, Gabon, Gambia, German Democratic Republic, Federal Republic of Germany, Ghana, Greece, Grenada, Guatemala, Guinea, Guinea-Bissau, Haiti, Holy See, Hungary, Iceland, India, Indonesia, Iran, Iraq, Ireland, Israel, Italy, Ivory Coast, Jamaica, Japan, Jordan, Kenya, Kuwait, Lao People's Democratic Republic, Lebanon, Lesotho, Liberia, Libyan Arab Jamahiriya, Luxembourg, Madagascar, Malawi, Malaysia, Mali, Malta, Mauritania, Mauritius, Mexico, Monaco, Mongolia, Morocco, Mozambique, Nepal, Netherlands, New Zealand, Nicaragua, Niger, Nigeria, Norway, Oman, Pakistan, Panama, Papua New Guinea, Paraguay, Peru, Philippines, Poland, Portugal, Qatar, Republic of Korea, Romania, Rwanda, Samoa, San Marino, Sao Tome and Principe, Saudi Arabia, Senegal, Seychelles, Sierra Leone, Somalia, South Africa, Spain, Sir Lanka, Sudan, Suriname, Swaziland, Sweden, Switzerland, Syrian Arab Republic, Thailand, Togo, Trinidad and Tobago, Tunisia, Turkey, Uganda, Union of Soviet Socialist Republics, United Arab Emirates, United Kingdom, United Republic of Tanzania, United States, Uruguay, Venezuela, Viet Nam, Yemen, Yugoslavia, Zaire, Zambia, and Zimbabwe.

No. 14

DECLARATION ON THE PROHIBITION OF THE USE OF NUCLEAR AND THERMO-NUCLEAR WEAPONS

Resolution 1653 (XVI) of the United Nations General Assembly adopted on 24 November 1961

INTRODUCTORY NOTE: In the Declaration reprinted below the General Assembly expresses its views on the question of the legality of the use of nuclear and thermo-nuclear weapons. The Declaration was submitted by twelve Asian and African states acting on the initiative of Ethiopia. In paragraph 2 the General Assembly requests the Secretary-General to ascertain the views of the member states on the possibility of convening a special conference for the purpose of signing a convention on the prohibition of such weapons. Of the 62 member states that replied to the Secretary-General in 1962, 33 viewed favourably the possibility of such a conference, 26 expressed negative views or doubts and three wished to await the results of the meetings of the Eighteen-Nation Committee on Disarmament before submitting their views. The General Assembly in later resolutions reaffirmed its view that the use of nuclear weapons is a direct violation of the Charter. See *No. 17* and Res. 46/37 D of 6 December 1991, with further references.

AUTHENTIC TEXTS: Chinese, English, French, Russian and Spanish.

TEXT PUBLISHED IN: *Resolutions adopted by the General Assembly during its Sixteenth session,* Vol. 1, *19 September 1961–23 February 1962,* General Assembly Official Records: Sixteenth session, Supplement No. 17 (A/5100), New York, United Nations, 1962, pp. 4–5 (Engl. – see also the Chinese, French, Russian and Spanish editions); *Droit des conflits armés*, pp. 137–139 (French).

* * *

The General Assembly,

Mindful *of its responsibility under the Charter of the United Nations in the maintenance of international peace and security, as well as in the consideration of principles governing disarmament,*

Gravely concerned *that while negotiations on disarmament have not so far achieved satisfactory results, the armaments race, particularly in the nuclear and thermo-nuclear fields, has reached a dangerous stage requiring all possible precautionary measures to protect humanity and civilization from the hazard of nuclear and thermo-nuclear catastrophe,*

Recalling *that the use of weapons of mass destruction, causing unnecessary human suffering, was in the past prohibited, as being contrary to the laws of humanity and to the principles of international law, by international declarations and binding agreements, such as the Declaration of St. Petesbury of 1868, the Declaration of the Brussels Conference of 1874, the Conventions of The Hague Peace Conferences of 1899 and 1907, and the Geneva Protocol of 1925, to which the majority of nations are still parties,*

Considering *that the use of nuclear and thermo-nuclear weapons would bring about indiscriminate suffering and destruction to mankind and civilization to an even greater extent than the use of those weapons declared by the aforementioned international declarations and agreements to be contrary to the laws of humanity and a crime under international law,*

Believing *that the use of weapons of mass destruction, such as nuclear and thermo-nuclear weapons, is a direct negation of the high ideals and objectives which the United Nations has been established to achieve through the protection of succeeding generations from the scourge of war and through the preservation and promotion of their cultures,*

1. Declares that:
   (a) The use of nuclear and thermo-nuclear weapons is contrary to the spirit, letter and aims of the United Nations and, as such, a direct violation of the Charter of the United Nations;
   (b) The use of nuclear and thermo-nuclear weapons would exceed even the scope of war and cause indiscriminate suffering and destruction to mankind and civilization and, as such, is contrary to the rule of international law and to the laws of humanity;
   (c) The use of nuclear and thermo-nuclear weapons is a war directed not against an enemy or enemies alone but also against mankind in general, since the peoples of the world not involved in such a war will be subjected to all the evils generated by the use of such weapons:
   (d) Any State using nuclear and thermo-nuclear weapons is to be considered as violating the Charter of the United Nations, as acting contrary to the laws of humanity and as committing a crime against mankind and civilization;
2. Requests *the Secretary-General to consult the Governments of Member States to ascertain their views on the possibility of convening a special conference for signing a convention on the prohibition of the use of nuclear and thermo-nuclear weapons for war purposes and to report on the results of such consultation to the General Assembly at its seventeenth session.*

VOTE

The Declaration was adopted by a vote of 55 in favour, 20 against and 26 abstentions.

RECORDED VOTE

In favour: Afghanistan, Albania, Bulgaria, Burma, Byelorussian SSR, Cambodia, Cameroon, Central African Republic, Ceylon, Chad, Congo (Brazzaville), Congo (Leopoldville), Cuba, Cyprus, Czechoslovakia, Dahomey, Ethiopia, Gabon, Ghana, Guinea, Hungary, India, Indonesia, Iraq, Ivory Coast, Japan, Jordan, Lebanon, Liberia, Libya, Madagascar, Mali, Mauritania, Mexico, Mongolia, Morocco, Nepal, Niger, Nigeria, Poland, Romania, Saudi Arabia, Senegal, Sierra Leone, Somalia, Sudan, Syria, Togo, Tunisia, Ukrainian SSR, USSR, United Arab Republic, Upper Volta, Yemen, Yugoslavia.

Against: Australia, Belgium, Canada, China, Costa Rica, France, Greece, Guatemala, Ireland, Italy, Luxemburg, Netherlands, New Zealand, Nicaragua, Portugal, South Africa, Spain, Turkey, United Kingdom, United States.

Abstaining: Argentina, Austria, Bolivia, Brazil, Chile, Colombia, Denmark, Ecuador, El Salvador, Federation of Malaya, Finland, Haiti, Honduras, Iceland, Iran, Israel, Norway, Pakistan, Panama, Paraguay, Peru, Philippines, Sweden, Thailand, Uruguay, Venezuela.

No. 15

QUESTIONS OF CHEMICAL AND BACTERIOLOGICAL (BIOLOGICAL) WEAPONS

Resolution 2603 A (XXIV) of the United Nations General Assembly adopted on 16 December 1969

INTRODUCTORY NOTE: The growing concern with the use of chemical and bacteriological (biological) weapons, including riot gases and herbicides, in recent armed conflicts induced the United Nations General Assembly to adopt a series of resolutions, of which the first dates from 1966, calling for strict observance by all states of the principles and objectives of the Geneva Protocol of 1925. In 1968, the Assembly requested the Secretary-General to appoint a group of experts to study the effects of chemical and bacteriological (biological) weapons (resolution 2454 A (XXIII)). In submitting the experts' report in July 1969, the Secretary-General recommended the members of the United Nations, *inter alia*, "to make a clear affirmation that the prohibition contained in the Geneva Protocol applies to the use in war of all chemical, bacteriological and biological agents (including tear gases and other harassing agents) which now exist or which may be developed in the future" (UN Doc. A/7575). Following this recommendation the General Assembly adopted the resolution reprinted below interpreting the Geneva Protocol of 1925. The resolution has, however, never been recited in the numerous resolutions adopted by the General Assembly in later years on the question of chemical and bacteriological (biological) weapons. This hints at a certain reserve existing in regard to it.

AUTHENTIC TEXTS: Chinese, English, French, Russian and Spanish.

TEXT PUBLISHED IN: *Resolutions adopted by the General Assembly during its Twenty-fourth session, 16 September – 17 December 1969.* General Assembly Official Records: Twenty-fourth session Supplement No. 30 (A/7630), New York, United Nations, 1970, p. 16 (Engl. – see also the Chinese, French, Russian and Spanish editions); *Droits des conflits armés*, pp. 141–43 (French).

* * *

The General Assembly,

Considering *that chemical and biological methods of warfare have always been viewed with horror and been justly condemned by the international community,*

Considering *that these methods of warfare are inherently reprehensible because their effects are often uncontrollable and unpredictable and may be injurious without distinction to combatants and non-combatants and because any use of such methods would entail a serious risk of escalation.*

Recalling *that successive international instruments have prohibited or sought to prevent the use of such methods of warfare,*

Noting specifically *in this regard that:*

(a) The majority of States then in existence adhered to the Protocol For the Prohibition of the Use in War of Asphyxiating, Poisonous or Other Gases, and of Bacteriological Methods of Warfare, signed at Geneva on 17 June 1925,

(b) Since then further States have become Parties to that Protocol,
(c) Still other States have declared that they will abide by its principles and objectives,
(d) These principles and objectives have commanded broad respect in the practice of States,
(e) The General Assembly, without any dissenting vote, has called for the strict observance by all States of the principles and objectives of the Geneva Protocol,

Recognizing therefore, *in the light of all the above circumstances, that the Geneva Protocol embodies the generally recognized rules of international law prohibiting the use in international armed conflicts of all biological and chemical methods of warfare, regardless of any technical developments,*

Mindful *of the report of the Secretary-General, prepared with the assistance of the Group of Consultant Experts appointed by him under General Assembly resolution 2454 A (XXIII) of 20 December 1968, and entitled Chemical and Bacteriological (Biological) Weapons and the Effects of Their Possible Use,*[1]

Considering *that this report and the foreword to it by the Secretary-General add further urgency for an affirmation of these rules and for dispelling, for the future, any uncertainty as to their scope and, by such affirmation, to assure the effectiveness of the rules and enable all States to demonstrate their determination to comply with them,*

Declares *as contrary to the generally recognized rules of international law, as embodied in the Protocol for the Prohibition of the Use in War of Asphyxiating, Poisonous or Other Gases, and of Bacteriological Methods of Warfare, signed at Geneva on 17 June 1925, the use in international armed conflicts of:*
(a) Any chemical agents of warfare – chemical substances, whether gaseous, liquid or solid – which might be employed because of their direct toxic effects on man, animals or plants;
(b) Any biological agents of warfare – living organisms, whatever their nature, or infective material derived from them – which are intended to cause disease or death in man, animals or plants, and which depend for their effects on their ability to multiply in the person, animal or plant attacked.

VOTE

Resolution 2603 A (XXIV) was adopted by a vote of 80 in favour, 3 against and 36 abstentions.

RECORDED VOTE

In favour: Afghanistan, Algeria, Argentina, Brazil, Bulgaria, Burma, Burundi, Byelorussia, Cameroon, Central African Republic, Ceylon, Chad, Colombia, Congo (Brazzaville), Congo (Democratic Republic of), Costa Rica, Cuba, Cyprus, Czechoslovakia, Dahomey, Dominican Republic, Ecuador, Equatorial Guinea, Ethiopia, Finland, Gabon, Ghana, Guatemala, Guinea, Guyana, Haiti, Honduras, Hungary, India, Indonesia, Iran, Iraq, Ireland, Ivory Coast, Jamaica, Jordan, Kenya, Kuwait, Lebanon, Lesotho, Libya, Maldives, Mali, Mauritania, Mauritius, Mexico, Mongolia, Morocco, Nepal, Niger, Nigeria, Pakistan, Panama, Peru, Poland Romania,

[1] United Nations Publication, Sales No. E.69.1.24.

Rwanda, Saudi Arabia, Senegal, Somalia, Southern Yemen, Spain, Sudan, Sweden, Syria, Togo, Trinidad and Tobago, Uganda, Ukraine, USSR, United Arab Republic, United Republic of Tanzania, Upper Volta, Yemen, Yugoslavia.

Against: Australia, Portugal, United States.

Abstaining: Austria, Belgium, Bolivia, Canada, Chile, China, Denmark, El Salvador, France, Greece, Iceland, Israel, Italy, Japan, Laos, Liberia, Luxembourg, Madagascar, Malawi, Malaysia, Netherlands, New Zealand, Nicaragua, Norway, Paraguay, Philippines, Sierra Leone, Singapore, South Africa, Swaziland, Thailand, Tunisia, Turkey, United Kingdom, Uruguay, Venezuela.

Absent: Albania, Barbados, Botswana, Cambodia,[2] Gambia, Malta, Zambia.

[2] Cambodia later announced it would have voted in favour.

No. 16

CONVENTION ON THE PROHIBITION OF DEVELOPMENT, PRODUCTION AND STOCKPILING OF BACTERIOLOGICAL (BIOLOGICAL) AND TOXIN WEAPONS AND ON THEIR DESTRUCTION

Opened for signature on 10 April 1972 at London, Moscow and Washington

INTRODUCTORY NOTE: Deficiencies of the Geneva Protocol of 17 June 1925 (*No. 13*) and the wish to prohibit not only the use but also the production and stockpiling of biological and chemical weapons induced the UN General Assembly and the Committee on Disarmament to take up this question. The Convention was drafted by the Committee on Disarmament and recommended for adherence by resolution 2826 (XXVI) of the General Assembly on 16 December 1971. It is limited to biological weapons. The inclusion of chemical weapons proved impossible, as no agreement on international supervision could be attained (but see now *No. 22*). With regard to biological weapons, international supervision of the production and stockpiling of such weapons seemed to be dispensable as it is assumed that the use of such weapons would have no immediate military advantage.

Although the present Convention deals with questions of disarmament and does not belong to the law of armed conflicts in its strict sense it is included in this collection in view of its close relationship with the Geneva Protocol of 1925.

ENTRY INTO FORCE: 26 March 1975.

AUTHENTIC TEXTS: Chinese, English, French, Russian, Spanish. The English text below is reprinted from *UNTS*, Vol. 1015, 1976, pp. 164–169.

TEXT PUBLISHED IN: *UNTS*, Vol. 1015, 1976, pp. 164–241 (Chinese, Engl., French, Russ., Span.); United Nations General Assembly resolution, A/RES/2826 (XXVI), annex (Chinese, Engl., French, Russ., Span.); *Arms Control and Disarmament Agreements: Texts and Histories of negotiations*, Washington DC, US Arms Control and Disarmament Agency, 1982, pp. 120–131 (Engl.); *Status of Multilateral Arms Regulation and Disarmament Agreements*, 4th edn., 1992, New York, United Nations, 1993 (sales No. E.93.IX.3 – Vol. I), pp. 191–216 (Engl.); *Etat des accords multilatéraux en matière de désarmement et du contrôle des armements*, 3ème édition, New York, Nations Unies, 1987 (F.88.IX.5), pp. 135–152 (French); *Situación de los acuerdos multilaterales de regulacion de armamentos y de desarme*, tercera edicion, 1987, Nueva York, Naciones Unidas, 1989 (S.89.IX.3), pp. 127–143 (Span.); *UST*, Vol. XXVI, Part 1, 1975, pp. 583–665 (Chinese, Engl., French, Russ., Span.); *TIAS* 8062; *AJIL*, Vol. 66, 1972, pp. 451–455 (Engl.); *ILM*, Vol. 11, No. 2, 1972, pp. 309–315 (Engl.); Goldblat, pp. 370–374 (Engl.); Ronzitti, pp. 623–639 (Engl.); *Droit des conflits armés*, pp. 145–170 (French); *RGDIP*, tome LXXVII, 1973, pp. 345–350 (French); *Sbornik dogovorov SSSR*, vyp. XXXI, 1975, pp. 58–61 (Russ.); Blatova, pp. 688–693

(Russ.); *Mezhdunarodnaya zhizn'*, No. 2, 1972, pp. 156–158 (Russ.); United Nations website: http://disarmament.un.org/TreatyStatus; ICRC website: www.icrc.org/ihl.nsf.

* * *

The States Parties to this Convention,

Determined to act with a view to achieving effective progress towards general and complete disarmament, including the prohibition and elimination of all types of weapons of mass destruction, and convinced that the prohibition of the development, production and stockpiling of chemical and bacteriological (biological) weapons and their elimination, through effective measures, will facilitate the achievement of general and complete disarmament under strict and effective international control.

Recognising the important significance of the Protocol for the Prohibition of the Use in War of Asphyxiating, Poisonous or Other Gases and of Bacteriological Methods of Warfare, signed at Geneva on 17 June 1925,[1] and conscious also of the contribution which the said Protocol has already made, and continues to make, to mitigating the horrors of war,

Reaffirming their adherence to the principles and objectives of that Protocol and calling upon all States to comply strictly with them,

Recalling that the General Assembly of the United Nations has repeatedly condemned all actions contrary to the principles and objectives of the Geneva Protocol of 17 June 1925,

Desiring to contribute to the strengthening of confidence between peoples and the general improvement of the international atmosphere,

Desiring also to contribute to the realisation of the purposes and principles of the Charter of the United Nations,

Convinced of the importance and urgency of eliminating from the arsenals of States, through effective measures, such dangerous weapons of mass destruction as those using chemical or bacteriological (biological) agents,

Recognising that an agreement on the prohibition of bacteriological (biological) and toxin weapons represents a first possible step towards the achievement of agreement on effective measures also for the prohibition of the development, production and stockpiling of chemical weapons, and determined to continue negotiations to that end,

Determined, for the sake of all mankind, to exclude completely the possibility of bacteriological (biological) agents and toxins being used as weapons,

Convinced that such use would be repugnant to the conscience of mankind and that no effort should be spared to minimise this risk,

Have agreed as follows:

Article I. Each State Party to this Convention undertakes never in any circumstances to develop, produce, stockpile or otherwise acquire or retain:

1. microbial or other biological agents, or toxins whatever their origin or method of production, of types and in quantities that have no justification for prophylactic, protective or other peaceful purposes;
2. weapons, equipment or means of delivery designed to use such agents or toxins for hostile purposes or in armed conflict.

[1] See document *No. 13*, p. 107.

Art II. Each State Party to this Convention undertakes to destroy, or to divert to peaceful purposes, as soon as possible but not later than nine months after the entry into force of the Convention, all agents, toxins, weapons, equipment and means of delivery specified in Article I of the Convention, which are in its possession or under its jurisdiction or control. In implementing the provisions of this Article all necessary safety precautions shall be observed to protect populations and the environment.

Art III. Each State Party to this Convention undertakes not to transfer to any recipient whatsover, directly or indirectly, and not in any way to assist, encourage, or induce any State, group of States or international organisations to manufacture or otherwise acquire any of the agents, toxins, weapons, equipment or means of delivery specified in Article I of the Convention.

Art IV. Each State Party to this Convention shall, in accordance with its constitutional processes, take any necessary measures to prohibit and prevent the development, production, stockpiling, acquisition or retention of the agents, toxins, weapons, equipment and means of delivery specified in Article I of the Convention, within the territory of such State, under its jurisdiction or under its control anywhere.

Art V. The States Parties to this Convention undertake to consult one another and to cooperate in solving any problems which may arise in relation to the objective of, or in the application of the provisions of, the Convention. Consultation and cooperation pursuant to this Article may also be undertaken through appropriate international procedures within the framework of the United Nations and in accordance with its Charter.

Art VI.

1. Any State Party to this Convention which finds that any other State Party is acting in breach of obligations deriving from the provisions of the Convention may lodge a complaint with the Security Council of the United Nations. Such a complaint should include all possible evidence confirming its validity, as well as a request for its consideration by the Security Council.
2. Each State Party to this Convention undertakes to co-operate in carrying out any investigation which the Security Council may initiate, in accordance with the provisions of the Charter of the United Nations, on the basis of the complaint received by the Council. The Security Council shall inform the States Parties to the Convention of the results of the investigation.

Art VII.[2] Each State Party to this Convention undertakes to provide or support assistance, in accordance with the United Nations Charter, to any Party to the Convention which so requests, if the Security Council decides that such Party has been exposed to danger a result of violation of the Convention.

---

[2] For reservations in respect of this article by Austria, Malaysia and Switzerland, see pp. 155, 157, 158. See also the objection of the United States to the reservation made by Switzerland, p. 159.

Art VIII. Nothing in this Convention shall be interpreted as in any way limiting or detracting from the obligations assumed by any State under the Protocol for the Prohibition of the Use in War of Asphyxiating, Poisonous or Other Gases, and of Bacteriological Methods of Warfare, signed at Geneva on 17 June 1925.

Art IX. Each State Party to this Convention affirms the recognised objective of effective prohibition of chemical weapons and, to this end, undertakes to continue negotiations in good faith with a view to reaching early agreement on effective measures for the prohibition of their development, production and stockpiling and for their destruction, and on appropriate measures concerning equipment and means of delivery specifically designed for the production or use of chemical agents for weapons purposes.

Art. X.

1. The State Parties to this Convention undertake to facilitate, and have the right to participate in, the fullest possible exchange of equipment, materials and scientific and technological information for the use of bacteriological (biological) agents and toxins for peaceful purposes. Parties to the Convention in a position to do so shall also co-operate in contributing individually or together with other States or international organisations to the further development and application of scientific discoveries in the field of bacteriology (biology) for the prevention of disease, or for other peaceful purposes.
2. This Convention shall be implemented in a manner designed to avoid hampering the economic or technological development of States Parties to the Convention or international co-operation in the field of peaceful bacteriological (biological) activities, including the international exchange of bacteriological (biological) agents and toxins and equipment for the processing, use or production of bacteriological (biological) agents and toxins for peaceful purposes in accordance with the provisions of the Convention.

Art XI. Any State Party may propose amendments to this Convention. Amendments shall enter into force for each State Party accepting the amendments upon their acceptance by a majority of the States Parties to the Convention and thereafter for each remaining State Party on the date of acceptance by it.

Art. XII. Five years after the entry into force of this Convention, or earlier if it is requested by a majority of Parties to the Convention by submitting a proposal to this effect to the Depositary Governments, a conference of States Parties to the Convention shall be held at Geneva, Switzerland, to review the operation of the Convention, with a view to assuring that the purposes of the preamble and the provisions of the Convention, including the provisions concerning negotiations on chemical weapons, are being realised. Such review shall take into account any new scientific and technological developments relevant to the Convention.

Art XIII.

1. This Convention shall be of unlimited duration.
2. Each State Party to this Convention shall in exercising its national sovereignty have the right to withdraw from the Convention if it decides that

extraordinary events, related to the subject matter of the Convention, have jeopardised the supreme interests of its country. It shall give notice of such withdrawal to all other States Parties to the Convention and to the United Nations Security Council three months in advance. Such notice shall include a statement of the extraordinary events it regards as having jeopardised its supreme interests.

Art XIV.

1. This Convention shall be open to all States for signature. Any State which does not sign the Convention before its entry into force in accordance with paragraph 3 of this Article may accede to it at any time.
2. This Convention shall be subject to ratification by signatory States. Instruments of ratification and instruments of accession shall be deposited with the Governments of the United Kingdom of Great Britain and Northern Ireland, the Union of Soviet Socialist Republics and the United States of America, which are hereby designated the Depositary Governments.
3. This Convention shall enter into force after the deposit of instruments of ratification by twenty-two Governments, including the Governments designated as Depositaries of the Convention.
4. For States whose instruments of ratification or accession are deposited subsequent to the entry into force of this Convention, it shall enter into force on the date of the deposit of their instruments of ratification or accession.
5. The Depositary Governments shall promptly inform all signatory and acceding States of the date of each signature, the date of deposit of each instrument of ratification or of accession and the date of the entry into force of this Convention, and of the receipt of other notices.
6. This Convention shall be registered by the Depositary Governments pursuant to Article 102 of the Charter of the United Nations.

Art XV. This Convention, the English, Russian, French, Spanish and Chinese texts of which are equally authentic, shall be deposited in the archives of the Depositary Governments. Duly certified copies of the Convention shall be transmitted by the Depositary Governments to the Governments of the signatory and acceding States.

SIGNATURES, RATIFICATIONS, ACCESSIONS AND NOTIFICATIONS OF SUCCESSION[1]

State	*Signature*[2]	*Ratification, Accession, Notification of Succession (C)*[3]
Afghanistan	(L) 10 April 1972 (M) 10 April 1972 (W) 10 April 1972	26 March 1975
Albania	(L) – (M) – (W) –	11 August 1992 26 March 1993 3 June 1992
Algeria	22 July 2001	22 July 2001
Argentina	(L) 3 August 1972 (M) 1 August 1972 (W) 7 August 1972	5 December 1979 27 December 1979 27 November 1979
Armenia	(L) – (M) – (W) –	* 7 June 1994 7 June 1994
Australia	(L) 10 April 1972 (M) 10 April 1972 (W) 10 April 1972	5 October 1977 5 October 1977 5 October 1977
Austria	(L) 10 April 1972 (M) 10 April 1972 (W) 10 April 1972	10 August 1973 *Res.* 10 August 1973 *Res.* 10 August 1973 *Res.*
Bahamas	(L) – (M) – (W) –	26 November 1986 * *
Bahrain	(L) – (M) – (W) –	28 October 1988 *Dec.* * *

[1] Based on the communications received from the Foreign and Commonwealth Office of Great Britain dated 7 December 2001, from the Embassy of the USSR in Berne of 20 November 1986 and United States Department of State, Office of the Legal Advisor of 23 June 1999 and verified also in *Status of Multilateral Arms Regulation and Disarmament Agreements*, 5th edn., 1996, New York, United Nations, 1997 (Sales No. E.97.IX.3), pp. 156–178, United Nations website: http://disarmament.un.org.TreatyStatus.nsf of 10 December 2001, and Foreign and Commonwealth Office website: www.fco.gov.uk; ICRC website: www.icrc.org/ihl.nsf.

A dash (–) after the name of a country indicates that the action has not been taken.

An asterisk (*) indicates that the action has not been taken with this depositary.

[2] Signatures affixed on the original of the Treaty deposited with the governments of the: Union of Soviet Socialist Republics (M), United Kingdom of Great Britain and Northern Ireland (L) and United States of America (W).

[3] Instruments of ratification, accession or notifications of succession or continuity (C) deposited with the governments of the Union of the Soviet Socialist Republics (M), United Kingdom of Great Britain and Northern Ireland (L) and United States of America (W).

State	*Signature*	*Ratification, Accession, Notification of Succession (C)*
Germany[10]	(L) 10 April 1972	7 April 1983
	(M) 10 April 1972	7 April 1983
	(W) 10 April 1972	7 April 1983
Ghana	(L) *	6 June 1975
	(M) 10 April 1972	*
	(W) 10 April 1972	*
Greece	(L) 10 April 1972	*
	(M) 14 April 1972	*
	(W) 12 April 1972	10 December 1975
Grenada	(L) –	22 October 1986
	(M)–	*
	(W) –	*
Guatemala	(L) *	*
	(M) *	*
	(W) 9 May 1972	19 September 1973
Guinea Bissau	(L) –	*
	(M) –	20 August 1976
	(W) –	*
Guyana	(L) *	–
	(M) *	–
	(W) 3 January 1973	–
Haiti	(L) *	–
	(M) *	–
	(W) 10 April 1972	–
Honduras	(L) *	*
	(M) *	*
	(W) 10 April 1972	14 March 1979
Hungary	(L) 10 April 1972	27 December 1972
	(M) 10 April 1972	27 December 1972
	(W) 10 April 1972	27 December 1972
Iceland	(L) 10 April 1972	15 February 1973
	(M) 10 April 1972	15 February 1973
	(W) 10 April 1972	15 February 1973

[10] The German Democratic Republic ratified the Convention on 28 November 1972.

Through the accession of the German Democratic Republic to the Federal Republic of Germany with effect from 3 October 1990, the German states have united to form one sovereign state (see note 3 in document *No. 18*, p. 170 and note 35 in document *Nos. 49–52*, p. 639. As regards treaties in respect of which formalities had been effected by both the Federal Republic of Germany and the former German Democratic Republic prior to unification, the entry indicates the type of formality effected by the Federal Republic of Germany, while the type of formality effected by the former German Democratic Republic appears in a footnote.

State	*Signature*	*Ratification, Accession, Notification of Succession (C)*
India	(L) 15 January 1973 *Dec.*	15 July 1974 *Dec.*
	(M) 15 January 1973 *Dec.*	15 July 1974 *Dec.*
	(W) 15 January 1973 *Dec.*	15 July 1974 *Dec.*
Indonesia	(L) 21 June 1972	19 February 1992
	(M) 20 June 1972	4 February 1992
	(W) 20 June 1972	1 April 1992
Iran	(L) 16 November 1972	22 August 1973
	(M) 10 April 1972	27 August 1973
	(W) 10 April 1972	22 August 1973
Iraq	(L) *	*
	(M) 11 May 1972	19 June 1991
	(W) *	*
Ireland	(L) 10 April 1972 *Dec.*	27 October 1972
	(M) *	*
	(W) 10 April 1972 *Dec.*	27 October 1972
Italy	(L) 10 April 1972	30 May 1975
	(M) 10 April 1972	30 May 1975
	(W) 10 April 1972	30 May 1975
Jamaica	(L) –	13 August 1975
	(M) –	*
	(W) –	*
Japan	(L) 10 April 1972	18 June 1982
	(M) 10 April 1972	18 June 1982
	(W) 10 April 1972	8 June 1982
Jordan	(L) 17 April 1972	27 June 1975
	(M) 24 April 1972	30 May 1975
	(W) 10 April 1972	2 June 1975
Kenya	(L) –	7 January 1976
	(M) –	*
	(W) –	*
Korea, Republic of	(L)10 April 1972 *Dec.*	25 June 1987
	(M) *	*
	(W) 10 April 1972	25 June 1987
Korea, People's Democratic Republic of	(L) –	*
	(M) –	13 March 1987
	(W) –	*
Kuwait	(L) 27 April 1972	26 July 1972 *Dec.*
	(M) 14 April 1972	1 August 1972 *Dec.*
	(W) 14 April 1972	18 July 1972 *Dec.*

State	*Signature*	*Ratification, Accession, Notification of Succession (C)*
Laos	(L) 10 April 1972	25 April 1973
	(M) 10 April 1972	20 March 1973
	(W) 10 April 1972	22 March 1973
Latvia	(L) –	6 February 1997
	(M)–	*
	(W) –	*
Lebanon	(L) 10 April 1972	26 March 1975
	(M) 21 April 1972	2 April 1975
	(W) 10 April 1972	13 June 1975
Lesotho	(L) *	6 September 1977
	(M) *	*
	(W) 10 April 1972	*
Liberia	(L) 14 April 1972	–
	(M) *	–
	(W) 10 April 1972	–
Libyan Arab Jamahiriya	(L) –	*
	(M) –	19 January 1982
	(W) –	*
Liechtenstein	(L) –	6 June 1991
	(M) –	31 May 1991
	(W) –	30 May 1991
Lithuania	(L) –	10 February 1998
	(M) –	
	(W) –	
Luxembourg	(L) 10 April 1972	23 March 1976
	(M) 10 April 1972	23 March 1976
	(W) 12 April 1972	23 March 1976
Madagascar	(L) 13 October 1972	–
	(M) *	–
	(W) *	–
Macedonia, The Former Yugoslav Republic of	(L) –	14 March 1997
	(M) –	24 December 1996 (C)
	(W) –	23 April 1997[11]
Malawi	(L) *	–
	(M) *	–
	(W) 10 April 1972	–

[11] Date of the receipt of notification of succession.

State	*Signature*	*Ratification, Accession, Notification of Succession (C)*
Malaysia	(L) 10 April 1972	6 September 1991 *Res.*
	(M) 10 April 1972	6 September 1991 *Res.*
	(W) 10 April 1972	26 September 1991 *Res.*
Maldives	(L) –	*
	(M) –	2 August 1993
	(W) –	*
Mali	(L) *	–
	(M) *	–
	(W) 10 April 1972	–
Malta	(L) 11 September 1972	7 April 1975
	(M) *	*
	(W) *	*
Mauritius	(L) *	11 January 1973
	(M) *	15 January 1973
	(W) 10 April 1972	7 August 1972
Mexico	(L) 10 April 1972 *Dec.*	8 April 1974
	(M) 10 April 1972	8 April 1974
	(W) 10 April 1972 Dec.	8 April 1974
Monaco	(L) –	30 April 1999
	(M) –	
	(W) –	
Mongolia	(L) 10 April 1972	14 September 1972
	(M) 10 April 1972	20 October 1972
	W) 10 April 1972	5 September 1972
Morocco	(L) 2 May 1972	–
	(M) 5 June 1972	–
	(W) 3 May 1972	–
Myanmar (Burma)	(L) 10 April 1972	–
	(M) 10 April 1972	–
	(W) 10 April 1972	–
Nepal	(L) 10 April 1972	–
	(M) 10 April 1972	–
	(W) 10 April 1972	–
Netherlands	(L) 10 April 1972	22 June 1981[12]
	(M) 10 April 1972	22 June 1981
	(W) 10 April 1972	22 June 1981[13]

[12] With the statement that ratification was also on behalf of the Netherlands Antilles.

[13] On 20 December 1985, the Netherlands informed the depositary government that as the island of Aruba, which on that date was still part of the Netherlands Antilles, would obtain internal autonomy as a country within the Kingdom of the Netherlands as of 1 January 1986

State	*Signature*	*Ratification, Accession, Notification of Succession (C)*
New Zealand	(L) 10 April 1972	18 December 1972
	(M) 10 April 1972	10 January 1973
	(W) 10 April 1972	13 December 1972
Nicaragua	(L) 10 April 1972	*
	(M) *	*
	(W) 10 April 1972	7 August 1975
Niger	(L) *	*
	(M) *	*
	(W) 21 April 1972	23 June 1972
Nigeria	(L) 10 July 1972	9 July 1973
	(M) 3 July 1972	20 July 1973
	(W) 6 December 1972	3 July 1973
Norway	(L) 10 April 1972	1 August 1973
	(M) 10 April 1972	23 August 1973
	(W) 10 April 1972	1 August 1973
Oman	(L) –	*
	(M) –	*
	(W) –	31 March 1992
Pakistan	(L) 10 April 1972	3 October 1974
	(M) 10 April 1972	25 September 1974
	(W) 10 April 1972	3 October 1974
Panama	(L) *	*
	(M) *	*
	(W) 2 May 1972	20 March 1974
Papua New Guinea	(L) –	27 October 1980
	(M) –	13 November 1980
	(W) –	16 March 1981
Paraguay	(L) –	*
	(M) –	*
	(W) –	9 June 1976
Peru	(L) 10 April 1972	5 June 1985
	(M) 10 April 1972	5 June 1985
	(W) 10 April 1972	11 June 1985
Philippines	(L) 10 April 1972	*
	(M) 21 June 1972	*
	(W) 10 April 1972	21 May 1973

cont.

the Convention would, as of 1 January 1986, as concerns the Kingdom of Netherlands, apply to the Netherlands Antilles (without Aruba) and Aruba.

State	*Signature*	*Ratification, Accession, Notification of Succession (C)*
Poland	(L) 10 April 1972	25 January 1973
	(M) 10 April 1972	25 January 1973
	(W) 10 April 1972	25 January 1973
Portugal	(L) *	15 May 1975
	(M) *	15 May 1975
	(W) 29 June 1972	15 May 1975
Qatar	(L) 14 November 1972	17 April 1975
	(M) *	*
	(W) *	*
Romania	(L) 10 April 1972	26 July 1979
	(M) 10 April 1972	27 July 1979
	(W) 10 April 1972	25 July 1979
Russian Federation (formerly Union of Soviet Socialist Republic)[14]	(L) 10 April 1972	26 March 1975 (C) *Dec.*
	(M) 10 April 1972	26 March 1975 (C) *Dec.*
	(W) 10 April 1972	26 March 1975 (C) *Dec.*
Rwanda	(L)	20 May 1975
	(M) 10 April 1972	20 May 1975
	(W) 10 April 1972	20 May 1975
Saint Kitts and Nevis	(L) –	2 April 1991
	(M) –	*
	(W) –	*
Saint Lucia	(L) –	26 November 1986 *(C)*
	(M) –	*
	(W) –	*
Saint Vincent and the Grenadines	(L) –	13 May 1999 *(C)*
	(M) –	
	(W) –	
San Marino	(L) 21 March 1973	11 March 1975
	(M) 30 January 1973	27 March 1975
	(W) 12 September 1972	17 March 1975
Sao Tome and Principe	(L) –	*
	(M) –	24 August 1979
	(W) –	*
Saudi Arabia	(L)*	*
	(M)*	*
	(W) 12 April 1972	24 May 1972

[14] As from 24 December 1991, the Russian Federation continues to exercise its rights and honour its commitments deriving from international treaties concluded by the USSR. For the view of the Government of the USSR in relation to the declaration made by the United Kingdom, see pp. 159–160.

State	*Signature*	*Ratification, Accession, Notification of Succession (C)*
Senegal	(L) *	*
	(M) *	*
	(W) 10 April 1972	26 March 1975
Seychelles	(L) –	11 October 1979
	(M) –	24 October 1979
	(W) –	16 October 1979
Sierra Leone	(L) 24 November 1972	29 June 1976
	(M) *	29 June 1976
	(W) 7 November 1972	29 June 1976
Singapore	(L) 19 June 1972	2 December 1975
	(M) 19 June 1972	2 December 1975
	(W) 19 June 1972	2 December 1975
Slovakia[15]	(L) –	17 May 1993 (C) *Dec.*
	(M) –	25 June 1993 (C) *Dec.*
	(W) –	10 June 1993 (C)[16] *Dec.*
Slovenia	(L) –	7 April 1992 (C)
	(M) –	*
	(W) –	20 August 1992 (C)[17]
Solomon Islands	(L) –	17 June 1981 (C)
	(M) –	*
	(W) –	*
Somalia	(L) *	–
	(M) 3 July 1973	–
	(W) *	–
South Africa	(L) *	–
	(M) *	–
	(W) 10 April 1972	3 November 1975
Spain	(L) 10 April 1972	20 June 1979
	(M) *	*
	(W) 10 April 1972	20 June 1979
Sri Lanka (formerly Ceylon)	(L) 10 April 1972	18 November 1986
	(M) 10 April 1972	18 November 1986
	(W) 10 April 1972	18 November 1986

[15] Czechoslovakia signed on 10 April 1972 and deposited an instrument of ratification on 30 April 1973. On 31 December 1992, at midnight, Czechoslovakia ceased to exist and was succeded by two separate and independent states, the Czech Republic and the Slovak Republic. See the declaration of succession on pp. 155 and 158.

[16] Effective date of notification of succession 1 January 1993.

[17] Date of receipt of notification of succession.

State	*Signature*	*Ratification, Accession, Notification of Succession (C)*
Suriname	(L) –	6 January 1993
	(M) –	*
	(W) –	9 April 1993
Swaziland	(L) –	18 June 1991
	(M) –	*
	(W) –	*
Sweden	(L) 27 February 1975	5 February 1976
	(M) 27 February 1975	5 February 1976
	(W) 27 February 1975	5 February 1976
Switzerland	(L) 10 April 1972 *Dec.*	4 May 1976 *Res.*[18]
	(M) 10 April 1972 *Dec.*	4 May 1976 *Res.*
	(W) 10 April 1972 *Dec.*	4 May 1976 *Res.*
Syria	(L) *	–
	(M) 14 April 1972	–
	(W) *	–
Tanzania, United Republic of	(L) 16 August 1972	–
	(M) *	–
	(W) *	–
Thailand	(L) *	*
	(M) *	*
	(W) 17 January 1973	28 May 1975
Togo	(L) *	*
	(M) *	*
	(W) 10 April 1972	10 November 1976
Tonga	(L) –	28 September 1976
	(M) –	*
	(W) –	*
Tunisia	(L) 10 April 1972	6 June 1973
	(M) 10 April 1972	30 May 1973
	(W) 10 April 1972	18 May 1973
Turkey	(L) 10 April 1972	4 November 1974
	(M) 10 April 1972	25 October 1974
	(W) 10 April 1972	5 November 1974
Turkmanistan	(L) –	11 January 1996
	(M) –	11 January 1996
	(W) –	8 March 1996

[18] For the view expressed by the Government of the United States of America in connection with the reservation made by the Government of Switzerland, see p. 159.

State	*Signature*	*Ratification, Accession, Notification of Succession (C)*
Uganda	(L) –	*
	(M) –	*
	(W) –	12 May 1992
Ukraine	(L) *	*
	(M) 10 April 1972	26 March 1975
	(W) *	*
Union of Soviet Socialist Republics *see Russian Federation*		
United Arab Emirates	(L) 28 September 1972	–
	(M) *	–
	(W) *	–
United Kingdom of Great Britain and Northern Ireland	(L) 10 April 1972	26 March 1975 *Dec.*[19]
	(M) 10 April 1972	26 March 1975
	(W) 10 April 1972	26 March 1975 *Dec.*[19]
United States of America[20]	(L) 10 April 1972	26 March 1975
	(M) 10 April 1972	26 March 1975
	(W) 10 April 1972	26 March 1975
Uruguay	(L) –	*
	(M) –	*
	(W) –	6 April 1981
Uzbekistan	(L) –	12 January 1996
	(M) –	12 January 1996
	(W) –	12 January 1996
Vanuatu	(L) –	12 October 1990
	(M) –	*
	(W) –	*
Venezuela	(L) *	18 October 1978
	(M) *	18 October 1978
	(W) 10 April 1972	18 October 1978
Viet Nam, the Socialist Republic of[21]	(L) –	*
	(M) –	20 June 1980
	(W) 10 April 1972	*

[19] The United Kingdom ratification was in respect of the United Kingdom of Great Britain and Northern Ireland, Dominica and territories under the territorial sovereignty of the United Kingdom, as well as the state of Brunei, the British Solomon Islands Protectorate and, within the limits of United Kingdom jurisdiction therein, the Condominium of New Hebrides.

[20] For the view expressed by the Government of the United States of America in connection with the reservation made by the Government of Switzerland, see p. 159.

[21] The Republic of Viet Nam signed the Convention in Washington on 10 April 1972. The Socialist Republic of Viet Nam deposited the instrument of accession in Moscow on 20 June 1980.

State	*Signature*	*Ratification, Accession, Notification of Succession (C)*
Yemen Arab Republic[22]	(L) 10 May 1972	–
	(M) 17 April 1972	–
	(W) 10 April 1972	–
Yemen Democratic[23]	(L) *	*
	(M) 26 April 1972	1 June 1979
	(W) *	*
Yugoslavia[24]	(L) 10 April 1972	25 October 1973
	(M) 10 April 1972	25 October 1973
	(W) 10 April 1972	25 October 1973
Zimbabwe	(L) –	5 November 1990
	(M) –	*
	(W) –	*

22 On 22 May 1990, the People's Democratic Republic of Yemen and the Yemen Arab Republic merged to form a single state with the name "Republic of Yemen". Since that date they have been represented as one member in the United Nations. In a letter dated 19 May 1990, the Ministers of Foreign Affairs of the Yemen Arab Republic and the People's Democratic Republic of Yemen informed the Secretary-General that "all treaties and agreements concluded between either the Yemen Arab Republic or the People's Democratic Republic of Yemen and other States and international organizations in accordance with international law which are in force on 22 May 1990 will remain in effect, and international relations existing on 22 May 1990 between the People's Democratic Republic of Yemen and the Yemen Arab Republic and other States will continue".

23 The signature and ratification on behalf of Democratic Yemen.

24 On 31 May 2001 the Government of the Federal Republic of Yugoslavia declared its succession to the Convention, with effect from 27 April 1992.

RESERVATIONS AND DECLARATIONS

AUSTRIA (*reservation made on ratification in London, Moscow and Washington*)
Considering the obligations resulting from its status as a permanently neutral state, the Republic of Austria declares a reservation to the effect that its cooperation within the framework of this Convention cannot exceed the limits determined by the status of permanent neutrality and membership with the United Nations.

This reservation refers in particular to Article VII of this Convention as well as to any similar provision replacing or supplementing this article.

BAHRAIN (*reservation made on accession in London*)
The accession by the State of Bahrain to the Convention on the Prohibition of the Development, Production and Stockpiling of Bacteriological (Biological) and Toxin Weapons and on their Destruction, 1972, shall in no way constitute recognition of Israel or be a cause for the establishment of any relations of any kind therewith.

CHINA, REPUBLIC OF (*declaration made on ratification in Washington, on 28 December 1973*)
As regards the statement of the Embassy of the USSR, the Ambassador wishes to express that the Republic of China is a sovereign State and its Government in exercising its sovereignty has the right to sign and to ratify the Convention. The said Soviet statement is malicious and invalid and should, therefore, be rejected.

CHINA, PEOPLE'S REPUBLIC OF (*statement made on accession in London, Moscow and Washington*)

1. The basic spirit of the Convention on the Prohibition of Biological Weapons conforms to China's consistent position and is conducive to the efforts of the world's peaceloving countries and peoples in fighting against aggression and maintaining world peace. China once was one of the victims of biological (bacteriological) weapons. China has not produced or possessed such weapons and will never do so in future. However, the Chinese Government considers that the Convention has its defects. For instance, it fails to provide in explicit terms for the 'prohibition of the use of' biological weapons and the concrete and effective measures for supervision and verification; it lacks forceful measures of sanctions in the procedure of complaint against instances of violation of the Convention. It is the hope of the Chinese Government that these defects may be made up or corrected at an appropriate time.
2. It is also the hope of the Chinese Government that a convention on complete prohibition and thorough destruction of chemical weapons will soon be concluded.
3. The signature and ratification of the Convention by the Taiwan authorities in the name of China on 10 April 1972 and 9 February 1973 are illegal and null and void.

CZECH REPUBLIC (*declaration made on succession*)
In a note dated 24 March 1993, received on 5 April 1993 the Minister of Foreign Affairs for the Czech Republic notified the Secretary of State for Foreign and Commonwealth Affairs of the following:
Upon the instruction of the Government of the Czech Republic and referring to the Declaration of the Czech National Council to All Parliaments and Nations of the World of 17 December 1992, 1 have the honour to communicate to Your Excellency the following:

In conformity with the valid principles of international law and to the extent defined by it, the Czech Republic, as a successor State to the Czech and Slovak Federal Republic, considers itself bound, as of 1 January 1993, i.e. the date of the dissolution of the Czech and Slovak Federal Republic, by multilateral international treaties to which the Czech and Slovak Federal Republic was a party on that date, including reservations and declarations to their provisions made earlier by the Czech and Slovak Federal Republic.

From among the treaties deposited with the Government of the United Kingdom of Great Britain and Northern Ireland this applies also to the following:

Convention on the Prohibition of the Development, Production and Stockpiling of Bacteriological (Biological) and Toxin Weapons and on their Destruction, done at London, Washington and Moscow on 10 April 1972.

INDIA (*statement made on signature and ratification*)

India has stood for the elimination of both chemical and bacteriological (biological) weapons. However, in view of the situation that developed in regard to the discussions concerning biological and chemical weapons, it became possible to reach agreement at the present moment on a Convention on the elimination of biological and toxin weapons only. Negotiations would need to be continued for the elimination of chemical weapons also. It has been recognised that, both in regard to the Convention on biological and toxin weapons and in respect of future negotiations concerning chemical weapons, the Geneva Protocol of 1925 should be safeguarded and the inseparable link between prohibition of biological and chemical weapons should be maintained.

India's position on the Convention on biological and toxin weapons has been outlined in the statements of the representative of India before the Conference of the Committee of Disarmament (CCD) and the First Committee of the General Assembly.

The Government of India would like to reiterate in particular its understanding that the objective of the Convention is to eliminate biological and toxin weapons, thereby excluding completely the possibility of their use, and that the exemption in regard to biological agents or toxins, which would be permitted for prophylactic protective or other peaceful purposes would not, in any way, create a loophole in regard to the production or retention of biological and toxic weapons. Also, any assistance which might be furnished under the terms of the Convention would be of medical or humanitarian nature and in conformity with the Charter of the United Nations.

India's support of the Convention on biological and toxin weapons is based on these main considerations. It is India's earnest hope that the Convention will be adhered to by all States, including all the major Powers, at a very early date.

On depositing the instrument of ratification the Government of India stated that its position on the Convention had already been made clear on the occasion of its signature.

IRELAND (*declaration made on signature*)

The accession on 29 August 1930, of the Government of the Irish Free State to the Protocol for the Prohibition of the Use in War of Asphyxiating, Poisonous or other Gases, and of Bacteriological Methods of Warfare, opened for signature at Geneva on 17 June, 1925, was subject to the reservations that they did not intend to assume, by this accession, any obligation except towards States which had signed and ratified this Protocol or which would have finally acceded thereto, and that in the event of the armed forces of any enemy State or of any ally of such State failing to respect the said Protocol, the Government of the Irish Free State would cease to be bound by the said Protocol towards any such State.

The Government of Ireland recognise that the value of the Convention on the Prohibition of the Development, Production and Stockpiling of Bacteriological (Biological) and Toxin Weapons and on their Destruction, which has been signed on their behalf today, could be undermined if reservations made by Parties to the 1925 Geneva Protocol were allowed to stand as the prohibition of possession is incompatible with the right to retaliate. As this Convention purports to strengthen the Geneva Protocol, there should be an absolute and universal prohibition of the use of the weapons in question.

The Government of Ireland, accordingly, have notified the depositary Government for the 1925 Geneva Protocol of the withdrawal of their reservations to the Protocol. The withdrawal of these reservations applies to chemical as well as to bacteriological (biological) and toxin agents of warfare.

KOREA (REPUBLIC OF) (*statement made on signature*)
The signing by the Government of the Republic of Korea of the present Convention does not in any way mean or imply the recognition of any territory or regime which has not been recognized by the Government of the Republic of Korea as a State or Government.

KUWAIT (*statement made on ratification*)
In London and in Washington
Understanding:
In ratifying the Convention on the Prohibition of Development, Production and Stockpiling of Bacteriological (Biological) and Toxin Weapons and their Destruction, 1972, the Government of the State of Kuwait takes the view that its ratification of the said Convention does not in any way imply its recognition of Israel, nor does it oblige it to apply the provisions of the aforementioned Convention in respect of the said country.

In tendering this "Understanding" the Government of the State of Kuwait reaffirms its position in accepting the obligations it has undertaken to assume by virtue of its ratification of the said Convention. It also confirms that the last clause of the 'Understanding' does not prejudice the said indivisible obligations.

In Moscow
In ratifying the Convention on the Prohibition of the Development, Production and Stockpiling of Bacteriological (Biological) and Toxin Weapons and on their Destruction, 1972, the Government of the State of Kuwait takes the view that its ratification of the said Convention does not in any way imply its recognition of Israel, nor does it oblige it to apply the provisions of the aforementioned Convention in respect of the said country.

MALAYSIA (*reservation made on ratification*)
Malaysia's ratification of this Convention does not in any way constitute recognition of the States of Israel and South Africa nor does it consider itself duty bound by Article VII to provide assistance to those two States.

MEXICO (*statement made on signature*)[1]

1. Continues to be convinced that the same reasons which made it advisable to prohibit biological and chemical weapons jointly in the Geneva Protocol of 1925 exist now to strive to pursue identical methods with respect to the prohibition of the development, production and stockpiling of the said weapons, as well as their elimination from the arsenals of all States.
2. Considers that the fact that the Convention now open to signature applies solely to biological and toxin weapons should be understood, as Resolution 2826 (XXVI) of the United Nations General Assembly, to which the Convention is annexed, explicitly indicates, to be merely a first step – the only one which has proved possible to take for the time being – towards an agreement prohibiting also the development, production and stockpiling of all chemical weapons.
3. Makes a note of the fact that the Convention contains an express commitment to continue negotiations in good faith with the aim of arriving at an early agreement on the prohibition of the development, production and stockpiling of chemical weapons and their destruction.

[1] Translation of the statement communicated by the depositary – the Government of the United Kingdom – on 29 June 1999.

4. Makes a note, furthermore, that the General Assembly, through its Resolution 2827 A (XXVI), has requested the Conference of the Disarmament Committee to continue as a high priority item, negotiations aimed at promptly reaching the agreement relative to chemical weapons which is being sought; and that, in Resolution 2827 B (XXVI), the General Assembly has urged all States to commit themselves, while the said agreement is being reached, to abstain from all additional development, production and stockpiling of those chemical substances capable of being used as weapons which, on account of their degree of toxicity, have the highest lethal effect and are not useable for peaceful purposes.
5. Is convinced that the success of the Convention relative to biological weapons will depend, in the last resort, on the manner in which the commitments under reference are honoured.

SLOVAKIA *(declaration made on succession)*

In a note dated 17 May 1993, received on 17 May 1993 the Ministry of Foreign Affairs of the Slovak Republic notified the Foreign and Commonwealth Office of the following:

In conformity with the valid principles of international law and to the extent defined by it, the Slovak Republic as one of the successor States to the Czech and Slovak Federal Republic, considers itself bound, as of 1 January 1993, i.e. the date of the dissolution of the Czech and Slovak Federal Republic, by multilateral international treaties to which the Czech and Slovak Federal Republic was a party on that date, including reservations and declarations to their provisions made earlier by the Czech and Slovak Federal Republic.

From among the treaties deposited with the Government of the United Kingdom of Great Britain and Northern Ireland this applies to the following:

Convention on the Prohibition of the Development, Production and Stockpiling of Bacteriological (Biological) and Toxin Weapons and on their Destruction, done at London, Moscow and Washington on 10 April 1972.

SWITZERLAND

Declaration made on signature[2]

1. In Switzerland, the Convention will not be submitted to the parliamentary procedure of approval preceding ratification until it has achieved the degree of universality deemed necessary by the Swiss Government.
2. Owing to the fact that the Convention also applies to weapons, equipment or means of delivery designed to use such biological agents or toxin, the delimitation of its scope of application can cause difficulties since there are scarcely any weapons, equipment or means of delivery peculiar to such use; therefore, Switzerland reserves the right to decide for itself what auxiliary means fall within that definition.
3. By reason of the obligations of its status as a perpetually neutral State, Switzerland is bound to make the general reservation that its collaboration within the framework of this Convention cannot go beyond the terms prescribed by that status. This reservation refers especially to Article VII of the Convention as well as to any similar clause that could replace or supplement that provision of the Convention (or any other arrangement).

On ratification of the aforesaid Convention, the last two declarations will be repeated as formal reservations.

Reservation made on ratification

1. Owing to the fact that the Convention also applies to weapons, equipment or means of delivery designed to use such biological agents or toxins, the delimitation of its scope of application can cause difficulties since there are scarcely any weapons, equipment or means of delivery peculiar to such use; therefore, Switzerland reserves the right to decide for itself what auxiliary means fall within that definition.

[2] Translation received from the US Department of State.

2. By reason of the obligations resulting from its status as a perpetually neutral State, Switzerland is bound to make the general reservation that its collaboration within the framework of this Convention cannot go beyond the terms prescribed by that status. This reservation refers especially to Article VII of the Convent I on as well as to any similar clause that could replace or supplement that provision of the Convention (or any other arrangement).

In a note, dated 4 October 1973, addressed to the Swiss Embassy, the Government of the United States of America expressed the following view in connection with the reservation made by the Government of Switzerland:

As is stated in the first Swiss reservation, the Convention prohibits the development, production, or stockpiling of weapons, equipment, or means of delivery designed to use the prohibited agents or toxins for hostile purposes or in armed conflict. In the view of the United States Government, this prohibition would apply only to (a) weapons, equipment and means of delivery the design of which indicated that *they* could have no other use than that specified, and (b) weapons, equipment and means of delivery the design of which indicated that they were specifically intended to be capable of the use specified. The Government of the United States shares the view of the Government of Switzerland that there are few weapons, equipment, or means of delivery peculiar to the uses referred to. It does not, however, believe that it would be appropriate, on this ground alone, for States to reserve unilaterally the right to decide which weapons, equipment or means of delivery fell within the definition. Therefore, while acknowledging the entry into force of the Convention between itself and the Government of Switzerland, the United States Government enters its objection to this reservation.

As provided by Article XIV, paragraph 5, the Government of the United States is informing the States signatory and acceding to the Convention at Washington of the deposit of the ratification by Switzerland and the accompanying reservations.

UNITED KINGDOM OF GREAT BRITAIN AND NORTHERN IRELAND

In a statement dated 27 April 1972, communicated to all states recognized by the United Kingdom, Her Majesty's Government recalled their view that if a regime is not recognised as the government of a state, neither signature nor the deposit of any instrument by it, nor notification of any of those acts will bring about recognition of that regime by any other state.

Declaration made on ratification

On depositing their instrument of ratification the Government of the United Kingdom made the following declaration:

that the provisions of the Convention shall not apply in regard to Southern Rhodesia unless and until the Government of the United Kingdom informs the other depositary Governments that it is in a position to ensure that the obligations imposed by the Convention in respect of that territory can be fully implemented.

Concerning this declaration, the Government of the Union of Soviet Socialist Republics expressed the following view:

The Soviet Government supports the view that the United Kingdom, as has been repeatedly noted in decisions of the General Assembly of the United Nations, bears full responsibility with regard to Southern Rhodesia until the people of that Territory obtain genuine independence. This fully applies also to the aforementioned Convention.

UNION OF SOVIET SOCIALIST REPUBLICS (*declarations made on ratification*)[3]

In Washington

The Embassy of the Union of Soviet Socialist Republics refers to the Department of State's Note dated April 6, 1973, regarding the deposit by a representative of Chiang-

[3] Translation from *UNTS*, Vol. 1015, p. 240.

Kai-Shek of an instrument of ratification of the Convention on the Prohibition of the Development, Production and Stockpiling of Bacteriological (Biological) and Toxin Weapons and on their Destruction, and hereby confirms the position of the Soviet Union regarding the illegality of the above-mentioned act, inasmuch as the Chiang-Kai-Shek clique does not represent anyone and does not have the right to act in the name of China; the Government of the Chinese People's Republic is the sole representative of China.

In Moscow
The Soviet Government is of the opinion that, as decisions of the General Assembly have repeatedly stated, the United Kingdom bears full responsibility with regard to Southern Rhodesia until the people of that Territory achieve real independence. This fully applies to the Convention in question also.

No. 17

NON-USE OF FORCE IN INTERNATIONAL RELATIONS AND PERMANENT PROHIBITION OF THE USE OF NUCLEAR WEAPONS

Resolution 2936 (XXVII) of the United Nations General Assembly adopted on 29 November 1972

INTRODUCTORY NOTE: The present resolution, initially sponsored by the Soviet Union, is the first one to link the non-use of force with the prohibition of the use of nuclear weapons. See also *No. 14*.

AUTHENTIC TEXTS: Chinese, English, French, Russian, Spanish.

TEXT PUBLISHED IN: *Resolutions adopted by the General Assembly during its Twenty-seventh session, 19 September – 19 December 1972*, General Assembly Official Records: Twenty-Seventh session Supplement No. 30 (A/8730), New York, United Nations, 1973, pp. 5–6; *Droit des conflits armés*, pp. 171–172.

* * *

The General Assembly,

Noting *that the renunciation of the use or threat of force as proclaimed in the Charter of the United Nations and reaffirmed in the Declaration on the Strengthening of International Security, contained in General Assembly resolution 2734 (XXV) of 16 December 1970, and the Declaration on Principles of International Law concerning Friendly Relations and Cooperation among States in accordance with the Charter of the United Nations, contained in Assembly resolution 2625 (XXV) of 24 October 1970, is an obligation that all States should respect,*

Noting with concern *that the use of force in various forms is still occurring in violation of the Charter,*

Bearing in mind *that the threat of the use of nuclear weapons continues to exist,*

Guided *by the desire of all peoples to eliminate war and above all to prevent a nuclear disaster,*

Reaffirming, *in accordance with Article 51 of the Charter, the inalienable right of States to self-defence against armed attack,*

Mindful *of the principle of the inadmissibility of acquisition of territory by force and the inherent right of States to recover such territories by all the means at their disposal,*

Reaffirming *its recognition of the legitimacy of the struggle of colonial peoples for their freedom by all appropriate means at their disposal,*

Recalling *the Declaration on the Prohibition of the Use of Nuclear and Thermonuclear Weapons, contained in General Assembly resolution 1653 (XVI) of 24 November 1961,*

Recalling further *its resolution 2160 (XXI) of 30 November 1966 on the strict observance of the prohibition of the threat or use of force in international relations, and of the right of peoples to self-determination,*

Believing *that renunciation of the use or threat of force and prohibition of the use of nuclear weapons should be fully observed as a law of international life,*

1. Solemnly declares, *on behalf of the States members of the Organization, their renunciation of the use or threat of force in all its forms and manifestations in international relations, in accordance with the Charter of the United Nations, and the permanent prohibition of the use of nuclear weapons;*
2. Recommends *that the Security Council should take, as soon as possible, appropriate measures for the full implementation of the present declaration of the General Assembly.*

VOTE

Resolution 2936 (XXVII) was adopted by 73 votes to 4, with 46 abstentions.

RECORDED VOTE

In favour: Afghanistan, Algeria, Bahrain, Barbados, Bhutan, Bulgaria, Burma, Byelorussian Soviet Socialist Republic, Cameroon, Chad, Chile, Congo, Cuba, Cyprus, Czechoslovakia, Democratic Yemen, Egypt, Ethiopia, Fiji, Finland, Gabon, Ghana, Guinea, Guyana, Hungary, India, Indonesia, Iran, Iraq, Jamaica, Jordan, Kenya, Khmer Republic, Kuwait, Laos, Lebanon, Lesotho, Libyan Arab Republic, Madagascar, Malaysia, Maldives, Mali, Malta, Mauritania, Mauritius, Mongolia, Nepal, Niger, Nigeria, Oman, Panama, Philippines, Poland, Qatar, Romania, Rwanda, Saudi Arabia, Senegal, Sierra Leone, Singapore, Sri Lanka, Sudan, Syrian Arab Republic, Trinidad and Tobago, Uganda, Ukrainian Soviet Socialist Republic, Union of Soviet Socialist Republics, United Arab Emirates, United Republic of Tanzania, Upper Volta, Yemen, Yugoslavia, Zambia.

Against: Albania, China, Portugal, South Africa.

Abstaining: Argentina, Australia, Austria, Belgium, Bolivia, Botswana, Brazil, Burundi, Canada, Central African Republic, Columbia, Costa Rica, Denmark, Dominican Republic, El Salvador, France, Greece, Guatemala, Honduras, Iceland, Ireland, Israel, Italy, Ivory Coast, Japan, Luxemburg, Malawi, Mexico, Morocco, Netherlands, New Zealand, Norway, Pakistan, Paraguay, Peru, Spain, Sweden, Thailand, Togo, Tunisia, Turkey, United Kingdom of Great Britain and Northern Ireland, United States of America, Uruguay, Venezuela, Zaire.

No. 18

CONVENTION ON THE PROHIBITION OF MILITARY OR ANY OTHER HOSTILE USE OF ENVIRONMENTAL MODIFICATION TECHNIQUES

Adopted by resolution 31/72 of the United Nations General Assembly on 10 December 1976

INTRODUCTORY NOTE: At the United Nations Conference on the Human Environment, held at Stockholm in 1972, the question of the use of environmental techniques for military purposes was hardly discussed. In 1974, the USSR submitted to the General Assembly of the United Nations a draft convention on the prohibition of the use of such techniques. The General Assembly hereupon requested the Conference of the Committee on Disarmament (CCD) to proceed as soon as possible to achieving agreement on the text of such a convention (resolution 3264 (XXIX) of 9 December 1974). Thereafter, the USSR and the USA submitted at the CCD identical drafts of a convention (see resolution 3475 (XXX) of 11 December 1975). After negotiations under the auspices of the CCD in which all thirty participating member states took part, the Conference transmitted the revised text to the United Nations General Assembly, together with a set of Understandings relating to Articles I, II, III and VIII of the Convention. (The Understandings are reproduced on pp. 168–169.)

The Convention was approved by the General Assembly of the United Nations in its resolution 31/72 of 10 December 1976. In application of paragraph 2 of the said resolution, the Secretary-General decided to open the Convention for signature and ratification by states from 18 to 31 May 1977 at Geneva. Subsequently, the Convention was transmitted to the Headquarters of the Organization of the United Nations, where it was open for signature by states until 4 October 1978. For further provisions relating to the protection of the natural environment in case of armed conflicts, see Protocol I additional to the Geneva Conventions (*No. 56*), Articles 35 (3) and 55, and Guidelines on the Protection of the Environment in Times of Armed Conflict (*No. 23A)*.

ENTRY INTO FORCE: 5 October 1978.

AUTHENTIC TEXT: Arabic, Chinese, English, French, Russian, Spanish. The text below is reproduced from the certified original text, which the editors received from the United Nations Treaty Section.

TEXT PUBLISHED IN: United Nations General Assembly resolution 31/72, Annex. *Resolutions and decisions adopted by the General Assembly during its Thirty-first session*, Vol. 1, *21 September–22 December 1976*. General Assembly Official Records: Thirty-first session, Supplement No. 39 (A/31/39), New York, United Nations, 1977, pp. 36–38 (Engl. – see also Chinese, French, Russian and Spanish editions); *UNTS*, Vol. 1108, pp. 151–210 (Arabic, Chinese, Engl., French, Span. Russ.); *Status of Multilateral Arms Regulations and Disarmament Agreements*, 4th edn., 1992, New York, United Nations, 1993 (Sales No. E.93.IX.5 (Vol. I)), pp. 217–230 (Engl.); *Etat des accords multilatéraux en matière de désarmement et de contrôle des armements*, 3ème édition, New

York, Nations Unies, 1987 (F.88.IX.5), pp. 153–162 (French); *Situación de los acuerdos multilaterales de regulacion de armamentos y de desarme*, tercera edicion, 1987, Nueva York, Naciones Unidas, 1989 (S.89.IX.3), pp. 144–153 (Span.); *Yearbook of the United Nations,* Vol. 30, 1976, pp. 45–47 (Engl.); *International Red Cross Handbook,* 1983, pp. 375–379 (Engl.); *Manuel de la Croix-Rouge internationale*, 1983, pp. 387–391 (French); *Manual de la Cruz Roja internacional*, 1983, pp. 379–383 (Span.); *Handbook of the International Movement*, 1994, pp. 352–368 (Engl.); *Manuel du Mouvement international*, 1994, pp. 364–368 (French); *Manual del Movimiento internacional*, 1994, pp. 356–360 (Span.); *RGDIP*, tome 81, 1977, pp. 1248–1252 (French); *ILM*, Vol. XVI, No. 1, 1977, pp. 88–94 (Engl.); *World Armaments and Disarmament, SIPRI Yearbook 1978*, pp. 392–397 (Engl.); *GBTS*, 1979, No. 24, Cmnd. 7469 (Engl.); Roberts and Guelff, pp. 407–417 (Engl.); Ronzitti, pp. 651–660 (Engl.); Goldblat, pp. 419–423 (Engl.); *UST,* Vol. 31, p. 333, TIAS 9614 (Engl.); *Sbornik dogovorov SSSR,* vyp. XXXIV, 1978, pp. 437–440 (Russ.); United Nations website: http://untreaty.un.org; http://disarmament.un.org/Treaty Status.nsf; ICRC website: www.icrc.org/ihl.nsf.

* * *

The States Parties to this Convention,

Guided by the interest of consolidating peace, and wishing to contribute to the cause of halting the arms race, and of bringing about general and complete disarmament under strict and effective international control, and of saving mankind from the danger of using new means of warefare, *Determined* to continue negotiations with a view to achieving effective progress toward further measures in the field of disarmament,

Recognizing that scientific and technical advances may open new possibilities with respect to modification of the environment,

Recalling the Declaration of the United Nations Conference on the Human Environment, adopted at Stockholm on 16 June 1972,

Realizing that the use of environmental modification techniques for peaceful purposes could improve the interrelationship of man and nature and contribute to the preservation and improvement of the environment for the benefit of present and future generations,

Recognizing, however, that military or any other hostile use of such techniques could have effects extremely harmful to human welfare,

Desiring to prohibit effectively military or any other hostile use of environmental modification techniques in order to eliminate the dangers to mankind from such use, and affirming their willingness to work towards the achievement of this objective,

Desiring also to contribute to the strengthening of trust among nations and to the further improvement of the international situation in accordance with the purposes and principles of the Charter of the United Nations,

Have agreed as follows:

Article I.[1]

1. Each State Party to this Convention undertakes not to engage in military or any other hostile use of environmental modification techniques having

[1] For declaration in respect of this article by the Netherlands, see p. 177.

widespread, longlasting or severe effects as the means of destruction, damage or injury to any other State Party.[2]

2. Each State Party to this Convention undertakes not to assist, encourage or induce any State, group of States or international organization to engage in activities contrary to the provisions of paragraph 1 of this article.

Art. II.[3] As used in article I, the term "environmental modification techniques" refers to any technique for changing – through the deliberate manipulation of natural processes – the dynamics, composition or structure of the Earth, including its biota, lithosphere, hydrosphere and atmosphere, or of outer space.

Art III.[4]

1. The provisions of this Convention shall not hinder the use of environmental modification techniques for peaceful purposes and shall be without prejudice to the generally recognized principles and applicable rules of international law concerning such use.
2. The States Parties to this Convention undertake to facilitate, and have the right to participate in, the fullest possible exchange of scientific and technological information on the use of environmental modification techniques for peaceful purposes. States Parties in a position to do so shall contribute, alone or together with other States or international organizations, to international economic and scientific co-operation in the preservation, improvement and peaceful utilization of the environment, with due consideration for the needs of the developing areas of the world.

Art. IV. Each State Party to this Convention undertakes to take any measures it considers necessary in accordance with its constitutional processes to prohibit and prevent any activity in violation of the provisions of the Convention anywhere under its jurisdiction or control.

Art. V.

1. The States Parties to this Convention undertake to consult one another and to co-operate in solving any problems which may arise in relation to the objectives of, or in the application of the provisions of, the Convention. Consultation and co-operation pursuant to this article may also be undertaken through appropriate international procedures within the framework of the United Nations and in accordance with its Charter. These international procedures may include the services of appropriate international organizations, as well as of a Consultative Committee of Experts as provided for in paragraph 2 of this article.
2. For the purposes set forth in paragraph 1 of this article, the Depositary shall, within one month of the receipt of a request from any State Party to this Convention, convene a Consultative Committee of Experts. Any State Party may appoint an expert to the Committee whose functions and rules of procedure are set out in the annex, which constitutes an integral part of this

---

[2] For interpretative declaration in respect of this paragraph by Argentina, see p. 173

[3] For declaration in respect of this article by Argentina and Republic of Korea, see pp. 173 and 176.

[4] For reservation by Guatemala and declaration by Argentina in respect of this article, see pp. 173 and 176.

Convention. The Committee shall transmit to the Depositary a summary of its findings of fact, incorporating all views and information presented to the Committee during its proceedings, The Depositary shall distribute the summary to all States Parties.
3. Any State Party to this Convention which has reason to believe that any other State Party is acting in breach of obligations deriving from the provisions of the Convention may lodge a complaint with the Security Council of the United Nations. Such a complaint should include all relevant information as well as all possible evidence supporting its validity.
4. Each State Party to this Convention undertakes to cooperate in carrying out any investigation which the Security Council may initiate, in accordance with the provisions of the Charter of the United Nations, on the basis of the complaint received by the Council. The Security Council shall inform the States Parties of the results of the investigation.
5. Each State Party to this Convention undertakes to provide or support assistance, in accordance with the provisions of the Charter of the United Nations, to any State Party which so requests, if the Security Council decides that such party has been harmed or is likely to be harmed as a result of violation of the Convention.[5]

Art. VI.
1. Any State Party to this Convention may propose amendments to the Convention. The text of any proposed amendment shall be submitted to the Depositary, who shall promptly circulate it to all States Parties.
2. An amendment shall enter into force for all States Parties to this Convention which have accepted it, upon the deposit with the Depositary of instruments of acceptance by a majority of States Parties. Thereafter it shall enter into force for any remaining State Party on the date of deposit of its instrument of acceptance.

Art. VII. This Convention shall be of unlimited duration.

Art. VIII.[6]
1. Five years after the entry into force of this Convention, a conference of the States Parties to the Convention shall be convened by the Depositary at Geneva, Switzerland. The conference shall review the operation of the Convention with a view to ensuring that its purposes and provisions are being realized, and shall in particular examine the effectiveness of the provisions of paragraph 1 of article I in eliminating the dangers of military or any other hostile use of environmental modification techniques.
2. At intervals of not less than five years thereafter, a majority of the States Parties to this Convention may obtain, by submitting a proposal to this effect to the Depositary, the convening of a conference with the same objectives.
3. If no conference has been convened pursuant to paragraph 2 of this article within ten years following the conclusion of a previous conference, the Depositary shall solicit the views of all States Parties to this Convention concerning the convening of such a conference. If one third or ten of the

---

[5] For declaration in respect of this paragraph by Switzerland, see p. 177.

[6] For declaration in respect of this article by Argentina, see p. 173.

States Parties, whichever number is less, respond affirmatively, the Depositary shall take immediate steps to convene the conference.

Art. IX.
1. This Convention shall be open to all States for signature. Any State which does not sign the Convention before its entry into force in accordance with paragraph 3 of this article may accede to it at any time.
2. This Convention shall be subject to ratification by signatory States. Instruments of ratification or accession shall be deposited with the Secretary-General of the United Nations.
3. This Convention shall enter into force upon the deposit of instruments of ratification by twenty Governments of accordance with paragraph 2 of this article.
4. For those States whose instruments of ratification or accession are deposited after the entry into force of this Convention, it shall enter into force on the date of the deposit of their instruments of ratification or accession.
5. The Depositary shall promptly inform all signatory and acceding States of the date of each signature, the date of deposit of each instrument of ratification or accession and the date of the entry into force of this Convention and of any amendments thereto, as well as the receipt of other notices.
6. This Convention shall be registered by the Depositary in accordance with Aricle 102 of the Charter of the United Nations.

Art. X. This Convention, of which the Arabic, Chinese, English, French, Russian and Spanish texts are equally authentic, shall be deposited with the Secretary-General of the United Nations, who shall send duly certified copies thereof to the Governments of the signatory and acceding States.

In witness whereof, the undersigned, being duly authorized thereto, have signed this Convention.

Done at Geneva, on the 18 day of May 1977

[Here follow signatures]

Annex to the Convention

Consultative Committee of Experts

1. The Consultative Committee of Experts shall undertake to make appropriate findings of fact and provide expert views relevant to any problem raised pursuant to paragraph 1 of article V of this Convention by the State Party requesting the convening of the Committee.
2. The work of the Consultative Committee of Experts shall be organized in such a way as to permit it to perform the functions set forth in paragraph 1 of this annex. The Committee shall decide procedural questions relative to the organization of its work, where possible by consensus, but otherwise by

a majority of those present and voting. There shall be no voting on matters of substance.

3. The Depositary or his representative shall serve as the Chairman of the Committee.
4. Each expert may be assisted at meetings by one or more advisers.
5. Each expert shall have the right, through the Chairman, to request from States, and from international organizations, such information and assistance as the expert considers desirable for the accomplishment of the Committee's work.

Understandings Regarding the Convention[1]

Understanding relating to Article I

It is the understanding of the Committee that, for the purposes of this Convention, the terms "widespread", "long-lasting" and "severe" shall be interpreted as follows:

(a) "widespread": encompassing an area on the scale of several hundred square kilometres;

(b) "long-lasting": lasting for a period of months, or approximately a season;

(c) "severe": involving serious or significant disruption or harm to human life, natural and economic resources or other assets.

It is further understood that the interpretation set forth above is intended exclusively for this Convention and is not intended to prejudice the interpretation of the same or similar terms if used in connexion with any other international agreement.

Understanding relating to Article II

It is the understanding of the Committee that the following examples are illustrative of phenomena that could be caused by the use of environmental modification techniques as defined in article II of the Convention: earthquakes; tsunamis; an upset in the ecological balance of a region; changes in weather patterns (clouds, precipitation, cyclones of various types and tornadic storms); changes in climate patterns; changes in ocean currents; changes in the state of the ozone layer; and changes in the state of the ionosphere.

It is further understood that all the phenomena listed above, when produced by a military or any other hostile use of environmental modification techniques, would result, or could reasonably be expected to result, in widespread, long-lasting or severe destruction, damage or injury. Thus, military or any other hostile use of environmental modification techniques as defined in article II, so as to cause those phenomena as a means of destruction, damage or injury to another State Party, would be prohibited.

[1] These understandings are not incorporated into the Convention but are part of the negotiating record and were included in the report transmitted by the Conference of the Committee on Disarmament to the United Nations General Assembly in September 1976 (*Report of the Conference of the Committee on Disarmament*, Vol. I, General Assembly Official Records: Thirty-first session, Supplement No. 27 (A/31/27), New York, United Nations, 1976, pp. 91–92).

It is recognized, moreover, that the list of examples set out above is not exhaustive. Other phenomena which could result from the use of environmental modification techniques as defined in article II could also be appropriately included. The absence of such phenomena from the list does not in any way imply that the undertaking contained in article I would not be applicable to those phenomena, provided the criteria set out in that article were met.

Understanding relating to Article III

It is the understanding of the Committee that this Convention does not deal with the question whether or not a given use of environmental modification techniques for peaceful purposes is in accordance with generally recognized principles and applicable rules of international law.

Understanding relating to Article VIII

It is the understanding of the Committee that a proposal to amend the Convention may also be considered at any conference of Parties held pursuant to article VIII. It is further understood that any proposed amendment that is intended for such consideration should, if possible, be submitted to the Depositary no less than 90 days before the commencement of the conference.

VOTE

Resolution 31/72, embodying the Convention, was adopted by a vote of 96 in favour, 8 against and with 30 abstentions.

RECORDED VOTE

In favour: Afghanistan, Algeria, Australia, Austria, Bahrain, Bangladesh, Belgium, Bhutan, Bolivia, Botswana, Brazil, Bulgaria, Burma, Byelorussian Soviet Socialist Republic, Canada, Central African Republic, Chad, Colombia, Cuba, Cyprus, Czechoslovakia, Democratic Yemen, Denmark, Egypt, El Salvador, Ethiopia, Fiji, Finland, German Democratic Republic, German (Federal Republic of), Ghana, Greece, Guinea-Bissau, Guyana, Hungary, Iceland, India, Indonesia, Iran, Ireland, Israel, Italy, Japan, Jordan, Lao People's Democratic Republic, Lebanon, Lesotho, Liberia, Libyan Arab Republic, Luxembourg, Madagascar, Malawi, Maldives, Mali, Malta, Mauritania, Mongolia, Morocco, Mozambique, Nepal, Netherlands, Nicaragua, Niger, Nigeria, Norway, Oman, Papua New Guinea, Philippines, Poland, Portugal, Qatar, Romania, Saudi Arabia, Senegal, Sierra Leone, Singapore, Somalia, Spain, Sri Lanka, Sudan, Surinam, Swaziland, Sweden, Syrian Arab Republic, Thailand, Tunisia, Turkey, Ukrainian Soviet Socialist Republic, Union of Soviet Socialist Republics, United Arab Emirates, United Kingdom of Great Britain and Northern Ireland, United States of America, Upper Volta, Uruguay, Yugoslavia, Zaire.

Against: Albania, Ecuador, Grenada, Kenya, Kuwait, Mexico, Panama, Zambia.

Abstaining: Argentina, Bahamas, Barbados, Burundi, Chile, Comoros, Congo, Costa Rica, Dominican Republic, Equatorial Guinea, France, Gabon, Gambia, Iraq, Ivory Coast, Jamaica, Malaysia, Mauritius, New Zealand, Pakistan, Paraguay, Peru, Rwanda, Togo, Trinidad and Tobago, Uganda, United Republic of Cameroon, United Republic of Tanzania, Venezuela, Yemen.

SIGNATURES, RATIFICATIONS AND ACCESSIONS[1]

State	*Signature*	*Ratification, Accession or Notification of Succession (C)*
Afghanistan	–	22 October 1985
Algeria	–	19 December 1991
Antigua and Barbuda	–	25 October 1988 (C)
Argentina	–	20 March 1987
Armenia	–	15 May 2002
Australia	31 May 1978	7 September 1984
Austria	–	17 January 1990
Bangladesh	–	3 October 1979
Belgium	18 May 1977	12 July 1982
Belarus	18 May 1977	7 June 1978
Belgium	18 May 1977	12 July 1982
Benin	10 June 1977	30 June 1986
Bolivia	18 May 1977	–
Brazil	9 November 1977	12 October 1984
Bulgaria	18 May 1977	31 May 1978
Canada	18 May 1977	11 June 1981
Cape Verde	–	3 October 1979
Chile	–	26 April 1994
Congo, Democratic Republic (Zaire)	28 February 1978	–
Costa Rica	–	7 February 1996
Cuba	23 September 1977	10 April 1978
Cyprus	7 October 1977	12 April 1978
[Czechoslovakia][2]	18 May 1977	12 May 1978
Czech Republic		22 February 1993 (C)
Denmark	18 May 1977	19 April 1978
Dominica		9 November 1992 (C)
Egypt	–	1 April 1982
Ethiopia	18 May 1977	–
Finland	18 May 1977	12 May 1978
Germany[3 4]	18 May 1977 *Dec.*	24 May 1983 *Dec.*

1 Based on the communication received on 29 June 1999 from the United Nations Treaty Section and on the indications in *Multilateral Treaties Deposited with the Secretary-General, New York, United Nations* (ST/LEG/SER.E) as available on http://untreaty.un.org/; ICRC website: www.icrc.org/ihl.nsf.

2 Following the dissolution of the Czech and Slovak Federal Republic on 31 December 1992, at midnight, both the Czech Republic and the Slovak Republic informed the depositaries concerned that they considered themselves bound, as of I January 1993, by multilateral international treaties to which the Czech and Slovak Federal Republic was a party on that date, including reservations and declarations to their provisions made earlier by the Czech and Slovak Federal Republic.

3 The German Democratic Republic had signed and ratified the Convention on 18 May 1977 and 25 May 1978, respectively. In a communication dated 3 October 1990, the Federal Minister for Foreign Affairs of the Federal Republic of Germany notified the Secretary-General of the following:

"Through the accession of the German Democratic Republic to the Federal Republic of Germany with effect from 3 October 1990, the two German States have united to form one sovereign State, which as a single Member of the United Nations remains bound by the provisions of the Charter in accordance with the solemn declaration of 12 June 1973. As from the date of unification, the Federal Republic of Germany will act in the United Nations under the designation 'Germany'."

State	*Signature*	*Ratification, Accession or Notification of Succession (C)*
Ghana	21 March 1978	22 June 1978
Greece	–	23 August 1983
Guatemala	–	21 March 1988
Holy See	27 May 1977	–
Hungary	18 May 1977	19 April 1978
Iceland	18 May 1977	–
India	15 December 1977	15 December 1978
Iran, Islamic Republic of	18 May 1977	–
Iraq	15 August 1977	–
Ireland	18 May 1977	16 December 1982
Italy	18 May 1977	27 November 1981
Japan	–	9 June 1982
Kuwait	–	2 January 1980
Lao People's Democratic Republic	13 April 1978	5 October 1978
Korea, Democratic People's Republic of	–	8 November 1984.
Korea, Republic of	–	2 December 1986
Kuwait	–	2 January 1980 *Dec.*[5]
Lao People's Democratic Republic	13 April 1978	5 October 1978
Lebanon	18 May 1977	–
Liberia	18 May 1977	–
Lithuania	–	16 April 2002
Luxembourg	18 May 1977	

cont.

The former German Democratic Republic was admitted to the Organization on 18 September 1973 by resolution 3050 (XXVIII). For the text of the declaration of acceptance of the obligations contained in the Charter dated 12 June 1973 made by the German Democratic Republic (registered under No. 12758), see *UNTS*, Vol. 891, p. 103.

Consequently, and in the light of Articles 11 and 12 of the Treaty of 31 August 1990 (Unification Treaty) between the Federal Republic of Germany and the German Democratic Republic, entries in status lists pertaining to formalities (i.e. signatures, ratifications, accessions, declarations and reservations, etc.) effected by the Federal Republic of Germany will now appear under "Germany" and indicate the dates of such formalities.

As regards treaties in respect of which formalities had been effected by both the Federal Republic of Germany and the former German Democratic Republic prior to unification, the entry will similarly indicate in the corresponding table the type of formality effected by the Federal Republic of Germany and the date on which it took place, while the type of formality effected by the former German Democratic Republic and the date thereof will appear in a footnote.

Finally, as regards the treatment of treaties in respect of which formalities were effected by the former German Democratic Republic alone, Article 12, para. 3 of the Unification Treaty contains the following provision: "Should the united Germany intend to accede to international organizations or other multilateral treaties of which the German Democratic Republic but not the Federal Republic of Germany is a member, agreement shall be reached with the respective contracting parties and with the European Communities where the latter's competence is affected" (*Multilateral Treaties Deposited with the Secretary-General, New York, United Nations* (ST/LEG/SER.E) as available on http://untreaty.un.org/ENGLISH, note 15, chapter I.2, of 30 November 2001).

4 See also the declaration of the Federal Republic of Germany concerning Berlin (West) and the communications of the USSR, France, United Kingdom and the United States of America. See pp. 173–176.

5 See also the communication of the Government of Israel in respect of the statement made by the Government of Kuwait, p. 176.

State	*Signature*	*Ratification, Accession or Notification of Succession (C)*
Malawi	–	5 October 1978
Mauritius	–	9 December 1992
Mongolia	18 May 1977	19 May 1978
Morocco	18 May 1977	–
Netherlands[6]	18 May 1977	15 April 1983 *Dec.*
New Zealand[7]	–	7 September 1984 *Dec.*
Nicaragua	11 August 1977	–
Niger	–	17 February 1993
Norway	18 May 1977	15 February 1979
Pakistan	–	27 February 1986
Papua New Guinea		28 October 1980
Poland	18 May 1977	8 June 1978
Portugal	18 May 1977	–
Romania	18 May 1977	6 May 1983
Russian Federation	18 May 1977	30 May 1978
Saint Lucia	–	27 May 1993
Saint Vincent and the Grenadines	–	27 April 1999 (C)
Sao Tome and Principe	–	5 October 1979
Sierra Leone	12 April 1978	–
Slovakia	–	28 May 1993 (C)
Solomon Islands	–	19 June 1981 (C)
Spain	18 May 1977	19 July 1978
Sri Lanka	8 June 1977	25 April 1978
Sweden	–	27 April 1984
Switzerland	–	5 August 1988
Syrian Arab Republic	4 August 1977	–
Tajikistan	–	12 October 1999
Tunisia	11 May 1978	11 May 1978
Turkey	18 May 1977 Dec.	–
Uganda	18 May 1977	–
Ukraine	18 May 1977	13 June 1978
[Union of Soviet Socialist Republics]	18 May 1977	30 May 1978
United Kingdom[8]	18 May 1977	16 May 1978
United States of America	18 May 1977	17 January 1980
Uruguay	–	16 September 1993

[6] For the Kingdom in Europe and the Netherlands Antilles. By a communication received on 30 December 1985, the Government of the Netherlands informed the Secretary-General that "the island of Aruba which was a part of the Netherlands Antilles would obtain internal autonomy as a separate country within the Kingdom of the Netherlands as of 1 January 1986". The said change would have no consequence in international law. The treaties concluded by the Kingdom which applied to the Netherlands Antilles, including Aruba would continue, after 1 January 1986, to apply to the Netherlands Antilles (of which Aruba is no longer a part) and to Aruba (*Multilateral Treaties Deposited with the Secretary-General, New York, United Nations* (ST/LEG/SER.E) as available on http://untreaty.un.org/ENGLISH, note 9 in chapter I.1 of 30 November 2001).

[7] The accession shall also apply to the Cook Islands and Niue.

[8] The instrument of ratification contains a declaration to the effect that the Convention is ratified in respect of the United Kingdom of Great Britain and Northern Ireland, the associated states (Antigua, Dominica, Saint Kitts, Nevis-Anguilla, Saint Lucia and Saint Vincent) and territories under the territorial sovereignty of the United Kingdom, as well as the Solomon Islands, the state of Brunei and the United Kingdom sovereign base areas of Akrotiri and Dhekelia in the island of Cyprus.

State	*Signature*	*Ratification, Accession or Notification of Succession (C)*
Uzbekistan	–	26 May 1993
Viet Nam	–	26 August 1980
Yemen[9]	18 May 1977	20 July 1971

RESERVATIONS AND DECLARATIONS

ARGENTINA (*declaration made on accession*)[10]
The Argentine Republic interprets the terms 'widespread, long-lasting or severe effects' in article I, paragraph 1, of the Convention in accordance with the definitions agreed upon in the understanding on that article. It likewise interprets articles II, III and VIII in accordance with the relevant understandings.

AUSTRIA (*reservation made on accession*)
Considering the obligations resulting from its status as a permanently neutral state, the Republic of Austria declares a reservation to the effect that its co-operation within the framework of this Convention cannot exceed the limits determined by the Status of permanent neutrality and membership with the United Nations.

GERMANY
declaration made on signature
With the proviso that the correct designation of the Federal Republic of Germany in the Russian language is "Federativnuju Respubliku Germaniju".

16 June 1977
The correct designation of the Federal Republic of Germany in the Russian language following the preposition "sa" in the Russian text was spelled out in the aforementioned proviso as "Federativnuju Respubliku Germaniu".

---

9 In a letter dated 19 May 1990, the Ministers of Foreign Affairs of the Yemen Arab Republic and the People's Democratic Republic of Yemen informed the Secretary-General of the following: "The Yemen signed the Convention on 18 May 1977 and ratified it on 20 July 1977. Democratic and People's Republic of Yemen acceded to the Convention on 12 June 1979. The People's Democratic Republic of Yemen and the Yemen Arab Republic merged in a single sovereign State called the Republic of Yemen (short form: Yemen) with Sana'a as its capital, on Tuesday, 22 May 1990."

In a letter dated 19 May 1990, the Ministers of Foreign Affairs of the Yemen Arab Republic and the People's Democratic Republic of Yemen informed the Secretary-General of the following: "All treaties and agreements concluded between either the Yemen Arab Republic or the People's Democratic Republic of Yemen and other States and international organizations in accordance with international law which are in force on 22 May 1990 will remain in effect, and international relations existing on 22 May 1990 between the People's Democratic Republic of Yemen and the Yemen Arab Republic and other States will continue." As concerns the treaties concluded prior to their union by the Yemen Arab Republic or the People's Democratic Republic of Yemen, the Republic of Yemen (as now united) is accordingly to be considered as a party to those treaties as from the date when one of these states first became a party to those treaties (*Multilateral Treaties Deposited with the Secretary-General, New York, United Nations* (ST/LEG/SER.E) as available on http://untreaty.un.org/ENGLISH, note 35 in chapter I.2, of 30 November 2001).

10 The Government of Argentina has specified that the understandings referred to in the declaration are the Understandings adopted as part of the report of the Conference of the Committee on Disarmament to the General Assembly at its thirty-first session, published under the symbol A/31/27. [*Report of the Conference of the Committee on Disarmament to the General Assembly* (Volume I, Annex I)].

Declaration on ratification
With effect from the day on which the Convention enters into force for the Federal Republic of Germany it shall also apply to Berlin (West) subject to the rights and responsibilities of the French Republic, the United Kingdom of Great Britain and Northern Ireland and the United States of America including those relating to disarmament and demilitarization.

In this regard, the Secretary-General received on the dates indicated, the following communications:

Union of Soviet Socialist Republics (5 December 1983)
The declaration by the Government of the Federal Republic of Germany that the application of the Convention on the Prohibition of Military or Any other Hostile Use of Environmental Modification Techniques extends to Berlin (West) is illegal. The aforesaid Convention, in all of its substance, directly affects agreements and arrangements whose application the Federal Republic of Germany, in accordance with the Quadripartite Agreement of 3 September 1971, has no right to extend to Berlin (West),

The stipulation contained in declaration of the Government of the Federal Republic of Germany to the effect that the Convention shall also apply to Berlin (West), subject to the rights and responsibilities of the French Republic, the United Kingdom of Great Britain and Northern Ireland and the United States of America, including those relating to disarmament and demilitarization is pointless, since all the main provisions of the Convention relate to questions of disarmament and demilitarization. This stipulation is intended merely to mask the illegality of the declaration made by the Government of the Federal Republic of Germany, which is nothing but a flagrant violation of the Quadripartite Agreement and cannot, of course, have any legal force.

As is known, the relevant Allied provisions relating to demilitariztion, which were confirmed upon the signature of the Quadripartite Agreement and the responsibility for whose practical observance lies with the authorities of France, United Kingdom and the United States, still remain in force in Berlin (West). This, of course, inevitably includes questions relating to the prohibition of the military use of environmental modification techniques.

German Democratic Republic (23 January 1984)
A communication, identical in essence to the communication of the USSR, *mutatis mutandis,* was received on 23 January 1984 by the Secretary-General.

France, the United Kingdom and the United States of America (2 July 1984)
In a communication to the Government of the Union of Soviet Socialist Republics, which is an integral part (Annex IV A) of the Quadripartite Agreement of 3 September 1971, the Governments of France, the United Kingdom and the United States, without prejudice to the maintenance of their rights and responsibilities relating to the representation abroad of the interests of the western sectors of Berlin, confirmed that, provided that matters of security and status are not affected and provided that the extension is specified in each case, international agreements and arrangements entered into by the Federal Republic of Germany may be extended to the Western sectors of Berlin in accordance with established procedures. For its part, the Government of the Union of Soviet Socialist Republics, in a communication to the Governments of the three powers which is similarly an integral part (Annex IV B) of the Quadripartite Agreement, affirmed that it would raise no objections to such extension.

The established procedures referred to above, which were endorsed in the Quadripartite Agreement, are designed *inter alia* to afford the authorities of the three powers the opportunity to ensure that international agreements and arrangements entered into by the Federal Republic of Germany which are to be extended to the western sectors of Berlin are extended in such a way that matters of security and status are not affected.

When authorizing the extension of the Convention on the Prohibition of Military or Any Other Hostile Use of Environmental Modification Techniques to the western sectors of Berlin, the authorities of the three powers took such steps as were necessary to ensure that matters of security and status were not affected. Accordingly, the Berlin declaration made by the Federal Republic of Germany in accordance with established procedures is valid and the Convention applies to the western sectors of Berlin, subject to Allied Rights and Responsibilities, including those in the Area of Disarmament and Demilitarization.

The three Governments wish further to recall that Quadripartite Legislation on Demilitarization applies to the whole of Greater Berlin.

With reference to the communication received on 23 January 1984 from the Government of the German Democratic Republic . . ., the three Governments wish to point out that States which are not parties to the Quadripartite Agreement of 3 September 1971 are not competent to comment authoritatively on its provisions. They do not consider it necessary, and do not intend, to respond to further communication on this matter from States which are not parties to the Quadripartite Agreement. This should not be taken to imply any change in the position of the three Governments in this matter.

Federal Republic of Germany (5 June 1985)
By their note of 2 July 1984, disseminated [. . .] on 20 July 1984, the Governments of France, the United Kingdom of Great Britain and Northern Ireland and the United States of America answered the assertions made in the communication referred to above. The Government of the Federal Republic of Germany wishes to confirm the position as set out by the three Powers in the above-mentioned note.

Union of Soviet Socialist Republics (2 December 1985)
The extension of the application of the Convention on the Prohibition of Military or Any other Hostile Use of Environmental Modification Techniques of 10 December 1976 to Berlin (West) is a gross violation of the Quadripartite Agreement of 3 September 1971 and therefore cannot have any legal effect.

At the same time, the Soviet side would like to draw attention to the fact that the Powers party to the Quadripartite Agreement of 3 September 1971 have formulated decisions in respect of Berlin (West) which have universal effect under international law. The extension of the Convention on the Prohibition of Military or Any other Hostile Use of Environmental Modification Techniques to Berlin (West) by the Federal Republic of Germany naturally affects the interests of the other parties to it, which have the right to express their opinion on this matter. That right cannot be disputed by anyone.

In this connection, the Soviet side rejects as unfounded the communication from France, the United Kingdom of Great Britain and Northern Ireland and the United States of America with respect to the declaration of the German Democratic Republic. The view set forth in that declaration by the Government of the German Democratic Republic as a party to the above-mentioned Convention is entirely in conformity with the Quadripartite Agreement of 3 September 1971.

As to the assertions about "Greater Berlin" in the same communication from the three Powers, they are pointless in that there has been no "Greater Berlin" for a long time. There is Berlin, capital of the German Democratic Republic, which is an inseparable component of the Republic and has the same status as any other territory of the German Democratic Republic, and there is Berlin (West) a city with a special status where the occupation régime still remains. It is from these *de jure* and *de facto* realities that the Quadripartite Agreement of 3 September 1971 stems.

France, United Kingdom and United States of America (6 October 1986)
The Government of the three powers reaffirm the statement in the note from the Permanent Representative of France of 28 June 1984 that the declaration made by the Federal Republic of Germany concerning the extension of the application of the Convention on the Prohibition of military or any other hostile use of environmental modification techniques of 10 December 1976 to the western sectors of Berlin is

valid and that the Convention applies to the western sectors of Berlin, subject to allied rights and responsibilities, including those in the area of disarmament and demilitarization.

The Government of France, the United Kingdom and the United States further reaffirm the statement in the same note of 28 June 1984 that States which are not parties to the quadripartite agreement are not competent to comment authoritatively on its provisions.

The quadripartite agreement of 3 September 1971 is an international agreement concluded between the four contracting parties and not open to participation by any other State. In concluding this agreement, the four powers acted on the basis of their quadripartite rights and responsibilities, and the corresponding wartime and post-war agreements and decisions of the four powers, which are not affected. The quadripartite agreement is a part of conventional and not customary international law.

The Governments of France, the United Kingdom and the United States cannot accept the assertions by the Permanent Mission of the Union of Soviet Socialist Republics that greater Berlin no longer exists and that Berlin is the capital of the German Democratic Republic.

The position of the three governments on the continuing quadripartite status of greater Berlin is well known and was set out for example in a letter to the Secretary-General of the United Nations of 14 April 1975 (A/10078 and Corr.).

GUATEMALA (*reservation made on accession*)
Guatemala accepts the text of article III, on condition that the use of environmental modification techniques for peaceful purposes does not adversely affect its territory or the use of its natural resources.

KOREA, REPUBLIC OF (*declaration made on accession*)
It is the understanding of the Government of the Republic of Korea that any technique for deliberately changing the natural state of rivers falls within the meaning of the term "environmental modification techniques" as defined in article II of the Convention.

It is further understood that military or any other hostile use of such techniques, which could cause flooding, inundation, reduction in the water-level, drying up, destruction of hydrotechnical installations or other harmful consequences, comes within the scope of the Convention, provided it meets the criteria set out in article I therefore.

KUWAIT (*reservation and understanding expressed at accession*)
Reservation
This Convention binds the State of Kuwait only towards States Parties thereto. Its obligatory character shall *ipso facto* terminate with respect to any hostile state which does not abide by the prohibition contained therein.

Understanding
It is understood that accession to the Convention on the Prohibition of Military or any other hostile use of Environmental Modification Techniques, done in Geneva, 1977, does not mean in any way recognition of Israel by the State of Kuwait. Furthermore, no treaty relation will arise between the State of Kuwait and Israel.

On 23 June 1980, the Secretary-General received from the Government of Israel the following communication concerning the above mentioned understanding:
The Government of Israel has noted the political character of the statement made by the Government of Kuwait. In the view of the Government of Israel, this Convention is not the proper place for making such political pronouncements. Moreover, the said declaration cannot in anyway affect whatever obligations are binding upon Kuwait, under general international law or under particular conventions. Insofar as concerns the substance of the matter, the Government of Israel will adopt towards the Government of Kuwait an attitude of complete reciprocity.

NETHERLANDS (*declaration made on ratification*)
The Kingdom of the Netherlands accepts the obligations laid down in article I of the said Convention as extending to states which are not a party to the Convention and which act in conformity with article I of the Convention.

NEW ZEALAND (*declaration made on accession*)
The Government of New Zealand hereby declares its interpretation that nothing in the Convention detracts from or limits the obligations of States to refrain from military or any other hostile use of environmental modification techniques which are contrary to international law.

SWITZERLAND (*reservation made on accession*)
Because of the obligation incumbent upon it by virtue of its status of perpetual neutrality, Switzerland must make a general reservation specifying that its co-operation in the framework of this Convention cannot go beyond the limits imposed by this status. This reservation refers, in particular, to article V, paragraph 5, of the Convention, and to any similar clause which may replace or supplement this provision in the Convention (or in any other arrangement).

TURKEY (*statement made on signature*)
Interpretative statement
In the opinion of the Turkish Government the terms "widespread", "long lasting" and "severe effects" contained in the Convention need to be more clearly defined. So long as this clarification is not made the Government of Turkey will be compelled to interpret itself the terms in question and consequently it reserves the right to do so as and when required.

Furthermore, the Government of Turkey believes that the difference between "military or any other hostile purposes" and "peaceful purposes" should be more clearly defined so as to prevent subjective evaluations.

No. 19

FINAL ACT OF THE UNITED NATIONS CONFERENCE ON PROHIBITIONS AND RESTRICTIONS ON THE USE OF CERTAIN CONVENTIONAL WEAPONS WHICH MAY BE DEEMED TO BE EXCESSIVELY INJURIOUS OR TO HAVE INDISCRIMINATE EFFECTS

Signed at Geneva, 10 October 1980

INTRODUCTORY NOTE: The need for additional conventions prohibiting or limiting the use of certain methods and means of warfare was emphasized in the resolutions of the International Red Cross Conference of 1965 (*No. 31*) and of the International Conference on Human Rights of 1968 (*No. 32*) as well as in Resolution 2444 (XXIII) of the United Nations General Assembly of 1968 (*No. 31*). At the conferences of government experts convened by the International Committee of the Red Cross in 1971 and 1972 to prepare the Protocols additional to the Geneva Conventions and at the Diplomatic Conference of 1974-1977 the opinion prevailed that an agreement on conventional weapons should be attempted, leaving aside weapons of mass destruction. Encouraged by the Diplomatic Conference, the ICRC convened two conferences of government experts on the use of certain conventional weapons, which met at Lucerne in 1974 and at Lugano in 1976. The Diplomatic Conference, on 9 June 1977, adopted resolution 221 (IV) (*No. 58*), which recommended that a conference of governments be convened not later than 1979 with a view to reaching agreements on prohibitions or restrictions of the use of specific conventional weapons. The UN General Assembly endorsed this recommendation and the Conference took place in Geneva from 10 to 28 September 1979, and from 15 September to 10 October 1980. The Convention and the three original Protocols (*No. 20*) were adopted by consensus on 10 October 1980 and opened for signature on 10 April 1981.

For Protocols adopted in 1995 and 1996 see *No. 20*.

The Final Act has no force of law.

AUTHENTIC TEXTS: Arabic, Chinese, English, French, Russian, Spanish. The text below is reprinted from the *United Nations Conference on Prohibitions or Restrictions of use of certain conventional weapons which may be deemed to be excessively injurious or to have indiscriminate effects*, Geneva, 10–28 September 1979, 15 September–10 October 1980, *Final report of the Conference to the General Assembly*, A/CONF.95/15, 27 October 1980, Annex 1.

TEXT PUBLISHED IN (*text of Final Act, Convention, three original Protocols and Resolution*): *United Nations Conference on Prohibitions or Restrictions of use of certain conventional weapons which may be deemed to be excessively injurious or to have indiscriminate effects*, Geneva, 10–28 September 1979, 15 September–10 October 1980, *Final report of the Conference to the General Assembly*, A/CONF. 95/15, 27 October 1980, Annex I (Arabic, Chinese, Engl., French, Russ. Span.); *UNTS*, Vol. 1342, pp. 137–246 (Arabic, Chinese, Engl., French, Russ., Span.); *United Nations Disarmament Yearbook*, Vol. V, 1980

(Sales No. E.81.IX.4), Appendix VII: *Status of Multilateral Arms Regulation and Disarmament of Agreements*, 3rd edn., New York, United Nations, 1988 (E.88.IX.5), (*Convention, Protocols, Resolutions*), pp. 151–168 (Engl.); *Etat des accords multilatéraux en matière de désarmement et de contrôle des armements*, 3ème édition, 1987, New York, Nations Unies, 1989 (F.88.IX.5) (*Convention, Protocols, Resolutions*), pp. 174–194 (French); *Situación de los acuerdos multilaterales de regulacion de armamentos y de desarme*, tercera edicion, 1987, Nueva York, Naciones Unidas, 1989 (S.88.IX.5) (*Convention, Protocols, Resolutions*), pp. 165–185 (Span.); *International Red Cross Handbook*, 1983, pp. 380–394 (Engl.); *Manuel de la Croix-Rouge internationale*, 1983, pp. 392–408 (French); *Manual de la Cruz Roja internacional*, 1983, pp. 384–399 (Span.); *Handbook of the International Movement*, 1994, pp. 357–371 (Engl.); *Manuel du Mouvement international*, 1994, pp. 369–385 (French); *Manual del Movimiento internacional*, 1994, pp. 361–376 (Span.); *ILM*, Vol. 19, 1980, (*Convention, Protocols, Resolutions)*, pp. 1524–1535 (Engl.); *IRRC*, No. 220, January-February 1981, pp. 41–55 (Engl.); *RICR*, No. 727, janvier–février 1981, pp. 43–58 (French); *RICR* (Span.), No. 43, enero–febrero de 1981, pp. 43–58 (Span.); Roberts and Guelff (*Convention, all Protocols*), pp. 515–560) (Engl.); *Droit des conflits armés*, pp. 191–222 (French); United Nations website: http://untreaty.un.org; http://disarmament.un.org/TreatyStatus.nsf; ICRC website: www.icrc.org/ihl.nsf.

* * *

The United Nations Conference on Prohibitions or Restrictions of Use of Certain Conventional Weapons Which May be Deemed to be Excessively Injurious or to have Indiscriminate Effects, convened on the basis of United Nations General Assembly resolutions 32/52 of 19 December 1977, 33/70 of 28 September 1978 and 34/82 of *11 December 1979, met at the Palais des Nations in Geneva from 10 to 28 September 1979 and from 15 September to 10 October 1980.*

Eighty-five States participated in the work of the Conference, 82 at the 1979 session, 76 at the 1980 session.

On 10 October 1980, the Conference adopted the following instruments:

1. *Convention on Prohibitions or Restrictions on the Use of Certain Conventional Weapons Which May be Deemed to be Excessively Injurious or to have Indiscriminate Effects (Appendix A).*
2. *Protocol on Non-Detectable Fragments (Protocol I) (Appendix B).*
3. *Protocol on Prohibitions or Restrictions on the Use of Mines, Booby- Traps and Other Devices (Protocol II) (Appendix C).*
4. *Protocol on Prohibitions or Restrictions on the Use of Incendiary Weapons (Protocol III) (Appendix D)*

In addition, the Conference at its 1979 session adopted the following resolution: Resolution on Small-Calibre Weapon Systems (Appendix E).

The texts of the above-mentioned instruments and resolution are appended to this Final Act.

in witness whereof, signed in Geneva, this tenth day of October 1980.

[Here follow signatures of the President and Executive Secretary of the Conference]

No. 20

CONVENTION ON PROHIBITIONS OR RESTRICTIONS ON THE USE OF CERTAIN CONVENTIONAL WEAPONS WHICH MAY BE DEEMED TO BE EXCESSIVELY INJURIOUS OR TO HAVE INDISCRIMINATE EFFECTS

Adopted at Geneva, 10 October 1980

INTRODUCTORY NOTE:
Convention: For historical origins, see note introducing the Final Act of the United Nations Conference of 1980 (*No. 19*). The Convention is a pure umbrella containing general provisions but no prohibition of weapons. Prohibitions of weapons are the object of the Protocols annexed to the Convention. The Convention can be adhered to only by states, which express their consent to be bound by at least two of the Protocols (Article 4, para. 3, of the Convention). On 21 December 2001 the Second Review Conference of states parties adopted an amendment to Article 1 which extends the application of the Convention and its Protocols to non-international armed conflicts, Previously, only Protocol I as amended on 3 May 1996 applied to such situations. The new version of Article 1 has not yet entered into force (see note 4 to Article 1 on p. 185).
Protocols I–III: In 1980, three Protocols were adopted and annexed to the Convention. Protocol I (p. 190) prohibits the use of any weapon whose primary effect is to injure by fragments that in the human body escape detection by X-rays. Protocol II (pp. 191–195) contains a set of restrictions on the use of mines, booby traps and similar devices. It was replaced by an Amended Protocol in 1996. Protocol III (pp. 210–211) restricts the use of incendiary weapons.
Protocol II as amended and Protocol IV were adopted at the First Review Conference, held in 1995 and 1996. Protocol II as amended on 3 May 1996 (pp. 196–209) replaces the original Protocol II in the relations between its parties. It introduces various improvements. However, no agreement could be reached on a total prohibition of the use of anti-personnel land mines. Such a prohibition was realized by the Ottawa Convention of 18 September 1997 (*No. 23*), concluded outside the framework of the 1980 Convention. Protocol IV on blinding laser weapons (p. 212) was adopted on 13 October 1995. Further protocols, among them one on explosive remnants of war, are in preparation.

ENTRY INTO FORCE:
Conventions and Protocols I–III: 2 December 1983. The amendment to Article 1, adopted on 21 December 2001, has not yet entered into force (see note 4 to Article 1 on p. 185). The Protocols enter into force as provided for in Article 5, paragraphs 3 and 4, of the Convention. Amendments are subject to the same rules (Article 8, para. I9(b) of the Convention).
Protocol II as amended on 3 May 1996: 3 December 1998.
Protocol IV: 30 July 1998.

AUTHENTIC TEXTS:
Convention and Protocols I–III: see indications under *No. 19*.

Protocol II as amended and Protocol IV: The text of Protocol II as amended on 3 May 1996 and of Protocol IV is reprinted from Doc. CCW/CONF.1/16 (Part I).

TEXT PUBLISHED IN:
Convention and Protocols I–III: see indications under *No. 19*.
Protocol II as amended: CCW/CONF.I/16/Part I (Arabic, Chinese, Engl., French, Russ., Span.); pp. xxx; *ILM*, Vol. 35, 1996, pp. 1205–1217 (Engl.); *IRRC*, Vol. 36, 1996, pp. 369–386 (Engl.); *RICR*, Vol. 78, 1996, pp. 399–417 (French); Roberts and Guelff, pp. 536–548 (Engl.); United Nations website: http://untreaty.un.org; http://disarmament.un.org/TreatyStatus.nsf.
Protocol IV: CCW/CONF.1/16/Part I (Arabic, Chinese, Engl., French, Russ., Span.); *ILM*, Vol. 35, 1996, p. 1218 (Engl.); *IRRC*, Vol. 36, 1996, p. 299 (Engl.); *RICR*, Vol. 78, 1996, p. 320–321 (French); Roberts and Guelff, p. 535 (Engl.). United Nations website: http://untreaty.un.org; http://disarmament.un.org/TreatyStatus.nsf.

TABLE OF CONTENTS

* * *

CONVENTION ON PROHIBITIONS OR RESTRICTIONS ON THE USE OF CERTAIN CONVENTIONAL WEAPONS WHICH MAY BE DEEMED TO BE EXCESSIVELY INJURIOUS OR TO HAVE INDISCRIMINATE EFFECTS

Adopted at Geneva, 10 October 1980

The High Contracting Parties,[1]

Recalling that every State has the duty, in conformity with the Charter of the United Nations, to refrain in its international relations from the threat or use of force against the sovereignty, territorial integrity or political independence of any State, or in any other manner inconsistent with the purposes of the United Nations.

Further recalling the general principle of the protection of the civilian population against the effects of hostilities,

Basing themselves on the principle of international law that the right of the parties to an armed conflict to choose methods or means of warfare is not unlimited, and on the principle that prohibits the employment in armed conflicts of weapons, projectiles and material and methods of warfare of a nature to cause superfluous injury or unnecessary suffering,

Also recalling that it is prohibited to employ methods or means of warfare which are intended, or may be expected, to cause widespread, long-term and severe damage to the natural environment,[2]

Confirming their determination that in cases not covered by this Convention and its annexed Protocols or by other international agreements, the civilian population and the combatants shall at all times remain under the protection and authority of the principles of international law derived from established custom, from the principles of humanity and from the dictates of public conscience,

Desiring to contribute to international détente, the ending of the arms race and the building of confidence among States, and hence to the realization of the aspiration of all peoples to live in peace,

Recognizing the importance of pursuing every effort which may contribute to progress towards general and complete disarmament under strict and effective international control,

Reaffirming the need to continue the codification and progressive development of the rules of international law applicable in armed conflict,

Wishing to prohibit or restrict further the use of certain conventional weapons and believing that the positive results achieved in this area may facilitate the main talks on disarmament with a view to putting an end to the production, stockpiling and proliferation of such weapons,

Emphasizing the desirability that all States become parties to this Convention and its annexed Protocols, especially the militarily significant States,

Bearing in mind that the General Assembly of the United Nations and the United Nations Disarmament Commission may decide to examine the question of a possible broadening of the scope of the prohibitions and restrictions contained in this Convention and its annexed Protocols,

---

1 For declarations by Argentina, Canada, France, Holy See, Israel, Italy, Romania, United Kingdom and United States of America, see pp. 216–221.

2 For reservation in respect of this paragraph by France (made on signature which was not confirmed at ratification) and the interpretative declaration of United States of America, see pp. 217, 221–222.

Further bearing in mind that the Committee on Disarmament may decide to consider the question of adopting further measures to prohibit or restrict the use of certain conventional weapons,

Have agreed as follows:

Article 1. Scope of application[3,4]
This Convention and its annexed Protocols shall apply in the situations referred to in Article 2 common to the Geneva Conventions of 12 August 1949 for the Protection of War Victims, including any situation described in paragraph 4 of Article 1 of Additional Protocol I to these Conventions.

Art. 2. Relations with other international agreements
Nothing in this Convention or its annexed Protocols shall be interpreted as detracting from other obligations imposed upon the High Contracting Parties by international humanitarian law applicable in armed conflict.

Art 3. Signature
This Convention shall be open for signature by all States at United Nations Headquarters in New York for a period of twelve months from 10 April 1981.

---

3 For reservation in respect of this article by France (made on signature, which was not confirmed on ratification) and declarations of Israel and the United States of America, see pp. 217,218,221.

4 The Second Review Conference on 21 December 2001 adopted the following new version of Article 1:

1. This Convention and its annexed Protocols shall apply in the situations referred to in Article 2 common to the Geneva Conventions of 12 August 1949 for the Protection of War Victims, including any situation described in paragraph 4 of Artcle I of Additional Protocol I to these Conventions.
2. This Convention and its annexed Protocols shall also apply, in addition to situations referred to in paragraph 1 of this Article, to situations referred to in Article 3 common to the Geneva Conventions of 12 August 1949. This Convention and its annexed Protocols shall not apply to situations of internal disturbances and tensions, such as riots, isolated and sporadic acts of violence, and other acts of a similar nature, as not being armed conflicts.
3. In case of armed conflicts not of an international character occurring in the territory of one of the High Contracting Parties, each party to the conflict shall be bound to apply the prohibitions and restrictions of this Convention and its annexed Protocols.
4. Nothing in this Convention or its annexed Protocols shall be invoked for the purpose of affecting the sovereignty of a State or the responsibility of the Government, by all legitimate means, to maintain or re-establish law and order in the State or to defend the national unity and territorial integrity of the State.
5. Nothing in this Convention or its annexed Protocols shall be invoked as a justification for intervening, directly or indirectly, for any reason whatsoever, in the armed conflict or in the internal or external affairs of the High Contracting Party in the territory of which that conflict occurs.
6. The application of the provisions of this Convention and its annexed Protocols to parties to a conflict which are not High Contracting Parties that have accepted this Convention or its annexed Protocols, shall not change their legal status of the legal status of a disputed territory, either explicitly or implicitly.
7. The provisions of Paragraphs 2–6 of this Article shall not prejudice additional Protocols adopted after 1 January 2002, which may apply, exclude or modify the scope of their application in relation to this Article.

This version will enter into force six months after the deposit of the twentieth instrument of acceptance. On 31 December 2002 it had not yet entered into force.

Art. 4. Ratification, acceptance, approval or accession

1. This Convention is subject to ratification, acceptance or approval by the Signatories. Any State which has not signed this Convention may accede to it.
2. The instruments of ratification, acceptance, approval or accession shall be deposited with the Depositary.
3.[5] Expressions of consent to be bound by any of the Protocols annexed to this Convention shall be optional for each State, provided that at the time of the deposit of its instrument of ratification, acceptance or approval of this Convention or of accession thereto, that State shall notify the Depositary of its consent to be bound by any two or more of these Protocols.
4. At any time after the deposit of its instrument of ratification, acceptance or approval of this Convention or of accession thereto, a State may notify the Depositary of its consent to be bound by any annexed Protocol by which it is not already bound.
5. Any Protocol by which a High Contracting Party is bound shall for that Party form an integral part of this Convention.

Art. 5. Entry into force

1. This Convention shall enter into force six months after the date of deposit of the twentieth instrument of ratification, acceptance, approval or accession.
2. For any State which deposits its instrument of ratification, acceptance, approval or accession after the date of the deposit of the twentieth instrument of ratification, acceptance, approval or accession, this Convention shall enter into force six months after the date on which that State has deposited its instrument of ratification, acceptance, approval or accession.
3. Each of the Protocols annexed to this Convention shall enter into force six months after the date by which twenty States have notified their consent to be bound by it in accordance with paragraph 3 or 4 of Article 4 of this Convention.
4. For any State which notifies its consent to be bound by a Protocol annexed to this Convention after the date by which twenty States have notified their consent to be bound by it, the Protocol shall enter into force six months after the date on which that State has notified its consent so to be bound.

Art. 6. Dissemination

The High Contracting Parties undertake, in time of peace as in time of armed conflict, to disseminate this Convention and those of its annexed Protocols by which they are bound as widely as possible in their respective countries and, in particular, to include the study thereof in their programmes of military instruction, so that those instruments may become known to their armed forces.

Art. 7. Treaty relations upon entry into force of this Convention

1. When one of the parties to a conflict is not bound by an annexed Protocol, the parties bound by this Convention and that annexed Protocol shall remain bound by them in their mutual relations.
2. Any High Contracting Party shall be bound by this Convention and any Protocol annexed thereto which is in force for it, in any situation contemplated by Article 1, in relation to any State which is not a party to this Convention or bound by the relevant annexed Protocol, if the latter accepts

[5] For reservation in respect of this paragraph by the United States of America, see p. 221.

and applies this Convention or the relevant Protocol, and so notifies the Depositary.

3. The Depositary shall immediately inform the High Contracting Parties concerned of any notification received under paragraph 2 of this Article.

4.[6] This Convention, and the annexed Protocols by which a High Contracting Party is bound, shall apply with respect to an armed conflict against that High Contracting Party of the type referred to in Article 1, paragraph 4, of Additional Protocol I to the Geneva Conventions of 12 August 1949 for the Protection of War Victims:

(a) where the High Contracting Party is also a party to Additional Protocol I and an authority referred to in Article 96, paragraph 3, of that Protocol has undertaken to apply the Geneva Conventions and Additional Protocol I in accordance with Article 96, paragraph 3, of the said Protocol, and undertakes to apply this Convention and the relevant annexed Protocols in relation to that conflict; or

(b)[7] where the High Contracting Party is not a party to Additional Protocol I and an authority of the type referred to in subparagraph (a) above accepts and applies the obligations of the Geneva Conventions and of this Convention and the relevant annexed Protocols in relation to that conflict. Such an acceptance and application shall have in relation to that conflict the following effects:

(i) the Geneva Conventions and this Convention and its relevant annexed Protocols are brought into force for the parties to the conflict with immediate effect;

(ii) the said authority assumes the same rights and obligations as those which have been assumed by a High Contracting Party to the Geneva Conventions, this Convention and its relevant annexed Protocols; and

(iii) the Geneva Conventions, this Convention and its relevant annexed Protocols are equally binding upon all parties to the conflict.

The High Contracting Party and the authority may also agree to accept and apply the obligations of Additional Protocol I to the Geneva Conventions on a reciprocal basis.

Art. 8.[8] *Review and amendments*

1. (a) At any time after the entry into force of this Convention any High Contracting Party may propose amendments to this Convention or any annexed Protocol by which it is bound. Any proposal for an amendment shall be communicated to the Depositary, who shall notify it to all the High Contracting Parties and shall seek their views on whether a conference should be convened to consider the proposal. If a majority, that shall not be less than eighteen of the High Contracting Parties so agree, he shall promptly convene a conference to which all High Contracting Parties shall be invited. States not parties to this Convention shall be invited to the conference as observers.

---

6 For reservations in respect of this paragraph by Israel, United Kingdom and United States of America, see pp. 218, 220.

7 For reservations in respect of this paragraph by France (made on signature and not confirmed on ratification) and the United States of America (made on ratification), see pp. 218, 221.

8 For declarations in respect of this article by Canada and France, see pp. 216, 217.

(b) Such a conference may agree upon amendments which shall be adopted and shall enter into force in the same manner as this Convention and the annexed Protocols, provided that amendments to this Convention may be adopted only by the High Contracting Parties and that amendments to a specific annexed Protocol may be adopted only by the High Contracting Parties which are bound by that Protocol.

2. (a) At any time after the entry into force of this Convention any High Contracting Party may propose additional protocols relating to other categories of conventional weapons not covered by the existing annexed Protocols. Any such proposal for an additional protocol shall be communicated to the Depositary, who shall notify it to all the High Contracting Parties in accordance with subparagraph 1 (a) of this Article. If a majority, that shall not be less than eighteen of the High Contracting Parties so agree, the Depositary shall promptly convene a conference to which all States shall be invited.

(b) Such a conference may agree, with the full participation of all States represented at the conference, upon additional protocols which shall be adopted in the same manner as this Convention, shall be annexed thereto and shall enter into force as provided in paragraphs 3 and 4 of Article 5 of this Convention.

3. (a) If, after a period of ten years following the entry into force of this Convention, no conference has been convened in accordance with subparagraph 1 (a) or 2 (a) of this Article, any High Contracting Party may request the Depositary to convene a conference to which all High Contracting Parties shall be invited to review the scope and operation of this Convention and the Protocols annexed thereto and to consider any proposal for amendments of this Convention or of the existing Protocols. States not parties to this Convention shall be invited as observers to the conference. The conference may agree upon amendments which shall be adopted and enter into force in accordance with subparagraph 1 (b) above.

(b) At such conference consideration may also be given to any proposal for additional protocols relating to other categories of conventional weapons not covered by the existing annexed Protocols. All States represented at the conference may participate fully in such consideration. Any additional protocols shall be adopted in the same manner as this Convention, shall be annexed thereto and shall enter into force as provided in paragraphs 3 and 4 of Article 5 of this Convention.

(c) Such a conference may consider whether provision should be made for the convening of a further conference at the request of any High Contracting Party if, after a similar period to that referred to in subparagraph 3 (a) of this Article, no conference has been convened in accordance with subparagraph 1 (a) or 2 (a) of this Article.

Art. 9. Denunciation

1. Any High Contracting Party may denounce this Convention or any of its annexed Protocols by so notifying the Depositary.
2. Any such denunciation shall only take effect one year after receipt by the Depositary of the notification of denunciation. If, however, on the expiry of that year the denouncing High Contracting Party is engaged in one of the situations referred to in Article 1, the Party shall continue to be bound by the

obligations of this Convention and of the relevant annexed Protocols until the end of the armed conflict or occupation and, in any case, until the termination of operations connected with the final release, repatriation or re-establishment of the person protected by the rules of international law applicable in armed conflict, and in the case of any annexed Protocol containing provisions concerning situations in which peace-keeping, observation or similar functions are performed by United Nations forces or missions in the area concerned, until the termination of those functions.

3. Any denunciation of this Convention shall be considered as also applying to all annexed Protocols by which the denouncing High Contracting Party is bound.
4. Any denunciation shall have effect only in respect of the denouncing High Contracting Party.
5. Any denunciation shall not affect the obligations already incurred, by reason of an armed conflict, under this Convention and its annexed Protocols by such denouncing High Contracting Party in respect of any act committed before this denunciation becomes effective.

Art. 10. Depositary

1. The Secretary-General of the United Nations shall be the Depositary of this Convention and of its annexed Protocols.
2. In addition to his usual functions, the Depositary shall inform all States of:
   (a) signatures affixed to this Convention under Article 3;
   (b) deposits of instruments of ratification, acceptance or approval of or accession to this Convention deposited under Article 4;
   (c) notifications of consent to be bound by annexed Protocols under Article 4;
   (d) the dates of entry into force of this Convention and of each of its annexed Protocols under Article 5; and
   (e) notifications of denunciation received under Article 9, and their effective date.

Art. 11. Authentic texts

The original of this Convention with the annexed Protocols, of which the Arabic, Chinese, English, French, Russian and Spanish texts are equally authentic, shall be deposited with the Depositary, who shall transmit certified true copies thereof to all States.

[Here follow signatures]

PROTOCOL ON NON-DETECTABLE FRAGMENTS (PROTOCOL I)[1]

Geneva, 10 October 1980

It is prohibited to use any weapon the primary effect of which is to injure by fragments which in the human body escape detection by X-rays.

[1] For declarations in respect of this Protocol by Argentina, Canada and Israel, see pp. 216, 218.

PROTOCOL ON PROHIBITIONS OR RESTRICTIONS ON THE USE OF MINES, BOOBY-TRAPS AND OTHER DEVICES (PROTOCOL II)[1]

Geneva, 10 October 1980

Article 1. Material scope of application
This Protocol relates to the use on land of the mines, booby-traps and other devices defined herein, including mines laid to interdict beaches, waterway crossings or river crossings, but does not apply to the use of anti-ship mines at sea or in inland waterways.

Art. 2.[2] *Definitions*
For the purpose of this Protocol:

1. "Mine" means any munition placed under, on or near the ground or other surface area and designed to be detonated or exploded by the presence, proximity or contact of a person or vehicle, and "remotely delivered mine" means any mine so defined delivered by artillery, rocket, mortar or similar means or dropped from an aircraft.
2. "Booby-trap" means any device or material which is designed, constructed or adapted to kill or injure and which functions unexpectedly when a person disturbs or approaches an apparently harmless object or performs an apparently safe act.
3. "Other devices" means manually-emplaced munitions and devices designed to kill, injure or damage and which are actuated by remote control or automatically after a lapse of time.
4.[3] "Military objective" means, so far as objects are concerned, any object which by its nature, location, purpose or use makes an effective contribution to military action and whose total or partial destruction, capture or neutralization, in the circumstances ruling at the time, offers a definite military advantage.
5. "Civilian objects" are all objects which are not military objectives as defined in paragraph 4.
6. "Recording" means a physical, administrative and technical operation designed to obtain, for the purpose of registration in the official records, all available information facilitating the location of minefields, mines and booby-traps.

Art. 3.[4] *General restrictions on the use of mines, booby-traps and other devices*

1. This Article applies to:
   (a) mines
   (b) booby-traps; and
   (c) other devices.

---

1 For declarations in respect of this Protocol by Argentina, Canada, the People's Republic of China and the Holy See, see pp. 216–218
2 For declaration in respect of this article by the United Kingdom, see p. 220.
3 For declaration in respect of this paragraph by the Netherlands, see p. 219.
4 For declaration in respect of this article by the United Kingdom, see p. 221.

2. It is prohibited in all circumstances to direct weapons to which this Article applies, either in offence, defence or by way of reprisals, against the civilian population as such or against individual civilians.
3. The indiscriminate use of weapons to which this Article applies is prohibited. Indiscriminate use is any placement of such weapons:
   (a) which is not on, or directed against, a military objective; or
   (b) which employs a method or means of delivery which cannot be directed at a specific military objective; or
   (c)[5] which may be expected to cause incidental loss of civilian life, injury to civilians, damage to civilian objects, or a combination thereof, which would be excessive in relation to the concrete and direct military advantage anticipated.
4. All feasible precautions shall be taken to protect civilians from the effects of weapons to which this Article applies. Feasible precautions are those precautions which are practicable or practically possible taking into account all circumstances ruling at the time, including humanitarian and military considerations.

Art. 4. Restrictions on the use of mines other than remotely delivered mines, booby-traps and other devices in populated areas

1. This Article applies to:
   (a) mines other than remotely delivered mines;
   (b) booby-traps; and
   (c) other devices.
2. It is prohibited to use weapons to which this Article applies in any city, town, village or other area containing a similar concentration of civilians in which combat between ground forces is not taking place or does not appear to be imminent, unless either:
   (a) they are placed on or in the close vicinity of a military objective belonging to or under the control of an adverse party; or
   (b) measures are taken to protect civilians from their effects, for example, the posting of warning signs, the posting of sentries, the issue of warnings or the provision of fences.

Art. 5. Restrictions on the use of remotely delivered mines

1. The use of remotely delivered mines is prohibited unless such mines are only used within an area which is itself a military objective or which contains military objectives, and unless:
   (a) their location can be accurately recorded in accordance with Article 7(1)(a);[6] or
   (b) an effective neutralizing mechanism is used on each such mine, that is to say, a self-actuating mechanism which is designed to render a mine harmless or cause it to destroy itself when it is anticipated that the mine will no longer serve the military purpose for which it was placed in position, or a remotely-controlled mechanism which is designed to render harmless or destroy a mine when the mine no longer serves the military purpose for which it was placed in position.

---

5 For declaration in respect of this paragraph by the Netherlands, see p. 219.

6 For declarations in respect of this paragraph by Canada and Israel, see pp. 216, 218.

2. Effective advance warning shall be given of any delivery or dropping of remotely delivered mines which may affect the civilian population, unless circumstances do not permit.

Art. 6. Prohibition on the use of certain booby-traps

1.[7] Without prejudice to the rules of international law applicable in armed conflict relating to treachery and perfidy, it is prohibited in all circumstances to use:
   (a) any booby-trap in the form of an apparently harmless portable object which is specifically designed and constructed to contain explosive material and to detonate when it is disturbed or approached, or
   (b) booby-traps which are in any way attached to or associated with:
      (i) internationally recognized protective emblems, signs or signals;
      (ii) sick, wounded or dead persons;
      (iii) burial or cremation sites or graves;
      (iv) medical facilities, medical equipment, medical supplies or medical transportation;
      (v) children's toys or other portable objects or products specially designed for the feeding, health, hygiene, clothing or education of children;
      (vi) food or drink;
      (vii) kitchen utensils or appliances except in military establishments, military locations or military supply depots;
      (viii) objects clearly of a religious nature;
      (ix) historic monuments, works of art or places or worship which constitute the cultural or spiritual heritage of peoples;
      (x) animals or their carcasses.
2. It is prohibited in all circumstances to use any booby-trap which is designed to cause superfluous injury or unnecessary suffering.

Art. 7. Recording and publication of the location of minefields, mines and booby-traps

1. The parties to a conflict shall record the location of:
   (a) all pre-planned minefields laid by them;[8] and
   (b) all areas in which they have made large-scale and pre-planned use of booby-traps.
2. The parties shall endeavour to ensure the recording of the location of all other minefields, mines and booby-traps which they have laid or placed in position.
3. All such records shall be retained by the parties who shall:
   (a) immediately after the cessation of active hostilities:
      (i) take all necessary and appropriate measures, including the use of such records, to protect civilians from the effects of minefields, mines and booby-traps; and either
      (ii) in cases where the forces of neither party are in the territory of the adverse party, make available to each other and to the Secretary-

[7] For the interpretative declaration in respect of this paragraph by the United States of America, see p. 221

[8] For declarations in respect of this paragraph by Canada and Israel, see pp. 216, 218.

General of the United Nations all information in their possession concerning the location of minefields, mines and booby-traps in the territory of the adverse party; or

(iii) once complete withdrawal of the forces of the parties from the territory of the adverse party has taken place, make available to the adverse party and to the Secretary-General of the United Nations all information in their possession concerning the location of minefields, mines and booby traps in the territory of the adverse party;

(b)[9] when a United Nations force or mission performs functions in any area, make available to the authority mentioned in Article 8 such information as is required by that Article;[10]

(c) whenever possible, by mutual agreement, provide for the release of information concerning the location of minefields, mines and booby traps, particularly in agreements governing the cessation of hostilities.

Art. 8.[10] *Protection of United Nations forces and missions from the effects of minefields, mines and booby-traps*[11]

1.[12] When a United Nations force or mission performs functions of peacekeeping, observation or similar functions in any area, each party to the conflict shall, if requested by the head of the United Nations force or mission in that area, as far as it is able:

(a) remove or render harmless all mines or booby traps in that area;

(b) take such measures as may be necessary to protect the force or mission from the effects of minefields, mines and booby traps while carrying out its duties; and

(c) make available to the head of the United Nations force or mission in that area, all information in the party's possession concerning the location of minefields, mines and booby traps in that area.

2. When a United Nations fact-finding mission performs functions in any area, any party to the conflict concerned shall provide protection to that mission except where, because of the size of such mission, it cannot adequately provide such protection. In that case it shall make available to the head of the mission the information in its possession concerning the location of minefields, mines and booby-traps in that area.

Art. 9. International co-operation in the removal of minefields, mines and booby-traps

After the cessation of active hostilities, the parties shall endeavour to reach agreement, both among themselves and, where appropriate, with other States and with international organizations, on the provision of information and technical and material assistance – including, in appropriate circumstances, joint operations – necessary to remove or otherwise render ineffective minefields, mines and booby-traps placed in position during the conflict.

9 For declaration in respect of this paragraph by Cyprus, see p. 217.

10 For declaration in respect of this article by Canada, see p. 216.

11 For declaration in respect of this article by Cyprus, see p. 217.

12 For declaration in respect of this paragraph by the Netherlands, see p. 219.

Technical Annex to the 1980 Protocol on Prohibitions or Restrictions on the Use of Mines, Booby-Traps and Other Devices (Protocol II)

Guidelines on recording

Whenever an obligation for the recording of the location of minefields, mines and booby traps arises under the Protocol, the following guidelines shall be taken into account.

1. With regard to pre-planned minefields and large-scale and pre-planned use of booby traps:
   (a) maps, diagrams or other records should be made in such a way as to indicate the extent of the minefield or booby-trapped area; and
   (b) the location of the minefield or booby-trapped area should be specified by relation to the co-ordinates of a single reference point and by the estimated dimensions of the area containing mines and booby traps in relation to that single reference point.
2. With regard to other minefields, mines and booby traps laid or placed in position: In so far as possible, the relevant information specified in paragraph I above should be recorded so as to enable the areas containing minefields, mines and booby traps to be identified.

PROTOCOL ON PROHIBITIONS OR RESTRICTIONS ON THE USE OF MINES, BOOBY-TRAPS AND OTHER DEVICES, AS AMENDED ON 3 MAY 1996 (PROTOCOL II AS AMENDED ON 3 MAY 1996)[1]

Adopted by the Conference of the States Parties at Geneva on 3 May 1996

Article 1. Scope of application[2]

1. This Protocol relates to the use on land of the mines, booby-traps and other devices, defined herein, including mines laid to interdict beaches, waterway crossings or river crossings, but does not apply to the use of anti-ship mines at sea or in inland waterways.

2.[3] This Protocol shall apply, in addition to situations referred to in Article I of this Convention, to situations referred to in Article 3 common to the Geneva Conventions of 12 August 1949. This Protocol shall not apply to situations of internal disturbances and tensions, such as riots, isolated and sporadic acts of violence and other acts of a similar nature, as not being armed conflicts.

3. In case of armed conflicts not of an international character occurring in the territory of one of the High Contracting Parties, each party to the conflict shall be bound to apply the prohibitions and restrictions of this Protocol.

4. Nothing in this Protocol shall be invoked for the purpose of affecting the sovereignty of a State or the responsibility of the Government, by all legitimate means, to maintain or re-establish law and order in the State or to defend the national unity and territorial integrity of the State.

5. Nothing in this Protocol shall be invoked as a justification for intervening, directly or indirectly, for any reason whatever, in the armed conflict or in the internal or external affairs of the High Contracting Party in the territory of which that conflict occurs.

6. The application of the provisions of this Protocol to parties to a conflict, which are not High Contracting Parties that have accepted this Protocol, shall not change their legal status or the legal status of a disputed territory, either explicitly or implicitly.

Art. 2. Definitions[4]

For the purpose of this Protocol:

1.[5] "Mine" means a munition placed under, on or near the ground or other surface area and designed to be exploded by the presence, proximity or contact of a person or vehicle.

---

1 For declarations and reservations in respect of this Protocol by Canada, France, Hungary, the United Kingdom and the United States of America, see pp. 224, 225, 226, 231–232.

2 For declarations in respect of this article by Austria, Belgium, Denmark, Finland, France, Germany, Greece, Ireland, Italy, Liechtenstein, Pakistan, South Africa and Sweden, see pp. 223, 224, 225, 226, 227, 228, 230.

3 For declaration in respect of this paragraph by the Netherlands, see pp. 228–229.

4 For the declarations in respect of this article by Italy and Sweden, see pp. 228, 230.

5 For declaration in respect of this paragraph by the United States of America, see p. 232.

2. "Remotely-delivered mine" means a mine not directly emplaced but delivered by artillery, missile, rocket, mortar, or similar means, or dropped from an aircraft. Mines delivered from a land-based system from less than 500 metres are not considered to be "remotely delivered", provided that they are used in accordance with Article 5 and other relevant Articles of this Protocol.
3.[6] "Anti-personnel mine" means a mine primarily designed to be exploded by the presence, proximity or contact of a person and that will incapacitate, injure or kill one or more persons.
4.[7] "Booby-trap" means any device or material which is designed, constructed or adapted to kill or injure, and which functions unexpectedly when a person disturbs or approaches an apparently harmless object or performs an apparently safe act.
5.[8] "Other devices" means manually-emplaced munitions and devices including improvised explosive devices designed to kill, injure or damage and which are actuated manually, by remote control or automatically after a lapse of time.
6.[9] "Military objective" means, so far as objects are concerned, any object which by its nature, location, purpose or use makes an effective contribution to military action and whose total or partial destruction, capture or neutralization, in the circumstances ruling at the time, offers a definite military advantage.
7. "Civilian objects" are all objects which are not military objectives as defined in paragraph 6 of this Article.
8. "Minefield" is a defined area in which mines have been emplaced and "mined area" is an area which is dangerous due to the presence of mines. "Phoney minefield" means an area free of mines that simulates a minefield. The term "minefield" includes phoney minefields.
9. "Recording" means a physical, administrative and technical operation designed to obtain, for the purpose of registration in official records, all available information facilitating the location of minefields, mined areas, mines, booby-traps and other devices.
10. "Self-destruction mechanism" means an incorporated or externally attached automatically-functioning mechanism which secures the destruction of the munition into which it is incorporated or to which it is attached.
11. "Self-neutralization mechanism" means an incorporated automatically-functioning mechanism which renders inoperable the munition into which it is incorporated.
12. "Self-deactivating" means automatically rendering a munition inoperable by means of the irreversible exhaustion of a component, for example, a battery, that is essential to the operation of the munition.
13. "Remote control" means control by commands from a distance.

---

6 For declarations in respect of this paragraph by Austria, Belgium, Canada, China, Denmark, Finland, France, Germany, Greece, Ireland, Israel, Italy, the Netherlands, Pakistan, South Africa, Sweden and the United States of America, see pp. 223–231.

7 For declaration in respect of this paragraph by the United States of America, see p. 232.

8 For reservation in respect of this paragraph by the United States of America, see pp. 231–232.

9 For declaration in respect of this paragraph by the Netherlands, see p. 229.

14.[10] "Antihandling device" means a device intended to protect a mine and which is part of, linked to, attached to or placed under the mine and which activates when an attempt is made to tamper with the mine.
15. "Transfer" involves, in addition to the physical movement of mines into or from national territory, the transfer of title to and control over the mines, but does not involve the transfer of territory containing emplaced mines.

Art. 3. General restrictions on the use of mines, booby-traps and other devices

1. This Article applies to:
   (a) mines;
   (b) booby-traps; and
   (c) other devices.
2. Each High Contracting Party or party to a conflict is, in accordance with the provisions of this Protocol, responsible for all mines, booby-traps, and other devices employed by it and undertakes to clear, remove, destroy or maintain them as specified in Article 10 of this Protocol.
3. It is prohibited in all circumstances to use any mine, booby-trap or other device which is designed or of a nature to cause superfluous injury or unnecessary suffering.
4. Weapons to which this Article applies shall strictly comply with the standards and limitations specified in the Technical Annex with respect to each particular category.
5. It is prohibited to use mines, booby-traps or other devices which employ a mechanism or device specifically designed to detonate the munition by the presence of commonly available mine detectors as a result of their magnetic or other non-contact influence during normal use in detection operations.
6. It is prohibited to use a self-deactivating mine equipped with an anti-handling device that is designed in such a manner that the anti-handling device is capable of functioning after the mine has ceased to be capable of functioning.
7. It is prohibited in all circumstances to direct weapons to which this Article applies, either in offence, defence or by way of reprisals, against the civilian population as such or against individual civilians or civilian objects.
8.[11] The indiscriminate use of weapons to which this Article applies is prohibited. Indiscriminate use is any placement of such weapons:
   (a) which is not on, or directed against, a military objective. In case of doubt as to whether an object which is normally dedicated to civilian purposes, such as a place of worship, a house or other dwelling or a school, is being used to make an effective contribution to military action, it shall be presumed not to be so used; or
   (b) which employs a method or means of delivery which cannot be directed at a specific military objective; or
   (c) which may be expected to cause incidental loss of civilian life, injury to civilians, damage to civilian objects, or a combination thereof,

[10] For declaration in respect of this paragraph by the United Kingdom, see p. 231.
[11] For declarations in respect of this paragraph by the Netherlands and the Republic of Korea, see pp. 228, 229.

which would be excessive in relation to the concrete and direct military advantage anticipated.

9.[12] Several clearly separated and distinct military objectives located in a city, town, village or other area containing a similar concentration of civilians or civilian objects are not to be treated as a single military objective.

10. All feasible precautions shall be taken to protect civilians from the effects of weapons to which this Article applies. Feasible precautions are those precautions which are practicable or practically possible taking into account all circumstances ruling at the time, including humanitarian and military considerations. These circumstances include, but are not limited to:
    (a) the short- and long-term effect of mines upon the local civilian population for the duration of the minefield;
    (b) possible measures to protect civilians (for example, fencing, signs, warning and monitoring);
    (c) the availability and feasibility of using alternatives; and
    (d) the short- and long-term military requirements for a minefield.

11. Effective advance warning shall be given of any emplacement of mines, booby-traps and other devices which may affect the civilian population, unless circumstances do not permit.

Art. 4. Restrictions on the use of anti-personnel mines[13]

It is prohibited to use anti-personnel mines which are not detectable, as specified in paragraph 2 of the Technical Annex.

Art. 5. Restrictions on the use of anti-personnel mines other than remotely-delivered mines

1. This Article applies to anti-personnel mines other than remotely-delivered mines.
2. It is prohibited to use weapons to which this Article applies which are not in compliance with the provisions on self-destruction and self-deactivation in the Technical Annex, unless:
    (a) such weapons are placed within a perimeter-marked area which is monitored by military personnel and protected by fencing or other means, to ensure the effective exclusion of civilians from the area. The marking must be of a distinct and durable character and must at least be visible to a person who is about to enter the perimeter-marked area; and
    (b)[14] such weapons are cleared before the area is abandoned, unless the area is turned over to the forces of another State which accept responsibility for the maintenance of the protections required by this Article and the subsequent clearance of those weapons.
3. A party to a conflict is relieved from further compliance with the provisions of sub-paragraphs 2 (a) and 2 (b) of this Article only if such compliance is not feasible due to forcible loss of control of the area as a result of

[12] For declarations in respect of this paragraph by Israel and Pakistan, see pp. 227, 229.

[13] For declarations in respect of this article by France, Israel and the Republic of Korea, see pp. 225, 227, 230.

[14] For declarations in respect of this paragraph by Germany, Greece, Israel, Italy, South Africa, Sweden and the United States of America, see pp. 225, 226, 227, 228, 230, 232.

enemy military action, including situations where direct enemy military action makes it impossible to comply. If that party regains control of the area, it shall resume compliance with the provisions of sub-paragraphs 2 (a) and 2 (b) of this Article.

4. If the forces of a party to a conflict gain control of an area in which weapons to which this Article applies have been laid, such forces shall, to the maximum extent feasible, maintain and, if necessary, establish the protections required by this Article until such weapons have been cleared.
5. All feasible measures shall be taken to prevent the unauthorized removal, defacement, destruction or concealment of any device, system or material used to establish the perimeter of a perimeter-marked area.
6. Weapons to which this Article applies which propel fragments in a horizontal arc of less than 90 degrees and which are placed on or above the ground may be used without the measures provided for in sub-paragraph 2 (a) of this Article for a maximum period of 72 hours, if:
   (a) they are located in immediate proximity to the military unit that emplaced them; and
   (b)[15] the area is monitored by military personnel to ensure the effective exclusion of civilians.

Art. 6. Restrictions on the use of remotely-delivered mines

1. It is prohibited to use remotely-delivered mines unless they are recorded in accordance with sub-paragraph I (b) of the Technical Annex.
2. It is prohibited to use remotely-delivered anti-personnel mines which are not in compliance with the provisions on self-destruction and self-deactivation in the Technical Annex.
3. It is prohibited to use remotely-delivered mines other than anti-personnel mines, unless, to the extent feasible, they are equipped with an effective self-destruction or self-neutralization mechanism and have a back-up self-deactivation feature, which is designed so that the mine will no longer function as a mine when the mine no longer serves the military purpose for which it was placed in position.
4. Effective advance warning shall be given of any delivery or dropping of remotely-delivered mines which may affect the civilian population, unless circumstances do not permit.

Art. 7. Prohibitions on the use of booby-traps and other devices

1. Without prejudice to the rules of international law applicable in armed conflict relating to treachery and perfidy, it is prohibited in all circumstances to use booby-traps and other devices which are in any way attached to or associated with:
   (a) internationally recognized protective emblems, signs or signals;
   (b) sick, wounded or dead persons;
   (c) burial or cremation sites or graves;
   (d) medical facilities, medical equipment, medical supplies or medical transportation;
   (e) children's toys or other portable objects or products specially designed for the feeding, health, hygiene, clothing or education of children;

[15] For declaration in respect of this paragraph by the United States of America, see p. 232.

(f)[16] food or drink;
(g) kitchen utensils or appliances except in military establishments, military locations or military supply depots;
(h) objects clearly of a religious nature;
(i)[17] historic monuments, works of art or places of worship which constitute the cultural or spiritual heritage of peoples; or
(j) animals or their carcasses.

2.[18] It is prohibited to use booby-traps or other devices in the form of apparently harmless portable objects which are specifically designed and constructed to contain explosive material.

3. Without prejudice to the provisions of Article 3, it is prohibited to use weapons to which this Article applies in any city, town, village or other area containing a similar concentration of civilians in which combat between ground forces is not taking place or does not appear to be imminent, unless either:
(a) they are placed on or in the close vicinity of a military objective; or
(b) measures are taken to protect civilians from their effects, for example, the posting of warning sentries, the issuing of warnings or the provision of fences.

Art. 8. Transfers

1. In order to promote the purposes of this Protocol, each High Contracting Party:
(a) undertakes not to transfer any mine the use of which is prohibited by this Protocol;
(b) undertakes not to transfer any mine to any recipient other than a State or a State agency authorized to receive such transfers;
(c) undertakes to exercise restraint in the transfer of any mine the use of which is restricted by this Protocol. In particular, each High Contracting Party undertakes not to transfer any anti-personnel mines to States which are not bound by this Protocol, unless the recipient State agrees to apply this Protocol; and
(d) undertakes to ensure that any transfer in accordance with this Article takes place in full compliance, by both the transferring and the recipient State, with the relevant provisions of this Protocol and the applicable norms of international humanitarian law.

2. In the event that a High Contracting Party declares that it will defer compliance with specific provisions on the use of certain mines, as provided for in the Technical Annex, sub-paragraph I (a) of this Article shall however apply to such mines.

3. All High Contracting Parties, pending the entry into force of this Protocol, will refrain from any actions which would be inconsistent with sub-paragraph I (a) of this Article.

[16] For declaration in respect of this paragraph by Israel, see p. 227
[17] For declarations in respect of this paragraph by the United States of America, see p. 232.
[18] For declarations in respect of this paragraph by the United States of America, see p. 232.

Art. 9. Recording and use of information on minefields, mined areas, mines, booby-traps and other devices

1. All information concerning minefields, mined areas, mines, booby-traps and other devices shall be recorded in accordance with the provisions of the Technical Annex.

2.[19] All such records shall be retained by the parties to a conflict, who shall, without delay after the cessation of active hostilities, take all necessary and appropriate measures, including the use of such information, to protect civilians from the effects of minefields, mined areas, mines, booby-traps and other devices in areas under their control.

At the same time, they shall also make available to the other party or parties to the conflict and to the Secretary-General of the United Nations all such information in their possession concerning minefields, mined areas, mines, booby-traps and other devices laid by them in areas no longer under their control; provided, however, subject to reciprocity, where the forces of a party to a conflict are in the territory of an adverse party, either party may withhold such information from the Secretary-General and the other party, to the extent that security interests require such withholding, until neither party is in the territory of the other. In the latter case, the information withheld shall be disclosed as soon as those security interests permit. Wherever possible, the parties to the conflict shall seek, by mutual agreement, to provide for the release of such information at the earliest possible time in a manner consistent with the security interests of each party.

3. This Article is without prejudice to the provisions of Articles 10 and 12 of this Protocol.

Art. 10. Removal of minefields, mined areas, mines, booby-traps and other devices and international cooperation[20]

1.[21] Without delay after the cessation of active hostilities, all minefields, mined areas, mines, booby-traps and other devices shall be cleared, removed, destroyed or maintained in accordance with Article 3 and paragraph 2 of Article 5 of this Protocol.

2. High Contracting Parties and parties to a conflict bear such responsibility with respect to minefields, mined areas, mines, booby-traps and other devices in areas under their control.

3. With respect to minefields, mined areas, mines, booby-traps and other devices laid by a party in areas over which it no longer exercises control, such party shall provide to the party in control of the area pursuant to paragraph 2 of this Article, to the extent permitted by such party, technical and material assistance necessary to fulfil such responsibility.

4. At all times necessary, the parties shall endeavour to reach agreement, both among themselves and, where appropriate, with other States and with international organizations, on the provision of technical and material assistance, including, in appropriate circumstances, the undertaking of joint operations necessary to fulfil such responsibilities.

---

[19] For declaration in respect of this paragraph by Republic of Korea, see p. 230.

[20] For declaration in respect of this article by Canada, see p. 224.

[21] For declaration in respect of this paragraph by Republic of Korea, see p. 230.

Art. 11. Technological cooperation and assistance

1. Each High Contracting Party undertakes to facilitate and shall have the right to participate in the fullest possible exchange of equipment, material and scientific and technological information concerning the implementation of this Protocol and means of mine clearance. In particular, High Contracting Parties shall not impose undue restrictions on the provision of mine clearance equipment and related technological information for humanitarian purposes.
2. Each High Contracting Party undertakes to provide information to the database on mine clearance established within the United Nations System, especially information concerning various means and technologies of mine clearance, and lists of experts, expert agencies or national points of contact on mine clearance.
3. Each high Contracting Party in a position to do so shall provide assistance for mine clearance through the United Nations System, other international bodies or on a bilateral basis, or contribute to the United Nations Voluntary Trust Fund for Assistance in Mine Clearance.
4. Requests by High Contracting Parties for assistance, substantiated by relevant information, may be submitted to the United Nations, to other appropriate bodies or to other States. These requests may be submitted to the Secretary-General of the United Nations, who shall transmit them to all High Contracting Parties and to relevant international organizations.
5. In the case of requests to the United Nations, the Secretary-General of the United Nations, within the resources available to the Secretary-General of the United Nations, may take appropriate steps to assess the situation and, in cooperation with the requesting High Contracting Party, determine the appropriate provision of assistance in mine clearance or implementation of the Protocol. The Secretary-General may also report to High Contracting Parties on any such assessment as well as on the type and scope of assistance required.
6. Without prejudice to their constitutional and other legal provisions, the High Contracting Parties undertake to cooperate and transfer technology to facilitate the implementation of the relevant prohibitions and restrictions set out in this Protocol.
7.[22] Each High Contracting Party has the right to seek and receive technical assistance, where appropriate, from another High Contracting Party on specific relevant technology, other than weapons technology, as necessary and feasible, with a view to reducing any period of deferral for which provision is made in the Technical Annex.

Art. 12. Protection from the effects of minefields, mined areas, mines, booby-traps and other devices

1. Application
   (a) With the exception of the forces and missions referred to in sub-paragraph 2(a) (i) of this Article, this Article applies only to missions which are performing functions in an area with the consent of the High Contracting Party on whose territory the functions are performed.

[22] For declaration in respect of this paragraph by Israel, see p. 227.

(b) The application of the provisions of this Article to parties to a conflict which are not High Contracting Parties shall not change their legal status or the legal status of a disputed territory, either explicitly or implicitly.

(c) The provisions of this Article are without prejudice to existing international humanitarian law, or other international instruments as applicable, or decisions by the Security Council of the United Nations, which provide for a higher level of protection to personnel functioning in accordance with this Article.

2. Peace-keeping and certain other forces and missions[23]

(a) This paragraph applies to:

(i) any United Nations force or mission performing peace-keeping, observation or similar functions in any area in accordance with the Charter of the United Nations;

(ii) any mission established pursuant to Chapter VIII of the Charter of the United Nations and performing its functions in the area of a conflict.

(b) Each High Contracting Party or party to a conflict, if so requested by the head of a force or mission to which this paragraph applies, shall:

(i) so far as it is able, take such measures as are necessary to protect the force or mission from the effects of mines, booby-traps and other devices in any area under its control;

(ii) if necessary in order effectively to protect such personnel, remove or render harmless, so far as it is able, all mines, booby-traps and other devices in that area; and

(iii) inform the head of the force or mission of the location of all known minefields, mined areas, mines, booby-traps and other devices in the area in which the force or mission is performing its functions and, so far as is feasible, make available to the head of the force or mission all information in its possession concerning such minefields, mined areas, mines, booby-traps and other devices.

3. Humanitarian and fact-finding missions of the United Nations System

(a) This paragraph applies to any humanitarian or fact-finding mission of the United Nations System.

(b) Each High Contracting Party or party to a conflict, if so requested by the head of a mission to which this paragraph applies, shall:

(i) provide the personnel of the mission with the protections set out in sub-paragraph 2(b) (i) of this Article; and

(ii) if access to or through any place under its control is necessary for the performance of the mission's functions and in order to provide the personnel of the mission with safe passage to or through that place:

(aa) unless on-going hostilities prevent, inform the head of the mission of a safe route to that place if such information is available; or

[23] For declarations in respect of this paragraph by the Netherlands and the United Kingdom, see pp. 229, 231.

(bb) if information identifying a safe route is not provided in accordance with sub-paragraph (aa), so far as is necessary and feasible, clear a lane through minefields.

4. Missions of the International Committee of the Red Cross
   (a) This paragraph applies to any mission of the International Committee of the Red Cross performing functions with the consent of the host State or States as provided for by the Geneva Conventions of 12 August 1949 and, where applicable, their Additional Protocols.
   (b) Each High Contracting Party or party to a conflict, if so requested by the head of a mission to which this paragraph applies, shall:
      (i) provide the personnel of the mission with the protections set out in sub-paragraph 2(b) (i) of this Article; and
      (ii) take the measures set out in sub-paragraph 3(b) (ii) of this Article.
5. Other humanitarian missions and missions of enquiry
   (a) Insofar as paragraphs 2, 3 and 4 above do not apply to them, this paragraph applies to the following missions when they are performing functions in the area of a conflict or to assist the victims of a conflict:
      (i) any humanitarian mission of a national Red Cross or Red Crescent Society or of their International Federation;
      (ii) any mission of an impartial humanitarian organization, including any impartial humanitarian demining mission; and
      (iii) any mission of enquiry established pursuant to the provisions of the Geneva Conventions of 12 August 1949 and, where applicable, their Additional Protocols.
   (b) Each High Contracting Party or party to a conflict, if so requested by the head of a mission to which this paragraph applies, shall, so far as is feasible:
      (i) provide the personnel of the mission with the protections set out in sub-paragraph 2(b) (i) of this Article, and
      (ii) take the measures set out in sub-paragraph 3(b) (ii) of this Article.
6. Confidentiality
   All information provided in confidence pursuant to this Article shall be treated by the recipient in strict confidence and shall not be released outside the force or mission concerned without the express authorization of the provider of the information.
7. Respect for laws and regulations
   Without prejudice to such privileges and immunities as they may enjoy or to the requirements of their duties, personnel participating in the forces and missions referred to in this Article shall:
   (a) respect the laws and regulations of the host State; and
   (b) refrain from any action or activity incompatible with the impartial and international nature of their duties.

Art. 13. Consultations of High Contracting Parties

1. The High Contracting Parties undertake to consult and cooperate with each other on all issues related to the operation of this Protocol. For this purpose, a conference of High Contracting Parties shall be held annually.

2. Participation in the annual conferences shall be determined by their agreed Rules of Procedure.
3. The work of the conference shall include:
   (a) review of the operation and status of this Protocol;
   (b) consideration of matters arising from reports by High Contracting Parties according to paragraph 4 of this Article;
   (c) preparation for review conferences; and
   (d) consideration of the development of technologies to protect civilians against indiscriminate effects of mines.
4. The High Contracting Parties shall provide annual reports to the Depositary, who shall circulate them to all High Contracting Parties in advance of the Conference, on any of the following matters:
   (a) dissemination of information on this Protocol to their armed forces and to the civilian population;
   (b) mine clearance and rehabilitation programmes;
   (c) steps taken to meet technical requirements of this Protocol and any other relevant information pertaining thereto;
   (d) legislation related to this Protocol;
   (e) measures taken on international technical information exchange, on international cooperation on mine clearance, and on technical cooperation and assistance; and
   (f) other relevant matters.
5. The cost of the Conference of High Contracting Parties shall be borne by the High Contracting Parties and States not parties participating in the work of the Conference, in accordance with the United Nations scale of assessment adjusted appropriately.

Art. 14. Compliance[24]

1. Each High Contracting Party shall take all appropriate steps, including legislative and other measures, to prevent and suppress violations of this Protocol by persons or on territory under its jurisdiction or control.
2. The measures envisaged in paragraph 1 of this Article include appropriate measures to ensure the imposition of penal sanctions against persons who, in relation to an armed conflict and contrary to the provisions of this Protocol, wilfully kill or cause serious injury to civilians and to bring such persons to justice.
3. Each High Contracting Party shall also require that its armed forces issue relevant military instructions and operating procedures and that armed forces personnel receive training commensurate with their duties and responsibilities to comply with the provisions of this Protocol.
4. The High Contracting Parties undertake to consult each other and to cooperate with each other bilaterally, through the Secretary-General of the United Nations or through other appropriate international procedures, to resolve any problems that may arise with regard to the interpretation and application of the provisions of this Protocol.

[24] For declaration in respect of this article by Israel and the United States of America, see pp. 228 and 232.

Technical Annex[25]

1. *Recording*
   (a) Recording of the location of mines other than remotely-delivered mines, minefields, mined areas, booby-traps and other devices shall be carried out in accordance with the following provisions:
      (i) the location of the minefields, mined areas and areas of booby-traps and other devices shall be specified accurately by relation to the coordinates of at least two reference points and the estimated dimensions of the area containing these weapons in relation to those reference points;
      (ii) maps, diagrams or other records shall be made in such a way as to indicate the location of minefields, mined areas, booby-traps and other devices in relation to reference points, and these records shall also indicate their perimeters and extent;
      (iii) for purposes of detection and clearance of mines, booby-traps and other devices, maps, diagrams or other records shall contain complete information on the type, number, emplacing method, type of fuse and life time, date and time of laying, anti-handling devices (if any) and other relevant information on all these weapons laid. Whenever feasible the minefield record shall show the exact location of every mine, except in row minefields where the row location is sufficient. The precise location and operating mechanism of each booby-trap laid shall be individually recorded.
   (b) The estimated location and area of remotely-delivered mines shall be specified by coordinates of reference points (normally corner points) and shall be ascertained and when feasible marked on the ground at the earliest opportunity. The total number and types of mines laid, the date and time of laying and the self-destruction time periods shall also be recorded.
   (c) Copies of records shall be held at a level of command sufficient to guarantee their safety as far as possible.
   (d) The use of mines produced after the entry into force of this Protocol is prohibited unless they are marked in English or in the respective national language or languages with the following information:
      (i) name of the country of origin;
      (ii) month and year of production; and
      (iii) serial number or lot number.

The marking should be visible, legible, durable and resistant to environmental effects, as far as possible.

2. *Specifications on detectability*
   (a) With respect to anti-personnel mines produced after 1 January 1997, such mines shall incorporate in their construction a material or device that enables the mine to be detected by commonly-available technical mine detection equipment and provides a response signal equivalent to a signal from 8 grammes or more of iron in a single coherent mass.

[25] For declaration in respect of the technical annexes by France and the Republic of Korea, see pp. 225 and 230.

(b) With respect to anti-personnel mines produced before 1 January 1997, such mines shall either incorporate in their construction, or have attached prior to their emplacement, in a manner not easily removable, a material or device that enables the mine to be detected by commonly-available technical mine detection equipment and provides a response signal equivalent to a signal from 8 grammes or more of iron in a single coherent mass.

(c)[26] In the event that a High Contracting Party determines that it cannot immediately comply with sub-paragraph (b), it may declare at the time of its notification of consent to be bound by this Protocol that it will defer compliance with sub-paragraph (b) for a period not to exceed 9 years from the entry into force of this Protocol. In the meantime it shall, to the extent feasible, minimize the use of anti-personnel mines that do not so comply.

3. *Specifications on self-destruction and self-deactivation*

(a) All remotely-delivered anti-personnel mines shall be designed and constructed so that no more than 10% of activated mines will fail to self-destruct within 30 days after emplacement, and each mine shall have a back-up self-deactivation feature designed and constructed so that, in combination with the self-destruction mechanism, no more than one in one thousand activated mines will function as a mine 120 days after emplacement.

(b) All non-remotely delivered anti-personnel mines, used outside marked areas, as defined in Article 5 of this Protocol, shall comply with the requirements for self-destruction and self-deactivation stated in sub-paragraph (a).

(c)[26] In the event that a High Contracting Party determines that it cannot immediately comply with sub-paragraphs (a) and/or (b), it may declare at the time of its notification of consent to be bound by this Protocol, that it will, with respect to mines produced prior to the entry into force of this Protocol defer compliance with sub-paragraphs (a) and/or (b) for a period not to exceed 9 years from the entry into force of this Protocol. During this period of deferral, the High Contracting Party shall:

(i) undertake to minimize, to the extent feasible, the use of anti-personnel mines that do not so comply, and

(ii) with respect to remotely-delivered anti-personnel mines, comply with either the requirements for self-destruction or the requirements for self-deactivation and, with respect to other anti-personnel mines comply with at least the requirements for self-deactivation.

4. *International signs for minefields and mined areas*

Signs similar to the example attached [1] and as specified below shall be utilized in the marking of minefields and mined areas to ensure their visibility and recognition by the civilian population:

(a) size and shape: a triangle or square no smaller than 28 centimetres (11 inches) by 20 centimetres (7.9 inches) for a triangle, and 15 centimetres (6 inches) per side for a square;

[26] For declarations in respect of these paragraphs by China, Hungary and Pakistan, see pp. 224, 226, 229.

(b) colour: red or orange with a yellow reflecting border;
(c) symbol: the symbol illustrated in the Attachment, or an alternative readily recognizable in the area in which the sign is to be displayed as identifying a dangerous area;
(d) language: the sign should contain the word "mines" in one of the six official languages of the Convention (Arabic, Chinese, English, French, Russian and Spanish) and the language or languages prevalent in that area;
(e) spacing: signs should be placed around the minefield or mined area at a distance sufficient to ensure their visibility at any point by a civilian approaching the area.

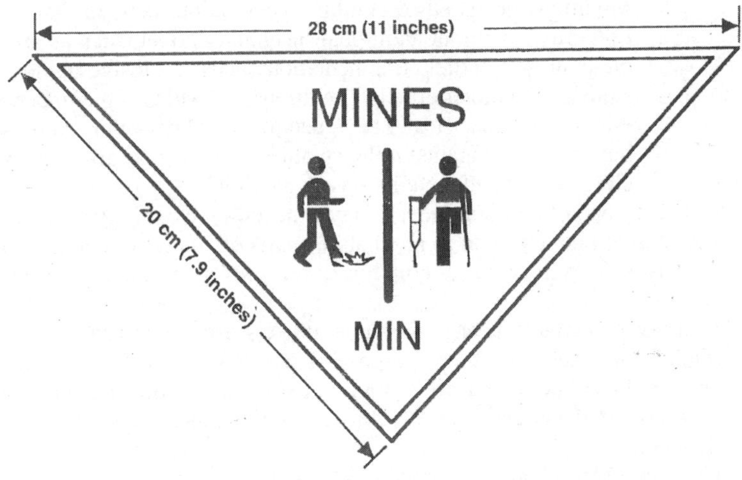

Symbol for mined areas

PROTOCOL ON PROHIBITIONS OR RESTRICTIONS ON THE USE OF INCENDIARY WEAPONS (PROTOCOL III)[1]

Geneva, 10 October 1980

Article 1.[2] *Definitions*

For the purpose of this Protocol:

1. "Incendiary weapon" means any weapon or munition which is primarily designed to set fire to objects or to cause burn injury to persons through the action of flame, heat, or combination thereof, produced by a chemical reaction of a substance delivered on the target.
   (a) Incendiary weapons can take the form of, for example, flame throwers, fougasses, shells, rockets, grenades, mines, bombs and other containers of incendiary substances.
   (b) Incendiary weapons do not include:
      (i) Munitions which may have incidental incendiary effects, such as illuminants, tracers, smoke or signalling systems;
      (ii) Munitions designed to combine penetration, blast or fragmentation effects with an additional incendiary effect, such as armour-piercing projectiles, fragmentation shells, explosive bombs and similar combined-effects munitions in which the incendiary effect is not specifically designed to cause burn injury to persons, but to be used against military objectives, such as armoured vehicles, aircraft and installations or facilities.
2. "Concentration of civilians" means any concentration of civilians, be it permanent or temporary, such as in inhabited parts of cities, or inhabited towns or villages, or as in camps or columns of refugees or evacuees, or groups of nomads.
3.[3] "Military objective" means, so far as objects are concerned, any object which by its nature, location, purpose or use makes an effective contribution to military action and whose total or partial destruction, capture or neutralization, in the circumstances ruling at the time, offers a definite military advantage.
4. "Civilian objects" are all objects which are not military objectives as defined in paragraph 3.
5. "Feasible precautions" are those precautions which are practicable or practically possible taking into account all circumstances ruling at the time, including humanitarian and military considerations.

Art. 2. Protection of civilians and civilian objects

1. It is prohibited in all circumstances to make the civilian population as such, individual civilians or civilian objects the object of attack by incendiary weapons.
2. It is prohibited in all circumstances to make any military objective located within a concentration of civilians the object of attack by air-delivered incendiary weapons.

---

[1] For declarations in respect of this Protocol by Argentina and the People's Republic of China, see pp. 216, 217.

[2] For declaration in respect of this article by the United Kingdom, see p. 220.

[3] For declaration in respect of this paragraph by the Netherlands, see p. 219.

3.[4] It is further prohibited to make any military objective located within a concentration of civilians the object of attack by means of incendiary weapons other than air-delivered incendiary weapons, except when such military objective is clearly separated from the concentration of civilians and all feasible precautions are taken with a view to limiting the incendiary effects to the military objective and to avoiding, and in any event to minimizing, incidental loss of civilian life, injury to civilians and damage to civilian objects.

4. It is prohibited to make forests or other kinds of plant cover the object of attack by incendiary weapons except when such natural elements are used to cover, conceal or camouflage combatants or other military objectives, or are themselves military objectives.

[4] For declarations in respect of paras. 2 and 3 by Canada and the United Kingdom, see pp. 216, 221.

PROTOCOL ON BLINDING LASER WEAPONS (PROTOCOL IV)[1]

Adopted by the Conference of the States Parties to the Convention at its 8th Plenary Meeting of the State Parties on 13 October 1995

Article 1.[2] It is prohibited to employ laser weapons specifically designed, as their sole combat function or as one of their combat functions, to cause permanent blindness to unenhanced vision, that is to the naked eye or to the eye with corrective eyesight devices. The High Contracting Parties shall not transfer such weapons to any State or non-State entity.

Art. 2. In the employment of laser systems, the High Contracting Parties shall take all feasible precautions to avoid the incidence of permanent blindness to unenhanced vision. Such precautions shall include training of their armed forces and other practical measures.

Art. 3. Blinding as an incidental or collateral effect of the legitimate military employment of laser systems, including laser systems used against optical equipment, is not covered by the prohibition of this Protocol.

Art. 4. For the purpose of this protocol "permanent blindness" means irreversible and uncorrectable loss of vision which is seriously disabling with no prospect of recovery. Serious disability is equivalent to visual acuity of less than 20/200 Snellen measured using both eyes.

[1] For declarations in respect of this Protocol by Australia, Belgium, South Africa, Sweden, Switzerland and the United Kingdom, see pp. 234–236.

[2] For declarations in respect of this article by Austria, Canada, Germany, Greece, Ireland, Italy, Liechtenstein and the Netherlands, see pp. 234–235.

SIGNATURES, RATIFICATIONS AND ACCESSIONS

TABLE OF CONTENTS

I. SIGNATURES, RATIFICATIONS AND ACCESSIONS TO THE CONVENTION AND THREE ORIGINAL PROTOCOLS OF 1980[1]

State	*Signature*	*Ratification, Accession, Notification of Succession (C)*	*Consent to be bound pursuant to Article 4 paragraphs 3 and 4 of Protocols*[2]		
			I	*II*	*III*
Afghanistan	10 Apr 1981	–			
Albania	–	28 Aug 2002	x	x	x
Argentina	2 Dec 1981	2 Oct 1995 *Res.*	x	x	x
Australia	8 Apr 1982	29 Sep 1983	x	x	x
Austria	10 Apr 1981	14 Mar 1983	x	x	x
Bangladesh	–	6 Sep 2000	x	x	x
Belarus	10 Apr 1981	23 Jun 1982	x	x	x
Belgium	10 Apr 1981	7 Feb 1995	x	x	x
Benin	–	27 Mar 1989	x	–	x
Bolivia	–	21 Sep 2001	x	x	x
Bosnia and Herzegovina	–	1 Sep 1993 (C)	x	x	x
Brazil		3 Oct 1995	x	x	x
Bulgaria	10 Apr 1981	15 Oct 1982	x	x	x
Cambodia	–	25 Mar 1997	x	x	x
Canada	10 Apr 1981	24 Jun 1994 *Dec.*	x	x	x
Cape Verde	–	16 Sep 1997	x	x	x
China	14 Sep 1981	7 Apr 1982 *Dec.*	x	x	x

[1] Based on the indications in *Multilateral Treaties Deposited with the Secretary-General, New York, United Nations* (ST/LEG/SER.E) as available on http://untreaty.un.org; http://disarmament.un.org/Treaty Status.nsf; ICRC website: www.icrc.org/ihl.nsf.

[2] The Protocols concerned are:
Protocol on non-detectable fragments (Protocol I);
Protocol on prohibitions or restrictions on the use of mines, booby-traps and other devices (Protocol II);
Protocol on prohibitions or restrictions on the use of incendiary weapons (Protocol III).
Each participant must consent to be bound by any two or more of the Protocols. Acceptance of a Protocol is denoted by an "x". Unless otherwise indicated, acceptance was notified upon ratification, acceptance, approval of, accession or succession to the Convention.

State	*Signature*	*Ratification, Accession, Notification of Succession (C)*	*Consent to be bound pursuant to Article 4 paragraphs 3 and 4 of Protocols[2]*		
			I	*II*	*III*
Colombia	–	6 Mar 2000	x	x	x
Costa Rica	–	17 Dec 1998	x	x	x
Croatia	–	2 Dec 1993 (C)	x	x	x
Cuba	10 Apr 1981	2 Mar 1987	x	x	x
Cyprus	–	12 Dec 1988 *Dec.*	x	x	x
Czech Republic[3]	–	22 Feb 1993 (C)	x	x	x
Denmark	10 Apr 1981	7 Jul 1982	x	x	x
Djibouti	–	29 Jul 1996	x	x	x
Ecuador	9 Sep 1981	4 May 1982	x	x	x
Egypt	10 Apr 1981	–			
El Salvador	–	26 Jan 2000	x	x	x
Estonia	–	20 Apr 2000	x	–	x
Finland	10 Apr 1981	8 May 1982	x	x	x
France	10 Apr 1981	4 Mar 1988 *Res.*	x	x	x
Georgia	–	29 Apr 1996	x	x	x
Germany[4]	10 Apr 1981	25 Nov 1992	x	x	x
Greece	10 Apr 1981	28 Jan 1992	x	x	x
Guatemala	–	21 Jul 1983	x	x	x
Holy See	–	22 July 1997 *Dec.*	x	x	x
Hungary	10 Apr 1981	14 Jun 1982	x	x	x
Iceland	10 Apr 1981	–	–	–	–
India	15 May 1981	1 Mar 1984	x	x	x
Ireland	10 Apr 1981	13 Mar 1995	x	x	x
Israel	–	22 Mar 1995 *Dec.*	x	x	–
Italy	10 Apr 1981	20 Jan 1995 *Dec.*	x	x	x
Japan	22 Sep 1981	9 Jun 1982	x	x	x
Jordan	–	19 Oct 1995	x	–	x
Lao People's Democratic Republic[5]	[2 Nov 1982]	3 Jan 1983	x	x	x
Latvia	–	4 Jan 1993	x	x	x
Lesotho	–	6 Sep 2000	x	x	x
Liechtenstein	11 Feb 1982	16 Aug 1989	x	x	x
Lithuania	–	3 Jun 1998	x	–	x
Luxembourg	10 Apr 1981	21 May 1996	x	x	x
Macedonia	–	30 Dec 1996 (C)	x	x	x
Maldives	–	7 Sep 2000	x	–	x
Mali	–	24 Oct 2001	x	x	x
Malta	–	26 Jun 1995	x	x	x
Mali	–	24 Oct 2001	x	x	x
Malta	–	26 Jun 1995	x	x	x
Mauritius	–	6 May 1996	x	x	x

3 Czechoslovakia had signed and ratified the Convention accepting Protocols I, II and III, on 10 April 1981 and 31 August 1982, respectively. See also note 2 in document *No. 18*, p. 170.

4 The German Democratic Republic had signed and ratified the Convention on 10 April 1981 and 20 July 1982, respectively, accepting all three Protocols. See also note 3 in the document *No. 18*, p. 170.

5 A signature was affixed on behalf of the Lao People's Democratic Republic on 2 November 1982, i.e. after the time-limit of 10 April 1982 prescribed by Article 3 of the Convention, as a result of an administrative oversight. The signature was cancelled; the Government of the Lao People's Democratic Republic subsequently acceded (on 3 January 1983) to the Convention, accepting the three Protocols.

State	*Signature*	*Ratification, Accession, Notification of Succession (C)*	*Consent to be bound pursuant to Article 4 paragraphs 3 and 4 of Protocols*[2] *I*	*II*	*III*
Mexico	10 Apr 1981	11 Feb 1982	x	x	x
Monaco		12 Aug 1997	x	–	–
Mongolia	10 Apr 1981	8 Jun 1982	x	x	x
Morocco	10 Apr 1981	19 March 2002	–	x	–
Nauru	–	12 Nov 2001	x	x	x
Netherlands[6]	10 Apr 1981	18 Jun 1987 *Dec.*	x	x	x
New Zealand	10 Apr 1981	18 Oct 1993	x	x	x
Nicaragua	20 May 1981	5 Dec 2000	x	–	x
Niger	–	10 Nov 1992	x	x	x
Nigeria	26 Jan 1982	–			
Norway	10 Apr 1981	7 Jun 1983	x	x	x
Pakistan	26 Jan 1982	1 Apr 1985	x	x	x
Panama	–	26 Mar 1997	x	x	x
Peru		3 Jul 1997	x	–	x
Philippines	15 May 1981	15 Jul 1996	x	x	x
Poland	10 Apr 1981	2 Jun 1983	x	x	x
Portugal	10 Apr 1981	4 Apr 1997	x	x	x
Republic of Korea	–	9 May 2001	x	–	–
Republic of Moldova	–	8 Sep 2000	x	x	x
Romania	8 Apr 1982	26 Jul 1995 *Dec.*	x	x	x
Russian Federation	10 Apr 1981	10 Jun 1982	x	x	x
Senegal	–	29 Nov 1999	–	–	x
Seychelles	–	8 Jun 2000	x	x	x
Sierra Leone	1 May 1981	–			
Slovakia[7]		28 May 1993 (C)	x	x	x
Slovenia		6 Jul 1992 (C)	x	x	x
South Africa		13 Sep 1995	x	x	x
Spain	10 Apr 1981	29 Dec 1993	x	x	x
Sudan	10 Apr 1981	–			
Sweden	10 Apr 1981	7 Jul 1982	x	x	x
Switzerland	18 Jun 1981	20 Aug 1982	x	x	x
Tajikistan		12 Oct 1999	x	x	x
Togo	15 Sep 1981	4 Dec 1995 A	x	x	x
Tunisia		15 May 1987	x	x	x
Turkey	26 Mar 1982	–			
Uganda		14 Nov 1995	x	x	x
Ukraine	10 Apr 1981	23 Jun 1982	x	x	x
United Kingdom of Great Britain and Northern Ireland	10 Apr 1981	13 Feb 1995 *Dec.*	x	x	x
United States of America	8 Apr 1982	24 Mar 1995 *Res.*	x	x	
Uruguay		6 Oct 1994	x	x	x
Uzbekistan		29 Sep 1997	x	x	x
Viet Nam	10 Apr 1981				
[Yugoslavia SFR	5 May 1981	24 May 1983	x	x	x]
Yugoslavia (Serbia and Montenegro)	–	12 Mar 2001 (C)	x	x	x

6 For the Kingdom in Europe.

7 See note 3.

II. RESERVATIONS AND DECLARATIONS TO THE CONVENTION AND THREE ORIGINAL PROTOCOLS OF 1980

ARGENTINA (*reservation made on ratification*)
The Argentine Republic makes the express reservation that any references to the 1977 Protocols Additional to the Geneva Conventions of 1949 that are contained in the [said Convention and its Protocols I, II and III] shall be interpreted in the light of the interpretative declarations in the instrument of accession of the Argentine Republic to the afore-mentioned Additional Protocols of 1977.

CANADA (*declaration made on ratification*)
1. It is the understanding of the Government of Canada that:
   (a) The compliance of commanders and others responsible for planning, deciding upon, or executing attacks to which the Conventions and its Protocols apply cannot be judged on the basis of information which subsequently comes to light but must be assessed on the basis of the information available to them at the time that such actions were taken; and
   (b) Where terms are not defined in the present Convention and its Protocols they shall, so far as is relevant, be construed in the same sense as terms contained in additional Protocol I to the Geneva Conventions of August 12, 1949.
2. With respect to Protocol I, it is the understanding of the Government of Canada that the use of plastics or similar materials for detonators or other weapons parts not designed to cause injury is not prohibited.
3. With respect to Protocol II, it is the understanding of the Government of Canada that:
   (a) Any obligation to record the location of remotely delivered mines pursuant to sub-paragraph 1 (a) of article 5 refers to the location of mine fields and not to the location of individual remotely delivered mines;
   (b) The term "pre-planned", as used in sub-paragraph 1 (a) of article 7 means that the position of the minefield in question should have been determined in advance so that an accurate record of the location of the minefield, when laid, can be made;
   (c) The phrase "similar functions" used in article 8, includes the concepts of "peace-making, preventive peace-keeping and peace enforcement" as defined in an agenda for peace (United Nations document A/47/277 S/2411 of 17 June 1992).
4. With respect to Protocol III, it is the understanding of the Government of Canada that the expression "clearly separated" in paragraph 3 of article 2 includes both spatial separation or separation by means of an effective physical barrier between the military objective and the concentration of civilians.

CHINA (*statement made on signature*)
1. The Government of the People's Republic of China has decided to sign the Convention on Prohibitions or Restrictions on the Use of Certain Conventional Weapons Which May be Deemed to be Excessively Injurious or to Have Indiscriminate Effects adopted at the United Nations Conference held in Geneva on 10 October 1980.
2. The Government of the People's Republic of China deems that the basic spirit of the Convention reflects the reasonable demand and good intention of numerous countries and peoples of the world regarding prohibitions or restrictions on the use of certain conventional weapons which are excessively injurious or have indiscriminate effects. This basic spirit conforms to China's consistent position and serves the interest of opposing aggression and maintaining peace.
3. However, it should be pointed out that the Convention fails to provide for supervision or verification of any violation of its clauses, thus weakening its binding force. The Protocol on Prohibitions or Restrictions on the Use of Mines, Booby Traps and

Other Devices fails to lay down strict restrictions on the use of such weapons by the aggressor on the territory of his victim and to provide adequately for the right of a state victim of an aggression to defend itself by all necessary means. The Protocol on Prohibitions or Restrictions on the Use of Incendiary Weapons does not stipulate restrictions on the use of such weapons against combat personnel. Furthermore, the Chinese texts of the Convention and Protocol are not accurate or satisfactory enough. It is the hope of the Chinese Government that these inadequacies can be remedied in due course.

CYPRUS (*declaration made on ratification*)
The provisions of article 7 paragraph (3b) and article 8 of the Protocol on Prohibitions or Restrictions on the Use of Mines, Booby-Traps and Other Devices (Protocol II) will be interpreted in such a way that neither the status of peace-keeping forces or missions of the United Nations in Cyprus will be affected nor will additional rights be, *ipso jure*, granted to them.

FRANCE (*declaration, interpretative statement and reservation made on signature but not confirmed on ratification*)
Declaration
After signing the Convention on Prohibitions or Restrictions on the Use of Certain Conventional Weapons Which May Be Deemed to Be excessively Injurious or to Have Indiscriminate Effects, the French Government, as it has already had occasion to state

- through its representative to the United Nations Conference on Prohibitions or Restrictions on the Use of Certain Conventional Weapons in Geneva, during the discussion of the proposal concerning verification arrangements submitted by the delegation of the Federal Republic of Germany and of which the French Government became a sponsor, and at the final meetings on 10 October 1980;
- on 20 November 1980 through the representative of the Netherlands, speaking on behalf of the nine States members of the European Community in the First Committee at the thirty-fifth session of the United Nations General Assembly;

Regrets that thus far it has not been possible for the States which participated in the negotiation of the Convention to reach agreement on the provisions concerning the verification of facts which might be alleged and that might constitute violations of the undertakings subscribed to.

It therefore reserves the right to submit, possibly in association with other States, proposals aimed at filling that gap at the first conference to be held pursuant to article 8 of the Convention and to utilize, as appropriate, procedures which would make it possible to bring before the international community facts and information which, if verified, could constitute violations of the provisions of the Convention and the Protocols annexed thereto.

Interpretative statement
The application of this Convention will have no effect on the legal status of the parties to a conflict.

Reservation
France, which is not bound by Additional Protocol I of 10 June 1977 to the Geneva Conventions of 12 August 1949:

Considers that the fourth paragraph of the preamble to the Convention on Prohibitions or Restrictions on the Use of Certain Conventional Weapons Which May Be Deemed to Be Excessively Injurious or to Have Indiscriminate Effects, which reproduces the provisions of article 35, paragraph 3, of Additional Protocol I, applies only to States parties to that Protocol;

States, with reference to the scope of application defined in article 1 of the Convention on Prohibitions or Restrictions on the Use of Certain Conventional Weapons, that it will apply the provisions of the Convention and its three Protocols to all the armed conflicts referred to in articles 2 and 3 common to the Geneva Conventions of 12 August 1949;

States that as regards the Geneva Conventions of 12 August 1949, the declaration of acceptance and application provided for in article 7, paragraph 4 (b), of the Convention on Prohibitions or Restrictions on the Use of Certain Conventional Weapons will have no effects other than those provided for in article 3 common to the Geneva Conventions, in so far as that article is applicable.

HOLY SEE (*declaration made on accession*)
The Holy See, as a signatory of the [said Convention and annexed Protocols], in keeping with its proper nature and with the particular condition of the Vatican City State, intends to renew its encouragement to the International Community to continue on the path it has taken for the reduction of human suffering caused by armed conflict.
Every step in this direction contributes to increasing awareness that war and the cruelty of war must be done away with in order to resolve tensions by dialogue and negotiation, and also by ensuring that international law is respected.

The Holy See, while maintaining that the above-mentioned Convention and Protocols constitute an important instrument for humanitarian international law, reiterates the objective hoped for by many parties: an agreement that would totally ban anti-personnel mines, the effects of which are tragically well-known.

In this regard, the Holy See considers that the modifications made so far in the second Protocol are insufficient and inadequate. It wishes, by means of its own accession to the Convention, to offer support to every effort aimed at effectively banning anti-personnel mines, in the conviction that all possible means must be used in order to build a safer and more fraternal world.

ISRAEL (*declarations made on accession*)
Declarations
(a) With reference to the scope of application defined in article 1 of the Convention, the Government of the State of Israel will apply the provisions of the Convention and those annexed Protocols to which Israel has agreed become bound to all armed conflicts involving regular armed forces of States referred to in article 2 common to the General Conventions of 12 August 1949, as well as to all armed conflicts referred to in article 3 common to the Geneva Conventions of 12 August 1949.
(b) Article 7, paragraph 4 of the Convention will have no effect.
(c) The application of this Convention will have no effect on the legal status of the parties to a conflict.

Understandings
(a) It is the understanding of the Government of the State of Israel that the compliance of commanders and others responsible for the planning, deciding upon, or executing attacks to which the Convention and its Protocols apply, cannot be judged on the basis of information which subsequently comes to light, but must be assessed on the basis of the information available to them at the time that such actions were taken.
(b) With respect to Protocol I, it is the understanding of the Government of Israel that the use of plastics or similar materials for detonators or other weapon parts not designed to cause injury is not prohibited.
(c) With respect to Protocol II, it is the understanding of the Government of Israel that:
    (i) Any obligation to record the location of remotely delivered mines pursuant to sub-paragraph 1 (a) of article 5 refers to the location of mine fields and not to the location of individual remotely delivered mines;
    (ii) the term pre-planned, as used in sub-paragraph 1 (a) of article 7 means that the position of the minefield in question should have been determined in advance so that an accurate record of the location of the minefield, when laid, can be made.

ITALY (*declaration made on signature*)
On 10 October 1980 in Geneva, the representative of Italy at the Conference speaking at the closing meeting, emphasized that the Conference, in an effort to reach a compromise between what was desirable and what was possible, had probably achieved the maximum results feasible in the circumstances prevailing at the time.

However, he observed in his statement that one of the objectives which had not been achieved at the Conference, to his Government's great regret, was the inclusion in the text of the Convention, in accordance with a proposal originated by the Federal Republic of Germany, of an article on the establishment of a consultative committee of experts competent to verify facts which might be alleged and which might constitute violations of the undertakings subscribed to.

On the same occasion, the representative of Italy expressed the wish that that proposal, which was aimed at strengthening the credibility and effectiveness of the Convention, should be reconsidered at the earliest opportunity within the framework of the mechanisms for the amendment of the Convention expressly provided for in that instrument.

Subsequently, through the representative of the Netherlands, speaking on behalf of nine States members of the European Community in the First Committee of the United Nations General Assembly on 20 November 1980, when it adopted draft resolution A/C.1/31/L.15 (subsequently adopted as General Assembly Resolution 35/153), Italy once again expressed regret that the States which had participated in the preparation of the texts of the Convention and its Protocols had been unable to reach agreement on provisions that would ensure respect for the obligations deriving from those texts.

In the same spirit, Italy – which has just signed the Convention in accordance with the wishes expressed by the General Assembly in its resolution 35/153 – wishes to confirm solemnly that it intends to undertake active efforts to ensure that the problem of the establishment of a mechanism that would make it possible to fill a gap in the Convention and thus ensure that it achieves maximum effectiveness and maximum credibility vis-à-vis the international community is taken up again at the earliest opportunity in every competent forum.

NETHERLANDS (*declaration made on ratification*)
1. With regard to article 2, paragraph 4, of Protocol II: It is the understanding of the Government of the Kingdom of the Netherlands that a specific area of land may also be a military objective if, because of its location or other reasons specified in paragraph 4, its total or partial destruction, capture, or neutralization in the circumstances ruling at the time, offers a definitive military advantage;
2. With regard to article 3, paragraph 3, under c, of Protocol II: It is the understanding of the Kingdom of the Netherlands that military advantage refers to the advantage anticipated from the attack considered as a whole and not only from isolated or particular parts of the attack;
3. With regard to article 8, paragraph 1, of Protocol II: It is the understanding of the Government of the Kingdom of the Netherlands that the words "as far as it is able" means "as far as it is technically able";
4. With regard to article 1, paragraph 3, of Protocol III: It is the understanding of the Government of the Kingdom of the Netherlands that a specific area of land may also be a military objective if, because of its location or other reasons specified in paragraph 3, its total or partial destruction, capture, or neutralization in the circumstances ruling at the time, offers a definite military advantage.

ROMANIA (*declaration made on signature*)
1. Romania considers that the Convention and the three Protocols annexed thereto constitute a positive step within the framework of the efforts which have been made for the gradual development of international humanitarian law applicable during armed conflicts and which aim at providing very broad and reliable protection for the civilian population and the combatants.

2. At the same time, Romania would like to emphasize that the provisions of the Convention and its Protocols have a restricted character and do not ensure adequate protection either to the civilian population or to the combatants as the fundamental principles of international humanitarian law require.
3. The Romanian Government wishes to state on this occasion also that real and effective protection for each individual and for peoples and assurance of their right to a free and independent life necessarily presuppose the elimination of all acts of aggression and the renunciation once and for all of the use of force and the threat of the use of force, of intervention in the domestic affairs of other States and of the policy of domination and diktat and strict observation of the sovereignty and independence of peoples and their legitimate right to self-determination.

   In the present circumstances, when a vast quantity of nuclear weapons has been accumulated in the world, the protection of each individual and of all peoples is closely linked with the struggle for peace and disarmament and with the adoption of authentic measures to halt the arms race and ensure the gradual reduction of nuclear weapons until they are totally eliminated.
4. The Romanian Government states once again its decision to act, together with other States, to ensure the prohibition or restriction of all conventional weapons which are excessively injurious or have indiscriminate effects, and the adoption of urgent and effective measures for nuclear disarmament which would protect peoples from the nuclear war which seriously threatens their right to life – a fundamental condition for the protection which international humanitarian law must ensure for the individual, the civilian population and the combatants.

UNITED KINGDOM OF GREAT BRITAIN AND NORTHERN IRELAND

Declaration made upon signature

The Government of the United Kingdom of Great Britain and Northern Ireland will give further consideration to certain provisions of the Convention, particularly in relation to the provisions of Protocol I additional to the Geneva Conventions of 12 August 1949, and may wish to make formal declarations in relation to these provisions at the time of ratification.

Ratification

(a) Generally
   (i) The term "armed conflict" of itself and in its context denotes a situation of a kind which is not constituted by the commission of ordinary crimes, including acts of terrorism, whether concerted or in isolation.
   (ii) The United Kingdom will not, in relation to any situation in which it is involved, consider itself bound in consequence of any declaration purporting to be made for the purposes of article 7 (4), unless the United Kingdom shall have expressly recognised that it has been made by a body which is genuinely and authority representing a people engaged in an armed conflict of the type to which that paragraph applies.
   (iii) The terms "civilian" and "civilian population" have the same meaning as in article 50 of the 1st Additional Protocol of 1977 to the 1949 Geneva Conventions. Civilians shall enjoy the protection afforded by this Convention unless and for such time as they take a direct part in hostilities.
   (iv) Military commanders and others responsible for planning, deciding upon, or executing attacks necessarily have to reach decisions on the basis of their assessment of the information from all sources which is reasonably available to them at the relevant time.

(b) *Re: Protocol II, article 2; and Protocol III, article 1*

   A specific area of land may be a military objective if, because of its location or other reasons specified in this article, its total or partial destruction, capture or neutralisation in the circumstances ruling at the time offers a definite military advantage.

(c) *Re: Protocol II, article 3*
In the view of the United Kingdom, the military advantage anticipated from an attack is intended to refer to the advantage anticipated from the attack considered as a whole and not only from isolated or particular parts of the attack.

(d) *Re: Protocol III, article 2*
The United Kingdom accepts the provisions of article 2 (2) and (3) on the understanding that the terms of those paragraphs of that article do not imply that the air-delivery of incendiary weapons, or of any other weapons, projectiles or munitions, is less accurate or less capable of being carried out discriminately than all or any other means of delivery.

UNITED STATES OF AMERICA (*declaration made upon signature*)
The United States Government welcomes the adoption of this Convention, and hopes that all States will give the most serious consideration to ratification or accession. We believe that the Convention represents a positive step forward in efforts to minimize injury or damage to the civilian population in time of armed conflict. Our signature of this Convention reflects the general willingness of the United States to adopt practical and reasonable provisions concerning the conduct of military operations, for the purpose of protecting noncombatants.

At the same time, we want to emphasize that formal adherence by States to agreements restricting the use of weapons in armed conflict would be of little purpose if the parties were not firmly committed to taking every appropriate step to ensure compliance with those restrictions after their entry into force. It would be the firm intention of the United States and, we trust, all other parties to utilize the procedures and remedies provided by this Convention, and by the general laws of war, to see to it that all parties to the Convention meet their obligations under it. The United States strongly supported proposals by other countries during the Conference to include special procedures for dealing with compliance matters, and reserves the right to propose at a later date additional procedures and remedies, should this prove necessary, to deal with such problems.

In addition, the United States of course reserves the right, at the time of ratification, to exercise the option provided by article 4 (3) of the Convention, and to make statements of understanding and/or reservations, to the extent that it may deem that to be necessary to ensure that the Convention and its Protocols conform to humanity and military requirements. As indicated in the negotiating record of the 1980 Conference, the prohibitions and restrictions contained in the Convention and its Protocols are of course new contractual rules (with the exception of certain provisions which restate existing international law) which will only bind States upon their ratification of, or accession to, the Convention and their consent to be bound by the Protocols in question.

Reservation, declaration and statement of understanding made upon ratification

Reservation
Article 7 (4) (b) of the Convention shall not apply with respect to the United States.

Declaration
The United States declares, with reference to the scope of application defined in article 1 of the Convention, that the United States will apply the provisions of the Convention, Protocol I, and Protocol II to all armed conflicts referred to in articles 2 and 3 common to the Geneva Conventions for the Protection of War Victims of August 12, 1949.

Understanding
The United States understands that article 6 (1) of the Protocol II does not prohibit the adaptation for use as booby-traps of portable objects created for a purpose other than as a booby-trap if the adaptation does not violate paragraph (1)(b) of the article.

The United States considers that the fourth paragraph of the preamble to the Convention, which refers to the substance of provisions of article 35 (3) and article 55 (1) of additional Protocol I to the Geneva Conventions for the Protection of War Victims of August 12, 1949, applies only to States which have accepted those provisions.

III. SIGNATURES, RATIFICATIONS AND ACCESSIONS TO PROTOCOL ON PROHIBITIONS OR RESTRICTIONS ON THE USE OF MINES, BOOBY-TRAPS AND OTHER DEVICES, AS AMENDED ON 3 MAY 1996 (PROTOCOL II AS AMENDED ON 3 MAY 1996)[7]

State	*Consent to be bound*
Albania	28 August 2002
Argentina	21 October 1998
Australia	22 August 1997
Austria	27 July 1998 *Dec.*
Bangladesh	6 September 2000
Belgium	10 March 1999 *Dec.*
Bolivia	21 September 2001
Bosnia and Herzegovina	7 September 2000
Brazil	4 October 1999
Bulgaria	3 December 1998
Cambodia	25 March 1997
Canada	5 January 1998 *Res.*
Cape Verde	16 September 1997
China	4 November 1998 *Dec.*
Colombia	6 March 2000
Costa Rica	17 December 1998
Croatia	25 April 2002
Czech Republic	10 August 1998
Denmark	30 April 1997 *Dec.*
Ecuador	14 August 2000
El Salvador	26 January 2000
Estonia	20 April 2000
Finland	3 April 1998 *Dec.*
France	23 July 1998 *Dec.*
Germany	2 May 1997 *Dec.*
Greece	20 January 1999 *Dec.*
Guatemala	29 October 2001
Holy See	22 July 1997
Hungary	30 January 1998 *Dec.*
India	2 September 1999
Ireland	27 March 1997 *Dec.*
Israel	30 October 2000 *Dec*
Italy	13 January 1999 *Dec.*
Japan	10 June 1997
Jordan	6 September 2000
Liechtenstein	19 November 1997 *Dec.*
Lithuania	3 June 1998
Luxembourg	5 August 1999
Maldives	7 September 2000

[7] Based on the communication received on 29 June 1999 from the United Nations Treaty Section and on the indications in *Multilateral Treaties Deposited with the Secretary-General, New York, United Nations* (ST/LEG/SER.E) as available on www.untreaty.un.org/; http://disarmament.un.org/TreatyStatus.nsf; ICRC website: www.icrc.org/ihl.nsf.

In keeping with the depositary practice followed in similar cases, the Secretary-General proposed to receive the declaration for deposit in the absence of any objection on the part of the contracting states, either to the deposit itself or to the procedure envisaged, within a period of 90 days from the date of its circulation (i.e. 21 July 1998). None of the contracting parties to the Protocol having notified the Secretary-General of an objection within the 90 days period, the declaration was deemed to have been accepted for deposit upon the expiration of the 90-day period in question, i.e. on 19 October 1998.

State	*Consent to be bound*
Mali	24 October 2001
Monaco	12 August 1997
Morrocco	19 March 2002
Nauru	12 November 2001
Netherlands[8]	25 March 1999 *Dec.*
New Zealand	8 January 1998
Nicaragua	5 December 2000
Norway	20 April 1998
Pakistan	9 March 1999 *Dec.*
Panama	3 November 1999
Peru	3 July 1997
Philippines	12 June 1997
Portugal	31 March 1999
Republic of Korea	9 May 2001 *Res.*
Republic of Moldova	16 July 2001
South Africa	26 June 1998 *Dec.*
Senegal	29 November 1999
Seychelles	8 June 2000
Slovakia	30 November 1999
Slovenia	3 December 2002
Spain	27 January 1998
Sweden	16 July 1997 *Dec.*
Switzerland	24 March 1998 *Dec.*
Tajikistan	12 October 1999
Ukraine	15 December 1999 *Dec.*
United Kingdom of Great Britain and Northern Ireland	11 February 1999 *Dec.*
United States of America	24 May 1999 R*es.*
Uruguay	18 August 1998

IV. RESERVATIONS AND DECLARATIONS TO PROTOCOL ON PROHIBITIONS OR RESTRICTIONS ON THE USE OF MINES, BOOBY-TRAPS AND OTHER DEVICES, AS AMENDED ON 3 MAY 1996 (PROTOCOL II AS AMENDED ON 3 MAY 1996)[9]

AUSTRIA (*declarations*)

Article 1

It is the understanding of Austria that the provisions of the amended Protocol which by their contents or nature may be applied also in peacetime, shall be observed at all times.

Article 2(3)

It is the understanding of Austria that the word "primarily" is included in article 2, paragraph 3 of the amended Protocol to clarify that mines designed to be detonated by

[8] For the Kingdom in Europe.

[9] Based on the indications in *Multilateral Treaties Deposited with the Secretary-General, New York, United Nations* (ST/LEG/SER.E) as available on http://untreaty.un.org; http://disarmament.un.org/TreatyStatus.nsf; ICRC website: www.icrc.org/ihl.nsf.

In keeping with the depositary practice followed in similar cases, the Secretary-General proposed to receive the declaration for deposit in the absence of any objection on the part of the contracting states, either to the deposit itself or to the procedure envisaged, within a period of 90 days from the date of its circulation (i.e. 21 July 1998). None of the contracting parties to the Protocol having notified the Secretary-General of an objection within the 90 days period, the declaration was deemed to have been accepted for deposit upon the expiration of the 90-day period in question, i.e. on 19 October 1998.

the presence, proximity or contact of a vehicle as opposed to a person, that are equipped with anti-handling devices, are not considered anti-personnel mines as a result of being so equipped.

BELGIUM (*declarations*)
Article 1
It is the understanding of the Government of the Kingdom of Belgium that the provisions of Protocol II as amended which by their contents or nature may be applied also in peacetime, shall be observed at all times.

Article 2
It is the understanding of the Government of the Kingdom of Belgium that the word "primarily" is included in article 2, paragraph 3 of amended Protocol II to clarify that mines designed to the detonated by the presence, proximity or contact of a vehicle as opposed to a person, that are equipped with anti-handling devices, are not considered anti-personnel mines as a result of being so equipped.

CANADA
Reservation 19 October 1998
Canada reserves the right to transfer and use a small number of mines prohibited under this Protocol to be used exclusively for training and testing purposes. Canada will ensure that the number of such mines shall not exceed that absolutely necessary for such purposes.

Statements of Understanding
1. It is understood that the provisions of Amended Protocol II shall, as the context requires, be observed at all times.
2. It is understood that the word "primarily" is included in Article 2, paragraph 3 of Amended Protocol II to clarify that mines designed to be detonated by the presence, proximity or contact of a vehicle as opposed to a person, that are equipped with anti-handling devices, are not considered anti-personnel mines as a result of being so equipped.
3. It is understood that the maintenance of a minefield referred to in Article 10, in accordance with the standards on marking, monitoring and protection by fencing or other means set out in Amended Protocol II, would not be considered as a use of the mines contained therein.

CHINA
Declaration
I. According to the provisions contained in Technical Annex 2 (c) and 3 (c) of the Amended Protocol II, China will defer compliance with 2 (b), 3 (a) and 3 (b);

Declaration in respect of Article 2(3)
It is the understanding of People's Republic of China that the word "primarily" is included in article 2, paragraph 3 of the amended Protocol to clarify that mines designed to be detonated by the presence, proximity or contact of a vehicle as opposed to a person, that are equipped with anti-handling devices, are not considered anti-personnel mines as a result of being so equipped.

DENMARK (*declarations*)
Article 1
It is the understanding of Denmark that the provisions of the amended Protocol which by their contents or nature may be applied also in peacetime, shall be observed at all times.

Article 2(3)
It is the understanding of Denmark that the word "primarily" is included in article 2, paragraph 3 of the amended Protocol to clarify that mines designed to be detonated by

the presence, proximity or contact of a vehicle as opposed to a person, that are equipped with anti-handling devices, are not considered anti-personnel mines as a result of being so equipped.

FINLAND (*declarations*)
Article 1
It is the understanding of Finland that the provisions of the amended Protocol which by their contents or nature may be applied also in peacetime, shall be observed at all times.

Article 2(3)
It is the understanding of Finland that the word "primarily" is included in article 2, paragraph 3 of the amended Protocol to clarify that mines designed to be detonated by the presence, proximity or contact of a vehicle as opposed to a person, that are equipped with anti-handling devices, are not considered anti-personnel mines as a result of being so equipped.

FRANCE
Declaration concerning the scope of amended Protocol II
Article 1
It is the understanding of France that the provisions of the amended Protocol which by their contents or nature may be applied also in peacetime, shall be observed at all times.

Article 2(3)
It is the understanding of France that the word "primarily" is included in article 2, paragraph 3 of the amended Protocol to clarify that mines designed to be detonated by the presence, proximity or contact of a vehicle as opposed to a person, that are equipped with anti-handling devices, are not considered anti-personnel mines as a result of being so equipped.

Article 4
France takes it that article 4 and the Technical Annex to amended Protocol II do not require the removal or replacement of mines that have already been laid.

Declaration concerning standards on marking, monitoring and protection
The provisions of amended Protocol II such as those concerning the marking, monitoring and protection of zones which contain anti-personnel mines and are under the control of a party, are applicable to all zones containing mines, irrespective of the date on which those mines were laid.

GERMANY (*declarations in respect of Articles 1, 2 and 5*)
Article 1
It is the understanding of Germany that the provisions of the amended Protocol which by their contents or nature may be applied also in peacetime, shall be observed at all times.

Article 2(3)
It is the understanding of Germany that the word "primarily" is included in article 2, paragraph 3 of the amended Protocol to clarify that mines designed to be detonated by the presence, proximity or contact of a vehicle as opposed to a person, that are equipped with anti-handling devices, are not considered anti-personnel mines as a result of being so equipped.

Article 5 para. 2 (b)
It is understood that article 5, paragraph 2 (b) does not preclude agreement among the states concerned, in connection with peace treaties or similar arrangements, to allocate responsibilities under paragraph 2 (b) in another manner which nevertheless respects the essential spirit and purpose of the article.

GREECE (*declarations*)
Article 1
It is understood that the provisions of the protocol shall, as the context requires, be observed at all times.

Article 2 (3)
It is the understanding of Greece that the word "primarily" is included in article 2, paragraph 3 of the amended Protocol to clarify that mines designed to be detonated by the presence, proximity or contact of a vehicle as opposed to a person, that are equipped with anti-handling devices, are not considered anti-personnel mines as a result of being so equipped.

Declaration in respect of Article 5, para. 2 (b)
It is understood that article 5, paragraph 2 (b) does not preclude agreement among the states concerned, in connection with peace treaties or similar arrangements, to allocate responsibilities under paragraph 2 (b) in another manner which nevertheless respects the essential spirit and purpose of the article.

HUNGARY (*declaration*)
The Republic of Hungary

1. declines to observe the 9 year period of deferral on compliance as allowed for in Paragraphs 2 (c) and 3 (c) of the Technical Annex to Amended Protocol II, and even prior to the entry into force of Amended Protocol II intends to be bound by its implementation measures as stipulated therein, as well as the rules of procedure regarding record keeping, detectability, self-destruction and self-deactivation and perimeter marking as stipulated in the Technical Annex;
2. intends to eliminate and eventually destroy its entire stockpile of anti-personnel landmines by December 31, 2000 the latest, in addition to the already undertaken destruction of stockpiled landmines, as initiated in August of 1996 and completed in 40%;
3. refrains from the emplacement of anti-personnel landmines and, for the duration of their complete destruction, intends to designate a central storage facility to pool the remainder stock of anti-personnel landmines as a way to facilitate inspection by international monitors;
4. announces a total ban on the development, production, acquisition, export and transfer of all types of anti-personnel landmines;
5. refrains from the operational use of anti-personnel landmines, unless a policy-revision becomes necessitated by a significant deterioration in the national security environment of the country, in which case due attention shall be paid to compliance with laws governing international warfare;
6. stands ready to engage in implementing appropriate confidence building measures, as a way to be enabled to present the implementation of the measures announced unilaterally by the Republic of Hungary in the course of joint military, educational, and training and other cooperational activities conducted with other armed forces;
7. offers appropriate technical and training assistance to international organizations engaged in de-mining activities;
8. urges her neighbours and other countries in the region to seek unilateral or coordinated measures designed to achieve the total elimination of all types of anti-personnel landmines from the weapons arsenal of the countries in the region, and expresses her readiness to engage in further negotiations to advance this cause;
9. reiterates her commitment to promote the early conclusion of and wide adherence to an international convention stipulating a total and comprehensive ban on anti-personnel landmines, by reaffirming her determination to contribute actively to the success of international efforts furthering this goal.

IRELAND (*declarations*)
Article 1
It is the understanding of Ireland that the provisions of the amended Protocol which by their contents or nature may be applied also in peacetime, shall be observed at all times.

Article 2(3)
It is the understanding of Ireland that the word "primarily" is included in article 2, paragraph 3 of the amended Protocol to clarify that mines designed to be detonated by the presence, proximity or contact of a vehicle as opposed to a person, that are equipped with anti-handling devices, are not considered anti-personnel mines as a result of being so equipped.

ISRAEL (*declaration*)
Article 1
The declaration made by Israel upon accession to the [Convention], shall be equally applicable regarding the Amended Protocol II.

Article 2(3)
Israel understands that the word "primarily" is included in article 2, paragraph 3 of the Amended Protocol II, to clarify that mines designed to be detonated by the presence, proximity or contact of vehicles as opposed to persons, that are equipped with anti-handling devices are not considered Anti-personnel mines as a result of being so equipped.

Article 3(9)
Israel understands, regarding article 3, paragraph 9, that an area of land can itself be a legitimate military objective for the purpose of the use of landmines, if its neutralization or denial of its use, in the circumstances ruling at the time, offers a definite military advantage.

Article 4
It is the understanding of the State of Israel, regarding article 4 of the Amended Protocol II and the Technical Annex, that article 4 of the Amended Protocol II shall not apply to mines already emplaced. However, provisions of the Amended Protocol II, such as those regarding marking, monitoring and protection of areas containing mines under the control of a high contracting party, shall apply to all areas containing mines, regardless of when the mines were emplaced.

Article 5(2)(b)
Israel understands that article 5 paragraph 2(b) does not apply to the transfer of areas pursuant to peace treaties, agreements on the cessation of hostlilities, or as part of a peace process or steps leading thereto.

Article 7(1)(f)
Israel reserves the right to use other devices (as defined in Article 2(5) of the Amended Protocol II) to destroy any stock of food or drink that is judged likely to be used by an enemy military force, if due preparations are taken for the safety of the civilian population.

Article 11(7)
(a) Israel understands that the provision on technical assistance mentioned in article 11 paragraph 7, will be without prejudice to a High contracting Party's constitutional and other legal provisions.
(b) No provision of the .Amended Protocol II may be construed as affecting the discretion of the state of Israel to refuse assistance or to restrict or deny permission for the export equipment, material or scientific or technological information for any reason.

Article 14

(a) It is the understanding of the Government of the State of Israel that the compliance of commanders and others responsible for planning, deciding upon, or executing military actions to which the Convention on Conventional Weapons and its Protocols apply, cannot be judged on the basis of information which subsequently comes to light, but must be assessed on the basis of the information available to them at the time that such actions were taken.

(b) Article 14 of the Amended Protocol II (insofar as it relates to penal sanctions) shall apply only in a situation in which an individual

1) knew, or should have known, that his action was prohibited under the Amended Protocol II,
2) intended to kill or cause serious injury to a civilian; and
3) knew, or should have known, that the person he intended to kill or cause serious injury to was a civilian.

(c) Israel understands that the provisions of article 14 of the Amended Protocol II relating to penal sanctions refer to measures by authorities of States Parties to the Protocol and do not authorize the trial of any person before an international criminal tribunal. Israel shall not recognize the jurisiction of any international tribunal to prosecute an Israel citizen for violation of the Protocol or the Convention on Conventional Weapons.

General

Israel understands that nothing in the Amended Protocol II may be construed as restriction or affecting in any way non-lethal weapon technology that is designed to temporarily disable, stun, signal the presence of a person, or operate in any other fashion, but not to cause permanent incapacity

ITALY (*declarations*)

Article 1

It is the understanding of Italy that the provisions of the amended Protocol which by their contents or nature may be applied also in peacetime, shall be observed at all times.

Article 2

Under article 2 of the amended Protocol II, in order to fully address the humanitarian concerns raised by anti-personnel land-mines, the Italian Parliament has enacted and brought into force a legislation containing a far more stringent definition of those devices. In this regard, while reaffirming its commitment to promote the further development of international humanitarian law, the Italian Government confirms its understanding that the word "primarily" is included in article 2, paragraph 3 of the amended Protocol II to clarify that mines designed to be detonated by the presence, proximity or contact of a vehicle as opposed to a person, that are equipped with anti-handling devices, are not considered anti-personnel mines as a result of being so equipped.

Article 5, para. 2(b)

Under article 5 of the amended Protocol II, it is the understanding of the Italian Government that article 5 (paragraph 2 b) does not preclude agreement in connection with peace treaties and related agreements among concerned states to allocate responsibilities under this paragraph in another manner which reflects the spirit and purpose of the article.

LIECHTENSTEIN (*declaration in respect of Article 1*)

It is the understanding of Liechtenstein that the provisions of the amended Protocol which by their contents or nature may be applied also in peacetime, shall be observed at all times.

NETHERLANDS (*declarations*)

Article 1, para. 2

The Government of the Kingdom of the Netherlands takes the view that the provisions of the Protocol which, given their content or nature, can also be applied in peacetime, must be observed in all circumstances.

With regard to
The Government of the Kingdom of the Netherlands takes the view that the word "primarily" means only that mines that are designed to be exploded by the presence, proximity or contact of a vehicle and that are equipped with an anti-handling device are not regarded as anti-personnel mines because of that device.

Article 2, para. 6
The Government of the Kingdom of the Netherlands takes the view that a specific area of land may also be a military objective if, because of its location or other reasons specified in paragraph six, its total or partial destruction, capture, or neutralization in the circumstances ruling at the time, offers a definitive military advantage.

Article 3, para. 8
The Government of the Kingdom of the Netherlands takes the view that military advantage refers to the advantage anticipated from the attack considered as a whole and not only from isolated or particular parts of the attack.

Article 12, para. 2
The Government of the Kingdom of the Netherlands takes the view that the words "as far as it is able" mean "as far as it is technically able".

PAKISTAN (*declarations*)
Article 1
- It is understood that for the purposes of interpretation the provisions of article 1 take precedence over provisions or undertakings in any other article.
- The rights and obligations arising from situations described in article 1 are absolute and immutable and the observance of any other provision of the Protocol cannot be construed, either directly or indirectly, as affecting the right of peoples struggling against colonial or other forms of alien domination and foreign occupation in the exercise of their inalienable right of self-determination, as enshrined in the Charter of the United Nations and the Declaration on Principles of International Law Concerning Friendly Relations and Co-operation among states in accordance with the Charter of the United Nations.
- The provisions of the Protocol must be observed at all times, depending on the circumstances.

Article 2 (para. 3)
- In the context of the word "primarily", it is understood that such anti-tank mines which use anti-personnel mines as a fuse but do not explode on contact with a person are not anti-personnel mines.

Article 3 (para. 9)
- It is understood that an area of land can itself be a legitimate military objective for the purposes of the use of landmines, if its neutralisation or denial, in the circumstances ruling at the time, offers a definite military advantage.

Sub-paras 2(c) and 3(c) of Technical Annex
- It is declared that compliance with sub-paras 2(b) and 3(a) and (b) is deferred as provided for in sub-paras 2(c) and 3(c), respectively.

REPUBLIC OF KOREA (*reservation and declarations*)
I. *Reservation*
With respect to the application of Protocol II to the 1980 Convention, as amended on 3 May 1996 ("Amended Mines Protocol"), the Republic of Korea reserves the right to use a small number of mines prohibited under this Protocol exclusively for training and testing purposes.

II. *Declarations*
It is the understanding of the Republic of Korea that
1. With respect to Article 3(8)(a) of the Amended Mines Protocol, in case there is an evidentindication that an object which is normally dedicated to civilian purposes,

such as a place of worship, a house or other dwelling or a school, is being used to make an effective contribution to military action, it shall be considered as a miltary object.
2. Article 4 and the Technical Annex of the Amended Mines Protocol do not require the removal or replacement of mines that have alreasdy been laid.
3. "Cessation of active hostilities" provided for in Articles 9(2) and 10(1) of the Amended Mines Protocol is interpreted as meaning the time when the present Armistice regime on the Korean peninsula has been transformed into a peace regime, establishing a stable peace on the Korean peninsula.
4. Any decision by any military commander, military personnel, or any other person responsible for planning, authorizing, or executing military action shall only be judged on the basis of that person's assessment of the information reasonably available to the person at the time the person planned, authorized or executed that action under review, and shall not be judged on the basis of information that comes to light after the action under review was taken.

SOUTH AFRICA (*declarations*)
Article 1
It is the understanding of South Africa that the provisions of the amended Protocol which by their contents or nature may be applied also in peacetime, shall be observed at all times.

Article 2(3)
It is the understanding of South Africa that the word "primarily" is included in article 2, paragraph 3 of the amended Protocol to clarify that mines designed to be detonated by the presence, proximity or contact of a vehicle as opposed to a person, that are equipped with anti-handling devices, are not considered anti-personnel mines as a result of being so equipped.

Article 5 para. 2 (b)
It is understood that Article 5 (2) (b) does not preclude agreement among the States concerned, in connection with peace treaties or similar arrangements, to alloctate responsibilities under this paragraph in another manner which nevertheless respects the essential spirit and purpose of the Article.

SWEDEN (*declarations*)
Articles 1 and 2)
Sweden intends to apply the Protocol also in time of peace.

Article 2(3)
It is the understanding of Sweden that the word "primarily" is included in article 2, paragraph 3 of the amended Protocol to clarify that mines designed to be detonated by the presence, proximity or contact of a vehicle as opposed to a person, that are equipped with anti-handling devices, are not considered anti-personnel mines as a result of being so equipped.

Article 5, para. 2
Sweden is of the opinion that the obligations ensuing from article 5, paragraph 2 shall not be interpreted to the effect that the High Contracting Parties or parties in a conflict are prevented from entering into an agreement allowing another party to conduct mine clearance.

SWITZERLAND (*declaration in respect of Article 2(3)*)
Switzerland interprets the definition of "anti-personnel mine" as excluding any mine designed to explode in the presence or proximity of, or upon contact with, a vehicle, when such mine is equipped with an anti-handling device.

UKRAINE (*declaration*)
Ukraine declares that it shall defer implementation of the provisions of subparagraphs 3(a) and 3(b) of the technical annex for a period of nine years from the date on which this Protocol enters into force.

UNITED KINGDOM OF GREAT BRITAIN AND NORTHERN IRELAND (*declarations*)
(a) the [declaration conveying consent to be bound by Protocols I, II and III to the Convention on Prohibitions or Restrictions on the Use of Certain Conventional Weapons which may be Deemed to be Excessively Injurious or to have Indiscriminate Effects, concluded at Geneva on 10 October 1980], in so far as it applies to Protocol II to the [1980] Convention, continues to apply to Protocol II as amended;
(b) the [declaration dated 28 January 1998 accompanying the United Kingdom's ratification of Additional Protocol I to the Geneva Conventions of 12 August 1949 relating to the Protection of Victims of Armed Conflicts, opened for signature at Geneva on 12 December 1977], in so far as it is relevant, also applies to the provisions of Protocol II as amended;
(c) nothing in the present declaration or in Protocol II as amended shall be taken as limiting the obligations of the United Kingdom under the [Convention on the Prohibition of the Use, Stockpiling, Production and Transfer of Anti-Personnel Mines and on their Destruction concluded at Oslo on 18 September 1997 (the "Ottawa Convention")] nor its rights in relation to other Parties to that Convention;
(d) Article 2(14) is interpreted to have the same meaning as Article 2(3) of the "Ottawa Convention";
(e) the references in Article 12(2) to "force" and "mission" are interpreted as including forces and missions authorised by the United Nations Security Council under Chapter VII or Chapter VIII of the Charter of the United Nations which are deployed by a regional arrangement or agency. This applies to all such forces or missions, whether or not they include contingents contributed by non-member States of the regional arrangement or agency.

UNITED STATES OF AMERICA
I. The Senate's advice and consent is subject to the following reservation:
The United States reserves the right to use other devices (as defined in Article 2(5) of the Amended Mines Protocol) to destroy any stock of food or drink that is judged likely to be used by an enemy military force, if due precautions are taken for the safety of the civilian population.
II. The Senate's advice and consent is subject to the following understandings:
(1) UNITED STATES COMPLIANCE,
– The United States understands that –
(A) any decision by any military commander, military personnel, or any other person responsible for planning, authorizing, or executing military action shall only be judged on the basis of that person's assessment of the information reasonably available to the person at the time the person planned, authorized, or executed the action under review, and shall not be judged on the basis of information that comes to light after the action under review was taken; and
(B) Article 14 of the Amended Mines Protocol (insofar as it relates to penal sanctions) shall apply only in a situation in which an individual –
(i) knew, or should have known, that his action was prohibited under the Amended Mines Protocol;
(ii) intended to kill or cause serious injury to a civilian; and
(iii) knew or should have known, that the person he intended to kill or cause serious injury was a civilian.

(2) EFFECTIVE EXCLUSION.
– The United States understands that, for the purposes of Article 5(6)(b) of the Amended Mines Protocol, the maintenance of observation over avenues of approach where mines subject to that Article are deployed constitutes one acceptable form of monitoring to ensure the effective exclusion of civilians.

(3) HISTORIC MONUMENTS.
– The United states understands that Article 7(1)(i) of the Amended Mines Protocol refers only to a limited class of objects that, because of their clearly recognizable characteristics and because of their widely recognized importance, constitute a part of the cultural or spiritual heritage of peoples.

(4) LEGITIMATE MILITARY OBJECTIVES.
– The United States understands that an area of land itself can be a legitimate military objective for the purpose of the use of landmines, if its neutralization or denial, in the circumstances applicable at the time, offers a military advantage.

(5) PEACE TREATIES.
– The United States understands that the allocation of responsibilities for landmines in Article 5(2)(b) of the Amended Mines Protocol does not preclude agreement, in connection with peace treaties or similar arrangements, to allocate responsibilities under that Article in a manner that respects the essential spirit and purpose of the Article.

(6) BOOBY-TRAPS AND OTHER DEVICES.
– For the purposes of the Amended Mines Protocol, the United States understands that –
  (A) the prohibition contained in Article 7(2) of the Amended Mines Protocol does not preclude the expedient adaptation or adaptation in advance of other objects for use as booby-traps or other devices;
  (B) a trip-wired hand grenade shall be considered a "booby-trap" under Article 2(4) of the Amended Mines Protocol and shall not be considered a "mine" or an "anti-personnel mine" under Article 2(1) or Article 2(3), respectively; and
  (C) none of the provisions of the Amended Mines Protocol, including Article 2(5), applies to hand grenades other than trip-wired hand grenades.

(7) NON-LETHAL CAPABILITIES.
– The United States understands that nothing in the Amended Mines Protocol may be construed as restricting or affecting in any way non-lethal weapon technology that is designed to temporarily disable, stun, signal the presence of a person, or operate in any other fashion, but not to cause permanent incapacity.

(8) INTERNATIONAL TRIBUNAL JURISDICTION.
– The United States understands that the provisions of Article 14 of the Amended Mines Protocol relating to penal sanctions refer to measures by the authorities of States Parties to the Protocol and do not authorize the trial of any person before an international criminal tribunal. The United States shall not recognize the jurisdiction of any international tribunal to prosecute a United States citizen for a violation of the Protocol or the Convention on Conventional Weapons.

(9) TECHNICAL COOPERATION AND ASSISTANCE.
– The United States understands that –
  (A) no provision of the Protocol may be construed as affecting the discretion of the United States to refuse assistance or to restrict or deny permission for the export of equipment, material, or scientific or technological information for any reason; and
  (B) the Amended Mines Protocol may not be used as a pretext for the transfer of weapons technology or the provision of assistance to the military mining or military counter-mining capabilities of a State Party to the Protocol.

V. SIGNATURES, RATIFICATIONS AND ACCESSIONS TO THE PROTOCOL ON BLINDING LASER WEAPONS (PROTOCOL IV)[10]

State	*Consent to be bound*
Albania	28 August 2002
Argentina	21 October 1998
Australia	22 August 1997 *Dec.*
Austria	27 July 1998 *Dec.*
Bangladesh	6 September 2000
Belarus	13 September 2000
Belgium	10 March 1999 *Dec.*
Bolivia	21 September 2001
Bosnia and Herzegovina	11 October 2001
Brazil	4 October 1999
Bulgaria	3 December 1998
Cambodia	25 March 1997
Canada	5 January 1998 *Dec.*
Cape Verde	16 September 1997
China	4 November 1998
Colombia	6 March 2000
Costa Rica	17 December 1998
Croatia	25 April 2002
Czech Republic	10 August 1998
Denmark	30 April 1997
El Salvador	26 January 2000
Estonia	20 April 2000
Finland	11 January 1996
France	30 June 1998
Germany	27 June 1997 *Dec.*
Greece	5 August 1997 *Dec.*
Guatamala	30 August 2002
Holy See	22 July 1997
Hungary	30 January 1998
India	2 September 1999
Ireland	27 March 1997 *Dec.*
Israel	30 October 2000 *Dec.*
Italy	13 January 1999 *Dec.*
Japan	10 June 1997
Latvia	11 March 1998
Liechtenstein	19 November 1997 *Dec.*
Lithuania	3 June 1998
Luxembourg	5 August 1999
Maldives	7 September 2000
Mali	24 October 2001
Mauritius	24 December 2002

[10] Based on the indications in *Multilateral Treaties Deposited with the Secretary-General, New York, United Nations*, (ST/LEG/SER.E) as available on http://untreaty.un.org.

In keeping with the depositary practice followed in similar cases, the Secretary-General proposed to receive the declaration for deposit in the absence of any objection on the part of the contracting states, either to the deposit itself or to the procedure envisaged, within a period of 90 days from the date of its circulation (i.e. 21 July 1998). None of the contracting parties to the Protocol having notified the Secretary-General of an objection within the 90 days period, the declaration was deemed to have been accepted for deposit upon the expiration of the 90-day period in question, i.e. on 19 October 1998.

State	*Consent to be bound*
Mexico	10 March 1998
Mongolia	6 April 1999
Morrocco	19 March 2002
Nauru	12 November 2001
Netherlands[11]	25 March 1999 *Dec.*
New Zealand	8 January 1998
Nicaragua	5 December 2000
Norway	20 April 1998
Pakistan	5 December 2000
Panama	26 March 1997
Peru	3 July 1997
Philippines	12 June 1997
Portugal	12 November 2001
Republic of Moldova	8 September 2000
Russian Federation	9 September 1999
Seychelles	8 June 2000
Slovakia	30 November 1999
Slovenia	3 December 2002
South Africa	26 June 1998 *Dec.*
Spain	19 January 1998
Sweden	15 January 1997 *Dec.*
Switzerland	24 March 1998
Tajikistan	12 October 1999
United Kingdom of Great Britain and Northern Ireland	11 February 1999 *Dec.*
Uruguay	18 August 1998
Uzbekistan	29 September 1997

VI. RESERVATIONS AND DECLARATIONS TO PROTOCOL ON BLINDING LASER WEAPONS (PROTOCOL IV)[12]

AUSTRALIA (*declaration*)
It is the understanding of the Government of Australia that the provisions of Protocol IV shall apply in all circumstances.

AUSTRIA (*declaration in relation to Article 1*)
It is the understanding of Austria that the provisions of the Additional Protocol which by their contents or nature may also be applied in peacetime, shall be observed at all times.

BELGIUM (*declaration*)
It is the understanding of the Government of the Kingdom of Belgium that the provisions of Protocol IV which by their contents or nature may also be applied in peacetime, shall be observed at all times.

[11] For the Kingdom in Europe.

[12] Based on a communication received on 29 June 1999 from the United Nations Treaty Section and on the indications in *Multilateral Treaties Deposited with the Secretary-General, New York, United Nations* (ST/LEG/SER.E) as available on http://www.untreaty.un.org.
Unless otherwise indicated, the declarations and reservations were made upon acceptance.

CANADA (*declaration in relation to Article 1 19 October 1998*)
It is the understanding of Canada that the provisions of the Additional Protocol which by their contents or nature may also be applied in peacetime, shall be observed at all times.

GERMANY (*declaration in relation to Article 1*)
It is the understanding of Germany that the provisions of the Additional Protocol which by their contents or nature may also be applied in peacetime, shall be observed at all times.

GREECE (*declaration in relation to Article 1*)
It is the understanding of Greece that the provisions of the Additional Protocol which by their contents or nature may also be applied in peacetime, shall be observed at all times.

IRELAND (*declaration in relation to Article 1*)
It is the understanding of Ireland that the provisions of the Additional Protocol which by their contents or nature may also be applied in peacetime, shall be observed at all times.

ISRAEL (*declaration*)
With reference to the scope of application defined in Article 1 of the Convention, the Government of the State of Israel will apply the provisions of the Protocol on Blinding Laser Weapons as well as the Convention and those annexed Protocols to which Israel has agreed to become bound, to all armed conflicts involving regular armed forces of States referred to in article 2 common to the Geneva Convention of 12 August 1949, as well as to all armed conflicts referred to in Article 3 common to the Geneva Convention of 12 August 1949.

ITALY (*declaration in relation to Article 1*)
It is the understanding of Italy that the provisions of the Additional Protocol which by their contents or nature may also be applied in peacetime, shall be observed at all times.

LIECHTENSTEIN (*declaration in relation to Article 1*)
It is the understanding of Liechtenstein that the provisions of the Additional Protocol which by their contents or nature may also be applied in peacetime, shall be observed at all times.

NETHERLANDS (*declaration with regard to Article 1*)
The Government of the Kingdom of the Netherlands takes the view that the provisions of Protocol IV which, given their content or nature, can also be applied in peacetime must be observed in all circumstances.

SOUTH AFRICA (*declaration*)
It is the understanding of the Government of South Africa that the provisions of Protocol IV shall apply in all circumstances.

SWEDEN (*declarations*)
- Sweden intends to apply the Protocol to all types of armed conflict;
- Sweden intends to pursue an international agreement by which the provisions of the Protocol shall be applicable to all types of armed conflict;
- Sweden has since long strived for explicit prohibition of the use of blinding laser which would risk causing permanent blindness to soldiers. Such an effect, in Sweden's view is contrary to the principle of international law prohibiting means and methods of warfare which cause unnecessary suffering.

SWITZERLAND (*declaration*)
It is the understanding of the Government of Switzerland that the provisions of Protocol IV shall apply in all circumstances.

UNITED KINGDOM OF GREAT BRITAIN AND NORTHERN IRELAND (*declaration*)
In relation to Protocol IV, the Government of the United Kingdom declare that their application of its provisions will not be limited to the situations set out in Article 1 of the [1980] Convention.

No. 21

RESOLUTION ON SMALL-CALIBRE WEAPON SYSTEMS

Adopted by the United Nations Conference on Prohibitions or Restrictions on the Use of Certain Conventional Weapons, 28 September 1979

INTRODUCTORY NOTE: The UN Conference of 1979 and 1980 did not reach agreement on a Protocol on small-calibre weapon systems. The resolution reprinted below was adopted at the 1979 session of the Conference and annexed to the Final Act of 1980 as Appendix E.

AUTHENTIC TEXTS: See indications under *No. 19.*

TEXT PUBLISHED IN: See indications under *No. 19.*

* * *

The United Nations Conference on Prohibitions or Restrictions of Use of Certain Conventional Weapons,

Recalling *United Nations General Assembly resolution 32/152 of 19 December 1977,*

Aware *of the continuous development of small-calibre weapon systems (i.e., arms and projectiles),*

Anxious *to prevent an unnecessary increase of the injurious effects of such weapon systems,*

Recalling *the agreement embodied in The Hague Declaration of 29 July 1899, to abstain, in international armed conflict, from the use of bullets which expand or flatten easily in the human body,*

Convinced *that it is desirable to establish accurately the wounding effects of current and new generations of small calibre weapon systems including the various parameters that affect the energy transfer and the wounding mechanism of such systems,*

1. Takes note *with appreciation of the intensive research carried out nationally and internationally in the area of wound ballistics, in particular relating to small-calibre weapon systems, as documented during the Conference;*
2. Considers *that this research and the international discussion on the subject has led to an increased understanding of the wounding effects of small-calibre weapon systems and of the parameters involved;*
3. Believes *that such research, including testing of small-calibre weapon systems, should be continued with a view to developing standardized assessment methodology relative to ballistic parameters and medical effects of such systems;*
4. Invites *Governments to carry out further research, jointly or individually on the wounding effects of small-calibre weapon systems and to communicate, where possible, their findings and conclusions;*
5. Welcomes *the announcement that an international scientific symposium on wound ballistics will be held in Gothenburg, Sweden, in late 1980 or in*

TABLE OF CONTENTS

* * *

[1] For the text of the Annexes, see the United Nations Document CD/CW/WP.400/Rev.2, pp. 59–221. See also OPCW website: www.opcw.nl/ptshome.htm (Engl., French, Span.).

Preamble

The States Parties to this Convention,

Determined to act with a view to achieving effective progress towards general and complete disarmament under strict and effective international control, including the prohibition and elimination of all types of weapons of mass destruction,

Desiring to contribute to the realization of the purposes and principles of the Charter of the United Nations,

Recalling that the General Assembly of the United Nations has repeatedly condemned all actions contrary to the principles and objectives of the Protocol for the Prohibition of the Use in War of Asphyxiating, Poisonous or Other Gases, and of Bacteriological Methods of Warfare, signed at Geneva on 17 June 1925 (the Geneva Protocol of 1925),

Recognizing that this Convention reaffirms principles and objectives of and obligations assumed under the Geneva Protocol of 1925, and the Convention on the Prohibition of the Development, Production and Stockpiling of Bacteriological (Biological) and Toxin Weapons and on their Destruction signed at London, Moscow and Washington on 10 April 1972,

Bearing in mind the objective contained in Article IX of the Convention on the Prohibition of the Development, Production and Stockpiling of Bacteriological (Biological) and Toxin Weapons and on their Destruction,

Determined for the sake of all mankind, to exclude completely the possibility of the use of chemical weapons, through the implementation of the provisions of this Convention, thereby complementing the obligations assumed under the Geneva Protocol of 1925,

Recognizing the prohibition, embodied in the pertinent agreements and relevant principles of international law, of the use of herbicides as a method of warfare,

Considering that achievements in the field of chemistry should be used exclusively for the benefit of mankind,

Desiring to promote free trade in chemicals as well as international cooperation and exchange of scientific and technical information in the field of chemical activities for purposes not prohibited under this Convention in order to enhance the economic and technological development of all States Parties,

Convinced that the complete and effective prohibition of the development, production, acquisition, stockpiling, retention, transfer and use of chemical weapons, and their destruction, represent a necessary step towards the achievement of these common objectives,

Have agreed as follows:

Art. I. General Obligations

1. Each State Party to this Convention undertakes never under any circumstances:
   (a) To develop, produce, otherwise acquire, stockpile or retain chemical weapons, or transfer, directly or indirectly, chemical weapons to anyone;
   (b) To use chemical weapons;
   (c) To engage in any military preparations to use chemical weapons;
   (d) To assist, encourage or induce, in any way, anyone to engage in any activity prohibited to a State Party under this Convention.

2. Each State Party undertakes to destroy chemical weapons it owns or possesses, or that are located in any place under its jurisdiction or control, in accordance with the provisions of this Convention.
3. Each State Party undertakes to destroy all chemical weapons it abandoned on the territory of another State Party, in accordance with the provisions of this Convention.
4. Each State Party undertakes to destroy any chemical weapons production facilities it owns or possesses, or that are located in any place under its jurisdiction or control, in accordance with the provisions of this Convention.
5. Each State Party undertakes not to use riot control agents as a method of warfare.

Art. II. Definitions and Criteria

For the purposes of this Convention:

1. "Chemical Weapons" means the following, together or separately:
   (a) Toxic chemicals and their precursors, except where intended for purposes not prohibited under this Convention, as long as the types and quantities are consistent with such purposes;
   (b) Munitions and devices, specifically designed to cause death or other harm through the toxic properties of those toxic chemicals specified in subparagraph (a), which would be released as a result of the employment of such munitions and devices;
   (c) Any equipment specifically designed for use directly in connection with the employment of munitions and devices specified in subparagraph (b).
2. "Toxic Chemical" means:
   Any chemical which through its chemical action on life processes can cause death, temporary incapacitation or permanent harm to humans or animals. This includes all such chemicals, regardless of their origin or of their method of production, and regardless of whether they are produced in facilities, in munitions or elsewhere.
   (For the purpose of implementing this Convention, toxic chemicals which have been identified for the application of verification measures are listed in Schedules contained in the Annex on Chemicals.)
3. "Precursor" means:
   Any chemical reactant which takes part at any stage in the production by whatever method of a toxic chemical. This includes any key component of a binary or multicomponent chemical system.
   (For the purpose of implementing this Convention, precursors which have been identified for the application of verification measures are listed in Schedules contained in the Annex on Chemicals.)
4. "Key Component of Binary or Multicomponent Chemical Systems" (hereinafter referred to as "key component") means:
   The precursor which plays the most important role in determining the toxic properties of the final product and reacts rapidly with other chemicals in the binary or multicomponent system.
5. "Old Chemical Weapons" means:
   (a) Chemical weapons which were produced before 1925; or

(b) Chemical weapons produced in the period between 1925 and 1946 that have deteriorated to such extent that they can no longer be used as chemical weapons.

6. "Abandoned Chemical Weapons" means:
Chemical weapons, including old chemical weapons, abandoned by a State after 1 January 1925 on the territory of another State without the consent of the latter.

7. "Riot Control Agent" means:
Any chemical not listed in a Schedule, which can produce rapidly in humans sensory irritation or disabling physical effects which disappear within a short time following termination of exposure.

8. "Chemical Weapons Production Facility":

(a) Means any equipment, as well as any building housing such equipment, that was designed, constructed or used at any time since 1 January 1946:

    (i) As part of the stage in the production of chemicals ("final technological stage") where the material flows would contain, when the equipment is in operation:

        (1) Any chemical listed in Schedule 1 in the Annex on Chemicals; or

        (2) Any other chemical that has no use, above 1 tonne per year on the territory of a State Party or in any other place under the jurisdiction or control of a State Party, for purposes not prohibited under this Convention, but can be used for chemical weapons purposes; or

    (ii) For filling chemical weapons, including, inter alia, the filling of chemicals listed in Schedule 1 into munitions, devices or bulk storage containers; the filling of chemicals into containers that form part of assembled binary munitions and devices or into chemical submunitions that form part of assembled unitary munitions and devices, and the loading of the containers and chemical submunitions into the respective munitions and devices;

(b) Does not mean:

    (i) Any facility having a production capacity for synthesis of chemicals specified in subparagraph (a) (i) that is less than 1 tonne;

    (ii) Any facility in which a chemical specified in subparagraph (a) (i) is or was produced as an unavoidable byproduct of activities for purposes not prohibited under this Convention, provided that the chemical does not exceed 3 per cent of the total product and that the facility is subject to declaration and inspection under the Annex on Implementation and Verification (hereinafter referred to as "Verification Annex"); or

    (iii) The single small-scale facility for production of chemicals listed in Schedule 1 for purposes not prohibited under this Convention as referred to in Part VI of the Verification Annex.

9. "Purposes Not Prohibited Under this Convention" means:

(a) Industrial, agricultural, research, medical, pharmaceutical or other peaceful purposes;

(b) Protective purposes, namely those purposes directly related to protection against toxic chemicals and to protection against chemical weapons;

(c) Military purposes not connected with the use of chemical weapons and not dependent on the use of the toxic properties of chemicals as a method of warfare;

(d) Law enforcement including domestic riot control purposes.

10. "Production Capacity" means:
The annual quantitative potential for manufacturing a specific chemical based on the technological process actually used or, if the process is not yet operational, planned to be used at the relevant facility. It shall be deemed to be equal to the nameplate capacity or, if the nameplate capacity is not available, to the design capacity. The nameplate capacity is the product output under conditions optimized for maximum quantity for the production facility, as demonstrated by one or more test-runs. The design capacity is the corresponding theoretically calculated product output.

11. "Organization" means the Organization for the Prohibition of Chemical Weapons established pursuant to Article VIII of this Convention.

12. For the purposes of Article VI:
    (a) "Production" of a chemical means its formation through chemical reaction;
    (b) "Processing" of a chemical means a physical process, such as formulation, extraction and purification, in which a chemical is not converted into another chemical;
    (c) "Consumption" of a chemical means its conversion into another chemical via a chemical reaction.

Art. III. Declarations

1. Each State Party shall submit to the Organization, not later than 30 days after this Convention enters into force for it, the following declarations, in which it shall:
    (a) With respect to chemical weapons:
        (i) Declare whether it owns or possesses any chemical weapons, or whether there are any chemical weapons located in any place under its jurisdiction or control;
        (ii) Specify the precise location, aggregate quantity and detailed inventory of chemical weapons it owns or possesses, or that are located in any place under its jurisdiction or control, in accordance with Part IV (A), paragraphs 1 to 3, of the Verification Annex, except for those chemical weapons referred to in sub-subparagraph (iii);
        (iii) Report any chemical weapons on its territory that are owned and possessed by another State and located in any place under the jurisdiction or control of another State, in accordance with Part IV (A), paragraph 4, of the Verification Annex;
        (iv) Declare whether it has transferred or received, directly or indirectly, any chemical weapons since 1 January 1946 and specify the transfer or receipt of such weapons, in accordance with Part IV (A), paragraph 5, of the Verification Annex;
        (v) Provide its general plan for destruction of chemical weapons that it owns or possesses, or that are located in any place under its

jurisdiction or control, in accordance with Part IV (A), paragraph 6, of the Verification Annex;

(b) With respect to old chemical weapons and abandoned chemical weapons:

(i) Declare whether it has on its territory old chemical weapons and provide all available information in accordance with Part IV (B), paragraph 3, of the Verification Annex;

(ii) Declare whether there are abandoned chemical weapons on its territory and provide all available information in accordance with Part IV (B), paragraph 8, of the Verification Annex;

(iii) Declare whether it has abandoned chemical weapons on the territory of other States and provide all available information in accordance with Part IV (B), paragraph 10, of the Verification Annex;

(c) With respect to chemical weapons production facilities:

(i) Declare whether it has or has had any chemical weapons production facility under its ownership or possession, or that is or has been located in any place under its jurisdiction or control at any time since 1 January 1946;

(ii) Specify any chemical weapons production facility it has or has had under its ownership or possession or that is or has been located in any place under its jurisdiction or control at any time since 1 January 1946, in accordance with Part V, paragraph 1, of the Verification Annex, except for those facilities referred to in subsubparagraph (iii);

(iii) Report any chemical weapons production facility on its territory that another State has or has had under its ownership and possession and that is or has been located in any place under the jurisdiction or control of another State at any time since 1 January 1946, in accordance with Part V, paragraph 2, of the Verification Annex;

(iv) Declare whether it has transferred or received, directly or indirectly, any equipment for the production of chemical weapons since 1 January 1946 and specify the transfer or receipt of such equipment, in accordance with Part V, paragraphs 3 to 5, of the Verification Annex;

(v) Provide its general plan for destruction of any chemical weapons production facility it owns or possesses, or that is located in any place under its jurisdiction or control, in accordance with Part V, paragraph 6, of the Verification Annex;

(vi) Specify actions to be taken for closure of any chemical weapons production facility it owns or possesses, or that is located in any place under its jurisdiction or control, in accordance with Part V, paragraph 1 (i), of the Verification Annex;

(vii) Provide its general plan for any temporary conversion of any chemical weapons production facility it owns or possesses, or that is located in any place under its jurisdiction or control, into a chemical weapons destruction facility, in accordance with Part V, paragraph 7, of the Verification Annex;

(d) With respect to other facilities:
Specify the precise location, nature and general scope of activities of any facility or establishment under its ownership or possession, or located in any place under its jurisdiction or control, and that has been designed, constructed or used since 1 January 1946 primarily for development of chemical weapons. Such declaration shall include, inter alia, laboratories and test and evaluation sites;

(e) With respect to riot control agents: Specify the chemical name, structural formula and Chemical Abstracts Service (CAS) registry number, if assigned, of each chemical it holds for riot control purposes. This declaration shall be updated not later than 30 days after any change becomes effective.

2. The provisions of this Article and the relevant provisions of Part IV of the Verification Annex shall not, at the discretion of a State Party, apply to chemical weapons buried on its territory before 1 January 1977 and which remain buried, or which had been dumped at sea before 1 January 1985.

Art. IV. Chemical Weapons

1. The provisions of this Article and the detailed procedures for its implementation shall apply to all chemical weapons owned or possessed by a State Party, or that are located in any place under its jurisdiction or control, except old chemical weapons and abandoned chemical weapons to which Part IV (B) of the Verification Annex applies.
2. Detailed procedures for the implementation of this Article are set forth in the Verification Annex.
3. All locations at which chemical weapons specified in paragraph 1 are stored or destroyed shall be subject to systematic verification through on-site inspection and monitoring with on-site instruments, in accordance with Part IV (A) of the Verification Annex.
4. Each State Party shall, immediately after the declaration under Article III, paragraph 1 (a), has been submitted, provide access to chemical weapons specified in paragraph 1 for the purpose of systematic verification of the declaration through on-site inspection. Thereafter, each State Party shall not remove any of these chemical weapons, except to a chemical weapons destruction facility. It shall provide access to such chemical weapons, for the purpose of systematic on-site verification.
5. Each State Party shall provide access to any chemical weapons destruction facilities and their storage areas, that it owns or possesses, or that are located in any place under its jurisdiction or control, for the purpose of systematic verification through on-site inspection and monitoring with on-site instruments.
6. Each State Party shall destroy all chemical weapons specified in paragraph 1 pursuant to the Verification Annex and in accordance with the agreed rate and sequence of destruction (hereinafter referred to as “order of destruction”). Such destruction shall begin not later than two years after this Convention enters into force for it and shall finish not later than 10 years after entry into force of this Convention. A State Party is not precluded from destroying such chemical weapons at a faster rate.

7. Each State Party shall:
   (a) Submit detailed plans for the destruction of chemical weapons specified in paragraph 1 not later than 60 days before each annual destruction period begins, in accordance with Part IV(A), paragraph 29, of the Verification Annex; the detailed plans shall encompass all stocks to be destroyed during the next annual destruction period;
   (b) Submit declarations annually regarding the implementation of its plans for destruction of chemical weapons specified in paragraph 1, not later than 60 days after the end of each annual destruction period; and
   (c) Certify, not later than 30 days after the destruction process has been completed, that all chemical weapons specified in paragraph 1 have been destroyed.
8. If a State ratifies or accedes to this Convention after the 10-year period for destruction set forth in paragraph 6, it shall destroy chemical weapons specified in paragraph 1 as soon as possible. The order of destruction and procedures for stringent verification for such a State Party shall be determined by the Executive Council.
9. Any chemical weapons discovered by a State Party after the initial declaration of chemical weapons shall be reported, secured and destroyed in accordance with Part IV (A) of the Verification Annex.
10. Each State Party, during transportation, sampling, storage and destruction of chemical weapons, shall assign the highest priority to ensuring the safety of people and to protecting the environment. Each State Party shall transport, sample, store and destroy chemical weapons in accordance with its national standards for safety and emissions.
11. Any State Party which has on its territory chemical weapons that are owned or possessed by another State, or that are located in any place under the jurisdiction or control of another State, shall make the fullest efforts to ensure that these chemical weapons are removed from its territory not later than one year after this Convention enters into force for it. If they are not removed within one year, the State Party may request the Organization and other States Parties to provide assistance in the destruction of these chemical weapons.
12. Each State Party undertakes to cooperate with other States Parties that request information or assistance on a bilateral basis or through the Technical Secretariat regarding methods and technologies for the safe and efficient destruction of chemical weapons.
13. In carrying out verification activities pursuant to this Article and Part IV (A) of the Verification Annex, the Organization shall consider measures to avoid unnecessary duplication of bilateral or multilateral agreements on verification of chemical weapons storage and their destruction among States Parties.

    To this end, the Executive Council shall decide to limit verification to measures complementary to those undertaken pursuant to such a bilateral or multilateral agreement, if it considers that:

   (a) Verification provisions of such an agreement are consistent with the verification provisions of this Article and Part IV (A) of the Verification Annex;

(b) Implementation of such an agreement provides for sufficient assurance of compliance with the relevant provisions of this Convention; and
(c) Parties to the bilateral or multilateral agreement keep the Organization fully informed about their verification activities.

14. If the Executive Council takes a decision pursuant to paragraph 13, the Organization shall have the right to monitor the implementation of the bilateral or multilateral agreement.
15. Nothing in paragraphs 13 and 14 shall affect the obligation of a State Party to provide declarations pursuant to Article III, this Article and Part IV (A) of the Verification Annex.
16. Each State Party shall meet the costs of destruction of chemical weapons it is obliged to destroy. It shall also meet the costs of verification of storage and destruction of these chemical weapons unless the Executive Council decides otherwise. If the Executive Council decides to limit verification measures of the Organization pursuant to paragraph 13, the costs of complementary verification and monitoring by the Organization shall be paid in accordance with the United Nations scale of assessment, as specified in Article VIII, paragraph 7.
17. The provisions of this Article and the relevant provisions of Part IV of the Verification Annex shall not, at the discretion of a State Party, apply to chemical weapons buried on its territory before 1 January 1977 and which remain buried, or which had been dumped at sea before 1 January 1985.

Art. V. Chemical Weapons Production Facilities

1. The provisions of this Article and the detailed procedures for its implementation shall apply to any and all chemical weapons production facilities owned or possessed by a State Party, or that are located in any place under its jurisdiction or control.
2. Detailed procedures for the implementation of this Article are set forth in the Verification Annex.
3. All chemical weapons production facilities specified in paragraph 1 shall be subject to systematic verification through on-site inspection and monitoring with on-site instruments in accordance with Part V of the Verification Annex.
4. Each State Party shall cease immediately all activity at chemical weapons production facilities specified in paragraph 1, except activity required for closure.
5. No State Party shall construct any new chemical weapons production facilities or modify any existing facilities for the purpose of chemical weapons production or for any other activity prohibited under this Convention.
6. Each State Party shall, immediately after the declaration under Article III, paragraph 1 (c), has been submitted, provide access to chemical weapons production facilities specified in paragraph 1, for the purpose of systematic verification of the declaration through on-site inspection.
7. Each State Party shall:
   (a) Close, not later than 90 days after this Convention enters into force for it, all chemical weapons production facilities specified in paragraph 1,

in accordance with Part V of the Verification Annex, and give notice thereof; and

(b) Provide access to chemical weapons production facilities specified in paragraph 1, subsequent to closure, for the purpose of systematic verification through on-site inspection and monitoring with on-site instruments in order to ensure that the facility remains closed and is subsequently destroyed.

8. Each State Party shall destroy all chemical weapons production facilities specified in paragraph 1 and related facilities and equipment, pursuant to the Verification Annex and in accordance with an agreed rate and sequence of destruction (hereinafter referred to as "order of destruction"). Such destruction shall begin not later than one year after this Convention enters into force for it, and shall finish not later than 10 years after entry into force of this Convention. A State Party is not precluded from destroying such facilities at a faster rate.

9. Each State Party shall:

(a) Submit detailed plans for destruction of chemical weapons production facilities specified in paragraph 1, not later than 180 days before the destruction of each facility begins;

(b) Submit declarations annually regarding the implementation of its plans for the destruction of all chemical weapons production facilities specified in paragraph 1, not later than 90 days after the end of each annual destruction period; and

(c) Certify, not later than 30 days after the destruction process has been completed, that all chemical weapons production facilities specified in paragraph 1 have been destroyed.

10. If a State ratifies or accedes to this Convention after the 10-year period for destruction set forth in paragraph 8, it shall destroy chemical weapons production facilities specified in paragraph 1 as soon as possible. The order of destruction and procedures for stringent verification for such a State Party shall be determined by the Executive Council.

11. Each State Party, during the destruction of chemical weapons production facilities, shall assign the highest priority to ensuring the safety of people and to protecting the environment. Each State Party shall destroy chemical weapons production facilities in accordance with its national standards for safety and emissions.

12. Chemical weapons production facilities specified in paragraph 1 may be temporarily converted for destruction of chemical weapons in accordance with Part V, paragraphs 18 to 25, of the Verification Annex. Such a converted facility must be destroyed as soon as it is no longer in use for destruction of chemical weapons but, in any case, not later than 10 years after entry into force of this Convention.

13. A State Party may request, in exceptional cases of compelling need, permission to use a chemical weapons production facility specified in paragraph 1 for purposes not prohibited under this Convention. Upon the recommendation of the Executive Council, the Conference of the States Parties shall decide whether or not to approve the request and shall establish the conditions upon which approval is contingent in accordance with Part V, Section D, of the Verification Annex.

14. The chemical weapons production facility shall be converted in such a manner that the converted facility is not more capable of being reconverted into a chemical weapons production facility than any other facility used for industrial, agricultural, research, medical, pharmaceutical or other peaceful purposes not involving chemicals listed in Schedule 1.
15. All converted facilities shall be subject to systematic verification through on-site inspection and monitoring with on-site instruments in accordance with Part V, Section D, of the Verification Annex.
16. In carrying out verification activities pursuant to this Article and Part V of the Verification Annex, the Organization shall consider measures to avoid unnecessary duplication of bilateral or multilateral agreements on verification of chemical weapons production facilities and their destruction among States Parties.

    To this end, the Executive Council shall decide to limit the verification to measures complementary to those undertaken pursuant to such a bilateral or multilateral agreement, if it considers that:
    (a) Verification provisions of such an agreement are consistent with the verification provisions of this Article and Part V of the Verification Annex;
    (b) Implementation of the agreement provides for sufficient assurance of compliance with the relevant provisions of this Convention; and
    (c) Parties to the bilateral or multilateral agreement keep the Organization fully informed about their verification activities.
17. If the Executive Council takes a decision pursuant to paragraph 16, the Organization shall have the right to monitor the implementation of the bilateral or multilateral agreement.
18. Nothing in paragraphs 16 and 17 shall affect the obligation of a State Party to make declarations pursuant to Article III, this Article and Part V of the Verification Annex.
19. Each State Party shall meet the costs of destruction of chemical weapons production facilities it is obliged to destroy. It shall also meet the costs of verification under this Article unless the Executive Council decides otherwise. If the Executive Council decides to limit verification measures of the Organization pursuant to paragraph 16, the costs of complementary verification and monitoring by the Organization shall be paid in accordance with the United Nations scale of assessment, as specified in Article VIII, paragraph 7.

Art. VI. Activities not Prohibited Under This Convention

1. Each State Party has the right, subject to the provisions of this Convention, to develop, produce, otherwise acquire, retain, transfer and use toxic chemicals and their precursors for purposes not prohibited under this Convention.
2. Each State Party shall adopt the necessary measures to ensure that toxic chemicals and their precursors are only developed, produced, otherwise acquired, retained, transferred, or used within its territory or in any other place under its jurisdiction or control for purposes not prohibited under this Convention. To this end, and in order to verify that activities are in accordance with obligations under this Convention, each State Party shall subject toxic chemicals and their precursors listed in Schedules 1, 2 and 3 of

the Annex on Chemicals, facilities related to such chemicals, and other facilities as specified in the Verification Annex, that are located on its territory or in any other place under its jurisdiction or control, to verification measures as provided in the Verification Annex.

3. Each State Party shall subject chemicals listed in Schedule 1 (hereinafter referred to as "Schedule 1 chemicals") to the prohibitions on production, acquisition, retention, transfer and use as specified in Part VI of the Verification Annex. It shall subject Schedule 1 chemicals and facilities specified in Part VI of the Verification Annex to systematic verification through on-site inspection and monitoring with on-site instruments in accordance with that Part of the Verification Annex.
4. Each State Party shall subject chemicals listed in Schedule 2 (hereinafter referred to as "Schedule 2 chemicals") and facilities specified in Part VII of the Verification Annex to data monitoring and on-site verification in accordance with that Part of the Verification Annex.
5. Each State Party shall subject chemicals listed in Schedule 3 (hereinafter referred to as "Schedule 3 chemicals") and facilities specified in Part VIII of the Verification Annex to data monitoring and on-site verification in accordance with that Part of the Verification Annex.
6. Each State Party shall subject facilities specified in Part IX of the Verification Annex to data monitoring and eventual on-site verification in accordance with that Part of theVerification Annex unless decided otherwise by the Conference of the States Parties pursuant to Part IX, paragraph 22, of the Verification Annex.
7. Not later than 30 days after this Convention enters into force for it, each State Party shall make an initial declaration on relevant chemicals and facilities in accordance with the Verification Annex.
8. Each State Party shall make annual declarations regarding the relevant chemicals and facilities in accordance with the Verification Annex.
9. For the purpose of on-site verification, each State Party shall grant to the inspectors access to facilities as required in the Verification Annex.
10. In conducting verification activities, the Technical Secretariat shall avoid undue intrusion into the State Party's chemical activities for purposes not prohibited under this Convention and, in particular, abide by the provisions set forth in the Annex on the Protection of Confidential Information (hereinafter referred to as "Confidentiality Annex").
11. The provisions of this Article shall be implemented in a manner which avoids hampering the economic or technological development of States Parties, and international cooperation in the field of chemical activities for purposes not prohibited under this Convention including the international exchange of scientific and technical information and chemicals and equipment for the production, processing or use of chemicals for purposes not prohibited under this Convention.

Art. VII. National Implementation Measures

General undertakings

1. Each State Party shall, in accordance with its constitutional processes, adopt the necessary measures to implement its obligations under this Convention. In particular, it shall:

(a) Prohibit natural and legal persons anywhere on its territory or in any other place under its jurisdiction as recognized by international law from undertaking any activity prohibited to a State Party under this Convention, including enacting penal legislation with respect to such activity;
(b) Not permit in any place under its control any activity prohibited to a State Party under this Convention; and
(c) Extend its penal legislation enacted under subparagraph (a) to any activity prohibited to a State Party under this Convention undertaken anywhere by natural persons, possessing its nationality, in conformity with international law.

2. Each State Party shall cooperate with other States Parties and afford the appropriate form of legal assistance to facilitate the implementation of the obligations under paragraph 1.
3. Each State Party, during the implementation of its obligations under this Convention, shall assign the highest priority to ensuring the safety of people and to protecting the environment, and shall cooperate as appropriate with other States Parties in this regard.

Relations between the State Party and the Organization

4. In order to fulfil its obligations under this Convention, each State Party shall designate or establish a National Authority to serve as the national focal point for effective liaison with the Organization and other States Parties. Each State Party shall notify the Organization of its National Authority at the time that this Convention enters into force for it.
5. Each State Party shall inform the Organization of the legislative and administrative measures taken to implement this Convention.
6. Each State Party shall treat as confidential and afford special handling to information and data that it receives in confidence from the Organization in connection with the implementation of this Convention.

   It shall treat such information and data exclusively in connection with its rights and obligations under this Convention and in accordance with the provisions set forth in the Confidentiality Annex.
7. Each State Party undertakes to cooperate with the Organization in the exercise of all its functions and in particular to provide assistance to the Technical Secretariat.

Art. VIII. The Organization

A. General Provisions

1. The States Parties to this Convention hereby establish the Organization for the Prohibition of Chemical Weapons to achieve the object and purpose of this Convention, to ensure the implementation of its provisions, including those for international verification of compliance with it, and to provide a forum for consultation and cooperation among States Parties.
2. All States Parties to this Convention shall be members of the Organization. A State Party shall not be deprived of its membership in the Organization.
3. The seat of the Headquarters of the Organization shall be The Hague, Kingdom of the Netherlands.

4. There are hereby established as the organs of the Organization: the Conference of the States Parties, the Executive Council, and the Technical Secretariat.
5. The Organization shall conduct its verification activities provided for under this Convention in the least intrusive manner possible consistent with the timely and efficient accomplishment of their objectives. It shall request only the information and data necessary to fulfil its responsibilities under this Convention. It shall take every precaution to protect the confidentiality of information on civil and military activities and facilities coming to its knowledge in the implementation of this Convention and, in particular, shall abide by the provisions set forth in the Confidentiality Annex.
6. In undertaking its verification activities the Organization shall consider measures to make use of advances in science and technology.
7. The costs of the Organization's activities shall be paid by States Parties in accordance with the United Nations scale of assessment adjusted to take into account differences in membership between the United Nations and this Organization, and subject to the provisions of Articles IV and V. Financial contributions of States Parties to the Preparatory Commission shall be deducted in an appropriate way from their contributions to the regular budget. The budget of the Organization shall comprise two separate chapters, one relating to administrative and other costs, and one relating to verification costs.
8. A member of the Organization which is in arrears in the payment of its financial contribution to the Organization shall have no vote in the Organization if the amount of its arrears equals or exceeds the amount of the contribution due from it for the preceding two full years. The Conference of the States Parties may, nevertheless, permit such a member to vote if it is satisfied that the failure to pay is due to conditions beyond the control of the member.

B. The Conference of the States Parties

Composition, procedures and decision-making

9. The Conference of the States Parties (hereinafter referred to as "the Conference") shall be composed of all members of this Organization. Each member shall have one representative in the Conference, who may be accompanied by alternates and advisers.
10. The first session of the Conference shall be convened by the depositary not later than 30 days after the entry into force of this Convention.
11. The Conference shall meet in regular sessions which shall be held annually unless it decides otherwise.
12. Special sessions of the Conference shall be convened:
    (a) When decided by the Conference;
    (b) When requested by the Executive Council;
    (c) When requested by any member and supported by one third of the members; or
    (d) In accordance with paragraph 22 to undertake reviews of the operation of this Convention. Except in the case of subparagraph (d), the special session shall be convened not later than 30 days after receipt of the

request by the Director-General of the Technical Secretariat, unless specified otherwise in the request.

13. The Conference shall also be convened in the form of an Amendment Conference in accordance with Article XV, paragraph 2.
14. Sessions of the Conference shall take place at the seat of the Organization unless the Conference decides otherwise.
15. The Conference shall adopt its rules of procedure. At the beginning of each regular session, it shall elect its Chairman and such other officers as may be required. They shall hold office until a new Chairman and other officers are elected at the next regular session.
16. A majority of the members of the Organization shall constitute a quorum for the Conference.
17. Each member of the Organization shall have one vote in the Conference.
18. The Conference shall take decisions on questions of procedure by a simple majority of the members present and voting. Decisions on matters of substance should be taken as far as possible by consensus. If consensus is not attainable when an issue comes up for decision, the Chairman shall defer any vote for 24 hours and during this period of deferment shall make every effort to facilitate achievement of consensus, and shall report to the Conference before the end of this period. If consensus is not possible at the end of 24 hours, the Conference shall take the decision by a two-thirds majority of members present and voting unless specified otherwise in this Convention. When the issue arises as to whether the question is one of substance or not, that question shall be treated as a matter of substance unless otherwise decided by the Conference by the majority required for decisions on matters of substance.

Powers and functions

19. The Conference shall be the principal organ of the Organization. It shall consider any questions, matters or issues within the scope of this Convention, including those relating to the powers and functions of the Executive Council and the Technical Secretariat. It may make recommendations and take decisions on any questions, matters or issues related to this Convention raised by a State Party or brought to its attention by the Executive Council.
20. The Conference shall oversee the implementation of this Convention, and act in order to promote its object and purpose. The Conference shall review compliance with this Convention. It shall also oversee the activities of the Executive Council and the Technical Secretariat and may issue guidelines in accordance with this Convention to either of them in the exercise of their functions.
21. The Conference shall:
    (a) Consider and adopt at its regular sessions the report, programme and budget of the Organization, submitted by the Executive Council, as well as consider other reports;
    (b) Decide on the scale of financial contributions to be paid by States Parties in accordance with paragraph 7;
    (c) Elect the members of the Executive Council;
    (d) Appoint the Director-General of the Technical Secretariat (hereinafter referred to as "the Director-General");

(e) Approve the rules of procedure of the Executive Council submitted by the latter;
(f) Establish such subsidiary organs as it finds necessary for the exercise of its functions in accordance with this Convention;
(g) Foster international cooperation for peaceful purposes in the field of chemical activities;
(h) Review scientific and technological developments that could affect the operation of this Convention and, in this context, direct the Director-General to establish a Scientific Advisory Board to enable him, in the performance of his functions, to render specialized advice in areas of science and technology relevant to this Convention, to the Conference, the Executive Council or States Parties. The Scientific Advisory Board shall be composed of independent experts appointed in accordance with terms of reference adopted by the Conference;
(i) Consider and approve at its first session any draft agreements, provisions and guidelines developed by the Preparatory Commission;
(j) Establish at its first session the voluntary fund for assistance in accordance with Article X;
(k) Take the necessary measures to ensure compliance with this Convention and to redress and remedy any situation which contravenes the provisions of this Convention, in accordance with Article XII.

22. The Conference shall not later than one year after the expiry of the fifth and the tenth year after the entry into force of this Convention, and at such other times within that time period as may be decided upon, convene in special sessions to undertake reviews of the operation of this Convention. Such reviews shall take into account any relevant scientific and technological developments. At intervals of five years thereafter, unless otherwise decided upon, further sessions of the Conference shall be convened with the same objective.

C. The Executive Council

Composition, procedure and decision-making

23. The Executive Council shall consist of 41 members. Each State Party shall have the right, in accordance with the principle of rotation, to serve on the Executive Council. The members of the Executive Council shall be elected by the Conference for a term of two years. In order to ensure the effective functioning of this Convention, due regard being specially paid to equitable geographical distribution, to the importance of chemical industry, as well as to political and security interests, the Executive Council shall be composed as follows:
(a) Nine States Parties from Africa to be designated by States Parties located in this region. As a basis for this designation it is understood that, out of these nine States Parties, three members shall, as a rule, be the States Parties with the most significant national chemical industry in the region as determined by internationally reported and published data; in addition, the regional group shall agree also to take into account other regional factors in designating these three members;
(b) Nine States Parties from Asia to be designated by States Parties located in this region. As a basis for this designation it is understood that, out of

these nine States Parties, four members shall, as a rule, be the States Parties with the most significant national chemical industry in the region as determined by internationally reported and published data; in addition, the regional group shall agree also to take into account other regional factors in designating these four members;

(c) Five States Parties from Eastern Europe to be designated by States Parties located in this region. As a basis for this designation it is understood that, out of these five States Parties, one member shall, as a rule, be the State Party with the most significant national chemical industry in the region as determined by internationally reported and published data; in addition, the regional group shall agree also to take into account other regional factors in designating this one member;

(d) Seven States Parties from Latin America and the Caribbean to be designated by States Parties located in this region. As a basis for this designation it is understood that, out of these seven States Parties, three members shall, as a rule, be the States Parties with the most significant national chemical industry in the region as determined by internationally reported and published data; in addition, the regional group shall agree also to take into account other regional factors in designating these three members;

(e) Ten States Parties from among Western European and other States to be designated by States Parties located in this region. As a basis for this designation it is understood that, out of these 10 States Parties, 5 members shall, as a rule, be the States Parties with the most significant national chemical industry in the region as determined by internationally reported and published data; in addition, the regional group shall agree also to take into account other regional factors in designating these five members;

(f) One further State Party to be designated consecutively by States Parties located in the regions of Asia and Latin America and the Caribbean. As a basis for this designation it is understood that this State Party shall be a rotating member from these regions.

24. For the first election of the Executive Council 20 members shall be elected for a term of one year, due regard being paid to the established numerical proportions as described in paragraph 23.

25. After the full implementation of Articles IV and V the Conference may, upon the request of a majority of the members of the Executive Council, review the composition of the Executive Council taking into account developments related to the principles specified in paragraph 23 that are governing its composition.

26. The Executive Council shall elaborate its rules of procedure and submit them to the Conference for approval.

27. The Executive Council shall elect its Chairman from among its members.

28. The Executive Council shall meet for regular sessions. Between regular sessions it shall meet as often as may be required for the fulfilment of its powers and functions.

29. Each member of the Executive Council shall have one vote. Unless otherwise specified in this Convention, the Executive Council shall take

decisions on matters of substance by a two-thirds majority of all its members. The Executive Council shall take decisions on questions of procedure by a simple majority of all its members. When the issue arises as to whether the question is one of substance or not, that question shall be treated as a matter of substance unless otherwise decided by the Executive Council by the majority required for decisions on matters of substance.

Powers and functions

30. The Executive Council shall be the executive organ of the Organization. It shall be responsible to the Conference. The Executive Council shall carry out the powers and functions entrusted to it under this Convention, as well as those functions delegated to it by the Conference. In so doing, it shall act in conformity with the recommendations, decisions and guidelines of the Conference and assure their proper and continuous implementation.
31. The Executive Council shall promote the effective implementation of, and compliance with, this Convention. It shall supervise the activities of the Technical Secretariat, cooperate with the National Authority of each State Party and facilitate consultations and cooperation among States Parties at their request.
32. The Executive Council shall:
    (a) Consider and submit to the Conference the draft programme and budget of the Organization;
    (b) Consider and submit to the Conference the draft report of the Organization on the implementation of this Convention, the report on the performance of its own activities and such special reports as it deems necessary or which the Conference may request;
    (c) Make arrangements for the sessions of the Conference including the preparation of the draft agenda.
33. The Executive Council may request the convening of a special session of the Conference.
34. The Executive Council shall:
    (a) Conclude agreements or arrangements with States and international organizations on behalf of the Organization, subject to prior approval by the Conference;
    (b) Conclude agreements with States Parties on behalf of the Organization in connection with Article X and supervise the voluntary fund referred to in Article X;
    (c) Approve agreements or arrangements relating to the implementation of verification activities, negotiated by the Technical Secretariat with States Parties.
35. The Executive Council shall consider any issue or matter within its competence affecting this Convention and its implementation, including concerns regarding compliance, and cases of non-compliance, and, as appropriate, inform States Parties and bring the issue or matter to the attention of the Conference.
36. In its consideration of doubts or concerns regarding compliance and cases of non-compliance, including, inter alia, abuse of the rights provided for under this Convention, the Executive Council shall consult with the States

Parties involved and, as appropriate, request the State Party to take measures to redress the situation within a specified time. To the extent that the Executive Council considers further action to be necessary, it shall take, inter alia, one or more of the following measures:

(a) Inform all States Parties of the issue or matter;

(b) Bring the issue or matter to the attention of the Conference;

(c) Make recommendations to the Conference regarding measures to redress the situation and to ensure compliance.

The Executive Council shall, in cases of particular gravity and urgency, bring the issue or matter, including relevant information and conclusions, directly to the attention of the United Nations General Assembly and the United Nations Security Council. It shall at the same time inform all States Parties of this step.

D. The Technical Secretariat

37. The Technical Secretariat shall assist the Conference and the Executive Council in the performance of their functions. The Technical Secretariat shall carry out the verification measures provided for in this Convention. It shall carry out the other functions entrusted to it under this Convention as well as those functions delegated to it by the Conference and the Executive Council.

38. The Technical Secretariat shall:

(a) Prepare and submit to the Executive Council the draft programme and budget of the Organization;

(b) Prepare and submit to the Executive Council the draft report of the Organization on the implementation of this Convention and such other reports as the Conference or the Executive Council may request;

(c) Provide administrative and technical support to the Conference, the Executive Council and subsidiary organs;

(d) Address and receive communications on behalf of the Organization to and from States Parties on matters pertaining to the implementation of this Convention;

(e) Provide technical assistance and technical evaluation to States Parties in the implementation of the provisions of this Convention, including evaluation of scheduled and unscheduled chemicals.

39. The Technical Secretariat shall:

(a) Negotiate agreements or arrangements relating to the implementation of verification activities with States Parties, subject to approval by the Executive Council;

(b) Not later than 180 days after entry into force of this Convention, coordinate the establishment and maintenance of permanent stockpiles of emergency and humanitarian assistance by States Parties in accordance with Article X, paragraphs 7 (b) and (c). The Technical Secretariat may inspect the items maintained for serviceability. Lists of items to be stockpiled shall be considered and approved by the Conference pursuant to paragraph 21 (i) above;

(c) Administer the voluntary fund referred to in Article X, compile declarations made by the States Parties and register, when requested, bilateral agreements concluded between States Parties or between a State Party and the Organization for the purposes of Article X.

40. The Technical Secretariat shall inform the Executive Council of any problem that has arisen with regard to the discharge of its functions, including doubts, ambiguities or uncertainties about compliance with this Convention that have come to its notice in the performance of its verification activities and that it has been unable to resolve or clarify through its consultations with the State Party concerned.
41. The Technical Secretariat shall comprise a Director-General, who shall be its head and chief administrative officer, inspectors and such scientific, technical and other personnel as may be required.
42. The Inspectorate shall be a unit of the Technical Secretariat and shall act under the supervision of the Director-General.
43. The Director-General shall be appointed by the Conference upon the recommendation of the Executive Council for a term of four years, renewable for one further term, but not thereafter.
44. The Director-General shall be responsible to the Conference and the Executive Council for the appointment of the staff and the organization and functioning of the Technical Secretariat. The paramount consideration in the employment of the staff and in the determination of the conditions of service shall be the necessity of securing the highest standards of efficiency, competence and integrity. Only citizens of States Parties shall serve as the Director-General, as inspectors or as other members of the professional and clerical staff.

    Due regard shall be paid to the importance of recruiting the staff on as wide a geographical basis as possible. Recruitment shall be guided by the principle that the staff shall be kept to a minimum necessary for the proper discharge of the responsibilities of the Technical Secretariat.
45. The Director-General shall be responsible for the organization and functioning of the Scientific Advisory Board referred to in paragraph 21 (h). The Director-General shall, in consultation with States Parties, appoint members of the Scientific Advisory Board, who shall serve in their individual capacity. The members of the Board shall be appointed on the basis of their expertise in the particular scientific fields relevant to the implementation of this Convention. The Director-General may also, as appropriate, in consultation with members of the Board, establish temporary working groups of scientific experts to provide recommendations on specific issues. In regard to the above, States Parties may submit lists of experts to the Director-General.
46. In the performance of their duties, the Director-General, the inspectors and the other members of the staff shall not seek or receive instructions from any Government or from any other source external to the Organization. They shall refrain from any action that might reflect on their positions as international officers responsible only to the Conference and the Executive Council.
47. Each State Party shall respect the exclusively international character of the responsibilities of the Director-General, the inspectors and the other members of the staff and not seek to influence them in the discharge of their responsibilities.

E. Privileges and Immunities

48. The Organization shall enjoy on the territory and in any other place under the jurisdiction or control of a State Party such legal capacity and such privileges and immunities as are necessary for the exercise of its functions.
49. Delegates of States Parties, together with their alternates and advisers, representatives appointed to the Executive Council together with their alternates and advisers, the Director-General and the staff of the Organization shall enjoy such privileges and immunities as are necessary in the independent exercise of their functions in connection with the Organization.
50. The legal capacity, privileges, and immunities referred to in this Article shall be defined in agreements between the Organization and the States Parties as well as in an agreement between the Organization and the State in which the headquarters of the Organization is seated. These agreements shall be considered and approved by the Conference pursuant to paragraph 21 (i).
51. Notwithstanding paragraphs 48 and 49, the privileges and immunities enjoyed by the Director-General and the staff of the Technical Secretariat during the conduct of verification activities shall be those set forth in Part II, Section B, of the Verification Annex.

Art. IX. Consultations, Cooperation and Fact-Finding

1. States Parties shall consult and cooperate, directly among themselves, or through the Organization or other appropriate international procedures, including procedures within the framework of the United Nations and in accordance with its Charter, on any matter which may be raised relating to the object and purpose, or the implementation of the provisions, of this Convention.
2. Without prejudice to the right of any State Party to request a challenge inspection, States Parties should, whenever possible, first make every effort to clarify and resolve, through exchange of information and consultations among themselves, any matter which may cause doubt about compliance with this Convention, or which gives rise to concerns about a related matter which may be considered ambiguous. A State Party which receives a request from another State Party for clarification of any matter which the requesting State Party believes causes such a doubt or concern shall provide the requesting State Party as soon as possible, but in any case not later than 10 days after the request, with information sufficient to answer the doubt or concern raised along with an explanation of how the information provided resolves the matter. Nothing in this Convention shall affect the right of any two or more States Parties to arrange by mutual consent for inspections or any other procedures among themselves to clarify and resolve any matter which may cause doubt about compliance or gives rise to a concern about a related matter which may be considered ambiguous. Such arrangements shall not affect the rights and obligations of any State Party under other provisions of this Convention.

Procedure for requesting clarification

3. A State Party shall have the right to request the Executive Council to assist in clarifying any situation which may be considered ambiguous or

which gives rise to a concern about the possible non-compliance of another State Party with this Convention. The Executive Council shall provide appropriate information in its possession relevant to such a concern.

4. A State Party shall have the right to request the Executive Council to obtain clarification from another State Party on any situation which may be considered ambiguous or which gives rise to a concern about its possible non-compliance with this Convention. In such a case, the following shall apply:
   (a) The Executive Council shall forward the request for clarification to the State Party concerned through the Director-General not later than 24 hours after its receipt;
   (b) The requested State Party shall provide the clarification to the Executive Council as soon as possible, but in any case not later than 10 days after the receipt of the request;
   (c) The Executive Council shall take note of the clarification and forward it to the requesting State Party not later than 24 hours after its receipt;
   (d) If the requesting State Party deems the clarification to be inadequate, it shall have the right to request the Executive Council to obtain from the requested State Party further clarification;
   (e) For the purpose of obtaining further clarification requested under subparagraph (d), the Executive Council may call on the Director-General to establish a group of experts from the Technical Secretariat, or if appropriate staff are not available in the Technical Secretariat, from elsewhere, to examine all available information and data relevant to the situation causing the concern. The group of experts shall submit a factual report to the Executive Council on its findings;
   (f) If the requesting State Party considers the clarification obtained under subparagraphs (d) and (e) to be unsatisfactory, it shall have the right to request a special session of the Executive Council in which States Parties involved that are not members of the Executive Council shall be entitled to take part. In such a special session, the Executive Council shall consider the matter and may recommend any measure it deems appropriate to resolve the situation.
5. A State Party shall also have the right to request the Executive Council to clarify any situation which has been considered ambiguous or has given rise to a concern about its possible non-compliance with this Convention. The Executive Council shall respond by providing such assistance as appropriate.
6. The Executive Council shall inform the States Parties about any request for clarification provided in this Article.
7. If the doubt or concern of a State Party about a possible non-compliance has not been resolved within 60 days after the submission of the request for clarification to the Executive Council, or it believes its doubts warrant urgent consideration, notwithstanding its right to request a challenge inspection, it may request a special session of the Conference in accordance with Article VIII, paragraph 12 (c). At such a special session, the Conference shall consider the matter and may recommend any measure it deems appropriate to resolve the situation.

Procedures for challenge inspections

8. Each State Party has the right to request an on-site challenge inspection of any facility or location in the territory or in any other place under the jurisdiction or control of any other State Party for the sole purpose of clarifying and resolving any questions concerning possible non-compliance with the provisions of this Convention, and to have this inspection conducted anywhere without delay by an inspection team designated by the Director-General and in accordance with the Verification Annex.
9. Each State Party is under the obligation to keep the inspection request within the scope of this Convention and to provide in the inspection request all appropriate information on the basis of which a concern has arisen regarding possible non-compliance with this Convention as specified in the Verification Annex. Each State Party shall refrain from unfounded inspection requests, care being taken to avoid abuse. The challenge inspection shall be carried out for the sole purpose of determining facts relating to the possible non-compliance.
10. For the purpose of verifying compliance with the provisions of this Convention, each State Party shall permit the Technical Secretariat to conduct the on-site challenge inspection pursuant to paragraph 8.
11. Pursuant to a request for a challenge inspection of a facility or location, and in accordance with the procedures provided for in the Verification Annex, the inspected State Party shall have:
    (a) The right and the obligation to make every reasonable effort to demonstrate its compliance with this Convention and, to this end, to enable the inspection team to fulfil its mandate;
    (b) The obligation to provide access within the requested site for the sole purpose of establishing facts relevant to the concern regarding possible non-compliance; and
    (c) The right to take measures to protect sensitive installations, and to prevent disclosure of confidential information and data, not related to this Convention.
12. With regard to an observer, the following shall apply:
    (a) The requesting State Party may, subject to the agreement of the inspected State Party, send a representative who may be a national either of the requesting State Party or of a third State Party, to observe the conduct of the challenge inspection.
    (b) The inspected State Party shall then grant access to the observer in accordance with the Verification Annex.
    (c) The inspected State Party shall, as a rule, accept the proposed observer, but if the inspected State Party exercises a refusal, that fact shall be recorded in the final report.
13. The requesting State Party shall present an inspection request for an on-site challenge inspection to the Executive Council and at the same time to the Director-General for immediate processing.
14. The Director-General shall immediately ascertain that the inspection request meets the requirements specified in Part X, paragraph 4, of the Verification Annex, and, if necessary, assist the requesting State Party in filing the inspection request accordingly. When the inspection request fulfils the requirements, preparations for the challenge inspection shall begin.

15. The Director-General shall transmit the inspection request to the inspected State Party not less than 12 hours before the planned arrival of the inspection team at the point of entry.
16. After having received the inspection request, the Executive Council shall take cognizance of the Director-General's actions on the request and shall keep the case under its consideration throughout the inspection procedure. However, its deliberations shall not delay the inspection process.
17. The Executive Council may, not later than 12 hours after having received the inspection request, decide by a three-quarter majority of all its members against carrying out the challenge inspection, if it considers the inspection request to be frivolous, abusive or clearly beyond the scope of this Convention as described in paragraph 8. Neither the requesting nor the inspected State Party shall participate in such a decision. If the Executive Council decides against the challenge inspection, preparations shall be stopped, no further action on the inspection request shall be taken, and the States Parties concerned shall be informed accordingly.
18. The Director-General shall issue an inspection mandate for the conduct of the challenge inspection. The inspection mandate shall be the inspection request referred to in paragraphs 8 and 9 put into operational terms, and shall conform with the inspection request.
19. The challenge inspection shall be conducted in accordance with Part X or, in the case of alleged use, in accordance with Part XI of the Verification Annex. The inspection team shall be guided by the principle of conducting the challenge inspection in the least intrusive manner possible, consistent with the effective and timely accomplishment of its mission.
20. The inspected State Party shall assist the inspection team throughout the challenge inspection and facilitate its task. If the inspected State Party proposes, pursuant to Part X, Section C, of the Verification Annex, arrangements to demonstrate compliance with this Convention, alternative to full and comprehensive access, it shall make every reasonable effort, through consultations with the inspection team, to reach agreement on the modalities for establishing the facts with the aim of demonstrating its compliance.
21. The final report shall contain the factual findings as well as an assessment by the inspection team of the degree and nature of access and cooperation granted for the satisfactory implementation of the challenge inspection. The Director-General shall promptly transmit the final report of the inspection team to the requesting State Party, to the inspected State Party, to the Executive Council and to all other States Parties. The Director-General shall further transmit promptly to the Executive Council the assessments of the requesting and of the inspected States Parties, as well as the views of other States Parties which may be conveyed to the Director-General for that purpose, and then provide them to all States Parties.
22. The Executive Council shall, in accordance with its powers and functions, review the final report of the inspection team as soon as it is presented, and address any concerns as to:
    (a) Whether any non-compliance has occurred;
    (b) Whether the request had been within the scope of this Convention; and
    (c) Whether the right to request a challenge inspection had been abused.

23. If the Executive Council reaches the conclusion, in keeping with its powers and functions, that further action may be necessary with regard to paragraph 22, it shall take the appropriate measures to redress the situation and to ensure compliance with this Convention, including specific recommendations to the Conference. In the case of abuse, the Executive Council shall examine whether the requesting State Party should bear any of the financial implications of the challenge inspection.
24. The requesting State Party and the inspected State Party shall have the right to participate in the review process. The Executive Council shall inform the States Parties and the next session of the Conference of the outcome of the process.
25. If the Executive Council has made specific recommendations to the Conference, the Conference shall consider action in accordance with Article XII.

Art. X. Assistance and Protection against Chemical Weapons

1. For the purposes of this Article, "Assistance" means the coordination and delivery to States Parties of protection against chemical weapons, including, inter alia, the following: detection equipment and alarm systems; protective equipment; decontamination equipment and decontaminants; medical antidotes and treatments; and advice on any of these protective measures.
2. Nothing in this Convention shall be interpreted as impeding the right of any State Party to conduct research into, develop, produce, acquire, transfer or use means of protection against chemical weapons, for purposes not prohibited under this Convention.
3. Each State Party undertakes to facilitate, and shall have the right to participate in, the fullest possible exchange of equipment, material and scientific and technological information concerning means of protection against chemical weapons.
4. For the purposes of increasing the transparency of national programmes related to protective purposes, each State Party shall provide annually to the Technical Secretariat information on its programme, in accordance with procedures to be considered and approved by the Conference pursuant to Article VIII, paragraph 21 (i).
5. The Technical Secretariat shall establish, not later than 180 days after entry into force of this Convention and maintain, for the use of any requesting State Party, a data bank containing freely available information concerning various means of protection against chemical weapons as well as such information as may be provided by States Parties.

   The Technical Secretariat shall also, within the resources available to it, and at the request of a State Party, provide expert advice and assist the State Party in identifying how its programmes for the development and improvement of a protective capacity against chemical weapons could be implemented.
6. Nothing in this Convention shall be interpreted as impeding the right of States Parties to request and provide assistance bilaterally and to conclude individual agreements with other States Parties concerning the emergency procurement of assistance.

7. Each State Party undertakes to provide assistance through the Organization and to this end to elect to take one or more of the following measures:
   (a) To contribute to the voluntary fund for assistance to be established by the Conference at its first session;
   (b) To conclude, if possible not later than 180 days after this Convention enters into force for it, agreements with the Organization concerning the procurement, upon demand, of assistance;
   (c) To declare, not later than 180 days after this Convention enters into force for it, the kind of assistance it might provide in response to an appeal by the Organization. If, however, a State Party subsequently is unable to provide the assistance envisaged in its declaration, it is still under the obligation to provide assistance in accordance with this paragraph.
8. Each State Party has the right to request and, subject to the procedures set forth in paragraphs 9, 10 and 11, to receive assistance and protection against the use or threat of use of chemical weapons if it considers that:
   (a) Chemical weapons have been used against it;
   (b) Riot control agents have been used against it as a method of warfare; or
   (c) It is threatened by actions or activities of any State that are prohibited for States Parties by Article I.
9. The request, substantiated by relevant information, shall be submitted to the Director-General, who shall transmit it immediately to the Executive Council and to all States Parties.The Director-General shall immediately forward the request to States Parties which have volunteered, in accordance with paragraphs 7 (b) and (c), to dispatch emergency assistance in case of use of chemical weapons or use of riot control agents as a method of warfare, or humanitarian assistance in case of serious threat of use of chemical weapons or serious threat of use of riot control agents as a method of warfare to the State Party concerned not later than 12 hours after receipt of the request. The Director-General shall initiate, not later than 24 hours after receipt of the request, an investigation in order to provide foundation for further action. He shall complete the investigation within 72 hours and forward a report to the Executive Council. If additional time is required for completion of the investigation, an interim report shall be submitted within the same time-frame. The additional time required for investigation shall not exceed 72 hours. It may, however, be further extended by similar periods. Reports at the end of each additional period shall be submitted to the Executive Council. The investigation shall, as appropriate and in conformity with the request and the information accompanying the request, establish relevant facts related to the request as well as the type and scope of supplementary assistance and protection needed.
10. The Executive Council shall meet not later than 24 hours after receiving an investigation report to consider the situation and shall take a decision by simple majority within the following 24 hours on whether to instruct the Technical Secretariat to provide supplementary assistance. The Technical Secretariat shall immediately transmit to all States Parties and relevant international organizations the investigation report and the decision taken by the Executive Council. When so decided by the Executive Council, the

Director-General shall provide assistance immediately. For this purpose, the Director-General may cooperate with the requesting State Party, other States Parties and relevant international organizations. The States Parties shall make the fullest possible efforts to provide assistance.

11. If the information available from the ongoing investigation or other reliable sources would give sufficient proof that there are victims of use of chemical weapons and immediate action is indispensable, the Director-General shall notify all States Parties and shall take emergency measures of assistance, using the resources the Conference has placed at his disposal for such contingencies. The Director-General shall keep the Executive Council informed of actions undertaken pursuant to this paragraph.

Art. XI. Economic and Technological Development

1. The provisions of this Convention shall be implemented in a manner which avoids hampering the economic or technological development of States Parties, and international cooperation in the field of chemical activities for purposes not prohibited under this Convention including the international exchange of scientific and technical information and chemicals and equipment for the production, processing or use of chemicals for purposes not prohibited under this Convention.
2. Subject to the provisions of this Convention and without prejudice to the principles and applicable rules of international law, the States Parties shall:
   (a) Have the right, individually or collectively, to conduct research with, to develop, produce,acquire, retain, transfer, and use chemicals;
   (b) Undertake to facilitate, and have the right to participate in, the fullest possible exchange of chemicals, equipment and scientific and technical information relating to the development and application of chemistry for purposes not prohibited under this Convention;
   (c) Not maintain among themselves any restrictions, including those in any international agreements, incompatible with the obligations undertaken under this Convention, which would restrict or impede trade and the development and promotion of scientific and technological knowledge in the field of chemistry for industrial, agricultural, research, medical, pharmaceutical or other peaceful purposes;
   (d) Not use this Convention as grounds for applying any measures other than those provided for, or permitted, under this Convention nor use any other international agreement for pursuing an objective inconsistent with this Convention;
   (e) Undertake to review their existing national regulations in the field of trade in chemicals in order to render them consistent with the object and purpose of this Convention.

Art. XII. Measures to Redress a Situation and to Ensure Compliance, Including Sanctions

1. The Conference shall take the necessary measures, as set forth in paragraphs 2, 3 and 4, to ensure compliance with this Convention and to redress and remedy any situation which contravenes the provisions of this Convention. In considering action pursuant to this paragraph, the Conference shall take

into account all information and recommendations on the issues submitted by the Executive Council.

2. In cases where a State Party has been requested by the Executive Council to take measures to redress a situation raising problems with regard to its compliance, and where the State Party fails to fulfil the request within the specified time, the Conference may, *inter alia*, upon the recommendation of the Executive Council, restrict or suspend the State Party's rights and privileges under this Convention until it undertakes the necessary action to conform with its obligations under this Convention.
3. In cases where serious damage to the object and purpose of this Convention may result from activities prohibited under this Convention, in particular by Article I, the Conference may recommend collective measures to States Parties in conformity with international law.
4. The Conference shall, in cases of particular gravity, bring the issue, including relevant information and conclusions, to the attention of the United Nations General Assembly and the United Nations Security Council.

Art. XIII. Relation to Other International Agreements

Nothing in this Convention shall be interpreted as in any way limiting or detracting from the obligations assumed by any State under the Protocol for the Prohibition of the Use in War of Asphyxiating, Poisonous or Other Gases, and of Bacteriological Methods of Warfare, signed at Geneva on 17 June 1925, and under the Convention on the Prohibition of the Development, Production and Stockpiling of Bacteriological (Biological) and Toxin Weapons and on Their Destruction, signed at London, Moscow and Washington on 10 April 1972.

Art. XIV. Settlement of Disputes

1. Disputes that may arise concerning the application or the interpretation of this Convention shall be settled in accordance with the relevant provisions of this Convention and in conformity with the provisions of the Charter of the United Nations.
2. When a dispute arises between two or more States Parties, or between one or more States Parties and the Organization, relating to the interpretation or application of this Convention, the parties concerned shall consult together with a view to the expeditious settlement of the dispute by negotiation or by other peaceful means of the parties' choice, including recourse to appropriate organs of this Convention and, by mutual consent, referral to the International Court of Justice in conformity with the Statute of the Court. The States Parties involved shall keep the Executive Council informed of actions being taken.
3. The Executive Council may contribute to the settlement of a dispute by whatever means it deems appropriate, including offering its good offices, calling upon the States Parties to a dispute to start the settlement process of their choice and recommending a time-limit for any agreed procedure.
4. The Conference shall consider questions related to disputes raised by States Parties or brought to its attention by the Executive Council. The Conference shall, as it finds necessary, establish or entrust organs with tasks related to the settlement of these disputes in conformity with Article VIII, paragraph 21 (f).

5. The Conference and the Executive Council are separately empowered, subject to authorization from the General Assembly of the United Nations, to request the International Court of Justice to give an advisory opinion on any legal question arising within the scope of the activities of the Organization. An agreement between the Organization and the United Nations shall be concluded for this purpose in accordance with Article VIII, paragraph 34 (a).
6. This Article is without prejudice to Article IX or to the provisions on measures to redress asituation and to ensure compliance, including sanctions.

Art. XV. Amendments

1. Any State Party may propose amendments to this Convention. Any State Party may also propose changes, as specified in paragraph 4, to the Annexes of this Convention. Proposals for amendments shall be subject to the procedures in paragraphs 2 and 3. Proposals for changes, as specified in paragraph 4, shall be subject to the procedures in paragraph 5.
2. The text of a proposed amendment shall be submitted to the Director-General for circulation to all States Parties and to the Depositary. The proposed amendment shall be considered only by an Amendment Conference. Such an Amendment Conference shall be convened if one third or more of the States Parties notify the Director-General not later than 30 days after its circulation that they support further consideration of the proposal. The Amendment Conference shall be held immediately following a regular session of the Conference unless the requesting States Parties ask for an earlier meeting. In no case shall an Amendment Conference be held less than 60 days after the circulation of the proposed amendment.
3. Amendments shall enter into force for all States Parties 30 days after deposit of the instruments of ratification or acceptance by all the States Parties referred to under subparagraph (b) below:
   (a) When adopted by the Amendment Conference by a positive vote of a majority of all States Parties with no State Party casting a negative vote; and
   (b) Ratified or accepted by all those States Parties casting a positive vote at the Amendment Conference.
4. In order to ensure the viability and the effectiveness of this Convention, provisions in the Annexes shall be subject to changes in accordance with paragraph 5, if proposed changes are related only to matters of an administrative or technical nature. All changes to the Annex on Chemicals shall be made in accordance with paragraph 5. Sections A and C of the Confidentiality Annex, Part X of the Verification Annex, and those definitions in Part I of the Verification Annex which relate exclusively to challenge inspections, shall not be subject to changes in accordance with paragraph 5.
5. Proposed changes referred to in paragraph 4 shall be made in accordance with the following procedures:
   (a) The text of the proposed changes shall be transmitted together with the necessary information to the Director-General. Additional information for the evaluation of the proposal may be provided by any State Party and the Director-General. The Director-General shall promptly com-

municate any such proposals and information to all States Parties, the Executive Council and the Depositary;

(b) Not later than 60 days after its receipt, the Director-General shall evaluate the proposal to determine all its possible consequences for the provisions of this Convention and its implementation and shall communicate any such information to all States Parties and the Executive Council;

(c) The Executive Council shall examine the proposal in the light of all information available to it, including whether the proposal fulfils the requirements of paragraph 4. Not later than 90 days after its receipt, the Executive Council shall notify its recommendation, with appropriate explanations, to all States Parties for consideration. States Parties shall acknowledge receipt within 10 days;

(d) If the Executive Council recommends to all States Parties that the proposal be adopted, it shall be considered approved if no State Party objects to it within 90 days after receipt of the recommendation. If the Executive Council recommends that the proposal be rejected, it shall be considered rejected if no State Party objects to the rejection within 90 days after receipt of the recommendation;

(e) If a recommendation of the Executive Council does not meet with the acceptance required under subparagraph (d), a decision on the proposal, including whether it fulfils the requirements of paragraph 4, shall be taken as a matter of substance by the Conference at its next session;

(f) The Director-General shall notify all States Parties and the Depositary of any decision under this paragraph;

(g) Changes approved under this procedure shall enter into force for all States Parties 180 days after the date of notification by the Director-General of their approval unless another time period is recommended by the Executive Council or decided by the Conference.

Art. XVI. Duration and Withdrawal

1. This Convention shall be of unlimited duration.
2. Each State Party shall, in exercising its national sovereignty, have the right to withdraw from this Convention if it decides that extraordinary events, related to the subject-matter of this Convention, have jeopardized the supreme interests of its country. It shall give notice of such withdrawal 90 days in advance to all other States Parties, the Executive Council, the Depositary and the United Nations Security Council. Such notice shall include a statement of the extraordinary events it regards as having jeopardized its supreme interests.
3. The withdrawal of a State Party from this Convention shall not in any way affect the duty of States to continue fulfilling the obligations assumed under any relevant rules of international law, particularly the Geneva Protocol of 1925.

Art. XVII. Status of the Annexes

The Annexes form an integral part of this Convention. Any reference to this Convention includes the Annexes.

Art. XVIII. Signature

This Convention shall be open for signature for all States before its entry into force.

Art. XIX. Ratification

This Convention shall be subject to ratification by States Signatories according to their respective constitutional processes.

Art. XX. Accession

Any State which does not sign this Convention before its entry into force may accede to it at any time thereafter.

Art. XXI. Entry into Force

1. This Convention shall enter into force 180 days after the date of the deposit of the 65th instrument of ratification, but in no case earlier than two years after its opening for signature.
2. For States whose instruments of ratification or accession are deposited subsequent to the entry into force of this Convention, it shall enter into force on the 30th day following the date of deposit of their instrument of ratification or accession.

Art. XXII. Reservations

The Articles of this Convention shall not be subject to reservations. The Annexes of this Convention shall not be subject to reservations incompatible with its object and purpose.

Art XXIII. Depositary

The Secretary-General of the United Nations is hereby designated as the Depositary of this Convention and shall, *inter alia*:

(a) Promptly inform all signatory and acceding States of the date of each signature, the date of deposit of each instrument of ratification or accession and the date of the entry into force of this Convention, and of the receipt of other notices;
(b) Transmit duly certified copies of this Convention to the Governments of all signatory and acceding States; and
(c) Register this Convention pursuant to Article 102 of the Charter of the United Nations.

Art. XXIV. Authentic Texts

This Convention, of which the Arabic, Chinese, English, French, Russian and Spanish texts are equally authentic, shall be deposited with the Secretary-General of the United Nations.

In Witness Whereof the undersigned, being duly authorized to that effect, have signed this Convention.

Done at Paris on the thirteenth day of January, one thousand nine hundred and ninety-three.

ANNEXES

(The Annexes form an integral part of this Convention, but are not reproduced in the present collection, except the tables of contents, which follow.)

Annex on Chemicals

Contents

Annex on Implementation and Verification ("Verification Annex")

Contents

Modification of intermediate destruction deadlines
Extension of the deadline for completion of destruction
Detailed annual plans for destruction
Annual reports on destruction

D. Verification
Verification of declarations of chemical weapons through on-site inspection
Systematic verification of storage facilities
Inspections and visits
Systematic verification of the destruction of chemical weapons
Chemical weapons storage facilities at chemical weapons destruction facilities
Systematic on-site verification measures at chemical weapons destruction facilities

Part IV (B): Old Chemical Weapons and Abandoned Chemical Weapons

A. General
B. Regime for Old Chemical Weapons
C. Regime for Abandoned Chemical Weapons

Part V: Destruction of Chemical Weapons Production Facilities and its Verification Pursuant to Article V

A. Declarations
Declarations of chemical weapons production facilities
Declarations of chemical weapons production facilities pursuant to Article III, para.1 (c) (iii)
Declarations of past transfers and receipts
Submission of general plans for destruction
Submission of annual plans for destruction and annual reports on destruction

B. Destruction
General principles for destruction of chemical weapons production facilities
Principles and methods for closure of a chemical weapons production facility
Technical maintenance of chemical weapons production facilities prior to their destruction
Principles and methods for temporary conversion of chemical weaponsproduction facilities into chemical weapons destruction facilities
Principles and methods related to destruction of a chemical weapons production facility
Order of destruction
Detailed plans for destruction
Review of detailed plans

C. Verification
Verification of declarations of chemical weapons production facilities through on-site inspection
Systematic verification of chemical weapons production facilities and cessation of their activities
Verification of destruction of chemical weapons production facilities
Verification of temporary conversion of a chemical weapons production facility into a chemical weapons destruction facility

D. Conversion of Chemical Weapons Production Facilities to Purposes Not Prohibited under this Convention
Procedures for requesting conversion

Actions pending a decision
Conditions for conversion
Decisions by the Executive Council and the Conference
Detailed plans for conversion
Review of detailed plans

Part VI: Activities Not Prohibited under this Convention in Accordance with Article VI:
Regime for Schedule 1 Chemicals and Facilities Related to such Chemicals
A. General Provisions
B. Transfers
C. Production
General principles for production
Single small-scale facility
Other facilities
D. Declarations
Single small-scale facility
Other facilities referred to in paragraphs 10 and 11
E. Verification
Single small-scale facility
Other facilities referred to in paragraphs 10 and 11

Part VII: Activities Not Prohibited under this Convention in Accordance with Article VI:
Regime for Schedule 2 Chemicals and Facilities Related to such Chemicals
A. Declarations
Declarations of aggregate national data
Declarations of plant sites producing, processing or consuming Schedule 2 chemicals
Declarations on past production of Schedule 2 chemicals for chemical weapons purposes
Information to States Parties
B. Verification
General
Inspection aims
Initial inspections
Inspections
Inspection procedures
Notification of inspection
C. Transfers to States Not Party to this Convention

Part VIII: Activities Not Prohibited under this Convention in Accordance with Article VI:
Regime for Schedule 3 Chemicals and Facilities Related to such Chemicals
A. Declarations
Declarations of aggregate national data
Declarations of plant sites producing Schedule 3 chemicals
Declarations on past production of Schedule 3 chemicals for chemical weapons purposes
Information to States Parties
B. Verification
General
Inspection aims
Inspection procedures
Notification of inspection
C. Transfers to States Not Party to this Convention

Annex on the Protection of Confidential Information ("Confidentiality Annex")

Contents

TABLE OF SIGNATURES, RATIFICATIONS AND ACCESSIONS[1]

State	*Signature*	*Ratification, Accession*
Afghanistan	14 January 1993	–
Albania	14 January 1993	11 May 1994
Algeria	13 January 1993	14 August 1995
Argentina	13 January 1993	2 October 1995
Armenia	19 March 1993	27 January 1995
Australia	13 January 1993	6 May 1994
Austria	13 January 1993	17 August 1995 *Dec.*
Azerbaijan	13 January 1993	29 February 2000
Bahamas	2 March 1994	–
Bahrain	24 February 1993	28 April 1997
Bangladesh	14 January 1993	25 April 1997
Belarus	14 January 1993	11 July 1996
Belgium	13 January 1993 *Dec.*	27 January 1997 *Dec.*
Benin	14 January 1993	14 May 1998
Bhutan	24 April 1997	–
Bolivia	14 January 1993	14 August 1998
Bosnia and Herzegovina	16 January 1997	25 February 1997
Botswana	–	31 August 1998
Brazil	13 January 1993	13 March 1996
Brunei Darussalam	13 January 1993	28 July 1997
Bulgaria	13 January 1993	10 August 1994
Burkina Faso	14 January 1993	8 July 1997
Burundi	15 January 1993	4 September 1998
Cambodia	15 January 1993	–
Cameroon	14 January 1993	16 September 1996
Canada	13 January 1993	26 September 1995
Cape Verde	15 January 1993	–
Central African Republic	14 January 1993	–
Chad	11 October 1994	–
Chile	14 January 1993	12 July 1996
China	13 January 1993 *Dec.*	25 April 1997 *Dec.*
Colombia	13 January 1993	5 April 2000
Comoros	13 January 1993	–
Congo	15 January 1993	–
Cook Islands	14 January 1993	15 July 1994
Costa Rica	14 January 1993	31 May 1996
Côte d'Ivoire	13 January 1993	18 December 1995
Croatia	13 January 1993	23 May 1995
Cuba	13 January 1993	29 April 1997 *Dec.*

[1] Based on indications in *Multilateral Treaties Deposited with the Secretary-General, New York, United Nations* (ST/LEG/SER.E), as available on http://untreaty.un.org. See also ICRC website: www.icrc.org/ihl.nsf.

State	*Signature*	*Ratification, Accession*
Cyprus	13 January 1993	28 August 1998
Czech Republic	14 January 1993	6 March 1996
Democratic Republic of the Congo	14 January 1993	–
Denmark	14 January 1993 *Dec.*	13 July 1995
Djibouti	28 September 1993	–
Dominica	2 August 1993	12 February 2001
Dominican Republic	13 January 1993	–
Ecuador	14 January 1993	6 September 1995
El Salvador	14 January 1993	30 October 1995
Equatorial Guinea	14 January 1993	25 April 1997
Eritrea	–	14 February 2000
Estonia	14 January 1993	26 May 1999
Ethiopia	14 January 1993	13 May 1996
Fiji	14 January 1993	20 January 1993
Finland	14 January 1993	7 February 1995
France	13 January 1993 *Dec.*	2 March 1995
Gabon	13 January 1993	8 September 2000
Gambia	13 January 1993	19 May 1998
Georgia	14 January 1993	27 November 1995
Germany	13 January 1993 *Dec.*	12 August 1994 *Dec.*
Ghana	14 January 1993	9 July 1997
Greece	13 January 1993 *Dec.*	22 December 1994 *Dec.*
Grenada	9 April 1997	–
Guatemala	14 January 1993	–
Guinea	14 January 1993	9 June 1997
Guinea-Bissau	14 January 1993	–
Guyana	6 October 1993	12 September 1997
Haiti	4 January 1993	–
Holy See	14 January 1993	12 May 1999 *Dec.*
Honduras	13 January 1993	–
Hungary	13 January 1993	31 October 1996
Iceland	13 January 1993	28 April 1997
India	14 January 1993	3 September 1996
Indonesia	13 January 1993	12 November 1998
Iran (Islamic Republic of)	13 January 1993	3 November 1997 *Dec.*
Ireland	14 January 1993 *Dec.*	24 June 1996 *Dec.*
Israel	13 January 1993	–
Italy	13 January 1993 *Dec.*	8 December 1995 *Dec.*
Jamaica	18 April 1997	8 September 2000
Japan	13 January 1993	15 September 1995
Jordan	–	29 October 1997
Kazakhstan	14 January 1993	23 March 2000
Kenya	15 January 1993	25 April 1997
Kiribati	–	7 September 2000
Kuwait	27 January 1993	29 May 1997
Kyrgyzstan	22 February 1993	–
Lao People's Democratic Republic	13 May 1993	25 February 1997
Latvia	6 May 1993	23 July 1996
Lesotho	7 December 1994	7 December 1994
Liberia	15 January 1993	–
Liechtenstein	21 July 1993	24 November 1999
Lithuania	13 January 1993	15 April 1998
Luxembourg	13 January 1993 *Dec.*	15 April 1997 *Dec.*

State	*Signature*	*Ratification, Accession*
Madagascar	15 January 1993	–
Malawi	14 January 1993	11 June 1998
Malaysia	13 January 1993	20 April 2000
Maldives	4 October 1993	31 May 1994
Mali	13 January 1993	28 April 1997
Malta	13 January 1993	28 April 1997
Marshall Islands	13 January 1993	–
Mauritania	13 January 1993	9 February 1998
Mauritius	14 January 1993	9 February 1993
Mexico	13 January 1993	29 August 1994
Micronesia (Federated States of)	13 January 1993	21 June 1999
Monaco	13 January 1993	1 June 1995
Mongolia	14 January 1993	17 January 1995
Morocco	13 January 1993	28 December 1995
Mozambique	–	15 August 2000
Myanmar	14 January 1993	–
Namibia	13 January 1993	24 November 1995
Nauru	13 January 1993	12 November 2001
Nepal	19 January 1993	18 November 1997
Netherlands[2]	14 January 1993 *Dec.*	30 June 1995
New Zealand	14 January 1993	15 July 1996
Nicaragua	9 March 1993	5 November 1999
Niger	14 January 1993	9 April 1997
Nigeria	13 January 1993	20 May 1999
Norway	13 January 1993	7 April 1994
Oman	2 February 1993	8 February 1995
Pakistan	13 January 1993	28 October 1997 *Dec.*
Panama	16 June 1993	7 October 1998
Papua New Guinea	14 January 1993	17 April 1996
Paraguay	14 January 1993	1 December 1994
Peru	14 January 1993	20 July 1995
Philippines	13 January 1993	11 December 1996
Poland	13 January 1993	23 August 1995
Portugal	13 January 1993 *Dec.*	10 September 1996 *Dec.*
Qatar	1 February 1993	3 September 1997
Republic of Korea	14 January 1993	28 April 1997
Republic of Moldova	13 January 1993	8 July 1996
Romania	13 January 1993	15 February 1995
Russian Federation	13 January 1993	5 November 1997
Rwanda	17 May 1993	–
Saint Kitts and Nevis	16 March 1994	–
Saint Lucia	29 March 1993	9 April 1997
Saint Vincent and the Grenadines	20 September 1993	–
Samoa	14 January 1993	–
San Marino	13 January 1993	10 December 1999
Saudi Arabia	20 January 1993	9 August 1996
Senegal	13 January 1993	20 July 1998
Seychelles	15 January 1993	7 April 1993
Sierra Leone	15 January 1993	–
Singapore	14 January 1993	21 May 1997
Slovakia	14 January 1993	27 October 1995

[2] For the Kingdom in Europe. On 28 April 1997: For the Netherlands Antilles and Aruba.

State	*Signature*	*Ratification, Accession*
Slovenia	14 January 1993	11 June 1997
South Africa	14 January 1993	13 September 1995
Spain	13 January 1993 *Dec.*	3 August 1994 *Dec.*
Sri Lanka	14 January 1993	19 August 1994
Sudan	–	24 May 1999 *Dec.*
Suriname	28 April 1997	28 April 1997
Swaziland	23 September 1993	20 November 1996
Sweden	13 January 1993	17 June 1993
Switzerland	14 January 1993	10 March 1995
Tajikistan	14 January 1993	11 January 1995
Thailand	14 January 1993	10 December 2002
The former Yugoslav Republic of Macedonia		20 June 1997
Togo	13 January 1993	23 April 1997
Trinidad and Tobago	–	24 June 1997
Tunisia	13 January 1993	15 April 1997
Turkey	14 January 1993	12 May 1997
Turkmenistan	12 October 1993	29 September 1994
Uganda	14 January 1993	30 November 2001
Ukraine	13 January 1993	16 October 1998
United Arab Emirates	2 February 1993	28 November 2000
United Kingdom	13 January 1993 *Dec.*	13 May 1996
United Republic of Tanzania	25 February 1994	25 June 1998
United States of America	13 January 1993	25 April 1997 *Dec.*
Uruguay	15 January 1993	6 October 1994
Uzbekistan	24 November 1995	23 July 1996
Venezuela	14 January 1993	3 December 1997
Viet Nam	13 January 1993	30 September 1998
Yemen	8 February 1993	2 October 2000
Yugoslavia	–	20 April 2000
Zambia	13 January 1993	9 February 2001
Zimbabwe	13 January 1993	25 April 1997

RESERVATIONS AND DECLARATIONS

AUSTRIA (*declaration made on ratification*)
As a Member State of the European Community, the Government of Austria will implement the provisions of the Convention on the Prohibition of Chemical Weapons, in accordance with its obligations arising from the rules of the Treaties establishing the European Communities to the extent that such rules are applicable.

BELGIUM (*declaration made upon signature and confirmed upon ratification*)
As a Member State of the European Community, the Government of Belgium will implement the provisions of the Convention on the Prohibition of Chemical Weapons, in accordance with its obligations arising from the rules of the Treaties establishing the European Communities to the extent that such rules are applicable.

CHINA
Declarations made upon signature

I. China has consistently stood for the complete prohibition and thorough destruction of all chemical weapons and their production facilities. The Convention constitutes the legal basis for the realization of this goal. China therefore supports the object and purpose and principles of the Convention.

II. The object and purpose and principles of the Convention should be strictly abided by. The relevant provisions on challenge inspection should not be abused to the detriment of the security interests of States Parties unrelated to chemical weapons. Otherwise, the universality of the Convention is bound to be adversely affected.

III. States Parties that have abandoned chemical weapons on the territories of other States parties should implement in earnest the relevant provisions of the Convention and undertake the obligation to destroy the abandoned chemical weapons.

IV. The Convention should effectively facilitate trade, scientific and technological exchanges and cooperation in the field of chemistry for peaceful purposes. All export controls inconsistent with the Convention should be abolished.

Declarations made upon ratification

1. China has always stood for complete prohibition and thorough destruction of chemical weapons. As CWC has laid an international legal foundation for the realization of this goal, China supports the purpose, objectives and principles of the CWC.
2. China calls upon the countries with the largest chemical weapons arsenals to ratify CWC without delay with a view to attaining its purposes and objectives at an early date.
3. The purposes, objectives and principles of CWC should be strictly observed. The provisions concerning challenge inspection shall not be abused and the national security interests of States parties not related to chemical weapons shall not be compromised. China is firmly opposed to any act of abusing the verification provisions which endangers its sovereignty and security.
4. Any country which has abandoned chemical weapons on the territory of another country should effectively implement the relevant CWC provisions, undertake the obligations to destroy those chemical weapons and ensure the earliest complete destruction of all the chemical weapons it has abandoned on another state's territory.
5. CWC should play a sound role in promoting international trade, scientific and technological exchanges and cooperation for peaceful purposes in the field of chemical industry. It should become the effective legal basis for regulating trade and exchange among the state parties in the field of chemical industry.

CUBA (*declarations made upon ratification*)

The Government of the Republic of Cuba declares, in conformity with article III (a) (iii) of the Convention, that there is a colonial enclave in its territory – the Guantanamo Naval Base – a part of Cuban national territory over which the Cuban State does not exercise its rightful jurisdiction, owing to its illegal occupation by the United States of America by reason of a deceitful and fraudulent Treaty.

Consequently, for the purposes of the Convention, the Government of the Republic of Cuba does not assume any responsibility with respect to the aforesaid territory, since it does not know whether or not the United States has installed, possesses, maintains or intends to possess chemical weapons in the part of Cuban territory that it illegally occupies.

The Government of the Republic of Cuba also considers that it has the right to require that the entry of any inspection group mandated by the Organization for the Prohibition of Chemical Weapons, to carry out in the territory of Guantanamo Naval Base the verification activities provided for in the Convention, should be effected through a point of entry in Cuban national territory to be determined by the Cuban Government.

The Government of the Republic of Cuba considers that, under the provisions of article XI of the Convention, the unilateral application by a State party to the Convention against another State party of any restriction which would restrict or impede trade and the development and promotion of scientific and technological knowledge in the field of chemistry for industrial, agricultural, research, medical, pharmaceutical or other purposes not prohibited under the Convention, would be incompatible with the object and purpose of the Convention.

The Government of Cuba designates the Ministry of Science, Technology and Environment, in its capacity as the national authority of the Republic of Cuba for the Convention on the Prohibition of the Development, Production, Stockpiling and Use of Chemical Weapons and on Their Destruction, as the body of the central administration of the State responsible for organizing, directing, monitoring and supervising the activities aimed at preparing the Republic of Cuba to fulfil the obligations it is assuming as a State party to the aforementioned Convention.

DENMARK (*declaration made upon signature*)
As a Member State of the European Community, the Government of Denmark will implement the provisions of the Convention on the Prohibition of Chemical Weapons, in accordance with its obligations arising from the rules of the Treaties establishing the European Communities to the extent that such rules are applicable.

FRANCE (*declaration made upon signature*)
As a Member State of the European Community, the Government of France will implement the provisions of the Convention on the Prohibition of Chemical Weapons, in accordance with its obligations arising from the rules of the Treaties establishing the European Communities to the extent that such rules are applicable.

GERMANY (*declaration made upon signature and confirmed upon ratification*)
As a Member State of the European Community, the Government of Germany will implement the provisions of the Convention on the Prohibition of Chemical Weapons, in accordance with its obligations arising from the rules of the Treaties establishing the European Communities to the extent that such rules are applicable.

GREECE (*declaration made upon signature and confirmed upon ratification*)
As a Member State of the European Community, the Government of Greece will implement the provisions of the Convention on the Prohibition of Chemical Weapons, in accordance with its obligations arising from the rules of the Treaties establishing the European Communities to the extent that such rules are applicable.

HOLY SEE (*declaration made upon ratification*)
[...] the Holy See, in conformity with the nature and particular condition of Vatican City State, intends to renew its encouragement to the International Community to continue on the path towards a situation of general and complete disarmament, capable of promoting peace and cooperation at world level.

Dialogue and multilateral negotiation are essential values in this process. Through the instruments of international law, they facilitate the peaceful resolution of controversies and help better mutual understanding. In this way they promote the effective affirmation of the culture of life and peace.

While not possessing chemical weapons of any kind, the Holy See accedes to the solemn act of ratification of the Convention in order to lend its moral support to this important area of international relations which seeks to ban weapons which are particularly cruel and inhuman and aimed at producing long-term traumatic effects among the defenceless civilian population."

IRAN (ISLAMIC REPUBLIC OF) (*declarations made upon ratification*)
The Islamic Republic of Iran, on the basis of the Islamic principles and beliefs, considers chemical weapons inhuman, and has consistently been on the vanguard of the international efforts to abolish these weapons and prevent their use.

1. The Islamic Consultative Assembly (the Parliament) of the Islamic Republic of Iran approved the bill presented by the Government to join the [said Convention] on 27 July 1997, and the Guardian Council found the legislation compatible with the Constitution and the Islamic Tenets on 30 July 1997, in accordance with its required Constitutional process. The Islamic Consultative Assembly decided that:

- The Government is hereby authorized, at an appropriate time, to accede to the [said Convention] – as annexed to this legislation and to deposit its relevant instrument.
- The Ministry of Foreign Affairs must pursue in all negotiations and within the framework of the Organization of the Convention, the full and indiscriminate implementation of the Convention, particularly in the areas of inspection and transfer of technology and chemicals for peaceful purposes. In case the afore-mentioned requirements are not materialized, upon the recommendation of the Cabinet and approval of the Supreme National Security Council, steps aimed at withdrawing from the Convention will be put in motion.

2. The Islamic Republic of Iran attaches vital significance to the full, unconditional and indiscriminate implementation of all provisions of the Convention. It reserves the right to withdraw from the Convention under the following circumstances:
   - non-compliance with the principle of equal treatment of all States Parties in implementation of all relevant provisions of the Convention;
   - disclosure of its confidential information contrary to the provisions of the Convention;
   - imposition of restrictions incompatible with the obligations under the Convention.
3. As stipulated in article XI, exclusive and non-transparent regimes impeding free international trade in chemicals and chemical technology for peaceful purposes should be disbanded. The Islamic Republic of Iran rejects any chemical export control mechanism not envisaged in the Convention.
4. The Organization for Prohibition of Chemical Weapons (OPCW) is the sole international authority to determine the compliance of States Parties regarding chemical weapons. Accusations by States Parties against other States Parties in the absence of a determination of non-compliance by OPCW will seriously undermine the Convention and its repetition may make the Convention meaningless.
5. One of the objectives of the Convention as stipulated in its preamble is to promote free trade in chemicals as well as international cooperation and exchange of scientific and technical information in the field of chemical activities for purposes not prohibited under the Convention in order to enhance the economic and technological development of all States Parties.' This fundamental objective of the Convention should be respected and embraced by all States Parties to the Convention. Any form of undermining, either in words or in action, of this overriding objective is considered by the Islamic Republic fo Iran a grave breach of the provisions of the Convention.
6. In line with the provisions of the Convention regarding non-discriminatory treatment of States Parties:
   - inspection equipment should be commercially available to all States Parties without condition or limitation.
   - the OPCW should maintain its international character by ensuring fair and balanced geographical distribution of the personnel of its Technical Secretariat, provision of assistance to and cooperation with States Parties, and equitable membership of States Parties in subsidiary organs of the Organization,
7. The implementation of the Convention should contribute to international peace and security and should not in any way diminish or harm national security or territorial integrity of the States Parties."

IRELAND (*declaration made upon signature and confirmed upon ratification*)
As a Member State of the European Community, the Government of Ireland will implement the provisions of the Convention on the Prohibition of Chemical Weapons, in accordance with its obligations arising from the rules of the Treaties establishing the European Communities to the extent that such rules are applicable.

ITALY (*declaration made upon signature and confirmed upon ratification*)
As a Member State of the European Community, the Government of Italy will implement the provisions of the Convention on the Prohibition of Chemical Weapons, in accordance with its obligations arising from the rules of the Treaties establishing the European Communities to the extent that such rules are applicable.

LUXEMBOURG (*declaration made upon signature and confirmed upon ratification*)
As a Member State of the European Community, the Government of Luxembourg will implement the provisions of the Convention on the Prohibition of Chemical Weapons, in accordance with its obligations arising from the rules of the Treaties establishing the European Communities to the extent that such rules are applicable.

NETHERLANDS (*declaration made upon signature*)
As a Member State of the European Community, the Government of the Netherlands will implement the provisions of the Convention on the Prohibition of Chemical Weapons, in accordance with its obligations arising from the rules of the Treaties establishing the European Communities to the extent that such rules are applicable.

PAKISTAN (*declaration made upon ratification*)
1. Pakistan has consistently stood for the complete prohibition and thorough destruction of all chemical weapons and their production facilities. The Convention constitutes an international legal framework for the realization of this goal. Pakistan, therefore, supports the objectives and purposes of the Convention.
2. The objectives and purposes of the Convention must be strictly adhered to by all states. The relevant provisions on Challenge Inspections must not be abused to the detriment of the economic and security interests of the States Parties unrelated to chemical weapons. Otherwise, the universality and effectiveness of the Convention is bound to be jeopardized.
3. Abuse of the verification provisions of the Convention, for purposes unrelated to the Convention, will not be acceptable. Pakistan will never allow its sovereignty and national security to be compromised.
4. The Convention should effectively facilitate trade, scientific and technological exchanges and co-operation in the field of chemistry for peaceful purposes. All export control regimes inconsistent with the Convention must be abolished.

PORTUGAL (*declaration made upon signature and confirmed upon ratification*)
As a Member State of the European Community, the Government of Portugal will implement the provisions of the Convention on the Prohibition of Chemical Weapons, in accordance with its obligations arising from the rules of the Treaties establishing the European Communities to the extent that such rules are applicable.

SPAIN (*declaration made upon signature and confirmed upon ratification*)
As a Member State of the European Community, the Government of Spain will implement the provisions of the Convention on the Prohibition of Chemical Weapons, in accordance with its obligations arising from the rules of the Treaties establishing the European Communities to the extent that such rules are applicable.

SUDAN (*declaration of understanding made upon accession*)
Firstly, the unilateral application by a State Party to the Convention, runs counter to the objectives and purposes of the Convention.

Secondly, the Convention must be fully and indiscriminately implemented particularly in the areas of inspection and transfer of technology for peaceful purposes.

Thirdly, no restrictions incompatible with the obligations under the Convention shall be imposed.

Fourthly, the Organization for Prohibition of Chemical Weapons (OPCW), is the sole international authority to determine the compliance of States Parties with the provisions of the Convention.

United Kingdom (*declaration made upon signature*)
As a Member State of the European Community, the Government of United Kingdom will implement the provisions of the Convention on the Prohibition of Chemical Weapons, in accordance with its obligations arising from the rules of the Treaties establishing the European Communities to the extent that such rules are applicable.

United States of America (*declaration made upon ratification*)
Subject to the condition which relates to the Annex on Implementation and Verification, that no sample collected in the United States pursuant to the Convention will be transferred for analysis to any laboratory outside the territory of the United States.

No. 23

CONVENTION ON THE PROHIBITION OF THE USE, STOCKPILING, PRODUCTION AND TRANSFER OF ANTI-PERSONNEL MINES AND ON THEIR DESTRUCTION

Adopted at Oslo on 18 September 1997

INTRODUCTORY NOTE: The amended Protocol II on prohibitions or restrictions on the use of mines, booby-traps and other devices (*No. 20*, Annex, of 3 May 1996), did not meet the expectations of those who aimed at a total prohibition of anti-personnel land mines. The problem of these weapons – of which more than 100 million are scattered in many states that had experienced civil wars, killing about 800 people every month – had still to be resolved. On the initiative of the Canadian government, the states interested in a total prohibition of anti-personnel land mines met in Ottawa from 3 to 5 October 1996. Following further meetings, a diplomatic conference took place in Oslo from 1 to 18 September 1997, which adopted the present Convention (often called the "Ottawa Convention").

ENTRY INTO FORCE: 1 March 1999.

AUTHENTIC TEXTS: Arabic, Chinese, English, French, Russian, Spanish.

TEXT PUBLISHED IN: *Conference of Disarmament* CD/1478 (Arabic, Chinese, Engl. French, Russ., Span.); *ILM*, Vol. 36, 1997, pp. 1509–1519 (Engl.); *IRRC*, Vol. 37, 1997, pp. 563–578 (Engl.); *RICR*, Vol. 79, 1997, No. 827, pp. 603–619 (French); *RICR* (Span.), 1997, (Span.); Roberts and Guelff, pp. 645–666 (Engl.). ICRC website: http://www.icrc.org/ihl.nsf (Engl., French); UN website: http://untreaty.un.org; http://disarmament.un.org/TreatyStatus.nsf; GRIP data: www.ib.be/grip/ bdg/g1653.html (Engl., French).

TABLE OF CONTENTS

* * *

Preamble[1]

The States Parties,

Determined to put an end to the suffering and casualties caused by anti-personnel mines, that kill or maim hundreds of people every week, mostly innocent and defenceless civilians and especially children, obstruct economic development and reconstruction, inhibit the repatriation of refugees and internally displaced persons, and have other severe consequences for years after emplacement,

Believing it necessary to do their utmost to contribute in an efficient and coordinated manner to face the challenge of removing anti-personnel mines placed throughout the world, and to assure their destruction,

Wishing to do their utmost in providing assistance for the care and rehabilitation, including the social and economic reintegration of mine victims,

Recognizing that a total ban of anti-personnel mines would also be an important confidence-building measure,

Welcoming the adoption of the Protocol on Prohibitions or Restrictions on the Use of Mines, Booby-Traps and Other Devices, as amended on 3 May 1996, annexed to the Convention on Prohibitions or Restrictions on the Use of Certain Conventional Weapons Which May Be Deemed to Be Excessively Injurious or to Have Indiscriminate Effects, and calling for the early ratification of this Protocol by all States which have not yet done so,

Welcoming also United Nations General Assembly Resolution 51/45 S of 10 December 1996 urging all States to pursue vigorously an effective, legally-binding international agreement to ban the use, stockpiling, production and transfer of anti-personnel landmines,

Welcoming furthermore the measures taken over the past years, both unilaterally and multilaterally, aiming at prohibiting, restricting or suspending the use, stockpiling, production and transfer of anti-personnel mines,

Stressing the role of public conscience in furthering the principles of humanity as evidenced by the call for a total ban of anti-personnel mines and recognizing the efforts to that end undertaken by the International Red Cross and Red Crescent Movement, the International Campaign to Ban Landmines and numerous other non-governmental organizations around the world,

---

[1] For declarations in respect of this Convention by Australia, Greece and Lithuania, see pp. 301–302.

Recalling the Ottawa Declaration of 5 October 1996 and the Brussels Declaration of 27 June 1997 urging the international community to negotiate an international and legally binding agreement prohibiting the use, stockpiling, production and transfer of anti-personnel mines,

Emphasizing the desirability of attracting the adherence of all States to this Convention, and determined to work strenuously towards the promotion of its universalization in all relevant fora including, inter alia, the United Nations, the Conference on Disarmament, regional organizations, and groupings, and review conferences of the Convention on Prohibitions or Restrictions on the Use of Certain Conventional Weapons Which May Be Deemed to Be Excessively Injurious or to Have Indiscriminate Effects,

Basing themselves on the principle of international humanitarian law that the right of the parties to an armed conflict to choose methods or means of warfare is not unlimited, on the principle that prohibits the employment in armed conflicts of weapons, projectiles and materials and methods of warfare of a nature to cause superfluous injury or unnecessary suffering and on the principle that a distinction must be made between civilians and combatants,

Have agreed as follows:

Article 1. General obligations

1. Each State Party undertakes never under any circumstances:
   (a)[2] To use anti-personnel mines;
   (b) To develop, produce, otherwise acquire, stockpile, retain or transfer to anyone, directly or indirectly, anti-personnel mines;
   (c) To assist, encourage or induce, in any way, anyone to engage in any activity prohibited to a State Party under this Convention.[3]
2. Each State Party undertakes to destroy or ensure the destruction of all anti-personnel mines in accordance with the provisions of this Convention.

Art. 2. Definitions

1.[4] "Anti-personnel mine" means a mine designed to be exploded by the presence, proximity or contact of a person and that will incapacitate, injure or kill one or more persons. Mines designed to be detonated by the presence, proximity or contact of a vehicle as opposed to a person, that are equipped with anti-handling devices, are not considered anti-personnel mines as a result of being so equipped.

2. "Mine" means a munition designed to be placed under, on or near the ground or other surface area and to be exploded by the presence, proximity or contact of a person or a vehicle.

3. "Anti-handling device" means a device intended to protect a mine and which is part of, linked to, attached to or placed under the mine and which activates when an attempt is made to tamper with or otherwise intentionally disturb the mine.

4. "Transfer" involves, in addition to the physical movement of anti-personnel mines into or from national territory, the transfer of title to and control over

---

[2] For declaration of understanding in respect of this paragraph by Australia, see p. 301.

[3] For declaration of understanding in respect of this paragraph by Australia, Canada, the Czech Republic and the United Kingdom, see pp. 301–302.

[4] For declaration of understanding in respect of this paragraph by Australia, see p. 301.

the mines, but does not involve the transfer of territory containing emplaced anti-personnel mines.

5. "Mined area" means an area which is dangerous due to the presence or suspected presence of mines.

Art. 3. Exceptions

1. Notwithstanding the general obligations under Article 1, the retention or transfer of a number of anti-personnel mines for the development of and training in mine detection, mine clearance, or mine destruction techniques is permitted. The amount of such mines shall not exceed the minimum number absolutely necessary for the above-mentioned purposes.
2. The transfer of anti-personnel mines for the purpose of destruction is permitted.

Art. 4.[5] Destruction of stockpiled anti-personnel mines

Except as provided for in Article 3, each State Party undertakes to destroy or ensure the destruction of all stockpiled anti-personnel mines it owns or possesses, or that are under its jurisdiction or control, as soon as possible but not later than four years after the entry into force of this Convention for that State Party.

Art. 5. Destruction of anti-personnel mines in mined areas

1.[6] Each State Party undertakes to destroy or ensure the destruction of all anti-personnel mines in mined areas under its jurisdiction or control, as soon as possible but not later than ten years after the entry into force of this Convention for that State Party.

2.[7] Each State Party shall make every effort to identify all areas under its jurisdiction or control in which anti-personnel mines are known or suspected to be emplaced and shall ensure as soon as possible that all anti-personnel mines in mined areas under its jurisdiction or control are perimeter-marked, monitored and protected by fencing or other means, to ensure the effective exclusion of civilians, until all anti-personnel mines contained therein have been destroyed. The marking shall at least be to the standards set out in the Protocol on Prohibitions or Restrictions on the Use of Mines, Booby-Traps and Other Devices, as amended on 3 May 1996, annexed to the Convention on Prohibitions or Restrictions on the Use of Certain Conventional Weapons Which May Be Deemed to Be Excessively Injurious or to Have Indiscriminate Effects.

3. If a State Party believes that it will be unable to destroy or ensure the destruction of all anti-personnel mines referred to in paragraph 1 within that time period, it may submit a request to a Meeting of the States Parties or a Review Conference for an extension of the deadline for completing the destruction of such anti-personnel mines, for a period of up to ten years.

4. Each request shall contain:
   (a) The duration of the proposed extension;

---

[5] For declaration of understanding in respect of this paragraph by Australia, see p. 301.
[6] For declaration of understanding in respect of this paragraph by Australia, see p. 301.
[7] For declaration of understanding in respect of this paragraph by Australia, see p. 301.

(b) A detailed explanation of the reasons for the proposed extension, including:
   (i) The preparation and status of work conducted under national demining programs;
   (ii) The financial and technical means available to the State Party for the destruction of all the anti-personnel mines; and
   (iii) Circumstances which impede the ability of the State Party to destroy all the anti-personnel mines in mined areas;
(c) The humanitarian, social, economic, and environmental implications of the extension; and
(d) Any other information relevant to the request for the proposed extension.

5. The Meeting of the States Parties or the Review Conference shall, taking into consideration the factors contained in paragraph 4, assess the request and decide by a majority of votes of States Parties present and voting whether to grant the request for an extension period.
6. Such an extension may be renewed upon the submission of a new request in accordance with paragraphs 3, 4 and 5 of this Article. In requesting a further extension period a State Party shall submit relevant additional information on what has been undertaken in the previous extension period pursuant to this Article.

Art. 6. International cooperation and assistance

1. In fulfilling its obligations under this Convention each State Party has the right to seek and receive assistance, where feasible, from other States Parties to the extent possible.
2. Each State Party undertakes to facilitate and shall have the right to participate in the fullest possible exchange of equipment, material and scientific and technological information concerning the implementation of this Convention. The States Parties shall not impose undue restrictions on the provision of mine clearance equipment and related technological information for humanitarian purposes.
3. Each State Party in a position to do so shall provide assistance for the care and rehabilitation, and social and economic reintegration, of mine victims and for mine awareness programs. Such assistance may be provided, inter alia, through the United Nations system, international, regional or national organizations or institutions, the International Committee of the Red Cross, national Red Cross and Red Crescent societies and their International Federation, non-governmental organizations, or on a bilateral basis.
4. Each State Party in a position to do so shall provide assistance for mine clearance and related activities. Such assistance may be provided, inter alia, through the United Nations system, international or regional organizations or institutions, non-governmental organizations or institutions, or on a bilateral basis, or by contributing to the United Nations Voluntary Trust Fund for Assistance in Mine Clearance, or other regional funds that deal with demining.
5. Each State Party in a position to do so shall provide assistance for the destruction of stockpiled anti-personnel mines.
6. Each State Party undertakes to provide information to the database on mine clearance established within the United Nations system, especially

information concerning various means and technologies of mine clearance, and lists of experts, expert agencies or national points of contact on mine clearance.

7. States Parties may request the United Nations, regional organizations, other States Parties or other competent intergovernmental or non-governmental fora to assist its authorities in the elaboration of a national demining program to determine, inter alia:
   (a) The extent and scope of the anti-personnel mine problem;
   (b) The financial, technological and human resources that are required for the implementation of the program;
   (c) The estimated number of years necessary to destroy all anti-personnel mines in mined areas under the jurisdiction or control of the concerned State Party;
   (d) Mine awareness activities to reduce the incidence of mine-related injuries or deaths;
   (e) Assistance to mine victims;
   (f) The relationship between the Government of the concerned State Party and the relevant governmental, inter-governmental or non-governmental entities that will work in the implementation of the program.
8. Each State Party giving and receiving assistance under the provisions of this Article shall cooperate with a view to ensuring the full and prompt implementation of agreed assistance programs.

Art. 7. Transparency measures

1. Each State Party shall report to the Secretary-General of the United Nations as soon as practicable, and in any event not later than 180 days after the entry into force of this Convention for that State Party on:
   (a) The national implementation measures referred to in Article 9;
   (b)[8] The total of all stockpiled anti-personnel mines owned or possessed by it, or under its jurisdiction or control, to include a breakdown of the type, quantity and, if possible, lot numbers of each type of anti-personnel mine stockpiled;
   (c)[9] To the extent possible, the location of all mined areas that contain, or are suspected to contain, anti-personnel mines under its jurisdiction or control, to include as much detail as possible regarding the type and quantity of each type of anti-personnel mine in each mined area and when they were emplaced;
   (d) The types, quantities and, if possible, lot numbers of all anti-personnel mines retained or transferred for the development of and training in mine detection, mine clearance or mine destruction techniques, or transferred for the purpose of destruction, as well as the institutions authorized by a State Party to retain or transfer anti-personnel mines, in accordance with Article 3;
   (e) The status of programs for the conversion or de-commissioning of anti-personnel mine production facilities;
   (f) The status of programs for the destruction of anti-personnel mines in accordance with Articles 4 and 5, including details of the methods

8 For declaration of understanding in respect of this paragraph by Australia, see p. 301.

9 For declaration of understanding in respect of this paragraph by Australia, see p. 301.

which will be used in destruction, the location of all destruction sites and the applicable safety and environmental standards to be observed;

(g) The types and quantities of all anti-personnel mines destroyed after the entry into force of this Convention for that State Party, to include a breakdown of the quantity of each type of anti-personnel mine destroyed, in accordance with Articles 4 and 5, respectively, along with, if possible, the lot numbers of each type of anti-personnel mine in the case of destruction in accordance with Article 4;

(h) The technical characteristics of each type of anti-personnel mine produced, to the extent known, and those currently owned or possessed by a State Party, giving, where reasonably possible, such categories of information as may facilitate identification and clearance of anti-personnel mines; at a minimum, this information shall include the dimensions, fusing, explosive content, metallic content, colour photographs and other information which may facilitate mine clearance; and

(i) The measures taken to provide an immediate and effective warning to the population in relation to all areas identified under paragraph 2 of Article 5.

2. The information provided in accordance with this Article shall be updated by the States Parties annually, covering the last calendar year, and reported to the Secretary-General of the United Nations not later than 30 April of each year.
3. The Secretary-General of the United Nations shall transmit all such reports received to the States Parties.

Art. 8. Facilitation and clarification of compliance

1. The States Parties agree to consult and cooperate with each other regarding the implementation of the provisions of this Convention, and to work together in a spirit of cooperation to facilitate compliance by States Parties with their obligations under this Convention.
2. If one or more States Parties wish to clarify and seek to resolve questions relating to compliance with the provisions of this Convention by another State Party, it may submit, through the Secretary-General of the United Nations, a Request for Clarification of that matter to that State Party. Such a request shall be accompanied by all appropriate information. Each State Party shall refrain from unfounded Requests for Clarification, care being taken to avoid abuse. A State Party that receives a Request for Clarification shall provide, through the Secretary-General of the United Nations, within 28 days to the requesting State Party all information which would assist in clarifying this matter.
3. If the requesting State Party does not receive a response through the Secretary-General of the United Nations within that time period, or deems the response to the Request for Clarification to be unsatisfactory, it may submit the matter through the Secretary-General of the United Nations to the next Meeting of the States Parties. The Secretary-General of the United Nations shall transmit the submission, accompanied by all appropriate information pertaining to the Request for Clarification, to all States Parties. All such information shall be presented to the requested State Party which shall have the right to respond.

4. Pending the convening of any meeting of the States Parties, any of the States Parties concerned may request the Secretary-General of the United Nations to exercise his or her good offices to facilitate the clarification requested.
5. The requesting State Party may propose through the Secretary-General of the United Nations the convening of a Special Meeting of the States Parties to consider the matter. The Secretary-General of the United Nations shall thereupon communicate this proposal and all information submitted by the States Parties concerned, to all States Parties with a request that they indicate whether they favour a Special Meeting of the States Parties, for the purpose of considering the matter. In the event that within 14 days from the date of such communication, at least one-third of the States Parties favours such a Special Meeting, the Secretary-General of the United Nations shall convene this Special Meeting of the States Parties within a further 14 days. A quorum for this Meeting shall consist of a majority of States Parties.
6. The Meeting of the States Parties or the Special Meeting of the States Parties, as the case may be, shall first determine whether to consider the matter further, taking into account all information submitted by the States Parties concerned. The Meeting of the States Parties or the Special Meeting of the States Parties shall make every effort to reach a decision by consensus. If despite all efforts to that end no agreement has been reached, it shall take this decision by a majority of States Parties present and voting.
7. All States Parties shall cooperate fully with the Meeting of the States Parties or the Special Meeting of the States Parties in the fulfilment of its review of the matter, including any fact-finding missions that are authorized in accordance with paragraph 8.
8. If further clarification is required, the Meeting of the States Parties or the Special Meeting of the States Parties shall authorize a fact-finding mission and decide on its mandate by a majority of States Parties present and voting. At any time the requested State Party may invite a fact-finding mission to its territory. Such a mission shall take place without a decision by a Meeting of the States Parties or a Special Meeting of the States Parties to authorize such a mission. The mission, consisting of up to 9 experts, designated and approved in accordance with paragraphs 9 and 10, may collect additional information on the spot or in other places directly related to the alleged compliance issue under the jurisdiction or control of the requested State Party.
9. The Secretary-General of the United Nations shall prepare and update a list of the names, nationalities and other relevant data of qualified experts provided by States Parties and communicate it to all States Parties. Any expert included on this list shall be regarded as designated for all fact-finding missions unless a State Party declares its non-acceptance in writing. In the event of non-acceptance, the expert shall not participate in fact-finding missions on the territory or any other place under the jurisdiction or control of the objecting State Party, if the non-acceptance was declared prior to the appointment of the expert to such missions.
10. Upon receiving a request from the Meeting of the States Parties or a Special Meeting of the States Parties, the Secretary-General of the United Nations shall, after consultations with the requested State Party, appoint

the members of the mission, including its leader. Nationals of States Parties requesting the fact-finding mission or directly affected by it shall not be appointed to the mission. The members of the fact-finding mission shall enjoy privileges and immunities under Article VI of the Convention on the Privileges and Immunities of the United Nations, adopted on 13 February 1946.

11. Upon at least 72 hours notice, the members of the fact-finding mission shall arrive in the territory of the requested State Party at the earliest opportunity. The requested State Party shall take the necessary administrative measures to receive, transport and accommodate the mission, and shall be responsible for ensuring the security of the mission to the maximum extent possible while they are on territory under its control.
12. Without prejudice to the sovereignty of the requested State Party, the fact-finding mission may bring into the territory of the requested State Party the necessary equipment which shall be used exclusively for gathering information on the alleged compliance issue. Prior to its arrival, the mission will advise the requested State Party of the equipment that it intends to utilize in the course of its fact-finding mission.
13. The requested State Party shall make all efforts to ensure that the fact-finding mission is given the opportunity to speak with all relevant persons who may be able to provide information related to the alleged compliance issue.
14. The requested State Party shall grant access for the fact-finding mission to all areas and installations under its control where facts relevant to the compliance issue could be expected to be collected. This shall be subject to any arrangements that the requested State Party considers necessary for:
    (a) The protection of sensitive equipment, information and areas;
    (b) The protection of any constitutional obligations the requested State Party may have with regard to proprietary rights, searches and seizures, or other constitutional rights; or
    (c) The physical protection and safety of the members of the fact-finding mission.

    In the event that the requested State Party makes such arrangements, it shall make every reasonable effort to demonstrate through alternative means its compliance with this Convention.
15. The fact-finding mission may remain in the territory of the State Party concerned for no more than 14 days, and at any particular site no more than 7 days, unless otherwise agreed.
16. All information provided in confidence and not related to the subject matter of the fact-finding mission shall be treated on a confidential basis.
17. The fact-finding mission shall report, through the Secretary-General of the United Nations, to the Meeting of the States Parties or the Special Meeting of the States Parties the results of its findings.
18. The Meeting of the States Parties or the Special Meeting of the States Parties shall consider all relevant information, including the report submitted by the fact-finding mission, and may request the requested State Party to take measures to address the compliance issue within a specified period of time. The requested State Party shall report on all measures taken in response to this request.
19. The Meeting of the States Parties or the Special Meeting of the States Parties may suggest to the States Parties concerned ways and means to fur-

ther clarify or resolve the matter under consideration, including the initiation of appropriate procedures in conformity with international law. In circumstances where the issue at hand is determined to be due to circumstances beyond the control of the requested State Party, the Meeting of the States Parties or the Special Meeting of the States Parties may recommend appropriate measures, including the use of cooperative measures referred to in Article 6.

20. The Meeting of the States Parties or the Special Meeting of the States Parties shall make every effort to reach its decisions referred to in paragraphs 18 and 19 by consensus, otherwise by a two-thirds majority of States Parties present and voting.

Art. 9. National implementation measures

Each State Party shall take all appropriate legal, administrative and other measures, including the imposition of penal sanctions, to prevent and suppress any activity prohibited to a State Party under this Convention undertaken by persons or on territory under its jurisdiction or control.

Art. 10. Settlement of disputes

1. The States Parties shall consult and cooperate with each other to settle any dispute that may arise with regard to the application or the interpretation of this Convention. Each State Party may bring any such dispute before the Meeting of the States Parties.
2. The Meeting of the States Parties may contribute to the settlement of the dispute by whatever means it deems appropriate, including offering its good offices, calling upon the States parties to a dispute to start the settlement procedure of their choice and recommending a time-limit for any agreed procedure.
3. This Article is without prejudice to the provisions of this Convention on facilitation and clarification of compliance.

Art. 11. Meetings of the States Parties

1. The States Parties shall meet regularly in order to consider any matter with regard to the application or implementation of this Convention, including:
   (a) The operation and status of this Convention;
   (b) Matters arising from the reports submitted under the provisions of this Convention;
   (c) International cooperation and assistance in accordance with Article 6;
   (d) The development of technologies to clear anti-personnel mines;
   (e) Submissions of States Parties under Article 8; and
   (f) Decisions relating to submissions of States Parties as provided for in Article 5.
2. The First Meeting of the States Parties shall be convened by the Secretary-General of the United Nations within one year after the entry into force of this Convention. The subsequent meetings shall be convened by the Secretary-General of the United Nations annually until the first Review Conference.
3. Under the conditions set out in Article 8, the Secretary-General of the United Nations shall convene a Special Meeting of the States Parties.

4. States not parties to this Convention, as well as the United Nations, other relevant international organizations or institutions, regional organizations, the International Committee of the Red Cross and relevant non-governmental organizations may be invited to attend these meetings as observers in accordance with the agreed Rules of Procedure.

Art. 12. Review Conferences

1. A Review Conference shall be convened by the Secretary-General of the United Nations five years after the entry into force of this Convention. Further Review Conferences shall be convened by the Secretary-General of the United Nations if so requested by one or more States Parties, provided that the interval between Review Conferences shall in no case be less than five years. All States Parties to this Convention shall be invited to each Review Conference.
2. The purpose of the Review Conference shall be:
   (a) To review the operation and status of this Convention;
   (b) To consider the need for and the interval between further Meetings of the States Parties referred to in paragraph 2 of Article 11;
   (c) To take decisions on submissions of States Parties as provided for in Article 5; and
   (d) To adopt, if necessary, in its final report conclusions related to the implementation of this Convention.
3. States not parties to this Convention, as well as the United Nations, other relevant international organizations or institutions, regional organizations, the International Committee of the Red Cross and relevant non-governmental organizations may be invited to attend each Review Conference as observers in accordance with the agreed Rules of Procedure.

Art. 13. Amendments

1. At any time after the entry into force of this Convention any State Party may propose amendments to this Convention. Any proposal for an amendment shall be communicated to the Depositary, who shall circulate it to all States Parties and shall seek their views on whether an Amendment Conference should be convened to consider the proposal. If a majority of the States Parties notify the Depositary no later than 30 days after its circulation that they support further consideration of the proposal, the Depositary shall convene an Amendment Conference to which all States Parties shall be invited.
2. States not parties to this Convention, as well as the United Nations, other relevant international organizations or institutions, regional organizations, the International Committee of the Red Cross and relevant non-governmental organizations may be invited to attend each Amendment Conference as observers in accordance with the agreed Rules of Procedure.
3. The Amendment Conference shall be held immediately following a Meeting of the States Parties or a Review Conference unless a majority of the States Parties request that it be held earlier.
4. Any amendment to this Convention shall be adopted by a majority of two-thirds of the States Parties present and voting at the Amendment Conference. The Depositary shall communicate any amendment so adopted to the States Parties.

5. An amendment to this Convention shall enter into force for all States Parties to this Convention which have accepted it, upon the deposit with the Depositary of instruments of acceptance by a majority of States Parties. Thereafter it shall enter into force for any remaining State Party on the date of deposit of its instrument of acceptance.

Art. 14. Costs

1. The costs of the Meetings of the States Parties, the Special Meetings of the States Parties, the Review Conferences and the Amendment Conferences shall be borne by the States Parties and States not parties to this Convention participating therein, in accordance with the United Nations scale of assessment adjusted appropriately.
2. The costs incurred by the Secretary-General of the United Nations under Articles 7 and 8 and the costs of any fact-finding mission shall be borne by the States Parties in accordance with the United Nations scale of assessment adjusted appropriately.

Art. 15. Signature

This Convention, done at Oslo, Norway, on 18 September 1997, shall be open for signature at Ottawa, Canada, by all States from 3 December 1997 until 4 December 1997, and at the United Nations Headquarters in New York from 5 December 1997 until its entry into force.

Art. 16. Ratification, acceptance, approval or accession

1. This Convention is subject to ratification, acceptance or approval of the Signatories.
2. It shall be open for accession by any State which has not signed the Convention.
3. The instruments of ratification, acceptance, approval or accession shall be deposited with the Depositary.

Art. 17. Entry into force

1. This Convention shall enter into force on the first day of the sixth month after the month in which the 40th instrument of ratification, acceptance, approval or accession has been deposited.
2. For any State which deposits its instrument of ratification, acceptance, approval or accession after the date of the deposit of the 40th instrument of ratification, acceptance, approval or accession, this Convention shall enter into force on the first day of the sixth month after the date on which that State has deposited its instrument of ratification, acceptance, approval or accession.

Art. 18. Provisional application

Any State may at the time of its ratification, acceptance, approval or accession, declare that it will apply provisionally paragraph 1 of Article 1 of this Convention pending its entry into force.

Art. 19. Reservations

The Articles of this Convention shall not be subject to reservations.

Art. 20. Duration and withdrawal

1. This Convention shall be of unlimited duration.

2. Each State Party shall, in exercising its national sovereignty, have the right to withdraw from this Convention. It shall give notice of such withdrawal to all other States Parties, to the Depositary and to the United Nations Security Council. Such instrument of withdrawal shall include a full explanation of the reasons motivating this withdrawal.
3. Such withdrawal shall only take effect six months after the receipt of the instrument of withdrawal by the Depositary. If, however, on the expiry of that six-month period, the withdrawing State Party is engaged in an armed conflict, the withdrawal shall not take effect before the end of the armed conflict.
4. The withdrawal of a State Party from this Convention shall not in any way affect the duty of States to continue fulfilling the obligations assumed under any relevant rules of international law.

Art. 21. Depositary
The Secretary-General of the United Nations is hereby designated as the Depositary of this Convention.

Art. 22. Authentic texts
The original of this Convention, of which the Arabic, Chinese, English, French, Russian and Spanish texts are equally authentic, shall be deposited with the Secretary-General of the United Nations.

[Here follow signatures]

SIGNATURES, RATIFICATIONS AND ACCESSIONS[1]

State	*Signature*	*Ratification, Accession Acceptance (A) Approval (AA)*
Afghanistan	–	11 September 2002
Albania	8 September 1998	29 February 2000
Algeria	3 December 1997	9 October 2001
Andorra	3 December 1997	29 June 1998
Angola	4 December 1997	5 July 2002
Antigua and Barbuda	3 December 1997	3 May 1999
Argentina	4 December 1997	14 September 1999 *Dec.*
Australia	3 December 1997	14 January 1999 *Dec.*
Austria*	3 December 1997	29 June 1998
Bahamas	3 December 1997	31 July 1998
Bangladesh	7 May 1998	6 September 2000
Barbados	3 December 1997	26 January 1999
Belgium	3 December 1997	4 September 1998
Belize	27 February 1998	23 April 1998
Benin	3 December 1997	25 September 1998

1 Based on the indications in *Multilateral Treaties Deposited with the Secretary-General, New York, United Nations* (ST/LEG/SER.E) as available on http://untreaty.un.org; http://disarmament.un.org/TreatyStatus.nsf; www.icrc.org/ihl.nsf. An asterisk attached to the name of the state indicates the provisional application of Article 1(1) in accordance with Article 18 of the Convention.

State	*Signature*	*Ratification, Accession Acceptance (A) Approval (AA)*
Bolivia	3 December 1997	9 June 1998
Bosnia and Herzegovina	3 December 1997	8 September 1998
Botswana	3 December 1997	1 March 2000
Brazil	3 December 1997	30 April 1999
Brunei Darussalam	4 December 1997	–
Bulgaria	3 December 1997	4 September 1998
Burkina Faso	3 December 1997	16 September 1998
Burundi	3 December 1997	–
Cambodia	3 December 1997	28 July 1999
Cameroon	3 December 1997	19 September 2002
Canada	3 December 1997	3 December 1997 *Dec.*
Cape Verde	4 December 1997	14 May 2001
Central African Republic	–	8 November 2002
Chad	6 July 1998	6 May 1999
Chile*	3 December 1997	10 September 2001
Colombia	3 December 1997	6 September 2000
Comoros	–	19 September 2002
Congo	–	4 May 2001
Cook Islands	3 December 1997	–
Costa Rica	3 December 1997	17 March 1999
Côte d'Ivoire	3 December 1997	20 June 2000
Croatia	4 December 1997	20 May 1998
Cyprus	4 December 1997	17 January 2003
Czech Republic	3 December 1997	26 October 1999 *Dec.*
Democratic Republic of the Congo	–	2 May 2002
Denmark	4 December 1997	8 June 1998
Djibouti	3 December 1997	18 May 1998
Dominica	3 December 1997	26 March 1999
Dominican Republic	3 December 1997	30 June 2000
Ecuador	4 December 1997	29 April 1999
El Salvador	4 December 1997	27 January 1999
Equatorial Guinea	–	16 September 1998
Eritrea	–	27 August 2001
Ethiopia	3 December 1997	–
Fiji	3 December 1997	10 June 1998
France	3 December 1997	23 July 1998
Gabon	3 December 1997	8 September 2000
Gambia	4 December 1997	23 September 2002
Germany	3 December 1997	23 July 1998
Ghana	4 December 1997	30 June 2000
Greece	3 December 1997 *Dec.*	–
Grenada	3 December 1997	19 August 1998
Guatemala	3 December 1997	26 March 1999
Guinea	4 December 1997	8 October 1998
Guinea-Bissau	3 December 1997	22 May 2001
Guyana	4 December 1997	–
Haiti	3 December 1997	–
Holy See	4 December 1997	17 February 1998
Honduras	3 December 1997	24 September 1998
Hungary	3 December 1997	6 April 1998
Iceland	4 December 1997	5 May 1999
Indonesia	4 December 1997	–

State	*Signature*	*Ratification, Accession Acceptance (A) Approval (AA)*
Ireland	3 December 1997	3 December 1997
Italy	3 December 1997	23 April 1999
Jamaica	3 December 1997	17 July 1998
Japan	3 December 1997	30 September 1998 (A)
Jordan	11 August 1998	13 November 1998
Kenya	5 December 1997	23 January 2001
Kiribati	–	7 September 2000
Lesotho	4 December 1997	2 December 1998
Liberia	–	23 December 1999
Liechtenstein	3 December 1997	5 October 1999
Lithuania	26 February 1999 *Dec.*	–
Luxembourg	4 December 1997	14 June 1999
Macedonia	–	9 September 1998
Madagascar	4 December 1997	16 September 1999
Malawi	4 December 1997	13 August 1998
Malaysia	3 December 1997	22 April 1999
Maldives	1 October 1998	7 September 2000
Mali	3 December 1997	2 June 1998
Malta	4 December 1997	7 May 2001
Marshall Islands	4 December 1997	–
Mauritania	3 December 1997	21 July 2001
Mauritius*	3 December 1997	3 December 1997
Mexico	3 December 1997	9 June 1998
Monaco	4 December 1997	17 November 1998
Mozambique	3 December 1997	25 August 1998
Namibia	3 December 1997	21 September 1998
Nauru	–	7 August 2000
Netherlands[2]	3 December 1997	12 April 1999 (A)
New Zealand	3 December 1997	27 January 1999
Nicaragua	4 December 1997	30 November 1998
Niger	4 December 1997	23 March 1999
Nigeria	–	27 September 2001
Niue	3 December 1997	15 April 1998
Norway	3 December 1997	9 July 1998
Panama	4 December 1997	7 October 1998
Paraguay	3 December 1997	13 November 1998
Peru	3 December 1997	17 June 1998
Philippines	3 December 1997	15 Febriary 2000
Poland	4 December 1997	–
Portugal	3 December 1997	19 February 1999
Qatar	4 December 1997	13 October 1998
Republic of Moldova	3 December 1997	8 September 2000
Romania	3 December 1997	30 November 2000
Rwanda	3 December 1997	8 June 2000
Saint Kitts and Nevis	3 December 1997	2 December 1998
Saint Lucia	3 December 1997	13 April 1999
Saint Vincent and the Grenadines	3 December 1997	1 August 2001
Samoa	3 December 1997	23 July 1998
San Marino	3 December 1997	18 March 1998
Sao Tome and Principe	30 April 1998	–

[2] For the Kingdom in Europe.

State	*Signature*	*Ratification, Accession Acceptance (A) Approval (AA)*
Senegal	3 December 1997	24 Sep 1998
Seychelles	4 December 1997	2 June 2000
Sierra Leone	29 July 1998	25 April 2001
Slovakia	3 December 1997	25 February 1999 (AA)
Slovenia	3 December 1997	27 October 1998
Solomon Islands	4 December 1997	26 January 1999
South Africa*	3 December 1997	26 June 1998
Spain	3 December 1997	19 January 1999
Sudan	4 December 1997	–
Suriname	4 December 1997	23 May 2002
Swaziland	4 December 1997	22 December 1998
Sweden*	4 December 1997	30 November 1998
Switzerland*	3 December 1997	24 March 1998
Tajikistan	–	12 October 1999
Thailand	3 December 1997	27 November 1998
Togo	4 December 1997	9 March 2000
Trinidad and Tobago	4 December 1997	27 April 1998
Tunisia	4 December 1997	9 July 1999
Turkmenistan	3 December 1997	19 January 1998
Uganda	3 December 1997	25 February 1999
Ukraine	24 February 1999	–
United Kingdom	3 December 1997	31 July 1998 *Dec.*
United Republicof Tanzania	3 December 1997	13 November 2000
Uruguay	3 December 1997	7 June 2001
Vanuatu	4 December 1997	–
Venezuela	3 December 1997	14 April 1999
Yemen	4 December 1997	1 September 1998
Zambia	12 December 1997	23 February 2001
Zimbabwe	3 December 1997	18 June 1998

RESERVATIONS AND DECLARATIONS[1]

ARGENTINA (*interpretative declaration made on ratification*)
The Argentine Republic declares that in its territory, in the Malvinas, there are anti-personnel mines. This situation was brought to the attention of the Secretary-General of the United Nations when providing information within the framework of General Assembly resolutions 48/7, 49/215, 50/82 and 51/149 concerning "Assistance in mine clearance".

Since this part of the Argentine territory is under illegal occupation by the United Kingdom of Great Britain and Northern Ireland, the Argentine Republic is effectively prevented from having access to the anti-personnel mines placed in the Malvinas in order to fulfil the obligations undertaken in the present Convention.

The United Nations General Assembly has recognized the existence of a dispute concerning sovereignty over the Malvinas, South Georgia and South Sandwich and has urged the Argentine Republic and the United Kingdom of Great Britain and Northern Ireland to maintain negotiations in order to find as soon as possible a peaceful and lasting solution to the dispute, with the good offices of the Secretary-General of the United Nations, who is to report to the General Assembly on the progress made (resolutions

[1] Unless otherwise indicated, the declarations were made upon ratification, acceptance, approval or accession.

2065 (XX), 3160 (XXVIII), 31/49, 37/9, 38/12, 39/6, 40/21, 41/40, 42/19 and 43/25). The Special Commitee on decolonization has taken the same position, and has adopted a resolution every year stating that the way to put an end to this colonial situation is the lasting settlement, on a peaceful and negotiated basis, of the sovereignty dispute, and requesting both Governments to resume negotiations to that end. The most recent of these resolutions was adopted on 1 July 1999.

The Argentine Republic reaffirms its rights of sovereignty over the Malvinas, South Georgia and South Sandwich and the surrounding maritime areas which form an integral part of its national territory.

AUSTRALIA (*declarations made on ratification*)
It is the understanding of Australia that, in the context of operations, exercises or other military activity authorised by the United Nations or otherwise conducted in accordance with international law, the participation by the Australian Defence Force, or individual Australian citizens or residents, in such operations, exercises or other military activity conducted in combination with the armed forces of States not party to the Convention which engage in activity prohibited under the Convention would not, by itself, be considered to be in violation of the Convention.

It is the understanding of Australia that, in relation to Article 1(a), the term "use" means the actual physical emplacement of anti-personnel mines and does not include receiving an indirect or incidental benefit from anti-personnel mines laid by another State or person. In Article 1(c) Australia will interpret the word "assist" to mean the actual and direct physical participation in any activity prohibited by the Convention but does not include permissible indirect support such as the provision of security for the personnel of a State not party to the Convention engaging in such activities, "encourage" to mean the actual request for the commission of any activity prohibited by the Convention, and "induce" to mean the active engagement in the offering of threats or incentives to obtain the commission of any activity prohibited by the Convention.

It is the understanding of Australia that in relation to Article 2(1), the definition of "anti-personnel mines" does not include command detonated munitions.

In relation to Articles 4, 5(1) and (2), and 7(1)(b) and (c), it is the understanding of Australia that the phrase "jurisdiction or control" is intended to mean within the sovereign territory of a State Party or over which it exercises legal responsibility by virtue of a United Nations mandate or arrangement with another State and the ownership or physical possession of anti-personnel mines, but does not include the temporary occupation of, or presence on, foreign territory where anti-personnel mines have been laid by other States or persons.

CANADA (*declaration of understanding made upon ratification*)
It is the understanding of the Government of Canada that, in the context of operations, exercises or other military activity sanctioned by the United Nations or otherwise conducted in accordance with international law, the mere participation by the Canadian Forces, or individual Canadians, in operations, exercises or other military activity conducted in combination with the armed forces of States not party to the Convention which engage in activity prohibited under the Convention would not, by itself, be considered to be assistance, encouragement or inducement in accordance with the meaning of those terms in article 1, paragraph 1(c).

CZECH REPUBLIC (*declaration made upon ratification*)
It is the understanding of the Government of the Czech Republic that, in the mere participation in the planning or execution of operations, exercises or other military activities by the Armed Forces of the Czech Republic, or individual Czech Republic nationals, conducted in combination with the armed forces of States not party to the [Convention], which engage in activities prohibited under the Convention, is not, by itself, assistance, encouragement or inducement for the purposes of Article 1, paragraph 1(c) of the Convention.

Greece (*declaration made upon signature*)
Greece fully subscribes to the principles enshrined within the [Convention] and declares that ratification of this Convention will take place as soon as conditions relating to the implementation of its relevant provisions are fulfilled.

Lithuania (*declaration made upon signature*)
The Republic of Lithuania subscribes to the principles and purposes of the [Convention] and declares that ratification of the Convention will take place as soon as the relevant conditions relating to the implementation of [the] provisions of the Convention are fulfilled.

United Kingdom of Great Britain and Northern Ireland (*declaration made upon ratification*)
It is the understanding of the Government of the United Kingdom that the mere participation in the planning or execution of operations, exercises or other military activity by the United Kingdom's Armed Forces, or individual United Kingdom nationals, conducted in combination with the armed forces of States not party to the [said Convention], which engage in activity prohibited under that Convention, is not, by itself, assistance, encouragement or inducement for the purposes of Article 1, paragraph (c) of the Convention.

DECLARATIONS OF PROVISIONAL APPLICATION

Declaration of provisional application of article 1(1) in accordance with Article 18 of the Convention (indicated by asterisk on the list of states parties to the Convention):

Austria
Chile
Mauritius
South Africa
Sweden
Switzerland

No. 23A

GUIDELINES FOR MILITARY MANUALS AND INSTRUCTIONS ON THE PROTECTION OF THE ENVIRONMENT IN TIMES OF ARMED CONFLICT

Prepared by the International Committee of the Red Cross and recommended for dissemination by resolution 49/50 of the United Nations General Assembly, 9 December 1994

INTRODUCTORY NOTE: During the Operation Desert Storm designed to end Iraq's occupation of Kuwait in 1991, Iraqi forces set Kuwaiti oil wells on fire, destroyed oil installations and discharged crude oil into the Gulf, thereby causing enormous damage to the natural environment. These acts awakened wide concern about the possibilties of international law to protect the environment in case of armed conflicts. The only two conventions of the law of war expressly referring to the "natural environment", the ENMOD Convention of 1976 (*No. 18*) and Protocol I of 1977 to the Geneva Conventions (*No. 56*, Articles 35(3) and 55) were not formally applicable in the Gulf War, as not all belligerents were party to them. It was realized, however, that there were other provisions of the law of armed conflicts limiting the right to cause environmental damage. All relevant provisions which were in force in 1994 are compiled in the present Guidelines.

The ICRC took up the matter in a report to the International Conference of the Red Cross and Red Crescent which was to be held in Budapest in late 1991 but was called off. Particular conferences on the subject took place in London, Munich and Ottawa in 1991 and 1992. The UN General Assembly, on 9 December 1991, adopted resolution 46/417 requesting the Secretary-General to report to the General Assembly "on activities undertaken in the framework of the International Committee of the Red Cross with regard to that issue". The ICRC, in 1992, after consultation of experts, submitted a first report to the UN Secretary-General (UN Doc. A/47/328, 1992). In resolution 47/37 of 25 November 1992 (para. 3) the General Assembly urged states "to incorporate the provisions of international law applicable to the protection of the environment into their military manuals and to ensure that they are effectively disseminated". It invited the ICRC to continue its work. The ICRC, after having again consulted experts, submitted a second report together with a draft of the present guidelines in 1993 (UN Doc. A/48/269. ch. II. 193). The General Assembly, in its resolution 48/30 of 9 December 1993 (paras. 11–14) invited govemments to comment on the draft guidelines and asked the ICRC to submit a revised text. After new consultations the ICRC revised the text and submitted it to the Secretary-General. It was annexed to the Secretary-General's report of 19 August 1994 (UN Doc. A/49/323). Without formally approving the guidelines, the General Assembly, in its resolution 49/50 of 9 December 1994, entitled "United Nations Decade of International Law", adopted the following paragraph:

"The General Assembly

11. *Invites* all States to disseminate widely the revised guidelines for military manuals and instructions on the protection of the environment in times of armed conflict received from the International Committee of the Red

Cross and to give due consideration to the possibility of incorporating them into their military manuals and other instructions addressed to their militarv personnel."

AUTHENTIC TEXT: Arabic, Chinese, English, French, Russian and Spanish.

TEXT PUBLISHED IN: UN Doc. A/49/323 of 19 August 1994, Annex (Arabic, Chinese, Engl., French, Russ., Span.); *AJIL,* Vol. 89, 1995, pp. 641–644 (Engl.); Richard J. Grunawalt, John E. King and Ronald S. McClain (eds.), *Protection of the Environment During Armed Conflict,* US Naval War College, *International Legal Studies*, Vol. 69, Newport, R.I., 1996, pp. 641–645 (Engl.); Roberts and Guelff, pp. 607–614 (Engl.).

* * *

I. Preliminary Remarks

1. The present Guidelines are drawn from existing international legal obligations and from State practice concerning the protection of the environment against the effects of armed conflict. They have been compiled to promote an active interest in, and concern for, the protection of the environment within the armed forces of all States.
2. Domestic legislation and other measures taken at the national level are essential means of ensuring that international law protecting the environment in times of armed conflict is indeed put into practice.
3. To the extent that the Guidelines are the expression of international customary law or of treaty law binding a particular State, they must be included in military manuals and instructions on the laws of war. Where they reflect national policy, it is suggested that they be included in such documents.

II. General Principles of International Law

4. In addition to the specific rules set out below, the general principles of international law applicable in armed conflict – such as the principle of distinction and the principle of proportionality – provide protection to the environment. In particular, only military objectives may be attacked and no methods or means of warfare which cause excessive damage shall be employed. Precautions shall be taken in military operations as required by international law. (G.P.I. Arts. 35, 48, 52 and 57)
5. International environmental agreements and relevant rules of customary law may continue to be applicable in times of armed conflict to the extent that they are not inconsistent with the applicable law of armed conflict.

   Obligations relating to the protection of the environment towards States not party to an armed conflict (e.g., neighbouring States) and in relation to areas beyond the limits of national jurisdiction (e.g., the High Seas) are not affected by the existence of the armed conflict to the extent that they are not inconsistent with the applicable law of armed conflict.
6. Parties to a non-international armed conflict are encouraged to apply the same rules that provide protection to the environment as those which prevail in international armed conflict and, accordingly, States are urged to incorporate such rules in their military manuals and instructions on the laws of war in a way that does not discriminate on the basis of how the conflict is characterized.
7. In cases not covered by rules of international agreements, the environment remains under the protection and authority of the principles of international law derived from established custom, from the principles of humanity and from the dictates of public conscience. (H.IV preamble, G.P.I, Art. 1.2, G.P.II preamble)

III. Specific Rules on the Protection of the Environment

8. Destruction of the environment not justified by military necessity violates international humanitarian law. Under certain circumstances, such destruction is punish-

able as a grave breach of international humanitarian law. (H.IV.R Art. 23 (g), G.IV Arts. 53 and 147, G.P.I Arts. 35.3 and 55)

9. The general prohibition to destroy civilian objects, unless such destruction is justified by military necessity, also protects the environment. (H.IV.R Art. 23(g), G.IV Art. 53, G.P.I Art. 52, G.P.II Art. 14)

   In particular, States should take all measures required by international law to avoid:

   (a) making forests or other kinds of plant cover the object of attack by incendiary weapons except when such natural elements are used to cover, conceal or camouflage combatants or other military objectives, or are themselves military objectives; (CW.P.III)

   (b) attacks on objects indispensable to the survival of the civilian population, such as foodstuffs, agricultural areas or drinking water installations, if carried out for the purpose of denying such objects to the civilian population; (G.P.I Art. 54, G.P.II Art. 14)

   (c) attacks on works or installations containing dangerous forces, namely dams, dykes and nuclear electrical generating stations, even where they are military objectives, if such attack may cause the release of dangerous forces and consequent severe losses among the civilian population and as long as such works or installations are entitled to special protection under Protocol I additional to the Geneva Conventions; (G.P.I Art. 56, G.P.II Art. 15)

   (d) attacks on historic monuments, works of art or places of worship which constitute the cultural or spiritual heritage of peoples. (H.CP, G.P.I Art. 53, G.P.II Art. 16)

10. The indiscriminate laying of landmines is prohibited. The location of all preplanned minefields must be recorded. Any unrecorded laying of remotely delivered non-self neutralizing landmines is prohibited. Special rules limit the emplacement and use of naval mines. (G.P.I Arts. 51.4 and 51.5, CW.P.II Art. 3, H.VIII)

11. Care shall be taken in warfare to protect and preserve the natural environment. It is prohibited to employ methods or means of warfare which are intended, or may be expected, to cause widespread, long-term and severe damage to the natural environment and thereby prejudice the health or survival of the population. (G.P.I Arts. 35.3 and 55)

12. The military or any other hostile use of environmental modification techniques having widespread, long-lasting or severe effects as the means of destruction, damage or injury to any other State party is prohibited. The term 'environmental modification techniques' refers to any technique for changing – through the deliberate manipulation of natural processes – the dynamics, composition or structure of the Earth, including its biota, lithosphere, hydrosphere and atmosphere, or of outer space.(ENMOD Arts. I and II)

13. Attacks against the natural environment by way of reprisals are prohibited for States party to Protocol I additional to the Geneva Conventions. (G.P.I Arts. 55.2)

14. States are urged to enter into further agreements providing additional protection to the natural environment in times of armed conflict.(G.P.I Art. 56.6)

15. Works or installations containing dangerous forces, and cultural property shall be clearly marked and identified in accordance with applicable international rules. Parties to an armed conflict are encouraged to mark and identify also works or installations where hazardous activities are being carried out, as well as sites which are essential to human health or the environment. (e.g. G.P.I Art. 56.7; H.CP. Art. 6)

IV. Implementation and Dissemination

16. States shall respect and ensure respect for the obligations under international law applicable in armed conflict, including the rules providing protection for the environment in times of armed conflict. (G.IV Art.1, G.P.I Art. 1.1)

17. States shall disseminate these rules and make them known as widely as possible in their respective countries and include them in their programmes of military and civil instruction. (H.IV.R. Art. 1, G.IV Art. 144, G.P.I Art. 83, G.P.II Art. 19)

18. In the study, development, acquisition or adoption of a new weapon, means or method of warfare, States are under an obligation to determine whether its employment would, in some or all circumstances, be prohibited by applicable rules of international law, including those providing protection to the environment in times of armed conflict. (G.P. I Art. 36)
19. In the event of armed conflict, parties to such a conflict are encouraged to facilitate and protect the work of impartial organizations contributing to prevent or repair damage to the environment, pursuant to special agreements between the parties concerned or, as the case may be, the permission granted by one of them. Such work should be performed with due regard to the security interests of the parties concerned. (e.g. G.IV Art. 63.2, G.P.1 Arts. 61–67)
20. In the event of breaches of rules of international humanitarian law protecting the environment, measures shall be taken to stop any such violation and to prevent further breaches. Military commanders are required to prevent and, where necessary, to suppress and to report to competent authorities breaches of these rules. In serious cases, offenders shall be brought to justice. (G.IV Arts. 146 and 147, G.P.I Arts. 86 and 87)

SOURCES OF INTERNATIONAL OBLIGATIONS CONCERNING THE PROTECTION OF THE ENVIRONMENT IN TIMES OF ARMED CONFLICT

1. General principles of law and international customary law
2. International conventions

Main international treaties with rules on the protection of the environment in times of armed conflict

Hague Convention (IV) respecting the Laws and Customs of War on Land of 1907 (H.IV) and Regulations Respecting the Laws and Customs of War on Land (H.IV.R)

Hague Convention (VIII) relative to the Laying of Automatic Submarine Contact Mines of 1907 (H.VIII)

Geneva Convention relative to the Protection of Civilian Persons in Time of War, of 1949 (G.IV)

Hague Convention for the Protection of Cultural Property in the Event of Armed Conflict, of 1954 (H.CP)

Convention on the Prohibition of Military or any Other Hostile Use of Environmental Modification Techniques, of 1976 (ENMOD)

Protocol Additional to the Geneva Conventions of 12 August 1949, and relating to the Protection of Victims of International Armed Conflicts (Protocol I), of 1977 (G.P.I)

Protocol Additional to the Geneva Conventions of 12 August 1949, and relating to the Protection of Victims of Non-International Armed Conflicts (Protocol II), of 1977 (G.P.II)

Convention on Prohibitions or Restrictions on the Use of Certain Conventional Weapons Which May be Deemed to be Excessively Injurious or to Have Indiscriminate Effects. of 1980 (CW), with:

- Protocol on Prohibitions or Restrictions on the Use of Mines, Booby Traps and Other Devices (CW.P.II)
- Protocol on Prohibitions or Restrictions on the Use of Incendiary Weapons (CW.P.III)

* * *

See also Nos. 1–3, 7, 8, 56, 58

III

AIR WARFARE

Nos. 24-25

No. 24. DECLARATION (IV,1) TO PROHIBIT, FOR THE TERM OF FIVE YEARS, THE LAUNCHING OF PROJECTILES AND EXPLOSIVES FROM BALLOONS, AND OTHER METHODS OF A SIMILAR NATURE

Signed at The Hague, 29 July 1899

No. 25. DECLARATION (XIV) PROHIBITING THE DISCHARGE OF PROJECTILES AND EXPLOSIVES FROM BALLOONS

Signed at The Hague, 18 October 1907

INTRODUCTORY NOTE: The Russian circular note of 30 December 1898, proposing the programme of the First Hague Peace Conference, suggested as one of the topics "the prohibition of the discharge of any kind of projectile or explosive from balloons or by similar means". Balloons had been used on a small scale in previous wars, and there was much speculation about the future use of aircraft in war. At the First Hague Conference the prohibition was accepted for a period of five years, which expired on 4 September 1905. Between the two Hague Conferences progress was made in aerial navigation, which induced many states, especially the great powers, to adopt a more reserved attitude. The Declaration of 1907 was to remain in force until the projected Third Peace Conference. This Conference never having met, the Declaration of 1907 is still formally in force today. Many of the important states, however, such as France, Germany, Italy, Japan and Russia, did not sign or ratify it. Austria-Hungary signed but did not ratify it. Of the great powers, only Great Britain and the United States ratified the Declaration.

The attempts, in 1907, to adopt a permanent prohibition of the discharge of projectiles from the air led to the insertion in Article 25 of the Hague Regulations on land warfare, which prohibits the attack or bombardment of undefended towns, villages, etc., of the words "by whatever means" in order to cover attack or bombardment from the air.

ENTRY INTO FORCE: September 1900 (Declaration of 1899); 27 November 1909 (Declaration of 1907).

AUTHENTIC TEXT: French. The English translation below is reprinted from Scott, *Hague Conventions*, pp. 220–224. It reproduces the translation of the United States Department of State.

TEXT PUBLISHED IN:
Declaration of 1899: Conférence internationale de la Paix 1899, pp. 252–253 (French); *Les deux Conférences de la Paix*, p. 43 (French); Scott, *Hague Conventions*, pp. 220–223 (Engl.); Scott, *Les Conventions de La Haye*, pp. 220–223 (French); Scott, *Les Conférences de La Haye*, pp. 26–27 (French); Martens, *NRGT*, 2ème série, Vol. XXVI, pp. 994–998 (French, German); Deltenre, pp.

134–137 (Engl., French, German, Dutch); Olivart, Vol. XII, pp. 639–642 (French, Span.); *BFSP*, Vol. 91, 1898–1899, pp. 1011–1013 (French); *US Statutes at Large*, Vol. 32, pp. 1839–1842 (Engl., French); Malloy, Vol. II, pp. 2032–2034 (Engl.); Bevans, Vol. 1, pp. 270–272 (Engl.); *CTS*, Vol. 187, 1898–1899, pp. 456–458 (French); *AJIL*, Vol. 1, 1907, Suppl., pp. 153–155 (Engl., French); Friedman, pp. 244–246 (Engl.); *Droit des conflits armés*, pp. 279–282 (French); De Clercq, Vol. 21, pp. 737–741 (French); Bustamante, pp. 229–231 (Span.). *Declaration of 1907: Conférence internationale de la Paix 1907*, pp. 687–688 (French); *Les deux Conférences de la Paix,* pp. 173–174 (French); Scott, *Hague Conventions*, pp. 220–224 (Engl.); Scott, *Les Conventions de La Haye*, pp. 220–224 (French); Scott, *Les Conférences de La Haye*, pp. 101–102 (French); Martens, *NRGT*, 3ème série, Vol. III, pp. 745–750 (French, German); Deltenre, pp. 416–419 (Engl., French, German, Dutch); *GBTS*, 1910, No. 15, Cd. 5119 (Engl., French); *BFSP*, Vol. 100, 1906–1907, pp. 455–459 (French); *US Statutes at Large*, Vol. 36, pp. 2439–2443 (Engl., French); Malloy, Vol. II, pp. 2366–2368 (Engl.); *CTS*, Vol. 205, 1907, pp. 403–408 (French); *AJIL*, Vol. 2, 1908, Suppl., pp. 216–218 (Engl., French); Friedman, pp. 395–397 (Engl.,); *Droit des conflits armés*, pp. 279–282 (French); Bustamante, pp. 385–386 (Span.); *Revista de Derecho Internacional y politica exterior*, Cronica, Año III, pp. 116–117 (Span.); Korovin, pp. 391 (Russ.); *Mezhdunarodnoe pravo,* Vol. III, pp. 39–40 (Russ.); ICRC website: www.icrc.org/ihl.nsf.

DECLARATION (IV, 1), TO PROHIBIT, FOR THE TERM OF FIVE YEARS, THE LAUNCHING OF PROJECTILES AND EXPLOSIVES FROM BALLOONS, AND OTHER METHODS OF SIMILAR NATURE.

Signed at The Hague, 29 July 1899

The undersigned, Plenipotentiaries of the Powers represented at the International Peace Conference at The Hague, duly authorized to that effect by their Governments, inspired by the sentiments which found expression in the Declaration of St. Petersburg of 29 November (11 December) 1868,

Declare that:

The Contracting Powers agree to prohibit, for a term of five years, the

DECLARATION (XIV) PROHIBITING THE DISCHARGE OF PROJECTILES AND EXPLOSIVES FROM BALLOONS

Signed at The Hague, 18 October 1907

The undersigned, Plenipotentiaries of the Powers *invited to the Second* International Peace Conference at The Hague, duly authorized to that effect by their Governments, inspired by the sentiments which found expression in the Declaration of St. Petersburg of 29 November (11 December) 1868, *and being desirous of renewing the declaration of The Hague of 29 July 1899, which has now expired,*

Declare:

The Contracting Powers agree to prohibit, *for a period extending to the*

launching of projectiles and explosives from balloons, or by other new methods of a similar nature.

The present Declaration is only binding on the Contracting Powers in case of war between two or more of them.

It shall cease to be binding from the time when, in a war between the Contracting Powers, one of the belligerents is joined by a non-Contracting Power.

The present Declaration shall be ratified as soon as possible.

The ratifications shall be deposited at The Hague.

A *procès-verbal* shall be drawn up on the receipt of each ratification, of which a copy, duly certified, shall be sent through the diplomatic channel, to all the Contracting Powers.

The non-Signatory Powers may adhere to the present Declaration. For this purpose they must make their adhesion known to the Contracting Powers by means of a written notification addressed to the Netherlands Government, and communicated by it to all the other Contracting Powers.

In the event of one of the High Contracting Parties denouncing the present Declaration, such denunciation shall not take effect until a year after the notification made in writing to the Netherlands Government, and by it forthwith communicated to all the other Contracting Powers.

This denunciation shall only affect the notifying Power.

In faith of which the Plenipotentiaries have signed the present Declaration, and affixed their seals thereto.

Done at The Hague, 29 July 1899, in a single copy, which shall be kept in the archives of the Netherlands Government, and of which copies, duly certified, shall be sent through the diplomatic channel to the Contracting Powers.

close of the Third Peace Conference, the discharge of projectiles and explosives from balloons or by other new methods of a similar nature.

The present Declaration is only binding on the Contracting Powers in case of war between two or more of them. It shall cease to be binding from the time when, in a war between the Contracting Powers, one of the belligerents is joined by a non-Contracting Power.

The present Declaration shall be ratified as soon as possible. The ratifications shall be deposited at The Hague. A *procès-verbal* shall be drawn up recording the receipt of the ratifications, of which a duly certified copy shall be sent, through the diplomatic channel, to all the Contracting Powers.

Non-Signatory Powers may adhere to the present Declaration. To do so, they must make known their adhesion to the Contracting Powers by means of a written notification, addressed to the Netherlands Government, and communicated by it to all the other Contracting Powers.

In the event of one of the High Contracting Parties denouncing the present Declaration, such denunciation shall not take effect until a year after the notification made in writing to the Netherlands Government, and forthwith communicated by it to all the other Contracting Powers.

This denunciation shall only have effect in regard to the notifying Power.

In faith whereof the Plenipotentiaries have *appended their signatures* to the present Declaration.

Done at The Hague, *18 October 1907* in a single copy, which shall remain deposited in the archives of the Netherlands Government, and duly certified copies of which shall be sent through the diplomatic channel, to the Contracting Powers.

DECLARATION OF 1899
SIGNATURES, RATIFICATIONS AND ACCESSIONS[1]

State	*Signature*	*Ratification, Accession*
Austria-Hungary	29 July 1899	4 September 1900
Belgium	29 July 1899	4 September 1900
Bulgaria	29 July 1899	4 September 1900
China	29 July 1899	21 November 1904
Denmark	29 July 1899	4 September 1900
France	29 July 1899	4 September 1900
Germany	29 July 1899	4 September 1900
Greece	29 July 1899	4 April 1901
Italy	29 July 1899	4 September 1900
Japan	29 July 1899	6 October 1900
Luxemburg	29 July 1899	12 July 1901
Mexico	29 July 1899	17 April 1901
Montenegro	29 July 1899	16 October 1900
Netherlands	29 July 1899	4 September 1900
Norway[2]	29 July 1899	4 September 1900
Persia	29 July 1899	4 September 1900
Portugal	29 July 1899	4 September 1900
Romania	29 July 1899	4 September 1900
Russia	29 July 1899	4 September 1900
Serbia	29 July 1899	11 May 1901
Siam	29 July 1899	4 September 1900
Spain	29 July 1899	4 September 1900
Sweden	29 July 1899	4 September 1900
Switzerland	29 July 1899	29 December 1900
Turkey	29 July 1899	–
United States of America	29 July 1899	–

RESERVATIONS

None

[1] Based on a communication received from the Ministry of Foreign Affairs of the Netherlands of 12 December 2001.

[2] Sweden and Norway constituted a Union until 1905. Action taken by them prior to that date was taken as a single power.

DECLARATION OF 1907
SIGNATURES, RATIFICATIONS AND ACCESSIONS[1]

State	*Signature*	*Ratification, Accession, Notification of Continuity (C)*
Argentine Republic	18 October 1907	–
Austria-Hungary	18 October 1907	
Belgium	18 October 1907	8 August 1910
Bolivia	18 October 1907	27 November 1909
Brazil	18 October 1907	5 January 1914
Bulgaria	18 October 1907	–
China	18 October 1907	27 November 1909
Colombia	18 October 1907	–
Cuba	18 October 1907	–
Dominican Republic	18 October 1907	–
Ecuador	18 October 1907	–
El Salvador	18 October 1907	27 November 1909
Ethiopia	–	2 August 1935
Fiji	–	2 April 1973
Finland	–	9 June 1922[2]
Great Britain	18 October 1907	27 November 1909
Greece	18 October 1907	–
Haiti	18 October 1907	2 February 1910
Liberia	–	4 February 1914
Luxemburg	18 October 1907	5 September 1912
Netherlands	18 October 1907	27 November 1909
Nicaragua	–	16 December 1909
Norway	18 October 1907	19 September 1910
Panama	18 October 1907	11 September 1911
Persia	18 October 1907	–
Peru	18 October 1907	–
Portugal	18 October 1907	13 April 1911
Siam	18 October 1907	12 March 1910
Switzerland	18 October 1907	12 May 1910
Turkey	18 October 1907	–
United States of America	18 October 1907	27 November 1909
Uruguay	18 October 1907	–

RESERVATIONS

None

[1] Based on a communication received from the Ministry of Foreign Affairs of the Netherlands of 12 December 2001. See also ICRC website: www.icrc.org/ihl.nsf.

[2] By letter dated 12 May 1980, the Netherlands Ministry of Foreign Affairs stated (a) Finland's accession on 30 December 1918 to this and other 1907 Hague Conventions and to the 1907 Hague Declaration was initially regarded as provisional, pending the final resolution of Finland's international status; (b) after consultation with the other contracting powers, the depositary stated on 9 June 1922 that Finland's accession should be regarded as final and complete, and (c) the Conventions and the Declaration entered into force for Finland on 9 June 1922.

No. 26

HAGUE RULES CONCERNING THE CONTROL OF WIRELESS TELEGRAPHY IN TIME OF WAR AND AIR WARFARE

Drafted by a Commission of Jurists at The Hague, 11 December 1922 – 17 February 1923

INTRODUCTORY NOTE: The Washington Conference of 1922 on the Limitation of Armaments adopted a resolution for the appointment of a Commission of Jurists charged with the preparation of rules relating to aerial warfare and rules concerning the use of radio in time of war. The Commission, presided over by John Bassett Moore, was composed of representatives of the United States, Great Britain, France, Italy, Japan, and the Netherlands. It was to report its conclusions to each of the governments of the six countries. The Commission met from December 1922 to February 1923 at The Hague. The rules were never adopted in legally binding form, but are of importance "as an authoritative attempt to clarify and formulate rules of law governing the use of aircraft in war" (Oppenheim/Lauterpacht, *International Law,* 7th edn., Vol. II, p. 519). To a great extent, they correspond to the customary rules and general principles underlying the conventions on the law of war on land and at sea.

AUTHENTIC TEXT: English. The text below is reprinted from *Parliamentary Papers,* Cmd. 2201, Miscellaneous No. 14 (1924).

TEXT PUBLISHED IN: Deltenre, pp. 819–849 (Engl., French, German, Dutch); *Parliamentary Papers,* Cmd. 2201, Miscellaneous No. 14 (1924) pp. 15–16 (Engl.); *AJIL,* Vol. 17, 1923, Suppl., pp. 245–260; and Vol. 32, 1938, Suppl., pp. 1–56 (Engl.); J. M. Spaight, *Air Power and War Rights,* 3rd edn., 1947, Appendix, pp. 498–508 (air warfare only) (Engl.); Friedman, pp. 437–449 (air warfare only) (Engl.); Roberts and Guelff, pp. 139–153 (air warfare only) (Engl.); Ronzitti, pp. 367–370, 381–395 (Engl.); Morris Greenspan, *The Modern Law of Land Warfare,* Berkeley, University of California Press, 1959, pp. 650–667 (air warfare only) (Engl.); *RGDIP,* Vol. 30, 1923, Documents, pp. 1–9 (air warfare only) (French); *La Guerre Aerienne. Revision des Lois de la Guerre, La Haye 1922–1923*, Paris, 1930, pp. 285–295 (air warfare only) (French); *Droit des conflits armés*, pp. 283–296 (French); R.A. Foglia, *Derecho Aeronautico de guerra,* Circulo de Aeronautica, Coleccion Aeronautica Argentina, Vol. 28, Buenos Aires, 1952, pp. 149–157 (air warfare only) (Span.); ICRC website: www.icrc.org/ihl.nsf.

TABLE OF CONTENTS

* * *

PART I. RULES FOR THE CONTROL OF WIRELESS TELEGRAPHY IN TIME OF WAR

Article 1. In time of war, the operation of wireless stations continues to be organized, so far as possible, in such manner as not to interfere with the service of other wireless stations. This rule does not apply to the wireless stations of the enemy.

Art. 2. The belligerent and neutral Powers may regulate or forbid the use of the wireless stations within their jurisdiction.

Art. 3. The installation or the operation of wireless stations, within a neutral jurisdiction, by a belligerent Power or by persons in its services, constitutes a violation of neutrality on the part of that belligerent as well as a breach of neutrality on the part of the neutral Power which permits the installation or the operation of such stations.

Art. 4. A neutral Power is not bound to restrict or to forbid the use of the wireless stations situated within its jurisdiction, save as far as this may be necessary to prevent the transmission of information, intended for a belligerent, concerning the military forces or military operations, and save the case provided for in Article 5.

Any restriction or prohibition enacted by a neutral Power shall apply to the belligerents uniformly.

Art. 5. Belligerent mobile wireless stations, when they are within a neutral jurisdiction, must abstain from any use of their wireless apparatus. The neutral governments are bound to employ the means at their disposal in order to prevent such use.

Art. 6.

1. The wireless transmission, by an enemy or neutral vessel or aircraft while being on or above the high seas, of any military information intended for a belligerent's immediate use, shall be considered a hostile act exposing the vessel or aircraft to be fired at;
2. A neutral vessel or a neutral aircraft which, while being on the high seas or above the high seas, transmits an information destined to a belligerent concerning the military forces or operations, is liable to capture. The prize court may pronounce the confiscation of the ship or the aircraft if it deems the confiscation justified by the circumstances;
3. The period within which a neutral vessel or aircraft may be captured on account of the acts referred to in paragraphs 1. and 2. shall not end with the current voyage or flight, but only after the expiration of one year, reckoning from the day on which the incriminated act was committed.

Art.7. If a belligerent commander is of the opinion that the presence of vessels or aircraft provided with wireless apparatus in the immediate vicinity of his armed force or the use of such installations will endanger the success of the operations in which he is engaged, he may order the neutral vessels or aircraft on the high seas or above the high seas:

1. To alter their course so far as necessary in order to prevent them from approaching the armed force operating under his command;
2. To abstain from making use of their wireless apparatus when they are in the immediate vicinity of that force.

A neutral ship or a neutral aircraft which does not comply with the directions that it has received, exposes itself to be fired at. It shall also liable to capture and can be confiscated if the prize court deems the confiscation justified by circumstances.

Art. 8. Neutral mobile wireless stations shall abstain from keeping a written copy of wireless messages received from belligerent military wireless stations, unless such messages are destined for the said neutral stations.

The violation of this rule entitles the belligerents to confiscate the texts in question.

Art. 9. Belligerents are bound to conform to the rules contained in the international conventions regarding distress signals and distress messages, so far as their military operations permit them to do so.

The provisions contained in the present regulations cannot dispense the belligerents from such obligation, or forbid the transmission of distress signals, distress messages and messages which are indispensable for the safety of navigation.

Art. 10. Diverting wireless distress signals or distress messages, prescribed by the international conventions, from their normal and legitimate use, constitutes a violation of the laws of war for which its author is personally responsible in accordance with international Law.

Art. 11. Acts which, in others respects, do not constitute acts of espionage, are not considered as such for the mere fact that they imply an infringement of the present rules.

Art. 12. Wireless operators incur no personal responsibility for merely carrying out the orders received in the exercise of their functions.

PART II. RULES OF AIR WARFARE

Chapter I. Domain of Application: Classification and Marks

Article 1. The rules of air warfare apply to all aircraft, whether lighter or heavier than air, without discriminating whether or not they are capable of floating on water.

Art. 2. Are to be considered as public aircraft:
(a) Military aircraft;
(b) Non-military aircraft, assigned exclusively to a public service.

Any other aircraft is considered as private aircraft.

Art. 3. A military aircraft must carry an exterior mark indicating its nationality and its military character.

Art. 4. A non-military public aircraft assigned to customs or police service must carry papers attesting that it is exclusively used for a public service. Such aircraft must carry an exterior mark indicating its nationality and its non-military public character.

Art. 5. Non-military public aircraft other than those assigned to customs or police service must, in time of war, carry the same exterior marks and shall be treated, as regards the present rules, in the same manner as private aircraft.

Art. 6. Aircraft not contemplated in Articles 3 and 4 and considered as private aircraft shall carry such papers and exterior marks as are required by the rules in force in their own country. Such marks must indicate their nationality and their character.

Art. 7. The exterior marks required by the above articles shall be affixed in such manner as to make it impossible for them to be altered during flight. They shall be as large as possible and shall be visible from above, from below and from either side.

Art. 8. The exterior marks required by the regulations in force in each State shall be brought without delay to the knowledge of all the other Powers.

Modifications made in time of peace in the regulations requiring exterior marks shall be brought to the knowledge of all the other Powers before being put in force.

Modifications made in such regulations at the outbreak or in course of hostilities shall be brought by each Power to the knowledge of all the other Powers as soon as possible and at the latest when they are communicated to its fighting forces.

Art. 9. A belligerent non-military aircraft, whether public or private, may be transformed into a military aircraft provided that such transformation be made within the jurisdiction of the belligerent State to which the aircraft belongs, and not on the high seas.

Art. 10. No aircraft can possess more than one nationality.

Chapter II. General Principles

Art. 11. Outside the jurisdiction of any State, whether belligerent or neutral, all aircraft have full liberty to pass and to alight on water.

Art. 12. In time of war, every State, whether belligerent or neutral, may forbid or regulate the entry, the movements or the sojourn of aircrafts within its jurisdiction.

Chapter III. Belligerents

Art. 13. Only military aircraft may exercise the rights of belligerents.

Art. 14. A military aircraft must be under the command of a person duly commissioned or matriculated in the military rolls of the State; the crew must be exclusively military.

Art. 15. The crews of military aircraft shall bear a fixed distinctive emblem of such a nature as to be recognizable at a distance in the event of crews finding themselves separated from the aircraft.

Art. 16. No aircraft other than a belligerent military aircraft may take part in hostilities in any form whatever.

The term "hostilities" includes the transmission, during a flight, of military information for the immediate use of a belligerent.

No private aircraft may be armed in time of war outside the jurisdiction of its own country.

Art. 17. The principles laid down by the Geneva Conference of 1906 and under the Convention for the adaptation of the said Convention to maritime warfare (Convention X of 1907) shall apply to air warfare and to ambulance planes as well as to the control of such ambulance planes by belligerent commanders.

In order to enjoy the protection and the privileges granted to mobile sanitary units by the Geneva Convention of 1906, the ambulance planes must carry, in addition to their normal distinctive marks, the distinctive emblem of the Red Cross.

Chapter IV. Hostilities

Art. 18. The use of tracer projectiles, whether incendiary or explosive, by or against an aircraft is not forbidden.

This rule applies as well to the States which are parties to the Declaration of St.Petersburg of 1866, as to those which are not.

Art. 19. The use of false exterior marks is forbidden.

Art. 20. In the event of an aircraft being disabled, the persons trying to escape by means of parachutes must not be attacked during their descent.

Art. 21. The use of aircraft for propaganda purposes shall not be considered as an illicit means of warfare. The members of the crew of such aircraft are not to be deprived of their rights as prisoners of war on the ground that they have committed such an act.

Bombardment

Art. 22. Any air bombardment for the purpose of terrorizing the civil population or destroying or damaging private property without military character or injuring non-combatants, is forbidden.

Art. 23. Any air bombardment carried out for the purpose of enforcing requisitions in kind or payments of contributions in ready money, is forbidden.

Art. 24.

1. An air bombardment is legitimate only when is directed against a military objective, i.e. an objective whereof the total or partial destruction would constitute an obvious military advantage for the belligerent;
2. Such bombardment is legitimate only when directed exclusively against the following objectives: military forces, military works, military establishments or depots, manufacturing plants constituting important and well-known centres for the production of arms, ammunition or characterized military supplies, lines of communication or of transport which are used for military purposes.
3. Any bombardment of cities, towns, villages, habitations and buildings which are not situated in the immediate vicinity of the operations of the land forces, is forbidden. Should the objectives specified in paragraph 2 be so situated that they could not be bombed but that an indiscriminating bombardment of the civil population would result therefrom, the aircraft must abstain from bombing;
4. In the immediate vicinity of the operations of the land forces, the bombardment of cities, towns, villages, habitations and buildings is legitimate, provided there is a reasonable presumption that the military concentration is important enough to justify the bombardment, taking into account the danger to which the civil population will thus be exposed;
5. The belligerent State is bound to pay compensation for damage caused to persons or property, in violation of the provisions of this Article, by any one of his agents or any one of its military forces.

Art. 25. In bombardments by aircraft, all necessary steps should be taken by the commander to spare, as far as possible, buildings dedicated to public worship, art, science, and charitable purposes, historic monuments, hospital ships, hospitals and other places where the sick and wounded are gathered, provided that such buildings, objectives and places are not being used at the same time for military purposes. Such monuments, objects and places must be indicated, during the day, by signs visible from the aircraft. Using such signs to indicate buildings, objects or places other than those hereinbefore specified shall be considered a perfidious act. The signs of which the above mentioned use is to be made, shall be, in the case of buildings protected under the Geneva Convention, the red cross on a white ground and, in the case of the other protected buildings, a large rectangular panel divided diagonally into two triangles, the one white and the other black.

A belligerent who desires to ensure by night the protection of hospitals and other above mentioned privileged buildings, must take the necessary steps to make the aforesaid special signs sufficiently visible.

Art. 26. The following special rules have been adopted to permit the States to ensure a more efficient protection of monuments of great historic value situated on their territory provided they are disposed to abstain from using for military purposes not only such monuments and also the area surrounding them and to accept a special system for control to this end.

1. A State, if it deems it suitable, may establish a protected area around such monuments situated on its territory. In time of war, such areas shall be sheltered from bombardments;
2. Monuments around which such area is to be established, shall already be, in time of peace, the object of a notification addressed to the other Powers through the diplomatic channel; the notification shall also state the limits of such areas. This notification cannot be revoked in time of war;
3. The protected area may include, in addition to the space occupied by the monument or the group of monuments, a surrounding zone, the width of which may not exceed 500 metres from the periphery of the said space;
4. Marks well visible from the aircraft, both by day and by night, shall be employed to enable the belligerent aeronauts to identify the limits of the areas;
5. The marks placed on the monuments themselves shall be those mentioned in Article 25. The marks employed to indicate the areas surrounding the monuments shall be fixed by every State which accepts the provisions of this Article and shall be notified to the other Powers together with the list of the monuments and areas;
6. Every improper use of the marks referred to in paragraph 5 shall be considered an act of perfidy;
7. A State which accepts the provisions of this Article should abstain from making use of the historic monuments and the zone surrounding them for military purposes or for the benefit of its military organization in any manner whatsoever and should also abstain from committing, in the interior of such monument or within such zone, any act for military purposes;
8. A commission of control, composed of three neutral representatives accredited to the State which has accepted the provisions of the present Article, or of their delegates, shall be appointed for the purpose of ascertaining that no violation of the provisions of paragraph 7 has been committed. One of the members of this commission of control shall be the representative, or his delegate, of the State which has been entrusted with the interests of the other belligerent.

Espionage

Art. 27. An individual, found on board a belligerent or neutral aircraft, can be considered as a spy only when, during a flight acting clandestinely or on false pretences, he obtains or endeavours to obtain information within the belligerent jurisdiction or in the zone of operations of a belligerent, with the intention of communicating it to the hostile party.

Art. 28. Acts of espionage committed, after leaving the aircraft, by members of the crew of an aircraft or by passengers transported by it, remain subject to the provisions of the Regulations concerning the laws and customs of war on land.

Art. 29. The repression of acts of espionage referred to in Articles 27 and 28 is subject to Articles 30 and 31 of the Regulations respecting the laws and customs of war on land.

Chapter V. On Military Authority over Enemy and Neutral Aircraft and Persons on Board

Art. 30. When a belligerent commander deems the presence of aircraft to be able to endanger the success of the operations in which he is engaged, he may forbid the passage of neutral aircraft in the immediate vicinity of his own forces or impose on them an itinerary. A neutral aircraft which does not comply with such prescription of which it has cognizance through a publication of the belligerent commander, exposes itself to being fired at.

Art. 31. In accordance with the principles of Article 53 of the Regulations respecting the laws and customs of war on land, private neutral aircraft found by a belligerent occupying force when entering an enemy jurisdiction, may be requisitioned under payment of a full indemnity.

Art. 32. Enemy public aircraft other than those which are treated on the same footing as private aircraft are liable to confiscation without prize proceedings.

Art. 33. Belligerent non-military aircraft, whether public or private, flying within the jurisdiction of their State, are exposed to being fired at if they do not land at the nearest suitable point when an enemy military aircraft is approaching.

Art. 34. Belligerent non-military aircraft, whether public or private, are exposed to being fired at, when they are flying:
1. Within the jurisdiction of the enemy;
2. In the immediate vicinity of such jurisdiction and outside that of their own country;
3. In the immediate vicinity of the military land and sea operations of the enemy.

Art. 35. Neutral aircraft flying within the jurisdiction of a belligerent and warned of the approaching of military aircraft belonging to the other belligerent, must land at the nearest suitable point, failing which they expose themselves to being fired at.

Art. 36. When an enemy military aircraft falls into the hands of a belligerent, the members of the crew and the passengers, if any, may be made prisoners of war. The same rule applies to members of the crew and to the passengers, if any, of an enemy non-military aircraft, except that in the case of public non-military aircraft exclusively employed for the transport of passengers, the latter are entitled to being released unless they be in the enemy's service or enemy subjects fit for military service.

If an enemy private aircraft falls into the hands of a belligerent, the members of the crew who are enemy subjects or neutral subjects in the enemy's service, may be made prisoners of war. The neutrals, members of the crew, who are not in the enemy's service, are entitled to being released, if they sign a written engagement to the effect that they will not serve on an enemy aircraft until the end of the hostilities. The passengers must be released unless they be in the enemy's service or enemy subjects fit for military service, in which cases they may be made prisoners of war.

The release may, in all cases, be postponed if the military interests of the belligerent require it.

The belligerent may keep as a prisoner of war every member of the crew or every passenger whose conduct during the flight at the end of which he has been arrested has been of a special and active assistance for the enemy.

The names of the persons released after signing the written engagement provided for in the third paragraph of the present article, shall be communicated to the other belligerent, who shall not employ them wittingly in violation of their engagement.

Art. 37. The members of the crew of a neutral aircraft who have been arrested by a belligerent shall be released unconditionally if they are neutral subjects and if they are not in the enemy's service. If they are enemy subjects or if they are in the enemy's service, they may be made prisoners of war.

The passengers must be released unless they are in the enemy's service or enemy subjects fit for military service, in which case they may be made prisoners of war.

The release may, in all cases, be postponed if the military interests of the belligerent require it.

The belligerent may retain as a prisoner of war every member of the crew or every passenger whose conduct during the flight at the end of which he has been arrested, was of a special active assistance to the enemy.

Art. 38. When the rules of Articles 36 and 37 provide that the members of the crew and the passengers may be made prisoners of war, it must be understood that, if they do not belong to the armed forces, they are entitled to a treatment which shall not be less favourable than that which is granted to prisoners of war.

Chapter VI. Duties of Belligerents towards Neutral States and Duties of Neutrals towards Belligerent States

Art. 39. Belligerent aircraft are bound to respect the rights of neutral Powers and to abstain, within the jurisdiction of a neutral State, from all acts which it is the duty of such State to prevent.

Art. 40. Belligerent military aircraft are forbidden to penetrate into the jurisdiction of a neutral State.

Art. 41. Aircraft on board of warships, aircraft-carriers included, are considered as forming part of such ships.

Art. 42. A neutral Government is bound to use the means at its disposal to prevent belligerent military aircraft from entering its jurisdiction and to compel them to land or to alight on water if they have penetrated therein.

A neutral government is bound to employ the means at its disposal to intern every belligerent military aircraft which is found within its jurisdiction after landing or watering for whatever cause, as well as its crew and its passengers, if any.

Art. 43. The personnel of a disabled belligerent military aircraft who have been rescued outside the neutral territorial waters and brought into the jurisdiction of a neutral State by a neutral military aircraft and who have been landed there, shall be interned.

Art. 44. It is forbidden to a neutral government to supply a belligerent Power, whether directly or indirectly, with aircraft, component parts thereof or material or ammunition for aircraft.

Art. 45. Subject to the provisions of Article 46, a neutral Power is not bound to prevent the export or the transit of aircraft, component parts thereof or material or ammunition for aircraft, for the account of a belligerent.

Art. 46. A neutral government is bound to use the means at its disposal to:

1. Prevent the departure from its jurisdiction of an aircraft capable of perpetrating an attack against a belligerent Power, or carrying or accompanied by apparatus or material which could be assembled or utilized in such a way to enable it to perpetrate an attack, if there are reasons to believe that such aircraft is intended to be utilized against a belligerent Power;
2. Prevent the departure of an aircraft the crew of which includes any member of the fighting forces of a belligerent Power;
3. Prevent any work being carried out on an aircraft for the purpose of preparing its departure contrary to the objects of the present Article.

At the time of departure of any aircraft forwarded by airway to a belligerent Power by persons or corporations established within a neutral jurisdiction, the neutral government must prescribe for such aircraft a flying route avoiding the vicinity of the military operations of the other belligerent and must demand all the necessary guarantees to asceratin the itinerary followed by the aircraft to be the prescribed one.

Art. 47. A neutral State is bound to take the measures at its disposal to prevent aerial observations of the movements, operations and defense works of a belligerent from being made within its jurisdiction for the purpose of giving information to the other belligerent.

This rule also applies to a belligerent military aircraft on board a warship.

Art. 48. When a neutral Power, exercising its rights and performing its duties according to the present provisions, uses violence or any other means at its disposal, this cannot be considered as an act of hostility.

Chapter VII. Search, Capture and Confiscation

Art. 49. Private aircraft are liable to search and capture by belligerent military aircraft.

Art. 50. Belligerent military aircraft have the right to give order to public non-military aircraft to land or to alight on water, or to repair to a suitable and reasonably accessible place for the purpose of being searched.

The refusal, after warning, to obey the order to land or to alight on water at such place for the purpose of being searched, exposes the aircraft to being fired at.

Art. 51. Neutral non-military public aircraft other than those which must be treated as private aircraft are only subject to the investigation of their papers.

Art. 52. An enemy private aircraft is liable to capture in all circumstances.

Art. 53. A neutral private aircraft is liable to capture:
(a) If it resists the legitimate exercise of the rights of the belligerents;
(b) If it violates an interdiction whereof it has cognizance through a publication of a belligerent commander under the provision of Article 30:
(c) If it is guilty of assistance to the enemy;
(d) If it is armed, in time of war, outside the jurisdiction of its own country;
(e) If it has no exterior marks or if it makes use of false marks;
(f) If it has no papers or if its papers are insufficient or irregular;
(g) If it is clearly out of the route between the point of departure and the point of destination indicated by its papers and if after such inquest as the belligerent may deem necessary, no reasons are given to justify such deviation. The aircraft as well as the members of the crew and the passengers, if any, may be retained by the belligerent during the inquest;
(h) If it carries war contraband or must be considered as such itself;
(i) If it tries to force a blockade duly established and effectively maintained;
(k) If it has been transferred from the belligerent nationality to the neutral nationality at a date and under circumstances indicating the intention of escaping the risks to which an enemy aircraft is exposed as such.

Nevertheless, in each case, except that indicated under k), the reason of the capture must be an act committed during the flight in the course of which the aircraft has fallen into the hands of the belligerent, i.e. since it has left its point of departure and before it has reached its point of destination.

Art. 54. The papers of a private aircraft shall be considered insufficient or irregular if they do not establish the nationality of the aircraft and if they do not show the names and the nationality of each of the members of the crew and of the passengers, the point of departure and the destination of the flight, as well as precisions concerning the cargo and the condition on which it is conveyed. The books of the aircraft are included therein,

Art. 55. The capture of an aircraft or of goods on board an aircraft shall be submitted to a prize court in order that any neutral complaint may be duly examined and judged.

Art. 56. A private aircraft captured because it has no exterior marks or because it has made use of false marks or because it is armed, in time of war, outside the jurisdiction of its own country, is liable to confiscation.

A neutral private aircraft captured on account of having violated the order given by a belligerent commander in virtue of the provisions of Article 30, is liable to confiscation unless it justifies its presence in the forbidden zone.

In all other case, the prize court adjudicating upon the validity of the capture of an aircraft, shall apply the same rules as it would to a merchant ship or to its cargo or to postal correspondence on board a merchant ship.

Art. 57. A private aircraft which after being searched turns out to be an enemy aircraft,may be destroyed if the belligerent commander deems it necessary, provided that all persons on board are previously placed in safety and all the papers of the aircraft are put in a safe place.

Art. 58. A private aircraft which after having been searched turns out to be neutral aircraft liable to confiscation on account of being guilty of hostile assistance or of being without exterior marks or of having carried false marks, may be destroyed if it is impossible to conduct it to the prize court or if such conduction might imperil the safety of the belligerent aircraft or the success of the operations in which it is engaged. In all cases other than those mentioned above, a neutral private aircraft may not be destroyed except in the event of a military necessity of extreme urgency which does not permit the commander to release it or to send it to the prize court for judgment.

Art. 59. Before a private aircraft is destroyed, all persons on board must be placed in safety and all the papers of the aircraft must be put in a safe place. The captor who destroys a neutral private aircraft must submit the validity of the capture to the prize court and must, first of all, prove that he was entitled to destroy the aircraft under Article 58. If he fails to do so, the parties interested in the aircraft or in its cargo are entitled to compensation. If the capture of an aircraft the destruction of which has been held justified, is declared invalid, an indemnity must be paid to the parties interested in place of the restitution to which they would have been entitled.

Art. 60. If a neutral private aircraft has been captured for having carried contraband, the captor is at liberty to demand the handing over of the absolute contraband found on board or to proceed to the destruction of such absolute contraband, when the circumstances are such as to make it impossible to send the aircraft for judgment or if this would endanger the safety of the belligerent aircraft or the success of the operations in which it is engaged. The captor must enter the goods surrendered or destroyed in the logbook of the aircraft and, after having obtained the originals or the duplicates of the papers of the aircraft referring thereto, must allow the neutral aircraft to continue its flight.

The provisions of the second paragraph of Article 59 are applicable in the event of the absolute contraband on board of a neutral private aircraft having been surrendered or destroyed.

Chapter VIII. Definitions

Art. 61. In the presents rules, the term "military" must be understood as referring to all elements of the armed forces, i.e. land, naval and air forces.

Art. 62. Except in so far as special provisions are laid down in the present regulations and save the provisions of Chapter VII of the present regulations or the international conventions indicating that maritime law and its proceedings are applicable, the aeronautical personnel taking part in the hostilities is subject to the laws of war and of neutrality applicable to the land troops in virtue of the custom and practice on International Law as well as of the various declarations and conventions to which interested States are parties.

* * *

See also Nos. 27–36, 55–58, 69–74

IV

PROTECTION OF POPULATIONS AGAINST EFFECTS OF HOSTILITIES

No. 27

PROTECTION OF CIVILIAN POPULATIONS AGAINST BOMBING FROM THE AIR IN CASE OF WAR

Resolution of the League of Nations Assembly adopted on 30 September 1938

INTRODUCTORY NOTE: The attempt to codify the rules of air warfare in the early 1920s (see *No. 26*) not having induced the adoption of a legally binding convention, the question of bombing from the air was brought up again at the Disarmament Conference at Geneva in 1932–34, but no agreement was reached. The bombardments that took place in Ethiopia, Spain and China occasioned new initiatives with a view to adopting regulations on bombing from the air and the protection of civilian populations. On 21 June 1938, the British Prime Minister, Neville Chamberlain, stated in the House of Commons that three principles of international law were applicable to warfare from the air. When the Assembly of the League of Nations met in the following autumn, it adopted without dissent the resolution printed below, which reproduces in substance the three principles put forward by Mr. Chamberlain.

AUTHENTIC TEXTS: English, French.

TEXT PUBLISHED IN: *League of Nations Official Journal*, Special Supplement No. 182, October 1938, Resolutions adopted by the Assembly during its 19th Ordinary Session (12–30 September 1938), pp. 15–16 (Engl.); *Journal Officiel de la Société des Nations*, Supplement spécial No. 182, October 1938, Résolutions adoptées par l'Assemblée à sa douzième séance, pp. 135–136 (French); *Droit des conflits armés*, pp. 299–300 (French).

* * *

The Assembly,

Considering that on numerous occasions public opinion has expressed through the most authoritative channels its horror of the bombing of civilian populations;

Considering that this practice, for which there is no military necessity and which, as experience shows, only causes needless suffering, is condemned under the recognized principles of international law;

Considering, further, that, though this principle ought to be respected by all States and does not require further reaffirmation, it urgently needs to be made the subject of regulations specially adapted to air warfare and taking account of the lessons of experience;

Considering that the solution of this problem, which is of concern to all States, whether Members of the League of Nations or not, calls for technical investigation and thorough consideration;

Considering that the Bureau of the Conference for the Reduction and Limitation of Armaments is to meet in the near future and that it is for the

Bureau to consider practical means of undertaking the necessary work under conditions most likely to lead to as general an agreement as possible:

I. Recognizes the following principles as a necessary basis for any subsequent regulations:
(1) The intentional bombing of civilian populations is illegal;
(2) Objectives aimed at from the air must be legitimate military objectives and must be identifiable;
(3) Any attack on legitimate military objectives must be carried out in such a way that civilian populations in the neighbourhood are not bombed through negligence;

II. Also takes the opportunity to reaffirm that the use of chemical or bacterial methods in the conduct of war is contrary to international law, as recalled more particularly in the resolution of the General Commission of the Conference for the Reduction and Limitation of Armaments of 23 July 1932, and the resolution of the Council of 14 May 1938.

No. 28

DRAFT CONVENTION FOR THE PROTECTION OF CIVILIAN POPULATIONS AGAINST NEW ENGINES OF WAR

Adopted by the International Law Association at its Fortieth Conference held at Amsterdam, on 3 September 1938

INTRODUCTORY NOTE: This draft convention, which was prepared by a committee of the International Law Association and approved in principle by the Fortieth Conference of the Association in 1938, represents one of the notable instances of the efforts of the interwar period to define and improve the protection of the civilian population in armed conflict. Its main object was the establishment of safety zones for certain non-combatant classes of the population.

AUTHENTIC TEXTS: English, French.

TEXT PUBLISHED IN: The International Law Association, *Report on the Fortieth Conference held at Amsterdam, 29 August to 2 September 1938*, pp. 41–54 (Engl., French); *Droit des conflits armés*, pp. 301–307 (French); ICRC website: www.icrc.org/ihl.nsf.

TABLE OF CONTENTS

* * *

All the High Contracting Parties,

Affirming their fidelity to their obligations under the Pact of Paris of 27 August 1928,

Declaring that in any war which they may wage they would necessarily be the victims of aggression, or such war would on their part be a war of legitimate assistance to a victim of aggression,

Undertaking to observe the following rules, which they acknowledge to embody principles of humanity demanded by the conscience of civilization,

Have decided to conclude a Treaty and for that purpose have appointed as their respective Plenipotentiaries ....

Who, having communicated to one another their full powers, found in good and due form, have agreed upon the following articles:

Article 1. The civilian population of a State shall not form the object of an act of war. The phrase "civilian population" within the meaning of this Convention shall include all those not enlisted in any branch of the combatant services nor for the time being employed or occupied in any belligerent establishment as defined in Article 2.

Attack or Bombardment of Undefended Towns

Art. 2. The bombardment by whatever means of towns, ports, villages or buildings which are undefended is prohibited in all circumstances. A town, port, village or isolated building shall be considered undefended provided that not only (a) no combatant troops, but also (b) no military, naval or air establishment, or barracks, arsenal, munition stores or factories, aerodromes or aeroplane workshops or ships of war, naval dockyards, forts, or fortifications for defensive or offensive purposes, or entrenchments (in this Convention referred to as "belligerent establishments") exist within its boundaries or within a radius of "x" kilometres from such boundaries.

Bombardment of Defended Towns

Art. 3. The bombardment by whatever means of towns, ports, villages or buildings which are defended is prohibited at any time (whether at night or day) when objects of military character cannot be clearly recognized.

Art. 4. Aerial bombardment for the purpose of terrorising the civilian population is expressly prohibited.

Art. 5.

1. Aerial bombardment is prohibited unless directed at combatant forces or belligerent establishments or lines of communication or transportation used for military purposes.
2. In cases where the objectives above specified are so situated that they cannot be bombarded without the indiscriminate bombardment of the civilian population, the aircraft must abstain from bombardment.

Chemical, Incendiary or Bacterial Weapons

Art. 6. The use of chemical, incendiary or bacterial weapons as against any State, whether or not a party to the present Convention, and in any war, whatever its character, is prohibited. The application of this rule shall be regulated by the following three articles.

Art. 7.

(a) The prohibition of the use of chemical weapons shall apply to the use, by any method whatsoever, for the purpose of injuring an adversary, of any natural or synthetic substance (whether solid, liquid or gaseous) which is harmful to the human or animal organism by reason of its being a toxic, asphyxiating, irritant or vesicant substance.

(b) The said prohibition shall not apply:

- I. to explosives that are not in the last-mentioned category;
- II. to the noxious substances arising from the combustion or detonation of such explosives, provided that such explosives have not been designed or used with the object of producing such noxious substances;
- III. to smoke or fog used to screen objectives or for other military purpose, provided that such smoke or fog is not liable to produce harmful effects under normal conditions of use;
- IV. to gas that is merely lachrymatory.

Art. 8. The prohibition of the use of incendiary weapons shall apply to projectiles specifically intended to cause fires except when used for defence against aircraft. The prohibition shall not apply:

I. to projectiles specially constructed to give light or to be luminous;
II. to pyrotechnics not normally likely to cause fires;
III. to projectiles of all kinds which, though capable of producing incendiary effects accidentally, are not normally likely to produce such effects;
IV. to incendiary projectiles designed specifically for defence against aircraft when used exclusively for that purpose;
V. to appliances, such as flame-projectors, used to attack individual combatants by fire.

Art. 9. The prohibition of the use of bacterial weapons shall apply to the use for the purpose of injuring an adversary of all methods for the dissemination of pathogenic microbes or of filter-passing viruses, or of infected substances, whether for the purpose of bringing them into immediate contact with human beings, animals or plants, or for the purpose of affecting any of the latter in any manner whatsoever, as, for example, by polluting the atmosphere, water, foodstuffs or any other objects of human use or consumption.

Safety Zones

Art. 10. For the purpose of better enabling a State to obtain protection for the non-belligerent part of its civil population, a State may, if it thinks fit, declare a specified part or parts of its territory to be a "safety zone" or "safety zones" and, subject to the conditions following, such safety zones shall enjoy immunity from attack or bombardment by whatsoever means, and shall not form the legitimate object of any act of war.

Art. 11. A safety zone shall consist of either:
(a) a camp specially erected for that purpose and so situated as to ensure that there is no defended town, port, village or building within "x" kilometres of any part of such camp, or
(b) an undefended town, port, village or building as defined in Article 2.

Art. 12. The inhabitants of a safety zone shall consist of persons who form part of the non-combatant civil population of the State concerned, and shall comprise only the following classes of persons:
(a) persons over the age of 60 years,
(b) persons under the age of 15 years,
(c) persons between 15 and 60 years of age who, by reason of physical or mental infirmity, or by reason of their being expectant mothers or mothers who are suckling infants, are unfit or unable to take part in any work that would enable the State concerned to carry on the war. The question whether any person is or is not within this category is one for the decision of the Controlling Authority hereafter referred to, and
(d) such other persons (not exceeding in the aggregate five percent of the number of such non-combatants) as shall be necessary for the purpose of tending such non-combatants and maintaining law and order within the safety zone, as well as the Controlling Authority hereafter referred to.

Art. 13. The situation of any such safety zone and the road, permanent way, river or canal whereby supplies will be brought to such safety zone shall be notified to other Powers in time of peace through diplomatic channels by means of a map and written description, and such notification shall indicate the precise site and limits of the zone. In time of war such notification shall be given through the agency of one of the States signatory to this Convention and not participating in the war. It shall be the duty of such State forthwith to inform directly the Governments of all States actively concerned in any such war of the contents of such notification, and as soon as may be to acquaint therewith the representatives of all States accredited to its Government and not actively participating in such war. A safety zone notified in time of war shall not be deemed to be such until the expiration of 48 hours after such State as aforesaid has informed the Governments of all States actively concerned in any such war as aforesaid.

Art. 14. Such safety zones must be circular in shape and clearly indicated by marks visible by day to aircraft, and the nature of such marks shall be set out in the notification to other Powers as provided in the last-mentioned Article. The marks used for its safety zones by a State must all be of the same size, colour and pattern. The distinctive flag of the Geneva Convention shall not be used as a mark for such safety zones, nor shall the national flag of any State be so used.

Art. 15. It shall be unlawful during time of war to export any article whatsoever from any such safety zone.

Art. 16. No person other than those specified in Article 12 shall during time of war be permitted to enter any such safety zone. It shall be lawful for the purposes of providing food, clothing and other necessaries of life to those within the zones for transport services (whether by land, sea or air) to proceed as far as the limits of the safety zone as indicated in the notification to other Powers, but not to enter within or fly over such limits, and to remain there for such period only as shall enable the articles transported to be unloaded. For such period as it is engaged upon or returning from such service, and provided it bears the same distinctive marks as those by which such safety zone is indicated, any railway, motor, steam or electric vehicle, ship or aircraft shall whilst within "x" kilometres of any part of the safety zone enjoy the same immunity as such safety zone, and such immunity shall extend to the road, permanent way, river or canal (so far as the same is within the said "x" kilometres of any part of the safety zone) along which such railway, vehicle or ship must necessarily travel in bringing supplies to or returning from the safety zone. No road, permanent way, river or canal which shall have been used for military purposes at any time whilst the safety zone existed as such shall be entitled to the immunity aforesaid.

Art. 17. Every safety zone shall in time of war be subject to the supervision of a Controlling Authority composed of one or more nationals of a non-belligerent State, and it shall be the duty of such Controlling Authority to satisfy itself that the rules herein contained relating to the establishment of safety zones are in all respects complied with. The Controlling Authority shall be accorded every facility for the carrying out of its duties by the Government of the State concerned, and shall enjoy diplomatic privileges.

Art. 18. The Controlling Authority shall be chosen by and be responsible to a Commission of Control appointed to any State which desires to avail itself of the protection hereby afforded to safety zones by the President of the Permanent Court of International Justice, and may be so appointed in time of peace as well as in time of war. Such Commission of Control shall consist of not less than three nationals of non-belligerent States, and shall be accorded every facility for the carrying out of its duties by the Government of the State to which it is appointed, and shall enjoy diplomatic privileges, but shall not interfere with the territorial sovereignty of such State.

Art. 19. The Controlling Authority of a safety zone shall also satisfy itself that the provisions of Article 16 are complied with by any transport service proceeding to or from such safety zone, and that the permanent way, road, river or canal used by such transport service had not been used for military purposes whilst such safety zone existed as such.

Art. 20. It shall be the duty of a Controlling Authority which becomes aware of any breach of any of the provisions of this Convention by any belligerent forthwith to notify the Commission of Control to which it is responsible, and the Commission of

Control, if satisfied that such breach has occurred shall forthwith notify the President of the Permanent Court of International Justice, specifying the breach and naming the State by which such breach is committed, and shall also forthwith notify the Governments of all belligerents.

Art. 21. If any State seeking to avail itself of the protection hereby afforded to safety zones commits a breach of any of the provisions relating to safety zones contained in this Convention in respect of one or more of its own safety zones, and such breach is notified as provided in the preceding article, and the safety zone or safety zones affected by such breach are specified in such notice, it shall be lawful for any other belligerent to give notice to such State that the safety zone or safety zones concerned will after the receipt of such notice no longer be recognized as such, but it shall not be lawful to cause any injury to civilian populations by way of reprisals for such breach.

Sanctions

Art. 22. Any party claiming that a breach of any of the provisions of this Convention (other than a breach of the provisions relating to the establishment of safety zones committed by a State seeking to obtain the protection hereby afforded to such safety zones, for which breach the provisions of the last preceding Article shall be the sole remedy) has occurred shall notify the President of the Permanent Court of International Justice with a view to the immediate constitution of a Commission of Investigation.

Art. 23. The Commission of Investigation shall proceed with all possible speed to make such inquiries as are necessary to determine whether any such breach has occurred. It shall report to the Permanent Court of International Justice.

Art. 24. The Permanent Court of International Justice shall invite the party[(1)] against which the complaint has been made to furnish explanations. It may send commissioners to the territory under the control of that party or of the party making such complaint for the purpose of proceeding to an inquiry, to determine whether any such breach has occurred.

Art. 25. The Permanent Court of International Justice may also carry out any other inquiry with the same object, and may determine any question which may arise requiring determination by a judicial tribunal, such decision to be given with all possible speed.

Art. 26. The parties involved in the above-mentioned operations, and, in general, all the parties to the present Convention, shall take the necessary measures to facilitate these operations, particularly as regards the rapid transport of persons and correspondence.

Art. 27. According to the result of the above-mentioned operations, the Permanent Court of International Justice, acting with all possible speed, shall establish whether any such breach has occurred.

Art. 28. In the event of any such breach being established to its satisfaction the Permanent Court of International Justice shall publish its findings, specifying the State or States which has or have committed such breach, and thereupon it shall be lawful for any Signatory State not being a party to such breach without thereby committing any breach of its treaty obligations or of International Law to do all or any of the following things:

(1) Signatory States not already adhering to the Statute of the Permanent Court would have to undertake to do so (*note in the original*).

(a) assist with armed forces the State against which such breach shall have been committed,
(b) supply such last-mentioned State with financial or material assistance, including munitions of war,
(c) refuse to admit the exercise by the State or States committing such breach of belligerent rights,
(d) decline to observe towards the State or States committing such breach the duties prescribed by International Law for a neutral in relation to a belligerent.

Art. 29. Any State committing a breach of this Convention is liable to pay compensation for all damage caused by such breach to a State injured thereby or any of its nationals.

Art. 30. Each of the High Contracting Parties agrees that it will without delay enact such domestic legislation as may be required to carry into effect the obligations entered into by it hereunder.

Art. 31. This Convention is in addition to, and not in substitution for, the humanitarian obligation imposed upon any Signatory State by any general treaty such as the Hague Conventions of 1899 and 1907 and the International Convention relating to the Treatment of Prisoners of War, 1929.

Art. 32. Non-Signatory Powers may adhere to this Convention. To do so they must make known their adhesion to the High Contracting Parties by means of a written notification addressed to all the High Contracting Parties.

No. 29

CONVENTION ON THE PREVENTION AND PUNISHMENT OF THE CRIME OF GENOCIDE

Adopted by resolution 260 (III) A of the United Nations General Assembly on 9 December 1948

Text reprinted below at *No. 61*.

No. 30

DRAFT RULES FOR THE LIMITATION OF THE DANGERS INCURRED BY THE CIVILIAN POPULATION IN TIME OF WAR

International Committee of the Red Cross, 1956

INTRODUCTORY NOTE. The International Committee of the Red Cross, convinced that the existing conventions did not provide sufficient protection of the civilian population against indiscriminate warfare, drafted the rules reprinted below. They were approved by the XIXth International Conference of the Red Cross in New Delhi in 1957 and thereupon submitted to the governments for examination. As there was virtually no response from governments, no further action was taken with a view to adopting a convention on the basis of this draft. However, the draft had some influence on the later attempts to define and develop the international law relating to armed conflicts. To a large extent, its provisions correspond to customary international law.

AUTHENTIC TEXT: French.

TEXT PUBLISHED IN: *Draft Rules for the Limitation of the Dangers Incurred by the Civilian Population in Time of War*, 2nd edn., Geneva, International Committee of the Red Cross, 1958 (Engl., French, German and Spanish editions); *Droit des conflits armés*, pp. 311–317 (French); ICRC website: www.icrc.org/ihl.nsf.

* * *

TABLE OF CONTENTS

Preamble

All nations are deeply convinced that war should be banned as a means of settling disputes between human communities.

However, in view of the need, should hostilities once more break out, of safeguarding the civilian population

from the destruction with which it is threatened as a result of technical developments in weapons and methods of warfare,

The limits placed by the requirements of humanity and the safety of the population on the use of armed force are restated and defined in the following rules.

In cases not specifically provided for, the civilian population shall continue to enjoy the protection of the general rule set forth in Article 1, and of the principles of international law.

Chapter I. Object and Field of Application

Object

Article 1. Since the right of Parties to the conflict to adopt means of injuring the enemy is not unlimited, they shall confine their operations to the destruction of his military resources, and leave the civilian population outside the sphere of armed attacks.

This general rule is given detailed expression in the following provisions:

Field of application

Art. 2. The present rules shall apply:
(a) In the event of declared war or of any other armed conflict, even if the state of war is not recognized by one of the Parties to the conflict.
(b) In the event of an armed conflict not of an international character.

Definition of term "attacks"

Art. 3. The present rules shall apply to acts of violence committed against the adverse Party by force of arms, whether in defence or offence. Such acts shall be referred to hereafter as "attacks."

Definition of term "civilian population"

Art. 4. For the purpose of the present rules, the civilian population consists of all persons not belonging to one or other of the following categories:
(a) Members of the armed forces, or of their auxiliary or complementary organizations.
(b) Persons who do not belong to the forces referred to above, but nevertheless take part in the fighting.

Relation with previous Conventions

Art. 5. The obligations imposed upon the Parties to the conflict in regard to the civilian population, under the present rules, are complementary to those which already devolve expressly upon the Parties by virtue of other rules in international law, deriving in particular from the instruments of Geneva and The Hague.

Chapter II. Objectives Barred from Attack

Art. 6. Attacks directed against the civilian population, as such, whether with the object of terrorizing it or for any other reason, are prohibited. This prohibition applies both to attacks on individuals and to those directed against groups.

Immunity of the civilian population

In consequence, it is also forbidden to attack dwellings, installations or means of transport, which are for the exclusive use of, and occupied by, the civilian population.

Nevertheless, should members of the civilian population, Article 11 notwithstanding, be within or in close proximity to a military objective they must accept the risks resulting from an attack directed against that objective.

Art. 7. In order to limit the dangers incurred by the civilian population, attacks may only be directed against military objectives.

Limitation of objectives which may be attacked

Only objectives belonging to the categories of objective which, in view of their essential characteristics, are generally acknowledged to be of military importance, may be considered as military objectives. Those categories are listed in an annex to the present rules [1].

However, even if they belong to one of those categories, they cannot be considered as a military objective where their total or partial destruction, in the circumstances ruling at the time, offers no military advantage.

Chapter III. Precautions in Attacks on Military Objectives

Art. 8. The person responsible for ordering or launching an attack shall, first of all:

Precautions to be taken in planning attacks

(a) make sure that the objective, or objectives, to be attacked are military objectives within the meaning of the present rules, and are duly identified.

When the military advantage to be gained leaves the choice open between several objectives, he is required to select the one, an attack on which involves least danger for the civilian population:

(b) take into account the loss and destruction which the attack, even if carried out with the precautions prescribed under Article 9, is liable to inflict upon the civilian population.

He is required to refrain from the attack if, after due consideration, it is apparent that the loss and destruction would be disproportionate to the military advantage anticipated:

(c) whenever the circumstances allow, warn the civilian population in jeopardy, to enable it to take shelter.

Art. 9. All possible precautions shall be taken, both in the choice of the weapons and methods to be used, and in the carrying out of an attack, to ensure that no losses or damage are caused to the civilian population in the vicinity of the objective, or to its dwellings, or that such losses or damage are at least reduced to a minimum.

Precautions to be taken in carrying out the attack

In particular, in towns and other places with a large civilian population, which are not in the vicinity of military or naval operations, the attack shall be conducted with the greatest degree of precision. It must not cause losses or destruction beyond the immediate surroundings of the objective attacked.

---

1 A tentative list of military objectives can be found in the commentary added to the Draft Rules (not reproduced in this volume).

The person responsible for carrying out the attack must abandon or break off the operation if he perceives that the conditions set forth above cannot be respected.

Target-area bombing

Art. 10. It is forbidden to attack without distinction, as a single objective, an area including several military objectives at a distance from one another where elements of the civilian population, or dwellings, are situated in between the said military objectives.

"Passive" precautions

Art. 11. The Parties to the conflict shall, so far as possible, take all necessary steps to protect the civilian population subject to their authority from the dangers to which they would be exposed in an attack – in particular by removing them from the vicinity of military objectives and from threatened areas. However, the rights conferred upon the population in the event of transfer or evacuation under Article 49 of the Fourth Geneva Convention of 12 August 1949 are expressly reserved.

Similarly, the Parties to the conflict shall, so far as possible, avoid the permanent presence of armed forces, military material, mobile military establishments or installations, in towns or other places with a large civilian population.

Civil Defence bodies

Art. 12. The Parties to the conflict shall facilitate the work of the civilian bodies exclusively engaged in protecting and assisting the civilian population in case of attack.

They can agree to confer special immunity upon the personnel of those bodies, their equipment and installations, by means of a special emblem.

Intentional exposure to danger

Art. 13. Parties to the conflict are prohibited from placing or keeping members of the civilian population subject to their authority in or near military objectives, with the idea of inducing the enemy to refrain from attacking those objectives.

Chapter IV. Weapons with Uncontrollable Effects

Prohibited methods of warfare

Art. 14. Without prejudice to the present or future prohibition of certain specific weapons, the use is prohibited of weapons whose harmful effects – resulting in particular from the dissemination of incendiary, chemical, bacteriological, radioactive or other agents – could spread to an unforeseen degree or escape, either in space or in time, from the control of those who employ them, thus endangering the civilian population.

This prohibition also applies to delayed-action weapons, the dangerous effects of which are liable to be felt by the civilian population.

Safety measures and devices

Art. 15. If the Parties to the conflict make use of mines, they are bound, without prejudice to the stipulations of the VIIIth Hague Convention of 1907, to chart the mine-fields. The charts shall be handed over, at the close of active hostilities, to the adverse Party, and also to all other authorities responsible for the safety of the population.

Without prejudice to the precautions specified under Article 9, weapons capable of causing serious damage to the civilian population shall, so far as possible, be equipped with a safety device which renders them harmless when they escape from the control of those who employ them.

Chapter V. Special Cases

Art. 16. When, on the outbreak or in the course of hostilities, a locality is declared to be an "open town" the adverse Party shall be duly notified. The latter is bound to reply, and if it agrees to recognize the locality in question as an open town, shall cease from all attacks on the said town, and refrain from any military operation the sole object of which is its occupation.

"Open towns"

In the absence of any special conditions which may, in any particular case, be agreed upon with the adverse Party, a locality, in order to be declared an "open town," must satisfy the following conditions:

(a) it must not be defended or contain any armed force;
(b) it must discontinue all relations with any national or allied armed forces;
(c) it must stop all activities of a military nature or for a military purpose in those of its installations or industries which might be regarded as military objectives;
(d) it must stop all military transit through the town.

The adverse Party may make the recognition of the status of "open town" conditional upon verification of the fulfilment of the conditions stipulated above. All attacks shall be suspended during the institution and operation of the investigatory measures.

The presence in the locality of civil defence services, or of the services responsible for maintaining public order, shall not be considered as contrary to the conditions laid down in paragraph 2. If the locality is situated in occupied territory, this provision applies also to the military occupation forces essential for the maintenance of public law and order.

When an "open town" passes into other hands, the new authorities are bound, if they cannot maintain its status, to inform the civilian population accordingly.

None of the above provisions shall be interpreted in such a manner as to diminish the protection which the civilian population should enjoy by virtue of the other provisions of the present rules, even when not living in localities recognized as "open towns."

Art. 17. In order to safeguard the civilian population from the dangers that might result from the destruction of engineering works or installations – such as hydro-electric dams, nuclear power stations or dikes – through the releasing of natural or artificial forces, the States or Parties concerned are invited:

Installations containing dangerous forces

(a) to agree, in time of peace, on a special procedure to ensure in all circumstances the general immunity of such works where intended essentially for peaceful purposes:
(b) to agree, in time of war, to confer special immunity, possibly on the basis of the stipulations of Article 16, on works and installations which have not, or no longer have, any connexion with the conduct of military operations.

The preceding stipulations shall not, in any way, release the Parties to the conflict from the obligation to take the precautions required by the general provisions of the present rules, under Articles 8 to 11 in particular.

Chapter VI. Application of the Rules [1]

Assistance of third parties

Art. 18. States not involved in the conflict, and also all appropriate organizations, are invited to co-operate, by lending their good offices, in ensuring the observance of the present rules and preventing either of the Parties to the conflict from resorting to measures contrary to those rules.

Trial and judicial safeguards

Art. 19. All States or Parties concerned are under the obligation to search for and bring to trial any person having committed, or ordered to be committed, an infringement of the present rules, unless they prefer to hand the person over for trial to another State or Party concerned with the case.

The accused persons shall be tried only by regular civil or military courts; they shall, in all circumstances, benefit by safeguards of proper trial and defence at least equal to those provided under Articles 105 and those following of the Geneva Convention relative to the Treatment of Prisoners of War of 12 August 1949.

Diffusion and details of application

Art. 20. All States or Parties concerned shall make the terms of the provisions of the present rules known to their armed forces and provide for their application in accordance with the general principles of these rules, not only in the instances specifically envisaged in the rules, but also in unforeseen cases.

(1) Articles 18 and 19, dealing with the procedure for supervision and sanctions, are merely given as a rough guide and in outline; they will naturally have to be elaborated and supplemented at a later stage (*note in the original*).

No. 31

PROTECTION OF CIVILIAN POPULATIONS AGAINST THE DANGERS OF INDISCRIMINATE WARFARE

Resolution XXVIII adopted by the XXth International Conference of the Red Cross, Vienna, 1965

INTRODUCTORY NOTE: This resolution is of importance in view of its restatement of four principles of international law which are to be observed in case of armed conflict. The resolution was affirmed by the United Nations General Assembly in resolution 2444 (XXIII) of 19 December 1968 (*No. 33*).

AUTHENTIC TEXT: French (English being recognized as a working language at the Conference).

TEXT PUBLISHED IN: *XXth International Conference of the Red Cross, Report*, Vienna, 2–9 October 1965, Neue Hofburg, pp. 108–109 (Engl.); *XXe Conférence Internationale de la Croix-Rouge, Compte Rendu*, Vienne, 2–9 Octobre 1965, Neue Hofburg, pp. 110–111 (French); *XX Conferencia Internacional de la Cruz Roja, Informe Final*, Viena, 2 al 9 de Octubre de 1965, Neue Hofburg, p. 114 (Span.); *International Red Cross Handbook*, 1983, pp. 626–627 (Engl.); *Manuel de la Croix-Rouge internationale*, 1983, pp. 647–648 (French); *Manual de la Cruz Roja internacional*, 1983, pp. 634–635 (Span.); *Handbook of the International Movement*, 1994, pp. 773–774 (Engl.); *Manuel du Mouvement internacional*, 1994, pp. 793–794 (French); *Manual del Movimiento internacional*, 1994, pp. 798–799 (Span); *XXth International Conference of the Red Cross, Vienna, October 1965, Resolutions*, pp. 21–23 (English, French, German and Spanish editions); *Droit des conflits armés*, pp. 319–320 (French).

* * *

The XXth International Conference of the Red Cross,

in its endeavours for the protection of the civilian populations, reaffirms Resolution No. XVIII of the XVIIIth International Conference of the Red Cross (Toronto, 1952), which, in consideration of Resolution No. XXIV of the XVIIth International Conference of the Red Cross (Stockholm, 1948) requested Governments to agree, within the framework of general disarmament, to a plan for the international control of atomic energy which would ensure the prohibition of atomic weapons and the use of atomic energy solely for peaceful purposes,

thanks the International Committee of the Red Cross for the initiative taken and the comprehensive work done by it in defining and further developing international humanitarian law in this sphere,

states that indiscriminate warfare constitutes a danger to the civilian population and the future of civilization,

solemnly declares that all Governments and other authorities responsible for action in armed conflicts should conform at least to the following principles:

- *that the right of parties to a conflict to adopt means of injuring the enemy is not unlimited;*
- *that it is prohibited to launch attacks against the civilian population as such;*

- *that distinction must be made at all times between persons taking part in the hostilities and members of the civilian population to the effect that the latter be spared as much as possible;*
- *that the general principles of the Law of War apply to nuclear and similar weapons;*

expressly invites all Governments who have not yet done so to accede to the Geneva Protocol of 1925 which prohibits the use of asphyxiating, poisonous, or other gases, all analogous liquids, materials or devices, and bacteriological methods of warfare,

urges the ICRC to pursue the development of International Humanitarian Law in accordance with Resolution No. XIII of the XIXth International Conference of the Red Cross, with particular reference to the need for protecting the civilian population against the sufferings caused by indiscriminate warfare,

requests the ICRC to take into consideration all possible means and to take all appropriate steps, including the creation of a committee of experts, with a view to obtaining a rapid and practical solution of this problem,

requests National Societies to intervene with their Governments in order to obtain their collaboration for an early solution of this question and urges all Governments to support the efforts of the International Red Cross in this respect,

requests all National Societies to do all in their power to persuade their Governments to reach fruitful agreements in the field of general disarmament.

VOTE

The resolution was adopted by 64 votes in favour, none against, and with two abstentions.

No. 32

HUMAN RIGHTS IN ARMED CONFLICTS

Resolution XXIII adopted by the International Conference on Human Rights, Teheran, 12 May 1968

INTRODUCTORY NOTE: This resolution reaffirms, in paragraph 2, the famous de Martens clause included in the preambles of the Hague Conventions of 1899 and 1907 concerning the laws and customs of war according to which states in armed conflict shall apply "the principles of the law of nations derived from the usages established among civilized peoples, from the laws of humanity and from the dictates of the public conscience". The Martens clause was subsequently reaffirmed in Article 1(4) of the 1977 Protocol Additional to the Geneva Conventions (*No. 56*) and in paragraph 5 of the Preamble of the 1980 Convention on Conventional Weapons (*No. 20*). The International Conference on Human Rights, which adopted the present resolution, was convened by the United Nations on the occasion of the International Year for Human Rights (twentieth anniversary of the Universal Declaration of Human Rights).

AUTHENTIC TEXTS: English, French, Russian, Spanish.

TEXT PUBLISHED IN: *Final Act of the International Conference on Human Rights*, Teheran, 22 April to 13 May 1968, United Nations, Document A/Conf. 32/41 (Sales No. 68.XIV.2), (also in French, Russ. and Span.); *Droits des conflits armés*, pp. 321–323 (French); ICRC website: www.icrc.org/ihl.nsf.

* * *

The International Conference on Human Rights,

Considering *that peace is the underlying condition for the full observance of human rights and war is their negation,*

Believing *that the purpose of the United Nations Organization is to prevent all conflicts and to institute an effective system for the peaceful settlement of disputes,*

Observing *that nevertheless armed conflicts continue to plague humanity,*

Considering, *also, that the widespread violence and brutality of our times, including massacres, summary executions, tortures, inhuman treatment of prisoners, killing of civilians in armed conflicts and the use of chemical and biological means of warfare, including napalm bombing, erode human rights land engender counter-brutality,*

Convinced *that even during the periods of armed conflict, humanitarian principles must prevail,*

Noting *that the provisions of the Hague Conventions of 1899 and 1907 were intended to be only a first step in the provision of a code prohibiting or limiting the use of certain methods of warfare and that they were adopted at a time when the present means and methods of warfare did not exist,*

Considering *that the provisions of the Geneva Protocol of 1925 prohibiting the use of "asphyxiating, poisonous or other gases and of all analogous liquids materials and devices" have not been universally accepted or applied and may need a revision in the light of modern development,*

Considering *further that the Red Cross Geneva Conventions of 1949 are not sufficiently broad in scope to cover all armed conflicts,*

Noting *that States parties to the Red Cross Geneva Conventions sometimes fail to appreciate their responsibility to take steps to ensure the respect of these humanitarian rules in all circumstances by other States, even if they are not themselves directly involved in an armed conflict,*

Noting also *that minority racist or colonial régimes which refuse to comply with the decisions of the United Nations and the principles of the Universal Declaration of Human Rights frequently resort to executions and inhuman treatment of those who struggle against such régimes and considering that such persons should be protected against inhuman or brutal treatment and also that such persons if detained should be treated as prisoners of war or political prisoners under international law,*

1. Requests *the General Assembly to invite the Secretary-General to study:*
   (a) Steps which could be taken to secure the better application of existing humanitarian international conventions and rules in all armed conflicts;
   (b) The need for additional humanitarian international conventions or for possible revision of existing Conventions to ensure the better protection of civilians, prisoners and combatants in all armed conflicts and the prohibition and limitation of the use of certain methods and means of warfare;

2. Requests *the Secretary-General, after consultation with the International Committee of the Red Cross, to draw the attention of all States members of the United Nations system to the existing rules of international law on the subject and urge them, pending the adoption of new rules of international law relating to armed conflicts, to ensure that in all armed conflicts the inhabitants and belligerents are protected in accordance with "the principles of the law of nations derived from the usages established among civilized peoples, from the laws of humanity and from the dictates of the public conscience;*

3. Calls *on all States which have not yet done so to become parties to the Hague Conventions of 1899 and 1907, the Geneva Protocol of 1925, and the Geneva Conventions of 1949.*

No. 33

RESPECT FOR HUMAN RIGHTS IN ARMED CONFLICTS

Resolution 2444 (XXIII) of the United Nations General Assembly adopted on 19 December 1968

INTRODUCTORY NOTE: Resolution 2444 (XXIII) affirms, in paragraph 1, the resolution on the protection of civilian populations against the dangers of indiscriminate warfare, which was adopted by the International Conference of the Red Cross in Vienna in 1965 (*No. 29*). However, of the four principles of international law laid down in the Red Cross resolution, only three are expressly repeated in the UN resolution.

AUTHENTIC TEXTS: Chinese, English, French, Russian, Spanish.

TEXT PUBLISHED IN: *Resolutions adopted by the General Assembly during its Twenty-third Session, 24 September–21 December 1968.* General Assembly Official Records: Twenty-third Session, Supplement No. 18 (A/7218), New York, United Nations, 1969, pp. 50–51 (Engl. – see also Chinese, French, Russian and Spanish editions); *International Red Cross Handbook*, 1983, pp. 396–397 (Engl.); *Manuel de la Croix-Rouge internationale*, 1983, pp. 410–411 (French); *Manual de la Cruz Roja internacional*, 1983, pp. 401–402 (Span.); *Handbook of the International Movement*, 1994, pp. 373–374 (Engl.); *Manuel du Mouvement international*, 1994, pp. 387–388 (French); *Manual del Movimiento internacional*, 1994, pp. 378–379 (Span); *Droit des conflits armés*, pp. 325–326 (French); ICRC website: www.icrc.org/ihl.nsf.

* * *

The General Assembly,

Recognizing *the necessity of applying basic humanitarian principles in all armed conflicts,*

Taking note *of resolution XXIII on human rights in armed conflicts, adopted on 12 May 1968 by the International Conference on Human Rights,*

Affirming *that the provisions of that resolution need to be implemented effectively as soon as possible,*

1. Affirms *resolution XXVIII of the XXth International Conference of the Red Cross held at Vienna in 1965, which laid down, inter alia, the following principles for observance by all governmental and other authorities responsible for action in armed conflicts:*
   (a) That the right of the parties to a conflict to adopt means of injuring the enemy is not unlimited;
   (b) That it is prohibited to launch attacks against the civilian populations as such;
   (c) That distinction must be made at all times between persons taking part in the hostilities and members of the civilian population to the effect that the latter be spared as much as possible;

2. Invites *the Secretary-General, in consultation with the International Committee of the Red Cross and other appropriate international organizations, to study:*
   (a) Steps which could be taken to secure the better application of existing humanitarian international conventions and rules in all armed conflicts;
   (b) The need for additional humanitarian international conventions or for other appropriate legal instruments to ensure the better protection of civilians, prisoners and combatants in all armed conflicts and the prohibition and limitation of the use of certain methods and means of warfare;
3. Requests *the Secretary-General to take all other necessary steps to give effect to the provisions of the present resolution and to report to the General Assembly at its twenty-fourth session on the steps he has taken;*
4. Further requests *Member States to extend all possible assistance to the Secretary-General in the preparation of the study requested in paragraph 2 above;*
5. Calls upon *all States which have not yet done so to become parties to the Hague Conventions of 1899 and 1907, the Geneva Protocol of 1925 and the Geneva Conventions of 1949.*

VOTE

Resolution 2444 (XXIII) was adopted by unanimous vote of 111 votes to none.[1]

[1] A roll-call vote did not take place.

No. 34

THE DISTINCTION BETWEEN MILITARY OBJECTIVES AND NON-MILITARY OBJECTIVES IN GENERAL AND PARTICULARLY THE PROBLEMS ASSOCIATED WITH WEAPONS OF MASS DESTRUCTION

Resolution adopted by the Institute of International Law at its session at Edinburgh, 9 September 1969

INTRODUCTORY NOTE: This resolution is intended to state the existing law. It was adopted by 60 votes to one, with two abstentions.

AUTHENTIC TEXT: French.

TEXT PUBLISHED IN: *Annuaire de l'Institut de Droit international*, Session d'Edimbourg, 1969, Vol. 53, II, p. 358 (French), p. 375 (English); Institut de Droit international, *Tableau des Résolutions adoptées, 1957–1991*, 1992, pp. 66–69 (Engl., French); *Droit des conflits armés*, pp. 327–328 (French); *AJIL*, Vol. 66, pp. 470–471 (Engl.); ICRC website: www.icrc.org/ihl.nsf.

* * *

The Institute of International Law,

Reaffirming the existing rules of international law whereby the recourse to force is prohibited in international relations,

Considering that, if an armed conflict occurs in spite of these rules, the protection of civilian populations is one of the essential obligations of the parties,

Having in mind the general principles of international law, the customary rules and the conventions and agreements which clearly restrict the extent to which the parties engaged in a conflict may harm the adversary,

Having also in mind that these rules, which are enforced by international and national courts, have been formally confirmed on several occasions by a large number of international organizations and especially by the United Nations Organization,

Being of the opinion that these rules have kept their full validity notwithstanding the infringements suffered,

Having in mind that the consequences which the indiscriminate conduct of hostilities and particularly the use of nuclear, chemical and bacteriological weapons, may involve for civilian populations and for mankind as a whole,

Notes that the following rules form part of the principles to be observed in armed conflicts by any *de jure* or *de facto* government, or by any other authority responsible for the conduct of hostilities:

1. The obligation to respect the distinction between military objectives and non-military objects as well as between persons participating in the hostilities and members of the civilian population remains a fundamental principle of the international law in force.
2. There can be considered as military objectives only those which, by their very nature or purpose or use, make an effective contribution to military action, or exhibit a generally recognized military significance, such that their total or partial

destruction in the actual circumstances gives a substantial, specific and immediate military advantage to those who are in a position to destroy them.

3. Neither the civilian population nor any of the objects expressly protected by conventions or agreements can be considered as military objectives, nor yet
   (a) under whatsoever circumstances the means indispensable for the survival of the civilian population,
   (b) those objects which, by their nature or use, serve primarily humanitarian or peaceful purposes such as religious or cultural needs.
4. Existing international law prohibits all armed attacks on the civilian population as such, as well as on non-military objects, notably dwellings or other buildings sheltering the civilian population, so long as these are not used for military purposes to such an extent as to justify action against them under the rules regarding military objectives as set forth in the second paragraph hereof.
5. The provisions of the preceding paragraphs do not affect the application of the existing rules of international law which prohibit the exposure of civilian populations and of non-military objects to the destructive effects of military means.
6. Existing international law prohibits, irrespective of the type of weapon used, any action whatsoever designed to terrorize the civilian population.
7. Existing international law prohibits the use of all weapons which, by their nature, affect indiscriminately both military objectives and non-military objects, or both armed forces and civilian populations. In particular, it prohibits the use of weapons the destructive effect of which is so great that it cannot be limited to specific military objectives or is otherwise uncontrollable (self-generating weapons), as well as of "blind" weapons.
8. Existing international law prohibits all attacks for whatsoever motive or by whatsoever means for the annihilation of any group, region or urban centre with no possible distinction between armed forces and civilian populations or between military objectives and non-military objects.

No. 35

BASIC PRINCIPLES FOR THE PROTECTION OF CIVILIAN POPULATIONS IN ARMED CONFLICTS

Resolution 2675 (XXV) of the United Nations General Assembly adopted on 9 December 1970

INTRODUCTORY NOTE: After the adoption of Resolution 2444 (XXIII) in 1968 (*No. 31*), which invited the Secretary-General, in consultation with the International Committee of the Red Cross and other appropriate international organizations, to study steps for the better application of existing conventions and the need for additional conventions, the General Assembly adopted further resolutions concerning human rights in armed conflicts every year. Most of these have a procedural character only or call upon states to apply existing conventions in particular situations. The following resolution restates rules of international law.

AUTHENTIC TEXTS: Chinese, English, French, Russian, Spanish.

TEXT PUBLISHED IN: *Resolutions adopted by the General Assembly during its Twenty-fifth Session, 15 September–17 December 1970,* General Assembly Official Records: Twenty-fifth Session Supplement No. 28 (A/8028), New York, United Nations, 1971, pp. 76 (Engl. – see also Chinese, French, Russian and Spanish editions); *Droit des conflits armés*, pp. 329–330 (French).

* * *

The General Assembly,

Noting *that in the present century the international community has accepted an increased role and new responsibilities for the alleviation of human suffering in any form and in particular during armed conflicts,*

Recalling *that to this end a series of international instruments has been adopted, including the four Geneva Conventions of 1949,*

Recalling further *its resolution 2444 (XXIII) of 19 December 1968 on respect for human rights in armed conflicts,*

Bearing in mind *the need for measures to ensure the better protection of human rights in armed conflicts of all types,*

Noting with appreciation *the work that is being undertaken in this respect by the International Committee of the Red Cross,*

Noting with appreciation *the reports of the Secretary-General on respect for human rights in armed conflicts,*

Convinced *that civilian populations are in special need of increased protection in time of armed conflicts,*

Recognizing *the importance of the strict application of the Geneva Convention relative to the Protection of Civilian Persons in Time of War, of 12 August 1949,*

Affirms *the following basic principles for the protection of civilian populations in armed conflicts, without prejudice to their future elaboration within the framework of progressive development of the international law of armed conflict:*

1. *Fundamental human rights, as accepted in international law and laid down in international instruments, continue to apply fully in situations of armed conflict.*
2. *In the conduct of military operations during armed conflicts, a distinction must be made at all times between persons actively taking part in the hostilities and civilian populations.*
3. *In the conduct of military operations, every effort should be made to spare civilian populations from the ravages of war, and all necessary precautions should be taken to avoid injury, loss or damage to civilian populations.*
4. *Civilian populations as such should not be the object of military operations.*
5. *Dwellings and other installations that are used only by civilian populations should not be the object of military operations.*
6. *Places or areas designated for the sole protection of civilians, such as hospital zones or similar refuges, should not be the object of military operations.*
7. *Civilian populations, or individual members thereof, should not be the object of reprisals, forcible transfers or other assaults on their integrity.*
8. *The provision of international relief to civilian populations is in conformity with the humanitarian principles of the Charter of the United Nations, the Universal Declaration of Human Rights and other international instruments in the field of human rights. The Declaration of Principles for International Humanitarian Relief to the Civilian Population in Disaster Situations, as laid down in resolution XXVI adopted by the twenty-first International Conference of the Red Cross, shall apply in situations of armed conflict, and all parties to a conflict shall make every effort to facilitate this application.*

VOTE

Resolution 2675 (XXV) was adopted by 109 votes to none, with 18 states abstaining or absent.[1]

[1] A roll-call vote did not take place.

No. 36

DECLARATION ON THE PROTECTION OF WOMEN AND CHILDREN IN EMERGENCY AND ARMED CONFLICT

Resolution 3318 (XXIX) of the United Nations General Assembly adopted on 14 December 1974

INTRODUCTORY NOTE: The present declaration originated in the UN Commission on the Status of Women and was recommended to the General Assembly by the Economic and Social Council.

AUTHENTIC TEXTS: Chinese, English, French, Russian, Spanish.

TEXT PUBLISHED IN: *Resolutions adopted by the General Assembly during its Twenty-Ninth Session,* Vol. 1, *17 September–18 December 1974*, General Assembly Official Records: Twenty-ninth Session Supplement No. 31 (A/9631), New York, United Nations, 1975, p. 146 (Engl. – see also Chinese, French, Russian and Spanish editions); *Human Rights – A Compilation of International Instruments*, Vol. I (First Part), New York, United Nations, 1993, pp. 167–169 (Engl.); *Droits de l'homme – Recueil d'instruments internationaux*, New York, Nations Unies, 1988, pp. 370–372 (French); *Derechos Humanos – Recopilación de instrumentos internacionales*, Nueva York, Naciones Unidas, 1988, pp. 369–371 (Span.); *Prava cheloveka – Sbornik mezhdunarodnykh dokumentov*, Nyu York, OON, 1989, pp. 420–422 (Russ.); *Droit des conflits armés*, pp. 331–333 (French); UN website: http://www.unhcr.ch.

* * *

The General Assembly,

Having considered *the recommendation of the Economic and Social Council contained in its resolution 1861 (LVI) of 16 May 1974,*

Expressing its deep concern *over the sufferings of women and children belonging to the civilian population who in periods of emergency and armed conflict in the struggle for peace, self-determination, national liberation and independence are too often the victims of inhuman acts and consequently suffer serious harm,*

Aware *of the suffering of women and children in many areas of the world, especially in those areas subject to suppression, aggression, colonialism, racism, alien domination and foreign subjugation,*

Deeply concerned *by the fact that, despite general and unequivocal condemnation, colonialism, racism and alien and foreign domination continue to subject many peoples under their yoke, cruelly suppressing the national liberation movements and inflicting heavy losses and incalculable sufferings on the populations under their domination, including women and children,*

Deploring *the fact that grave attacks are still being made on fundamental freedoms and the dignity of the human person and that colonial and racist foreign domination Powers continue to violate international humanitarian law,*

Recalling *the relevant provisions contained in the instruments of international humanitarian law relative to the protection of women and children in time of peace and war,*

Recalling, *among other important documents, its resolutions 2444 (XXIII) of 19 December 1968, 2597 (XXIV) of 16 December 1969 and 2674 (XXV) and 2675 (XXV) of 9 December 1970, on respect for human rights and on basic principles for the protection of civilian populations in armed conflicts, as well as Economic and Social Council resolution 1515 (XLVIII) of 28 May 1970 in which the Council requested the General Assembly to consider the possibility of drafting a declaration on the protection of women and children in emergency or wartime,*

Conscious *of its responsibility for the destiny of the rising generation and for the destiny of mothers, who play an important role in society, in the family and particularly in the upbringing of children,*

Bearing in mind *the need to provide special protection of women and children belonging to the civilian population,*

Solemnly proclaims *this Declaration on the Protection of Women and Children in Emergency and Armed Conflict and calls for the strict observance of the Declaration by all Member States:*

1. *Attacks and bombings on the civilian population, inflicting incalculable suffering, especially on women and children, who are the most vulnerable members of the population, shall be prohibited, and such acts shall be condemned.*
2. *The use of chemical and bacteriological weapons in the course of military operations constitutes one of the most flagrant violations of the Geneva Protocol of 1925, the Geneva Conventions of 1949 and the principles of international humanitarian law and inflicts heavy losses on civilian populations, including defenceless women and children, and shall be severely condemned.*
3. *All States shall abide fully by their obligations under the Geneva Protocol of 1925 and the Geneva Conventions of 1949, as well as other instruments of international law relative to respect for human rights in armed conflicts, which offer important guarantees for the protection of women and children.*
4. *All efforts shall be made by States involved in armed conflicts, military operations in foreign territories or military operations in territories still under colonial domination to spare women and children from the ravages of war. All the necessary steps shall be taken to ensure the prohibition of measures such as persecution, torture, punitive measures, degrading treatment and violence, particularly against that part of the civilian population that consists of women and children.*
5. *All forms of repression and cruel and inhuman treatment of women and children, including imprisonment, torture, shooting, mass arrests, collective punishment, destruction of dwellings and forcible eviction, committed by belligerents in the course of military operations or in occupied territories shall be considered criminal.*
6. *Women and children belonging to the civilian population and finding themselves in circumstances of emergency and armed conflict in the struggle for peace, self-determination, national liberation and independence, or who live in occupied territories, shall not be deprived of shelter, food, medical aid or other inalienable rights, in accordance with the provisions of the*

Universal Declaration of Human Rights, the International Covenant on Civil and Political Rights, the International Covenant on Economic, Social and Cultural Rights, the Declaration of the Rights of the Child or other instruments of international law.

VOTE

The Declaration was adopted by a vote of 110 in favour, none against and 14 abstentions.[1]

* * *

See also Nos. 1-3, 7 and 8, 52, 56-60

1 A roll-call vote did not take place.

V

VICTIMS OF WAR
(WOUNDED, SICK, PRISONERS, CIVILIANS)

No. 37

RESOLUTIONS OF THE GENEVA INTERNATIONAL CONFERENCE

Geneva, 26–29 October 1863

INTRODUCTORY NOTE: The Geneva International Conference of 1863 was the founding Conference of the Red Cross and gave the impetus to the development of the humanitarian laws of war embodied in the Geneva Conventions of 1864, 1906, 1929, 1949 and in the Additional Protocols of 1977.

The movement was initiated by Henry Dunant, a citizen of Geneva, who, in 1859, was an eyewitness of the battle of Solférino where thousands of wounded died without care who could have been saved if sufficient medical services had existed. In 1862, Dunant published his book *Un souvenir de Solférino* in which, after an impressive description of the battle, he proposed to set up in time of peace relief societies in each country for the care of the wounded in time of war. He furthermore suggested the adoption of an international agreement recognizing the inviolability of medical services and of the wounded. The book aroused much discussion all over Europe. The Geneva Society of Public Welfare, under the presidency of Gustave Moynier, took up Dunant's ideas and, on 9 February 1863, appointed a committee, consisting of General G.H. Dufour as president, Gustave Moynier, Henry Dunant, Theodore Maunoir and Louis Appia, to examine the questions involved, This "Committee of Five" which later was to become the International Committee of the Red Cross, convened on a private basis the International Conference of 1863 at which 16 states were represented. The Conference adopted Dunant's and the Committee's proposals for the creation of national committees and decided that a red cross on a white ground should be the distinctive sign of the medical personnel. In the Recommendations attached to the Resolutions the Conference expressed its wish that the governments conclude a corresponding agreement.

AUTHENTIC TEXT: French. The translation below is reprinted from the *Handbook of the International Red Cross and Red Crescent Movement,* 13th edn., Geneva, 1994, pp. 613–615.

TEXT PUBLISHED IN: *Secours aux blessés. Communication du Comité international faisant suite au compte-rendu de la Conférence internationale de Genève*, Genève, Imprimerie de Jules-Guillaume Fick, 1864, pp. 41–43 (French); *La Charité internationale sur les champs de bataille – Le Traité de Genève et un Souvenir de Solférino*, Paris, Hachette, 1865, pp. 144–147 (French); P. Fauchille and N. Politis, *Manuel de la Croix-Rouge à l'usage des militaires de terre et de mer et des sociétés de secours aux blessés,* Paris, Société française d'imprimerie et de librairie, 1908, pp. 161–163 (French); Deltenre, pp. 718–721 (Engl., French, German, Dutch); *Manuel de la Croix-Rouge internationale*, 1983, pp. 563–564 (French); *International Red Cross Handbook*, 1983, pp. 547–548 (Engl.); *Manual de la Cruz Roja internacional*, 1983, pp. 551–552 (Span.); *Handbook of the International Movement*, 1994, pp. 613–615 (Engl.); *Manuel du Mouvement international*, 1994, pp.631–633 (French); *Manual del Movimiento internacional*, 1994, pp.

625–627 (Span.); *Droit des conflits armés*, pp. 337–339 (French); I.A. Ivanovskii, *Zhenevskaya konventsiya 10/22 avgusta 1864*, Kiev, 1884, pp. 31–32 (Russ.); ICRC website: www.icrc.org/ihl.nsf.

* * *

The International Conference, desirous of coming to the aid of the wounded should the Military Medical Services prove inadequate, adopts the following Resolutions:

Article 1. *Each country shall have a Committee whose duty it shall be, in time of war and if the need arises, to assist the Army Medical Services by every means in its power. The Committee shall organize itself in the manner which seems to it most useful and appropriate.*

Art. 2. *An unlimited number of Sections may be formed to assist the Committee, which shall be the central directing body.*

Art. 3. *Each Committee shall get in touch with the Government of its country, so that its services may be accepted should the occasion arise.*

Art. 4. *In peacetime, the Committees and Sections shall take steps to ensure their real usefulness in time of war, especially by preparing material relief of all sorts and by seeking to train and instruct voluntary medical personnel.*

Art. 5. *In time of war, the Committees of belligerent nations shall supply relief to their respective armies as far as their means permit: in particular, they shall organize voluntary personnel and place them on an active footing and, in agreement with the military authorities, shall have premises made available for the care of the wounded.*

They may call for assistance upon the Committees of neutral countries.

Art. 6. *On the request or with the consent of the military authorities, Committees may send voluntary medical personnel to the battlefield where they shall be placed under military command.*

Art. 7. *Voluntary medical personnel attached to armies shall be supplied by the respective Committees with everything necessary for their upkeep.*

Art. 8. *They shall wear in all countries, as a uniform distinctive sign, a white armlet with a red cross.*

Art. 9. *The Committees and Sections of different countries may meet in international assemblies to communicate the results of their experience and to agree on measures to be taken in the interest of the work.*

Art. 10. *The exchange of communications between the Committees of the various countries shall be made for the time being through the intermediary of the Geneva Committee.*

Independently of the above Resolutions, the Conference makes the following Recommendations:

(a) that Governments should extend their patronage to Relief Committees which may be formed, and facilitate as far as possible the accomplishment of their task.

(b) that in time of war the belligerent nations should proclaim the neutrality of ambulances and military hospitals, and that neutrality should likewise be recognized, fully and absolutely, in respect of official medical personnel, voluntary medical

personnel, inhabitants of the country who go to the relief of the wounded, and the wounded themselves;

(c) *that a uniform distinctive sign be recognized for the Medical Corps of all armies, or at least for all persons of the same army belonging to this Service; and, that a uniform flag also be adopted in all countries for ambulances and hospitals.*

No. 38

CONVENTION FOR THE AMELIORATION OF THE CONDITION OF THE WOUNDED IN ARMIES IN THE FIELD

Signed at Geneva, 22 August 1864

INTRODUCTORY NOTE: After the successful termination of the Geneva Conference of 1863, the Swiss Federal Council, on the initiative of the Geneva Committee, invited the governments of all European and several American states to a diplomatic conference for the purpose of adopting a convention for the amelioration of the condition of the wounded in war. The conference, at which 16 states were represented, lasted from 8 to 22 August 1864. The draft convention submitted to the conference, which was prepared by the Geneva Committee, was adopted by the Conference without major alterations. The main principles laid down in the Convention and maintained by the later Geneva Conventions are:

- relief to the wounded without any distinction as to nationality;
- neutrality (inviolability) of medical personnel and medical establishments and units;
- the distinctive sign of the red cross on a white ground.

A second diplomatic conference was convened at Geneva in October 1868 in order to clarify some provisions of the Convention of 1864 and, particularly, to adapt the principles of the Convention to sea warfare. The Additional Articles, which were adopted on 20 October 1868 (*No. 39*), were, however, not ratified, and did not enter into force.

The Convention of 1864 was replaced by the Geneva Conventions of 1906, 1929 and 1949 on the same subject (*Nos. 42, 45 and 49*). However, it ceased to have effect only in 1966 when the last state party to it which had not yet acceded to a later Convention (Republic of Korea) acceded to the Conventions of 1949.

ENTRY INTO FORCE: 22 June 1865.

AUTHENTIC TEXT: French. The translation below is reprinted from Edward Hertslet, *The Map of Europe by Treaty*, Vol. III, *1864–1875*, London, Butterworths, 1875, pp. 1621–1626.

TEXT PUBLISHED IN: Martens, *NRGT*, 1ère série, Vol. XVIII, pp. 612–619 (French); *Fontes Historiae Juris Gentium*, Vol. III/1, pp. 551–556 (Engl., French, German); Edward Hertslet, *The Map of Europe by Treaty*, Vol. III, *1864–1875*, London, Butterworths, 1875, pp. 1621–1626 (Engl.); *Manual of Military Law*, London, War Office, 1884, pp. 885–889 (French, Engl.); Deltenre, pp. 30–39 (Engl., French, German, Dutch); *International Red Cross Handbook*, 1983, pp. 19–20 (Engl.); *Manuel de la Croix-Rouge internationale*, 1983, pp. 19–20 (French); *Manual de la Cruz Roja internacional*, 1983, pp. 19–20 (Span.); *BFSP*, Vol. 55, 1864–1865, pp. 43–48 (French); *US Statutes at Large*, Vol. 22, pp. 940–945, 950–51 (Engl., French); Higgins, pp. 8–12 (Engl., French); Malloy, Vol. II, pp. 1903–1906 (Engl.); Bevans, Vol. I, pp. 7–11

(Engl.); *CTS*, Vol. 129, 1864, pp. 361–367 (French); *AJIL*, Vol. 1, 1907, Suppl. pp. 90–95 (Engl.); Freidman, pp. 187–191 (Engl.); *Droit des conflits armés*, pp. 341–345 (French); Arellano, pp. 350–351 (Span.); Bustamante, pp. 163–166 (Span.); *Polnoe sobranie zakanov*, tome XLII, otd. 2, No. 44992 (Russ.); Heffter-Taube, pp. 98–100 (Russ.); I.A. Ivanovskii, *Zhenevskaya konventsiya 10/22 avgusta 1864*, Kiev, 1884, pp. 37–39 (Russ.); ICRC website: www.icrc.org/ihl.nsf.

* * *

[List of contracting parties]

Who, after having exchanged their Powers, found in good and due form, have agreed upon the following Articles.

Article 1. Ambulances and military hospitals shall be recognized as neutral, and, as such, protected and respected by the belligerents as long as they accommodate wounded and sick.

Neutrality shall end if the said ambulances or hospitals should be held by a military force.

Art. 2. Hospital and ambulance personnel, including the quarter-master's staff, the medical, administrative and transport services, and the chaplains, shall have the benefit of the same neutrality when on duty, and while there remain any wounded to be brought in or assisted.

Art. 3. The persons designated in the preceding Article may, even after enemy occupation, continue to discharge their functions in the hospital or ambulance with which they serve, or may withdraw to rejoin the units to which they belong.

When in these circumstances they cease from their functions, such persons shall be delivered to the enemy outposts by the occupying forces.

Art. 4. The material of military hospitals being subject to the laws of war, the persons attached to such hospitals may take with them, on withdrawing, only the articles which are their own personal property.

Ambulances, on the contrary, under similar circumstances, shall retain their equipment.

Art. 5. Inhabitants of the country who bring help to the wounded shall be respected and shall remain free. Generals of the belligerent Powers shall make it their duty to notify the inhabitants of the appeal made to their humanity, and of the neutrality which humane conduct will confer.

The presence of any wounded combatant receiving shelter and care in a house shall ensure its protection. An inhabitant who has given shelter to the wounded shall be exempted from billeting and from a portion of such war contributions as may be levied.

Art. 6. Wounded or sick combatants, to whatever nation they may belong, shall be collected and cared for.

Commanders-in-Chief may hand over immediately to the enemy outposts enemy combatants wounded during an engagement, when circumstances allow and subject to the agreement of both parties.

Those who, after their recovery, are recognized as being unfit for further service, shall be repatriated.

The others may likewise be sent back, on condition that they shall not again, for the duration of hostilities, take up arms.

Evacuation parties, and the personnel conducting them, shall be considered as being absolutely neutral.

Art. 7. A distinctive and uniform flag shall be adopted for hospitals, ambulances and evacuation parties. It should in all circumstances be accompanied by the national flag. An armlet may also be worn by personnel enjoying neutrality but its issue shall be left to the military authorities.

Both flag and armlet shall bear a red cross on a white ground.

Art. 8. The implementing of the present Convention shall be arranged by the Commanders-in-Chief of the belligerent armies following the instructions of their respective Governments and in accordance with the general principles set forth in this Convention.

Art. 9. The High Contracting Parties have agreed to communicate the present Convention with an invitation to accede thereto to Governments unable to appoint Plenipotentiaries to the International Conference at Geneva. The Protocol has accordingly been left open.

Art. 10. The present Convention shall be ratified and the ratifications exchanged at Berne, within the next four months, or sooner if possible.

In faith whereof, the respective Plenipotentiaries have signed the Convention and thereto affixed their seals.

Done at Geneva, this twenty-second day of August, in the year one thousand eight hundred and sixty-four.

[Here follow signatures]

SIGNATURES, RATIFICATIONS AND ACCESSIONS[1]

State	*Signature*	*Ratification, Accession*
Argentina	–	25 November 1879
Austria	–	21 July 1866
Baden	22 August 1864	16 December 1864
Bavaria	–	30 June 1866
Belgium	22 August 1864	14 October 1864
Bolivia	–	16 October 1879
Brazil	–	30 April 1906
Bulgaria	–	1 March 1884
Chile	–	15 November 1879
China	–	29 June 1904
Columbia	–	7 June 1906
Congo	–	27 December 1888
Cuba	–	25 June 1907
Denmark	22 August 1864	15 December 1864
Dominican Republic	–	25 June 1907
Ecuador	–	3 August 1907
El Salvador	–	30 December 1874
France	22 August 1864	22 September 1864

[1] Based on indications received from the Swiss Federal Department of Foreign Affairs, 25 June 1999 and on ICRC website: www, icrc.org/ihl.nsf.

State	*Signature*	*Ratification, Accession*
Germany	–	12 June 1906
Great Britain	–	18 February 1865
Greece	–	5-17 January 1865
Guatemala	–	24 March 1903
Haiti	–	24 June 1907
Hesse	22 August 1864	22 June 1866
Holy See	–	9 May 1868
Honduras	–	16 May 1898
Italy	22 August 1864	4 December 1864
Japan	–	6 June 1886
Korea	–	8 January 1903
Luxemburg	–	5 October 1888
Mecklenburg-Schwerin	–	9 March 1895
Mexico	–	25 April 1905
Montenegro	–	29 November 1875
Netherlands	22 August 1864	29 November 1864
Nicaragua	–	16 May 1898
Norway *(see Sweden & Norway)*	–	13 December 1864
Orange Free State	–	28 September 1897
Panama	–	24 July 1907
Paraguay	–	31 May 1907
Persia	–	5 December 1874
Peru	–	22 April 1880
Portugal	22 August 1864	9 August 1866
Prussia	22 August 1864	4 January 1865
Romania	–	18-30 November 1874
Russia	–	10-22 May 1867
Saxony	–	25 October 1866
Serbia	–	24 March 1876
Siam	–	29 June 1895
South African Republic	–	30 September 1896
Spain	22 August 1864	5 December 1864
Sweden & Norway[2]	–	13 December 1864
Turkey	–	5 July 1865
United States of America	–	1 March 1882
Uruguay	–	3 May 1900
Venezuela	–	9 July 1894
Wurttemberg	22 August 1864	2 June 1866

RESERVATIONS

None.

[2] Sweden and Norway constituted a Union until 1905. Action taken by them prior to that date was taken as a single power.

No. 39

ADDITIONAL ARTICLES RELATING TO THE CONDITION OF THE WOUNDED IN WAR

Signed at Geneva, 20 October 1868

INTRODUCTORY NOTE: The Additional Articles of 1868 were adopted at a Diplomatic Conference convened by the Swiss Federal Council in Geneva in order to clarify some provisions of the Geneva Convention of 1864 and, particularly, to extend to naval forces the advantages of this Convention. They failed, however, to secure any ratifications and never entered into force. Nevertheless, in the Franco-German War of 1870–71 and in the Spanish-American War of 1898 the parties agreed to observe their provisions. It was not before the First Hague Peace Conference of 1899 that a Convention for the Adaptation to Maritime Warfare of the Principles of the Geneva Convention was finally adopted (*No. 40*).

ENTRY INTO FORCE: Did not enter into force.

AUTHENTIC TEXT: French. The translation below is reprinted from Edward Hertslet, *The Map of Europe by Treaty*, Vol. III, London, Butterworths, 1875, pp. 1853–1859.

TEXT PUBLISHED IN: *Projet d'Articles additionels à la Convention du 22 août 1864 pour l'amélioration du sort des militaires blessés dans les armées en campagne*, Geneva, 1868 (French); Martens, *NRGT*, 1ère série, Vol. XVIII, pp. 612–619 (French); Deltenre, pp. 41–47 (Engl., French, German, Dutch); *CTS*, Vol. 138, 1868–1869, pp. 189–194 (French); *Droits des conflits armés*, pp. 347–351 (French); Edward Hertslet, *The Map of Europe by Treaty*, Vol. III, London, Butterworths, 1875, pp. 1853–1859 (Engl.); *BFSP*, Vol. 73, 1881–1882, pp. 1113–1123 (Engl., French); Higgins, pp. 14–17 (Engl.); *US Statutes at Large*, Vol. 22, pp. 946–951 (Engl., French); Malloy, Vol. II, p. 1907 (Engl.); *Les deux Conférences de la Paix*, pp. 179–181 (French); Genet, pp. 517–520 (French); Heffter-Taube, pp. 101–104 (Russ.); I.A. Ivanovskii, *Zhenevskaya konventsiya 10/22 avgusta 1864*, Kiev, 1884, pp. 56–61 (Russ.); ICRC website: www.icrc.org/ihl.nsf.

* * *

[List of contracting parties]

Desiring to extend to naval forces the advantages of the Convention concluded at Geneva on 22 August 1864, for the amelioration of the condition of wounded soldiers in armies in the field, and to further particularize some of the stipulations of the said Convention, have named for their Commissioners:

[Here follow the names of plenipotentiaries]

Who, having been duly authorized to that effect, agreed, under reserve of approbation from their governments, on the following dispositions:

Article 1. The persons designated in Article 2 of the Convention shall, after the occupation by the enemy, continue to fulfil their duties, according to their wants, to the sick and wounded in the ambulance or the hospital which they serve.

When they request to withdraw, the commander of the occupying troops shall fix the time of departure, which he shall only be allowed to delay for a short time in case of military necessity.

Art. 2. Arrangements will have to be made by the belligerent powers to ensure to the neutralized persons, fallen into the hands of the army of the enemy, the entire enjoyment of his salary.

Art. 3. Under the conditions provided for in Articles 1 and 4 of the Convention, the name "ambulance" applies to field hospitals and other temporary establishments, which follow the troops on the fields of battle to receive the sick and wounded.

Art. 4. In conformity with the spirit of Article 5 of the Convention, and with the reservations contained in the Protocol of 1864, it is explained that for the apportionment of the charges relative to the quartering of troops, and of the contributions of war, account shall only be taken in an equitable manner of the charitable zeal displayed by the inhabitants.

Art. 5. In addition to Article 6 of the Convention, it is stipulated that, with the reservation of officers whose detention might be important to the fate of arms and within limits fixed by the second paragraph of the article, the wounded fallen into the hands of the enemy shall be sent back to their country after they are cured, or sooner if possible, on condition, nevertheless, of not again bearing arms during the continuance of the war.

Art. 6. The boats which, at their own risk and peril, during and after an engagement pick up the shipwrecked or wounded, or which, having picked them up convey them on board a neutral or hospital ship shall enjoy, until the accomplishment of their mission, the character of neutrality, so far as the circumstances of the engagement and the position of the ships engaged will permit.

The appreciation of these circumstances is entrusted to the humanity of all the combatants.

The wrecked and wounded thus picked up and saved must not serve again during the continuance of the war.

Art. 7. The religious, medical, and hospital staff of any captured vessel are declared neutral, and, on leaving the ship, may remove the articles and surgical instruments which are their private property.

Art. 8. The staff designated in the preceding article must continue to fulfil their functions in the captured ship, assisting in the removal of the wounded made by the victorious party; they will then be at liberty to return to their country, in conformity with the second paragraph of the first Additional Article. The stipulations of the second additional article are applicable to the pay and allowance of the staff.

Art. 9. The military hospital ships remain under Martial Law in all that concerns their stores; they become the property of the captor, but the latter must not divert them from their special appropriation during the continuance of the war.

The vessels not equipped for fighting which, during peace, the government shall have officially declared to be intended to serve as floating hospital ships, shall, however, enjoy during the war complete neutrality, both as regards stores, and also as regards their staff, provided their equipment is exclusively appropriated to the special service on which they are employed.

Art. 10. Any merchantman regardless of their nationality charged exclusively with removal of sick and wounded, is protected by neutrality, but the mere fact, noted on the ship's books, of the vessel having been visited by an enemy's cruiser, renders the sick and wounded incapable of serving during the continuance of the war. The cruiser shall even have the right of putting on board an officer in order to accompany the convoy, and thus verify the good faith of the operation.

If the merchant-ship also carries a cargo, her neutrality will still protect it, provided that such cargo is not of a nature to be confiscated by the belligerent.

The belligerents retain the right to interdict neutralized vessels from all communication, and from any course which they may deem prejudicial to the secrecy of their operations.

In urgent cases special conventions may be entered into between the commanders-in-chief, in order to neutralize temporarily and in a special manner the vessels intended for the removal of the sick and wounded.

Art. 11. Wounded or sick sailors and soldiers, when embarked, to whatever nation they may belong, shall be protected and taken care of by their captors.

Their return to their own country is subject to the provisions of Article 6 of the Convention and the Additional Article 5.

Art. 12. The distinctive flag to be used with the national flag, in order to indicated any vessel or boat which may claim the benefits of neutrality, in virtue of the principles of this Convention, is a white flag with a red cross.

The belligerents may exercise in this respect any mode of verification which they may deem necessary.

Military hospital ships shall be distinguished by being painted white outside, with green strake.

Art. 13. The hospital ships which are equipped at the expense of the aid societies, recognized by the governments signing this Convention, and which are furnished with a commission emanating form the Sovereign, who shall have given express authority for their being fitted out, and with a certificate from the proper naval authority that they have been placed under his control during their fitting out and on their final departure and that they were then appropriated solely to the purpose of their mission, shall be considered neutral as well as the whole of their staff.

They shall be recognized and protected by the belligerents.

They shall make themselves known by hoisting, together with their national flag, the white flag with a red cross. The distinctive mark of their staff, while performing their duties, shall be an armlet of the same colours.

The outer painting of these hospital ships shall be white, with red strake.

These ships shall bear aid and assistance to the wounded and wrecked belligerents, without distinction of nationality.

They must take care not to interfere in any way with movements of the combatants. During and after the battle they must do their duty at their own risk and peril.

The belligerents shall have the right of controlling and visiting them; they will be at liberty to refuse their assistance, to order them to depart, and to detain them if the exigencies of the case require such a step.

The wounded and wrecked picked up by these ships cannot be reclaimed by either of the combatants, and they will be required not to serve during the continuance of the war.

Art. 14. In naval wars any strong presumption that either belligerent takes advantage of the benefits of neutrality, with any other view than the interest of the sick and wounded, gives to the other belligerent, until proof to the contrary, the right of suspending the Convention as regards such belligerent.

Should this presumption become a certainty, notice may be given to such belligerent that the Convention is suspended with regard to him during the whole continuance of the war.

Art. 15. The present Act shall be drawn up in a single original copy, which shall be deposited in the archives of the Swiss Confederation.

An authentic copy of this Act shall be delivered, with an invitation to adhere to it, to each of the Signatory Powers of the Convention of 22 August 1864, as well as to those that have acceded to it.

In faith whereof the undersigned Commissioners have drawn up the present project of Additional Articles, and have affixed thereto the seal of their Arms.

Done at Geneva, the twentieth day of the month of October, of the year one thousand eight hundred and sixty-eight.

[Here follow signatures]

SIGNATURES

Austria
Baden
Bavaria
Belgium
Denmark
France
Great Britain
Italy
Netherlands
North German Confederation
Sweden and Norway
Switzerland
Turkey
Wurttemberg

RATIFICATIONS

None

ACCESSIONS

United States of America[1] 1 March 1882

RESERVATIONS

None

[1] The United States acceded to the Additional Articles of 20 October 1868. After the text was approved by the Senate, the US President announced that his country would accede to both the Geneva Convention of 22 August 1864 and to the Additional Articles. The instrument of accession was deposited with the Swiss Federal Council on 9 June 1882 but the Federal Council informed the US Government that as none of the signatories had yet ratified the Additional Articles they could not be considered to be in force or otherwise producing any effect. In his announcement of 26 July 1882, the US President took formal note of this fact (*US Statutes at Large*, Vol. 22, 1883, pp. 950–951).

No. 40

CONVENTION (III) FOR THE ADAPTATION TO MARITIME WARFARE OF THE PRINCIPLES OF THE GENEVA CONVENTION OF 22 AUGUST 1864

Signed at The Hague, 29 July 1899

INTRODUCTORY NOTE: The Additional Articles to the Geneva Convention, which were drafted in 1868 in order to adapt the principles of the Geneva Convention to sea warfare (*No. 39*), failed to secure any ratifications. It was not before the end of the nineteenth century that the question of the revision of the Geneva Convention and especially of the adoption of supplementary articles concerning sea warfare gained new support. The International Committee of the Red Cross, at the request of the Swiss Federal Council, prepared a new draft, but before a diplomatic conference could be convened at Geneva, the Czar of Russia took the initiative to convene the First Hague Peace Conference of 1899 and proposed as one of the subjects the "adaptation to naval war of the stipulations of the Geneva Convention of 1864". The Convention which was adopted at The Hague in 1899 was replaced by the Hague Convention (X) of 1907 (*No. 43*). It is no longer in force.

ENTRY INTO FORCE: 4 September 1900. No longer in force.

AUTHENTIC TEXT: French. The translation below is reprinted from Scott, *Hague Conventions*, pp. 163–181. It reproduces the translation of the United States Department of State.

TEXT PUBLISHED IN: *Conférence internationale de la Paix, 1899*, pp. 235–238 (French); *Les deux Conférences de la Paix*, pp. 39–42 (French); Scott, *Hague Conventions*, pp. 163–181 (Engl.); Scott, *Les Conventions de La Haye*, pp. 163–181 (French); Scott, *Les Conférences de La Haye*, pp. 24–26 (French); Bustamante, pp. 203–208 (Span.); Martens, *NRGT*, 2ème série, Vol. XXVI, pp. 979–993 (French, German); Deltenre, pp. 124–133 (Engl., French, German, Dutch); Olivart, Vol. XII, pp. 626–637 (French, Span.); *CTS*, Vol. 187, 1898–1899, pp. 443–452 (French); *Handbook of the International Red Cross*, 1953, pp. 11–15 (Engl.); *Manuel de la Croix-Rouge internationale*, 1953, pp. 15–19 (French); *Manual de la Cruz Roja internacional*, 1953, pp. 11–15 (Span.); *Droit des conflits armés*, pp. 353–359 (French); *GBTS*, 1901, No. 10, Cd. 799 (Engl., French); *BFSP*, Vol. 91, 1898–1899, pp. 1002–1010 (French); *US Statutes at Large*, Vol. 32, pp. 1827–1838 (Engl., French); Malloy, Vol. II, pp. 2035–2042 (Engl.); Bevans, Vol. I, pp. 263–269 (Engl.); *AJIL*, Vol. 1, 1907, Suppl. pp. 159–166 (Engl., French). Friedman, pp. 236–243 (Engl.); Arellano, pp. 357–359 (Span. – extract); ICRC website: www.icrc.org/ihl.nsf.

* * *

[List of contracting parties]

Alike animated by the desire to diminish, as far as depends on them the evils inseparable from warfare, and wishing with this object to adapt to maritime warfare the principles of the Geneva Convention of 22 August 1864, have decided to conclude a convention to this effect:

They have, in consequence, appointed as their Plenipotentiaries, to wit:

[Here follow the names of plenipotentiaries]

Who, after communication of their full powers, found in good and due form, have agreed on the following provisions:

Article 1. Military hospital ships, that is to say, ships constructed or assigned by States specially and solely for the purpose of assisting the wounded, sick or shipwrecked, and the names of which shall have been communicated to the belligerent Powers at the beginning or during the course of hostilities, and in any case before they are employed, shall be respected and cannot be captured while hostilities last.

These ships, moreover, are not on the same footing as men-of-war as regards their stay in a neutral port.

Art. 2. Hospital ships, equipped wholly or in part at the cost of private individuals or officially recognized relief societies, shall likewise be respected and exempt from capture, provided the belligerent Power to whom they belong has given them an official commission and has notified their names to the hostile Power at the commencement of or during hostilities, and in any case before they are employed.

These ships should be furnished with a certificate from the competent authorities, declaring that they have been under their control while fitting out and on final departure.

Art. 3. Hospital ships, equipped wholly or in part at the cost of private individuals or officially recognized societies of neutral countries, shall be respected and exempt from capture, if the neutral Power to whom they belong has given them an official commission and notified their names to the belligerent Powers at the commencement of or during hostilities, and in any case before they are employed.

Art. 4. The ships mentioned in Articles 1, 2 and 3 shall afford relief and assistance to the wounded, sick, and shipwrecked of the belligerents independently of their nationality.

The Governments engage not to use these ships for any military purpose.

These ships must not in any way hamper the movements of the combatants.

During and after an engagement they will act at their own risk and peril.

The belligerents will have the right to control and visit them; they can refuse to help them, order them off, make them take a certain course, and put a commissioner on board; they can even detain them, if important circumstances require it.

As far as possible the belligerents shall inscribe in the sailing papers of the hospital ships the orders they give them.

Art. 5. The military hospital ships shall be distinguished by being painted white outside with a horizontal band of green about a metre and a half in breadth.

The ships mentioned in Articles 2 and 3 shall be distinguished by being painted white outside with a horizontal band of red about a metre and a half in breadth.

The boats of the ships above mentioned, as also small craft which may be used for hospital work, shall be distinguished by similar painting.

All hospital ships shall make themselves known by hoisting, together with their national flag, the white flag with a red cross provided by the Geneva Convention.

Art. 6. Neutral merchantmen, yachts, or vessels, having, or taking on board, sick, wounded, or shipwrecked of the belligerents, cannot be captured for so doing, but they are liable to capture for any violation of neutrality they may have committed.

Art. 7. The religious, medical, or hospital staff of any captured ship is inviolable, and its members cannot be made prisoners of war. On leaving the ship they take with them the objects and surgical instruments which are their own private property.

This staff shall continue to discharge its duties while necessary, and can afterwards leave when the commander-in-chief considers it possible.

The belligerents must guarantee to the staff that has fallen into their hands the enjoyment of their salaries intact.

Art. 8. Sailors and soldiers who are taken on board when sick or wounded, to whatever nation they belong, shall be protected and looked after by the captors.

Art. 9. The shipwrecked, wounded, or sick of one of the belligerents who fall into the hands of the other, are prisoners of war. The captor must decide, according to circumstances, if it is best to keep them or send them to a port of his own country, to a neutral port, or even to a hostile port. In the last case, prisoners thus repatriated cannot serve as long as the war lasts.

Art. 10.[1] The shipwrecked, wounded, or sick, who are landed at a neutral port with the consent of the local authorities, must, failing a contrary arrangement between the neutral State and the belligerents, be guarded by the neutral State, so that they can not again take part in the military operations.

The expenses of tending them in hospital and internment shall be borne by the State to which the shipwrecked, wounded, or sick belong.

Art. 11. The rules contained in the above articles are binding only on the Contracting Powers, in case of war between two or more of them.

The said rules shall cease to be binding from the time when, in a war between the Contracting Powers, one of the belligerents is joined by a non-Contracting Power.

Art. 12. The present Convention shall be ratified as soon as possible.

The ratifications shall be deposited at The Hague.

On the receipt of each ratification a *procès-verbal* shall be drawn up, a copy of which, duly certified, shall be sent through the diplomatic channel to all the Contracting Powers.

Art. 13. The non-Signatory Powers who accepted the Geneva Convention of 22 August 1864, are allowed to adhere to the present Convention.

For this purpose they must make their adhesion known to the Contracting Powers by means of a written notification addressed to the Netherlands Government, and by it communicated to all the other Contracting Powers.

Art. 14. In the event of one of the High Contracting Parties denouncing the present Convention, such denunciation shall not take effect until a year after the notification made in writing to the Netherlands Government, and forthwith communicated by it to all the other Contracting Powers.

This denunciation shall only affect the notifying Power.

In testimony whereof the respective Plenipotentiaries have signed the present Convention and affixed their seals thereto.

---

[1] For reservations in respect of this article by Germany, Great Britain, Turkey and the United States, see p. 377.

Done at The Hague, 29 July 1899, in a single copy, which shall be kept in the archives of the Government of the Netherlands, and copies of which duly certified, shall be sent through the diplomatic channel to the Contracting Powers.

[Here follow signatures]

SIGNATURES, RATIFICATIONS AND ACCESSIONS[1]

State	*Signature*	*Ratification, Accession Notification of Continuity (C)*
Argentine Republic	–	17 June 1907
Austria-Hungary	29 July 1899	4 September 1900
Belgium	29 July 1899	4 September 1900
Bolivia	–	7 February 1907
Brazil	–	25 February 1907
Bulgaria	29 July 1899	4 September 1900
Chile	–	19 June 1907
China	29 July 1899	21 November 1904
Colombia	–	30 January 190 7
Cuba	–	29 June 1907
Denmark	29 July 1899	4 September 1900
Dominican Republic	–	29 June 1907
Ecuador	–	5 August 1907
El Salvador	–	20 June 1902
Fiji	–	2 April 1973 (C)
France	29 July 1899	4 September 1900
Germany	29 July 1899 *Res.*	4 September 1900
Great Britain and Ireland	29 July 1899 *Res.*	4 September 1900
Greece	29 July 1899	4 April 1901
Guatemala	–	6 April 1903
Haiti	–	29 June 1907
Honduras	–	21 August 1906
Italy	29 July 1899	4 September 1900
Japan	29 July 1899	6 October 1900
Korea	–	7 February 1903
Luxembourg	29 July 1899	12 July 1901
Mexico	29 July 1899	17 April 1901
Montenegro	29 July 1899	16 October 1900
Netherlands	29 July 1899	4 September 1900
Nicaragua	–	17 May 1907
Norway[2]	29 July 1899	4 September 1900
Panama	–	22 July 1907
Paraguay	–	29 June 1907
Persia	29 July 1899	4 September 1900
Peru	–	24 November 1903
Portugal	29 July 1899	4 September 1900
Romania	29 July 1899	4 September 1900
Russia[3]	29 July 1899	4 September 1900

1 Based on a communication received from the Ministry of Foreign Affairs of the Netherlands of 12 December 2001. See also ICRC website: www.icrc.org/ihl.nsf.

2 Sweden and Norway constituted a Union until 1905. Action taken by them prior to that date was taken as a single power.

3 By the note of the Foreign Ministry of the USSR of 7 March 1955 "The Government of the USSR recognizes the Conventions and Declarations of The Hague from 1899 and 1907,

State	*Signature*	*Ratification, Accession Notification of Continuity (C)*
Serbia[4]	29 July 1899	11 May 1901
Siam	29 July 1899	4 September 1900
South Africa	–	10 March 1978
Spain	29 July 1899	4 September 1900
Sweden	29 July 1899	4 September 1900
Switzerland	29 July 1899	29 December, 1900
Turkey	29 July 1899 *Res.*	12 June 1907
United States of America	29 July 1899 *Res.*	4 September 1900
Uruguay	–	21 June 1906
Venezuela	–	1 March 1907

RESERVATIONS[5]

GERMANY (*reservation made on signature*)
Signed with reservations in respect of Article 10.

GREAT BRITAIN (*reservation made on signature*)
Signed with reservations in respect of Article 10.

TURKEY (*reservation made on signature*)
Signed with reservations in respect of Article 10.

UNITED STATES OF AMERICA (*reservation made on signature*)
Signed with reservations in respect of Article 10.

cont.
which were ratified by Russia to the extent that the Conventions and Declarations do not contradict the United Nations Charter and if they are not amended or replaced by ulteriorinternational agreements to which the USSR is a Party, such as the 1925 Geneva Protocol for the Prohibition of Use of Asphyxiating, Poisonous and Other Gases and of Bacteriological Methods of Warfare and the 1949 Geneva Conventions for the Protection of Victims of War" (*Izvestiya*, 9 March 1955).

In January 1992, the Ministry of Foreign Affairs of the Russian Federation informed the heads of diplomatic missions in Moscow, that the Russian Federation continues to be a party to all conventions, which are in force for the Soviet Union. The Ministry of Foreign Affairs of the Kingdom of the Netherlands considers therefore that the Russian Federation is bound by the conventions to which the Soviet Union was party (communication of a depositary to the Henry Dunant Institute of 6 November 1992).

On 4 June 1962, the Byelorussian Soviet Socialist Republic made a declaration similar to that made by the USSR.

4 The Government of the Socialist Federative Republic of Yugoslavia confirmed by its note of 27 March 1969, received by the Ministry of Foreign Affairs of the Netherlands on 8 April 1969, that it considers itself to be a party to the Treaties and Declarations of The Hague of 29 July 1899, ratified by Serbia.

5 It was subsequently agreed, on an understanding reached by the Government of the Netherlands with the signatory powers, to exclude Article 10 from all ratifications of the Convention. This understanding was proposed by the Kingdom of Netherlands to signatory powers by a note of 31 January 1900. The purpose of this proposal was the following: to avoid internal difficulties which may constitute an obstacle to ratification and to ensure a uniformity in the obligations of contracting parties when four of them signed the Convention under the reservation to Article 10. The signatory powers unanimously accepted this proposal (letter of the Ministry of Foreign Affairs of the Netherlands dated of 23 October 1992 addressed to the Henry Dunant Institute).

No. 41

HAGUE CONVENTION ON HOSPITAL SHIPS

I. CONVENTION FOR THE EXEMPTION OF HOSPITAL SHIPS, IN TIME OF WAR, FROM THE PAYMENT OF ALL DUES AND TAXES IMPOSED FOR THE BENEFIT OF THE STATE

Signed at The Hague on 21 December 1904

II. FINAL ACT OF THE HAGUE CONFERENCE

Signed at The Hague on 21 December 1904

INTRODUCTORY NOTE: This Convention was adopted at a Conference convened by the Government of the Netherlands on the initiative of the Government of France. It is still in force today. No later convention has been concluded on the same subject.

ENTRY INTO FORCE: 26 March 1907.

AUTHENTIC TEXT: French. The translation below is reprinted from *US Statutes at Large*, Vol. 35, Part 2, pp. 1854–1862.

TEXT PUBLISHED IN: Martens, *NRGT*, 3ème série, Vol. II, pp. 213–222 (French, German); Deltenre, pp. 153–159 (Engl., French, German, Dutch); *CTS*, Vol. 197, 1904–1905, pp. 331–337 (French); *Handbook of the International Red Cross*, 1953, pp. 16–17 (Engl.); *Manuel de la Croix-Rouge internationale*, 1953, pp. 20–21 (French); *Manual de la Cruz Roja internacional*, 1953, pp. 16–17 (Span.); *BFSP*, Vol. 98, 1904–1905, pp. 624–632 (French); *US Statutes at Large*, Vol. 35, pp. 1854–1862 (Engl., French); Malloy, Vol. II, pp. 2135–2138 (Engl.); Bevans, Vol. I, pp. 430–435 (Engl.); *AJIL*, Vol. 1, 1907, Suppl., pp. 272–277 (Engl.); Friedman, pp. 251–256 (Engl.); Ronzitti, pp. 77–83 (Engl., French); *Droit des conflits armés*, pp. 361–365 (French); *Les deux Conférences de la Paix*, pp. 191–192 (French); *Sbornik dogovorov RSFSR*, vyp. I, 1921, pp. 228–229, No. 36 (Russ.); *Sobranie zakonov*, 1926, Vol. II, No. 38, st. 227, pp. 638–641 (French, Russ.); *Mezhdunarodnoe pravo*, Vol. III, p. 162 (Russ.); ICRC website: www.icrc.org/ihl.nsf.

* * *

I. CONVENTION FOR THE EXEMPTION OF HOSPITAL SHIPS, IN TIME OF WAR, FROM THE PAYMENT OF ALL DUES AND TAXES IMPOSED FOR THE BENEFIT OF THE STATE

[List of Contracting Parties]

Taking into consideration that the Convention concluded at The Hague on 29 July 1899 for the adaptation to Maritime Warfare of the Principles of the

Geneva Convention of 22 August 1864, has sanctioned the principle of the intervention of the Red Cross in naval wars by provisions in favour of hospital ships;

Desirous of concluding a convention to the end of facilitating by additional provisions the mission of such ships;

Have appointed as their Plenipotentiaries, to wit:

[Here follow the names of plenipotentiaries]

Who, after communication of their full powers, found to be in good and due form, have agreed on the following provisions:

Article 1. Hospital ships, concerning which the conditions set forth in Articles 1, 2 and 3 of the Convention concluded at The Hague on 29 July 1899, for the adaptation to Maritime Warfare of the principles of the Geneva Convention of 22 August 1864, are fulfilled shall be exempted, in time of war, from all dues and taxes imposed on vessels for the benefit of the State, in the ports of the Contracting Parties.

Art. 2. The provision of the foregoing article does not prevent the application, by means of visitation or other formalities of fiscal or other laws in force at said ports.

Art. 3. The rule laid down in Article 1 is binding only on the Contracting Powers in case of war between two or more of them.

The said rule shall cease to be binding from the time when a non-Contracting Power shall join one of the belligerents, in a war between Contracting Powers.

Art. 4. The present Convention which bearing the date of this day, may be signed until 1 October 1905 by the Powers expressing their desire to do so, shall be ratified as soon as possible.

The ratifications shall be deposited at The Hague.

A *procès-verbal* of the deposit of the ratifications shall be drawn up and a copy thereof, duly certified, shall be delivered through the diplomatic channel to all the Contracting Powers.

Art. 5. The non-Signatory Powers are permitted to adhere to the present Convention after 1 October 1905.

They shall, to that end, make their adhesion known to the Contracting Powers by means of a written notification addressed to the Government of the Netherlands and communicated by the latter to the other Contracting Powers.

Art. 6. In the event of one of the High Contracting Powers denouncing the present Convention, such denunciation shall not take effect until one year after the notification made in writing to the Government of the Netherlands and immediately communicated by the latter to all the other Contracting Powers. This denunciation shall only affect the notifying Power.

In testimony whereof the Plenipotentiaries have signed the present Convention and affixed their seals thereto.

Done at The Hague the twenty-first of December one thousand nine hundred and four, in a single copy which shall remain filed in the archives of the Government of the Netherlands and copies of which, duly certified shall be delivered through the diplomatic channel to the Contracting Powers.

[Here follow signatures]

II. FINAL ACT

At the moment of proceeding to sign the Convention having for its object the exemption of hospital ships in time of war in the ports of the Contracting Parties from all dues and taxes imposed on vessels for the benefit of the State, the Plenipotentiaries signing the present Act express the wish that, in view of the highly humanitarian mission of these ships, the Contracting Governments may take the measures necessary in order to exempt these ships within a short time also from the payment of the dues and taxes collected in their ports for the benefit of others than the State, especially those collected for the benefit of municipalities or of private companies or persons.

In witness whereof the Plenipotentiaries have signed the present procès-verbal, *which, bearing the date of this day, may be signed up to the first October, 1905.*

Done at The Hague, the twenty-first of December, nineteen hundred and four, in a single copy, which shall remain on file in the archives of the Government of the Netherlands, and of which certified copies shall be delivered through the diplomatic channel to the Powers signing the aforementioned Convention.

[Here follow signatures]

SIGNATURES, RATIFICATIONS AND ACCESSIONS[1]

State	*Signature*	*Ratification, Accession*
Austria-Hungary[2] [3]	21 December 1904	26 March 1907
Belgium	21 December 1904	26 March 1907
China	21 December 1904	26 March 1907
Cuba	–	6 September 1965
Danzig	–	31 October 1921

[1] Based on a communication received from the Ministry of Foreign Affairs of the Netherlands of 12 December 2001. See also ICRC website: www.icrc.org/ihl.nsf.

[2] On 27 July 1927, the Austrian Republic declared that, to avoid the difficulties which might arise from differences of opinion on the question as to whether pre-war treaties were binding on the states created as a result of the dismemberment of the Austro-Hungarian monarchy, it recognized, without prejudice to its origin independent of the former monarchy, that it was bound by the Convention in relation to all other states parties to it.

[3] Hungary declared on 24 June 1922, that in spite of the dissolution of the Austro-Hungarian monarchy and irrespective of Article 221 of the Treaty of Trianon it recognized that it was bound by the Convention and intended to apply it in the future in relation to all other states parties to it.

State	*Signature*	*Ratification, Accession*
Denmark	21 December 1904	26 March 1907
France	21 December 1904	10 April, 1907
Germany[4]	21 December 1904 *Res.*	26 March 1907
Greece	21 December 1904	26 March 1907
Guatemala	–	24 March 1906
Italy	21 December 1904	14 August 1907
Japan	21 December 1904	26 March1907
Korea	21 December 1904	26 March1907
Luxembourg	21 December 1904	26 March1907
Mexico	21 December 1904	26 March1907
Montenegro	21 December 1904	26 March1907
Netherlands	21 December 1904	26 March1907
Norway	–	8 January 1907
Persia	21 December 1904	26 February 1908
Peru	21 December 1904	26 March 1907
Poland	–	31 October 1921
Portugal	21 December 1904	26 March 1907
Romania	21 December 1904 *Res.*	26 March 1907
Russia	21 December 1904	26 March1907
Serbia	21 December 1904	–
Siam	11 December 1904	26 March1907
Spain	21 December 1904	10 May 1907
Sweden	–	1 January 1908
Switzerland	21 December 1904	26 March 1907
Turkey	–	8 June 1932
United States of America	21 December 1904	26 March 1907

RESERVATIONS

GERMANY (*reservation made on signature*)
Under reservation of the declaration made at the meeting of the Conference held 21 December 1904.
At the meeting of 21 December 1904, the delegate for Germany made the following declaration:
The Imperial Government reserves to itself the option to refuse to apply the present Convention to States in whose ports duties and taxes are imposed upon German hospital ships for the benefit of others than the State.

ROMANIA (*reservation made on signature*)
Under reservation of reciprocity and of pilotage dues.

SIGNATORIES OF THE FINAL ACT

The Final act of 21 December 1904 was signed by the representatives of the Powers represented at the Conference:

[4] By a letter received at the Ministry of Foreign Affairs of the Kingdom of the Netherlands on 9 February 1959, the Government of the German Democratic Republic has informed the Ministry that it reapplies the Convention.

Austria-Hungary
Belgium
China
Denmark
France
Germany
Greece
Italy
Japan
Korea
Luxembourg
Mexico (United States of)
Netherlands
Persia
Portugal
Romania
Russia
Serbia
Siam
Spain
Switzerland
United States of America

No. 42

CONVENTION FOR THE AMELIORATION OF THE CONDITION OF THE WOUNDED AND SICK IN ARMIES IN THE FIELD

Signed at Geneva, 6 July 1906

INTRODUCTORY NOTE: Several proposals were made after 1864, especially by the International Conferences of the Red Cross societies, for the revision of the Convention of 1864. They led first to the adoption of the Additional Articles of 1868 (*No. 37*) and the Convention of 1899 concerning maritime warfare (*No. 38*). The Hague Peace Conference of 1899, in its Final Act, expressed the wish that a special conference be convened for the revision of the Geneva Convention of 1864. In 1906 this conference was organized by the Swiss Government and attended by 35 states. On the basis of proposals submitted to it by the International Committee of the Red Cross the conference adopted the new Convention, which replaced the 1864 Convention in the relations between the contracting states.

With 33 articles divided into eight chapters, the Convention of 1906 is more detailed and more precise in its terminology than the Convention of 1864. New provisions were included concerning the burial of the dead and the transmission of information. The voluntary aid societies were for the first time expressly recognized. On the other hand, provisions that had proved to be impracticable were altered. The prerogatives of the inhabitants bringing help to the wounded were reduced to more reasonable proportions, and the duty to repatriate the wounded who are unfit for further service was transformed into a mere recommendation.

The Convention of 1906 was replaced by the Geneva Convention of 1929 (*No. 43*), but remained in force until 1970, when the last state party to it which had not yet adhered to one of the later Conventions (Costa Rica) acceded to the Conventions of 1949.

ENTRY INTO FORCE: 9 August 1907. No longer in force.

AUTHENTIC TEXT: French. The translation below is reprinted from *US Statutes at Large*, Vol. 35, pp. 1885–1911.

TEXT PUBLISHED IN: *Actes de la Conférence de Révision, réunie à Genève du 11 juin au 6 juillet 1906*, Genève 1906, pp. 277–293 (French); Deltentre, pp. 161–185 (Engl., French, German, Dutch); *CTS*, Vol. 202, 1906, pp. 144–162 (French); *Handbook of the International Red Cross*, 1953, pp. 18–27 (Engl.); *Manuel de la Croix-Rouge internationale*, 1953, pp. 22–31 (French); *Manual de la Cruz Roja internacional*, 1953, pp. 18–27 (Span.); *Droit des conflits armés*, pp. 367–380 (French); *GBTS*, 1907, No. 15, Cd. 3502 (Engl., French); Higgins, pp. 18–35 (Engl., French); *US Statutes at Large*, Vol. 35 pp. 1885–1911 (Engl.); Malloy, Vol. II, pp. 2183–2205 (Engl.); Bevans, Vol. I, pp. 516–534 (Engl.); *AJIL*, Vol. 1, 1907, Suppl., pp. 201–209 (Engl.); Friedman, pp. 257–269 (Engl.); *Les deux Conférences de la Paix*, pp. 183–189 (French); Arellano, pp. 359–361 (Span. – extracts); Bustamante, pp. 167–181 (Span.);

Ceppi, pp. 328–336 (Span.); *Sbornik zakonov*, 1926, Vol. II, No. 38, str. 228, pp. 641–657 (French, Russ.); *Sbornik dogovorov RSFSR*, vyp. 1, 1921, No. 37, pp. 230–238 (Russ.); Korovin, pp. 359–367 (Russ.); Liszt, pp. LXXXVI–XCIII (Russ.);ICRC website: www.icrc.org/ihl.nsf.

TABLE OF CONTENTS

* * *

I. CONVENTION

[List of contracting parties]

Being equally animated by the desire to lessen the inherent evils of warfare as far as is within their power, and wishing for this purpose to improve and supplement the provisions agreed upon at Geneva on 22 August 1864, for the amelioration of the condition of the wounded or sick in armies in the field,

Have decided to conclude a new convention to that effect, and have appointed as their Plenipotentiaries:

[Here follow the names of plenipotentiaries]

Who, after having communicated to each other their full powers, found in good and due form, have agreed on the following:

Chapter I. The Sick and Wounded

Article 1. Officers, soldiers, and other persons officially attached to armies, who are sick or wounded, shall be respected and cared for, without distinction of nationality, by the belligerent in whose power they are. A belligerent, however, when compelled to leave his wounded in the hands of his adversary, shall leave with them, so far as military conditions permit, a portion of the personnel and *matériel* of his sanitary service to assist in caring for them.

Art. 2. Subject to the care that must be taken of them under the preceding Article, the sick and wounded of an army who fall into the power of the other belligerent become prisoners of war, and the general rules of international law in respect to prisoners become applicable to them.

The belligerents remain free, however, to mutually agree upon such clauses, by way of exception or favor, in relation to the wounded or sick as they may deem proper. They shall especially have authority to agree:

1. To mutually return the sick and wounded left on the field of battle after an engagement.
2. To send back to their own country the sick and wounded who have recovered, or who are in a condition to be transported and whom they do not desire to retain as prisoners.

   To send the sick and wounded of the enemy to a neutral state, with the consent of the latter and on condition that it shall charge itself with their internment until the close of hostilities.

Art. 3. After every engagement the belligerent who remains in possession of the field of battle shall take measures to search for the wounded and to protect the wounded and dead from robbery and ill treatment.

He will see that a careful examination is made of the bodies of the dead prior to their interment or incineration.

Art. 4. As soon as possible each belligerent shall forward to the authorities of their country or army the marks or military papers of identification found upon the bodies of the dead, together with a list of names of the sick and wounded taken in charge by him.

Belligerents will keep each other mutually advised of internments and transfers, together with admissions to hospitals and deaths which occur among the sick and wounded in their hands. They will collect all objects of personal use, valuables, letters, etc., which are found upon the field of battle, or have been left by the sick or wounded who have died in sanitary formations or other establishments, for transmission to persons in interest through the authorities of their own country.

Art. 5. Military authority may make an appeal to the charitable zeal of the inhabitants to receive and, under its supervision, to care for the sick and wounded of the armies, granting to persons responding to such appeals special protection and certain immunities.

Chapter II. Sanitary Formations and Establishments

Art. 6. Mobile sanitary formations (*i.e.*, those which are intended to accompany armies in the field) and the fixed establishments belonging to the sanitary service shall be protected and respected by belligerents.

Art. 7. The protection due to sanitary formations and establishments ceases if they are used to commit acts injurious to the enemy.

Art. 8. A sanitary formation or establishment shall not be deprived of the protection accorded by Article 6 by the fact:

1. That the personnel of a formation or establishment is armed and uses its arms in self-defense or in defense of its sick and wounded.
2. That in the absence of armed hospital attendants, the formation is guarded by an armed detachment or by sentinels acting under competent orders.
3. That arms or cartridges, taken from the wounded and not yet turned over to the proper authorities, are found in the formation or establishment.

Chapter III. Personnel

Art. 9. The personnel charged exclusively with the removal, transportation, and treatment of the sick and wounded, as well as with the administration of sanitary formations and establishments, and the chaplains attached to armies, shall be respected and protected under all circumstances. If they fall into the hands of the enemy they shall not be considered as prisoners of war.

These provisions apply to the guards of sanitary formations and establishments in the case provided for in section 2 of Article 8.

Art. 10. The personnel of volunteer aid societies, duly recognized and authorized by their own governments, who are employed in the sanitary formations and establishments of armies, are assimilated to the personnel contemplated in the preceding article, upon condition that the said personnel shall be subject to military laws and regulations. Each state shall make known to the other, either in time of peace or at the opening, or during the progress of hostilities, and in any case before actual employment, the names of the societies which it has authorized to render assistance, under its responsibility, in the official sanitary service of its armies.

Art. 11. A recognized society of a neutral state can only lend the services of its sanitary personnel and formations to a belligerent with the prior consent of its own government and the authority of such belligerent. The belligerent who has accepted such assistance is required to notify the enemy before making any use thereof.

Art. 12. Persons described in Articles 9, 10, and 11 will continue in the exercise of their functions, under the direction of the enemy, after they have fallen into his power.

When their assistance is no longer indispensable they will be sent back to their army or country, within such period and by such route as may accord with military necessity.

They will carry with them such effects, instruments, arms, and horses as are their private property.

Art. 13. While they remain in his power, the enemy will secure to the personnel mentioned in Article 9 the same pay and allowances to which persons of the same grade in his own army are entitled.

Chapter IV. *Matériel*

Art. 14. If mobile sanitary formations fall into the power of the enemy, they shall retain their *matériel*, including the teams, whatever may be the means of transportation and the conducting personnel. Competent military authority, however, shall have the right to employ it in caring for the sick and wounded. The restitution of the *matériel* shall take place in accordance with the conditions prescribed for the sanitary personnel, and, as far as possible, at the same time.

Art. 15. Buildings and *matériel* pertaining to fixed establishments shall remain subject to the laws of war, but cannot be diverted from their use so long as they are necessary for the sick and wounded. Commanders of troops engaged in operations, however, may use them, in case of important military necessity, if, before such use, the sick and wounded who are in them have been provided for.

Art. 16. The *matériel* of aid societies admitted to the benefits of this convention, in conformity to the conditions therein established, is regarded as private property and, as such, will be respected under all circumstances, save that it is subject to the recognized right of requisition by belligerents in conformity to the laws and usages of war.

Chapter V. Convoys of Evacuation

Art. 17. Convoys of evacuation shall be treated as mobile sanitary formations subject to the following special provisions:

1. A belligerent intercepting a convoy may, if required by military necessity, break up such convoy, charging himself with the care of the sick and wounded whom it contains.
2. In this case the obligation to return the sanitary personnel, as provided for in Article 12, shall be extended to include the entire military personnel employed, under competent orders, in the transportation and protection of the convoy.

The obligation to return the sanitary *matériel* as provided for in Article 14, shall apply to railway trains and vessels intended for interior navigation which have been especially equipped for evacuation purposes, as well as to the ordinary vehicles, trains, and vessels which belong to the sanitary service.

Military vehicles, with their teams, other than those belonging to the sanitary service, may be captured.

The civil personnel and the various means of transportation obtained by requisition, including railway *matériel* and vessels utilized for convoys, are subject to the general rules of international law.

Chapter VI. Distinctive Emblem

Art. 18.[1] Out of respect to Switzerland the heraldic emblem of the red cross on a white ground, formed by the reversal of the federal colors, is continued as the emblem and distinctive sign of the sanitary service of armies.

[1] For reservations in respect of this article by Egypt, Persia and Turkey, see pp. 394–395.

Art. 19. This emblem appears on flags and brassards, as well as upon all *matériel* appertaining to the sanitary service, with the permission of the competent military authority.

Art. 20. The personnel protected in virtue of the first paragraph of Article 9, and Articles 10 and 11, will wear attached to the left arm a brassard bearing a red cross on a white ground, which will be issued and stamped by competent military authority, and accompanied by a certificate of identity in the case of persons attached to the sanitary service of armies who do not have military uniform.

Art. 21. The distinctive flag of the convention can only be displayed over the sanitary formations and establishments which the convention provides shall be respected, and with the consent of the military authorities. It shall be accompanied by the national flag of the belligerent to whose service the formation or establishment is attached.

Sanitary formations which have fallen into the power of the enemy, however, shall fly no other flag than that of the Red Cross so long as they continue in that situation.

Art. 22. The sanitary formations of neutral countries which, under the conditions set forth in Article 11, have been authorized to render their services, shall fly, with the flag of the convention, the national flag of the belligerent to which they are attached. The provisions of the second paragraph of the preceding article are applicable to them.

Art. 23.[2] The emblem of the red cross on a white ground and the words "Red Cross" or "Geneva Cross" may only be used, whether in time of peace or war, to protect or designate sanitary formations and establishments, the personnel and *matériel* protected by the convention.

Chapter VII. Application and Execution of the Convention

Art. 24. The provisions of the present Convention are obligatory only on the Contracting Powers, in case of war between two or more of them. The said provisions shall cease to be obligatory if one of the belligerent Powers should not be signatory to the Convention.

Art. 25. It shall be the duty of the commanders in chief of the belligerent armies to provide for the details of execution of the foregoing articles, as well as for unforeseen cases, in accordance with the instructions of their respective governments, and conformably to the general principles of this convention.

Art. 26. The signatory governments shall take the necessary steps to acquaint their troops, and particularly the protected personnel, with the provisions of this convention and to make them known to the people at large.

Chapter VIII. Repression of Abuses and Infractions

Art. 27.[3] The signatory powers whose legislation may not now be adequate engage to take or recommend to their legislatures such measures as may be necessary to prevent the use, by private persons or by societies other than those upon which this convention confers the right thereto, of the emblem or name of the Red Cross or Geneva Cross, particularly for commercial purposes by means of trade-marks or commercial labels.

The prohibition of the use of the emblem or name in question shall take effect from the time set in each act of legislation, and at the latest five years after this convention goes into effect. After such going into effect, it shall be unlawful to use a trade-mark or commercial label contrary to such prohibition.

---

[2] For reservations in respect of this article by Great Britain and Ireland, see p. 394.

[3] For reservations in respect of this article by Great Britain and Ireland, see p. 394.

Art 28.[4] In the event of their military penal laws being insufficient, the signatory governments also engage to take, or to recommend to their legislatures, the necessary measures to repress, in time of war, individual acts of robbery and ill treatment of the sick and wounded of the armies, as well as to punish, as usurpations of military insignia, the wrongful use of the flag and brassard of the Red Cross by military persons or private individuals not protected by the present convention.

They will communicate to each other through the Swiss Federal Council the measures taken with a view to such repression, not later than five years from the ratification of the present convention.

General Provisions

Art. 29. The present convention shall be ratified as soon as possible. The ratifications will be deposited at Berne.

A record of the deposit of each act of ratification shall be prepared, of which a duly certified copy shall be sent, through diplomatic channels, to each of the contracting powers.

Art. 30. The present convention shall become operative, as to each power, six months after the date of deposit of its ratification.

Art. 31. The present convention, when duly ratified, shall supersede the Convention of August 22, 1864, in the relations between the contracting states.

The Convention of 1864 remains in force in the relations between the parties who signed it but who may not also ratify the present convention.

Art. 32. The present convention may, until December 31, proximo, be signed by the powers represented at the conference which opened at Geneva on June 11, 1906, as well as by the powers not represented at the conference who have signed the Convention of 1864.

Such of these powers as shall not have signed the present convention on or before December 31, 1906, will remain at liberty to accede to it after that date. They shall signify their adherence in a written notification addressed to the Swiss Federal Council, and communicated to all the contracting powers by the said Council.

Other powers may request to adhere in the same manner, but their request shall only be effective if, within the period of one year from its notification to the Federal Council, such Council has not been advised of any opposition on the part of any of the contracting powers.

Art. 33. Each of the contracting parties shall have the right to denounce the present convention. This denunciation shall only become operative one year after a notification in writing shall have been made to the Swiss Federal Council, which shall forthwith communicate such notification to all the other contracting parties. This denunciation shall only become operative in respect to the power which has given it.

In faith whereof the plenipotentiaries have signed the present convention and affixed their seals thereto.

Done at Geneva, the sixth day of July, one thousand nine hundred and six, in a single copy, which shall remain in the archives of the Swiss Confederation and certified copies of which shall be delivered to the Contracting Parties through diplomatic channels.

[Here follow signatures]

---

4 For reservations in respect of this article by Great Britain and Ireland and by Japan, see pp. 394–395.

II. FINAL PROTOCOL

[List of the contracting parties]

The Conference called by the Swiss Federal Council, with a view to revising the International Convention of 22 August 1864, for the Amelioration of the Condition of Soldiers wounded in Armies in the field, met at Geneva on 11 June 1906. The Powers herein below enumerated took part in the Conference to which they had designated the delegates herein below named:

[Here follow the names of plenipotentiaries]

In a series of meetings held from 11 June to 5 July 1906, the Conference discussed and framed, for the signatures of the Plenipotentiaries, the text of a Convention which will bear the date of 6 July 1906. In addition, and conformably to Article 16 of the Convention for the peaceful settlement of international disputes, of 29 July 1899, which recognized arbitration as the most effective and, at the same time, most equitable means of adjusting differences that have not been resolved through the diplomatic channel, the Conference uttered the following wish:

The Conference expressed the wish that, in order to arrive at as exact as possible an interpretation and application of the Geneva Convention, the Contracting Powers will refer to the Permanent Court at The Hague, if permitted by the cases and circumstances, such differences as may arise among them, in time of peace, concerning the interpretation of the said Convention.

This wish was adopted by the following States:

Argentine Republic
Austria-Hungary
Belgium
Brazil
Bulgaria
Chile
China
Congo
Denmark
France
Germany
Greece
Guatemala
Honduras
Italy
Luxemburg
Mexico
Montenegro
Nicaragua
Netherlands
Norway
Persia
Peru
Portugal
Romania
Russia
Serbia
Siam
Spain (*ad referendum*)
Sweden
Switzerland
United States of America
Uruguay

The wish was rejected by the following States:

Great Britain
Japan and Korea

In witness whereof, the Delegates have signed the present Protocol.

Done at Geneva, the sixth day of July, one thousand nine hundred and six, in a single copy which shall be deposited in the archives of the Swiss Confederation and certified copies of which shall be delivered to all the Powers represented at the Conference.

[Here follow signatures]

SIGNATURES, RATIFICATIONS AND ACCESSIONS[1]

State	*Signature*	*Ratification, Accession*
Afghanistan	–	4 April 1922
Albania	–	13 September 1922
Argentina	6 July 1906	–
Austria-Hungary[2]	6 July 1906[3]	27 March 1908
Belgium	6 July 1906	27 August 1907
Brazil	6 July 1906	18 June 1907
Bulgaria	6 July 1906	3 June 1912
Chile	6 July 1906	6 September 1909
China	6 July 1906	–
Colombia	–	28 October 1907
Congo Free State	6 July 1906	16 April 1907
Costa Rica	–	29 July 1910
Cuba	–	17 March 1908
Czechoslovakia	–	17 November 1919
Danzig	–	6 October 1921
Denmark	6 July 1906	11 June 1907
Dominican Republic	–	25 August 1926
Ecuardo	–	13 April 1923
Egypt	–	17 December 1923 *Res.*
El Salvador	–	28 September 1911
Estonia	–	10 March 1921
Finland	–	27 January 1920
France	6 July 1906	19 July 1913
Germany	6 July 1906	27 May 1907
Great Britain and Ireland	6 July 1906 *Res.*	16 April 1907
Greece	6 July 1906	27 May 1921
Guatemala	6 July 1906	25/26 March 1912
Haiti	–	22 September 1918
Honduras	6 July 1906	27 November 1911
Hungary[4]	6 July 1906	27 March 1908

[1] Based on a communication from the Swiss Federal Department of Foreign Affairs of 25 June 1999. ee also ICRC website: www.icrc.org/ihl.nsf.

[2] See note 4 under Hungary.

[3] Signature *ad referendum*.

[4] Communication of 1 May 1923 from the Hungarian Chargé d'Affaires at Berne concerning the participation of the Kingdom of Hungary in the Convention of Geneva dated 6 July 1906:

"In accordance with instructions received from my Government, I have the honour to bring the following facts to the notice of the Federal Political Department, Section for Foreign Affairs: Although the Treaty of Trianon and the other Treaties of Peace do not contain any express provisions concerning the application of the Red Cross Conventions of Geneva, these Conventions will no doubt remain in force in the future.

In order, therefore, to avoid any misunderstanding due to differences of opinion regarding the continued observance by Hungary of the above mentioned Conventions, the Undersigned has the honour to declare on behalf of the Royal Hungarian Government that in spite of the dissolution of the Austro-Hungarian Monarchy Hungary recognizes that she is bound by the Red Cross Conventions of Geneva and will continue in the future to apply the provisions of the Convention of 1906 in respect of States which are Contracting Parties, and also the Convention of 1864 as regards all Contracting States which have not ratified the Convention of 1906.

The present statement should be regarded as merely in the nature of a declaration in order not to leave any doubt as to Hungary's continued observance of the provisions in question. Although reduced in area by the Treaty of Peace, Hungary is from the point of view of

State	*Signature*	*Ratification, Accession*
Iceland	–	25 March 1925
Italy	6 July 1906	9 March 1907
Japan and Korea	6 July 1906 *Res.*	23 April 1908
Latvia	–	8 April 1922
Lithuania	–	3 September 1921
Luxemburg	6 July 1906	27 August 1907
Mexico	6 July 1906	4 June 1907
Montenegro	6 July 1906	–
Netherlands	6 July 1906	31 July 1908
Nicaragua	–	17 June 1907
Norway	6 July 1906	24/29 November 1909
Paraguay	–	4 December 1909
Peru	6 July 1906	–
Persia	6 July 1906 *Res.*	–
Poland	–	15 July 1919
Portugal	6 July 1906	12 July 1911
Romania	6 July 1906	3 August 1911
Russia	6 July 1906	9 February 1907
Serbia	6 July 1906	17 September/19 October 1909
Siam (Thailand)	6 July 1906	29 January 1907
Spain	6 July 1906	11 October 1907
Sweden	6 July 1906	11/13 July 1911
Switzerland	6 July 1906	16 April 1907
Turkey	–	24 August 1907 *Res.*
United States of America	6 July 1906	9 February 1907
Uruguay	6 July 1906	25 November 1919
Venezuela	–	8 July 1907

RESERVATIONS

EGYPT

Accession "subject to the reservation that the Egyptian emblem shall consist of the red crescent on a white ground, with the two horns (points) facing towards the right, when seen from the front or facing towards the left on the brassards of the personnel" (*LNTS*, Vol. 19, p. 293).

GREAT BRITAIN AND IRELAND

Reservation made on signature in respect of Articles 23, 27 and 28. Great Britain waived this reservation by a declaration signed on 7 July 1914.

---

cont.

Hungarian constitutional law identical with the former Kingdom of Hungary, which, in the time of Dual Monarchy, constituted with Austria the second component part of the Austro-Hungarian Monarchy. Consequently the dissolution of the Monarchy, that is to say the abolition of the constitutional connection between Austria and Hungary, has not in itself modified the force of treaties, conventions and agreements concluded in the time of the Dual Monarchy in virtue of Hungary's constitutional adherence thereto.

In bringing the foregoing to the notice of the Federal Political Department, Section for Foreign Affairs, I have the honour to request the Department to be good enough to communicate this declaration to the States which are Parties to the Convention in question, and to transmit to me in due course the replies received."

The Government of Austria declared itself bound by this Convention in its note of 29 January 1923 (translated by the Secretariat of the League of Nations, *LNTS*, Vol. 15, pp. 329–331).

JAPAN AND KOREA
Reservation made on signature in respect of Article 28.

PERSIA
Reservation made on signature in respect of Article 18.

TURKEY
Reservation made on accession concerning the use of the red crescent (Article 18).

No. 43

CONVENTION (X) FOR THE ADAPTATION TO MARITIME WARFARE OF THE PRINCIPLES OF THE GENEVA CONVENTION

Signed at The Hague, 18 October 1907

INTRODUCTORY NOTE: The Second Hague Peace Conference of 1907 revised and enlarged Convention (III) of 1899 concerning the adaptation to maritime warfare of the principles of the Geneva Convention of 1864 (*No. 40*). Most of the 14 articles of the 1899 Convention were taken over without change in the 1907 version, but several new articles were added. The number of articles was doubled to 28. The new Convention was based on the Geneva Convention of 1906, whereas the earlier one had been based on the less developed Convention of 1864. New provisions are contained especially in Articles 5–9, 13, 15–17 and 19–23.

The Convention remained in force during both world wars. It was replaced in 1949 by the Geneva Convention (II) (*No. 49*).

ENTRY INTO FORCE: 26 January 1910.

AUTHENTIC TEXT: French. The translation below is reprinted from Scott, *Hague Conventions*, pp. 163–181. It reproduces the translation of the United States Department of State.

TEXT PUBLISHED IN: *Conférence internationale de la Paix, 1907*, pp. 658–663 (French); *Les deux Conférences de la Paix*, pp. 139–145 (French); Scott, *Hague Conventions*, pp. 163–181 (Engl.); Scott, *Les Conventions de La Haye*, pp. 163–181 (French); Scott, *Les Conférences de La Haye*, pp. 79–84 (French); Martens, *NRGT*, 3ème série, Vol. III, pp. 630–662 (French, German); Deltenre, pp. 338–353 (Engl., French, German, Dutch); *CTS*, Vol. 205, 1907, pp. 359–366 (French); *Handbook of the International Red Cross*, 1953, pp. 42–49 (Engl.); *Manuel de la Croix-Rouge internationale*, 1953, pp. 46–53 (French); *Manual de la Cruz Roja internacional*, 1953, pp. 43–50 (Span.); *Droit des conflits armés*, pp. 381–392 (French); *BFSP*, Vol. 100, 1906–1907, pp. 415–421 (French); *US Statutes at Large*, Vol. 36, pp. 2371–2395 (Engl., French); Malloy, Vol. II, pp. 2326–2340 (Engl.); Bevans, Vol. I, pp. 694–710 (Engl.); *AJIL*, Vol. 2, 1908, Suppl., pp. 153–167 (Engl., French); Friedman, pp. 354–363 (Engl.); Genet, pp. 527–532 (French); Arellano, pp. 377–379 (Span. – extracts); Bustamante, pp. 336–346 (Span.); Ceppi, pp. 367–373 (Span.); *Revista de Derecho Internacional y politica exterior*, Cronicá, Año III, 1907, pp. 93–98 (Span.); *Sbornik dogovorov RSFSR*, vyp. I, 1921, No. 38, pp. 239–246 (Russ.); Korovin, pp. 389 (Russ.); *Sobranie zakonov*, 1929, Section II, st. 229, pp. 658–673 (French, Russ.); ICRC website: www.icrc.org/ihl.nsf.

TABLE OF CONTENTS

* * *

[List of contracting parties]

Animated alike by the desire to diminish, as far as depends on them, the inevitable evils of war;

And wishing with this object to adapt to maritime warfare the principles of the Geneva Convention of 6 July 1906.

Have resolved to conclude a Convention for the purpose of revising the Convention of 29 July 1899, relative to this question, and have appointed the following as their Plenipotentiaries:

[Here follow the names of plenipotentiaries]

Who, after having deposited their full powers, found in good and due form, have agreed upon the following provisions:

Article 1. Military hospital ships, that is to say, ships constructed or assigned by States specially and solely with a view to assisting the wounded, sick and shipwrecked, the names of which have been communicated to the belligerent Powers at the commencement or during the course of hostilities, and in any case before they are employed, shall be respected, and cannot be captured while hostilities last.

These ships, moreover, are not on the same footing as war-ships as regards their stay in a neutral port.

Art. 2. Hospital ships, equipped wholly or in part at the expense of private individuals or officially recognized relief societies, shall likewise be respected and exempt from capture, if the belligerent Power to whom they belong has given them an official commission and has notified their names to the hostile Power at the commencement of or during hostilities, and in any case before they are employed.

These ships must be provided with a certificate from the competent authorities declaring that the vessels have been under their control while fitting out and on final departure.

Art. 3. Hospital ships, equipped wholly or in part at the expense of private individuals or officially recognized societies of neutral countries shall be respected and exempt from capture, on condition that they are placed under the control of one of the belligerents, with the previous consent of their own Government and with the authorization of the belligerent himself, and that the latter has notified their names to his adversary at the commencement of or during hostilities, and in any case, before they are employed.

Art. 4. The ships mentioned in Articles 1, 2, and 3 shall afford relief and assistance to the wounded, sick, and shipwrecked of the belligerents without distinction of nationality.

The Governments undertake not to use these ships for any military purpose.

These vessels must in no wise hamper the movements of the combatants.

During and after an engagement they will act at their own risk and peril.

The belligerents shall have the right to control and search them; they can refuse to help them, order them off, make them take a certain course, and put a commissioner on board; they can even detain them, if important circumstances require it.

As far as possible, the belligerents shall enter in the log of the hospital ships the orders which they give them.

Art. 5. Military hospital ships shall be distinguished by being painted white outside with a horizontal band of green about a metre and a half in breadth.

The ships mentioned in Articles 2 and 3 shall be distinguished by being painted white outside with a horizontal band of red about a metre and a half in breadth.

The boats of the ships above mentioned, as also small craft which may be used for hospital work, shall be distinguished by similar painting.

All hospital ships shall make themselves known by hoisting, with their national flag, the white flag with a red cross provided by the Geneva Convention,[1] and further, if they belong to a neutral State, by flying at the mainmast the national flag of the belligerent under whose control they are placed.

Hospital ships which, in the terms of Article 4, are detained by the enemy must haul down the national flag of the belligerent to whom they belong.

The ships and boats above mentioned which wish to ensure by night the freedom from interference to which they are entitled, must, subject to the assent of the belligerent they are accompanying, take the necessary measures to render their special painting sufficiently plain.

Art. 6.[2] The distinguishing signs referred to in Article 5 can only be used, whether in time of peace or war, for protecting or indicating the ships therein mentioned.

Art. 7. In the case of a fight on board a war-ship, the sick wards shall be respected and spared as far as possible.

The said sick wards and the material belonging to them remain subject to the laws of war; they cannot, however, be used for any purpose other than that for which they were originally intended, so long as they are required for the sick and wounded.

The commander, however, into whose power they have fallen may apply them to other purposes, if the military situation requires it, after seeing that the sick and wounded on board are properly provided for.

Art. 8. Hospital ships and sick wards of vessels are no longer entitled to protection if they are employed for the purpose of injuring the enemy.

The fact of the staff of the said ships and sick wards being armed for maintaining order and for defending the sick and wounded, and the presence of wireless telegraphy apparatus on board, is not a sufficient reason for withdrawing protection.

Art. 9. Belligerents may appeal to the charity of the commanders of neutral merchant ships, yachts, or boats to take on board and tend the sick and wounded.

Vessels responding to the appeal, and also vessels which have of their own accord rescued sick, wounded, or ship-wrecked men, shall enjoy special protection and certain immunities. In no case can they be captured for having such persons on board, but, apart from special undertakings that have been made to them, they remain liable to capture for any violations of neutrality they may have committed.

Art. 10. The religious, medical, and hospital staff of any captured ship is inviolable, and its members cannot be made prisoners of war. On leaving the ship they take away with them the objects and surgical instruments which are their own private property.

This staff shall continue to discharge its duties while necessary, and can afterwards leave, when the commander-in-chief considers it possible.

The belligerents must guarantee to the said staff, when it has fallen into their hands, the same allowances and pay which are given to the staff of corresponding rank in their own navy.

Art. 11. Sailors and soldiers on board, when sick or wounded, as well as other persons officially attached to fleets or armies, whatever their nationality, shall be respected and tended by the captors.

---

[1] For reservation in respect of this provision by Persia and Turkey, see p. 404.

[2] For reservation in respect of this article by Great Britain, see p. 404.

Art. 12.[3]Any war-ship belonging to a belligerent may demand that sick, wounded, or shipwrecked men on board military hospital ships, hospital ships belonging to relief societies or to private individuals, merchant ships, yachts, or boats, whatever the nationality of these vessels, should be handed over.

Art. 13. If sick, wounded, or shipwrecked persons are taken on board a neutral warship, every possible precaution must be taken that they do not again take part in the operations of the war.

Art. 14. The shipwrecked, wounded, or sick of one of the belligerents who fall into the power of the other belligerent are prisoners of war. The captor must decide, according to circumstances, whether to keep them, send them to a port of his own country, to a neutral port, or even to an enemy port. In this last case, prisoners thus repatriated cannot serve again while the war lasts.

Art. 15. The shipwrecked, sick, or wounded, who are landed at a neutral port with the consent of the local authorities, must, unless an arrangement is made to the contrary between the neutral State and the belligerent States, be guarded by the neutral State, so as to prevent them again taking part in the operations of the war.

The expenses of tending them in hospital and interning them shall be borne by the State to which the shipwrecked, sick, or wounded persons belong.

Art. 16. After every engagement, the two belligerents, so far as military interests permit, shall take steps to look for the shipwrecked, sick, and wounded, and to protect them, as well as the dead, against pillage and ill-treatment.

They shall see that the burial, whether by land or sea, or cremation of the dead shall be preceded by a careful examination of the corpse.

Art. 17. Each belligerent shall send, as early as possible, to the authorities of their country, navy, or army the military marks or documents of identity found on the dead and the description of the sick and wounded picked up by him.

The belligerents shall keep each other informed as to internments and transfers as well as to the admissions into hospital and deaths which have occurred among the sick and wounded in their hands. They shall collect all the objects of personal use, valuables, letters, etc., which are found in the captured ships, or which have been left by the sick or wounded who died in hospital, in order to have them forwarded to the persons concerned by the authorities of their own country.

Art. 18. The provisions of the present Convention do not apply except between Contracting Powers, and then only if all the belligerents are parties to the Convention.

Art. 19. The commanders-in-chief of the belligerent fleets must see that the above articles are properly carried out; they will have also to see to cases not covered thereby, in accordance with the instructions of their respective Governments and in conformity with the general principles of the present Convention.

Art. 20. The signatory Powers shall take the necessary measures for bringing the provisions of the present Convention to the knowledge of their naval forces, and especially of the members entitled thereunder to immunity, and for making them known to the public.

Art. 21.[4]The Signatory Powers likewise undertake to enact or to propose to their legislatures, if their criminal laws are inadequate, the measures necessary for checking in time of war individual acts of pillage and ill-treatment in respect to the sick and

[3] For declaration in respect of this article by Great Britain, see p. 404.

[4] For reservations in respect of this article by China and Great Britain, see p. 404.

wounded in the fleet, as well as for punishing, as an unjustifiable adoption of naval or military marks, the unauthorized use of the distinctive marks mentioned in Article 5 by vessels not protected by the present Convention.

They will communicate to each other, through the Netherlands Government, the enactments for preventing such acts at the latest within five years of the ratification of the present Convention.

Art. 22. In the case of operations of war between the land and sea forces of belligerents, the provisions of the present Convention do not apply except between the forces actually on board ship.

Art. 23. The present Convention shall be ratified as soon as possible.

The ratifications shall be deposited at The Hague.

The first deposit of ratifications shall be recorded in a *procès-verbal* signed by the representatives of the Powers taking part therein and by the Netherlands Minister for Foreign Affairs.

Subsequent deposits of ratifications shall be made by means of a written notification addressed to the Netherlands Government and accompanied by the instrument of ratification.

A certified copy of the *procès-verbal* relative to the first deposit of ratifications, of the notifications mentioned in the preceding paragraph, as well as of the instruments of ratification, shall be at once sent by the Netherlands Government through the diplomatic channel to the Powers invited to the Second Peace Conference, as well as to the other Powers which have adhered to the Convention. In the cases contemplated in the preceding paragraph the said Government shall inform them at the same time of the date on which it received the notification.

Art. 24. Non-signatory Powers which have accepted the Geneva Convention of 6 July 1906 may adhere to the present Convention.

The Power which desires to adhere notifies its intention to the Netherlands Government in writing, forwarding to it the act of adhesion, which shall be deposited in the archives of the said Government.

The said Government shall at once transmit to all the other Powers a duly certified copy of the notification as well as of the act of adhesion, mentioning the date on which it received the notification.

Art. 25. The present Convention, duly ratified, shall replace as between Contracting Powers, the Convention of 29 July 1899, for the adaptation to maritime warfare of the principles of the Geneva Convention.

The Convention of 1899 remains in force as between the Powers which signed it but which do not also ratify the present Convention.

Art. 26. The present Convention shall come into force, in the case of the Powers which were a party to the first deposit of ratifications, sixty days after the date of the *procès-verbal* of this deposit, and, in the case of the Powers which ratify subsequently or which adhere, sixty days after the notification of their ratification or of their adhesion has been received by the Netherlands Government.

Art. 27. In the event of one of the Contracting Powers wishing to denounce the present Convention, the denunciation shall be notified in writing to the Netherlands Government, which shall at once communicate a duly certified copy of the notification to all the other Powers, informing them at the same time of the date on which it was received.

The denunciation shall only have effect in regard to the notifying Power, and one year after the notification has reached the Netherlands Government.

Art. 28. A register kept by the Netherlands Ministry for Foreign Affairs shall give the date of the deposit of ratifications made in virtue of Article 23, paragraphs 3 and 4, as well as the date on which the notifications of adhesion (Article 24, paragraph 2) or of denunciation (Article 27, paragraph 1) have been received.

Each Contracting Power is entitled to have access to this register and to be supplied with duly certified extracts from it. In faith whereof the Plenipotentiaries have appended their signatures to the Convention.

Done at The Hague, 18 October 1907, in a single copy, which shall remain deposited in the archives of the Netherlands Government, and duly certified copies of which shall be sent, through the diplomatic channel, to the Powers which have been invited to the Second Peace Conference.

[Here follow signatures]

SIGNATURES, RATIFICATIONS AND ACCESSIONS[1]

State	*Signature*	*Ratification, Accession*
Argentine Republic	18 October 1907	–
Austria-Hungary	18 October 1907	27 November 1909
Belgium	18 October 1907	8 August 1910
Bolivia	18 October 1907	27 November 1909
Brazil	18 October 1907	5 January 1914
Bulgaria	18 October 1907	–
Chile	18 October 1907	–
China	18 October 1907 *Res.*	27 November 1909 *Res.*
Colombia	18 October 1907	–
Cuba	18 October 1907	22 February 1912
Denmark	18 October 1907	27 November 1909
Dominican Republic	18 October 1907	–
Ecuador	18 October 1907	–
El Salvador	18 October 1907	27 November 1909
Ethiopia	–	5 August 1935
Finland[2]	–	–
France	18 October 1907	7 October 1910
Germany	18 October 1907	27 November 1909
Great Britain	18 October 1907 *Res.*	–
Greece	18 October 1907	–
Guatemala	18 October 1907	15 March 1911
Haiti	18 October 1907	2 February 1910
Italy	18 October 1907	15 February 1937
Japan	18 October 1907	13 December 1911
Latvia	–	8 April 1923
Luxembourg	18 October 1907	5 September 1912
Mexico	18 October 1907	27 November 1909
Montenegro	18 October 1907	–
Netherlands	18 October 1907	27 November 1909

1 Based on a communication received from the Ministry of Foreign Affairs of the Netherlands of 12 December 2001. See also ICRC website: www.icrc.org/ihl.nsf.

2 By letter dated 12 May 1980, the Netherlands Ministry of Foreign Affairs stated (a) Finland's accession on 30 December 1918 to this and other 1907 Hague Conventions and to the 1907 Hague Declaration was initially regarded as provisional, pending the final resolution of Finland's international status; (b) after consultation with the other contracting powers, the depositary stated on 9 June 1922 that Finland's accession should be regarded as final and complete, and (c) the Conventions and the Declaration entered into force for Finland on 9 June 1922.

State	*Signature*	*Ratification, Accession*
Nicaragua	–	16 December 1909
Norway	18 October 1907	19 September 1910
Panama	18 October 1907	11 September 1911
Paraguay	18 October 1907	–
Persia	18 October 1907 *Res.*	–
Peru	18 October 1907	–
Poland	–	31 May 1935
Portugal	18 October 1907	13 April 1911
Romania	18 October 1907	1 March 1912
Russia[3]	18 October 1907	27 November 1909
Serbia	18 October 1907	–
Siam	18 October 1907	12 March 1910
Spain	18 October 1907	18 March 1913
Sweden	18 October 1907	27 November 1909
Switzerland	18 October 1907	12 May 1910
Turkey	18 October 1907 *Res.*	–
United States of America	18 October 1907	27 November 1909
Uruguay	18 October 1907	–
Venezuela	18 October 1907	–

RESERVATIONS

CHINA (*reservation made on signature and maintained on ratification*)
Under reservation of Article 21.

GREAT BRITAIN (*reservation made on signature*)

Under reservation of Articles 6 and 21 and of the following declaration
In affixing their signatures to the above Convention, the British Plenipotentiaries declare that His Majesty's Government understands Article 12 to apply only to the case of combatants rescued during or after a naval engagement in which they have taken part.

PERSIA (*reservation made on signature*)
Under reservation of the right, admitted by the Conference, to use the lion and red sun instead of and in place of the red cross.

TURKEY (*reservation made on signature*)
Under reservation of the right admitted by the Peace Conference to use the red crescent.

[3] By the note of the Foreign Ministry of the USSR of 7 March 1955 "The Government of the USSR recognises the Conventions and Declarations of The Hague from 1899 and 1907, which were ratified by Russia to the extent that the Conventions and Declarations do not contradict the United Nations Charter and if they are not amended or replaced by ulterior international agreements to which the USSR is a Party, such as the 1925 Geneva Protocol for the Prohibition of Use of Asphyxiating, Poisonous and Other Gases and of Bacteriological Methods of Warfare and the 1949 Geneva Conventions for the Protection of Victims of War" (*Izvestiya*, 9 March 1955).

In January 1992, the Ministry of Foreign Affairs of the Russian Federation informed the heads of diplomatic missions in Moscow, that the Russian Federation continues to be a party to all conventions which are in force for the Soviet Union. The Ministry of Foreign Affairs of the Kingdom of the Netherlands considers therefore that the Russian Federation is bound by the conventions to which the Soviet Union was party (communication of the depositary to the Henry Dunant Institute of 6 November 1992).

On 4 June 1962, the Byelorussian Soviet Socialist Republic made a declaration similar to that made by the USSR.

No. 44

FINAL ACT OF THE DIPLOMATIC CONFERENCE 1929

Signed at Geneva, 27 July 1929

INTRODUCTORY NOTE: The Diplomatic Conference of 1929 was convened by the Swiss Federal Council for the purpose of revising the Geneva Convention of 1906 (*No. 42*) and of adopting a new convention relative to the treatment of prisoners of war. The Conference, at which 47 governments were represented, lasted from 1 to 27 July 1929. For further indications see the introductory notes to the two Conventions (*Nos. 44 and 45*). The Final Act has no force of law.

AUTHENTIC TEXT: French. The translation below is reprinted from Cmd. 3795 (1931).

TEXT PUBLISHED IN: *Actes de la Conférence diplomatique convoquée par le Conseil fédéral suisse pour la revision de la Convention du 6 Juillet 1906 pour l'amélioration du sort des blessés et malades dans les armées en campagne et pour l'élaboration d'une Convention relative au traitemenet des prisonniers de guerre et reunie à Genève du 1 au 27 Juillet 1929*, Genève 1930, pp. 725–740 (French); Cmd. 3795 (1931) (Engl.); Deltenre, pp. 558–561 (Engl., French, German, Dutch); *Manuel de la Croix-Rouge internationale*, 1938, 7ème édition, Genève, Paris, pp. 145–147 (French); *Handbook of the International Red Cross*, 1953, p. 98 (Engl.); *Manuel de la Croix-Rouge internationale*, 1953, pp. 107–108 (French); *Manual de la Cruz Roja internacional*, 1953, p. 103, (Span.); *Droit des conflits armés*, pp. 393–395 (French); ICRC website: www.icrc.irg/ihl.nsf.

* * *

The Conference convened by the Swiss Federal Council with a view to the revision of the Geneva Convention for the Amelioration of the Condition of the Wounded and Sick in Armies in the Field of 6 July 1906, and the elaboration of a Code relating to Prisoners of War, deliberated at Geneva from 1–27 July 1929, on the basis of two draft Conventions which had been examined and approved by the 10th and 11th International Conferences of the Red Cross.

The countries enumerated below took part in the Conference for which the Delegates hereinafter named had been appointed:

[Here follow the names of delegates]

The Conference was presided over by Mr. Paul Dinichert, Minister Plenipotentiary, Delegate of Switzerland.

The Conference appointed two Commissions.

The First Commission, charged with the revision of the Geneva Convention, was presided over by M. Paul Dinichert, the Second, charged with the elaboration of a Code relating to Prisoners of War, by M. Harald Scavenius. The Second Commission was divided into two Sub-Commissions, one presided over by Mr. Hugh R. Wilson, Delegate of the United States of America, the other by the Right Honourable Sir Horace Rumbold, Delegate of Great Britain.

The Conference has drawn up, for signature by the Plenipotentiaries, two Conventions bearing this day's date:

The Geneva Convention for the Amelioration of the Condition of the Wounded and Sick in Armies in the Field; and

The Convention relative to the Treatment of Prisoners of War.

The Conference further made the following recommendations and expressed the following views:

I. The Conference recommends that the question be examined whether fresh safeguards lasting until the end of their treatment in hospital could not be established for the benefit of persons who are badly wounded or seriously ill and have fallen into the hands of the enemy.

II. In view of a request by the Sovereign and Military Order of the Hospitallers of St. John of Jerusalem, called the Order of Malta, the Conference considers that the provisions laid down by the Geneva Convention governing the position of Aid Societies with armies in the field are applicable to the national organizations of this Order. The same applies as regards the Grand Priory of St. John of Jerusalem in England, the Orders of St. John (Johanniter) and of St. George in Germany, and similar nursing Orders in all countries.

III. The Conference recommends that the countries participating in the Geneva Conventions should meet in conference in the near future, with the view to regulate as comprehensively as may be necessary the use of medical aircraft in time of war.

IV. The Conference recommends that the consideration and establishment of an uniform pattern of identity certificate for all Red Cross personnel not provided with military uniform should be referred to the International Commission for the Standardization of Medical Material.

V.. The Conference, recognizing the importance of the mission entrusted to the National Societies of the Red Cross and the voluntary aid societies in their work of solidarity among nations, considers that it is highly desirable that all facilities and immunities for the exercise of their functions in time of peace should be accorded in the widest measure permissible under the national legislations, particularly as regards their establishment, the circulation of their personnel and material, and their nursing activities.

VI. The Conference, adopting the unanimous resolutions of its two Commissions, recommends that an exhaustive study should be made with a view to the conclusion of an international Convention regarding the condition and protection of civilians of enemy nationality in the territory of a belligerent or in territory occupied by a belligerent.

In witness whereof the delegates have signed the present Final Act.

Done at Geneva, 27 July 1929, in a single copy, which shall be deposited in the archives of the Swiss Federation, and of which copies, certified to be correct, shall be transmitted to all the countries represented at the Conference.

[Here follow signatures]

SIGNATURES

The Final Act was signed by the representatives of the following states:

Australia
Austria
Belgium
Bolivia

Italy
Japan
Latvia
Luxemburg

Brazil
Bulgaria
Canada
Chile
China
Columbia
Cuba
Czechoslovakia
Denmark
Dominican Republic
Egypt
Siam
South Africa
Spain *(ad referendum)*
Sweden
Switzerland
Greece
Hungary
Uruguay
Venezuela

Mexico
Netherlands *Res.*
New Zealand
Nicaragua
Norway
Persia
Poland
Portugal
Romania
Kingdom of the Serbs, Croats and Slovenes
Estonia
Finland
France
Germany
Great Britain and Northern Ireland
Turkey
United States of America
India
Irish Free State

RESERVATION

NETHERLANDS (*reservation made on signature of the Final Act*)
In signing this Final Act the Netherlands Delegation makes the following reservation: the Netherlands' regulations require that in time of war or of mobilization all the voluntary aid organizations in the Netherlands be subordinated to the direction of the Association of the Netherlands Red Cross.

No. 45

CONVENTION FOR THE AMELIORATION OF THE CONDITION OF THE WOUNDED AND SICK IN ARMIES IN THE FIELD

Signed at Geneva, 27 July 1929

INTRODUCTORY NOTE: The Convention on the wounded and sick of 1929 represents the third version of the Geneva Convention after those of 1864 and 1906 (see *Nos. 38 and 42*). It was based on the experience of World War I. The alterations that were adopted were of lesser importance than those of 1906. The division into chapter and articles remained essentially unchanged. New provisions were inserted concerning the protection of medical aircraft and the use of the distinctive emblem in time of peace. Furthermore, the emblems of the red crescent and of the red lion and sun were recognized for countries which already used those signs in place of the red cross. The provision concerning repatriation of the seriously wounded and seriously sick prisoners were transferred to the Convention on prisoners of war.

The Convention of 1929 was replaced by the Geneva Convention (I) of 1949 (*No. 49*).

ENTRY INTO FORCE: 19 June 1931.

AUTHENTIC TEXT: French. The translation below is reprinted from *LNTS*, Vol. 118, pp. 303–341.

TEXT PUBLISHED IN: *Actes de la Conférence diplomatique convoquée par le Conseil fédéral suisse pour la révision de la Convention du 6 juillet 1906 pour l'amélioration du sort des blessés et malades dans les armées en campagne et pour l'élaboration d'une Convention relative au traitement des prisonniers de guerre et réunie à Genève du 1 au 27 juillet 1929*, Genève 1930, pp. 655–680 (French); *LNTS*, Vol. 118, pp. 303–341, No. 2733 (Eng., French); Martens, *NRGT*, 3ème série, Vol. XXX, pp. 827–846 (French); Deltenre, pp. 460–489 (Engl., French, German, Dutch); Hudson, Vol. V, pp. 1–20 (Engl., French); *Fontes Historiae Juris Gentium*, Vol. III/2, pp. 1202–1211 (Engl., French, German – extract); *Handbook of the International Red Cross*, 1953, pp. 59–70 (Engl.); *Manuel de la Croix-Rouge internationale*, 1953, pp. 64–70 (French); *Manual de la Cruz Roja internacional*, 1953, pp. 61–72 (Span.); *GBTS*, 1931, No. 36, Cmd. 3940 (Engl., French); Wilson-Tucker, pp. CXXXIV–CXIIV (Engl.); *US Statutes at Large*, Vol. 47, pp. 2074–2101 (Engl., French); *Droit des conflits armés*, pp. 397–413 (French); Malloy, Vol. IV, pp. 5209–5223 (Engl.); Bevans, Vol. II, pp. 965–982 (Engl.); *AJIL*, Vol. 27, 1933, Suppl., pp. 43–59 (Engl.); Friedman, pp. 471–487 (Engl.); *Sobranie zakonov*, 10 March 1932, No. 4, Vol. II, No. 60, 1932 (Russ.); Arellano, pp. 388–390 (Span. – extracts); ICRC website: www.icrc.org/ihl.nsf.

TABLE OF CONTENTS

* * *

[List of contracting parties]

Being equally animated by the desire to lessen, so far as lies in their power, the evils inseparable from war and desiring, for this purpose, to perfect and complete the provisions agreed to at Geneva on 22 August 1864, and 6 July 1906, for the amelioration of the condition of the wounded and sick in armies in the field,

Have resolved to conclude a new Convention for that purpose and have appointed as their Plenipotentiaries:

[Here follow the names of plenipotentiaries]

Who, after having communicated to each other their full powers, found in good and due form, have agreed as follows.

Chapter I. Wounded and Sick

Article 1. Officers and soldiers and other persons officially attached to the armed forces who are wounded or sick shall be respected and protected in all circumstances; they shall be treated with humanity and cared for medically, without distinction of nationality, by the belligerent in whose power they may be.

Nevertheless, the belligerent who is compelled to abandon wounded or sick to the enemy, shall, as far as military exigencies permit, leave with them a portion of his medical personnel and material to help with their treatment.

Art. 2. Except as regards the treatment to be provided for them in virtue of the preceding Article, the wounded and sick of an army who fall into the hands of the enemy shall be prisoners of war, and the general provisions of international law concerning prisoners of war shall be applicable to them.

Belligerents shall, however, be free to prescribe, for the benefit of wounded or sick prisoners such arrangements as they may think fit beyond the limits of the existing obligations.

Art. 3. After each engagement the occupant of the field of battle shall take measures to search for the wounded and dead, and to protect them against pillage and maltreatment. Whenever circumstances permit, a local armistice or a suspension of fire shall be arranged to permit the removal of the wounded remaining between the lines.

Art. 4. Belligerents shall communicate to each other reciprocally, as soon as possible, the names of the wounded, sick and dead, collected or discovered, together with any indications which may assist in their identification.

They shall establish and transmit to each other the certificates of death.

They shall likewise collect and transmit to each other all articles of a personal nature found on the field of battle or on the dead, especially one half of their identity discs, the other hall to remain attached to the body.

They shall ensure that the burial or cremation of the dead is preceded by a careful, and if possible medical, examination of the bodies, with a view to confirming death, establishing identity and enabling a report to be made.

They shall further ensure that the dead are honourably interred, that their graves are respected and marked so that they may always be found.

To this end, at the commencement of hostilities, they shall organize officially a graves registration service, to render eventual exhumations possible, and to ensure the identification of bodies whatever may be the subsequent site of the grave.

After the cessation of hostilities they shall exchange the list of graves and of dead interred in their cemeteries and elsewhere.

Art. 5. The military authorities may appeal to the charitable zeal of the inhabitants to collect and afford medical assistance under their direction to the wounded or sick of armies, and may accord to persons who have responded to this appeal special protection and certain facilities.

Chapter II. Medical Formations and Establishments

Art. 6. Mobile medical formations, that is to say, those which are intended to accompany armies in the field, and the fixed establishments of the medical service shall be respected and protected by the belligerents.

Art. 7. The protection to which medical formations and establishments are entitled shall cease if they are made use of to commit acts harmful to the enemy.

Art. 8. The following conditions are not considered to be of such a nature as to deprive a medical formation or establishment of the protection guaranteed by Article 6:

1. That the personnel of the formation or establishment is armed, and that they use the arms in their own defence or in that of the sick and wounded in charge;
2. That in the absence of armed orderlies the formation or establishment is protected by a piquet or by sentries;
3. That small arms and ammunition taken from the wounded and sick, which have not yet been transferred to the proper service, are found in the formation or establishment;
4. That personnel and material of the veterinary service are found in the formation or establishment, without forming an integral part of the same.

Chapter III. Personnel

Art. 9.[1] The personnel engaged exclusively in the collection, transport and treatment of the wounded and sick, and in the administration of medical formations and establishments, and chaplains attached to armies, shall be respected and protected under all circumstances. If they fall into the hands of the enemy they shall not be treated as prisoners of war.

Soldiers specially trained to be employed, in case of necessity, as auxiliary nurses or stretcher-bearers for the collection, transport and treatment of the wounded and sick, and furnished with a proof of identity, shall enjoy the same treatment as the permanent medical personnel if they are taken prisoners while carrying out these functions.

Art. 10. The personnel of Voluntary Aid Societies, duly recognized and authorized by their Government, who may be employed on the same duties as those of the personnel mentioned in the first paragraph of Article 9, are placed on the same footing as the personnel contemplated in that paragraph, provided that the personnel of such societies are subject to military law and regulations.

Each High Contracting Party shall notify to the other, either in time of peace or at the commencement of or during the course of hostilities, but in every case before actually employing them, the names of the societies which it has authorized, under its responsibility, to render assistance to the regular medical service of its armed forces.

Art. 11. A recognized society of a neutral country can only afford the assistance of its medical personnel and formations to a belligerent with the previous consent of its own Government and the authorization of the belligerent concerned.

The belligerent who accepts such assistance is bound to notify the enemy thereof before making any use of it.

Art. 12. The persons designated in Articles 9, 10 and 11 may not be retained after they have fallen into the hands of the enemy.

---

[1] For declaration in respect of this article by the Union of Soviet Socialist Republics, see p. 420.

In the absence of an agreement to the contrary, they shall be sent back to the belligerent to which they belong as soon as a route for their return shall be open and military considerations permit.

Pending their return they shall continue to carry out their duties under the direction of the enemy; they shall preferably be engaged in the care of the wounded and sick of the belligerent to which they belong.

On their departure, they shall take with them the effects, instruments, arms and means of transport belonging to them.

Art. 13. Belligerents shall secure to the personnel mentioned in Articles 9, 10 and 11, while in their hands, the same food, the same lodging, the same allowances and the same pay as are granted to the corresponding personnel of their own armed forces.

At the outbreak of hostilities the belligerents will notify one another of the grades of their respective medical personnel.

Chapter IV. Buildings and Material

Art. 14. Mobile medical formations, of whatsoever kind, shall retain, if they fall into the hands of the enemy, their equipment and stores, their means of transport and the drivers employed.

Nevertheless, the competent military authority shall be free to use the equipment and stores for the care of the wounded and sick; it shall be restored under the conditions laid down for the medical personnel, and as far as possible at the same time.

Art. 15. The buildings and material of the fixed medical establishments of the army shall be subject to the laws of war, but may not be diverted from their purpose so long as they are necessary for the wounded and sick.

Nevertheless, the commanders of troops in the field may make use of them, in case of urgent military necessity, provided that they make previous arrangements for the welfare of the wounded and sick who are being treated therein.

Art. 16. The buildings of aid societies which are admitted to the privileges of the Convention shall be regarded as private property.

The material of these societies, wherever it may be, shall similarly be considered as private property.

The right of requisition, recognized for belligerents by the laws and customs of war, shall only be exercised in case of urgent necessity and only after the welfare of the wounded and sick has been secured.

Chapter V. Medical Transport

Art. 17. Vehicles equipped for the evacuation of wounded and sick, proceeding singly or in convoy, shall be treated as mobile medical formations, subject to the following special provisions:

A belligerent intercepting vehicles of medical transport, singly or in convoy, may, if military exigencies demand, stop them, and break up the convoy, provided he takes charge in every case of the wounded and sick who are in it. He can only use the vehicles in the sector where they have been intercepted, and exclusively for medical requirements. These vehicles, as soon as they are no longer required for local use, shall be given up in accordance with the conditions laid down in Article 14.

The military personnel in charge of the transport and furnished for this purpose with authority in due form, shall be sent back in accordance with the conditions prescribed in Article 12 for medical personnel, subject to the condition of the last paragraph of Article 18.

All means of transport specially organized for evacuation and the material used in equipping these means of transport belonging to the medical service shall be restored in accordance with the provisions of Chapter IV.

Military means of transport other than those of the medical service may be captured, with their teams.

The civilian personnel and all means of transport obtained by requisition shall be subject to the general rules of international law.

Art. 18. Aircraft used as means of medical transport shall enjoy the protection of the Convention during the period in which they are reserved exclusively for the evacuation of wounded and sick and the transport of medical personnel and material.

They shall be painted white and shall bear, clearly marked, the distinctive emblem prescribed in Article 19, side by side with their national colours, on their lower and upper surfaces.

In the absence of special and express permission, flying over the firing line, and over the zone situated in front of clearing or dressing stations, and generally over all enemy territory or territory occupied by the enemy, is prohibited.

Medical aircraft shall obey every summons to land.

In the event of a landing thus imposed, or of an involuntary landing in enemy territory and territory occupied by the enemy, the wounded and sick, as well as the medical personnel and material, including the aircraft, shall enjoy the privileges of the present Convention.

The pilot, mechanics and wireless telegraph operators captured shall be sent back, on condition that they shall be employed until the close of hostilities in the medical service only.

Chapter VI. The Distinctive Emblem

Art. 19. As compliment to Switzerland, the heraldic emblem of the red cross on a white ground, formed by reversing the Federal colours, is retained as the emblem and distinctive sign of the medical service of armed forces.

Nevertheless, in the case of countries which already use, in place of the red cross, the red crescent or the red lion and sun on a white ground as a distinctive sign, these emblems are also recognized by the terms of the present Convention.

Art. 20. The emblem shall figure on the flags, armlets, and on all material belonging to the medical service, with the permission of the competent military authority.

Art. 21. The personnel protected in pursuance of Articles 9 (paragraph 1), 10 and 11, shall wear, affixed to the left arm, an armlet bearing the distinctive sign, issued and stamped by military authority.

The personnel mentioned in Article 9, paragraphs 1 and 2, shall be provided with a certificate of identity, consisting either of an entry in their small book (paybook) or a special document.

The persons mentioned in Articles 10 and 11 who have no military uniform shall be furnished by the competent military authority with a certificate of identity with photograph, certifying their status as medical personnel.

The certificates of identity shall be uniform and of the same pattern in each army.

In no case may the medical personnel be deprived of their armlets or the certificates of identity belonging to them.

In case of loss they have the right to obtain duplicates.

Art. 22. The distinctive flag of the Convention shall be hoisted only over such medical formations and establishments as are entitled to be respected under the Convention and with the consent of the military authorities. In fixed establishments it shall be, and in mobile formations it may be, accompanied by the national flag of the belligerent to whom the formation or establishment belongs.

Nevertheless, medical formations which have fallen into the hands of the enemy, so long as they are in that situation, shall not fly any other flag than that of the Convention.

Belligerents shall take the necessary steps, so far as military exigencies permit, to make clearly visible to the enemy forces, whether land, air or sea, the distinctive emblems indicating medical formations and establishments, in order to avoid the possibility of any offensive action.

Art. 23. The medical units belonging to neutral countries which shall have been authorized to lend their services under the conditions laid down in Article 11, shall fly, along with the flag of the Convention, the national flag of the belligerent to whose army they are attached.

They shall also have the right, so long as they shall lend their services to a belligerent, to fly their national flag.

The provisions of the second paragraph of the preceding article are applicable to them.

Art. 24. The emblem of the red cross on a white ground and the words "Red Cross" or "Geneva Cross" shall not be used either in time of peace or in time of war, except to protect or to indicate the medical formations and establishments and the personnel and material protected by the Convention.

The same shall apply, as regards the emblems mentioned in Article 19, paragraph 2, in respect of the countries which use them.

The Voluntary Aid Societies mentioned in Article 10, may, in accordance with their national legislation, use the distinctive emblem in connection with their humanitarian activities in time of peace.

As an exceptional measure, and with the express authority of one of the national societies of the Red Cross (Red Crescent, Red Lion and Sun), use may be made of the emblem of the Convention in time of peace to mark the position of aid stations exclusively reserved for the purpose of giving free treatment to the wounded or the sick.

Chapter VII. Application and Execution of the Convention

Art. 25. The provisions of the present Convention shall be respected by the High Contracting Parties in all circumstances.

If, in time of war, a belligerent is not a party to the Convention, its provisions shall, nevertheless, be binding as between all the belligerents who are parties thereto.

Art 26. The Commanders-in-Chief of belligerent armies shall arrange the details for carrying out the preceding articles as well as for cases not provided for in accordance with the instructions of their respective Governments and in conformity with the general principles of the present Convention.

Art. 27. The High Contracting Parties shall take the necessary steps to instruct their troops, and in particular the personnel protected, in the provisions of the present Convention, and to bring them to the notice of the civil population.

Chapter VIII. Suppression of Abuses and Infractions

Art. 28.[2] The Governments of the High Contracting Parties whose legislation is not at present adequate for the purpose, shall adopt or propose to their legislatures the measures necessary to prevent at all times:

(a) The use of the emblem or designation "Red Cross" or "Geneva Cross" by private individuals or associations, firms or companies, other than those entitled thereto under the present Convention, as well as the use of any sign or designation constituting an imitation, for commercial or any other purposes;

(b) By reason of the compliment paid to Switzerland by the adoption of the reversed Federal colours, the use by private individuals or associations, firms or companies

[2] For reservations in respect of this article by Australia, Canada, Great Britain, India, Ireland, Japan and New Zealand. see pp. 419–420.

of the arms of the Swiss Confederation or marks constituting an imitation, whether as trademarks or as parts of such marks, for a purpose contrary to commercial honesty, or in circumstances capable of wounding Swiss national sentiment.

The prohibition in (a) of the use of marks or designations constituting an imitation of the emblem or designation of "Red Cross" or "Geneva Cross," as well as the prohibition in (b) of the use of the arms of the Swiss Confederation or marks constituting an imitation, shall take effect as from the date fixed by each legislature, and not later than five years after the coming into force of the present Convention. From the date of such coming into force, it shall no longer be lawful to adopt a trademark in contravention of these rules.

Art. 29. The Governments of the High Contracting Parties shall also propose to their legislatures should their penal laws be inadequate, the necessary measures for the repression in time of war of any act contrary to the provisions of the present Convention.

They shall communicate to one another, through the Swiss Federal Council, the provisions relative to such repression not later than five years from the ratification of the present Convention.

Art. 30. On the request of a belligerent, an enquiry shall be instituted, in a manner to be decided between the interested parties, concerning any alleged violation of the Convention; when such violation has been established the belligerents shall put an end to and repress it as promptly as possible.

Final Provisions

Art. 31. The present Convention, which shall bear this day's date, may be signed, up to the 1 February 1930, on behalf of all the countries represented at the Conference which opened at Geneva on 1 July 1929, as well as by countries not represented at that Conference but which were parties to the Geneva Conventions of 1864 and 1906.

Art. 32. The present Convention shall be ratified as soon as possible.

The ratifications shall be deposited at Berne.

A *procès-verbal* of the deposit of each instrument of ratification shall be drawn up, one copy of which, certified to be correct, shall be transmitted by the Swiss Federal Council to the Governments of all countries on whose behalf the Convention has been signed, or whose accession has been notified.

Art. 33. The present Convention shall come into force six months after not less than two instruments of ratification have been deposited.

Thereafter, it shall enter into force for each High Contracting Party six months after the deposit of its instrument of ratification.

Art. 34. The present Convention shall replace the Conventions of 22 August 1864, and 6 July 1906, in relations between the High Contracting Parties.

Art. 35. From the date of its coming into force, the present Convention shall be open to accession duly notified on behalf of any country on whose behalf this Convention has not been signed.

Art. 36. Accessions shall be notified in writing to the Swiss Federal Council, and shall take effect six months after the date on which they are received.

The Swiss Federal Council shall communicate the accessions to the Governments of all the countries on whose behalf the Convention has been signed or whose accession has been notified.

Art. 37. A state of war shall give immediate effect to ratifications deposited and accessions notified by the belligerent Powers before or after the outbreak of hostilities. The communication of ratifications or accessions received from Powers in a state of war shall be made by the Swiss Federal Council by the quickest method.

Art. 38. Each of the High Contracting Parties shall be at liberty to denounce the present Convention. The denunciation shall not take effect until one year after the notification thereof in writing has been made to the Swiss Federal Council. The latter shall communicate such notification to the Governments of all the High Contracting Parties.

The denunciation shall only have effect in respect of the High Contracting Party which has made notification thereof.

Moreover, this denunciation shall not take effect during a war in which the denouncing Power is involved. In such a case the present Convention shall continue to be binding beyond the period of one year, until the conclusion of peace.

Art. 39. A certified copy of the present Convention shall be deposited in the archives of the League of Nations by the Swiss Federal Council. Similarly, ratifications, accessions and denunciations which shall be notified to the Swiss Federal Council shall be communicated by them to the League of Nations.

In witness whereof, the above-named Plenipotentiaries have signed the present Convention.

Done at Geneva the twenty-seventh July, one thousand nine hundred and twenty-nine, in a single copy, which shall remain deposited in the archives of the Swiss Confederation, and of which copies, certified to be correct, shall be transmitted to the Governments of all the countries invited to the Conference.

[Here follow signatures]

SIGNATURES, RATIFICATIONS AND ACCESSIONS[1]

State	*Signature*	*Ratification, Accession or Notification of Continuity (C)*
Argentina	–	5 March 1945
Australia	27 July 1929 *Res.*	23 June 1931 *Res.*
Austria	27 July 1929	13 March 1936
Belgium	27 July 1929	12 May 1932
Bolivia	27 July 1929	13 August 1940
Brazil	27 July 1929	23 March 1932
Bulgaria	27 July 1929	13 October 1937
Burma[2]	–	1 April 1937 (C)
Canada	27 July 1929	20 February 1933
Chile	27 July 1929	1 June 1933
China	27 July 1929	19 November 1935
Colombia	27 July 1929	–
Cuba	27 July 1929	–
Czechoslovakia	27 July 1929	12 October 1937
Denmark	27 July 1929	5 August 1932
Dominican Republic	27 July 1929	–
Egypt	27 July 1929	25 July 1933
El Salvador	–	22 April 1942

1 Based on a communication from the Swiss Federal Department of Foreign Affairs of 25 June 1999. See also ICRC website: www.icrc.org/ihl.nsf.

2 Burma, formerly a party to this Convention by reason of its inclusion in India, was separated from the Indian Empire on 1 April 1937. Having on that date acquired the status of a British overseas territory, it is now to be considered a party to the Convention in virtue of the United Kingdom's signature and ratification thereof. (Registered at the Secretariat of the League of Nations on 26 November 1938 on the request of the Swiss Federal Council in its capacity of depositary (*LNTS*, Vol. 193, 1938, p. 270).)

State	*Signature*	*Ratification, Accession or Notification of Continuity (C)*
Estonia	27 July 1929	11 June 1936[3]
Ethiopia	–	15 July 1935
Fiji	–	9 August 1971 (C)[4]
Finland	27 July 1929	8 February 1936
France	27 July 1929	21 August 1935
Germany	27 July 1929	21 February 1934
Great Britain and Northern Ireland[5]	27 July 1929	23 June 1931
Greece	27 July 1929	28 May 1935
Hungary	27 July 1929	10 September 1936
India	27 July 1929	23 June 1931
Indonesia	–	5 June 1950 (C)[6]
Iraq	–	25 May 1934
Ireland (Irish Free State)	27 July 1929	–
Israel	–	3 August 1948
Italy	27 July 1929	24 March 1931
Japan	27 July 1929	18 December 1934
Latvia	27 July 1929	14 October 1931[7]
Lebanon	–	12 June 1946
Liechtenstein	–	11 January 1944
Lithuania	–	27 February 1939[8]
Luxemburg	27 July 1929	–
Mexico	27 July 1929	1 August 1932
*S*Monaco	–	6 January 1948
Netherlands	27 July 1929	5 October 1932
New Zealand	27 July 1929	23 June 1931
Nicaragua	27 July 1929	–

3 On 19 November 1991, Estonia deposited a declaration of continuity which took effect retroactively on 6 September 1991, the date on which the Soviet Union recognized the independence of the Baltic states (Note of 8 January 1992 from the Swiss Federal Department of Foreign Affairs to the ICRC and Notification from the Swiss Federal Department of Foreign Affairs to the governments of state parties to the Geneva Conventions of 1929 and 1949, of 10 February 1992). On 18 January 1993, Estonia deposited the instrument of accession to the Geneva Conventions of 1949 which took effect from 18 July 1993 and is from that date party to the Geneva Convention (I) for the amelioration of the Condition of the Wounded and Sick in Armed Forces in the Field. It replaces from that date the present 1929 Convention.

4 With effect from 10 October 1970.

5 The instrument of ratification was deposited in the name of Great Britain and Northern Ireland and all parts of the British Empire not separate members of the League of Nations.

6 Application on the territory of Indonesia and on its behalf. Declaration signed at the Swiss Political Department on 5 June 1950 (*UNTS*, Vol. 76, 1950, p. 286).

7 On 26 November 1991, Latvia deposited a declaration of continuity dated 15 November 1991, which took effect retroactively on 6 September 1991, the date on which the Soviet Union recognized the independence of the Baltic states (note of 8 January 1992 from the Swiss Federal Department of Foreign Affairs to the ICRC and notification from the Swiss Federal Department of Foreign Affairs to the governments of states parties to the Geneva Conventions of 1929 and 1949, of 10 February 1992). On 24 December 1991, Latvia deposited the instrument of accession to the Geneva Conventions of 1949 which took effect from 24 June 1992 and is from that date party to the Geneva Convention (I) for the amelioration of the Condition of the Wounded and Sick in Armed Forces in the Field. It replaces from that date the present 1929 Convention (Letter of the Swiss Federal Department of Foreign Affairs to the ICRC of 28 January 1992).

8 On 20 December 1991, Lithuania deposited a declaration of continuity dated 10 October 1991, which took effect retroactively on 6 September 1991, the date on which the Soviet Union recognized the independence of the Baltic states (note of 8 January 1992 from the Swiss Federal Department of Foreign Affairs to the ICRC and notification from the Swiss

State	*Signature*	*Ratification, Accession or Notification of Continuity (C)*
Norway	27 July 1929	24 June 1931
Pakistan	–	2 February 1948
Papua New Guinea	–	26 May 1976 (C)[9]
Persia	27 July 1929	–
Peru	–	10 March 1933
Philippines	–	1 April 1947
Poland	27 July 1929	29 June 1932
Portugal	27 July 1929	8 June 1931
Romania	27 July 1929	24 October 1931
San Marino	–	12 October 1950
Siam (Thailand)	27 July 1929	3 June 1939
Spain	27 July 1929[10]	6 August 1930
Sweden	27 July 1929	3 July 1931
Switzerland	27 July 1929[11]	19 December 1930
Syria	–	4 July 1946
Transjordan	–	20 November 1948 (C)
Turkey	27 July 1929	10 March 1934
Union of South Africa	27 July 1929	23 June 1931
Union of Soviet Socialist Republics	–	26 September 1931
United States of America	27 July 1929	4 February 1932
Uruguay	27 July 1929	–
Venezuela	27 July 1929	15 July 1944
Yugoslavia	27 July 1929	20 May 1931

RESERVATIONS

AUSTRALIA (*reservation made on signature and confirmed on ratification*)
I declare that my signature of this Convention in respect of the Commonwealth of Australia is subject to the understanding that the Government of the Commonwealth of Australia will interpret Article 28 of the Convention in the sense that the legislative measures contemplated by that Article may provide that private individuals, associations, firms or companies who have used the Arms of the Swiss Confederation, or marks constituting an imitation thereof, for any lawful purpose before the coming into force of the present Convention shall not be prevented from continuing to use such Arms or marks for the same purpose.

CANADA (*reservation made on signature*)
I declare that my signature of this Convention in respect of *Canada* is subject to the understanding that the Government of the Dominion of Canada will interpret Article 28

cont.
Federal Department of Foreign Affairs to the governments of states parties to the Geneva Conventions of 1929 and 1949, of 10 February 1992). On 3 October 1996, Lithuania deposited the instrument of accession to the Geneva Conventions of 1949 which took effect from 4 April 1997 and is from that date party to the Geneva Convention (I) for the Amelioration of the Condition of the Wounded and Sick in Armed Forces in the Field. It replaces from that date the present 1929 Convention (letter of the Swiss Federal Department of Foreign Affairs to the ICRC).

9 With effect from 16 September 1975.

10 Signed *ad referendum*.

11 In application of Article 10 of the present Convention, the Swiss Federal Political Department informed the Secretariat of the League of Nations by a note of 30 January 1937 that the Swiss Federal Council authorized the Swiss Red Cross to render assistance to the official medical service of the Swiss Army (*LNTS*, Vol. 177, 1937, p. 407).

of the Convention in the sense that the legislative measures contemplated by that article may provide that private individuals, associations, firms or companies who have used the Arms of the Swiss Confederation, or marks constituting an imitation thereof, for any lawful purpose before the coming into force of the present Convention shall not be prevented from continuing to use such Arms or marks for the same purpose.

GREAT BRITAIN (*reservation made on signature*)
I declare that my signature of this Convention in respect of *Great Britain and Northern Ireland* and all parts of the British Empire which are not separate Members of the League of Nations is subject to the understanding that His Britannic Majesty will interpret Article 28 of the Convention in the sense that the legislative measures contemplated by that article may provide that private individuals, associations, firms or companies who have used the Arms of the Swiss Confederation, or marks constituting an imitation thereof, for any lawful purpose before the coming into force of the present Convention shall not be prevented from continuing to use such Arms or marks for the same purpose.

INDIA (*reservation made on signature*)
I declare that my signature of this Convention in respect of *India* is subject to the understanding that the Government of India will interpret Article 28 of the Convention in the sense that the legislative measures contemplated by that article may provide that private individuals, associations, firms or companies who have used the Arms of the Swiss Confederation, or marks constituting an imitation thereof, for any lawful purpose before the coming into force of the present Convention shall not be prevented from continuing to use such Arms or marks for the same purpose.

IRISH FREE STATE (*reservation made on signature*)
I declare that my signature of this Convention in respect of the *Irish Free State* is subject to the understanding that the Irish Free State will interpret Article 28 of the Convention in the sense that the legislative measures contemplated by that article may provide that private individuals, associations, firms or companies who have used the Arms of the Swiss Confederation, or marks constituting an imitation thereof, for any lawful purpose before the coming into force of the present Convention shall not be prevented from continuing to use such Arms or marks for the same purpose.

JAPAN (*reservation made on signature*)
While accepting the provisions of Article 28, *Japan* makes reservations as regards the date of the coming into force of the prohibitioncontemplated by clause (b) of the said Article.

Japan understands that this prohibition does not apply to Arms and marks which have been in use or registered before its coming into force.

The delegates of Japan sign the present Convention subject to the above-mentioned reservations.

NEW ZEALAND (*reservation made on signature*)
I declare that my signature of this Convention in respect of *New Zealand*, is subject to the understanding that the Government of New Zealand will interpret Article 28 of the Convention in the sense that the legislative measures contemplated by that article may provide that private individuals, associations, firms or companies who have used the Arms of the Swiss Confederation, or marks constituting an imitation thereof, for any lawful purpose before the coming into force of the present Convention shall not be prevented from continuing to use such Arms or marks for the same purpose.

UNION OF SOVIET SOCIALIST REPUBLICS (*declaration made on accession*)
The act of accession was accompanied by the following declaration by which Article 9 of the Convention is understood by the Government of the Union in the sense that all military personnel on active service but affected to medical formations and establishments will be subject to the treatment provided for in the above-mentioned Article.

No. 46

CONVENTION RELATIVE TO THE TREATMENT OF PRISONERS OF WAR

Signed at Geneva, 27 July 1929

INTRODUCTORY NOTE: Provisions concerning the treatment of prisoners of war are contained in the Hague Regulations of 1899 and 1907 (*Nos. 7 and 8*). In the course of World War I they proved to be insufficient. Their deficiencies could partly be overcome by special agreements made by belligerents in Berne in 1917 and 1918. In 1921, the International Red Cross Conference held at Geneva expressed the wish that a special convention on the treatment of prisoners of war be adopted. The International Committee of the Red Cross drew up a draft convention which was submitted to the Diplomatic Conference convened at Geneva in 1929.

The Convention does not replace but only completes the provisions of the Hague Regulations. The most important innovations consisted in the prohibition of reprisals and collective penalties, the organization of prisoners' work, the designation, by the prisoners, of representatives and the control exercised by protecting powers.

The Convention of 1929 was replaced by the Geneva Convention (III) of 1949 (see *No. 51*).

ENTRY INTO FORCE: 19 June 1931.

AUTHENTIC TEXT: French. The translation below is reprinted from *LNTS*, Vol. 118, pp. 343–411.

TEXT PUBLISHED IN: *Actes de la Conférence diplomatique convoquée par le Conseil fédéral suisse pour la révision de la Convention du 6 juillet 1906 pour l'amélioration du sort des blessés et malades dans les armées en campagne et pour l'élaboration d'une convention relative au traitement des prisonniers de guerre et réunie à Genève du 1 au 27 juillet 1929*, Genève 1930, pp. 681–724 (French); *LNTS*, Vol. 118, pp. 343–411, No. 2734 (Engl., French); Martens, *NRGT*, 3ème série, Vol. XXX, pp. 846–881 (French); Deltenre, pp. 490–557 (Engl., French, German, Dutch); Hudson, Vol. V, pp. 20–63 (Engl., French); *Fontes Historiae Juris Gentium*, Vol. III/2, pp. 1201–1202 (Engl., French, German – extract); *Handbook of the International Red Cross*, 1953, pp. 71–97 (Engl.); *Manuel de la Croix-Rouge internationale*, 1953, pp. 77–106 (French); *Manual de la Cruz Roja internacional*, 1953, pp. 73–102 (Span.); *GBTS*, 1931, Vol. 37, Cmd. 3941 (Engl., French); *BFSP*, Vol. 130, pp. 239–265 (French); *US Statutes at Large*, Vol. 47, pp. 2021–2073 (Engl., French); *Droit des conflits armés*, pp. 415–447 (French); Malloy, Vol. IV, pp. 5524–5250 (Engl.); Bevans, Vol. II, pp. 932–964 (Engl.); *AJIL*, Vol. 27, 1933, Supp., pp. 59–91 (Engl.); Friedman, pp. 488–522 (Engl.); Arellano, pp. 390–394 (Span.– extract); ICRC website: www.icrc.org/ihl.nsf.

TABLE OF CONTENTS

ANNEX TO THE CONVENTION OF 27 JULY 1929 RELATIVE TO THE TREATMENT OF PRISONERS OF WAR

* * *

[List of contracting parties]

Recognizing that, in the extreme event of a war, it will be the duty of every Power, to mitigate as far as possible, the inevitable rigours thereof and to alleviate the condition of prisoners of war;

Being desirous of developing the principles which have inspired the international conventions of The Hague, in particular the Convention concerning the Laws and Customs of War and the Regulations thereunto annexed,

Have resolved to conclude a Convention for that purpose and have appointed as their Plenipotentiaries:

[Here follow the names of plenipotentiaries]

Who, having communicated their full powers, found in good and due form, have agreed as follows.

PART I. GENERAL PROVISIONS

Article 1. The present Convention shall apply without prejudice to the stipulations of Part VII:

(1) To all persons referred to in Articles 1, 2 and 3 of the Regulations annexed to the Hague Convention (IV) of 18 October 1907, concerning the Laws and Customs of War on Land, who are captured by the enemy.

(2) To all persons belonging to the armed forces of belligerents who are captured by the enemy in the course of operations of maritime or aerial war, subject to such exceptions (derogations) as the conditions of such capture render inevitable. Nevertheless these exceptions shall not infringe the fundamental principles of the present Convention; they shall cease from the moment when the captured persons shall have reached a prisoners of war camp.

Art. 2. Prisoners of war are in the power of the hostile Government, but not of the individuals or formation which captured them.

They shall at all times be humanely treated and protected, particularly against acts of violence, from insults and from public curiosity.

Measures of reprisal against them are forbidden.

Art. 3. Prisoners of war are entitled to respect for their persons and honour. Women shall be treated with all consideration due to their sex.

Prisoners retain their full civil capacity.

Art. 4. The detaining Power is required to provide for the maintenance of prisoners of war in its charge.

Differences of treatment between prisoners are permissible only if such differences are based on the military rank, the state of physical or mental health, the professional abilities, or the sex of those who benefit from them.

PART II. CAPTURE

Art. 5. Every prisoner of war is required to declare, if he is interrogated on the subject, his true names and rank, or his regimental number.

If he infringes this rule, he exposes himself to a restriction of the privileges accorded to prisoners of his category.

No pressure shall be exercised on prisoners to obtain information regarding the situation in their armed forces or their country. Prisoners who refuse to reply may not be threatened, insulted, or exposed to unpleasantness or disadvantages of any kind whatsoever.

If, by reason of his physical or mental condition, a prisoner is incapable of stating his identity, he shall be handed over to the Medical Service.

Art. 6. All personal effects and articles in personal use – except arms, horses, military equipment and military papers – shall remain in the possession of prisoners of war, as well as their metal helmets and gas-masks.

Sums of money carried by prisoners may only be taken from them on the order of an officer and after the amount has been recorded. A receipt shall be given for them. Sums thus impounded shall be placed to the account of each prisoner.

Their identity tokens, badges of rank, decorations and articles of value may not be taken from prisoners.

PART III. CAPTIVITY

Section I. Evacuation of Prisoners of War

Art. 7. As soon as possible after their capture, prisoners of war shall be evacuated to depots sufficiently removed from the fighting zone for them to be out of danger.

Only prisoners who, by reason of their wounds or maladies, would run greater risks by being evacuated than by remaining may be kept temporarily in a dangerous zone.

Prisoners shall not be unnecessarily exposed to danger while awaiting evacuation from a fighting zone.

The evacuation of prisoners on foot shall in normal circumstances be effected by stages of not more than 20 kilometres per day, unless the necessity for reaching water and food depôts requires longer stages.

Art. 8. Belligerents are required to notify each other of all captures of prisoners as soon as possible, through the intermediary of the Information Bureaux organised in accordance with Article 77. They are likewise required to inform each other of the official addresses to which letter from the prisoners' families may be addressed to the prisoners of war.

As soon as possible, every prisoner shall be enabled to correspond personally with his family, in accordance with the conditions prescribed in Article 36 and the following Articles.

As regards prisoners captured at sea, the provisions of the present article shall be observed as soon as possible after arrival in port.

Section II. Prisoners of War Camps

Art. 9. Prisoners of war may be interned in a town, fortress or other place, and may be required not to go beyond certain fixed limits. They may also be interned in fenced camps; they shall not be confined or imprisoned except as a measure indispensable for safety or health, and only so long as circumstances exist which necessitate such a measure.

Prisoners captured in districts which are unhealthy or whose climate is deleterious to persons coming from temperate climates shall be removed as soon as possible to a more favourable climate.

Belligerents shall as far as possible avoid bringing together in the same camp prisoners of different races or nationalities.

No prisoner may at any time be sent to an area where he would be exposed to the fire of the fighting zone, or be employed to render by his presence certain points or areas immune from bombardment.

Chapter 1. Installation of camps

Art. 10. Prisoners of war shall be lodged in buildings or huts which afford all possible safeguards as regards hygiene and salubrity.

The premises must be entirely free from damp, and adequately heated and lighted. All precautions shall be taken against the danger of fire.

As regards dormitories, their total area, minimum cubic air space, fittings and bedding material, the conditions shall be the same as for the depot troops of the detaining Power.

Chapter 2. Food and clothing of prisoners of war

Art. 11. The food ration of prisoners of war shall be equivalent in quantity and quality to that of the depot troops.

Prisoners shall also be afforded the means of preparing for themselves such additional articles of food as they may possess.

Sufficient drinking water shall be supplied to them. The use of tobacco shall be authorized. Prisoners may be employed in the kitchens.

All collective disciplinary measures affecting food are prohibited.

Art. 12. Clothing, underwear and footwear shall be supplied to prisoners of war by the detaining Power. The regular replacement and repair of such articles shall be assured. Workers shall also receive working kit wherever the nature of the work requires it.

In all camps, canteens shall be installed at which prisoners shall be able to procure, at the local market price, food commodities and ordinary articles.

The profits accruing to the administrations of the camps from the canteens shall be utilised for the benefit of the prisoners.

Chapter 3. Hygiene in camps

Art. 13. Belligerents shall be required to take all necessary hygienic measures to ensure the cleanliness and salubrity of camps and to prevent epidemics.

Prisoners of war shall have for their use, day and night, conveniences which conform to the rules of hygiene and are maintained in a constant state of cleanliness.

In addition and without prejudice to the provision as far as possible of baths and shower-baths in the camps, the prisoners shall be provided with a sufficient quantity of water for their bodily cleanliness.

They shall have facilities for engaging in physical exercises and obtaining the benefit of being out of doors.

Art. 14. Each camp shall possess an infirmary, where prisoners of war shall receive attention of any kind of which they may be in need. If necessary, isolation establishments shall be reserved for patients suffering from infectious and contagious diseases.

The expenses of treatment, including those of temporary remedial apparatus, shall be borne by the detaining Power.

Belligerents shall be required to issue, on demand, to any prisoner treated, an official statement indicating the nature and duration of his illness and of the treatment received.

It shall be permissible for belligerents mutually to authorize each other, by means of special agreements, to retain in the camps doctors and medical orderlies for the purpose of caring for their prisoner compatriots.

Prisoners who have contracted a serious malady, or whose condition necessitates important surgical treatment, shall be admitted, at the expense of the detaining Power, to any military or civil institution qualified to treat them.

Art. 15. Medical inspections of prisoners of war shall be arranged at least once a month. Their object shall be the supervision of the general state of health and cleanliness, and the detection of infectious and contagious diseases., particularly tuberculosis and venereal complaints.

Chapter 4. Intellectual and moral needs of prisoners of war

Art. 16. Prisoners of war shall be permitted complete freedom in the performance of their religious duties, including attendance at the services of their faith, on the sole condition that they comply with the routine and police regulations prescribed by the military authorities.

Ministers of religion, who are prisoners of war, whatever may be their denomination, shall be allowed freely to minister to their co-religionists.

Art. 17. Belligerents shall encourage as much as possible the organization of intellectual and sporting pursuits by the prisoners of war.

Chapter 5. Internal discipline of camps
Art. 18. Each prisoners of war camp shall be placed under the authority of a responsible officer.

In addition to external marks of respect required by the regulations in force in their own armed forces with regard to their nationals, prisoners of war shall be required to salute all officers of the detaining Power.

Officer prisoners of war shall be required to salute only officers of that Power who are their superiors or equals in rank.

Art. 19. The wearing of badges of rank and decorations shall be permitted.

Art. 20. Regulations, orders, announcements and publications of any kind shall be communicated to prisoners of war in a language which they understand. The same principle shall be applied to questions.

Chapter 6. Special provisions concerning officers and persons of equivalent status
Art. 21. At the commencement of hostilities, belligerents shall be required reciprocally to inform each other of the titles and ranks in use in their respective armed forces, with the view of ensuring equality of treatment between the corresponding ranks of officers and persons of equivalent status.

Officers and persons of equivalent status who are prisoners of war shall be treated with due regard to their rank and age.

Art. 22. In order to ensure the service of officers' camps, soldier prisoners of war of the same armed forces, and as far as possible speaking the same language, shall be detached for service therein in sufficient number, having regard to the rank of the officers and persons of equivalent status.

Officers and persons of equivalent status shall procure their food and clothing from the pay to be paid to them by the detaining Power. The management of a mess by officers themselves shall be facilitated in every way.

Chapter 7. Pecuniary resources of prisoners of war
Art. 23. Subject to any special arrangements made between the belligerent Powers, and particularly those contemplated in Article 24, officers and persons of equivalent status who are prisoners of war shall receive from the detaining Power the same pay as officers of corresponding rank in the armed forces of that Power, provided, however, that such pay does not exceed that to which they are entitled in the armed forces of the country in whose service they have been. This pay shall be paid to them in full, once a month if possible, and no deduction therefrom shall be made for expenditure devolving upon the detaining Power, even if such expenditure is incurred on their behalf.

An agreement between the belligerents shall prescribe the rate of exchange applicable to this payment; in default of such agreement, the rate of exchange adopted shall be that in force at the moment of the commencement of hostilities.

All advances made to prisoners of war by way of pay shall be reimbursed, at the end of hostilities, by the Power in whose service they were.

Art. 24. At the commencement of hostilities, belligerents shall determine by common accord the maximum amount of cash which prisoners of war of various ranks and categories shall be permitted to retain in their possession. Any excess withdrawn or withheld from a prisoner, and any deposit of money effected by him, shall be carried to his account, and may not be converted into another currency without his consent.

The credit balances of their accounts shall be paid to the prisoners of war at the end of their captivity.

During the continuance of the latter, facilities shall be accorded to them for the transfer of these amounts, wholly or in part, to banks or private individuals in their country of origin.

Chapter 8. Transfer of prisoners of war
Art. 25. Unless the course of military operations demands it, sick and wounded prisoners of war shall not be transferred if their recovery might be prejudiced by the journey.

Art. 26. In the event of transfer, prisoners of war shall be officially informed in advance of their new destination; they shall be authorized to take with them their personal effects, their correspondence and parcels which have arrived for them.

All necessary arrangements shall be made so that correspondence and parcels addressed to their former camp shall be sent on to them without delay.

The sums credited to the account of transferred prisoners shall be transmitted to the competent authority of their new place of residence.

Expenses incurred by the transfers shall be borne by the detaining Power.

Section III. Work of Prisoners of War

Chapter 1. General
Art. 27. Belligerents may employ as workmen prisoners of war who are physically fit, other than officers and persons of equivalent statue, according to their rank and their ability.

Nevertheless, if officers or persons of equivalent status ask for suitable work, this shall be found for them as far as possible.

Non-commissioned officers who are prisoners of war may be compelled to undertake only supervisory work, unless they expressly request remunerative occupation.

During the whole period of captivity, belligerents are required to admit prisoners of war who are victims of accidents at work to the benefit of provisions applicable to workmen of the same category under the legislation of the detaining Power. As regards prisoners of war to whom these legal provisions could not be applied by reason of the legislation of that Power, the latter undertakes to recommend to its legislative body all proper measures for the equitable compensation of the victims.

Chapter 2. Organization of work
Art. 28. The detaining Power shall assume entire responsibility for the maintenance, care, treatment and the payment of the wages of prisoners of war working for private individuals.

Art. 29. No prisoner of war may be employed on work for which he is physically unsuited.

Art. 30. The duration of the daily work of prisoners of war, including the time of the journey to and from work, shall not be excessive and shall in no case exceed that permitted for civil workers of the locality employed on the same work. Each prisoner shall be allowed a rest of twenty-four consecutive hours each week, preferably on Sunday.

Chapter 3. Prohibited work
Art. 31. Work done by prisoners of war shall have no direct connection with the operations of the war. In particular, it is forbidden to employ prisoners in the manufacture or transport of arms or munitions of any kind, or on the transport of material destined for combatant units.

In the event of violation of the provisions of the preceding paragraph, prisoners are at liberty, after performing or commencing to perform the order, to have their complaints presented through the intermediary of the prisoners' representatives whose functions are described in Articles 43 an 44, or, in the absence of a prisoners' representative, through the intermediary of the representatives of the protecting Power.

Art. 32. It is forbidden to employ prisoners of war on unhealthy or dangerous work. Conditions of work shall not be rendered more arduous by disciplinary measures.

Chapter 4. Labour detachments

Art. 33. Conditions governing labour detachments shall be similar to those of prisoners-of-war camps, particularly as concerns hygienic conditions, food, care in case of accidents or sickness, correspondence, and the reception of parcels.

Every labour detachment shall be attached to a prisoners' camp. The commander of this camp shall be responsible for the observance in the labour detachment of the provisions of the present Convention.

Chapter 5. Pay

Art. 34. Prisoners of war shall not receive pay for work in connection with the administration, internal arrangement and maintenance of camps.

Prisoners employed on other work shall be entitled to a rate of pay, to be fixed by agreements between the belligerents.

These agreements shall also specify the portion which may be retained by the camp administration, the amount which shall belong to the prisoner of war and the manner in which this amount shall be placed at his disposal during the period of his captivity.

Pending the conclusion of the said agreements, remuneration of the work of prisoners shall be fixed according to the following standards:

(a) Work done for the State shall be paid for according to the rates in force for soldiers of the national forces doing the same work, or, if no such rates exist, according to a tariff corresponding to the work executed.

(b) When the work is done for other public administrations or for private individuals, the conditions shall be settled in agreement with the military authorities.

The pay which remains to the credit of a prisoner shall be remitted to him on the termination of his captivity. In case of death, it shall be remitted through the diplomatic channel to the heirs of the deceased.

Section IV. Relations of Prisoners of War with the Exterior

Art. 35. On the commencement of hostilities, belligerents shall publish the measures prescribed for the execution of the provisions of the present section.

Art. 36. Each of the belligerents shall fix periodically the number of letters and postcards which prisoners of war of different categories shall be permitted to send per month, and shall notify that number to the other belligerent. These letters and cards shall be sent by post by the shortest route. They may not be delayed or withheld for disciplinary motives.

Not later than one week after his arrival in camp, and similarly in case of sickness, each prisoner shall be enabled to send a postcard to his family informing them of his capture and the state of his health. The said postcards shall be forwarded as quickly as possible and shall not be delayed in any manner.

As a general rule, the correspondence of prisoners shall be written in their native language. Belligerents may authorize correspondence in other languages.

Art. 37. Prisoners of war shall be authorized to receive individually postal parcels containing foodstuffs and other articles intended for consumption or clothing. The parcels shall be delivered to the addressees and a receipt given.

Art. 38. Letters and remittances of money or valuables, as well as postal parcels addressed to prisoners of war, or despatched by them, either directly or through the intermediary of the information bureaux mentioned in Article 77, shall be exempt from all postal charges in the countries of origin and destination and in the countries through which they pass.

Presents and relief in kind intended for prisoners of war shall also be exempt from all import or other duties, as well as any charges for carriage on railways operated by the State.

Prisoners may, in cases of recognized urgency, be authorized to send telegrams on payment of the usual charges.

Art. 39. Prisoners of war shall be permitted to receive individually consignments of books which may be subject to censorship.

Representatives of the protecting Powers and of duly recognized and authorized relief societies may send works and collections of books to the libraries of prisoners' camps. The transmission of such consignments to libraries may not be delayed under pretext of difficulties of censorship.

Art. 40. The censoring of correspondence shall be accomplished as quickly as possible. The examination of postal parcels shall, moreover, be effected under such conditions as will ensure the preservation of any foodstuffs which they may contain, and, if possible, be done in the presence of the addressee or of a representative duly recognized by him. Any prohibition of correspondence ordered by the belligerents, for military or political reasons, shall only be of a temporary character and shall also be for as brief a time as possible.

Art. 41. Belligerents shall accord all facilities for the transmission of documents destined for prisoners of war or signed by them, in particular powers of attorney and wills. They shall take the necessary measures to secure, in case of need, the legalisation of signatures of prisoners.

Section V. Relations between Prisoners of War and the Authorities

Chapter 1. Complaints of prisoners of war respecting the conditions of captivity

Art. 42. Prisoners of war shall have the right to bring to the notice of the military authorities, in whose hands they are, their petitions concerning the conditions of captivity to which they are subjected.

They shall also have the right to communicate with the representatives of the protecting Powers in order to draw their attention to the points on which they have complaints to make with regard to the conditions of captivity.

Such petitions and complaints shall be transmitted immediately.

Even though they are found to be groundless, they shall not give rise to any punishment.

Chapter 2. Representatives of prisoners of war

Art. 43. In any locality where there may be prisoners of war, they shall be authorized to appoint representatives to represent them before the military authorities and the protecting Powers.

Such appointments shall be subject to the approval of the military authorities.

The prisoners' representatives shall be charged with the reception and distribution of collective consignments. Similarly, in the event of the prisoners deciding to organize amongst themselves a system of mutual aid, such organization shall be one of the functions of the prisoners" representatives. On the other hand, the latter may offer their services to prisoners to facilitate their relations with the relief societies mentioned in Article 78.

In camps of officers and persons of equivalent status the senior officer prisoner of the highest rank shall be recognized as intermediary between the camp authorities and the officers and similar persons who are prisoners, for this purpose he shall have the power to appoint an officer prisoner to assist him as interpreter in the course of conferences with the authorities of the camp.

Art. 44. When the prisoners' representatives are employed as workmen, their work as representatives of the prisoners of war shall be reckoned in the compulsory period of labour.

All facilities shall be accorded to the prisoners' representatives for their correspondence with the military authorities and the protecting Power. Such correspondence shall not be subject to any limitation.

No prisoners' representative may be transferred without his having been allowed the time necessary to acquaint his successors with the current business.

Chapter 3. Penal sanctions with regard to prisoners of war

I. General provisions

Art. 45. Prisoners of war shall be subject to the laws, regulations and orders in force in the armed forces of the detaining Power.

Any act of insubordination shall render them liable to the measures prescribed by such laws, regulations, and orders, except as otherwise provided in this Chapter.

Art. 46. Prisoners of war shall not be subjected by the military authorities or the tribunals of the detaining Power to penalties other than those which are prescribed for similar acts by members of the national forces.

Officers, non-commissioned officers or private soldiers, prisoners of war, undergoing disciplinary punishment shall not be subjected to treatment less favourable than that prescribed, as regards the same punishment, for similar ranks in the armed forces of the detaining Power.

All forms of corporal punishment, confinement in premises not lighted by daylight and, in general, all forms of cruelty whatsoever are prohibited.

Collective penalties for individual acts are also prohibited.

Art. 47. A statement of the facts in cases of acts constituting a breach of discipline, and particularly an attempt to escape, shall be drawn up in writing without delay. The period during which prisoners of war of whatever rank are detained in custody (pending the investigation of such offences) shall be reduced to a strict minimum.

The judicial proceedings against a prisoner of war shall be conducted as quickly as circumstances will allow. The period during which prisoners shall be detained in custody shall be as short as possible.

In all cases the period during which a prisoner is under arrest (awaiting punishment or trial) shall be deducted from the sentence, whether disciplinary or judicial, provided such deduction is permitted in the case of members of the national forces.

Art. 48. After undergoing the judicial or disciplinary punishment which has been inflicted on them, prisoners of war shall not be treated differently from other prisoners.

Nevertheless, prisoners who have been punished as the result of an attempt to escape may be subjected to a special régime of surveillance, but this shall not involve the suppression of any of the safeguards accorded to prisoners by the present Convention.

Art. 49. No prisoner of war may be deprived of his rank by the detaining Power. Prisoners on whom disciplinary punishment is inflicted shall not be deprived of the privileges attaching to their rank. In particular, officers and persons of equivalent status who suffer penalties entailing deprivation of liberty shall not be placed in the same premises as non-commissioned officers or private soldiers undergoing punishment.

Art. 50. Escaped prisoners of war who are re-captured before they have been able to rejoin their own armed forces or to leave the territory occupied by the armed forces which captured them shall be liable only to disciplinary punishment.

Prisoners who, after succeeding in rejoining their armed forces or in leaving the territory occupied by the armed forces which captured them, are again taken prisoner shall not be liable to any punishment for their previous escape.

Art. 51. Attempted escape, even if it is not a first offence, shall not be considered as an aggravation of the offence in the event of the prisoner of war being brought before the courts for crimes or offences against persons or property committed in the course of such attempt.

After an attempted or successful escape, the comrades of the escaped person who aided the escape shall incur only disciplinary punishment therefor.

Art. 52. Belligerents shall ensure that the competent authorities exercise the greatest leniency in considering the question whether an offence committed by a prisoner of war should be punished by disciplinary or by judicial measures.

This provision shall be observed in particular in appraising facts in connexion with escape or attempted escape.

A prisoner shall not be punished more than once for the same act or on the same charge.

Art. 53. No prisoner who has been awarded any disciplinary punishment for an offence and who fulfils the conditions laid down for repatriation shall be retained on the ground that he has not undergone his punishment.

Prisoners qualified for repatriation against whom any prosecution for a criminal offence has been brought may be excluded from repatriation until the termination of the proceedings and until fulfilment of their sentence, if any; prisoners already serving a sentence of imprisonment may be retained until the expiry of the sentence.

Belligerents shall communicate to each other lists of those who cannot be repatriated for the reasons indicated in the preceding paragraph.

II. Disciplinary punishments

Art. 54. Imprisonment is the most severe disciplinary punishment which may be inflicted on a prisoner of war.

The duration of any single punishment shall not exceed thirty days.

This maximum of thirty days shall, moreover, not be exceeded in the event of there being several acts for which the prisoner is answerable to discipline at the time when his case is disposed of, whether such acts are connected or not.

Where, during the course or after the termination of a period of imprisonment, a prisoner is sentenced to a fresh disciplinary penalty, a period of at least three days shall intervene between each of the periods of imprisonment, if one of such periods is of ten days or over.

Art. 55. Subject to the provisions of the last paragraph of Article 11, the restrictions in regard to food permitted in the armed forces of the detaining Power may be applied, as an additional penalty, to prisoners of war undergoing disciplinary punishment.

Such restrictions shall, however, only be ordered if the state of the prisoner's health permits.

Art. 56. In no case shall prisoners of war be transferred to penitentiary establishments (prisons, penitentiaries, convict establishments, etc.) in order to undergo disciplinary sentence there.

Establishments in which disciplinary sentences are undergone shall conform to the requirements of hygiene.

Facilities shall be afforded to prisoners undergoing sentence to keep themselves in a state of cleanliness.

Every day, such prisoners shall have facilities for taking exercise or for remaining out of doors for at least two hours.

Art. 57. Prisoners of war undergoing disciplinary punishment shall be permitted to read and write and to send and receive letters.

On the other hand, it shall be permissible not to deliver parcels and remittances of money to the addressees until the expiration of the sentence. If the undelivered parcels contain perishable foodstuffs, these shall be handed over to the infirmary or to the camp kitchen.

Art. 58. Prisoners of war undergoing disciplinary punishment shall be permitted, on their request, to present themselves for daily medical inspection. They shall receive such attention as the medical officers may consider necessary, and, if need be, shall be evacuated to the camp infirmary or to hospital.

Art. 59. Without prejudice to the competency of the courts and the superior military authorities, disciplinary sentences may only be awarded by an officer vested with disciplinary powers in his capacity as commander of the camp or detachment, or by the responsible officer acting as his substitute.

III. Judicial proceedings

Art. 60. At the commencement of a judicial hearing against a prisoner of war, the detaining Power shall notify the representative of the protecting Power as soon as possible, and in any case before the date fixed for the opening of the hearing.

The said notification shall contain the following particulars:

(a) Civil status and rank of the prisoner.
(b) Place of residence or detention.
(c) Statement of the charge or charges, and of the legal provisions applicable.

If it is not possible in this notification to indicate particulars of the court which will try the case, the date of the opening of the hearing and the place where it will take place, these particulars shall be furnished to the representative of the protecting Power at a later date, but as soon as possible and in any case at least three weeks before the opening of the hearing.

Art. 61. No prisoner of war shall be sentenced without being given the opportunity to defend himself.

No prisoner shall be compelled to admit that he is guilty of the offence of which he is accused.

Art. 62. The prisoner of war shall have the right to be assisted by a qualified. advocate of his own choice and, if necessary, to have recourse to the offices of a competent interpreter. He shall be informed of his right by the detaining Power in good time before the hearing.

Failing a choice on the part of the prisoner, the protecting Power may procure an advocate for him. The detaining Power shall, on the request of the protecting Power, furnish to the latter a list of persons qualified to conduct the defence.

The representatives of the protecting Power shall have the right to attend the hearing of the case.

The only exception to this rule is where the hearing has to be kept secret in the interests of the safety of the State. The detaining Power would then notify the protecting Power accordingly.

Art. 63. A sentence shall only be pronounced on a prisoner of war by the same tribunals and in accordance with the same procedure as in the case of persons belonging to the armed forces of the detaining Power.

Art. 64. Every prisoner of war shall have the right of appeal against any sentence against him in the same manner as persons belonging to the armed forces of the detaining Power.

Art. 65. Sentences pronounced against prisoners of war shall be communicated immediately to the protecting Power.

Art. 66. If sentence of death is passed on a prisoner of war, a communication setting forth in detail the nature and the circumstances of the offence shall be addressed as soon as possible to the representative of the protecting Power for transmission to the Power in whose armed forces the prisoner served.

The sentence shall not be carried out before the expiration of a period of at least three months from the date of the receipt of this communication by the protecting Power.

Art. 67. No prisoner of war may be deprived of the benefit of the provisions of Article 42 of the present Convention as the result of a judgment or otherwise.

PART IV. END OF CAPTIVITY

Section I. Direct Repatriation and Accommodation in a Neutral Country

Art. 68. Belligerents shall be required to send back to their own country, without regard to rank or numbers, after rendering them in a fit condition for transport, prisoners of war who are seriously ill or seriously wounded.

Agreements between the belligerents shall therefore determine, as soon as possible, the forms of disablement or sickness requiring direct repatriation and cases which may necessitate accommodation in a neutral country. Pending the conclusion of such agreements, the belligerents may refer to the model draft agreement annexed to the present Convention.

Art. 69. On the opening of hostilities, belligerents shall come to an understanding as to the appointment of mixed medical commissions. These commissions shall consist of three members, two of whom shall belong to a neutral country and one appointed by the detaining Power; one of the medical officers of the neutral country shall preside. These mixed medical commissions shall proceed to the examination of sick or wounded prisoners and shall make all appropriate decisions with regard to them.

The decisions of these commissions shall be decided by majority and shall be carried into effect as soon as possible.

Art. 70. In addition to those prisoners of war selected by the medical officer of the camp, the following shall be inspected by the mixed medical Commission mentioned in Article 69, with a view to their direct repatriation or accommodation in a neutral country:

(a) Prisoners who make a direct request to that effect to the medical officer of the camp;

(b) Prisoners presented by the prisoners' representatives mentioned in Article 43, the latter acting on their own initiative or on the request of the prisoners themselves;

(c) Prisoners nominated by the Power in whose armed forces they served or by a relief society duly recognized and authorized by that Power.

Art. 71. Prisoners of war who meet with accidents at work, unless the injury is self-inflicted, shall have the benefit of the same provisions as regards repatriation or accommodation in a neutral country.

Art. 72. During the continuance of hostilities, and for humanitarian reasons, belligerents may conclude agreements with a view to the direct repatriation or accommodation in a neutral country of prisoners of war in good health who have been in captivity for a long time.

Art. 73. The expenses of repatriation or transport to a neutral country of prisoners of war shall be borne, as from the frontier of the detaining Power, by the Power in whose armed forces such prisoners served.

Art. 74. No repatriated person shall be employed on active military service.

Section II. Liberation and Repatriation at the End of Hostilities

Art. 75. When belligerents conclude an armistice convention, they shall normally cause to be included therein provisions concerning the repatriation of prisoners of war. If it has not been possible to insert in that convention such stipulations, the belligerents shall, nevertheless, enter into communication with each other on the question as soon as possible. In any case, the repatriation of prisoners shall be effected as soon as possible after the conclusion of peace.

Prisoners of war who are subject to criminal proceedings for a crime or offence at common law may, however, be detained until the end of the proceedings, and, if need be, until the expiration of the sentence. The same applies to prisoners convicted for a crime or offence at common law.

By agreement between the belligerents, commissions may be instituted for the purpose of searching for scattered prisoners and ensuring their repatriation.

PART V. DEATHS OF PRISONERS OF WAR

Art. 76. The wills of prisoners of war shall be received and drawn up under the same conditions as for soldiers of the national armed forces.

The same rules shall be followed as regards the documents relative to the certification of the death.

The belligerents shall ensure that prisoners of war who have died in captivity are honourably buried, and that the graves bear the necessary indications and are treated with respect and suitably maintained.

PART VI. BUREAUX OF RELIEF AND INFORMATION CONCERNING PRISONERS OF WAR

Art. 77. At the commencement of hostilities, each of the belligerent Powers and the neutral Powers who have belligerents in their care, shall institute an official bureau to give information about the prisoners of war in their territory.

Each of the belligerent Powers shall inform its Information Bureau as soon as possible of all captures of prisoners effected by its armed forces, furnishing them with all particulars of identity at its disposal to enable the families concerned to be quickly notified, and stating the official addresses to which families may write to the prisoners.

The Information Bureau shall transmit all such information immediately to the Powers concerned, on the one hand through the intermediary of the protecting Powers, and on the other through the Central Agency contemplated in Article 79.

The Information Bureau, being charged with replying to all enquiries relative to prisoners of war, shall receive from the various services concerned all particulars respecting internments and transfers, releases on parole, repatriations, escapes, stays in hospitals, and deaths, together with all other particulars necessary for establishing and keeping up to date an individual record for each prisoner of war.

The Bureau shall note in this record, as far as possible, and subject to the provisions of Article 5, the regimental number, names and surnames, date and place of birth, rank and unit of the prisoner, the surname of the father and name of the mother, the address of the person to be notified in case of accident, wounds, dates and places of capture, of internment, of wounds, of death, together with all other important particulars.

Weekly lists containing all additional particulars capable of facilitating the identification of each prisoner shall be transmitted to the interested Powers.

The individual record of a prisoner of war shall be sent after the conclusion of peace to the Power in whose service he was.

The Information Bureau shall also be required to collect all personal effects, valuables, correspondence, pay-books, identity tokens, etc., which have been left by prisoners of war who have been repatriated or released on parole, or who have escaped or died, and to transmit them to the countries concerned.

Art. 78. Societies for the relief of prisoners of war, regularly constituted in accordance with the laws of their country, and having for their object to serve as intermediaries for charitable purposes, shall receive from the belligerents, for themselves and their duly accredited agents, all facilities for the efficacious performance of their humane task within the limits imposed by military exigencies. Representatives of these societies shall be permitted to distribute relief in the camps and at the halting places of repatriated prisoners under a personal permit issued by the military authority, and on giving an undertaking in writing to comply with all routine and police orders which the said authority shall prescribe.

Art. 79. A Central Agency of information regarding prisoners of war shall be established in a neutral country. The International Red Cross Committee shall, if they consider it necessary, propose to the Powers concerned the organization of such an agency.

This agency shall be charged with the duty of collecting all information regarding prisoners which they may be able to obtain through official or private channels, and the agency shall transmit the information as rapidly as possible to the prisoners' own country or the Power in whose service they have been.

These provisions shall not be interpreted as restricting the humanitarian work of the International Red Cross Committee.

Art. 80. Information Bureaux shall enjoy exemption from fees on postal matter as well as all the exemptions prescribed in Article 38.

PART VII. APPLICATION OF THE CONVENTION TO CERTAIN CATEGORIES OF CIVILIANS

Art. 81. Persons who follow the armed forces without directly belonging thereto, such as correspondents, newspaper reporters, sutlers, or contractors, who fall into the hands of the enemy, and whom the latter think fit to detain, shall be entitled to be treated as prisoners of war, provided they are in possession of an authorization from the military authorities of the armed forces which they were following.

PART VIII. EXECUTION OF THE CONVENTION

Section I. General Provisions

Art. 82. The provisions of the present Convention shall be respected by the High Contracting Parties in all circumstances.

In time of war if one of the belligerents is not a party to the Convention, its provisions shall, nevertheless, remain binding as between the belligerents who are parties thereto.

Art. 83. The High Contracting Parties reserve to themselves the right to conclude special conventions on all questions relating to prisoners of war concerning which they may consider it desirable to make special provisions.

Prisoners of war shall continue to enjoy the benefits of these agreements until their repatriation has been effected, subject to any provisions expressly to the contrary contained in the above-mentioned agreements or in subsequent agreements, and subject to any more favourable measures by one or the other of the belligerent Powers concerning the prisoners detained by that Power.

In order to ensure the application, on both sides, of the provisions of the present Convention, and to facilitate the conclusion of the special conventions mentioned above, the belligerents may, at the commencement of hostilities, authorize meetings of representatives of the respective authorities charged with the administration of prisoners of war.

Art. 84. The text of the present Convention and of the special conventions mentioned in the preceding Article shall be posted, whenever possible, in the native language of the prisoners of war, in places where it may be consulted by all the prisoners.

The text of these conventions shall be communicated, on their request, to prisoners who are unable to inform themselves of the text posted.

Art. 85. The High Contracting Parties shall communicate to each other, through the intermediary of the Swiss Federal Council, the official translations of the present Convention, together with such laws and regulations as they may adopt to ensure the application of the present Convention.

Section II. Organization of Control

Art. 86. The High Contracting Parties recognize that a guarantee of the regular application of the present Convention will be found in the possibility of collaboration between the protecting Powers charged with the protection of the interests of the belligerents; in this connexion, the protecting Powers may, apart from their diplomatic personnel, appoint delegates from among their own nationals or the nationals of other neutral Powers. The appointment of these delegates shall be subject to the approval of the belligerent with whom they are to carry out their mission.

The representatives of the protecting Power or their recognized delegates shall be authorized to proceed to any place, without exception, where prisoners of war are interned. They shall have access to all premises occupied by prisoners and may hold conversation with prisoners, as a general rule without witnesses, either personally or through the intermediary of interpreters.

Belligerents shall facilitate as much as possible the task of the representatives or recognized delegates of the protecting Power. The military authorities shall be informed of their visits.

Belligerents may mutually agree to allow persons of the prisoners own nationality to participate in the tours of inspection.

Art. 87. In the event of dispute between the belligerents regarding the application of the provisions of the present Convention, the protecting Powers shall, as far as possible, lend their good offices with the object of settling the dispute.

To this end, each of the protecting Powers may, for instance, propose to the belligerents concerned that a conference of representatives of the latter should be held, on suitably chosen neutral territory. The belligerents shall be required to give effect to proposals made to them with this object. The protecting Power may, if necessary, submit fur the approval of the Powers in dispute the name of a person belonging to a neutral

Power or nominated by the International Red Cross Committee, who shall be invited to take part in this conference.

Art. 88. The foregoing provisions do not constitute any obstacle to the humanitarian work which the International Red Cross Committee may perform for the protection of prisoners of war with the consent of the belligerents concerned.

Section III. Final Provisions

Art. 89. In the relations between the Powers who are bound either by The Hague Convention concerning the Laws and Customs of War on Land of 29 July 1899, or that of 18 October 1907, and are parties to the present Convention, the latter shall be complementary to Chapter 2 of the Regulations annexed to the above-mentioned Conventions of The Hague.

Art. 90. The present Convention, which shall bear this day's date, may be signed up to 1 February 1930, on behalf of any of the countries represented at the Conference which opened at Geneva on 1 July 1929.

Art. 91. The present Convention shall be ratified as soon as possible.

The ratifications shall be deposited at Berne.

In respect of the deposit of each instrument of ratification, a *procès-verbal* shall be drawn up, and copy thereof, certified correct, shall be sent by the Swiss Federal Council to the Governments of all the countries on whose behalf the Convention has been signed or whose accession has been notified.

Art. 92. The present Convention shall enter into force six months after at least two instruments of ratification have been deposited.

Thereafter it shall enter into force for each High Contracting Party six months after the deposit of its instrument of ratification.

Art. 93. As from the date of its entry into force, the present Convention shall be open to accession notified in respect of any country on whose behalf this Convention has not been signed.

Art. 94. Accessions shall be notified in writing to the Swiss Federal Council and shall take effect six months after the date on which they have been received.

The Swiss Federal Council shall notify the accessions to the Governments of all the countries on whose behalf the Convention has been signed or whose accession has been notified.

Art. 95. A state of war shall give immediate effect to ratifications deposited and to accessions notified by the belligerent Powers before or after the commencement of hostilities. The communication of ratifications or accessions received from Powers in a state of war shall be effected by the Swiss Federal Council by the quickest method.

Art. 96. Each of the High Contracting Parties shall have the right to denounce the present Convention. The denunciation shall only take effect one year after notification thereof has been made in writing to the Swiss Federal Council. The latter shall communicate this notification to the Governments of all the High Contracting Parties.

The denunciation shall only be valid in respect of the High Contracting Party which has made notification thereof.

Such denunciation shall, moreover, not take effect during a war in which the denouncing Power is involved. In this case, the present Convention shall continue binding, beyond the period of one year, until the conclusion of peace and, in any case, until operations of repatriation shall have terminated.

Art. 97. A copy of the present Convention, certified to be correct, shall be deposited by the Swiss Federal Council in the archives of the League of Nations. Similarly, ratifications, accessions and denunciations notified to the Swiss Federal Council shall be communicated by them to the League of Nations.

In faith whereof the above-mentioned Plenipotentiaries have signed the present Convention.

Done at Geneva the twenty-seventh July, one thousand nine hundred and twenty-nine, in a single copy, which shall remain deposited in the archives of the Swiss Confederation, and of which copies, certified correct, shall be transmitted to the Governments of all the countries invited to the Conference.

[Here follow signatures]

ANNEX TO THE CONVENTION OF 27 JULY 1929, RELATIVE TO THE TREATMENT OF PRISONERS OF WAR

Model draft agreement concerning the direct repatriation or accommodation in a neutral country of prisoners of war for reasons of health

I. Guiding Principles for Direct Repatriation or Accommodation in a Neutral Country

A. Guiding Principles for Direct Repatriation
The following shall be repatriated directly:
1 Sick and wounded whose recovery within one year is not probable according to medical prognosis, whose condition requires treatment, and whose intellectual or bodily powers appear to have undergone a considerable diminution.
2. Incurable sick and wounded whose intellectual or bodily powers appear to have undergone a considerable diminution.
3. Convalescent sick and wounded, whose intellectual or bodily powers appear to have undergone a considerable diminution.

B. Guiding Principles for Accommodation in a Neutral Country.
The following shall be accommodated in a neutral country:
1. Sick and wounded whose recovery is presumable within the period of one year, when it appears that such recovery would be more certain and more rapid if the sick and wounded were given the benefit of the resources offered by the neutral country than if their captivity, properly so called, were prolonged.
2. Prisoners of war whose intellectual or physical health appears, according to medical opinion, to be seriously threatened by continuance in captivity, while accommodation in a neutral country would probably diminish that risk.

C. Guiding Principles for the Repatriation of Prisoners in a Neutral Country
Prisoners of war who have been accommodated in a neutral country, and belong to the following categories, shall be repatriated:
1. Those whose state of health appears to be, or likely to become such that they would fall into the categories of those to be repatriated for reasons of health.
2. Those who are convalescent, whose intellectual or physical powers appear to have undergone a considerable diminution.

II. Special Principles for Direct Repatriation or Accommodation in a Neutral Country
A. Special Principles for Repatriation
The following shall be repatriated:
1. All prisoners of war suffering the following effective or functional disabilities as the result of organic injuries: loss of a limb, paralysis, articular or other disabilities,

when the defect is at least the loss of a foot or a hand, or the equivalent of the loss of a foot or a hand.

2. All wounded or injured prisoners of war whose condition is such as to render them invalids whose cure within a year cannot be medically foreseen.
3. All sick prisoners whose condition is such as to render them invalids whose cure within a year cannot be medically foreseen. The following in particular belong to this category:
   (a) Progressive tuberculosis of any organ which, according to medical prognosis, cannot be cured or at least considerably improved by treatment in a neutral country;
   (b) Non-tubercular affections of the respiratory organs which are presumed to be incurable (in particular, strongly developed pulmonary emphysema, with or without bronchitis, bronchiectasis, serious asthma, gas poisoning, etc.):
   (c) Grave chronic affections of the circulatory organs (for example: valvular affections with a tendency to compensatory troubles, relatively gave affections of the myocardium, pericardium or the vessels, in particular, aneurism of the larger vessels which cannot be operated on, etc.);
   (d) Grave chronic affections of the digestive organs;
   (e) Grave chronic affections of the urinary and sexual organs, in particular, for example: any case of chronic nephritis, confirmed by symptoms, and especially when cardiac and vascular deterioration already exists; the same applies to chronic pyelitis and cystitis, etc.;
   (f) Grave chronic maladies of the central and peripheral nervous system; in particular grave neurasthenia and hysteria, any indisputable case of epilepsy, grave Basedow's disease, etc.;
   (g) Blindness of both eyes, or of one eye when the vision of the other is less than 1 in spite of the use of corrective glasses. Diminution of visual acuteness in cases where it is impossible to restore it by correction to an acuteness of 1/2 in at least one eye. The other ocular affections falling within the present category (glaucoma, iritis, choroiditis, etc.);
   (h) Total bilateral deafness, and total unilateral deafness in cases where the ear which is not completely deaf cannot hear ordinary speaking voice at a distance of one metre;
   (i) Any indisputable case of mental affection;
   (k) Grave cases of chronic poisoning by metals or other causes (lead poisoning, mercury poisoning, morphinism, cocainism, alcoholism, gas poisoning, etc.);
   (l) Chronic affections of the locomotive organs (arthritis deformans, gout, or rheumatism with impairment, which can be ascertained clinically), provided that they are serious;
   (m) Malignant growths, if they are not amenable to relatively mild operations without danger to the life of the person operated upon;
   (n) All cases of malaria with appreciable organic deterioration (serious chronic enlargement of the liver or spleen, cachexy, etc.);
   (o) Grave chronic cutaneous affections, when their nature does not constitute a medical reason for treatment in a neutral country;
   (p) Serious avitaminosis (beri-beri, pellagra, chronic scurvy).

B. Special Principles for Accommodation in a Neutral Country

Prisoners of war shall be accommodated in a neutral country if they suffer from the following affections:

1. All forms of tuberculosis of any organ, if, according to present medical knowledge, they can be cured or their condition considerably improved by methods applicable in a neutral country (altitude, treatment in sanatoria, etc.).
2. All forms necessitating treatment of affections of the respiratory, circulatory, digestive, genito-urinary, or nervous organs, of the organs of the senses, or of the locomotive or cutaneous functions, provided that such forms of affection do not belong to the categories necessitating direct repatriation, or that they are not acute mal-

adies (properly so called) susceptible of complete cure. The affections referred to in this paragraph are such as admit, by the application of methods of treatment available in the neutral country, of really better chances of the patient's recovery than if he were treated in captivity.

Special consideration should be given to nervous troubles, the effective or determining causes of which are the effects of the war or of captivity, such as psychasthenia of prisoners of war or other analogous cases.

All duly established cases of this nature must be treated in neutral countries when their gravity or their constitutional character does not render them cases for direct repatriation. Cases of psychasthenia of prisoners of war who are not cured after three months' sojourn in a neutral country, or which after that period are not manifestly on the way to complete recovery, shall be repatriated.

3. All cases of wounds or injuries or their consequences which offer better prospects of cure in a neutral country than in captivity, provided that such cases are neither such as justify direct repatriation, nor insignificant cases.
4. All duly established cases of malaria which do not show organic deterioration clinically ascertainable (chronic enlargement of the liver or spleen, cachexy, etc.), if sojourn in a neutral country offers particularly favourable prospects of final cure.
5. All cases of poisoning (in particular by gas, metals, or alkaloids) for which the prospects of cure in a neutral country are especially favourable. The following are excluded from accommodation in a neutral country:
   1. All cases of duly established mental affections.
   2. All organic or functional nervous affections which are reputed to be incurable. (These two categories belong to those which entitle direct repatriation).
   3. Grave chronic alcoholism.
4. All contagious affections during the period when they are transmissible (acute infectious diseases, primary and secondary (syphilis, trachoma, leprosy, etc.).

III. General Observations

The conditions stated above must, in a general way, be interpreted and applied in as broad a spirit as possible.

This breadth of interpretation must especially be applied in neuropathic or psychopathic cases caused or aggravated by the effects of war or captivity (psychasthenia of prisoners of war), and in cases of tuberculosis in all degrees.

It is obvious that camp doctors and mixed medical commissions may find themselves faced with many cases not mentioned amongst the examples given under Section II above, or with cases that cannot be assimilated to these examples. The above-mentioned examples are only given as typical examples; a similar list of surgical disabilities has not been drawn up because, apart from cases which are indisputable on account of their very nature (amputations), it is difficult to draw up a list of specified types; experience has shown that a list of such specified cases was not without inconvenience in practice.

Cases not conforming exactly with the examples quoted shall be determined in the spirit of the guiding principles given above.

SIGNATURES, RATIFICATIONS AND ACCESSIONS[1]

State	*Signature*	*Ratification, Accession or Notification of Continuity* (C)
Argentina	–	5 March 1945
Australia	27 July 1929	23 June 1931
Austria	27 July 1929	13 March 1936

[1] Based on a communication from the Swiss Federal Department of Foreign Affairs of 25 June 1999. See also ICRC website: www.org/ihl.nsf.

State	*Signature*	*Ratification, Accession or Notification of Continuity* (C)
Belgium	27 July 1929	12 May 1932
Bolivia	27 July 1929	13 August 1940
Brazil	27 July 1929	23 March 1932
Bulgaria	27 July 1929	13 October 1937
Burma[2]		1 April 1937 (C)
Canada	27 July 1929	20 February 1933
Chile	27 July 1929	1 June 1933
China	27 July 1929	19 November 1935
Columbia	27 July 1929	5 June 1941
Cuba	27 July 1929	–
Czechoslovakia	27 July 1929	12 October 1937
Denmark	27 July 1929	5 August 1932
Dominican Republic	27 July 1929	–
Egypt	27 July 1929	25 July 1933
El Salvador	–	22 April 1942
Estonia	27 July 1929	11 June 1936[3]
Finland	27 July 1929	–
Fiji	–	9 August 1971 (C)[4]
France	27 July 1929	21 August 1935
Germany	27 July 1929	21 February 1934
Great Britain and Northern Ireland[5]	27 July 1929	23 June 1931
Greece	27 July 1929	28 May 1935
Hungary	27 July 1929	10 September 1936
India	27 July 1929	23 June 1931
Indonesia	–	5 June 1950 (C)[6]
Iraq	–	29 May 1934
Ireland (Irish Free State)	27 July 1929	–
Israel	–	3 August 1948
Italy	27 July 1929	24 March 1931
Japan	27 July 1929	–

2 Burma, formerly a Party to this Convention by reason of her inclusion in India, was separated from the Indian Empire on 1 April 1937. Having on that date acquired the status of a British overseas territory, she is now to be considered a party to the Convention in virtue of the United Kingdom's signature and ratification thereof. (Registered at the Secretariat of the League of Nations on 26 November 1938 on the request of the Swiss Federal Council in its capacity of depositary (*LNTS*, Vol. 193, 1938, p. 270).

3 On 19 November 1991, Estonia deposited a declaration of continuity which took effect retroactively on 6 September 1991, the date on which the Soviet Union recognized the independence of the Baltic States (Note of 8 January 1992 from the Swiss Federal Department of Foreign Affairs to the ICRC and Notification from the Swiss Federal Department of Foreign Affairs to the governments of State Parties to the Geneva Conventions of 1929 and 1949, of 10 February 1992). On 18 January 1993, Estonia deposited the instrument of accession to the Geneva Conventions of 1949 which took effect from 18 July 1993 and is from that date party to the Geneva Convention (III) relative to the treatment of prisoners of war. It replaces from that date the present 1929 Convention.

4 With effect from 10 October 1970.

5 The instrument of ratification was deposited in the name of Great Britain and Northern Ireland and all parts of the British Empire not separate members of the League of Nations.

6 Application on the territory of Indonesia and on its behalf. Declaration signed at the Swiss Political Department on 5 June 1950 (*UNTS*, Vol. 76, 1950, p. 286).

State	*Signature*	*Ratification, Accession or Notification of Continuity (C)*
Latvia	27 July 1929	14 October 1931[7]
Liechtenstein	–	11 January 1944
Lithuania	–	27 February 1939[8]
Luxemburg	27 July 1929	–
Mexico	27 July 1929	1 August 1932
Monaco	–	17 March 1948
Netherlands	27 July 1929	5 October 1932
New Zealand	27 July 1929	23 June 1931
Nicaragua	27 July 1929	–
Norway	27 July 1929	24 June 1931
Pakistan	–	2 February 1948
Papua New Guinea	–	26 May 1976 (C)[9]
Persia	27 July 1929	–
Philippines	–	1 April 1947
Poland	27 July 1929	29 June 1932
Portugal	27 July 1929	8 June 1931
Romania	27 July 1929	24 October 1931
Siam (Thailand)	27 July 1929	3 June 1939
Spain	27 July 1929[10]	6 August 1930
Sweden	27 July 1929	3 July 1931
Switzerland	27 July 1929	19 December 1930
Transjordan	–	9 March 1949 (C)
Turkey	27 July 1929	10 March 1934
Union of South Africa	27 July 1929	23 June 1931
United States of America	27 July 1929	4 February 1932
Uruguay	27 July 1929	–
Venezuela	–	15 July 1944
Yugoslavia	27 July 1929	20 May 1931

RESERVATIONS

None

7 On 26 November 1991, Latvia deposited a declaration of continuity dated 15 November 1991, which took effect retroactively on 6 September 1991, the date on which the Soviet Union recognized the independence of the Baltic states (note of 8 January 1992 from the Swiss Federal Department of Foreign Affairs to the ICRC and notification from the Swiss Federal Department of Foreign Affairs to the governments of states parties to the Geneva Conventions of 1929 and 1949, of 10 February 1992). On 24 December 1991, Latvia deposited the instrument of accession to the Geneva Conventions of 1949 which took effect from 24 June 1992 and is from that date party to the Geneva Convention (III) relative to the treatment of prisoners of war. It replaces from that date the present 1929 convention (letter of the Swiss Federal Department of Foreign Affairs to the ICRC of 28 January 1992).

8 On 20 December 1991, Lithuania deposited a declaration of continuity dated 10 October 1991, which took effect retroactively on 6 September 1991, the date on which the Soviet Union recognized the independence of the Baltic states (note of 8 January 1992 from the Swiss Federal Department of Foreign Affairs to the ICRC and notification from the Swiss Federal Department of Foreign Affairs to the governments of states parties to the Geneva Conventions of 1929 and 1949, of 10 February 1992). On 3 October 1996, Lithuania deposited the instrument of accession to the Geneva Conventions of 1949 which took effect from 4 April 1997 and is from that date party to the Geneva Convention (III) relative to the treatment of prisoners of war. It replaces from that date the present 1929 convention (letter of the Swiss Federal Department of Foreign Affairs to the ICRC of 8 January 1992).

9 With the effect from 16 September 1975.

No. 47

DRAFT INTERNATIONAL CONVENTION ON THE CONDITION AND PROTECTION OF CIVILIANS OF ENEMY NATIONALITY WHO ARE ON TERRITORY BELONGING TO OR OCCUPIED BY A BELLIGERENT

Recommended by the XVth International Red Cross Conference, Tokyo, 1934

INTRODUCTORY NOTE: The law of war, until World War 1, was based on the assumption that civilians enjoyed complete immunity from war operations. No provisions with respect to civilians existed except those on their treatment in occupied territory, contained in the Hague Regulations of 1899 and 1907 (*Nos. 7 and 8*, Annexes). World War I fundamentally altered the situation. Enemy civilians in the territories of belligerents were interned in great numbers notwithstanding the lack of relevant provisions. Moreover, the provisions of the Hague Regulations on occupied territories proved to be insufficient in view of changed circumstances. After the war, the ICRC, invited by several International Red Cross Conferences, prepared drafts for a convention on the protection of civilians in the territory of belligerents and in occupied territories. These efforts, however, for several years, did not find the necessary support of governments. Some governments feared that a new convention relating to war would undermine the cause of peace. As a consequence, no draft on civilians was submitted to the Diplomatic Conference of 1929. Yet this Conference recommended "that an exhaustive study should be made with a view to the conclusion of an international Convention regarding the condition and protection of civilians of enemy nationality in the territory of a belligerent or in the territory occupied by a belligerent" (see *No.44*, Recommendation V1). In response to this request, the ICRC prepared the draft reproduced below, which was approved by the International Red Cross Conference in Tokyo in 1934 with a view to its submission to a diplomatic conference convened by the Swiss government. Due to the slowness of government reactions, the date of the conference could not be set until 1939. It was fixed for the beginning of 1940. The outbreak of the war in September 1939 prevented its taking place. From the outset of the war, the ICRC proposed to belligerents to apply the rules of the draft, yet belligerents preferred to apply the Prisoners of War Convention of 1929 (*No. 46*) by analogy to interned civilians.

AUTHENTIC TEXT: French. The translation below is an inofficial translation by the ICRC.

TEXT PUBLISHED IN: *Quinzième Conférence internationale de la Croix Rouge, tenue à Tokyo du 20 au 29 octobre 1934, Compte rendu*, Tokyo 1934, pp. 262–268 (French). ICRC web site: www.icrc.org/ihl.nsf; University of Minnesota Human Rights Library: www1.umn.edu/humanrts/instree/ 1934b.htm.

TABLE OF CONTENTS

* * *

CHAPTER I. QUALIFICATION OF ENEMY CIVILIAN (ENEMY ALIEN)

Definition
Article 1. Enemy civilians in the sense of the present Convention are persons fulfilling the two following conditions:
(a) that of not belonging to the land, maritime or air armed forces of the belligerents, as defined by international law, and in particular by Articles 1, 2 and 3 of the Regulations attached to the Fourth Hague Convention, of October 18, 1907, concerning the Laws and Customs of War on Land;
(b) that of being the national of an enemy country in the territory of a belligerent, or in a territory occupied by the latter.

CHAPTER II. ENEMY CIVILIANS IN THE TERRITORY OF A BELLIGERENT

Section I. General Provisions

Permission to leave
Art. 2. Subject to the provisions of Article 4, enemy civilians who may desire to leave the territory at the outset of military operations shall be granted, as rapidly as possible, the necessary authorizations, as well as all facilities compatible with such operations.

They will have the right to provide themselves with the necessary funds for their journey and to take with them at least their personal effects.

Administrative evacuation
Art. 3. In the event of the departure of civilians being administratively organized, they shall be conducted to the frontier of their country or of the nearest neutral country.

These repatriations shall be effected with due regard to all humanitarian considerations.

The manner of such repatriations may form the subject of special agreements between belligerents.

Detention of civilians
Art. 4. Only civilians falling within the following categories may be held:
(a) Those who are eligible for immediate mobilization or mobilization within a year, under the laws of their country of origin or of the country of residence;
(b) those whose departure may reasonably be opposed on grounds involving the security of the Detaining Power.

In either case, appeal to the Protecting Power shall always be admitted. This Power shall have the right to demand that an inquiry be opened and the result communicated to it within three months of its request.

Detainees
Art. 5. Those who are in preventive imprisonment or condemned to a sentence depriving them of liberty shall, on their liberation, benefit by the provisions of the present Convention.

The fact that they belong to an enemy State shall not increase the severity of the regime to which they are subjected.

Treatment of civilians
Art. 6. Enemy aliens who have remained in the territory, as those who have been held in application of Article 4, shall receive the treatment to which aliens are ordinarily entitled, except for measures of control or security which may be ordered, and subject to the provisions of Section III.

With these reservations, and in so far as military operations permit, they will have the possibility of carrying on their occupations.

News and relief
Art. 7. Subject to the measures applied to the population in general, enemy civilians shall have the possibility of giving news of a strictly private character to next of kin, and of receiving such news.

With the same reservation they shall also have the possibility of receiving relief.

Recognized relief societies
Art. 8. Enemy civilians shall have every facility for application to duly recognized relief societies, whose object is to act as intermediaries in welfare activities.

These societies shall receive, for this purpose, all facilities from the authorities, within the limits compatible with military necessities.

Protection
Art. 9. Enemy civilians shall be protected against measures of violence, insults and public curiosity.

Prohibitions
Art. 10. Measures of reprisal directed against them are prohibited.

Art. 11. The taking of hostages is forbidden.

Section II. Enemy civilians brought into the territory of a belligerent

Newcomers
Art. 12. Enemy civilians who for any reason may be brought into the territory of a belligerent during hostilities shall benefit by the same guarantees as those who were in the territory at the outset of military operations.

Section III. Compulsory residence and internment

General principles
Art. 13. Should a belligerent country judge the measures of control or security mentioned in Article 6 as inadequate, it may have recourse to compulsory residence or internment, in conformity with the provisions of the present Section.

Confinement
Art. 14. As a general rule, the compulsory residence of enemy civilians in a specified district shall be preferred to their internment. In particular, those who are established in the territory of the belligerent shall, subject to the security of the State, be thus restricted.

Internment
Art. 15. The internment of enemy civilians in fenced-in camps may only be ordered in one of the following cases:
(a) where civilians eligible for mobilization under the conditions set forth in Article 4 (a) of the present Convention are concerned;
(b) where the security of the Detaining Power is involved;
(c) where the situation of the enemy civilians renders it necessary.

Separate camps and health conditions
Art. 16. Internment camps for enemy civilians shall be separate from internment camps for prisoners of war.

These camps cannot be set up in unhealthy districts, nor where the climate would be harmful to the internees' health.

Application of PoW Convention
Art.17. Furthermore, the Convention of July 27, 1929, concerning the treatment of Prisoners of War is by analogy applicable to civilian internees.

The treatment of civilian internees shall in no case be inferior to that laid down in the said Convention.

CHAPTER III. ENEMY CIVILIANS IN TERRITORY OCCUPIED BY A BELLIGERENT

Observation of the Hague Regulations
Art. 18. The High Contracting Parties undertake to observe, as regards the condition and protection of enemy civilians in territory occupied by a belligerent, the provisions of Section III of the Regulations annexed to the Fourth Hague Convention, of 1907.

Additional Provisions
Art. 19. The High Contracting Parties further undertake to observe the following provisions:

(a) In the event of it appearing, in an exceptional case, indispensable for an occupying Power to take hostages, the latter shall always be treated humanely. Under no pretext shall they be put to death or submitted to corporal punishments;

(b) Deportations outside the territory of the occupied State are forbidden, unless they are evacuations intended, on account of the extension of military operations, to ensure the security of the inhabitants;

(c) Enemy civilians shall have the possibility of giving news of a strictly private character to next of kin in the interior of occupied territory and of receiving such news. The same possibility shall be granted for correspondence with the exterior, subject to the measures applied to the population of the occupying Power, in general.

With the same reservation enemy civilians shall have the possibility of receiving relief.

(d) Enemy civilians shall also benefit by the provisions of Article 8 of the present Convention.

CHAPTER IV. EXECUTION OF THE CONVENTION

Section I. Application and Execution of the Convention

In general
Art. 20. The provisions of the present Convention shall be respected by the High Contracting Parties in all circumstances.

In the event that, in time of war, one of the belligerents should not be a party to the Convention, its provisions shall nevertheless remain obligatory between the belligerents parties thereto.

Text posted
Art. 21. The text of the present Convention and of the special Conventions foreseen in Article 3 shall be posted up in all civilian internment centres and shall be communicated, at their request, to those who are unable to consult it.

Translations and regulations
Art. 22. The High Contracting Powers shall exchange, through the intermediary of the Swiss Federal Council, the official translations of the present Convention, as well as the laws and regulations which they may be called upon to adopt to ensure its application.

Section II. Organization of Control

Protecting Power, Delegates
Art. 23. The High Contracting Parties recognize that the full execution of the present Convention implies the cooperation of Protecting Powers; they declare themselves ready to accept the good offices of these Powers.

To this end, the Protecting Powers may nominate delegates, apart from their diplomatic staff, among their own nationals or among the nationals of other neutral Powers. These delegates shall be subject to the agreement of the belligerent to which their mission accredits them.

The representatives of the Protecting Power or its accepted delegates shall be authorized to visit all places of civilian internment, without exception. They shall have access to all buildings occupied by civilian internees and be allowed to converse with them, as a general rule without witnesses, personally or by the intermediary of interpreters.

The belligerents shall facilitate to the greatest possible extent the task of the representatives or of the recognized delegates of the Protecting Power. The military authorities shall be informed of their visits.

The belligerents may agree between themselves to allow persons of the same nationality as that of the civilian internees to participate in the journeys of inspection.

Interpretation of the Convention; Conferences
Art. 24. In case of disagreement between belligerents concerning the application of the provisions of the present Convention, the Protecting Powers shall, as far as possible, exercise their good offices with a view to settling the difference.

To this end, each of the Protecting Powers may, in particular, propose to the belligerents concerned a meeting of their representatives, possibly on properly selected neutral territory. The belligerents shall be under the obligation to take action on the proposals made to them to this effect. The Protecting Power may, if judged desirable, submit to the approval of the Powers concerned the name of a person belonging to a neutral Power, or of a personality delegated by the International Committee of the Red Cross, who shall be called upon to participate in this meeting.

International Committee of the Red Cross
Art. 25. The above provisions do not constitute an obstacle to the humanitarian activity which the International Committee of the Red Cross may exercise for the protection of enemy civilians, with the approval of the belligerents concerned.

Section III. Final provisions

Signature
Art. 26. The present Convention, which bears the date of this day, is open for signature until ...., in the name of all countries represented at the Conference.

Ratification
Art. 27. The present Convention shall be ratified as soon as possible. The ratifications shall be deposited in Bern.

A record shall be drawn up of the deposit of each instrument of ratification and certified copies of this record shall be transmitted by the Swiss Federal Council to the Governments of all the countries in whose name the Convention has been signed or whose accession has been notified.

Entry into force
Art. 28. The present Convention shall come into force six months after not less than two instruments of ratification have been deposited.

Thereafter, it shall come into force for each High Contracting Party six months after the deposit of the instrument of ratification.

Accession
Art. 29. From the date of its coming into force, the present Convention shall be open for accession in the name of any country in whose name the Convention has not been signed.

Notification
Art. 30. Accessions shall be notified in writing to the Swiss Federal Council and shall take effect six months after the date on which they are received. The Swiss Federal Council shall communicate the accessions to the Governments of all the countries in whose name the Convention has been signed or whose accession has been notified.

State of war, immediate effect
Art. 31. A state of war shall give immediate effect to the ratifications deposited and accessions notified by the belligerent Powers before or after the beginning of hostilities. The Swiss Federal Council shall communicate by the quickest method any ratifications or accessions received from belligerent Powers.

Denunciation
Art. 32. Each of the High Contracting Parties shall be at liberty to denounce the present Convention. The denunciation shall not take effect until one year after the notification thereof has been made in writing to the Swiss Federal Council.

The Swiss Federal Council shall transmit the notification to the Governments of all the High Contracting Parties.

The denunciation shall have effect only in respect of the denouncing High Contracting Party.

Moreover, the denunciation shall not take effect during a war in which the denouncing Power is involved. In such a case, the present Convention shall continue to have effect, beyond the period of one year, until peace has been concluded and, in any event, until repatriation operations have been completed.

Deposit
Art. 33. The Swiss Federal Council shall deposit a certified copy of the present Convention in the archives of the League of Nations. The Swiss Federal Council shall also inform the League of Nations of the ratifications, accessions and denunciations that have been notified to it.

No. 48

FINAL ACT OF THE DIPLOMATIC CONFERENCE 1949

Signed at Geneva, 12 August 1949

INTRODUCTORY NOTE: After the adoption of the two Geneva Conventions of 1929 attempts were made to supplement them by new regulations. The Geneva Conference of 1929, in its Final Act (*No. 42*), expressed the wish that a conference be convened with a view to regulating more comprehensively the use of medical aircraft in time of war and that an exhaustive study be made in order to prepare an international convention regarding the condition and protection of civilians of enemy nationality in the territory of a belligerent or in the territory occupied by a belligerent. The International Red Cross Conferences of Brussels (1930), Tokyo (1934) and London (1938) suggested the preparation of projects on further subjects (see *No. 47*). In January 1939, the Swiss Federal Council transmitted to all governments preliminary drafts, prepared by the International Committee of the Red Cross, as a basis for a diplomatic conference that was planned to be convened in Geneva early in 1940 but could not take place due to the outbreak of World War II.

The preliminary drafts dealt with the following subjects:

1. revision of the Geneva Convention of 1929 for the Amelioration of the Condition of the Wounded and Sick;
2. revision of the Hague Convention of 1907 for the Adaptation to Maritime Warfare of the Principles of the Geneva Convention;
3. Draft Convention for the Adaptation to Air Warfare of the Principles of the Geneva Convention;
4. Draft Convention for the Establishment of Hospital and Safety Zones in Time of War;
5. Draft Convention concerning the Condition and Protection of Civilians of Enemy Nationality in the Territory of a Belligerent or in the Territory Occupied by a Belligerent (cf. *No. 47*).

After the end of World War II new drafts were prepared that took account of the experience gained during the war. The two Geneva Conventions of 1929 as well as the Hague Convention of 1907 for the Adaptation to Maritime Warfare of the Principles of the Geneva Convention were included in the revision. A new draft for the protection of civilians was drawn up. The four draft conventions were prepared by the International Committee of the Red Cross with the assistance of a conference of government experts and were submitted to the International Red Cross Conference held at Stockholm in 1948. The Diplomatic Conference that adopted them in their final form took place from 21 April to 12 August 1949 in Geneva and assembled representatives of 63 governments.

The Conference made an innovation by grouping together the common provisions of the four Conventions. They embrace the general provisions, which are placed at the beginning of each Convention, the provisions on the repression of breaches of the Conventions and the final provisions.

Nearly all the states existing at present have ratified the four Conventions or adhered to them.

The Final Act has no force of law.

AUTHENTIC TEXTS: English and French. The text below is reprinted from the *Final Record of the Diplomatic Conference of Geneva of 1949*, Vol. I, Federal Political Department, Berne, pp. 195–199.

TEXT PUBLISHED IN: (Indications are given for the Final Act as well as for the four Conventions (*Nos. 45–49*)): *Final Record of the Diplomatic Conference of Geneva of 1949*, Vol. I, Federal Political Department, Berne, *Final Act*, pp. 195–199, *1st Convention*, pp. 205–224, *2nd Convention*, pp. 225–242, *3rd Convention*, pp. 243–296, *4th Convention*, pp. 297–341 (*Reservations*, pp. 342–357) (Engl.); *Actes de la Conférence Diplomatique de Genève de 1949*, tome I, Département Politique Fédéral, Berne, *Final Act*, pp. 195–200, *1st Convention*, pp. 205–224, *2nd Convention*, pp. 225–242, *3rd Convention*, pp. 243–293, *4th Convention*, pp. 294–335 (*Reservations*, pp. 336–351) (French); – *UNTS*, Vol. 75, *Final Act*, pp. 5–29, *1st Convention*, pp. 31–83, *2nd Convention*, pp. 85–133, *3rd Convention*, pp. 135–285, *4th Convention*, pp. 287–417 (*Reservations*, pp. 419–468) (Engl., French); *The Geneva Conventions of 12 August 1949*, 2nd revised edn., International Committee of the Red Cross, Geneva, July 1950, *1st Convention*, pp. 23–50, *2nd Convention*, pp. 51–74, *3rd Convention*, pp. 75–152, *4th Convention*, pp. 153–222 (Engl.); *Les Conventions de Genève du 12 août 1949*, 3ème édition, Comité international de la Croix-Rouge, Genève 1951, *1st Convention*, pp. 25–52, *2nd Convention*, pp. 53–76, *3rd Convention*, pp. 77–156, *4th Convention*, pp. 157–227 (French); *Los Conenios de Ginebra del 12 de Agosto de 1949*, Comité Internacional de la Cruz Roja, Ginebra 1950, *1st Convention*, pp. 27–56, *2nd Convention*, pp. 57–80, *3rd Convention*, pp. 81–160, *4th Convention*, pp. 161–230 (Span.); *International Red Cross Handbook*, 1983, *1st Convention*, pp. 23–46, *2nd Convention*, pp. 47–66, *3rd Convention*, pp. 67–135, *4th Convention*, pp. 136–194 (Engl.); *Manuel de la Croix-Rouge internationale*, 1983, *1st Convention*, pp. 23–47, *2nd Convention*, pp. 48–68, *3rd Convention*, pp. 69–140, *4th Convention*, pp. 141–202 (French); *Manual de la Cruz Roja internacional*, 1983, *1st Convention*, pp. 23–46, *2nd Convention*, pp. 47–67, *3rd Convention*, pp. 68–137, *4th Convention*, pp. 138–196 (Span.); *Handbook of the International Movement 1994*, *1st Convention*, pp. 23–46, *2nd Convention*, pp. 47–66, *3rd Convention*, pp. 67–135, *4th Convention*, pp. 136–194 (Engl.); *Manuel du Mouvement international*, 1994, *1st Convention*, pp. 23–47; *2nd Convention*, pp. 48–68, *3rd Convention*, pp. 69–140, *4th Convention*, pp. 141–203 (French); *Manual del Movimiento internacional*, 1994, *1st Convention*, pp. 23–47, *2nd Convention*, pp. 48–67, *3rd Convention*, pp. 68–137, *4th Convention*, pp. 138–196 (Span.); *GBTS*, 1958, No. 39, Cmnd. 550, *1st Convention*, pp. 4–51, *2nd Convention*, pp. 52–93, *3rd Convention*, pp. 94–215, *4th Convention*, pp. 355–423 (Engl.); *US Treaties and Other International Agreements*, *1st Convention*, *TIAS* 3362, *UST* 6, pp. 3114–3216, *2nd Convention*, *TIAS* 3363, *UST* 6, pp. 3217–3315, *3rd Convention*, *TIAS* 3364 *UST* 6 pp. 3316–3515, *4th Convention*, *TIAS* 3365 *UST* 6 pp. 3516–3695 (Engl., French); *Human Rights: A Compilation of International Instruments*, Vol. I (Second Part), New York, United Nations, 1993, *1st Convention*, pp. 681–706, *2nd Convention*, pp. 707–727, *3rd Convention*, pp. 728–798, *4th Convention*, pp. 799–861 (Engl.); *Droit des conflits armés*, pp. 457–731 (French); Ronzitti, *2nd Convention*, pp. 503–533 (Engl.); *AJIL*, *3rd Convention* (*with Reservations*), Vol. 47, 1953, Suppl., pp. 119–177 (Engl.); *4th Convention* (*with Reservations*), Vol. 50, 1956, Suppl., pp. 724–783 (Engl.); Friedman, pp. 525–691 (Engl.); Roberts and

Guelff, *1st Convention*, pp. 195–215, *2nd Convention*, pp. 221–241, *3rd Convention*, pp. 243–298, *4th Convention*, pp. 299–355 (Engl.); *Sbornik dogovorov SSSR*, vyp. XVI, 1957, *1st Convention*, pp. 71–100, *2nd Convention*, pp. 101–124, *3rd Convention*, pp. 125– 204, *4th Convention*, pp. 204–278 (Russ.); *Mezhdunarodnoe pravo*, Tom III, *1st Convention*, pp. 163–185, *2nd Convention*, pp. 185–206, *3rd Convention*, pp. 206–261, *4th Convention*, pp. 53–112 (Russ. – extracts); *Zhenevskie konventsii o zaschite zhertv voiny ot 12 avgusta 1949 goda*, Moskva, Izdatel'stvo *Izvestiya Sovetov deputatov trudyashchikhsya SSSR*, 1969, *1-aya Konventsiya*, pp. 29–57; *2-aya Konventsiya*, pp. 59–83, *3-aya Konventsiya*, pp. 85–162, *4-aya Konventsiya*, pp. 163–235 (Russ.); Blatova, *1st Convention*, pp. 734–746, *2nd Convention*, pp. 746–751, *3rd Convention*, pp. 751–772, *4th Convention*, pp. 772–794 (Russ. – extracts); ICRC website: www.icrc.org/ihl.nsf.

* * *

The Conference convened by the Swiss Federal Council for the purpose of revising:

the Geneva Convention of 27 July 1929 for the Relief of the Wounded and Sick in Armies in the Field,

the Xth Hague Convention of 18 October 1907 for the Adaptation to Maritime Warfare of the Principles of the Geneva Convention of 6 July 1906,

the Geneva Convention of 27 July 1929 relative to the Treatment of Prisoners of War, and

to establish

a Convention for the Protection of Civilian Persons in Time of War,

deliberated from 21 April to 12 August 1949, at Geneva, on the basis of the four Draft Conventions examined and approved by the XVIIth international Red Cross Conference held at Stockholm.

The Conference established the texts of the following Conventions:

I. *Geneva Convention for the Amelioration of the Condition of the Wounded and Sick in Armed Forces in the Field.*

II. *Geneva Convention for the Amelioration of the Condition of Wounded, Sick and Shipwrecked Members of Armed Forces at Sea.*

III. *Geneva Convention relative to the Treatment of Prisoners of War.*

IV. *Geneva Convention relative to the Protection of Civilian Persons in Time of War.*

These Conventions, the text of which has been established in the English and French languages, are attached to the present Act. The official translation of the same Conventions into Russian and Spanish will be made through the good offices of the Swiss Federal Council.

The Conference further adopted 11 resolutions which are also attached to the present Act:

In witness whereof, the undersigned, duly authorized by their respective Governments, have signed this present Final Act.

Done at Geneva, this twelfth day of August 1949, in the English and French languages. The original and the documents accompanying it shall be deposited in the Archives of the Swiss Confederation.

[Here follow signatures]

SIGNATURES

Afghanistan
Albania
Argentina
Australia
Austria
Belgium
Brazil
Bulgaria
Burma
Byelorussian Soviet Socialist Republic[1]
Canada
Chile
China
Colombia
Costa Rica
Cuba
Czechoslovakia
Denmark
Ecuador
Egypt
Ethiopia
Finland
France
Greece
Guatemala
Holy See
Hungary
India
Iran
Ireland
Israel
Italy
Lebanon
Liechtenstein
Luxemburg
Mexico
Monaco
Netherlands
New Zealand
Nicaragua
Pakistan
Peru
PolandSpain
Portugal
Romania
Sweden
Switzerland
Syria
Turkey
Thailand
Ukrainian Soviet Socialist Republic[1]
Union of Soviet Socialist Republics[1]
United Kingdom of Great Britain and Northern Ireland
UnitedStates of America
Uruguay
Venezuela
Yugoslavia

RESERVATIONS AND DECLARATIONS

BYELORUSSIAN SOVIET SOCIALIST REPUBLIC
The Delegation of the Byelorussian Soviet Socialist Republic regrets the fact that the resolution submitted by the Delegation of the Union of Soviet Socialist Republics, condemning the use of methods of mass extermination, was rejected by the Conference. The adoption of this resolution, which was in the interests of all freedom-loving nations of the world, would have helped to render as effective as possible the protection of war victims against the most disastrous consequences of war.

UKRAINIAN SOVIET SOCIALIST REPUBLIC
The Delegation of the Ukrainian Soviet Socialist Republic regrets the fact that the resolution submitted by the Delegation of the Union of Soviet Socialist Republics, condemning the use of methods of mass extermination, was rejected by the Conference. The adoption of this resolution, which was in the interests of all freedom-loving nations of the world, would have helped to render as effective as possible the protection of war victims against the most disastrous consequences of war.

[1] Signed subject to the attached reservation.

Union of Soviet Socialist Republics

On signing the Final Act of the Diplomatic Conference, the Delegation of the Union of Soviet Socialist Republics makes the following reservations:

1. The Soviet Delegation regrets the fact that the resolution which it submitted, condemning the use of methods of mass extermination, was rejected by the Conference. The adoption of this resolution, which was in the interests of all freedom-loving nations of the world, would have considerably enhanced the role and influence of this Conference and would have helped to render as effective as possible the protection of war victims against the most disastrous consequences of war.
2. As regards the adoption by the Conference of a resolution recommending that consideration be given to the advisability of setting up an international body to replace the Protecting Power, the Soviet Delegation sees no need to consider this question or to create such a body, since the problem of the Protecting Powers has been satisfactorily solved by the Conventions established at the present Conference.

No. 49

CONVENTION (I) FOR THE AMELIORATION OF THE CONDITION OF THE WOUNDED AND SICK IN ARMED FORCES IN THE FIELD

Signed at Geneva, 12 August 1949

INTRODUCTORY NOTE: This Convention represents the fourth version of the Geneva Convention on the wounded and sick after those adopted in 1864, 1906 and 1929 (see *Nos. 38, 42 and 45*). The fundamental principles as well as the division into chapters remained the same as in the preceding version with the exception of the new introductory chapter on general provisions. Changes were made especially in Chapter IV (personnel). Hitherto, medical personnel and chaplains falling into enemy hands had to be immediately repatriated. The 1949 Convention, taking account of changed conditions of warfare, provides that they may in certain circumstances be retained to care for prisoners of war. The provisions on medical equipment were correspondingly altered. In the chapter on medical transports it was provided that medical aircraft may in certain circumstances fly over neutral territory. Some clarifications were made as regards the article on the use of the emblem (Article 44).

ENTRY INTO FORCE: 21 October 1950.

AUTHENTIC TEXTS: English and French. The text below is reprinted from the *Final Record of the Diplomatic Conference of Geneva of 1949*, Vol. I, Federal Political Department, Berne, pp. 205–224.

The marginal titles added to the articles of the present Convention have no official character and were not adopted by the Diplomatic Conference. They were drafted by the Conference Secretariat and are used in the edition of the Geneva Convention published by the International Committee of the Red Cross.

TEXT PUBLISHED IN: See indications under *No. 48*.

TABLE OF CONTENTS

* * *

The undersigned Plenipotentiaries of the Governments represented at the Diplomatic Conference held at Geneva from April 21 to August 12, 1949, for the purpose of revising the Geneva Convention for the Relief of the Wounded and Sick in Armies in the Field of July 27, 1929, have agreed as follows:[1]

Chapter I. General Provisions

Article 1. The High Contracting Parties undertake to respect and to ensure respect for the present Convention in all circumstances. Respect for the Convention

Art. 2. In addition to the provisions which shall be implemented in peacetime, the present Convention shall apply to all cases of declared war or of any other armed conflict which may arise between two or more of the High Contracting Parties, even if the state of war is not recognized by one of them. Application of the Conventions

The Convention shall also apply to all cases of partial or total occupation of the territory of a High Contracting Party, even if the said occupation meets with no armed resistance.

Although one of the Powers in conflict may not be a party to the present Convention, the Powers who are parties thereto shall remain bound by it in their mutual relations. They shall furthermore be bound by the Convention in relation to the said Power, if the latter accepts and applies the provisions thereof.

Art. 3.[2] In the case of armed conflict not of an international character occurring in the territory of one of the High Contracting Conflicts not of an international character

[1] For objection by the United States of America to reservations made by other states with respect to this Convention, see pp. 680–681.

[2] For reservation in respect of this article by Argentina and Portugal (withdrawn) see pp. 651, 671 and 672.

Parties, each Party to the conflict shall be bound to apply, as a minimum, the following provisions:

(1) Persons taking no active part in the hostilities, including members of armed forces who have laid down their arms and those placed *hors de combat* by sickness, wounds, detention, or any other cause, shall in all circumstances be treated humanely, without any adverse distinction founded on race, colour, religion or faith, sex, birth or wealth, or any other similar criteria.

To this end, the following acts are and shall remain prohibited at any time and in any place whatsoever with respect to the above-mentioned persons:

(a) violence to life and person, in particular murder of all kinds, mutilation, cruel treatment and torture;

(b) taking of hostages;

(c) outrages upon personal dignity, in particular humiliating and degrading treatment;

(d) the passing of sentences and the carrying out of executions without previous judgment pronounced by a regularly constituted court, affording all the judicial guarantees which are recognized as indispensable by civilized peoples.

(2) The wounded and sick shall be collected and cared for. An impartial humanitarian body, such as the International Committee of the Red Cross, may offer its services to the Parties to the conflict.

The Parties to the conflict should further endeavour to bring into force, by means of special agreements, all or part of the other provisions of the present Convention. The application of the preceding provisions shall not affect the legal status of the Parties to the conflict.

Application by neutral Powers

Art. 4. Neutral Powers shall apply by analogy the provisions of the present Convention to the wounded and sick, and to members of the medical personnel and to chaplains of the armed forces of the Parties to the conflict, received or interned in their territory, as well as to dead persons found.

Duration of application

Art. 5. For the protected persons who have fallen into the hands of the enemy, the present Convention shall apply until their final repatriation.

Special agreements

Art. 6. In addition to the agreements expressly provided for in Articles 10, 15, 23, 28, 31, 36, 37 and 52, the High Contracting Parties may conclude other special agreements for all matters concerning which they may deem it suitable to make separate provision. No special agreement shall adversely affect the situation of the wounded and sick, of members of the medical personnel or of chaplains, as defined by the present Convention, nor restrict the rights which it confers upon them.

Wounded and sick, as well as medical personnel and chaplains, shall continue to have the benefit of such agreements as long as the Convention is applicable to them, except where express provisions to the contrary are contained in the aforesaid or in subsequent agreements, or where more favourable measures have been taken with regard to them by one or other of the Parties to the conflict.

Non-renunciation of rights

Art. 7. Wounded and sick, as well as members of the medical personnel and chaplains, may in no circumstances renounce in part or in entirety the rights secured to them by the present Convention, and by the special agreements referred to in the foregoing Article, if such there be.

Protecting Powers

Art. 8. The present Convention shall be applied with the cooperation and under the scrutiny of the Protecting Powers whose duty it is to safeguard the interests of the Parties to the conflict. For this purpose, the Protecting Powers may appoint, apart from their diplomatic or consular staff, delegates from amongst their own nationals or the nationals of other neutral Powers. The said delegates shall be subject to the approval of the Power with which they are to carry out their duties.

The Parties to the conflict shall facilitate, to the greatest extent possible, the task of the representatives or delegates of the Protecting Powers.

The representatives or delegates of the Protecting Powers shall not in any case exceed their mission under the present Convention. They shall, in particular, take account of the imperative necessities of security of the State wherein they carry out their duties. Their activities shall only be restricted as an exceptional and temporary measure when this is rendered necessary by imperative military necessities.

Activities of the International Committee of the Red Cross

Art. 9. The provisions of the present Convention constitute no obstacle to the humanitarian activities which the International Committee of the Red Cross or any other impartial humanitarian organization may, subject to the consent of the Parties to the conflict concerned, undertake for the protection of wounded and sick, medical personnel and chaplains, and for their relief.

Substitutes for the Protecting Powers

Art. 10.[3] [4] The High Contracting Parties may at any time agree to entrust to an organization which offers all guarantees of impartiality and efficacy the duties incumbent on the Protecting Powers by virtue of the present Convention.

---

3 For reservation in respect of this article by Albania, Bulgaria, Byelorussian SSR, China, Czechoslovakia, Germany (Democratic Republic of), Guinea-Bissau. Hungary, Korea (People's Democratic Republic of), Poland, Portugal, Romania, Ukrainian SSR, USSR, Vietnam (Socialist Republic of) and Yugoslavia, see pp. 650–688.

4 In connection with this article see resolution 2 of the Diplomatic Conference of Geneva, 1949, p. 690.

When wounded and sick, or medical personnel and chaplains do not benefit or cease to benefit, no matter for what reason, by the activities of a Protecting Power or of an organization provided for in the first paragraph above, the Detaining Power shall request a neutral State, or such an organization, to undertake the functions performed under the present Convention by a Protecting Power designated by the Parties to a conflict.

If protection cannot be arranged accordingly, the Detaining Power shall request or shall accept, subject to the provisions of this Article, the offer of the services of a humanitarian organization, such as the International Committee of the Red Cross, to assume the humanitarian functions performed by Protecting Powers under the present Convention.

Any neutral Power, or any organization invited by the Power concerned or offering itself for these purposes, shall be required to act with a sense of responsibility towards the Party to the conflict on which persons protected by the present Convention depend, and shall be required to furnish sufficient assurances that it is in a position to undertake the appropriate functions and to discharge them impartially.

No derogation from the preceding provisions shall be made by special agreements between Powers one of which is restricted, even temporarily, in its freedom to negotiate with the other Power or its allies by reason of military events, more particularly where the whole, or a substantial part, of the territory of the said Power is occupied.

Whenever in the present Convention mention is made of a Protecting Power, such mention also applies to substitute organizations in the sense of the present Article.

Conciliation procedure

Art. 11.[5] In cases where they deem it advisable in the interest of protected persons, particularly in cases of disagreement between the Parties to the conflict as to the application or interpretation of the provisions of the present Convention, the Protecting Powers shall lend their good offices with a view to settling the disagreement.

For this purpose, each of the Protecting Powers may, either at the invitation of one Party or on its own initiative, propose to the Parties to the conflict a meeting of their representatives, in particular of the authorities responsible for the wounded and sick, members of medical personnel and chaplains, possibly on neutral territory suitably chosen. The Parties to the conflict shall be bound to give effect to the proposals made to them for this purpose. The Protecting Powers may, if necessary, propose for approval by the Parties to the conflict a person belonging to a neutral Power or delegated by the International Committee of the Red Cross, who shall be invited to take part in such a meeting.

[5] For reservation in respect of this article by Hungary, see pp. 662–663.

Chapter II. Wounded and Sick

Art. 12. Members of the armed forces and other persons mentioned in the following Article, who are wounded or sick, shall be respected and protected in all circumstances.

Protection and care

They shall be treated humanely and cared for by the Party to the conflict in whose power they may be, without any adverse distinction founded on sex, race, nationality, religion, political opinions, or any other similar criteria. Any attempts upon their lives, or violence to their persons, shall be strictly prohibited; in particular, they shall not be murdered or exterminated, subjected to torture or to biological experiments; they shall not wilfully be left without medical assistance and care, nor shall conditions exposing them to contagion or infection be created.

Only urgent medical reasons will authorize priority in the order of treatment to be administered.

Women shall be treated with all consideration due to their sex.

The Party to the conflict which is compelled to abandon wounded or sick to the enemy shall, as far as military considerations permit, leave with them a part of its medical personnel and material to assist in their care.

Art. 13.[6] The present Convention shall apply to the wounded and sick belonging to the following categories:

Protected persons

(1) Members of the armed forces of a Party to the conflict as well as members of militias or volunteer corps forming part of such armed forces.

(2) Members of other militias and members of other volunteer corps, including those of organized resistance movements, belonging to a Party to the conflict and operating in or outside their own territory, even if this territory is occupied, provided that such militias or volunteer corps, including such organized resistance movements, fulfil the following conditions:
   (a) that of being commanded by a person responsible for his subordinates;
   (b) that of having a fixed distinctive sign recognizable at a distance;
   (c) that of carrying arms openly;
   (d) that of conducting their operations in accordance with the laws and customs of war.

(3) Members of regular armed forces who profess allegiance to a Government or an authority not recognized by the Detaining Power.

6 For reservation in respect of this article by Guinea-Bissau (and objection to this reservation by the Federal Republic of Germany) and Portugal (withdrawn), see pp. 660, 661, 671.

(4) Persons who accompany the armed forces without actually being members thereof, such as civil members of military aircraft crews, war correspondents, supply contractors, members of labour units or of services responsible for the welfare of the armed forces, provided that they have received authorization from the armed forces which they accompany.

(5) Members of crews, including masters, pilots and apprentices of the merchant marine and the crews of civil aircraft of the Parties to the conflict, who do not benefit by more favourable treatment under any other provisions in international law.

(6) Inhabitants of a non-occupied territory who on the approach of the enemy spontaneously take up arms to resist the invading forces, without having had time to form themselves into regular armed units, provided they carry arms openly and respect the laws and customs of war.

Status

Art. 14. Subject to the provisions of Article 12 the wounded and sick of a belligerent who fall into enemy hands shall be prisoners of war, and the provisions of international law concerning prisoners of war shall apply to them.

Search for casualties. Evacuation

Art. 15. At all times, and particularly after an engagement, Parties to the conflict shall, without delay, take all possible measures to search for and collect the wounded and sick, to protect them against pillage and ill-treatment, to ensure their adequate care, and to search for the dead and prevent their being despoiled.

Whenever circumstances permit, an armistice or a suspension of fire shall be arranged, or local arrangements made, to permit the removal, exchange and transport of the wounded left on the battlefield.

Likewise, local arrangements may be concluded between Parties to the conflict for the removal or exchange of wounded and sick from a besieged or encircled area, and for the passage of medical and religious personnel and equipment on their way to that area.

Recording and forwarding of information

Art. 16. Parties to the conflict shall record as soon as possible, in respect of each wounded, sick or dead person of the adverse Party falling into their hands, any particulars which may assist in his identification.

These records should if possible include:

(a) designation of the Power on which he depends;
(b) army, regimental, personal or serial number;
(c) surname;
(d) first name or names;
(e) date of birth;
(f) any other particulars shown on his identity card or disc;

(g) date and place of capture or death;
(h) particulars concerning wounds or illness, or cause of death.

As soon as possible the above mentioned information shall be forwarded to the Information Bureau described in Article 122 of the Geneva Convention relative to the Treatment of Prisoners of War of August 12, 1949, which shall transmit this information to the Power on which these persons depend through the intermediary of the Protecting Power and of the Central Prisoners of War Agency.

Parties to the conflict shall prepare and forward to each other through the same bureau, certificates of death or duly authenticated lists of the dead. They shall likewise collect and forward through the same bureau one half of a double identity disc, last wills or other documents of importance to the next of kin, money and in general all articles of an intrinsic or sentimental value, which are found on the dead. These articles, together with unidentified articles, shall be sent in sealed packets, accompanied by statements giving all particulars necessary for the identification of the deceased owners, as well as by a complete list of the contents of the parcel.

Prescriptions regarding the dead. Graves Registration Service

Art. 17. Parties to the conflict shall ensure that burial or cremation of the dead, carried out individually as far as circumstances permit, is preceded by a careful examination, if possible by a medical examination, of the bodies, with a view to confirming death, establishing identity and enabling a report to be made. One half of the double identity disc, or the identity disc itself if it is a single disc, should remain on the body.

Bodies shall not be cremated except for imperative reasons of hygiene or for motives based on the religion of the deceased. In case of cremation, the circumstances and reasons for cremation shall be stated in detail in the death certificate or on the authenticated list of the dead.

They shall further ensure that the dead are honourably interred, if possible according to the rites of the religion to which they belonged, that their graves are respected, grouped if possible according to the nationality of the deceased, properly maintained and marked so that they may always be found. For this purpose, they shall organize at the commencement of hostilities an Official Graves Registration Service, to allow subsequent exhumations and to ensure the identification of bodies, whatever the site of the graves, and the possible transportation to the home country. These provisions shall likewise apply to the ashes, which shall be kept by the Graves Registration Service until proper disposal thereof in accordance with the wishes of the home country.

As soon as circumstances permit, and at latest at the end of hostilities, these Services shall exchange, through the Information Bureau mentioned in the second paragraph of Article 16, lists showing the exact location and markings of the graves together with particulars of the dead interred therein.

Role of the population

Art. 18. The military authorities may appeal to the charity of the inhabitants voluntarily to collect and care for, under their direction, the wounded and sick, granting persons who have responded to this appeal the necessary protection and facilities. Should the adverse party take or retake control of the area, he shall likewise grant these persons the same protection and the same facilities.

The military authorities shall permit the inhabitants and relief societies, even in invaded or occupied areas, spontaneously to collect and care for wounded or sick of whatever nationality. The civilian population shall respect these wounded and sick, and in particular abstain from offering them violence.

No one may ever be molested or convicted for having nursed the wounded or sick.

The provisions of the present Article do not relieve the occupying Power of its obligation to give both physical and moral care to the wounded and sick.

Chapter III. Medical Units and Establishments

Protection

Art. 19. Fixed establishments and mobile medical units of the Medical Service may in no circumstances be attacked, but shall at all times be respected and protected by the Parties to the conflict. Should they fall into the hands of the adverse Party, their personnel shall be free to pursue their duties, as long as the capturing Power has not itself ensured the necessary care of the wounded and sick found in such establishments and units.

The responsible authorities shall ensure that the said medical establishments and units are, as far as possible, situated in such a manner that attacks against military objectives cannot imperil their safety.

Protection of hospital ships

Art. 20. Hospital ships entitled to the protection of the Geneva Convention for the Amelioration of the Condition of Wounded, Sick and Shipwrecked Members of Armed Forces at Sea of August 12, 1949, shall not be attacked from the land.

Discontinuance of protection of medical establishments and units

Art. 21. The protection to which fixed establishments and mobile medical units of the Medical Service are entitled shall not cease unless they are used to commit, outside their humanitarian duties, acts harmful to the enemy. Protection may, however, cease only after a due warning has been given, naming, in all appropriate cases, a reasonable time limit and after such warning has remained unheeded.

Art. 22. The following conditions shall not be considered as depriving a medical unit or establishment of the protection guaranteed by Article 19:

Conditions not depriving medical units and establishments of protection

(1) That the personnel of the unit or establishment are armed, and that they use the arms in their own defence, or in that of the wounded and sick in their charge.
(2) That in the absence of armed orderlies, the unit or establishment is protected by a picket or by sentries or by an escort.
(3) That small arms and ammunition taken from the wounded and sick and not yet handed to the proper service, are found in the unit or establishment.
(4) That personnel and material of the veterinary service are found in the unit or establishment, without forming an integral part thereof.
(5) That the humanitarian activities of medical units and establishments or of their personnel extend to the care of civilian wounded or sick.

Hospital zones and localities

Art. 23. In time of peace, the High Contracting Parties and, after the outbreak of hostilities, the Parties to the conflict, may establish in their own territory and, if the need arises, in occupied areas, hospital zones and localities so organized as to protect the wounded and sick from the effects of war, as well as the personnel entrusted with the organization and administration of these zones and localities and with the care of the persons therein assembled.

Upon the outbreak and during the course of hostilities, the Parties concerned may conclude agreements on mutual recognition of the hospital zones and localities they have created. They may for this purpose implement the provisions of the Draft Agreement annexed to the present Convention, with such amendments as they may consider necessary.

The Protecting Powers and the International Committee of the Red Cross are invited to lend their good offices in order to facilitate the institution and recognition of these hospital zones and localities.

Chapter IV. Personnel

Protection of permanent personnel

Art. 24. Medical personnel exclusively engaged in the search for, or the collection, transport or treatment of the wounded or sick, or in the prevention of disease, staff exclusively engaged in the administration of medical units and establishments, as well as chaplains attached to the armed forces, shall be respected and protected in all circumstances.

Protection of auxiliary personnel

Art. 25. Members of the armed forces specially trained for employment, should the need arise, as hospital orderlies, nurses or auxiliary stretcher-bearers, in the search for or the collection, transport or treatment of the wounded and sick shall likewise be respected and protected if they are carrying out these duties at the time when they come into contact with the enemy or fall into his hands.

Personnel of aid societies

Art. 26. The staff of National Red Cross Societies and that of other Voluntary Aid Societies, duly recognized and authorized by their Governments, who may be employed on the same duties as the personnel named in Article 24, are placed on the same footing as the personnel named in the said Article, provided that the staff of such societies are subject to military laws and regulations.

Each High Contracting Party shall notify to the other, either in time of peace or at the commencement of or during hostilities, but in any case before actually employing them, the names of the societies which it has authorized, under its responsibility, to render assistance to the regular medical service of its armed forces.

Societies of neutral countries

Art. 27. A recognized Society of a neutral country can only lend the assistance of its medical personnel and units to a Party to the conflict with the previous consent of its own Government and the authorization of the Party to the conflict concerned. That personnel and those units shall be placed under the control of that Party to the conflict.

The neutral Government shall notify this consent to the adversary of the State which accepts such assistance. The Party to the conflict who accepts such assistance is bound to notify the adverse Party thereof before making any use of it.

In no circumstances shall this assistance be considered as interference in the conflict.

The members of the personnel named in the first paragraph shall be duly furnished with the identity cards provided for in Article 40 before leaving the neutral country to which they belong.

Retained personnel

Art. 28.[7] Personnel designated in Articles 24 and 26 who fall into the hands of the adverse Party, shall be retained only in so far as the state of health, the spiritual needs and the number of prisoners of war require.

Personnel thus retained shall not be deemed prisoners of war. Nevertheless they shall at least benefit by all the provisions of the Geneva Convention relative to the Treatment of Prisoners of War of August 12, 1949. Within the framework of the military laws and regulations of the Detaining Power, and under the authority of its competent service, they shall continue to carry out, in accordance with their professional ethics, their medical and spiritual duties on behalf of prisoners of war, preferably those of the armed forces to which they themselves belong. They shall further enjoy the following facilities for carrying out their medical or spiritual duties:

(a) They shall be authorized to visit periodically the prisoners of war in labour units or hospitals outside the camp. The

[7] In connection with this article, see resolution 3 of the Diplomatic Conference of Geneva, 1949, p. 690.

Detaining Power shall put at their disposal the means of transport required.

(b) In each camp the senior medical officer of the highest rank shall be responsible to the military authorities of the camp for the professional activity of the retained medical personnel. For this purpose, from the outbreak of hostilities, the Parties to the conflict shall agree regarding the corresponding seniority of the ranks of their medical personnel, including those of the societies designated in Article 26. In all questions arising out of their duties, this medical officer, and the chaplains, shall have direct access to the military and medical authorities of the camp who shall grant them the facilities they may require for correspondence relating to these questions.

(c) Although retained personnel in a camp shall be subject to its internal discipline, they shall not, however, be required to perform any work outside their medical or religious duties.

During hostilities the Parties to the conflict shall make arrangements for relieving where possible retained personnel, and shall settle the procedure of such relief.

None of the preceding provisions shall relieve the Detaining Power of the obligations imposed upon it with regard to the medical and spiritual welfare of the prisoners of war.

Status of auxiliary personnel

Art. 29. Members of the personnel designated in Article 25 who have fallen into the hands of the enemy, shall be prisoners of war but shall be employed on their medical duties in so far as the need arises.

Return of medical & religious personnel

Art. 30. Personnel whose retention is not indispensable by virtue of the provisions of Article 28 shall be returned to the Party to the conflict to whom they belong, as soon as a road is open for their return and military requirements permit.

Pending their return, they shall not be deemed prisoners of war. Nevertheless they shall at least benefit by all the provisions of the Geneva Convention relative to the Treatment of Prisoners of War of August 12, 1949. They shall continue to fulfil their duties under the orders of the adverse Party and shall preferably be engaged in the care of the wounded and sick of the Party to the conflict to which they themselves belong.

On their departure, they shall take with them the effects, personal belongings, valuables and instruments belonging to them.

Selection of personnel for return

Art. 31.[8] The selection of personnel for return under Article 30 shall be made irrespective of any consideration of race, religion or political opinion, but preferably according to the chronological order of their capture and their state of health.

[8] In connection with this article, see resolution 3 of the Diplomatic Conference of Geneva, 1949, p. 690.

As from the outbreak of hostilities, Parties to the conflict may determine by special agreement the percentage of personnel to be retained, in proportion to the number of prisoners and the distribution of the said personnel in the camps.

Return of personnel belonging to neutral countries

Art. 32. Persons designated in Article 27 who have fallen into the hands of the adverse Party may not be detained.

Unless otherwise agreed, they shall have permission to return to their country, or if this is not possible, to the territory of the Party to the conflict in whose service they were, as soon as a route for their return is open and military considerations permit.

Pending their release, they shall continue their work under the direction of the adverse Party; they shall preferably be engaged in the care of the wounded and sick of the Party to the conflict in whose service they were.

On their departure, they shall take with them their effects, personal articles and valuables and the instruments, arms and if possible the means of transport belonging to them.

The Parties to the conflict shall secure to this personnel, while in their power, the same food, lodging, allowances and pay as are granted to the corresponding personnel of their armed forces. The food shall in any case be sufficient as regards quantity, quality and variety to keep the said personnel in a normal state of health.

Chapter V. Buildings and Material

Buildings and stores

Art. 33. The material of mobile medical units of the armed forces which fall into the hands of the enemy, shall be reserved for the care of wounded and sick.

The buildings, material and stores of fixed medical establishments of the armed forces shall remain subject to the laws of war, but may not be diverted from that purpose as long as they are required for the care of wounded and sick. Nevertheless, the commanders of forces in the field may make use of them, in case of urgent military necessity, provided that they make previous arrangements for the welfare of the wounded and sick who are nursed in them.

The material and stores defined in the present Article shall not be intentionally destroyed.

Property of aid societies

Art. 34. The real and personal property of aid societies which are admitted to the privileges of the Convention shall be regarded as private property.

The right of requisition recognized for belligerents by the laws and customs of war shall not be exercised except in case of urgent necessity, and only after the welfare of the wounded and sick has been ensured.

Chapter VI. Medical Transports

Art. 35. Transports of wounded and sick or of medical equipment shall be respected and protected in the same way as mobile medical units. Protection

Should such transports or vehicles fall into the hands of the adverse Party, they shall be subject to the laws of war, on condition that the Party to the conflict who captures them shall in all cases ensure the care of the wounded and sick they contain.

The civilian personnel and all means of transport obtained by requisition shall be subject to the general rules of international law.

Art. 36. Medical aircraft, that is to say, aircraft exclusively employed for the removal of wounded and sick and for the transport of medical personnel and equipment, shall not be attacked, but shall be respected by the belligerents, while flying at heights, times and on routes specifically agreed upon between the belligerents concerned. Medical aircraft

They shall bear, clearly marked, the distinctive emblem prescribed in Article 38, together with their national colours, on their lower, upper and lateral surfaces. They shall be provided with any other markings or means of identification that may be agreed upon between the belligerents upon the outbreak or during the course of hostilities.

Unless agreed otherwise, flights over enemy or enemy-occupied territory are prohibited.

Medical aircraft shall obey every summons to land. In the event of a landing thus imposed, the aircraft with its occupants may continue its flight after examination, if any.

In the event of an involuntary landing in enemy or enemy-occupied territory, the wounded and sick, as well as the crew of the aircraft shall be prisoners of war. The medical personnel shall be treated according to Article 24, and the Articles following.

Art. 37. Subject to the provisions of the second paragraph, medical aircraft of Parties to the conflict may fly over the territory of neutral Powers, land on it in case of necessity, or use it as a port of call. They shall give the neutral Powers previous notice of their passage over the said territory and obey all summons to alight, on land or water. They will be immune from attack only when flying on routes, at heights and at times specifically agreed upon between the Parties to the conflict and the neutral Power concerned. Flight over neutral countries. Landing of wounded

The neutral Powers may, however, place conditions or restrictions on the passage or landing of medical aircraft on their territory. Such possible conditions or restrictions shall be applied equally to all Parties to the conflict.

Unless agreed otherwise between the neutral Power and the Parties to the conflict, the wounded and sick who are disembarked, with the consent of the local authorities, on neutral territory by medical aircraft, shall be detained by the neutral Power, where so required by international law, in such a manner that they cannot again take part in operations of war. The cost of their accommodation and internment shall be borne by the Power on which they depend.

Chapter VII. The Distinctive Emblem[9]

Emblem of the Convention

Art. 38. As a compliment to Switzerland, the heraldic emblem of the red cross on a white ground, formed by reversing the Federal colours, is retained as the emblem and distinctive sign of the Medical Service of armed forces.

Nevertheless, in the case of countries which already use as emblem, in place of the red cross, the red crescent or the red lion and sun on a white ground, those emblems are also recognized by the terms of the present Convention.

Use of the emblem

Art. 39. Under the direction of the competent military authority, the emblem shall be displayed on the flags, armlets and on all equipment employed in the Medical Service.

Identification of medical and religious personnel

Art. 40.[10] The personnel designated in Article 24 and in Articles 26 and 27 shall wear, affixed to the left arm, a water-resistant armlet bearing the distinctive emblem, issued and stamped by the military authority.

Such personnel, in addition to wearing the identity disc mentioned in Article 16, shall also carry a special identity card bearing the distinctive emblem. This card shall be water-resistant and of such size that it can be carried in the pocket. It shall be worded in the national language, shall mention at least the surname and first names, the date of birth, the rank and the service number of the bearer, and shall state in what capacity he is entitled to the protection of the present Convention. The card shall bear the photograph of the owner and also either his signature or his finger-prints or both. It shall be embossed with the stamp of the military authority.

The identity card shall be uniform throughout the same armed forces and, as far as possible, of a similar type in the armed forces of the High Contracting Parties. The Parties to the conflict may be guided by the model which is annexed, by way of example, to the present Convention. They shall inform each other, at the outbreak of hostilities, of the model they are using. Identity cards should be made out, if possible, at least in duplicate, one copy being kept by the home country.

[9] For declaration and reservation with respect to the distinctive emblem by Iran and Israel, see p. 663.

[10] In connection with this article, see resolution 4 of the Diplomatic Conference of Geneva, 1949, p. 691.

In no circumstances may the said personnel be deprived of their insignia or identity cards nor of the right to wear the armlet. In case of loss, they shall be entitled to receive duplicates of the cards and to have the insignia replaced.

Art. 41. The personnel designated in Article 25 shall wear, but only while carrying out medical duties, a white armlet bearing in its centre the distinctive sign in miniature; the armlet shall be issued and stamped by the military authority.

Identification of auxiliary personnel

Military identity documents to be carried by this type of personnel shall specify what special training they have received, the temporary character of the duties they are engaged upon, and their authority for wearing the armlet.

Art. 42. The distinctive flag of the Convention shall be hoisted only over such medical units and establishments as are entitled to be respected under the Convention, and only with the consent of the military authorities.

Marking of medical units and establishments

In mobile units, as in fixed establishments, it may be accompanied by the national flag of the Party to the conflict to which the unit or establishment belongs.

Nevertheless, medical units which have fallen into the hands of the enemy shall not fly any flag other than that of the Convention.

Parties to the conflict shall take the necessary steps, in so far as military considerations permit, to make the distinctive emblems indicating medical units and establishments clearly visible to the enemy land, air or naval forces, in order to obviate the possibility of any hostile action.

Art. 43. The medical units belonging to neutral countries, which may have been authorized to lend their services to a belligerent under the conditions laid down in Article 27, shall fly, along with the flag of the Convention, the national flag of that belligerent, wherever the latter makes use of the faculty conferred on him by Article 42.

Marking of units of neutral countries

Subject to orders to the contrary by the responsible military authorities, they may, on all occasions, fly their national flag, even if they fall into the hands of the adverse Party.

Art. 44.[11] With the exception of the cases mentioned in the following paragraphs of the present Article, the emblem of the Red Cross on a white ground and the words "Red Cross", or "Geneva Cross" may not be employed, either in time of peace or in time of war, except to indicate or to protect the medical units and establishments, the personnel and material protected by the present Convention and other Conventions dealing with similar matters. The same shall apply to the emblems mentioned in Article 38, second paragraph, in respect of the countries

Restrictions in the use of the emblem.

11 For reservation in respect of this article by the United States of America, see p. 680.

which use them. The National Red Cross Societies and other Societies designated in Article 26 shall have the right to use the distinctive emblem conferring the protection of the Convention only within the framework of the present paragraph.

Furthermore, National Red Cross (Red Crescent, Red Lion and Sun) Societies may, in time of peace, in accordance with their national legislation, make use of the name and emblem of the Red Cross for their other activities which are in conformity with the principles laid down by the International Red Cross Conferences. When those activities are carried out in time of war, the conditions for the use of the emblem shall be such that it cannot be considered as conferring the protection of the Convention; the emblem shall be comparatively small in size and may not be placed on armlets or on the roofs of buildings.

The international Red Cross organizations and their duly authorized personnel shall be permitted to make use, at all times, of the emblem of the Red Cross on a white ground.

Exceptions

As an exceptional measure, in conformity with national legislation and with the express permission of one of the National Red Cross (Red Crescent, Red Lion and Sun) Societies, the emblem of the Convention may be employed in time of peace to identify vehicles used as ambulances and to mark the position of aid stations exclusively assigned to the purpose of giving free treatment to the wounded or sick.

Chapter VIII. Execution of the Convention

Detailed execution. Unforeseen cases

Art. 45. Each Party to the conflict, acting through its commanders-in-chief, shall ensure the detailed execution of the preceding Articles and provide for unforeseen cases, in conformity with the general principles of the present Convention.

Prohibition of reprisals

Art. 46. Reprisals against the wounded, sick, personnel, buildings or equipment protected by the Convention are prohibited.

Dissemination of the Convention

Art. 47. The High Contracting Parties undertake, in time of peace as in time of war, to disseminate the text of the present Convention as widely as possible in their respective countries, and, in particular, to include the study thereof in their programmes of military and, if possible, civil instruction, so that the principles thereof may become known to the entire population, in particular to the armed fighting forces, the medical personnel and the chaplains.

Translations. Rules of Application

Art. 48. The High Contracting Parties shall communicate to one another through the Swiss Federal Council and, during hostilities, through the Protecting Powers, the official translations of the present Convention, as well as the laws and regulations which they may adopt to ensure the application thereof.

Chapter IX. Repression of Abuses and Infractions

Penal sanctions
I.
General observations

Art. 49. The High Contracting Parties undertake to enact any legislation necessary to provide effective penal sanctions for persons committing, or ordering to be committed, any of the grave breaches of the present Convention defined in the following Article.

Each High Contracting Party shall be under the obligation to search for persons alleged to have committed, or to have ordered to be committed, such grave breaches, and shall bring such persons, regardless of their nationality, before its own courts. It may also, if it prefers, and in accordance with the provisions of its own legislation, hand such persons over for trial to another High Contracting Party concerned, provided such High Contracting Party has made out a *prima facie* case.

Each High Contracting Party shall take measures necessary for the suppression of all acts contrary to the provisions of the present Convention other than the grave breaches defined in the following Article.

In all circumstances, the accused persons shall benefit by safeguards of proper trial and defence, which shall not be less favourable than those provided by Article 105 and those following of the Geneva Convention relative to the Treatment of Prisoners of War of August 12, 1949.

II.
Grave breaches

Art. 50. Grave breaches to which the preceding Article relates shall be those involving any of the following acts, if committed against persons or property protected by the Convention: wilful killing, torture or inhuman treatment, including biological experiments, wilfully causing great suffering or serious injury to body or health, and extensive destruction and appropriation of property, not justified by military necessity and carried out unlawfully and wantonly.

III.
Responsibilities of the Contracting Parties

Art. 51. No High Contracting Party shall be allowed to absolve itself or any other High Contracting Party of any liability incurred by itself or by another High Contracting Party in respect of breaches referred to in the preceding Article.

Enquiry procedure

Art. 52. At the request of a Party to the conflict, an enquiry shall be instituted, in a manner to be decided between the interested Parties, concerning any alleged violation of the Convention.

If agreement has not been reached concerning the procedure for the enquiry, the Parties should agree on the choice of an umpire who will decide upon the procedure to be followed.

Once the violation has been established, the Parties to the conflict shall put an end to it and shall repress it with the least possible delay.

Misuse of the emblem

Art. 53.[12] [13] The use by individuals, societies, firms or companies either public or private, other than those entitled thereto under the present Convention, of the emblem or the designation "Red Cross" or "Geneva Cross", or any sign or designation constituting an imitation thereof, whatever the object of such use, and irrespective of the date of its adoption, shall be prohibited at all times.

By reason of the tribute paid to Switzerland by the adoption of the reversed Federal colours, and of the confusion which may arise between the arms of Switzerland and the distinctive emblem of the Convention, the use by private individuals, societies or firms, of the arms of the Swiss Confederation, or of marks constituting an imitation thereof, whether as trademarks or commercial marks, or as parts of such marks, or for a purpose contrary to commercial honesty, or in circumstances capable of wounding Swiss national sentiment, shall be prohibited at all times.

Nevertheless, such High Contracting Parties as were not party to the Geneva Convention of July 27, 1929, may grant to prior users of the emblems, designations, signs or marks designated in the first paragraph, a time limit not to exceed three years from the coming into force of the present Convention to discontinue such use, provided that the said use shall not be such as would appear, in time of war, to confer the protection of the Convention.

The prohibition laid down in the first paragraph of the present Article shall also apply, without effect on any rights acquired through prior use, to the emblems and marks mentioned in the second paragraph of Article 38

Prevention of misuse

Art. 54. The High Contracting Parties shall, if their legislation is not already adequate, take measures necessary for the prevention and repression, at all times, of the abuses referred to under Article 53.

Final Provisions

Languages

Art. 55. The present Convention is established in English and in French. Both texts are equally authentic.

The Swiss Federal Council shall arrange for official translations of the Convention to be made in the Russian and Spanish languages.

Signature

Art. 56. The present Convention, which bears the date of this day, is open to signature until February 12, 1950, in the name of the Powers represented at the Conference which opened at

[12] For reservation in respect of this article by the United States of America, see p. 680.

[13] In connection with this article, see resolution 5 of the Diplomatic Conference of Geneva, 1949, p. 691.

Geneva on April 21, 1949; furthermore, by Powers not represented at that Conference but which are parties to the Geneva Conventions of 1864, 1906 or 1929 for the Relief of the Wounded and Sick in Armies in the Field.

Art. 57. The present Convention shall be ratified as soon as possible and the ratifications shall be deposited at Berne. Ratification

A record shall be drawn up of the deposit of each instrument of ratification and certified copies of this record shall be transmitted by the Swiss Federal Council to all the Powers in whose name the Convention has been signed, or whose accession has been notified.

Art. 58. The present Convention shall come into force six months after not less than two instruments of ratification have been deposited. Coming into force

Thereafter, it shall come into force for each High Contracting Party six months after the deposit of the instrument of ratification.

Art. 59. The present Convention replaces the Conventions of August 22, 1864, July 6, 1906, and July 27, 1929, in relations between the High Contracting Parties. Relation to previous Conventions

Art. 60. From the date of its coming into force, it shall be open to any Power in whose name the present Convention has not been signed, to accede to this Convention. Accession

Art. 61. Accessions shall be notified in writing to the Swiss Federal Council, and shall take effect six months after the date on which they are received. Notification of accessions

The Swiss Federal Council shall communicate the accessions to all the Powers in whose name the Convention has been signed, or whose accession has been notified.

Art. 62. The situations provided for in Articles 2 and 3 shall give immediate effect to ratifications deposited and accessions notified by the Parties to the conflict before or after the beginning of hostilities or occupation. The Swiss Federal Council shall communicate by the quickest method any ratifications or accessions received from Parties to the conflict. Immediate effect

Art. 63. Each of the High Contracting Parties shall be at liberty to denounce the present Convention. Denunciation

The denunciation shall be notified in writing to the Swiss Federal Council, which shall transmit it to the Governments of all the High Contracting Parties.

The denunciation shall take effect one year after the notification thereof has been made to the Swiss Federal Council. However, a denunciation of which notification has been made at a time when the denouncing Power is involved in a conflict shall not take effect until peace has been concluded, and until after operations connected with the release and repatriation of the persons protected by the present Convention have been terminated.

The denunciation shall have effect only in respect of the denouncing Power. It shall in no way impair the obligations which the Parties to the conflict shall remain bound to fulfil by virtue of the principles of the law of nations, as they result from the usages established among civilized peoples, from the laws of humanity and the dictates of the public conscience.

Registration with the United Nations

Art. 64. The Swiss Federal Council shall register the present Convention with the Secretariat of the United Nations. The Swiss Federal Council shall also inform the Secretariat of the United Nations of all ratifications, accessions and denunciations received by it with respect to the present Convention.

In witness whereof the undersigned, having deposited their respective full powers, have signed the present Convention.

Done at Geneva this twelfth day of August 1949, in the English and French languages. The original shall be deposited in the Archives of the Swiss Confederation. The Swiss Federal Council shall transmit certified copies thereof to each of the signatory and acceding States.

[Here follow signatures]

ANNEX I: DRAFT AGREEMENT RELATING TO HOSPITAL ZONES AND LOCALITIES

Article 1. Hospital zones shall be strictly reserved for the persons named in Article 23 of the Geneva Convention for the Amelioration of the Condition of the Wounded and Sick in Armed Forces in the Field of August 12, 1949, and for the personnel entrusted with the organization and administration of these zones and localities and with the care of the persons therein assembled.

Nevertheless, persons whose permanent residence is within such zones shall have the right to stay there.

Art. 2. No persons residing, in whatever capacity, in a hospital zone shall perform any work, either within or without the zone, directly connected with military operations or the production of war material.

Art. 3. The Power establishing a hospital zone shall take all necessary measures to prohibit access to all persons who have no right of residence or entry therein.

Art. 4. Hospital zones shall fulfil the following conditions:
(a) They shall comprise only a small part of the territory governed by the Power which has established them.
(b) They shall be thinly populated in relation to the possibilities of accommodation.
(c) They shall be far removed and free from all military objectives, or large industrial or administrative establishments.
(d) They shall not be situated in areas which, according to every probability, may become important for the conduct of the war.

Art. 5. Hospital zones shall be subject to the following obligations:
(a) The lines of communication and means of transport which they possess shall not be used for the transport of military personnel or material, even in transit.
(b) They shall in no case be defended by military means.

Art. 6. Hospital zones shall be marked by means of red crosses (red crescents, red lions and suns) on a white background placed on the outer precincts and on the buildings. They may be similarly marked at night by means of appropriate illumination.

Art. 7. The Powers shall communicate to all the High Contracting Parties in peacetime or on the outbreak of hostilities, a list of the hospital zones in the territories governed by them. They shall also give notice of any new zones set up during hostilities.

As soon as the adverse Party has received the above-mentioned notification, the zone shall be regularly constituted.

If, however, the adverse Party considers that the conditions of the present agreement have not been fulfilled, it may refuse to recognise the zone by giving immediate notice thereof to the Party responsible for the said zone, or may make its recognition of such zone dependent upon the institution of the control provided for in Article 8.

Art. 8. Any Power having recognized one or several hospital zones instituted by the adverse Party shall be entitled to demand control by one or more Special Commissions, for the purpose of ascertaining if the zones fulfil the conditions and obligations stipulated in the present agreement.

For this purpose, the members of the Special Commissions shall at all times have free access to the various zones and may even reside there permanently. They shall be given all facilities for their duties of inspection.

Art. 9. Should the Special Commissions note any facts which they consider contrary to the stipulations of the present agreement, they shall at once draw the attention of the Power governing the said zone to these facts, and shall fix a time limit of five days within which the matter should be rectified. They shall duly notify the Power who has recognised the zone.

If, when the time limit has expired, the Power governing the zone has not complied with the warning, the adverse Party may declare that it is no longer bound by the present agreement in respect of the said zone.

Art. 10. Any Power setting up one or more hospital zones and localities, and the adverse Parties to whom their existence has been notified, shall nominate or have nominated by neutral Powers, the persons who shall be members of the Special Commissions mentioned in Articles 8 and 9.

Art. 11. In no circumstances may hospital zones be the object of attack. They shall be protected and respected at all times by the Parties to the conflict.

Art. 12. In the case of occupation of a territory, the hospital zones therein shall continue to be respected and utilized as such.

Their purpose may, however, be modified by the Occupying Power, on condition that all measures are taken to ensure the safety of the persons accommodated.

Art. 13. The present agreement shall also apply to localities which the Powers may utilize for the same purposes as hospital zones.

ANNEX II. IDENTITY CARD FOR MEMBERS OF MEDICAL AND RELIGIOUS PERSONNEL ATTACHED TO THE ARMED FORCES

Front

(Space reserved for the name of the country and military authority issuing this card)

IDENTITY CARD

for members of medical and religious personnel attached to the armed forces

Surname ....
First names ....
Date of birth ....
Rank ....
Army Number ....

The bearer of this card is protected by the Geneva Convention for the Amelioration of the Condition of the Wounded and Sick in Armed Forces in the Field of August 12, 1949, in his capacity as

....

Date of issue	Number of Card
....	....

Reverse Side

Photo of bearer

Signature of bearer or finger-prints or both

Embossed stamp of military authority issuing card

Height	Eyes	Hair
....	....	....

Other distinguishing marks:

....
....
....
....
....

SIGNATURES, RATIFICATIONS AND ACCESSIONS

See list on pp. 635–649.

RESERVATIONS

See list on pp. 650–688.

No. 50

CONVENTION (II) FOR THE AMELIORATION OF THE CONDITION OF WOUNDED, SICK AND SHIPWRECKED MEMBERS OF ARMED FORCES AT SEA

Signed at Geneva, 12 August 1949

INTRODUCTORY NOTE: The present Convention replaced Hague Convention (X) of 1907 for the Adaptation to Maritime Warfare of the Principles of the Geneva Convention (*No. 43*). It contains 63 articles, whereas the 1907 Convention had only 28. This extension is mainly due to the fact that the present Convention is conceived as a complete and independent Convention whereas the 1907 Convention restricted itself to adapting to maritime warfare the principles of the Convention on the wounded and sick in land warfare. In its structure the 1949 Convention closely follows the provisions of Geneva Convention (I) of 1949 (*No. 49*).

ENTRY INTO FORCE: 21 October 1950.

AUTHENTIC TEXTS: English and French. The text below is reprinted from the *Final Record of the Diplomatic Conference of Geneva of 1949*, Vol. I, Federal Political Department, Berne, pp. 225–242.

The marginal titles added to the articles of the present Convention have no official character and were not adopted by the Diplomatic Conference. They were drafted by the Conference Secretariat and are used in the edition of the Geneva Conventions published by the International Committee of the Red Cross.

TEXT PUBLISHED IN: See indications under *No. 48*.

TABLE OF CONTENTS

* * *

The undersigned Plenipotentiaries of the Governments represented at the Diplomatic Conference held at Geneva from April 21 to August 12, 1949, for the purpose of revising the Xth Hague Convention of October 18, 1907 for the Adaptation to Maritime Warfare of the Principles of the Geneva Convention of 1906, have agreed as follows:[1]

Chapter I. General Provisions

Art. 1. The High Contracting Parties undertake to respect and to ensure respect for the present Convention in all circumstances. Respect for the Convention

Art. 2. In addition to the provisions which shall be implemented in peacetime, the present Convention shall apply to all cases of declared war or of any other armed conflict which may arise between two or more of the High Contracting Parties, even if the state of war is not recognized by one of them. Application of the Convention

The Convention shall also apply to all cases of partial or total occupation of the territory of a High Contracting Party, even if the said occupation meets with no armed resistance.

Although one of the Powers in conflict may not be a party to the present Convention, the Powers who are parties thereto shall remain bound by it in their mutual relations. They shall furthermore be bound by the Convention in relation to the said Power, if the latter accepts and applies the provisions thereof.

Art. 3.[2] In the case of armed conflict not of an international character occurring in the territory of one of the High Contracting Parties, each Party to the conflict shall be bound to apply, as a minimum, the following provisions: Conflicts not of an international character

(1) Persons taking no active part in the hostilities, including members of armed forces who have laid down their arms and those placed *hors de combat* by sickness, wounds,

---

1 For objection by the United States of America to reservations made by other states with respect to the Convention, see p. 681.

2 For reservations in respect of this article by Argentina and Portugal (withdrawn), see pp. 651 and 671.

detention, or any other cause, shall in all circumstances be treated humanely, without any adverse distinction founded on race, colour, religion or faith, sex, birth or wealth, or any other similar criteria.

To this end, the following acts are and shall remain prohibited at any time and in any place whatsoever with respect to the above-mentioned persons:

(a) violence to life and person, in particular murder of all kinds, mutilation, cruel treatment and torture;
(b) taking of hostages;
(c) outrages upon personal dignity, in particular, humiliating and degrading treatment;
(d) the passing of sentences and the carrying out of executions without previous judgment pronounced by a regularly constituted court, affording all the judicial guarantees which are recognized as indispensable by civilized peoples.

(2) The wounded, sick and shipwrecked shall be collected and cared for.

An impartial humanitarian body, such as the International Committee of the Red Cross, may offer its services to the Parties to the conflict.

The Parties to the conflict should further endeavour to bring into force, by means of special agreements, all or part of the other provisions of the present Convention.

The application of the preceding provisions shall not affect the legal status of the Parties to the conflict.

Field of application

Art. 4. In case of hostilities between land and naval forces of Parties to the conflict, the provisions of the present Convention shall apply only to forces on board ship.

Forces put ashore shall immediately become subject to the provisions of the Geneva Convention for the Amelioration of the Condition of the Wounded and Sick in Armed Forces in the Field of August 12, 1949.

Application by neutral Powers

Art. 5. Neutral Powers shall apply by analogy the provisions of the present Convention to the wounded, sick and shipwrecked, and to members of the medical personnel and to chaplains of the armed forces of the Parties to the conflict received or interned in their territory, as well as to dead persons found.

Special agreements

Art. 6. In addition to the agreements expressly provided for in Articles 10, 18, 31, 38, 39, 40, 43 and 53, the High Contracting Parties may conclude other special agreements for all matters concerning which they may deem it suitable to make separate provision. No special agreement shall adversely affect the situation of wounded, sick and shipwrecked persons, of members of the medical personnel or of chaplains, as defined by the present Convention, nor restrict the rights which it confers upon them.

Wounded, sick, and shipwrecked persons, as well as medical personnel and chaplains, shall continue to have the benefit of such agreements as long as the Convention is applicable to them, except where express provisions to the contrary are contained in the aforesaid or in subsequent agreements, or where more favourable measures have been taken with regard to them by one or other of the Parties to the conflict.

Non-renunciation of rights

Art. 7. Wounded, sick and shipwrecked persons, as well as members of the medical personnel and chaplains, may in no circumstances renounce in part or in entirety the rights secured to them by the present Convention, and by the special agreements referred to in the foregoing Article, if such there be.

Protecting Powers

Art. 8. The present Convention shall be applied with the cooperation and under the scrutiny of the Protecting Powers whose duty it is to safeguard the interests of the Parties to the conflict. For this purpose, the Protecting Powers may appoint, apart from their diplomatic or consular staff, delegates from amongst their own nationals or the nationals of other neutral Powers. The said delegates shall be subject to the approval of the Power with which they are to carry out their duties.

The Parties to the conflict shall facilitate to the greatest extent possible the task of the representatives or delegates of the Protecting Powers.

The representatives or delegates of the Protecting Powers shall not in any case exceed their mission under the present Convention. They shall, in particular, take account of the imperative necessities of security of the State wherein they carry out their duties. Their activities shall only be restricted as an exceptional and temporary measure when this is rendered necessary by imperative military necessities.

Activities of the International Committee of the Red Cross

Art. 9. The provisions of the present Convention constitute no obstacle to the humanitarian activities which the International Committee of the Red Cross or any other impartial humanitarian organization may, subject to the consent of the Parties to the conflict concerned, undertake for the protection of wounded, sick and shipwrecked persons, medical personnel and chaplains, and for their relief.

Substitutes for Protecting Powers

Art. 10.[3] The High Contracting Parties may at any time agree to entrust to an organization which offers all guarantees of impartiality and efficacy the duties incumbent on the Protecting Powers by virtue of the present Convention.

When wounded, sick and shipwrecked, or medical personnel and chaplains do not benefit or cease to benefit, no matter for what reason, by the activities of a Protecting Power or of an

---

3 For reservations in respect of this article by Albania, Bulgaria, Byelorussian SSR, China, Czechoslovakia, Germany (Democratic Republic of), Guinea-Bissau, Hungary, Korea (Demo-

organization provided for in the first paragraph above, the Detaining Power shall request a neutral State, or such an organization, to undertake the functions performed under the present Convention by a Protecting Power designated by the Parties to a conflict.

If protection cannot be arranged accordingly, the Detaining Power shall request or shall accept, subject to the provisions of this Article, the offer of the services of a humanitarian organization, such as the International Committee of the Red Cross, to assume the humanitarian functions performed by Protecting Powers under the present Convention.

Any neutral Power, or any organization invited by the Power concerned or offering itself for these purposes, shall be required to act with a sense of responsibility towards the Party to the conflict on which persons protected by the present Convention depend, and shall be required to furnish sufficient assurances that it is in a position to undertake the appropriate functions and to discharge them impartially.

No derogation from the preceding provisions shall be made by special agreements between Powers one of which is restricted, even temporarily, in its freedom to negotiate with the other Power or its allies by reason of military events, more particularly where the whole, or a substantial part, of the territory of the said Power is occupied.

Whenever, in the present Convention, mention is made of a Protecting Power, such mention also applies to substitute organizations in the sense of the present Article.

Conciliation procedure

Art. 11.[4] In cases where they deem it advisable in the interest of protected persons, particularly in cases of disagreement between the Parties to the conflict as to the application or interpretation of the provisions of the present Convention, the Protecting Powers shall lend their good offices with a view to settling the disagreement.

For this purpose, each of the Protecting Powers may, either at the invitation of one Party or on its own initiative, propose to the Parties to the conflict a meeting of their representatives, in particular of the authorities responsible for the wounded, sick and shipwrecked, medical personnel and chaplains, possibly on neutral territory suitably chosen. The Parties to the conflict shall be bound to give effect to the proposals made to them for this purpose. The Protecting Powers may, if necessary, propose for approval by the Parties to the conflict, a person belonging to a neutral Power or delegated by the International Committee of the Red Cross, who shall be invited to take part in such a meeting.

---

cont.
cratic People's Republic of), Poland, Portugal, Romania, Ukrainian SSR, USSR, Vietnam (Socialist Republic of) and Yugoslavia, see pp. 650–688.

[4] For reservation in respect of this article by Hungary, see p. 662.

Chapter II. Wounded, Sick and Shipwrecked

Art. 12. Members of the armed forces and other persons mentioned in the following Article, who are at sea and who are wounded, sick or shipwrecked, shall be respected and protected in all circumstances, it being understood that the term "shipwreck" means shipwreck from any cause and includes forced landings at sea by or from aircraft.

Protection and care

Such persons shall be treated humanely and cared for by the Parties to the conflict in whose power they may be, without any adverse distinction founded on sex, race, nationality, religion, political opinions, or any other similar criteria. Any attempts upon their lives, or violence to their persons, shall be strictly prohibited; in particular, they shall not be murdered or exterminated, subjected to torture or to biological experiments; they shall not wilfully be left without medical assistance and care, nor shall conditions exposing them to contagion or infection be created.

Only urgent medical reasons will authorize priority in the order of treatment to be administered.

Women shall be treated with all consideration due to their sex.

Art. 13.[5] The present Convention shall apply to the wounded, sick and shipwrecked at sea belonging to the following categories:

Protected persons

(1) Members of the armed forces of a Party to the conflict, as well as members of militias or volunteer corps forming part of such armed forces.

(2) Members of other militias and members of other volunteer corps, including those of organized resistance movements, belonging to a Party to the conflict and operating in or outside their own territory, even if this territory is occupied, provided that such militias or volunteer corps, including such organized resistance movements, fulfil the following conditions:
   (a) that of being commanded by a person responsible for his subordinates;
   (b) that of having a fixed distinctive sign recognizable at a distance;
   (c) that of carrying arms openly;
   (d) that of conducting their operations in accordance with the laws and customs of war.

(3) Members of regular armed forces who profess allegiance to a Government or an authority not recognized by the Detaining Power.

(4) Persons who accompany the armed forces without actually being members thereof, such as civilian members of mili-

5 For reservation in respect of this article by Guinea-Bissau and objection to this reservation by the Federal Republic of Germany, see pp. 660, 661.

tary aircraft crews, war correspondents, supply contractors, members of labour units or of services responsible for the welfare of the armed forces, provided that they have received authorization from the armed forces which they accompany.

(5) Members of crews, including masters, pilots and apprentices of the merchant marine and the crews of civil aircraft of the Parties to the conflict, who not benefit by more favourable treatment under any other provisions of international law.

(6) Inhabitants of a non-occupied territory who, on the approach of the enemy, spontaneously take up arms to resist the invading forces, without having had time to form themselves into regular armed units, provided they carry arms openly and respect the laws and customs of war.

Handing over to a belligerent

Art. 14. All warships of a belligerent Party shall have the right to demand that the wounded, sick or shipwrecked on board military hospital ships, and hospital ships belonging to relief societies or to private individuals, as well as merchant vessels, yachts and other craft shall be surrendered, whatever their nationality, provided that the wounded and sick are in a fit state to be moved and that the warship can provide adequate facilities for necessary medical treatment.

Wounded taken on board a neutral warship

Art. 15. If wounded, sick or shipwrecked persons are taken on board a neutral warship or a neutral military aircraft, it shall be ensured, where so required by international law, that they can take no further part in operations of war.

Wounded falling into enemy hands

Art. 16. Subject to the provisions of Article 12, the wounded, sick and shipwrecked of a belligerent who fall into enemy hands shall be prisoners of war, and the provisions of international law concerning prisoners of war shall apply to them. The captor may decide, according to circumstances, whether it is expedient to hold them, or to convey them to a port in the captor's own country, to a neutral port or even to a port in enemy territory. In the last case, prisoners of war thus returned to their home country may not serve for the duration of the war.

Wounded landed in a neutral port

Art. 17. Wounded, sick or shipwrecked persons who are landed in neutral ports with the consent of the local authorities, shall, failing arrangements to the contrary between the neutral and the belligerent Powers, be so guarded by the neutral Power, where so required by international law, that the said persons cannot again take part in operations of war.

The costs of hospital accommodation and internment shall be borne by the Power on whom the wounded, sick or shipwrecked persons depend.

Art. 18. After each engagement, Parties to the conflict shall, without delay, take all possible measures to search for and collect the shipwrecked, wounded and sick, to protect them against pillage and ill-treatment, to ensure their adequate care, and to search for the dead and prevent their being despoiled.

Search for casualties after an engagement

Whenever circumstances permit, the Parties to the conflict shall conclude local arrangements for the removal of the wounded and sick by sea from a besieged or encircled area and for the passage of medical and religious personnel and equipment on their way to that area.

Art. 19. The Parties to the conflict shall record as soon as possible, in respect of each shipwrecked, wounded, sick or dead person of the adverse Party falling into their hands, any particulars which may assist in his identification. These records should if possible include:

Recording and forwarding of information

(a) designation of the Power on which he depends;
(b) army, regimental, personal or serial number;
(c) surname;
(d) first name or names;
(e) date of birth;
(f) any other particulars shown on his identity card or disc;
(g) date and place of capture or death;
(h) particulars concerning wounds or illness, or cause of death.

As soon as possible the above-mentioned information shall be forwarded to the information bureau described in Article 122 of the Geneva Convention relative to the Treatment of Prisoners of War of August 12, 1949, which shall transmit this information to the Power on which these persons depend through the intermediary of the Protecting Power and of the Central Prisoners of War Agency.

Parties to the conflict shall prepare and forward to each other through the same bureau, certificates of death or duly authenticated lists of the dead. They shall likewise collect and forward through the same bureau one half of the double identity disc, or the identity disc itself if it is a single disc, last wills or other documents of importance to the next of kin, money and in general all articles of an intrinsic or sentimental value, which are found on the dead. These articles, together with unidentified articles, shall be sent in sealed packets, accompanied by statements giving all particulars necessary for the identification of the deceased owners, as well as by a complete list of the contents of the parcel.

Art. 20. Parties to the conflict shall ensure that burial at sea of the dead, carried out individually as far as circumstances permit, is preceded by a careful examination, if possible by a medical examination, of the bodies, with a view to confirming death, establishing identity and enabling a report to be made.

Prescriptions regarding the dead

Where a double identity disc is used, one half of the disc should remain on the body.

If dead persons are landed, the provisions of the Geneva Convention for the Amelioration of the Condition of the Wounded and Sick in Armed Forces in the Field of August 12, 1949, shall be applicable.

Appeals to neutral vessels

Art. 21. The Parties to the conflict may appeal to the charity of commanders of neutral merchant vessels, yachts or other craft, to take on board and care for wounded, sick or shipwrecked persons, and to collect the dead.

Vessels of any kind responding to this appeal, and those having of their own accord collected wounded, sick or shipwrecked persons, shall enjoy special protection and facilities to carry out such assistance.

They may, in no case, be captured on account of any such transport; but, in the absence of any promise to the contrary, they shall remain liable to capture for any violations of neutrality they may have committed.

Chapter III. Hospital Ships[6]

Notification and protection of military hospital ships

Art. 22. Military hospital ships, that is to say, ships built or equipped by the Powers specially and solely with a view to assisting the wounded, sick and shipwrecked, to treating them and to transporting them, may in no circumstances be attacked or captured, but shall at all times be respected and protected, on condition that their names and descriptions have been notified to the Parties to the conflict ten days before those ships are employed.

The characteristics which must appear in the notification shall include registered gross tonnage, the length from stem to stern and the number of masts and funnels.

Protection of medical establishments ashore

Art. 23. Establishments ashore entitled to the protection of the Geneva Convention for the Amelioration of the Condition of the Wounded and Sick in Armed Forces in the Field of August 12, 1949, shall be protected from bombardment or attack from the sea.

Hospital ships utilized by relief societies and private individuals of
I. Parties to the conflict

Art. 24. Hospital ships utilized by National Red Cross Societies, by officially recognized relief societies or by private persons shall have the same protection as military hospital ships and shall be exempt from capture, if the Party to the conflict on which they depend has given them an official commission and in so far as the provisions of Article 22 concerning notification have been complied with.

---

[6] In connection with this chapter, see resolutions 6 and 7 of the Diplomatic Conference of Geneva, 1949, pp. 691–692.

These ships must be provided with certificates from the responsible authorities, stating that the vessels have been under their control while fitting out and on departure.

Art. 25. Hospital ships utilized by National Red Cross Societies, officially recognised relief societies, or private persons of neutral countries shall have the same protection as military hospital ships and shall be exempt from capture, on condition that they have placed themselves under the control of one of the Parties to the conflict, with the previous consent of their own governments and with the authorization of the Party to the conflict concerned, in so far as the provisions of Article 22 concerning notification have been complied with.

II. Neutral countries

Art. 26. The protection mentioned in Articles 22, 24 and 25 shall apply to hospital ships of any tonnage and to their lifeboats, wherever they are operating. Nevertheless, to ensure the maximum comfort and security, the Parties to the conflict shall endeavour to utilize, for the transport of wounded, sick and shipwrecked over long distances and on the high seas, only hospital ships of over 2,000 tons gross.

Tonnage

Art. 27. Under the same conditions as those provided for in Articles 22 and 24, small craft employed by the State or by the officially recognized lifeboat institutions for coastal rescue operations, shall also be respected and protected, so far as operational requirements permit.

The same shall apply so far as possible to fixed coastal installations used exclusively by these craft for their humanitarian missions.

Coastal rescue craft

Art. 28. Should fighting occur on board a warship, the sick-bays shall be respected and spared as far possible. Sick-bays and their equipment shall remain subject to the laws of warfare, but may not be diverted from their purpose so long as they are required for the wounded and sick. Nevertheless, the commander into whose power they have fallen may, after ensuring the proper care of the wounded and sick who are accommodated therein, apply them to other purposes in case of urgent military necessity.

Protection of sick-bays

Art. 29. Any hospital ship in a port which falls into the hands of the enemy shall be authorised to leave the said port.

Hospital ships in occupied ports

Art. 30. The vessels described in Articles 22, 24, 25 and 27 shall afford relief and assistance to the wounded, sick and shipwrecked without distinction of nationality.

The High Contracting Parties undertake not to use these vessels for any military purpose.

Employment of hospital ships and small craft

Such vessels shall in no wise hamper the movements of the combatants.

During and after an engagement, they will act at their own risk.

Right of control and search

Art. 31. The Parties to the conflict shall have the right to control and search the vessels mentioned in Articles 22, 24, 25 and 27. They can refuse assistance from these vessels, order them off, make them take a certain course, control the use of their wireless and other means of communication, and even detain them for a period not exceeding seven days from the time of interception, if the gravity of the circumstances so requires.

They may put a commissioner temporarily on board whose sole task shall be to see that orders given in virtue of the provisions of the preceding paragraph are carried out.

As far as possible, the Parties to the conflict shall enter in the log of the hospital ship, in a language he can understand, the orders they have given the captain of the vessel.

Parties to the conflict may, either unilaterally or by particular agreements, put on board their ships neutral observers who shall verify the strict observation of the provisions contained in the present Convention.

Stay in a neutral port

Art. 32. Vessels described in Articles 22, 24, 25 and 27 are not classed as warships as regards their stay in a neutral port.

Converted merchant vessels

Art. 33. Merchant vessels which have been transformed into hospital ships cannot be put to any other use throughout the duration of hostilities.

Discontinuance of protection

Art. 34. The protection to which hospital ships and sick-bays are entitled shall not cease unless they are used to commit, outside their humanitarian duties, acts harmful to the enemy. Protection may, however, cease only after due warning has been given, naming in all appropriate cases a reasonable time limit, and after such warning has remained unheeded.

In particular, hospital ships may not possess or use a secret code for their wireless or other means of communication.

Conditions not depriving hospital ships of protection

Art. 35. The following conditions shall not be considered as depriving hospital ships or sick-bays of vessels of the protection due to them:

(1) The fact that the crews of ships or sick-bays are armed for the maintenance of order, for their own defence or that of the sick and wounded.

(2) The presence on board of apparatus exclusively intended to facilitate navigation or communication.

(3) The discovery on board hospital ships or in sick-bays of portable arms and ammunition taken from the wounded, sick and shipwrecked and not yet handed to the proper service.

(4) The fact that the humanitarian activities of hospital ships and sick-bays of vessels or of the crews extend to the care of wounded, sick or shipwrecked civilians.
(5) The transport of equipment and of personnel intended exclusively for medical duties, over and above the normal requirements.

Chapter IV. Personnel

Art. 36. The religious, medical and hospital personnel of hospital ships and their crews shall be respected and protected; they may not be captured during the time they are in the service of the hospital ship, whether or not there are wounded and sick on board.

Protection of the personnel of hospital ships

Art. 37. The religious, medical and hospital personnel assigned to the medical or spiritual care of the persons designated in Articles 12 and 13 shall, if they fall into the hands of the enemy, be respected and protected; they may continue to carry out their duties as long as this is necessary for the care of the wounded and sick. They shall afterwards be sent back as soon as the Commander-in-Chief, under whose authority they are, considers it practicable. They may take with them, on leaving the ship, their personal property.

Medical and religious personnel of other ships

If, however, it proves necessary to retain some of this personnel owing to the medical or spiritual needs of prisoners of war, everything possible shall be done for their earliest possible landing.

Retained personnel shall be subject, on landing, to the provisions of the Geneva Convention for the Amelioration of the Condition of the Wounded and Sick in Armed Forces in the Field of August 12, 1949.

Chapter V. Medical Transports

Art. 38. Ships chartered for that purpose shall be authorized to transport equipment exclusively intended for the treatment of wounded and sick members of armed forces or for the prevention of disease, provided that the particulars regarding their voyage have been notified to the adverse Power and approved by the latter. The adverse Power shall preserve the right to board the carrier ships, but not to capture them or seize the equipment carried.

Ships used for the conveyance of medical equipment

By agreement amongst the Parties to the conflict, neutral observers may be placed on board such ships to verify the equipment carried. For this purpose, free access to the equipment shall be given.

Art. 39. Medical aircraft, that is to say, aircraft exclusively employed for the removal of wounded, sick and shipwrecked, and for the transport of medical personnel and equipment,

Medical aircraft

may not be the object of attack, but shall be respected by the Parties to the conflict, while flying at heights, at times and on routes specifically agreed upon between the Parties to the conflict concerned.

They shall be clearly marked with the distinctive emblem prescribed in Article 41, together with their national colours, on their lower, upper and lateral surfaces. They shall be provided with any other markings or means of identification which may be agreed upon between the Parties to the conflict upon the outbreak or during the course of hostilities.

Unless agreed otherwise, flights over enemy or enemy-occupied territory are prohibited.

Medical aircraft shall obey every summons to alight on land or water. In the event of having thus to alight, the aircraft with its occupants may continue its flight after examination, if any.

Flight over neutral countries. Landing of wounded

In the event of alighting involuntarily on land or water in enemy or enemy-occupied territory, the wounded, sick and shipwrecked, as well as the crew of the aircraft shall be prisoners of war. The medical personnel shall be treated according to Articles 36 and 37.

Art. 40. Subject to the provisions of the second paragraph, medical aircraft of Parties to the conflict may fly over the territory of neutral Powers, land thereon in case of necessity, or use it as a port of call. They shall give neutral Powers prior notice of their passage over the said territory, and obey every summons to alight, on land or water. They will be immune from attack only when flying on routes, at heights and at times specifically agreed upon between the Parties to the conflict and the neutral Power concerned.

The neutral Powers may, however, place conditions or restrictions on the passage or landing of medical aircraft on their territory. Such possible conditions or restrictions shall be applied equally to all Parties to the conflict.

Unless otherwise agreed between the neutral Powers and the Parties to the conflict, the wounded, sick or shipwrecked who are disembarked with the consent of the local authorities on neutral territory by medical aircraft shall be detained by the neutral Power, where so required by international law, in such a manner that they cannot again take part in operations of war. The cost of their accommodation and internment shall be borne by the Power on which they depend.

Chapter VI. The Distinctive Emblem[7]

Use of the emblem.

Art. 41. Under the direction of the competent military authority, the emblem of the red cross on a white ground shall be dis-

[7] For declaration and reservation with respect to the distinctive emblem by Iran and Israel, see p. 663.

played on the flags, armlets and on all equipment employed in the Medical Service.

Nevertheless, in the case of countries which already use as emblem, in place of the red cross, the red crescent or the red lion and sun on a white ground, these emblems are also recognized by the terms of the present Convention.

Identification of medical and religious personnel

Art. 42. The personnel designated in Articles 36 and 37 shall wear, affixed to the left arm, a water-resistant armlet bearing the distinctive emblem, issued and stamped by the military authority.

Such personnel, in addition to wearing the identity disc mentioned in Article 19, shall also carry a special identity card bearing the distinctive emblem. This card shall be water-resistant and of such size that it can be carried in the pocket. It shall be worded in the national language, shall mention at least the surname and first names, the date of birth, the rank and the service number of the bearer, and shall state in what capacity he is entitled to the protection of the present Convention. The card shall bear the photograph of the owner and also either his signature or his finger-prints or both. It shall be embossed with the stamp of the military authority.

The identity card shall be uniform throughout the same armed forces and, as far as possible, of a similar type in the armed forces of the High Contracting Parties. The Parties to the conflict may be guided by the model which is annexed, by way of example, to the present Convention. They shall inform each other, at the outbreak of hostilities, of the model they are using. Identity cards should be made out, if possible, at least in duplicate, one copy being kept by the home country.

In no circumstances may the said personnel be deprived of their insignia or identity cards nor of the right to wear the armlet. In cases of loss they shall be entitled to receive duplicates of the cards and to have the insignia replaced.

Marking of hospital ships and small craft

Art. 43. The ships designated in Articles 22, 24, 25 and 27 shall be distinctively marked as follows:

(a) All exterior surfaces shall be white.

(b) One or more dark red crosses, as large as possible, shall be painted and displayed on each side of the hull and on the horizontal surfaces, so placed as to afford the greatest possible visibility from the sea and from the air.

All hospital ships shall make themselves known by hoisting their national flag and further, if they belong to a neutral state, the flag of the Party to the conflict whose direction they have accepted. A white flag with a red cross shall be flown at the mainmast as high as possible.

Lifeboats of hospital ships, coastal lifeboats and all small craft used by the Medical Service shall be painted white with dark red crosses prominently displayed and shall, in general, comply with the identification system prescribed above for hospital ships.

The above-mentioned ships and craft, which may wish to ensure by night and in times of reduced visibility the protection to which they are entitled, must, subject to the assent of the Party to the conflict under whose power they are, take the necessary measures to render their painting and distinctive emblems sufficiently apparent.

Hospital ships which, in accordance with Article 31, are provisionally detained by the enemy, must haul down the flag of the Party to the conflict in whose service they are or whose direction they have accepted.

Coastal lifeboats, if they continue to operate with the consent of the Occupying Power from a base which is occupied, may be allowed, when away from their base, to continue to fly their own national colours along with a flag carrying a red cross on a white ground, subject to prior notification to all the Parties to the conflict concerned.

All the provisions in this Article relating to the red cross shall apply equally to the other emblems mentioned in Article 41.

Parties to the conflict shall at all times endeavour to conclude mutual agreements, in order to use the most modern methods available to facilitate the identification of hospital ships.

Limitation in the use of markings

Art. 44. The distinguishing signs referred to in Article 43 can only be used, whether in time of peace or war, for indicating or protecting the ships therein mentioned, except as may be provided in any other international Convention or by agreement between all the Parties to the conflict concerned.

Prevention of misuse

Art. 45. The High Contracting Parties shall, if their legislation is not already adequate, take the measures necessary for the prevention and repression, at all times, of any abuse of the distinctive signs provided for under Article 43.

Chapter VII. Execution of the Convention

Detailed execution. Unforeseen cases

Art. 46. Each Party to the conflict, acting through its Commanders-in-Chief, shall ensure the detailed execution of the preceding Articles and provide for unforeseen cases, in conformity with the general principles of the present Convention.

Prohibition of reprisals

Art. 47. Reprisals against the wounded, sick and shipwrecked persons, the personnel, the vessels or the equipment protected by the Convention are prohibited.

Dissemination of the Convention

Art. 48. The High Contracting Parties undertake, in time of peace as in time of war, to disseminate the text of the present Convention as widely as possible in their respective countries, and, in particular, to include the study thereof in their programmes of military and, if possible, civil instruction, so that the principles thereof may become known to the entire population, in particular to the armed fighting forces, the medical personnel and the chaplains.

Translations. Rules of application

Art. 49. The High Contracting Parties shall communicate to one another through the Swiss Federal Council and, during hostilities, through the Protecting Powers, the official translations of the present Convention, as well as the laws and regulations which they may adopt to ensure the application thereof.

Chapter VIII. Repression of Abuses and Infractions

Penal sanctions
I. General observations

Art. 50. The High Contracting Parties undertake to enact any legislation necessary to provide effective penal sanctions for persons committing, or ordering to be committed, any of the grave breaches of the present Convention defined in the following Article.

Each High Contracting Party shall be under the obligation to search for persons alleged to have committed, or to have ordered to be committed, such grave breaches, and shall bring such persons, regardless of their nationality, before its own courts. It may also, if it prefers, and in accordance with the provisions of its own legislation, hand such persons over for trial to another High Contracting Party concerned, provided such High Contracting Party has made out a *prima facie* case.

Each High Contracting Party shall take measures necessary for the suppression of all acts contrary to the provisions of the present Convention other than the grave breaches defined in the following Article.

In all circumstances, the accused persons shall benefit by safeguards of proper trial and defence, which shall not be less favourable than those provided by Article 105 and those following of the Geneva Convention relative to the Treatment of Prisoners of War of August 12, 1949.

II. Grave breaches

Art. 51. Grave breaches to which the preceding Article relates shall be those involving any of the following acts, if committed against persons or property protected by the Convention: wilful killing, torture or inhuman treatment, including biological experiments, wilfully causing great suffering or serious injury to body or health, and extensive destruction and appropriation of property, not justified by military necessity and carried out unlawfully and wantonly.

III. Responsibilities of the Contracting Parties

Art. 52. No High Contracting Party shall be allowed to absolve itself or any other High Contracting Party of any liability incurred by itself or by another High Contracting Party in respect of breaches referred to in the preceding Article.

Enquiry procedure

Art. 53. At the request of a Party to the conflict, an enquiry shall be instituted, in a manner to be decided between the interested Parties, concerning any alleged violation of the Convention.

If agreement has not been reached concerning the procedure for the enquiry, the Parties should agree on the choice of an umpire, who will decide upon the procedure to be followed.

Once the violation has been established, the Parties to the conflict shall put an end to it and shall repress it with the least possible delay.

Final Provisions

Languages

Art. 54. The present Convention is established in English and in French. Both texts are equally authentic.

The Swiss Federal Council shall arrange for official translations of the Convention to be made in the Russian and Spanish languages.

Signature

Art. 55. The present Convention, which bears the date of this day, is open to signature until February 12, 1950, in the name of the Powers represented at the Conference which opened at Geneva on April 21, 1949; furthermore, by Powers not represented at that Conference, but which are parties to the Xth Hague Convention of October 18, 1907, for the adaptation to Maritime Warfare of the principles of the Geneva Convention of 1906, or to the Geneva Conventions of 1864, 1906 or 1929 for the Relief of the Wounded and Sick in Armies in the Field.

Ratification

Art. 56. The present Convention shall be ratified as soon as possible and the ratifications shall be deposited at Berne.

A record shall be drawn up of the deposit of each instrument of ratification and certified copies of this record shall be transmitted by the Swiss Federal Council to all the Powers in whose name the Convention has been signed, or whose accession has been notified.

Coming into force

Art. 57. The present Convention shall come into force six months after not less than two instruments of ratification have been deposited.

Thereafter, it shall come into force for each High Contracting Party six months after the deposit of the instruments of ratification.

Relation to the 1907 Convention

Art. 58 The present Convention replaces the Xth Hague Convention of October 18, 1907, for the adaptation to Maritime Warfare of the principles of the Geneva Convention of 1906, in relations between the High Contracting Parties.

Accession

Art. 59. From the date of its coming into force, it shall be open to any Power in whose name the present Convention has not been signed, to accede to this Convention.

Art. 60. Accessions shall be notified in writing to the Swiss Federal Council, and shall take effect six months after the date on which they are received.

Notification of accessions

The Swiss Federal Council shall communicate the accessions to all the Powers in whose name the Convention has been signed, or whose accession has been notified.

Art. 61. The situations provided for in Articles 2 and 3 shall give immediate effect to ratifications deposited and accessions notified by the Parties to the conflict before or after the beginning of hostilities or occupation. The Swiss Federal Council shall communicate by the quickest method any ratifications or accessions received from Parties to the conflict.

Immediate effect

Art. 62. Each of the High Contracting Parties shall be at liberty to denounce the present Convention.

Denunciation

The denunciation shall be notified in writing to the Swiss Federal Council, which shall transmit it to the Governments of all the High Contracting Parties.

The denunciation shall take effect one year after the notification thereof has been made to the Swiss Federal Council. However, a denunciation of which notification has been made at a time when the denouncing Power is involved in a conflict shall not take effect until peace has been concluded, and until after operations connected with the release and repatriation of the persons protected by the present Convention have been terminated.

The denunciation shall have effect only in respect of the denouncing Power. It shall in no way impair the obligations which the Parties to the conflict shall remain bound to fulfil by virtue of the principles of the law of nations, as they result from the usages established among civilized peoples, from the laws of humanity and the dictates of the public conscience.

Art. 63 The Swiss Federal Council shall register the present Convention with the Secretariat of the United Nations. The Swiss Federal Council shall also inform the Secretariat of the United Nations of all ratifications, accessions and denunciations received by it with respect to the present Convention.

Registration with the United Nations

In witness whereof the undersigned, having deposited their respective full powers, have signed the present Convention.

Done at Geneva this twelfth day of August 1949, in the English and French languages. The original shall be deposited in the Archives of the Swiss Confederation. The Swiss Federal Council shall transmit certified copies thereof to each of the signatory and acceding States.

[Here follow signatures]

ANNEX IDENTITY CARD FOR MEMBERS OF MEDICAL AND RELIGIOUS PERSONNEL ATTACHED TO THE ARMED FORCES AT SEA

Front

(Space reserved for the name of the country and military authority issuing this card)

IDENTITY CARD

for members of medical and religious personnel attached to the armed forces at sea

Surname ....

First names ....

Date of birth ....

Rank ....

Army Number ....

The bearer of this card is protected by the Geneva Convention for the Amelioration of the Condition of the Wounded, Sick and Shipwrecked Members of Armed Forces at Sea of August 12, 1949, in his capacity as

....

Date of issue ....

Number of Card ....

Reverse side

Photo of bearer

Signature of bearer or finger-prints or both

Embossed stamp of military authority issuing card

Height	Eyes	Hair

Other distinguishing marks:

....

....

....

....

....

SIGNATURES, RATIFICATIONS AND ACCESSIONS

See list of pp. 635–649.

RESERVATIONS

See list on pp. 650–688.

No. 51

CONVENTION (III) RELATIVE TO THE TREATMENT OF PRISONERS OF WAR

Signed at Geneva, 12 August 1949

INTRODUCTORY NOTE: The present Convention replaced the Prisoners of War Convention of 1929 (*No. 46*). It contains 143 articles whereas the 1929 Convention had only 97. Experience had shown that it was necessary to give certain regulations a more explicit form in order to preclude misinterpretation, to which certain of the former provisions were open. Since the text of the Convention is to be posted in all prisoner of war camps (see Article 41) it has to be comprehensible not only to the authorities but also to the ordinary reader. The categories of persons entitled to prisoner of war status were broadened in accordance with Conventions I and II. The conditions of captivity were more precisely defined, in particular with regard to the labour of prisoners of war, their financial resources, the relief they receive and the judicial proceedings instituted against them. The Convention establishes the principle that prisoners of war shall be released and repatriated without delay after the cessation of active hostilities (Article 118).

ENTRY INTO FORCE: 21 October 1950.

AUTHENTIC TEXTS: English and French. The text below is reprinted from the *Final Record of the Diplomatic Conference of Geneva of 1949*, Vol. I, Federal Political Department, Berne, pp. 243–296.

The marginal titles added to the articles of the present Convention have no official character and were not adopted by the Diplomatic Conference. They were drafted by the Conference Secretariat and are used in the edition of the Geneva Conventions published by the International Committee of the Red Cross.

TEXT PUBLISHED IN: See indications under *No. 48*.

TABLE OF CONTENTS

* * *

The undersigned Plenipotentiaries of the Governments represented at the Diplomatic Conference held at Geneva from April 21 to August 12, 1949, for the purpose of revising the Convention concluded at Geneva on July 27, 1929, relative to the Treatment of Prisoners of War, have agreed as follows:[1]

PART I. GENERAL PROVISIONS

Respect for the Convention

Article 1. The High Contracting Parties undertake to respect and to ensure respect for the present Convention in all circumstances.

Application of the Convention

Art. 2. In addition to the provisions which shall be implemented in peace time, the present Convention shall apply to all cases of declared war or of any other armed conflict which may arise between two or more of the High Contracting Parties, even if the state of war is not recognized by one of them.

The Convention shall also apply to all cases of partial or total occupation of the territory of a High Contracting Party, even if the said occupation meets with no armed resistance.

Although one of the Powers in conflict may not be a party to the present Convention, the Powers who are parties thereto shall remain bound by it in their mutual relations. They shall furthermore be bound by the Convention in relation to the said Power, if the latter accepts and applies the provisions thereof.

Conflicts not of an international character

Art. 3.[2] In the case of armed conflict not of an international character occurring in the territory of one of the High Contracting Parties, each Party to the conflict shall be bound to apply, as a minimum, the following provisions:

(1) Persons taking no active part in the hostilities, including members of armed forces who have laid down their arms and those placed *hors de combat* by sickness, wounds, detention, or any other cause, shall in all circumstances be treated humanely, without any adverse distinction founded on race, colour, religion or faith, sex, birth or wealth, or any other similar criteria.

To this end the following acts are and shall remain prohibited at any time and in any place whatsoever with respect to the above-mentioned persons:

(a) violence to life and person, in particular murder of all kinds, mutilation, cruel treatment and torture;
(b) taking of hostages;
(c) outrages upon personal dignity, in particular, humiliating and degrading treatment;

[1] For objection by the United States of America to reservations made by other states with respect to this Convention, see p. 681.

[2] For reservations in respect of this article by Argentina and Portugal (withdrawn), see pp. 651 and 671.

(d) the passing of sentences and the carrying out of executions without previous judgment pronounced by a regularly constituted court affording all the judicial guarantees which are recognized as indispensable by civilized peoples.

(2) The wounded and sick shall be collected and cared for. An impartial humanitarian body, such as the International Committee of the Red Cross, may offer its services to the Parties to the conflict.

The Parties to the conflict should further endeavour to bring into force, by means of special agreements, all or part of the other provisions of the present Convention.

The application of the preceding provisions shall not affect the legal status of the Parties to the conflict.

Art. 4.[3]

A. Prisoners of war, in the sense of the present Convention, are persons belonging to one of the following categories, who have fallen into the power of the enemy:

Prisoners of war

(1) Members of the armed forces of a Party to the conflict as well as members of militias or volunteer corps forming part of such armed forces.

(2) Members of other militias and members of other volunteer corps, including those of organized resistance movements, belonging to a Party to the conflict and operating in or outside their own territory, even if this territory is occupied, provided that such militias or volunteer corps, including such organized resistance movements, fulfil the following conditions:

(a) that of being commanded by a person responsible for his subordinates;

(b) that of having a fixed distinctive sign recognizable at a distance;

(c) that of carrying arms openly;

(d) that of conducting their operations in accordance with the laws and customs of war.

(3) Members of regular armed forces who profess allegiance to a government or an authority not recognized by the Detaining Power.

(4) Persons who accompany the armed forces without actually being members thereof, such as civilian members of military aircraft crews, war correspondents, supply contractors, members of labour units or of services responsible for the welfare of the armed forces, provided that they have received authorization from the armed forces which they accompany, who shall provide them for that purpose with an identity card similar to the annexed model.

[3] For reservations in respect of this article by Guinea-Bissau (and objection to this reservation by the Federal Republic of Germany) and Portugal (witdrawn), see pp. 661, 660, 671.

(5) Members of crews, including masters, pilots and apprentices, of the merchant marine and the crews of civil aircraft of the Parties to the conflict, who do not benefit by more favourable treatment under any other provisions of international law.

(6) Inhabitants of a non-occupied territory, who on the approach of the enemy spontaneously take up arms to resist the invading forces, without having had time to form themselves into regular armed units, provided they carry arms openly and respect the laws and customs of war.

B. The following shall likewise be treated as prisoners of war under the present Convention:

(1) Persons belonging, or having belonged, to the armed forces of the occupied country, if the occupying Power considers it necessary by reason of such allegiance to intern them, even though it has originally liberated them while hostilities were going on outside the territory it occupies, in particular where such persons have made an unsuccessful attempt to rejoin the armed forces to which they belong and which are engaged in combat, or where they fail to comply with a summons made to them with a view to internment.

(2) The persons belonging to one of the categories enumerated in the present Article, who have been received by neutral or non-belligerent Powers on their territory and whom these Powers are required to intern under international law, without prejudice to any more favourable treatment which these Powers may choose to give and with the exception of Articles 8, 10,15,30, fifth paragraph, 58-67, 92, 126 and, where diplomatic relations exist between the Parties to the conflict and the neutral or non-belligerent Power concerned, those Articles concerning the Protecting Power. Where such diplomatic relations exist, the Parties to a conflict on whom these persons depend shall be allowed to perform towards them the functions of a Protecting Power as provided in the present Convention, without prejudice to the functions which these Parties normally exercise in conformity with diplomatic and consular usage and treaties.

C. This Article shall in no way affect the status of medical personnel and chaplains as provided for in Article 33 of the present Convention.

Beginning and end of application

Art. 5. The present Convention shall apply to the persons referred to in Article 4 from the time they fall into the power of the enemy and until their final release and repatriation.

Should any doubt arise as to whether persons, having committed a belligerent act and having fallen into the hands of the enemy, belong to any of the categories enumerated in Article 4, such persons shall enjoy the protection of the present Convention until such time as their status has been determined by a competent tribunal.

Special agreements

Art. 6. In addition to the agreements expressly provided for in Articles 10, 23, 28, 33, 60, 65, 66, 67, 72, 73, 75, 109, 110, 118, 119, 122 and 132, the High Contracting Parties may conclude other special agreements for all matters concerning which they may deem it suitable to make separate provision. No special agreement shall adversely affect the situation of prisoners of war, as defined by the present Convention, nor restrict the rights which it confers upon them.

Prisoners of war shall continue to have the benefit of such agreements as long as the Convention is applicable to them, except where express provisions to the contrary are contained in the aforesaid or in subsequent agreements, or where more favourable measures have been taken with regard to them by one or other of the Parties to the conflict.

Non-renunciation of rights

Art. 7. Prisoners of war may in no circumstances renounce in part or in entirety the rights secured to them by the present Convention, and by the special agreements referred to in the foregoing Article, if such there be.

Protecting Powers

Art. 8. The present Convention shall be applied with the cooperation and under the scrutiny of the Protecting Powers whose duty it is to safeguard the interests of the Parties to the conflict. For this purpose, the Protecting Powers may appoint, apart from their diplomatic or consular staff, delegates from amongst their own nationals or the nationals of other neutral Powers. The said delegates shall be subject to the approval of the Power with which they are to carry out their duties.

The Parties to the conflict shall facilitate to the greatest extent possible the task of the representatives or delegates of the Protecting Powers.

The representatives or delegates of the Protecting Powers shall not in any case exceed their mission under the present Convention. They shall, in particular, take account of the imperative necessities of security of the State wherein they carry out their duties.

Activities of the International Committee of the Red Cross

Art. 9. The provisions of the present Convention constitute no obstacle to the humanitarian activities which the International Committee of the Red Cross or any other impartial humanitarian organization may, subject to the consent of the Parties to the conflict concerned, undertake for the protection of prisoners of war and for their relief.

Substitutes for Protecting Powers

Art. 10.[4] The High Contracting Parties may at any time agree to entrust to an organization which offers all guarantees of impartiality and efficacy the duties incumbent on the Protecting Powers by virtue of the present Convention.

When prisoners of war do not benefit or cease to benefit, no matter for what reason, by the activities of a Protecting Power or of an organization provided for in the first paragraph above, the Detaining Power shall request a neutral State, or such an organization, to undertake the functions performed under the present Convention by a Protecting Power designated by the Parties to a conflict.

If protection cannot be arranged accordingly, the Detaining Power shall request or shall accept, subject to the provisions of this Article, the offer of the services of a humanitarian organization, such as the International Committee of the Red Cross, to assume the humanitarian functions performed by Protecting Powers under the present Convention.

Any neutral Power or any organization invited by the Power concerned or offering itself for these purposes, shall be required to act with a sense of responsibility towards the Party to the conflict on which persons protected by the present Convention depend, and shall be required to furnish sufficient assurances that it is in a position to undertake the appropriate functions and to discharge them impartially.

No derogation from the preceding provisions shall be made by special agreements between Powers one of which is restricted, even temporarily, in its freedom to negotiate with the other Power or its allies by reason of military events, more particularly where the whole, or a substantial part, of the territory of the said Power is occupied.

Whenever in the present Convention mention is made of a Protecting Power, such mention applies to substitute organizations in the sense of the present Article.

Conciliation procedure

Art. 11.[5] In cases where they deem it advisable in the interest of protected persons, particularly in cases of disagreement between the Parties to the conflict as to the application or interpretation of the provisions of the present Convention, the protecting Powers shall lend their good offices with a view to settling the disagreement.

For this purpose, each of the Protecting Powers may, either at the invitation of one Party or on its own initiative, propose to the Parties to the conflict a meeting of their representatives, and in particular of the authorities responsible for prisoners of war, possibly on neutral territory suitably chosen. The Parties to the

4 For reservations in respect of this article by Albania, Bulgaria, Byelorussian SSR, China, Czechoslovakia, Germany (Democratic Republic of), Guinea-Bissau, Hungary, Korea (Democratic People's Republic of), Poland, Portugal, Romania, Ukrainian SSR, USSR, Vietnam (Socialist Republic of) and Yugoslavia, see pp. 650–688.

5 For reservations in respect of this article by Hungary, see p. 662.

conflict shall be bound to give effect to the proposals made to them for this purpose. The Protecting Powers may, if necessary, propose for approval by the Parties to the conflict a person belonging to a neutral Power, or delegated by the International Committee of the Red Cross, who shall be invited to take part in such a meeting.

PART II. GENERAL PROTECTION OF PRISONERS OF WAR

Art. 12.[6] Prisoners of war are in the hands of the enemy Power, but not of the individuals or military units who have captured them. Irrespective of the individual responsibilities that may exist, the Detaining Power is responsible for the treatment given them.

Responsibility for the treatment of prisoners

Prisoners of war may only be transferred by the Detaining Power to a Power which is a party to the Convention and after the Detaining Power has satisfied itself of the willingness and ability of such transferee Power to apply the Convention. When prisoners of war are transferred under such circumstances, responsibility for the application of the Convention rests on the Power accepting them while they are in its custody.

Nevertheless if that Power fails to carry out the provisions of the Convention in any important respect, the Power by whom the prisoners of war were transferred shall, upon being notified by the Protecting Power, take effective measures to correct the situation or shall request the return of the prisoners of war. Such requests must be complied with.

Art. 13. Prisoners of war must at all times be humanely treated. Any unlawful act or omission by the Detaining Power causing death or seriously endangering the health of a prisoner of war in its custody is prohibited, and will be regarded as a serious breach of the present Convention. In particular, no prisoner of war may be subjected to physical mutilation or to medical or scientific experiments of any kind which are not justified by the medical, dental or hospital treatment of the prisoner concerned and carried out in his interest.

Humane treatment of prisoners

Likewise, prisoners of war must at all times be protected, particularly against acts of violence or intimidation and against insults and public curiosity.

Measures of reprisal against prisoners of war are prohibited.

Art. 14. Prisoners of war are entitled in all circumstances to respect for their persons and their honour.

---

6 For reservations in respect of this article by Albania, Bulgaria, Byelorussian SSR, China, Czechoslovakia, Germany (Democratic Republic of), Hungary, Korea (Democratic People's Republic of), Poland, Portugal, Romania, Ukrainian SSR, USSR, Vietnam (Socialist Republic of) and Yugoslavia, and objections to these reservations by Australia, New Zealand, the United Kingdom and the United States of America, see pp. 650–683.

Respect for the person of prisoners

Women shall be treated with all the regard due to their sex and shall in all cases benefit by treatment as favourable as that granted to men.

Prisoners of war shall retain the full civil capacity which they enjoyed at the time of their capture. The Detaining Power may not restrict the exercise, either within or without its own territory, of the rights such capacity confers except in so far as the captivity requires.

Maintenance of prisoners

Art. 15. The Power detaining prisoners of war shall be bound to provide free of charge for their maintenance and for the medical attention required by their state of health.

Equality of treatment

Art. 16. Taking into consideration the provisions of the present Convention relating to rank and sex, and subject to any privileged treatment which may be accorded to them by reason of their state of health, age or professional qualifications, all prisoners of war shall be treated alike by the Detaining Power, without any adverse distinction based on race, nationality, religious belief or political opinions, or any other distinction founded on similar criteria.

PART III. CAPTIVITY

Section I. Beginning of Captivity

Questioning of prisoners

Art. 17. Every prisoner of war, when questioned on the subject, is bound to give only his surname, first names and rank, date of birth, and army, regimental, personal or serial number, or failing this, equivalent information.

If he wilfully infringes this rule, he may render himself liable to a restriction of the privileges accorded to his rank or status.

Each Party to a conflict is required to furnish the persons under its jurisdiction who are liable to become prisoners of war, with an identity card showing the owner's surname, first names, rank, army, regimental, personal or serial number or equivalent information, and date of birth. The identity card may, furthermore, bear the signature or the fingerprints, or both, of the owner, and may bear, as well, any other information the Party to the conflict may wish to add concerning persons belonging to its armed forces. As far as possible the card shall measure 6.5 x 10 cm. and shall be issued in duplicate. The identity card shall be shown by the prisoner of war upon demand, but may in no case be taken away from him.

No physical or mental torture, nor any other form of coercion, may be inflicted on prisoners of war to secure from them information of any kind whatever. Prisoners of war who refuse to answer may not be threatened, insulted, or exposed to any unpleasant or disadvantageous treatment of any kind.

Prisoners of war who, owing to their physical or mental condition, are unable to state their identity, shall be handed over to the medical service. The identity of such prisoners shall be established by all possible means, subject to the provisions of the preceding paragraph.

The questioning of prisoners of war shall be carried out in a language which they understand.

Art. 18. All effects and articles of personal use, except arms, horses, military equipment and military documents, shall remain in the possession of prisoners of war, likewise their metal helmets and gas masks and like articles issued for personal protection. Effects and articles used for their clothing or feeding shall likewise remain in their possession, even if such effects and articles belong to their regulation military equipment.

Property of prisoners

At no time should prisoners of war be without identity documents. The Detaining Power shall supply such documents to prisoners of war who possess none.

Badges of rank and nationality, decorations and articles having above all a personal or sentimental value may not be taken from prisoners of war.

Sums of money carried by prisoners of war may not be taken away from them except by order of an officer, and after the amount and particulars of the owner have been recorded in a special register and an itemized receipt has been given, legibly inscribed with the name, rank and unit of the person issuing the said receipt. Sums in the currency of the Detaining Power, or which are changed into such currency at the prisoner's request, shall be placed to the credit of the prisoner's account as provided in Article 64.

The Detaining Power may withdraw articles of value from prisoners of war only for reasons of security; when such articles are withdrawn, the procedure laid down for sums of money impounded shall apply.

Such objects, likewise the sums taken away in any currency other than that of the Detaining Power and the conversion of which has not been asked for by the owners, shall be kept in the custody of the Detaining Power and shall be returned in their initial shape to prisoners of war at the end of their captivity.

Art. 19. Prisoners of war shall be evacuated, as soon as possible after their capture, to camps situated in an area far enough from the combat zone for them to be out of danger.

Evacuation of prisoners

Only those prisoners of war who, owing to wounds or sickness, would run greater risks by being evacuated than by remaining where they are, may be temporarily kept back in a danger zone.

Prisoners of war shall not be unnecessarily exposed to danger while awaiting evacuation from a fighting zone.

Conditions of evacuation

Art. 20. The evacuation of prisoners of war shall always be effected humanely and in conditions similar to those for the forces of the Detaining Power in their changes of station.

The Detaining Power shall supply prisoners of war who are being evacuated with sufficient food and potable water, and with the necessary clothing and medical attention. The Detaining Power shall take all suitable precautions to ensure their safety during evacuation, and shall establish as soon as possible a list of the prisoners of war who are evacuated.

If prisoners of war must, during evacuation, pass through transit camps, their stay in such camps shall be as brief as possible.

Section II. Internment of Prisoners of War

Chapter I. General observations

Restriction of liberty of movement

Art. 21. The Detaining Power may subject prisoners of war to internment. It may impose on them the obligation of not leaving, beyond certain limits, the camp where they are interned, or if the said camp is fenced in, of not going outside its perimeter. Subject to the provisions of the present Convention relative to penal and disciplinary sanctions, prisoners of war may not be held in close confinement except where necessary to safeguard their health and then only during the continuation of the circumstances which make such confinement necessary.

Prisoners of war may be partially or wholly released on parole or promise, in so far as is allowed by the laws of the Power on which they depend. Such measures shall be taken particularly in cases where this may contribute to the improvement of their state of health. No prisoner of war shall be compelled to accept liberty on parole or promise.

Upon the outbreak of hostilities, each Party to the conflict shall notify the adverse Party of the laws and regulations allowing or forbidding its own nationals to accept liberty on parole or promise. Prisoners of war who are paroled or who have given their promise in conformity with the laws and regulations so notified, are bound on their personal honour scrupulously to fulfil, both towards the Power on which they depend and towards the power which has captured them, the engagements of their paroles or promises. In such cases, the Power on which they depend is bound neither to require nor to accept from them any service incompatible with the parole or promise given.

Places and conditions of internment

Art. 22. Prisoners of war may be interned only in premises located on land and affording every guarantee of hygiene and healthfulness. Except in particular cases which are justified by the interest of the prisoners themselves, they shall not be interned in penitentiaries.

Prisoners of war interned in unhealthy areas, or where the climate is injurious for them, shall be removed as soon as possible to a more favourable climate.

The Detaining Power shall assemble prisoners of war in camps or camp compounds according to their nationality, language and customs, provided that such prisoners shall not be separated from prisoners of war belonging to the armed forces with which they were serving at the time of their capture, except with their consent.

Art. 23. No prisoner of war may at any time be sent to, or detained in areas where he may be exposed to the fire of the combat zone, nor may his presence be used to render certain points or areas immune from military operations. Security of prisoners

Prisoners of war shall have shelters against air bombardment and other hazards of war, to the same extent as the local civilian population. With the exception of those engaged in the protection of their quarters against the aforesaid hazards, they may enter such shelters as soon as possible after the giving of the alarm. Any other protective measure taken in favour of the population shall also apply to them.

Detaining Powers shall give the Powers concerned, through the intermediary of the Protecting Powers, all useful information regarding the geographical location of prisoner of war camps.

Whenever military considerations permit, prisoner of war camps shall be indicated in the day-time by the letters PW or PG, placed so as to be clearly visible from the air. The Powers concerned may, however, agree upon any other system of marking. Only prisoner of war camps shall be marked as such.

Art. 24. Transit or screening camps of a permanent kind shall be fitted out under conditions similar to those described in the present Section, and the prisoners therein shall have the same treatment as in other camps. Permanent transit camps

Chapter II. Quarters, food and clothing of prisoners of war

Art. 25. Prisoners of war shall be quartered under conditions as favourable as those for the forces of the Detaining Power who are billeted in the same area. The said conditions shall make allowance for the habits and customs of the prisoners and shall in no case be prejudicial to their health. Quarters

The foregoing provisions shall apply in particular to the dormitories of prisoners of war as regards both total surface and minimum cubic space, and the general installations, bedding and blankets.

The premises provided for the use of prisoners of war individually or collectively, shall be entirely protected from dampness and adequately heated and lighted, in particular between dusk and lights out. All precautions must be taken against the danger of fire.

In any camps in which women prisoners of war, as well as men, are accommodated, separate dormitories shall be provided for them.

Food

Art. 26. The basic daily food rations shall be sufficient in quantity, quality and variety to keep prisoners of war in good health and to prevent loss of weight or the development of nutritional deficiencies. Account shall also be taken of the habitual diet of the prisoners.

The Detaining Power shall supply prisoners of war who work with such additional rations as are necessary for the labour on which they are employed.

Sufficient drinking water shall be supplied to prisoners of war. The use of tobacco shall be permitted.

Prisoners of war shall, as far as possible, be associated with the preparation of their meals; they may be employed for that purpose in the kitchens. Furthermore, they shall be given the means of preparing, themselves, the additional food in their possession.

Adequate premises shall be provided for messing.

Collective disciplinary measures affecting food are prohibited.

Clothing

Art. 27. Clothing, underwear and footwear shall be supplied to prisoners of war in sufficient quantities by the Detaining Power, which shall make allowance for the climate of the region where the prisoners are detained. Uniforms of enemy armed forces captured by the Detaining Power should, if suitable for the climate, be made available to clothe prisoners of war.

The regular replacement and repair of the above articles shall be assured by the Detaining Power. In addition, prisoners of war who work shall receive appropriate clothing, wherever the nature of the work demands.

Canteens

Art. 28. Canteens shall be installed in all camps, where prisoners of war may procure foodstuffs, soap and tobacco and ordinary articles in daily use. The tariff shall never be in excess of local market prices.

The profits made by camp canteens shall be used for the benefit of the prisoners; a special fund shall be created for this purpose. The prisoners' representative shall have the right to collaborate in the management of the canteen and of this fund.

When a camp is closed down, the credit balance of the special fund shall be handed to an international welfare organization, to be employed for the benefit of prisoners of war of the same nationality as those who have contributed to the fund. In case of a general repatriation, such profits shall be kept by the Detaining Power, subject to any agreement to the contrary between the Powers concerned.

Chapter III. Hygiene and medical attention

Hygiene

Art. 29. The Detaining Power shall be bound to take all sanitary measures necessary to ensure the cleanliness and healthfulness of camps and to prevent epidemics.

Prisoners of war shall have for their use, day and night, conveniences which conform to the rules of hygiene and are maintained in a constant state of cleanliness. In any camps in which women prisoners of war are accommodated, separate conveniences shall be provided for them.

Also, apart from the baths and showers with which the camps shall be furnished, prisoners of war shall be provided with sufficient water and soap for their personal toilet and for washing their personal laundry; the necessary installations, facilities and time shall be granted them for that purpose.

Art. 30. Every camp shall have an adequate infirmary where prisoners of war may have the attention they require, as well as appropriate diet. Isolation wards shall, if necessary, be set aside for cases of contagious or mental disease. Medical attention

Prisoners of war suffering from serious disease, or whose condition necessitates special treatment, a surgical operation or hospital care, must be admitted to any military or civilian medical unit where such treatment can be given, even if their repatriation is contemplated in the near future. Special facilities shall be afforded for the care to be given to the disabled, in particular to the blind, and for their rehabilitation, pending repatriation.

Prisoners of war shall have the attention, preferably, of medical personnel of the Power on which they depend and, if possible, of their nationality.

Prisoners of war may not be prevented from presenting themselves to the medical authorities for examination. The detaining authorities shall, upon request, issue to every prisoner who has undergone treatment, an official certificate indicating the nature of his illness or injury, and the duration and kind of treatment received. A duplicate of this certificate shall be forwarded to the Central Prisoners of War Agency.

The costs of treatment, including those of any apparatus necessary for the maintenance of prisoners of war in good health, particularly dentures and other artificial appliances, and spectacles, shall be borne by the Detaining Power.

Art. 31. Medical inspections of prisoners of war shall be held at least once a month. They shall include the checking and the recording of the weight of each prisoner of war. Their purpose shall be, in particular, to supervise the general state of health, nutrition and cleanliness of prisoners and to detect contagious diseases, especially tuberculosis, malaria and venereal disease. For this purpose the most efficient methods available shall be employed, e.g. periodic mass miniature radiography for the early detection of tuberculosis. Medical inspections

Art. 32. Prisoners of war who, though not attached to the medical service of their armed forces, are physicians, surgeons, dentists, nurses or medical orderlies, may be required by the Prisoners engaged on medical duties

Detaining Power to exercise their medical functions in the interests of prisoners of war dependent on the same Power. In that case they shall continue to be prisoners of war, but shall receive the same treatment as corresponding medical personnel retained by the Detaining Power. They shall be exempted from any other work under Article 49.

Chapter IV. Medical personnel and chaplains retained to assist prisoners of war

Rights and privileges of retained personnel

Art. 33. Members of the medical personnel and chaplains while retained by the Detaining Power with a view to assisting prisoners of war, shall not be considered as prisoners of war. They shall, however, receive as a minimum the benefits and protection of the present Convention, and shall also be granted all facilities necessary to provide for the medical care of, and religious ministration to prisoners of war.

They shall continue to exercise their medical and spiritual functions for the benefit of prisoners of war, preferably those belonging to the armed forces upon which they depend, within the scope of the military laws and regulations of the Detaining Power and under the control of its competent services, in accordance with their professional etiquette. They shall also benefit by the following facilities in the exercise of their medical or spiritual functions:

(a) They shall be authorized to visit periodically prisoners of war situated in working detachments or in hospitals outside the camp. For this purpose, the Detaining Power shall place at their disposal the necessary means of transport.

(b) The senior medical officer in each camp shall be responsible to the camp military authorities for everything connected with the activities of retained medical personnel. For this purpose, Parties to the conflict shall agree at the outbreak of hostilities on the subject of the corresponding ranks of the medical personnel, including that of societies mentioned in Article 26 of the Geneva Convention for the Amelioration of the Condition of the Wounded and Sick in Armed Forces in the Field of August 12, 1949. This senior medical officer, as well as chaplains, shall have the right to deal with the competent authorities of the camp on all questions relating to their duties. Such authorities shall afford them all necessary facilities for correspondence relating to these questions.

(c) Although they shall be subject to the internal discipline of the camp in which they are retained, such personnel may not be compelled to carry out any work other than that concerned with their medical or religious duties.

During hostilities, the Parties to the conflict shall agree concerning the possible relief of retained personnel and shall settle the procedure to be followed.

None of the preceding provisions shall relieve the Detaining Power of its obligations with regard to prisoners of war from the medical or spiritual point of view.

Chapter V. Religious, intellectual and physical activities

Religious duties

Art. 34. Prisoners of war shall enjoy complete latitude in the exercise of their religious duties, including attendance at the service of their faith, on condition that they comply with the disciplinary routine prescribed by the military authorities.

Adequate premises shall be provided where religious services may be held.

Retained chaplains

Art. 35. Chaplains who fall into the hands of the enemy Power and who remain or are retained with a view to assisting prisoners of war, shall be allowed to minister to them and to exercise freely their ministry amongst prisoners of war of the same religion, in accordance with their religious conscience. They shall be allocated among the various camps and labour detachments containing prisoners of war belonging to the same forces, speaking the same language or practising the same religion. They shall enjoy the necessary facilities, including the means of transport provided for in Article 33, for visiting the prisoners of war outside their camp. They shall be free to correspond, subject to censorship, on matters concerning their religious duties with the ecclesiastical authorities in the country of detention and with international religious organizations. Letters and cards which they may send for this purpose shall be in addition to the quota provided for in Article 71.

Prisoners who are ministers of religion

Art. 36. Prisoners of war who are ministers of religion, without having officiated as chaplains to their own forces, shall be at liberty, whatever their denomination, to minister freely to the members of their community. For this purpose, they shall receive the same treatment as the chaplains retained by the Detaining Power. They shall not be obliged to do any other work.

Prisoners without a minister of their religion

Art. 37. When prisoners of war have not the assistance of a retained chaplain or of a prisoner of war minister of their faith, a minister belonging to the prisoners' or a similar denomination, or in his absence a qualified layman, if such a course is feasible from a confessional point of view, shall be appointed, at the request of the prisoners concerned, to fill this office. This appointment, subject to the approval of the Detaining Power, shall take place with the agreement of the community of prisoners concerned and, wherever necessary, with the approval of the local religious authorities of the same faith. The person thus appointed shall comply with all regulations established by the Detaining Power in the interests of discipline and military security.

Recreation, study, sports and games

Art. 38. While respecting the individual preferences of every prisoner, the Detaining Power shall encourage the practice of intellectual, educational, and recreational pursuits, sports and games amongst prisoners, and shall take the measures necessary to ensure the exercise thereof by providing them with adequate premises and necessary equipment.

Prisoners shall have opportunities for taking physical exercise, including sports and games, and for being out of doors. Sufficient open spaces shall be provided for this purpose in all camps.

Chapter VI. Discipline

Administration. Saluting

Art. 39. Every prisoner of war camp shall be put under the immediate authority of a responsible commissioned officer belonging to the regular armed forces of the Detaining Power. Such officer shall have in his possession a copy of the present Convention; he shall ensure that its provisions are known to the camp staff and the guard and shall be responsible, under the direction of his government, for its application.

Prisoners of war, with the exception of officers, must salute and show to all officers of the Detaining Power the external marks of respect provided for by the regulations applying in their own forces.

Officer prisoners of war are bound to salute only officers of a higher rank of the Detaining Power; they must, however, salute the camp commander regardless of his rank.

Badges and decorations

Art. 40. The wearing of badges of rank and nationality, as well as of decorations, shall be permitted.

Posting of the Conventions, and of regulations and orders concerning prisoners

Art. 41. In every camp the text of the present Convention and its Annexes and the contents of any special agreement provided for in Article 6, shall be posted, in the prisoners' own language, at places where all may read them. Copies shall be supplied, on request, to the prisoners who cannot have access to the copy which has been posted.

Regulations, orders, notices and publications of every kind relating to the conduct of prisoners of war shall be issued to them in a language which they understand. Such regulations, orders and publications shall be posted in the manner described above and copies shall be handed to the prisoners' representative. Every order and command addressed to prisoners of war individually must likewise be given in a language which they understand.

Use of weapons

Art. 42. The use of weapons against prisoners of war, especially against those who are escaping or attempting to escape, shall constitute an extreme measure, which shall always be preceded by warnings appropriate to the circumstances.

Chapter VII. Rank of prisoners of war

Art. 43. Upon the outbreak of hostilities, the Parties to the conflict shall communicate to one another the titles and ranks of all the persons mentioned in Article 4 of the present Convention, in order to ensure equality of treatment between prisoners of equivalent rank. Titles and ranks which are subsequently created shall form the subject of similar communications.

Notification of ranks

The Detaining Power shall recognize promotions in rank which have been accorded to prisoners of war and which have been duly notified by the Power on which these prisoners depend.

Art. 44. Officers and prisoners of equivalent status shall be treated with the regard due to their rank and age.

Treatment of officers

In order to ensure service in officers' camps, other ranks of the same armed forces who, as far as possible, speak the same language, shall be assigned in sufficient numbers, account being taken of the rank of officers and prisoners of equivalent status. Such orderlies shall not be required to perform any other work.

Supervision of the mess by the officers themselves shall be facilitated in every way.

Art. 45. Prisoners of war other than officers and prisoners of equivalent status shall be treated with the regard due to their rank and age.

Treatment of other prisoners

Supervision of the mess by the prisoners themselves shall be facilitated in every way.

Chapter VIII. Transfer of prisoners of war after their arrival in camp

Art. 46. The Detaining Power, when deciding upon the transfer of prisoners of war, shall take into account the interests of the prisoners themselves, more especially so as not to increase the difficulty of their repatriation.

Conditions

The transfer of prisoners of war shall always be effected humanely and in conditions not less favourable than those under which the forces of the Detaining Power are transferred. Account shall always be taken of the climatic conditions to which the prisoners of war are accustomed and the conditions of transfer shall in no case be prejudicial to their health.

The Detaining Power shall supply prisoners of war during transfer with sufficient food and drinking water to keep them in good health, likewise with the necessary clothing, shelter and medical attention. The Detaining Power shall take adequate precautions especially in case of transport by sea or by air, to ensure their safety during transfer, and shall draw up a complete list of all transferred prisoners before their departure.

Circumstances precluding transfer

Art. 47. Sick or wounded prisoners of war shall not be transferred as long as their recovery may be endangered by the journey, unless their safety imperatively demands it.

If the combat zone draws closer to a camp, the prisoners of war in the said camp shall not be transferred unless their transfer can be carried out in adequate conditions of safety, or if they are exposed to greater risks by remaining on the spot than by being transferred.

Procedure for transfer

Art. 48. In the event of transfer, prisoners of war shall be officially advised of their departure and of their new postal address. Such notifications shall be given in time for them to pack their luggage and inform their next of kin.

They shall be allowed to take with them their personal effects, and the correspondence and parcels which have arrived for them. The weight of such baggage may be limited, if the conditions of transfer so require, to what each prisoner can reasonably carry, which shall in no case be more than twenty-five kilograms per head.

Mail and parcels addressed to their former camp shall be forwarded to them without delay. The camp commander shall take, in agreement with the prisoners' representative, any measures needed to ensure the transport of the prisoners, community property and of the luggage they are unable to take with them in consequence of restrictions imposed by virtue of the second paragraph of this Article.

The costs of transfers shall be borne by the Detaining Power.

Section III. Labour of Prisoners of War

General observations

Art. 49. The Detaining Power may utilize the labour of prisoners of war who are physically fit, taking into account their age, sex, lank and physical aptitude, and with a view particularly to maintaining them in a good state of physical and mental health. Non-commissioned officers who are prisoners of war shall only be required to do supervisory work. Those not so required may ask for other suitable work which shall, so far as possible, be found for them.

If officers or persons of equivalent status ask for suitable work, it shall be found for them, so far as possible, but they may in no circumstances be compelled to work.

Authorized work

Art. 50. Besides work connected with camp administration, installation or maintenance, prisoners of war may be compelled to do only such work as is included in the following classes:

(a) agriculture;

(b) industries connected with the production or the extraction of raw materials, and manufacturing industries, with the exception of metallurgical, machinery and chemical industries; public works and building operations which have no military character or purpose;

(c) transport and handling of stores which are not military in character or purpose;
(d) commercial business, and arts and crafts;
(e) domestic service;
(f) public utility services having no military character or purpose.

Should the above provisions be infringed, prisoners of war shall be allowed to exercise their right of complaint, in conformity with Article 78.

Working conditions

Art. 51. Prisoners of war must be granted suitable working conditions, especially as regards accommodation, food, clothing and equipment; such conditions shall not be inferior to those enjoyed by nationals of the Detaining Power employed in similar work; account shall also be taken of climatic conditions.

The Detaining Power, in utilizing the labour of prisoners of war, shall ensure that in areas in which prisoners are employed, the national legislation concerning the protection of labour, and, more particularly, the regulations for the safety of workers, are duly applied.

Prisoners of war shall receive training and be provided with the means of protection suitable to the work they will have to do and similar to those accorded to the nationals of the Detaining Power. Subject to the provisions of Article 52, prisoners may be submitted to the normal risks run by these civilian workers.

Conditions of labour shall in no case be rendered more arduous by disciplinary measures.

Dangerous or humiliating labour

Art. 52. Unless he be a volunteer, no prisoner of war maybe employed on labour which is of an unhealthy or dangerous nature.

No prisoner of war shall be assigned to labour which would be looked upon as humiliating for a member of the Detaining Power's own forces.

The removal of mines or similar devices shall be considered as dangerous labour.

Duration of labour

Art. 53. The duration of the daily labour of prisoners of war, including the time of the journey to and fro, shall not be excessive, and must in no case exceed that permitted for civilian workers in the district, who are nationals of the Detaining Power and employed on the same work.

Prisoners of war must be allowed, in the middle of the day's work, a rest of not less than one hour. This rest will be the same as that to which workers of the Detaining Power are entitled, if the latter is of longer duration. They shall be allowed in addition a rest of twenty-four consecutive hours every week, preferably on Sunday or the day of rest in their country of origin. Furthermore, every prisoner who has worked for one year shall be granted a rest of eight consecutive days, during which his working pay shall be paid him.

If methods of labour such as piece work are employed, the length of the working period shall not be rendered excessive thereby.

Working pay. Occupational accidents and diseases

Art. 54. The working pay due to prisoners of war shall be fixed in accordance with the provisions of Article 62 of the present Convention.

Prisoners of war who sustain accidents in connection with work, or who contract a disease in the course, or in consequence of their work, shall receive all the care their condition may require. The Detaining Power shall furthermore deliver to such prisoners of war a medical certificate enabling them to submit their claims to the Power on which they depend, and shall send a duplicate to the Central Prisoners of War Agency provided for in Article 123.

Medical supervision

Art. 55. The fitness of prisoners of war for work shall be periodically verified by medical examinations at least once a month. The examinations shall have particular regard to the nature of the work which prisoners of war are required to do.

If any prisoner of war considers himself incapable of working, he shall be permitted to appear before the medical authorities of his camp. Physicians or surgeons may recommend that the prisoners who are, in their opinion, unfit for work, be exempted therefrom.

Labour detachments

Art. 56. The organization and administration of labour detachments shall be similar to those of prisoner of war camps.

Every labour detachment shall remain under the control of and administratively part of a prisoner of war camp. The military authorities and the commander of the said camp shall be responsible, under the direction of their government, for the observance of the provisions of the present Convention in labour detachments.

The camp commander shall keep an up-to-date record of the labour detachments dependent on his camp, and shall communicate it to the delegates of the Protecting Power, of the International Committee of the Red Cross, or of other agencies giving relief to prisoners of war, who may visit the camp.

Prisoners working for private employers

Art. 57. The treatment of prisoners of war who work for private persons, even if the latter are responsible for guarding and protecting them, shall not be inferior to that which is provided for by the present Convention. The Detaining Power, the military authorities and the commander of the camp to which such prisoners belong shall be entirely responsible for the maintenance, care, treatment, and payment of the working pay of such prisoners of war.

Such prisoners of war shall have the right to remain in communication with the prisoners' representatives in the camps on which they depend.

Section IV. Financial Resources of Prisoners of War

Art. 58. Upon the outbreak of hostilities, and pending an arrangement on this matter with the Protecting Power, the Detaining Power may determine the maximum amount of money in cash or in any similar form, that prisoners may have in their possession. Any amount in excess, which was properly in their possession and which has been taken or withheld from them, shall be placed to their account, together with any monies deposited by them, and shall not be converted into any other currency without their consent.

Ready money

If prisoners of war are permitted to purchase services or commodities outside the camp against payment in cash, such payments shall be made by the prisoner himself or by the camp administration who will charge them to the accounts of the prisoners concerned. The Detaining Power will establish the necessary rules in this respect.

Art. 59. Cash which was taken from prisoners of war, in accordance with Article 18, at the time of their capture, and which is in the currency of the Detaining Power, shall be placed to their separate accounts, in accordance with the provisions of Article 64 of the present Section.

Amounts in cash taken from prisoners

The amounts, in the currency of the Detaining Power, due to the conversion of sums in other currencies that are taken from the prisoners of war at the same time, shall also be credited to their separate accounts.

Art. 60.[7] The Detaining Power shall grant all prisoners of war a monthly advance of pay, the amount of which shall be fixed by conversion, into the currency of the said Power, of the following amounts:

Advances of pay

Category I: Prisoners ranking below sergeants: eight Swiss francs.
Category II: Sergeants and other non-commissioned officers, or prisoners of equivalent rank: twelve Swiss francs.
Category III: Warrant officers and commissioned officers below the rank of major or prisoners of equivalent rank: fifty Swiss francs.
Category IV: Majors, lieutenant-colonels, colonels or prisoners of equivalent rank: sixty Swiss francs.
Category V: General officers or prisoners of war of equivalent rank: seventy-five Swiss francs.

However, the Parties to the conflict concerned may by special agreement modify the amount of advances of pay due to prisoners of the preceding categories.

Furthermore, if the amounts indicated in the first paragraph above would be unduly high compared with the pay of the

[7] For reservation in respect of this article by Portugal (withdrawn), see p. 671.

Detaining Power's armed forces or would, for any reason, seriously embarrass the Detaining Power, then, pending the conclusion of a special agreement with the Power on which the prisoners depend to vary the amounts indicated above, the Detaining Power:

(a) shall continue to credit the accounts of the prisoners with the amounts indicated in the first paragraph above;

(b) may temporarily limit the amount made available from these advances of pay to prisoners of war for their own use, to sums which are reasonable, but which, for Category I, shall never be inferior to the amount that the Detaining Power gives to the members of its own armed forces.

The reasons for any limitations will be given without delay to the Protecting Power.

Supplementary pay

Art. 61. The Detaining Power shall accept for distribution as supplementary pay to prisoners of war sums which the Power on which the prisoners depend may forward to them, on condition that the sums to be paid shall be the same for each prisoner of the same category, shall be payable to all prisoners of that category depending on that Power, and shall be placed in their separate accounts, at the earliest opportunity, in accordance with the provisions of Article 64. Such supplementary pay shall not relieve the Detaining Power of any obligation under this Convention.

Working pay

Art. 62. Prisoners of war shall be paid a fair working rate of pay by the detaining authorities direct. The rate shall be fixed by the said authorities, but shall at no time be less than one-fourth of one Swiss franc for a full working day. The Detaining Power shall inform prisoners of war, as well as the Power on which they depend, through the intermediary of the Protecting Power, of the rate of daily working pay that it has fixed.

Working pay shall likewise be paid by the detaining authorities to prisoners of war permanently detailed to duties or to a skilled or semi-skilled occupation in connection with the administration, installation or maintenance of camps, and to the prisoners who are required to carry out spiritual or medical duties on behalf of their comrades.

The working pay of the prisoners' representative, of his advisers, if any, and of his assistants, shall be paid out of the fund maintained by canteen profits. The scale of this working pay shall be fixed by the prisoners' representative and approved by the camp commander. If there is no such fund, the detaining authorities shall pay these prisoners a fair working rate of pay.

Transfer of funds

Art. 63. Prisoners of war shall be permitted to receive remittances of money addressed to them individually or collectively.

Every prisoner of war shall have at his disposal the credit balance of his account as provided for in the following Article, within the limits fixed by the Detaining Power, which shall make such payments as are requested. Subject to financial or monetary restrictions which the Detaining Power regards as essential, prisoners of war may also have payments made abroad. In this case payments addressed by prisoners of war to dependents shall be given priority.

In any event, and subject to the consent of the Power on which they depend, prisoners may have payments made in their own country, as follows: the Detaining Power shall send to the aforesaid Power through the Protecting Power, a notification giving all the necessary particulars concerning the prisoners of war, the beneficiaries of the payments, and the amount of the sums to be paid, expressed in the Detaining Power's currency. The said notification shall be signed by the prisoners and countersigned by the camp commander. The Detaining Power shall debit the prisoners' account by a corresponding amount; the sums thus debited shall be placed by it to the credit of the Power on which the prisoners depend.

To apply the foregoing provisions, the Detaining Power may usefully consult the Model Regulations in Annex V of the present Convention.

Prisoners' accounts

Art. 64. The Detaining Power shall hold an account for each prisoner of war, showing at least the following:

(1) The amounts due to the prisoner or received by him as advances of pay, as working pay or derived from any other source; the sums in the currency of the Detaining Power which were taken from him; the sums taken from him and converted at his request into the currency of the said Power.

(2) The payments made to the prisoner in cash, or in any other similar form; the payments made on his behalf and at his request; the sums transferred under Article 63, third paragraph.

Management of prisoners' accounts

Art. 65. Every item entered in the account of a prisoner of war shall be countersigned or initialled by him, or by the prisoners' representative acting on his behalf.

Prisoners of war shall at all times be afforded reasonable facilities for consulting and obtaining copies of their accounts, which may likewise be inspected by the representatives of the Protecting Powers at the time of visits to the camp.

When prisoners of war are transferred from one camp to another, their personal accounts will follow them. In case of transfer from one Detaining Power to another, the monies which are their property and are not in the currency of the Detaining Power will follow them. They shall be given certificates for any other monies standing to the credit of their accounts.

The Parties to the conflict concerned may agree to notify to each other at specific intervals through the Protecting Power, the amount of the accounts of the prisoners of war.

Winding up of accounts

Art. 66.[8] On the termination of captivity, through the release of a prisoner of war or his repatriation, the Detaining Power shall give him a statement, signed by an authorized officer of that Power, showing the credit balance then due to him. The Detaining Power shall also send through the Protecting Power to the government upon which the prisoner of war depends, lists giving all appropriate particulars of all prisoners of war whose captivity has been terminated by repatriation, release, escape, death or any other means, and showing the amount of their credit balances. Such lists shall be certified on each sheet by an authorized representative of the Detaining Power.

Any of the above provisions of this Article may be varied by mutual agreement between any two Parties to the conflict.

The Power on which the prisoner of war depends shall be responsible for settling with him any credit balance due to him from the Detaining Power on the termination of his captivity.

Adjustment between Parties to the conflict

Art. 67. Advances of pay, issued to prisoners of war in conformity with Article 60, shall be considered as made on behalf of the Power on which they depend. Such advances of pay, as well as all payments made by the said Power under Article 63, third paragraph, and Article 68, shall form the subject of arrangements between the Powers concerned, at the close of hostilities.

Claims for compensation

Art. 68. Any claim by a prisoner of war for compensation in respect of any injury or other disability arising out of work shall be referred to the Power on which he depends, through the Protecting Power. In accordance with Article 54, the Detaining Power will, in all cases, provide the prisoner of war concerned with a statement showing the nature of the injury or disability, the circumstances in which it arose and particulars of medical or hospital treatment given for it. This statement will be signed by a responsible officer of the Detaining Power and the medical particulars certified by a medical officer. Any claim by a prisoner of war for compensation in respect of personal effects, monies or valuables impounded by the Detaining Power under Article 18 and not forthcoming on his repatriation, or in respect of loss alleged to be due to the fault of the Detaining Power or any of its servants, shall likewise be referred to the Power on which he depends. Nevertheless, any such personal effects required for use by the prisoners of war whilst in captivity shall be replaced at the expense of the Detaining Power. The Detaining Power will, in all cases, provide the prisoner of war with a statement, signed by a responsible officer, showing all available

[8] For reservation in respect of paragraph 3 of this article by Italy, see p. 665.

information regarding the reasons why such effects, monies or valuables have not been restored to him. A copy of this statement will be forwarded to the Power on which he depends through the Central Prisoners of War Agency provided for in Article 123.

Section V. Relations of Prisoners of War with the Exterior

Notification of measures taken

Art. 69. Immediately upon prisoners of war falling into its power, the Detaining Power shall inform them and the Powers on which they depend, through the Protecting Power, of the measures taken to carry out the provisions of the present Section. They shall likewise inform the parties concerned of any subsequent modifications of such measures.

Capture card

Art. 70. Immediately upon capture, or not more than one week after arrival at a camp, even if it is a transit camp, likewise in case of sickness or transfer to hospital or another camp, every prisoner of war shall be enabled to write direct to his family, on the one hand, and to the Central Prisoners of War Agency provided for in Article 123, on the other hand, a card similar, if possible, to the model annexed to the present Convention, informing his relatives of his capture, address and state of health. The said cards shall be forwarded as rapidly as possible and may not be delayed in any manner.

Correspondence

Art. 71.[9] Prisoners of war shall be allowed to send and receive letters and cards. If the Detaining Power deems it necessary to limit the number of letters and cards sent by each prisoner of war, the said number shall not be less than two letters and four cards monthly, exclusive of the capture cards provided for in Article 70, and conforming as closely as possible to the models annexed to the present Convention. Further limitations may be imposed only if the Protecting Power is satisfied that it would be in the interests of the prisoners of war concerned to do so owing to difficulties of translation caused by the Detaining Power's inability to find sufficient qualified linguists to carry nut the necessary censorship. If limitations must be placed on the correspondence addressed to prisoners of war, they may be ordered only by the Power on which the prisoners depend, possibly at the request of the Detaining Power. Such letters and cards must be conveyed by the most rapid method at the disposal of the Detaining Power; they may not be delayed or retained for disciplinary reasons.

Prisoners of war who have been without news for a long period, or who are unable to receive news from their next of kin or to give them news by the ordinary postal route, as well as

[9] In connection with this article, see resolution 9 of the Diplomatic Conference of Geneva, 1949, p. 692.

those who are at a great distance from their homes, shall be permitted to send telegrams, the fees being charged against the prisoners of war's accounts with the Detaining Power, or paid in the currency at their disposal. They shall likewise benefit by this measure in cases of urgency.

As a general rule, the correspondence of prisoners of war shall be written in their native language. The Parties to the conflict may allow correspondence in other languages.

Sacks containing prisoner of war mail must be securely sealed and labelled so as clearly to indicate their contents, and must be addressed to offices of destination.

Relief shipments
I. General principles

Art. 72. Prisoners of war shall be allowed to receive by post or by any other means individual parcels or collective shipments containing, in particular, foodstuffs, clothing, medical supplies and articles of a religious, educational or recreational character which may meet their needs, including books, devotional articles, scientific equipment, examination papers, musical instruments, sports outfits and materials allowing prisoners of war to pursue their studies or their cultural activities.

Such shipments shall in no way free the Detaining Power from the obligations imposed upon it by virtue of the present Convention.

The only limits which may be placed on these shipments shall be those proposed by the Protecting Power in the interest of the prisoners themselves, or by the International Committee of the Red Cross or any other organization giving assistance to the prisoners, in respect of their own shipments only, on account of exceptional strain on transport or communications.

The conditions for the sending of individual parcels and collective relief shall, if necessary, be the subject of special agreements between the Powers concerned, which may in no case delay the receipt by the prisoners of relief supplies. Books may not be included in parcels of clothing and foodstuffs. Medical supplies shall, as a rule, be sent in collective parcels.

II. Collective relief

Art. 73. In the absence of special agreements between the Powers concerned on the conditions for the receipt and distribution of collective relief shipments, the rules and regulations concerning collective shipments, which are annexed to the present Convention, shall be applied.

The special agreements referred to above shall in no case restrict the right of prisoners' representatives to take possession of collective relief shipments intended for prisoners of war, to proceed to their distribution or to dispose of them in the interest of the prisoners.

Nor shall such agreements restrict the right of representatives of the Protecting Power, the International Committee of the Red Cross or any other organization giving assistance to prisoners of war and responsible for the forwarding of collective shipments, to supervise their distribution to the recipients.

Art. 74. All relief shipments for prisoners of war shall be exempt from import, customs and other dues.

Exemptions from postal and transport charges

Correspondence, relief shipments and authorized remittances of money addressed to prisoners of war or despatched by them through the post office, either direct or through the Information Bureaux provided for in Article 122 and the Central Prisoners of War Agency provided for in Article 123, shall be exempt from any postal dues, both in the countries of origin and destination, and in intermediate countries.

If relief shipments intended for prisoners of war cannot be sent through the post office by reason of weight or for any other cause, the cost of transportation shall be borne by the Detaining Power in all the territories under its control. The other Powers party to the Convention shall bear the cost of transport in their respective territories.

In the absence of special agreements between the Parties concerned, the costs connected with transport of such shipments, other than costs covered by the above exemption, shall be charged to the senders.

The High Contracting Parties shall endeavour to reduce, so far as possible, the rates charged for telegrams sent by prisoners of war, or addressed to them.

Art. 75. Should military operations prevent the Powers concerned from fulfilling their obligation to assure the transport of the shipments referred to in Articles 70, 71, 72 and 77, the Protecting Powers concerned, the International Committee of the Red Cross or any other organization duly approved by the Parties to the conflict may undertake to ensure the conveyance of such shipments by suitable means (railway wagons, motor vehicles, vessels or aircraft, etc.). For this purpose, the High Contracting Parties shall endeavour to supply them with such transport and to allow its circulation, especially by granting the necessary safe-conducts.

Special means of transport

Such transport may also be used to convey:

(a) correspondence, lists and reports exchanged between the Central Information Agency referred to in Article 123 and the National Bureaux referred to in Article 122;

(b) correspondence and reports relating to prisoners of war which the Protecting Powers, the International Committee of the Red Cross or any other body assisting the prisoners, exchange either with their own delegates or with the Parties to the conflict.

These provisions in no way detract from the right of any Party to the conflict to arrange other means of transport, if it should so prefer, nor preclude the granting of safe-conducts, under mutually agreed conditions, to such means of transport.

In the absence of special agreements, the costs occasioned by the use of such means of transport shall be borne proportionally by the Parties to the conflict whose nationals are benefited thereby.

Censorship and examination

Art. 76. The censoring of correspondence addressed to prisoners of war or despatched by them shall be done as quickly as possible. Mail shall be censored only by the despatching State and the receiving State, and once only by each.

The examination of consignments intended for prisoners of war shall not be carried out under conditions that will expose the goods contained in them to deterioration; except in the case of written or printed matter, it shall be done in the presence of the addressee, or of a fellow-prisoner duly delegated by him. The delivery to prisoners of individual or collective consignments shall not be delayed under the pretext of difficulties of censorship.

Any prohibition of correspondence ordered by Parties to the conflict, either for military or political reasons, shall be only temporary and its duration shall be as short as possible.

Preparation, execution and transmission of legal documents

Art. 77. The Detaining Powers shall provide all facilities for the transmission, through the Protecting Power or the Central Prisoners of War Agency provided for in Article 123, of instruments, papers or documents intended for prisoners of war or despatched by them, especially powers of attorney and wills.

In all cases they shall facilitate the preparation and execution of such documents on behalf of prisoners of war; in particular, they shall allow them to consult a lawyer and shall take what measures are necessary for the authentication of their signatures.

Section VI. Relations between Prisoners of War and the Authorities

Chapter I. Complaints of prisoners of war respecting the conditions of captivity

Complaints and requests

Art. 78. Prisoners of war shall have the right to make known to the military authorities in whose power they are, their requests regarding the conditions of captivity to which they are subjected.

They shall also have the unrestricted right to apply to the representatives of the Protecting Powers either through their prisoners' representative or, if they consider it necessary, direct, in order to draw their attention to any points on which they may have complaints to make regarding their conditions of captivity.

These requests and complaints shall not be limited nor considered to be a part of the correspondence quota referred to in Article 71. They must be transmitted immediately. Even if they are recognized to be unfounded, they may not give rise to any punishment.

Prisoners' representatives may send periodic reports on the situation in the camps and the needs of the prisoners of war to the representatives of the Protecting Powers.

Chapter II. Prisoner of war representatives

Art. 79. In all places where there are prisoners of war, except in those where there are officers, the prisoners shall freely elect by secret ballot, every six months, and also in case of vacancies, prisoners' representatives entrusted with representing them before the military authorities, the Protecting Powers, the International Committee of the Red Cross and any other organization which may assist them. These prisoners' representatives shall be eligible for re-election. Election

In camps for officers and persons of equivalent status or in mixed camps, the senior officer among the prisoners of war shall be recognized as the camp prisoners' representative. In camps for officers, he shall be assisted by one or more advisers chosen by the officers; in mixed camps, his assistants shall be chosen from among the prisoners of war who are not officers and shall be elected by them.

Officer prisoners of war of the same nationality shall be stationed in labour camps for prisoners of war, for the purpose of carrying out the camp administration duties for which the prisoners of war are responsible. These officers may be elected as prisoners' representatives under the first paragraph of this Article. In such a case the assistants to the prisoners' representatives shall be chosen from among those prisoners of war who are not officers.

Every representative elected must be approved by the Detaining Power before he has the right to commence his duties. Where the Detaining Power refuses to approve a prisoner of war elected by his fellow prisoners of war, it must inform the Protecting Power of the reason for such refusal.

In all cases the prisoners' representative must have the same nationality, language and customs as the prisoners of war whom he represents. Thus, prisoners of war distributed in different sections of a camp, according to their nationality, language or customs, shall have for each section their own prisoners' representative, in accordance with the foregoing paragraphs.

Art. 80. Prisoners' representatives shall further the physical, spiritual and intellectual well-being of prisoners of war. Duties

In particular, where the prisoners decide to organize amongst themselves a system of mutual assistance, this organization will be within the province of the prisoners' representative, in addition to the special duties entrusted to him by other provisions of the present Convention.

Prisoners' representatives shall not be held responsible, simply by reason of their duties, for any offences committed by prisoners of war.

Art. 81. Prisoners' representatives shall not be required to perform any other work, if the accomplishment of their duties is thereby made more difficult. Prerogatives

Prisoners' representatives may appoint from amongst the prisoners such assistants as they may require. All material facilities shall be granted them, particularly a certain freedom of movement necessary for the accomplishment of their duties (inspection of labour detachments, receipt of supplies, etc.).

Prisoners' representatives shall be permitted to visit premises where prisoners of war are detained, and every prisoner of war shall have the right to consult freely his prisoners' representative.

All facilities shall likewise be accorded to the prisoners' representatives for communication by post and telegraph with the detaining authorities, the Protecting Powers, the International Committee of the Red Cross and their delegates, the Mixed Medical Commissions and with the bodies which give assistance to prisoners of war. Prisoners' representatives of labour detachments shall enjoy the same facilities for communication with the prisoners' representatives of the principal camp. Such communications shall not be restricted, nor considered as forming a part of the quota mentioned in Article 71.

Prisoners' representatives who are transferred shall be allowed a reasonable time to acquaint their successors with current affairs.

In case of dismissal, the reasons therefor shall be communicated to the Protecting Power.

Chapter III. Penal and disciplinary sanctions

I. General provisions

Applicable legislation

Art. 82. A prisoner of war shall be subject to the laws, regulations and orders in force in the armed forces of the Detaining Power; the Detaining Power shall be justified in taking judicial or disciplinary measures in respect of any offence committed by a prisoner of war against such laws, regulations or orders. However, no proceedings or punishments contrary to the provisions of this Chapter shall be allowed.

If any law, regulation or order of the Detaining Power shall declare acts committed by a prisoner of war to be punishable, whereas the same acts would not be punishable if committed by a member of the forces of the Detaining Power, such acts shall entail disciplinary punishments only.

Choice of disciplinary or judicial proceedings

Art. 83. In deciding whether proceedings in respect of an offence alleged to have been committed by a prisoner of war shall be judicial or disciplinary, the Detaining Power shall ensure that the competent authorities exercise the greatest leniency and adopt, wherever possible, disciplinary rather than judicial measures.

Courts

Art. 84. A prisoner of war shall be tried only by a military court, unless the existing laws of the Detaining Power expressly permit the civil courts to try a member of the armed forces of the Detaining Power in respect of the particular offence alleged to have been committed by the prisoner of war.

In no circumstances whatever shall a prisoner of war be tried by a court of any kind which does not offer the essential guarantees of independence and impartiality as generally recognized, and, in particular, the procedure of which does not afford the accused the rights and means of defence provided for in Article 105.

Offences committed before capture

Art. 85.[9] Prisoners of war prosecuted under the laws of the Detaining Power for acts committed prior to capture shall retain, even if convicted, the benefits of the present Convention.

Non bis in idem

Art. 86. No prisoner of war may be punished more than once for the same act, or on the same charge.

Penalties

Art. 87.[10] Prisoners of war may not be sentenced by the military authorities and courts of the Detaining Power to any penalties except those provided for in respect of members of the armed forces of the said Power who have committed the same acts.

When fixing the penalty, the courts or authorities of the Detaining Power shall take into consideration, to the widest extent possible, the fact that the accused, not being a national of the Detaining Power, is not bound to it by any duty of allegiance, and that he is in its power as the result of circumstances independent of his own will. The said courts or authorities shall be at liberty to reduce the penalty provided for the violation of which the prisoner of war is accused, and shall therefore not be bound to apply the minimum penalty prescribed.

Collective punishment for individual acts, corporal punishments, imprisonment in premises without daylight and, in general, any form of torture or cruelty, are forbidden.

No prisoner of war may be deprived of his rank by the Detaining Power, or prevented from wearing his badges.

Execution of penalties

Art. 88. Officers, non-commissioned officers and men who are prisoners of war undergoing a disciplinary or judicial punishment, shall not be subjected to more severe treatment than that applied in respect of the same punishment to members of the armed forces of the Detaining Power of equivalent rank.

A woman prisoner of war shall not be awarded or sentenced to a punishment more severe, or treated whilst undergoing pun-

---

9 For reservations in respect of this article by Albania, Angola, Bulgaria, Byelorussian SSR, China, Czechoslovakia, Germany (Democratic Republic of), Hungary, Korea (Democratic People's Republic of), Poland, Romania, Ukrainian SSR, USSR and Vietnam (Socialist Republic of), see pp. 650–684. For objections to these reservations by Australia, New Zealand, the United Kingdom and the United States of America, see pp. 651–681.

10 For reservation in respect of this article by Uruguay, see p. 683.

ishment more severely, than a woman member of the armed forces of the Detaining Power dealt with for a similar offence.

In no case may a woman prisoner of war be awarded or sentenced to a punishment more severe, or treated whilst undergoing punishment more severely, than a male member of the armed forces of the Detaining Power dealt with for a similar offence.

Prisoners of war who have served disciplinary or judicial sentences may not be treated differently from other prisoners of war.

II. Disciplinary sanctions

General observations
I. Forms of punishment

Art. 89. The disciplinary punishments applicable to prisoners of war are the following:

(1) A fine which shall not exceed 50 per cent of the advances of pay and working pay which the prisoner of war would otherwise receive under the provisions of Articles 60 and 62 during a period of not more than thirty days.
(2) Discontinuance of privileges granted over and above the treatment provided for by the present Convention.
(3) Fatigue duties not exceeding two hours daily.
(4) Confinement.

The punishment referred to under (3) shall not be applied to officers.

In no case shall disciplinary punishments be inhuman, brutal or dangerous to the health of prisoners of war.

II. Duration of punishments

Art. 90. The duration of any single punishment shall in no case exceed thirty days. Any period of confinement awaiting the hearing of a disciplinary offence or the award of disciplinary punishment shall be deducted from an award pronounced against a prisoner of war.

The maximum of thirty days provided above may not be exceeded, even if the prisoner of war is answerable for several acts at the same time when he is awarded punishment, whether such acts are related or not.

The period between the pronouncing of an aware of disciplinary punishment and its execution shall not exceed one month.

When a prisoner of war is awarded a further disciplinary punishment, a period of at least three days shall elapse between the execution of any two of the punishments, if the duration of one of these is ten days or more.

Escapes
I. Successful escape

Art. 91. The escape of a prisoner of war shall be deemed to have succeeded when:

(1) he has joined the armed forces of the Power on which he depends, or those of an allied Power;
(2) he has left the territory under the control of the Detaining Power, or of an ally of the said Power;
(3) he has joined a ship flying the flag of the Power on which he depends, or of an allied Power, in the territorial waters

of the Detaining Power, the said ship not being under the control of the last named Power.

Prisoners of war who have made good their escape in the sense of this Article and who are recaptured, shall not be liable to any punishment in respect of their previous escape.

II. Unsuccessful escape

Art. 92. A prisoner of war who attempts to escape and is recaptured before having made good his escape in the sense of Article 91 shall be liable only to a disciplinary punishment in respect of this act, even if it is a repeated offence.

A prisoner of war who is recaptured shall be handed over without delay to the competent military authority.

Article 88, fourth paragraph, notwithstanding, prisoners of war punished as a result of an unsuccessful escape may be subjected to special surveillance. Such surveillance must not affect the state of their health, must be undergone in a prisoner of war camp, and must not entail the suppression of any of the safeguards granted them by the present Convention.

III. Connected offences

Art. 93. Escape or attempt to escape, even if it is a repeated offence, shall not be deemed an aggravating circumstance if the prisoner of war is subjected to trial by judicial proceedings in respect of an offence committed during his escape or attempt to escape.

In conformity with the principle stated in Article 83, offences committed by prisoners of war with the sole intention of facilitating their escape and which do not entail any violence against life or limb, such as offences against public property, theft without intention of self-enrichment, the drawing up or use of false papers, the wearing of civilian clothing, shall occasion disciplinary punishment only.

Prisoners of war who aid or abet an escape or an attempt to escape shall be liable on this count to disciplinary punishment only.

IV. Notification of recapture

Art. 94. If an escaped prisoner of war is recaptured, the Power on which he depends shall be notified thereof in the manner defined in Article 122, provided notification of his escape has been made.

Procedure
I. Confinement awaiting hearing

Art. 95. A prisoner of war accused of an offence against discipline shall not be kept in confinement pending the hearing unless a member of the armed forces of the Detaining Power would be so kept if he were accused of a similar offence, or if it is essential in the interests of camp order and discipline.

Any period spent by a prisoner of war in confinement awaiting the disposal of an offence against discipline shall be reduced to an absolute minimum and shall not exceed fourteen days.

The provisions of Articles 97 and 98 of this Chapter shall apply to prisoners of war who are in confinement awaiting the disposal of offences against discipline.

II. Competent authorities and right of defence

Art. 96. Acts which constitute offences against discipline shall be investigated immediately.

Without prejudice to the competence of courts and superior military authorities, disciplinary punishment may be ordered only by an officer having disciplinary powers in his capacity as camp commander, or by a responsible officer who replaces him or to whom he has delegated his disciplinary powers.

In no case may such powers be delegated to a prisoner of war or be exercised by a prisoner of war.

Before any disciplinary award is pronounced, the accused shall be given precise information regarding the offences of which he is accused, and given an opportunity of explaining his conduct and of defending himself. He shall be permitted, in particular, to call witnesses and to have recourse, if necessary, to the services of a qualified interpreter. The decision shall be announced to the accused prisoner of war and to the prisoners' representative.

A record of disciplinary punishments shall be maintained by the camp commander and shall be open to inspection by representatives of the Protecting Power.

Execution of punishment
I. Premises

Art. 97. Prisoners of war shall not in any case be transferred to penitentiary establishments (prisons, penitentiaries, convict prisons, etc.) to undergo disciplinary punishment therein.

All premises in which disciplinary punishments are undergone shall conform to the sanitary requirements set forth in Article 25. A prisoner of war undergoing punishment shall be enabled to keep himself in a state of cleanliness, in conformity with Article 29.

Officers and persons of equivalent status shall not be lodged in the same quarters as non-commissioned officers or men.

Women prisoners of war undergoing disciplinary punishment shall be confined in separate quarters from male prisoners of war and shall be under the immediate supervision of women.

II. Essential safeguards

Art. 98. A prisoner of war undergoing confinement as a disciplinary punishment, shall continue to enjoy the benefits of the provisions of this Convention except in so far as these are necessarily rendered inapplicable by the mere fact that he is confined. In no case may he be deprived of the benefits of the provisions of Articles 78 and 126.

A prisoner of war awarded disciplinary punishment may not be deprived of the prerogatives attached to his rank.

Prisoners of war awarded disciplinary punishment shall be allowed to exercise and to stay in the open air at least two hours daily.

They shall be allowed, on their request, to be present at the daily medical inspections.

They shall receive the attention which their state of health requires and, if necessary, shall be removed to the camp infirmary or to a hospital. They shall have permission to read and write, likewise to send and receive letters. Parcels and remittances of money however, may be withheld from them until the completion of the punishment; they shall meanwhile be entrusted to the prisoners' representative, who will hand over to the infirmary the perishable goods contained in such parcels.

III. Judicial proceedings

Art. 99.[11] No prisoner of war may be tried or sentenced for an act which is not forbidden by the law of the Detaining Power or by international law, in force at the time the said act was committed.

Essential rules
I. General principles

No moral or physical coercion may be exerted on a prisoner of war in order to induce him to admit himself guilty of the act of which he is accused.

No prisoner of war may be convicted without having had an opportunity to present his defence and the assistance of a qualified advocate or counsel.

Art. 100.[12] Prisoners of war and the Protecting Powers shall be informed as soon as possible of the offences which are punishable by the death sentence under the laws of the Detaining Power.

II. Death penalty

Other offences shall not thereafter be made punishable by the death penalty without the concurrence of the Power upon which the prisoners of war depend.

The death sentence cannot be pronounced on a prisoner of war unless the attention of the court has, in accordance with Article 87, second paragraph, been particularly called to the fact that since the accused is not a national of the Detaining Power, he is not bound to it by any duty of allegiance, and that he is in its power as the result of circumstances independent of his own will.

Art. 101.[13] If the death penalty is pronounced on a prisoner of war, the sentence shall not be executed before the expiration of a period of at least six months from the date when the Protecting Power receives, at an indicated address, the detailed communication provided for in Article 107.

III. Delay in execution of the death penalty

Art. 102. A prisoner of war can be validly sentenced only if the sentence has been pronounced by the same courts according to the same procedure as in the case of members of the armed forces of the Detaining Power, and if, furthermore, the provisions of the present Chapter have been observed.

Procedure
I. Conditions for validity of sentence

Art. 103. Judicial investigations relating to a prisoner of war shall be conducted as rapidly as circumstances permit and so

II. Confinement awaiting trial (Deduction from sentence, treatment)

[11] For reservation in respect of this article by Spain, see p. 674.
[12] For reservation in respect of this article by Uruguay, see p. 683.
[13] For reservation in respect of this article by Uruguay, see p. 683.

that his trial shall take place as soon as possible. A prisoner of war shall not be confined while awaiting trial unless a member of the armed forces of the Detaining Power would be so confined if he were accused of a similar offence, or if it is essential to do so in the interests of national security. In no circumstances shall this confinement exceed three months.

Any period spent by a prisoner of war in confinement awaiting trial shall be deducted from any sentence of imprisonment passed upon him and taken into account in fixing any penalty.

The provisions of Articles 97 and 98 of this Chapter shall apply to a prisoner of war whilst in confinement awaiting trial.

III. Notification of proceedings

Art. 104. In any case in which the Detaining Power has decided to institute judicial proceedings against a prisoner of war, it shall notify the Protecting Power as soon as possible and at least three weeks before the opening of the trial. This period of three weeks shall run as from the day on which such notification reaches the Protecting Power at the address previously indicated by the latter to the Detaining Power. The said notification shall contain the following information:

(1) surname and first names of the prisoner of war, his rank, his army, regimental, personal or serial number, his date of birth, and his profession or trade, if any;
(2) place of internment or confinement;
(3) specification of the charge or charges on which the prisoner of war is to be arraigned, giving the legal provisions applicable;
(4) designation of the court which will try the case, likewise the date and place fixed for the opening of the trial.

The same communication shall be made by the Detaining Power to the prisoners' representative.

If no evidence is submitted, at the opening of a trial, that the notification referred to above was received by the Protecting Power, by the prisoner of war and by the prisoners' representative concerned, at least three weeks before the opening of the trial, then the latter cannot take place and must be adjourned.

IV. Rights and means of defence

Art. 105. The prisoner of war shall be entitled to assistance by one of his prisoner comrades, to defence by a qualified advocate or counsel of his own choice, to the calling of witnesses and, if he deems necessary, to the services of a competent interpreter. He shall be advised of these rights by the Detaining Power in due time before the trial.

Failing a choice by the prisoner of war, the Protecting Power shall find him an advocate or counsel, and shall have at least one week at its disposal for the purpose. The Detaining Power shall deliver to the said Power, on request, a list of persons qualified to present the defence. Failing a choice of an advocate or counsel by the prisoner of war or the Protecting Power, the Detaining Power shall appoint a competent advocate or counsel to conduct the defence.

The advocate or counsel conducting the defence on behalf of the prisoner of war shall have at his disposal a period of two weeks at least before the opening of the trial, as well as the necessary facilities to prepare the defence of the accused. He may, in particular, freely visit the accused and interview him in private. He may also confer with any witnesses for the defence, including prisoners of war. He shall have the benefit of these facilities until the term of appeal or petition has expired.

Particulars of the charge or charges on which the prisoner of war is to be arraigned, as well as the documents which are generally communicated to the accused by virtue of the laws in force in the armed forces of the Detaining Power, shall be communicated to the accused prisoner of war in a language which he understands, and in good time before the opening of the trial. The same communication in the same circumstances shall be made to the advocate or counsel conducting the defence on behalf of the prisoner of war.

The representatives of the Protecting Power shall be entitled to attend the trial of the case, unless, exceptionally, this is held *in camera* in the interest of State security. In such a case the Detaining Power shall advise the Protecting Power accordingly.

V. Appeals

Art. 106. Every prisoner of war shall have, in the same manner as the members of the armed forces of the Detaining Power, the right of appeal or petition from any sentence pronounced upon him, with a view to the quashing or revising of the sentence or the reopening of the trial. He shall be fully informed of his right to appeal or petition and of the time limit within which he may do so.

VI. Notification of findings and sentence

Art. 107. Any judgment and sentence pronounced upon a prisoner of war shall be immediately reported to the Protecting Power in the form of a summary communication, which shall also indicate whether he has the right of appeal with a view to the quashing of the sentence or the reopening of the trial. This communication shall likewise be sent to the prisoners' representative concerned. It shall also be sent to the accused prisoner of war in a language he understands, if the sentence was not pronounced in his presence. The Detaining Power shall also immediately communicate to the Protecting Power the decision of the prisoner of war to use or to waive his right of appeal.

Furthermore, if a prisoner of war is finally convicted or if a sentence pronounced on a prisoner of war in the first instance is a death sentence, the Detaining Power shall as soon as possible address to the Protecting Power a detailed communication containing:

(1) the precise wording of the finding and sentence;
(2) a summarized report of any preliminary investigation and of the trial, emphasizing in particular the elements of the prosecution and the defence;

(3) notification, where applicable, of the establishment where the sentence will be served.

The communications provided for in the foregoing subparagraphs shall be sent to the Protecting Power at the address previously made known to the Detaining Power.

Execution of penalties. Penal regulations

Art. 108. Sentences pronounced on prisoners of war after a conviction has become duly enforceable, shall be served in the same establishments and under the same conditions as in the case of members of the armed forces of the Detaining Power. These conditions shall in all cases conform to the requirements of health and humanity.

A woman prisoner of war on whom such a sentence has been pronounced shall be confined in separate quarters and shall be under the supervision of women.

In any case, prisoners of war sentenced to a penalty depriving them of their liberty shall retain the benefit of the provisions of Articles 78 and 126 of the present Convention. Furthermore, they shall be entitled to receive and despatch correspondence, to receive at least one relief parcel monthly, to take regular exercise in the open air, to have the medical care required by their state of health, and the spiritual assistance they may desire. Penalties to which they may be subjected shall be in accordance with the provisions of Article 87, third paragraph.

PART IV. TERMINATION OF CAPTIVITY

Section I. Direct Repatriation and Accommodation in Neutral Countries

General observations

Art. 109. Subject to the provisions of the third paragraph of this Article, Parties to the conflict are bound to send back to their own country, regardless of number or rank, seriously wounded and seriously sick prisoners of war, after having cared for them until they are fit to travel, in accordance with the first paragraph of the following Article.

Throughout the duration of hostilities, Parties to the conflict shall endeavour, with the cooperation of the neutral Powers concerned, to make arrangements for the accommodation in neutral countries of the sick and wounded prisoners of war referred to in the second paragraph of the following Article. They may, in addition, conclude agreements with a view to the direct repatriation or internment in a neutral country of able-bodied prisoners of war who have undergone a long period of captivity.

No sick or injured prisoner of war who is eligible for repatriation under the first paragraph of this Article, may be repatriated against his will during hostilities.

Art. 110. The following shall be repatriated direct:

(1) Incurably wounded and sick whose mental or physical fitness seems to have been gravely diminished.

Cases of repatriation and accommodation

(2) Wounded and sick who, according to medical opinion, are not likely to recover within one year, whose condition requires treatment and whose mental or physical fitness seems to have been gravely diminished.

(3) Wounded and sick who have recovered, but whose mental or physical fitness seems to have been gravely and permanently diminished.

The following may be accommodated in a neutral country:

(1) Wounded and sick whose recovery may be expected within one year of the date of the wound or the beginning of the illness, if treatment in a neutral country might increase the prospects of a more certain and speedy recovery.

(2) Prisoners of war whose mental or physical health, according to medical opinion, is seriously threatened by continued captivity, but whose accommodation in a neutral country might remove such a threat.

The conditions which prisoners of war accommodated in a neutral country must fulfil in order to permit their repatriation shall be fixed, as shall likewise their status, by agreement between the Powers concerned. In general, prisoners of war who have been accommodated in a neutral country, and who belong to the following categories, should be repatriated:

(1) those whose state of health has deteriorated so as to fulfil the conditions laid down for direct repatriation;

(2) those whose mental or physical powers remain, even after treatment, considerably impaired.

If no special agreements are concluded between the Parties to the conflict concerned, to determine the cases of disablement or sickness entailing direct repatriation or accommodation in a neutral country, such cases shall be settled in accordance with the principles laid down in the Model Agreement concerning direct repatriation and accommodation in neutral countries of wounded and sick prisoners of war and in the Regulations concerning Mixed Medical Commissions annexed to the present Convention.

Art. 111. The Detaining Power, the Power on which the prisoners of war depend, and a neutral Power agreed upon by these two Powers, shall endeavour to conclude agreements which will enable prisoners of war to be interned in the territory of the said neutral Power until the close of hostilities.

Internment in a neutral country

Art. 112. Upon the outbreak of hostilities, Mixed Medical Commissions shall be appointed to examine sick and wounded prisoners of war, and to make all appropriate decisions regarding them. The appointment, duties and functioning of these Commissions shall be in conformity with the provisions of the Regulations annexed to the present Convention.

Mixed Medical Commissions

However, prisoners of war who, in the opinion of the medical authorities of the Detaining Power, are manifestly seriously injured or seriously sick, may be repatriated without having to be examined by a Mixed Medical Commission.

Prisoners entitled to examination by Mixed Medical Commissions

Art. 113. Besides those who are designated by the medical authorities of the Detaining Power, wounded or sick prisoners of war belonging to the categories listed below shall be entitled to present themselves for examination by the Mixed Medical Commissions provided for in the foregoing Article:

(1) Wounded and sick proposed by a physician or surgeon who is of the same nationality, or a national of a Party to the conflict allied with the Power on which the said prisoners depend, and who exercises his functions in the camp.
(2) Wounded and sick proposed by their prisoners' representative.
(3) Wounded and sick proposed by the Power on which they depend, or by an organization duly recognized by the said Power and giving assistance to the prisoners.

Prisoners of war who do not belong to one of the three foregoing categories may nevertheless present themselves for examination by Mixed Medical Commissions, but shall be examined only after those belonging to the said categories.

The physician or surgeon of the same nationality as the prisoners who present themselves for examination by the Mixed Medical Commission, likewise the prisoners' representative of the said prisoners, shall have permission to be present at the examination.

Prisoners meeting with accidents

Art. 114. Prisoners of war who meet with accidents shall, unless the injury is self-inflicted, have the benefit of the provisions of this Convention as regards repatriation or accommodation in a neutral country.

Prisoners serving a sentence

Art. 115. No prisoner of war on whom a disciplinary punishment has been imposed and who is eligible for repatriation or for accommodation in a neutral country, may be kept back on the plea that he has not undergone his punishment.

Prisoners of war detained in connection with a judicial prosecution or conviction and who are designated for repatriation or accommodation in a neutral country, may benefit by such measures before the end of the proceedings or the completion of the punishment, if the Detaining Power consents.

Parties to the conflict shall communicate to each other the names of those who will be detained until the end of the proceedings or the completion of the punishment.

Costs of repatriation

Art. 116. The costs of repatriating prisoners of war or of transporting them to a neutral country shall be borne, from the frontiers of the Detaining Power, by the Power on which the said prisoners depend.

Art. 117. No repatriated person may be employed on active military service.

Activity after repatriation

Section II. Release and Repatriation of Prisoners of War at the Close of Hostilities

Art. 118.[14] Prisoners of war shall be released and repatriated without delay after the cessation of active hostilities.

Release and repatriation

In the absence of stipulations to the above effect in any agreement concluded between the Parties to the conflict with a view to the cessation of hostilities, or failing any such agreement, each of the Detaining Powers shall itself establish and execute without delay a plan of repatriation in conformity with the principle laid down in the foregoing paragraph.

In either case, the measures adopted shall be brought to the knowledge of the prisoners of war.

The costs of repatriation of prisoners of war shall in all cases be equitably apportioned between the Detaining Power and the Power on which the prisoners depend. This apportionment shall be carried out on the following basis:

(a) If the two Powers are contiguous, the Power on which the prisoners of war depend shall bear the costs of repatriation from the frontiers of the Detaining Power.

(b) If the two Powers are not contiguous, the Detaining Power shall bear the costs of transport of prisoners of war over its own territory as far as its frontier or its port of embarkation nearest to the territory of the Power on which the prisoners of war depend. The Parties concerned shall agree between themselves as to the equitable apportionment of the remaining costs of the repatriation. The conclusion of this agreement shall in no circumstances justify any delay in the repatriation of the prisoners of war.

Art. 119. Repatriation shall be effected in conditions similar to those laid down in Articles 46 to 48 inclusive of the present Convention for the transfer of prisoners of war, having regard to the provisions of Article 118 and to those of the following paragraphs.

Details of procedure

On repatriation, any articles of value impounded from prisoners of war under Article 18, and any foreign currency which has not been converted into the currency of the Detaining Power, shall be restored to them. Articles of value and foreign currency which, for any reason whatever, are not restored to prisoners of war on repatriation, shall be despatched to the Information Bureau set up under Article 122.

Prisoners of war shall be allowed to take with them their personal effects, and any correspondence and parcels which have arrived for them. The weight of such baggage may be limited, if the conditions of repatriation so require, to what each

[14] For reservation in respect of this article by Korea (Republic of), see p. 666.

prisoner can reasonably carry. Each prisoner shall in all cases be authorized to carry at least twenty-five kilograms.

The other personal effects of the repatriated prisoner shall be left in the charge of the Detaining Power which shall have them forwarded to him as soon as it has concluded an agreement to this effect, regulating the conditions of transport and the payment of the costs involved, with the Power on which the prisoner depends.

Prisoners of war against whom criminal proceedings for an indictable offence are pending may be detained until the end of such proceedings, and, if necessary, until the completion of the punishment. The same shall apply to prisoners of war already convicted for an indictable offence.

Parties to the conflict shall communicate to each other the names of any prisoners of war who are detained until the end of the proceedings or until punishment has been completed.

By agreement between the Parties to the conflict, commissions shall be established for the purpose of searching for dispersed prisoners of war and of assuring their repatriation with the least possible delay.

Section III. Death of Prisoners of War

Wills, death certificates, burial, cremation

Art. 120. Wills of prisoners of war shall be drawn up so as to satisfy the conditions of validity required by the legislation of their country of origin, which will take steps to inform the Detaining Power of its requirements in this respect. At the request of the prisoner of war and, in all cases, after death, the will shall be transmitted without delay to the Protecting Power; a certified copy shall be sent to the Central Agency.

Death certificates in the form annexed to the present Convention, or lists certified by a responsible officer, of all persons who die as prisoners of war shall be forwarded as rapidly as possible to the Prisoner of War Information Bureau established in accordance with Article 122. The death certificates or certified lists shall show particulars of identity as set out in the third paragraph of Article 17, and also the date and place of death, the cause of death, the date and place of burial and all particulars necessary to identify the graves.

The burial or cremation of a prisoner of war shall be preceded by a medical examination of the body with a view to confirming death and enabling a report to be made and, where necessary, establishing identity.

The detaining authorities shall ensure that prisoners of war who have died in captivity are honourably buried, if possible according to the rites of the religion to which they belonged, and that their graves are respected, suitably maintained and marked so as to be found at any time. Wherever possible, deceased prisoners of war who depended on the same Power shall be interred in the same place.

Deceased prisoners of war shall be buried in individual graves unless unavoidable circumstances require the use of collective graves. Bodies may be cremated only for imperative reasons of hygiene, on account of the religion of the deceased or in accordance with his express wish to this effect. In case of cremation, the fact shall be stated and the reasons given in the death certificate of the deceased.

In order that graves may always be found, all particulars of burials and graves shall be recorded with a Graves Registration Service established by the Detaining Power. Lists of graves and particulars of the prisoners of war interred in cemeteries and elsewhere shall be transmitted to the Power on which such prisoners of war depended. Responsibility for the care of these graves and for records of any subsequent moves of the bodies shall rest on the Power controlling the territory, if a Party to the present Convention. These provisions shall also apply to the ashes, which shall be kept by the Graves Registration Service until proper disposal thereof in accordance with the wishes of the home country.

Prisoners killed or injured in special circumstances

Art. 121. Every death or serious injury of a prisoner of war caused or suspected to have been caused by a sentry, another prisoner of war, or any other person, as well as any death the cause of which is unknown, shall be immediately followed by an official enquiry by the Detaining Power.

A communication on this subject shall be sent immediately to the Protecting Power. Statements shall be taken from witnesses, especially from those who are prisoners of war, and a report including such statements shall be forwarded to the Protecting Power.

If the enquiry indicates the guilt of one or more persons, the Detaining Power shall take all measures for the prosecution of the person or persons responsible.

PART V. INFORMATION BUREAUX AND RELIEF SOCIETIES FOR PRISONERS OF WAR

National Bureaux

Art. 122. Upon the outbreak of a conflict and in all cases of occupation, each of the Parties to the conflict shall institute an official Information Bureau for prisoners of war who are in its power. Neutral or non-belligerent Powers who may have received within their territory persons belonging to one of the categories referred to in Article 4, shall take the same action with respect to such persons. The Power concerned shall ensure that the Prisoners of War Information Bureau is provided with the necessary accommodation, equipment and staff to ensure its efficient working. It shall be at liberty to employ prisoners of war in such a Bureau under the conditions laid down in the Section of the present Convention dealing with work by prisoners of war.

Within the shortest possible period, each of the Parties to the conflict shall give its Bureau the information referred to in the fourth, fifth and sixth paragraphs of this Article regarding any enemy person belonging to one of the categories referred to in Article 4, who has fallen into its power. Neutral or non-belligerent Powers shall take the same action with regard to persons belonging to such categories whom they have received within their territory.

The Bureau shall immediately forward such information by the most rapid means to the Powers concerned, through the intermediary of the Protecting Powers and likewise of the Central Agency provided for in Article 123.

This information shall make it possible quickly to advise the next of kin concerned. Subject to the provisions of Article 17, the information shall include, in so far as available to the Information Bureau, in respect of each prisoner of war, his surname, first names, rank, army, regimental, personal or serial number, place and full date of birth, indication of the Power on which he depends, first name of the father and maiden name of the mother, name and address of the person to be informed and the address to which correspondence for the prisoner may be sent.

The Information Bureau shall receive from the various departments concerned information regarding transfers, releases, repatriations, escapes, admissions to hospital, and deaths, and shall transmit such information in the manner described in the third paragraph above.

Likewise, information regarding the state of health of prisoners of war who are seriously ill or seriously wounded shall be supplied regularly, every week if possible.

The Information Bureau shall also be responsible for replying to all enquiries sent to it concerning prisoners of war, including those who have died in captivity; it will make any enquiries necessary to obtain the information which is asked for if this is not in its possession.

All written communications made by the Bureau shall be authenticated by a signature or a seal.

The Information Bureau shall furthermore be charged with collecting all personal valuables, including sums in currencies other than that of the Detaining Power and documents of importance to the next of kin, left by prisoners of war who have been repatriated or released, or who have escaped or died, and shall forward the said valuables to the Powers concerned. Such articles shall be sent by the Bureau in sealed packets which shall be accompanied by statements giving clear and full particulars of the identity of the person to whom the articles belonged, and by a complete list of the contents of the parcel. Other personal effects of such prisoners of war shall be transmitted under arrangements agreed upon between the Parties to the conflict concerned.

Art. 123. A Central Prisoners of War Information Agency shall be created in a neutral country. The International Committee of the Red Cross shall, if it deems necessary, propose to the Powers concerned the organization of such an Agency.

Central Agency

The function of the Agency shall be to collect all the information it may obtain through official or private channels respecting prisoners of war, and to transmit it as rapidly as possible to the country of origin of the prisoners of war or to the Power on which they depend. It shall receive from the Parties to the conflict all facilities for effecting such transmissions.

The High Contracting Parties, and in particular those whose nationals benefit by the services of the Central Agency, are requested to give the said Agency the financial aid it may require.

The foregoing provisions shall in no way be interpreted as restricting the humanitarian activities of the International Committee of the Red Cross, or of the relief Societies provided for in Article 125.

Art. 124. The national Information Bureaux and the Central Information Agency shall enjoy free postage for mail, likewise all the exemptions provided for in Article 74, and further, so far as possible, exemption from telegraphic charges or, at least, greatly reduced rates.

Exemption from charges

Art. 125. Subject to the measures which the Detaining Powers may consider essential to ensure their security or to meet any other reasonable need, the representatives of religious organizations, relief societies, or any other organization assisting prisoners of war, shall receive from the said Powers, for themselves and their duly accredited agents, all necessary facilities for visiting the prisoners, distributing relief supplies and material, from any source, intended for religious, educational or recreative purposes, and for assisting them in organizing their leisure time within the camps. Such societies or organizations may be constituted in the territory of the Detaining Power or in any other country, or they may have an international character.

Relief societies and other organisations

The Detaining Power may limit the number of societies and organizations whose delegates are allowed to carry out their activities in its territory and under its supervision, on condition, however, that such limitation shall not hinder the effective operation of adequate relief to all prisoners of war.

The special position of the International Committee of the Red Cross in this field shall be recognized and respected at all times.

As soon as relief supplies or material intended for the abovementioned purposes are handed over to prisoners of war, or very shortly afterwards, receipts for each consignment, signed by the prisoners' representative, shall be forwarded to the relief society or organization making the shipment. At the same time, receipts for these consignments shall be supplied by the administrative authorities responsible for guarding the prisoners.

PART VI. EXECUTION OF THE CONVENTION

Section I. General Provisions

Supervision

Art. 126. Representatives or delegates of the Protecting Powers shall have permission to go to all places where prisoners of war may be, particularly to places of internment, imprisonment and labour, and shall have access to all premises occupied by prisoners of war; they shall also be allowed to go to the places of departure, passage and arrival of prisoners who are being transferred. They shall he able to interview the prisoners, and in particular the prisoners' representatives, without witnesses, either personally or through an interpreter.

Representatives and delegates of the Protecting Powers shall have full liberty to select the places they wish to visit. The duration and frequency of these visits shall not be restricted. Visits may not be prohibited except for reasons of imperative military necessity, and then only as an exceptional and temporary measure.

The Detaining Power and the Power on which the said prisoners of war depend may agree, if necessary, that compatriots of these prisoners of war be permitted to participate in the visits.

The delegates of the International Committee of the Red Cross shall enjoy the same prerogatives. The appointment of such delegates shall be submitted to the approval of the Power detaining the prisoners of war to be visited.

Dissemination of the Convention

Art. 127. The High Contracting Parties undertake, in time of peace as in time of war, to disseminate the text of the present Convention as widely as possible in their respective countries, and, in particular, to include the study thereof in their programmes of military and, if possible, civil instruction, so that the principles thereof may become known to all their armed forces and to the entire population.

Any military or other authorities, who in time of war assume responsibilities in respect of prisoners of war, must possess the text of the Convention and be specially instructed as to its provisions.

Translations. Rules of application

Art. 128. The High Contracting Parties shall communicate to one another through the Swiss Federal Council and, during hostilities, through the Protecting Powers, the official translations of the present Convention, as well as the laws and regulations which they may adopt to ensure the application thereof.

Penal sanctions

Art. 129. The High Contracting Parties undertake to enact any legislation necessary to provide effective penal sanctions for persons committing, or ordering to be committed, any of the grave breaches of the present Convention defined in the following Article.

I. General observations

Each High Contracting Party shall be under the obligation to search for persons alleged to have committed, or to have ordered to be committed, such grave breaches, and shall bring such persons, regardless of their nationality, before its own courts. It may also, if it prefers, and in accordance with the provisions of its own legislation, hand such persons over for trial to another High Contracting Party concerned, provided such High Contracting Party has made out a prima facie case.

Each High Contracting Party shall take measures necessary for the suppression of all acts contrary to the provisions of the present Convention other than the grave breaches defined in the following Article.

In all circumstances, the accused persons shall benefit by safeguards of proper trial and defence, which shall not be less favourable than those provided by Article 105 and those following of the present Convention.

II. Grave breaches

Art. 130. Grave breaches to which the preceding Article relates shall be those involving any of the following acts, if committed against persons or property protected by the Convention: wilful killing, torture or inhuman treatment, including biological experiments, wilfully causing great suffering or serious injury to body or health, compelling a prisoner of war to serve in the forces of the hostile Power, or wilfully depriving a prisoner of war of the rights of fair and regular trial prescribed in this Convention.

III. Responsibilities of the Contracting Parties

Art. 131. No High Contracting Party shall be allowed to absolve itself or any other High Contracting Party of any liability incurred by itself or by another High Contracting Party in respect of breaches referred to in the preceding Article.

Enquiry procedure

Art. 132. At the request of a Party to the conflict, an enquiry shall be instituted, in a manner to be decided between the interested Parties, concerning any alleged violation of the Convention.

If agreement has not been reached concerning the procedure for the enquiry, the Parties should agree on the choice of an umpire who will decide upon the procedure to be followed.

Once the violation has been established, the Parties to the conflict shall put an end to it and shall repress it with the least possible delay.

Section II. Final Provisions

Languages

Art. 133. The present Convention is established in English and in French. Both texts are equally authentic.

The Swiss Federal Council shall arrange for official translations of the Convention to be made in the Russian and Spanish languages.

Relation to the 1929 Convention

Art. 134. The present Convention replaces the Convention of July 27, 1929, in relations between the High Contracting Parties.

Relation to the Hague Convention

Art. 135. In the relations between the Powers which are bound by the Hague Convention respecting the Laws and Customs of War on Land, whether that of July 29, 1899, or that of October 18, 1907, and which are parties to the present Convention, this last Convention shall be complementary to Chapter II of the Regulations annexed to the above-mentioned Conventions of the Hague.

Signature

Art. 136. The present Convention, which bears the date of this day, is open to signature until February 12, 1950, in the name of the Powers represented at the Conference which opened at Geneva on April 21, 1949; furthermore, by Powers not represented at that Conference, but which are parties to the Convention of July 27, 1929.

Ratification

Art. 137. The present Convention shall be ratified as soon as possible and the ratifications shall be deposited at Berne.

A record shall be drawn up of the deposit of each instrument of ratification and certified copies of this record shall be transmitted by the Swiss Federal Council to all the Powers in whose name the Convention has been signed, or whose accession has been notified.

Coming into force

Art. 138. The present Convention shall come into force six months after not less than two instruments of ratification have been deposited.

Thereafter, it shall come into force for each High Contracting Party six months after the deposit of the instrument of ratification.

Accession

Art. 139. From the date of its coming into force, it shall be open to any Power in whose name the present Convention has not been signed, to accede to this Convention.

Notification of accessions

Art. 140. Accessions shall be notified in writing to the Swiss Federal Council, and shall take effect six months after the date on which they are received.

The Swiss Federal Council shall communicate the accessions to all the Powers in whose name the Convention has been signed, or whose accession has been notified.

Immediate effect

Art. 141. The situations provided for in Articles 2 and 3 shall give immediate effect to ratifications deposited and accessions notified by the Parties to the conflict before or after the beginning of hostilities or occupation. The Swiss Federal Council shall communicate by the quickest method any ratifications or accessions received from Parties to the conflict.

Denunciation

Art. 142. Each of the High Contracting Parties shall be at liberty to denounce the present Convention.

The denunciation shall be notified in writing to the Swiss Federal Council, which shall transmit it to the Governments of all the High Contracting Parties.

The denunciation shall take effect one year after the notification thereof has been made to the Swiss Federal Council. However, a denunciation of which notification has been made at a time when the denouncing Power is involved in a conflict shall not take effect until peace has been concluded, and until after operations connected with the release and repatriation of the persons protected by the present Convention have been terminated.

The denunciation shall have effect only in respect of the denouncing Power. It shall in no way impair the obligations which the Parties to the conflict shall remain bound to fulfil by virtue of the principles of the law of nations, as they result from the usages established among civilized peoples, from the laws of humanity and the dictates of the public conscience.

Registration with the United Nations

Art. 143. The Swiss Federal Council shall register the present Convention with the Secretariat of the United Nations. The Swiss Federal Council shall also inform the Secretariat of the United Nations of all ratifications, accessions and denunciations received by it with respect to the present Convention.

In witness whereof the undersigned, having deposited their respective full powers, have signed the present Convention.

Done at Geneva this twelfth day of August 1949, in the English and French languages. The original shall be deposited in the Archives of the Swiss Confederation. The Swiss Federal Council shall transmit certified copies thereof to each of the signatory and acceding States.

ANNEX I. MODEL AGREEMENT CONCERNING DIRECT REPATRIATION AND ACCOMMODATION IN NEUTRAL COUNTRIES OF WOUNDED AND SICK PRISONERS OF WAR

(see *Article 110*)

I. Principles for Direct Repatriation and Accommodation in Neutral Countries

A. Direct repatriation

The following shall be repatriated direct:

(1) All prisoners of war suffering from the following disabilities as the result of trauma: loss of limb, paralysis, articular or other disabilities, when this disability is at least the loss of a hand or a foot, or the equivalent of the loss of a hand or a foot. Without prejudice to a more generous interpretation, the following shall be considered as equivalent to the loss of a hand or a foot:

- (a) Loss of a hand or of all the fingers, or of the thumb and forefinger of one hand; loss of a foot, or of all the toes and metatarsals of one foot.
- (b) Ankylosis, loss of osseous tissue, cicatricial contracture preventing the functioning of one of the large articulations or of all the digital joints of one hand.
- (c) Pseudarthrosis of the long bones.
- (d) Deformities due to fracture or other injury which seriously interfere with function and weight-bearing power.

(2) All wounded prisoners of war whose condition has become chronic, to the extent that prognosis appears to exclude recovery – in spite of treatment – within one year from the date of the injury, as, for example, in case of:

- (a) Projectile in the heart, even if the Mixed Medical Commission should fail, at the time of their examination, to detect any serious disorders.
- (b) Metallic splinter in the brain or the lungs, even if the Mixed Medical Commission cannot, at the time of examination, detect any local or general reaction.
- (c) Osteomyelitis, when recovery cannot be foreseen in the course of the year following the injury, and which seems likely to result in ankylosis of a joint, or other impairments equivalent to the loss of a hand or a foot.
- (d) Perforating and suppurating injury to the large joints.
- (e) Injury to the skull, with loss or shifting of bony tissue.
- (f) Injury or burning of the face with loss of tissue and functional lesions.
- (g) Injury to the spinal cord.
- (h) Lesion of the peripheral nerves, the sequelae of which are equivalent to the loss of a hand or foot, and the cure of which requires more than a year from the date of injury, for example: injury to the brachial or lumbosacral plexus, the median or sciatic nerves, likewise combined injury to the radial and cubital nerves or to the lateral popliteal nerve (N. peroneus communis) and medial popliteal nerve (N. tibialis); etc. The separate injury of the radial (musculo-spiral), cubital, lateral or medial popliteal nerves shall not, however, warrant repatriation except in case of contractures or of serious neurotrophic disturbance.
- (i) Injury to the urinary system, with incapacitating results.

(3) All sick prisoners of war whose condition has become chronic to the extent that prognosis seems to exclude recovery – in spite of treatment – within one year from the inception of the disease, as, for example, in case of:

(a) Progressive tuberculosis of any organ which, according to medical prognosis, cannot be cured, or at least considerably improved, by treatment in a neutral country.

(b) Exudate pleurisy.

(c) Serious diseases of the respiratory organs of non-tubercular etiology, presumed incurable, for example: serious pulmonary emphysema, with or without bronchitis; chronic asthma;(*) chronic bronchitis(*) lasting more than one year in captivity; bronchiectasis;(*) etc.

(d) Serious chronic affections of the circulatory system, for example: valvular lesions and myocarditis,(*) which have shown signs of circulatory failure during captivity, even though the Mixed Medical Commission cannot detect any such signs at the time of examination; affections of the pericardium and the vessels (Buerger's disease, aneurism of the large vessels); etc.

(e) Serious chronic affections of the digestive organs, for example: gastric or duodenal ulcer; sequelae of gastric operations performed in captivity; chronic gastritis, enteritis or colitis, having lasted more than one year and seriously affecting the general condition; cirrhosis of the liver; chronic cholecystopathy;(*) etc.

(f) Serious chronic affections of the genito-urinary organs, for example: chronic diseases of the kidney with consequent disorders; nephrectomy because of a tubercular kidney; chronic pyelitis or chronic cystitis; hydronephrosis or pyonephrosis; chronic grave gynaecological conditions; normal pregnancy and obstetrical disorder, where it is impossible to accommodate in a neutral country; etc.

(g) Serious chronic diseases of the central and peripheral nervous system, for example: all obvious psychoses and psychoneuroses, such as serious hysteria, serious captivity psychoneurosis, etc., duly verified by a specialist;(*) any epilepsy duly verified by the camp physician;(*) cerebral arteriosclerosis; chronic neuritis lasting more than one year; etc.

(h) Serious chronic diseases of the neuro-vegetative system, with considerable diminution of mental or physical fitness, noticeable loss of weight and general asthenia.

(i) Blindness of both eyes, or of one eye when the vision of the other is less than 1 in spite of the use of corrective glasses; diminution of visual acuity in cases where it is impossible to restore it by correction to an acuity of 1/2 in at least one eye;(*) other grave ocular affections, for example: glaucoma, iritis, choroiditis; trachoma; etc.

(k) Auditive disorders, such as total unilateral deafness, if the other ear does not discern the ordinary spoken word at a distance of one metre;(*) etc.

(*) The decision of the Mixed Medical Commission shall be based and to a great extent on the records kept by the camp physicians and surgeons of the same nationality as the prisoners of war, or on an examination by medical specialists of the detaining power (*note in the original*).

(l) Serious affections of metabolism, for example: diabetes mellitus requiring insulin treatment; etc.
(m) Serious disorders of the endocrine glands, for example: thyrotoxicosis; hypotyrosis; Addison's disease; Simmonds' cachexia; tetany; etc.
(n) Grave and chronic disorders of the blood-forming organs.
(o) Serious cases of chronic intoxication, for example: lead poisoning, mercury poisoning, morphinism, cocainism, alcoholism; gas or radiation poisoning; etc.
(p) Chronic affections of locomotion, with obvious functional disorders, for example: arthritis deformans; primary and secondary progressive chronic polyarthritis; rheumatism with serious clinical symptoms; etc.
(q) Serious chronic skin diseases, not amenable to treatment.
(r) Any malignant growth.
(s) Serious chronic infectious diseases, persisting for one year after their inception, for example: malaria with decided organic impairment, amoebic or bacillary dysentery with grave disorders; tertiary visceral syphilis resistant to treatment; leprosy; etc.
(t) Serious avitaminosis or serious inanition.

B. Accommodation in Neutral Countries

The following shall be eligible for accommodation in a neutral country:
(1) All wounded prisoners of war who are not likely to recover in captivity, but who might be cured or whose condition might be considerably improved by accommodation in a neutral country.
(2) Prisoners of war suffering from any form of tuberculosis, of whatever organ, and whose treatment in a neutral country would be likely to lead to recovery or at least to considerable improvement, with the exception of primary tuberculosis cured before captivity.
(3) Prisoners of war suffering from affections requiring treatment of the respiratory, circulatory, digestive, nervous, sensory, genito-urinary, cutaneous, locomotive organs, etc., if such treatment would clearly have better results in a neutral country than in captivity.
(4) Prisoners of war who have undergone a nephrectomy in captivity for a non-tubercular renal affection; cases of osteomyelitis, on the way to recovery or latent; diabetes mellitus not requiring insulin treatment; etc.
(5) Prisoners of war suffering from war or captivity neuroses. Cases of captivity neurosis which are not cured after three months of accommodation in a neutral country, or which after that length of time are not clearly on the way to complete cure, shall be repatriated.
(6) All prisoners of war suffering from chronic intoxication (gases, metals, alkaloids, etc), for whom the prospects of cure in a neutral country are especially favourable.
(7) All women prisoners of war who are pregnant or mothers with infants and small children.

The following cases shall not be eligible for accommodation in a neutral country:
(1) All duly verified chronic psychoses.
(2) All organic or functional nervous affections considered to be incurable.
(3) All contagious diseases during the period in which they are transmissible, with the exception of tuberculosis.

II. General Observations

(1) The conditions given shall, in a general way, be interpreted and applied in as broad a spirit as possible. Neuropathic and psychopathic conditions caused by war or captivity, as well as cases of tuberculosis in all stages, shall above all benefit by such liberal interpretation. Prisoners of war who have sustained several wounds, none of which, considered by itself, justifies repatriation, shall be examined in the same spirit, with due regard for the psychic traumatism due to the number of their wounds.
(2) All unquestionable cases giving the right to direct repatriation (amputation, total blindness or deafness, open pulmonary tuberculosis, mental disorder, malignant growth, etc.) shall be examined and repatriated as soon as possible by the camp physicians or by military medical commissions appointed by the Detaining Power.
(3) Injuries and diseases which existed before the war and which have not become worse, as well as war injuries which have not prevented subsequent military service, shall not entitle to direct repatriation.
(4) The provisions of this Annex shall be interpreted and applied in a similar manner in all countries party to the conflict. The Powers and authorities concerned shall grant to Mixed Medical Commissions all the facilities necessary for the accomplishment of their task.
(5) The examples quoted under (I) above represent only typical cases. Cases which do not correspond exactly to these provisions shall be judged in the spirit of the provisions of Article 110 of the present Convention, and of the principles embodied in the present Agreement.

ANNEX II. REGULATIONS CONCERNING MIXED MEDICAL COMMISSIONS
(*see Article 112*)

Article 1. The Mixed Medical Commissions provided for in Article 112 of the Convention shall be composed of three members, two of whom shall belong to a neutral country, the third being appointed by the Detaining Power. One of the neutral members shall take the chair.

Art. 2. The two neutral members shall be appointed by the International Committee of the Red Cross, acting in agreement with the Protecting Power, at the request of the Detaining Power. They may be domiciled either in their country of origin, in any other neutral country, or in the territory of the Detaining Power.

Art. 3. The neutral members shall be approved by the Parties to the conflict concerned, who shall notify their approval to the International Committee of the Red Cross and to the Protecting Power. Upon such notification, the neutral members shall be considered as effectively appointed.

Art. 4. Deputy members shall also be appointed in sufficient number to replace the regular members in case of need. They shall be appointed at the same time as the regular members or, at least, as soon as possible.

Art. 5. If for any reason the International Committee of the Red Cross cannot arrange for the appointment of the neutral members, this shall be done by the Power protecting the interests of the prisoners of war to be examined.

Art. 6. So far as possible, one of the two neutral members shall be a surgeon and the other a physician.

Art. 7. The neutral members shall be entirely independent of the Parties to the conflict, which shall grant them all facilities in the accomplishment of their duties.

Art. 8. By agreement with the Detaining Power, the International Committee of the Red Cross, when making the appointments provided for in Articles 2 and 4 of the present Regulations, shall settle the terms of service of the nominees.

Art. 9. The Mixed Medical Commissions shall begin their work as soon as possible after the neutral members have been approved, and in any case within a period of three months from the date of such approval.

Art. 10. The Mixed Medical Commissions shall examine all the prisoners designated in Article 113 of the Convention. They shall propose repatriation, rejection, or reference to a later examination. Their decisions shall be made by a majority vote.

Art. 11. The decisions made by the Mixed Medical Commissions in each specific case shall be communicated, during the month following their visit, to the

Detaining Power, the Protecting Power and the International Committee of the Red Cross. The Mixed Medical Commissions shall also inform each prisoner of war examined of the decision made, and shall issue to those whose repatriation has been proposed, certificates similar to the model appended to the present Convention.

Art. 12. The Detaining Power shall be required to carry out the decisions of the Mixed Medical Commissions within three months of the time when it receives due notification of such decisions.

Art. 13. If there is no neutral physician in a country where the services of a Mixed Medical Commission seem to be required, and if it is for any reason impossible to appoint neutral doctors who are resident in another country, the Detaining Power, acting in agreement with the Protecting Power, shall set up a Medical Commission which shall undertake the same duties as a Mixed Medical Commission, subject to the provisions of Articles 1, 2, 3, 4, 5 and 8 of the present Regulations.

Art. 14. Mixed Medical Commissions shall function permanently and shall visit each camp at intervals of not more than six months.

ANNEX III. REGULATIONS CONCERNING COLLECTIVE RELIEF
(*see Article 73*)

Article 1. Prisoners' representatives shall be allowed to distribute collective relief shipments for which they are responsible, to all prisoners of war administered by their camp, including those who are in hospitals, or in prisons or other penal establishments.

Art. 2. The distribution of collective relief shipments shall be effected in accordance with the instructions of the donors and with a plan drawn up by the prisoners' representatives. The issue of medical stores shall, however, be made for preference in agreement with the senior medical officers, and the latter may, in hospitals and infirmaries, waive the said instructions, if the needs of their patients so demand. Within the limits thus defined, the distribution shall always be carried out equitably.

Art. 3. The said prisoners' representatives or their assistants shall be allowed to go to the points of arrival of relief supplies near their camps, so as to enable the prisoners' representatives or their assistants to verify the quality as well as the quantity of the goods received, and to make out detailed reports thereon for the donors.

Art. 4. Prisoners' representatives shall be given the facilities necessary for verifying whether the distribution of collective relief in all sub-divisions and annexes of their camps has been carried out in accordance with their instructions.

Art. 5. Prisoners' representatives shall be allowed to fill up, and cause to be filled up by the prisoners' representatives of labour detachments or by the senior medical officers of infirmaries and hospitals, forms or questionnaires intended for the donors, relating to collective relief supplies (distribution, requirements, quantities, etc.). Such forms and questionnaires, duly completed, shall be forwarded to the donors without delay.

Art. 6. In order to secure the regular issue of collective relief to the prisoners of war in their camp, and to meet any needs that may arise from the arrival of new contingents of prisoners, prisoners' representatives shall be allowed to build up and maintain adequate reserve stocks of collective relief. For this purpose, they shall have suitable warehouses at their disposal; each warehouse shall be provided with two locks, the prisoners' representative holding the keys of one lock and the camp commander the keys of the other.

Art. 7. When collective consignments of clothing are available each prisoner of war shall retain in his possession at least one complete set of clothes. If a prisoner has more than one set of clothes, the prisoners' representative shall be permitted to withdraw excess clothing from those with the largest number of sets, or particular articles in excess of one, if this is necessary in order to supply prisoners who are less well provided. He shall not, however, withdraw second sets of underclothing, socks or footwear, unless this is the only means of providing for prisoners of war with none.

Art. 8. The High Contracting Parties, and the Detaining Powers in particular, shall authorize, as far as possible and subject to the regulations governing the supply of the population, all purchases of goods made in their territories for the distribution of collective relief to prisoners of war. They shall similarly facilitate the transfer of funds and other financial measures of a technical or administrative nature taken for the purpose of making such purchases.

Art. 9. The foregoing provisions shall not constitute an obstacle to the right of prisoners of war to receive collective relief before their arrival in a camp or in the course of transfer, nor to the possibility of representatives of the Protecting Power, the International Committee of the Red Cross, or any other body giving assistance to prisoners which may be responsible for the forwarding of such supplies, ensuring the distribution thereof to the addressees by any other means that they may deem useful.

ANNEX IV

A. IDENTITY CARD

(*see Article 4*)

NOTICE

This identity card is issued to persons who accompany the Armed Forces of .... but are not part of them. The card must be carried at all times by the person to whom it is issued. If the bearer is taken prisoner, he shall at once hand the card to the Detaining Authorities, to assist in his identification.

Official seal imprint

Blood type ....

Religion ....

Finger-prints (optional)

(Left forefinger) (Right forefinger)

Any other mark of identification ....

Hair	Eyes	Weight	Height
....	....	....	....

Photograph of the bearer

(Name of the country and military authority issuing this card)

IDENTITY CARD

FOR A PERSON WHO ACCOMPANIES THE ARMED FORCES

Name ....

First names ....

Date and place of birth ....

Accompanies the Armed Forces as ....

Date of issue .... Signature of bearer ....

Remarks. — This card should be made out for preference in two or three languages, one of which is in international use. Actual size of the card: 13 by 10 centimetres. It should be folded along the dotted line.

ANNEX IV

B. CAPTURE CARD
(*see Article 70*)

1. Front

PRISONER OF WAR MAIL | Postage free

CAPTURE CARD FOR PRISONER OF WAR

IMPORTANT

This card must be completed by each prisoner immediately after being taken prisoner and each time his address is changed (by reason of transfer to a hospital or to another camp).

This card is distinct from the special card which each prisoner is allowed to send to his relatives.

CENTRAL PRISONERS OF WAR AGENCY

International Committee of the Red Cross

GENEVA

(Switzerland)

2. Reverse side

Write legibly and in block letters

1. Power on which the prisoner depends ....

2. Name 3. First names (in full) 4. First name of father ....

5. Date of birth .... 6. Place of birth ....

7. Rank ....

8. Service number ....

9. Address of next of kin ....

* 10. Taken prisoner on: (or) Coming from (Camp No., hospital, etc.) ....

* 11. *a*) Good health—*b*) Not wounded—*c*) Recovered—*d*) Convalescent—*e*) Sick—*f*) Slightly wounded—*g*) Seriously wounded.

12. My present address is: Prisoner No. ....

Name of camp ....

13. Date .... 14. Signature ....

* Strike out what is not applicable—Do not add any remarks—See explanations overleaf.

Remarks. — This form should be made out in two or three languages, particularly in the prisoner's own language and in that of the Detaining Power. Actual size of form: 15 by 10.5 centimetres.

ANNEX IV

C.1 CORRESPONDENCE CARD
(*see Article 71*)

1. Front

PRISONER OF WAR MAIL

| Postage free |

POST CARD

To ....

Sender:	
Name and first names	....
....	Place of Destination
Place and date of birth	....
....	
Prisoner of War No.	
....	
Name of camp	Street ....
....	Country ....
Country where posted	Province or Department ....
....	

2. Reverse side

NAME OF CAMP .... Date ....

....

....

....

....

....

....

....

....

Write on the dotted lines only and as legibly as possible.

Remarks.—This form should be made out in two or three languages, particularly in the prisoner's own language and in that of the Detaining Power. Actual size of form : 15 by 10 centimetres.

ANNEX IV

C.2 CORRESPONDENCE LETTER
(*see Article 71*)

PRISONER OF WAR MAIL

Postage free

To ....

....

Place ....

Street ....

Country ....

Department or Province ....

Sender:

Name and first names ....

Date and place of birth ....

Prisoner of War No. ....

Name of camp ....

Country where posted ....

* * * * * *

Remarks.—This form should be made out in two or three languages, particularly in the prisoner's own language and in that of the Detaining Power. It should be folded along the dotted line, the tab being inserted in the slit (marked by a line of asterisks); it then has the appearance of an envelope. Overleaf, it is lined like the postcard above (*Annex IV C1*); this space can contain about 250 words which the prisoner is free to write. Actual size of the folded form: 29 by 15 centimetres.

ANNEX IV

D. NOTIFICATION OF DEATH
(see Article 120)

(Title of responsible authority)	NOTIFICATION OF DEATH
	Power on which the prisoner depended ....
Name and first names	
First name of father	....
Place and date of birth	....
Place and date of death	....
Rank and service number (as given on identity disc)	....
Address of next of kin	....
Where and when taken prisoner	....
Cause and circumstances of death	....
Place of burial	....
Is the grave marked and can it be found later by the relatives?	....
Are the personal effects of the deceased in the keeping of the Detaining Power or are they being forwarded together with this notification?	....
If forwarded, through what agency?	....
Can the person who cared for the deceased during sickness or during his last moments (doctor, nurse, minister of religion, fellow prisoner) give here or on an attached sheet a short account of the circumstances of the death and burial?	....
(Date, seal and signature of responsible authority)	Signature and address of two witnesses
....	....

Remarks.—This form should be made out in two or three languages, particularly in the prisoner's own language and in that of the Detaining Power. Actual size of form: 21 by 30 centimetres.

ANNEX IV

E. REPATRIATION CERTIFICATE
(*see Annex II, Article 11*)

REPATRIATION CERTIFICATE

Date:

Camp:

Hospital:

Surname:

First names:

Date of birth:

Rank:

Army number:

P. W. number:

Injury-Disease:

Decision of the Commission:

Chairman of the
Mixed Medical Commission:

A = direct repatriation

B = accommodation in a neutral country

NC = re-examination by next Commission

ANNEX V

MODEL REGULATIONS CONCERNING PAYMENTS SENT BY PRISONERS TO THEIR OWN COUNTRY
(*see Article 63*)

(1) The notification referred to in the third paragraph of Article 63 will show:
  (a) number as specified in Article 17, rank, surname and first names of the prisoner of war who is the payer;
  (b) the name and address of the payee in the country of origin;
  (c) the amount to be so paid in the currency of the country in which he is detained.

(2) The notification will be signed by the prisoner of war, or his witnessed mark made upon it if he cannot write, and shall be countersigned by the prisoners' representative.

(3) The camp commander will add to this notification a certificate that the prisoner of war concerned has a credit balance of not less than the amount registered as payable.

(4) The notification may be made up in lists, each sheet of such lists witnessed by the prisoners' representative and certified by the camp commander.

SIGNATURES, RATIFICATIONS AND ACCESSIONS

See list on pp. 635–649.

RESERVATIONS AND DECLARATIONS

See list on pp. 650–688.

No. 52

CONVENTION (IV) RELATIVE TO THE PROTECTION OF CIVILIAN PERSONS IN TIME OF WAR

Signed at Geneva, 12 August 1949

INTRODUCTORY NOTE: The Geneva Conventions which were adopted before 1949 were concerned with combatants only, not with civilians. Some provisions concerning the protection of populations against the consequences of war and their protection in occupied territories are contained in the Hague Regulations of 1899 and 1907 (*Nos. 7 and 8, Annexes*). During World War I the Hague provisions proved to be insufficient in view of the dangers originating from air warfare and of the problems relating to the treatment of civilians in enemy territory and in occupied territories. The International Red Cross Conferences of the 1920s took the first steps towards laying down supplementary rules for the protection of civilians in time of war. The 1929 Diplomatic Conference, which revised the Convention on wounded and sick and drew up the Convention on prisoners of war, recommended that studies should be made with a view to concluding a convention on the protection of civilians in enemy territory and in enemy occupied territory. A draft convention prepared by the International Committee of the Red Cross was approved by the International Red Cross Conference in Tokyo in 1934 (*No. 47*). It was to be submitted to a diplomatic conference planned for 1940, but this was postponed on account of the war. The events of World War II showed the disastrous consequences of the absence of a convention for the protection of civilians in wartime. The Convention adopted in 1949 takes account of the experiences of World War II. It contains a rather short part concerning the general protection of populations against certain consequences of war (Part II) leaving aside the problem of the limitation of the use of weapons. The great bulk of the Convention deals with civilians in enemy territory and in occupied territory. The Convention does not invalidate the provisions of the Hague Regulations of 1907 on the same subjects but is supplementary to them (see Article 154 of the Convention).

ENTRY INTO FORCE: 21 October 1950.

AUTHENTIC TEXTS: English and French. The text below is reprinted from the *Final Record of the Diplomatic Conference of Geneva of 1949*, Vol. I, Federal Political Department, Berne, pp. 297–341.

The marginal titles added to the articles of the present Convention have no official character and were not adopted by the Diplomatic Conference. They were drafted by the Conference Secretariat and are used in the edition of the Geneva Conventions published by the International Committee of the Red Cross.

TEXT PUBLISHED IN: See indications under *No. 48*.

TABLE OF CONTENTS

* * *

The undersigned Plenipotentiaries of the Governments represented at the Diplomatic Conference held at Geneva from April 21 to August 12, 1949, for the purpose of establishing a Convention for the Protection of Civilian Persons in Time of War, have agreed as follows:[1]

PART I. GENERAL PROVISIONS

Respect for the Convention

Art. 1. The High Contracting Parties undertake to respect and to ensure respect for the present Convention in all circumstances.

Application of the Convention

Art. 2. In addition to the provisions which shall be implemented in peacetime, the present Convention shall apply to all cases of declared war or of any other armed conflict which may arise between two or more of the High Contracting Parties, even if the state of war is not recognized by one of them.

The Convention shall also apply to all cases of partial or total occupation of the territory of a High Contracting Party, even if the said occupation meets with no armed resistance.

Although one of the Powers in conflict may not be a party to the present Convention, the Powers who are parties thereto shall remain bound by it in their mutual relations. They shall furthermore be bound by the Convention in relation to the said Power, if the latter accepts and applies the provisions thereof.

Conflicts not of an international character

Art. 3.[2] In the case of armed conflict not of an international character occurring in the territory of one of the High Contracting Parties, each Party to the conflict shall be bound to apply, as a minimum, the following provisions:

(1) Persons taking no active part in the hostilities, including members of armed forces who have laid down their arms and those placed *hors de combat* by sickness, wounds, detention, or any other cause, shall in all circumstances be treated humanely, without any adverse distinction founded on race, colour, religion or faith, sex, birth or wealth, or any other similar criteria.

To this end, the following acts are and shall remain prohibited at any time and in any place whatsoever with respect to the above-mentioned persons:

(a) violence to life and person, in particular murder of all kinds, mutilation, cruel treatment and torture;
(b) taking of hostages;
(c) outrages upon personal dignity, in particular humiliating and degrading treatment;
(d) the passing of sentences and the carrying out of executions without previous judgment pronounced by a reg-

1 For objection by the United States of America to reservations made by other states with respect to this Convention, see pp. 681.

2 For reservations in respect of this article by Argentina and Portugal (withdrawn), see pp. 651 and 671.

ularly constituted court, affording all the judicial guarantees which are recognized as indispensable by civilized peoples.

(2) The wounded and sick shall be collected and cared for. An impartial humanitarian body, such as the International Committee of the Red Cross, may offer its services to the Parties to the conflict.

The Parties to the conflict should further endeavour to bring into force, by means of special agreements, all or part of the other provisions of the present Convention.

The application of the preceding provisions shall not affect the legal status of the Parties to the conflict.

Art. 4.[3] Persons protected by the Convention are those who, at a given moment and in any manner whatsoever, find themselves, in case of a conflict or occupation, in the hands of a Party to the conflict or Occupying Power of which they are not nationals.

Definition of protected persons

Nationals of a State which is not bound by the Convention are not protected by it. Nationals of a neutral State who find themselves in the territory of a belligerent State, and nationals of a co-belligerent State, shall not be regarded as protected persons while the State of which they are nationals has normal diplomatic representation in the State in whose hands they are.

The provisions of Part II are, however, wider in application, as defined in Article 13.

Persons protected by the Geneva Convention for the Amelioration of the Condition of the Wounded and Sick in Armed Forces in the Field of August 12, 1949, or by the Geneva Convention for the Amelioration of the Condition of Wounded, Sick and Shipwrecked Members of Armed Forces at Sea of August 12, 1949, or by the Geneva Convention relative to the Treatment of Prisoners of War of August 12, 1949, shall not be considered as protected persons within the meaning of the present Convention.

Art. 5.[4] Where, in the territory of a Party to the conflict, the latter is satisfied that an individual protected person is definitely suspected of or engaged in activities hostile to the security of the State, such individual person shall not be entitled to claim such rights and privileges under the present Convention as would, if exercised in the favour of such individual person, be prejudicial to the security of such State.

Derogations

Where in occupied territory an individual protected person is detained as a spy or saboteur, or as a person under definite suspicion of activity hostile to the security of the Occupying Power, such person shall, in those cases where absolute military security so requires, be regarded as having forfeited rights of communication under the present Convention.

---

[3] For declaration in respect of this article by Hungary, see p. 662.

[4] For declaration in respect of this article by Hungary, see p. 662.

In each case, such persons shall nevertheless be treated with humanity, and in case of trial, shall not be deprived of the rights of fair and regular trial prescribed by the present Convention. They shall also be granted the full rights and privileges of a protected person under the present Convention at the earliest date consistent with the security of the State or Occupying Power, as the case may be.

Beginning and end of application

Art. 6. The present Convention shall apply from the outset of any conflict or occupation mentioned in Article 2.

In the territory of Parties to the conflict, the application of the present Convention shall cease on the general close of military operations.

In the case of occupied territory, the application of the present Convention shall cease one year after the general close of military operations; however, the Occupying Power shall be bound, for the duration of the occupation, to the extent that such Power exercises the functions of government in such territory, by the provisions of the following Articles of the present Convention: 1 to 12, 27, 29 to 34, 47, 49, 51, 52, 53, 59, 61 to 77, 143.

Protected persons whose release, repatriation or re-establishment may take place after such dates shall meanwhile continue to benefit by the present Convention.

Special agreements

Art. 7. In addition to the agreements expressly provided for in Articles 11, 14, 15, 17, 36, 108, 109, 132, 133 and 149, the High Contracting Parties may conclude other special agreements for all matters concerning which they may deem it suitable to make separate provision. No special agreement shall adversely affect the situation of protected persons, as defined by the present Convention, nor restrict the rights which it confers upon them.

Protected persons shall continue to have the benefit of such agreements as long as the Convention is applicable to them, except where express provisions to the contrary are contained in the aforesaid or in subsequent agreements, or where more favourable measures have been taken with regard to them by one or other of the Parties to the conflict.

Non-renunciation of rights

Art. 8. Protected persons may in no circumstances renounce in part or in entirety the rights secured to them by the present Convention, and by the special agreements referred to in the foregoing Article, if such there be.

Protecting Powers

Art. 9. The present Convention shall be applied with the cooperation and under the scrutiny of the Protecting Powers whose duty it is to safeguard the interests of the Parties to the conflict. For this purpose, the Protecting Powers may appoint, apart from their diplomatic or consular staff, delegates from amongst their own nationals or the nationals of other neutral Powers. The said delegates shall be subject to the approval of the Power with which they are to carry out their duties.

The Parties to the conflict shall facilitate to the greatest extent possible the task of the representatives or delegates of the Protecting Powers.

The representatives or delegates of the Protecting Powers shall not in any case exceed their mission under the present Convention. They shall, in particular, take account of the imperative necessities of security of the State wherein they carry out their duties.

Activities of the International Committee of the Red Cross

Art. 10. The provisions of the present Convention constitute no obstacle to the humanitarian activities which the International Committee of the Red Cross or any other impartial humanitarian organization may, subject to the consent of the Parties to the conflict concerned, undertake for the protection of civilian persons and for their relief.

Substitutes for Protecting Powers

Art. 11.[5] The High Contracting Parties may at any time agree to entrust to an organization which offers all guarantees of impartiality and efficacy the duties incumbent on the Protecting Powers by virtue of the present Convention.

When persons protected by the present Convention do not benefit or cease to benefit, no matter for what reason, by the activities of a Protecting Power or of an organization provided for in the first paragraph above, the Detaining Power shall request a neutral State, or such an organization, to undertake the functions performed under the present Convention by a Protecting Power designated by the Parties to a conflict.

If protection cannot be arranged accordingly, the Detaining Power shall request or shall accept, subject to the provisions of this Article, the offer of the services of a humanitarian organization, such as the International Committee of the Red Cross, to assume the humanitarian functions performed by Protecting Powers under the present Convention.

Any neutral Power, or any organization invited by the Power concerned or offering itself for these purposes, shall be required to act with a sense of responsibility towards the Party to the conflict on which persons protected by the present Convention depend, and shall be required to furnish sufficient assurances that it is in a position to undertake the appropriate functions and to discharge them impartially.

No derogation from the preceding provisions shall be made by special agreements between Powers one of which is

[5] For reservations in respect of this article by Albania, Bulgaria, Byelorussian SSR, China, Czechoslovakia, Germany (Democratic Republic of), Guinea-Bissau, Hungary, Korea (Democratic People's Republic of), Poland, Portugal, Romania, Ukrainian SSR, USSR, Vietnam (Socialist Republic of) and Yugoslavia, see pp. 650–688.

restricted, even temporarily, in its freedom to negotiate with the other Power or its allies by reason of military events, more particularly where the whole, or a substantial part, of the territory of the said Power is occupied.

Whenever in the present Convention mention is made of a Protecting Power, such mention applies to substitute organizations in the sense of the present Article.

The provisions of this Article shall extend and be adapted to cases of nationals of a neutral State who are in occupied territory or who find themselves in the territory of a belligerent State in which the State of which they are nationals has not normal diplomatic representation.

Conciliation procedure

Art. 12.[6] In cases where they deem it advisable in the interest of protected persons, particularly in cases of disagreement between the Parties to the conflict as to the application or interpretation of the provisions of the present Convention, the Protecting Powers shall lend their good offices with a view to settling the disagreement.

For this purpose, each of the Protecting Powers may, either at the invitation of one Party or on its own initiative, propose to the Parties to the conflict a meeting of their representatives, and in particular of the authorities responsible for protected persons, possibly on neutral territory suitably chosen. The Parties to the conflict shall be bound to give effect to the proposals made to them for this purpose. The Protecting Powers may, if necessary, propose for approval by the Parties to the conflict, a person belonging to a neutral Power or delegated by the International Committee of the Red Cross, who shall be invited to take part in such a meeting.

PART II. GENERAL PROTECTION OF POPULATIONS AGAINST CERTAIN CONSEQUENCES OF WAR

Field of application Part II

Art. 13. The provisions of Part II cover the whole of the populations of the countries in conflict, without any adverse distinction based, in particular, on race, nationality, religion or political opinion, and are intended to alleviate the sufferings caused by war.

Hospital and safety zones and localities

Art. 14. In time of peace, the High Contracting Parties and, after the outbreak of hostilities, the Parties thereto, may establish in their own territory and, if the need arises, in occupied areas, hospital and safety zones and localities so organized as to protect from the effects of war, wounded, sick and aged persons, children under fifteen, expectant mothers and mothers of children under seven.

Upon the outbreak and during the course of hostilities, the Parties concerned may conclude agreements on mutual recogni-

6 For reservation in respect of this article by Hungary, see p. 662.

tion of the zones and localities they have created. They may for this purpose implement the provisions of the Draft Agreement annexed to the present Convention, with such amendments as they may consider necessary.

The Protecting Powers and the International Committee of the Red Cross are invited to lend their good offices in order to facilitate the institution and recognition of these hospital and safety zones and localities.

Neutralized zones

Art. 15. Any Party to the conflict may, either direct or through a neutral State or some humanitarian organization, propose to the adverse Party to establish, in the regions where fighting is taking place, neutralized zones intended to shelter from the effects of war the following persons, without distinction:
(a) wounded and sick combatants or non-combatants;
(b) civilian persons who take no part in hostilities, and who, while they reside in the zones, perform no work of a military character.

When the Parties concerned have agreed upon the geographical position, administration, food supply and supervision of the proposed neutralized zone, a written agreement shall be concluded and signed by the representatives of the Parties to the conflict. The agreement shall fix the beginning and the duration of the neutralization of the zone.

Wounded and sick
I. General provisions

Art. 16. The wounded and sick, as well as the infirm, and expectant mothers, shall be the object of particular protection and respect.

As far as military considerations allow, each Party to the conflict shall facilitate the steps taken to search for the killed and wounded, to assist the shipwrecked and other persons exposed to grave danger, and to protect them against pillage and ill-treatment.

II. Evacuation

Art. 17. The Parties to the conflict shall endeavour to conclude local agreements for the removal from besieged or encircled areas, of wounded, sick, infirm, and aged persons, children and maternity cases, and for the passage of ministers of all religions, medical personnel and medical equipment on their way to such areas.

III. Protection of hospitals

Art. 18.[7] Civilian hospitals organized to give care to the wounded and sick, the infirm and maternity cases, may in no circumstances be the object of attack, but shall at all times be respected and protected by the Parties to the conflict.

States which are Parties to a conflict shall provide all civilian hospitals with certificates showing that they are civilian hospitals and that the buildings which they occupy are not used

7 For declaration and reservation with respect to the distinctive emblem by Iran and Israel, see p. 663.

for any purpose which would deprive these hospitals of protection in accordance with Article 19.

Civilian hospitals shall be marked by means of the emblem provided for in Article 38 of the Geneva Convention for the Amelioration of the Condition of the Wounded and Sick in Armed Forces in the Field of August 12, 1949, but only if so authorized by the State.

The Parties to the conflict shall, in so far as military considerations permit, take the necessary steps to make the distinctive emblems indicating civilian hospitals clearly visible to the enemy land, air and naval forces in order to obviate the possibility of any hostile action.

In view of the dangers to which hospitals may be exposed by being close to military objectives, it is recommended that such hospitals be situated as far as possible from such objectives.

IV. Discontinuance of protection of hospitals

Art. 19. The protection to which civilian hospitals are entitled shall not cease unless they are used to commit, outside their humanitarian duties, acts harmful to the enemy. Protection may, however, cease only after due warning has been given, naming, in all appropriate cases, a reasonable time limit, and after such warning has remained unheeded.

The fact that sick or wounded members of the armed forces are nursed in these hospitals, or the presence of small arms and ammunition taken from such combatants which have not yet handed to the proper service, shall not be considered to be acts harmful to the enemy.

V. Hospital staff

Art. 20.[8] Persons regularly and solely engaged in the operation and administration of civilian hospitals, including the personnel engaged in the search for, removal and transporting of and caring for wounded and sick civilians, the infirm and maternity cases, shall be respected and protected.

In occupied territory and in zones of military operations, the above personnel shall be recognisable by means of an identity card certifying their status, bearing the photograph of the holder and embossed with the stamp of the responsible authority, and also by means of a stamped, water-resistant armlet which they shall wear on the left arm while carrying out their duties. This armlet shall be issued by the State and shall bear the emblem provided for in Article 38 of the Geneva Convention for the Amelioration of the Condition of the Wounded and Sick in Armed Forces in the Field of August 12, 1949.

Other personnel who are engaged in the operation and administration of civilian hospitals shall be entitled to respect and protection and to wear the armlet, as provided in and under the conditions prescribed in this Article, while they are employed on

[8] For declaration and reservation with respect to the distinctive emblem by Iran and Israel, see pp. 663 and 664.

such duties. The identity card shall state the duties on which they are employed.

The management of each hospital shall at all times hold at the disposal of the competent national or occupying authorities an up-to-date list of such personnel.

VI. Land and sea transport

Art. 21.[9] Convoys of vehicles or hospital trains on land or specially provided vessels on sea, conveying wounded and sick civilians, the infirm and maternity cases, shall be respected and protected in the same manner as the hospitals provided for in Article 18, and shall be marked, with the consent of the State, by the display of the distinctive emblem provided for in Article 38 of the Geneva Convention for the Amelioration of the Condition of the Wounded and Sick in Armed Forces in the Field of August 12, 1949.

VII. Air transport

Art. 22.[10] Aircraft exclusively employed for the removal of wounded and sick civilians, the infirm and maternity cases, or for the transport of medical personnel and equipment, shall not be attacked, but shall be respected while flying at heights, times and on routes specifically agreed upon between all the Parties to the conflict concerned.

They may be marked with the distinctive emblem provided for in Article 38 of the Geneva Convention for the Amelioration of the Condition of the Wounded and Sick in Armed Forces in the Field of August 12, 1949.

Unless agreed otherwise, flights over enemy or enemy-occupied territory are prohibited.

Such aircraft shall obey every summons to land. In the event of a landing thus imposed, the aircraft with its occupants may continue its flight after examination, if any.

Consignment of medical supplies, food and clothing

Art. 23.[11] Each High Contracting Party shall allow the free passage of all consignments of medical and hospital stores and objects necessary for religious worship intended only for civilians of another High Contracting Party, even if the latter is its adversary. It shall likewise permit the free passage of all consignments of essential foodstuffs, clothing and tonics intended for children under fifteen, expectant mothers and maternity cases.

The obligation of a High Contracting Party to allow the free passage of the consignments indicated in the preceding paragraph is subject to the condition that this Party is satisfied that there are no serious reasons for fearing:

(a) that the consignments may be diverted from their destination,

---

9 For declaration and reservation with respect to the distinctive emblem by Iran and Israel, see pp. 663 and 664.

10 For declaration and reservation with respect to the distinctive emblem by Iran and Israel, see pp. 663 and 664.

11 For declaration and reservation with respect to the distinctive emblem by Iran and Israel, see pp. 663 and 664.

(b) that the control may not be effective, or
(c) that a definite advantage may accrue to the military efforts or economy of the enemy through the substitution of the above-mentioned consignments for goods which would otherwise be provided or produced by the enemy or through the release of such material, services or facilities as would otherwise be required for the production of such goods.

The Power which allows the passage of the consignments indicated in the first paragraph of this Article may ma permission conditional on the distribution to the persons benefited thereby being made under the local supervision of the Protecting Powers.

Such consignments shall be forwarded as rapidly as possible, and the Power which permits their free passage shall have the right to prescribe the technical arrangements under which such passage is allowed.

Measures relating to child welfare

Art. 24. The Parties to the conflict shall take the necessary measures to ensure that children under fifteen, who are orphaned or are separated from their families as a result of the war, are not left to their own resources, and that their maintenance, the exercise of their religion and their education are facilitated in all circumstances. Their education shall, as far as possible, be entrusted to persons of a similar cultural tradition.

The Parties to the conflict shall facilitate the reception of such children in a neutral country for the duration of the conflict with the consent of the Protecting Power, if any, and under due safeguards for the observance of the principles stated in the first paragraph.

They shall, furthermore, endeavour to arrange for all children under twelve to be identified by the wearing of identity discs, or by some other means.

Family news

Art. 25. All persons in the territory of a Party to the conflict, or in a territory occupied by it, shall be enabled to give news of a strictly personal nature to members of their families, wherever they may be, and to receive news from them. This correspondence shall be forwarded speedily and without undue delay.

If, as a result of circumstances, it becomes difficult or impossible to exchange family correspondence by the ordinary post, the Parties to the conflict concerned shall apply to a neutral intermediary, such as the Central Agency provided for in Article 140, and shall decide in consultation with it how to ensure the fulfilment of their obligations under the best possible conditions, in particular with the cooperation of the National Red Cross (Red Crescent, Red Lion and Sun) Societies.

If the Parties to the conflict deem it necessary to restrict family correspondence, such restrictions shall be confined to the compulsory use of standard forms containing twenty-five freely chosen words, and to the limitation of the number of these forms despatched to one each month.

Art. 26. Each Party to the conflict shall facilitate enquiries made by members of families dispersed owing to the war, with the object of renewing contact with one another and of meeting, if possible. It shall encourage, in particular, the work of organizations engaged on this task provided they are acceptable to it and conform to its security regulations.

Dispersed families

PART III. STATUS AND TREATMENT OF PROTECTED PERSONS

Section I. Provisions Common to the Territories of the Parties to the Conflict and to Occupied Territories

Art. 27. Protected persons are entitled, in all circumstances, to respect for their persons, their honour, their family rights, their religious convictions and practices, and their manners and customs. They shall at all times be humanely treated, and shall be protected especially against all acts of violence or threats thereof and against insults and public curiosity.

Treatment I. General observations

Women shall be especially protected against any attack on their honour, in particular against rape, enforced prostitution, or any form of indecent assault.

Without prejudice to the provisions relating to their state of health, age and sex, all protected persons shall be treated with the same consideration by the Party to the conflict in whose power they are, without any adverse distinction based, in particular, on race, religion or political opinion.

However, the Parties to the conflict may take such measures of control and security in regard to protected persons as may be necessary as a result of the war.

Art. 28. The presence of a protected person may not be used to render certain points or areas immune from military operations.

II. Danger zones

Art. 29. The Party to the conflict in whose hands protected persons may be, is responsible for the treatment accorded to them by its agents, irrespective of any individual responsibility which may be incurred.

III. Responsibilities

Art. 30. Protected persons shall have every facility for making application to the Protecting Powers, the International Committee of the Red Cross, the National Red Cross (Red Crescent, Red Lion and Sun) Society of the country where they may be, as well as to any organization that might assist them.

Application to Protecting Powers and relief organizations

These several organizations shall be granted all facilities for that purpose by the authorities, within the bounds set by military or security considerations.

Apart from the visits of the delegates of the Protecting Powers and of the International Committee of the Red Cross, provided for by Article 143, the Detaining or Occupying Powers shall facilitate as much as possible visits to protected persons by the representatives of other organizations whose object is to give spiritual aid or material relief to such persons.

Prohibition of coercion

Art. 31. No physical or moral coercion shall be exercised against protected persons, in particular to obtain information from them or from third parties.

Prohibition of corporal punishment, torture, etc.

Art. 32. The High Contracting Parties specifically agree that each of them is prohibited from taking any measure of such a character as to cause the physical suffering or extermination of protected persons in their hands. This prohibition applies not only to murder, torture, corporal punishment, mutilation and medical or scientific experiments not necessitated by the medical treatment of a protected person, but also to any other measures of brutality whether applied by civilian or military agents.

Individual responsibility, collective penalties, pillage, reprisals

Art. 33. No protected person may be punished for an offence he or she has not personally committed. Collective penalties and likewise all measures of intimidation or of terrorism are prohibited.

Pillage is prohibited.

Reprisals against protected persons and their property are prohibited.

Hostages

Art. 34 The taking of hostages is prohibited.

Section II. Aliens in the Territory of a Party to the Conflict

Right to leave the territory

Art. 35. All protected persons who may desire to leave the territory at the outset of, or during a conflict, shall be entitled to do so, unless their departure is contrary to the national interests of the State. The applications of such persons to leave shall be decided in accordance with regularly established procedures and the decision shall be taken as rapidly as possible. Those persons permitted to leave may provide themselves with the necessary funds for their journey and take with them a reasonable amount of their effects and articles of personal use.

If any such person is refused permission to leave the territory, he shall be entitled to have such refusal reconsidered as soon as possible by an appropriate court or administrative board designated by the Detaining Power for that purpose.

Upon request, representatives of the Protecting Power shall, unless reasons of security prevent it, or the persons concerned object, be furnished with the reasons for refusal of any request for permission to leave the territory and be given, as expeditiously as possible, the names of all persons who have been denied permission to leave.

Method of repatriation

Art. 36. Departures permitted under the foregoing Article shall be carried out in satisfactory conditions as regards safety, hygiene, sanitation and food. All costs in connection therewith, from the point of exit in the territory of the Detaining Power, shall be borne by the country of destination, or, in the case of accommodation in a neutral country, by the Power whose nationals are benefited. The practical details of such movements may, if necessary, be settled by special agreements between the Powers concerned.

The foregoing shall not prejudice such special agreements as may be concluded between Parties to the conflict concerning the exchange and repatriation of their nationals in enemy hands.

Art. 37. Protected persons who are confined pending proceedings or serving a sentence involving loss of liberty, shall during their confinement be humanely treated.

Persons in confinement

As soon as they are released, they may ask to leave the territory in conformity with the foregoing Articles.

Art. 38. With the exception of special measures authorized by the present Convention, in particular by Articles 27 and 41 thereof, the situation of protected persons shall continue to be regulated, in principle, by the provisions concerning aliens in time of peace. In any case, the following rights shall be granted to them:

Non-repatriated persons
I. General observations

(1) they shall be enabled to receive the individual or collective relief that may be sent to them.
(2) they shall, if their state of health so requires, receive medical attention and hospital treatment to the same extent as the nationals of the State concerned.
(3) they shall be allowed to practise their religion and to receive spiritual assistance from ministers of their faith.
(4) if they reside in an area particularly exposed to the dangers of war, they shall be authorized to move from that area to the same extent as the nationals of the State concerned.
(5) children under fifteen years, pregnant women and mothers of children under seven years shall benefit by any preferential treatment to the same extent as the nationals of the State concerned.

Art. 39. Protected persons who, as a result of the war, have lost their gainful employment, shall be granted the opportunity to find paid employment. That opportunity shall, subject to security considerations and to the provisions of Article 40, be equal to that enjoyed by the nationals of the Power in whose territory they are.

II. Means of existence

Where a Party to the conflict applies to a protected person methods of control which result in his being unable to support himself, and especially if such a person is prevented for reasons of security from finding paid employment on reasonable conditions, the said Party shall ensure his support and that of his dependents.

Protected persons may in any case receive allowances from their home country, the Protecting Power, or the relief societies referred to in Article 30.

III. Employment

Art. 40. Protected persons may be compelled to work only to the same extent as nationals of the Party to the conflict in whose territory they are.

If protected persons are of enemy nationality, they may only be compelled to do work which is normally necessary to ensure the feeding, sheltering, clothing, transport and health of human beings and which is not directly related to the conduct of military operations.

In the cases mentioned in the two preceding paragraphs, protected persons compelled to work shall have the benefit of the same working conditions and of the same safeguards as national workers, in particular as regards wages, hours of labour, clothing and equipment, previous training and compensation for occupational accidents and diseases.

If the above provisions are infringed, protected persons shall be allowed to exercise their right of complaint in accordance with Article 30.

IV. Assigned residence. Internment

Art. 41. Should the Power in whose hands protected persons may be consider the measures of control mentioned in the present Convention to be inadequate, it may not have recourse to any other measure of control more severe than that of assigned residence or internment, in accordance with the provisions of Articles 42 and 43.

In applying the provisions of Article 39, second paragraph, to the cases of persons required to leave their usual places of residence by virtue of a decision placing them in assigned residence elsewhere, the Detaining Power shall be guided as closely as possible by the standards of welfare set forth in Part III, Section IV of this Convention.

V. Ground for internment or assigned residence. Voluntary internment

Art. 42. The internment or placing in assigned residence of protected persons may be ordered only if the security of the Detaining Power makes it absolutely necessary.

If any person, acting through the representatives of the Protecting Power, voluntarily demands internment and if his situation renders this step necessary, he shall be interned by the Power in whose hands he may be.

VI. Procedure

Art. 43. Any protected person who has been interned or placed in assigned residence shall be entitled to have such action reconsidered as soon as possible by an appropriate court or administrative board designated by the Detaining Power for that purpose. If the internment or placing in assigned residence is maintained, the court or administrative board shall periodically, and at least twice yearly, give consideration to his or her case, with a view to the favourable amendment of the initial decision, if circumstances permit.

Unless the protected persons concerned object, the Detaining Power shall, as rapidly as possible, give the Protecting Power the names of any protected persons who have been interned or subjected to assigned residence, or who have been released from internment or assigned residence. The decisions of the courts or boards mentioned in the first paragraph of the present Article shall also, subject to the same conditions, be notified as rapidly as possible to the Protecting Power.

VII. Refugees

Art. 44.[12] In applying the measures of control mentioned in the present Convention, the Detaining Power shall not treat as enemy aliens exclusively on the basis of their nationality nationality *de jure* of an enemy State, refugees who do not, in fact, enjoy the protection of any government.

VIII. Transfer to another Power

Art. 45.[13] Protected persons shall not be transferred to a Power which is not a party to the Convention.

This provision shall in no way constitute an obstacle to the repatriation of protected persons, or to their return to their country of residence after the cessation of hostilities.

Protected persons may be transferred by the Detaining Power only to a Power which is a party to the present Convention and after the Detaining Power has satisfied itself of the willingness and ability of such transferee Power to apply the present Convention. If protected persons are transferred under such circumstances, responsibility for the application of the present Convention rests on the Power accepting them, while they are in its custody. Nevertheless, if that Power fails to carry out the provisions of the present Convention in any important respect, the Power by which the protected persons were transferred shall, upon being so notified by the Protecting Power, take effective measures to correct the situation or shall request the return of the protected persons. Such request must be complied with.

In no circumstances shall a protected person be transferred to a country where he or she may have reason to fear persecution for his or her political opinions or religious beliefs.

The provisions of this Article do not constitute an obstacle to the extradition, in pursuance of extradition treaties concluded before the outbreak of hostilities, of protected persons accused of offences against ordinary criminal law.

Cancellation of restrictive measures

Art. 46.[14] In so far as they have not been previously withdrawn, restrictive measures taken regarding protected persons shall be cancelled as soon as possible after the close of hostilities.

---

[12] For reservation in respect of this article by Brazil and Pakistan, see pp. 654 and 659.

[13] For reservations in respect of this article by Albania, Bulgaria, Byelorussian SSR, China, Czechoslovakia, Germany (Democratic Republic of), Guinea-Bissau, Hungary, Korea (Democratic People's Republic of), Poland, Romania, Ukrainian SSR, USSR, Vietnam (Socialist Republic of) and Yugoslavia, see pp. 650–658. For objections to those reservations by Australia, New Zealand, United Kingdom and United States of America, see pp. 652, 668, 678, 681.

[14] For reservation in respect of paragraph 2 of this article by Brazil, see p. 654.

Restrictive measures affecting their property shall be cancelled, in accordance with the law of the Detaining Power, as soon as possible after the close of hostilities.

Section III. Occupied Territories

Inviolability of rights

Art. 47. Protected persons who are in occupied territory shall not be deprived, in any case or in any manner whatsoever, of the benefits of the present Convention by any change introduced, as the result of the occupation of a territory, into the institutions or government of the said territory, nor by any agreement concluded between the authorities of the occupied territories and the Occupying Power, nor by any annexation by the latter of the whole or part of the occupied territory.

Special cases of repatriation

Art. 48. Protected persons who are not nationals of the Power whose territory is occupied, may avail themselves of the right to leave the territory subject to the provisions of Article 35, and decisions thereon shall be taken according to the procedure which the Occupying Power shall establish in accordance with the said Article.

Deportation, transfers, evacuation

Art. 49. Individual or mass forcible transfers, as well as deportations of protected persons from occupied territory to the territory of the Occupying Power or to that of any other country, occupied or not, are prohibited, regardless of their motive.

Nevertheless, the Occupying Power may undertake total or partial evacuation of a given area if the security of the population or imperative military reasons so demand. Such evacuations may not involve the displacement of protected persons outside the bounds of the occupied territory except when for material reasons it is impossible to avoid such displacement. Persons thus evacuated shall be transferred back to their homes as soon as hostilities in the area in question have ceased.

The Occupying Power undertaking such transfers or evacuations shall ensure, to the greatest practicable extent, that proper accommodation is provided to receive the protected persons, that the removals are effected in satisfactory conditions of hygiene, health, safety and nutrition, and that members of the same family are not separated.

The Protecting Power shall be informed of any transfers and evacuations as soon as they have taken place.

The Occupying Power shall not detain protected persons in an area particularly exposed to the dangers of war unless the security of the population or imperative military reasons so demand.

The Occupying Power shall not deport or transfer parts of its own civilian population into the territory it occupies.

Children

Art. 50. The Occupying Power shall, with the cooperation of the national and local authorities, facilitate the proper working of all institutions devoted to the care and education of children.

The Occupying Power shall take all necessary steps to facilitate the identification of children and the registration of their parentage. It may not, in any case, change their personal status, nor enlist them in formations or organizations subordinate to it.

Should the local institutions be inadequate for the purpose, the Occupying Power shall make arrangements for the maintenance and education, if possible by persons of their own nationality, language and religion, of children who are orphaned or separated from their parents as a result of the war and who cannot be adequately cared for by a near relative or friend.

A special section of the Bureau set up in accordance with Article 136 shall be responsible for taking all necessary steps to identify children whose identity is in doubt. Particulars of their parents or other near relatives should always be recorded if available.

The Occupying Power shall not hinder the application of any preferential measures in regard to food, medical care and protection against the effects of war, which may have been adopted prior to the occupation in favour of children under fifteen years, expectant mothers, and mothers of children under seven years.

Enlistment. Labour

Art. 51. The Occupying Power may not compel protected persons to serve in its armed or auxiliary forces. No pressure or propaganda which aims at securing voluntary enlistment is permitted.

The Occupying Power may not compel protected persons to work unless they are over eighteen years of age, and then only on work which is necessary either for the needs of the army of occupation, or for the public utility services, or for the feeding, sheltering, clothing, transportation or health of the population of the occupied country. Protected persons may not be compelled to undertake any work which would involve them in the obligation of taking part in military operations. The Occupying Power may not compel protected persons to employ forcible means to ensure the security of the installations where they are performing compulsory labour.

The work shall be carried out only in the occupied territory where the persons whose services have been requisitioned are. Every such person shall, so far as possible, be kept in his usual place of employment. Workers shall be paid a fair wage and the work shall be proportionate to their physical and intellectual capacities. The legislation in force in the occupied country concerning working conditions, and safeguards as regards, in particular, such matters as wages, hours of work, equipment, preliminary training and compensation for occupational accidents and diseases, shall be applicable to the protected persons assigned to the work referred to in this Article.

In no case shall requisition of labour lead to a mobilization of workers in an organization of a military or semi-military character.

Protection of workers

Art. 52. No contract, agreement or regulation shall impair the right of any worker, whether voluntary or not and wherever he may be, to apply to the representatives of the Protecting Power in order to request the said Power's intervention.

All measures aiming at creating unemployment or at restricting the opportunities offered to workers in an occupied territory, in order to induce them to work for the Occupying Power, are prohibited.

Prohibited destruction

Art. 53. Any destruction by the Occupying Power of real or personal property belonging individually or collectively to private persons, or to the State, or to other public authorities, or to social or cooperative organizations, is prohibited, except where such destruction is rendered absolutely necessary by military operations.

Judges and public officials

Art. 54. The Occupying Power may not alter the status of public officials or judges in the occupied territories, or in any way apply sanctions to or take any measures of coercion or discrimination against them, should they abstain from fulfilling their functions for reasons of conscience.

This prohibition does not prejudice the application of the second paragraph of Article 51. It does not affect the right of the Occupying Power to remove public officials from their posts.

Food and medical supplies for the population

Art. 55. To the fullest extent of the means available to it, the Occupying Power has the duty of ensuring the food and medical supplies of the population; it should, in particular, bring in the necessary foodstuffs, medical stores and other articles if the resources of the occupied territory are inadequate.

The Occupying Power may not requisition foodstuffs, articles or medical supplies available in the occupied territory, except for use by the occupation forces and administration personnel, and then only if the requirements of the civilian population have been taken into account. Subject to the provisions of other international Conventions, the Occupying Power shall make arrangements to ensure that fair value is paid for any requisitioned goods.

The Protecting Power shall, at any time, be at liberty to verify the state of the food and medical supplies in occupied territories, except where temporary restrictions are made necessary by imperative military requirements.

Hygiene and public health

Art. 56. To the fullest extent of the means available to it, the Occupying Power has the duty of ensuring and maintaining, with the cooperation of national and local authorities, the medical and hospital establishments and services, public health and hygiene in the occupied territory, with particular reference to the adoption and application of the prophylactic and preventive measures necessary to combat the spread of contagious diseases and epidemics. Medical personnel of all categories shall be allowed to carry out their duties.

If new hospitals are set up in occupied territory and if the competent organs of the occupied State are not operating there, the occupying authorities shall, if necessary, grant them the recognition provided for in Article 18. In similar circumstances, the occupying authorities shall also grant recognition to hospital personnel and transport vehicles under the provisions of Articles 20 and 21.

In adopting measures of health and hygiene and in their implementation, the Occupying Power shall take into consideration the moral and ethical susceptibilities of the population of the occupied territory.

Requisition of hospitals

Art. 57. The Occupying Power may requisition civilian hospitals only temporarily and only in cases of urgent necessity for the care of military wounded and sick, and then on condition that suitable arrangements are made in due time for the care and treatment of the patients and for the needs of the civilian population for hospital accommodation.

The material and stores of civilian hospitals cannot be requisitioned so long as they are necessary for the needs of the civilian population.

Spiritual assistance

Art. 58. The Occupying Power shall permit ministers of religion to give spiritual assistance to the members of their religious communities.

The Occupying Power shall also accept consignments of books and articles required for religious needs and shall facilitate their distribution in occupied territory.

Relief
I. Collective relief

Art. 59. If the whole or part of the population of an occupied territory is inadequately supplied, the Occupying Power shall agree to relief schemes on behalf of the said population, and shall facilitate them by all the means at its disposal.

Such schemes, which may be undertaken either by States or by impartial humanitarian organizations such as the International Committee of the Red Cross, shall consist, in particular, of the provision of consignments of foodstuffs, medical supplies and clothing.

All Contracting Parties shall permit the free passage of these consignments and shall guarantee their protection.

A Power granting free passage to consignments on their way to territory occupied by an adverse Party to the conflict shall, however, have the right to search the consignments, to regulate their passage according to prescribed times and routes, and to be reasonably satisfied through the Protecting Power that these consignments are to be used for the relief of the needy population and are not to be used for the benefit of the Occupying Power.

II. Responsibilities of the Occupying Power

Art. 60. Relief consignments shall in no way relieve the Occupying Power of any of its responsibilities under Articles 55, 56 and 59. The Occupying Power shall in no way whatsoever divert relief consignments from the purpose for which they are intended, except in cases of urgent necessity, in the interests of the population of the occupied territory and with the consent of the Protecting Power.

III. Distribution

Art. 61. The distribution of the relief consignments referred to in the foregoing Articles shall be carried out with the cooperation and under the supervision of the Protecting Power. This duty may also be delegated, by agreement between the Occupying Power and the Protecting Power, to a neutral Power, to the International Committee of the Red Cross or to any other impartial humanitarian body.

Such consignments shall be exempt in occupied territory from all charges, taxes or customs duties unless these are necessary in the interests of the economy of the territory. The Occupying Power shall facilitate the rapid distribution of these consignments.

All Contracting Parties shall endeavour to permit the transit and transport, free of charge, of such relief consignments on their way to occupied territories.

IV. Individual relief

Art. 62. Subject to imperative reasons of security, protected persons in occupied territories shall be permitted to receive the individual relief consignments sent to them.

National Red Cross and other relief societies

Art. 63. Subject to temporary and exceptional measures imposed for urgent reasons of security by the Occupying Power:

(a) recognized National Red Cross (Red Crescent, Red Lion and Sun) Societies shall be able to pursue their activities in accordance with Red Cross principles, as defined by the International Red Cross Conferences. Other relief societies shall be permitted to continue their humanitarian activities under similar conditions;

(b) the Occupying Power may not require any changes in the personnel or structure of these societies, which would prejudice the aforesaid activities.

The same principles shall apply to the activities and personnel of special organizations of a non-military character, which already exist or which may be established, for the purpose of ensuring the living conditions of the civilian population by the maintenance of the essential public utility services, by the distribution of relief and by the organization of rescues.

Penal legislation
I. General observations

Art. 64. The penal laws of the occupied territory shall remain in force, with the exception that they may be repealed or suspended by the Occupying Power in cases where they constitute a threat to its security or an obstacle to the application of the present Convention. Subject to the latter consideration and to the necessity for ensuring the effective administration of justice, the tribunals of the occupied territory shall continue to function in respect of all offences covered by the said laws.

The Occupying Power may, however, subject the population of the occupied territory to provisions which are essential to enable the Occupying Power to fulfil its obligations under the present Convention, to maintain the orderly government of the territory, and to ensure the security of the Occupying Power, of the members and property of the occupying forces or administration, and likewise of the establishments and lines of communication used by them.

II. Publications

Art. 65. The penal provisions enacted by the Occupying Power shall not come into force before they have been published and brought to the knowledge of the inhabitants in their own language. The effect of these penal provisions shall not be retroactive.

III. Competent courts

Art. 66. In case of a breach of the penal provisions promulgated by it by virtue of the second paragraph of Article 64, the Occupying Power may hand over the accused to its properly constituted, non-political military courts, on condition that the said courts sit in the occupied country. Courts of appeal shall preferably sit in the occupied country.

IV. Applicable provisions

Art. 67. The courts shall apply only those provisions of law which were applicable prior to the offence, and which are in accordance with general principles of law, in particular the principle that the penalty shall be proportioned to the offence. They shall take into consideration the fact that the accused is not a national of the Occupying Power.

V. Penalties. Death penalty

Art. 68.[15] Protected persons who commit an offence which is solely intended to harm the Occupying Power, but which does not constitute an attempt on the life or limb of members of the occupying forces or administration, nor a grave collective danger, nor seriously damage the property of the occupying forces or administration or the installations used by them, shall be liable to internment or simple imprisonment, provided the duration of such internment or imprisonment is proportionate to the offence committed. Furthermore, internment or imprisonment shall, for such offences, be the only measure adopted for depriving protected persons of liberty. The courts provided for under Article 66 of the present Convention may at their discretion convert a sentence of imprisonment to one of internment for the same period.

---

[15] For reservations in respect of this article by Argentina, Australia, Canada (withdrawn), Korea (Republic of), Netherlands, New Zealand, Pakistan, Surinam, United Kingdom, United States of America and Uruguay, see pp. 651–683.

The death penalty may not be pronounced against a protected person unless the attention of the court has been particularly called to the fact that since the accused is not a national of the Occupying Power, he is not bound to it by any duty of allegiance.

In any case, the death penalty may not be pronounced against a protected person who was under eighteen years of age at the time of the offence.

VI. Deduction from sentence of period under arrest

Art. 69. In all cases, the duration of the period during which a protected person accused of an offence is under arrest awaiting trial or punishment shall be deducted from any period of imprisonment awarded.

VII. Offence committed before occupation

Art. 70.[16] Protected persons shall not be arrested, prosecuted or convicted by the Occupying Power for acts committed or for opinions expressed before the occupation, or during a temporary interruption thereof, with the exception of breaches of the laws and customs of war.

Nationals of the occupying Power who, before the outbreak of hostilities, have sought refuge in the territory of the occupied State, shall not be arrested, prosecuted, convicted or deported from the occupied territory, except for offences committed after the outbreak of hostilities, or for offences under common law committed before the outbreak of hostilities which, according to the law of the occupied State, would have justified extradition in time of peace.

Penal procedure I. General observations

Art. 71. No sentence shall be pronounced by the competent courts of the Occupying Power except after a regular trial.

Accused persons who are prosecuted by the Occupying Power shall be promptly informed, in writing, in a language which they understand, of the particulars of the charges preferred against them, and shall be brought to trial as rapidly as possible. The Protecting Power shall be informed of all proceedings instituted by the Occupying Power against protected persons in respect of charges involving the death penalty or imprisonment for two years or more; it shall be enabled, at any time, to obtain information regarding the state of such proceedings. Furthermore, the Protecting Power shall be entitled, on request, to be furnished with all particulars of these and of any other proceedings instituted by the Occupying Power against protected persons.

The notification to the Protecting Power, as provided for in the second paragraph above, shall be sent immediately, and shall in any case reach the Protecting Power three weeks before the date of the first hearing. Unless, at the opening of the trial, evidence is submitted that the provisions of this Article are

[16] For reservation in respect of paragraph 1 of this article by New Zealand (withdrawn), see p. 668.

fully complied with, the trial shall not proceed. The notification shall include the following particulars:

(a) description of the accused;
(b) place of residence or detention;
(c) specification of the charge or charges (with mention of the penal provisions under which it is brought);
(d) designation of the court which will hear the case;
(e) place and date of the first hearing.

Art. 72. Accused persons shall have the right to present evidence necessary to their defence and may, in particular, call witnesses. They shall have the right to be assisted by a qualified advocate or counsel of their own choice, who shall be able to visit them freely and shall enjoy the necessary facilities for preparing the defence.

II. Rights of defence

Failing a choice by the accused, the Protecting Power may provide him with an advocate or counsel. When an accused person has to meet a serious charge and the Protecting Power is not functioning, the Occupying Power, subject to the consent of the accused, shall provide an advocate or counsel.

Accused persons shall, unless they freely waive such assistance, be aided by an interpreter, both during preliminary investigation and during the hearing in court. They shall have the right at any time to object to the interpreter and to ask for his replacement.

Art. 73. A convicted person shall have the right of appeal provided for by the laws applied by the court. He shall be fully informed of his right to appeal or petition and of the time limit within which he may do so.

III. Right of appeal

The penal procedure provided in the present Section shall apply, as far as it is applicable, to appeals. Where the laws applied by the Court make no provision for appeals, the convicted person shall have the right to petition against the finding and sentence to the competent authority of the Occupying Power.

Art. 74. Representatives of the Protecting Power shall have the right to attend the trial of any protected person, unless the hearing has, as an exceptional measure, to be held held "in camera" in the interests of the security of the Occupying Power, which shall then notify the Protecting Power. A notification in respect of the date and place of trial shall be sent to the Protecting Power.

IV. Assistance by the Protecting Power

Any judgment involving a sentence of death, or imprisonment for two years or more, shall be communicated, with the relevant grounds, as rapidly as possible to the Protecting Power. The notification shall contain a reference to the notification made under Article 71, and, in the case of sentences of imprisonment, the name of the place where the sentence is to be served. A record of judgments other than those referred to above shall be kept by the court and shall be open to inspection by representatives of the Protecting Power. Any period allowed for appeal in the case of sentences involving the death penalty, or imprisonment of two years or more, shall not run until notification of judgment has been received by the Protecting Power.

V. Death sentence

Art. 75. In no case shall persons condemned to death be deprived of the right of petition for pardon or reprieve.

No death sentence shall be carried out before the expiration of a period of at least six months from the date of receipt by the Protecting Power of the notification of the final judgment confirming such death sentence, or of an order denying pardon or reprieve.

The six months period of suspension of the death sentence herein prescribed may be reduced in individual cases in circumstances of grave emergency involving an organized threat to the security of the Occupying Power or its forces, provided always that the Protecting Power is notified of such reduction and is given reasonable time and opportunity to make representations to the competent occupying authorities in respect of such death sentences.

Treatment of detainees

Art. 76. Protected persons accused of offences shall be detained in the occupied country, and if convicted they shall serve their sentences therein. They shall, if possible, be separated from other detainees and shall enjoy conditions of food and hygiene which will be sufficient to keep them in good health, and which will be at least equal to those obtaining in prisons in the occupied country.

They shall receive the medical attention required by their state of health.

They shall also have the right to receive any spiritual assistance which they may require.

Women shall be confined in separate quarters and shall be under the direct supervision of women.

Proper regard shall be paid to the special treatment due to minors.

Protected persons who are detained shall have the right to be visited by delegates of the Protecting Power and of the International Committee of the Red Cross, in accordance with the provisions of Article 143.

Such persons shall have the right to receive at least one relief parcel monthly.

Handing over of detainees at the close of occupation

Art. 77. Protected persons who have been accused of offences or convicted by the courts in occupied territory, shall be handed over at the close of occupation, with the relevant records, to the authorities of the liberated territory.

Security measures.

Art. 78. If the Occupying Power considers it necessary, for imperative reasons of security, to take safety measures concerning protected persons, it may, at the most, subject them to assigned residence or to internment.

Internment and assigned residence. Right of appeal

Decisions regarding such assigned residence or internment shall be made according to a regular procedure to be prescribed by the Occupying Power in accordance with the provisions of the present Convention. This procedure shall include the right of appeal for the parties concerned. Appeals shall be decided with the least possible delay. In the event of the decision being upheld, it shall be subject to periodical review, if possible every six months, by a competent body set up by the said Power.

Protected persons made subject to assigned residence and thus required to leave their homes shall enjoy the full benefit of Article 39 of the present Convention.

Section IV. Regulations for the Treatment of Internees

Chapter I. General provisions

Art. 79. The Parties to the conflict shall not intern protected persons, except in accordance with the provisions of Articles 41, 42, 43, 68 and 78.

Cases of internment and applicable provisions

Art. 80. Internees shall retain their full civil capacity and shall exercise such attendant rights as may be compatible with their status.

Civil capacity

Art. 81. Parties to the conflict who intern protected persons shall be bound to provide free of charge for their maintenance, and to grant them also the medical attention required by their state of health.

Maintenance

No deduction from the allowances, salaries or credits due to the internees shall be made for the repayment of these costs.

The Detaining Power shall provide for the support of those dependent on the internees, if such dependents are without adequate means of support or are unable to earn a living.

Art. 82. The Detaining Power shall, as far as possible, accommodate the internees according to their nationality, language and customs. Internees who are nationals of the same country shall not be separated merely because they have different languages.

Grouping of internees

Throughout the duration of their internment, members of the same family, and in particular parents and children, shall be lodged together in the same place of internment, except when separation of a temporary nature is necessitated for reasons of employment or health or for the purposes of enforcement of the provisions of Chapter IX of the present Section. Internees may request that their children who are left at liberty without parental care shall be interned with them.

Wherever possible, interned members of the same family shall be housed in the same premises and given separate accommodation from other internees, together with facilities for leading a proper family life.

Chapter II. Places of internment

Location of places of internment. Marking of camps

Art. 83. The Detaining Power shall not set up places of internment in areas particularly exposed to the dangers of war.

The Detaining Power shall give the enemy Powers, through the intermediary of the Protecting Powers, all useful information regarding the geographical location of places of internment.

Whenever military considerations permit, internment camps shall be indicated by the letters IC, placed so as to be clearly visible in the daytime from the air. The Powers concerned may, however, agree upon any other system of marking. No place other than an internment camp shall be marked as such.

Separate internment

Art. 84. Internees shall be accommodated and administered separately from prisoners of war and from persons deprived of liberty for any other reason.

Accommodation, hygiene

Art. 85. The Detaining Power is bound to take all necessary and possible measures to ensure that protected persons shall, from the outset of their internment, be accommodated in buildings or quarters which afford every possible safeguard as regards hygiene and health, and provide efficient protection against the rigours of the climate and the effects of the war. In no case shall permanent places of internment be situated in unhealthy areas or in districts the climate of which is injurious to the internees. In all cases where the district, in which a protected person is temporarily interned,is in an unhealthy area or has a climate which is harmful to his health, he shall be removed to a more suitable place of internment as rapidly as circumstances permit.

The premises shall be fully protected from dampness, adequately heated and lighted, in particular between dusk and lights out. The sleeping quarters shall be sufficiently spacious and well ventilated, and the internees shall have suitable bedding and sufficient blankets, account being taken of the climate, and the age, sex, and state of health of the internees.

Internees shall have for their use, day and night, sanitary conveniences which conform to the rules of hygiene and are constantly maintained in a state of cleanliness. They shall be provided with sufficient water and soap for their daily personal toilet and for washing their personal laundry; installations and facilities necessary for this purpose shall be granted to them. Showers or baths shall also be available. The necessary time shall be set aside for washing and for cleaning.

Whenever it is necessary, as an exceptional and temporary measure, to accommodate women internees who are not members of a family unit in the same place of internment as men, the provision of separate sleeping quarters and sanitary conveniences for the use of such women internees shall be obligatory.

Art. 86. The Detaining Power shall place at the disposal of interned persons, of whatever denomination, premises suitable for the holding of their religious services. Premises for religious services

Art. 87. Canteens shall be installed in every place of internment, except where other suitable facilities are available. Their purpose shall be to enable internees to make purchases, at prices not higher than local market prices, of foodstuffs and articles of everyday use, including soap and tobacco, such as would increase their personal well-being and comfort. Canteens

Profits made by canteens shall be credited to a welfare fund to be set up for each place of internment, and administered for the benefit of the internees attached to such place of internment. The Internee Committee provided for in Article 102 shall have the right to check the management of the canteen and of the said fund.

When a place of internment is closed down, the balance of the welfare fund shall be transferred to the welfare fund of a place of internment for internees of the same nationality, or, if such a place does not exist, to a central welfare fund which shall be administered for the benefit of all internees remaining in the custody of the Detaining Power. In case of a general release, the said profits shall be kept by the Detaining Power, subject to any agreement to the contrary between the Powers concerned.

Art. 88. In all places of internment exposed to air raids and other hazards of war, shelters adequate in number and structure to ensure the necessary protection shall be installed. In case of alarms, the internees shall be free to enter such shelters as quickly as possible, excepting those who remain for the protection of their quarters against the aforesaid hazards. Any protective measures taken in favour of the population shall also apply to them. Air raid shelters, Protective measures

All due precautions must be taken in places of internment against the danger of fire.

Chapter III. Food and clothing

Art. 89. Daily food rations for internees shall be sufficient in quantity, quality and variety to keep internees in a good state of health and prevent the development of nutritional deficiencies. Account shall also be taken of the customary diet of the internees. Food

Internees shall also be given the means by which they can prepare for themselves any additional food in their possession.

Sufficient drinking water shall be supplied to internees. The use of tobacco shall be permitted.

Internees who work shall receive additional rations in proportion to the kind of labour which they perform.

Expectant and nursing mothers and children under fifteen years of age, shall be given additional food, in proportion to their physiological needs.

Clothing

Art. 90. When taken into custody, internees shall be given all facilities to provide themselves with the necessary clothing, footwear and change of underwear, and later on, to procure further supplies if required. Should any internees not have sufficient clothing, account being taken of the climate, and be unable to procure any, it shall be provided free of charge to them by the Detaining Power.

The clothing supplied by the Detaining Power to internees and the outward markings placed on their own clothes shall not be ignominious nor expose them to ridicule.

Workers shall receive suitable working outfits, including protective clothing, whenever the nature of their work so requires.

Chapter IV. Hygiene and medical attention

Medical attention

Art. 91. Every place of internment shall have an adequate infirmary, under the direction of a qualified doctor, where internees may have the attention they require, as well as an appropriate diet. Isolation wards shall be set aside for cases of contagious or mental diseases.

Maternity cases and internees suffering from serious diseases, or whose condition requires special treatment, a surgical operation or hospital care, must be admitted to any institution where adequate treatment can be given and shall receive care not inferior to that provided for the general population.

Internees shall, for preference, have the attention of medical personnel of their own nationality.

Internees may not be prevented from presenting themselves to the medical authorities for examination. The medical authorities of the Detaining Power shall, upon request, issue to every internee who has undergone treatment an official certificate showing the nature of his illness or injury, and the duration and nature of the treatment given. A duplicate of this certificate shall be forwarded to the Central Agency provided for in Article 140.

Treatment, including the provision of any apparatus necessary for the maintenance of internees in good health, particularly dentures and other artificial appliances and spectacles, shall be free of charge to the internee.

Medical inspections

Art. 92. Medical inspections of internees shall be made at least once a month. Their purpose shall be, in particular, to supervise the general state of health, nutrition and cleanliness of internees, and to detect contagious diseases, especially tuberculosis, malaria, and venereal diseases. Such inspections shall include, in particular, the checking of weight of each internee and, at least once a year, radioscopic examination.

Chapter V. Religious, intellectual and physical activities

Religious duties

Art. 93. Internees shall enjoy complete latitude in the exercise of their religious duties, including attendance at the services of their faith, on condition that they comply with the disciplinary routine prescribed by the detaining authorities.

Ministers of religion who are interned shall be allowed to minister freely to the members of their community. For this purpose, the Detaining Power shall ensure their equitable allocation amongst the various places of internment in which there are internees speaking the same language and belonging to the same religion. Should such ministers be too few in number, the Detaining Power shall provide them with the necessary facilities, including means of transport, for moving from one place to another, and they shall be authorized to visit any internees who are in hospital. Ministers of religion shall be at liberty to correspond on matters concerning their ministry with the religious authorities in the country of detention and, as far as possible, with the international religious organizations of their faith. Such correspondence shall not be considered as forming a part of the quota mentioned in Article 107. It shall, however, be subject to the provisions of Article 112.

When internees do not have at their disposal the assistance of ministers of their faith, or should these latter be too few in number, the local religious authorities of the same faith may appoint, in agreement with the Detaining Power, a minister of the internees' faith or, if such a course is feasible from a denominational point of view, a minister of similar religion or a qualified layman. The latter shall enjoy the facilities granted to the ministry he has assumed. Persons so appointed shall comply with all regulations laid down by the Detaining Power in the interests of discipline and security.

Recreation, study, sports and games

Art. 94. The Detaining Power shall encourage intellectual, educational and recreational pursuits, sports and games amongst internees, whilst leaving them free to take part in them or not. It shall take all practicable measures to ensure the exercise thereof, in particular by providing suitable premises.

All possible facilities shall be granted to internees to continue their studies or to take up new subjects. The education of children and young people shall be ensured; they shall be allowed to attend schools either within the place of internment or outside.

Internees shall be given opportunities for physical exercise, sports and outdoor games. For this purpose, sufficient open spaces shall be set aside in all places of internment. Special playgrounds shall be reserved for children and young people.

Working conditions

Art. 95. The Detaining Power shall not employ internees as workers, unless they so desire. Employment which, if undertaken under compulsion by a protected person not in internment, would involve a breach of Articles 40 or 51 of the present

Convention, and employment on work which is of a degrading or humiliating character are in any case prohibited.

After a working period of six weeks, internees shall be free to give up work at any moment, subject to eight days' notice.

These provisions constitute no obstacle to the right of the Detaining Power to employ interned doctors, dentists and other medical personnel in their professional capacity on behalf of their fellow internees, or to employ internees for administrative and maintenance work in places of internment and to detail such persons for work in the kitchens or for other domestic tasks, or to require such persons to undertake duties connected with the protection of internees against aerial bombardment or other war risks. No internee may, however, be required to perform tasks for which he is, in the opinion of a medical officer, physically unsuited.

The Detaining Power shall take entire responsibility for all working conditions, for medical attention, for the payment of wages, and for ensuring that all employed internees receive compensation for occupational accidents and diseases. The standards prescribed for the said working conditions and for compensation shall be in accordance with the national laws and regulations, and with the existing practice; they shall in no case be inferior to those obtaining for work of the same nature in the same district. Wages for work done shall be determined on an equitable basis by special agreements between the internees, the Detaining Power, and, if the case arises, employers other than the Detaining Power, due regard being paid to the obligation of the Detaining Power to provide for free maintenance of internees and for the medical attention which their state of health may require. Internees permanently detailed for categories of work mentioned in the third paragraph of this Article, shall be paid fair wages by the Detaining Power. The working conditions and the scale of compensation for occupational accidents and diseases to internees thus detailed, shall not be inferior to those applicable to work of the same nature in the same district.

Labour detachments

Art. 96. All labour detachments shall remain part of and dependent upon a place of internment. The competent authorities of the Detaining Power and the commandant of a place of internment shall be responsible for the observance in a labour detachment of the provisions of the present Convention. The commandant shall keep an up-to-date list of the labour detachments subordinate to him and shall communicate it to the delegates of the Protecting Power, of the International Committee of the Red Cross and of other humanitarian organisations who may visit the places of internment.

Chapter VI. Personal property and financial resources

Valuables and personal effects

Art. 97. Internees shall be permitted to retain articles of personal use. Monies, cheques, bonds, etc., and valuables in their possession may not be taken from them except in accordance with established procedure. Detailed receipts shall be given therefor.

The amounts shall be paid into the account of every internee as provided for in Article 98. Such amounts may not be converted into any other currency unless legislation in force in the territory in which the owner is interned so requires or the internee gives his consent.

Articles which have above all a personal or sentimental value may not be taken away.

A woman internee shall not be searched except by a woman.

On release or repatriation, internees shall be given all articles, monies or other valuables taken from them during internment and shall receive in currency the balance of any credit to their accounts kept in accordance with Article 98, with the exception of any articles or amounts withheld by the Detaining power by virtue of its legislation in force. If the property of an internee is so withheld, the owner shall receive a detailed receipt.

Family or identity documents in the possession of internees may not be taken away without a receipt being given. At no time shall internees be left without identity documents. If they have none, they shall be issued with special documents drawn up by the detaining authorities, which will serve as their identity papers until the end of their internment.

Internees may keep on their persons a certain amount of money, in cash or in the shape of purchase coupons, to enable them to make purchases.

Financial resources and individual accounts

Art. 98. All internees shall receive regular allowances, sufficient to enable them to purchase goods and articles, such as tobacco, toilet requisites, etc. Such allowances may take the form of credits or purchase coupons.

Furthermore, internees may receive allowances from the Power to which they owe allegiance, the Protecting Powers, the organizations which may assist them, or their families, as well as the income on their property in accordance with the law of the Detaining Power. The amount of allowances granted by the Power to which they owe allegiance shall be the same for each category of internees (infirm, sick, pregnant women, etc.), but may not be allocated by that Power or distributed by the Detaining Power on the basis of discriminations between internees which are prohibited by Article 27 of the present Convention.

The Detaining Power shall open a regular account for every internee, to which shall be credited the allowances named in the present Article, the wages earned and the remittances received, together with such sums taken from him as may be available under the legislation in force in the territory in which he is interned. Internees shall be granted all facilities consistent with the legislation in force in such territory to make remittances to their families and to other dependants. They may draw from their accounts the amounts necessary for their personal expenses, within the limits fixed by the Detaining Power. They shall at all times be afforded reasonable facilities for consulting and obtaining copies of their accounts. A statement of accounts shall be furnished to the Protecting Power on request, and shall accompany the internee in case of transfer.

Chapter VII. Administration and discipline

Camp administration. Posting of the Convention and orders

Art. 99. Every place of internment shall be put under the authority of a responsible officer, chosen from the regular military forces or the regular civil administration of the Detaining Power. The officer in charge of the place of internment must have in his possession a copy of the present Convention in the official language, or one of the official languages, of his country and shall be responsible for its application. The staff in control of internees shall be instructed in the provisions of the present Convention and of the administrative measures adopted to ensure its application.

The text of the present Convention and the texts of special agreements concluded under the said Convention shall be posted inside the place of internment, in a language which the internees understand, or shall be in the possession of the Internee Committee.

Regulations, orders, notices and publications of every kind shall be communicated to the internees and posted inside the places of internment, in a language which they understand.

Every order and command addressed to internees individually, must likewise be given in a language which they understand.

General discipline

Art. 100. The disciplinary regime in places of internment shall be consistent which humanitarian principles, and shall in no circumstances include regulations imposing on internees any physical exertion dangerous to their health or involving physical or moral victimization. Identification by tattooing or imprinting signs or markings on the body, is prohibited.

In particular, prolonged standing and roll-calls, punishment drill, military drill and manoeuvres, or the reduction of food rations, are prohibited.

Complaints and petitions

Art. 101. Internees shall have the right to present to the authorities in whose power they are, any petition with regard to the conditions of internment to which they are subjected.

They shall also have the right to apply without restriction through the Internee Committee or, if they consider it necessary, direct to the representatives of the Protecting Power, in order to indicate to them any points on which they may have complaints to make with regard to the conditions of internment.

Such petitions and complaints shall be transmitted forthwith and without alteration, and even if the latter are recognized to be unfounded, they may not occasion any punishment.

Periodic reports on the situation in places of internment and as to the needs of the internees, may be sent by the Internee Committees to the representatives of the Protecting Powers.

Art. 102. In every place of internment, the internees shall freely elect by secret ballot every six months, the members of a Committee empowered to represent them before the Detaining and the Protecting Powers, the International Committee of the Red Cross and any other organization which may assist them. The members of the Committee shall be eligible for re-election.

Internee committees
I. Election of members

Internees so elected shall enter upon their duties after their election has been approved by the detaining authorities. The reasons for any refusals or dismissals shall be communicated to the Protecting Powers concerned.

Art. 103. The Internee Committees shall further the physical, spiritual and intellectual well-being of the internees.

II. Duties

In case the internees decide, in particular, to organize a system of mutual assistance amongst themselves, this organization would be within the competence of the Committees in addition to the special duties entrusted to them under other provisions of the present Convention.

Art. 104. Members of Internee Committees shall not be required to perform any other work, if the accomplishment of their duties is rendered more difficult thereby.

III. Prerogatives

Members of Internee Committees may appoint from amongst the internees such assistants as they may require. All material facilities shall be granted to them, particularly a certain freedom of movement necessary for the accomplishment of their duties (visits to labour detachments, receipt of supplies, etc.).

All facilities shall likewise be accorded to members of Internee Committees for communication by post and telegraph with the detaining authorities, the protecting Powers, the International Committee of the Red Cross and their delegates, and with the organizations which give assistance to internees. Committee members in labour detachments shall enjoy similar facilities for communication with their Internee Committee in the principal place of internment. Such communications shall not be limited, nor considered as forming a part of the quota mentioned in Article 107.

Members of Internee Committees who are transferred shall be allowed a reasonable time to acquaint their successors with current affairs.

Chapter VIII. Relations with the exterior

Art. 105. Immediately upon interning protected persons, the Detaining Powers shall inform them, the Power to which they owe allegiance and their Protecting Power of the measures taken for executing the provisions of the present Chapter. The

Notification of measures taken

Detaining Powers shall likewise inform the Parties concerned of any subsequent modifications of such measures.

Internment card

Art. 106. As soon as he is interned, or at the latest not more than one week after his arrival in a place of internment, and likewise in cases of sickness or transfer to another place of internment or to a hospital, every internee shall be enabled to send direct to his family, on the one hand, and to the Central Agency provided for by Article 140, on the other, an internment card similar, if possible, to the model annexed to the present Convention, informing his relatives of his detention, address and state of health. The said cards shall be forwarded as rapidly as possible and may not be delayed in any way.

Correspondence

Art. 107. Internees shall be allowed to send and receive letters and cards. If the Detaining power deems it necessary to limit the number of letters and cards sent by each internee, the said number shall not be less than two letters and four cards monthly; these shall be drawn up so as to conform as closely as possible to the models annexed to the present Convention. If limitations must be placed on the correspondence addressed to internees, they may be ordered only by the Power to which such internees owe allegiance, possibly at the request of the Detaining Power. Such letters and cards must be conveyed with reasonable despatch; they may not be delayed or retained for disciplinary reasons.

Internees who have been a long time without news, or who find it impossible to receive news from their relatives, or to give them news by the ordinary postal route, as well as those who are at a considerable distance from their homes, shall be allowed to send telegrams, the charges being paid by them in the currency at their disposal. They shall likewise benefit by this provision in cases which are recognized to be urgent.

As a rule, internees' mail shall be written in their own language. The Parties to the conflict may authorize correspondence in other languages.

Relief shipments
I. General principles

Art. 108. Internees shall be allowed to receive, by post or by any other means, individual parcels or collective shipments containing in particular foodstuffs, clothing, medical supplies, as well as books and objects of a devotional, educational or recreational character which may meet their needs. Such shipments shall in no way free the Detaining Power from the obligations imposed upon it by virtue of the present Convention.

The conditions for the sending of individual parcels and collective shipments shall, if necessary, be the subject of special agreements between the Powers concerned, which may in no case delay the receipt by the internees of relief supplies. Parcels of clothing and foodstuffs may not include books. Medical relief supplies shall, as a rule, be sent in collective parcels.

Art. 109. In the absence of special agreements between Parties to the conflict regarding the conditions for the receipt and distribution of collective relief shipments, the regulations concerning collective relief which are annexed to the present Convention shall be applied.

II. Collective relief

The special agreements provided for above shall in no case restrict the right of Internee Committees to take possession of collective relief shipments intended for internees, to undertake their distribution and to dispose of them in the interests of the recipients.

Nor shall such agreements restrict the right of representatives of the Protecting Powers, the International Committee of the Red Cross, or any other organization giving assistance to internees and responsible for the forwarding of collective shipments, to supervise their distribution to the recipients.

Art. 110. All relief shipments for internees shall be exempt from import, customs and other dues.

III. Exemption from postal and transport charges

All matter sent by mail, including relief parcels sent by parcel post and remittances of money, addressed from other countries to internees or despatched by them through the post office, either direct or through the Information Bureaux provided for in Article 136 and the Central Information Agency provided for in Article 140, shall be exempt from all postal dues both in the countries of origin and destination and in intermediate countries. To this end, in particular, the exemption provided by the Universal Postal Convention of 1947 and by the agreements of the Universal Postal Union in favour of civilians of enemy nationality detained in camps or civilian prisons, shall be extended to the other interned persons protected by the present Convention. The countries not signatory to the above-mentioned agreements shall be bound to grant freedom from charges in the same circumstances.

The cost of transporting relief shipments which are intended for internees and which, by reason of their weight or any other cause, cannot be sent through the post office, shall be borne by the Detaining power in all the territories under its control. Other Powers which are Parties to the present Convention shall bear the cost of transport in their respective territories.

Costs connected with the transport of such shipments, which are not covered by the above paragraphs, shall be charged to the senders.

The High Contracting Parties shall endeavour to reduce, so far as possible, the charges for telegrams sent by internees, or addressed to them.

Art. 111. Should military operations prevent the Powers concerned from fulfilling their obligation to ensure the conveyance of the mail and relief shipments provided for in Articles 106, 107, 108 and 113, the Protecting Powers concerned, the Inter-

Special means of transport

national Committee of the Red Cross or any other organization duly approved by the Parties to the conflict may undertake the conveyance of such shipments by suitable means (rail, motor vehicles, vessels or aircraft, etc.). For this purpose, the High Contracting parties shall endeavour to supply them with such transport, and to allow its circulation, especially by granting the necessary safe-conducts.

Such transport may also be used to convey:

(a) correspondence, lists and reports exchanged between the Central Information Agency referred to in Article 140 and the National Bureaux referred to in Article 136;

(b) correspondence and reports relating to internees which the Protecting Powers, the International Committee of the Red Cross or any other organization assisting the internees exchange either with their own delegates or with the Parties to the conflict.

These provisions in no way detract from the right of any Party to the conflict to arrange other means of transport if it should so prefer, nor preclude the granting of safe-conducts, under mutually agreed conditions, to such means of transport.

The costs occasioned by the use of such means of transport shall be borne, in proportion to the importance of the shipments, by the Parties to the conflict whose nationals are benefited thereby.

Censorship and examination

Art. 112. The censoring of correspondence addressed to internees or despatched by them shall be done as quickly as possible.

The examination of consignments intended for internees shall not be carried out under conditions that will expose the goods contained in them to deterioration. It shall be done in the presence of the addressee, or of a fellow-internee duly delegated by him. The delivery to internees of individual or collective consignments shall not be delayed under the pretext of difficulties of censorship.

Any prohibition of correspondence ordered by the Parties to the conflict either for military or political reasons, shall be only temporary and its duration shall be as short as possible.

Execution and transmission of legal documents

Art. 113. The Detaining Powers shall provide all reasonable facilities for the transmission, through the protecting Power or the Central Agency provided for in Article 140, or as otherwise required, of wills, powers of attorney, letters of authority, or any other documents intended for internees or despatched by them.

In all cases the Detaining Powers shall facilitate the execution and authentication in due legal form of such documents on behalf of internees, in particular by allowing them to consult a lawyer.

Management of property

Art. 114. The Detaining Power shall afford internees all facilities to enable them to manage their property, provided this is not incompatible with the conditions of internment and the law which is applicable. For this purpose, the said Power may give them permission to leave the place of internment in urgent cases and if circumstances allow.

Art. 115. In all cases where an internee is a party to proceedings in any court, the Detaining Power shall, if he so requests, cause the court to be informed of his detention and shall, within legal limits, ensure that all necessary steps are taken to prevent him from being in any way prejudiced, by reason of his internment, as regards the preparation and conduct of his case or as regards the execution of any judgment of the court.

Facilities for preparation and conduct of cases

Art. 116. Every internee shall be allowed to receive visitors, especially near relatives, at regular intervals and as frequently as possible.

Visits

As far as is possible, internees shall be permitted to visit their homes in urgent cases, particularly in cases of death or serious illness of relatives.

Chapter IX. Penal and disciplinary sanctions

Art. 117. Subject to the provisions of the present Chapter, the laws in force in the territory in which they are detained will continue to apply to internees who commit offences during internment.

General provisions. Applicable legislation

If general laws, regulations or orders declare acts committed by internees to be punishable, whereas the same acts are not punishable when committed by persons who are not internees, such acts shall entail disciplinary punishments only.

No internee may be punished more than once for the same act, or on the same count.

Art. 118. The courts or authorities shall in passing sentence take as far as possible into account the fact that the defendant is not a national of the Detaining Power. They shall be free to reduce the penalty prescribed for the offence with which the internee is charged and shall not be obliged, to this end, to apply the minimum sentence prescribed.

Penalties

Imprisonment in premises without daylight, and, in general, all forms of cruelty without exception are forbidden.

Internees who have served disciplinary or judicial sentences shall not be treated differently from other internees.

The duration of preventive detention undergone by an internee shall be deducted from any disciplinary or judicial penalty involving confinement to which he may be sentenced.

Internee Committees shall be informed of all judicial proceedings instituted against internees whom they represent, and of their result.

Art. 119. The disciplinary punishments applicable to internees shall be the following:

Disciplinary punishments

(1) A fine which shall not exceed 50 per cent of the wages which the internee would otherwise receive under the provisions of Article 95 during a period of not more than thirty days.
(2) Discontinuance of privileges granted over and above the treatment provided for by the present Convention.
(3) Fatigue duties, not exceeding two hours daily, in connection with the maintenance of the place of internment.
(4) Confinement.

In no case shall disciplinary penalties be inhuman, brutal or dangerous for the health of internees. Account shall be taken of the internee's age, sex and state of health.

The duration of any single punishment shall in no case exceed a maximum of thirty consecutive days, even if the internee is answerable for several breaches of discipline when his case is dealt with, whether such breaches are connected or not.

Escapes

Art. 120. Internees who are recaptured after having escaped or when attempting to escape, shall be liable only to disciplinary punishment in respect of this act, even if it is a repeated offence.

Article 118, paragraph 3, notwithstanding, internees punished as a result of escape or attempt to escape, may be subjected to special surveillance, on condition that such surveillance does not affect the state of their health, that it is exercised in a place of internment and that it does not entail the abolition of any of the safeguards granted by the present Convention.

Internees who aid and abet an escape, or attempt to escape, shall be liable on this count to disciplinary punishment only.

Connected offences

Art. 121. Escape, or attempt to escape, even if it is a repeated offence, shall not be deemed an aggravating circumstance in cases where an internee is prosecuted for offences committed during his escape.

The Parties to the conflict shall ensure that the competent authorities exercise leniency in deciding whether punishment inflicted for an offence shall be of a disciplinary or judicial nature, especially in respect of acts committed in connection with an escape, whether successful or not.

Investigations. Confinement awaiting hearing

Art. 122. Acts which constitute offences against discipline shall be investigated immediately. This rule shall be applied, in particular, in cases of escape or attempt to escape. Recaptured internees shall be handed over to the competent authorities as soon as possible.

In case of offences against discipline, confinement awaiting trial shall be reduced to an absolute minimum for all internees, and shall not exceed fourteen days. Its duration shall in any case be deducted from any sentence of confinement.

The provisions of Articles 124 and 125 shall apply to internees who are in confinement awaiting trial for offences against discipline.

Art. 123. Without prejudice to the competence of courts and higher authorities, disciplinary punishment may be ordered only by the commandant of the place of internment, or by a responsible officer or official who replaces him, or to whom he has delegated his disciplinary powers.

Competent authorities. Procedure

Before any disciplinary punishment is awarded, the accused internee shall be given precise information regarding the offences of which he is accused, and given an opportunity of explaining his conduct and of defending himself. He shall be permitted, in particular, to call witnesses and to have recourse, if necessary, to the services of a qualified interpreter. The decision shall be announced in the presence of the accused and of a member of the Internee Committee.

The period elapsing between the time of award of a disciplinary punishment and its execution shall not exceed one month.

When an internee is awarded a further disciplinary punishment, a period of at least three days shall elapse between the execution of any two of the punishments, if the duration of one of these is ten days or more.

A record of disciplinary punishments shall be maintained by the commandant of the place of internment and shall be open to inspection by representatives of the Protecting Power.

Art. 124. Internees shall not in any case be transferred to penitentiary establishments (prisons, penitentiaries, convict prisons, etc.) to undergo disciplinary punishment therein.

Premises for disciplinary punishments

The premises in which disciplinary punishments are undergone shall conform to sanitary requirements; they shall in particular be provided with adequate bedding. Internees undergoing punishment shall be enabled to keep themselves in a state of cleanliness.

Women internees undergoing disciplinary punishment shall be confined in separate quarters from male internees and shall be under the immediate supervision of women.

Art. 125. Internees awarded disciplinary punishment shall be allowed to exercise and to stay in the open air at least two hours daily.

Essential safeguards

They shall be allowed, if they so request, to be present at the daily medical inspections. They shall receive the attention which their state of health requires and, if necessary, shall be removed to the infirmary of the place of internment or to a hospital.

They shall have permission to read and write, likewise to send and receive letters. Parcels and remittances of money, however, may be withheld from them until the completion of their punishment; such consignments shall meanwhile be entrusted to the Internee Committee, who will hand over to the infirmary the perishable goods contained in the parcels.

No internee given a disciplinary punishment may be deprived of the benefit of the provisions of Articles 107 and 143 of the present Convention.

Provisions applicable to judicial proceedings

Art. 126. The provisions of Articles 71 to 76 inclusive shall apply, by analogy, to proceedings against internees who are in the national territory of the Detaining Power.

Chapter X. Transfers of internees

Conditions

Art. 127. The transfer of internees shall always be effected humanely. As a general rule, it shall be carried out by rail or other means of transport, and under conditions at least equal to those obtaining for the forces of the Detaining Power in their changes of station. If, as an exceptional measure, such removals have to be effected on foot, they may not take place unless the internees are in a fit state of health, and may not in any case expose them to excessive fatigue.

The Detaining Power shall supply internees during transfer with drinking water and food sufficient in quantity, quality and variety to maintain them in good health, and also with the necessary clothing, adequate shelter and the necessary medical attention. The Detaining Power shall take all suitable precautions to ensure their safety during transfer, and shall establish before their departure a complete list of all internees transferred.

Sick, wounded or infirm internees and maternity cases shall not be transferred if the journey would be seriously detrimental to them, unless their safety imperatively so demands.

If the combat zone draws close to a place of internment, the internees in the said place shall not be transferred unless their removal can be carried out in adequate conditions of safety, or unless they are exposed to greater risks by remaining on the spot than by being transferred.

When making decisions regarding the transfer of internees, the Detaining Power shall take their interests into account and, in particular, shall not do anything to increase the difficulties of repatriating them or returning them to their own homes.

Method

Art. 128. In the event of transfer, internees shall be officially advised of their departure and of their new postal address. Such notification shall be given in time for them to pack their luggage and inform their next of kin.

They shall be allowed to take with them their personal effects, and the correspondence and parcels which have arrived for them. The weight of such baggage may be limited if the conditions of transfer so require, but in no case to less than twenty-five kilograms per internee.

Mail and parcels addressed to their former place of internment shall be forwarded to them without delay.

The commandant of the place of internment shall take, in agreement with the Internee Committee, any measures needed to ensure the transport of the internees' community property and of the luggage the internees are unable to take with them in consequence of restrictions imposed by virtue of the second paragraph.

Chapter XI. Deaths

Art. 129. The wills of internees shall be received for safe-keeping by the responsible authorities; and in the event of the death of an internee his will shall be transmitted without delay to a person whom he has previously designated.

Wills. Death certificates

Deaths of internees shall be certified in every case by a doctor, and a death certificate shall be made out, showing the causes of death and the conditions under which it occurred.

An official record of the death, duly registered, shall be drawn up in accordance with the procedure relating thereto in force in the territory where the place of internment is situated, and a duly certified copy of such record shall be transmitted without delay to the Protecting Power as well as to the Central Agency referred to in Article 140.

Art. 130. The detaining authorities shall ensure that internees who die while interned are honourably buried, if possible according to the rites of the religion to which they belonged, and that their graves are respected, properly maintained, and marked in such a way that they can always be recognized.

Burial. Cremation

Deceased internees shall be buried in individual graves unless unavoidable circumstances require the use of collective graves. Bodies may be cremated only for imperative reasons of hygiene, on account of the religion of the deceased or in accordance with his expressed wish to this effect. In case of cremation, the fact shall be stated and the reasons given in the death certificate of the deceased. The ashes shall be retained for safe-keeping by the detaining authorities and shall be transferred as soon as possible to the next of kin on their request.

As soon as circumstances permit, and not later than the close of hostilities, the Detaining Power shall forward lists of graves of deceased internees to the Powers on whom the deceased internees depended, through the Information Bureaux provided for in Article 136. Such lists shall include all particulars necessary for the identification of the deceased internees, as well as the exact location of their graves.

Art. 131. Every death or serious injury of an internee, caused or suspected to have been caused by a sentry, another internee or any other person, as well as any death the cause of which is unknown, shall be immediately followed by an official enquiry by the Detaining Power.

Internees killed or injured in special circumstances

A communication on this subject shall be sent immediately to the Protecting Power. The evidence of any witnesses shall be taken, and a report including such evidence shall be prepared and forwarded to the said Protecting Power.

If the enquiry indicates the guilt of one or more persons, the Detaining Power shall take all necessary steps to ensure the prosecution of the person or persons responsible.

Chapter XII. Release, repatriation and accommodation in neutral countries

During hostilities or occupation

Art. 132. Each interned person shall be released by the Detaining Power as soon as the reasons which necessitated his internment no longer exist.

The Parties to the conflict shall, moreover, endeavour during the course of hostilities, to conclude agreements for the release, the repatriation, the return to places of residence or the accommodation in a neutral country of certain classes of internees, in particular children, pregnant women and mothers with infants and young children, wounded and sick, and internees who have been detained for a long time.

After the close of hostilities

Art. 133. Internment shall cease as soon as possible after the close of hostilities.

Internees in the territory of a Party to the conflict, against whom penal proceedings are pending for offences not exclusively subject to disciplinary penalties, may be detained until the close of such proceedings and, if circumstances require, until the completion of the penalty. The same shall apply to internees who have been previously sentenced to a punishment depriving them of liberty.

By agreement between the Detaining Power and the Powers concerned, committees may be set up after the close of hostilities, or of the occupation of territories, to search for dispersed internees.

Repatriation and return to last place of residence

Art. 134. The High Contracting Parties shall endeavour, upon the close of hostilities or occupation, to ensure the return of all internees to their last place of residence, or to facilitate their repatriation.

Costs

Art. 135. The Detaining Power shall bear the expense of returning released internees to the places where they were residing when interned, or, if it took them into custody while they were in transit or on the high seas, the cost of completing their journey or of their return to their point of departure.

Where a Detaining Power refuses permission to reside in its territory to a released internee who previously had his permanent domicile therein, such Detaining Power shall pay the cost of the said internee's repatriation. If, however, the internee elects to return to his country on his own responsibility or in obedience to the Government of the Power to which he owes allegiance, the Detaining Power need not pay the expenses of his journey beyond the point of his departure from its territory.

The Detaining Power need not pay the costs of repatriation of an internee who was interned at his own request.

If internees are transferred in accordance with Article 45, the transferring and receiving Powers shall agree on the portion of the above costs to be borne by each.

The foregoing shall not prejudice such special agreements as may be concluded between Parties to the conflict concerning the exchange and repatriation of their nationals in enemy hands.

Section V. Information Bureaux and Central Agency

National Bureaux

Art. 136. Upon the outbreak of a conflict and in all cases of occupation, each of the Parties to the conflict shall establish an official Information Bureau responsible for receiving and transmitting information in respect of the protected persons who are in its power.

Each of the Parties to the conflict shall, within the shortest possible period, give its Bureau information of any measure taken by it concerning any protected persons who are kept in custody for more than two weeks, who are subjected to assigned residence or who are interned. It shall, furthermore, require its various departments concerned with such matters to provide the aforesaid Bureau promptly with information concerning all changes pertaining to these protected persons, as, for example, transfers, releases, repatriations, escapes, admittances to hospitals, births and deaths.

Transmission of information

Art. 137. Each national Bureau shall immediately forward information concerning protected persons by the most rapid means to the Powers of whom the aforesaid persons are nationals, or to Powers in whose territory they resided, through the intermediary of the Protecting Powers and likewise through the Central Agency provided for in Article 140. The Bureaux shall also reply to all enquiries which may be received regarding protected persons.

Information Bureaux shall transmit information concerning a protected person unless its transmission might be detrimental to the person concerned or to his or her relatives in such a case, the information may not be withheld from the Central Agency which, upon being notified of the circumstances, will take the necessary precautions indicated in Article 140.

All communications in writing made by any Bureau shall be authenticated by a signature or a seal.

Particulars required

Art. 138. The information received by the national Bureau and transmitted by it shall be of such a character as to make it possible to identify the protected person exactly and to advise his next of kin quickly. The information in respect of each person shall include at least his surname, first names, place and date of birth, nationality, last residence and distinguishing characteristics, the first name of the father and the maiden name of the mother, the date, place and nature of the action taken with regard to the individual, the address at which correspondence may be sent to him and the name and address of the person to be informed.

Likewise, information regarding the state of health of internees who are seriously ill or seriously wounded shall be supplied regularly and if possible every week.

Forwarding of personal valuables

Art. 139. Each national Information Bureau shall, furthermore, be responsible for collecting all personal valuables left by protected persons mentioned in Article 136, in particular those who have been repatriated or released, or who have escaped or died; it shall forward the said valuables to those concerned, either direct, or, if necessary, through the Central Agency. Such articles shall be sent by the Bureau in sealed packets which shall be accompanied by statements giving clear and full identity particulars of the person to whom the articles belonged, and by a complete list of the contents of the parcel. Detailed records shall be maintained of the receipt and despatch of all such valuables.

Central Agency

Art. 140. A Central Information Agency for protected persons, in particular for internees, shall be created in a neutral country. The International Committee of the Red Cross shall, if it deems necessary, propose to the Powers concerned the organization of such an Agency, which may be the same as that provided for in Article 123 of the Geneva Convention relative to the Treatment of Prisoners of War of August 12, 1949.

The function of the Agency shall be to collect all information of the type set forth in Article 136 which it may obtain through official or private channels and to transmit it as rapidly as possible to the countries of origin or of residence of the persons concerned, except in cases where such transmissions might be detrimental to the persons whom the said information concerns, or to their relatives. It shall receive from the Parties to the conflict all reasonable facilities for effecting such transmissions.

The High Contracting Parties, and in particular those whose nationals benefit by the services of the Central Agency, are requested to give the said Agency the financial aid it may require.

The foregoing provisions shall in no way be interpreted as restricting the humanitarian activities of the International Committee of the Red Cross and of the relief Societies described in Article 142.

Exemption from charges

Art. 141. The national Information Bureaux and the Central Information Agency shall enjoy free postage for all mail, likewise the exemptions provided for in Article 110, and further, so far as possible, exemption from telegraphic charges or, at least, greatly reduced rates.

PART IV. EXECUTION OF THE CONVENTION

Section I. General Provisions

Relief societies and other organizations

Art. 142. Subject to the measures which the Detaining Powers may consider essential to ensure their security or to meet any other reasonable need, the representatives of religious organizations, relief societies, or any other organizations assisting the protected persons, shall receive from these Powers, for themselves or their duly accredited agents, all facilities for visiting the protected persons, for distributing relief supplies and material from any source, intended for educational, recreational or religious purposes, or for assisting them in organizing their leisure time within the places of internment. Such societies or organizations may be constituted in the territory of the Detaining Power, or in any other country, or they may have an international character.

The Detaining Power may limit the number of societies and organizations whose delegates are allowed to carry out their activities in its territory and under its supervision, on condition, however, that such limitation shall not hinder the supply of effective and adequate relief to all protected persons.

The special position of the International Committee of the Red Cross in this field shall be recognized and respected at all times.

Supervision

Art. 143. Representatives or delegates of the Protecting Powers shall have permission to go to all places where protected persons are, particularly to places of internment, detention and work.

They shall have access to all premises occupied by protected persons and shall be able to interview the latter without witnesses, personally or through an interpreter.

Such visits may not be prohibited except for reasons of imperative military necessity, and then only as an exceptional and temporary measure. Their duration and frequency shall not be restricted.

Such representatives and delegates shall have full liberty to select the places they wish to visit. The Detaining or Occupying Power, the Protecting Power and when occasion arises the Power of origin of the persons to be visited, may agree that compatriots of the internees shall be permitted to participate in the visits.

The delegates of the International Committee of the Red Cross shall also enjoy the above prerogatives. The appointment of such delegates shall be submitted to the approval of the Power governing the territories where they will carry out their duties.

Dissemination of the Convention

Art. 144. The High Contracting Parties undertake, in time of peace as in time of war, to disseminate the text of the present

Convention as widely as possible in their respective countries, and, in particular, to include the study thereof in their programmes of military and, if possible, civil instruction, so that the principles thereof may become known to the entire population.

Any civilian, military, police or other authorities, who in time of war assume responsibilities in respect of protected persons, must possess the text of the Convention and be specially instructed as to its provisions.

Translations. Rules of application

Art. 145. The High Contracting Parties shall communicate to one another through the Swiss Federal Council and, during hostilities, through the Protecting Powers, the official translations of the present Convention, as well as the laws and regulations which they may adopt to ensure the application thereof.

Penal sanctions
I. General observations

Art. 146. The High Contracting Parties undertake to enact any legislation necessary to provide effective penal sanctions for persons committing, or ordering to be committed, any of the grave breaches of the present Convention defined in the following Article.

Each High Contracting Party shall be under the obligation to search for persons alleged to have committed, or to have ordered to be committed, such grave breaches, and shall bring such persons, regardless of their nationality, before its own courts. It may also, if it prefers, and in accordance with the provisions of its own legislation, hand such persons over for trial to another High Contracting Party concerned, provided such High Contracting Party has made out a ' prima facie ' case.

Each High Contracting Party shall take measures necessary for the suppression of all acts contrary to the provisions of the present Convention other than the grave breaches defined in the following Article.

In all circumstances, the accused persons shall benefit by safeguards of proper trial and defence, which shall not be less favourable than those provided by Article 105 and those following of the Geneva Convention relative to the Treatment of Prisoners of War of August 12, 1949.

II. Grave breaches

Art. 147. Grave breaches to which the preceding Article relates shall be those involving any of the following acts, if committed against persons or property protected by the present Convention: wilful killing, torture or inhuman treatment, including biological experiments, wilfully causing great suffering or serious injury to body or health, unlawful deportation or transfer or unlawful confinement of a protected person, compelling a protected person to serve in the forces of a hostile Power, or wilfully depriving a protected person of the rights of fair and regular trial prescribed in the present Convention, taking of hostages and extensive destruction and appropriation of property, not justified by military necessity and carried out unlawfully and wantonly.

Art. 148. No High Contracting Party shall be allowed to absolve itself or any other High Contracting Party of any liability incurred by itself or by another High Contracting Party in respect of breaches referred to in the preceding Article.

Art. 149. At the request of a Party to the conflict, an enquiry shall be instituted, in a manner to be decided between the interested Parties, concerning any alleged violation of the Convention.

Enquiry procedure

If agreement has not been reached concerning the procedure for the enquiry, the Parties should agree on the choice of an umpire who will decide upon the procedure to be followed.

Once the violation has been established, the Parties to the conflict shall put an end to it and shall repress it with the least possible delay.

Section II. Final Provisions

Art. 150. The present Convention is established in English and in French. Both texts are equally authentic. The Swiss Federal Council shall arrange for official translations of the Convention to be made in the Russian and Spanish languages.

Languages

Art. 151. The present Convention, which bears the date of this day, is open to signature until February 12, 1950, in the name of the Powers represented at the Conference which opened at Geneva on April 21, 1949.

Signature

Art. 152. The present Convention shall be ratified as soon as possible and the ratifications shall be deposited at Berne.

Ratification

A record shall be drawn up of the deposit of each instrument of ratification and certified copies of this record shall be transmitted by the Swiss Federal Council to all the Powers in whose name the Convention has been signed, or whose accession has been notified.

Art. 153. The present Convention shall come into force six months after not less than two instruments of ratification have been deposited.

Coming into force

Thereafter, it shall come into force for each High Contracting Party six months after the deposit of the instrument of ratification.

Art. 154. In the relations between the Powers who are bound by the Hague Conventions respecting the Laws and Customs of War on Land, whether that of July 29, 1899, or that of October 18, 1907, and who are parties to the present Convention, this

Relation with the Hague Conventions

last Convention shall be supplementary to Sections II and III of the Regulations annexed to the above-mentioned Conventions of The Hague.

Accession

Art. 155. From the date of its coming into force, it shall be open to any Power in whose name the present Convention has not been signed, to accede to this Convention.

Notification of accessions

Art. 156. Accessions shall be notified in writing to the Swiss Federal Council, and shall take effect six months after the date on which they are received.

The Swiss Federal Council shall communicate the accessions to all the Powers in whose name the Convention has been signed, or whose accession has been notified.

Immediate effect

Art. 157. The situations provided for in Articles 2 and 3 shall give immediate effect to ratifications deposited and accessions notified by the Parties to the conflict before or after the beginning of hostilities or occupation. The Swiss Federal Council shall communicate by the quickest method any ratifications or accessions received from Parties to the conflict.

Denunciation

Art. 158. Each of the High Contracting Parties shall be at liberty to denounce the present Convention.

The denunciation shall be notified in writing to the Swiss Federal Council, which shall transmit it to the Governments of all the High Contracting Parties.

The denunciation shall take effect one year after the notification thereof has been made to the Swiss Federal Council. However, a denunciation of which notification has been made at a time when the denouncing Power is involved in a conflict shall not take effect until peace has been concluded, and until after operations connected with the release, repatriation and reestablishment of the persons protected by the present Convention have been terminated.

The denunciation shall have effect only in respect of the denouncing Power. It shall in no way impair the obligations which the Parties to the conflict shall remain bound to fulfil by virtue of the principles of the law of nations, as they result from the usages established among civilized peoples, from the laws of humanity and the dictates of the public conscience.

Registration with the United Nations

Art. 159. The Swiss Federal Council shall register the present Convention with the Secretariat of the United Nations. The Swiss Federal Council shall also inform the Secretariat of the United Nations of all ratifications, accessions and denunciations received by it with respect to the present Convention.

In witness whereof the undersigned, having deposited their respective full powers, have signed the present Convention.

Done at Geneva this twelfth day of August 1949, in the English and French languages. The original shall be deposited in the Archives of the Swiss Confederation. The Swiss Federal Council shall transmit certified copies thereof to each of the signatory and acceding States.

ANNEX I. DRAFT AGREEMENT RELATING TO HOSPITAL AND SAFETY ZONES AND LOCALITIES

Article 1. Hospital and safety zones shall be strictly reserved for the persons mentioned in Article 23 of the Geneva Convention for the Amelioration of the Condition of the Wounded and Sick in Armed Forces in the Field of August 12, 1949, and in Article 14 of the Geneva Convention relative to the Protection of Civilian Persons in Time of War of August 12, 1949, and for the personnel entrusted with the organization and administration of these zones and localities and with the care of the persons therein assembled.

Nevertheless, persons whose permanent residence is within such zones shall have the right to stay there.

Art. 2. No persons residing, in whatever capacity, in a hospital and safety zone shall perform any work, either within or without the zone, directly connected with military operations or the production of war material.

Art. 3. The Power establishing a hospital and safety zone shall take all necessary measures to prohibit access to all persons who have no right of residence or entry therein.

Art. 4. Hospital and safety zones shall fulfil the following conditions:

(a) They shall comprise only a small part of the territory governed by the Power which has established them.

(b) They shall be thinly populated in relation to the possibilities of accommodation.

(c) They shall be far removed and free from all military objectives, or large industrial or administrative establishments.

(d) They shall not be situated in areas which, according to every probability, may become important for the conduct of the war.

Art. 5. Hospital and safety zones shall be subject to the following obligations:

(a) The lines of communication and means of transport which they possess shall not be used for the transport of military personnel or material, even in transit.

(b) They shall in no case be defended by military means.

Art. 6. Hospital and safety zones shall be marked by means of oblique red bands on a white ground, placed on the buildings and outer precincts.

Zones reserved exclusively for the wounded and sick may be marked by means of the Red Cross (Red Crescent, Red Lion and Sun) emblem on a white ground.

They may be similarly marked at night by means of appropriate illumination.

Art. 7. The Powers shall communicate to all the High Contracting Parties in peacetime or on the outbreak of hostilities, a list of the hospital and safety zones in the territories governed by them. They shall also give notice of any new zones set up during hostilities.

As soon as the adverse Party has received the above-mentioned notification, the zone shall be regularly established.

If, however, the adverse Party considers that the conditions of the present agreement have not been fulfilled, it may refuse to recognize the zone by giving immediate notice thereof to the Party responsible for the said zone, or may make its recognition of such zone dependent upon the institution of the control provided for in Article 8.

Art. 8. Any Power having recognized one or several hospital and safety zones instituted by the adverse Party shall be entitled to demand control by one or more Special Commissions, for the purpose of ascertaining if the zones fulfil the conditions and obligations stipulated in the present agreement.

For this purpose, members of the Special Commissions shall at all times have free access to the various zones and may even reside there permanently. They shall be given all facilities for their duties of inspection.

Art. 9. Should the Special Commissions note any facts which they consider contrary to the stipulations of the present agreement, they shall at once draw the attention of the Power governing the said zone to these facts, and shall fix a time limit of five days within which the matter should be rectified. They shall duly notify the Power who has recognized the zone.

If, when the time limit has expired, the Power governing the zone has not complied with the warning, the adverse Party may declare that it is no longer bound by the present agreement in respect of the said zone.

Art. 10. Any Power setting up one or more hospital and safety zones, and the adverse Parties to whom their existence has been notified, shall nominate or have nominated by the Protecting Powers or by other neutral Powers, persons eligible to be members of the Special Commissions mentioned in Articles 8 and 9.

Art. 11. In no circumstances may hospital and safety zones be the object of attack. They shall be protected and respected at all times by the Parties to the conflict.

Art. 12. In the case of occupation of a territory, the hospital and safety zones therein shall continue to be respected and utilized as such.

Their purpose may, however, be modified by the Occupying Power, on condition that all measures are taken to ensure the safety of the persons accommodated.

Art. 13. The present agreement shall also apply to localities which the Powers may utilize for the same purposes as hospital and safety zones.

ANNEX II DRAFT REGULATIONS CONCERNING COLLECTIVE RELIEF

Article 1. The Internee Committees shall be allowed to distribute collective relief shipments for which they are responsible, to all internees who are dependent for administration on the said Committee's place of internment, including those internees who are in hospitals, or in prisons or other penitentiary establishments.

Art. 2. The distribution of collective relief shipments shall be effected in accordance with the instructions of the donors and with a plan drawn up by the Internee Committees. The issue of medical stores shall, however, be made for preference in agreement with the senior medical officers, and the latter may, in hospitals and infirmaries, waive the said instructions, if the needs of their patients so demand. Within the limits thus defined, the distribution shall always be carried out equitably.

Art. 3. Members of Internee Committees shall be allowed to go to the railway stations or other points of arrival of relief supplies near their places of internment so as to enable them to verify the quantity as well as the quality of the goods received and to make out detailed reports thereon for the donors.

Art. 4. Internee Committees shall be given the facilities necessary for verifying whether the distribution of collective relief in all subdivisions and annexes of their places of internment has been carried out in accordance with their instructions.

Art. 5. Internee Committees shall be allowed to complete, and to cause to be completed by members of the Internee Committees in labour detachments or by the senior medical officers of infirmaries and hospitals, forms or questionnaires intended for the donors, relating to collective relief supplies (distribution, requirements, quantities, etc.). Such forms and questionnaires, duly completed, shall be forwarded to the donors without delay.

Art. 6. In order to secure the regular distribution of collective relief supplies to the internees in their place of internment, and to meet any needs that may arise through the arrival of fresh parties of internees, the Internee Committees shall be allowed to create and maintain sufficient reserve stocks of collective relief. For this purpose, they shall have suitable warehouses at their disposal; each warehouse shall be provided with two locks, the Internee Committee holding the keys of one lock, and the commandant of the place of internment the keys of the other.

Art. 7. The High Contracting Parties, and the Detaining Powers in particular, shall, so far as is in any way possible and subject to the regulations governing the food supply of the population, authorize purchases of goods to be made in their territories for the distribution of collective relief to the internees. They shall likewise facilitate the transfer of funds and other financial measures of a technical or administrative nature taken for the purpose of making such purchases.

Art. 8. The foregoing provisions shall not constitute an obstacle to the right of internees to receive collective relief before their arrival in a place of internment or in the course of their transfer, nor to the possibility of representatives of the Protecting Power, or of the International Committee of the Red Cross or any other humanitarian organization giving assistance to internees and responsible for forwarding such supplies, ensuring the distribution thereof to the recipients by any other means they may deem suitable.

ANNEX III I. INTERNMENT CARD

1. Front

CIVILIAN INTERNEE MAIL

Postage free

POST CARD

IMPORTANT

This card must be completed by each internee immediately on being interned and each time his address is altered by reason of transfer to another place of internment or to a hospital.
This card is not the same as the special card which each internee is allowed to send to his relatives.

CENTRAL INFORMATION AGENCY FOR PROTECTED PERSONS

INTERNATIONAL COMMITTEE OF THE RED CROSS

2. Reverse side

Write legibly and in block letters —1. Nationality ....

2. Surname 3. First names *(in full)* 4. First name of father

....

5. Date of birth .... 6. Place of birth ....
7. Occupation ....
8. Address before detention ....
9. Address of next of kin ....
....

10. Interned on: * ....
(or)
Coming from (hospital, etc.) on: ....
11. State of health * ....

12. Present address ....
13. Date .... 14. Signature ....

* Strike out what is not applicable—Do not add any remarks— See explanations on other side of card.

(Size of internment card—10×15 cm)

ANNEX III II. LETTER

CIVILIAN INTERNEE SERVICE

Postage free

To

Street and number

Place of destination *(in block capitals)*

Province or Department

Country *(in block capitals)*

Sender:

Surname and first names

Date and place of birth

Internment address

(Size of letter—29×15 cm)

ANNEX III. CORRESPONDENCE CARD

Front

CIVILIAN INTERNEE MAIL

Postage free

POST CARD

Sender:

Surname and first names

Place and date of birth

Internment address

To

Street and number

Place of destination *(in block capitals)*

Province or Department

Country *(in block capitals)*

Reverse side

Date:

....

....

....

....

....

....

Write on the dotted lines only and as legibly as possible.

(Size of correspondence card—10 × 15 cm.)

Nos. 49–52

SIGNATURES, RATIFICATIONS, ACCESSIONS AND NOTIFICATIONS OF SUCCESSION AND CONTINUITY[1]

concerning the four Geneva Conventions of 12 August 1949

State	*Signature*[2]	*Ratification, Accession or Notification of Succession (C)*[3]
Afghanistan	8 December 1949	26 September 1956
Albania	12 December 1949 *Res.*	27 May 1957 *Res.*
Algeria	–	20 June 1960/3 July 1962[4]
Andorra	–	17 September 1993
Angola	–	20 September 1984 *Res.*
Antigua and Barbuda	–	6 October 1986 (C)[5]
Argentina	8 December 1949 *Res.*[6]	18 September 1956
Armenia	–	7 June 1993
Australia	4 January 1950 *Res.*	14 October 1958 *Res.*[7]

[1] Based on communication received from the Swiss Federal Department of Foreign Affairs, on 25 June 1999 and completed by indications published in the *United Nations Treaty Series* and on the ICRC website: www.icrc.org.ihl.nsf. The texts of reservations, declarations and communications are published on pp. 650 ff.

The reservations, declarations and communications are indicated in the table by abbreviations "*Res.*" or "*Dec.*" placed after the dates of signatures, ratifications, accessions or notifications of succession or continuity. The withdrawal of a reservation is indicated by a footnote. The depositary renounced in principle to notify certain declarations and communications that do not modify the scope of application of the 1949 Geneva Conventions; these declarations and communications are mentioned in the footnotes, but are not, in principle, reproduced in the texts of the reservations, declarations and communications.

[2] According to common Articles 56/55/136/151, the 1949 Geneva Conventions were open to signature until 12 February 1950, in the name of the powers represented at the Conference. Furthermore, they were open to signature by powers not represented at the Conference that are parties to the Geneva Conventions of 1864, 1906 or 1929 (for the first and second Conventions), to the Hague Convention (X) of 1907 (for the second Convention) and to the 1929 Convention relative to the treatment of prisoners of war (third Convention).

[3] The dates indicated in this table are the dates of the deposit of the instruments of ratification or accession or the dates of the deposit of the notification of succession or continuity with the depositary, the Swiss Federal Council.

[4] On 20 June 1960 the Provisional Government of the Algerian Republic, not recognized by the majority of states, including Switzerland, deposited an instrument of accession to the four 1949 Geneva Convention. Algeria became independent on 3 July 1962. The depositary lists Algeria's accession as entering into force on 20 December 1960, but states that it is equally open to parties to the Conventions to consider that this accession took effect on 3 July 1962.

[5] On 6 October 1986, Antigua and Barbuda deposited with the Swiss Government its declaration of succession to the four Geneva Conventions of 1949 with effect retroactively as from 1 November 1981, the date on which that country became independent.

[6] Argentina made a reservation on signature, which was not maintained at ratification. Argentina expressed objection to the accession of the People's Republic of Mongolia to the Geneva Conventions. This declaration is not reproduced in this collection.

[7] By an act dated 20 February 1974, received on the 21 of the same month, the Minister of Foreign Affairs of the Commonwealth of Australia notified the Federal Political Department of the partial withdrawal of the reservation made by the Government of Australia at the time of ratification, the 14 October 1958, of the Convention relative to the Protection of Civilian Persons in Time of War (*UNTS*, Vol. 914, 1974, p. 310). For the text of the withdrawn reservation, see p. 652. On ratification, Australia also expressed objections to the reservations presented by Albania, Byelorussian SSR, Bulgaria, Czechoslovakia, Hungary, Poland,

State	*Signature*[2]	*Ratification, Accession or Notification of Succession (C)*[3]
Austria[8]	12 August 1949 (*Conv. I, III, IV*)	27 August 1953
	8 December 1949 (*Conv. II*)	27 August 1953
Azerbaijan	–	1 June 1993
Bahamas	–	11 July 1975 (C)[9]
Bahrain	–	30 November 1971
Bangladesh	–	4 April 1972 (C)[10]
Barbados	–	10 September 1968 (C) *Dec.*[11]
Belarus[12]	12 December 1949 *Res.*	3 August 1954 *Res.*
Belgium[13]	8 December 1949	3 September 1952
Belize	–	29 June 1984
Benin	–	14 December 1961 (C)[14]
Bhutan	–	10 January 1991

cont.

Romania, Ukrainian SSR, USSR and Federal People's Republic of Yugoslavia. See p. 652. At the same time, Australia, taking note of the acceptance of the Conventions by The German Democratic Republic, The Democratic People's Republic of Korea, the Democratic Republic of Viet Nam and the People's Republic of China, declared that it does not recognize these states and objects to their reservations. See p. 652.

8 The Austrian Ministry of Foreign Affairs took note of the accession of the Democratic Republic of Viet Nam to the Geneva Conventions, but it does not imply the recognition of the Democratic Republic of Viet Nam by Austria (declaration not reproduced in the present collection).

9 In a letter dated 27 June 1975 and received by the Swiss Federal Council on 11 July 1975, the Minister of Foreign Affairs of the Commonwealth of Bahamas declared that that state considered itself bound by the four Geneva Conventions of 12 August 1949 for the Protection of War Victims, this by virtue of their previous ratification by Great Britain. This declaration of continuity made the Commonwealth of Bahamas party to those Conventions as from 10 July 1973, the date of accession to independence.

10 In a letter dated 27 March 1972 and received by the Swiss Federal Council on 4 April of that year, the Minister of Foreign Affairs of the People's Republic of Bangladesh declared that that state considered itself bound by the four Geneva Conventions of 12 August 1949 for the Protection of War Victims, this by virtue of their previous ratification by the Islamic Republic of Pakistan. This declaration of continuity made the People's Republic of Bangladesh party to those Conventions retroactively as from 26 March 1971, the date on which Bangladesh became independent.

By a communication to the states parties to the Geneva Conventions of 12 August 1949, the Swiss Federal Department of Foreign Affairs informed the states parties to the Convention that the Permanent Mission of Bangladesh to the United Nations in Geneva informed the Swiss Government by a note of 20 December 1988 of the decision of the Government of the People's Republic of Bangladesh to use henceforth the red crescent instead of the red cross as distinctive emblem and sign (communication of the depositary of 9 January 1989, see p. 652).

11 In a letter dated 20 August 1968 and received by the Swiss Federal Council on 10 September of that year, the Barbadian Prime Minister and Minister of Foreign Affairs stated that Barbados considered itself bound by the four Geneva Conventions of 12 August 1949 for the Protection of War Victims by virtue of their previous ratification by Great Britain. Under this declaration of succession, therefore, those Conventions came into force retroactively for Barbados as from 30 November 1966, the date on which that country became independent.

12 The Soviet Socialist Republic of Byelorussia made a declaration relating to the accession of the Republic of Korea that is not reproduced in this collection.

13 Belgium attached to the instrument of ratification a document extending the application of the four Geneva Conventions to the territories of the Belgian Congo and Rwanda-Urundi (communication addressed to the ICRC on 15 September 1952).

14 In a note dated 14 December 1961 and received by the Swiss Federal Council on 12 January 1962, the Government of Dahomey (now Benin) declared that state to be party to the Conventions by virtue of their ratification by France on 28 June 1951. This declaration took effect retroactively as from 1 August 1960, the date on which Dahomey achieved independence.

State	*Signature*[2]	*Ratification, Accession or Notification of Succession (C)*[3]
Bolivia	8 December 1949	10 December 1976
Bosnia and Herzegovina	–	31 December 1992 (C)[15]
Botswana	–	29 March 1968
Brazil	8 December 1949 *Res.*[16]	29 June 1957
Brunei Darussalam	–	14 October 1991
Bulgaria	28 December 1949 *Res.*	22 July 1954[17]
Burkina Faso	–	7 November 1961 (C)[18]
Burundi	–	27 December 1971 (C)[19]
Cambodia	–	8 December 1958
Cameroon	–	16 September 1963 (C)[20]
Canada	8 December 1949 *Res.*[21]	14 May 1965
Cape Verde	–	11 May 1984
Central African Republic	–	1 August 1966 (C)[22]
Chad	–	5 August 1970
Chile	12 August 1949	12 October 1950
China (People's Republic)[23]	10 December 1949	28 December 1956 *Res.*
Colombia	12 August 1949	8 November 1961

[15] The succession of Bosnia and Herzegovina took effect retroactively on 6 March 1992, the day of accession to independence (communication of the depositary to the ICRC of 5 January 1993).

[16] Brazil made two reservations on signature, which were not maintained on ratification. Brazil also made a declaration concerning the accession of the Republic of Guinea-Bissau and of the Provisional Revolutionary Government of the Republic of South Viet Nam. See p. 654.

[17] By a letter of 19 April 1994, received on 9 May 1994, the Ministry of Foreign Affairs of the Republic of Bulgaria informed the Swiss Federal Department of Foreign Affairs of the withdrawal of its declarations and reservations concerning the 1949 Geneva Conventions, i.e. the declaration concerning the Article 10 of the Convention I, II and III, as well as Article II of the Convention IV, and the reservations concerning Article 12 of the Convention III, Article 85 of the Convention III and Article 45 of the Convention IV (communication of the depositary of 11 May 1994 addressed to the ICRC). See p. 656.

[18] In a note received by the Swiss Federal Council on 7 November 1961, the Government of Upper Volta (now Burkina Faso) declared itself party to the Geneva Conventions by virtue of their ratification by France on 28 June 1951. This declaration took effect retroactively as from 5 August 1960, the date on which Upper Volta achieved independence.

[19] In a letter dated 21 December 1971 and received by the Swiss Federal Council on 27 December of that year, the Republic of Burundi's Minister of External Relations, Cooperation and Planning stated that Burundi considered itself bound by the four Geneva Conventions of 12 August 1949 for the Protection of War Victims by virtue of their previous ratification by Belgium. According to this declaration of continuity, the Republic of Burundi considers itself bound by those Conventions since 1 July 1962, the date on which it became independent.

[20] In a note sent to the Swiss Federal Council on 16 September 1963, the Government of Cameroon declared that country to be party to the Conventions by virtue of their ratification by France on 28 June 1951. This declaration took effect retroactively as from 1 January 1960, the date on which Cameroon became independent.

[21] Canada made the reservation on signature and withdrew it on ratification. See p. 656.

[22] In a letter (declaration of succession) dated 23 July 1966 and received on 1 August of that year, the Minister of Foreign Affairs of the Central African Republic informed the Swiss Federal Council of that state's participation in the four Geneva Conventions of 12 August 1949 for the Protection of War Victims. The Conventions came into force for the Central African Republic retroactively as from 13 August 1960, the date on which that country became independent.

[23] The Republic of China signed the Conventions on 12 August 1949. However, they were never ratified. In 1952, the People's Republic of China made known that, with certain reservations, it recognized that signature. In 1956, the People's Republic of China ratified the Conventions with reservations.

The United States of America made a declaration concerning the ratification of the Conventions by the People's Republic of China. The depositary indicated that as the scope of application of the Geneva Conventions is not modified, it will not proceed to the notification to the states parties to the Conventions (the declaration is not reproduced in the present collection).

State	*Signature*[2]	*Ratification, Accession or Notification of Succession (C)*[3]
Comoros	–	21 November 1985
Congo, Democratic Republic of (formally Zaire)	–	20 February 1961 (C)[24]
Congo (People's Republic, Brazzaville)	–	4 February 1967 (C)[25]
Cook Island	–	7 May 2002(C)
Costa Rica	–	15 October 1969
Côte d'Ivoire	–	28 December 1961 (C)[26]
Croatia	–	11 May 1992 (C)[27]
Cuba	12 August 1949	15 April 1954
Cyprus	–	23 May 1962[28]
[Czechoslovakia	8 December 1949 *Res.*	19 December 1950 *Res.*]
Czech Republic	–	5 February 1993 (C) *Res.*[29]
Denmark	12 August 1949	27 June 1951
Djibouti	–	26 January 1978 (C) (*Convention I*) 6 March 1978 (C)[30] (*Conventions II, III, IV*)

cont.

On 14 April 1999, the People's Republic of China notified the depositary the following: "The Government of the People's Republic of China hereby confirms that the four Geneva Conventions of 1949 and the 1977 Additional Protocols I and II apply to the Hong Kong Special Administrative Region of the People's Republic of China (HKSAR) with the effect from 1 July 1997, as they apply to the whole territory of the People's Republic of China."

24 In a note date 20 February 1961 and received by the Swiss Federal Council on 24 February of that year, the Government of the Republic of the Congo (Léopoldville) declared that it considered itself bound by the Conventions, which were extended to cover the territory of the Congo when Belgium ratified them. This declaration took effect retroactively as from 30 June 1960, the date on which the Congo became independent.

25 In a letter dated 30 January 1967 and received by the Swiss Government on 4 February of that year, the Ministry of Foreign Affairs of the Republic of the Congo informed the Swiss Federal Council that that state considered itself bound by the four Geneva Conventions of 12 August 1949 for the Protection of War Victims, this by virtue of the Conventions' previous ratification by France. Under this declaration of succession the Conventions entered into force retroactively for the Republic of the Congo as from 15 August 1960, the date on which that country became independent.

26 In a note dated 28 December 1961 and received by the Swiss Federal Council on 30 December of that year, the Government of the Côte d'Ivoire declared itself party to the Conventions by virtue of their ratification by France on 28 June 1951. This declaration took effect retroactively for the Côte d'Ivoire as from 7 August 1960.

27 By a letter of 29 April 1992 addressed to the Swiss Federal Council and received on 11 May 1992, the Ministry of Foreign Affairs of the Republic of Croatia deposited the notification of succession to the four Geneva Conventions and two Additional Protocols of 1977, without reservations and declarations made by the Socialist Federal Republic of Yugoslavia and without new reservations, with the retroactive effect as from 8 October 1991, day of the accession to independence.

28 On 3 May 1962, the Government of the Republic of Cyprus declared that that state was acceding to the Geneva Conventions with the reservation that it would use the ratification procedure provided for in Article 169 of the Constitution of the Republic of Cyprus. On 18 July 1966, the approval by the Cypriot House of Representatives was published in the Republic's Official Gazette.

29 The Czech Republic made on 5 February 1993 a declaration of succession to the 1949 Geneva Conventions and maintained the reservations made by Czechoslovakia. The succession took effect on 1 January 1993, the date of the accession to independence (communication of the depositary to the ICRC of 10 February 1993).

30 In a letter of 5 January 1978 addressed to the Swiss Federal Council and received on 26 January 1978, the Minister of Foreign Affairs of the Republic of Djibouti declared that this state con-

State	*Signature*[2]	*Ratification, Accession or Notification of Succession (C)*[3]
Dominica	–	28 September 1981 (C)[31]
Dominican Republic	–	22 January 1958
Ecuador	12 August 1949	11 August 1954
Egypt	8 December 1949	10 November 1952
El Salvador	8 December 1949	17 June 1953
Equatorial Guinea	–	24 July 1986
Eritrea	–	14 December 2000
Estonia	–	18 January 1993
Ethiopia	8 December 1949	2 October 1969
Fiji Islands	–	9 August 1971 (C)[32]
Finland	8 December 1949	22 February 1955
France	8 December 1949	28 June 1951
Gabon	–	20 February 1965 (C)[33]
Gambia	–	11 October 1966 (C)[34]
Georgia	–	14 September 1993
Germany	–	3 September 1954 *Dec.*[35]

cont.
sidered itself bound by the Convention for the Amelioration of the condition of the wounded and sick in armed forces in the field, by virtue of its ratification by France. In a letter of 1 March, received on the 6 March, the same Minister declared that Djibouti considered itself bound by three other Geneva Conventions by virtue of the previous ratification by France and with the retroactive effect as from 27 June 1977, date of its accession to independence.

[31] On 28 September 1981, the Swiss Government received an instrument by which the Commonwealth of Dominica declared its succession to the four Geneva Conventions of 12 August 1949 for the Protection of War Victims, this by virtue of their previous ratification by the United Kingdom of Great Britain and Northern Ireland. The Conventions came into force retroactively as from 3 November 1978, the date on which Dominica became independent.

[32] In a letter dated 28 June 1971 and received by the Swiss Federal Council on 9 August 1971, the Minister of Foreign Affairs of Fiji declared that that state considered itself bound by the four Geneva Conventions of 12 August 1949 for the Protection of War Victims, this by virtue of those Conventions' previous ratification by the United Kingdom. Under that declaration of succession Fiji became bound by the Geneva Conventions as from 10 October 1970, the date on which that country became independent.

[33] On 20 February 1965, the President of the Gabonese Republic sent a letter to the President of the Swiss Confederation (which the latter received on 26 February of the same year) confirming to the Swiss Government that the Gabonese Republic was party to the four Geneva Conventions of 12 August 1949 for the Protection of War Victims, this by virtue of those Conventions' previous ratification by France on 28 June 1951. This declaration of succession meant that the Gabonese Republic became bound by the Geneva Conventions retroactively as from 17 August 1960, the date on which that country reached independence.

[34] In a letter dated 11 October 1966 to the President of the Swiss Confederation and received by him on 20 October of that year, the Gambian Government declared that it considered Gambia to be bound by the four Geneva Conventions of 12 August 1949 for the Protection of War Victims, this by virtue of their previous ratification by the United Kingdom of Great Britain and Northern Ireland. The Gambian Government further declared that it did not wish to retain the United Kingdom's reservation concerning the Geneva Convention relative to the Protection of Civilian Persons in Time of War. Gambia thus became party to the Geneva Conventions retroactively as from 18 February 1965, the date on which that country became independent.

[35] At accession, the Federal Republic of Germany stated that the Conventions are also applicable to *Land Berlin.* See p. 660.

The Federal Republic of Germany made a declaration relating to the accession of the Provisional Revolutionary Government of the Republic of South Viet Nam and expressed objection to the reservation made upon accession by Guinea-Bissau; see p.660.

The German Democratic Republic acceded to the 1949 Geneva Conventions on 30 November 1956 with reservations, see p. 659.

The United States of America made a declaration concerning the accession of the German Democratic Republic to the Geneva Conventions. The depositary indicated that as the scope

State	*Signature*[2]	*Ratification, Accession or Notification of Succession (C)*[3]
Ghana	–	2 August 1958
Greece	22 December 1949	5 June 1956
Grenada	–	13 April 1981 (C)[36]
Guatemala	12 August 1949	14 May 1952
Guinea	–	11 July 1984
Guinea-Bissau	–	21 February 1974 *Res.*[37]
Guyana	–	22 July 1968 (C)[38]

cont.
of application of the Geneva Conventions was not modified, it would not proceed to the notification of this declaration to the states parties to the Conventions.

Australia and United Kingdom made objections to some reservations made by the German Democratic Republic on its accession. See pp. 652, 679–680.

The German Democratic Republic transmitted to the depositary a declaration of 3 July 1974 concerning the objections to the accession of the Provisional Revolutionary Government of the Republic of South Viet Nam made by Federal Republic of Brazil, Portugal and the Republic of Viet Nam.

In a letter of 3 October 1990 to the Secretary-General of the United Nations, the foreign minister of the Federal Republic of Germany stated: "Through the accession of the German Democratic Republic to the Federal Republic of Germany with effect from 3 October 1990, the two German States have united to form one sovereign State, which as a single Member of the United Nations remains bound by the provisions of the Charter in accordance with the solemn declaration of 12 June 1973. As from the date of unification, the Federal Republic of Germany will act in the United Nations under the designation 'Germany'."

Consequently, and in the light of Articles 11 and 12 of the Treaty of 31 August 1990 (Unification Treaty) between the Federal Republic of Germany and the German Democratic Republic, entries in status lists pertaining to formalities (i.e. signatures, ratifications, accessions, declarations and reservations, etc.) effected by the Federal Republic of Germany will now appear under "Germany" and indicate the dates of such formalities.

As regards treaties in respect of which formalities had been effected by both the Federal Republic of Germany and the former German Democratic Republic prior to unification, the entry will similarly indicate in the corresponding table the type of formality effected by the Federal Republic of Germany and the date on which it took place, while the type of formality effected by the former German Democratic Republic and the date thereof will appear in a footnote.

Finally, as regards the treatment of treaties in respect of which formalities were effected by the former German Democratic Republic alone, Article 12, paragraph 3 of the Unification Treaty contains the following provision: "Should the united Germany intend to accede to international organizations or other multilateral treaties of which the German Democratic Republic but not the Federal Republic of Germany is a member, agreement shall be reached with the respective contracting parties and with the European Communities where the latter's competence is affected".

36 In a letter dated 25 March 1981 to the Swiss Federal Council and received by it on 13 April of that year, the Government of Grenada declared that that state considered itself bound by the four Geneva Conventions of 12 August 1949 for the Protection of War Victims, this by virtue of those Conventions' previous ratification by the United Kingdom of Great Britain and Northern Ireland. Grenada thus became party to the Conventions retroactively as from 7 February 1974, the date on which it became independent.

37 When the Government of the Republic of Guinea-Bissau notified the Swiss Government, on 26 February 1974, that it was acceding to the Geneva Conventions of 1949, Switzerland issued a declaration to the effect that it was taking note of the accession in its capacity as depositary of those Conventions, but that in its capacity as a state party to the Conventions it refrained from making any pronouncement on the status of Guinea-Bissau under international law. Brazil and Portugal both made declarations regarding Guinea-Bissau's accession. See pp. 654–655, 672. Poland and Mongolia expressed objections to those declarations. See pp. 667, 671. The Federal Republic of Germany, United Kingdom and United States of America made objections to the reservations formulated by the Republic of Guinea-Bissau in time of its accession. See pp. 660, 679, 682–683.

38 In a letter dated 11 July 1968 and received by the Swiss Federal Council on 22 July of that year, the Prime Minister of Guyana declared that that state considered itself bound by the

State	*Signature*[2]	*Ratification, Accession or Notification of Succession (C)*[3]
Haiti	–	11 April 1957
Holy See	8 December 1949	22 February 1951
Honduras	–	31 December 1965
Hungary[39]	8 December 1949 *Res.*	3 August 1954 *Res.*
Iceland	–	10 August 1965
India	16 December 1949	9 November 1950
Indonesia	–	30 September 1958
Iran	8 December 1949	20 February 1957 *Dec*[40]
Iraq	–	14 February 1956
Ireland	19 December 1949	27 September 1962
Israel	8 December 1949 *Res.*	6 July 1951 *Res.*[41]
Italy[42]	8 December 1949 *Res.*	17 December 1951
Jamaica	–	20 July 1964 (C)[43]
Japan	–	21 April 1953
Jordan	–	29 May 1951
Kazakhstan	–	5 May 1992 (C)[44]
Kenya	–	20 September 1966
Kiribati	–	5 January 1989 (C)[45]
Korea (Democratic People's Republic of)[46]	–	27 August 1957 *Res.*

cont.

four Geneva Conventions of 12 August 1949 for the Protection of War Victims, this by virtue of their previous ratification by the United Kingdom of Great Britain and Northern Ireland. Guyana thus became party to the four Conventions retroactively as from 26 May 1966, the date on which it achieved independence.

39 The People's Republic of Hungary transmitted to the depositary a declaration of 23 December 1974 concerning the objections to the accession of the Provisional Revolutionary Government of the Republic of South Viet Nam, made by the Republic of Viet Nam and some other states (*UNTS*, Vol. 972, 1975, p. 404). See p. 663.

40 On 4 September 1980 the Government of the Islamic Republic of Iran declared that henceforth it wishes to use the red crescent as the distinctive emblem and sign instead of the red lion and sun (notification of the depositary to the ICRC of 26 September 1980).

41 Kuwait, the Democratic People's Republic of Yemen and Qatar made a declaration concerning Israel. See p. 664. The State of Israel made a declaration in respect of these communications, see p. 664. See also note 67 on p. 644.

42 By a verbal note of 9 August 1977, the Italian Government informed the depositary that it does not recognize the Democratic Republic of Viet Nam and that it cannot accept the notification of the depositary in this respect (communication of the depositary to the ICRC of 22 August 1957).

43 In a note dated 17 July 1964 and received by the Swiss Federal Council on 20 July of that year, the Government of Jamaica declared that state to be bound by the Conventions by virtue of their ratification, on 23 September 1957, by the United Kingdom of Great Britain and Northern Ireland. The Conventions entered into force for Jamaica retroactively as from 6 August 1962, the date on which it became independent.

44 On 5 May 1992, the Republic of Kazakhstan deposited with the Swiss Government the declaration of succession to the four Conventions of Geneva and Additional Protocols I and II, without any comment on the reservations and declarations made by the former USSR, and without new reservations or declarations. The Conventions and Protocols entered into forece on 21 December 1991, the date of signature of the Declaration of Alma-Ata creating the Commonwealth of Independent States (communication of the depositary to the ICRC of 15 July and 24 September 1992 and to the states parties of 14 October 1992).

45 On 5 January 1989, the Republic of Kiribati deposited with the Swiss Government a declaration of succession to the four Geneva Conventions of 1949 and thus became party to those Conventions retroactively as from 12 July 1979, the date on which it became independent.

46 The People's Democratic Republic of Korea made a declaration concerning the accession of the Republic of Korea to the Conventions. This declaration is not reproduced in the present collection.

State	*Signature*[2]	*Ratification, Accession or Notification of Succession (C)*[3]
Korea (Republic of)[47]	–	16 August 1966 *Res.*
Kuwait	–	2 September 1967 *Dec.*
Kyrghyzstan	–	18 September 1992 (C)[48]
Lao People's Democratic Republic	–	29 October 1956
Latvia	–	24 December 1991
Lebanon	8 December 1949	10 April 1951
Lesotho	–	20 May 1968 (C)[49]
Liberia	–	29 March 1954
Libyan Arab Jamahiriya	–	22 May 1956
Liechtenstein	12 August 1949	21 September 1950
Lithuania	–	3 October 1996
Luxembourg	12 August 1949 *Res.*[50]	1 July 1953
Macedonia	–	1 September 1993 (C) *Res.*[51]
Madagascar	–	18 July 1963 (C)[52]
Malawi	–	5 January 1968
Malaysia (Federation)	–	24 August 1962
Maldives	–	18 June 1991
Mali	–	24 May 1965

47 On the request of the Government of the Republic of Korea and in application of Articles 62/61/141/157 common to the Geneva Conventions, the accession took immediate effect. The depositary indicates 16 August 1966 as the date of entry into force of the Conventions for the Republic of Korea.

The following states made a declaration on the accession of the Republic of Korea to the Conventions: Soviet Socialist Republic of Byelorussia, People's Democratic Republic of Korea, Poland, Soviet Socialist Republic of Ukraine and the URRS. The depositary indicated that as the scope of application of the Geneva Conventions was not modified, it would not proceed to the notification of this declaration to the States parties to the Conventions. These declarations are not reproduced in the present collection.

Romania made objections to the reservations of the Republic of Korea at its accession and these objections were communicated by the depositary to the states parties to the Geneva Conventions. See pp. 673–674.

48 On 18 September 1992, the Republic of Kyrghyzstan deposited with the Swiss Government the declaration of succession to the four Conventions of Geneva and Additional Protocols I and II, without any comment on the reservations and declarations made by the former USSR, and without new reservations or declarations. The Conventions and Protocols entered into forece on 21 December 1991, the date of signature of the Declaration of Alma-Ata creating the Commonwealth of Independent States (communication of the depositary to the states parties of 14 October 1992).

49 In a note (declaration of succession) dated 10 May 1968 and received by the Swiss Federal Council on 20 May of that year, the Minister of Foreign Affairs of the Kingdom of Lesotho confirmed that that state was party to the four Geneva Conventions of 12 August 1949 for the Protection of War Victims, by virtue of their previous ratification by the United Kingdom of Great Britain and Northern Ireland. Lesotho thus became bound by those Conventions retroactively as from 4 October 1966, the date on which it became independent.

50 Luxembourg made a reservation upon signature and withdrew it on ratification. See p. 667.

51 The former Yugoslav Republic of Macedonia deposited on 1 September 1993 the notification of succession to the 1949 Geneva Conventions dated of 25 August 1993. The succession took effect at 8 September 1991, the date of the independence. On 19 September 1996, the Minister of Foreign Affairs of Macedonia informed the depositary that the Government of the Republic of Macedonia wishes to maintain the reservations by Former Socialist Federal Republic of Yugoslavia made in 1950 to the Conventions and in 1979 to the Protocols.

52 In a note dated 13 July 1963 and received by the Swiss Federal Council on 18 July of that year, the Malagasy Government declared that state to be party to the Conventions by virtue of their ratification by France on 28 June 1951. This declaration took effect retroactively as from 26 June 1960, the date on which Madagascar became independent.

State	*Signature*[2]	*Ratification, Accession or Notification of Succession (C)*[3]
Malaysia (Federation)	–	24 August 1962
Malta	–	22 August 1968 (C)[53]
Mauritania	–	30 October 1962 (C)[54]
Mauritius	–	18 August 1970 (C)[55]
Mexico	8 December 1949	29 October 1952
Micronesia	–	19 September 1995
Moldova	–	24 May 1993
Monaco	12 August 1949	5 July 1950
Mongolia[56]	–	20 December 1958 (C)[57]
Morocco	–	26 July 1956
Mozambique	–	14 March 1983
Myanmar	–	25 August 1992
Namibia[58]	–	22 August 1991 (C)
Nepal	–	7 February 1964
Netherlands[59]	8 December 1949 *Res.*	3 August 1954[60]

[53] In a note (declaration of succession) dated 20 August 1968, delivered to the Swiss Embassy in London and forwarded to the Swiss Government on 22 August of that year, the Maltese Minister for Commonwealth and Foreign Affairs declared that Malta was bound by the four Geneva Conventions of 12 August for the Protection of the War Victims, this by virtue of their ratification by Great Britain. Those Conventions entered into force for Malta retroactively on 21 September 1964, the date on which that country became independent.

[54] In a note dated 27 October 1962 and received by the Swiss Federal Council on 30 October of that year, the Mauritanian Government declared that country to be party to the Conventions by virtue of their ratification by France on 28 June 1951. This declaration took effect retroactively as from 28 November 1960, the date on which Mauritania became independent.

[55] In a note dated 12 August 1970 and received by the Swiss Federal Council on 18 August of that year, the Government of Mauritius declared that state to be bound by the Geneva Conventions of 12 August 1949 for the Protection of War Victims. This declaration took effect retroactively as from 12 March 1968, the date on which Mauritius became independent.

[56] The People's Republic of Mongolia made a declaration dated 13 August 1974 concerning the objections made by Federal Republic of Brazil and Portugal to the accession of the Government of the Provisional Revolutionary Republic of South Viet Nam and of the Republic of Guinea-Bissau. See p. 667.

[57] The following states made objections to the accession of the People's Republic of Mongolia: Argentina, South Africa and United States of America. As the scope of application of the Geneva Conventions was not modified, the depositary did not proceed to the notification of these objections to the states parties to the Conventions. These objections are not reproduced in the present collection.

[58] An instrument of accession to the Geneva Conventions and their additional Protocols was deposited by the United Nations Council for Namibia on 18 October 1983 and entered into force on 18 April 1984. South Africa made a communication relating to this aaccession, see p. 675. In an instrument deposited on 22 August 1991, Namibia declared its succession to the Geneva Conventions, which were previously applicable pursuant to South Africa's accession on 31 March 1952. Following the usual practice, the Convention entered into force on 21 March 1990, date of Namibia'a accession to independence.

[59] For the Kingdom in Europe and the Netherlands Antilles. The island of Aruba, which was a part of the Netherlands Antilles, obtained internal autonomy as a separate country within the Kingdom of the Netherlands as of 1 January 1986. The treaties concluded by the Kingdom which applied to the Netherlands Antilles, including Aruba continue, after 1 January 1986 to apply to the Netherlands Antilles (of which Aruba is no longer a part) and to Aruba.

[60] In a note of 5 February 1983, received on 7 February 1983, the Government of the Kingdom of Netherlands addressed to the Swiss Federal Department of Foreign Affairs a declaration dated 25 January 1983 by which it withdrew for the Kingdom in Europe and the Netherlands Antilles the reservation made to Article 68, paragraph 2 of the Geneva Convention (IV) relative to the Protection of Civilian Persons in time of war. See p. 667.

State	*Signature*[2]	*Ratification, Accession or Notification of Succession (C)*[3]
New Zealand	11 February 1950 *Res.*	2 May 1959 *Res.*[61]
Nicaragua	12 August 1949	17 December 1953
Niger	–	21 April 1964 (C)[62]
Nigeria	–	9 June 1961 (C)[63]
Norway	12 August 1949	3 August 1951
Oman	–	31 January 1974
Pakistan	12 August 1949	12 June 1951 *Res.*
Palau	–	25 June 1996
Palestine *See PLO (Palestine Liberation Organization) at the end of the list)*		
Panama	–	10 February 1956
Papua New Guinea	–	26 May 1976 (C)[64]
Paraguay	10 December 1949	23 October 1961
Peru	12 August 1949	15 February 1956
Philippines	8 December 1949	7 March 1951 (*Convention I*) 6 October 1952 (*Conventions II, III, IV*)
Poland[65]	8 December 1949 *Res.*	26 November 1954 *Res.*
Portugal[66]	11 February 1950 *Res.*	14 March 1961 *Res.*
Qatar	–	15 October 1975[67]

[61] On ratification, New Zealand expressed objections to the reservations presented by Albania, Byelorussian SSR, Bulgaria, Czechoslovakia, Hungary, Poland, Romania, Ukrainian SSR, USSR and Federal People's Republic of Yugoslavia. See p. 668.

By a letter of 1 December 1975, received on 2 March 1976, the Ministry of Foreign Affairs of New Zealand notified the Federal Political Department of the partial withdrawal of the reservation made by the Government of New Zealand at the time of ratification, the 2 May 1959, of the Convention relative to the Protection of Civilian Persons in Time of War. See p. 669.

[62] In a note dated 16 April 1964 and received by the Swiss Federal Council on 21 April of that year, the Government of Niger declared that state to be party to the Conventions by virtue of their ratification by France on 28 June 1951. This declaration took effect retroactively as from 3 August 1960, the date on which Niger became independent.

[63] In a note dated 9 June 1961 and received by the Swiss Federal Council on 20 June of that year, the Nigerian Government declared that it considered that the ratification of the Geneva Conventions by the United Kingdom of Great Britain and Northern Ireland on 23 September 1957 made those Conventions binding on the Federal Republic of Nigeria as from 1 October 1960, the date on which that country became independent.

[64] In a note dated 7 April 1976 and received by the Swiss Federal Political Department on 26 May of that year, the Minister of Foreign Affairs of Papua New Guinea declared that that state considered itself to be party to the Geneva Conventions of 12 August 1949 for the Protection of War Victims, by virtue of their previous ratification by Australia. This declaration took effect retroactively as from 16 September 1975, the date on which Papua New Guinea became independent.

[65] Poland made a declaration concerning the accession of the Republic of Korea, see p. 670. On 18 July 1974, the Poland made another declaration concerning the objections of some states to the accession of the Provisional Revolutionary Government of the Republic of South Viet Nam and the Republic of Guinea-Bissau. See p. 671.

[66] The Government of Portugal made objections to the accession of the Provisional Revolutionary Government of the Republic of South Viet Nam and Guinea-Bissau (notification of the depositary of 28 March 1974). See p. 672.

[67] On 24 September 1991, the state of Qatar deposited to the Swiss Federal Council an instrument containing the declaration of recognition of the competence of the International Fact-Finding Commission, according to Article 90 of the Additional Protocol I to the Geneva Conventions (notification of the depositary to the ICRC of 10 January 1992). This declaration includes a reservation concerning the recognition of the state of Israel. As the International Fact-Finding Commission is competent to enquire into any facts alleged to be a grave

State	*Signature*[2]	*Ratification, Accession or Notification of Succession (C)*[3]
Romania	10 February 1950 *Res.*	1 June 1954 *Res.*[68]
Russian Federation[69]	12 December 1949 Res.	10 May 1954 (C) *Res.*[70]
Rwanda	–	21 March 1964 (C)[71]
Saint Kitts and Nevis	–	14 February 1986[72]
Saint Lucia	–	18 September 1981 (C)[73]
Saint Vincent and the Grenadine	–	1 April 1981
Samoa	–	23 August 1984 (C)[74]
San Marino	–	29 August 1953
Sao Tome and Principe	–	21 May 1976
Saudi Arabia	–	18 May 1963
Senegal	–	18 May 1963 (C)[75]

cont.
breach as defined in the Conventions and in the Protocol I (Article 90, paragraph 2 (c) of the Protocol I) and as the declaration of the state of Israel refers to the Geneva Conventions, we reproduce this declaration in this collection. See p. 664.

68 The People's Republic of Romania made objections to the reservations and declaration of the Republic of Korea (see pp. .673–674). On 18 July 1974, Romania made a declaration to the objections relating to the accession of the Provisional Revolutionary Government of the Republic of South Viet Nam (*UNTS*, Vol. 949, 1974, p. 307 and 311). See pp. 674.

69 According to a note of the Ministry for Foreign Affairs of the Russian Federation of 13 January 1992: "The Russian Federation continues to exercise the rights and carry out the obligations resulting from the international agreements signed by the Union of Soviet Socialist Republics. Accordingly the Government of the Russian Federation will carry out, instead of the Government of the USSR, functions of depositary of the corresponding multilateral treaties. In this connection the Ministry asks to consider the Russian Federation as a Party to all international agreements in force, instead of the USSR" (note from the Permanent Mission of the Russian Federation in Geneva transmitted to the ICRC on 15 January 1992).

70 At its time, the USSR made a declaration concerning the accession of the Republic of Korea. (This declaration is not reproduced in the present collection.) On 6 August 1974, the USSR also made a declaration concerning the objections of some states to the accession of the Provisional Revolutionary Government of the Republic of South Viet Nam. See pp. 677–678.

71 In a note date 21 March 1964 and which the Swiss Federal Council received on 5 May of that year, the Rwandese Government declared Rwanda to be party to the Conventions by virtue of the ratification of those instruments by Belgium on 3 September 1952. The Conventions came into force for Rwanda retroactively as from 1 July 1962, the date on which that country became independent.

72 On 14 February 1986, Saint Kitts and Nevis deposited with the Swiss Government a declaration of succession to the four Geneva Conventions of 12 August 1949 for the Protection of War Victims. The declaration took effect retroactively as from 19 September 1983, the date on which Saint Kitts and Nevis became independent (notification of the depositary to the ICRC of 17 February 1986).

73 On 18 September 1981, the Swiss Government received an instrument dated 14 September of that year by which Saint Lucia declared its succession to the four Geneva Conventions of 12 August 1949 for the Protection of War Victims, by virtue of their ratification by the United Kingdom of Great Britain and Northern Ireland. This declaration took effect retroactively as from 22 February 1979, the date on which Saint Lucia became independent.

74 The Swiss Government received from the independent state of Western Samoa an instrument of succession, without reservations, to the four Geneva Conventions of 1949. This instrument was dated 1 August 1984 and was registered on 23 August of that year. The four Geneva Conventions took effect for Western Samoa retroactively as from 1 January 1962, the date on which that country became independent.

75 In a note dated 23 April 1963 and which the Swiss Federal Council received on 18 May of that year, the Senegalese Government declared that state to be party to the Conventions by virtue of those instruments' ratification by France on 28 June 1951. The Conventions came into force for Senegal retroactively as from 20 June 1960, the date on which that country became independent.

State	*Signature*[2]	*Ratification, Accession or Notification of Succession (C)*[3]
Seychelles	–	8 November 1984
Sierra Leone	–	31 May 1965 (C)[76]
Singapore	–	27 April 1973
Slovakia	–	2 April 1993 (C) *Res.*[77]
Slovenia	–	26 March 1992 (C)[78]
Solomon Islands	–	6 July 1981 (C)[79]
Somalia	–	12 July 1962
South Africa	–	31 March 1952[80]
Spain	8 December 1949 *Res.*	4 August 1952[81]
Sri Lanka	8 December 1949 (*Conventions I, II, III*)	28 February 1959 (*Conventions I, II, III*) 23 February 1959 (*Convention IV*)
Sudan	–	23 September 1957
Surinam	–	13 October 1976 (C) *Res.*[82]
Swaziland	–	28 June 1973
Sweden	8 December 1949	28 December 1953

[76] In a note dated 31 May 1965 and received by the Swiss Federal Council on 10 June of that year, the Government of Sierra Leone declared that state to be party to the four Conventions by virtue of their ratification by the United Kingdom of Great Britain and Northern Ireland on 23 September 1957. The Conventions entered into force for Sierra Leone retroactively as from 27 April 1961, the date on which that country became independent.

[77] Slovakia made on 2 April 1993 a declaration of succession to the 1949 Geneva Conventions and maintained the reservations made formally by Czechoslovakia. The succession took effect on 1 January 1993, the date of the accession to independence (communication of the depositary to the ICRC of 5 April 1993).

[78] On 26 March 1992, Slovenia transmitted to the Swiss Federal Council its notification of succession to the four 1949 Geneva Conventions and to the two Additional Protocols by virtue of their ratification by Yugoslavia, without the reservations and declarations made by Yugoslavia at the moment of ratification and without formulating new reservations. The Republic of Slovenia became party to the Conventions and Protocols retroactively as from 25 June 1991, the date of accession to independence.

[79] By depositing instruments with the Swiss Government on 6 July 1981, the Solomon Islands declared that state's succession to the four Geneva Conventions of 12 August 1949 for the Protection of War Victims, by virtue of their previous ratification by the United Kingdom of Great Britain and Northern Ireland. This declaration took effect retroactively as from 7 July 1978, the date on which the Solomon Islands became independent.

[80] For the communication of South Africa concerning the accession of the United Nations Council for Namibia, see note 58 and p. 675.

South Africa made also objections to the accession of the People' Republic of Mongolia to the Conventions. The South African Department for Foreign Affairs notified the depositary that the South Africa does not recognize the Democratic Republic of Viet Nam and does not accept its accession to the Geneva Conventions (communication of the depositary to the ICRC of 27 August 1957). These two declarations are not reproduced in the present collection.

[81] Spain made two reservations at the signature of the third 1949 Geneva Convention relative to the treatment of prisoners of war (see p. 674). On ratification, it maintained the second reservation concerning the Article 99 of the third Convention. Later it withdrew this reservation by a communication received by the depositary on 5 January 1979. See p. 674.

[82] In a letter of 30 September 1976 addressed to the Swiss Federal Council and received on 13 October 1976, the Prime Minister of the Republic of Surinam declared that his State considered itself bound by the Geneva Conventions by virtue of the previous ratification by the Netherlands, with effect as from 25 November 1975, date of accession to independence. By notification of 25 October 1979, the Swiss Federal Department of Foreign Affairs informed the states parties that the declaration of succession includes the same reservation as the reservation of the Kingdom of the Netherlands. See p. 674.

State	*Signature*[2]	*Ratification, Accession or Notification of Succession (C)*[3]
Switzerland[83]	12 August 1949	31 March 1950
Syrian Arab Republic	12 August 1949	2 November 1953
Tajikistan	–	13 January 1993 (C)[84]
Tanzania, United Republic of	–	12 December 1962 (C)[85]
Thailand	–	29 December 1954
Togo	–	6 January 1962 (C)[86]
Tonga	–	13 April 1978 (C)[87]
Trinidad and Tobago	–	17 May 1963 (*Convention I*) 24 September 1963 (*Conventions II, III, IV*)
Tunisia	–	4 May 1957
Turkey	12 August 1949	10 February 1954
Turkmenistan	–	10 April 1992 (C)[88]
Tuvalu	–	19 February 1981 (C)[89]
Uganda	–	18 May 1964
Ukraine[90]	12 December 1949 *Res.*	3 August 1954 *Res.*

83 Switzerland, as party to the Geneva Conventions, made a declaration concerning the accession of the Republic of Guinea-Bissau (see note 37).

84 By a letter of 13 January 1993, the Ministry of Foreign Affairs of Tajikistan informed the Swiss Federal Department of Foreign Affairs that the Republic of Tajikistan succeed to the four Conventions of Geneva. No comment on the reservations and declaration made by the former Soviet Union, and no new reservations or declarations were made. As the date of succession was not mentioned, the depositary considers that the Conventions entered into force on 21December 1991, the date of signature of the Declaration of Alma-Ata creating the Commonwealth of Independent States (communication of the depositary to the ICRC of 14 January 1993).

85 In a note received by the Swiss Federal Council on 12 December 1962, the Government of Tanganyika declared that country to be party to the Conventions by virtue of those instruments' ratification by the United Kingdom of Great Britain and Northern Ireland on 23 September 1957. The Conventions came into force for Tanganyika (now United Republic of Tanzania) retroactively as from 9 December 1961, the date on which that country became independent.

86 In a note received by the Swiss Federal Council on 6 January 1962, the Government of Togo declared that country to be party to the Conventions by virtue of their ratification by France on 28 June 1951. This declaration took effect for Togo retroactively as from 27 April 1960, the date on which that country became independent.

87 In a note dated 22 March 1978 and received by the President of the Swiss Confederation on 13 April of that year, the Kingdom of Tonga declared that State to be bound by the four Geneva Conventions of 12 August 1949 for the Protection of War Victims, by virtue of their previous ratification by the United Kingdom of Great Britain and Northern Ireland. The Conventions came into force for Tonga retroactively on 4 June 1970, the date on which that country became independent.

88 On 10 April 1992, the Republic of Turkmenistan deposited with the Swiss Government the declaration of succession to the four Conventions of Geneva and Additional Protocols I and II, without any comment on the reservations and declarations made by the former USSR, and without new reservations or declarations. The succession became effective on 21 December 1991, the date of signature of the Declaration of Alma-Ata creating the Commonwealth of Independent States (communication of the depositary to the ICRC of 15 July and 24 September 1992 and to the states parties of 14 October 1992).

89 In a letter dated 9 February 1981 and received by the Swiss Federal Council on 19 February of that year, the Government of Tuvalu declared that that State considered itself bound by the four Geneva Conventions of 12 August 1949 for the Protection of War Victims, by virtue of their previous ratification by the United Kingdom of Great Britain and Northern Ireland. This declaration took effect retroactively as from 1 October 1978, the date on which Tuvalu became independent.

90 The Soviet Socialist Republic of Ukraine made a declaration on the accession of the Republic of Korea (this declaration is not reproduced in the present collection). On 16 August 1974,

State	Signature[2]	Ratification, Accession or Notification of Succession (C)[3]
[USSR[91]	12 December 1949 *Res.*	10 May 1954 *Res*]
United Arab Emirates	–	10 May 1972
United Kingdom[92]	8 December 1949 *Res.*	23 September 1957[93]
United States of America[94]	12 August 1949 (*Conventions I, II, III*)	2 August 1949 *Res.*
	8 December 1949 *Res.* (*Convention IV*)	2 August 1949 *Res.*
Uruguay	12 August 1949	5 March 1969 *Res.*
Uzbekistan	–	8 October 1993
Vanuatu	–	27 October 1982
Venezuela	10 February 1950	13 February 1956
Vietnam, Socialist Republic of[95]	–	4 July 1976 (C) *Res.*

cont.
it transmitted to the depositary a declaration concerning the objections of some States to the accession of the Provisional Revolutionary Government of the Republic of South Viet Nam. See p. 676.

91 See note 69 on p. 645.

92 This ratification was also applicable in respect of Bahrain, Kuwait, Qatar, and the Trucial States to the extent of Her Majesty's powers in relation to those territories.

93 On ratification, United Kingdom expressed objections to the reservations presented by Albania, Byelorussian SSR, Bulgaria, Czechoslovakia, Hungary, Poland, Romania, Ukrainian SSR, USSR and Federal People's Republic of Yugoslavia. See p. 678.

By a note dated 14 December 1971, received on 15th of the same month, Her Britannic Majesty's Embassy in Berne notified the Federal Political Department of the withdrawal of the reservation made by the United Kingdom of Great Britain and Northern Ireland at the time of signature on 12 August 1949 of the Convention relative to the Protection of Civilian Persons in Time of War which was confirmed on its ratification. See pp. 678–679.

The Government of the United Kingdom made objections to reservations made by the People's Republic of Angola, Guinea-Bissau, Provisional Revolutionary Government of South Viet Nam, the German Democratic Republic and the Democratic Republic of Viet Nam (notification addressed to the Swiss Government on 19 November 1975). See p. 679.

On 13 June 1997, the British Ambassador to Switzerland deposited with the Swiss Government a declaration concerning the responsibility for Hong Kong. See p. 680.

94 See note of the Embassy of the United States of America of 2 September 1955 concerning the reservations to the Conventions. See p. 681.

The United States made a declaration concerning the accession of the Democratic Republic of Viet Nam, of the Provisions Revolutionary Government of the Republic of South Viet Nam and made objections to the reservations made upon accession by Guinea-Bissau, see p. 682.

The United States of America also made declarations concerning the ratification of the Conventions by German Democratic Republic, People's Republic of China, and concerning the accession of the People's Republic of Mongolia. The depositary indicated that as the scope of application of the Geneva Conventions was not modified, it will not proceed to the notification of this declaration to the states parties to the Conventions. These declarations are not reproduced in the present collection.

95 On 4 July 1976, following the unification of Viet Nam, the Minister of Foreign Affairs of the Socialist Republic of Viet Nam sent a letter to the head of the Swiss Federal Political Department containing the following declaration: "The Socialist Republic of Viet Nam will continue the participation of the Democratic Republic of Viet Nam and of the Republic of South Viet Nam in the four Geneva Conventions of 1949 concerning the Protection of War Victims with the same reservations as those set forth by the Democratic Republic of Viet Nam and the Republic of South Viet Nam" (*UNTS*, Vol. 1028, 1976, p. 438). On 3 December 1973, the Provisional Revolutionary Government in the Republic of Vietnam acceded to the Conventions. This elicited declarations from the following states: the Federal Republic of Germany, Brazil, the United States, Portugal and the Republic of Vietnam. Other states made objections to those declarations: Hungary, Mongolia, Poland, the German Democratic Republic, Romania, the Ukrainian SSR and the USSR.

State	*Signature*[2]	*Ratification, Accession or Notification of Succession (C)*[3]
Yemen[96]	–	16 July 1970
Yugoslavia[97]	–	16 October 2001
Zambia	–	19 October 1966
Zimbabwe	–	7 March 1983

* * *

Palestine Liberation Organization	–	21 June 1989[98]

---

cont.

See also the text of the reservations made by the Socialist Republic of Viet-Nam (pp. 683–684), the Provisional Revolutionary Government of South Viet Nam (pp. 684–685), the Republic of Viet Nam (pp. 683–684) and the Republic of South Viet Nam (pp. 686–687).

96 The Arab Republic of Yemen acceded to the Geneva Conventions on 16 July 1970. The People's Democratic Republic of Yemen acceded to the Conventions on 25 May 1977 with a declaration. See p. 687. In a letter dated 19 May 1990, the Ministers of Foreign Affairs of the Yemen Arab Republic and the People's Democratic Republic of Yemen informed the Secretary-General of the United Nations of the following: " All treaties and agreements concluded between either the Yemen Arab Republic or the People's Democratic Republic of Yemen and other States and international organizations in accordance with international law which are in force on 22 May 1990 will remain in effect, and international relations existing on 22 May 1990 between the People's Democratic Republic of Yemen and the Yemen Arab Republic and other States will continue." As concerns the treaties concluded prior to their union by the Yemen Arab Republic or the People's Democratic Republic of Yemen, theRepublic of Yemen (as now united) is accordingly to be considered as a party to those treaties as from the date when one of these states first became a party to those treaties (*Multilateral Treaties Deposited with the Secretary-General, New York, United Nations* (ST/LEG/SER.E).

97 See explanatory note in document *No. 61*, note 16, p. 850.

98 On 21 June 1989, the Swiss Federal Department of Foreign Affairs received a letter from the Permanent observer of Palestine to the United Nations Office at Geneva informing the Swiss Federal Council "that the Executive Committee of the Palestine Liberation Organization, entrusted with the functions of the Government of the State of Palestine by decision of the Palestine National Council, decided, on 4 May 1989, to adhere to the Four Geneva Conventions of 12 August 1949 and the two Protocols additional thereto." On 13 September 1989, the Federal Department sent a note of information concerning this letter to the governments of the states parties to the Geneva Conventions, together with the text of the letter. The text of the note of information reads as follows:

"On 21 June 1989, the Permanent observer of Palestine to the Office of the United Nations at Geneva transmitted to the Federal Department of Foreign Affairs, through the intermediary of the Permanent Mission of Switzerland to the international organizations in Geneva, a communication concerning the participation of Palestine in the four Geneva Conventions of 12 August 1949 and their two Additional Protocols of 8 June 1977.

Due to the uncertainty within the international community as to the existence or non-existence of a State of Palestine, and as long as the issue has not been settled in an appropriate framework, the Swiss Government, in its capacity as depositary of the Geneva Conventions and their Additional Protocols, is not in a position to decide whether this communication can be considered as an instrument of accession in the sense of the relevant provisions of the Conventions and their Additional Protocols.

The Federal Department of Foreign Affaits, following the practice relating to the functions of the depositary State as codified in the Vienna Convention on the Law of Treaties of 23 May 1969, transmits to the Governments of the States parties to the Geneva Conventions, for their information, a copy of this communication attached hereto, in the original Arabic and in an English translation.

The unilateral declaration of application of the four Geneva Conventions and of Additional Protocol I made on 7 June 1982 by the Palestine Liberation Organization remains valid.

Berne, 13 September 1989."

RESERVATIONS AND DECLARATIONS[1]

concerning the four Geneva Conventions of 12 August 1949

PEOPLE'S REPUBLIC OF ALBANIA (*reservation made on signature and maintained on ratification*)[2]
Mr. Malo, First Secretary of the Albanian Legation in Paris:

1. *Convention for the Amelioration of the Condition of the Wounded and Sick in Armed Forces in the Field*
   Article 10: The People's Republic of Albania will not recognize a request by a Detaining Power to a humanitarian organization or to a neutral State to take the place of a Protecting Power, as being in order, unless the Power of which the protected persons are nationals has given its consent.
2. *Convention for the Amelioration of the Condition of Wounded, Sick and Shipwrecked Members of Armed Forces at Sea*
   Article 10: The People's Republic of Albania will not recognize a request by a Detaining Power to a humanitarian organization or to a neutral State to take the place of a Protecting Power, as being in order, unless the Power of which the protected persons are nationals has given its consent.
3. *Convention relative to the Treatment of Prisoners of War*
   Article 10: The People's Republic of Albania will not recognize a request by a Detaining Power to a humanitarian organization or to a neutral State to take the place of a Protecting Power, as being in order, unless the Power of which the prisoners of war are nationals has given its consent.
   Article 12: The People's Republic of Albania considers that in the case of prisoners of war being transferred to another Power by the Detaining Power, the responsibility for the application of the Convention to such prisoners of war will continue to rest with the Power which captured them.
   Article 85: The People's Republic of Albania considers that persons convicted under the law of the Detaining Power in accordance with the principles of the Nuremberg trial, of war crimes and crimes against humanity, must be treated in the same manner as persons convicted in the country in question. Albania does not, therefore, consider herself bound by Article 85 so far as the category of persons mentioned in the present reservation is concerned.
4. *Convention relative to the Protection of Civilian Persons in Time of War*
   Article 11: The People's Republic of Albania will not recognize a request by a Detaining Power to a humanitarian organization or to a neutral State to take the place of a Protecting Power, as being in order, unless the Power of which the protected persons are nationals has given its consent.
   Article 45: The People's Republic of Albania considers that in the case of protected persons being transferred to another Power by the Detaining Power, the responsibility for the application of the Convention to such protected persons will continue to rest with the Detaining Power.

ANGOLA (*reservation made on accession*)[3] [4]
In acceding to the Geneva Conventions of 12 August 1949, the People's Republic of Angola reserves the right not to extend the benefits deriving from Article 85 of the Convention concerning the treatment of prisoners of war to persons who have commit-

---

1 Unless otherwise indicated, the English text of the reservations and declarations is reproduced from *Final Record of the Diplomatic Conference of Geneva of 1949*, Vol. I, Berne, Federal Political Department, 1950.

2 For objections to this reservation made by Australia, Barbados, New Zealand and United Kingdom, see pp. 651, 653, 668 and 678.

3 *IRRC,* September-October 1984, No. 242, p. 287; *UNTS,* Vol. 1372, 1984, p. 49.

4 For objections of the United Kingdom of 28 March 1985, see p. 679.

ted war crimes and crimes against humanity as defined in Article VI of the Nuremberg Principles as formulated in 1950 by the International Law Commission on the instructions of the United Nations General Assembly.

ARGENTINA (*reservation made on signature*)
Mr. Speroni, First Secretary of the Argentine Legation in Berne, made the following reservation to the four Geneva Conventions:
The Argentine Government has followed the work of the Conference with interest and the Argentine Delegation has taken part in it with pleasure. The task was a difficult one, but as our President said at the closing meeting, we have succeeded.

Argentina, Gentlemen, has always taken a leading place among many other nations on the questions which have formed the subject of our discussions. I shall, therefore, sign the four Conventions in the name of my Government and subject to ratification with the reservation that Article 3, common to all four Conventions, shall be the only Article, to the exclusion of all others, which shall be applicable in the case of armed conflicts not of an international character. I shall likewise sign the Convention relative to the Protection of Civilian Persons with a reservation in respect of Article 68.
This reservation made on signature was not maintained at ratification.[5]

AUSTRALIA
Reservation made on signature
When signing, the Australian plenipotentiary declared that his government retained the right to enter reservations at the time of ratification.

Reservations and statement made when depositing the instrument of ratification[6]
Whereas at Berne on the fourth day of January, One thousand nine hundred and fifty the duly accredited Plenipotentiary of the Government of the Commonwealth of Australia signed for and on behalf of and subject to ratification by the said Government the following Conventions which were concluded at Geneva on the twelfth day of August, One thousand nine hundred and forty-nine:

And whereas the said Plenipotentiary declared at the time of signing the said Conventions that the Government of the Commonwealth of Australia reserved the right to enter reservations at the time of ratification;

The Government of the Commonwealth of Australia having considered the said Conventions hereby, subject to the reservation and declaration herein made, confirms and ratifies the same and undertakes faithfully to carry out all the stipulations therein contained.

In ratifying the *Geneva Convention relative to the Protection of Civilian Persons in Time of War*, the Government of the Commonwealth of Australia reserves the right to impose the death penalty in accordance with the provisions of paragraph 2 of Article 68 of the said Convention without regard to whether the offences referred to therein are punishable by death under the law of the occupied territory at the time the occupation begins and declares that it interprets the term “military installations” in paragraph 2 of Article 68 of the said Convention as meaning installations having an essential military interest for an Occupying Power.

Statement
On depositing the Ratification by the Commonwealth of Australia of the following Conventions which were concluded at Geneva on the twelfth day of August, One thousand nine hundred and forty-nine:

I am instructed by the Government of the Commonwealth of Australia to refer to the reservations made to Article 85 of the *Convention relative to the Treatment of Prisoners of War* by the following:

The People’s Republic of Albania
The Byelorussian Soviet Socialist Republic

---

5 Notification of the depositary to ICRC of 18 October 1976.
6 Original: English. *UNTS*, Vol. 314, 1958, pp. 333–334.

The Bulgarian People's Republic
The Czechoslovak Republic
The Hungarian People's Republic
The Polish Republic
The Romanian People's Republic
The Ukrainian Soviet Socialist Republic
The Union of Soviet Socialist Republics

and to the reservations to *Article 12* of the *Convention relative to the Treatment of Prisoners of War* and to *Article 45* of the *Convention relative to the Treatment of Civilian Persons in Time of War* made by all the above-mentioned and by the Federal People's Republic of Yugoslavia.

I am instructed by the Government of the Commonwealth of Australia to state that whilst they regard all the above-mentioned as being parties to the above-mentioned Conventions they do not regard the above-mentioned reservations as valid and will therefore regard any application of any of those reservations as constituting a breach of the Convention to which the reservation relates.

I am further instructed by the Government of the Commonwealth of Australia to refer to notifications concerning the "German Democratic Republic", the "Democratic People's Republic of Korea", the "Democratic Republic of Vietnam" and the "People's Republic of China". While the Government of the Commonwealth of Australia does not recognize any of the foregoing it has taken note of their acceptance of the provisions of the Conventions and their intention to apply them. The position of the Government of the Commonwealth of Australia towards the reservations referred to above applies equally in relation to the similar reservations attached to such acceptance.

By an act dated 20 February 1974, received on 21st of the same month, the Minister of Foreign Affairs of the Commonwealth of Australia notified the Swiss Federal Political Department of the partial withdrawal of the reservation[7] *made by the Government of Australia at the time of ratification, on 14 October 1958, of the Convention relative to the Protection of Civilian Persons in Time of War. The reservation withdrawn was as follows*:
In ratifying the *Geneva Convention relative to the Protection of Civilian Persons in Time of War*, the Government of the Commonwealth of Australia reserves the right to impose the death penalty in accordance with the provisions of paragraph 2 of Article 68 of the said Convention without regard to whether the offences referred to therein are punishable by death under the law of the occupied territory at the time the occupation begins.

BANGLADESH (*note of the Permanent Mission of the People's Republic of Bangladesh in Geneva, of 20 December 1988, addressed to the Permanent Mission of Switzerland in Geneva*)[8]
The Permanent Mission of the People's Republic of Bangladesh to the United Nations Office and other International Organisations in Geneva presents its compliments to the Permanent Mission of Switzerland and has the honour to inform that the Government of Bangladesh has decided sometime ago that henceforth the Bangladesh Red Cross Society will be known as Bangladesh Red Crescent Society. The Government of Bangladesh has also adopted the Red Crescent emblem in place of Red Cross for the Bangladesh National Society and for the medical services of the Bangladesh Armed Forces. This has already been communicated to the International Committee of Red Cross and the League of Red Cross. Copies of the relevant ordinance and the specimen of the changed emblem are enclosed.[9]

It will be highly appreciated if the concerned authorities in Switzerland, as the depository State of the Geneva Conventions of August 12, 1949 could make the necessary announcement to all States parties to the Convention in this regard.

---

7 Notification of the depositary to the ICRC of 30 August 1974; *UNTS*, Vol. 914, p. 310.
8 Original: English. Notification of the depositary to the ICRC of 9 January 1989.
9 The ordinance was published in the Bangladesh Gazette on 4 April 1988. It is not reproduced in this collection.

BARBADOS (*declaration made at succession*)[10]
The Government of Barbados notes that the following countries have made reservations with respect to *Article 85* of the *Convention Relative to the Treatment of Prisoners of War*, Albania, Byelorussia, Bulgaria, Czechoslovakia, Poland, Rumania, Ukraine, and Soviet Union; and Yugoslavia has made reservations with respect to *Article 12* of the *Convention Relative to the Treatment of Prisoners of War* and to *Article 45* of the *Convention Relative to the Treatment of Civilian Persons in Time of War*. The Government of Barbados states that whilst it regards all the above mentioned States as being parties to above mentioned Conventions it does not regard the above mentioned reservations thereto made by those States as valid and will therefore regard any application of any of those reservations as constituting a breach of the Convention to which the reservation relates.

The Government of Barbados notes that the People's Republic of China has deposited a reservation in respect to *Article 85* of the *Convention Relative to the treatment of Prisoners of War* but considers that China is a party to the Convention and does not accept the validity of any reservations made the Government of the People Republic.

BELARUS (*reservations made on signature and maintained on ratification*)[11]
Mr. Kouteinikov, Head of the Delegation of the Soviet Socialist Republic of Byelorussia:

1. On signing the *Convention for the Amelioration of the Condition of the Wounded and Sick in Armed Forces in the Field*, the Government of the Byelorussian Soviet Socialist Republic makes the following reservation:
   Article 10: The Byelorussian Soviet Socialist Republic will not recognize the validity of requests by the Detaining Power to a neutral State or to a humanitarian organization, to undertake the functions performed by a Protecting Power, unless the consent of the Government of the country of which the protected persons are nationals has been obtained.
2. On signing the *Convention for the Amelioration of the Condition of Wounded, Sick and Shipwrecked Members of Armed Forces at Sea*, the Government of the Byelorussian Soviet Socialist Republic makes the following reservation:
   Article 10: The Byelorussian Soviet Socialist Republic will not recognize the validity of requests by the Detaining Power to a neutral State or to a humanitarian organization, to undertake the functions performed by a Protecting Power, unless the consent of the Government of the country of which the protected persons are nationals has been obtained.
3. On signing the *Convention relative to the Treatment of Prisoners of War*, the Government of the Byelorussian Soviet Socialist Republic makes the following reservations:
   Article 10: The Byelorussian Soviet Socialist Republic will not recognize the validity of requests by the Detaining Power to a neutral State or to a humanitarian organization, to undertake the functions performed by a Protecting Power, unless the consent of the Government of the country of which the prisoners of war are nationals has been obtained.
   Article 12: The Byelorussian Soviet Socialist Republic does not consider as valid the freeing of a Detaining Power, which has transfer-red prisoners of war to another Power, from responsibility for the application of the Convention to such prisoners of war while the latter are in the custody of the Power accepting them.
   Article 85: The Byelorussian Soviet Socialist Republic does not consider itself bound by the obligation, which follows from Article 85, to extend the application of the Convention to prisoners of war who have been convicted under the law of the Detaining Power, in accordance with the principles of the Nuremberg trial, for war crimes and crimes against humanity, it being understood that persons convicted of

[10] Notification by the depositary addressed to the ICRC on 12 Deceember 1968: *UNTS*, Vol. 653, 1968, p. 454.

[11] For the objections of Australia, Barbados, New Zealand and United Kingdom, see pp. 652, 653, 668 and 678.

such crimes must be subject to the conditions obtaining in the country in question for those who undergo their punishment.

4. On signing the *Convention relative to the Protection of Civilian Persons in Time of War*, the Government of the Byelorussian Soviet Socialist Republic feels called upon to make the following declaration:

   Although the present Convention does not cover the civilian population in territory not occupied by the enemy and does not, therefore, completely meet humanitarian requirements, the Byelorussian Delegation, recognizing that the said Convention makes satisfactory provision for the protection of the civilian population in occupied territory and in certain other cases, declares that it is authorized by the Government of the Byelorussian Soviet Socialist Republic to sign the present Convention with the following reservations:

   Article 11: The Byelorussian Soviet Socialist Republic will not recognize the validity of requests by the Detaining Power to a neutral State or to a humanitarian organization, to undertake the functions performed by a Protecting Power, unless the consent of the Government of the country of which the protected persons are nationals has been obtained.

   Article 45: The Byelorussian Soviet Socialist Republic will not consider as valid the freeing of a Detaining Power, which has transferred protected persons to another Power, from responsibility for the application of the Convention to the persons transferred, while the latter are in the custody of the Power accepting them.

The Republic of Belarus has withdrawn on 7 August 2001 the reservations made at the signature of the four Geneva Conventions.

BRAZIL (*reservation made on signature*)
Mr. Pinto da Silva, Consul-General of Brazil at Geneva, made the following reservations to the Geneva Convention relative to the Protection of Civilian Persons in Time of War:
On signing the *Convention relative to the Protection of Civilian Persons in Time of War*, Brazil wishes to make two express reservations in regard to *Article 44* because it is liable to hamper the action of the Detaining Power and in regard to *Article 46* because the matter dealt with in its second paragraph is outside the scope of the Convention, the essential and specific purpose of which is the protection of persons and not of their property.

Objection to the accession of the Republic of South Viet Nam in respect of the 1949 Geneva Conventions, notified by the Swiss Government on 21 March 1974: [12] [13]
[S]ince the Government of the Federative Republic of Brazil does not recognize the "Revolutionary Government of Viet Nam" as constituting a State, the declaration of accession to the 1949 Geneva Conventions made by that entity can in no circumstances be invoked vis-a-vis the Government of the Federative Republic of Brazil as creating any rights or duties.

Objection to the accession of the Republic of Guinea-Bissau in respect of the 1949 Geneva Conventions, notified by the Swiss Government on 21 March 1974: [14] [15]
[S]ince the Government of the Federative Republic of Brazil does not recognize the existence of the "Republic of Guinea-Bissau as a State, the declaration of accession to

[12] Translation supplied by the Government of Switzerland and published in *UNTS*, Vol. 941, 1974, pp. 320–321.

[13] Several states made declarations in respect of the objection to the accession of the Revolutionary Government of South Viet Nam; see in particular the declarations of [German Democratic Republic], Hungary, Mongolia, Poland, Romania, Ukraine and [USSR], see pp. 660, 663, 667, 671, 674, 676–678.

[14] Translation supplied by the Government of Switzerland and published in *UNTS*, Vol. 941, 1974, pp. 321–322.

[15] Several states made declarations in respect of the objection to the accession of the Government of Guinea-Bissau; see in particular the declarations of Mongolia and Poland.

the 1949 Geneva Conventions made by that entity can in no circumstances be invoked vis-a-vis the Government of the Federative Republic of Brazil as creating any rights or duties.

BULGARIAN PEOPLE'S REPUBLIC (*reservation made on signature and maintained on* ratification)[16]
Mr. Kosta B. Svetlov, Bulgarian Minister in Switzerland, made the following declaration: In my capacity as representative of the Government of the Bulgarian People's Republic, I have the pleasant duty of expressing here its satisfaction at having been able to take part in drawing up a humanitarian instrument of the highest international importance – a group of conventions for the protection of war victims.

Nevertheless, my wish is that there shall be no need to apply them, that – is to say – that we may exert every effort to prevent a new war, so that there may be no victims to be helped in accordance with the provisions of a convention.

I must, first of all, express my Government's deep regret that the majority of the Diplomatic Conference did not accept the Soviet Delegation's proposal for the unconditional banning of atomic weapons and other weapons for the mass extermination of the population.

Therefore, on signing the Conventions the Government of the Bulgarian People's Republic makes the following reservations, which constitute an integral part of the Conventions:

1. *Convention relative to the Protection of Civilian Persons in Time of War* of 12 August 1949
   On signing the present Convention, the Government of the Bulgarian People's Republic makes the following reservations, which constitute an integral part of the Convention:
   With regard to Article 11: The Bulgarian People's Republic will not recognize as valid the action of a Detaining Power of civilian persons in time of war, in approaching a neutral Power or a humanitarian organization with a view to entrusting it with the protection of such persons without the consent of the Government of the country of which the latter are nationals.
   With regard to Article 45: The Bulgarian People's Republic will not consider the Detaining Power of civilian persons in time of war, which has transferred such persons to another Power which has agreed to accept them, as being freed from responsibility for applying the provisions of the Convention to such persons during the time that they are detained by the other Power.
2. *Convention for the Amelioration of the Condition of Wounded, Sick and Shipwrecked Members of Armed Forces at Sea* of 12 August 1949
   On signing the present Convention, the Government of the Bulgarian People's Republic makes the following reservation which constitutes an integral part of the Convention:
   With regard to Article 10: The Bulgarian People's Republic will not recognize as valid the action of a Detaining Power of wounded, sick and shipwrecked persons or of medical personnel of armed forces at sea, in approaching a neutral Power or a humanitarian organization, with a view to entrusting it with the protection of such persons without the consent of the Government of the country of which the latter are nationals.
3. *Convention relative to the Treatment of Prisoners of War* of 12 August 1949
   On signing the present Convention, the Government of the Bulgarian People's Republic makes the following reservations, which constitute an integral part of the Convention:
   With regard to Article 10: The Bulgarian People's Republic will not recognize as valid the action of a Detaining Power of prisoners of war, in approaching a neutral

[16] For the objections made by Australia, Barbados, New Zealand and United Kingdom, see pp. 652, 653, 668 and 678.

Power or a humanitarian organization with a view to entrusting it with the protection of such persons without the consent of the Government of the country of which the latter are nationals.

With regard to Article 12: The Bulgarian People's Republic will not consider the Detaining Power of prisoners of war, which has transferred such persons to another Power which has agreed to accept them, as being freed from responsibility for applying the provisions of the Convention to such persons during the time that they are detained by the other Power.

With regard to Article 85: The Bulgarian People's Republic does not consider itself bound to extend the application of the provisions derived from Article 85 to prisoners of war convicted, under the law of the Detaining Power and in accordance with the principles of the Nuremberg trial, of war crimes or crimes against humanity which they committed before being taken prisoner, because those thus convicted must be subject to the regulations of the country in which they have to serve their sentence.

4. *Convention for the Amelioration of the Condition of the Wounded and Sick in Armed Forces in the Field* of 12 August 1949

On signing the present Convention, the Government of the Bulgarian People's Republic makes the following reservation, which constitutes an integral part of the Convention.

With regard to Article 10: The Bulgarian People's Republic will not recognize as valid the action of a Detaining Power of wounded and sick persons or of medical personnel in armed forces in the field, in approaching a neutral Power or a humanitarian organization with a view to entrusting it with the protection of such persons without the consent of the Government of the country of which the latter are nationals.

Withdrawal of the reservations made on signature and ratification

The letter of the Minister of Foreign Affairs of the Republic of Bulgaria of 19 April 1994, received by the depositary on 9 May 1994:[17]

On behalf of the Republic of Bulgaria, I have an honour to declare that the National Assembly by its Law of 16 February 1994 decided to withdraw the reservations mentioned below, which were made by the Republic of Bulgaria at ratification of the Geneva Conventions of 12 August 1949, for which the Swiss Federal Council exercises the function of depositary:

Reservation concerning *Article 10* of the *Convention for the Amelioration of the Condition of the Wounded and Sick in Armed Forces in the Field.*

Reservation concerning *Article 10* of the *Convention for the Amelioration of the Condition of Wounded, Sick and Shipwrecked Members of Armed Forces at Sea.*

Reservations concerning *Articles 10, 12 and 85* of the *Convention relative to the Treatment of Prisoners of War.*

Reservations concerning *Articles 11 and 45* of the *Convention relative to the Protection of Civilian Persons in Time of War.*

CANADA (*reservation made when signing Geneva Convention IV relative to the Protection of Civilian Persons in Time of War*)

Mr. Wershof, Counsellor, Office of the High Commissioner for Canada in London, made the following reservation to the Geneva Convention for the Protection of Civilian Persons in Time of War:

Canada reserves the right to impose the death penalty in accordance with the provisions of *Article 68*, paragraph 2, without regard to whether the offences referred to therein are punishable by death under the law of the occupied territory at the time the occupation begins.

This reservation was withdrawn on ratification.[18]

[17] Notification of the depositary to the ICRC of 11 May 1994. Translated by editors from French.

[18] Notification of the depositary to the ICRC of 31 May 1965.

CHINA, PEOPLE'S REPUBLIC of (*reservation made on ratification*)[19] [20]

1. *Regarding Article 10* of the *Geneva Convention for the Amelioration of the Condition of the Wounded and Sick in Armed Forces in the Field* of 12 August 1949, the People's Republic of China will not recognize as valid a request by the Detaining Power of the wounded and sick, or medical personnel and chaplains to a neutral State or to a humanitarian organization, to undertake the functions which should be performed by a Protecting Power, unless the consent has been obtained of the government of the State of which the protected persons are nationals.
2. *Regarding Article 10* of the *Geneva Convention for the Amelioration of the Condition of the Wounded, Sick and Shipwrecked Members of Armed Forces at Sea* of 12 August 1949, the People's Republic of China will not recognize as valid a request by the Detaining Power of the wounded, sick and shipwrecked, or medical personnel and chaplains to a neutral State or to a humanitarian organization, to undertake the functions which should be performed by a Protecting Power, unless the consent has been obtained of the government of the State of which the protected persons are nationals.
3. *Regarding Article 10* of the *Geneva Convention relative to the Treatment of Prisoners of War* of 12 August 1949, the People's Republic of China will not recognize as valid a request by the Detaining Power of prisoners of war to a neutral State or to a humanitarian organization, to undertake the functions which should be performed by a Protecting Power, unless the consent has been obtained of the government of the State of which the prisoners of war are nationals.

   Regarding Article 12, the People's Republic of China holds that the original Detaining Power which has transferred prisoners of war to another Contracting Power, is not for that reason freed from its responsibility for the application of the Convention while such prisoners of war are in the custody of the Power accepting them. *Regarding Article 85*, the People's Republic of China is not bound by Article 85 in respect of the treatment of prisoners of war convicted under the laws of the Detaining Power in accordance with the principles laid down in the trials of war crimes or crimes against humanity by the Nuremberg and the Tokyo International Military Tribunals.
4. Although the *Geneva Convention relative to the Protection of Civilian Persons in Time of War* of 12 August 1949 does not apply to civilian persons outside enemy-occupied areas and consequently does not completely meet humanitarian requirements, it is found to be in accord with the interest of protecting civilian persons in occupied territory and in certain other cases, hence it is ratified with the following reservations:

   Regarding Article 11: The People's Republic of China will not recognize as valid a request by the Detaining Power of protected persons to a neutral State or to a humanitarian organization, to undertake the functions which should be performed by a Protecting Power, unless the consent has been obtained of the government of the State of which the protected persons are nationals.

   Regarding Article 45: The People's Republic of China holds that the original Detaining Power which has transferred protected persons to another Contracting Power, is not for that reason freed from its responsibility for the application of the Convention while such protected persons are in the custody of the Power accepting them."

[CZECHOSLOVAKIA] (*reservation made on signature and maintained on ratification*)[21]
Mr. Tsauber, Minister of Czechoslovakia in Switzerland, made the following reservations:

1. On proceeding to sign the *Geneva Convention for the Amelioration of the Condition of the Wounded and Sick in Armed Forces in the Field*, I declare that the Govern-

[19] *UNTS*, Vol. 260, 1957, pp. 438–444.
[20] For the objections made by Australia and United Kingdom, see pp. 652 and 678.
[21] For the objections made by Australia, Barbados, New Zealand and United Kingdom, see pp. 652, 653, 668 and 678.

ment of the Czechoslovakian Republic adheres to the said Convention, with a reservation in respect of Article 10.

The Government of the Czechoslovakian Republic will not consider as legal a request by the Detaining Power that a neutral State or an international organization or a humanitarian organization should undertake the functions performed under the present Convention by the Protecting Powers, on behalf of the wounded and sick, or medical personnel and chaplains, unless the Government whose nationals they are has given its consent.

2. On proceeding to sign the *Geneva Convention for the Amelioration of the Condition of Wounded, Sick and Shipwrecked Members of Armed Forces at Sea*, I declare that the Government of the Czechoslovakian Republic adheres to the said Convention, with a reservation in respect of Article 10.
   The Government of the Czechoslovakian Republic will not consider as legal a request by the Detaining Power that a neutral State or an international organization or a humanitarian organization should undertake the functions performed under the present Convention by the Protecting Powers, on behalf of the wounded, sick and shipwrecked, or medical personnel and chaplains, unless the Government whose nationals they are has given its consent.
3. On proceeding to sign the *Geneva Convention relative to the Treatment of Prisoners of War*, I declare that the Government of the Czechoslovakian Republic adheres to the said Convention, with reservations in respect of Articles 10, 12 and 85.
   In regard to Article 10: The Government of the Czechoslovakian Republic will not consider as legal a request by the Detaining Power that a neutral State or an international organization or a humanitarian organization should undertake the functions performed under the present Convention by the Protecting Powers, on behalf of prisoners of war, unless the Government whose nationals they are has given its consent.
   In regard to Article 12: The Government of the Czechoslovakian Republic will not consider it legal for a Power, which effects a transfer of prisoners of war, to be freed from its responsibility for applying the Convention, even for the time during which such prisoners of war are in the custody of the Power accepting them.
   In regard to Article 85: The Government of the Czechoslovakian Republic will not consider it legal for prisoners of war convicted of war crimes and crimes against humanity in accordance with the principles set forth at the time of the Nuremberg trials, to continue to enjoy protection under the present Convention, it being understood that prisoners of war convicted of such crimes must be subject to the regulations for the execution of punishments, in force in the State concerned.
4. On proceeding to sign the *Geneva Convention relative to the Protection of Civilian Persons in Time of War*, I declare that the Government of the Czechoslovakian Republic adheres to the said Convention, with reservations in respect of Articles 11 and 45.
   In regard to Article 11: The Government of the Czechoslovakian Republic will not consider as legal a request by the Detaining Power that a neutral State or an international organization or a humanitarian organization should undertake the functions performed under the present Convention by the Protecting Powers, on behalf of protected persons, unless the Government whose nationals they are has given its consent.
   In regard to Article 45: The Government of the Czechoslovakian Republic will not consider it legal for a Power, which effects a transfer of protected persons, to be freed from its responsibility for applying the Convention, even for the time during which such protected persons are in the custody of the Power accepting them."

CZECH REPUBLIC (*reservations maintained on succession*)
See the text of the reservations made by Czechoslovakia, pp. 657–658.

[GERMAN DEMOCRATIC REPUBLIC] (*reservations made on accession*)[22 23 24]
To the Geneva Convention of 12 August 1949 for the Amelioration of the Condition of the Wounded and Sick in Armed Forces in the Field,
To the Geneva Convention of 12 August 1949 for the Amelioration of the Condition of Wounded, Sick and Shipwrecked Members of Armed Forces at Sea,
To the Geneva Convention of 12 August 1949 relative to the Treatment of Prisoners of War,
To the Geneva Convention relative to the Protection of Civilian Persons in Time of War,
The German Democratic Republic makes the following reservations:

1. *Geneva Convention of 12 August 1949 for the Amelioration of the Condition of the Wounded and Sick in Armed Forces in the Field.*
   Ad Article 10: A request by the Detaining Power to a neutral State or an international or humanitarian organization, to undertake the functions entrusted to Protecting Powers by the provisions of the Convention will not be accepted as valid by the German Democratic Republic unless the consent of the Government of the country of which the protected persons are nationals has been obtained.
2. *Geneva Convention of 12 August 1949 for the Amelioration of the Condition of Wounded, Sick and Shipwrecked Members of Armed Forces at Sea.*
   Ad Article 10: A request by the Detaining Power to a neutral State or an international or humanitarian organization, to undertake the functions entrusted to Protecting Powers by the provisions of the Convention will not be accepted as valid by 'the German Democratic Republic unless the consent of the Government of the country of which the protected persons are nationals has been obtained.
3. *Geneva Convention of 12 August 1949 relative to the Treatment of Prisoners of War.*
   Ad Article 10*:* A request by the Detaining Power to a neutral State or an international or humanitarian organization, to undertake the functions entrusted to Protecting Powers by the provisions of the Convention will not be accepted as valid by the German Democratic Republic unless the consent of the Government of the country of which the protected persons are nationals has been obtained.
   Ad Article 12: The Government of the German Democratic Republic declares that the transfer of prisoners of war to another Power which is a Party to the Convention does not free the Detaining Power from responsibility for the application of the provisions of the Convention to such prisoners of war.
   Ad Article 85: The German Democratic Republic will not grant the benefit of Article 85 to prisoners of war who have been convicted of war crimes or crimes against humanity in accordance with the principles of the Nuremberg Judicial Tribunal and whose sentence is immediately enforceable.
4. *Geneva Convention of 12 August 1949 relative to the Protection of Civilian Persons in Time of War.*
   Ad Article 11: A request by the Detaining Power to a neutral State or an international or humanitarian organization to undertake the functions entrusted to Protecting Powers by the provisions of the Convention will not be accepted as valid by the German Democratic Republic unless the consent of the Government of the country of which the protected persons are nationals has been obtained.
   Ad Article 45: The Government of the German Democratic Republic declares that the transfer of protected persons to another Power which is a party to the Convention does not free the Detaining Power from responsibility for the application of the provisions of the Convention to such protected persons.

---

22 *UNTS*, Vol. 257, 1957, pp. 364–371.
23 See also note 35 on p. 640.
24 For objections made by Australia and United Kingdom, see pp. 652 and 678.

Declaration of 3 July 1974 relating to objections made in respect of the accession by the Provisional Revolutionary Government of the Republic of South Viet Nam[25] [26]
The notifications of the Embassy of the so-called Republic of Viet Nam in Berne, of the Ministry of Foreign Affairs of the Federative Republic of Brazil and of the Ministry of Foreign Affairs of the Portuguese Republic concerning the declaration made by the Provisional Revolutionary Government of South Viet Nam concerning its accession to the Geneva Conventions of 12 August 1949 for the protection of war victims have been transmitted to the Ministry of Foreign Affairs of the German Democratic Republic through the Swiss Embassy in Berlin with its notes of 15 February 1974 and 17 May 1974. In these notifications the Republic of South Viet Nam is denied the right to accede to the above-named Conventions and the declaration of accession is described as invalid. The Government of the German Democratic Republic is of the opinion that the assertions contained in the above mentioned notifications can in no way alter the legal position, which is that the Provisional Revolutionary Government of the Republic of South Viet Nam is a party, having equality of rights, to the Geneva Conventions of 1949.

GERMANY, FEDERAL REPUBLIC[27]
Declaration made on accession[28]
At accession on 3 December 1954, the Federal Republic of Germany stated that the Conventions are also applicable to Land Berlin.

Declaration relating to the accession of the Provisional Revolutionary Government of the Republic of South Viet Nam to 1949 Geneva Conventions, effected with the Government of Switzerland on 29 March 1974 and notified on 31 October 1974[29]
[T]hat the Federal Government /of FRG/ does not recognize the Provisional Revolutionary Government as being a body competent to represent a State and that, consequently, it is unable to consider the Provisional Revolutionary Government as a Party to the Geneva Conventions of 12 August 1949.

Objection to the reservation made upon accession by Guinea-Bissau to the Geneva Conventions I, II and III. Notification effected with the Government of Switzerland on 3 March 1975[30]
The reservation formulated in this connection by the Republic of Guinea-Bissau concerning
Article 13(2) of the first *Geneva Convention for the Amelioration of the Condition of the Wounded and Sick in Armed Forces in the Field*
Article 13(2) of the second *Geneva Convention for the Amelioration of the Condition of Wounded, Sick and Shipwrecked Members of Armed Forces at Sea*
Article 4(2) of the third *Geneva Convention relative to the Treatment of Prisoners of War*
exceeds, in the opinion of the Government of the Federal Republic of Germany, the purpose and intent of these Conventions and are therefore unacceptable to it. This declaration shall not otherwise affect the validity of the said Geneva Conventions under international law as between the Federal Republic of Germany and the Republic of Guinea-Bissau.

---

[25] See p. 684.
[26] For English text see *UNTS,* Vol. 949, 1974, p. 305.
[27] See also the reservation made by the German Democratic Republic (p. 659) and the explanatory note 35 on p. 640.
[28] Notification of the depositary to the ICRC of 22 December 1954; *UNTS*, Vol. 202, 1954–1955, pp. 330–333.
[29] Translation supplied by the Government of Switzerland and published in *UNTS*, Vol. 954, 1974, pp. 458–459.
[30] *UNTS*, Vol. 970, 1975, p. 367.

GUINEA-BISSAU (*reservation made on accession*)[31 32 33]

1. *Geneva Convention for the Amelioration of the Condition of the Wounded and Sick in Armed Forces of 12 August 1949.*
   To Article 10: The Council of State of the Republic of Guinea-Bissau does not recognize the legality of the request of a Detaining Power to a neutral country or to a humanitarian organization to undertake the functions of a Protecting Power unless the State on which the sick and wounded of armed forces in the field depend has, agreed to that request.
   To Article 13: The Council of State of the Republic of Guinea-Bissau does not recognize the "conditions" laid down in sub-paragraph 2 of this article concerning "members of other militias and members of other volunteer corps, including those of organized resistance movements", because those conditions are unsuited to wars conducted today by the people.
2. *Geneva Convention for the Amelioration of the Condition of the Wounded, Sick and Shipwrecked Members of Armed Forces in the Field of 12 August 1949.*
   To Article 10: The Council of State of the Republic of Guinea-Bissau does not recognize the legality of the request of a Detaining Power to a neutral country or to a humanitarian organization to undertake the functions of a Protecting Power unless the State on which the sick, wounded and shipwrecked persons depend, has agreed to that request.
   To Article 13: The Council of State of the Republic of Guinea-Bissau does not recognize the "conditions" laid down in sub-paragraph 2 of this article concerning "members of other militias and members of other volunteer corps, including those of organized resistance movements", because those conditions are unsuited to wars conducted today by the people.
3. *Geneva Convention relative to the Treatment of. Prisoners of War of 12 August 1949.*
   To Article 4: The Council of State of the Republic of Guinea-Bissau does not recognize the "conditions" laid down in sub-paragraph 2 of this article concerning "members of other militias and members of other volunteer corps, including those of organized resistance movements", because those conditions are unsuited to wars conducted today by the people.
   To Article 10: The Council of State of the Republic of Guinea-Bissau does not recognize the legality of the request of a Detaining Power to a neutral country or to a humanitarian organization to undertake the functions of a Protecting Power unless the State on which the prisoners depend has agreed to that request.
4. *Geneva Convention relative to the Protection of Civilian Persons in Time of War of 12 August 1949.*
   To Article 11: The Council of State of the Republic of Guinea-Bissau does not recognize the legality of the request of a Detaining Power to a neutral country or to a humanitarian organization to undertake the functions of a Protecting Power unless the State on which the said civilian persons depend has agreed to that request.

---

[31] Notification of the depositary to the ICRC of 26 February 1974; *UNTS*, Vol. 920, 1974, pp. 280–282.

[32] When the Government of the Republic of Guinea-Bissau notified the Swiss Government, on 26 February 1974, that it was acceding to the Geneva Conventions of 1949, Switzerland issued a declaration to the effect that it was taking note of the accession in its capacity as depositary of those Conventions, but that in its capacity as a state party to the Conventions it refrained from making any pronouncement on the status of Guinea-Bissau under international law.

[33] Brazil and Portugal both made declarations regarding Guinea-Bissau's accession. See pp. 654 and 672. Mongolia and Poland expressed objections to those declarations. See pp. 667 and 671. The Federal Republic of Germany, United Kingdom and United States of America made objections to the reservations formulated by the Republic of Guinea-Bissau in time of its accession. See pp. 660, 679, 682.

To Article 45: The Council of State of the Republic of Guinea-Bissau declares that the transfer of civilian persons protected by the present Convention to a Power which is a party to the Convention does not release the Detaining Power from the application of the provisions of this Convention.

HUNGARY (*reservation made on signature and maintained on ratification*)[34]
Mrs. Kara made the following reservations:
At the meeting of the Diplomatic Conference on 12 August 1949, the Delegation of the Hungarian People's Republic reserved the right to make express reservations on signing the Conventions, after having examined them. In their speech at the above meeting the Hungarian Delegation observed that they were not in agreement with all the provisions of the Conventions. After a thorough study of the text of the Conventions, the Government of the Hungarian People's Republic decided to sign the Conventions in spite of their obvious defects, as it considered that the Conventions constituted an advance in comparison with the existing situation from the point of view of the practical application of humanitarian principles and the protection of war victims.

The Government of the Hungarian People's Republic is obliged to state that the concrete results achieved by the Diplomatic Conference which ended on 12 August do not come up to expectations, since the majority of the members of the Conference did not adopt the proposals of the Soviet Delegation concerning the atomic weapon and other means of mass extermination of the population.

The Delegation of the Hungarian People's Republic noted with regret the point of view of the majority of the Conference, which was contrary to the wishes of the nations engaged in the struggle for peace and liberty. The Delegation of the Hungarian People's Republic is convinced that the adoption of the Soviet proposals would have been the most effective means of protecting war victims. The Delegation of the Hungarian People's Republic wishes, in particular, to point out the essential defects of the Convention relative to the Protection of Civilian Persons in Time of War; they drew the attention of the States taking part in the Conference to those defects during the meetings. A particular case in point is that of Article 4 of the Convention; by virtue of that Article the provisions of the Civilians Convention do not apply to certain persons, because the States whose nationals they are, have not adhered to the Convention. The Government of the Hungarian People's Republic considers that the above provision is contrary to the humanitarian principles which the Convention is intended to uphold.

The Hungarian People's Government has also serious objections to Article 5 of the said Convention: according to the terms of that Article, if protected persons are definitely suspected of activities hostile to the security of the State, that is enough to deprive them of protection under the Convention. The Government of the Hungarian People's Republic considers that that provision has already made any hope of realizing the fundamental principles of the Convention illusory.

The express reservations made by the Government of the Hungarian People's Republic on signing the Conventions, are as follows:

1. In the opinion of the Government of the Hungarian People's Republic, the provisions of *Article 10* of the *Wounded and Sick, Maritime Warfare and Prisoners of War Conventions* and of *Article 11* of the *Civilians Convention*, concerning the replacement of the Protecting Power, can only be applied if the Government of the State of which the protected persons are nationals, no longer exists.
2. The Government of the Hungarian People's Republic cannot approve the provisions of *Article 11* of the *Wounded and Sick, Maritime Warfare and Prisoners of War Conventions* and of *Article 12* of the *Civilians Convention*, according to which the competence of the Protecting Power extends to the interpretation of the Convention.
3. In regard to *Article 12* of the *Convention relative to the Treatment of Prisoners of War*, the Government of the Hungarian People's Republic maintains its point of view that in the case of the transfer of prisoners of war from one Power to another,

[34] For the objections to the reservations by Australia, New Zealand and the United Kingdom, see pp. 652, 668 and 678.

the responsibility for the application of the provisions of the Conventions must rest with both of those Powers.

4. The Delegation of the Hungarian People's Republic repeats the objection which it made, in the course of the meetings at which *Article 85* of the *Prisoners of War Convention* was discussed, to the effect that prisoners of war convicted of war crimes and crimes against humanity in accordance with the principles of Nuremberg, must be subject to the same treatment as criminals convicted of other crimes.
5. Lastly, the Government of the Hungarian People's Republic maintains the point of view which it expressed in regard to *Article 45* of the *Civilians Convention*, namely that, in the case of the transfer of protected persons from one Power to another, the responsibility for the application of the Convention must rest with both of those Powers.

Declaration relating to objections made in respect of the accession of the Provisional Revolutionary Government of the Republic of South Viet Nam to 1949 Geneva Conventions, effected with the Government of Switzerland on 23 December 1974[35]

The Ministry of Foreign Affairs of Hungary deems it necessary to state that the declarations by the Ministries of Foreign Affairs of a number of States and by the Saigon Administration opposing the accession of the Provisional Revolutionary Government of the Republic of South Viet Nam to the Geneva Conventions are entirely without foundation or legal validity.

The contestation of this right of the Provisional Revolutionary Government of the Republic of South Viet Nam is contrary to the Paris Agreement on ending the war and restoring peace in Viet Nam of 27 January 1973, which recognizes that there now exist two administrations in South Viet Nam and to which the Provisional Revolutionary Government of the Republic of South Viet Nam is a party possessed of equal rights.

Inasmuch as the Provisional Revolutionary Government of the Republic of South Viet Nam in a member of the community of States possessed of equal rights, its accession to the Geneva Conventions is fully grounded in international law.

IRAN (*declaration*)[36]

On 4 September 1980 the Government of the Islamic Republic of Iran declared that henceforth it wishes to use the red crescent as the distinctive emblem and sign instead of the red lion and sun.

ISRAEL (*reservation made on signature and maintained on ratification*)

Mr. Kahany, Delegate of Israel to the European Office of the United Nations and to the ICRC, made the following declaration:

In accordance with instructions received from my Government, I shall sign the Geneva Convention relative to the Treatment of Prisoners of War without any reservation. But in the case of each of the other three Conventions, our signature will be given with reservations the purport of which is as follows

1. *Geneva Convention for the Amelioration of the Condition of the Wounded and Sick in Armed Forces in the Field.*
   Subject to the reservation that, while respecting the inviolability of the distinctive signs and emblems of the Convention. Israel will use the Red Shield of David as the emblem and distinctive sign of the medical services of her armed forces.
2. *Geneva Convention for the Amelioration of the Condition of Wounded, Sick and Shipwrecked 'Members of Armed Forces at Sea.*
   Subject to the reservation that, while respecting the inviolability of the distinctive signs and emblems of the Convention, Israel will use the Red Shield of David on the flags, armlets and on all equipment (including hospital ships), employed in the medical service.

---

35 Notification of the depositary of 6 June 1975. Translation published in *UNTS*, Vol. 972, 1975, p. 402.

36 Notification of the depositary to the ICRC of 26 September 1980.

3. *Geneva Convention relative to the Protection of Civilian Persons in Time of War.* Subject to the reservation that, while respecting the inviolability of the distinctive signs and emblems provided for in Article 38 of the Geneva Convention for the Amelioration of the Condition of the Wounded and Sick in Armed Forces in the Field of 12 August 1949, Israel will use the Red Shield of David as the emblem and distinctive sign provided for in this Convention.

Declaration received by the depositary on 22 January 1968 in respect of the declaration made by Kuwait on the accession to 1949 Geneva Conventions[37 38]
The Ministry of Foreign Affairs presents its compliments to the Swiss Embassy, and with regard to the Embassy's Note from the Ministry of Foreign Affairs of Kuwait dated 31 August 1967, has the honour to state that the Government of Israel has noted the political character of the declaration made by the Government of Kuwait on the occasion of its accession to the Geneva Conventions of 1949 for the Protection of War Victims. In the view of the Government of Israel that statement is inadmissible, and the Government of Israel formally objects to it while reserving its rights to act in relation to Kuwait, as regards the matters with which the Conventions deal, on the basis of strict reciprocity.

The Government of Israel request that the text of this note be communicated to all States signatory to the Conventions and to all States ratifying or acceding thereto.

Declaration of the state of Israel relating to the declaration made upon accession by Democratic Yemen,[39] *received by the depositary on 10 February 1978*[40]
The Government of Israel takes note that by declaration dated 10 February 1977, and received by the Swiss Government on 25 May 1977, the Popular Democratic Republic of Yemen adhered to the four Geneva Conventions of 12 August 1949 relating to the Protection of War Victims.

The said instruments were accompanied by a declaration of a political character in respect to Israel. In the view of the Government of Israel, this is not the proper place for making such political pronouncements, which are, moreover, in flagrant contradiction to the principles, objects and purposes of the said Conventions. The said declaration cannot in any way affect whatever obligations are binding upon the Popular Democratic Republic of Yemen under general international law or under particular treaties.

Declaration of the state of Israel relating to the declaration of Qatar concerning the recognition of competence of the International Fact-Finding Commission according to the Article 90, paragraph 2 a) of the Protocol Additional to the Geneva Conventions of 12 August 1949, and relating to the Protection of Victims of International Armed Conflicts (Protocol I) of 8 June 1977, received by the depositary on 24 September 1991
The Ministry of Foreign Affairs presents its compliments to the Embassy of Switzerland and has the honour to refer to the Embassy's Note of 22 February 1992 referring, among others, to the Geneva Conventions of 12 August 1949 for the Protection of War Victims and to the declaration with respect to Israel by Qatar concerning the Additional Protocol 1.

In the view of the Government of the State of Israel such declaration, which is explicitly of political character, is incompatible with the purposes and objectives of this Convention and cannot in any way affect whatever obligations are binding upon Qatar under general International Law or under particular Conventions.

The Government of the State of Israel will, in so far as concerns the substance of the matter, adopt towards Qatar an attitude of complete reciprocity.

---

[37] For the declaration of Kuwait, see p. 667.

[38] Original: English. Notification of the depositary to the ICRC of 6 February 1968.

[39] For the declaration of the Democratric People's Republic of Yemen concerning the accession of Israel, see p. 687.

[40] Notification of the depositary to the ICRC of 16 March 1978 and *UNTS*, Vol. 1080, 1978, p. 370.

ITALY (*reservations made on signature*)

Mr. Auriti, Ambassador, made the following declaration concerning the Convention relative to the Treatment of Prisoners of War and Resolutions 6, 7 and 9 of the Diplomatic Conference of Geneva:

1. *Geneva Convention relative to the Treatment of Prisoners of War.*
   The Italian Government declares that it makes a reservation in respect of the last paragraph of Article 66 of the Convention relative to the Treatment of Prisoners of War.
2. *Resolution 6* of the Diplomatic Conference of Geneva
   Whereas the Conference has recommended "that the High Contracting Parties will, in the near future, instruct a Committee of Experts to examine technical improvements of modern means of communication between hospital ships, on the one hand, and warships and military aircraft, on the other" the Italian Government expresses the hope that the said Committee of Experts may be convoked, if possible, during the coming months in order that they may draw tip an international code of rules for the use of the above means of communication.
   The Italian Armed Forces are at present engaged in making a thorough study of the above subject and will, if necessary, be ready to submit concrete proposals of a technical nature as a basis for discussion.
3. *Resolution 7* of the Diplomatic Conference of Geneva
   The Italian Government is prepared to arrange that, whenever conveniently practicable, hospital ships shall frequently and regularly broadcast particulars of their position, route and speed.
4. *Resolution 9* of the Diplomatic Conference of Geneva
   In regard to the second paragraph of Resolution 9, The Italian Government considers that the departments dealing with telecommunications in the countries of the High Contracting Parties must collaborate in drawing up some method of grouping telegrams of prisoners of war, so as to facilitate the transmission of numbered messages and thus avoid errors and the duplication of international transmissions and the consequent increase in their cost."

KOREA, DEMOCRATIC PEOPLE'S REPUBLIC OF (*reservations made on accession*)[41] [42]

1. On *Article 10* of the *Geneva Convention for the Amelioration of the Condition of the Wounded and Sick in Armed Forces in the Field* of 12 August 1949:
   In the event of a Power detaining wounded and sick, or medical personnel, requesting a neutral State, or a humanitarian organization, to undertake the functions incumbent on a Protecting Power, the Government of the Democratic People's Republic of Korea will not consider it a legal request unless an approval is obtained from the Government of the State on which the protected persons concerned depend.
2. On *Article 10* of the *Geneva Convention for the Amelioration of the Condition of Wounded, Sick and Shipwrecked Members of Armed Forces at Sea* of 12 August 1949:
   In the event of a Power detaining wounded, sick and shipwrecked, or medical personnel, requesting a neutral State, or a humanitarian organization, to undertake the functions incumbent on a Protecting Power, the Government of the Democratic People's Republic of Korea will not consider it a legal request unless an approval is obtained from the Government of the State on which the protected persons concerned depend.
3. On *Article 10* of the *Geneva Convention relative to the Treatment of Prisoners of War* of 12 August 1949:
   In the event of a Power detaining prisoners of war requesting a neutral State, or a humanitarian organization, to undertake the functions incumbent on a Protecting Power, the Government of the Democratic People's Republic of Korea will not con-

[41] Notification of the depositary to the ICRC of 18 September 1957, and *UNTS*, Vol. 276, 1957, pp. 263–264

[42] For the objection made by Australia, see p. 652.

sider it a legal request unless an approval is obtained from the Government of the State on which the prisoners of war concerned depend.

On Article 12 of the same Convention:

The Government of the Democratic People's Republic of Korea considers that, even during the period in which the Power detaining prisoners of war has transferred the prisoners of war to other Powers which are parties to the present Convention to be in their custody, responsibility as an original Detaining Power for the application of the present Convention towards the prisoners of war concerned will not be released.

On Article 85 of the same Convention:

The Government of the Democratic People's Republic of Korea will not be bound by Article 85, in regard to the treatment of the prisoners of war convicted under the laws of the Detaining Power of prisoners of war for having committed war crimes or inhumane offences, based on the principles of Nuremberg and the Tokyo Far East International Military Tribunal.

4. *On the Geneva Convention relative to the Protection of Civilian Persons in Time of War* of 12 August 1949:

The Government of the Democratic People's Republic of Korea considers that the present Convention cannot fully meet humanitarian requirements, inasmuch as it does not apply to civilian persons outside the territory occupied by the enemy.

But, considering that the present Convention has a positive aspect of protecting the interests of civilian persons in the territory of occupation and in a series of other cases, the Government of the Democratic People's Republic of Korea accedes to it with reservations on the following articles.

On Article 11 of the same Convention:

In the event of a Power detaining protected persons requesting a neutral State, or a humanitarian organization, to undertake the functions incumbent on a Protecting Power, the Government of the Democratic People's Republic of Korea will not consider it a legal request unless an approval is obtained from the Government of the State on which the protected persons concerned depend.

On Article 45 of the same Convention:

The Government of the Democratic People's Republic of Korea considers that, even during the period in which the Power detaining protected persons has transferred the protected persons to other Powers which are parties to the present Convention to be in their custody, responsibility as an original Detaining Power for the application of the present Convention towards the protected persons concerned will not be released.

KOREA, REPUBLIC OF (*reservations made on accession*)[43] [44]

Ad Article 118 of the *Geneva Convention relative to the Treatment of Prisoners of War*:

The Republic of Korea interprets the provisions of Article 118, paragraph 1, as not binding upon a Power detaining prisoners of war to forcibly repatriate its prisoners against their openly and freely expressed will.

Ad Article 68 of the *Geneva Convention relative to the Protection of Civilian Persons in Time of War*:

The Republic of Korea reserves the right to impose the death penalty in accordance with the provisions of Article 68, paragraph 2, without regard to whether the offences referred to therein are punishable by death under the law of the occupied territory at the time the occupation begins.

And, furthermore, the Government of the Republic of Korea do hereby declare that it is the only lawful Government in Korea as set forth in General Assembly Resolution No. 195 (111) of 12 December 1948, and its accession to the present Convention shall not be construed as recognizing any Contracting Party thereto which the Republic of Korea has not hitherto recognized.

---

[43] Notification of the depositary to the ICRC of 17 August 1966 and *UNTS*, Vol. 575, 1966, pp. 285–287.

[44] For the objections made by Romania, see pp. 672–673.

KUWAIT (*reservation made on accession*)[45] [46]
This accession ... does not imply recognition of Israel or entering with it into relations governed by the Convention ...

LUXEMBOURG (*reservations made on signature*)
Mr. Sturm, chargé d'affaires of Luxembourg in Switzerland, made the following reservation:
The undersigned Delegate of the Grand Duchy of Luxembourg, duly empowered by its Government, has this eighth day of December 1949, signed the *Convention* established by the Diplomatic Conference of Geneva *relative to the Treatment of Prisoners of War*, with the reservation: "that its existing national law shall continue to be applied to cases now under consideration".
This reservation was withdrawn on ratification.

MACEDONIA
The former Yugoslav Republic of Macedonia deposited on 18 October 1996 the instrument of succession and maintains the reservations and declarations made by the former Federal People's Republic of Yugoslavia. See Yugoslavia, p. 687.

MONGOLIA (*declaration of 13 August 1974 relating to objections made in respect of the accession by the Republic of Guinea-Bissau, and by the Provisional Revolutionary Government of the Republic of South Viet Nam*)[47]
The Government of Mongolia supports the declaration of the Ministry of Foreign Affairs of the Republic of South Viet Nam and is of the opinion that the Republic of South Viet Nam is a full party to the Geneva Conventions of 12 August 1949 for the Protection of War Victims in conformity with the rules of public international law.

The Government of Mongolia regrets that it cannot share the opinion of the Federative Republic of Brazil and of Portugal and is categorically opposed to any discrimination on the part of States Parties to the Geneva Conventions of 12 August 1949 for the Protection of War Victims against the Republic of South Viet Nam and of the Republic of Guinea-Bissau.

NETHERLANDS (*reservation made on signature and maintained on ratification*)
Mr. Bosch, Chevalier Van Rosenthal, Minister of the Netherlands in Switzerland, made the following declaration:
My Government has instructed me to sign the four Conventions established at the Diplomatic Conference held at Geneva from 21 April to 12 August 1949, but my Government wishes to make the following reservation regarding the *Convention relative to the Protection of Civilian Persons in Time of War*, which reservation reads as follows:
"The Kingdom of the Netherlands reserves the right to impose the death penalty in accordance with the provisions of Article 68, paragraph 2 without regard to whether the offences referred to therein are punishable by death under the law of the occupied territory at the time the occupation begins."

Withdrawal of the reservation made on ratification[48]
By a note of 4 February 1983 addressed to the Federal Department of Foreign Affairs and received on 7 February 1983, the Government of the Netherlands withdrew the reservation made on ratification.

---

[45] Notification of the depositary to the ICRC of 7 September 1976 and *UNTS*, Vol. 608, p. 353.
[46] For the objection of Israel, see p. 664.
[47] *UNTS*, Vol. 949, 1974, pp. 308–309, 311–312.
[48] Notification of the depositary to the ICRC of 8 February 1983.

New Zealand (*reservation made on signature*)
Mr. George Robert Laking, Counsellor to the New Zealand Embassy in Washington made the following declaration:
In signing the four Conventions established by the Diplomatic Conference at Geneva 1949, the New Zealand Government desire me to state that as there has been insufficient opportunity to study the reservations made on behalf of other States, the Government for the present reserve their view in regard to such reservations.

In signing the *Convention relating to the Protection of Civilian Persons in Time of War*, the New Zealand Government desire me to make the following reservations:

1. New Zealand reserves the right to impose the death penalty in accordance with the provisions of *Article 68*, paragraph 2, without regard to whether the offences referred to therein are punishable by death under the law of the occupied territory at the time the occupation begins.
2. In view of the fact that the General Assembly of the United Nations, having approved the principles established by the Charter and judgment of the Nuremberg Tribunal, has directed the International Law Commission to include these principles in a general codification of offences against the peace and security of mankind, New Zealand reserves the right to take such action as may be necessary to ensure that such offences are punished, notwithstanding the provisions of Article 70, paragraph 1.

Declaration made on depositing the instrument of ratification[49]
On authorizing me to deposit the instruments of ratification by the Government of New Zealand of the following Conventions concluded at Geneva on 12 August 1949: ....

Her Majesty's Government in New Zealand have requested me to notify you that in ratifying the *Geneva Convention relative to the Protection of Civilian Persons in Time of War*, they do not desire to maintain the reservation to Article 70 paragraph 1, of that Convention, made by the Government of New Zealand at the time of signature. Her Majesty's Government in New Zealand desire, however, to maintain the reservation recorded at the time of signature in respect of Article 68, paragraph 2, of the same Convention, and have included a statement to this effect in the relevant instrument of ratification.

Her Majesty's Government in New Zealand also desire me to refer to the reservations made to Article 85 of the *Geneva Convention relative to the Treatment of Prisoners of War* by the following States:

The People's Republic of Albania
The Byelorussian Soviet Socialist Republic
The Bulgarian People's Republic
The Czechoslovak Republic
The Hungarian People's Republic
The Polish Republic
The Romanian People's Republic
The Ukrainian Soviet Socialist Republic
The Union of Soviet Socialist Republics

and to the reservations to *Article 12* of the *Geneva Convention relative to the Treatment of Prisoners of War* and to *Article 45* of the *Geneva Convention relative to the Protection of Civilian Persons in Time of War* made by all the above-mentioned and by the Federal People's Republic of Yugoslavia.

I am requested to state that Her Majesty's Government in New Zealand do not regard as valid reservations in the terms of those recorded by the above-mentioned States. Whilst Her Majesty's Government in New Zealand regard those States as parties to the Conventions in question, they will regard any application of such a reservation as constituting a breach of the Convention to which the reservation relates.

[49] Notification of the depositary to the ICRC of 26 May 1959; *UNTS*, Vol. 330, 1959, pp. 354–359.

By a letter of 1 December 1975,[50] *received on 2 March 1976, the Ministry of Foreign Affairs of New Zealand notified the Federal Political Department of the partial withdrawal of the reservation made by the Government of New Zealand at the time of ratification, on 6 May 19-59, of the Convention relative to the Protection of Civilian Persons in Time of War. The reservation withdrawn was as follows*:
New Zealand reserves the right to impose the death penalty in accordance with the provisions of Article 68, paragraph 2, without regard to whether the offences referred to therein are punishable by death under the law of the occupied territory at the time the occupation begins.

PAKISTAN (*reservations made on ratification concerning Convention IV relative to the Protection of Civilian Persons in Time of War*)[51]

1. Reservation concerning *Article 44* of the Convention:
   Every protected person who is a national *de jure* of an enemy State, against whom action is taken or sought to be taken under Article 41 by assignment of residence or internment, or in accordance with any law, on the ground of his being an enemy alien, shall be entitled to submit proofs to the Detaining Power, or as the case may be, to any appropriate Court or administrative board which may review his case, that he does not enjoy the protection of any enemy State, and full weight shall be given to this circumstance, if it is established whether with or without further enquiry by the Detaining Power, in deciding appropriate action,. by way of an initial order or, as the case may be, by amendment thereof.
2. Reservation concerning *Article 68, paragraph 2*, of the Convention
   The Government of Pakistan associate themselves with the reservation made by the United Kingdom of Great Britain and Northern Ireland and reserve the right to impose the death penalty in accordance with the provision of Article 68, paragraph 2, without regard to whether the offences referred to therein are punishable by death under the law of the occupied territory at the time the occupation begins.

POLAND (*reservation made on signature and maintained at ratification*)[52]
Mr. Przybos, Polish Minister in Switzerland, made the following reservation concerning the four Geneva Conventions:

1. On signing the *Geneva Convention for the Amelioration of the Condition of the Wounded and Sick in Armed Forces in the Field*, I declare that the Government of the Polish Republic adheres to the said Convention, with a reservation in respect of Article 10.
   The Government of the Polish Republic will not consider as legal a request by the Detaining Power that a neutral State or an international organization or a humanitarian organization should undertake the functions performed under the present Convention by the Protecting Powers, on behalf of the wounded and sick, or medical personnel and chaplains unless the Government whose nationals they are has given its consent.
2. On signing the *Geneva Convention for the Amelioration of the Condition of Wounded, Sick and Shipwrecked Members of Armed Forces at Sea*, I declare that the Government of the Polish Republic adheres to the said Convention, with a reservation in respect of Article 10.
   The Government of the Polish Republic will not consider as legal a request by the Detaining Power that a neutral State or an international organization or a humanitarian organization should undertake the functions performed under the present Convention to the Protecting Powers, on behalf of the wounded, sick and ship-

[50] Notification of the depositary to the ICRC of 28 June 1976; *UNTS*, Vol. 1015, 1976, p. 345.
[51] Notification of the depositary to the ICRC of 20 June 1951.
[52] For objections made by Australia, Barbados, New Zealand and United Kingdom, see pp. 652, 653, 668 and 678.

wrecked, or medical personnel and chaplains, unless the Government whose nationals they are has given its consent.

3. On signing the *Geneva Convention relative to the Treatment of Prisoners of War*, I declare that the Government of the Polish Republic adheres to the said Convention with reservations in respect of Articles 10, 12 and 85.
   In regard to Article 10: The Government of the Polish Republic will not consider as legal a request by the Detaining Power that a neutral State or an international organization or a humanitarian organization should undertake the functions performed under the present Convention by the Protecting Powers, on behalf of prisoners of war, unless the Government whose nationals they are has given its consent.
   In regard to Article 12: The Government of the Polish Republic will not consider as legal for a Power, which effects a transfer of prisoners of war, to be freed from its responsibility for applying the Convention, even for the time during which such prisoners of war are in the custody of the Power accepting them,
   In regard to Article 85: The Government of the Polish Republic will not consider as legal for prisoners of war convicted of war crimes and crimes against humanity in accordance with the principles set forth at the time of the Nuremberg trials, to continue to enjoy protection under the present Convention, it being understood that prisoners of war convicted of such crimes must be subject to the regulations for the execution of punishments, in force in the State concerned.
4. On signing the *Geneva Convention relative to the Protection of Civilian Persons in Time of War*, I declare that the Government of the Polish Republic adheres to the said Convention, with reservations in respect of Articles 11 and 45.
   In regard to Article 11: The Government of the Polish Republic will not consider as legal a request by the Detaining Power that a neutral State or an international organization or a humanitarian organization should undertake the functions performed under the present Convention by the Protecting Powers, on behalf of protected persons, unless the Government whose nationals they are has given its consent.
   In regard to Article 45: The Government of the Polish Republic will not consider it legal for a Power, which effects a transfer of protected persons, to be freed from its responsibility for applying the Convention, even for the time during which such protected persons are in the custody of the Power accepting them."

Declaration of 15 November 1966 in respect of the accession of the Republic of Korea[53]

The Ministry of Foreign Affairs of the People's Republic of Poland … refers to the note of 29 September concerning the accession of the South Korea to Geneva Conventions of 12 August 1949 and has an honour to communicate the following:

The People's Republic of Poland does not recognize the Government of South Korea and recognizes only the Government of the People's Democratic Republic of Korea, which acceded to the Geneva Conventions in 1957. The pretensions of the Government of South Korea to represent all Korean people as expressed in the instrument of accession have no basis and are contrary to the facts and legal situation. For this reason, the Ministry of Foreign Affairs is obliged to return the copy of the document annexed to the above-mentioned note of Swiss Embassy of 29 September.

In the moment when its armed forces participate in the aggression against the people of Viet Nam, the accession of South Korea to above-named Conventions needs no commentary.

The Government of South Korea sends a great number of soldiers to South Viet Nam. Its mercenary troops commit barbarous acts against towns and villages of Viet Nam, create victims among the civilian population and use terror and cruel methods against the prisoners of war who participate in the war of national liberation. All these acts constitute the flagrant violation of international law, and in particular of the text and spirit of Geneva Conventions.

[53] Note of the Ministry of Foreign Affairs of Poland addressed to the Swiss Embassy in Warsaw (Editors' translation).

The accession of the Government of South Korea to the Geneva Conventions must be seen in connection with these acts, which are in flagrant contradiction with the provisions of these Conventions and with the humanitarian spirit they express.

In view of this situation, when the Government acceding to the Geneva Conventions continues systematically to commit the acts contrary to the provisions of these Conventions, the Government of the People's Republic of Poland expresses its objections as well as the fear of the reduction of the value of Geneva Conventions in international relations.

Declaration of 18 July 1974 relating to objections made in respect of the accession by the Provisional Revolutionary Government of the Republic of South Viet Nam and the Republic of Guinea-Bissau[54]

The Ministry of Foreign Affairs of the Polish People's Republic supports the position taken by the Ministry of Foreign Affairs of the Republic of South Viet Nam in its note of 19 March 1974 and wishes to stress that the notifications received against the accession of the Provisional Revolutionary Government of the Republic of South Viet Nam to the Geneva Conventions can in no way influence its status as a party to those Conventions.

The Provisional Revolutionary Government of the Republic of South Viet Nam is a subject of international law recognized by a considerable number of States. It is a party to the Paris Agreement on ending the war and restoring peace in Viet Nam of 27 January 1973 and the accompanying international legal instruments having taken part in the Paris Conference on the same footing as the other participants. Furthermore, that Government's accession to the Geneva Conventions cannot be challenged without calling into question the participation of the Saigon Government in those Conventions.

Accordingly, the Ministry of Foreign Affairs emphatically affirms the full right of the Provisional Revolutionary Government of the Republic of South Viet Nam to be a party to the Geneva Convention.

The accession of the Republic of Guinea-Bissau to the above-mentioned Conventions is likewise, in the light of law and international reality, not open to question.

PORTUGAL (*reservation made on signature*)

Mr. Gonçalo Caldeira Coelho, chargé d'affaires of Portugal in Switzerland made the following declaration:

(a) *Article 3, common to the four Conventions*: As there is no actual definition of what is meant by a conflict not of an international character, and as, in case this term is intended to refer solely to civil war, it is not clearly laid down at what moment an armed rebellion within a country should be considered as having become a civil war, Portugal reserves the right not to apply the provisions of Article 3, in so far as they may be contrary to the provisions of Portuguese law, in all territories subject to her sovereignty in any part of the world.

(b) *Article 10 of Conventions I, II and III and Article 11 of Convention IV*: The Portuguese Government only accepts the above Articles with the reservation that requests by the Detaining Power to a neutral State or to a humanitarian organization to undertake the functions normally performed by protecting Powers are made with the consent or agreement of the government of the country of which the persons to be protected are nationals (Countries of origin).

(c) *Article 13 of Convention I and Article 4 of Convention III*: The Portuguese Government makes a reservation regarding the application of the above Articles in all cases in which the legitimate Government has already asked for and agreed to an armistice or the suspension of military operations of no matter what character, even if the armed forces in the field have not yet capitulated.

(d) *Article 60 of Convention III*: The Portuguese Government accepts this Article with the reservation that it in no case binds itself to grant prisoners a monthly rate of pay in excess of fifty per cent of the pay due to Portuguese soldiers of equivalent appointment or rank, on active service in the combat zone.

[54] *UNTS*, Vol. 949, 1974, p. 306.

Declaration made on ratification[55]
At the time of deposit of the instrument of ratification, the Ambassador Extraordinary and Plenipotentiary of Portugal in Switzerland communicated to the Federal Political Department the following declaration:
At the time of deposit with the Swiss Federal Council of the instrument of ratification of the Geneva Conventions for the Protection of War Victims of 12 August 1949, the undersigned, Ruy Teixeira Guerra, Ambassador of Portugal to Switzerland, declares that his Government has decided to withdraw the reservations made at the time of signature of these Conventions in respect of Article 3, common to the four Conventions, Article 13 of Convention I and Article 4 of Convention III, and Article 60 of Convention III.

On the other hand, the Portuguese Government only accepts Article 10 of Conventions I, II and III and Article 11 of Convention IV with the reservation that requests by the Detaining Power to a neutral State or to a humanitarian organization to undertake the functions normally performed by Protecting Powers are made with the consent or agreement of the Government of the country of which the persons to be protected are nationals (Countries of origin).

Objections to the accession of the Revolutionary Government of the Republic of South Viet Nam to the 1949 Geneva Conventions. Notification effected with the Government of Switzerland on 28 March 1974[56] [57]
[T]he Portuguese Government considers that, in the light of the 1949 Geneva Conventions, the accession of the so-called Revolutionary Government of the South Viet Nam to the said Conventions is totally invalid.

Objections to the accession of the Republic of Guinea-Bissau in respect of the 1949 Geneva Conventions[58] [59]
The so-called "Republic of Guinea-Bissau" is a mere fiction, since it has neither population nor territory. Contrary to the claim asserted by this fiction, it is the Portuguese State that exercises full sovereignty over that territory and its populations assuming at the international level the obligations, which follow from that situation.

Such being the case, it is not possible, in the light of international law, to attribute statehood or any other legal status to this supposed acceder.

The Portuguese Government therefore considers [this] application [for accession] entirely inoperative and legally non-existent.

ROMANIA (*reservation made on signature and maintained on ratification*)[60]
Mr. Ioan Dragomir, chargé d'affaires of Romania in Switzerland, made the following declaration:

1. On signing the *Convention for the Amelioration of the Condition of the Wounded and Sick in Armed Forces in the Field*, the Government of the Romanian People's Republic makes the following reservation:
   Article 10: The Romanian People's Republic will not recognize the validity of requests by the Detaining Power to a neutral State or to a humanitarian organization, to undertake the functions performed by a Protecting Power, unless the consent of the Government of the country of which the protected persons are nationals has been obtained.
2. On signing the *Convention for the Amelioration of the Condition of Wounded, Sick and Shipwrecked Members of Armed Forces at Sea*, the Government of the Romanian People's Republic makes the following reservation:

[55] Notification of the depositary to the ICRC of 13 April 1961; *UNTS*, Vol. 394, 1961, p. 258.
[56] *UNTS*, Vol. 941, 1974, p. 321.
[57] Several states made declarations in respect of these objections: [German Democratic Republic], Hungary, Poland, Romania, Ukraine, [USSR]. See pp. 660, 663, 671, 674, 676, 677.
[58] *UNTS*, Vol. 941, 1974, p. 322.
[59] For declarations in respect of these objections made by Mongolia and Poland, see pp. 667, 671.
[60] For objections made by Australia, Barbados, New Zealand and the United Kingdom, see pp. 652, 653, 668 and 678.

Article 10: The Romanian People's Republic will not recognize the validity of requests by the Detaining Power to a neutral State or to a humanitarian organization, to undertake the functions performed by a Protecting Power, unless the consent of the Government of the country of which the protected persons are nationals has been obtained.

3. On signing the *Convention relative to the Treatment of Prisoners of War*, the Government of the Romanian People's Republic makes the following reservations:
Article 10: The Romanian People's Republic will not recognize the validity of requests by the Detaining Power to a neutral State or to a humanitarian organization, to undertake the functions performed by a Protecting Power, unless the consent of the Government of the country of which the prisoners of war are nationals has been obtained.
Article 12: The Romanian People's Republic does not consider as valid the freeing of a Detaining Power, which has transferred prisoners of war to another Power, from responsibility for the application of the Convention to such prisoners of war while the latter are under the protection of the Power accepting them.
Article 85: The Romanian People's Republic does not consider itself bound by the obligation, which follows from Article 85, to extend the application of the Convention to prisoners of war who have been convicted under the law of the Detaining Power, in accordance with the principles of the Nuremberg trial, for war crimes and crimes against humanity, it being understood that persons convicted of such crimes must be subject to the conditions obtaining in the country in question for those who undergo their punishment.
4. I am authorized to make the following declaration on signing the *Convention relative to the Protection of Civilian Persons in Time of War*.
The Government of the Romanian People's Republic considers that this Convention does not completely meet humanitarian requirements, owing to the fact that it does not apply to the civilian population in territory not occupied by the enemy.
Nevertheless, taking into consideration the fact that the Convention is intended to protect the interests of the civilian population in occupied territory, I am authorized by the Romanian People's Government to sign the said Convention with the following reservations:
Article 11: The Romanian People's Republic will not recognize the validity of requests by the Detaining Power to a neutral State or to a humanitarian organization, to undertake the functions performed by a Protecting Power, unless the consent of the Government of the country of which the protected persons are nationals has been obtained.
Article 45: The Romanian People's Republic will not consider as valid the freeing of a Detaining Power, which has transferred protected persons to another Power, from responsibility for the application of the Convention to the persons transferred, while the latter are under the protection of the Power accepting them."

Objection to the reservations and the declaration made by the Government of the Republic of Korea in its instrument of accession[61]
In a note dated Bucharest, 18 January 1967, the Minister of Foreign Affairs of the Socialist Republic of Romania transmitted to the Swiss Embassy the following comments on the reservations and the declaration contained in the above-mentioned instrument of accession:
The Government of the Socialist Republic of Romania cannot accept the reservations made by the South Korean authorities with regard to *Article 118* of the *Convention relative to the treatment of prisoners of war* and to *Article 68* of the *Convention relative to the protection of civilian persons in time of war*. It regards those reservations as incompatible with the purposes of the aforementioned Conventions. The Government of the Socialist Republic of Romania also rejects the declaration of the South Korean authori-

[61] Notification of the depositary to the ICRC of 20 September 1967; *UNTS*, Vol. 609, 1967, pp. 254–255.

ties in which the latter claim to be the only lawful Government in Korea. This assertion is unfounded since it is contradicted by the indisputable fact that the Democratic People's Republic of Korea exists as a sovereign and independent State.

Declaration relating to objections made in respect of the accession by the Provisional Revolutionary Government of the Republic of South Viet Nam[62]
The Ministry of Foreign Affairs of the Socialist Republic of Romania considers that the accession of the Provisional Revolutionary Government of South Viet Nam to the Geneva Conventions of 1949 for the Protection of War Victims is legal since the Saigon authorities certainly cannot unilaterally represent South Viet Nam, where two administrations recognized by the Paris Agreement on Peace in Viet Nam, signed in 1972,[63] exist.

RUSSIAN FEDERATION [64] *See Union of Soviet Socialist Republics.*

SOUTH AFRICA
Communication concerning the accession of the United Nations Council for Namibia[65] [66]
Accession to the aforementioned Geneva Conventions and Protocols is governed by an identically worded article which stipulates that "From the date of its coming into force, it shall be open to any Power in whose name the present Convention has not been signed, to accede to this Convention". Since South West Africa/Namibia cannot, in terms of international law, be regarded as such a Power and since neither it nor the UN Council for Namibia is able to assume the obligations imposed upon such Power by the four Geneva Conventions, the South African Government rejects the so-called instruments of accession of the UN Council for Namibia to the four Geneva Conventions and its two Additional Protocols as having no legal effect.

SPAIN (*reservation made when signing the Geneva Convention relative to the Treatment of Prisoners of War; the text of the reservation being submitted in the Spanish, French and English languages)*
Mr. Calderon y Martin, Spanish Minister in Switzerland, made the following reservation to the Geneva Convention relative to the Treatment of Prisoners of War:
In matters regarding procedural guarantees and penal and disciplinary sanctions, Spain will grant prisoners of war the same treatment as is provided by her legislation for members of her own national forces.

Under "International Law in Force" (Article 99) Spain understands she only accepts that which arises from contractual sources or which has been previously elaborated by Organizations in which she participates.

On ratification, Spain maintained only the second reservation concerning Article 99 of the Geneva Convention relative to the Treatment of Prisoners of War.
By a communication to the depositary of 5 January 1979, Spain withdrew the reservation made on ratification, concerning *Article 99* of the *Geneva Convention relative to the Treatment of Prisoners of War*.

---

62 *UNTS*, Vol. 949, 1974, p. 311.

63 *UNTS*, Vol. 935, 1974, p. 3.

64 Note of the Ministry for Foreign Affairs of the Russian Federation: "The Russian Federation continues to exercise the rights and carry out the obligations resulting from the international agreements signed by the Union of Soviet Socialist Republics.Accordingly the Government of the Russian Federation will carry out, instead of the Government of the USSR, functions of depositary of the corresponding multilateral treaties. In this connection the Ministry asks to consider the Russian Federation as the Party to all international agreements in force, instead of the USSR" (note from the Permanent Mission of the Russian Federation in Geneva transmitted to the ICRC on 15 January 1992).

65 *UNTS*, Vol. 1360, 1984, p. 357.

66 United Nations Council for Namibia deposited on 18 October 1983 the instrument of accession to four Geneva Conventions and two additional Protocols. This accession entered into force on 18 April 1984.

SLOVAKIA (*reservation maintained on succession*) *see the text of the reservations made by Czechoslovakia, pp. 657–658.*

SURINAM (*reservation made at succession identical with the reservation made by Netherlands to the Convention relative to the Protection of Civilian Persons in Time of War*)[67]
Surinam reserves the right to impose the death penalty in accordance with the provisions of Article 68, paragraph 2, without regard to whether the offences referred to therein are punishable by death under the law of the occupied territory at the time the occupation begins.

UKRAINE (*reservation made by Ukrainian Soviet Socialist Republic on signature and maintained on* ratification)[68]
Mr. Bogomoletz, Head of the Delegation of the Ukrainian Soviet Socialist Republic:

1. On signing the *Convention for the Amelioration of the Condition of the Wounded and Sick in Armed Forces in the Field*, the Government of the Ukrainian Soviet Socialist Republic makes the following reservation:
   Article 10: The Ukrainian Soviet Socialist Republic will not recognize the validity of requests by the Detaining Power to a neutral State or to a humanitarian organization, to undertake the functions performed by a Protecting Power, unless the consent of the Government of the country of which the protected persons are nationals has been obtained.
2. On signing the *Convention for the Amelioration of the Condition of Wounded, Sick and Shipwrecked Members of Armed Forces at Sea*, the Government of the Ukrainian Soviet Socialist Republic makes the following reservation:
   Article 10: The Ukrainian Soviet Socialist Republic will not recognize the validity of requests by the Detaining Power to a neutral State or to a humanitarian organization, to undertake the functions performed by a Protecting Power, unless the consent of the Government of the country of which the protected persons are nationals has been obtained.
3. On signing the *Convention relative to the Treatment of Prisoners of War*, the Government of the Ukrainian Soviet Socialist Republic makes the following reservations:
   Article 10: The Ukrainian Soviet Socialist Republic will not recognize the validity of requests by the Detaining Power to a neutral State or to a humanitarian organization, to undertake the functions performed by a Protecting Power, unless the consent of the Government of the country of which the prisoners of war are nationals has been obtained.
   Article 12: The Ukrainian Soviet Socialist Republic does not consider as valid the freeing of a Detaining Power, which has transferred prisoners of war to another Power, from responsibility for the application of the Convention to such prisoners of war while the latter are in the custody of the Power accepting them.
   Article 85: The Ukrainian Soviet Socialist Republic does not consider itself bound by the obligation, which follows from Article 85, to extend the application of the Convention to prisoners of war who have been convicted under the law of the Detaining Power, in accordance with the principles of the Nuremberg trial, for war crimes and crimes against humanity, it being understood that persons convicted of such crimes must be subject to the conditions obtaining in the country in question for those who undergo their punishment.
4. On signing the *Convention relative to the Protection of Civilian Persons in Time of War*, the Government of the Ukrainian Soviet Socialist Republic feels called upon to make the following declaration:
   Although the present Convention does not cover the civilian population in territory not occupied by the enemy and does not, therefore, completely meet humanitarian

[67] Notification of the depositary to ICRC of 25 October 1979.
[68] For objections made by Australia, Barbados, New Zealand and United Kingdom, see pp. 652, 653, 668 and 678.

requirements, the Ukrainian Delegation, recognizing that the said Convention makes satisfactory provision for the protection of the civilian population in occupied territory and in certain other cases, declares that it is authorized by the Government of the Ukrainian Soviet Socialist Republic to sign the present Convention with the following reservations:

Article 11: The Ukrainian Soviet Socialist Republic will not recognize the validity of requests by the Detaining Power to a neutral State or to a humanitarian organization to undertake the functions performed by a Protecting Power, unless the consent of the Government of the country of which the protected persons are nationals has been obtained.

Article 45: The Ukrainian Soviet Socialist Republic will not consider as valid the freeing of a Detaining Power, which has transferred protected persons to another Power, from responsibility for the application of the Convention to the persons transferred, while the latter are in the custody of the Power accepting them.

Declaration relating to the accession of the Provisional Revolutionary Government of the Republic of South Viet Nam, effected with the Government of Switzerland on 16 August 1974[69]

There are no political or juridical grounds whatsoever for the declarations made by a number of States and by the Saigon Administration in relation to the accession of the Provisional Revolutionary Government of the Republic of South Viet Nam. In accordance with the 1973 Paris Agreement,[70] these are two zones and two administrations in South Viet Nam, namely the Provisional Revolutionary Government of South Viet Nam and the Saigon Administration. In no case, therefore, can the Saigon authorities claim to be acting on behalf of South Viet Nam. Consequently, the Provisional Revolutionary Government has the right to represent South Viet Nam for the purposes of all agreements and conventions of a universal character and matters relating to international humanitarian law.

UNION OF SOVIET SOCIALIST REPUBLICS (*reservation made on signature and maintained on* ratification)[71]

General Slavin, Head of the Delegation of the Union of Soviet Socialist Republic:

1. On signing the *Convention for the Amelioration of the Condition of the Wounded and Sick in Armed Forces in the Field*, the Government of the Union of Soviet Socialist Republics makes the following reservation:
   Article 10: The Union of Soviet Socialist Republics will not recognize the validity of requests by the Detaining Power to a neutral State or to a humanitarian organization, to undertake the functions performed by a Protecting Power, unless the consent of the Government of the country of which the protected persons are nationals has been obtained.
2. On signing the *Convention for the Amelioration of the Condition of Wounded, Sick and Shipwrecked Members of Armed Forces at Sea*, the Government of the Union of Soviet Socialist Republics makes the following reservation:
   Article 10: The Union of Soviet Socialist Republics will not recognize the validity of requests by the Detaining Power to a neutral State or to a humanitarian organization, to undertake the functions performed by a Protecting Power, unless the consent of the Government of the country of which the protected persons are nationals has been obtained.
3. On signing the *Convention relative to the Treatment of Prisoners of War*, the Government of the Union of Soviet Socialist Republics makes the following reservations:

---

69 Notification of the depositary of 31 October 1974; *UNTS*, Vol. 954, 1974, p. 459.

70 *UNTS*, Vol. 935, p. 2.

71 For the objections made by Australia, Barbados, New Zealand and the United Kingdom, see pp. 652, 653, 668 and 678.

Article 10: The Union of Soviet Socialist Republics will not recognize the validity of requests by the Detaining Power to a neutral State or to a humanitarian organization, to undertake the functions performed by a Protecting Power, unless the consent of the Government of the country of which the prisoners of war are nationals has been obtained.

Article 12: The Union of Soviet Socialist Republics does not consider as valid the freeing of a Detaining Power, which has transferred prisoners of war to another Power, from responsibility' for the application of the Convention to such prisoners of war while the latter are in the custody of the Power accepting them.

Article 85: The Union of Soviet Socialist Republics does not consider itself bound by the obligation, which follows from Article 85, to extend the application of the Convention to prisoners of war who have been convicted under the law of the Detaining Power, in accordance with the principles of the Nuremberg trial, for war crimes and crimes against humanity, it being understood that persons convicted of such crimes must be subject to the conditions obtaining in the country in question for those who undergo their punishment.

4. On signing the *Convention relative to the Protection of Civilian Persons in Time of War*, the Government of the Union of Soviet Socialist Republics feels called upon to make the following declaration:

Although the present Convention does not cover the civilian population in territory not occupied by the enemy and does not, therefore, completely meet humanitarian requirements, the Soviet Delegation, recognizing that the said Convention makes satisfactory provision for the protection of the civilian population in occupied territory and in certain other cases, declares that it is authorized by the Government of the Union of Soviet Socialist Republics to sign the present Convention with the following reservations:

Article 11: The Union of Soviet, Socialist Republics will not recognize the validity of requests by the Detaining Power to a neutral State or to a humanitarian organization, to undertaken the functions performed by a Protecting Power, unless the consent of the Government of the country of which the protected persons are nationals has been obtained.

Article 45: The Union of Soviet Socialist Republics will not consider as valid the freeing of a Detaining Power, which has transferred protected persons to another Power, from responsibility for the application of the Convention to the persons transferred, while the latter are in the custody of the Power accepting them."

Declaration of the USSR of 6 August 1974 relating to objections made in respect of the accession by the Provisional Revolutionary Government of the Republic of South Viet Nam[72]

The Ministry of Foreign Affairs of the Union of Soviet Socialist Republics states with reference to the Embassy's note No. 126 of 14 June 1974 concerning the Geneva Conventions of 12 August 1949 for the Protection of War Victims, that the statements made in the declaration of the ministries of Foreign Affairs of certain States and of the Saigon Administration, which were annexed to the said note, on the subject of the accession of the Provisional Revolutionary Government of the Republic of South Viet Nam to the Geneva Conventions are irrelevant.

The Ministry feels it necessary to draw attention to the fact that the Saigon authorities can in no case claim to be acting on behalf of South Viet Nam, because according to the Paris Agreement of 1973, two zones and two administrations exists in South Viet Nam (the Provisional Revolutionary Government of the Republic of South Viet Nam and the Saigon Administration). Consequently, the Provisional Revolutionary Government of the Republic of South Viet Nam has the right to represent South Viet

[72] *UNTS*, Vol. 949, 1974, p. 308.

Nam in all conventions of a universal nature, such as those dealing with humanitarian questions.

UNITED KINGDOM OF GREAT BRITAIN AND NORTHERN IRELAND
Reservation made on signature and maintained on ratification)
The Rt. Hon. Sir Robert Craigie, Foreign Office, made the following declaration:
In signing the *Convention relative to the Protection of Civilian Persons in Time of War*, His Majesty's Government in the United Kingdom desire me to make the following reservation:
The United Kingdom of Great Britain and Northern Ireland reserve the right to impose the death penalty in accordance with the provisions of *Article 68*, paragraph 2, without regard to whether the offences referred to therein are punishable by death under the law of the occupied territory at the time the occupation begins.

Declaration made on ratification
On depositing the instrument of ratification by the United Kingdom of Great Britain and Northern Ireland of the four Conventions, I am instructed by Her Majesty's Government in the United Kingdom to make the following declaration:
The United Kingdom of Great Britain and Northern Ireland will apply each of the above-mentioned Conventions in the British Protected States of Bahrain, Kuwait, Qatar and the Trucial States to the extent of Her Majesty's powers in relation to those territories.

I am also instructed by Her Majesty's Government in the United Kingdom to state that the reservation to the second paragraph of *Article 68* of the *Convention relative to the Protection of Civilian Persons in Time of War* which was made by the United Kingdom on signature of that Convention is maintained.

I am further instructed by Her Majesty's Government in the United Kingdom to refer to the reservations made to *Article 85* of the *Convention relative to the Treatment of Prisoners of War* by the following States:

The People's Republic of Albania
The Byelorussian Soviet Socialist Republic
The Bulgarian People's Republic
The People's Republic of China
The Czechoslovak Republic
The Hungarian People's Republic
The Polish Republic
The Romanian People's Republic
The Ukrainian Soviet Socialist Republic
The Union of Soviet Socialist Republics

and to the reservations to *Article 12* of the *Convention relative to the Treatment of Prisoners of War* and to *Article 45* of the *Convention relative to the Treatment of Civilian Persons in Time of War* made by all the above-mentioned States and by the Federal People's Republic of Yugoslavia.

I am instructed by Her Majesty's Government to state that whilst they regard all the above-mentioned States as being parties to the above-mentioned Conventions, they do not regard the above-mentioned reservations thereto made by those States as valid, and will therefore regard any application of any of those reservations as constituting a breach of the Convention to which the reservation relates.

By a note dated 14 December 1971,[73] *received on 15th of the same month, Her Britannic Majesty's Embassy in Berne notified the Federal Political Department of the withdrawal of the reservation made by the United Kingdom of Great Britain and Northern Ireland at the time of signature on 12 August 1949 of the Convention relative to the Protection of Civilian Persons in Time of War which was confirmed on its ratification. The reservation withdrawn was as follows*:

[73] Notification of the depositary to the ICRC of 20 January 1972; *UNTS*, Vol. 811, 1972, p. 376.

The United Kingdom of Great Britain and Northern Ireland reserve the right to impose the death penalty in accordance with the provisions of Article 68, paragraph 2, without regard to whether the offences referred to therein are punishable by death under the law of the occupied territory at the time the. occupation begins.

Objection to the reservation of the People's Republic of Angola[74]
With reference to the reservation made by the Government of the People's Republic of Angola to *Article 85* of the *Convention relative to the Treatment of Prisoners of War*, Her Majesty's Government, recalling their previous declarations in relations to similar reservations by other States, wish to state that, whilst they do not oppose the entry into force of the Convention in question between the United Kingdom and the People's Republic of Angola, they are unable to accept the reservation because, in the view of the Government of the United Kingdom, this reservation is not of the kind which intending parties to the Convention are entitled to make."

Declaration concerning the accession of the Democratic Republic of Viet Nam[75]
Her Majesty's Government does not recognize the Viet Nam authorities in North Viet Nam as a Government, nor do they recognize the so-called "Democratic Republic of Viet Nam" as a State. While, therefore, they have noted the contents of the enclosure to His Excellency's note under reference in so far as they relate to the application of the provisions of the Geneva Conventions in North Viet Nam, they are unable to accept that the so-called "Democratic Republic of Viet Nam" has the right to accede to those Conventions.

Objections to the reservations made to the accessions of Guinea-Bissau, Provisional Revolutionary Government of the Republic of South Viet Nam, [German Democratic Republic], and Democratic Republic of Viet Nam, effected with the Government of Switzerland on 19 November 1975[76] [77]
In relation with the reservations made by the Provisional Revolutionary Government of the Republic of South Vietnam to *Articles 12* and *85* of the *Convention relative to the Treatment of Prisoners of War* and *Article 45* of the *Convention relative to the Protection of Civilian Persons in Time of War* and in relation with the reservation to *Article 45* of the *Convention relative to the Protection of Civilian Persons in Time of War* made by the Republic of Guinea-Bissau, the Government of the United Kingdom of Great Britain and Northern Ireland, recalling their declaration on ratification in relation to similar reservations by other States, wish to state that, whilst they do not oppose the entry into force of the two Conventions in question between the United Kingdom and the Republic of South Vietnam and the Republic of Guinea-Bissau, they are unable to accept the above-mentioned reservations thereto made by those States because, in the view of the Government of the United Kingdom, these reservations are not of the kind that intending Parties to the Convention are entitled to make.

The Government of the United Kingdom wish also to place on record that they take the same view of the similar reservations made by [the German Democratic Republic], notified by the Swiss Minister in London on 8 January 1957, and by the Democratic Republic of Vietnam, notified by the Swiss Ambassador in London on 24 August 1957. In relation to the reservation made by the Provisional Revolutionary Government of the Republic of South Vietnam and the Republic of Guinea-Bissau to *Article 4* of the *Convention relative to the Treatment of Prisoners of War* and by the Republic of Guinea-Bissau to *Article 13* of the *Convention for the Amelioration of the Condition of*

74 Objection of 28 March 1985, notified by the depositary to the ICRC on 18 June 1985.

75 Notification of the depositary to the ICRC of 5 October 1957.

76 Notification of the depositary to the ICRC of 12 January 1976; *UNTS*, Vol. 995, 1976, pp. 394–397.

77 After the reunification of two Viet Nams, and the accession of the German Democratic Republic to Federal Republic of Germany, these objections became void.

the Wounded and Sick in Armed Forces in the Field and *Article 13* of the *Convention for the Amelioration of the Condition of Wounded, Sick and Shipwrecked Members of Armed Forces at Sea*, the Government of the United Kingdom wish to state that they are likewise unable to accept those reservations.

By a letter of 13 June 1997, the British Ambassador to Switzerland deposited the following declaration:[78]

I am instructed by Her Majesty's Principal Secretary of State for Foreign and Commonwealth Affairs to refer to the [four Geneva Conventions] (hereinafter referred to as the "Convention") which apply to Hong Kong at present.

I am also instructed to state that, in accordance with the Joint Declaration of the Government of the United Kingdom of Great Britain and Northern Ireland and the Government of the People's Republic of China on the Question of Hong Kong signed on 19 December 1984, the Government of the United Kingdom will restore Hong Kong to the People's Republic of China with effect from 1 July 1997. The Government of the United Kingdom will continue to have international responsibility for Hong Kong until that date. Therefore, from that date the Government of the United Kingdom will cease to be responsible for the international rights and obligations arising from application of the Convention to Hong Kong.

UNITED STATES OF AMERICA

Reservation made when signing Geneva Convention IV relative to the Protection of Civilian Persons in Time of War

Mr. Vincent, Minister of the United States of America in Switzerland, on signing the Geneva Convention relative to the Protection of Civilian Persons in Time of War of 12 August 1949, made the following declaration:

The Government of the United States fully supports the objectives of this Convention.

1 am instructed by my Government to sign, making the following reservation to Article 68:

The United States reserve the right to impose the death penalty in accordance with the provisions of Article 68, paragraph 2, without regard to whether the offences referred to therein are punishable by death under the law of the occupied territory at the time the occupation begins.

Reservations made on ratification[79] [80]

1. *Convention I for the Amelioration of the Wounded and Sick in Armed Forces in the Field*:

   The United States in ratifying the Geneva Convention for the Amelioration of the Condition of the Wounded and Sick in Armed Forces in the Field does so with the reservation that irrespective of any provision or provisions in said Convention to the contrary, nothing contained therein shall make unlawful, or obligate the United States of America to make unlawful, any use or right of use within the United States of America and its territories and possessions of the Red Cross emblem, sign, insignia, or words as was lawful by reason of domestic law and a use begun prior to 5 January 1905, provided such use by pre-1905 users does not extend to the placing of the Red Cross emblem, sign, or insignia upon aircraft, vessels, vehicles, buildings or other structures, or upon the ground.

   Rejecting the reservations which States have made with respect to the Geneva Convention for the Amelioration of the Condition of the Wounded and Sick in Armed Forces in the Field, the United States accepts treaty relations with all parties to that Convention, except as to the changes proposed by such reservations.

---

[78] Notification by the Swiss Government to the governments of the states parties to the Geneva Conventions of 12 August 1949 for the protection of War Victims, Berne, 24 June 1997.

[79] See Explanatory note of 2 September 1955, p. 681.

[80] Notification of the depositary to the ICRC of 8 August 1955; *UNTS*, Vol. 213, 1955, pp. 378–384.

2. *Convention II for the Amelioration of the Condition of Wounded, Sick and Shipwrecked Members of Armed Forces at Sea*:
Rejecting the reservations which States have made with respect to the Geneva Convention for the Amelioration of the Condition of Wounded, Sick and Shipwrecked Members of Armed Forces at Sea, the United States accepts treaty relations with all Parties to that Convention, except as to the changes proposed by such reservations.
3. *Convention III relative to the Treatment of Prisoners of War*:
Rejecting the reservations which States have made with respect to the Geneva Convention relative to the Treatment of Prisoners of War, the United States accepts treaty relations with all Parties to that Convention, except as to the changes proposed by such reservations.
4. *Convention IV relative to the Protection of Civilian Persons in Time of War*:
The United States reserves the right to impose the death penalty in accordance with the provisions of Article 68, paragraph 2, without regard to whether the offences referred to therein are punishable by death under the law of the occupied territory at the time the occupation begins.
Rejecting the reservations - other than to Article 68, paragraph 2 - which States have made with respect to the Geneva Convention relative to the Protection of Civilian Persons in Time of War, the United States accepts treaty relations with all Parties to that Convention, except as to the changes proposed by such reservations."

Note of the Embassy of the United States of America of 2 September 1955[81]
By a note of 22 September 1955, the Permanent Observer of Switzerland transmitted to the Secretariat of the United Nations a copy of the note addressed by the Embassy of the United States of America in Berne to the Political Department of the Swiss Confederation, the text of which reads as follows:

"AMERICAN EMBARRY, BERNE
No. 119
The Embassy of the United States of America presents its compliments to the Federal Political Department and has the honor to invite the attention of the Department to a clarification which the United States Government considers it necessary to make with respect to the *procès-verbal* signed on August 2, 1955 on the occasion of the deposit with the Swiss Government of the instruments of ratification by the United States of America of the Geneva Conventions of 1949 for the Protection of War Victims.

The Embassy has the honor to inform the Department that the statement regarding the reservations of other states which is embodied in each of the four ratifications is not considered by the United States Government to be a reservation to the convention. The Embassy is instructed to point out that only two reservations were made by the United States: the first relates to the use of the Red Cross emblem in so far as the Convention for the Amelioration of the Condition of the Wounded and Sick in Armed Forces in the Field is concerned, and the second, made at the time of signature, relates to the right to impose the death penalty, in so far as the Convention Relative to the Protection of Civilian Persons in Time of War is concerned. It is believed that this clarification of the distinction made by the United States Government between the actual reservations and the statements which accompanied the ratifications by the United States will forestall thed possibility of the future complications or misinterpretation which may arise if other Governments parties to the Conventions, on the basis of the *procès-verbal*, should be led to believe that the above-mentioned statements are themselves considered to be reservations by the United States.

The Embassy avails itself of this opportunity to renew to the Federal Political Department the assurance of its high consideration.

Berne, September 2, 1955"

---

[81] Notification of the depositary to the ICRC of 17 September 1955; *UNTS*, Vol. 213, 1955, p. 378.

Declaration concerning the accession of the Democratic Republic of Viet Nam[82]
The Government of the United States of America does not recognize the "Democratic Republic of Viet Nam". Bearing in mind, however, the purpose of the Geneva Conventions that their provisions should protect war victims in armed conflict, the Government of the United States of America notes that the 'Democratic Republic of Viet Nam' has accepted the provisions of the Geneva Conventions for the Protection of War Victims of 12 August 1949, and has indicated its intention to apply them, subject to certain reservations expressed by the "Democratic Republic of Viet Nam" as to which the attitude of the Government of the United States parallels its attitude towards reservations to the Conventions as communicated at the time of deposit of the United States instruments of ratification.

Declaration in respect of the accession of the Provisional Revolutionary Government of the Republic of South Viet Nam, effected with the Government of Switzerland of 31 December 1974[83]
Reference is made to a telegram dated January 18, 1974, and a note of the same date by which The Federal Political Department of the Swiss Confederation informed the Department of State of the deposit by the Provisional Revolutionary Government of The Republic of South Viet-Nam of its instruments of accession to the four Geneva Conventions of 1949 for the Protection of War Victims, subject to certain stated reservations.

The Government of the United States of America recognizes the Government of the Republic of Viet-Nam and does not recognize the "Provisional Revolutionary Government of the Republic of South Viet-Nam" as a government. The United States Government therefore does not recognize that the "Provisional Revolutionary Government of the Republic of South Viet-Nam" is qualified to accede to the Geneva Conventions. Bearing in mind, however, that it is the purpose of the Geneva Conventions that their provisions should protect war victims in armed conflict, the Government of the United States of America notes that the "Provisional Revolutionary Government of the Republic of South Viet-Nam" has indicated its intention to apply them subject to certain reservations. The reservations expressed with respect to the Third Geneva Convention go far beyond previous reservations, and are directed against the object and purpose of the Convention. Other reservations are similar to reservations expressed by others previously and concerning which the Government of the United States has previously declared its views. The Government of the United States rejects all the expressed reservations.

The Government of the United States notes that the views expressed in this note should not be understood as implying any withdrawal from the policy heretofore pursued by its armed forces in according the treatment provided by the Conventions to hostile armed forces.

Objection to the reservations made upon accession by Guinea-Bissau to the Geneva Conventions I, II and III. Notification effected with the Government of Switzerland on 4 March 1975[84]
The Department of State refers to the note of March 5, 1974 from the Embassy of Switzerland enclosing the notification of the Swiss Federal Political Department concerning the accession of the Republic of Guinea-Bissau to the Geneva Conventions of August 12, 1949 for the protection of war victims, subject to certain reservations. The reservations are similar to the reservations expressed by others previously with respect to the same or different conventions and concerning which the government of the United States has previously declared its views. The attitude of the Government of the United States with respect to all the reservations by the Republic of Guinea-Bissau par-

[82] Notification of the depositary to the ICRC of 2 October 1957.
[83] Notification of the depositary to the ICRC of 6 June 1975; *UNTS*, Vol. 972, 1975, p. 403.
[84] Notification of the depositary to the ICRC of 7 May 1975; *UNTS*, Vol. 970, 1975, pp. 367–368.

allels its attitude toward such other reservations. The Government of the United States, while rejecting the reservations, accepts treaty relations with the Republic of Guinea-Bissau.

URUGUAY (*reservation made on ratification to Articles 87, 100, and 101 of Convention III and to Article 68 of Convention* IV)[85]
With express reservations in respect of Articles 87, 100 and 101, third paragraph, and of Article 68, final paragraph, in so far as they involve the imposition and execution of the death penalty.

VIET-NAM, SOCIALIST REPUBLIC OF (*reservations made on accession of the Democratic Republic of Vietnam of 28 June* 1957)[86] [87]
In acceding to:
1. The Geneva Convention of 12 August 1949 for the Amelioration of the Wounded and Sick in Armed Forces in the Field,
2. The Geneva Convention of 12 August 1949 for the Amelioration of the Condition of Wounded, Sick and Shipwrecked Members of Armed Forces at Sea,
3. The Geneva Convention of 12 August 1949 relative to the Treatment of Prisoners of War,
4. The Geneva Convention relative to the Protection of Civilian Persons in Time of War, the Democratic Republic of Vietnam makes the following reservations:
1. As regards the *Geneva Convention of 12 August 1949 for the Amelioration of the Conditions of the Wounded and Sick in Armed Forces in the Field*:
   Article 10: A request by the Detaining Power to a neutral Power or to an organization providing guarantees of impartiality and effectiveness, to undertake the functions entrusted to the Protecting Powers by the Convention, will not be recognized as lawful by the Democratic Republic of Vietnam unless the State of which the wounded and sick in armed forces in the field are nationals has approved the request.
2. As regards the *Geneva Convention of 12 August 1949 for the Amelioration of the Condition of Wounded, Sick and Shipwrecked Members of Armed Forces at Sea*:
   Article 10: A request by the Detaining Power to a neutral Power or to an organization providing guarantees of impartiality and effectiveness, to undertake the functions entrusted to the Protecting Powers by the Convention, will not be recognized as lawful by the Democratic Republic of Vietnam unless the State of which the wounded and sick in armed forces in the field are nationals has approved the request.
3. As regards the *Geneva Convention of 12 August 1949 relative to the Treatment of Prisoners of War*:
   Article 4: The Provisional Revolutionary Government of the Republic of South Viet Nam does not recognize the provisions set forth in section 2 of said article relative to members of other militias and members of other volunteer corps, including those of organized resistance movements, because these provisions do not apply to the people's wars in the contemporary world.
   Article 10: A request by the Detaining Power, to a neutral Power or to an organization providing guarantees of impartiality and effectiveness, to undertake the functions entrusted to the Protecting Powers by the Convention, will not be recognized as lawful by the Democratic Republic of Vietnam unless the State of which the wounded and sick in armed forces in the field are nationals has approved the request.
   Article 12: The Democratic Republic of Vietnam declares that the transfer by the Detaining Power of prisoners of war to a Power which is a party to the Convention does not release the Detaining Power from its responsibility for the application of the provisions of the Convention to such prisoners.

[85] Notification of the depositary to the ICRC of 10 March 1969.
[86] Notification of the depositary to the ICRC of 23 July 1957.
[87] For objections by Australia and United Kingdom, see p. 652 and 679.

Article 85: The Democratic Republic of Vietnam declares that prisoners of war tried and convicted of war crimes or crimes against humanity, in accordance with the principles laid down by the Nuremberg Judicial Tribunal, shall not benefit from the provisions of the present Convention as is specified in Article 85,

4. *Geneva Convention of 12 August 1949 relative to the Protection of Civilian Persons in Time of War*:
Article 11: A request by the Detaining Power, to a neutral Power or to an organization providing guarantees of impartiality and effectiveness, to undertake the functions entrusted to the Protecting Powers by the Convention, will not be recognized as lawful by the Democratic Republic of Vietnam unless the State of which the wounded and sick in armed forces in the field are nationals has approved the request.
Article 45: The Democratic Republic of Vietnam declares that the transfer by the Detaining Power of protected persons to a Power which is a party to the Convention does not release the Detaining Power from its responsibility for the application of the provisions of the Convention relating to civilian persons in time of war.

By a letter dated 4 July 1976, the Minister of Foreign Affairs of the Socialist Republic of Vietnam addressed to the Chief of the Federal Political Department the following declaration
The Socialist Republic of Vietnam continues the participation of the Democratic Republic of Vietnam and of the Republic of South Vietnam in the four Geneva Conventions of 1949 on the protection of the victims of war, with the reservations specified by the Democratic Republic of Vietnam and the Republic of South Vietnam.[88]

[VIET NAM, PROVISIONAL REVOLUTIONARY GOVERNMENT OF SOUTH VIET NAM] (*reservations made upon accession on 3 December 1973*)[89] [90]

1. With regard to the *Geneva Convention for the Amelioration of the Condition of the Wounded and Sick in Armed Forces in the Field of 12 August 1949*:
Ad article 10.: The Provisional Revolutionary Government of the Republic of South Viet Nam recognizes as lawful a request by the Detaining Power to a neutral country or a humanitarian organization, to assume the functions performed by protecting Powers only when the State on which the wounded and sick members of armed forces in the field depend shall have given prior consent to such a request.
2. With regard to the *Geneva Convention for the Amelioration of the Condition of the Wounded, Sick and Shipwrecked Members of Armed Forces at Sea of 12 August 1949*:
Ad Article 10: The Provisional Revolutionary Government of the Republic of South Viet-Nam recognizes as lawful a request by the Detaining Power to a neutral country, or a humanitarian organization, to assume the functions performed by Protecting Powers only when the State on which the wounded, sick and shipwrecked members of armed forces at sea depend shall have given prior consent to such a request.
3. With regard to the *Geneva Convention relative to the Treatment of Prisoners of War of 12 August 1949*:
Ad Article 4: The Provisional Revolutionary Government of the Republic of South Viet Nam does not recognize the "conditions" lay down in item (2) of this article concerning "members of other militias and members of other volunteer corps, including those of organized resistance movements", because these conditions are not suited to cases of people's wars in the world of today.

---

[88] *UNTS*, Vol. 1028, 1976, p. 438.

[89] *UNTS*, Vol. 913, 1974, pp. 175–176. The Swiss Government made a declaration taking note of the accession to the Geneva Conventions, but without pronouncing the attitude on the status of the Provisional Revolutionary Government of the Republic of South Viet Nam.

[90] See also objections to the reservations made by the United Kingdom and the United States of America, pp. 679 and 682.

Ad Article 10: The Provisional Revolutionary Government of the Republic of South Viet Nam recognizes as lawful a request by the Detaining Power to a neutral country, or a humanitarian organization, to assume the functions performed by Protecting Powers only when the State on which the prisoners of war depend shall have given prior consent to such a request

Ad Article 12: The Provisional Revolutionary Government of the Republic of South Viet Nam declares that the transfer of prisoners of war by the Detaining Power to a Power which is a party to the Convention does not release the Detaining Power from its responsibility for the application of the provisions of the Convention.

Ad Article 85: The Provisional Revolutionary Government of the Republic of South Viet Nam declares that prisoners of war prosecuted and convicted for crimes of aggression, crimes of genocide or war crimes, and crimes against humanity in accordance with the principles established by the Nuremberg Tribunal shall not benefit from the provisions of the present Convention.

4. With regard to the *Geneva Convention relative to the Protection of Civilian Persons in Time of War of 12 August 1949*:

Ad article 11: The Provisional Revolutionary Government of the Republic of South Viet Nam recognizes as lawful a request by the Detaining Power to a neutral country, or a humanitarian organization, to assume the functions performed by Protecting Powers only when the State on which the civilian persons in question depend shall have given prior consent to such a request

Ad Article 45: The Provisional Revolutionary Government of the Republic of South Viet Nam declares that the transfer of civilian persons protected by this Convention to a Power which is a party to the Convention does not release the Detaining Power from its responsibility for the application of the provisions of the Convention."

VIET NAM (REPUBLIC OF)

Objections to the accession of the Provisional Revolutionary Government of South Viet Nam to 1949 Geneva Conventions, notified to the Government of Switzerland on 6 and 18 February 1974[91]

6 February 1974:

The so-called "Provisional Revolutionary Government of South Viet-Nam" can in no way be considered a Government. That name is merely a way of referring to the "National Liberation Front of South Viet-Nam", a body established by North Viet-Nam during the third Congress of the Lao-Dông Party (Communist Party) in September 1960 in order to camouflage its aggression against the Republic of Viet-Nam. The name "NLF" or "PRG" in no way changes the nature of that Organization, which entirely owes its existence to the direct support of the North Vietnamese forces.

Furthermore, the 1973 Paris Agreement[92] did not set up the "PRG" as a Government either in spirit or in letter. On the contrary, that Agreement specifically recognized the sovereignty of South Viet-Nam. The Government of the Republic of Viet-Nam, which was elected by its people in conformity with the country's Constitution, is the sole Government that legally represents that people.

The so-called "PRG", which does not constitute a Government and does not represent a State, therefore does not meet the definition of a Power referred to in articles 60, 59, 139 and 155, respectively of the four Geneva Conventions of 1949 and is therefore in no way qualified to request accession to the said Conventions.

For the above-mentioned reasons the Government of the Republic of Viet-Nam considers null and void the deposit of the instruments of accession of the so-called "PRG" to the four Geneva Conventions of 1949 for the protection of war victims.

---

91 *UNTS*, Vol. 917, 1974, pp. 296–297.

92 *UNTS*, Vol. 935, p. 2.

18 February 1974:
The Ministry would be grateful if the Embassy would kindly draw its Government's attention to the fact that the so-called Provisional Revolutionary Government of the Republic of South Viet Nam does not meet the requirements for being considered as representing a State and that it is therefore not competent to deposit the instruments of accession to the four above-mentioned Conventions, under articles 59, 60, 139 and 155 of the said Conventions.

In the event that deposit has been automatically registered by the Swiss Federal Government, in its capacity as depositary State of the Geneva Conventions in question, it shall be regarded as null and void by the Government of the Republic of Viet Nam. Furthermore, such deposit can in no way affect the position of the Government of the Republic of Viet Nam, stated on many occasions, concerning the so-called Provisional Revolutionary Government of the Republic of South Viet-Nam, which can in no way claim any governmental status whatsoever.

VIET NAM (REPUBLIC OF SOUTH) (*declaration relating to the objection made by the Republic of Viet Nam to the accession of the Provisions Revolutionary Government of the Republic of South Viet Nam in respect of 1949 Geneva Conventions. Effected with the Government of Switzerland on 19 March* 1974)[93]
The Ministry of Foreign Affairs of the Republic of South Viet Nam presents its compliments to the Swiss Federal Political Department and has the honour to inform it of its regret at the transmittal by the Federal Political Department, by notes of 15 February and 26 February 1974 to the Governments of the States parties to the 1949 Geneva Conventions, of the two notes dated 6 February 1974 from the Saigon administration addressed to the Federal Political Department and the Embassy of Switzerland in Saigon respectively, in which that administration claims to be the sole representative of South Viet Nam and declares that it objects to the accession of the Provisional Revolutionary Government of the Republic of South Viet Nam to the said Conventions.
....

As every one knows, the Paris Agreement on Viet Nam,[94] to which the Saigon administration is a signatory, recognizes the existence in South Viet Nam of two authorities and two zones under different control. In claiming to be the sole Government of South Viet Nam, that administration is acting contrary to international law and to reality, distorting, the facts with the aim of confusing public opinion about the situation in South Viet Nam since the signing of the Paris Agreement.

Created by the United States imperialists to serve their neo-colonialist war policy in South Viet Nam, it is nothing but a warmongering fascist clique which can survive only through military force and American to commit innumerable barbarous crimes against the population of South Viet Nam. It does not and cannot represent the South Vietnamese people, who are struggling against its regime of oppression, exploitation and police repression.

The Saigon administration therefore has neither any grounds nor any right to prevent the Provisional Revolutionary Government from acceding to the 1949 Geneva Conventions. Its objection to the perfectly proper and legal accession of the Provisional Revolutionary Government simply makes even more apparent its evil intentions of sabotaging the Paris Agreement on Viet Nam and preventing the restoration of peace and national reconciliation and concord in South Viet Nam.

It should be pointed out that the Provisional Revolutionary Government of the Republic of South Viet Nam is the government which led the just struggle for peace, independence and freedom for the South Vietnamese people, of which it is the sole authentic representative. As a signatory to the Paris Agreement on Viet Nam, a full member of the group of non-aligned countries and a Government recognized by 38 States, it has the right to accede to the Geneva Conventions with the requisite qualifi-

[93] *UNTS*, Vol. 941, 1974, pp. 319–320.
[94] *UNTS,* Vol. 913, p. 172.

cations, whether or not this is to the liking of the Saigon administration. Its accession, which is fully valid from the legal standpoint, has been officially registered by the Swiss Federal Government, the depositary of the said Conventions."

YEMEN, PEOPLE'S DEMOCRATIC REPUBLIC OF (SOUTH) (*declaration made on accession*)[95] [96]
The Government of the People's Democratic Republic of Yemen declares that the accession of the People's Democratic Republic of Yemen to these Conventions by no means implies recognition of Israel.

YUGOSLAVIA, FEDERAL PEOPLE'S REPUBLIC OF (*reservation made on signature and maintained on ratification*)[97]
Mr. Milan Ristic, Minister in Switzerland, made the following declaration:[98]

1. On signing the *Geneva Convention for the Amelioration of the Condition of the Wounded and Sick in Armed Forces in the Field*, I declare that the Government of the Federal People's Republic of Yugoslavia adheres to the said Convention, with a reservation in respect of Article 10.
   The Government of the Federal People's Republic of Yugoslavia will not consider as legal a request by the Detaining Power that a neutral State or an international organization or a humanitarian organization should undertake the functions performed under the present Convention by the Protecting Powers, on behalf of the wounded and sick, or medical personnel and chaplains, unless the Government whose nationals they are has given its consent.
2. On signing the *Geneva Convention for the Amelioration of the Condition of Wounded, Sick and Shipwrecked Members of Armed Forces at Sea*, I declare that the Government of the Federal People's Republic of Yugoslavia adheres to the said Convention with a reservation in respect of Article 10.
   The Government of the Federal People's Republic of Yugoslavia win not consider as legal a request by the Detaining Power that a neutral State or an international organization or a humanitarian organization should undertake the functions performed under the present Convention by the Protecting Powers, on behalf of the wounded, sick and shipwrecked, or medical personnel and chaplains, unless the Government whose nationals they are has given its consent.
3. On signing the *Geneva Convention relative to the Treatment of Prisoners of War*, I declare that the Government of the Federal People's Republic of Yugoslavia adheres to the said Convention, with reservations in respect of Articles 10 and 12.
   In regard to Article 10: The Government of the Federal People's Republic of Yugoslavia will not consider as legal a request by the Detaining Power that a neutral State or an international organization or a humanitarian organization should undertake the functions performed under the present Convention by the Protecting Powers, on behalf of prisoners of war, unless the Government whose nationals they are has given its consent.
   In regard to Article 12: The Government of the Federal People's Republic of Yugoslavia will not consider that the Power, which has effected the transfer of prisoners of war, is freed from its responsibility f6r the application of the Convention for the whole of the time during which such prisoners of war are in the custody of the Power accepting them.
4. On signing the *Geneva Convention relative to the Protection of Civilian Persons in Time of War*, I declare that the Government of the Federal People's Republic of Yugoslavia adheres to the said Convention, with reservations in respect of Articles 11 and 45.

[95] Notification of the depositary to the ICRC of 27 June 1991; *UNTS*, Vol. 1049, 1977, p. 32.
[96] See also the declaration of Israel, p. 664.
[97] See explanatory note in the document *No. 61*, note 16, p. 850.
[98] For objections by Australia, Barbados, New Zealand and United Kingdom, see pp. 652, 653, 668 and 678.

In regard to Article 11: The Government of the Federal People's Republic of Yugoslavia will not consider as legal a request by the Detaining Power that a neutral State or an international organization or a humanitarian organization should undertake the functions performed under the present Convention by the Protecting Powers, on behalf of protected persons unless the Government whose nationals they are has given its consent.

In regard to Article 45: The Government of the Federal People's Republic of Yugoslavia will not consider it legal for a Power, which effects a transfer of protected persons to another' Power, to be freed from its responsibility for applying the Convention for the whole of the time during which such protected persons are in the custody of the Power accepting them.

No. 53

RESOLUTIONS OF THE DIPLOMATIC CONFERENCE OF GENEVA, 1949

INTRODUCTORY NOTE: The Resolutions of the Diplomatic Conference of Geneva of 1949 have no force of law. They were adopted by a majority vote.

The titles given for the Resolutions have no official character and were not adopted by the Diplomatic Conference. They were drafted by the Conference Secretariat and are used in the edition of the Geneva Conventions published by the International Committee of the Red Cross.

See also note introducing the Final Act of the Diplomatic Conference 1949 (*No. 45*).

AUTHENTIC TEXTS: English and French. The text below is reprinted from the *Final Record of the Diplomatic Conference of Geneva of 1949*, Vol. I, Federal Political Department, Berne, pp. 361–362.

TEXT PUBLISHED IN: *Final Record of the Diplomatic Conference of Geneva of 1949*, Vol. I, Berne, Federal Political Department, pp. 361–362 (Engl.); *Actes de la Conférence Diplomatique de Genève de 1949*, tome I, Berne, Département Politique Fédéral, pp. 355–356 (French); *UNTS*, Vol. 75, p. 21 (Engl., French); *The Geneva Conventions of 12 August 1949*, 2nd revised edn., Geneva, International Committee of the Red Cross, July 1950, pp. 223–226 (Engl.); *Les Conventions de Genève du 12 août 1949*, 3ème édition, Genève, Comité international de la Croix-Rouge, 1951, pp. 228–231 (French); *Los Convenios de Ginebra del 12 de Agosto de 1949*, Ginebra, Comité Internacional de la Cruz Roja, 1950, pp. 231–234 (Span.); *International Red Cross Handbook*, 1983, pp. 213–215 (Engl.); *Manuel de la Croix-Rouge internationale*, 1983, pp. 221–223 (French); *Manual de la Cruz Roja internacional*, 1983, pp. 214–216 (Span.); *Handbook of the International Movement*, 1994, pp. 195–197 (Engl.); *Manuel du Mouvement internacional*, 1994, pp. 203–205 (French); *Manual del Movimiento internacional*, 1994, pp. 197–199 (Span.); *Droit des conflits armés*, pp. 725–731 (French); ICRC website: www.icrc.org/ihl.nsf.

* * *

TABLE OF CONTENTS

Resolution 1. Submission of Disputes to the International Court of Justice

The Conference recommends that, in the case of a dispute relating to the interpretation or application of the present Conventions which cannot be settled by other means, the High Contracting Parties concerned endeavour to agree between themselves to refer such dispute to the International Court of Justice.

Resolution 2.[1] Creation of an International Body in the Absence of a Protecting Power

Whereas circumstances may arise in the event of the outbreak of a future international conflict in which there will be no Protecting Power with whose cooperation and under whose scrutiny the Conventions for the Protection of Victims of War can be applied; and

whereas Article 10 of the Geneva Convention for the Amelioration of the Condition of the Wounded and Sick in Armed Forces in the Field of August 12, 1949, Article 10 of the Geneva Convention for the Amelioration of the Condition of Wounded, Sick and Shipwrecked Members of Armed Forces at Sea of August 12, 1949, Article 10 of the Geneva Convention relative to the Treatment of Prisoners of War of August 12, 1949, and Article 11 of the Geneva Convention relative to the Protection of Civilian Persons in Time of War of August 12, 1949, provide that the High Contracting Parties may at any time agree to entrust to a body which offers all guarantees of impartiality and efficacy the duties incumbent on the Protecting Powers by virtue of the aforesaid Conventions,

the Conference recommends that consideration be given as soon as possible to the advisability of setting up an international body, the functions of which shall be, in the absence of a Protecting Power, to fulfil the duties performed by Protecting Powers in regard to the application of the Conventions for the Protection of War Victims.

Resolution 3. Preparation of a Model Agreement on the Percentage and Relief of Retained Personnel

Whereas agreements may only with difficulty be concluded during hostilities;

whereas Article 28 of the Geneva Convention for the Amelioration of the Condition of the Wounded and Sick in Armed Forces in the Field of August 12, 1949, provides that the Parties to the conflict shall, during hostilities, make

[1] For declaration in respect of this resolution by the USSR see p. 457 (paragraph 2).

arrangements for relieving where possible retained personnel, and shall settle the procedure of such relief;

whereas Article 31 of the same Convention provides that, as from the outbreak of hostilities, Parties to the conflict may determine by special arrangement the percentage of personnel to be retained, in proportion to the number of prisoners and the distribution of the said personnel in the camps,

the Conference requests the International Committee of the Red Cross to prepare a model agreement on the two questions referred to in the two Articles mentioned above and to submit it to the High Contracting Parties for their approval.

Resolution 4. Badges and Identity Cards of Medical Personnel

Whereas Article 33 of the Geneva Convention of July 27, 1929, for the Relief of the Wounded and Sick in Armies in the Field, concerning the identity documents to be carried by medical personnel, was only partially observed during the course of the recent war, thus creating serious difficulties for many members of such personnel,

the Conference recommends that States and National Red Cross Societies take all necessary steps in time of peace to have medical personnel duly provided with the badges and identity cards prescribed in Article 40 of the new Convention.

Resolution 5. Misuse of the Red Cross Emblem

Whereas misuse has frequently been made of the Red Cross emblem,

the Conference recommends that States take strict measures to ensure that the said emblem, as well as other emblems referred to in Article 38 of the Geneva Convention for the Amelioration of the Condition of the Wounded and Sick in Armed Forces in the Field of August 12, 1949, is used only within the limits prescribed by the Geneva Conventions, in order to safeguard their authority and protect their high significance.

Resolution 6.[2] Improvement of Means of Communication between Hospital Ships and Warships, and Preparation of International Regulations for the Use of such Means

Whereas the present Conference has not been able to raise the question of the technical study of means of communication between hospital ships, on the one hand, and warships and military aircraft on the other, since that study went beyond its terms of reference;

whereas this question is of the greatest importance for the safety and efficient operation of hospital ships,

the Conference recommends that the High Contracting Parties will, in the near future, instruct a Committee of Experts to examine technical improvements of modern means of communication between hospital ships, on the one hand, and warships and military aircraft, on the other, and also to study the pos-

[2] For declaration in respect of this resolution by Italy, see p. 665.

sibility of drawing up an International Code laying down precise regulations for the use of those means, in order that hospital ships may be assured of the maximum protection and be enabled to operate with the maximum efficiency.

Resolution 7. Notification by Hospital Ships of their Position by Wireless

The Conference, being desirous of securing the maximum protection for hospital ships, expresses the hope that all High Contracting Parties to the Geneva Convention for the Amelioration of the Condition of Wounded, Sick and Shipwrecked Members of Armed forces at Sea of August 12, 1949, will arrange that, when ever conveniently practicable, such ships shall frequently and regularly broadcast particulars of their position, route and speed.

Resolution 8. Pacific Settlement of International Differences

The Conference wishes to affirm before all nations:

that, its work having been inspired solely by humanitarian aims, its earnest hope is that, in the future, Governments may never have to apply the Geneva Conventions for the Protection of War Victims;

that its strongest desire is that the Powers, great and small, may always reach a friendly settlement of their differences through cooperation and understanding between nations, so that peace shall reign on earth for ever.

Resolution 9. Specimen Telegraphic Messages for Prisoners of War

Whereas Article 71 of the Geneva Convention relative to the Treatment of Prisoners of War of August 12, 1949, provides that prisoners of war who have been without news for a long period, or who are unable to receive news from their next of kin or to give them news by the ordinary postal route, as well as those who are at a great distance from their home, shall be permitted to send telegrams, the fees being charged against the prisoners of war's account with the Detaining Power or paid in the currency at their disposal, and that prisoners of war shall likewise benefit by these facilities in cases of urgency; and

whereas to reduce the cost, often prohibitive, of such telegrams or cables, it appears necessary that some method of grouping messages should be introduced whereby a series of short specimen messages concerning personal health, health of relatives at home, schooling, finance, etc., could be drawn up and numbered, for use by prisoners of war in the aforesaid circumstances,

the Conference, therefore, requests the International Committee of the Red Cross to prepare a series of specimen messages covering these requirements and to submit them to the High Contracting Parties for their approval.

Resolution 10. Recognition of a Party to a Conflict by Powers not Taking Part in such Conflict

The Conference considers that the conditions under which a Party to a conflict can be recognized as a belligerent by Powers not taking part in this conflict, are governed by the general rules of international law on the subject and are in no way modified by the Geneva Conventions.

Resolution 11. Financial Support for the International Committee of the Red Cross

Whereas the Geneva Conventions require the International Committee of the Red Cross to be ready at all times and in all circumstances to fulfil the humanitarian tasks entrusted to it by these Conventions,

the Conference recognizes the necessity of providing regular financial support for the International Committee of the Red Cross.

No. 54

BASIC PRINCIPLES OF THE LEGAL STATUS OF THE COMBATANTS STRUGGLING AGAINST COLONIAL AND ALIEN DOMINATION AND RACIST REGIMES

Resolution 3103 (XXVIII) of the United Nations General Assembly adopted on 12 December 1973

INTRODUCTORY NOTE: Beginning in 1968, the General Assembly adopted yearly resolutions urging governments to ensure that the Geneva Conventions of 1949 would be applied to fighters against colonial and alien domination and against racist régimes. The following resolution attempts a general regulation of the legal status of combatants in such struggles. Since its adoption, Protocol I Additional to the Geneva Conventions was signed in 1977 (*No. 53*) which puts struggles of this kind on a par with international armed conflicts.

AUTHENTIC TEXTS: Chinese, English, French, Russian, Spanish.

TEXT PUBLISHED IN: *Resolutions adopted by the General Assembly during its Twenty-eighth session,* Vol. I, *18 September–18 December 1973*, General Assembly Official Records: Twenty-eighth session, Supplement No. 30 (A/9030), New York, United Nations, 1974, pp. 142–143 (Engl. – see also Chinese, French, Russian and Spanish editions); *Droit des conflits armés*, pp. 733–736 (French).

* * *

The General Assembly,

Recalling *that the Charter of the United Nations reaffirms faith in the dignity and worth of the human person,*

Recalling *resolution 2444 (XXIII) of 19 December 1968 in which the General Assembly,* inter alia, *recognized the need for applying basic humanitarian principles in all armed conflicts,*

Recognizing further *the importance of respecting the Hague Convention of 1907, the Geneva Protocol of 1925, the Geneva Conventions of 1949 and other universally recognized norms of modern international law for the protection of human rights in armed conflicts,*

Reaffirming *that the continuation of colonialism in all its forms and manifestations, as noted in General Assembly resolution 2621 (XXV) of 12 October 1970, is a crime and that colonial peoples have the inherent right to struggle by all necessary means at their disposal against colonial Powers and alien domination in exercise of their right of self-determination recognized in the Charter of the United Nations and the Declaration on Principles of International Law concerning Friendly Relations and Co-operation among States in accordance with the Charter of the United Nations.*[1]

[1] Resolution 2625 (XXV), annex.

Stressing *that the policy of* apartheid *and racial oppression has been condemned by all countries and peoples, and that the pursuing of such a policy has been recognized as an international crime,*

Reaffirming *the declarations made in General Assembly resolutions 2548 (XXIV) of 11 December 1969 and 2708 (XXV) of 14 December 1970 that the practice of using mercenaries against national liberation movements in the colonial Territories constitutes a criminal act,*

Recalling *the numerous appeals of the General Assembly to the colonial Powers, and those occupying foreign territories as well as to the racist régimes set forth,* inter alia, *in resolutions 2383 (XXIII) of 7 November 1968, 2508 (XXIV) of 21 November 1969, 2547 (XXIV) of 11 December 1969, 2652 (XXV) of 3 December 1970, 2678 (XXV) of 9 December 1970, 2707 (XXV) of 14 December 1970, 2795 (XXVI) and 2796 (XXVI) of 10 December 1971 and 2871 (XXVI) of 20 December 1971, to ensure the application to the fighters for freedom and self-determination of the provisions of the Geneva Convention relative to the Treatment of Prisoners of War, of 12 August 1949, and the Geneva Convention relative to the Protection of Civilian Persons in Time of War, of 12 August 1949,*

Deeply concerned *at the fact that, despite the numerous appeals of the General Assembly, compliance with the provisions of the said Conventions has not yet been ensured,*

Noting *that the treatment of the combatants struggling against colonial and alien domination and racist régimes captured as prisoners still remains inhuman,*

Recalling *its resolutions 2674 (XXV) of 9 December 1970 and 2852 (XXVI) of 20 December 1971, in which it pointed out the need for the elaboration of additional international instruments and norms envisaging,* inter alia, *the increase of the protection of persons struggling for freedom against colonial and alien domination and racist régimes,*

Solemnly proclaims *the following basic principles of the legal status of the combatants struggling against colonial and alien domination and racist régimes without prejudice to their elaboration in future within the framework of the development of international law applying to the protection of human rights in armed conflicts:*

1. *The struggle of peoples under colonial and alien domination and racist régimes for the implementation of their right to self-determination and independence is legitimate and in full accordance with the principles of international law.*
2. *Any attempt to suppress the struggle against colonial and alien domination and racist régimes is incompatible with the Charter of the United Nations, the Declaration on Principles of International Law concerning Friendly Relations and Co-operation among States in accordance with the Charter of the United Nations, the Universal Declaration of Human Rights and the Declaration on the Granting of Independence to Colonial Countries and Peoples*[2] *and constitutes a threat to international peace and security.*
3. *The armed conflicts involving the struggle of peoples against colonial and alien domination and racist régimes are to be regarded as international armed conflicts in the sense of the 1949 Geneva Conventions, and the legal*

2 Resolution 1514 (XV).

status envisaged to apply to the combatants in the 1949 Geneva Conventions and other international instruments is to apply to the persons engaged in armed struggle against colonial and alien domination and racist régimes.

4. *The combatants struggling against colonial and alien domination and racist régimes captured as prisoners are to be accorded the status of prisoners of war and their treatment should be in accordance with the provisions of the Geneva Convention relative to the Treatment of Prisoners of War, of 12 August 1949.*
5. *The use of mercenaries by colonial and racist régimes against the national liberation movements struggling for their freedom and independence from the yoke of colonialism and alien domination is considered to be a criminal act and the mercenaries should accordingly be punished as criminals.*
6. *The violation of the legal status of the combatants struggling against colonial and alien domination and racist régimes in the course of armed conflicts entails full responsibility in accordance with the norms of international law.*

VOTE

Resolution 3103 (XXVIII) was adopted by a vote of 83 in favour, 13 against and 19 abstentions.

RECORDED VOTE

In favour: Afghanistan, Algeria, Argentina, Bahrain, Barbados, Bhutan, Botswana, Bulgaria, Burma, Burundi, Byelorussian Soviet Socialist Republic, Cameroon, Central African Republic, Chad, China, Congo, Cuba, Cyprus, Czechoslovakia, Dahomey, Democratic Yemen, Ecuador, Egypt, El Salvador, Equatorial Guinea, Ethiopia, Gabon, German Democratic Republic, Ghana, Guinea, Guyana, Hungary, India, Indonesia, Iraq, Ireland, Ivory Coast, Jamaica, Kenya, Kuwait, Laos, Lebanon, Lesotho, Liberia, Libyan Arab Republic, Madagascar, Malaysia, Mali, Mauritania, Mexico, Mongolia, Nepal, Nicaragua, Niger, Nigeria, Oman, Pakistan, Panama, Peru, Philippines, Poland, Qatar, Romania, Rwanda, Senegal, Sierra Leone, Singapore, Sri Lanka, Sudan, Syrian Arab Republic, Thailand, Togo, Trinidad and Tobago, Tunisia, Uganda, Ukrainian Soviet Socialist Republic, Union of Soviet Socialist Republics, United Arab Emirates, United Republic of Tanzania, Yemen, Yugoslavia, Zaire, Zambia.

Against: Austria, Belgium, Brazil, France, Germany (Federal Republic of), Israel, Italy, Luxembourg, Portugal, South Africa, United Kingdom of Great Britain and Northern Ireland, United States of America, Uruguay.

Abstaining: Australia, Canada, Costa Rica, Denmark, Finland, Greece, Guatemala, Honduras, Iceland, Iran, Japan, Malawi, Netherlands, New Zealand, Norway, Paraguay, Spain, Sweden, Turkey.

No. 55

FINAL ACT OF THE DIPLOMATIC CONFERENCE ON THE REAFFIRMATION AND DEVELOPMENT OF INTERNATIONAL HUMANITARIAN LAW APPLICABLE IN ARMED CONFLICTS

Signed at Geneva, 10 June 1977

INTRODUCTORY NOTE: Soon after the adoption of the four Geneva Conventions of 1949 it became clear that additional rules would be necessary for the protection of the civilian population against the effects of hostilities. The Geneva Conventions are concerned only with persons in the power of a party to a conflict, the only exception being Part II (Articles 13–26) of the Fourth Geneva Convention (*No. 52*), which deals with the protection of the population against certain consequences of war.

In 1956, the ICRC, with the approval of the International Conference of the Red Cross, submitted to the governments the Draft Rules for the Limitation of the Dangers Incurred by the Civilian Population in Time of War (*No. 30*). The time was not ready, however, for their adoption as an international convention. It was only in the mid-1960s that the interest in the law of arrned conflicts awoke as a consequence of the conflicts in Vietnam, the Middle East, Nigeria and other parts of the world, later also in connection with the struggles against colonial and alien domination and racist regimes. In 1965, the International Conference of the Red Cross adopted a resolution urging the ICRC to pursue the development of international humanitarian law (*No. 31*). In 1968, the International Conference on Human Rights at Teheran, convened by the United Nations General Assembly, emphasized the need for additional humanitarian conventions (*No. 32*), and in the same year, the General Assembly supported this request (*No. 33*). In 1969, the International Conference of the Red Cross asked the ICRC to work out proposals for the completion of the humanitarian law and to convene government and other experts for consultation on such proposals.

On the basis of these and later resolutions, the ICRC convened two successive conferences of government experts in Geneva (24 May to 12 June 1971, and 3 May to 3 June 1972) in order to prepare two draft protocols additional to the Geneva Conventions, one on international armed conflicts, the other on non-international armed conflicts. In 1973, the ICRC published the two draft protocols and the Swiss Federal Council convened the Diplomatic Conference which held four sessions from 1974 to 1977. The dates of the sessions and the states represented at them are indicated in the Final Act. The two Protocols were adopted by consensus on 8 June 1977. The Final Act was adopted at the plenary meeting of the Conference on 9 June 1977 by 78 votes to one, with 12 abstentions. It was signed on 10 June 1977 by the representatives of 102 states and of 3 national liberation movements. The two Protocols were opened for signature on 12 December 1977.

The Final Act has no force of law.

AUTHENTIC TEXTS: Arabic, English, French, Russian and Spanish.

TEXT PUBLISHED IN: (The indications are given for the Final Act as well as for the two Protocols and resolutions.) *Official Records of the Diplomatic Con-*

ference on the Reaffirmation and Development of International Humanitarian Law applicable in Armed Conflicts, Geneva (1974-1977), Vol. 1, Bern, Federal Political Department, 1978, *Final Act*, pp. 3–114, *Protocols*, pp. 115–198, *Resolutions 17–24*, pp. 194–218. *Resolutions 1–16*, on pages following p. 219 (Engl. – see also the Arabic, French, Russian and Spanish editions); *UNTS*, Vol. 1125, 1979, *Final Act*, pp. 435–535, *Protocol I*, pp. 3–434, *Protocol II*, pp. 609–699, *Resolutions*, pp. 536–608 (Arabic, Engl., French, Russ., Span.); *United Nations General Assembly, Respect for Human Rights in Armed Conflicts. Fourth session of the Diplomatic Conference on the Reaffirmation and Development of International Humanitarian Law Applicable in Armed Conflicts, Report of the Secretary General,* United Nations document A/32/144, 15 August 1977, *Protocols, Annex I and II* (Engl. – See also Arabic, Chinese, French, Russian and Spanish texts); *Commentary on the Additional Protocols of 8 June 1977 to the Geneva Conventions of 12 August 1949*, Yves Sandoz, Christophe Swiniarski and Bruno Zimmermann, eds., Geneva, ICRC, Martinus Nijhoff Publishers, 1987, *Protocols* pp. 19–1509, *Resolutions*, pp 1511–1529, *Final Act*, p. 1531 (Engl.); *Commentaire des Protocoles additionnales du 8 juin 1977 aux Conventions de Genève du 12 août 1949,* Yves Sandoz, Christophe Swiniarski and Bruno Zimmermann, eds., Genève, CICR, Martinus Nijhoff Publishers, 1986, *Protocols*, pp. 19–1531, *Resolutions*, pp. 1533–1551, *Final Act*, p. 1553 (French); M. Bothe, K. J. Partsch and W. A. Solf, *New Rules for Victims of Armed Conflicts. Commentary on the two 1977 Protocols Additional to the Geneva Conventions of 1949*, The Hague, Martinus Nijhoff Publishers, 1982, *Protocols*, pp. 31–705 (Engl.); *International Red Cross Handbook,* 1983, *Final Act*, pp. 317–318 (extracts), *Protocols*, pp. 216–296, *Resolutions*, pp. 304–316 (Engl.); *Manual de la Cruz Roja Internacional,* 1983, *Final Act*, pp. 321–322 (extracts), *Protocols*, pp. 217–307, *Resolutions*, pp. 308–320 (Span.); *Manuel de la Croix-Rouge Internationale,* 1983, *Final Act*, pp. 329–330, *Protocols*, pp. 224–315, *Resolutions*, pp. 316–328 (French); *International Review of the Red Cross*, No. 197–198, August–September 1977, Special double issue, *Final Act*, pp. 123–124 (extracts), *Protocols*, pp. 3–101, *Resolutions*, pp. 103–121 (Engl.); *Revue Internationale de la Croix-Rouge*, No. 704–705, août–septembre 1977, Numéro spécial double, Final (French); *Revista Internacional de la Cruz Roja*, No. 20–21, agosto–septiembre de 1977, Numero especial doble, *Final Act*, pp. 125–126 (extracts), *Protocols*, pp. 3–103, *Resolutions*, pp. 105–124 (Span.); *Handbook of the International Movement*, 1994, *Final Act*, pp. 294–295 (extracts); *Protocols*, pp. 198–280; *Resolutions*, pp. 281–293 (Engl.); *Manuel du Mouvement international*, 1994, *Final Act*, pp. 306–307 (extracts); *Protocols*, pp. 206–292; *Resolutions*, pp. 293–305 (French); *Manual del Movimiento internacional*, 1994, *Final Act*, pp. 298–299 (extracts); *Protocols*, pp. 200–284; *Resolutions*, pp. 285–297 (Span.); *ILM*, Vol. 16, No. 6, 1977, pp. 1391–1449 (Engl.); *AJIL*, Vol. 72, 1978, pp. 457–509 (Engl.); Roberts and Guelff, *Protocols*, pp. 387–458 (Engl.); Ronzitti, *Protocol I*, pp. 673–759 (Engl.); *Droit des conflits armés*, pp. 737–894 (French); *RGDIP,* tome XXXII, No. 1, 1978, *Protocols*, pp. 329–398 (French); *Handbuch des Deutschen Roten Kreuzes zum IV. Genfer Rotkreuz-Abkommen und zu den Zusatzprotokollen*, Bonn, Deutsches Rotes Kreuz, 1981, *Protocols*, pp. 18–379, *Resolutions*, pp. 381–416 (Engl., French, German, Russ.); ICRC website: www.icrc.org/ihl.nsf.

* * *

1. The Diplomatic Conference on the Reaffirmation and Development of International Humanitarian Law Applicable in Armed Conflicts, convened by the Swiss Federal Council, held four sessions in Geneva (from 20 February to 29 March 1974, from 3 February to 18 April 1975, from 21 April to 11 June 1976 and from 17 March to 10 June 1977). The object of the Conference was to study two draft Additional Protocols prepared, after official and private consultations, by the International Committee of the Red Cross and intended to supplement the four Geneva Conventions of 12 August 1949:

Geneva Convention for the Amelioration of the Condition of the Wounded and Sick in Armed Forces in the Field (I);
Geneva Convention for the Amelioration of the Condition of Wounded, Sick and Shipwrecked Members of Armed Forces at Sea (II);
Geneva Convention relative to the Treatment of Prisoners of War (III);
Geneva Convention relative to the Protection of Civilian Persons in Time of War (IV).

The United Nations General Assembly supported the efforts of the Diplomatic Conference by adopting successive resolutions relating to human rights in periods of armed conflict:

2444 (XXIII) Respect for human rights in armed conflicts
2597 (XXIV) Respect for human rights in armed conflicts
2673 (XXV) Protection of journalists engaged in dangerous missions in areas of armed conflict
2674 (XXV) Respect for human rights in armed conflicts
2675 (XXV) Basic principles for the protection of civilian populations in armed conflicts
2676 (XXV) Respect for human rights in armed conflicts
2677 (XXV) Respect for human rights in armed conflicts
2852 (XXVI) Respect for human rights in armed conflicts
2853 (XXVI) Respect for human rights in armed conflicts
2854 (XXVI) Protection of journalists engaged in dangerous missions in areas of armed conflict
3032 (XXVII) Respect for human rights in armed conflicts
3058 (XXVIII) Protection of journalists engaged in dangerous missions in areas of armed conflict
3076 (XXVIII) Napalm and other incendiary weapons and all aspects of their possible use
3102 (XXVIII) Respect for human rights in armed conflicts
3220 (XXIX) Assistance and co-operation in accounting for persons who are missing or dead in armed conflicts
3245 (XXIX) Human rights in armed conflicts: protection of journalists engaged in dangerous missions in areas of armed conflict
3255 (XXIX) Napalm and other incendiary weapons and all aspects of their possible use
3318 (XXIX) Declaration on the protection of women and children in emergency and armed conflict
3319 (XXIX) Respect for human rights in armed conflicts
3464 (XXX) Napalm and other incendiary weapons and all aspects of their possible use
3500 (XXX) Respect for human rights in armed conflicts

31/19	*Respect for human rights in armed conflicts*
31/64	*Incendiary and other specific conventional weapons which may be the subject of prohibitions or restrictions of use for humanitarian reasons*

2. One hundred and twenty-six States were represented at the first session of the Conference, 121 States at the second session, 106 States at the third session and 109 States at the fourth session. Representatives of the following States were present at the Conference.

Afghanistan
Albania (First Session)
Algeria
Argentina
Australia
Austria
Bangladesh
Belgium
Benin[1] *(First and Second Sessions)*
Bolivia
Botswana (First and Second Sessions)
Brazil
Bulgaria
Burma (First Session)
Burundi (First and Second Sessions)
Byelorussian Soviet Socialist Republic
Canada
Cape Verde (Fourth Session)
Central African Empire[2]
Chad (First and Second Sessions)
Chile
China (First Session)
Colombia
Congo (First and Second Sessions)
Costa Rica
Cuba
Cyprus
Czechoslovakia
Democratic Kampuchea[3]*(First and Second Sessions)*
Democratic People's Republic of Korea
Democratic Republic of Viet-Nam (First, Second and Third Sessions)
Democratic Yemen (First and Fourth Sessions)
Denmark
Dominican Republic (First, Second and Fourth Sessions)
Ecuador
Liechtenstein
Luxembourg
Madagascar
Malaysia (First, Second and Fourth Sessions)
Mali (First, Second and Fourth Sessions)
Malta
Mauritania
Mauritius
Mexico
Monaco
Mongolia
Morocco
Mozambique (Third and Fourth Sessions)
Netherlands
New Zealand
Nicaragua
Niger (First and Second Sessions)
Nigeria
Norway
Oman
Pakistan
Panama
Paraguay (First and Second Sessions)
Peru
Philippines
Poland
Portugal
Qatar
Republic of Korea
Republic of South Viet-Nam (Third Session)
Republic of Viet-Nam (First and Second Sessions)
Romania
San Marino
Saudi Arabia
Senegal

1 Formerly Dahomey.
2 Formerly Central African Republic.
3 Formerly Khmer Republic.

Egypt
El Salvador (First and Second Sessions)
Finland
France
Gabon (First, Second and Third Sessions)
Gambia (First, Second and Fourth Sessions)
German Democratic Republic
Germany, Federal Republic of
China
Greece
Guatemala
Guinea (Second Session)
Guinea-Bissau (First and Second Sessions)
Haiti (First and Second Sessions)
Holy See
Honduras
Hungary
Iceland
India
Indonesia
Iran
Iraq
Ireland
Israel
Italy
Ivory Coast
Jamaica (Third and Fourth Sessions)
Japan
Jordan
Kenya (First and Fourth Sessions)
Kuwait
Lebanon
Lesotho (Second Session)
Liberia (First, Second and Third Sessions)
Socialist People's Libyan Arab Jamahiriya[4]
Socialist Republic of Viet Nam (Fourth Session)
Somalia (Fourth Session)
South Africa (First Session)
Spain
Sri Lanka
Sudan
Swaziland (Second, Third and Fourth Sessions)
Sweden
Switzerland
Syrian Arab Republic
Thailand
Togo (First Session)
Trinidad And Tobago (First, Second and Third Sessions)
Tunisia
Turkey
Uganda
Ukrainian Soviet Socialist Republic
Union of Soviet Socialist Republics
United Arab Emirates
United Kingdom of Great Britain and Northern Ireland
United Republic of Cameroon[5]
United Republic of Tanzania
United States of America
Upper Volta (First, Second and Third Sessions)
Uruguay
Venezuela
Yemen
Yugoslavia
Zaire
Zambia (First Session)

3. In view of the paramount importance of ensuring broad participation in the work of the Conference, which was of a fundamentally humanitarian nature, and because the progressive development and codification of international humanitarian law applicable in armed conflicts is a universal task in which the national liberation movements can contribute positively, the Conference by its resolution 3 (I) decided to invite also the national liberation movements recognized by the regional intergovernmental organizations concerned to participate fully in the deliberations of the Conference and its Main Committees, it being understood that only delegations representing States were entitled to vote. The national liberation movements listed below accepted that invitation and were represented at the Conference:

[4] Formerly Libyan Arab Republic.
[5] Formerly Cameroon.

African National Congress (South Africa) (ANC) (first, second and third sessions)
African National Council of Zimbabwe (Rhodesia) (ANCZ) (third and fourth sessions)
Angola National Liberation Front (FNLA) (first and second sessions)
Mozambique Liberation Front (FRELIMO) (first session)
Palestine Liberation Organization (PLO)
Panafricanist Congress (South Africa) (PAC) (first, second and fourth sessions)
People's Movement for the Liberation of Angola (MPLA) (first and second sessions)
Seychelles People's United Party (SPUP) (first session)
South West Africa People's Organization (SWAPO)
Zimbabwe African National Union (ZANU) (first and second sessions)
Zimbabwe African People's Union (ZAPU) (first and second sessions)

4. The following organizations were represented at the Conference with observer status:

Council of Europe
Institut Henry-Dunant
Inter-Governmental Maritime Consultative Organization (IMCO)
International Civil Aviation Organization (ICAO)
International Civil Defence Organization (ICDO)
International Committee of Military Medicine and Pharmacy (ICMMP)
International Federation for Human Rights
International Frequency Registration Board
International Institute of Humanitarian Law
International Labour Organisation (ILO)
International Telecommunication Union (ITU)
League of Arab States
League of Red Cross Societies
Office of the United Nations High Commissioner for Refugees (UNHCR)
Organization of African Unity (OAU)
Organization of American States (OAS)
Sovereign Order of Malta
United Nations
United Nations Children's Fund (UNICEF)
United Nations Education, Scientific and Cultural Organization (UNESCO)
United Nations Environment Programme (UNEP)
World Food Programme (WFP)
World Health Organization (WHO)
World Medical Association

Working Group for the Development of Humanitarian Law, comprising

Amnesty International
Arab Lawyers Union
Association for the Study of the World Refugee Problem
Carnegie Endowment for International Peace
Christian Peace Conference
Commission of the Churches on International Affairs (World Council of Churches)

Consultative Council on Jewish Organizations
Friends World Committee for Consultation
International Association of Democratic Lawyers
International Association of Lighthouse Authorities
International Commission of Jurists
International Commission on Illumination
International Confederation of Catholic Charities (Caritas Internationalis)
International Confederation of former Prisoners of War
International Electro-Technical Commission
International Secretariat of Catholic Jurists (Pax Romana)
International Union for Child Welfare
International Union of Socialist Youth
World Confederation of Religions for Peace
World Federation of Democratic Youth
World Federation of Scientific Workers
World Federation of United Nations Associations
World Jewish Congress
World Muslim Congress
World Peace Council
World Veterans Federation
World Young Women's Christian Association

5. The International Committee of the Red Cross, which had prepared the two draft Additional Protocols, participated in the work of the Conference in an expert capacity.

6. The Conference elected as its President, Mr. Pierre Graber, Federal Councillor, Head of the Federal Political Department of the Swiss Confederation.

7. The Conference elected as Vice-Presidents the representatives of the following States:

Austria; Belgium; Canada; China; Germany; Federal Republic of Guinea-Bissau; Honduras (fourth session); Italy; Mauritania; Morocco; Panama; Philippines; Romania; Sri Lanka; Syrian Arab Republic; Trinidad and Tobago (first, second and third sessions); Uganda; Union of Soviet Socialist Republics; Uruguay; Zaire.

8. The Conference established the following organs:

General Committee of the Conference:

Chairman: *The President of the Conference*

Members: *The President and Vice-Presidents of the Conference, the Chairmen of the Main Committees, the* Ad Hoc *Committee of the whole on Conventional Weapons, the Drafting Committee and the Credentials Committee, and the Secretary-General*

Committee I:

Chairmen:

Mr. Edward Hambro (Norway) (first and second sessions)
Mr. Einar-Fredeik Ofstad (Norway) (third and fourth sessions)

Vice-Chairmen:

Mr. B. Akporode Clark (Nigeria)
Mr. Konstantin Obradović (Yugoslavia)

Rapporteurs:
Mr. Miguel Marin Bosch (Mexico) (first session)
Mr. Antonio Eusebio de leaza (Mexico) (second, third and fourth sessions)

Committee II:

Chairmen:
Mr. Tadeusz Mallik (Poland) (first session)
Mr. Stanislaw-Edward Nahlik (Poland) (second, third and fourth sessions)

Vice-Chairmen:
Mr. Osvaldo Salas (Chile) (first, second and fourth sessions)
Mr. Carlos Makenney (Chile) (third session)
Mr. Nasim Shah (Pakistan) (first session)
Mr. Javed Khan (Pakistan) (first session)
Mr. Khalid Saleem (Pakistan) (second and third sessions)
Mr. Chaudhri Khurshid Hasan (Pakistan) (fourth session)

Rapporteurs:
Mr. Djibrilla Maiga (Mali) (first and second sessions)
Mr. El Hussein El Hassan (Sudan) (third and fourth sessions)

Committee III:

Chairman:
Mr. Hamed Sultan (Egypt)

Vice-Chairmen:
Mr. Géza Herczegh (Hungary)
Mr. Mangalyn Dugersuren (Mongolia) (first, second and third sessions)
Mr. Dugersurengiin Erdembileg (Mongolia) (fourth session)

Rapporteurs:
Mr. Richard Baxter (United States of America) (first, second and third sessions)
Mr. George H. Aldrich (United States of America) (second, third and fourth sessions)

Ad Hoc Committee of the whole on Conventional Weapons:

Chairmen:
Mr. Diego Garcés (Colombia) (first, second and third sessions)
Mr. Héctor Charry Samper (Colombia) (fourth session)

Vice-Chairmen:
Mr. Houchang Amir-Mokri (Iran)
Mr. Mustapha Chelbi (Tunisia)
Mr. Nkeke Ndongo Mangbau (Zaire) (second session)

Rapporteurs:
Mr. Frits Kalshoven (Netherlands) (first, second and third sessions)
Mr. Robert J. Akkerman (Netherlands) (third session)
Mr. John G. Taylor (United Kingdom of Great Britain and Northern Ireland) (fourth session)
Mr. Martin R. Eaton (United Kingdom of Great Britain and Northern Ireland) (fourth session)

Drafting Committee:

Chairmen:
Mr. Abu Sayed Chowdhury (Bangladesh) (first and second sessions)
Mr. Iqbal Abdul Qarim Al-Fallouji (Iraq) (third and fourth sessions)

Vice-Chairmen:
Mr. Mario Carias (Honduras) (first, second and third sessions)
Mr. Rodrigo Valdez Baquero (Ecuador) (fourth session)
Mr. M. Sinkutu Kabuaye (United Republic of Tanzania)
Members representatives of the following States:
Algeria, Brazil, France, German Democratic Republic, Indonesia, Lebanon, Sweden, Union of Soviet Socialist Republics, United Kingdom of Great Britain and Northern Ireland
Ex officio members under rule 47 of the rules of procedures:
The Rapporteurs of the Main Committees
Credentials Committee:
Chairmen:
Mr. Danilo Sansón Román (Nicaragua) (first, second and third sessions)
Mr. Gastón Cajina Mejicano (Nicaragua) (fourth session)
Members representatives of the following States:
Australia, Czechoslovakia, Iraq, Madagascar, Peru, Senegal, Thailand, United Republic of Cameroon, United States of America

9. Mr. Jean Humbert, Ambassador (Switzerland), held the office of Secretary-General.

10. The Conference referred to the Main Committees for consideration the text of the two draft Additional Protocols to the Geneva Conventions of 12 August 1949. The Conference also established an Ad Hoc Committee of the whole on Conventional Weapons to consider the question of the prohibition or restriction of the use of conventional weapons likely to cause unnecessary suffering or to produce indiscriminate effects. The Drafting Committee was responsible for co-ordinating and reviewing the drafting of all the texts adopted by the Main Committees.

11. On the basis of the discussions reported in the summary records of the plenary meetings of the Conference (CDDH/SR.1-59) and in the summary records of the meetings of the Main Committees (CDDH/I/SR.1-79, CDDH/II/SR.1-101, CDDH/III/SR.1-60) and of the Ad Hoc Committee (CDDH/IV/SR.1-42), and in the reports of all the Committees:
First session
CDDH/47/Rev.1
CDDH/48/Rev.1
CDDH/49/Rev.1
CDDH/50/Rev.1
CDDH/51/Rev.1
Second session
CDDH/219/Rev.1
CDDH/221/Rev.1
CDDH/215/Rev.1
CDDH/220/Rev.1
CDDH/218/Rev.2
Third session
CDDH/234/Rev.1

CDDH/235/Rev.1
CDDH/236/Rev.1
CDDH/237/Rev.1
CDDH/233/Rev.1

Fourth session

CDDH/404/Rev.1
CDDH/405/Rev.1
CDDH/406/Rev.1
CDDH/407/Rev.1
CDDH/408/Rev.1
CDDH/409/Rev.1

The Conference drew up the following instruments:

Protocol Additional to the Geneva Conventions of 12 August 1949, and relating to the Protection of Victims of International Armed Conflicts (Protocol I) and Annexes I and II;

Protocol Additional to the Geneva Conventions of 12 August 1949, and relating to the Protection of Victims of Non-International Armed Conflicts (Protocol II).

12. These Additional Protocols were adopted by the Conference on 8 June 1977. They will be submitted to Governments for consideration and will be open for signature on 12 December 1977, at Berne, for a period of twelve months, in accordance with their provisions. These instruments will also be open for accession, in accordance with their provisions.

13. These Additional Protocols, the text of which has been established in Arabic, English, French, Russian and Spanish, are annexed to this Final Act. The Chinese text of the Additional Protocols will be established later.

14. The Conference further adopted the following resolutions, which are annexed to this Final Act:

17 (IV) Use of certain electronic and visual means of identification by medical aircraft protected under the Geneva Conventions of 1949 and under the Protocol Additional to the Geneva Conventions of 12 August 1949, and relating to the Protection of Victims of International Armed Conflicts (Protocol I)

18 (IV) Use of visual signalling for identification of medical transports protected under the Geneva Conventions of 1949 and under the Protocol Additional to the Geneva Conventions of 12 August 1949, and relating to the Protocol of Victims of International Armed Conflicts (Protocol I)

19 (IV) Use of radiocommunications for announcing and identifying medical transports protected under the Geneva Conventions of 1949 and under the Protocol Additional to the Geneva Conventions of 12 August 1949, and relating to the Protocol of Victims of International Armed Conflicts (Protocol I)

20 (IV) Protection of cultural property

21 (IV) Dissemination of knowledge of international humanitarian law applicable in armed conflicts

22 (IV) Follow-up regarding prohibition or restriction of use of certain conventional weapons

23 (IV) Report of the Credentials Committee
24 (IV) Expression of gratitude to the host country.

Done at Geneva, on 10 June 1977, in Arabic, English, French, Russian and Spanish, the original and the accompanying documents to be deposited in the Archives of the Swiss Confederation.

In witness whereof, the representatives have signed this Final Act, on behalf of:

[Here follow signatures]

SIGNATURES

Afghanistan
Algeria
Argentina
Australia
Austria
Bangladesh
Belgium
Bolivia
Brazil
Bulgaria
Byelorussian Soviet Socialist Republic
Canada
Cape Verde
Central African Empire
Chile
Colombia
Cyprus
Czechoslovakia
Democratic People's Republic of Korea
Democratic Yemen
Denmark
Dominican Republic
Ecuador
Egypt
Finland
France
German Democratic Republic
Germany (Federal Republic of)
Ghana
Greece
Guatemala
Holy See
Honduras
Hungary
India
Indonesia
Iran
Iraq
Ireland
Italy
Ivory Coast
Mauritania
Mauritius
Mexico
Monaco
Mongolia
Morocco
Mozambique
Netherlands
New Zealand
Nicaragua
Nigeria
Norway
Oman
Pakistan
Panama
Peru
Philippines
Poland
Portugal
Qatar
Republic of Korea
Romania
San Morino
Saudi Arabia
Senegal
Socialist People's Libyan Arab Jamahiriya
Socialist Republic of Viet-Nam
Spain
Sri Lanka
Sudan
Sweden
Switzerland
Syrian Arab Republic
Thailand
Tunisia
Turkey
Uganda
Ukrainian Soviet Socialist Republic
Union of Soviet Socialist Republic
United Arab Emirates

Jamaica
Japan
Jordan
Kenya
Kuwait
Lebanon
Liechtenstein
Luxembourg
Madagascar
Mali
Malta
United Kingdom of Great Britain and Northern Ireland
United Republic of Cameroon
United Republic of Tanzania
United States of America
Upper Volta
Uruguay
Venezuela
Yemen
Yugoslavia
Zaire

*National Liberation Movements recognized by the Regional Intergovernmental Organizations concerned and invited by the Conference to participate in its work.**

Palestine Liberation Organization (PLO)
Panafricanist Congress (South Africa) (PAC)
South West Africa People's Organization (SWAPO)

* It is understood that the signature by these movements is without prejudice to the position of participating states on the question of precedent.

No. 56

PROTOCOL ADDITIONAL TO THE GENEVA CONVENTIONS OF 12 AUGUST 1949, AND RELATING TO THE PROTECTION OF VICTIMS OF INTERNATIONAL ARMED CONFLICTS (PROTOCOL I)

Adopted at Geneva, 8 June 1977

INTRODUCTORY NOTE: For the historical background of the Protocol, see the introductory note to *No. 55*. The present Protocol mainly brings the following innovations.

Article 1(4) provides that armed conflicts in which peoples are fighting against colonial domination, alien occupation or racist regimes are to be considered international conflicts.

Part II (Articles 8–34) develops the rules of the First and the Second Geneva Conventions on the wounded, sick and shipwrecked. It extends the protection of the Conventions to civilian medical personnel, equipment and supplies and to civilian units and transports and contains detailed provisions on medical transportation.

Part III and several chapters of Part IV (Articles 35–60) deal with the conduct of hostilities, i.e. questions that hitherto were regulated by the Hague Conventions of 1899 and 1907 (*Nos. 7 and 8*) and by customary international law. Their reaffirmation and development is important in view of the age of the Hague Conventions and of the new states which had no part in their elaboration. Article 43 and 44 give a new definition of armed forces and combatants. Among the most important articles are those on the protection of the civilian population against the effects of hostilities. They contain a definition of military objectives and prohibitions of attack on civilian persons and objects. Further articles (61–79) deal with the protection of civil defence organizations, relief actions and the treatment of persons in the power of a party to a conflict.

Part V (Articles 80–91) brings some new elements to the problem of the execution of the Conventions and the Protocol.

Annex I to Protocol I (Regulations concerning identification) was amended on 30 November 1993 (see p. 762). The amendments entered into force on 1 March 1994.

ENTRY INTO FORCE: 7 December 1978.

AUTHENTIC TEXTS: Arabic, Chinese, English, French, Russian and Spanish. The text below is reprinted from *Official Records of the Diplomatic Conference on the Reaffirmation and Development of International Humanitarian Law applicable in Armed Conflicts, Geneva (1974-1977)*, Berne, Federal Political Department, 1978, Vol. I, pp. 115–183.

TEXT PUBLISHED IN: See indications under *No. 55*.

TABLE OF CONTENTS

* * *

PREAMBLE[1]

The High Contracting Parties,

Proclaiming their earnest wish to see peace prevail among peoples,

Recalling that every State has the duty, in conformity with the Charter of the United Nations, to refrain in its international relations from the threat or use of force against the sovereignty, territorial integrity or political independence of any State, or in any other manner inconsistent with the purposes of the United Nations,

Believing it necessary nevertheless to reaffirm and develop the provisions protecting the victims of armed conflicts and to supplement measures intended to reinforce their application,

Expressing their conviction that nothing in this Protocol or in the Geneva Conventions of 12 August 1949 can be construed as legitimizing or authorizing any act of aggression or any other use of force inconsistent with the Charter of the United Nations,

Reaffirming further that the provisions of the Geneva Conventions of 12 August 1949 and of this Protocol must be fully applied in all circumstances to all persons who are protected by those instruments, without any adverse distinction based on the nature or origin of the armed conflict or on the causes espoused by or attributed to the Parties to the conflict,

Have agreed on the following:

PART I. GENERAL PROVISIONS

Article 1.[2] *General principles and scope of application*

1. The High Contracting Parties undertake to respect and to ensure respect for this Protocol in all circumstances.
2 In cases not covered by this Protocol or by other international agreements, civilians and combatants remain under the protection and authority of the principles of international law derived from established custom, from the principles of humanity and from the dictates of public conscience.
3. This Protocol, which supplements the Geneva Conventions of 12 August 1949 for the protection of war victims, shall apply in the situations referred to in Article 2 common to those Conventions.
4.[3] The situations referred to in the preceding paragraph include armed conflicts in which peoples are fighting against colonial domination and alien occupation and against racist régimes in the exercise of their right of self-determination, as enshrined in the Charter of the United Nations and the Declaration on Principles of International Law concerning Friendly Relations and Co-operation among States in accordance with the Charter of the United Nations.

---

[1] Some states made declarations concerning all provisions of the Protocol. See in particular the declaration of the Holy See, Ireland and [USSR], pp. 803, 804, 811–812. Declarations concerning the use of certain weapons were made on ratification or accession by the following states: Belgium, Canada, Germany, Italy, Netherlands, Spain, United Kingdom (on signature and ratification) and United States (on signature), pp. 795, 796, 802, 807, 809–810, 812–816. Angola made a declaration concerning the crime of mercenarism, see p. 792. The Socialist Federal Republic of Yugoslavia made a declaration concerning occupation, see p. 818. (This declaration is also binding on Macedonia.

[2] For declaration in respect of this article by the United Kingdom, see p. 816.

[3] For declaration in respect of this paragraph by France, Spain and the United Kingdom, see pp. 800, 813, 816.

Art. 2. Definitions

For the purposes of this Protocol:

(a) "First Convention", "Second Convention", "Third Convention" and "Fourth Convention" mean, respectively, the Geneva Convention for the Amelioration of the Condition of the Wounded and Sick in Armed Forces in the Field of 12 August 1949; the Geneva Convention for the Amelioration of the Condition of Wounded, Sick and Shipwrecked Members of Armed Forces at Sea of 12 August 1949; the Geneva Convention relative to the Treatment of Prisoners of War of 12 August 1949; the Geneva Convention relative to the Protection of Civilian Persons in Time of War of 12 August 1949; "the Conventions" means the four Geneva Conventions of 12 August 1949 for the protection of war victims;

(b) "rules of international law applicable in armed conflict" means the rules applicable in armed conflict set forth in international agreements to which the Parties to the conflict are Parties and the generally recognized principles and rules of international law which are applicable to armed conflict;

(c) "Protecting Power" means a neutral or other State not a Party to the conflict which has been designated by a Party to the conflict and accepted by the adverse Party and has agreed to carry out the functions assigned to a Protecting Power under the Conventions and this Protocol;

(d) "substitute" means an organization acting in place of a Protecting Power in accordance with Article 5.

Art. 3. Beginning and end of application

Without prejudice to the provisions which are applicable at all times:

(a) the Conventions and this Protocol shall apply from the beginning of any situation referred to in Article 1 of this Protocol;

(b) the application of the Conventions and of this Protocol shall cease, in the territory of Parties to the conflict, on the general close of military operations and, in the case of occupied territories, on the termination of the occupation, except, in either circumstance, for those persons whose final release, repatriation or re-establishment takes place thereafter. These persons shall continue to benefit from the relevant provisions of the Conventions and of this Protocol until their final release, repatriation or re-establishment.

Art. 4. Legal status of the Parties to the conflict

The application of the Conventions and of this Protocol, as well as the conclusion of the agreements provided for therein, shall not affect the legal status of the Parties to the conflict. Neither the occupation of a territory nor the application of the Conventions and this Protocol shall affect the legal status of the territory in question.

Art. 5. Appointment of Protecting Powers and of their substitute[4]

1. It is the duty of the Parties to a conflict from the beginning of that conflict to secure the supervision and implementation of the Conventions and of this Protocol by the application of the system of Protecting Powers, including

[4] For reservation and declaration in respect of this article by Australia and Saudi Arabia, see pp. 793, 812.

inter alia the designation and acceptance of those Powers, in accordance with the following paragraphs. Protecting Powers shall have the duty of safeguarding the interests of the Parties to the conflict.

2. From the beginning of a situation referred to in Article 1, each Party to the conflict shall without delay designate a Protecting Power for the purpose of applying the Conventions and this Protocol and shall, likewise without delay and for the same purpose, permit the activities of a Protecting Power which has been accepted by it as such after designation by the adverse Party.
3. If a Protecting Power has not been designated or accepted from the beginning of a situation referred to in Article 1, the International Committee of the Red Cross, without prejudice to the right of any other impartial humanitarian organization to do likewise, shall offer its good offices to the Parties to the conflict with a view to the designation without delay of a Protecting Power to which the Parties to the conflict consent. For that purpose it may, *inter alia*, ask each Party to provide it with a list of at least five States which that Party considers acceptable to act as Protecting Power on its behalf in relation to an adverse Party, and ask each adverse Party to provide a list of at least five States which it would accept as the Protecting Power of the first Party; these lists shall be communicated to the Committee within two weeks after the receipt of the request; it shall compare them and seek the agreement of any proposed State named on both lists.
4. If, despite the foregoing, there is no Protecting Power, the Parties to the conflict shall accept without delay an offer which may be made by the International Committee of the Red Cross or by any other organization which offers all guarantees of impartiality and efficacy, after due consultations with the said Parties and taking into account the result of these consultations, to act as a substitute. The functioning of such a substitute is subject to the consent of the Parties to the conflict; every effort shall be made by the Parties to the conflict to facilitate the operations of the substitute in the performance of its tasks under the Conventions and this Protocol.
5. In accordance with Article 4, the designation and acceptance of Protecting Powers for the purpose of applying the Conventions and this Protocol shall not affect the legal status of the Parties to the conflict or of any territory, including occupied territory.
6. The maintenance of diplomatic relations between Parties to the conflict or the entrusting of the protection of a Party's interests and those of its nationals to a third State in accordance with the rules of international law relating to diplomatic relations is no obstacle to the designation of Protecting Powers for the purpose of applying the Conventions and this Protocol.
7. Any subsequent mention in this Protocol of a Protecting Power includes also a substitute.

Art. 6. Qualified persons

1. The High Contracting Parties shall, also in peacetime, endeavour, with the assistance of the national Red Cross (Red Crescent, Red Lion and Sun) Societies, to train qualified personnel to facilitate the application of the Conventions and of this Protocol, and in particular the activities of the Protecting Powers.

2. The recruitment and training of such personnel are within domestic jurisdiction.
3. The International Committee of the Red Cross shall hold at the disposal of the High Contracting Parties the lists of persons so trained which the High Contracting Parties may have established and may have transmitted to it for that purpose.
4. The conditions governing the employment of such personnel outside the national territory shall, in each case, be the subject of special agreements between the Parties concerned.

Art. 7. Meetings
The depositary of this Protocol shall convene a meeting of the High Contracting Parties, at the request of one or more of the said Parties and upon the approval of the majority of the said Parties, to consider general problems concerning the application of the Conventions and of the Protocol.

PART II. WOUNDED, SICK AND SHIPWRECKED

Section I. General Protection

Art. 8. Terminology
For the purposes of this Protocol:
(a) "wounded" and "sick" mean persons, whether military or civilian, who, because of trauma, disease or other physical or mental disorder or disability, are in need of medical assistance or care and who refrain from any act of hostility. These terms also cover maternity cases, new-born babies and other persons who may be in need of immediate medical assistance or care, such as the infirm or expectant mothers, and who refrain from any act of hostility;
(b) "shipwrecked" means persons, whether military or civilian, who are in peril at sea or in other waters as a result of misfortune affecting them or the vessel or aircraft carrying them and who refrain from any act of hostility. These persons, provided that they continue to refrain from any act of hostility, shall continue to be considered shipwrecked during their rescue until they acquire another status under the Conventions or this Protocol;
(c) "medical personnel" means those persons assigned, by a Party to the conflict, exclusively to the medical purposes enumerated under sub-paragraph (e) or to the administration of medical units or to the operation or administration of medical transports. Such assignments may be either permanent or temporary. The term includes:
   (i) medical personnel of a Party to the conflict, whether military or civilian, including those described in the First and Second Conventions, and those assigned to civil defence organizations;
   (ii) medical personnel of national Red Cross (Red Crescent, Red Lion and Sun) Societies and other national voluntary aid societies duly recognized and authorized by a Party to the conflict;
   (iii) medical personnel of medical units or medical transports described in Article 9, paragraph 2;
(d) "religious personnel" means military or civilian persons, such as chaplains, who are exclusively engaged in the work of their ministry and attached:
   (i) to the armed forces of a Party to the conflict;

(ii) to medical units or medical transports of a Party to the conflict;
(iii) to medical units or medical transports described in Article 9, paragraph 2; or
(iv) to civil defence organizations of a Party to the conflict.

The attachment of religious personnel may be either permanent or temporary, and the relevant provisions mentioned under subparagraph (k) apply to them;

(e) "medical units" means establishments and other units, whether military or civilian, organized for medical purposes, namely the search for, collection, transportation, diagnosis or treatment – including first-aid treatment – of the wounded, sick and shipwrecked, or for the prevention of disease. The term includes, for example, hospitals and other similar units, blood transfusion centres, preventive medicine centres and institutes, medical depots and the medical and pharmaceutical stores of such units. Medical units may be fixed or mobile, permanent or temporary;
(f) "medical transportation" means the conveyance by land, water or air of the wounded, sick, shipwrecked, medical personnel, religious personnel, medical equipment or medical supplies protected by the Conventions and by this Protocol;
(g) "medical transports" means any means of transportation, whether military or civilian, permanent or temporary, assigned exclusively to medical transportation and under the control of a competent authority of a Party to the conflict;
(h) "medical vehicles" means any medical transports by land;
(i) "medical ships and craft" means any medical transports by water;
(j) "medical aircraft" means any medical transports by air;
(k) "permanent medical personnel", "permanent medical units" and "permanent medical transports" mean those assigned exclusively to medical purposes for an indeterminate period. "Temporary medical personnel", "temporary medical units" and "temporary medical transports" mean those devoted exclusively to medical purposes for limited periods during the whole of such periods. Unless otherwise specified, the terms "medical personnel", "medical units" and "medical transports" cover both permanent and temporary categories;
(l) "distinctive emblem" means the distinctive emblem of the red cross, red crescent or red lion and sun on a white ground when used for the protection of medical units and transports, or medical and religious personnel, equipment or supplies;
(m) "distinctive signal" means any signal or message specified for the identification exclusively of medical units or transports in Chapter III of Annex I to this Protocol.

Art. 9. Field of application

1. This Part, the provisions of which are intended to ameliorate the condition of the wounded, sick and shipwrecked, shall apply to all those affected by a situation referred to in Article 1, without any adverse distinction founded on race, colour, sex, language, religion or belief, political or other opinion, national or social origin, wealth, birth or other status, or on any other similar criteria.
2. The relevant provisions of Articles 27 and 32 of the First Convention shall apply to permanent medical units and transports (other than hos-

pital ships, to which Article 25 of the Second Convention applies) and their personnel made available to a Party to the conflict for humanitarian purposes:

(a) by a neutral or other State which is not a Party to that conflict;
(b) by a recognized and authorized aid society of such a State;
(c) by an impartial international humanitarian organization.

Art. 10. Protection and care

1. All the wounded, sick and shipwrecked, to whichever Party they belong, shall be respected and protected.
2. In all circumstances they shall be treated humanely and shall receive, to the fullest extent practicable and with the least possible delay, the medical care and attention required by their condition. There shall be no distinction among them founded on any grounds other than medical ones.

Art. 11. Protection of persons[5]

1. The physical or mental health and integrity of persons who are in the power of the adverse Party or who are interned, detained or otherwise deprived of liberty as a result of a situation referred to in Article 1 shall not be endangered by any unjustified act or omission. Accordingly, it is prohibited to subject the persons described in this Article to any medical procedure which is not indicated by the state of health of the person concerned and which is not consistent with generally accepted medical standards which would be applied under similar medical circumstances to persons who are nationals of the Party conducting the procedure and who are in no way deprived of liberty.
2. It is, in particular, prohibited to carry out on such persons, even with their consent:
   (a) physical mutilations;
   (b) medical or scientific experiments;
   (c)[6] removal of tissue or organs for transplantation, except where these acts are justified in conformity with the conditions provided for in paragraph 1.
3. Exceptions to the prohibition in paragraph 2(c) may be made only in the case of donations of blood for transfusion or of skin for grafting, provided that they are given voluntarily and without any coercion or inducement, and then only for therapeutic purposes, under conditions consistent with generally accepted medical standards and controls designed for the benefit of both the donor and the recipient.
4. Any wilful act or omission which seriously endangers the physical or mental health or integrity of any person who is in the power of a Party other than the one on which he depends and which either violates any of the prohibitions in paragraphs 1 and 2 or fails to comply with the requirements of paragraph 3 shall be a grave breach of this Protocol.
5. The persons described in paragraph 1 have the right to refuse any surgical operation. In case of refusal, medical personnel shall endeavour to obtain a written statement to that effect, signed or acknowledged by the patient.

---

[5] For reservation in respect of this article by Ireland, see p. 804.

[6] For reservation in respect of this paragraph by Canada and Ireland, see pp. 797, 804.

6. Each Party to the conflict shall keep a medical record for every donation of blood for transfusion or skin for grafting by persons referred to in paragraph 1, if that donation is made under the responsibility of that Party. In addition, each Party to the conflict shall endeavour to keep a record of all medical procedures undertaken with respect to any person who is interned, detained or otherwise deprived of liberty as a result of a situation referred to in Article 1. These records shall be available at all times for inspection by the Protecting Power.

Art. 12. Protection of medical units

1. Medical units shall be respected and protected at all times and shall not be the object of attack.
2. Paragraph 1 shall apply to civilian medical units, provided that they:
   (a) belong to one of the Parties to the conflict;
   (b) are recognized and authorized by the competent authority of one of the Parties to the conflict; or
   (c) are authorized in conformity with Article 9, paragraph 2, of this Protocol or Article 27 of the First Convention.
3. The Parties to the conflict are invited to notify each other of the location of their fixed medical units. The absence of such notification shall not exempt any of the Parties from the obligation to comply with the provisions of paragraph 1.
4. Under no circumstances shall medical units be used in an attempt to shield military objectives from attack. Whenever possible, the Parties to the conflict shall ensure that medical units are so sited that attacks against military objectives do not imperil their safety.

Art. 13. Discontinuance of protection of civilian medical units

1. The protection to which civilian medical units are entitled shall not cease unless they are used to commit, outside their humanitarian function, acts harmful to the enemy. Protection may, however, cease only after a warning has been given setting, whenever appropriate, a reasonable time-limit, and after such warning has remained unheeded.
2. The following shall not be considered as acts harmful to the enemy:
   (a) that the personnel of the unit are equipped with light individual weapons for their own defence or for that of the wounded and sick in their charge;
   (b) that the unit is guarded by a picket or by sentries or by an escort;
   (c) that small arms and ammunition taken from the wounded and sick, and not yet handed to the proper service, are found in the units;
   (d) that members of the armed forces or other combatants are in the unit for medical reasons.

Art. 14. Limitations on requisition of civilian medical units

1. The Occupying Power has the duty to ensure that the medical needs of the civilian population in occupied territory continue to be satisfied.
2. The Occupying Power shall not, therefore, requisition civilian medical units, their equipment, their *matériel* or the services of their personnel, so long as these resources are necessary for the provision of adequate medical services for the civilian population and for the continuing medical care of any wounded and sick already under treatment.

3. Provided that the general rule in paragraph 2 continues to be observed, the Occupying Power may requisition the said resources, subject to the following particular conditions:
   (a) that the resources are necessary for the adequate and immediate medical treatment of the wounded and sick members of the armed forces of the Occupying Power or of prisoners of war;
   (b) that the requisition continues only while such necessity exists; and
   (c) that immediate arrangements are made to ensure that the medical needs of the civilian population, as well as those of any wounded and sick under treatment who are affected by the requisition, continue to be satisfied.

Art. 15. Protection of civilian medical and religious personnel

1. Civilian medical personnel shall be respected and protected.
2. If needed, all available help shall be afforded to civilian medical personnel in an area where civilian medical services are disrupted by reason of combat activity.
3. The Occupying Power shall afford civilian medical personnel in occupied territories every assistance to enable them to perform, to the best of their ability, their humanitarian functions. The Occupying Power may not require that, in the performance of those functions, such personnel shall give priority to the treatment of any person except on medical grounds. They shall not be compelled to carry out tasks which are not compatible with their humanitarian mission.
4. Civilian medical personnel shall have access to any place where their services are essential, subject to such supervisory and safety measures as the relevant Party to the conflict may deem necessary.
5. Civilian religious personnel shall be respected and protected. The provisions of the Conventions and of this Protocol concerning the protection and identification of medical personnel shall apply equally to such persons.

Art. 16. General protection of medical duties

1. Under no circumstances shall any person be punished for carrying out medical activities compatible with medical ethics, regardless of the person benefiting therefrom.
2. Persons engaged in medical activities shall not be compelled to perform acts or to carry out work contrary to the rules of medical ethics or to other medical rules designed for the benefit of the wounded and sick or to the provisions of the Conventions or of this Protocol, or to refrain from performing acts or from carrying out work required by those rules and provisions.
3. No person engaged in medical activities shall be compelled to give to anyone belonging either to an adverse Party, or to his own Party except as required by the law of the latter Party, any information concerning the wounded and sick who are, or who have been, under his care, if such information would, in his opinion, prove harmful to the patients concerned or to their families. Regulations for the compulsory notification of communicable diseases shall, however, be respected.

Art. 17. Role of the civilian population and of aid societies

1. The civilian population shall respect the wounded, sick and shipwrecked, even if they belong to the adverse Party, and shall commit no act of vio-

lence against them. The civilian population and aid societies, such as national Red Cross (Red Crescent, Red Lion and Sun) Societies, shall be permitted, even on their own initiative, to collect and care for the wounded, sick and shipwrecked, even in invaded or occupied areas. No one shall be harmed, prosecuted, convicted or punished for such humanitarian acts.

2. The Parties to the conflict may appeal to the civilian population and the aid societies referred to in paragraph 1 to collect and care for the wounded, sick and shipwrecked, and to search for the dead and report their location; they shall grant both protection and the necessary facilities to those who respond to this appeal. If the adverse Party gains or regains control of the area, that Party also shall afford the same protection and facilities for so long as they are needed.

Art. 18. Identification

1. Each Party to the conflict shall endeavour to ensure that medical and religious personnel and medical units and transports are identifiable.
2. Each Party to the conflict shall also endeavour to adopt and to implement methods and procedures which will make it possible to recognize medical units and transports which use the distinctive emblem and distinctive signals.
3. In occupied territory and in areas where fighting is taking place or is likely to take place, civilian medical personnel and civilian religious personnel should be recognizable by the distinctive emblem and an identity card certifying their status.
4. With the consent of the competent authority, medical units and transports shall be marked by the distinctive emblem. The ships and craft referred to in Article 22 of this Protocol shall be marked in accordance with the provisions of the Second Convention.
5. In addition to the distinctive emblem, a Party to the conflict may, as provided in Chapter III of Annex I to this Protocol, authorize the use of distinctive signals to identify medical units and transports. Exceptionally, in the special cases covered in that Chapter, medical transports may use distinctive signals without displaying the distinctive emblem.
6. The application of the provisions of paragraphs 1 to 5 of this Article is governed by Chapters I to III of Annex I to this Protocol. Signals designated in Chapter III of the Annex for the exclusive use of medical units and transports shall not, except as provided therein, be used for any purpose other than to identify the medical units and transports specified in that Chapter.
7. This Article does not authorize any wider use of the distinctive emblem in peacetime than is prescribed in Article 44 of the First Convention.
8. The provisions of the Conventions and of this Protocol relating to supervision of the use of the distinctive emblem and to the prevention and repression of any misuse thereof shall be applicable to distinctive signals.

Art. 19. Neutral and other States not Parties to the conflict

Neutral and other States not Parties to the conflict shall apply the relevant provisions of this Protocol to persons protected by this Part who may be received or interned within their territory, and to any dead of the Parties to that conflict whom they may find.

Art. 20. Prohibition of reprisals
Reprisals against the persons and objects protected by this Part are prohibited.

Section II. Medical Transportation

Article 21. Medical vehicles
Medical vehicles shall be respected and protected in the same way as mobile medical units under the Conventions and this Protocol.

Art. 22. Hospitals ships and coastal rescue craft
1. The provisions of the Conventions relating to:
   (a) vessels described in Articles 22,24,25 and 27 of the Second Convention,
   (b) their lifeboats and small craft,
   (c) their personnel and crews, and
   (d) the wounded, sick and shipwrecked on board,

shall also apply where these vessels carry civilian wounded, sick and shipwrecked who do not belong to any of the categories mentioned in Article 13 of the Second Convention. Such civilians shall not, however, be subject to surrender to any Party which is not their own, or to capture at sea. If they find themselves in the power of a Party to the conflict other than their own they shall be covered by the Fourth Convention and by this Protocol.

2. The protection provided by the Conventions to vessels described in Article 25 of the Second Convention shall extend to hospital ships made available for humanitarian purposes to a Party to the conflict:
   (a) by a neutral or other State which is not a Party to that conflict; or
   (b) by an impartial international humanitarian organization, provided that, in either case, the requirements set out in that Article are complied with.
3. Small craft described in Article 27 of the Second Convention shall be protected even if the notification envisaged by that Article has not been made. The Parties to the conflict are, nevertheless, invited to inform each other of any details of such craft which will facilitate their identification and recognition.

Art. 23. Other medical ships and craft
1. Medical ships and craft other than those referred to in Article 22 of this Protocol and Article 38 of the Second Convention shall, whether at sea or in other waters, be respected and protected in the same way as mobile medical units under the Conventions and this Protocol. Since this protection can only be effective if they can be identified and recognized as medical ships or craft, such vessels should be marked with the distinctive emblem and as far as possible comply with the second paragraph of Article 43 of the Second Convention.
2. The ships and craft referred to in paragraph 1 shall remain subject to the laws of war. Any warship on the surface able immediately to enforce its command may order them to stop, order them off, or make them take a certain course, and they shall obey every such command. Such ships and craft may not in any other way be diverted from their medical mission so long as they are needed for the wounded, sick and shipwrecked on board.
3. The protection provided in paragraph 1 shall cease only under the conditions set out in Articles 34 and 35 of the Second Convention. A clear refusal

to obey a command given in accordance with paragraph 2 shall be an act harmful to the enemy under Article 34 of the Second Convention.

4. A Party to the conflict may notify any adverse Party as far in advance of sailing as possible of the name, description, expected time of sailing, course and estimated speed of the medical ship or craft, particularly in the case of ships of over 2,000 gross tons, and may provide any other information which would facilitate identification and recognition. The adverse Party shall acknowledge receipt of such information.
5. The provisions of Article 37 of the Second Convention shall apply to medical and religious personnel in such ships and craft.
6. The provisions of the Second Convention shall apply to the wounded, sick and shipwrecked belonging to the categories referred to in Article 13 of the Second Convention and in Article 44 of this Protocol who may be on board such medical ships and craft. Wounded, sick and shipwrecked civilians who do not belong to any of the categories mentioned in Article 13 of the Second Convention shall not be subject, at sea, either to surrender to any Party which is not their own, or to removal from such ships or craft; if they find themselves in the power of a Party to the conflict other than their own, they shall be covered by the Fourth Convention and by this Protocol.

Art. 24. Protection of medical aircraft
Medical aircraft shall be respected and protected, subject to the provisions of this Part.

Art. 25. Medical aircraft in areas not controlled by an adverse Party
In and over land areas physically controlled by friendly forces, or in and over sea areas not physically controlled by an adverse Party, the respect and protection of medical aircraft of a Party to the conflict is not dependent on any agreement with an adverse Party. For greater safety, however, a Party to the conflict operating its medical aircraft in these areas may notify the adverse Party, as provided in Article 29, in particular when such aircraft are making flights bringing them within range of surface-to-air weapons systems of the adverse Party.

Art. 26. Medical aircraft in contact or similar zones

1. In and over those parts of the contact zone which are physically controlled by friendly forces and in and over those areas the physical control of which is not clearly established, protection for medical aircraft can be fully effective only by prior agreement between the competent military authorities of the Parties to the conflict, as provided for in Article 29. Although, in the absence of such an agreement, medical aircraft operate at their own risk, they shall nevertheless be respected after they have been recognized as such.
2. "Contact zone" means any area on land where the forward elements of opposing forces are in contact with each other, especially where they are exposed to direct fire from the ground.

Art. 27. Medical aircraft in areas controlled by an adverse Party

1. The medical aircraft of a Party to the conflict shall continue to be protected while flying over land or sea areas physically controlled by an adverse Party, provided that prior agreement to such flights has been obtained from the competent authority of that adverse Party.

2. A medical aircraft which flies over an area physically controlled by an adverse Party without, or in deviation from the terms of, an agreement provided for in paragraph 1, either through navigational error or because of an emergency affecting the safety of the flight, shall make every effort to identify itself and to inform the adverse Party of the circumstances. As soon as such medical aircraft has been recognized by the adverse Party, that Party shall make all reasonable efforts to give the order to land or to alight on water, referred to in Article 30, paragraph 1, or to take other measures to safeguard its own interests, and, in either case, to allow the aircraft time for compliance, before resorting to an attack against the aircraft.

Art. 28. Restrictions on operations of medical aircraft

1. The Parties to the conflict are prohibited from using their medical aircraft to attempt to acquire any military advantage over an adverse Party. The presence of medical aircraft shall not be used in an attempt to render military objectives immune from attack.
2.[7] Medical aircraft shall not be used to collect or transmit intelligence data and shall not carry any equipment intended for such purposes. They are prohibited from carrying any persons or cargo not included within the definition in Article 8, subparagraph (f). The carrying on board of the personal effects of the occupants or of equipment intended solely to facilitate navigation, communication or identification shall not be considered as prohibited.
3. Medical aircraft shall not carry any armament except small arms and ammunition taken from the wounded, sick and shipwrecked on board and not yet handed to the proper service, and such light individual weapons as may be necessary to enable the medical personnel on board to defend themselves and the wounded, sick and shipwrecked in their charge.
4. While carrying out the flights referred to in Articles 26 and 27, medical aircraft shall not, except by prior agreement with the adverse Party, be used to search for the wounded, sick and shipwrecked.

Art. 29. Notifications and agreements concerning medical aircraft

1. Notifications under Article 25, or requests for prior agreement under Articles 26, 27, 28 (paragraph 4), or 31 shall state the proposed number of medical aircraft, their flight plans and means of identification, and shall be understood to mean that every flight will be carried out in compliance with Article 28.
2. A Party which receives a notification given under Article 25 shall at once acknowledge receipt of such notification.
3. A Party which receives a request for prior agreement under Articles 26, 27, 28 (paragraph 4), or 31 shall, as rapidly as possible, notify the requesting Party:
   (a) that the request is agreed to;
   (b) that the request is denied; or
   (c) of reasonable alternative proposals to the request. It may also propose a prohibition or restriction of other flights in the area during the time involved. If the Party which submitted the request accepts the alternative proposals, it shall notify the other Party of such acceptance.

[7] For declaration in respect of this paragraph by France, Ireland and United Kingdom, see pp. 800, 804, 816.

4. The Parties shall take the necessary measures to ensure that notifications and agreements can be made rapidly.
5. The Parties shall also take the necessary measures to disseminate rapidly the substance of any such notifications and agreements to the military units concerned and shall instruct those units regarding the means of identification that will be used by the medical aircraft in question.

Art. 30. Landing and inspection of medical aircraft

1. Medical aircraft flying over areas which are physically controlled by an adverse Party, or over areas the physical control of which is not clearly established, may be ordered to land or to alight on water, as appropriate, to permit inspection in accordance with the following paragraphs. Medical aircraft shall obey any such order.
2. If such an aircraft lands or alights on water, whether ordered to do so or for other reasons, it may be subjected to inspection solely to determine the matters referred to in paragraphs 3 and 4. Any such inspection shall be commenced without delay and shall be conducted expeditiously. The inspecting Party shall not require the wounded and sick to be removed from the aircraft unless their removal is essential for the inspection. That Party shall in any event ensure that the condition of the wounded and sick is not adversely affected by the inspection or by the removal.
3. If the inspection discloses that the aircraft:
   (a) is a medical aircraft within the meaning of Article 8, subparagraph (j),
   (b) is not in violation of the conditions prescribed in Article 28, and
   (c) has not flown without or in breach of a prior agreement where such agreement is required, the aircraft and those of its occupants who belong to the adverse Party or to a neutral or other State not a Party to the conflict shall be authorized to continue the flight without delay.
4. If the inspection discloses that the aircraft:
   (a) is not a medical aircraft within the meaning of Article 8, sub-paragraph (j),
   (b) is in violation of the conditions prescribed in Article 28, or
   (c) has flown without or in breach of a prior agreement where such agreement is required,

   the aircraft may be seized. Its occupants shall be treated in conformity with the relevant provisions of the Conventions and of this Protocol. Any aircraft seized which had been assigned as a permanent medical aircraft may be used thereafter only as a medical aircraft.

Art. 31. Neutral or other States not Parties to the conflict

1. Except by prior agreement, medical aircraft shall not fly over or land in the territory of a neutral or other State not a Party to the conflict. However, with such an agreement, they shall be respected throughout their flight and also for the duration of any calls in the territory. Nevertheless they shall obey any summons to land or to alight on water, as appropriate.
2. Should a medical aircraft, in the absence of an agreement or in deviation from the terms of an agreement, fly over the territory of a neutral or other State not a Party to the conflict, either through navigational error or because of an emergency affecting the safety of the flight, it shall make every effort to give notice of the flight and to identify itself. As soon as such medical aircraft is recognized, that State shall make all reasonable

efforts to give the order to land or to alight on water referred to in Article 30, paragraph 1, or to take other measures to safeguard its own interests, and, in either case, to allow the aircraft time for compliance, before resorting to an attack against the aircraft.

3. If a medical aircraft, either by agreement or in the circumstances mentioned in paragraph 2, lands or alights on water in the territory of a neutral or other State not Party to the conflict, whether ordered to do so or for other reasons, the aircraft shall be subject to inspection for the purposes of determining whether it is in fact a medical aircraft. The inspection shall be commenced without delay and shall be conducted expeditiously. The inspecting Party shall not require the wounded and sick of the Party operating the aircraft to be removed from it unless their removal is essential for the inspection. The inspecting Party shall in any event ensure that the condition of the wounded and sick is not adversely affected by the inspection or the removal. If the inspection discloses that the aircraft is in fact a medical aircraft, the aircraft with its occupants, other than those who must be detained in accordance with the rules of international law applicable in armed conflict, shall be allowed to resume its flight, and reasonable facilities shall be given for the continuation of the flight. If the inspection discloses that the aircraft is not a medical aircraft, it shall be seized and the occupants treated in accordance with paragraph 4.
4. The wounded, sick and shipwrecked disembarked, otherwise than temporarily, from a medical aircraft with the consent of the local authorities in the territory of a neutral or other State not a Party to the conflict shall, unless agreed otherwise between that State and the Parties to the conflict, be detained by that State where so required by the rules of international law applicable in armed conflict, in such a manner that they cannot again take part in the hostilities. The cost of hospital treatment and internment shall be borne by the State to which those persons belong.
5. Neutral or other States not Parties to the conflict shall apply any conditions and restrictions on the passage of medical aircraft over, or on the landing of medical aircraft in, their territory equally to all Parties to the conflict.

Section III. Missing and Dead Persons

Art. 32. General principle

In the implementation of this Section, the activities of the High Contracting Parties, of the Parties to the conflict and of the international humanitarian organizations mentioned in the Conventions and in this Protocol shall be prompted mainly by the right of families to know the fate of their relatives.

Art. 33. Missing persons

1. As soon as circumstances permit, and at the latest from the end of active hostilities, each Party to the conflict shall search for the persons who have been reported missing by an adverse Party. Such adverse Party shall transmit all relevant information concerning such persons in order to facilitate such searches.
2. In order to facilitate the gathering of information pursuant to the preceding paragraph, each Party to the conflict shall, with respect to persons who would not receive more favourable consideration under the Conventions and this Protocol:

(a) record the information specified in Article 138 of the Fourth Convention in respect of such persons who have been detained, imprisoned or otherwise held in captivity for more than two weeks as a result of hostilities or occupation, or who have died during any period of detention;
(b) to the fullest extent possible, facilitate and, if need be, carry out the search for and the recording of information concerning such persons if they have died in other circumstances as a result of hostilities or occupation.

3. Information concerning persons reported missing pursuant to paragraph 1 and requests for such information shall be transmitted either directly or through the Protecting Power or the Central Tracing Agency of the International Committee of the Red Cross or national Red Cross (Red Crescent, Red Lion and Sun) Societies. Where the information is not transmitted through the International Committee of the Red Cross and its Central Tracing Agency, each Party to the conflict shall ensure that such information is also supplied to the Central Tracing Agency.
4. The Parties to the conflict shall endeavour to agree on arrangements for teams to search for, identify and recover the dead from battlefield areas, including arrangements, if appropriate, for such teams to be accompanied by personnel of the adverse Party while carrying out these missions in areas controlled by the adverse Party. Personnel of such teams shall be respected and protected while exclusively carrying out these duties.

Art. 34. Remains of deceased

1. The remains of persons who have died for reasons related to occupation or in detention resulting from occupation or hostilities and those of persons not nationals of the country in which they have died as a result of hostilities shall be respected, and the gravesites of all such persons shall be respected, maintained and marked as provided for in Article 130 of the Fourth Convention, where their remains or gravesites would not receive more favourable consideration under the Conventions and this Protocol.
2. As soon as circumstances and the relations between the adverse Parties permit, the High Contracting Parties in whose territories graves and, as the case may be, other locations of the remains of persons who have died as a result of hostilities or during occupation or in detention are situated, shall conclude agreements in order:
   (a) to facilitate access to the gravesites by relatives of the deceased and by representatives of official graves registration services and to regulate the practical arrangements for such access;
   (b) to protect and maintain such gravesites permanently;
   (c) to facilitate the return of the remains of the deceased and of personal effects to the home country upon its request or, unless that country objects, upon the request of the next of kin.
3. In the absence of the agreements provided for in paragraph 2(b) or (c) and if the home country of such deceased is not willing to arrange at its expense for the maintenance of such gravesites, the High Contracting Party in whose territory the gravesites are situated may offer to facilitate the return of the remains of the deceased to the home country. Where such an offer has not been accepted the High Contracting Party may, after the expiry of five years from the date of the offer and upon due notice to the

home country, adopt the arrangements laid down in its own laws relating to cemeteries and graves.

4. A High Contracting Party in whose territory the gravesites referred to in this Article are situated shall be permitted to exhume the remains only:
   (a) in accordance with paragraphs 2(c) and 3, or
   (b) where exhumation is a matter of overriding public necessity, including cases of medical and investigative necessity, in which case the High Contracting Party shall at all times respect the remains, and shall give notice to the home country of its intention to exhume the remains together with details of the intended place of reinterment.

PART III. METHODS AND MEANS OF WARFARE, COMBATANT AND PRISONER-OF-WAR STATUS

Section I. Methods and Means of Warfare

Art. 35. Basic rules[8]

1. In any armed conflict, the right of the Parties to the conflict to choose methods or means of warfare is not unlimited.
2. It is prohibited to employ weapons, projectiles and material and methods of warfare of a nature to cause superfluous injury or unnecessary suffering.
3.[9] It is prohibited to employ methods or means of warfare which are intended, or may be expected, to cause widespread, long-term and severe damage to the natural environment.

Art. 36. New weapons

In the study, development, acquisition or adoption of a new weapon, means or method of warfare, a High Contracting Party is under an obligation to determine whether its employment would, in some or all circumstances, be prohibited by this Protocol or by any other rule of international law applicable to the High Contracting Party.

Art. 37. Prohibition of perfidy

1. It is prohibited to kill, injure or capture an adversary by resort to perfidy. Acts inviting the confidence of an adversary to lead him to believe that he is entitled to, or is obliged to accord, protection under the rules of international law applicable in armed conflict, with intent to betray that confidence, shall constitute perfidy. The following acts are examples of perfidy:
   (a) the feigning of an intent to negotiate under a flag of truce or of a surrender;
   (b) the feigning of an incapacitation by wounds or sickness;
   (c) the feigning of civilian, non-combatant status; and
   (d) the feigning of protected status by the use of signs, emblems or uniforms of the United Nations or of neutral or other States not Parties to the conflict.
2. Ruses of war are not prohibited. Such ruses are acts which are intended to mislead an adversary or to induce him to act recklessly but which infringe no rule of international law applicable in armed conflict and

8 For declaration in respect of this article by France and Ireland, see pp. 800, 804.

9 For declaration in respect of this paragraph by United Kingdom, see p. 816.

which are not perfidious because they do not invite the confidence of an adversary with respect to protection under that law. The following are examples of such ruses: the use of camouflage, decoys, mock operations and misinformation.

Art. 38. Recognized emblems[10]

1. It is prohibited to make improper use of the distinctive emblem of the red cross, red crescent or red lion and sun or of other emblems, signs or signals provided for by the Conventions or by this Protocol. It is also prohibited to misuse deliberately in an armed conflict other internationally recognized protective emblems, signs or signals, including the flag of truce, and the protective emblem of cultural property.
2. It is prohibited to make use of the distinctive emblem of the United Nations, except as authorized by that Organization.

Art. 39. Emblems of nationality

1. It is prohibited to make use in an armed conflict of the flags or military emblems, insignia or uniforms of neutral or other States not Parties to the conflict.
2.[11] It is prohibited to make use of the flags or military emblems, insignia or uniforms of adverse Parties while engaging in attacks or in order to shield, favour, protect or impede military operations.
3. Nothing in this Article or in Article 37, paragraph 1(d), shall affect the existing generally recognized rules of international law applicable to espionage or to the use of flags in the conduct of armed conflict at sea.

Art. 40. Quarter

It is prohibited to order that there shall be no survivors, to threaten an adversary therewith or to conduct hostilities on this basis.

Art. 41. Safeguard of an enemy hors de combat[12]

1. A person who is recognized or who, in the circumstances, should be recognized to be *hors de combat* shall not be made the object of attack.
2. A person is *hors de combat* if:
   (a) he is in the power of an adverse Party;
   (b) he clearly expresses an intention to surrender; or
   (c) he has been rendered unconscious or is otherwise incapacitated by wounds or sickness, and therefore is incapable of defending himself, provided that in any of these cases he abstains from any hostile act and does not attempt to escape.
3.[13] When persons entitled to protection as prisoners of war have fallen into the power of an adverse Party under unusual conditions of combat which prevent their evacuation as provided for in Part III, Section I, of the Third Convention, they shall be released and all feasible precautions shall be taken to ensure their safety.

[10] For statement of understanding in respect of this article by Canada, see p. 797.

[11] For reservation in respect of this paragraph by Canada, see p. 797.

[12] For declaration in respect of this article by Belgium, Canada, Germany, Ireland, Italy, Netherlands, Spain and United Kingdom, see pp. 796, 797, 802, 805, 807, 810, 813, 815.

[13] For declaration in respect of this paragraph by Algeria and the Netherlands, see pp. 792, 810.

Art. 42. Occupants of aircraft

1. No person parachuting from an aircraft in distress shall be made the object of attack during his descent.
2. Upon reaching the ground in territory controlled by an adverse Party, a person who has parachuted from an aircraft in distress shall be given an opportunity to surrender before being made the object of attack, unless it is apparent that he is engaging in a hostile act.
3. Airborne troops are not protected by this Article.

Section II. Combatant and Prisoner-of-War Status

Art. 43. Armed forces

1.[14] The armed forces of a Party to a conflict consist of all organized armed forces, groups and units which are under a command responsible to that Party for the conduct of its subordinates, even if that Party is represented by a government or an authority not recognized by an adverse Party. Such armed forces shall be subject to an internal disciplinary system which, *inter alia*, shall enforce compliance with the rules of international law applicable in armed conflict.

2. Members of the armed forces of a Party to a conflict (other than medical personnel and chaplains covered by Article 33 of the Third Convention) are combatants, that is to say, they have the right to participate directly in hostilities.

3.[15] Whenever a Party to a conflict incorporates a paramilitary or armed law enforcement agency into its armed forces it shall so notify the other Parties to the conflict.

Art. 44. Combatants and prisoners of war[16]

1.[17] Any combatant, as defined in Article 43, who falls into the power of an adverse Party shall be a prisoner of war.

2.[18] While all combatants are obliged to comply with the rules of international law applicable in armed conflict, violations of these rules shall not deprive a combatant of his right to be a combatant or, if he falls into the power of an adverse Party, of his right to be a prisoner of war, except as provided in paragraphs 3 and 4.

3.[19] In order to promote the protection of the civilian population from the effects of hostilities, combatants are obliged to distinguish themselves from the civilian population while they are engaged in an attack or in a military operation preparatory to an attack. Recognizing, however, that there are situations in armed conflicts where, owing to the nature of the hostilities an armed combatant cannot so distinguish himself, he shall retain his status as a combatant, provided that, in such situations, he carries his arms openly:

---

14 For declaration in respect of this paragraph by Argentina, see p. 793.

15 For declaration in respect of this paragraph by Belgium and France, see pp. 796, 803.

16 For declaration in respect of this article by Argentina, Belgium, Ireland and the United Kingdom, see pp. 792, 796, 805, 815.

17 For interpretative statement in respect of this paragraph by Argentina, see p. 792.

18 For interpretative statement in respect of this paragraph by Argentina, see p. 792.

19 For declarations in respect of this paragraph by Argentina, Australia, Belgium, Canada, Germany, Italy, the Netherlands, New Zealand, Republic of Korea, Spain and United Kingdom, see pp. 792, 793, 796, 797, 802, 807, 808, 810, 813, 816, 818. See also the declaration of United States of America made on signature, p. 818.

(a) during each military engagement, and
(b)[20] during such time as he is visible to the adversary while he is engaged in a military deployment preceding the launching of an attack in which he is to participate. Acts which comply with the requirements of this paragraph shall not be considered as perfidious within the meaning of Article 37, paragraph 1(c).

4.[21] A combatant who falls into the power of an adverse Party while failing to meet the requirements set forth in the second sentence of paragraph 3 shall forfeit his right to be a prisoner of war, but he shall, nevertheless, be given protections equivalent in all respects to those accorded to prisoners of war by the Third Convention and by this Protocol. This protection includes protections equivalent to those accorded to prisoners of war by the Third Convention in the case where such a person is tried and punished for any offences he has committed.
5. Any combatant who falls into the power of an adverse Party while not engaged in an attack or in a military operation preparatory to an attack shall not forfeit his rights to be a combatant and a prisoner of war by virtue of his prior activities.
6. This Article is without prejudice to the right of any person to be a prisoner of war pursuant to Article 4 of the Third Convention.
7. This Article is not intended to change the generally accepted practice of States with respect to the wearing of the uniform by combatants assigned to the regular, uniformed armed units of a Party to the conflict.
8. In addition to the categories of persons mentioned in Article 13 of the First and Second Conventions, all members of the armed forces of a Party to the conflict, as defined in Article 43 of this Protocol, shall be entitled to protection under those Conventions if they are wounded or sick or, in the case of the Second Convention, shipwrecked at sea or in other waters.

Art. 45. Protection of persons who have taken part in hostilities

1. A person who takes part in hostilities and falls into the power of an adverse Party shall be presumed to be a prisoner of war, and therefore shall be protected by the Third Convention, if he claims the status of prisoner of war, or if he appears to be entitled to such status, or if the Party on which he depends claims such status on his behalf by notification to the detaining Power or to the Protecting Power. Should any doubt arise as to whether any such person is entitled to the status of prisoner of war, he shall continue to have such status and, therefore, to be protected by the Third Convention and this Protocol until such time as his status has been determined by a competent tribunal.
2. If a person who has fallen into the power of an adverse Party is not held as a prisoner of war and is to be tried by that Party for an offence arising out of the hostilities, he shall have the right to assert his entitlement to prisoner-of-war status before a judicial tribunal and to have that question adjudicated. Whenever possible under the applicable procedure, this adjudication shall occur before the trial for the offence. The representatives of

[20] For declarations in respect of this paragraph made by Australia, Belgium, Canada, France, Germany, Italy, the Netherlands, New Zealand, Republic of Korea and Spain, see pp. 793, 796, 797, 801, 802, 807, 808, 810, 813. See also the declaration by the United Kingdom made on signature, p. 815.

[21] For interpretative statement in respect of this paragraph by Argentina, see p. 792.

the Protecting Power shall be entitled to attend the proceedings in which that question is adjudicated, unless, exceptionally, the proceedings are held *in camera* in the interest of State security. In such a case the detaining Power shall advise the Protecting Power accordingly.

3. Any person who has taken part in hostilities, who is not entitled to prisoner-of-war status and who does not benefit from more favourable treatment in accordance with the Fourth Convention shall have the right at all times to the protection of Article 75 of this Protocol. In occupied territory, any such person, unless he is held as a spy, shall also be entitled, notwithstanding Article 5 of the Fourth Convention, to his rights of communication under that Convention.

Art. 46. Spies

1. Notwithstanding any other provision of the Conventions or of this Protocol, any member of the armed forces of a Party to the conflict who falls into the power of an adverse Party while engaging in espionage shall not have the right to the status of prisoner of war and may be treated as a spy.
2. A member of the armed forces of a Party to the conflict who, on behalf of that Party and in territory controlled by an adverse Party, gathers or attempts to gather information shall not be considered as engaging in espionage if, while so acting, he is in the uniform of his armed forces.
3. A member of the armed forces of a Party to the conflict who is a resident of territory occupied by an adverse Party and who, on behalf of the Party on which he depends, gathers or attempts to gather information of military value within that territory shall not be considered as engaging in espionage unless he does so through an act of false pretences or deliberately in a clandestine manner. Moreover, such a resident shall not lose his right to the status of prisoner of war and may not be treated as a spy unless he is captured while engaging in espionage.
4. A member of the armed forces of a Party to the conflict who is not a resident of territory occupied by an adverse Party and who has engaged in espionage in that territory shall not lose his right to the status of prisoner of war and may not be treated as a spy unless he is captured before he has rejoined the armed forces to which he belongs.

Art. 47. Mercenaries[22]

1. A mercenary shall not have the right to be a combatant or a prisoner of war.
2.[23] A mercenary is any person who:
   (a) is specially recruited locally or abroad in order to fight in an armed conflict;
   (b) does, in fact, take a direct part in the hostilities;
   (c) is motivated to take part in the hostilities essentially by the desire for private gain and, in fact, is promised, by or on behalf of a Party to the conflict, material compensation substantially in excess of that promised or paid to combatants of similar ranks and functions in the armed forces of that Party;

[22] For declaration in respect of this article by Angola, Ireland and Netherlands, see pp. 792, 805, 810.

[23] For reservation in respect of this paragraph by Algeria, see p. 792.

(d) is neither a national of a Party to the conflict nor a resident of territory controlled by a Party to the conflict;
(e) is not a member of the armed forces of a Party to the conflict; and
(f) has not been sent by a State which is not a Party to the conflict on official duty as a member of its armed forces.

PART IV. CIVILIAN POPULATION

Section I. General Protection against Effects of Hostilities[24]

Chapter I. Basic rule and field of application

Art. 48. Basic rule[25]
In order to ensure respect for and protection of the civilian population and civilian objects, the Parties to the conflict shall at all times distinguish between the civilian population and combatants and between civilian objects and military objectives and accordingly shall direct their operations only against military objectives.

Art. 49. Definition of attacks and scope of application
1. "Attacks" means acts of violence against the adversary, whether in offence or in defence.
2. The provisions of this Protocol with respect to attacks apply to all attacks in whatever territory conducted, including the national territory belonging to a Party to the conflict but under the control of an adverse Party.
3. The provisions of this Section apply to any land, air or sea warfare which may affect the civilian population, individual civilians or civilian objects on land. They further apply to all attacks from the sea or from the air against objectives on land but do not otherwise affect the rules of international law applicable in armed conflict at sea or in the air.
4. The provisions of this Section are additional to the rules concerning humanitarian protection contained in the Fourth Convention, particularly in Part II thereof, and in other international agreements binding upon the High Contracting Parties, as well as to other rules of international law relating to the protection of civilians and civilian objects on land, at sea or in the air against the effects of hostilities.

Chapter II. Civilians and civilian population

Art. 50. Definition of civilians and civilian population[26]
1. A civilian is any person who does not belong to one of the categories of persons referred to in Article 4 A (1), (2), (3) and (6) of the Third Convention and in Article 43 of this Protocol. In case of doubt whether a person is a civilian, that person shall be considered to be a civilian.
2. The civilian population comprises all persons who are civilians.

---

[24] For declarations in respect of this section by Belgium, Canada and Germany, see pp. 796, 797–798, 802.
[25] For statement of understanding in respect of this article by Canada, see p. 797.
[26] For declaration in respect of this article by France and the United Kingdom, see pp. 803, 816.

3. The presence within the civilian population of individuals who do not come within the definition of civilians does not deprive the population of its civilian character.

Art. 51. Protection of the civilian population[27]

1. The civilian population and individual civilians shall enjoy general protection against dangers arising from military operations. To give effect to this protection, the following rules, which are additional to other applicable rules of international law, shall be observed in all circumstances.
2. The civilian population as such, as well as individual civilians, shall not be the object of attack. Acts or threats of violence the primary purpose of which is to spread terror among the civilian population are prohibited.
3. Civilians shall enjoy the protection afforded by this Section, unless and for such time as they take a direct part in hostilities.
4. Indiscriminate attacks are prohibited. Indiscriminate attacks are:
   (a) those which are not directed at a specific military objective;
   (b) those which employ a method or means of combat which cannot be directed at a specific military objective; or
   (c) those which employ a method or means of combat the effects of which cannot be limited as required by this Protocol; and consequently, in each such case, are of a nature to strike military objectives and civilians or civilian objects without distinction.
5.[28] Among others, the following types of attacks are to be considered as indiscriminate:
   (a) an attack by bombardment by any methods or means which treats as a single military objective a number of clearly separated and distinct military objectives located in a city, town, village or other area containing a similar concentration of civilians or civilian objects; and
   (b)[29] an attack which may be expected to cause incidental loss of civilian life, injury to civilians, damage to civilian objects, or a combination thereof, which would be excessive in relation to the concrete and direct military advantage anticipated.
6. Attacks against the civilian population or civilians by way of reprisals are prohibited.
7. The presence or movements of the civilian population or individual civilians shall not be used to render certain points or areas immune from military operations, in particular in attempts to shield military objectives from attacks or to shield, favour or impede military operations. The Parties to the conflict shall not direct the movement of the civilian population or individual civilians in order to attempt to shield military objectives from attacks or to shield military operations.
8. Any violation of these prohibitions shall not release the Parties to the conflict from their legal obligations with respect to the civilian population and

[27] For declarations in respect of this article by Australia, Belgium, Canada, France, Germany, Ireland, Italy, Netherlands, New Zealand, Spain and United Kingdom, see pp. 793, 796, 797, 801, 802, 805, 807, 810–811, 813, 816–817. See also the declaration of the United Kingdom made on signature, p. 815.

[28] For declaration in respect of this paragraph by the Netherlands, see p. 810.

[29] For declarations in respect of this paragraph by Australia, Canada, France, Italy and New Zealand, see pp. 793, 798, 801, 807, 810. See also the declaration of the United Kingdom made on signature, p. 815.

civilians, including the obligation to take the precautionary measures provided for in Article 57.

Chapter III. Civilian objects[30]

Art. 52. General protection of civilian objects

1. Civilian objects shall not be the object of attack or of reprisals. Civilian objects are all objects which are not military objectives as defined in paragraph 2.
2.[31] Attacks shall be limited strictly to military objectives. In so far as objects are concerned, military objectives are limited to those objects which by their nature, location, purpose or use make an effective contribution to military action and whose total or partial destruction, capture or neutralization, in the circumstances ruling at the time, offers a definite military advantage.
3. In case of doubt whether an object which is normally dedicated to civilian purposes, such as a place of worship, a house or other dwelling or a school, is being used to make an effective contribution to military action, it shall be presumed not to be so used.

Art. 53. Protection of cultural objects and of places of worship[32]

Without prejudice to the provisions of the Hague Convention for the Protection of Cultural Property in the Event of Armed Conflict of 14 May 1954, and of other relevant international instruments, it is prohibited:

(a) to commit any acts of hostility directed against the historic monuments, works of art or places of worship which constitute the cultural or spiritual heritage of peoples;
(b) to use such objects in support of the military effort;
(c) to make such objects the object of reprisals.

Art. 54. Protection of objects indispensable to the survival of the civilian population[33]

1. Starvation of civilians as a method of warfare is prohibited.
2. It is prohibited to attack, destroy, remove or render useless objects indispensable to the survival of the civilian population, such as foodstuffs, agricultural areas for the production of foodstuffs, crops, livestock, drinking water installations and supplies and irrigation works, for the specific purpose of denying them for their sustenance value to the civilian population or to the adverse Party, whatever the motive, whether in order to starve out civilians, to cause them to move away, or for any other motive.
3. The prohibitions in paragraph 2 shall not apply to such of the objects covered by it as are used by an adverse Party:

---

[30] For declarations in respect of the articles of this chapter by Australia, Canada, Germany, Ireland, Italy, Netherlands, New Zealand, Spain and United Kingdom, see pp. 793, 797–798, 802, 805, 807–808, 810–811, 813, 815–817.

[31] For declarations in respect of this paragraph by Australia, Canada, Italy, France, Netherlands, New Zealand and Spain, see pp. 793, 798, 801, 808, 810, 811, 813.

[32] For declarations in respect of this article by Australia, Canada, France, Ireland, Italy, Netherlands, New Zealand, Spain and United Kingdom (made on signature and ratification), see pp. 793, 798, 801, 805, 808, 810, 813, 815, 817.

[33] For declarations in respect of this article by Australia, Canada, France, Ireland, Italy, Netherlands, New Zealand, Spain and United Kingdom (made on signature and ratification), see pp. 793, 797, 801, 805, 807, 810, 813, 815, 817.

(a) as sustenance solely for the members of its armed forces; or
(b) if not as sustenance, then in direct support of military action, provided, however, that in no event shall actions against these objects be taken which may be expected to leave the civilian population with such inadequate food or water as to cause its starvation or force its movement.

4. These objects shall not be made the object of reprisals.
5. In recognition of the vital requirements of any Party to the conflict in the defence of its national territory against invasion, derogation from the prohibitions contained in paragraph 2 may be made by a Party to the conflict within such territory under its own control where required by imperative military necessity.

Art. 55. Protection of the natural environment[34]

1. Care shall be taken in warfare to protect the natural environment against widespread, long-term and severe damage. This protection includes a prohibition of the use of methods or means of warfare which are intended or may be expected to cause such damage to the natural environment and thereby to prejudice the health or survival of the population.
2. Attacks against the natural environment by way of reprisals are prohibited.

Art. 56. Protection of works and installations containing dangerous forces[35]

1. Works or installations containing dangerous forces, namely dams, dykes and nuclear electrical generating stations, shall not be made the object of attack, even where these objects are military objectives, if such attack may cause the release of dangerous forces and consequent severe losses among the civilian population. Other military objectives located at or in the vicinity of these works or installations shall not be made the object of attack if such attack may cause the release of dangerous forces from the works or installations and consequent severe losses among the civilian population.

2.[36] The special protection against attack provided by paragraph 1 shall cease:
(a) for a dam or a dyke only if it is used for other than its normal function and in regular, significant and direct support of military operations and if such attack is the only feasible way to terminate such support;
(b) for a nuclear electrical generating station only if it provides electric power in regular, significant and direct support of military operations and if such attack is the only feasible way to terminate such support;
(c) for other military objectives located at or in the vicinity of these works or installations only if they are used in regular, significant and direct support of military operations and if such attack is the only feasible way to terminate such support.

3. In all cases, the civilian population and individual civilians shall remain entitled to all the protection accorded them by international law, including the protection of the precautionary measures provided for in Article 57. If the protection ceases and any of the works, installations or military objec-

[34] For declarations in respect of this article by Australia, Canada, France, Ireland, Italy, Netherlands, New Zealand, Spain and United Kingdom (made on signature and ratification, see pp. 793, 797, 800, 805, 807, 810, 813, 815–817.

[35] For declarations in respect of this article by Australia, Canada, France, Germany, Ireland, Italy, Netherlands, New Zealand, Spain and United Kingdom (made on signature and ratification), see pp. 793, 797, 802, 803, 805, 807, 810, 813, 815, 817.

[36] For declaration in respect of this paragraph by the Netherlands, see p. 810.

tives mentioned in paragraph 1 is attacked, all practical precautions shall be taken to avoid the release of the dangerous forces.

4. It is prohibited to make any of the works, installations or military objectives mentioned in paragraph 1 the object of reprisals.
5. The Parties to the conflict shall endeavour to avoid locating any military objectives in the vicinity of the works or installations mentioned in paragraph 1. Nevertheless, installations erected for the sole purpose of defending the protected works or installations from attack are permissible and shall not themselves be made the object of attack, provided that they are not used in hostilities except for defensive actions necessary to respond to attacks against the protected works or installations and that their armament is limited to weapons capable only of repelling hostile action against the protected works or installations.
6. The High Contracting Parties and the Parties to the conflict are urged to conclude further agreements among themselves to provide additional protection for objects containing dangerous forces.
7. In order to facilitate the identification of the objects protected by this article, the Parties to the conflict may mark them with a special sign consisting of a group of three bright orange circles placed on the same axis, as specified in Article 17[37] of Annex I to this Protocol. The absence of such marking in no way relieves any Party to the conflict of its obligations under this Article.

Chapter IV. Precautionary measures

Art. 57. Precautions in attack[38]

1. In the conduct of military operations, constant care shall be taken to spare the civilian population, civilians and civilian objects.

2.[39] With respect to attacks, the following precautions shall be taken:
   (a) those who plan or decide upon an attack shall:
      (i) do everything feasible to verify that the objectives to be attacked are neither civilians nor civilian objects and are not subject to special protection but are military objectives within the meaning of paragraph 2 of Article 52 and that it is not prohibited by the provisions of this Protocol to attack them;
      (ii) take all feasible precautions in the choice of means and methods of attack with a view to avoiding, and in any event to minimizing, incidental loss of civilian life, injury to civilians and damage to civilian objects;
      (iii)[40] refrain from deciding to launch any attack which may be expected to cause incidental loss of civilian life, injury to civilians, damage to civilian objects, or a combination thereof, which

---

[37] See notes 1 and 2 on p. 770.

[38] For declarations in respect of this article by Australia, Austria, Belgium, Canada, France, Germany, Ireland, Italy, Netherlands, New Zealand, Spain and United Kingdom (made on signature and ratification), see pp. 793, 794, 796, 797, 801, 802, 805, 807, 810–811, 813, 815–817.

[39] For declarations in respect of this paragraph by Algeria, Austria, Canada, Germany, Netherlands and Switzerland, see pp. 792, 794, 798, 802, 810, 814.

[40] For declarations in respect of this paragraph by Australia, Canada, France, Germany, Italy, New Zealand and United Kingdom (made on signature and ratification), see pp. 793, 798, 801, 802, 807, 811, 815–816.

would be excessive in relation to the concrete and direct military advantage anticipated;

(b) an attack shall be cancelled or suspended if it becomes apparent that the objective is not a military one or is subject to special protection or that the attack may be expected to cause incidental loss of civilian life, injury to civilians, damage to civilian objects, or a combination thereof, which would be excessive in relation to the concrete and direct military advantage anticipated;

(c) effective advance warning shall be given of attacks which may affect the civilian population, unless circumstances do not permit.

3.[41] When a choice is possible between several military objectives for obtaining a similar military advantage, the objective to be selected shall be that the attack on which may be expected to cause the least danger to civilian lives and to civilian objects.

4. In the conduct of military operations at sea or in the air, each Party to the conflict shall, in conformity with its rights and duties under the rules of international law applicable in armed conflict, take all reasonable precautions to avoid losses of civilian lives and damage to civilian objects.

5. No provision of this Article may be construed as authorizing any attacks against the civilian population, civilians or civilian objects.

Art. 58. Precautions against the effects of attacks[42]

The Parties to the conflict shall, to the maximum extent feasible:

(a) without prejudice to Article 49 of the Fourth Convention, endeavour to remove the civilian population, individual civilians and civilian objects under their control from the vicinity of military objectives;

(b) avoid locating military objectives within or near densely populated areas;

(c) take the other necessary precautions to protect the civilian population, individual civilians and civilian objects under their control against the dangers resulting from military operations.

Chapter V. Localities and zones under special protection

Art. 59. Non-defended localities[43]

1. It is prohibited for the Parties to the conflict to attack, by any means whatsoever, non-defended localities.

2. The appropriate authorities of a Party to the conflict may declare as a non-defended locality any inhabited place near or in a zone where armed forces are in contact which is open for occupation by an adverse Party. Such a locality shall fulfil the following conditions:

(a) all combatants, as well as mobile weapons and mobile military equipment must have been evacuated;

(b) no hostile use shall be made of fixed military installations or establishments;

---

[41] For declaration in respect of this paragraph by Netherlands, see p. 810.

[42] For declarations in respect of this article by Algeria, Australia, Austria, Belgium, Canada, Germany, Ireland, Italy, Netherlands, New Zealand, Spain and Switzerland, see pp. 792, 793, 794, 796, 797, 802, 805, 807, 810, 813, 814. See also the declaration of the United Kingdom made on signature, p. 815.

[43] For statement of understanding in respect of this article by Canada, see p. 797–798.

(c) no acts of hostility shall be committed by the authorities or by the population; and
(d) no activities in support of military operations shall be undertaken.

3. The presence, in this locality, of persons specially protected under the Conventions and this Protocol, and of police forces retained for the sole purpose of maintaining law and order, is not contrary to the conditions laid down in paragraph 2.
4. The declaration made under paragraph 2 shall be addressed to the adverse Party and shall define and describe, as precisely as possible, the limits of the non-defended locality. The Party to the conflict to which the declaration is addressed shall acknowledge its receipt and shall treat the locality as a non-defended locality unless the conditions laid down in paragraph 2 are not in fact fulfilled, in which event it shall immediately so inform the Party making the declaration. Even if the conditions laid down in paragraph 2 are not fulfilled, the locality shall continue to enjoy the protection provided by the other provisions of this Protocol and the other rules of international law applicable in armed conflict.
5. The Parties to the conflict may agree on the establishment of non-defended localities even if such localities do not fulfil the conditions laid down in paragraph 2. The agreement should define and describe, as precisely as possible, the limits of the non-defended locality; if necessary, it may lay down the methods of supervision.
6. The Party which is in control of a locality governed by such an agreement shall mark it, so far as possible, by such signs as may be agreed upon with the other Party, which shall be displayed where they are clearly visible, especially on its perimeter and limits and on highways.
7. A locality loses its status as a non-defended locality when it ceases to fulfil the conditions laid down in paragraph 2 or in the agreement referred to in paragraph 5. In such an eventuality, the locality shall continue to enjoy the protection provided by the other provisions of this Protocol and the other rules of international law applicable in armed conflict.

Art. 60. Demilitarized zones[44]

1. It is prohibited for the Parties to the conflict to extend their military operations to zones on which they have conferred by agreement the status of demilitarized zone, if such extension is contrary to the terms of this agreement.
2. The agreement shall be an express agreement, may be concluded verbally or in writing, either directly or through a Protecting Power or any impartial humanitarian organization, and may consist of reciprocal and concordant declarations. The agreement may be concluded in peacetime, as well as after the outbreak of hostilities, and should define and describe, as precisely as possible, the limits of the demilitarized zone and, if necessary, lay down the methods of supervision.
3. The subject of such an agreement shall normally be any zone which fulfils the following conditions:
   (a) all combatants, as well as mobile weapons and mobile military equipment, must have been evacuated;

---

[44] For statement of understanding in respect of this article by Canada, see p. 797.

(b) no hostile use shall be made of fixed military installations or establishments;
(c) no acts of hostility shall be committed by the authorities or by the population; and
(d) any activity linked to the military effort must have ceased.

The Parties to the conflict shall agree upon the interpretation to be given to the condition laid down in sub-paragraph (d) and upon persons to be admitted to the demilitarized zone other than those mentioned in paragraph 4.

4. The presence, in this zone, of persons specially protected under the Conventions and this Protocol, and of police forces retained for the sole purpose of maintaining law and order, is not contrary to the conditions laid down in paragraph 3.
5. The Party which is in control of such a zone shall mark it, so far as possible, by such signs as may be agreed upon with the other Party, which shall be displayed where they are clearly visible, especially on its perimeter and limits and on highways.
6. If the fighting draws near to a demilitarized zone, and if the Parties to the conflict have so agreed, none of them may use the zone for purposes related to the conduct of military operations or unilaterally revoke its status.
7. If one of the Parties to the conflict commits a material breach of the provisions of paragraphs 3 or 6, the other Party shall be released from its obligations under the agreement conferring upon the zone the status of demilitarized zone. In such an eventuality, the zone loses its status but shall continue to enjoy the protection provided by the other provisions of this Protocol and the other rules of international law applicable in armed conflict.

Chapter VI. Civil defence

Art. 61. Definitions and scope

For the purposes of this Protocol:

(a) "civil defence" means the performance of some or all of the undermentioned humanitarian tasks intended to protect the civilian population against the dangers, and to help it to recover from the immediate effects of hostilities or disasters and also to provide the conditions necessary for its survival. These tasks are:
  (i) warning;
  (ii) evacuation;
  (iii) management of shelters;
  (iv) management of blackout measures;
  (v) rescue;
  (vi) medical services, including first aid, and religious assistance;
  (vii) fire-fighting;
  (viii) detection and marking of danger areas;
  (ix) decontamination and similar protective measures;
  (x) provision of emergency accommodation and supplies;
  (xi) emergency assistance in the restoration and maintenance of order in distressed areas;
  (xii) emergency repair of indispensable public utilities;
  (xiii) emergency disposal of the dead;
  (xiv) assistance in the preservation of objects essential for survival;

(xv) complementary activities necessary to carry out any of the tasks mentioned above, including, but not limited to, planning and organization;

(b) "civil defence organizations" means those establishments and other units which are organized or authorized by the competent authorities of a Party to the conflict to perform any of the tasks mentioned under sub-paragraph (a), and which are assigned and devoted exclusively to such tasks;

(c) "personnel" of civil defence organizations means those persons assigned by a Party to the conflict exclusively to the performance of the tasks mentioned under sub-paragraph (a), including personnel assigned by the competent authority of that Party exclusively to the administration of these organizations;

(d) "*matériel*" of civil defence organizations means equipment, supplies and transports used by these organizations for the performance of the tasks mentioned under sub-paragraph (a).

Art. 62. General protection[45]

1. Civilian civil defence organizations and their personnel shall be respected and protected, subject to the provisions of this Protocol, particularly the provisions of this Section. They shall be entitled to perform their civil defence tasks except in case of imperative military necessity.
2. The provisions of paragraph 1 shall also apply to civilians who, although not members of civilian civil defence organizations, respond to an appeal from the competent authorities and perform civil defence tasks under their control.
3. Buildings and *matériel* used for civil defence purposes and shelters provided for the civilian population are covered by Article 52. Objects used for civil defence purposes may not be destroyed or diverted from their proper use except by the Party to which they belong.

Art. 63. Civil defence in occupied territories

1. In occupied territories, civilian civil defence organizations shall receive from the authorities the facilities necessary for the performance of their tasks. In no circumstances shall their personnel be compelled to perform activities which would interfere with the proper performance of these tasks. The Occupying Power shall not change the structure or personnel of such organizations in any way which might jeopardize the efficient performance of their mission. These organizations shall not be required to give priority to the nationals or interests of that Power.
2. The Occupying Power shall not compel, coerce or induce civilian civil defence organizations to perform their tasks in any manner prejudicial to the interests of the civilian population.
3. The Occupying Power may disarm civil defence personnel for reasons of security.
4. The Occupying Power shall neither divert from their proper use nor requisition buildings or *matériel* belonging to or used by civil defence organizations if such diversion or requisition would be harmful to the civilian population.
5. Provided that the general rule in paragraph 4 continues to be observed, the Occupying Power may requisition or divert these resources, subject to the following particular conditions:

[45] For statement of understanding in respect of this article by Canada and Ireland, see pp. 797, 805.

(a) that the buildings or *matériel* are necessary for other needs of the civilian population; and
(b) that the requisition or diversion continues only while such necessity exists.

6. The Occupying Power shall neither divert nor requisition shelters provided for the use of the civilian population or needed by such population.

Art. 64. Civilian civil defence organizations of neutral or other States not Parties to the conflict and international co-ordinating organizations

1. Articles 62, 63, 65 and 66 shall also apply to the personnel and *matériel* of civilian civil defence organizations of neutral or other States not Parties to the conflict which perform civil defence tasks mentioned in Article 61 in the territory of a Party to the conflict, with the consent and under the control of that Party. Notification of such assistance shall be given as soon as possible to any adverse Party concerned. In no circumstances shall this activity be deemed to be an interference in the conflict. This activity should, however, be performed with due regard to the security interests of the Parties to the conflict concerned.
2. The Parties to the conflict receiving the assistance referred to in paragraph 1 and the High Contracting Parties granting it should facilitate international co-ordination of such civil defence actions when appropriate. In such cases the relevant international organizations are covered by the provisions of this Chapter.
3. In occupied territories, the Occupying Power may only exclude or restrict the activities of civilian civil defence organizations of neutral or other States not Parties to the conflict and of international co-ordinating organizations if it can ensure the adequate performance of civil defence tasks from its own resources or those of the occupied territory.

Art. 65. Cessation of protection

1. The protection to which civilian civil defence organizations, their personnel, buildings, shelters and *matériel* are entitled shall not cease unless they commit or are used to commit, outside their proper tasks, acts harmful to the enemy. Protection may, however, cease only after a warning has been given setting, whenever appropriate, a reasonable time-limit, and after such warning has remained unheeded.
2. The following shall not be considered as acts harmful to the enemy:
   (a) that civil defence tasks are carried out under the direction or control of military authorities;
   (b) that civilian civil defence personnel co-operate with military personnel in the performance of civil defence tasks, or that some military personnel are attached to civilian civil defence organizations;
   (c) that the performance of civil defence tasks may incidentally benefit military victims, particularly those who are *hors de combat*.
3. It shall also not be considered as an act harmful to the enemy that civilian civil defence personnel bear light individual weapons for the purpose of maintaining order or for self-defence. However, in areas where land fighting is taking place or is likely to take place, the Parties to the conflict shall undertake the appropriate measures to limit these weapons to handguns, such as pistols or revolvers, in order to assist in distinguishing

between civil defence personnel and combatants. Although civil defence personnel bear other light individual weapons in such areas, they shall nevertheless be respected and protected as soon as they have been recognized as such.

4. The formation of civilian civil defence organizations along military lines, and compulsory service in them, shall also not deprive them of the protection conferred by this Chapter.

Art. 66. Identification

1. Each Party to the conflict shall endeavour to ensure that its civil defence organizations, their personnel, buildings and *matériel*, are identifiable while they are exclusively devoted to the performance of civil defence tasks. Shelters provided for the civilian population should be similarly identifiable.
2. Each Party to the conflict shall also endeavour to adopt and implement methods and procedures which will make it possible to recognize civilian shelters as well as civil defence personnel, buildings and *matériel* on which the international distinctive sign of civil defence is displayed.
3. In occupied territories and in areas where fighting is taking place or is likely to take place, civilian civil defence personnel should be recognizable by the international distinctive sign of civil defence and by an identity card certifying their status.
4. The international distinctive sign of civil defence is an equilateral blue triangle on an orange ground when used for the protection of civil defence organizations, their personnel, buildings and *matériel* and for civilian shelters.
5. In addition to the distinctive sign, Parties to the conflict may agree upon the use of distinctive signals for civil defence identification purposes.
6. The application of the provisions of paragraphs 1 to 4 is governed by Chapter V of Annex I to this Protocol.
7. In time of peace, the sign described in paragraph 4 may, with the consent of the competent national authorities, be used for civil defence identification purposes.
8. The High Contracting Parties and the Parties to the conflict shall take the measures necessary to supervise the display of the international distinctive sign of civil defence and to prevent and repress any misuse thereof.
9. The identification of civil defence medical and religious personnel, medical units and medical transports is also governed by Article 18.

Art. 67. Members of the armed forces and military units assigned to civil defence organizations[46]

1. Members of the armed forces and military units assigned to civil defence organizations shall be respected and protected, provided that:
   (a) such personnel and such units are permanently assigned and exclusively devoted to the performance of any of the tasks mentioned in Article 61;
   (b) if so assigned, such personnel do not perform any other military duties during the conflict;
   (c) such personnel are clearly distinguishable from the other members of the armed forces by prominently displaying the international distinctive

[46] For statement of understanding in respect of this article by Canada, see p. 797.

sign of civil defence, which shall be as large as appropriate, and such personnel are provided with the identity card referred to in Chapter V of Annex I to this Protocol certifying their status;

(d) such personnel and such units are equipped only with light individual weapons for the purpose of maintaining order or for self-defence. The provisions of Article 65, paragraph 3 shall also apply in this case;

(e) such personnel do not participate directly in hostilities, and do not commit, or are not used to commit, outside their civil defence tasks, acts harmful to the adverse Party;

(f) such personnel and such units perform their civil defence tasks only within the national territory of their Party.

The non-observance of the conditions stated in (e) above by any member of the armed forces who is bound by the conditions prescribed in (a) and (b) above is prohibited.

2. Military personnel serving within civil defence organizations shall, if they fall into the power of an adverse Party, be prisoners of war. In occupied territory they may, but only in the interest of the civilian population of that territory, be employed on civil defence tasks in so far as the need arises, provided however that, if such work is dangerous, they volunteer for such tasks.
3. The buildings and major items of equipment and transports of military units assigned to civil defence organizations shall be clearly marked with the international distinctive sign of civil defence. This distinctive sign shall be as large as appropriate.
4. The *matériel* and buildings of military units permanently assigned to civil defence organizations and exclusively devoted to the performance of civil defence tasks shall, if they fall into the hands of an adverse Party, remain subject to the laws of war. They may not be diverted from their civil defence purpose so long as they are required for the performance of civil defence tasks, except in case of imperative military necessity, unless previous arrangements have been made for adequate provision for the needs of the civilian population.

Section II. Relief in Favour of the Civilian Population

Art. 68. Field of application

The provisions of this Section apply to the civilian population as defined in this Protocol and are supplementary to Articles 23, 55, 59, 60, 61 and 62 and other relevant provisions of the Fourth Convention.

Art. 69. Basic needs in occupied territories

1. In addition to the duties specified in Article 55 of the Fourth Convention concerning food and medical supplies, the Occupying Power shall, to the fullest extent of the means available to it and without any adverse distinction, also ensure the provision of clothing, bedding, means of shelter, other supplies essential to the survival of the civilian population of the occupied territory and objects necessary for religious worship.
2. Relief actions for the benefit of the civilian population of occupied territories are governed by Articles 59, 60, 61, 62, 108, 109, 110 and 111 of the Fourth Convention, and by Article 71 of this Protocol, and shall be implemented without delay.

Art. 70. Relief actions[47]

1. If the civilian population of any territory under the control of a Party to the conflict, other than occupied territory, is not adequately provided with the supplies mentioned in Article 69, relief actions which are humanitarian and impartial in character and conducted without any adverse distinction shall be undertaken, subject to the agreement of the Parties concerned in such relief actions. Offers of such relief shall not be regarded as interference in the armed conflict or as unfriendly acts. In the distribution of relief consignments, priority shall be given to those persons, such as children, expectant mothers, maternity cases and nursing mothers, who, under the Fourth Convention or under this Protocol, are to be accorded privileged treatment or special protection.
2. The Parties to the conflict and each High Contracting Party shall allow and facilitate rapid and unimpeded passage of all relief consignments, equipment and personnel provided in accordance with this Section, even if such assistance is destined for the civilian population of the adverse Party.
3. The Parties to the conflict and each High Contracting Party which allow the passage of relief consignments, equipment and personnel in accordance with paragraph 2:
   (a) shall have the right to prescribe the technical arrangements, including search, under which such passage is permitted;
   (b) may make such permission conditional on the distribution of this assistance being made under the local supervision of a Protecting Power;
   (c) shall, in no way whatsoever, divert relief consignments from the purpose for which they are intended nor delay their forwarding, except in cases of urgent necessity in the interest of the civilian population concerned.
4. The Parties to the conflict shall protect relief consignments and facilitate their rapid distribution.
5. The Parties to the conflict and each High Contracting Party concerned shall encourage and facilitate effective international co-ordination of the relief actions referred to in paragraph 1.

Art. 71. Personnel participating in relief actions

1. Where necessary, relief personnel may form part of the assistance provided in any relief action, in particular for the transportation and distribution of relief consignments; the participation of such personnel shall be subject to the approval of the Party in whose territory they will carry out their duties.
2. Such personnel shall be respected and protected.
3. Each Party in receipt of relief consignments shall, to the fullest extent practicable, assist the relief personnel referred to in paragraph 1 in carrying out their relief mission. Only in case of imperative military necessity may the activities of the relief personnel be limited or their movements temporarily restricted.
4. Under no circumstances may relief personnel exceed the terms of their mission under this Protocol. In particular they shall take account of the security requirements of the Party in whose territory they are carrying out their duties. The mission of any of the personnel who do not respect these conditions may be terminated.

[47] For declaration in respect of this article by France and the United Kingdom, see pp. 801, 817.

Section III. Treatment of Persons in the Power of a Party to the Conflict

Chapter I. Field of application and protection of persons and objects

Art. 72. Field of application
The provisions of this Section are additional to the rules concerning humanitarian protection of civilians and civilian objects in the power of a Party to the conflict contained in the Fourth Convention, particularly Parts I and III thereof, as well as to other applicable rules of international law relating to the protection of fundamental human rights during international armed conflict.

Art. 73. Refugees and stateless persons
Persons who, before the beginning of hostilities, were considered as stateless persons or refugees under the relevant international instruments accepted by the Parties concerned or under the national legislation of the State of refuge or State of residence shall be protected persons within the meaning of Parts I and III of the Fourth Convention, in all circumstances and without any adverse distinction.

Art. 74. Reunion of dispersed families
The High Contracting Parties and the Parties to the conflict shall facilitate in every possible way the reunion of families dispersed as a result of armed conflicts and shall encourage in particular the work of the humanitarian organizations engaged in this task in accordance with the provisions of the Conventions and of this Protocol and in conformity with their respective security regulations.

Art. 75. Fundamental guarantees[48]

1. In so far as they are affected by a situation referred to in Article 1 of this Protocol, persons who are in the power of a Party to the conflict and who do not benefit from more favourable treatment under the Conventions or under this Protocol shall be treated humanely in all circumstances and shall enjoy, as a minimum, the protection provided by this Article without any adverse distinction based upon race, colour, sex, language, religion or belief, political or other opinion, national or social origin, wealth, birth or other status, or on any other similar criteria. Each Party shall respect the person, honour, convictions and religious practices of all such persons.
2. The following acts are and shall remain prohibited at any time and in any place whatsoever, whether committed by civilian or by military agents:
   (a) violence to the life, health, or physical or mental well-being of persons, in particular:
      (i) murder;
      (ii) torture of all kinds, whether physical or mental;
      (iii) corporal punishment; and
      (iv) mutilation;
   (b) outrages upon personal dignity, in particular humiliating and degrading treatment, enforced prostitution and any form of indecent assault;
   (c) the taking of hostages;

[48] For declaration in respect of this article by Finland, see pp. 799-800.

(d) collective punishments; and
(e) threats to commit any of the foregoing acts.

3. Any person arrested, detained or interned for actions related to the armed conflict shall be informed promptly, in a language he understands, of the reasons why these measures have been taken. Except in cases of arrest or detention for penal offences, such persons shall be released with the minimum delay possible and in any event as soon as the circumstances justifying the arrest, detention or internment have ceased to exist.
4. No sentence may be passed and no penalty may be executed on a person found guilty of a penal offence related to the armed conflict except pursuant to a conviction pronounced by an impartial and regularly constituted court respecting the generally recognized principles of regular judicial procedure, which include the following:
   (a) the procedure shall provide for an accused to be informed without delay of the particulars of the offence alleged against him and shall afford the accused before and during his trial all necessary rights and means of defence;
   (b) no one shall be convicted of an offence except on the basis of individual penal responsibility;
   (c) no one shall be accused or convicted of a criminal offence on account of any act or omission which did not constitute a criminal offence under the national or international law to which he was subject at the time when it was committed; nor shall a heavier penalty be imposed than that which was applicable at the time when the criminal offence was committed; if, after the commission of the offence, provision is made by law for the imposition of a lighter penalty, the offender shall benefit thereby;
   (d) anyone charged with an offence is presumed innocent until proved guilty according to law;
   (e)[49] anyone charged with an offence shall have the right to be tried in his presence;
   (f) no one shall be compelled to testify against himself or to confess guilt;
   (g) anyone charged with an offence shall have the right to examine, or have examined, the witnesses against him and to obtain the attendance and examination of witnesses on his behalf under the same conditions as witnesses against him;
   (h)[50] no one shall be prosecuted or punished by the same Party for an offence in respect of which a final judgement acquitting or convicting that person has been previously pronounced under the same law and judicial procedure;
   (i)[51] anyone prosecuted for an offence shall have the right to have the judgement pronounced publicly; and

[49] For declarations and reservations in respect of this paragraph by Austria, Germany, Ireland, Liechtenstein and Malta, see pp. 794, 802, 805, 808, 809.

[50] For declarations and reservations in respect of this paragraph by Austria, Denmark, Finland, Germany, Iceland, Liechtenstein, Malta and Sweden, see pp. 794, 799, 800, 802, 804, 808, 809, 813.

[51] For reservation in respect of this paragraph by Liechtenstein, see p. 808. Finland made a reservation to this paragraph, but withdrew it with immediate effect on 16 February 1987, see p. 799.

(j) a convicted person shall be advised on conviction of his judicial and other remedies and of the time-limits within which they may be exercised.

5. Women whose liberty has been restricted for reasons related to the armed conflict shall be held in quarters separated from men's quarters. They shall be under the immediate supervision of women. Nevertheless, in cases where families are detained or interned, they shall, whenever possible, be held in the same place and accommodated as family units.
6. Persons who are arrested, detained or interned for reasons related to the armed conflict shall enjoy the protection provided by this Article until their final release, repatriation or re-establishment, even after the end of the armed conflict.
7. In order to avoid any doubt concerning the prosecution and trial of persons accused of war crimes or crimes against humanity, the following principles shall apply:
   (a) persons who are accused of such crimes should be submitted for the purpose of prosecution and trial in accordance with the applicable rules of international law; and
   (b) any such persons who do not benefit from more favourable treatment under the Conventions or this Protocol shall be accorded the treatment provided by this Article, whether or not the crimes of which they are accused constitute grave breaches of the Conventions or of this Protocol.
8. No provision of this Article may be construed as limiting or infringing any other more favourable provision granting greater protection, under any applicable rules of international law, to persons covered by paragraph 1.

Chapter II. Measures in favour of women and children

Art. 76. Protection of women

1. Women shall be the object of special respect and shall be protected in particular against rape, forced prostitution and any other form of indecent assault.
2. Pregnant women and mothers having dependent infants who are arrested, detained or interned for reasons related to the armed conflict, shall have their cases considered with the utmost priority.
3. To the maximum extent feasible, the Parties to the conflict shall endeavour to avoid the pronouncement of the death penalty on pregnant women or mothers having dependent infants, for an offence related to the armed conflict. The death penalty for such offences shall not be executed on such women.

Art. 77. Protection of children

1. Children shall be the object of special respect and shall be protected against any form of indecent assault. The Parties to the conflict shall provide them with the care and aid they require, whether because of their age or for any other reason.
2. The Parties to the conflict shall take all feasible measures in order that children who have not attained the age of fifteen years do not take a direct part in hostilities and, in particular, they shall refrain from recruiting them into their armed forces. In recruiting among those persons who have attained the age of fifteen years but who have not attained the age of eighteen years, the Parties to the conflict shall endeavour to give priority to those who are oldest.

3. If, in exceptional cases, despite the provisions of paragraph 2, children who have not attained the age of fifteen years take a direct part in hostilities and fall into the power of an adverse Party, they shall continue to benefit from the special protection accorded by this Article, whether or not they are prisoners of war.
4. If arrested, detained or interned for reasons related to the armed conflict, children shall be held in quarters separate from the quarters of adults, except where families are accommodated as family units as provided in Article 75, paragraph 5.
5. The death penalty for an offence related to the armed conflict shall not be executed on persons who had not attained the age of eighteen years at the time the offence was committed.

Art. 78. Evacuation of children[52]

1.[53] No Party to the conflict shall arrange for the evacuation of children, other than its own nationals, to a foreign country except for a temporary evacuation where compelling reasons of the health or medical treatment of the children or, except in occupied territory, their safety, so require. Where the parents or legal guardians can be found, their written consent to such evacuation is required. If these persons cannot be found, the written consent to such evacuation of the persons who by law or custom are primarily responsible for the care of the children is required. Any such evacuation shall be supervised by the Protecting Power in agreement with the Parties concerned, namely, the Party arranging for the evacuation, the Party receiving the children and any Parties whose nationals are being evacuated. In each case, all Parties to the conflict shall take all feasible precautions to avoid endangering the evacuation.
2. Whenever an evacuation occurs pursuant to paragraph 1, each child's education, including his religious and moral education as his parents desire, shall be provided while he is away with the greatest possible continuity.
3. With a view to facilitating the return to their families and country of children evacuated pursuant to this Article, the authorities of the Party arranging for the evacuation and, as appropriate, the authorities of the receiving country shall establish for each child a card with photographs, which they shall send to the Central Tracing Agency of the International Committee of the Red Cross. Each card shall bear, whenever possible, and whenever it involves no risk of harm to the child, the following information:
   (a) surname(s) of the child;
   (b) the child's first name(s);
   (c) the child's sex;
   (d) the place and date of birth (or, if that date is not known, the approximate age);
   (e) the father's full name;
   (f) the mother's full name and her maiden name;
   (g) the child's next-of-kin;
   (h) the child's nationality;
   (i) the child's native language, and any other languages he speaks;
   (j) the address of the child's family;

[52] For declarations in respect of this article by Canada, Germany, Ireland, Italy and Spain, see pp. 797, 802, 805, 807, 813.

[53] For declaration in respect of this paragraph by Netherlands, see p. 810.

(k) any identification number for the child;
(l) the child's state of health;
(m) the child's blood group;
(n) any distinguishing features;
(o) the date on which and the place where the child was found;
(p) the date on which and the place from which the child left the country;
(q) the child's religion, if any;
(r) the child's present address in the receiving country;
(s) should the child die before his return, the date, place and circumstances of death and place of interment.

Chapter III. Journalists

Art. 79. Measures of protection for journalists

1. Journalists engaged in dangerous professional missions in areas of armed conflict shall be considered as civilians within the meaning of Article 50, paragraph 1.
2. They shall be protected as such under the Conventions and this Protocol, provided that they take no action adversely affecting their status as civilians, and without prejudice to the right of war correspondents accredited to the armed forces to the status provided for in Article 4 A (4) of the Third Convention.
3. They may obtain an identity card similar to the model in Annex II of this Protocol. This card, which shall be issued by the government of the State of which the journalist is a national or in whose territory he resides or in which the news medium employing him is located, shall attest to his status as a journalist.

PART V. EXECUTION OF THE CONVENTIONS AND OF THIS PROTOCOL

Section I. General Provisions

Art. 80. Measures for execution

1. The High Contracting Parties and the Parties to the conflict shall without delay take all necessary measures for the execution of their obligations under the Conventions and this Protocol.
2. The High Contracting Parties and the Parties to the conflict shall give orders and instructions to ensure observance of the Conventions and this Protocol, and shall supervise their execution.

Art. 81. Activities of the Red Cross and other humanitarian organizations

1. The Parties to the conflict shall grant to the International Committee of the Red Cross all facilities within their power so as to enable it to carry out the humanitarian functions assigned to it by the Conventions and this Protocol in order to ensure protection and assistance to the victims of conflicts; the International Committee of the Red Cross may also carry out any other humanitarian activities in favour of these victims, subject to the consent of the Parties to the conflict concerned.
2. The Parties to the conflict shall grant to their respective Red Cross (Red Crescent, Red Lion and Sun) organizations the facilities necessary for car-

rying out their humanitarian activities in favour of the victims of the conflict, in accordance with the provisions of the Conventions and this Protocol and the fundamental principles of the Red Cross as formulated by the International Conferences of the Red Cross.

3. The High Contracting Parties and the Parties to the conflict shall facilitate in every possible way the assistance which Red Cross (Red Crescent, Red Lion and Sun) organizations and the League of Red Cross Societies extend to the victims of conflicts in accordance with the provisions of the Conventions and this Protocol and with the fundamental principles of the Red Cross as formulated by the International Conferences of the Red Cross.
4. The High Contracting Parties and the Parties to the conflict shall, as far as possible, make facilities similar to those mentioned in paragraphs 2 and 3 available to the other humanitarian organizations referred to in the Conventions and this Protocol which are duly authorized by the respective Parties to the conflict and which perform their humanitarian activities in accordance with the provisions of the Conventions and this Protocol.

Art. 82. Legal advisers in armed forces

The High Contracting Parties at all times, and the Parties to the conflict in time of armed conflict, shall ensure that legal advisers are available, when necessary, to advise military commanders at the appropriate level on the application of the Conventions and this Protocol and on the appropriate instruction to be given to the armed forces on this subject.

Art. 83. Dissemination

1. The High Contracting Parties undertake, in time of peace as in time of armed conflict, to disseminate the Conventions and this Protocol as widely as possible in their respective countries and, in particular, to include the study thereof in their programmes of military instruction and to encourage the study thereof by the civilian population, so that those instruments may become known to the armed forces and to the civilian population.
2. Any military or civilian authorities who, in time of armed conflict, assume responsibilities in respect of the application of the Conventions and this Protocol shall be fully acquainted with the text thereof.

Art. 84. Rules of application

The High Contracting Parties shall communicate to one another, as soon as possible, through the depositary and, as appropriate, through the Protecting Powers, their official translations of this Protocol, as well as the laws and regulations which they may adopt to ensure its application.

Section II. Repression of Breaches of the Conventions and of this Protocol

Art. 85. Repression of breaches of this Protocol[54]

1. The provisions of the Conventions relating to the repression of breaches and grave breaches, supplemented by this Section, shall apply to the repression of breaches and grave breaches of this Protocol.

[54] For declarations and reservations in respect of this article by Algeria, Austria and Finland, see pp. 792, 794, 799.

2. Acts described as grave breaches in the Conventions are grave breaches of this Protocol if committed against persons in the power of an adverse Party protected by Articles 44, 45 and 73 of this Protocol, or against the wounded, sick and shipwrecked of the adverse Party who are protected by this Protocol, or against those medical or religious personnel, medical units or medical transports which are under the control of the adverse Party and are protected by this Protocol.
3. In addition to the grave breaches defined in Article 11, the following acts shall be regarded as grave breaches of this Protocol, when committed wilfully, in violation of the relevant provisions of this Protocol, and causing death or serious injury to body or health:
   (a) making the civilian population or individual civilians the object of attack;
   (b) launching an indiscriminate attack affecting the civilian population or civilian objects in the knowledge that such attack will cause excessive loss of life, injury to civilians or damage to civilian objects, as defined in Article 57, paragraph 2(a)(iii);
   (c)[55] launching an attack against works or installations containing dangerous forces in the knowledge that such attack will cause excessive loss of life, injury to civilians or damage to civilian objects, as defined in Article 57, paragraph 2(a)(iii);
   (d) making non-defended localities and demilitarized zones the object of attack;
   (e) making a person the object of attack in the knowledge that he is *hors de combat*;
   (f) the perfidious use, in violation of Article 37, of the distinctive emblem of the red cross, red crescent or red lion and sun or of other protective signs recognized by the Conventions or this Protocol.
4. In addition to the grave breaches defined in the preceding paragraphs and in the Conventions, the following shall be regarded as grave breaches of this Protocol, when committed wilfully and in violation of the Conventions or the Protocol:
   (a) the transfer by the Occupying Power of parts of its own civilian population into the territory it occupies, or the deportation or transfer of all or parts of the population of the occupied territory within or outside this territory, in violation of Article 49 of the Fourth Convention;
   (b)[56] unjustifiable delay in the repatriation of prisoners of war or civilians;
   (c) practices of *apartheid* and other inhuman and degrading practices involving outrages upon personal dignity, based on racial discrimination;
   (d) making the clearly-recognized historic monuments, works of art or places of worship which constitute the cultural or spiritual heritage of peoples and to which special protection has been given by special arrangement, for example, within the framework of a competent international organization, the object of attack, causing as a result extensive destruction thereof, where there is no evidence of the violation by the adverse Party of Article 53, sub-paragraph (b), and when such his-

[55] For declaration in respect of this paragraph by France and the United Kingdom, see pp. 801, 817.

[56] For declaration in respect of this paragraph by the Republic of Korea, see p. 808.

toric monuments, works of art and places of worship are not located in the immediate proximity of military objectives;

(e) depriving a person protected by the Conventions or referred to in paragraph 2 of this Article of the rights of fair and regular trial.

5. Without prejudice to the application of the Conventions and of this Protocol, grave breaches of these instruments shall be regarded as war crimes.

Art. 86. Failure to act[57]

1. The High Contracting Parties and the Parties to the conflict shall repress grave breaches, and take measures necessary to suppress all other breaches, of the Conventions or of this Protocol which result from a failure to act when under a duty to do so.

2.[58] The fact that a breach of the Conventions or of this Protocol was committed by a subordinate does not absolve his superiors from penal or disciplinary responsibility, as the case may be, if they knew, or had information which should have enabled them to conclude in the circumstances at the time, that he was committing or was going to commit such a breach and if they did not take all feasible measures within their power to prevent or repress the breach.

Art. 87. Duty of commanders

1. The High Contracting Parties and the Parties to the conflict shall require military commanders, with respect to members of the armed forces under their command and other persons under their control, to prevent and, where necessary, to suppress and to report to competent authorities breaches of the Conventions and of this Protocol.
2. In order to prevent and suppress breaches, High Contracting Parties and Parties to the conflict shall require that, commensurate with their level of responsibility, commanders ensure that members of the armed forces under their command are aware of their obligations under the Conventions and this Protocol.
3. The High Contracting Parties and Parties to the conflict shall require any commander who is aware that subordinates or other persons under his control are going to commit or have committed a breach of the Conventions or of this Protocol, to initiate such steps as are necessary to prevent such violations of the Conventions or this Protocol, and, where appropriate, to initiate disciplinary or penal action against violators thereof.

Art. 88. Mutual assistance in criminal matters

1. The High Contracting Parties shall afford one another the greatest measure of assistance in connexion with criminal proceedings brought in respect of grave breaches of the Conventions or of this Protocol.

2.[59] Subject to the rights and obligations established in the Conventions and in Article 85, paragraph 1, of this Protocol, and when circumstances permit, the High Contracting Parties shall co-operate in the matter of extradition.

---

[57] For declarations and reservations in respect of this article by Algeria, Austria, Canada, Germany, Ireland, Italy and Spain, see pp. 792, 794, 797, 802, 805, 807, 813.

[58] For declaration in respect of this paragraph by the Netherlands, see p. 810.

[59] For reservation in respect of this paragraph by China and Mongolia, see pp. 798, 809.

They shall give due consideration to the request of the State in whose territory the alleged offence has occurred.

3. The law of the High Contracting Party requested shall apply in all cases. The provisions of the preceding paragraphs shall not, however, affect the obligations arising from the provisions of any other treaty of a bilateral or multilateral nature which governs or will govern the whole or part of the subject of mutual assistance in criminal matters.

Art. 89. Co-operation

In situations of serious violations of the Conventions or of this Protocol, the High Contracting Parties undertake to act, jointly or individually, in co-operation with the United Nations and in conformity with the United Nations Charter.

Art. 90. International Fact-Finding Commission

1. (a) An International Fact-Finding Commission (hereinafter referred to as "the Commission") consisting of fifteen members of high moral standing and acknowledged impartiality shall be established.
   (b)[60] When not less than twenty High Contracting Parties have agreed to accept the competence of the Commission pursuant to paragraph 2, the depositary shall then, and at intervals of five years thereafter, convene a meeting of representatives of those High Contracting Parties for the purpose of electing the members of the Commission. At the meeting, the representatives shall elect the members of the Commission by secret ballot from a list of persons to which each of those High Contracting Parties may nominate one person.
   (c) The members of the Commission shall serve in their personal capacity and shall hold office until the election of new members at the ensuing meeting.
   (d) At the election, the High Contracting Parties shall ensure that the persons to be elected to the Commission individually possess the qualifications required and that, in the Commission as a whole, equitable geographical representation is assured.
   (e) In the case of a casual vacancy, the Commission itself shall fill the vacancy, having due regard to the provisions of the preceding subparagraphs.
   (f) The depositary shall make available to the Commission the necessary administrative facilities for the performance of its functions.
2. (a)[61] The High Contracting Parties may at the time of signing, ratifying or acceding to the Protocol, or at any other subsequent time, declare that

[60] A meeting to elect the fifteen members of the International Fact-Finding Commission was convened in Bern on 25 June 1991, by the Swiss Federal Council, the depositary of the 1949 Geneva Conventions and their Additional Protocols. Only the first 20 States which made the formal declaration accepting the Commission's competence were entitled to elect members. On 12 and 13 March 1992, the Commission held its first meeting in Bern, where it has established its headquarters. On 8 July 1992, the Commission adopted its Rules (*IRRC*, 1993, pp. 170 ff.).

[61] On 5 June 2002, the following 61 states had made the declaration according to Article 90, paragraph 2(a) of Protocol I recognizing the competence of the International Fact-Finding Commission: Algeria, Argentina, Australia, Austria, Belarus, Belgium, Bolivia, Bosnia-Herzegovina, Brazil, Bulgaria, Canada, Cape-Verde, Chile, Colombia, Cook Islands Costa Rica, Croatia, Czech Republic, Denmark, Finland, Germany, Greece, Guinea, Hungary, Iceland, Ireland, Italy, Lao (People's Dem. Rep.), Liechtenstein, Lithuania Luxembourg, Macedonia,

they recognize *ipso facto* and without special agreement, in relation to any other High Contracting Party accepting the same obligation, the competence of the Commission to enquire into allegations by such other Party, as authorized by this Article.

(b) The declarations referred to above shall be deposited with the depositary, which shall transmit copies thereof to the High Contracting Parties.

(c) The Commission shall be competent to:
   (i) enquire into any facts alleged to be a grave breach as defined in the Conventions and this Protocol or other serious violation of the Conventions or of this Protocol;
   (ii) facilitate, through its good offices, the restoration of an attitude of respect for the Conventions and this Protocol.

(d) In other situations, the Commission shall institute an enquiry at the request of a Party to the conflict only with the consent of the other Party or Parties concerned.

(e) Subject to the foregoing provisions of this paragraph, the provisions of Article 52 of the First Convention, Article 53 of the Second Convention, Article 132 of the Third Convention and Article 149 of the Fourth Convention shall continue to apply to any alleged violation of the Conventions and shall extend to any alleged violation of this Protocol.

3. (a) Unless otherwise agreed by the Parties concerned, all enquiries shall be undertaken by a Chamber consisting of seven members appointed as follows:
   (i) five members of the Commission, not nationals of any Party to the conflict, appointed by the President of the Commission on the basis of equitable representation of the geographical areas, after consultation with the Parties to the conflict;
   (ii) two *ad hoc* members, not nationals of any Party to the conflict, one to be appointed by each side.

(b) Upon receipt of the request for an enquiry, the President of the Commission shall specify an appropriate time limit for setting up a Chamber. If any *ad hoc* member has not been appointed within the time limit, the President shall immediately appoint such additional member or members of the Commission as may be necessary to complete the membership of the Chamber.

4. (a) The Chamber set up under paragraph 3 to undertake an enquiry shall invite the Parties to the conflict to assist it and to present evidence. The Chamber may also seek such other evidence as it deems appropriate and may carry out an investigation of the situation *in loco*.

(b) All evidence shall be fully disclosed to the Parties, which shall have the right to comment on it to the Commission.

(c) Each Party shall have the right to challenge such evidence.

5. (a) The Commission shall submit to the Parties a report on the findings of fact of the Chamber, with such recommendations as it may deem appropriate.

---

cont.

Madagascar, Malta, Mongolia, Namibia, Netherlands, New Zealand, Norway, Panama, Paraguay, Poland, Portugal, Qatar, Romania, Russian Federation, Rwanda, Seychelles, Slovakia, Slovenia, Spain, Sweden, Switzerland, Tajikistan, Togo, Trinidad and Tobago, Ukraine, United Arab Emirates, United Kingdom, Uruguay, Yugoslavia.

(b) If the Chamber is unable to secure sufficient evidence for factual and impartial findings, the Commission shall state the reasons for that inability.
(c) The Commission shall not report its findings publicly, unless all the Parties to the conflict have requested the Commission to do so.

6. The Commission shall establish its own rules, including rules for the presidency of the Commission and the presidency of the Chamber. Those rules shall ensure that the functions of the President of the Commission are exercised at all times and that, in the case of an enquiry, they are exercised by a person who is not a national of a Party to the conflict.
7. The administrative expenses of the Commission shall be met by contributions from the High Contracting Parties which made declarations under paragraph 2, and by voluntary contributions. The Party or Parties to the conflict requesting an enquiry shall advance the necessary funds for expenses incurred by a Chamber and shall be reimbursed by the Party or Parties against which the allegations are made to the extent of fifty per-cent of the costs of the Chamber. Where there are counter-allegations before the Chamber each side shall advance fifty per cent of the necessary funds.

Art. 91. Responsibility[62]

A Party to the conflict which violates the provisions of the Conventions or of this Protocol shall, if the case demands, be liable to pay compensation. It shall be responsible for all acts committed by persons forming part of its armed forces.

PART VI. FINAL PROVISIONS

Art. 92. Signature

This Protocol shall be open for signature by the Parties to the Conventions six months after the signing of the Final Act and will remain open for a period of twelve months.

Art. 93. Ratification

This Protocol shall be ratified as soon as possible. The instruments of ratification shall be deposited with the Swiss Federal Council, depositary of the Conventions.

Art. 94. Accession

This Protocol shall be open for accession by any Party to the Conventions which has not signed it. The instruments of accession shall be deposited with the depositary.

Art. 95. Entry into force

1. This Protocol shall enter into force six months after two instruments of ratification or accession have been deposited.
2. For each Party to the Conventions thereafter ratifying or acceding to this Protocol, it shall enter into force six months after the deposit by such Party of its instrument of ratification or accession.

[62] For declaration in respect of this article by the Republic of Korea, see p. 808.

Art. 96. Treaty relations upon entry into force of this Protocol

1. When the Parties to the Conventions are also Parties to this Protocol, the Conventions shall apply as supplemented by this Protocol.
2. When one of the Parties to the conflict is not bound by this Protocol, the Parties to the Protocol shall remain bound by it in their mutual relations. They shall furthermore be bound by this Protocol in relation to each of the Parties which are not bound by it, if the latter accepts and applies the provisions thereof.
3.[63] The authority representing a people engaged against a High Contracting Party in an armed conflict of the type referred to in Article 1, paragraph 4, may undertake to apply the Conventions and this Protocol in relation to that conflict by means of a unilateral declaration addressed to the depositary. Such declaration shall, upon its receipt by the depositary, have in relation to that conflict the following effects:
   (a) the Conventions and this Protocol are brought into force for the said authority as a Party to the conflict with immediate effect;
   (b) the said authority assumes the same rights and obligations as those which have been assumed by a High Contracting Party to the Conventions and this Protocol; and
   (c) the Conventions and this Protocol are equally binding upon all Parties to the conflict.

Art. 97. Amendment

1. Any High Contracting Party may propose amendments to this Protocol. The text of any proposed amendment shall be communicated to the depositary, which shall decide, after consultation with all the High Contracting Parties and the International Committee of the Red Cross, whether a conference should be convened to consider the proposed amendment.
2. The depositary shall invite to that conference all the High Contracting Parties as well as the Parties to the Conventions, whether or not they are signatories of this Protocol.

Art. 98. Revision of Annex I

1. Not later than four years after the entry into force of this Protocol and thereafter at intervals of not less than four years, the International Committee of the Red Cross shall consult the High Contracting Parties concerning Annex I to this Protocol and, if it considers it necessary, may propose a meeting of technical experts to review Annex I and to propose such amendments to it as may appear to be desirable. Unless, within six months of the communication of a proposal for such a meeting to the High Contracting Parties, one third of them object, the International Committee of the Red Cross shall convene the meeting, inviting also observers of appropriate international organizations. Such a meeting shall also be convened by the International Committee of the Red Cross at any time at the request of one third of the High Contracting Parties.
2. The depositary shall convene a conference of the High Contracting Parties and the Parties to the Conventions to consider amendments proposed by

[63] For declarations in respect of this paragraph by Belgium, Canada, France, Germany, Ireland, Republic of Korea, Spain and United Kingdom (made on signature and ratification), see pp. 796, 798, 801, 803, 805, 808, 813, 815–816.

the meeting of technical experts if, after that meeting, the International Committee of the Red Cross or one third of the High Contracting Parties so request.

3. Amendments to Annex I may be adopted at such a conference by a two-thirds majority of the High Contracting Parties present and voting.
4. The depositary shall communicate any amendment so adopted to the High Contracting Parties and to the Parties to the Conventions. The amendment shall be considered to have been accepted at the end of a period of one year after it has been so communicated, unless within that period a declaration of nonacceptance of the amendment has been communicated to the depositary by not less than one third of the High Contracting Parties.
5. An amendment considered to have been accepted in accordance with paragraph 4 shall enter into force three months after its acceptance for all High Contracting Parties other than those which have made a declaration of non-acceptance in accordance with that paragraph. Any Party making such a declaration may at any time withdraw it and the amendment shall then enter into force for that Party three months thereafter.
6. The depositary shall notify the High Contracting Parties and the Parties to the Conventions of the entry into force of any amendment, of the Parties bound thereby, of the date of its entry into force in relation to each Party, of declarations of non-acceptance made in accordance with paragraph 4, and of withdrawals of such declarations.

Art. 99. Denunciation

1. In case a High Contracting Party should denounce this Protocol, the denunciation shall only take effect one year after receipt of the instrument of denunciation. If, however, on the expiry of that year the denouncing Party is engaged in one of the situations referred to in Article 1, the denunciation shall not take effect before the end of the armed conflict or occupation and not, in any case, before operations connected with the final release, repatriation or re-establishment of the persons protected by the Conventions or this Protocol have been terminated.
2. The denunciation shall be notified in writing to the depositary, which shall transmit it to all the High Contracting Parties.
3. The denunciation shall have effect only in respect of the denouncing Party.
4. Any denunciation under paragraph 1 shall not affect the obligations already incurred, by reason of the armed conflict, under this Protocol by such denouncing Party in respect of any act committed before this denunciation becomes effective.

Art. 100. Notifications

The depositary shall inform the High Contracting Parties as well as the Parties to the Conventions, whether or not they are signatories of this Protocol, of:

(a) signatures affixed to this Protocol and the deposit of instruments of ratification and accession under Articles 93 and 94;
(b) the date of entry into force of this Protocol under Article 95;
(c) communications and declarations received under Articles 84, 90 and 97;
(d) declarations received under Article 96, paragraph 3, which shall be communicated by the quickest methods; and
(e) denunciations under Article 99.

Art. 101. Registration

1. After its entry into force, this Protocol shall be transmitted by the depositary to the Secretariat of the United Nations for registration and publication, in accordance with Article 102 of the Charter of the United Nations.
2. The depositary shall also inform the Secretariat of the United Nations of all ratifications, accessions and denunciations received by it with respect to this Protocol.

Art. 102. Authentic texts

The original of this Protocol, of which the Arabic, Chinese, English, French, Russian and Spanish texts are equally authentic, shall be deposited with the depositary, which shall transmit certified true copies thereof to all the Parties to the Conventions.

ANNEX I

Regulations Concerning Identification[1, 2]

(as amended on 30 November 1993)

Article 1. General provisions (New article)

1. *The regulations concerning identification in this Annex implement the relevant provisions of the Geneva Conventions and the Protocol; they are intended to facilitate the identification of personnel, material, units, transports and installations protected under the Geneva Conventions and the Protocol.*

---

1 *Presentation of the text of Annex 1.*

1. New texts are written in *italics*.
2. Existing texts *transferred from* one article to another are written in bold.
3. Article 1 of the proposed text is new, meaning that the numbering of all the other articles has changed (existing Article 1 is now Article 2, and so on). The changed numbering has also been taken into consideration in the references to other articles contained in some of the Annex's provisions.
4. Article 56 of Protocol I contains a reference to Article 16 of Annex 1. This reference should now be to Article 17.

The text of the Annex I as amended is published in *International Review of the Red Cross*, No. 298, January–February 1994, pp. 27–41 (Engl.); *Revue internationale de la Croix-Rouge*, No. 805, janvier–fevrier 1994, pp. 29–32 (French).

2 On the basis of Article 98 of 1977 Protocol I additional to the 1949 Geneva Conventions, and after consulting the states party to the said Protocol, the ICRC in 1989 called a meeting of technical experts to review Annex I (Regulations concerning identification) to this Protocol.

At the end of the meeting, which was held in Geneva in August 1990, the experts proposed a number of amendments. In accordance with the provisions of Article 98 of Protocol I, the ICRC requested the Swiss Confederation, depositary state of the Geneva Conventions and their Additional Protocols, to initiate the procedure laid down for inviting States party to adopt the proposed amendments. The main purpose of the latter was to incorporate into Annex I of Protocol I certain technical provisions already adopted by the competent international organizations.

To simplify matters, and bearing in mind that these amendments reflect the points of view of a large number of experts from many countries, the depositary suggested that instead of holding a diplomatic conference the amendments be adopted by correspondence. After consultation, the states party to Protocol I agreed to the suggested procedure. These same states were then asked to declare whether they accepted or rejected the amendments to Annex I to Additional Protocol I proposed by the technical experts in 1990.

On 21 October 1992, the Swiss Confederation informed the ICRC that, of the twenty-two states party to Protocol I which had replied, nineteen were in favour of the proposed amendments. Only Hungary, Jordan and Sweden had expressed reservations.

When more than two thirds of the high contracting parties *which replied* (Article 98, para. 3) had decided in favour of the amendments, the latter would be considered to have been adopted at the end of a period of one year after the date on which they had been officially communicated by the Swiss Confederation to the states party, i.e. 30 November 1992, unless within that period a declaration of non-acceptance of the amendments had been communicated to the authorities by not less than one third of all the parties to Protocol I (Article 98, para. 4).

This one-year period ended on 30 November 1993 and, since no further declarations of non-acceptance of the amendments were communicated to the depositary during the period, *the amendments in the form proposed by the experts* were accepted and entered into force on 1 March 1994 for *all parties* to Protocol I. (With the exception of those parties which made reservations or declarations of non acceptance during the one-year period, i.e. Sweden, which rejected the *wording* of Articles 7 and 8 (former Articles 6 and 7), and Jordan, which wishes to retain the original wording of paragraph I (c) of Article 2 (formerly Article 1). Hungary has since withdrawn its reservation.)

2. *These rules do not in and of themselves establish the right to protection. This right is governed by the relevant articles in the Conventions and the Protocol.*
3. *The competent authorities may, subject to the relevant provisions of the Geneva Conventions and the Protocol, at all times regulate the use, display, illumination and detectability of the distinctive emblems and signals.*
4. *The High Contracting Parties and in particular the Parties to the conflict are invited at all times to agree upon additional or other signals, means or systems which enhance the possibility of identification and take full advantage of technological developments in this field.*

Chapter I. Identity cards

Art. 2. Identity card for permanent civilian medical and religious personnel

1. The identity card for permanent civilian medical and religious personnel referred to in Article 18, paragraph 3, of the Protocol should:
   (a) bear the distinctive emblem and be of such size that it can be carried in the pocket;
   (b) be as durable as practicable;
   (c) be worded in the national or official language and, *in addition and when appropriate, in the local language of the region concerned*;
   (d) mention the name, the date of birth (or, if that date is not available, the age at the time of issue) and the identity number, if any, of the holder;
   (e) state in what capacity the holder is entitled to the protection of the Conventions and of the Protocol;
   (f) bear the photograph of the holder as well as his signature or his thumbprint, or both;
   (g) bear the stamp and signature of the competent authority;
   (h) state the date of issue and date of expiry of the card;
   (i) *indicate, whenever possible, the holder's blood group, on the reverse side of the card.*

2. The identity card shall be uniform throughout the territory of each High Contracting Party and, as far as possible, of the same type for all Parties to the conflict. The Parties to the conflict may be guided by the single-language model shown in Figure 1. At the outbreak of hostilities, they shall transmit to each other a specimen of the model they are using, if such model differs from that shown in Figure 1. The identity card shall be made out, if possible, in duplicate, one copy being kept by the issuing authority, which should maintain control of the cards which it has issued.
3. In no circumstances may permanent civilian medical and religious personnel be deprived of their identity cards. In the event of the loss of a card, they shall be entitled to obtain a duplicate copy.

Art. 3. Identity card for temporary civilian medical and religious personnel

1. The identity card for temporary civilian medical and religious personnel should, whenever possible, be similar to that provided for in Article 2 of these Regulations. The Parties to the conflict may be guided by the model shown in Figure 1.
2. When circumstances preclude the provision to temporary civilian medical and religious personnel of identity cards similar to those described in

(space reserved for the name of the country and authority issuing this card)

IDENTITY CARD

for PERMANENT / TEMPORARY civilian medical / religious personnel

Name . . . .

. . . .

Date of birth (or age) . . . .

Identity No. (if any) . . . .

The holder of this card is protected by the Geneva Conventions of 12 August 1949 and by the Protocol Additional to the Geneva Conventions of 12 August 1949, and relating to the Protection of Victims of International Armed Conflicts (Protocol I) in his capacity as

. . . .

Date of issue . . . . . . No. of card . . . . . .

Signature of issuing authority

Date of expiry . . . .

Height	Eyes	Hair . . . .

Other distinguishing marks or information:

. . . .

. . . .

. . . .

PHOTO OF HOLDER

Stamp	Signature of holder or thumbprint or both

Fig. 1. Sample of identity card (size: 74 mm x 105 mm).

Article 2 of these Regulations, the said personnel may be provided with a certificate signed by the competent authority certifying that the person to whom it is issued is assigned to duty as temporary personnel and stating, if possible, the duration of such assignment and his right to wear the distinctive emblem. The certificate should mention the holder's name and date of birth (or if that is not available, his age at the time when the certificate was issued), his function and identity number, if any. It shall bear his signature or his thumbprint, or both.

Chapter II. The distinctive emblem

Art. 4. Shape
The distinctive emblem (red on a white ground) shall be as large as appropriate under the circumstances. For the shapes of the cross, the crescent or the lion and sun,* the High Contracting Parties may be guided by the models shown in Figure 2.

Fig. 2. Distinctive emblems in red on a white background.

Art. 5. Use

1. The distinctive emblem shall, whenever possible, be displayed on a flat surface, on flags *or in any other way appropriate to the lay of the land, so that it is* visible from as many directions and from as far away as possible, *and in particular from the air.*
2. **At night or when visibility is reduced, the distinctive emblem may be lighted or illuminated.**
3. *The distinctive emblem may be made of materials which make it recognizable by technical means of detecting. The red part should be painted on top of black primer paint in order to facilitate its identification, in particular by infrared instruments.*
4. Medical and religious personnel carrying out their duties in the battle area shall, as far as possible, wear headgear and clothing bearing the distinctive emblem.

Chapter III. Distinctive signals

Art. 6. Use

1. *All distinctive signals specified in this Chapter may be used by medical units or transports.*

* No state has used the emblem of the lion and sun since 1980.

2. *These signals, at the exclusive disposal of medical units and transports, shall not be used for any other purpose, the use of the light signal being reserved (see paragraph 3 below).*
3. **In the absence of a special agreement between the Parties to the conflict reserving the use of flashing blue lights for the identification of medical vehicles, ships and craft, the use of such signals for other vehicles, ships and** ***craft*** **is not prohibited.**
4. Temporary medical aircraft which cannot, either for lack of time or because of their characteristics, be marked with the distinctive emblem, may use the distinctive signals authorized in this Chapter.

Art. 7. Light signal

1. The light signal, consisting of a flashing blue light *as defined in the Airworthiness Technical Manual of the International Civil Aviation Organization (ICAO) Doc. 9051*, is established for the use of medical aircraft to signal their identity. No other aircraft shall use this signal. *Medical aircraft using the flashing blue light should exhibit such lights as may be necessary to make the light visible from as many directions as possible.*
2. *In accordance with the provisions of Chapter XIV, para. 4 of the International Maritime Organization (IMO) International Code of Signals, vessels protected by the Geneva Conventions of 1949 and the Protocol should exhibit one or more flashing blue lights visible from any direction.*
3. *Medical vehicles should exhibit one or more flashing blue lights visible from as far away as possible. The High Contracting Parties and, in particular, the Parties to the conflict which use lights of other colours should give notification of this.*
4. The recommended blue colour is obtained *when its chromaticity is within the boundaries of the International Commission on Illumination (ICI) chromaticity diagram defined by the following equations:*

   green boundary $y = 0.065 + 0.805\,x$;
   white boundary $y = 0.400 - x$;
   purple boundary $x = 0.133 + 0.600\,y$.

   The recommended flashing rate of the blue light is between sixty and one hundred flashes per minute.

Art. 8. Radio signal

1. *The radio signal shall consist of the urgency signal and the distinctive signal as described in the International Telecommunication Union (ITU) Radio Regulations (RR Articles 40 and N 40).*
2. *The radio message preceded by the urgency and distinctive signals mentioned in paragraph 1 shall be transmitted in English at appropriate intervals on a frequency or frequencies specified for this purpose in the Radio Regulations, and shall convey the following data relating to the medical transports concerned:*
   - *(a) call sign or other recognized means of identification;*
   - *(b) position;*
   - *(c) number and type of vehicles;*
   - *(d) intended route;*
   - *(e) estimated time* en route *and of departure and arrival, as appropriate;*
   - *(f) any other information, such as flight altitude, guarded radio frequencies, languages used and secondary surveillance radar modes and codes.*

3. In order to facilitate the communications referred to in paragraphs 1 and 2, as well as the communications referred to in Articles 22, 23 and 25 to 31 of the Protocol, the High Contracting Parties, the Parties to a conflict, or one of the Parties to a conflict, acting in agreement or alone, may designate, in accordance with the Table of Frequency Allocations in the Radio Regulations annexed to the International Telecommunication Convention, and publish selected national frequencies to be used by them for such communications. The International Telecommunication Union shall be notified of these frequencies in accordance with procedures approved by a World Administrative Radio Conference.

Art. 9. Electronic identification

1. The Secondary Surveillance Radar (SSR) system, as specified in Annex 10 to the Chicago Convention on International Civil Aviation of 7 December 1944, as amended from time to time, may be used to identify and to follow the course of medical aircraft. The SSR mode and code to be reserved for the exclusive use of medical aircraft shall be established by the High Contracting Parties, the Parties to a conflict, or one of the Parties to a conflict, acting in agreement or alone, in accordance with procedures to be recommended by the International Civil Aviation Organization.
2. *Protected medical transports may, for their identification and location, use standard aeronautical radar transponders and/or maritime search and rescue radar transponders.*

   It should be possible for protected medical transports to be identified by other vessels or aircraft equipped with secondary surveillance radar by means of a code transmitted by a radar transponder, e.g. in mode 3/A, fitted on the medical transports.

   The code transmitted by the medical transport transponder should be assigned to that transport by the competent authorities and notified to all the Parties to the conflict.
3. *It should be possible for medical transports to be identified by submarines by the appropriate underwater acoustic signals transmitted by the medical transports.*

   The underwater acoustic signal shall consist of the call sign (or any other recognized means of identification of medical transport) of the ship preceded by the single group YYY transmitted in morse on an appropriate acoustic frequency, e.g. 5kHz.

   Parties to a conflict wishing to use the underwater acoustic identification signal described above shall inform the Parties concerned of the signal as soon as possible, and shall, when notifying the use of their hospital ships, confirm the frequency to be employed.
4. Parties to a conflict may, by special agreement between them, establish for their use a similar electronic system for the identification of medical vehicles, and medical ships and craft.

Chapter IV. Communications

Art. 10. Radiocommunications

1. *The urgency signal and the distinctive signal provided for in Article 8 may* precede appropriate radiocommunications by medical units and transports

in the application of the procedures carried out under Articles 22, 23 and 25 to 31 of the Protocol.

2. *The medical transports referred to in Articles 40 (Section II, No. 3209) and N 40 (Section III, No. 3214) of the ITU Radio Regulations may also transmit their communications by satellite systems, in accordance with the provisions of Articles 37, N 37 and 59 of the ITU Radio Regulations for the Mobile-Satellite Services.*

Art. 11. Use of international codes

Medical units and transports may also use the codes and signals laid down by the International Telecommunication Union, the International Civil Aviation Organization and the *International Maritime Organization*. These codes and signals shall be used in accordance with the standards, practices and procedures established by these Organizations.

Art. 12. Other means of communication

When two-way radiocommunication is not possible, the signals provided for in the International Code of Signals adopted by the *International Maritime Organization* or in the appropriate Annex to the Chicago Convention on International Civil Aviation of 7 December 1944, as amended from time to time, may be used.

Art. 13. Flight plans

The agreements and notifications relating to flight plans provided for in Article 29 of the Protocol shall as far as possible be formulated in accordance with procedures laid down by the International Civil Aviation Organization.

Art. 14. Signals and procedures for the interception of medical aircraft

If an intercepting aircraft is used to verify the identity of a medical aircraft in flight or to require it to land in accordance with Articles 30 and 31 of the Protocol, the standard visual and radio interception procedures prescribed by Annex 2 to the Chicago Convention on International Civil Aviation of 7 December 1944, as amended from time to time, should be used by the intercepting and the medical aircraft.

Chapter V. Civil defence

Art. 15. Identity card

1. The identity card of the civil defence personnel provided for in Article 66, paragraph 3, of the Protocol is governed by the relevant provisions of Article 2 of these Regulations.
2. The identity card for civil defence personnel may follow the model shown in Figure 3.
3. If civil defence personnel are permitted to carry light individual weapons, an entry to that effect should be made on the card mentioned.

Art. 16. International distinctive sign

1. The international distinctive sign of civil defence provided for in Article 66, paragraph 4, of the Protocol is an equilateral blue triangle on an orange background. A model is shown in Figure 4:

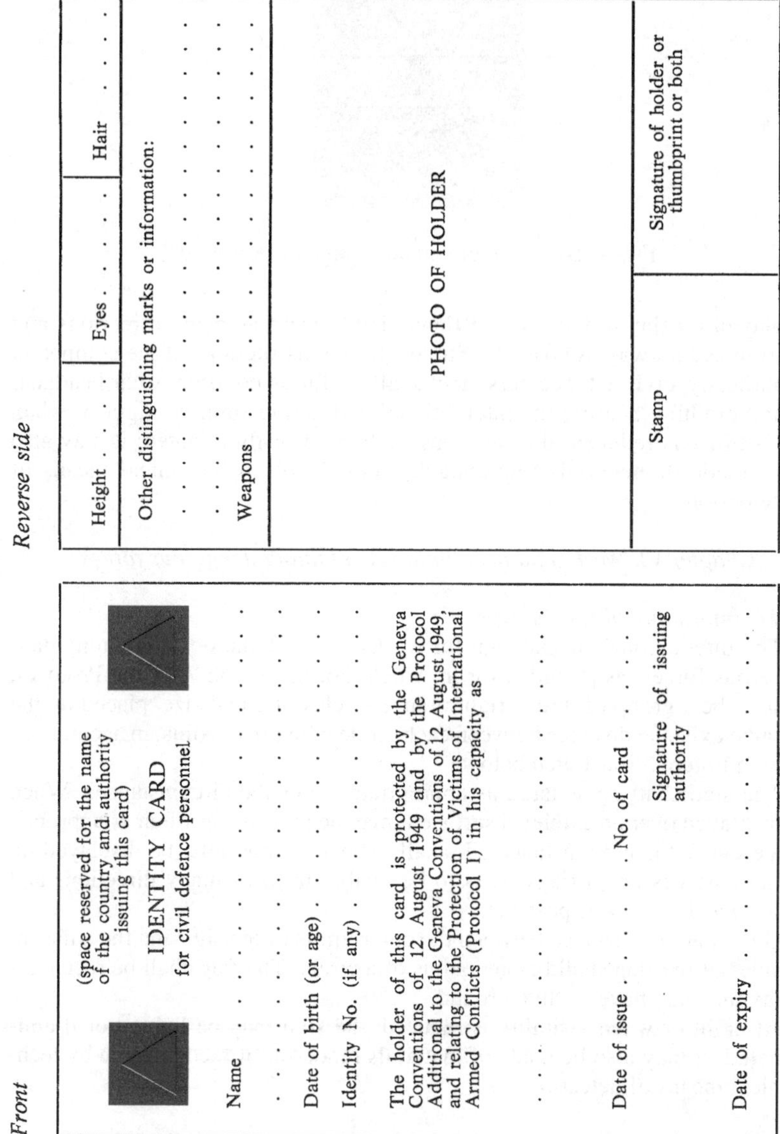

Front

(space reserved for the name of the country and authority issuing this card)

IDENTITY CARD
for civil defence personnel

Name . . . .

. . . .

Date of birth (or age) . . . .

Identity No. (if any) . . . .

The holder of this card is protected by the Geneva Conventions of 12 August 1949 and by the Protocol Additional to the Geneva Conventions of 12 August 1949, and relating to the Protection of Victims of International Armed Conflicts (Protocol I) in his capacity as

. . . .

Date of issue . . . . No. of card . . . .

Signature of issuing authority

Date of expiry . . . .

Reverse side

Height . . . . . . Eyes . . . . . . Hair . . . . . .

Other distinguishing marks or information: . . . .

. . . .

. . . .

Weapons . . . .

PHOTO OF HOLDER

Stamp	Signature of holder or thumbprint or both

Fig. 3. Model of identity card for civil defence personnel (size: 74 x 105 mm).

2. It is recommended that:
   (a) if the blue triangle is on a flag or armlet or tabard, the ground to the triangle be the orange flag, armlet or tabard;
   (b) one of the angles of the triangle be pointed vertically upwards;
   (c) no angle of the triangle touch the edge of the orange ground.
3. The international distinctive sign shall be as large as appropriate under the circumstances. The distinctive sign shall, whenever possible, be dis-

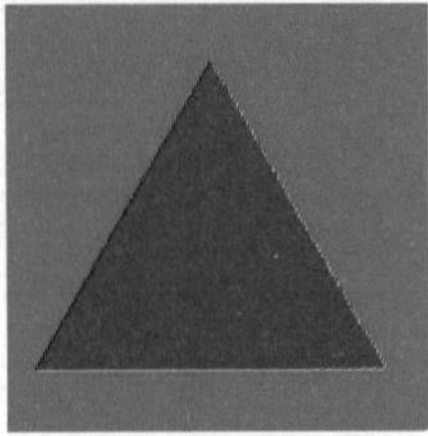

Fig. 4. Blue triangle on an orange background

played on flat surfaces or on flags visible from as many directions and from as far away as possible. Subject to the instructions of the competent authority, civil defence personnel shall, as far as possible, wear headgear and clothing bearing the international distinctive sign. At night or when visibility is reduced, the sign may be lighted or illuminated; it may also be made of materials rendering it recognizable by technical means of detection.

Chapter VI. Works and installations containing dangerous forces

Art. 17. International special sign

1. The international special sign for works and installations containing dangerous forces, as provided for in Article 56, paragraph 7, of the Protocol, shall be a group of three bright orange circles of equal size, placed on the same axis, the distance between each circle being one radius, in accordance with Figure 5 illustrated below.
2. The sign shall be as large as appropriate under the circumstances. When displayed over an extended surface it may be repeated as often as appropriate under the circumstances. It shall, whenever possible, be displayed on flat surfaces or on flags so as to be visible from as many directions and from as far away as possible.
3. On a flag, the distance between the outer limits of the sign and the adjacent sides of the flag shall be one radius of a circle. The flag shall be rectangular and shall have a white ground.
4. At night or when visibility is reduced, the sign may be lighted or illuminated. It may also be made of materials rendering it recognizable by technical means of detection.

Fig. 5. International special sign for works and installations containing dangerous forces

ANNEX II. IDENTITY CARD FOR JOURNALISTS ON DANGEROUS PROFESSIONAL MISSIONS

FRONT

NOTICE

This identity card is issued to journalists on dangerous professional missions in areas of armed conflicts. The holder is entitled to be treated as a civilian under the Geneva Conventions of 12 August 1949, and their Additional Protocol I. The card must be carried at all times by the bearer. If he is detained, he shall at once hand it to the Detaining Authorities, to assist in his identification.

ملحوظة

تصرف هذه البطاقة للصحفيين المكلفين بمهمات مهنية خطرة في مناطق النازعات المسلحة ويحق لصاحبها أن يعامل معاملة الشخص المدني وفقاً لاتفاقيات جنيف المؤرخة ١٢ آب / أغسطس ١٩٤٩ ولحقها (بروتوكولها) الإضافي الأول . ويجب أن يحتفظ صاحب البطاقة بها دوما وإذا اعتقل فيجب أن يسلمها فوراً إلى سلطة الاعتقال لتساعد على تحديد هويته

NOTA

La presente tarjeta de identidad se expide a los periodistas en misión profesional peligrosa en zonas de conflictos armados. Su titular tiene derecho a ser tratado como persona civil conforme a los Convenios de Ginebra del 12 de agosto de 1949 y su Protocolo adicional I. El titular debe llevar la tarjeta consigo, en todo momento. En caso de ser detenido, la entregará inmediatamente a las autoridades que lo detengan a fin de facilitar su identificación.

AVIS

La présente carte d'identité est délivrée aux journalistes en mission professionnelle périlleuse dans des zones de conflit armé. Le porteur a le droit d'être traité comme une personne civile aux termes des Conventions de Genève du 12 août 1949 et de leur Protocole additionnel I. La carte doit être portée en tout temps par son titulaire. Si celui-ci est arrêté, il la remettra immédiatement aux autorités qui le détiennent afin qu'elles puissent l'identifier.

ПРИМЕЧАНИЕ

Настоящее удостоверение выдается журналистам, находящимся в опасных профессиональных командировках в районах вооруженного конфликта. Его обладатель имеет право на обращение с ним как с гражданским лицом в соответствии с Женевскими Конвенциями от 12 августа 1949 г. и Дополнительным Протоколом I к ним. Владелец настоящего удостоверения должен постоянно иметь его при себе. В случае задержания он немедленно вручает его задерживающим властям для содействия установлению его личности.

(Name of country issuing this card)

(اسم القطر المصدر لهذه البطاقة)

(Nombre del país que expide esta tarjeta)

(Nom du pays qui a délivré cette carte)

(Название страны, выдавшей настоящее удостоверение)

IDENTITY CARD FOR JOURNALISTS ON DANGEROUS PROFESSIONAL MISSIONS

بطاقة الهوية الخاصة بالصحفين المكلفين بمهمات مهنية خطرة

TARJETA DE IDENTIDAD DE PERIODISTA EN MISION PELIGROSA

CARTE D'IDENTITÉ DE JOURNALISTE EN MISSION PÉRILLEUSE

УДОСТОВЕРЕНИЕ ЖУРНАЛИСТА, НАХОДЯЩЕГОСЯ В ОПАСНОЙ КОМАНДИРОВКЕ

REVERSE SIDE

Issued by (competent authority)
(صدرت من (السلطة المختصة
Expedida por (autoridad competente)
Délivrée par (autorité compétente) ....
Видано (компетентными властями)

Photograph of bearer
صورة صاحب البطاقة
Fotografía del titular
Photographie du porteur
Фотография предъявителя

Place
المكان
Lugar
Lieu ....
Место

Date
التاريخ
Fecha
Date ....
Дата

(Official seal imprint)
(الخاتم الرسمي)
(Sello oficial)
(Timbre de l'autorité délivrant la carte)
(Официальная печать)

(Signature of bearer)
(توقيع صاحب البطاقة)
(Firma del titular)
.... (Signature du porteur)
(Подпись владельца)

Name
اسم الشهرة
Apellidos
Nom ....
Фамилия

First names
الاسم
Nombre
Prénoms ....
Имя, Отчество

Place & date of birth
مكان وتاريخ الميلاد
Lugar y fecha de nacimiento
Lieu & date de naissance ....
Дата и место рождения

Correspondent of
مراسل
Corresponsal de
Correspondant de ....
Корреспондент

Specific occupation
المهمة المحددة
Categoría profesional
Catégorie professionnelle ....
Род занятий

Valid for
ينتهي العمل بها في
Válido por
Durée de validité ....
Действительно

Height
الطول
Estatura
Taille ....
Рост

Eyes
العينان
Ojos
Yeux ....
Глаза

Weight
الوزن
Peso
Poids ....
Вес

Hair
الشعر
Cabello
Cheveux ....
Волосы

Blood type
فصيلة الدم
Grupo sanguíneo
Groupe sanguin ....
Группа крови

Rh factor
عامل الجلط
Factor Rh
Facteur Rh ....
Rh- фактор

Religion (optional)
الديانة (اختياري)
Religión (optativo)
Religion (facultatif) ....
Религия (факультативно)

Fingerprints (optional)
البصمة (اختياري)
Huellas dactilares (optativo)
Empreintes digitales (facultatif)
Отпечатки пальцев (факультативно)

(Left forefinger)
(السبابة اليسرى)
(Dedo índice izquierdo)
(Index gauche)
(Левый указательный палец)

(Right forefinger)
(السبابة اليمنى)
(Dedo índice derecho)
(Index droit)
(Правый указательный палец)

Special marks of identification
العلامات المميزة لتحديد الهوية
Señas particulares
Signes particuliers
Особые приметы
....
....
....

SIGNATURES, RATIFICATIONS AND ACCESSIONS

See list on pp. 785–791.

RESERVATIONS AND DECLARATIONS

See list on pp. 792–818.

No. 57

PROTOCOL ADDITIONAL TO THE GENEVA CONVENTIONS OF 12 AUGUST 1949, AND RELATING TO THE PROTECTION OF VICTIMS OF NON-INTERNATIONAL ARMED CONFLICTS (PROTOCOL II)

Adopted at Geneva, 8 June 1977

INTRODUCTORY NOTE: The only provision applicable to non-international armed conflicts before the adoption of the present Protocol was Article 3 common to all four Geneva Conventions of 1949. This article proved to be inadequate in view of the fact that about 80 per cent of the victims of armed conflicts since 1945 have been victims of non-international conflicts and that non-international conflicts are often fought with more cruelty than international conflicts. The aim of the present Protocol is to extend the essential rules of the law of armed conflicts to internal wars. The fear that the Protocol might affect state sovereignty, prevent governments from effectively maintaining law and order within their borders and that it might be invoked to justify outside intervention led to the decision of the Diplomatic Conference at its fourth session to shorten and simplify the Protocol. Instead of the 47 articles proposed by the ICRC the Conference adopted only 28. The essential substance of the draft was, however, maintained. The part on methods and means of combat was deleted, but its basic principles are to be found in Article 4 (fundamental guarantees). The provisions on the activity of impartial humanitarian organizations were adopted in a less binding form than originally foreseen. The restrictive definition of the material field of application in Article 1 has the effect that Protocol II is applicable to a smaller range of internal conflicts than Article 3 common to the Conventions of 1949.

ENTRY INTO FORCE: 7 December 1978.

AUTHENTIC TEXTS: Arabic, Chinese, English, French, Russian and Spanish. The text below is reprinted from the *Official Records of the Diplomatic Conference on the Reaffirmation and Development of International Humanitarian Law applicable in Armed Conflicts*, Geneva (1974–1977), Berne, Federal Political Department, 1978, Vol. 1, pp. 185–198.

TEXT PUBLISHED IN: See indications under *No. 52*.

TABLE OF CONTENTS

* * *

PREAMBLE[1]

The High Contracting Parties,

Recalling that the humanitarian principles enshrined in Article 3 common to the Geneva Conventions of 12 August 1949, constitute the foundation of respect for the human person in cases of armed conflict not of an international character,

Recalling furthermore that international instruments relating to human rights offer a basic protection to the human person,

Emphasizing the need to ensure a better protection for the victims of those armed conflicts,

Recalling that, in cases not covered by the law in force, the human person remains under the protection of the principles of humanity and the dictates of the public conscience,

Have agreed on the following:

---

[1] Some states made general declarations concerning all provisions of the Protocol. See in particular the declaration of Ireland, pp. 806.
For the statement of understanding by Canada relating to the undefined terms used in the present Protocol II, see p. 798.

PART I. SCOPE OF THIS PROTOCOL

Art. 1. Material field of application[2]

1. This Protocol, which develops and supplements Article 3 common to the Geneva Conventions of 12 August 1949 without modifying its existing conditions of application, shall apply to all armed conflicts which are not covered by Article 1 of the Protocol Additional to the Geneva Conventions of 12 August 1949, and relating to the Protection of Victims of International Armed Conflicts (Protocol I) and which take place in the territory of a High Contracting Party between its armed forces and dissident armed forces or other organized armed groups which, under responsible command, exercise such control over a part of its territory as to enable them to carry out sustained and concerted military operations and to implement this Protocol.
2. This Protocol shall not apply to situations of internal disturbances and tensions, such as riots, isolated and sporadic acts of violence and other acts of a similar nature, as not being armed conflicts.

Art. 2. Personal field of application

1. This Protocol shall be applied without any adverse distinction founded on race, colour, sex, language, religion or belief, political or other opinion, national or social origin, wealth, birth or other status, or on any other similar criteria (hereinafter referred to as "adverse distinction") to all persons affected by an armed conflict as defined in Article 1.
2. At the end of the armed conflict, all the persons who have been deprived of their liberty or whose liberty has been restricted for reasons related to such conflict, as well as those deprived of their liberty or whose liberty is restricted after the conflict for the same reasons, shall enjoy the protection of Articles 5 and 6 until the end of such deprivation or restriction of liberty.

Art. 3. Non-intervention

1. Nothing in this Protocol shall be invoked for the purpose of affecting the sovereignty of a State or the responsibility of the government, by all legitimate means, to maintain or re-establish law and order in the State or to defend the national unity and territorial integrity of the State.
2. Nothing in this Protocol shall be invoked as a justification for intervening, directly or indirectly, for any reason whatever, in the armed conflict or in the internal or external affairs of the High Contracting Party in the territory of which that conflict occurs.

PART II. HUMANE TREATMENT

Art. 4. Fundamental guarantees

1. All persons who do not take a direct part or who have ceased to take part in hostilities, whether or not their liberty has been restricted, are entitled to respect for their person, honour and convictions and religious practices. They shall in all circumstances be treated humanely, without any adverse distinction. It is prohibited to order that there shall be no survivors.

---

2 For declaration in respect of this article by Argentina, see p. 793.

2. Without prejudice to the generality of the foregoing, the following acts against the persons referred to in paragraph 1 are and shall remain prohibited at any time and in any place whatsoever:
   (a) violence to the life, health and physical or mental well-being of persons, in particular murder as well as cruel treatment such as torture, mutilation or any form of corporal punishment;
   (b) collective punishments;
   (c) taking of hostages;
   (d) acts of terrorism;
   (e) outrages upon personal dignity, in particular humiliating and degrading treatment, rape, enforced prostitution and any form of indecent assault;
   (f) slavery and the slave trade in all their forms;
   (g) pillage;
   (h) threats to commit any of the foregoing acts.
3. Children shall be provided with the care and aid they require, and in particular:
   (a) they shall receive an education, including religious and moral education, in keeping with the wishes of their parents, or in the absence of parents, of those responsible for their care;
   (b) all appropriate steps shall be taken to facilitate the reunion of families temporarily separated;
   (c) children who have not attained the age of fifteen years shall neither be recruited in the armed forces or groups nor allowed to take part in hostilities;
   (d) the special protection provided by this Article to children who have not attained the age of fifteen years shall remain applicable to them if they take a direct part in hostilities despite the provisions of sub-paragraph (c) and are captured;
   (e) measures shall be taken, if necessary, and whenever possible with the consent of their parents or persons who by law or custom are primarily responsible for their care, to remove children temporarily from the area in which hostilities are taking place to a safer area within the country and ensure that they are accompanied by persons responsible for their safety and well-being.

Art. 5. Persons whose liberty has been restricted

1. In addition to the provisions of Article 4, the following provisions shall be respected as a minimum with regard to persons deprived of their liberty for reasons related to the armed conflict, whether they are interned or detained:
   (a) the wounded and the sick shall be treated in accordance with Article 7;
   (b) the persons referred to in this paragraph shall, to the same extent as the local civilian population, be provided with food and drinking water and be afforded safeguards as regards health and hygiene and protection against the rigours of the climate and the dangers of the armed conflict;
   (c) they shall be allowed to receive individual or collective relief;
   (d) they shall be allowed to practise their religion and, if requested and appropriate, to receive spiritual assistance from persons, such as chaplains, performing religious functions;

(e) they shall, if made to work, have the benefit of working conditions and safeguards similar to those enjoyed by the local civilian population.

2. Those who are responsible for the internment or detention of the persons referred to in paragraph 1 shall also, within the limits of their capabilities, respect the following provisions relating to such persons:
   (a) except when men and women of a family are accommodated together, women shall be held in quarters separated from those of men and shall be under the immediate supervision of women;
   (b) they shall be allowed to send and receive letters and cards, the number of which may be limited by competent authority if it deems necessary;
   (c) places of internment and detention shall not be located close to the combat zone. The persons referred to in paragraph 1 shall be evacuated when the places where they are interned or detained become particularly exposed to danger arising out of the armed conflict, if their evacuation can be carried out under adequate conditions of safety;
   (d) they shall have the benefit of medical examinations;
   (e) their physical or mental health and integrity shall not be endangered by any unjustified act or omission. Accordingly, it is prohibited to subject the persons described in this Article to any medical procedure which is not indicated by the state of health of the person concerned, and which is not consistent with the generally accepted medical standards applied to free persons under similar medical circumstances.
3. Persons who are not covered by paragraph 1 but whose liberty has been restricted in any way whatsoever for reasons related to the armed conflict shall be treated humanely in accordance with Article 4 and with paragraphs 1(a), (c) and (d), and 2(b) of this Article.
4. If it is decided to release persons deprived of their liberty, necessary measures to ensure their safety shall be taken by those so deciding.

Art. 6. Penal prosecutions

1. This Article applies to the prosecution and punishment of criminal offences related to the armed conflict.
2. No sentence shall be passed and no penalty shall be executed on a person found guilty of an offence except pursuant to a conviction pronounced by a court offering the essential guarantees of independence and impartiality. In particular:
   (a) the procedure shall provide for an accused to be informed without delay of the particulars of the offence alleged against him and shall afford the accused before and during his trial all necessary rights and means of defence;
   (b) no one shall be convicted of an offence except on the basis of individual penal responsibility;
   (c) no one shall be held guilty of any criminal offence on account of any act or omission which did not constitute a criminal offence, under the law, at the time when it was committed; nor shall a heavier penalty be imposed than that which was applicable at the time when the criminal offence was committed; if, after the commission of the offence, provision is made by law for the imposition of a lighter penalty, the offender shall benefit thereby;
   (d) anyone charged with an offence is presumed innocent until proved guilty according to law;

(e)[3] anyone charged with an offence shall have the right to be tried in his presence;

(f) no one shall be compelled to testify against himself or to confess guilt.

3. A convicted person shall be advised on conviction of his judicial and other remedies and of the time-limits within which they may be exercised.
4. The death penalty shall not be pronounced on persons who were under the age of eighteen years at the time of the offence and shall not be carried out on pregnant women or mothers of young children.
5. At the end of hostilities, the authorities in power shall endeavour to grant the broadest possible amnesty to persons who have participated in the armed conflict, or those deprived of their liberty for reasons related to the armed conflict, whether they are interned or detained.

PART III.[4] WOUNDED, SICK AND SHIPWRECKED

Art. 7. Protection and care

1. All the wounded, sick and shipwrecked, whether or not they have taken part in the armed conflict, shall be respected and protected.
2. In all circumstances they shall be treated humanely and shall receive, to the fullest extent practicable and with the least possible delay, the medical care and attention required by their condition. There shall be no distinction among them founded on any grounds other than medical ones.

Art. 8. Search

Whenever circumstances permit, and particularly after an engagement, all possible measure shall be taken, without delay, to search for and collect the wounded, sick and shipwrecked, to protect them against pillage and ill-treatment, to ensure their adequate care, and to search for the dead, prevent their being despoiled, and decently dispose of them.

Art. 9. Protection of medical and religious personnel

1. Medical and religious personnel shall be respected and protected and shall be granted all available help for the performance of their duties. They shall not be compelled to carry out tasks which are not compatible with their humanitarian mission.
2. In the performance of their duties medical personnel may not be required to give priority to any person except on medical grounds.

Art. 10. General protection of medical duties

1. Under no circumstances shall any person be punished for having carried out medical activities compatible with medical ethics, regardless of the person benefiting therefrom.
2. Persons engaged in medical activities shall neither be compelled to perform acts or to carry out work contrary to, nor be compelled to refrain from acts

---

3 For reservations and declarations in respect of this paragraph by Austria, Germany, Ireland, Liechtenstein and Malta, see pp. 794, 802, 806, 808, 809.

4 For declaration concerning the terms used in the present title by United States (on signature), see p. 818.

required by, the rules of medical ethics or other rules designed for the benefit of the wounded and sick, or this Protocol.

3. The professional obligations of persons engaged in medical activities regarding information which they may acquire concerning the wounded and sick under their care shall, subject to national law, be respected.
4. Subject to national law, no person engaged in medical activities may be penalized in anyway for refusing or failing to give information concerning the wounded and sick who are, or who have been, under his care.

Art. 11. Protection of medical units and transports

1. Medical units and transports shall be respected and protected at all times and shall not be the object of attack.
2. The protection to which medical units and transports are entitled shall not cease unless they are used to commit hostile acts, outside their humanitarian function. Protection may, however, cease only after a warning has been given setting, whenever appropriate, a reasonable time-limit, and after such warning has remained unheeded.

Art. 12. The distinctive emblem

Under the direction of the competent authority concerned, the distinctive emblem of the red cross, red crescent or red lion and sun on a white ground shall be displayed by medical and religious personnel and medical units, and on medical transports. It shall be respected in all circumstances. It shall not be used improperly.

PART IV. CIVILIAN POPULATION

Art. 13. Protection of the civilian population

1. The civilian population and individual civilians shall enjoy general protection against the dangers arising from military operations. To give effect to this protection, the following rules shall be observed in all circumstances.
2. The civilian population as such, as well as individual civilians, shall not be the object of attack. Acts or threats of violence the primary purpose of which is to spread terror among the civilian population are prohibited.
3. Civilians shall enjoy the protection afforded by this Part, unless and for such time as they take a direct part in hostilities.

Art. 14. Protection of objects indispensable to the survival of the civilian population

Starvation of civilians as a method of combat is prohibited. It is therefore prohibited to attack, destroy, remove or render useless, for that purpose, objects indispensable to the survival of the civilian population, such as foodstuffs, agricultural areas for the production of foodstuffs, crops, livestock, drinking water installations and supplies and irrigation works.

Art. 15. Protection of works and installations containing dangerous forces

Works or installations containing dangerous forces, namely dams, dykes and nuclear electrical generating stations, shall not be made the object of attack, even where these objects are military objectives, if such attack may cause the release of dangerous forces and consequent severe losses among the civilian population.

Art. 16. Protection of cultural objects and of places of worship
Without prejudice to the provisions of the Hague Convention for the Protection of Cultural Property in the Event of Armed Conflict of 14 May 1954, it is prohibited to commit any acts of hostility directed against historic monuments, works of art or places of worship which constitute the cultural or spiritual heritage of peoples, and to use them in support of the military effort.

Art. 17. Prohibition of forced movement of civilians
1. The displacement of the civilian population shall not be ordered for reasons related to the conflict unless the security of the civilians involved or imperative military reasons so demand. Should such displacements have to be carried out, all possible measures shall be taken in order that the civilian population may be received under satisfactory conditions of shelter, hygiene, health, safety and nutrition.
2. Civilians shall not be compelled to leave their own territory for reasons connected with the conflict.

Art. 18. Relief societies and relief actions
1. Relief societies located in the territory of the High Contracting Party, such as Red Cross (Red Crescent, Red Lion and Sun) organizations, may offer their services for the performance of their traditional functions in relation to the victims of the armed conflict. The civilian population may, even on its own initiative, offer to collect and care for the wounded, sick and shipwrecked.
2. If the civilian population is suffering undue hardship owing to a lack of the supplies essential for its survival, such as foodstuffs and medical supplies, relief actions for the civilian population which are of an exclusively humanitarian and impartial nature and which are conducted without any adverse distinction shall be undertaken subject to the consent of the High Contracting Party concerned.

PART V. FINAL PROVISIONS

Art. 19. Dissemination
This Protocol shall be disseminated as widely as possible.

Art. 20. Signature
This Protocol shall be open for signature by the Parties to the Conventions six months after the signing of the Final Act and will remain open for a period of twelve months.

Art. 21. Ratification
This Protocol shall be ratified as soon as possible. The instruments of ratification shall be deposited with the Swiss Federal Council, depositary of the Conventions.

Art. 22. Accession
This Protocol shall be open for accession by any Party to the Conventions which has not signed it. The instruments of accession shall be deposited with the depositary.

Art. 23. Entry into force

1. This Protocol shall enter into force six months after two instruments of ratification or accession have been deposited.
2. For each Party to the Conventions thereafter ratifying or acceding to this Protocol, it shall enter into force six months after the deposit by such Party of its instrument of ratification or accession.

Art. 24. Amendment

1. Any High Contracting Party may propose amendments to this Protocol. The text of any proposed amendment shall be communicated to the depositary which shall decide, after consultation with all the High Contracting Parties and the International Committee of the Red Cross, whether a conference should be convened to consider the proposed amendment.
2. The depositary shall invite to that conference all the High Contracting Parties as well as the Parties to the Conventions, whether or not they are signatories of this Protocol.

Art. 25. Denunciation

1. In case a High Contracting Party should denounce this Protocol, the denunciation shall only take effect six months after receipt of the instrument of denunciation. If, however, on the expiry of six months, the denouncing Party is engaged in the situation referred to in Article 1, the denunciation shall not take effect before the end of the armed conflict. Persons who have been deprived of liberty, or whose liberty has been restricted, for reasons related to the conflict shall nevertheless continue to benefit from the provisions of this Protocol until their final release.
2. The denunciation shall be notified in writing to the depositary, which shall transmit it to all the High Contracting Parties.

Art. 26. Notifications

The depositary shall inform the High Contracting Parties as well as the Parties to the Conventions, whether or not they are signatories of this Protocol, of:

(a) signatures affixed to this Protocol and the deposit of instruments of ratification and accession under Articles 21 and 22;
(b) the date of entry into force of this Protocol under Article 23; and
(c) communications and declarations received under Article 24.

Art. 27. Registration

1. After its entry into force, this Protocol shall be transmitted by the depositary to the Secretariat of the United Nations for registration and publication, in accordance with Article 102 of the Charter of the United Nations.
2. The depositary shall also inform the Secretariat of the United Nations of all ratifications and accessions received by it with respect to this Protocol.

Art. 28. Authentic texts

The original of this Protocol, of which the Arabic, Chinese, English, French, Russian and Spanish texts are equally authentic, shall be deposited with the depositary, which shall transmit certified true copies thereof to all the Parties to the Conventions.

SIGNATURES, RATIFICATIONS AND ACCESSIONS

See list on pp. 785–791.

DECLARATIONS AND RESERVATIONS

See list on pp. 792–818.

Nos. 56–57

SIGNATURES, RATIFICATIONS AND ACCESSIONS

concerning Protocols I and II Additional to the Geneva Conventions, 1977[1]

State[2]	*Signature*[3]	*Ratification, Accession, Notifications of Succession or Continuity (C)*[4]
Albania	–	16 July 1993
Algeria*	–	16 August 1989 *Dec.*
Angola	–	20 September 1984 *Dec.* (*Protocol I*)
Antigua and Barbuda	–	6 October 1986
Argentina*	–	26 November 1986 *Dec.*
Armenia	–	7 June 1993
Australia*	7 December 1978 *Dec.*	21 June 1991 *Dec.*
Austria*[5]	12 December 1977	13 August 1982 *Res.*
Azerbaijan	–	1 June 1993

1 Based on the communication received from the Swiss Federal Department of Foreign Affairs, 25 June 1999 and completed by the indications published in the *United Nations Treaty Series* and on the ICRC website: www.icrc.org/ihl.nsf. The texts of reservations, declarations and communications are published on pp. 792 ff. The reservations, declarations and communications are indicated in the table by abbreviations "*Res.*" or "*Dec.*" placed after the dates of signatures, ratifications, accessions or notifications of succession or continuity. The withdrawal of the reservation is indicated by a footnote.

2 * The asterisk which follows the name of the state means that this state made the declaration according to Article 90, paragraph 2, sub-paragraph (a) of the Protocol I recognizing *ipso facto* and without special agreement, in relation to any other high contracting party accepting the same obligation, the competence of the International Fact-Finding Commission to enquire into allegations by such other party. These declarations were made at the time of the deposit of the instruments of signature, ratification, accession or notification of succession or continuity. If the declaration was deposited at the later date, this date will be mentioned in the brackets after the name of the state. On 5 June 2002, the following states had made such a declaration: Algeria, Argentina (11 October 1996), Australia (23 September 1992), Austria, Belarus, Belgium (27 March 1987), Bolivia (10 August 1992), Bosnia and Herzegovina, Brazil (23 November 1993), Bulgaria (9 May 1994), Canada, Cape Verde, Chile, Colombia (17 April 1996), Cook Islands, Costa Rica (2 December 1999), Croatia, Czech Republic (2 May 1995), Denmark, Finland, Germany, Greece (4 February 1998), Guinea (20 December 1993), Hungary (23 September 1991), Iceland, Ireland, Italy, Lao People's Dem. Rep. (30 January 1998), Liechtenstein, Lithuania, Luxembourg (12 May 1993), Macedonia, Madagascar (27 July 1993), Malta, Mongolia, Namibia (21 July 1994), Netherlands, New Zealand, Norway, Panama (26 October 1999), Paraguay (30 January 1998), Poland (2 October 1992), Portugal (1 July 1994), Qatar (24 September 1991), Romania (31 May 1995), Russian Federation, Rwanda (8 July 1993 – notification: 17 January 1995), Seychelles (22 May 1992), Slovakia (13 March 1995), Slovenia, Spain, Sweden, Switzerland, Tajikistan (10 September 1997), Togo (21 November 1991), Trinidad and Tobago, Ukraine, United Arab Emirates (6 March 1992), United Kingdom (17 May 1999), Uruguay (17 July 1990), Yugoslavia.

3 According to Article 92 of the Protocol I and Article 20 of the Protocol II, the Protocols were open for signature by the parties to the Conventions six months after the signing of the Final Act and remained open during a period of twelve months. The Protocols were open for signature from 12 December 1977 to 12 December 1978. Sixty-two states signed the Protocol I during this period and fifty-eight states signed Protocol II.

4 The dates mentioned in this table indicate the deposit of the instruments of ratification, accession or of notifications of succession or continuity to the depositary, the Swiss Federal Council.

5 See also the communication of the Austrian Embassy in Berne of 27 March 1980, received by the Swiss Federal Department of Foreign Affairs on 28 March 1980 concerning the Order of Malta, see pp. 794–795.

State[2]	*Signature*[3]	*Ratification, Accession, Notifications of Succession or Continuity (C)*[4]
Bahamas	–	10 April 1980
Bahrain	–	30 October 1986
Bangladesh	–	8 September 1980[6]
Barbados	–	19 February 1990
Belarus*	12 December 1977	23 October 1989
Belgium*	12 December 1977	20 May 1986 *Dec.*
Belize	–	29 June 1984
Benin	–	28 May 1986
Bolivia*	–	8 December 1983
Bosnia and Herzegovina	–	31 December 1992 (C)[7]
Botswana	–	23 May 1979
Brazil*	–	5 May 1993
Brunei Darussalam	–	14 October 1991
Bulgaria*	11 December 1978	26 September 1989
Burkina Faso	11 January 1978	20 October 1987
Burundi	–	10 June 1993
Cambodia	–	14 January 1998
Cameroon	–	16 March 1984
Canada*	12 December 1977 *Dec.*	20 November 1990 *Res.*
Cape Verde	–	16 March 1995
Central African .Republic	–	17 July 1984
Chad	–	17 January 1997
Chile*	12 December 1977	24 April 1991
China, People's Republic[8]	–	14 September 1983 *Res.*
Colombia*	–	1 September 1993 (*Protocol I*) 14 August 1995 (*Protocol II*)
Comoros	–	21 November 1985
Congo	–	10 November 1983
Congo, Democratic Republic (formerly Zaire)	–	3 June 1982 (*Protocol I*) 12 December 2002 (*Protocol II*)
Costa Rica	–	15 December 1983
Côte d'Ivoire	–	20 September 1989
Croatia	–	11 May 1992 (C)[9]

6 By a communication to states parties to the Geneva Conventions of 12 August 1949 for the protection of victims of war, the Swiss Federal Department of Foreign Affairs informed the governments that the Permanent Mission of Bangladesh to the United Nations had informed the Swiss Government by a note of 20 December 1988 of the decision of the Government of the People's Republic of Bangladesh to use the red crescent instead of the red cross as distinctive emblem and sign. Communication of the depositary of 9 January 1989. See p. 652.

7 The succession of Bosnia and Herzegovina took place retroactively on 6 March 1992, the date of the independence of this state.

8 On 14 April 1999, the People's Republic of China notified to the depositary the following: "The Government of the People's Republic of China hereby confirms that the four Geneva Conventions of 1949 and the 1977 Additional Protocols I and II apply to the Hong Kong Special Administrative Region of the People's Republic of China (HKSAR) with effect from 1 July 1997, as they apply to the whole territory of the People's Republic of China."

9 Succession to the four Geneva Conventions and Protocols I and II, which were applicable to it by virtue of their ratification by Yugoslavia, without reservations, on 11 May 1992, with retroactive effect as from 8 October 1991, date of independence.

State[2]	*Signature*[3]	*Ratification, Accession, Notifications of Succession or Continuity (C)*[4]
Cuba	–	25 November 1982 (*Protocol I*)
Cyprus	12 July 1978 (*Protocol I*)	1 June 1979 (*Protocol I*)
[Czechoslovakia	6 December 1978	14 February 1990]
Czech Republic*	–	5 February 1993 (C)[10]
Denmark*	12 December 1977	17 June 1982 *Res.*
Djibouti	–	8 April 1991
Dominica	–	25 April 1996
Dominican Republic	–	26 May 1994
Ecuador	12 December 1977	10 April 1979
Egypt	12 December 1977	9 October 1992 *Dec.*
El Salvador	12 December 1977	23 November 1978
Equatorial Guinea	–	24 July 1986
Estonia	–	18 January 1993
Ethiopia	–	8 April 1994
Finland*	12 December 1977	7 August 1980 *Res.*
France	–	24 February 1984 *Dec.*[11] *(Protocol II)*
France	–	11 April 2001 *Res.* *(Protocol I)*
Gabon	–	8 April 1980
Gambia	–	12 January 1989
Georgia	–	14 September 1993
Germany*[12]	23 December 1977 *Dec.*	14 February 1991 *Dec.*
Ghana	12 December 1977	28 February 1978[13]
Greece*	22 March 1978 *Dec.*	31 March 1989 (*Protocol I*) 15 February 1993 (*Protocol II*)
Grenada	–	23 September 1998
Guatemala	12 December 1977	19 October 1987
Guinea *	–	11 July 1984
Guinea-Bissau	–	21 October 1986
Guyana	–	18 January 1988
Holy See	12 December 1977	21 November 1985 *Dec.*
Honduras	12 December 1977	16 February 1995
Hungary	12 December 1977	12 April 1989
Iceland	12 December 1977	10 April 1987 *Res.*
Iran	12 December 1977	–
Ireland*	12 December 1977	19 May 1999 *Res.*
Italy*	12 December 1977 *Dec.*	27 February 1986 *Dec.*

[10] Declaration of succession to the four Geneva Conventions and Additional Protocols I and II, retaining the reservations made previously by Czechoslovakia with regard to the Conventions.

[11] At the accession to Protocol II, France made a communication concerning Protocol I. See p. 800.

[12] The German Democratic Republic signed the Protocols on 12 December 1977, but did not ratify them.

[13] According to Article 95 of Protocol I and Article 23 of Protocol II, the Protocols came into force on 7 December 1978, six months after the deposit of the second instrument or ratification or accession. Ghana ratified the Protocols I and II on 28 February 1978 and Libya acceded to the Protocols on 7 June 1978. The Protocols came into force on 7 December 1978 for both states.

State[2]	*Signature*[3]	*Ratification, Accession, Notifications of Succession or Continuity (C)*[4]
Ivory Coast See Côte d'Ivoire		
Jamaica	–	29 July 1986
Jordan	12 December 1977	1 May 1979
Kazakhstan	–	5 May 1992 (C)[14]
Kenya	–	23 February 1999
Korea, Democratic. People's Republic	–	9 March 1988
Korea, Republic of	7 December 1978	15 January 1982 *Dec.*
Kuwait	–	17 January 1985
Kyrghyzstan	–	18 September 1992 (C)[15]
Lao People's Democratic. Republic*	18 April 1978	18 November 1980
Latvia	–	24 December 1991
Lebanon	–	23 July 1997
Lesotho	–	20 May 1994
Liberia	–	30 June 1988
Libyan Arab Jamahiriya	–	7 June 1978
Liechtenstein*	12 December 1977	10 August 1989 *Res.*
Lithuania	–	13 July 2000
Luxembourg*	12 December 1977	29 August 1989
Macedonia*	–	1 September 1993 (C)[16]
Madagascar*	13 October 1978	8 May 1992
Malawi	–	7 October 1991
Maldives	–	3 September 1991
Mali	–	8 February 1989
Malta*	–	17 April 1989 *Res.*
Mauritania	–	14 March 1980
Mauritius	–	22 March 1982
Mexico	–	10 March 1983 (*Protocol I*)
Micronesia	–	19 September 1995
Moldova	–	24 May 1993
Monaco	–	7 January 2000
Mongolia*	12 December 1977	6 December 1995 Res.
Morocco	12 December 1977	–
Mozambique	–	14 March 1983 (*Protocol I*) 12 December 2002 (*Protocol II*)

14 Declaration of succession to the four Conventions of Geneva and Additional Protocols I and II, on 5 May 1992. No comment on the reservations and declarations made by the former USSR, and no new reservations or declarations were made (notification of the depositary to ICRC of 15 July and 24 September 1992 and notification to states parties of 14 October 1992).

15 Declaration of succession to the four Conventions of Geneva and Additional Protocols I and II. No comment on the reservations and declarations made by the former USSR, and no new reservations or declarations were made (notification of the depositary to ICRC of 24 September 1992 and notification to states parties of 14 October 1992).

16 The Former Yugoslav Republic of Macedonia deposited on 1 September 1993 the instrument of succession to the 1949 Geneva Conventions and Additional Protocols, dated 25 August 1993. The succession took effect on 8 September 1991, the day of independence. The former Yugoslav Republic of Macedonia decided on 18 October 1996 to succeed to the reservations and declarations made by the Former Socialist Federal Republic of Yugoslavia (notification of the depositary to ICRC of 9 September 1993).

State[2]	*Signature*[3]	*Ratification, Accession, Notifications of Succession or Continuity (C)*[4]
Namibia*[17]	–	17 June 1994
Netherlands*[18]	12 December 1977	26 June 1987 *Dec.*
New Zealand*[19]	27 November 1978	6 February 1988 *Dec.*
Nicaragua	12 December 1977	19 July 1999
Niger	16 June 1978	8 June 1979
Nigeria	–	10 October 1988
Norway*	12 December 1977	14 December 1981 *Dec.*
Oman	–	29 March 1984 *Dec.*
Pakistan	12 December 1977	–
Palestine See Palestine Liberation Organization, at this end of this table		
Panama*	12 December 1977	18 September 1995
Paraguay*	–	30 November 1990
Palau	–	25 June 1996
Peru	12 December 1977	14 July 1989
Philippines	12 December 1977 (*Protocol I*)	–
		11 December 1986 (*Protocol II*)
Poland*	12 December 1977	23 October 1991
Portugal*	12 December 1977 *Dec.*	27 May 1992
Qatar*[20]	–	5 April 1988 (*Protocol I*)
Romania*	28 March 1978	21 June 1990
Russian Federation*[21]	12 December 1977 *Dec.*	29 September 1989 (C) *Dec.*
Rwanda*	–	19 November 1984
Saint Kitts and Nevis	–	14 February 1986

[17] United Nations Council for Namibia deposited the instruments of accession to the Geneva Conventions and Additional Protocols on 18 October 1983 (notification of the depositary to ICRC of 18 October 1983). South Africa made a declaration in this respect (see p. 814). After accession to independence, Namibia made a notification of succession on 6 June 1994, received by the depositary on 17 June 1994. The Protocols entered into force with the retroactive effect as from 21 March 1990, day of the accession to independence (communication of the ICRC from 23 June 1994).

[18] Covers the Kingdom's territory within Europe, plus the Netherlands Antilles and Aruba.

[19] When the Protocol was ratified, the government of New Zealand declared that the instrument did not apply to the Cook Islands, Niue and the Tokelau Islands.

[20] On 24 September 1991, the State of Qatar deposited with the Swiss Federal Council an instrument containing a declaration of recognition of the competence of the International Fact-Finding Commission, according to Article 90 of the Additional Protocol I to the Geneva Conventions (notification of the depositary to the ICRC of 10 January 1992). This declaration includes a reservation concerning the recognition of the state of Israel. As the International Fact-Finding Commission is competent to enquire into any facts alleged to be a grave breach as defined in the Conventions and in the Protocol I (Article 90, paragraph 2(c)) of Protocol I) and as the declaration of the state of Israel is referring to the Geneva Conventions, we reproduce this declaration in this collection, See p. 807.

[21] Note of the Ministry for Foreign Affairs of the Russian Federation: "The Russian Federation continues to exercise the rights and carry out the obligations resulting from the international agreements signed by the Union of Soviet Socialist Republics.

Accordingly the Government of the Russian Federation will carry out, instead of the Government of the USSR, functions of depositary of the corresponding multilateral treaties. In this connection the Ministry asks to consider the Russian Federation as a Party to all international agreements in force, instead of the USSR" (note from the Permanent Mission of the Russian Federation in Geneva transmitted to the ICRC on 15 January 1992).

State[2]	*Signature*[3]	*Ratification, Accession, Notifications of Succession or Continuity (C)*[4]
Saint Lucia	–	7 October 1982
Saint Vincent and the Grenadines	-	8 April 1983
Samoa	–	23 August 1984
San Marino	22 June 1978	5 April 1994
Sao Tome and Principe	–	5 July 1996
Saudi Arabia	–	21 August 1987 *Res.* (*Protocol I*)
Senegal	12 December 1977	7 May 1985
Seychelles*	–	8 November 1984
Sierra Leone	–	21 October 1986
Slovakia*	–	2 April 1993 (C)[22]
Slovenia*	–	26 March 1992 (C)[23]
Solomon Islands	–	19 September 1988
South Africa	–	21 November 1995
Spain*	7 November 1978 *Dec.*	21 April 1989 *Dec.*
Suriname	–	16 December 1985
Swaziland	–	2 November 1995
Sweden*	12 December 1977	31 August 1979 *Res.*
Switzerland*	12 December 1977 *Dec.*	17 February 1982 *Res.*
Syrian Arab Republic	–	14 November. 1983 *Dec.* (*Protocol I*)
Tajikistan	–	13 January 1993 (C)[24]
Tanzania United Republic of	–	15 February 1983
Togo*	12 December 1977	21 June 1984
Trinidad and Tobago*	–	20 July 2001
Tunisia	12 December 1977	9 August 1979
Turkmenistan	–	10 April 1992 (C)[25]
Uganda	–	13 March 1991
Ukraine*	12 December 1977	25 January 1990
[Union of Soviet Socialist. Republic]*[26]	12 December 1977	29 September 1989 *Dec.*
United Arab Emirates*	–	9 March 1983 *Dec.*

[22] Declaration of succession to the four Geneva Conventions and Additional Protocols I and II, retaining the reservations made previously by Czechoslovakia with regard to the Conventions.

[23] Succession to the four Geneva Conventions and Protocols I and II, which were applicable to it by virtue of their ratification by Yugoslavia, without reservations, on 26 March 1992 (notification of the depositary of 13 April 1992).

[24] Declaration of succession to the four Conventions of Geneva and Additional Protocols I and II. No comment on the reservations and declaration made by the former Soviet Union, and no new reservations or declarations (notification of the depositary to ICRC of 14 January 1993).

[25] Declaration of succession to the four Conventions of Geneva and Additional Protocols I and II. No comment on the reservations and declarations made by the former USSR, and no new reservations or declarations (notification of the depositary to the ICRC of 15 July and 24 September 1992 and to States Parties of 14 October 1992).

[26] Note of the Ministry for Foreign Affairs of the Russian Federation: "The Russian Federation continues to exercise the rights and carry out the obligations resulting from the international agreements signed by the Union of Soviet Socialist Republics.

Accordingly, the Government of the Russian Federation will carry out, instead of the Government of the USSR, functions of depositary of the corresponding multilateral treaties. In this connection the Ministry asks to consider the Russian Federation as the Party to all international agreements in force, instead of the USSR" (note from the Permanent Mission of the Russian Federation in Geneva transmitted to the ICRC on 15 January 1992).

State[2]	*Signature*[3]	*Ratification, Accession, Notifications of Succession or Continuity (C)*[4]
United Kingdom*	2 December 1977 *Dec.*[27]	28 January 1998
United States of America	12 December 1977 *Dec.*	
Uruguay*	–	13 December 1985
Uzbekistan	–	8 October 1993
Vanuatu	–	28 February 1985
Venezuela	–	23 July 1998
Vietnam (Soc. Rep.)	12 December 1977 (*Protocol I*)	19 October 1981 (*Protocol I*)
Yemen	14 February 1978	17 April 1990
Yugoslavia[28]	–	16 October 2001
Zambia	–	4 May 1995
Zimbabwe	–	19 October 1992
Palestine Liberation Organization		21 June 1989[29]

[27] On signing the Protocol Additional II, the Government of the United Kingdom declared that they have signed on the understanding that the provisions of the Protocol shall apply to Southern Rhodesia unless and until the Government of the United Kingdom inform the depositary that they are in a position to ensure that the obligations imposed by the Protocol in respect of that territory can be fully implemented.

[28] The Socialist Federal Republic of Yugoslavia signed the Protocols on 12 December 1977 and ratified them on 11 June 1979, with declarations reproduced below, see p. 820.

[29] On 21 June 1989, the Swiss Federal Department of Foreign Affairs received a letter from the Permanent Observer of Palestine to the United Nations Office at Geneva informing the Swiss Federal Council "that the Executive Committee of the Palestine Liberation Organization, entrusted with the functions of the Government of the State of Palestine by decision of the Palestine National Council, decided, on 4 May 1989, to adhere to the Four Geneva Conventions of 12 August 1949 and the two Protocols additional thereto." On 13 September 1989, the Swiss Federal Council informed the states that it was not in a position to decide whether the letter constituted an instrument of accession "due to the uncertainty within the international community as to the existence or non-existence of a State of Palestine".

RESERVATIONS AND DECLARATIONS

ALGERIA (*interpretative declaration made at the time of accession*)[1]

1. The Government of the People's Democratic Republic of Algeria declares that the expressions "feasible precautions" (Art. 41, para. 3), "everything feasible" (Art. 57, para. 2), and "to the maximum extent feasible" (Art. 58) are to be interpreted as referring to precautions and measures which are feasible in view of the circumstances and the information and means available at the time.
2. As concerns the repression of breaches of the Conventions and the present Protocol as defined in Articles 85 and 86 of Section II of Protocol I, the Government of the People's Democratic Republic of Algeria considers that to judge any decision, the circumstances, the means and the information available at the time the decision was made are determinant factors and elements in assessing the nature of the said decision.
3. The Government of the People's Democratic Republic of Algeria reserves judgement on the definition of mercenarism as set out in Article 47, para. 2 of the present Protocol, this definition being deemed restrictive.

ANGOLA (*declaration made on accession*)[2]

In acceding to Protocol I of 1977, additional to the Geneva Conventions of 12 August 1949, the People's Republic of Angola declares that, pending the entry into force of the International Convention on Mercenarism which is at present being drafted by the United Nations, and until such time as the State of Angola becomes a party to that Convention, the People's Republic of Angola will consider the following to be committing the crime of mercenarism:

(a) those who recruit, organise, finance, equip or train mercenaries or employ them in any other way;

(b) those who, in the territory under their jurisdiction or in any other place under their control, allow the performance of any of the acts referred to in the previous paragraph or afford facilities for the transit or transport of mercenaries;

(c) any alien who, on Angolan territory, commits any of the acts mentioned above against another country;

(d) any Angolan national who, with a view to subverting the sovereignty or the territorial integrity of a foreign country or to opposing the self-determination of a people, commits any of the acts referred to in the preceding articles.

ARGENTINA (*declaration made on accession*)[3]

Interpretative statements

With reference to Article 43, paragraph 1, and Article 44, paragraph 1, of the Protocol Additional to the Geneva Conventions of 12 August 1949, and relating to the Protection of Victims of International Armed Conflicts (Protocol 1), the Argentine Republic interprets these provisions as not implying any derogation of:

(a) the concept of the permanent regular armed forces of a Sovereign State;

(b) the conceptual distinction between regular armed forces, understood as being permanent army units under the authority of Governments of Sovereign States, and the resistance movements which are referred to in Article 4 of the Third Geneva Convention of 1949.

With reference to Article 44, paragraphs 2, 3 and 4, of the same Protocol, the Argentine Republic considers that these provisions cannot be interpreted:

(a) as conferring on persons who violate the rules of international law applicable in armed conflicts any kind of immunity exempting them from the system of sanctions which apply to each case;

---

[1] Notification by the depositary addressed to the ICRC on 25 August 1989.

[2] Original Portuguese. Notification by the depositary addressed to the ICRC on 27 September 1984.

[3] Original Spanish. Notification by the depositary addressed to the ICRC on 1 December 1986.

(b) as specifically favouring anyone who violates the rules the aim of which is the distinction between combatants and the civilian population;
(c) as weakening respect for the fundamental principle of the international law of war which requires that a distinction be made between combatants and the civilian population, with the prime purpose of protecting the latter.

With reference to Article 1 of the Protocol Additional to the Geneva Conventions of 12 August 1949, and relating to the Protection of Victims of Non-International Armed Conflicts (Protocol II), taken its context into account, the Argentine Republic considers that the term "organized armed groups" which is used in Article 1 of the said Protocol is not to be understood as equivalent to that used in Article 43, Protocol 1, to define the concept of armed forces, even if the aforementioned groups meet all the requirements set forth in the said Article 43.

AUSTRALIA

Declaration made on signature[4]

The Australian Embassy wishes to advise the Federal Political Department that the Australian Government is undertaking careful study of the interpretation of the provisions of Protocol I and their implications for the legitimate conduct of national defence and reserves the right to make declarations and reservations upon ratification.

Declarations made at the time of ratification[5]

In depositing its instrument of ratification for Protocol I, Australia hereby makes declarations of understanding in relation to Articles 5, 44 and 51 to 58 inclusive of the said Protocol.

It is Australia's understanding that in relation to Article 5, with regard to the issue whether, and in what measure, Protecting Powers may have to exercise any functions within the combat zone (such as may be implied by provisions in Parts II and IV of the Protocol), the role of the Protecting Power will be of a like character to that specified in the First and Second Conventions and Part II of the Fourth Convention, which apply mainly to the battlefield and its immediate surroundings.

It is the understanding of Australia that in relation to Article 44, the situation described in the second sentence of paragraph 3 can exist only in occupied territory or in armed conflicts covered by paragraph 4 of Article 1. Australia will interpret the word "deployment" in paragraph 3(b) of the Article as meaning any movement towards a place from which an attack is to be launched. It will interpret the words "visible to the adversary" in the same paragraph as including visible with the aid of binoculars, or by infra-red or image intensification devices.

In relation to Articles 51 to 58 inclusive it is the understanding of Australia that military commanders and others responsible for planning, deciding upon, or executing attacks, necessarily have to reach their decisions on the basis of their assessment of the information from all sources, which is available to them at the relevant time.

In relation to paragraph 5(b) of Article 51 and to paragraph 2(a)(iii) of Article 57, it is the understanding of Australia that references to the "military advantage" are intended to mean the advantage anticipated from the military attack considered as a whole and not only from isolated or particular parts of that attack and that the term "military advantage" involves a variety of considerations including the security of attacking forces. It is further the understanding of Australia that the term "concrete and direct military advantage anticipated", used in Articles 51 and 57, means a bona fide expectation that the attack will make a relevant and proportional contribution to the objective of the military attack involved.

It is the understanding of Australia that the first sentence of paragraph 2 of Article 52 is not intended to, nor does it, deal with the question of incidental or collateral damage resulting from an attack directed against a military objective.

---

4 *UNTS*, Vol. 1125, 1979, p. 429.
5 Notification by the depositary addressed to the ICRC on 24 June 1991.

AUSTRIA (*reservations made on ratification)*[6]

Reservation with regard to Article 57, paragraph 2, of Protocol I

Article 57, paragraph 2, of Protocol I will be applied on the understanding that, with respect to any decision taken by a military commander, the information actually available at the time of the decision is determinative.

Reservation with regard to Article 58 of Protocol I

In view of the fact that Article 58 of Protocol I contains the expression 'to the maximum extent feasible', sub-paragraphs (a) and (b) will be applied subject to the requirements of national defence.

Reservation with regard to Article 75 of Protocol I

Article 75 of Protocol I will be applied insofar as

(a) sub-paragraph (e) of paragraph 4 is not incompatible with legislation providing that any defendant, who causes a disturbance at the trial or whose presence is likely to impede the questioning of another defendant or the hearing of a witness or expert witness, may be removed from the courtroom;

(b) sub-paragraph (h) of paragraph 4 is not incompatible with legal provisions authorizing the reopening of proceedings that have resulted in a final declaration of conviction or acquittal.

Reservation with regard to Articles 85 and 86 of Protocol I

For the purposes of judging any decision taken by a military commander, Articles 85 and 86 of Protocol I will be applied on the understanding that military imperatives, the reasonable possibility of recognizing them and the information actually available at the time that decision was taken, are determinative.

Reservation with regard to Article 6 of Protocol II

Article 6, paragraph 2, sub-paragraph (e) of Protocol II will be applied insofar as it is not incompatible with legislation providing that any defendant, who causes a disturbance at the trial or whose presence is likely to impede the questioning of another defendant or the hearing of a witness or expert witness, may be removed from the courtroom.

Communication concerning the Sovereign Order of Malta addressed on 27 March 1980 by the Austrian Embassy in Bern and received by the Swiss Federal Department of Foreign Affairs on 28 March 1980[7]

During the Diplomatic Conference on the reaffirmation and development of international humanitarian law applicable in armed conflicts (CDDH), held in Geneva from 1974 to 1977, the Delegation of the Sovereign Order of Malta asked on 31 May 1977 the General Committee of the Conference what would be the most appropriate form to make known to the participating powers at this Conference the position of the Sovereign Order on the Geneva Conventions and their Additional Protocol. The Order wanted to make formally known that:

(a) the mission of the Order is accomplished by the relief societies as defined by the Geneva Conventions of 1949 and the Additional Protocols and the Order takes the engagement that these societies will observe the provisions of these legal instruments in this respect;

(b) the Order being a fully independent *sui generis* subject of international law has its functional sovereignty which gives it an opportunity to assume in all impartiality the mandate of the substitute of the Protection Power as defined in the Geneva Conventions and Additional Protocols;

(c) in front of the International Community, the Order wishes to affirm its availability to assume any humanitarian task which a party to the conflict may confer on it.

At the plenary session on 9 June 1977, the Order's Delegation expressed thanks to the General Committee of the Conference for accepting to study this question and unani-

---

6 Notification by the depositary addressed to the ICRC on 16 August 1982.

7 Notification by the depositary to the states parties to the Geneva Conventions of 2 May 1980 (editors' translation from French).

mously agreed that the Order's Delegation might make a statement on its position as regards the Geneva Conventions and Additional Protocols and that the Depositary state would kindly transmit these texts to the Powers which had participated in the present Conference.

The Sovereign Order of Malta has now asked the Government of Austria to kindly transmit this declaration to the Depositary Power of the said Additional Protocols to be made available to the Powers which participated in the CDDH.

BELGIUM (*declaration of interpretation made on ratification*)[8]
On depositing the instrument of ratification by Belgium of the Protocol Additional to the Geneva Conventions of 12 August 1949, and relating to the Protection of Victims of International Armed Conflicts (Protocol 1), done at Geneva on 8 June 1977, the Belgian Government makes the following declarations of interpretation:

1. The Belgian Government, in view of the *travaux préparatoires* for the international instrument herewith ratified, wishes to emphasize that the Protocol was established to broaden the protection conferred by humanitarian law solely when conventional weapons are used in armed conflicts, without prejudice to the provisions of international law relating to the use of other types of weapons.
2. The Belgian Government, in view of paragraph 3 of Article 43 (Armed forces) and the special status of the Belgian *Gendarmerie* (constabulary), has decided to notify the High Contracting Parties as follows of the duties assigned to the Belgian *Gendarmerie* in time of armed conflict. It considers that this notification fully satisfies any and all requirements of Article 43 pertaining to the *Gendarmerie.*
   (a) The Belgian *Gendarmerie,* which was formed to maintain law and order, is a police force stated by national legislation to be one of the armed forces and is therefore covered by the expression "armed forces of a Party to a conflict" within the meaning of Article 43 of Protocol I. Thus in time of international armed conflict members of the *Gendarmerie* have the status of 'combatant' within the meaning of this Protocol.
   (b) In addition to this notification the Belgian Government wishes to state exactly what duties the law entrusts to the *Gendarmerie* in time of war. Those duties are described in the "Act on the *Gendarmerie*" of 2 December 1957 (published in the *Moniteur belge* official gazette of 12 December 1957).

   Part VI of that Act, in its Articles 63, 64, 66 and 67, covers the special duties assigned to the *Gendarmerie* in time of war in addition to their peacetime duties. The said duties are as follows:

   63. The *Gendarmerie* shall take part in the internal defence of Belgian territory to the extent fixed by mutual agreement between the Minister of National Defence, the Minister of Justice and the Minister of the Interior.

   Territorial units shall not be required to perform any duties other than intelligence and warning duties.

   Mobile units may be placed in support of units of the other armed forces.

   64. Throughout the duration of the time of war the *Gendarmerie* shall provide detachments known as *prévôtés* (military police) to maintain order in and police the other armed forces.

   Each *prévôté* shall be under the command of a *prévôt* (Assistant Provost Marshal), who shall be an officer of the *Gendarmerie.*

   66. Throughout the duration of the time of war the *Gendarmerie* shall keep in constant touch with prosecuting officers at courts martial.

   The *Gendarmerie* shall report on events concerning security and public order.

   67. Throughout the duration of the time of war the *Gendarmerie* may be instructed by prosecuting officers at courts martial to serve subpoenas on the parties or witnesses.'

[8] Notification by the depositary addressed to the ICRC on 21 May 1986.

(c) The Belgian Government wishes to emphasize that even in time of war the *Gendarmerie's* principal duty is still the general one conferred on it by Article 1 of the "Act on the *Gendarmerie*".

Indeed the Royal Order of 14 March 1963 "respecting the organization of the general service of the *Gendarmerie*" (published in the *Moniteur belge* official gazette of 29 March 1963) stipulates in its Article 17:

"In time of war:

(a) The *Gendarmerie* shall retain its normal duties of maintaining law and order;

(b) Without prejudice to Article 63 on the *Gendarmerie* and the measures that shall result from its execution, all *Gendarmerie* forces, whether mobile or territorial, shall remain under the command of the Commanding Officer of the *Gendarmerie.* He shall use and distribute them as the maintenance of order and the judicial service shall require. Each subordinate echelon shall act similarly within the limits of its powers and responsibilities."

3. With respect to Articles 41, 57 and 58, the Belgian Government considers that, in view of the *travaux préparatoires,* the expression 'feasible precautions' in Article 41 must be interpreted in the same way as the "feasible precautions" mentioned in Articles 57 and 58,[9] that is, those that can be taken in the circumstances prevailing at the moment, which include military considerations as much as humanitarian ones.
4. With respect to Article 44, the Belgian Government declares that the armed conflict situations described in paragraph 3 can arise only in occupied territory or in the armed conflicts covered by Article 1, paragraph 4, of the Protocol. Furthermore the Belgian Government interprets the term "deployment" used in subparagraph (b) of the said paragraph 3 as comprising any individual or collective movement towards a position from which an attack is to be launched.
5. With respect to Articles 51 and 57, the Belgian Government interprets the "military advantage" mentioned therein as being that expected from an attack considered in its totality.
6. With respect to Part IV, Section 1, of the Protocol, the Belgian Government wishes to emphasize that, whenever a military commander is required to take a decision affecting the protection of civilians or civilian objects or objects assimilated therewith, the only information on which that decision can possibly be taken is such relevant information as is then available and that it has been feasible for him to obtain for that purpose.
7. With respect to Article 96, paragraph 3, the Belgian Government declares that the only authority that could address a declaration having the effects described in paragraph 3 of Article 96 would be an authority that in any case:
   (a) is recognized by the intergovernmental regional organization concerned, and
   (b) does in fact represent a people engaged in an armed conflict the characteristics of which strictly and exactly conform to the definition given by Article 1, paragraph 4, and to the interpretation given to the exercise of the right of self-determination at the time of the adoption of the Protocol.

CANADA

Declaration made on signature[10]

Some provisions (in Protocol I) are formulated in such a way that they give rise to different, even contradictory, interpretations. My Government does not wish at this juncture to raise these problems, but it reserves the right to do so before it ratifies the Protocol.

---

[9] Translator's note: whereas the term "feasible precautions" is used in all three articles in the English version of the Protocol, in the French version the term *précautions utiles* is used in Article 41 and the term *précautions pratiquement possibles* in Articles 57 and 58.

Reservations and declarations made at the time of ratification[11]

Protocol I
Protocol relating to the Protection of Victims of International Armed Conflicts
Article 11. Protection of persons (Medical procedures)
The Government of Canada does not intend to be bound by the prohibitions contained in Article 11, sub-paragraph 2(c), with respect to Canadian nationals or other persons ordinarily resident in Canada who may be interned, detained or otherwise deprived of liberty as a result of a situation referred to in Article 1, so long as the removal of tissue or organs for transplantation is in accordance with Canadian laws and applicable to the population generally and the operation is carried out in accordance with normal Canadian medical practices, standards and ethics.

Article 39. Emblems of nationality (enemy uniforms)
The Government of Canada does not intend to be bound by the prohibitions contained in paragraph 2 of Article 39 to make use of military emblems, insignia or uniforms of adverse parties in order to shield, favour, protect or impede military operations.

Statements of understanding (conventional weapons)
It is the understanding of the Government of Canada that the rules introduced by Protocol I were intended to apply exclusively to conventional weapons. In particular, the rules so introduced do not have any effect on and do not regulate or prohibit the use of nuclear weapons.

Article 38. Recognized emblems (protective emblems)
It is the understanding of the Government of Canada that, in relation to Article 38, in situations where the Medical Service of the armed forces of a party to an armed conflict is identified by another emblem than the emblems referred to in Article 38 of the First Geneva Convention of August 12, 1949, that other emblem, when notified, should be respected by the adverse party as a protective emblem in the conflict, under analogous conditions to those imposed by the Geneva Conventions of 1949 and the Additional Protocols of 1977 for the use of emblems referred to in Article 38 of the First Geneva Convention and Protocol I. In such situations, misuse of such an emblem should be considered as misuse of emblems referred to in Article 38 of the First Geneva Convention and Protocol I.

Articles 41, 56, 57, 58, 78 and 86 (meaning of "feasible")
It is the understanding of the Government of Canada that in relation to Article 41, 56, 57, 58, 78 and 86 the word "feasible" means that which is practicable or practically possible, taking into account all circumstances ruling at the time, including humanitarian and military considerations.

Article 44. Combatants and prisoners of war (combatant status)
It is understanding of the Government of Canada that:
a. the situation described in the second sentence of paragraph 3 of Article 44 can exist only in occupied territory or in armed conflicts covered by paragraph 4 of Article 1; and
b. the word "deployment" in paragraph 3 of Article 44 includes any movement towards a place from which an attack is to be launched.

Part IV, Section I: General protection against effects of hostilities (standard for decision-making)
It is the understanding of the Government of Canada that, in relation to Articles 48, 51 to 60 inclusive, 62 and 67, military commanders and others responsible for planning, deciding upon or executing attacks have to reach decisions on the basis of their assessment of

[10] *UNTS*, vol. 1125, 1979, p. 429
[11] Notification by the depositary to the ICRC on 22 November 1990.

the information reasonably available to them at the relevant time and that such decisions cannot be judged on the basis of information which has subsequently come to light.

Article 52. General protection of civilian objects (military objectives)
It is the understanding of the Government of Canada in relation to Article 52 that:
(a) a specific area of land may be a military objective if, because of its location or other reasons specified in the Article as to what constitutes a military objective, its total or partial destruction, capture or neutralization in the circumstances governing at the time offers a definite military advantage; and
(b) the first sentence of paragraph 2 of the Article is not intended to, nor does it, deal with the question of incidental or collateral damage resulting from an attack directed against a military objective.

Article 53. Protection of cultural objects and of places of worship (cultural objects)
It is the understanding of the Government of Canada in relation to Article 53 that:
(a) such protection as is afforded by the Article will be lost during such time as the protected property is used for military purposes; and
(b) the prohibitions contained in sub-paragraphs (a) and (b) of this Article can only be waived when military necessity imperatively requires such a waiver.

Article 51, sub-paragraph 5 (b), 52, paragraph 2, and 57, clause 2 (a) (iii) (military advantage)
It is the understanding of the Government of Canada in relation to sub-paragraph 5 (b) of Article 51, paragraph 2 of Article 52, and clause 2 (a) (iii) of Article 57 that the military advantage anticipated from an attack is intended to refer to the advantage anticipated from the attack considered as a whole and not from isolated or particular parts of the attack.

Article 62. General protection (protection of civil defence personnel)
It is the understanding of the Government of Canada that nothing in Article 62 will prevent Canada from using assigned civil defence personnel or volunteer civil defence workers in Canada in accordance with nationally established priorities regardless of the military situation.

Article 96. Treaty relations upon entry into force of this Protocol, paragraph 3 (declaration by national liberation movement)
It is the understanding of the Government of Canada that the making of a unilateral declaration does not, in itself, validate the credentials of the person or persons making such declaration and that States are entitled to satisfy themselves as to whether in fact the makers of such declaration constitute an authority referred to in Article 96. In this respect, the fact that such authority has or has not been recognized as such by an appropriate regional intergovernmental organization is relevant.

Protocol II
Protocol relating to the Protection of Victims of Non- International Armed Conflicts.
Statement of understanding
The Government of Canada understands that the undefined terms used in Additional Protocol II which are defined in Additional Protocol I shall, so far as relevant, be construed in the same sense as those definitions.

The understandings expressed by the Government of Canada with respect to Additional Protocol I shall, as far as relevant, be applicable to the comparable terms and provisions contained in Additional Protocol II.

CHINA (*reservation made on accession*)[12]
At present, Chinese legislation has no provisions concerning extradition and deals with this matter on a case-by-case basis. For this reason China does not accept the stipulations arising from Article 88, paragraph 2, of Protocol I.

---

[12] Notification by the depositary to the states parties of 21 October 1983.

DENMARK (*reservation made on ratification*)
Denmark makes a reservation with respect to the implementation of paragraph 4(h) of Article 75 (Protocol 1) so that the provisions set forth in that paragraph do not prevent the reopening of criminal proceedings in cases where the Rules of the Danish Code of Civil and Criminal Law procedure allow, in exceptional cases, for such a measure to be taken.

EGYPT
Reservation made upon ratification[13]
The Arab Republic of Egypt, in ratifying Protocols I and II of 1977 additional to the Geneva Conventions of 1949, wishes to express its conviction that the provisions of Additional Protocols I and II represent the minimum level of legal and actual protection that must be afforded to persons and civilian and cultural objects in armed conflict. On the basis of its strong conviction of the principles of the great Islamic Sharia, the Arab Republic of Egypt wishes at the same time to emphasize that it is the duties of all nations alike to refrain from the involvement of innocent civilians in armed conflict; furthermore they should make all efforts, to the maximum extent possible, to that end as this is indispensable for the survival of humanity and the cultural heritage and civilization of all countries and nations.

The Arab Republic of Egypt, while declaring its commitment to respecting all the provisions of Additional Protocols I and II, wishes to emphasize, on the basis of reciprocity, that it upholds the right to react against any violation by any party of the obligations imposed by Additional Protocols I and II with all means admissible under international law in order to prevent any further violation. In this context it wishes to assert that military commanders planning or executing attacks make their decisions on the basis of their assessment of all kinds of information available to them at the time of the military operations.

Notification made upon ratification[13]
The Arab Republic of Egypt, while welcoming the adoption by the Diplomatic Conference in June 1977 of Protocols I and II additional to the Geneva Conventions of 1949 in six languages, including the Arabic language, notes that all original texts are certified and equally authentic with no prevalence of one single language over the other. However, on comparison of the original Arabic text of Additional Protocols I and II with the other original texts, it became evident that in some respects the Arabic text does not fully correspond to the other original texts to the extent that it is at variance in terms of both expression and substance with some of the provisions of Additional Protocols I and II adopted by States in the field of international law and human relations. Hence the Arab Republic of Egypt, on the occasion of the deposit of its instrument of ratification of Protocols I and II additional to the Geneva Conventions of 1949 with the depositary, the Swiss Federal Council, wishes to declare that in that respect it shall adopt the meaning which best concurs with the original texts of Additional Protocols I and II.

FINLAND
Reservation made on ratification[14]
With regard to Article 75, paragraph 4 (i), Finland enters a reservation to the effect that under Finnish law a judgment can be declared secret if its publication could be an affront to morals or endanger national security.
Finland withdrew its reservation with immediate effect on 16 February 1987.[15]

Declaration made on ratification[14]
With reference to Articles 75 and 85 of the Protocol, the Finnish Government declare their understanding that, under Article 72, the field of application of Article 75 shall be

[13] Notification by the depositary to the states parties on 17 February 1993.
[14] *UNTS*, vol. 1202, 1980, p. 421.
[15] Notification by the depositary addressed to the ICRC on 18 February 1987.

interpreted to include also the nationals of the Contracting Party applying the provisions of that Article, as well as the nationals of neutral or other States not Parties to the conflict, and that the provisions of Article 85 shall be interpreted to apply to nationals of neutral or other States not Parties to the conflict as they apply to those mentioned in paragraph 2 of that Article.

With reference to Article 75, paragraph 4(h), of the Protocol, the Finnish Government wish to clarify that under Finnish law a judgment shall not be considered final until the time-limit for exercising any extraordinary legal remedies has expired.

FRANCE

Communication made on accession to Protocol II[16]

On the occasion of the deposit of the instrument of accession of France to Protocol II of 8 June 1977 to the Geneva Conventions of 12 August 1949, I have the honour to inform you that the Republic of France does not intend to accede to Protocol I of the same date to the said Conventions. The explanation for this decision can be found in the reasons indicated by the representative of France at the fourth session of the Geneva Diplomatic Conference on the Reaffirmation and Development of International Humanitarian Law applicable in Armed Conflicts, and particularly in the lack of consensus among the States signatories to Protocol I on the exact nature of the obligations undertaken by them concerning dissuasion.

Reservations and declarations made on accession to Protocol I:

After having seen and examined the Additional Protocol,

We declare to accede to it and promise that it will be inviolably observed.

The following reservations and declarations are made on this accession:

1. The provisions of 1977 Protocol I constitute no obstacle for France to exercise its inherent right of self-defense in conformity with Article 51 of the Charter of the United Nations.
2. Referring to the draft protocol drawn up by the International Committee of the Red Cross which constituted a basis of 1974-1977 Diplomatic Conference, the Government of the French Republic continues to consider that the Protocol's provisions concern exclusively conventional weapons and do not regulate or prohibit the use of nuclear weapons, nor should they constitute a prejudice to any other rules of international law applicable to other activities necessary for the exercise by France of its inherent right of self-defense.
3. It is the understanding of the Government of the French Republic that the expressions "possible" and "make every effort", used in the Protocol mean what is practicable or practically possible taking into account all circumstances at the time including those relevant to humanitarian and military considerations.
4. It is the understanding of the Government of the French Republic that the term "armed conflict" mentioned in paragraph 4 of Article 1, of itself and in its context denotes a situation of a kind which is not constituted by the commission of ordinary crimes including acts of terrorism whether concerted or in isolation.
5. Given the practical need to make use of non-dedicated aircraft for medical evacuation purposes, the Government of the French Republic does not interpret paragraph 2 of Article 28 as precluding the presence on board of communications equipment and encryption materials or the use thereof solely to facilitate navigation, identification or communication in support of medical transportation, as defined in Article 8.
6. It is the understanding of the Government of the French Republic that the risk of damage to the natural environment arising from the employment of methods or means of warfare as expressed in the provisions of paragraphs 2 and 3 of article 35 and those of article 55 is to be assessed objectively on the basis of the information available at the time under consideration.

[16] Notification by the depositary addressed to the ICRC on 12 March 1984; *UNTS*, Vol. 1125, 1979, pp. 429–430.

7. In view of the provisions of article 43, paragraph 3 of the Protocol concerning armed services charged with maintaining order, the Government of the French Republic notifies the States parties to the Protocol that its armed forces include permanently the national Gendarmerie ("Gendarmerie nationale").
8. The Government of the French Republic considers that the situation mentioned in the second phrase of paragraph 3 of article 44 can exist only if a territory is occupied or in case of an armed conflict in the sense of paragraph 4 of Article 1. The term "deployment" used in paragraph 3 (b) of the same Article means any movement toward a place from which an attack is susceptible to be launched.
9. It is the understanding of the Government of the French Republic that the rule contained in the second phrase of paragraph 1 of Article 50 cannot be interpreted as obligating the commander to take a decision, which, according to the circumstances and information available, would not be compatible with his duty to ensure the security of troops under his responsibility or to maintain its military situation in conformity with the other provisions of the Protocol.
10. It is the understanding of the Government of the French Republic that the expression "military advantage" contained in paragraphs 5 (b) of Article 51, 2 of Article 52 and 2 (a) (iii) of Article 57, is intended to refer to the advantage anticipated from the attack considered as a whole and not from isolated or particular parts of the attack.
11. The Government of the French Republic declares that it will apply the provisions of paragraph 8 of Article 51 insofar as their interpretation does not constitute an obstacle to the use, according to international law, of the means which it considers indispensable for the protection of its civilian population against grave, clear and deliberate violations of the Geneva Conventions and of the Protocol by the enemy.
12. It is the understanding of the Government of the French Republic that a specified area of land may be considered as a military objective if, because of its location or other reasons specified in Article 52, its total or partial destruction, its capture or neutralization in the circumstances governing at the time offers a definite military advantage. In addition, it is the understanding of the French Government that the first sentence of paragraph 2 of the Article 52 is not intended to deal with the question of collateral damage resulting from an attack directed against military objectives.
13. The Government of the French Republic declares that if the objects protected by Article 53 are used for military purposes, they will lose the protection which they would otherwise have according to the provisions of the Protocol.
14. It is the understanding of the Government of the French Republic that paragraph 2 of Article 54 does not prohibit attacks that are carried out for a specific purpose, with the exception of those which aim at depriving the civilian population of objects indispensable to its survival and those which are directed against objects which, even if used by the adverse Party do not serve solely for the sustenance of the members of its armed forces.
15. The Government of the French Republic cannot guarantee an absolute protection to the works and installations containing dangerous forces which may contribute to the opposing Party's war effort, or to the defenders of such installations, but will take all due precautions referred to in the provisions of Article 56, of Article 57, paragraph 2 (a) (iii) and of paragraph 3 (c) of Article 85 in order to avoid severe collateral losses among the civilian populations, including possible direct attacks.
16. It is the understanding of the Government of French Republic that the duty to cancel or suspend an attack according to the provisions of paragraph 2 (b) of Article 57 requires only the application of normal proceedings for cancellation or suspension of this attack on the basis of information available to those deciding on an attack.
17. It is the understanding of the Government of the French Republic that Article 70 concerning relief actions has no implication on the rules existing in the field of naval warfare concerning maritime blockade, submarine warfare and mine warfare.
18. The Government of the French Republic does not consider itself bound by a declaration made in application of paragraph 3 of Article 96 unless it has expressly recognized that such declaration was made by an authority truly representing the people engaged in a conflict as defined in paragraph 4 of Article 1.

GERMANY, FEDERAL REPUBLIC OF

Declaration made on signature[17]

The Federal Republic of Germany signs the Protocols in the conviction that this will serve a noble humanitarian aim to which it has always felt strongly committed.

In view of the not always clear wording of the first Additional Protocol it is, however, necessary to consider carefully whether and to what extend this Protocol impairs the right of individual or collective self-defense under Article 51 of the Charter of the United Nations. The Government of the Federal Republic of Germany must therefore reserve the right to make additional statements on the occasion of a subsequent ratification on order to define and make clear the commitments of the Federal Republic of Germany under International Law.

Declarations made at the time of ratification[18]

1. It is the understanding of the Federal Republic of Germany that the rules relating to the use of weapons introduced by Additional Protocol I were intended to apply exclusively to conventional weapons without prejudice to any other rules of international law applicable to other types of weapons.
2. The Federal Republic of Germany understands the word "feasible" in Articles 41, 56, 57, 58, 78 and 86 of Additional Protocol I to mean that which is practicable or practically possible, taking into account all circumstances ruling at the time including humanitarian and military considerations.
3. The criteria contained in the second sentence of Article 44, paragraph 3, of Additional Protocol I for distinction between combatants and the civilian population are understood by the Federal Republic of Germany to apply only in occupied territories and in the other armed conflicts described in Article 1, paragraph 4. The term "military deployment" is interpreted to mean any movements towards the place from which an attack is to be launched.
4. It is the understanding of the Federal Republic of Germany that in the application of the provisions of Part IV, Section I, of Additional Protocol I, to military commanders and others responsible for planning, deciding upon or executing attacks, the decision taken by the person responsible has to be judged on the basis of all information available to him at the relevant time, and not on the basis of hindsight.
5. In applying the rule of proportionality in Article 51 and Article 57, "military advantage" is understood to refer to the advantage anticipated from the attack considered as a whole and not only from isolated or particular parts of the attack.
6. The Federal Republic of Germany will react against serious and systematic violations of the obligations imposed by Additional Protocol I and in particular its Articles 51 and 52 with all means admissible under international law in order to prevent any further violation.
7. Article 52 of Additional Protocol I is understood by the Federal Republic of Germany to mean that a specific area of land may also be a military objective if it meets all requirements of Article 52, paragraph 2.
8. Article 75, paragraph 4, subparagraph (e) of Additional Protocol I and Article 6, paragraph 2, subparagraph (e) of Additional Protocol II will be applied in such manner that it is for the court to decide whether an accused person held in custody must appear in person at the hearing before the court of review.

   Article 75, paragraph 4, subparagraph (h) of Additional Protocol I will only be applied to the extent that it is in conformity with legal provisions which permit under special circumstances the re-opening of proceedings that had led to final conviction or acquittal.
9. [Declaration of recognition according to Article 90, paragraph 2 of Additional Protocol I.]

[17] *UNTS*, Vol. 1125, 1979, pp. 429–430.

[18] Notification by the depositary addressed to the ICRC on 15 February 1991 (translation provided by Germany upon ratification).

10. The Federal Republic of Germany understands paragraph 3 of Article 96 of Additional Protocol I to mean that only those declarations described in subparagraphs (a) and (c) of paragraph 3 of Article 96 that are issued by an authority which genuinely satisfies all the criteria contained in paragraph 4 of Article 1 can have legally binding effect.

GREECE (*declaration made on signature*)[19]
The Hellenic Government hereby states that it reserves the right to formulate reservations, in accordance with constitutional provisions, upon deposit of the instrument of ratification.

HOLY SEE (*declaration made on ratification*)[20]
By ratifying the two Protocols additional to the Geneva Conventions of 12 August 1949, relating to the Protection of Victims of International (Protocol I) and Non-International (Protocol II) Armed Conflicts and adopted in Geneva on 8 June 1977, the *Holy See* wishes, first of all, to acknowledge the merits and the positive results obtained by the "Diplomatic Conference on the Reaffirmation and Development of International Humanitarian Law, Applicable in Armed Conflicts", in which it played an active part.

The Holy See believes that, from an overall historical and legal point of view, the two Protocols represent and confirm a significant advance in humanitarian law applicable in armed conflicts, an advance that deserves approval and support.

At the same time, with regard to the provisions of the above-mentioned legal texts, the Holy See wishes to remind the Secretariat of the Conference of the considerations that were made known by its delegation at the end of the session. It is a source of great pleasure to recognize the value of provisions which, in certain sectors, increase the scope of humanitarian law, as for example: the protection of the civilian population, especially of women and children; the protection afforded to cultural objects and places of worship which are evidence and signs of the spiritual heritage of nations; the protection of objects indispensable to the survival of the civilian population; the respect and protection of medical and religious personnel; the ban on retaliation.

On the other hand, in the opinion of the Holy See, other provisions are less satisfactory in substance or are not very well formulated. Furthermore, uncertainties and omissions were found on important issues in relation to the development of humanitarian standards. With regard to Protocol II in particular, the Holy See regrets that, after having been stripped of a large part of its humanitarian substance by the plenary Assembly of the Conference, the Protocol has become the instrument of a rigorous legal system both in its text and in its spirit. Although the Holy See signed the Protocol, with serious reservations, and although it is now ratifying it, it is mainly because it looks upon the Protocol as an open door to future developments of humanitarian law in a crucial and, until now, much neglected sector.

The Holy See also announces that it has taken note of the reservations and declarations formulated by some State that have deposited an instrument of ratification or of adhesion to the Protocols.

Finally, the Holy See reasserts, on this occasion, its strong conviction as to the fundamentally inhumane nature of war. The humanization of the effects of armed conflicts, such as that undertaken by the two Protocols, is received with favour and encouraged by the Holy See in so far as it aims to alleviate human suffering and strives, amid unbridled passions and evil forces, to safeguard the basic principles of humanity and the supreme benefits of civilization. The Holy See expresses, moreover, its firm belief that the ultimate goal, that which is worthy of the calling of man and of human civilization, is the abolition of war. One cannot help thinking that the measures embodied in the Geneva Conventions and more recently by the two Additional Protocols – measures which are already in themselves frail instruments for the protection of vic-

[19] *UNTS*, vol. 1125, 1979, p. 430.
[20] Notification by the depositary addressed to the ICRC on 22 November 1985.

tims of conventional armed conflicts – would prove to be not only insufficient but totally inadequate in the face of the ruinous devastation of a nuclear war.

The Holy See, considering itself the spokesman for the fears and the hopes of nations, hopes that the encouraging start made in Geneva by the codification of humanitarian law in armed conflicts may not go unheeded or remain a purely formal commitment but that people may become aware of it, put it into practice and follow it to its final conclusion: the abolition of war, of any kind whatever.

ICELAND

Reservation made on ratification[21]

The President of Iceland proclaims:

That I have seen and examined Additional Protocols I and II to the Geneva Conventions of 12 August 1949 which were opened for signature at Berne on 12 December 1977 and hereby declare that Iceland through this document ratifies the aforementioned Protocols, subject to a reservation with respect to Article 75, paragraph 4 (h), of Protocol I regarding the resumption of cases which have already been tried, the Icelandic law of procedure containing detailed provisions on this matter.

IRELAND (*declarations and reservations made on ratification*)

Declarations and reservations in relation to Additional Protocol I

1. Ireland, in ratifying Protocol I Additional to the Geneva Conventions of 1949 adopted at Geneva on 8 June 1977, declares its belief that the provisions of this Protocol represent the minimum level of legal and actual protection bound to be afforded to persons and civilian and cultural objects in armed conflicts.
2. *Article 11*
   For the purposes of investigating any breach of the Geneva Conventions of 1949 or of the Protocols Additional to the Geneva Conventions of 1949 adopted at Geneva on 8 June 1977, Ireland reserves the right to take samples of blood, tissue, saliva or other bodily fluids for DNA comparisons from a person who is detained, interned or otherwise deprived of liberty as a result of a situation referred to in Article 1, in accordance with Irish law and normal Irish medical practice, standards and ethics.
3. *Article 11 paragraph 2(c)*
   Ireland declares that nothing in Article 11 paragraph 2(c) shall prohibit the donation of tissue, bone marrow or of an organ from a person who is detained, interned or otherwise deprived of liberty as a result of a situation referred to in Article 2 to a close relative who requires a donation of tissue, bone marrow or an organ from such a person for medical reasons, so long as the removal of tissue, bone marrow or organs for transplantation is in accordance with Irish law and the operation is carried out in accordance with normal Irish medical practice, standards and ethics.
4 *Article 28 paragraph 2*
   Given the practical need to make use of non-dedicated aircraft for medical evacuation purposes, Ireland does not interpret this paragraph as precluding the presence on board of communication equipment and encryption materials or the use thereof solely to facilitate navigation, identification or communication in support of medical transportation as defined in Article 8 (f).
5. *Article 35*
   Ireland accepts, as stated in Article 35 paragraph 1, that the right of Parties to the conflict to choose methods or means of warfare is not unlimited. In view of the potentially destructive effect of nuclear weapons, Ireland declares that nuclear weapons, even if not directly governed by Additional Protocol I, remain subject to existing rules of international law as confirmed in 1996 by the International Court of Justice in its Advisory Opinion on the Legality of the Threat or Use of Nuclear Weapons.

[21] Notification by the depositary addressed to the ICRC on 15 April 1987.

6. *Articles 41, 56, 57, 58, 78 and 86*
   It is the understanding of Ireland that in relation to Article 41, 56, 57, 58, 78 and 86 the word "feasible" means that which is practicable or practically possible, taking into account all circumstances at the time, including humanitarian and military considerations.
7. *Article 44*
   It is the understanding of Ireland that:
   (a) The situation described in the second sentence of paragraph 3 of Article 44 can exist only in occupied territory or in armed conflicts covered by paragraph 4 of Article 1, and
   (b) The word "deployment" in paragraph 3 of Article 44 includes any movement towards a place from which an attack is to be launched.
8. *Article 47*
   It is the understanding of Ireland that Article 47 in no way prejudices the application of Articles 45(3) and 75 of Protocol I to mercenaries as defined in this Article.
9. *Articles 51 to 58*
   In relation to Articles 51 to 58 inclusive, it is the understanding of Ireland that military commanders and others responsible for planning, deciding upon, or executing attacks necessarily have to reach decisions on the basis of their assessment of the information from all sources which is reasonably available to them at the relevant time.
10. *Article 53*
    It is the understanding of Ireland in relation to the protection of cultural objects in Article 53 that if the objects protected by this Article are unlawfully used for military purposes they will thereby lose protection from attacks directed against such unlawful military use.
11. *Article 55*
    In ensuring that care shall be taken in warfare to protect the natural environment against widespread, long-term and severe damage and taking account of the prohibition of the use of methods or means of warfare which are intended or may be expected to cause such damage to the natural environment thereby prejudicing the health or survival of the population, Ireland declares that nuclear weapons, even if not directly governed by Additional Protocol I, remain subject to existing rules of international law as confirmed in 1996 by the International Court of Justice in its Advisory Opinion on the Legality of the Threat or Use of Nuclear Weapons. Ireland will interpret and apply this Article in a way which leads to the best possible protection for the civilian population.
12. *Article 62*
    It is the understanding of Ireland that nothing in Article 62 will prevent Ireland from using assigned civil defence personnel or volunteer civil defence workers in Ireland in accordance with nationally established priorities regardless of the military situation.
13. *Article 75 paragraph 4(e)*
    Article 75 will be applied in Ireland insofar as paragraph 4(e) is not incompatible with the power enabling a judge, in exceptional circumstances, to order the removal of an accused from the court who causes a disturbance at the trial.
14. *Article 90*
    Ireland declares that it recognises ipso facto and without special agreement, in relation to any other High Contracting Party accepting the same obligation, the competence of the International Fact-Finding Commission to enquire into allegations by such other Party, as authorised by Article 90 of Protocol I Additional to the Geneva Conventions of 1949. The exercise by the Commission of powers and functions in Ireland shall be in accordance with Irish law.
15. *Article 96 paragraph 3*
    It is the understanding of Ireland that the making of a unilateral declaration does not in itself, validate the credentials of the persons making such a declaration and

that States are entitled to satisfy themselves as to whether in fact the makers of such a declaration, constitute an authority referred to in Article 96. In this respect, the fact that such authority has or has not been recognised as such by the UN or an appropriate regional intergovernmental organisation is relevant.

Additional Protocol II

1. Ireland, in ratifying Protocol II Additional to the Geneva Conventions of 1949 adopted at Geneva on 8 June 1977, declares its belief that the provisions of this Protocol represent the minimum level of legal and actual protection bound to be afforded to persons and civilian and cultural objects in armed conflicts.
2. *Article 6 paragraph 2(e)*
   Article 6 will be applied in Ireland insofar as paragraph 2(e) is not incompatible with the power enabling a judge, in exceptional circumstances, to order the removal of an accused from the court who causes a disturbance at the trial."

ISRAEL[22] (*communications made in relation to the declarations made in the instruments of accession by Oman, Syria, United Arab Emirates and Qatar*)

Sultanate of Oman (Note of 2 August 1984)[23]

The Government of Israel has taken note that an Instrument of Adhesion to the Additional Protocols (I and 11) to the Geneva Conventions of 12 August 1949 adopted on 8 June 1977, was received from the Sultanate of Oman and placed with the Government of Switzerland on 29 March 1984.

The Instrument deposited by the Sultanate of Oman includes a hostile declaration of a political character regarding Israel. In the view of the Government of Israel the Geneva Conventions and the Protocols are not the appropriate channel for making political pronouncements, which are, moreover, in flagrant contradiction to the principles, objects and purposes of the Conventions and the Protocols. The statement by the Sultanate of Oman cannot in any way affect whatever obligations are binding upon it under general international law or under particular conventions. In so far as the substance of the matter is concerned, the Government of Israel will adopt towards the Sultanate of Oman an attitude of complete reciprocity.

Arab Republic of Syria (Note of 14 January 1984)[24]

The Government of Israel takes note that an instrument of adhesion to the Additional Protocol (I) to the Geneva Conventions of 12 August 1949, adopted on 8 June 1977, was received from the Government of the Arab Republic of Syria and placed with the Government of Switzerland on 14 November 1983.

The instrument deposited by the Government of the Arab Republic of Syria contains a hostile statement of a political character in respect of Israel. In the view of the Government of Israel the Geneva Conventions and the Protocols are not the proper place for making such hostile political pronouncements, which are, moreover, in flagrant contradiction to the principles, objects and purposes of the Conventions and the Protocols. This statement by the Government of the Arab Republic of Syria cannot in any way affect whatever obligations are binding upon the Arab Republic of Syria under general international law or under particular conventions. The Government of the State of Israel will, in so far as concerns the substance of the matter, adopt towards the Government of the Arab Republic of Syria an attitude of complete reciprocity.

United Arab Emirates (Note of 14 June 1983)[25]

The Government of Israel takes note that an instrument of adhesion to the Additional Protocols (I and II) to the Geneva Conventions of 12 August 1949, adopted on 8 June 1977, was received from the Government of the United Arab Emirates and placed with the Government of Switzerland on 9 March 1983.

[22] State not party to the Protocols.
[23] Notification by the depositary addressed to the ICRC on 27 September 1984.
[24] Notification by the depositary addressed to the ICRC on 20 January 1984.
[25] Notification by the depositary addressed to the ICRC on 21 October 1983.

The instrument deposited by the Government of the United Arab Emirates contains a statement of a political character in respect of Israel. In the view of the Government of the State of Israel, the Geneva Conventions and the Protocols are not the proper place for making such political pronouncements, which are moreover, in flagrant contradiction to the principles, objects and purposes of the Conventions and the Protocols. This statement by the Government of the United Arab Emirates cannot in any way affect whatever obligations are binding upon the United Arab Emirates under general international law or under particular conventions. The Government of the State of Israel will, in so far as concerns the substance of the matter, adopt towards the Government of the United Arab Emirates an attitude of complete reciprocity.

Qatar (Note of 10 March 1992)[26]
In the view of the Government of the State of Israel such declaration, which is explicitly of a political character, is incompatible with the purposes and objectives of this Convention and cannot in any way affect whatever obligations are binding upon Qatar under general international law or under particular Conventions.

The Government of the State of Israel will, in so far as concerns the substance of the matter, adopt towards Qatar an attitude of complete reciprocity.

It is respectfully requested that the Embassy of Switzerland as the depositary to the said Protocol notify the text of this Note to all states signatory and/or party to the Geneva Conventions of 12 August 1949 for the Protection of War victims."

ITALY
Declaration made on signature[27]
On signing the Protocols with a reservation with regard to ratification, the Plenipotentiary of Italy declares that, owing to the different interpretations to which the wording of some of the provisions lends itself, Italy may take advantage, when depositing the instruments of ratification, of the faculty in Article 19 of the Vienna Convention on the Law of Treaties of 23 May 1969 on the basis of general principles of international law.

Declarations made on ratification[28]
It is the understanding of the Government of Italy that the rules relating to the use of weapons introduced by Additional Protocol I were intended to apply exclusively to conventional weapons. They do not prejudice any other rule of international law applicable to other types of weapons.

The Italian Government understands, in relation to Articles 41, 56, 57, 58, 78 and 86 that the word "feasible" is to be understood as practicable or practically possible taking into account all circumstances ruling at the time, including humanitarian and military considerations.

The situation described in the second sentence of paragraph 3 of Article 44 can exist only in occupied territory.

The word "deployment" in paragraph 3 (b) means any movement towards a place from which an attack is to be launched.

In relation to Articles 51 to 58 inclusive, the Italian Government understands that military commanders and other responsible for planning, deciding upon or executing attacks necessarily have to reach decisions on the basis of their assessment of the information from all sources which is available to them at the relevant time.

In relation to paragraph 5 (b) of Article 51 and paragraph 2(a) (iii) of Article 57, the Italian Government understands that the military advantage anticipated from an attack is intended to refer to the advantage anticipated from the attack considered as a whole and not only from isolated or particular parts of the attack.

---

26 Notification by the depositary addressed to the ICRC on 7 July 1992.
27 *UNTS*, Vol. 1125, 1979, p. 430.
28 Notification by the depositary addressed to the ICRC on 27 February 1986.

A specific area of land may be a "military objective" if, because of its location or other reasons specified in Article 52, its total or partial destruction, capture or neutralisation, in the circumstances ruling at the time, offers definite military advantage.

The first sentence of paragraph 2 of the Article prohibits only such attacks as may be directed against non-military objectives. Such a sentence does not deal with the question of collateral damage caused by attacks directed against military objectives.

If and so long as the objectives protected by Article 53 are unlawfully used for military purposes, they will thereby lose protection.

The Government of Italy declares that it recognizes *ipso facto* and without special agreement, in relation to any other High Contracting Party accepting the same obligation, the competence of the Commission to enquire, as authorised by Article 90, into allegations by such other Party that it has been the victim of violations or has otherwise suffered as a consequence of breaches of the Conventions or the Protocol by Italy.

Italy will react to serious and systematic violations by an enemy of the obligations imposed by Additional Protocol I and in particular its Articles 51 and 52 with all means admissible under international law in order to prevent any further violation."

KOREA, REPUBLIC OF (*declaration made on the ratification of Protocol I*)[29]

1. In relation to Article 44 of Protocol I, the "situation" described in the second sentence of paragraph 3 of the Article can exist only in occupied territory or in armed conflicts covered by paragraph 4 of Article 1, and the Government of the Republic of Korea will interpret the word "deployment" in paragraph 3 (b) of the Article as meaning "any movement towards a place from which an attack is to be launched";
2. in relation to paragraph 4 (b) of Article 85 of Protocol I, a party detaining prisoners of war may not repatriate its prisoners agreeably to their openly and freely expressed will, which shall not be regarded as unjustifiable delay in the repatriation of prisoners of war constituting a grave breach of this Protocol;
3. in relation to Article 91 of Protocol 1, a party to the conflict which violates the provisions of the Conventions or of this Protocol shall take the responsibility for paying compensation to the party damaged from the acts of violation, whether the damaged party is a legal party to the conflict or not; and
4. in relation to paragraph 3 of Article 96 of Protocol I, only a declaration made by an authority which genuinely fulfills the criteria of paragraph 4 of Article I can have the effects stated in paragraph 3 of Article 96, and it is also necessary that the authority concerned be recognized as such by the appropriate regional intergovernmental organization."

LIECHTENSTEIN

Reservations made at the time of ratification[30]

Reservation concerning Article 75 of Protocol I

Article 75 of Protocol I will be implemented provided that

(a) paragraph 4(e) is not incompatible with legislation under which any accused who causes a disturbance in court or whose presence could impede the questioning of another accused, a witness or expert may be excluded from the courtroom;
(b) paragraph 4(h) is not incompatible with legislation providing for the reopening of a trial which has already led to a person's conviction or acquittal;
(c) paragraph 4(i) is not incompatible with legislation relating to the public nature of hearings and of the pronouncement of judgement.

Reservation concerning Article 6 of Protocol II

Article 6, paragraph 2(e), of Protocol II will be implemented provided that it is not incompatible with legislation under which any accused who causes a disturbance in court or whose presence could impede the questioning of another accused or of a witness or expert may be excluded from the court room.

[29] Notification by the depositary addressed to the ICRC on 18 January 1982.

[30] Notification by the depositary addressed to the ICRC on 11 August 1989.

MACEDONIA
The former Yugoslav Republic of Macedonia decided on 18 October 1996 to succeed to the reservations and declarations made by the Former Republic of Yugoslavia.
Declaration made at the time of ratification[31]
The Socialist Federal Republic of Yugoslavia states hereby that the provisions of the Protocol Additional to the Geneva Conventions of 12 August 1949, and relating to the Protection of Victims of International Armed Conflicts (Protocol I) relating to occupation, shall be applied in keeping with Article 238 of the Constitution of the Socialist Federal Republic of Yugoslavia according to which no one shall have the right to acknowledge or sign an act of capitulation, nor to accept or recognize the occupation of the Socialist Federal Republic of Yugoslavia or any of its individual parts.

MALTA (*reservation made at the time of accession*)[32]
(1) Article 75 of Protocol I will be applied insofar as:
  (a) sub-paragraph (e) of paragraph 4 is not incompatible with legislation providing that any defendant, who causes a disturbance at the trial or whose presence is likely to impede the questioning of another defendant or the hearing or another witness or expert witness, may be removed from the courtroom;
  (b) sub-paragraph (h) of paragraph 4 is not incompatible with legal provisions authorizing the reopening of proceedings that have resulted in a final declaration of conviction or acquittal.
(2) Article 6, paragraph 2, sub-paragraph (e) of Protocol II will be applied insofar as it is not incompatible with legislation providing that any defendant, who causes a disturbance at the trial or whose presence is likely to impede the questioning of another defendant or the hearing of a witness or expert witness, may be removed from the courtroom.

MONGOLIA
Reservation made on ratification
In regard of Article 88, paragraph 2 of "the Additional Protocol on the Protection of Victims in the International Armed Conflicts ('Protocol I') which states "The High Contracting Parties shall co-operate in the matter of extradition", the Mongolian law which prohibits deprivation and extradition of its citizens from Mongolia shall be respected.

Declaration made on ratification
By a note verbale addressed on 26 February 1996 to the depositary, the government of Mongolia added the following clarification: The expression "deprivation" means "deprivation of one's rights as a citizen of Mongolia".

Pursuant to their provisions, the Protocols will come into force for Mongolia on 6 June 1996.

NETHERLANDS (*declarations made on ratification*)[33]
On the occasion of the deposit today by the Kingdom of the Netherlands (for the Kingdom in Europe, the Netherlands Antilles and Aruba) of the instrument of ratification of the
- Protocol Additional to the Geneva Conventions of 12 August 1949, and relating to the protection of victims of international armed conflicts (Protocol 1), and the
- Protocol Additional to the Geneva Conventions of 12 August 1949, and relating to the protection of victims of non-international armed conflicts (Protocol II),

both adopted in Berne on 12 December 1977,

I have the honour to declare on behalf of my Government the following:

[31] See [Yugoslavia, Socialist Federal Republic of], p. 820.
[32] Notification by the depositary addressed to the ICRC on 19 April 1989.
[33] Notification by the depositary addressed to the ICRC on 10 July 1987.

1. *With regard to Protocol I as a whole*
   It is the understanding of the Government of the Kingdom of the Netherlands that the rules introduced by Protocol I relating to the use of weapons were intended to apply and consequently do apply solely to conventional weapons, without prejudice to any other rules of international law applicable to other types of weapons;
2. *With regard to Article 41, paragraph 3, Article 56, paragraph 2, Article 57, paragraph 2, Article 58, Article 78, paragraph 1, and Article 86, paragraph 2 of Protocol I*
   It is the understanding of the Government of the Kingdom of the Netherlands that the word "feasible" means that which is practicable or practically possible, taking into account all circumstances ruling at the time, including humanitarian and military considerations;
3. *With regard to Article 44, paragraph 3 of Protocol 1*
   It is the understanding of the Government of the Kingdom of the Netherlands that the words "engaged in a military deployment" mean "any movement towards a place from which an attack may be launched";
4. *With regard to Article 47 of Protocol 1*
   It is the understanding of the Government of the Kingdom of the Netherlands that Article 47 in no way prejudices the application of Articles 45 and 75 of Protocol I to mercenaries as defined in this Article;
5. *With regard to Article 51, paragraph 5 and Article 57, paragraphs 2 and 3 of Protocol 1:*
   It is the understanding of the Government of the Kingdom of the Netherlands that military advantage refers to the advantage anticipated from the attack considered as a whole and not only from isolated or particular parts of the attack;
6. *With regard to Articles 51 to 58 inclusive of Protocol I*:
   It is the understanding of the Government of the Kingdom of the Netherlands that military commanders and others responsible for planning, deciding upon or executing attacks necessarily have to reach decisions on the basis of their assessment of the information from all sources which is available to them at the relevant time;
7. *With regard to Article 52, paragraph 2 of Protocol I*
   It is the understanding of the Government of the Kingdom of the Netherlands that a specific area of land may also be a military objective if, because of its location or other reasons specified in paragraph 2, its total or partial destruction, capture, or neutralization in the circumstances ruling at the time, offers a definite military advantage;
8. *With regard to Article 53 of Protocol I*
   It is the understanding of the Government of the Kingdom of the Netherlands that if and for so long as the objects and places protected by this Article, in violation of paragraph (b), are used in support of the military effort they will thereby lose such protection;

NEW ZEALAND (*declarations made at the time of ratification*)[34]
[The Government of New Zealand] *declares* that this ratification shall not extend to the Cook Islands, Niue and Tokelau; *and further declares* as follows:
1. It is the understanding of the Government of New Zealand that in relation to Article 44 of Protocol I, the situation described in the second sentence of paragraph 3 (b) of the Article as meaning any movement towards a place from which an attack is to be launched. It will interpret the words "visible to the adversary" in the same paragraph as including visible with the aid of any form of surveillance, electronic or otherwise, available to help keep a member of the armed forces of the adversary under observation.
2. In relation to Articles 51 to 58 inclusive, it is the understanding of the Government of New Zealand that military commanders and others responsible for planning, deciding upon, or executing attacks necessarily have to reach decisions on the basis of their assessment of the information from all sources which is reasonably available to them at the relevant time.

[34] Notification by the depositary addressed to the ICRC on 12 February 1988.

3. In relation to paragraph 5(b) of Article 51 and to paragraph 2(a)(iii) of Article 57, the Government of New Zealand understands that the military advantage anticipated from an attack is intended to refer to the advantage anticipated from the attack considered as a whole and not only from isolated or particular parts of that attack and that the term 'military advantage' involves a variety of considerations, including the security of attacking forces. It is further the understanding of the Government of New Zealand that the term "concrete and direct military advantage anticipated", used in Articles 51 and 57, means a bona fide expectation that the attack will make a relevant and proportional contribution to the objective of the military attack involved.
4. In relation to Article 52, it is the understanding of the Government of New Zealand that a specific area of land may be a military objective if, because of its location or other reasons specified in the Article, its total or partial destruction, capture or neutralisation in the circumstances ruling at the time offers a definite military advantage. The Government of New Zealand further understands that the first sentence of paragraph 2 of the Article is not intended to, and nor does it deal with, the question of incidental or collateral damage resulting from an attack directed against a military objective.

OMAN (*declaration made on accession*)[35]
While deposing these instruments, the Government of the Sultanate of Oman declares that these accessions shall in no way amount to recognition of nor the establishment of any relations with Israel with respect to the application of the provisions of the said protocols."

PORTUGAL (*declaration made on signature*)[36]
The Portuguese Government will defer until ratification the formulation of any reservations it might possibly judge to be appropriate.

QATAR
Declaration made upon accession[37]
This accession shall in no way imply recognition of Israel by the State of Qatar nor agreement to establish any relations whatsoever with it.

Declaration made on 24 September 1991[38]
Pursuant to the United Nations General Assembly Resolution No.45/38 dated November 28th, 1990 and Article (90) of Additional Protocol I.

The State of Qatar declares before any other High Contracting party accepting the same commitment, that it recognizes *ipso facto* and without special agreement the competence of the International Fact-Finding Commission to consider the allegations of such other Party.

Yet the State of Qatar expressing reservations that this declaration is by no means construed as a recognition of Israel by the State of Qatar or as consenting to enter into dealings with Israel.

RUSSIAN FEDERATION
Note of the Ministry for Foreign Affairs of the Russian Federation[39]
The Russian Federation continues to exercise the rights and carry out the obligations resulting from the international agreements signed by the Union of Soviet Socialist

35 Notification by the depositary addressed to the ICRC on 29 March 1981. See also the declaration of Israel, p. 806.
36 *UNTS*, Vol. 1125, 1979, p. 431.
37 Notification by the depositary addressed to the ICRC on 12 April 1988.
38 Notification by the depositary addressed to the ICRC on 10 February 1992. See also the declaration of Israel, p. 807.
39 Note from the Permanent Mission of the Russian Federation in Geneva transmitted to the ICRC on 15 January 1992.

Republics. Accordingly the Government of the Russian Federation will carry out, instead of the Government of the USSR, functions of depositary of the corresponding multilateral treaties. In this connection the Ministry asks to consider the Russian Federation as the Party to all international agreements in force, instead of the USSR.

Declaration made at the time of ratification[40]
The Soviet Union's ratification of the Protocols additional to the Geneva Conventions for the protection of the victims of war constitutes an unusual event in the recent diplomatic history of our country.

It reflects the spirit of new political thinking and demonstrates the Soviet State's commitment to humanizing international affairs and strengthening the system of international law.

At the same time, it exemplifies the spirit of continuity between Russian and Soviet diplomacy, extending back to the 1860s, in seeking to ensure that the principles of humanism and mercy are respected even in the tragic circumstances of war.

The Additional Protocols, in whose drafting the Soviet Union played a universally recognized role, were among the first international instruments presented for ratification to the new Soviet Parliament.

It should be pointed out that the Supreme Soviet of the USSR chose to ratify the Protocols without any reservation whatsoever. At the same time, our State recognized the competence of the International Fact-Finding Commission in cases where international humanitarian law is violated.

We in the Soviet Union hope that the ratification of the Additional Protocols will be duly appreciated by all those involved in the noble cause of humanism and the endeavour to free mankind from the horrors of war.

SAUDI ARABIA (*reservation made at the time of accession*)[41]
We declare hereby the accession of the Kingdom of Saudi Arabia, with a reservation in respect of article 5 stipulating "Appointment of protecting powers and of their substitute".

SOUTH AFRICA[42] (*communication made on accession of the United Nations Council for Namibia to the Additional Protocols*)

Accession to the aforementioned Geneva Conventions and Protocols is governed by an identically worded article which stipulates that

"From the date of its coming into force, it shall be open to any Power in whose name the present Convention has not been signed, to accede to this Convention".

Since South West Africa/Namibia cannot, in terms of international law, be regarded as such a Power and since neither it nor the UN Council for Namibia is able to assume the obligations imposed upon such Power by the four Geneva Conventions, the South African Government rejects the so-called instruments of accession of the UN Council for Namibia to the four Geneva Conventions and its two Additional Protocols as having no legal effect.

SPAIN

Declaration made on signature
Spain reserves the right to make any statements and reservations it deems appropriate at, the time of ratification of these two Protocols, in accordance with recognized international practice.

---

[40] Additional Protocols of 8 June 1977 to the Geneva Conventions of 12 August 1949; Reservations, declarations and communications made at the time of or in reference to ratification or accession as at 30 June 1992, ICRC, 15 July 1992, pp. 36–37.

[41] Notification by the depositary addressed to the states parties to the Geneva Conventions of 1949 on 27 November 1987 (original Arabic; official translation submitted by the Government of the Kingdom of Saudi Arabia).

[42] Notification by the depositary addressed to the ICRC on 15 November 1983.

Interpretative declarations made at the time of ratification[43]
With reference to Protocol I in its entirety:

It is the understanding [of the Government of Spain] that this Protocol, within its specific scope applies exclusively to conventional weapons, and without prejudice to the rules of International Law governing other types of weapons.

Article 1, paragraph 4, and Article 96, paragraph 3
These articles shall be interpreted in accordance with the Principle contained in Article 2, paragraph 4 of the United Nations Charter, as developed and reaffirmed in the following texts:

1. Operative paragraph 6 of Resolution 1514 (XV) of the United Nations General Assembly, 14 December 1960.
2. The final paragraph relative to the principle of equal rights and self-determination of peoples, of the Declaration on Principles of International Law concerning Friendly Relations and Co-operation among States in accordance with the Charter of the United Nations, approved in Resolution 2625 (XXV) of the United Nations General Assembly on 24 October 1970.

Articles 41, 56, 57, 58, 78 and 86
It is the understanding [of the Government of Spain] that in Articles 41, 56, 57, 58, 78 and 86 the word “feasible” means that the matter to which reference is made is practicable or practically possible taking into account all circumstances at the time when the situation arises, including humanitarian and military considerations.

Article 44, paragraph 3
It is understood that the criteria mentioned in sub-paragraph b of Article 44(3) on the distinction between combatants and civilians can be applied only in occupied territories. The Spanish Government also interprets the expression ‘military deployment’ to mean any movement towards a place from which or against which an attack is going to be launched.

Articles 51–58
It is the understanding [of the Spanish Government] that the decision made by military commanders, or others with the legal capacity to plan or execute attacks which may have repercussions on civilians or civilian objects or similar objects, shall not necessarily be based on anything more than the relevant information available at the time and which it has been possible to obtain to that effect.

Articles 51, 52 and 57
It is the understanding [of the Spanish Government] that the ‘military advantage’ which these articles mention refers to the advantage expected from the attack as a whole and not from isolated parts of it.

Article 52, paragraph 2
It is the understanding [of the Spanish Government] that the capture or holding of a specific area of territory constitutes a military objective when all the conditions set out in this paragraph together offer a concrete military advantage taking into account the circumstances at the relevant time.

SWEDEN (*reservation made on ratification*)[44]
Protocol I
I hereby declare on behalf of the Government that Sweden ratifies the said Protocol and undertakes faithfully to perform and carry out all the stipulations therein contained, subject to the reservation that Article 75, Paragraph 4, sub-paragraph (h) shall be applied only to the extent that it is not in conflict with legal provisions which allow, in

[43] Notification by the depositary addressed to the ICRC on 24 November 1989.
[44] Notification by the depositary addressed to the ICRC on 31 August 1979; *UNTS*, Vol. 1151, 1979, p. 423.

exceptional circumstances, the reopening of proceedings which have resulted in a final. conviction or acquittal.

SWITZERLAND
Declaration made on signature[45]
Re Article 57 of Protocol I. The provisions in paragraph 2 of this article impose obligations only upon commanders at batallion or group levels and those of higher rank.
Re Article 58 of Protocol I. Considering that this article contains the expression "to the maximum extent feasible", paragraphs (a) and (b) will be applied subject to the defence requirements of the national territory.

Reservations and declaration made on ratification of Protocol I[46]
The instrument of ratification of Protocol I contains two reservations and a declaration by the Swiss Government:

1. *Reservation with respect to Article 57*
   The provisions of Article 57 (2) are binding only on battalion or group commanders and higher echelons. The determinant factor shall be the information available to such commanders at the time of reaching a decision.
2. *Reservation with respect to Article 58*
   As Article 58 contains the phrase "to the maximum extent feasible", paragraphs a and b will be applied subject to the exigencies dictated by the defence of the national territory.

SYRIA (*declaration made on accession to Protocol I*)[47]
The present accession does not in any way constitute recognition of Israel or the establishment relations with Israel in respect of the implementation of the provisions of the said Protocol.

UNION OF SOVIET SOCIALIST REPUBLICS *see Russian Federation*

UNITED ARAB EMIRATES (*declaration made on accession*)[48]
On accepting the said protocol, the Government of the United Arab Emirates takes the view that its acceptance of the said protocol does not, in any way, imply its recognition of Israel, nor does it oblige to apply the provisions of the protocol in respect of the said country.

The Government of the United Arab Emirates wishes further to indicate that its understanding described above in conformity with general practice existing in the United Arab Emirates regarding signature, ratification, accession or acceptance of international conventions, treaties or protocols, of which a country not recognized by the United Arab Emirates is a party.

UNITED KINGDOM OF GREAT BRITAIN AND NORTHERN IRELAND
Declaration made on signature[49]

1. On signing the Protocol Additional to the Geneva Conventions of 12 August 1949 and relating to the Protection of Victims of International Armed Conflicts (Protocol I), the Government of the United Kingdom of Great Britain and Northern Ireland declare that they have signed on the basis of the following understandings:
   (a) in relation to Article 1, that the term "armed conflict" of itself and in its context implies a certain level of intensity of military operations which must be present

[45] *UNTS*, Vol. 1125, 1979, p. 431
[46] Notification by the depositary addressed to the ICRC on 17 February 1982.
[47] Notification by the depositary addressed to the ICRC on 23 November 1983. See also the declaration of Israel, p. 806.
[48] Notification by the depositary addressed to the ICRC on 11 March 1983. See also the declaration of Israel, pp. 806-807.
[49] *UNTS*, Vol. 1125, 1979, 432-433, 699.

before the Conventions or the Protocol are to apply to any given situation, and that this level of intensity cannot be less than that required for the application of Protocol II, by virtue of Article 1 of that Protocol, to internal conflicts;

(b) in relation to Articles 41, 57 and 58, that the word "feasible" means that which is practicable or practically possible, taking into account all circumstances at the time including those relevant to the success of military operations;

(c) in relation to Article 44, that the situation described in the second sentence of paragraph 3 of the Article can exist only in occupied territory or in armed conflicts covered by paragraph 4 of Article 1, and that the Government of the United Kingdom will interpret the word "deployment" in paragraph 3(b) of Article 44 as meaning any movement towards a place from which an attack is to be launched;

(d) in relation to Articles 51 to 58 inclusive, that military commanders and others responsible for planning, deciding upon or executing attacks necessarily have to reach decisions on the basis of their assessment of the information from all sources which is available to them at the relevant time;

(e) in relation to paragraph 5(b) of Article 51 and paragraph (2)(a)(iii) of Article 57, that the military advantage anticipated from an attack is intended to refer to the advantage anticipated from the attack considered as a whole and not only from isolated or particular parts of the attack;

(f) in relation to Article 52, that a specific area of land may be a military objective if, because of its location or other reasons specified in the Article, its total or partial destruction, capture or neutralisation in the circumstances ruling at the time offers definite military advantage;

(g) in relation to Article 53, that if the objects protected by the Article are unlawfully used for military purposes they will thereby lose protection from attacks directed against such unlawful military uses;

(h) in relation to paragraph 3 of Article 96, that only a declaration made by an authority which genuinely fulfils the criteria of paragraph 4 of Article 1 can have the effects stated in paragraph 3 of Article 96, and that, in the light of the negotiating history, it is to be regarded as necessary also that the authority concerned be recognised as such by the appropriate regional intergovernmental organisation;

(i) that the new rules introduced by the Protocol are not intended to have any effect on and do not regulate or prohibit the use of nuclear weapons; and

(j) that the provisions of the Protocol shall not apply to Southern Rhodesia unless and until the Government of the United Kingdom inform the depositary that they are in a position to ensure that the obligations imposed by the Protocol in respect of that territory can be fully implemented.

2. On signing the Protocol Additional to the Geneva Conventions of 12 August 1949, and relating to the Protection of Victims of Non-international Armed Conflicts (Protocol II), the Government of the United Kingdom of Great Britain and Northern Ireland declare that they have signed on the understanding that the provisions of the Protocol shall not apply to Southern Rhodesia unless and until the Government of the United Kingdom inform the depositary that they are in a position to ensure that the obligations imposed by the Protocol in respect of that territory can be fully implemented.

Reservations and declarations made on ratification[50]

I also have the honour to lodge with the Government of the Swiss Federation, as the depository of Additional Protocol I the following statements in respect of the ratification by the United Kingdom of that Protocol:

(a) It continues to be the understanding of the United Kingdom that the rules introduced by the Protocol apply exclusively to conventional weapons without preju-

[50] Corrected Letter of 28 January 1998 sent to the Swiss Government by Christopher Hulse, HM Ambassador of the United Kingdom.

dice to any other rules of international law applicable to other types of weapons. In particular, the rules so introduced do not have any effect on and do not regulate or prohibit the use of nuclear weapons.

(b) The United Kingdom understands the term "feasible" as used in the Protocol to mean that which is practicable or practically possible, taking into account all circumstances ruling at the time, including humanitarian and military considerations.

(c) Military commanders and others responsible for planning, deciding upon, or executing attacks necessarily have to reach decisions on the basis of their assessment of the information from all sources which is reasonably available to them at the relevant time.

(d) *Re: Article 1, paragraph 4, and Article 96, paragraph 3*
It is the understanding of the United Kingdom that the term "armed conflict" of itself and in its context denotes a situation of a kind which is not constituted by the commission of ordinary crimes including acts of terrorism whether concerted or in isolation.

The United Kingdom will not, in relation to any situation in which it is itself involved, consider itself bound in consequence of any declaration purporting to be made under paragraph 3 of Article 96 unless the United Kingdom shall have expressly recognised that it has been made by a body which is genuinely an authority representing a people engaged in an armed conflict of the type to which Article 1, paragraph 4, applies.

(e) *Re: Article 28, paragraph 2*
Given the practical need to make use of non-dedicated aircraft for medical evacuation purposes, the United Kingdom does not interpret this paragraph as precluding the presence on board of communications equipment and encryption materials or the use thereof solely to facilitate navigation, identification or communication in support of medical transportation as defined in Article 8(f).

(f) *Re: Article 35, paragraph 3 and Article 55*
The United Kingdom understands both of these provisions to cover the employment of methods and means of warfare and that the risk of environmental damage falling within the scope of these provisions arising from such methods and means of warfare is to be assessed objectively on the basis of the information available at the time.

(g) *Re Article 44, paragraph 3*
It is the understanding of the United Kingdom that:
- the situation in the second sentence of paragraph 3 can only exist in occupied territory or in armed conflicts covered by paragraph 4 of Article 1;
- 'deployment' in paragraph 3(b) means any movement towards a place from which an attack is to be launched.

(h) *Re: Article 50*
In the view of the United Kingdom the rule in the second sentence of paragraph 1 applies only in cases of substantial doubt still remaining after the assessment referred to at paragraph (c) above has been made, and not as overriding a commander's duty to protect the safety of troops under his command or to preserve his military situation, in conformity with other provisions of the Protocol.

(i) *Re: Article 51 and Article 57*
In the view of the United Kingdom, the military advantage anticipated from an attack is intended to refer to the advantage anticipated from the attack considered as a whole and not only from isolated or particular parts of the attack.

(j) *Re: Article 52*
It is the understanding of the United Kingdom that:
- a specific area of land may be a military objective if, because of its location or other reasons specified in this Article, its total or partial destruction, capture or neutralisation in the circumstances ruling at the time offers definite military advantage;
- the first sentence of paragraph 2 prohibits only such attacks as may be directed against non-military objectives; it does not deal with the question of collateral damage resulting from attacks directed against military objectives.

(k) *Re: Article 53*

The United Kingdom declares that if the objects protected by this Article are unlawfully used for military purposes they will thereby lose protection from attacks directed against such unlawful military uses.

(l) *Re: Article 54, paragraph 2*

The United Kingdom understands that paragraph 2 has no application to attacks that are carried out for a specific purpose other than denying sustenance to the civilian population or the adverse party.

(m) *Re: Articles 51–55*

The obligations of Articles 51 and 55 are accepted on the basis that any adverse party against which the United Kingdom might be engaged will itself scrupulously observe those obligations. If an adverse party makes serious and deliberate attacks, in violation of Article 51 or Article 52 against the civilian population or civilians or against civilian objects, or, in violation of Articles 53, 54 and 55, on objects or items protected by those Articles, the United Kingdom will regard itself as entitled to take measures otherwise prohibited by the Articles in question to the extent that it considers such measures necessary for the sole purpose of compelling the adverse party to cease committing violations under those Articles, but only after formal warning to the adverse party requiring cessation of the violations has been disregarded and then only after a decision taken at the highest level of government. Any measures thus taken by the United Kingdom will not be disproportionate to the violations giving rise there to and will not involve any action prohibited by the Geneva Conventions of 1949 nor will such measures be continued after the violations have ceased. The United Kingdom will notify the Protecting Powers of any such formal warning given to an adverse party, and if that warning has been disregarded, of any measures taken as a result.

(n) *Re: Article 56 and 85, paragraph 3c*

The United Kingdom cannot undertake to grant absolute protection to installations which may contribute to the opposing Party's war effort, or to the defenders of such installations, but will take all due precautions in military operations at or near the installations referred to in paragraph 1 of Article 56 in the light of the known facts, including any special marking which the installation may carry, to avoid sever collateral losses among the civilian populations; direct attacks on such installations will be launched only on authorisation at a high level of command.

(o) *Re: Article 57, paragraph 2*

The United Kingdom understands that the obligation to comply with paragraph 2(b) only extends to those who have the authority and practical possibility to cancel or suspend the attack.

(p) *Re: Article 70*

It is the understanding of the United Kingdom that this Article does not affect the existing rules of naval warfare regarding naval blockade, submarine warfare or mine warfare.

UNITED STATES OF AMERICA

Declaration made on signature[51]

The Embassy of the United States of America presents its compliments to the Federal Political Department and has the honor to inform it that the two protocols to the Geneva Conventions of August 12, 1949 relating to the protection of victims of armed conflicts will be signed today on behalf of the United States. This signature is subject to the following understandings:

A) *Protocol I*

1. It is the understanding of the United States of America that the rules established by this protocol were not intended to have any effect on and do not regulate or prohibit the use of nuclear weapons.

[51] *UNTS*, Vol. 1125, 1979, p. 434, 699.

2. It is the understanding of the United States of America that the phrase "military deployment preceding the launching of an attack" in Article 44, Paragraph 3, means any movement towards a place from which an attack is to be launched.

B) *Protocol II*

It is the understanding of the United States of America that the terms used in Part III of this protocol which are the same as the terms defined in Article 8 of Protocol I shall so far as relevant be construed in the same sense as those definitions.

The Embassy has the honor to request that you circulate the text of this note to the states party to the Geneva Convention.

[YUGOSLAVIA, SOCIALIST FEDERAL REPUBLIC OF (*Declaration made on ratification)*[52]
The Socialist Federal Republic of Yugoslavia states hereby that the provisions of the Protocol Additional to the Geneva Conventions of 12 August 1949, and relating to the Protection of Victims of International Armed Conflicts (Protocol I) relating to occupation, shall be applied in keeping with Article 238 of the Constitution of the Socialist Federal Republic of Yugoslavia according to which no one shall have the right to acknowledge or sign an act of capitulation, nor to accept or recognize the occupation of the Socialist Federal Republic of Yugoslavia or of any of its individual parts.]

[52] Notification by the depositary addressed to the ICRC on 25 June 1979.

No. 58

RESOLUTIONS OF THE DIPLOMATIC CONFERENCE ON THE REAFFIRMATION AND DEVELOPMENT OF INTERNATIONAL HUMANITARIAN LAW APPLICABLE IN ARMED CONFLICTS, 1977

INTRODUCTORY NOTE: The resolutions reproduced below were adopted at the end of the fourth session either by a two-thirds majority or by consensus. The resolutions adopted at the first three sessions (Nos. 1–16) concern the internal organization of the Conference and are not reproduced.

AUTHENTIC TEXTS: Arabic, Chinese, English, French, Russian, Spanish. The text below is reprinted from the *Official Records of the Diplomatic Conference on the Reaffirmation and Development of International Humanitarian Law applicable in Armed Conflicts*, Geneva (1974–1977), Berne, 1978, Vol. I, pp. 199–218.

TEXT PUBLISHED IN: See indications under *No. 55*.

TABLE OF CONTENTS

* * *

RESOLUTION 17.

USE OF CERTAIN ELECTRONIC AND VISUAL MEANS OF IDENTIFICATION BY MEDICAL AIRCRAFT PROTECTED UNDER THE GENEVA CONVENTIONS OF 1949 AND UNDER THE PROTOCOL ADDITIONAL TO THE GENEVA CONVENTIONS OF 12 AUGUST 1949, AND RELATING TO THE PROTECTION OF VICTIMS OF INTERNATIONAL ARMED CONFLICTS (PROTOCOL I)

The Diplomatic Conference on the Reaffirmation and Development of International Humanitarian Law Applicable in Armed Conflicts, Geneva, 1974–1977,

Considering *that:*

(a) in order to avoid their engagement by combatant forces there is an urgent need for both electronic and visual identification of medical aircraft in flight,

(b) the Secondary Surveillance Radar (SSR) systems has the capability of providing unique identification of aircraft and of en route flight details,

(c) the International Civil Aviation Organization is the most appropriate international body to designate SSR modes and codes in the range of circumstances envisaged,

(d) this Conference has agreed to the use of a flashing blue light as a means of visual identification to be employed only by aircraft exclusively engaged in medical transport,[1]

Recognizing *that the designation in advance of an exclusive, world-wide SSR mode and code for the identification of medical aircraft may not be possible owing to the extensive deployment of the SSR system,*

1. Requests the President of the Conference to transmit to the International Civil Aviation Organization this document, together with the attached documents of this Conference, inviting that Organization to:
   (a) establish appropriate procedures for the designation, in case of an international armed conflict, of an exclusive SSR mode and code to be employed by medical aircraft concerned; and,
   (b) note the agreement of this Conference to recognize the flashing blue light as a means of identification of medical aircraft, and provide for that use in the appropriate International Civil Aviation Organization documents;

2. Urges the Governments invited to the present Conference to lend their full co-operation to this endeavour in the consultative processes of the International Civil Aviation Organization. Fifty-fourth plenary meeting 7 June 1977

Annex. Articles 6 and 8 of the Regulations contained in Annex I to Protocol I[2]

Article 6. Light signal

1. The light signal, consisting of a blue flashing light, is established for the use of medical aircraft to signal their identity. No other aircraft shall use this signal. The recommended blue colour is obtained by using, as trichromatic co-ordinates:

[1] See Annex to this resolution.

[2] See the revised version of the Regulations of 30 November 1993, pp. 762 ff.

green boundary y = 0.065 + 0.805x
white boundary y= 0.400 – x
purple boundary x= 0.133 + 0.600y

The recommended flashing rate of the blue light is between sixty and one hundred flashed per minute.

2. *Medical aircraft should be equipped with such lights as may be necessary to make the light signal visible in as many directions as possible.*
3. *In the absence of a special agreement between the Parties to the conflict reserving the use of flashing blue lights for the identification of medical vehicles and medical ships and craft, the use of such signals for other vehicles or ships is not prohibited.*

Article 8. Electronic identification

1. *The Secondary Surveillance Radar (SSR) system as specified in Annex 10 to the Chicago Convention on International Civil Aviation of 7 December 1944, as amended from time to time, may be used to identify and to follow the course of medical aircraft. The SSR mode and code to be reserved for the exclusive use of medical aircraft shall be established by the High Contracting Parties, the Parties to the conflict, or one of the Parties to a conflict, acting in agreement or alone, in accordance with procedures to be recommended by the International Civil Aviation Organization*
2. *Parties to a conflict may, by special agreement between them, establish for their use a similar electronic system for the identification of medical vehicles and medical ships and craft.*

RESOLUTION 18.

USE OF VISUAL SIGNALLING FOR IDENTIFICATION OF MEDICAL TRANSPORTS PROTECTED UNDER THE GENEVA CONVENTIONS OF 1949 AND UNDER THE PROTOCOL ADDITIONAL TO THE GENEVA CONVENTIONS OF 12 AUGUST 1949, AND RELATING TO THE PROTECTION OF VICTIMS OF INTERNATIONAL ARMED CONFLICTS (PROTOCOL I)

The Diplomatic Conference on the Reaffirmation and Development of International Humanitarian Law Applicable in Armed Conflicts, Geneva, 1974-1977,

Considering *that:*

(a) *in order to avoid attacks upon them there is a need for the improved visual identification of medical transports,*
(b) *this Conference has agreed to the use of a flashing blue light as a means of visual identification to be employed only by aircraft exclusively engaged in medical transport,*
(c) *by special agreement, Parties to a conflict may reserve the use of a flashing blue light for the identification of medical vehicles and medical ships and craft, but, in the absence of such agreement, the use of such signals for other vehicles or ships is not prohibited,*

(d) in addition to the distinctive emblem and the flashing blue light, other means of visual identification, such as signal flags and combinations of flares, may be used eventually to identify medical transports,

(e) the Inter-Governmental Maritime Consultative Organization is the most appropriate international body to designate and promulgate visual signals to be employed within the maritime environment,

Having noted *that, though the Geneva Conventions of 12 August 1949 recognize the use of the distinctive emblem to be flown by hospital ships and medical craft, this use is not reflected in relevant documents of the Inter-Governmental Maritime Consultative Organization,*

1. Requests *the President of the Conference to transmit to the Inter-Governmental Maritime Consultative Organization this resolution, together with the documents of this Conference, inviting that Organization to:*

(a) consider introduction into the appropriate documents, such as the International Code of Signals, the flashing blue light as described in Article 6 of Chapter III of the Regulations contained in Annex I to Protocol I;

(b) provide for recognition of the distinctive emblem in the appropriate documents (see Article 3 of Chapter II of the said Regulations);

(c) consider the establishment both of unique flag signals and of a flare combination, such as white-red-white, which might be used for additional or alternative visual identification of medical transports;

2. Urges *the Governments invited to this Conference to lend their full co-operation to this endeavour in the consultative processes of the Inter-Governmental Maritime Consultative Organization. Fifty-fourth plenary meeting 7 June 1977*

ANNEX. Articles 3, 6, 10 and 11 of the Regulations contained in Annex I to Protocol I [3]

Article 3. Shape and nature

1. The distinctive emblem (red on a white ground) shall be as large as appropriate under the circumstances. For the shapes of the cross, the crescent or the lion and sun, the High Contracting Parties may be guided by the models shown in Figure 2.

2. At night or when visibility is reduced, the distinctive emblem may be lighted or illuminated; it may also be made of materials rendering it recognizable by technical means of detection.

Fig. 2. Distinctive emblems in red on a white background.

[3] See the revised version of the Regulations of 30 November 1993, pp. 762 ff.

Article 6. Light signal

1. *The light signal, consisting of a blue flashing light, is established for the use of medical aircraft to signal their identity. No other aircraft shall use this signal. The recommended blue colour is obtained by using, as trichromatic co-ordinates:*

   green boundary $y = 0.065 + 0.805x$
   white boundary $y = 0.400 - x$
   purple boundary $x = 0.133 + 0.600y$

   The recommended flashing rate of the blue light is between sixty and one hundred flashed per minute.
2. *Medical aircraft should be equipped with such lights as may be necessary to make the light signal visible in as many directions as possible.*
3. *In the absence of a special agreement between the Parties to the conflict reserving the use of flashing blue lights for the identification of medical vehicles and medical ships and craft, the use of such signals for other vehicles or ships is not prohibited.*

Article 10. Use of international codes
Medical units and transports may also use the codes and signals laid down by the International Telecommunications Union, the International Civil Aviation Organization and the Inter-Governmental Maritime Consultative Organization. These codes and signals shall be used in accordance with the standards, practices and procedures established by these Organizations.

Article 11. Other means of communication
When two-way radiocommunication is not possible, the signals provided for in the International Code of Signals adopted by the Inter-Governmental Maritime Consultative Organization or in the appropriate Annex to the Chicago Convention on International Civil Aviation of 7 December 1944, as amended from time to time, may be used.

RESOLUTION 19.

USE OF RADIOCOMMUNICATIONS FOR ANNOUNCING AND IDENTIFYING MEDICAL TRANSPORTS PROTECTED UNDER THE GENEVA CONVENTIONS OF 1949 AND UNDER THE PROTOCOL ADDITIONAL TO THE GENEVA CONVENTIONS OF 12 AUGUST 1949, AND RELATING TO THE PROTECTION OF VICTIMS OF INTERNATIONAL ARMED CONFLICTS (PROTOCOL I)

The Diplomatic Conference on the Reaffirmation and Development of International Humanitarian Law Applicable in Armed Conflicts, Geneva, 1974–1977,

Considering *that:*

(a) *it is vital that distinctive and reliable communications be used for identifying, and announcing the movement of, medical transports,*
(b) *adequate and appropriate consideration will be given to communications related to the movement of a medical transport only if it is identified by an*

internationally recognized priority signal such as "Red Cross", "Humanity", "Mercy" or other technically and phonetically recognizable term,

(c) the wide range of circumstances under which a conflict may occur makes it impossible to select in advance suitable radio frequencies for communications,

(d) the radio frequencies to be employed for communicating information relative to the identification and movement of medical transports must be made known to all parties who may use medical transports,

Having noted*:*

(a) Recommendation No. 2 of the International Telecommunication Union (ITU) Plenipotentiary Conference, 1973, relating to the use of radiocommunications for announcing and identifying hospital ships and medical aircraft protected under the Geneva Conventions of 1949,

(b) Recommendation No. Mar2 – 17 of the International Telecommunication Union World Maritime Administrative Radio Conference, Geneva, 1974, relating to the use of radio-communications for marking, identifying, locating, and communicating with the means of transport protected under the Geneva Conventions of 12 August 1949, concerning the protection of war victims and any additional instruments of those conventions, as well as for ensuring the safety of ships and aircraft of States not Parties to an armed conflict;

(c) the memorandum by the International Frequency Registration Board (IFRB), a permanent organ of the International Telecommunication Union (ITU), relating to the need for national co-ordination on radiocommunication matters;

Recognizing *that:*

(a) the designation and use of frequencies, including the use of distress frequencies,

– operating procedures in the Mobile Service,

– the distress, alarm, urgency and safety signals, and

– the order of priority of communications in the Mobile service

are governed by the Radio Regulations annexed to the International Telecommunication Convention;

(b) these Regulations may be revised only by a competent ITU World Administrative Radio Conference;

(c) the next competent World Administrative Radio Conference is planned for 1979 and that written proposals for the revision of the Radio Regulations should be submitted by Governments about one year before the opening of the Conference,

1. Takes note with appreciation *that a specific item has been included on the agenda of the World Administrative Radio Conference, Geneva, 1979, which reads:*

> *"2.6 to study the technical aspects of the use of radiocommunications for marking, identifying, locating and communicating with the means of medical transport protected under the 1949 Geneva Conventions and any additional instruments of these Conventions";*

2. Requests *the President of the Conference to transmit this document to all Governments and organizations invited to the present Conference, together with the attachments representing the requirements, both for radio frequencies and for international recognition of an appropriate priority signal, which must be satisfied in the proceedings of a competent World Administrative Radio Conference;*

3. Urges *the Governments invited to the present Conference to make, as a matter of urgency, the appropriate preparations for the World Administrative Radio Conference to be held in 1979 so that the vital requirements of communications for protected medical transports in armed conflicts may be adequately provided for in the Radio Regulations.*

Fifty-fourth plenary meeting
7 June 1977

Annex. Articles 7, 8 and 9 of the Regulations contained in Annex I to Protocol I [4]

Article 7. Radio signal

1. *The radio signal shall consist of a radiotelephonic or radiotelegraphic message preceded by a distinctive priority signal to be designated and approved by a World Administrative Radio Conference of the International Telecommunications Union. It shall be transmitted three times before the call sign of the medical transport involved. The message shall be transmitted in English at appropriate intervals on a frequency or frequencies specified pursuant to paragraph 3. The use of the priority signal shall be restricted exclusively to medical units and transports.*
2. *The radio message preceded by the distinctive priority signal mentioned in paragraph 1 shall convey the following data:*
   (a) call sign of the medical transport;
   (b) position of the medical transport;
   (c) number and type of medical transports;
   (d) intended route;
   (e) estimated time en route and of departure and arrival, as appropriate;
   (f) any other information such as flight altitude, radio frequencies guarded, languages and secondary surveillance radar modes and codes.
3. *In order to facilitate the communications referred to in paragraphs 1 and 2, as well as the communications referred to in Articles 22, 23, 25, 26, 27, 28, 30 and 31 of the Protocol, the High Contracting Parties, the Parties to a conflict, or one of the Parties to a conflict, acting in agreement or alone, may designate, in accordance with the Table of Frequency Allocations in the Radio Regulations annexed to the international Telecommunications Convention, and publish selected national frequencies to be used by them for such communications. These frequencies shall be notified to the International Telecommunications Union in accordance with procedures to be approved by a World Administrative Radio Conference.*

Article 8. Electronic identification

1. *The Secondary Surveillance Radar (SSR) system as specified in Annex 10 to the Chicago Convention on International Civil Aviation of 7 December 1944, as amended from time to time, may be used to identify and to follow the course of medical aircraft. The SSR mode and code to be reserved for the exclusive use of medical aircraft shall be established by the High Contracting Parties, the Parties to the conflict, or one of the Parties to a conflict, acting in agreement or alone, in accordance with*

4 See the revised version of the Regulations of 30 November 1993, pp. 762 ff.

procedures to be recommended by the International Civil Aviation Organization

2. *Parties to a conflict may, by special agreement between them, establish for their use a similar electronic system for the identification of medical vehicles and medical ships and craft.*

Article 9. Radiocommunications
The priority signal provided for in Article 7 of these Regulations may preceded appropriate radiocommunications by medical units and transports in the application of procedures carried out under Articles 22, 23, 25, 26, 27, 28, 29, 30 and 31 of the Protocol.

RESOLUTION 20.

PROTECTION OF CULTURAL PROPERTY

The Diplomatic Conference on the Reaffirmation and Development of International Humanitarian Law Applicable in Armed Conflicts, Geneva, 1974-1977,

Welcoming *the adoption of Article 53 relating to the protection of cultural objects and places of worship as defined in the said Article, contained in the Protocol Additional to the Geneva Conventions of 12 August 1949, and relating to the Protection of Victims of International Armed Conflicts (Protocol I),*

Acknowledging *that the Convention for the Protection of Cultural Property in the Event of Armed Conflict and its Additional Protocol, signed at The Hague on 14 May 1954, constitutes an instrument of paramount importance for the international protection of the cultural heritage of all mankind against the effects of armed conflict and that the application of this Convention will in no way be prejudiced by the adoption of the Article referred to in the preceding paragraph,*

Urges *States which have not yet done so to become Parties to the aforementioned Convention.*

Fifty-fifth plenary meeting
7 June 1977

RESOLUTION 21.

DISSEMINATION OF KNOWLEDGE OF INTERNATIONAL HUMANITARIAN LAW APPLICABLE IN ARMED CONFLICTS

The Diplomatic Conference on the Reaffirmation and Development of International Humanitarian Law Applicable in Armed Conflicts, Geneva, 1974-1977,

Convinced *that a sound knowledge of international humanitarian law is an essential factor for its effective application,*

Confident *that widespread knowledge of that law will contribute to the promotion of humanitarian ideals and a spirit of peace among nations,*

1. Reminds *the High Contracting Parties that under the four Geneva Conventions of 1949 they have undertaken to disseminate knowledge of those*

Conventions as widely as possible, and that the Protocols adopted by the Conference reaffirm and extend that obligation;

2. Invites *the signatory States to take all appropriate measures to ensure that knowledge of international humanitarian law applicable in armed conflicts, and of the fundamental principles on which that law is based, is effectively disseminated, particularly by:*
   (a) encouraging the authorities concerned to plan and give effect, if necessary with the assistance and advice of the International Committee of the Red Cross, to arrangements to teach international humanitarian law, particularly to the armed forces and to appropriate administrative authorities, in a manner suited to national circumstances;
   (b) undertaking in peacetime the training of suitable persons to teach international humanitarian law and to facilitate the application thereof, in accordance with Articles 6 and 82 of the Protocol Additional to the Geneva Conventions of 12 August 1949, and relating to the Protection of Victims of International Armed Conflicts (Protocol I);
   (c) recommending that the appropriate authorities intensify the teaching of international humanitarian law in universities (faculties of law, political science, medicine, etc.);
   (d) recommending to educational authorities the introduction of courses on the principles of international humanitarian law in secondary and similar schools;
3. Urges *National Red Cross, Red Crescent and Red Lion and Sun Societies to offer their service to the authorities in their own countries with a view to the effective dissemination of knowledge of international humanitarian law;*
4. Invites *the International Committee of the Red Cross to participate actively in the effort to disseminate knowledge of international humanitarian law by,* inter alia*:*
   (a) publishing material that will assist in teaching international humanitarian law, and circulating appropriate information for the dissemination of the Geneva Conventions and the Protocols,
   (b) organizing, on its own initiative or when requested by Governments or National Societies, seminars and courses on international humanitarian law, and co-operating for that purpose with States and appropriate institutions.

Fifty-fifth plenary meeting
7 June 1977

RESOLUTION 22.

FOLLOW-UP REGARDING PROHIBITION OR RESTRICTION OF USE OF CERTAIN CONVENTIONAL WEAPONS

The Diplomatic Conference on the Reaffirmation and Development of International Humanitarian Law Applicable in Armed Conflicts, Geneva, 1974-1977

Having met *at Geneva for four session, in 1974, 1975, 1976 and 1977, and having adopted new humanitarian rules relating to armed conflicts and methods and means of warfare,*

Convinced *that the suffering of the civilian population and combatants could be significantly reduced if agreements can be attained on the prohibition or restriction for humanitarian reasons of the use of specific conventional weapons, including any which may be deemed to be excessively injurious or to have indiscriminate effects,*

Recalling *that the issue of prohibitions or restrictions for humanitarian reasons of the use of specific conventional weapons has been the subject of substantive discussion in the Ad Hoc Committee on Conventional Weapons of the Conference at all its four sessions, and at the Conferences of Government Experts held under the auspices of the International Committee of the Red Cross in 1974 at Lucerne and in 1976 at Lugano,*

Recalling, *in this connexion, discussions and relevant resolutions of the General Assembly of the United Nations and appeals made by several Heads of State and Government,*

Having concluded, *from these discussions, that agreement exists on the desirability of prohibiting the use of conventional weapons, the primary effect of which is to injure by fragments not detectable by X-ray, and that there is a wide area of agreement with regard to land-mines and booby-traps,*

Having also devoted efforts *to the further narrowing down of divergent views on the desirability of prohibiting or restricting the use of incendiary weapons, including napalm,*

Having also considered *the effects of the use of other conventional weapons, such as small calibre projectiles and certain blast and fragmentation weapons, and having begun the consideration of the possibility of prohibiting or restricting the use of such weapons,*

Recognizing *that it is important that this work continue and be pursued with the urgency required by evident humanitarian considerations,*

Believing *that further work should both build upon the areas of agreement thus far identified and include the search for further areas of agreement and should, in each case, seek the broadest possible agreement,*

1. Resolves *to send the report of the Ad Hoc Committee and the proposals presented in that Committee to the Governments of States represented at the Conference and to the Secretary-General of the United Nations;*
2. Requests *that serious and early consideration be given to these documents and to the reports of the Conferences of Government Experts of Lucerne and Lugano;*
3. Recommends *that a Conference of Governments should be convened not later than 1979 with a view to reaching:*
   (a) *agreements on prohibitions or restrictions on the use of specific conventional weapons including those which may be deemed to be excessively injurious or have indiscriminate effects, taking into account humanitarian and military considerations; and*
   (b) *agreement on a mechanism for the review of any such agreements and for the consideration of proposals for further such agreements;*
4. Urges *that consultations be undertaken prior to the consideration of this question at the thirty-second session of the United Nations General Assembly for the purpose of reaching agreement on the steps to be taken in preparation for the Conference;*
5. Recommends *that a consultative meeting of all interested Governments be convened during September/October 1977 for this purpose;*

6. Recommends *further that the States participating in these consultations should consider* inter alia *the establishment of a Preparatory Committee which would seek to establish the best possible basis for the achievement at the Conference of agreements as envisaged in this resolution;*
7. Invites *the General Assembly of the United Nations at its thirty-second session, in the light of the results of the consultations undertaken pursuant to paragraph 4 of this resolution, to take any further action that may be necessary for the holding of the Conference in 1979.*

Fifty-seventh plenary meeting
9 June 1977

RESOLUTION 23.

REPORT OF THE CREDENTIALS COMMITTEE

The Diplomatic Conference on the Reaffirmation and Development of International Humanitarian Law Applicable in Armed Conflicts, Geneva, 1974–1977,

Approves *the report of the Credentials Committee.*[5]

Fifty-seventh plenary meeting
9 June 1977

RESOLUTION 24.

EXPRESSION OF GRATITUDE TO THE HOST COUNTRY

The Diplomatic Conference on the Reaffirmation and Development of International Humanitarian Law Applicable in Armed Conflicts, Geneva, 1974–1977,

Having been convened *at Geneva at the invitation of the Swiss Government,*

Having held *four sessions, in 1974, 1975, 1976 and 1977, during which it considered two draft Protocols additional to the Geneva Conventions of 12 August 1949, which had been prepared by the International Committee of the Red Cross,*

Having benefited *throughout its four sessions form the facilities placed at its disposal by the Government of Switzerland and by the authorities of the Republic and Canton and of the City of Geneva,*

Profoundly appreciative *of the hospitality and courtesy accorded to the participants of the Conference by the Government of Switzerland and by the authorities and the people of the Republic and Canton of Geneva and of the City of Geneva,*

Having concluded *its work by the adoption of two Protocols additional to the Geneva Conventions of 12 August 1949 and of various resolutions,*

1. Expresses *its sincere gratitude to the Government of Switzerland for its unfailing support for the work of the Conference and in particular to Mr. Pierre Graber, President of the Conference, Federal Councillor, Head of*

[5] Document CDDH/409/Rev. 1.

the Federal Political Department of the Swiss Confederation, whose wise and firm guidance has contributed so much to the Conference's success;

2. Expresses *its sincere gratitude to the authorities and the people of the Republic and Canton of Geneva and of the City of Geneva for the generous hospitality and courtesy which they showed the Conference and those participating in it;*
3. Pays a *tribute to the International Committee of the Red Cross and to its representatives and experts who devotedly and patiently advised the Conference on all matters arising in connexion with the draft Protocols and whose attachment to the principles of the Red Cross has served as an inspiration to the Conference;*
4. Expresses *its appreciation to Ambassador Jean Humbert, Secretary-General of the Conference, and to the entire staff of the Conference for the provision of efficient services at all times throughout the four years' duration of the Conference.*

Fifty-eighth plenary meeting
9 June 1977

VOTE

Resolution No. 17 was adopted by consensus.[6]

Resolution No. 18 was adopted by consensus.[7]

Resolution No. 19 was adopted by consensus.[8]

Resolution 20 was adopted by 53 to none, with 33 abstentions.[9]

Resolution 21 was adopted by 63 votes to 2, with 21 abstentions.[10]

Resolution 22 and Add. 1 was adopted by consensus.[11]

Resolution 23 was adopted by acclamation.[12]

---

6 CDDH/SR.54, para. 44. *Official records of the Diplomatic Conference on the Reaffirmation and Development of International Humanitarian Law applicable in Armed Conflicts, Geneva, 1974–1977*, Berne, Federal Political Department, 1978, Vol. VII, p. 171.
7 *Idem.*
8 *Idem.*
9 CDDH/SR. 55, para. 21, *Official records*, Vol. VII, p. 184.
10 CDDH/SR. 55, para. 48, *Official records*, Vol. VII, p. 187.
11 CDDH/SR. 57, para. 69, *Official records*, Vol. VII, p. 266.
12 CDDH/SR. 58, para. 189, *Official records*, Vol. VII, p. 318.

No. 59

FUNDAMENTAL RULES OF INTERNATIONAL HUMANITARIAN LAW APPLICABLE IN ARMED CONFLICTS

Published by the International Committee of the Red Cross and the League of Red Cross Societies, 1978

INTRODUCTORY NOTE: By the adoption of the 1977 Protocols Additional to the Geneva Conventions (*Nos. 56 and 57*) the law of armed conflicts had become so voluminous and complex that it seemed desirable to establish a short text containing the most essential rules of this law. This text was drafted by experts of the ICRC, the League of Red Cross Societies and of national Red Cross Societies. It has no official character and no force of law.

TEXT PUBLISHED IN: *International Review of the Red Cross*, Vol. 18, No. 206, September–October 1978, pp. 247–249 (Engl.); *Revue Internationale de la Croix-Rouge*, Vol. 60, No. 713, septembre–octobre 1978, pp. 247–249 (French); *Revista Internacional de la Cruz Roja*, Vol. III, No. 29, septiembre–octubre de 1978, pp. 247–249 (Span.); *Droit des conflits armés*, pp. 895–896 (French); Roberts and Guelff, pp. 513–514 (Engl.).

* * *

International humanitarian law is made up of all the international legal provisions, whether of written or customary law, ensuring respect for the individual in armed conflict. Taking its inspiration from the sentiment of humanity, it postulates the principle that belligerents must not inflict harm on their adversaries out of proportion with the object of warfare, which is to destroy or weaken the military strength of the enemy.

International humanitarian law comprises the "law of Geneva", which aims to safeguard military personnel *hors de combat* and persons who do not take part in the hostilities, and the "law of The Hague" which determines the rights and duties of belligerents in the conduct of operations and limits the choice of the means of harming an enemy.

The paper entitled "Fundamental Rules of International Humanitarian Law", which we give here, contains the essential parts of this law. Its authors have endeavoured, as far as possible, to use simple and concise terms.

These rules are not vested with the authority of an international legal instrument and are not intended to take the place of the treaties in force. Their sole purpose is to facilitate the dissemination of knowledge of international humanitarian law.

The ICRC and the League communicate this document to National Societies so that it might be used to instruct all those who, at different levels, are responsible for applying humanitarian law, or those who may wish to exercise their rights under that law or to grant their fellowmen the advantage of such rights.

1. Persons *hors de combat* and those who do not take a direct part in hostilities are entitled to respect for their lives and physical and moral integrity. They shall in all circumstances be protected and treated humanely without any adverse distinction.
2. It is forbidden to kill or injure an enemy who surrenders or who is *hors de combat*.
3. The wounded and sick shall be collected and cared for by the party to the conflict which has them in its power. Protection also covers medical personnel, establishments, transports and *matériel*. The emblem of the red cross (red crescent, red lion and sun) is the sign of such protection and must be respected.
4. Captured combatants and civilians under the authority of an adverse party are entitled to respect for their lives, dignity, personal rights and convictions. They shall be protected against all acts of violence and reprisals. They shall have the right to correspond with their families and to receive relief.
5. Everyone shall be entitled to benefit from fundamental judicial guarantees. No one shall be held responsible for an act he has not committed. No one shall be subjected to physical or mental torture, corporal punishment or cruel or degrading treatment.
6. Parties to a conflict and members of their armed forces do not have an unlimited choice of methods and means of warfare. It is prohibited to employ weapons or methods of warfare of a nature to cause unnecessary losses or excessive suffering.
7. Parties to a conflict shall at all times distinguish between the civilian population and combatants in order to spare civilian population and property. Neither the civilian population as such nor civilian persons shall be the object of attack. Attacks shall be directed solely against military objectives.

No. 60

DECLARATION OF THE INTERNATIONAL CONFERENCE FOR THE PROTECTION OF VICTIMS OF WAR

Adopted at Geneva, 1 September 1993

INTRODUCTORY NOTE: The International Conference for the Protection of War Victims was convened by the Swiss government on the initiative of the ICRC. It took place from 30 August to 1 September 1993. Its aim was to elicit a strong reaction to widespread violations of international humanitarian law and to mobilize the international community to give in-depth consideration to the measures that the states should undertake to ensure universal recognition of and respect for humanitarian law. The Conference was preceded by an intense preparation by diplomatic means and the mass media. 815 delegates representing 160 states as well as observers of intergovernmental and non-governmental organizations took part in it. More than 130 participants took the floor in order to emphasize the importance of the Conference and the interest governments attach to respect for humanitarian law. At the end of the Conference the participants adopted the present Declaration by consensus.

AUTHENTIC TEXT: Arabic, Chinese, English, French, German, Italian, Russian, Spanish.

TEXT PUBLISHED IN: Document of the United Nations General Assembly: A748/742, 8 December 1993 (Arabic, Chinese, Engl., French, Russ. Span.); *IRRC*, September–October 1993, Thirty-third year, No. 296, pp. 377–381 (Engl.); *RICR*, September–October 1993, 75 année, No. 803, pp. 401–405 (French); *Revista Internacional de la Cruz Roja*, septiembre–octubre de 1993, Decimoctavo ano, No. 119, pp. 398–402 (Span.); see also the Arabic and German editions of the *International Review of the Red Cross*; *Droit des conflits armés*, pp. 897–903 (French); *International Commission of Jurists Review*, No. 51, December 1993, pp. 56–58 (Engl.); *Handbook of the International Movement*, 1994, pp. 375–378 (Engl.); *Manuel du Mouvement international*, 1994, pp. 389–392 (French); *Manual del Movimiento internacional*, 1994, pp. 380–383 (Span.).

* * *

The participants in the International Conference for the Protection of War Victims, held in Geneva from 30 August to 1 September 1993, solemnly declare the following:

I

1. *We refuse to accept that war, violence and hatred spread throughout the world, and fundamental rights of persons are violated in an increasingly grave and systematic fashion. We refuse to accept that wounded are shown no mercy, children massacred, women raped, prisoners tortured, victims denied elementary humanitarian assistance, civilians starved as a method*

of warfare, obligations under international humanitarian law in territories under foreign occupation not respected, families of missing persons denied information about the fate of their relatives, populations illegally displaced, and countries laid to waste.

2. *We refuse to accept that, since war has not been eradicated, obligations under international humanitarian law aimed at limiting the suffering caused by armed conflicts are constantly violated. We vigorously condemn these violations which result in a continued deterioration of the situation of persons whom the law is intended to protect.*
3. *We refuse to accept that civilian populations should become more and more frequently the principal victim of hostilities and acts of violence perpetrated in the course of armed conflicts, for example where they are intentionally targeted or used as human shields, and particularly when they are victims of the odious practice of "ethnic cleansing". We are alarmed by the marked increase in acts of sexual violence directed notably against women and children and we reiterate that such acts constitute grave breaches of international humanitarian law.*
4. *We deplore the means and methods used in the conduct of hostilities which cause heavy suffering among civilians. In that context we reaffirm our determination to apply, to clarify and, where it is deemed necessary, to consider further developing the existing law governing armed conflicts, in particular non-international ones, in order to ensure more effective protection for their victims.*
5. *We affirm the necessity to reinforce, in accordance with international law, the bond of solidarity that must unite mankind against the tragedy of war and in all efforts to protect the victims thereof. In that spirit, we support peaceful bilateral and multilateral initiatives aimed at easing tensions and preventing the outbreak of armed conflicts.*
6. *We undertake to act in cooperation with the UN and in conformity with the UN Charter to ensure full compliance with international humanitarian law in the event of genocide and other serious violations of this law.*
7. *We demand that measures be taken at the national, regional and international levels to allow assistance and relief personnel to carry out in all safety their mandate in favour of the victims of an armed conflict. Stressing that peace-keeping forces are bound to act in accordance with international humanitarian law, we also demand that the members of peace-keeping forces be permitted to fulfil their mandate without hindrance and that their physical integrity be respected.*

II

We affirm our responsibility, in accordance with Article 1 common to the Geneva Conventions, to respect and ensure respect for international humanitarian law in order to protect the victims of war. We urge all States to make every effort to:

1. *Disseminate international humanitarian law in a systematic way by teaching its rules to the general population, including incorporating them in education programmes and by increasing media awareness, so that people may assimilate that law and have the strength to react in accordance with these rules to violations thereof.*
2. *Organize the teaching of international humanitarian law in the public administrations responsible for its application and incorporate the funda-*

mental rules in military training programmes, and military code books, handbooks and regulations, so that each combatant is aware of his or her obligation to observe and help enforce these rules.

3. *Study with utmost attention practical means of promoting understanding of and respect for international humanitarian law in armed conflicts in the event that State structures disintegrate so that a State cannot discharge its obligations under that law.*
4. *Consider or reconsider, in order to enhance the universal character of international humanitarian law, becoming party or confirming their succession, where appropriate, to the relevant treaties concluded since the adoption of the 1949 Geneva Conventions, in particular:*
   - *the Protocol Additional to the Geneva Conventions of 12 August 1949, and relating to the Protection of Victims of International Armed Conflicts of 8 June 1977 (Protocol I);*
   - *the Protocol Additional to the Geneva Conventions of 12 August 1949, and relating to the Protection of Victims of Non-International Armed Conflicts of 8 June 1977 (Protocol II);*
   - *the 1980 Convention on Prohibitions or Restrictions on the Use of Certain Conventional Weapons and its three Protocols;*
   - *the 1954 Convention for the Protection of Cultural Property in the Event of Armed Conflict;*
5. *Adopt and implement, at the national level, all appropriate regulations, laws and measures to ensure respect for international humanitarian law applicable in the event of armed conflict and to punish violations thereof.*
6. *Contribute to an impartial clarification of alleged violations of international humanitarian law and, in particular, consider recognizing the competence of the International Fact-Finding Commission according to Article 90 of Protocol I mentioned in Part II, paragraph 4 of this Declaration.*
7. *Ensure that war crimes are duly prosecuted and do not go unpunished, and accordingly implement the provisions on the punishment of grave breaches of international humanitarian law and encourage the timely establishment of appropriate international legal machinery, and in this connection acknowledge the substantial work accomplished by the International Law Commission on an international criminal court. We reaffirm that States which violate international humanitarian law shall, if the case demands, be liable to pay compensation.*
8. *Improve the coordination of emergency humanitarian actions in order to give them the necessary coherence and efficiency, provide the necessary support to the humanitarian organizations entrusted with granting protection and assistance to the victims of armed conflicts and supplying, in all impartiality, victims of armed conflicts with goods or services essential to their survival, facilitate speedy and effective relief operations by granting to those humanitarian organizations access to the affected areas, and take the appropriate measures to enhance the respect for their safety, security and integrity, in conformity with applicable rules of international humanitarian law.*
9. *Increase respect for the emblems of the red cross and red crescent as well as for the other emblems provided for by international humanitarian law and protecting medical personnel, objects, installations and means of transport, religious personnel and places of worship, and relief personnel, goods and convoys as defined in international humanitarian law.*

10. Reaffirm and ensure respect for the rules of international humanitarian law applicable during armed conflicts protecting cultural property, places of worship and the natural environment, either against attacks on the environment as such or against wanton destruction causing serious environmental damage; and continue to examine the opportunity of strengthening them.

11. Ensure the effectiveness of international humanitarian law and take resolute action, in accordance with that law, against States bearing responsibility for violations of international humanitarian law with a view to terminating such violations.

12. Take advantage of the forthcoming Conference for the review of the 1980 Convention on Prohibitions or Restrictions on the Use of Certain Conventional Weapons and the three Protocols thereto, which provides a platform for wider accession to this instrument, and to consider strengthening existing law with a view to finding effective solutions to the problem of the indiscriminate use of mines whose explosions maim civilians in different parts of the world.

With this Declaration in mind, we reaffirm the necessity to make the implementation of international humanitarian law more effective. In this spirit, we call upon the Swiss Government to convene an open-ended intergovernmental group of experts to study practical means of promoting full respect for and compliance with that law, and to prepare a report for submission to the States and to the next session of the International Conference of the Red Cross and Red Crescent.

In conclusion we affirm our conviction that, by preserving a spirit of humanity in the midst of armed conflicts, international humanitarian law keeps open the road to reconciliation, facilitates the restoration of peace between the belligerents, and fosters harmony between all peoples.

* * *

See also Nos. 7, 8, 20–36, 61–68

VI

PROTECTION OF HUMAN RIGHTS IN SITUATIONS OF ARMED CONFLICT

No. 61

CONVENTION ON THE PREVENTION AND PUNISHMENT OF THE CRIME OF GENOCIDE

Adopted by resolution 260 (III) A of the United Nations General Assembly on 9 December 1948

INTRODUCTORY NOTE: Although the Genocide Convention does not constitute a part of the law of armed conflicts in a strict sense, it is reprinted below in view of the fact that it is of particular importance in time of war. The Convention was adopted by resolution 260 (III) A of the United Nations General Assembly. By resolution 260 (III) B, the General Assembly invited the International Law Commission to study the desirability of establishing an international judicial organ for the trial of persons charged with genocide or other crimes. By resolution C the General Assembly recommended that parties to the Convention which administer dependent territories should take such measures as are necessary and feasible to enable the provisions of the Convention to be extended to those territories as soon as possible. Resolution A was adopted by 56 votes to none, resolution B by 43 votes to 6, with 3 abstentions, resolution C by 50 votes, with one abstention.

The reservations to the Convention and the objections raised in regard to them by several states induced the General Assembly, by resolution 478 (V) of 16 November 1950, to request the International Court of Justice to give an advisory opinion on the reservations to the Genocide Convention. The International Court gave its advisory opinion on 28 May 1951 (*International Court of Justice, Reports of Judgments, Advisory Opinions and Orders*, 1951, pp. 15 ff.). In this advisory opinion the Court stated that "the principles unterlying the Convention are principles which are recognized by civilized nations as binding on States, even without any conventional obligation" (p. 23).

ENTRY INTO FORCE: 12 January 1951.

AUTHENTIC TEXTS: Chinese, English, French, Russian, Spanish. The text below is reprinted from *UNTS,* Vol. 78, p. 277.

TEXT PUBLISHED IN: *United Nations, Official Records of the Third session of the General Assembly*, Part I, *September 21 – December 12, 1948, Resolutions,* Paris, Palais de Chaillot, UN Doc. A/810, December, 1948, pp. 174-177 (Engl., see also editions in Chinese, Russian and Spanish); *UNTS*, Vol. 78, p. 277 (Chinese, Engl., French, Russ., Span.); *GBTS*, 1970, No. 58, Cmnd. 4421 (Chinese, Engl., French, Russ., Span.); *BFSP*, Vol. 151, 1948, pp. 682–687 (Engl.); *AJIL*, Vol. 45, 1951, Suppl., pp. 7–13 (Engl.); *Human Rights – A Compilation of International Instruments,* Vol. I (Second Part), New York, United Nations, 1993, pp. 669–673 (Engl.); *Droits de l'Homme*, *Recueil d'instruments internationaux*, New York, Nations Unies, 1988, pp. 143–147 (French); *Derechos Humanos – Recopilacion de instrumentos internacionales*, Nueva York, Naciones Unidas, 1988, pp. 143–147 (Span.); *Prava cheloveka – Sbornik mezhdunarodnkyh dokumentov*, N'yu-York, OON, 1989, pp. 160–164 (Russ.); *Human Rights Documents, Compilation of Documents on Human Rights*, Washington, DC, US

Government Printing Office, 1983, pp. 105–108 (Engl.); *Droit des conflits armés*, pp. 907–936 (French); *Derechos humanos,* pp. 40–62 (Spanish); Ian Brownlie, *Basic Documents on Human Rights*, 74th ed., Oxford, 2002, pp. 108–111 (Engl.); Friedman, pp. 692–696 (Engl.); Lillich, 130.1 – 139.13 (Engl.); *Global War Crimes Tribunal Collection*, J. Oppenheim, W. van der Wolf, Nijmegen, Global Law Association, 1997–1999, Vol. I, pp. 219–221, Vol. Ic, pp. 163–166 (Engl.); Roberts and Guelff, pp. 179–194 (Engl.); *Vedomosti Verkhovnogo Soveta SSSR*, No. 12, 1954, pp. 406–409 (Russ.); *Sbornik dogovorov SSSR*, vyp. XVI, pp. 66–71 (Russ.); *Mezhdunarodnoe pravo*, Vol. I, pp. 213–217 (Russ.); Blatova, pp. 335–338 (Russ.); *Prava cheloveka. Sbornik mezhdunarodnykh dokumentov*, L.N. Shestakov (ed.), Moska, Izdatel'stvo Moskovskogo universiteta, 1986, pp. 82–88 (Russ.); *Droit des conflits armés*, pp. 909–936 (French); United Nations website: www.unhchr.ch/html; ICRC website: icrc.org/ihl.nsf (Engl., French, Span.).

* * *

The Contracting Parties,

Having considered the declaration made by the General Assembly of the United Nations in its resolution 96 (1) dated 11 December 1946 that genocide is a crime under international law, contrary to the spirit and aims of the United Nations and condemned by the civilized world;

Recognizing that at all periods of history genocide has inflicted great losses on humanity; and

Being convinced that, in order to liberate mankind from such an odious scourge, international co-operation is required;

Hereby agree as hereinafter provided.

Article 1. The Contracting Parties confirm that genocide, whether committed in time of peace or in time of war, is a crime under international law which they undertake to prevent and to punish.

Art. 2.[1] In the present Convention, genocide means any of the following acts committed with intent to destroy, in whole or in part, a national, ethnical, racial or religious group, as such:
(a) Killing members of the group;
(b) Causing serious bodily or mental harm to members of the group;
(c) Deliberately inflicting on the group conditions of life calculated to bring about its physical destruction in whole or in part;
(d) Imposing measures intended to prevent births within the group;
(e) Forcibly transferring children of the group to another group.

Art. 3. The following acts shall be punishable:
(a) Genocide;
(b) Conspiracy to commit genocide;
(c) Direct and public incitement to commit genocide;

[1] For understanding in respect of this article by the United States of America, see p. 855.

(d) Attempt to commit genocide;
(e) Complicity in genocide.

Art. 4.[2] Persons committing genocide or any of the other acts enumerated in Article 3 shall be punished, whether they are constitutionally responsible rulers, public officials or private individuals.

Art. 5. The Contracting Parties undertake to enact, in accordance with their respective Constitutions, the necessary legislation to give effect to the provisions of the present Convention and, in particular, to provide effective penalties for persons guilty of genocide or any of the other acts enumerated in Article 3.

Art. 6.[3] Persons charged with genocide or any of the other acts enumerated in Article 3 shall be tried by a competent tribunal of the State in the territory of which the act was committed, or by such international penal tribunal as may have jurisdiction with respect to those Contracting Parties which shall have accepted this jurisdiction.

Art. 7.[4] Genocide and the other acts enumerated in Article 3 shall not be considered as political crimes for the purpose of extradition.

The Contracting Parties pledge themselves in such cases to grant extradition in accordance with their laws and treaties in force.

Art. 8.[5] Any Contracting Party may call upon the competent organs of the United Nations to take such action under the Charter of the United Nations as they consider appropriate for the prevention and suppression of acts of genocide or any of the other acts enumerated in Article 3.

Art. 9.[6] Disputes between the Contracting Parties relating to the interpretation, application or fulfilment of the present Convention, including those relating to the responsibility of a State for genocide or any of the other acts enumerated in Article 3, shall be submitted to the International Court of Justice at the request of any of the parties to the dispute.

Art. 10. The present Convention, of which the Chinese, English, French, Russian and Spanish texts are equally authentic, shall bear the date of 9 December 1948.

---

[2] For reservations made in respect of this article by Finland (withdrawn) and Philippines, see pp. 851, 852–853.

[3] For reservations made in respect of this article by Algeria, Burma, Morocco, the Philippines, the United States of America and Venezuela, see pp. 848, 850, 852, 853, 855. For objections to these reservations, see pp. 856, 857, 862, 863, 865.

[4] For declarations in respect of this article made by Malaysia, Philippines, Portugal and Venezuela, see pp. 852, 853, 855.

[5] For declaration made in respect of this article by Burma, see p. 850.

[6] For reservations in respect of this article by Albania (withdrawn), Algeria, Belarus (withdrawn), Bulgaria (withdrawn), China, Czechoslovakia, German Democratic Republic, Hungary (withdrawn), India, Malaysia, Mongolia (withdrawn), Philippines, Poland (withdrawn), Romania (withdrawn), Rwanda, Singapore, Spain, Ukraine (withdrawn), United States of America, USSR (withdrawn), Viet Nam, Yemen and Yugoslavia, see pp. 849–856. For objections to these reservations, see pp. 856–863.

Art. 11.[7] The present Convention shall be open until 31 December 1949 for signature on behalf of any Member of the United Nations and of any non-member State to which an invitation to sign has been addressed by the General Assembly.

The present Convention shall be ratified, and the instruments of ratification shall be deposited with the Secretary-General of the United Nations.

After 1 January 1950, the present Convention may be acceded to on behalf of any Member of the United Nations and of any non-member State which has received an invitation as aforesaid.

Instruments of accession shall be deposited with the Secretary-General of the United Nations.

Art. 12.[8] Any Contracting Party may at any time, by notification addressed to the Secretary-General of the United Nations, extend the application of the present Convention to all or any of the territories for the conduct of whose foreign relations that Contracting Party is responsible.

Art. 13. On the day when the first twenty instruments of ratification or accession have been deposited, the Secretary-General shall draw up a *procès-verbal* and transmit a copy of it to each Member of the United Nations and to each of the non-member States contemplated in Article 11.

The present Convention shall come into force on the ninetieth day following the date of deposit of the twentieth instrument of ratification or accession.

Any ratification or accession effected subsequent to the latter date shall become effective on the ninetieth day following the deposit of the instrument of ratification or accession.

Art. 14. The present Convention shall remain in effect for a period of ten years as from the date of its coming into force.

It shall thereafter remain in force for successive periods of five years for such Contracting Parties as have not denounced it at least six months before the expiration of the current period.

Denunciation shall be effected by a written notification addressed to the Secretary-General of the United Nations.

Art. 15. If, as a result of denunciations, the number of Parties to the present Convention should become less than sixteen, the Convention shall cease to be in force as from the date on which the last of these denunciations shall become effective.

Art. 16. A request for the revision of the present Convention may be made at any time by any Contracting Party by means of a notification in writing addressed to the Secretary-General.

The General Assembly shall decide upon the steps, if any, to be taken in respect of such request.

---

7 For declaration in respect of this article made by the German Democratic Republic and Viet Nam, see pp. 851, 855.

8 For reservations in respect of this article made by Albania, Algeria, Argentina, Belarus, Bulgaria, Czechoslovakia, German Democratic Republic, Hungary, Mongolia, Poland, Romania, Ukraine, USSR, Viet Nam, see pp. 849–855. For objections to these reservations, see pp. 856–863.

Art. 17. The Secretary-General of the United Nations shall notify all Members of the United Nations and the non-member States contemplated in Article 11 of the following:

(a) Signatures, ratifications and accessions received in accordance with Article 11;
(b) Notifications received in accordance with Article 12;
(c) The date upon which the present Convention comes into force in accordance with Article 13;
(d) Denunciations received in accordance with Article 14;
(e) The abrogation of the Convention in accordance with Article 15;
(f) Notifications received in accordance with Article 16.

Art. 18. The original of the present Convention shall be deposited in the archives of the United Nations. A certified copy of the Convention shall be transmitted to all Members of the United Nations and to the non-member States contemplated in Article 11.

Art. 19. The present Convention shall be registered by the Secretary-General of the United Nations on the date of its coming into force.

SIGNATURES, RATIFICATIONS, ACCESSIONS AND NOTIFICATIONS OF SUCCESSION OR CONTINUITY[1]

State	*Signatures*	*Ratifications, Accessions, Notifications of Succession or Continuity (C)*
Afghanistan	–	22 March 1956
Albania	–	12 May 1955 *Res.*
Algeria	–	31 October 1963 *Res.*
Antigua and Barbuda	–	25 October 1988 (C)
Argentina	–	5 June 1956 *Res.*
Armenia	–	23 June 1993
Australia[2]	11 December 1948	8 July 1949
Austria	–	19 March 1958
Azerbaijan	–	16 August 1996
Bahamas	–	5 August 1975 (C)
Bahrain	–	27 March 1990 *Res.*[3]
Bangladesh	–	5 October 1998 *Dec.*

[1] Based on indications in Multilateral Treaties Deposited with the Secretary-General, New York, United Nations, (ST/LEG/SER.E) as available on http://untreaty.un.org, of 30 October 2002. See also ICRC website: www.icrc.org/ihl.nsf.

[2] Notification of territorial application by Australia received on 8 July 1949: all territories for the conduct of whose foreign relations Australia is responsible.

[3] On 25 June 1990, the Secretary-General received from the Government of Israel the following objection: "The Government of the State of Israel has noted that the instrument of accession of Bahrain to the [said] Convention contains a declaration in respect of Israel. In the view of the Government of the State of Israel, such declaration, which is explicitly of a political character, is incompatible with the purpose and objectives of this Convention and cannot in any way affect whatever obligations are binding upon Bahrain under general International Law or under particular Conventions. The Government of the State of Israel will, in so far as concerns the substance of the matter, adopt towards Bahrain an attitude of complete reciprocity."

State	*Signatures*	*Ratifications, Accessions, Notifications of Succession or Continuity (C)*
Barbados	–	14 January 1980
Belarus	16 December 1949	11 August 1954 *Res.*
Belgium[4]	12 December 1949	5 September 1951
Belize	–	10 March 1998
Bolivia	11 December 1948	–
Bosnia and Herzegovina[5]		29 December 1992 (C)
Brazil	11 December 1948	15 April 1952
Bulgaria		21 July 1950 *Res*
Burkina Faso	–	14 September 1965
Burundi	–	6 January 1997
Cambodia	–	14 October 1950
Canada	28 November 1949	3 September 1952
Chile	11 December 1948	3 June 1953
China[6 7]	20 July 1949	18 April 1983 *Res.*
Colombia	12 August 1949	27 October 1959
Costa Rica	–	14 October 1950
Côte d'Ivoire	–	18 December 1995

4 Notification of territorial application by Belgium received on 13 March 1952: Belgian Congo, Trust Territory of Rwanda-Urundi.

5 On 15 June 1993, the Secretary-General received from the Government of Yugoslavia the following communication: "Considering the fact that the replacement of sovereignty on the part of the territory of the Socialist Federal Republic of Yugoslavia previously comprising the Republic of Bosnia and Herzegovina was carried out contrary to the rules of international law, the Government of the Federal Republic of Yugoslavia herewith states that it does not consider the so-called Republic of Bosnia and Herzegovina a party to the [said] Convention, but does consider that the so-called Republic of Bosnia and Herzegovina is bound by the obligation to respect the norms on preventing and punishing the crime of genocide in accordance with general international law irrespective of the Convention on the Prevention and Punishment of the Crime of Genocide."

6 Ratified on behalf of the Republic of China on 19 July 1951.

7 On 6 June 1997, the Government of China notified the Secretary-General of the following: In accordance with the declaration of the Government of the People's Republic of China and the United Kingdom of Great Britain and Northern Ireland on the question of Hong Kong signed on 19 December 1984, the People's Republic of China will resume the exercise of sovereignty over Hong Kong with effect from 1 July 1997. Hong Kong will, with effect from that date, become a Special Administrative Region of the People's Republic of China and will enjoy a high degree of autonomy, except in foreign and defence affairs which are the responsibility of the Central People's Government of the People's Republic of China.

The [said] Convention, which the Government of the People's Republic of China ratified on [18] April 1983, will apply to Hong Kong Special Administrative Region with effect from 1 July 1997. (The notification also contained the following declaration): The reservation to article 9 of the said Convention made by the Government of the People's Republic of China will also apply to the Hong Kong Special Administrative Region.

The Government of the People's Republic of China will assume responsibility for the international rights and obligations arising from the application of the Convention to Hong Kong Special Administrative Region.

Subsequently, on 10 June 1997, the Government of the United Kingdom of Great Britain and Northern Ireland notified the Secretary-General of the following:

"In accordance with the Joint Declaration of the Government of the United Kingdom of Great Britain and Northern Ireland and the Government of the People's Republic of China on the Question of Hong Kong signed on 19 December 1984, the Government of the United Kingdom will restore Hong Kong to the People's Republic of China with effect from 1 July 1997. The Government of the United Kingdom will continue to have international responsibility for Hong Kong until that date. Therefore, from that date the Government of the United Kingdom will cease to be responsible for the international rights and obligations arising from the application of the [said Convention] to Hong Kong."

State	*Signatures*	*Ratifications, Accessions, Notifications of Succession or Continuity (C)*
Croatia	–	12 October 1992 (C)
Cuba	28 December 1949	4 March 1953
Cyprus[8]	–	29 March 1982
Czech Republic[9]	–	22 February 1993 (C) *Res.*
Democratic People's Republic of Korea	–	31 January 1989
Democratic Republic of the Congo	–	31 May 1962 (C)
Denmark	28 September 1949	15 June 1951
Dominican Republic	11 December 1948	–
Ecuador	11 December 1948	21 December 1949
Egypt	12 December 1948	8 February 1952
El Salvador	27 April 1949	28 September 1950
Estonia	–	21 October 1991
Ethiopia	11 December 1948	1 July 1949
Fiji	–	11 January 1973 (C)
Finland	–	18 December 1959 *Res.*
France	11 December 1948	14 October 1950
Gabon	–	21 January 1983
Gambia	–	29 December 1978
Georgia	–	11 October 1993
Germany[10 11]	–	24 November 1954
Ghana	–	24 December 1958
Greece	29 December 1949	8 December 1954
Guatemala	22 June 1949	13 January 1950
Guinea	–	7 September 2000
Haiti	11 December 1948	14 October 1950
Honduras	22 April 1949	5 March 1952
Hungary	–	7 January 1952 *Res.*
Iceland	14 May 1949	29 August 1949
India	29 November 1949	27 August 1959 *Res.*
Iran (Islamic Republic of)	8 December 1949	14 August 1956

[8] On 18 May 1998, the Government of Cyprus notified the Secretary-General of the following: "The Government of the Republic of Cyprus has taken note of the reservations made by a number of countries when acceding to the [Convention] and wishes to state that in its view these are not the kind of reservations which intending parties to the Convention have the right to make. Accordingly, the Government of the Republic of Cyprus does not accept any reservations entered by any Government with regard to any of the Articles of the Convention."

[9] Czechoslovakia had signed and ratified the Convention on 28 December 1949 and 21 December 1950, respectively, with a reservation. Subsequently, by a notification received on 26 April 1991, the Government of Czechoslovakia notified the Secretary-General of its decision to withdraw the reservation to Article 9 made upon signature and confirmed upon ratification. For the text of the reservation, see p. 851.

[10] The German Democratic Republic had acceded to the Convention with reservation and declaration on 27 March 1973. For the text of the reservation and the declarations see p. 851.

[11] In a note accompanying the instrument of accession, the Government of the Federal Republic of Germany stated that the Convention would also apply to Land Berlin. In a communication received by the Secretary-General on 27 December 1973, the German Democratic Republic objected to this. Subsequently, the Secretary-General received communications from the governments of France, the United Kingdom of Great Britain and Northern Ireland and the United States of America (17 June 1974 and 8 July 1975), the Federal Republic of Germany (15 July 1974 and 19 September 1975), the Union of Soviet Socialist Republics (12 September 1974 and 8 December 1975), and the Ukrainian Soviet Socialist Republic (19 September 1974). See also pp. 173–176 (under Germany)..

State	*Signatures*	*Ratifications, Accessions, Notifications of Succession or Continuity (C)*
Iraq	–	20 January 1959
Ireland	–	22 June 1976
Israel	17 August 1949	9 March 1950
Italy	–	4 June 1952
Jamaica	–	23 September 1968
Jordan	–	3 April 1950
Kazakhstan	–	26 August 1998
Kuwait	–	7 March 1995
Kyrgyzstan	–	5 September 1997
Lao People's Democratic Republic	–	8 December 1950
Latvia	–	14 April 1992
Lebanon	30 December 1949	17 December 1953
Lesotho	–	29 November 1974
Liberia	11 December 1948	9 June 1950
Libyan Arab Jamahiriya	–	16 May 1989
Liechtenstein	–	24 March 1994
Lithuania	–	1 February 1996
Luxembourg	–	7 October 1981
Malaysia	–	20 December 1994 *Res.*
Maldives	–	24 April 1984
Mali	–	16 July 1974
Mexico	4 December 1948	22 July 1952
Monaco	–	30 March 1950
Mongolia	–	5 January 1967 *Res.*
Morocco	–	24 January 1958 *Res.*
Mozambique	–	18 April 1983
Myanmar (formerly Burma)	30 December 1949	14 March 1956 *Res.*
Namibia		28 November 1994
Nepal	–	17 January 1969
Netherlands	–	20 June 1966
New Zealand	25 November 1949	28 December 1978
Nicaragua	–	29 January 1952
Norway	11 December 1948	22 July 1949
Pakistan	11 December 1948	12 October 1957
Panama	11 December 1948	11 January 1950
Papua New Guinea	–	27 January 1982
Paraguay	11 December 1948	–
Peru	11 December 1948	24 February 1960
Philippines	11 December 1948	7 July 1950 *Res.*
Poland	–	14 November 1950 *Res.*
Portugal[12]	–	9 February 1999 *Dec.*

[12] On 16 September 1999, the government of Portugal informed the Secretary-General that the Convention would apply to Macau.

Subsequently, the Secretary-General received the following communication on the date indicated hereinafter:

China (17 December 1999):

In accordance with the Joint Declaration of the Government of the People's Republic of China and the Government of the Republic of Portugal on the question of Macau (hereinafter referred to as the Joint Declaration), the Government of the People's Republic of China will resume the exercise of sovereignty over Macau with effect from 20 December 1999. Macau will, from that date, become a Special Administrative Region of the People's Republic of China and will enjoy a high degree of autonomy, except in foreign and defense

State	*Signatures*	*Ratifications, Accessions, Notifications of Succession or Continuity (C)*
Republic of Korea	–	14 October 1950
Republic of Moldova	–	26 January 1993
Romania	–	2 November 1950 *Res.*
Russian Federation	16 December 1949	3 May 1954 *Res.*
Rwanda	–	16 April 1975 *Res.*
Saint Vincent and the Grenadines	–	9 November 1981
Saudi Arabia	–	13 July 1950
Senegal	–	4 August 1983
Seychelles	–	5 May 1992
Singapore	–	18 August 1995 *Res.*
Slovakia	–	28 May 1993 (C)
Slovenia	–	6 July 1992 (C)
South Africa	–	10 December 1998
Spain	–	13 September 1968 *Res.*
Sri Lanka	–	12 October 1950
Sweden	30 December 1949	27 May 1952
Switzerland	–	7 September 2000
Syrian Arab Republic	–	25 June 1955
The Former Yugoslav Republic of Macedonia	–	18 January 1994 (C)
Togo	–	24 May 1984
Tonga	–	16 February 1972
Trinidad and Tobago	–	13 December 2002
Tunisia	–	29 November 1956
Turkey	–	31 July 1950
Uganda	–	14 November 1995
Ukraine	16 December 1949	15 November 1954 *Res.*
United Kingdom[13]	–	30 January 1970
United Republic of Tanzania	–	5 April 1984
United States of America	11 December 1948	25 November 1988 *Res.*
Uruguay	11 December 1948	11 July 1967
Uzbekistan	–	9 September 1999
Venezuela	–	12 July 1960 *Res.*

cont.

affairs which are the responsibilities of the Central People's Government of the People's Republic of China.

In this connection, [the Government of the People's Republic of China informs the Secretary-General of the following]:

The Convention on the Prevention and Punishment of the Crime of Genocide, adopted at Paris on 9 December 1948 (hereinafter referred to as the "Convention"), to which the Government of the People's Republic of China deposited the instrument of ratification on 18 April 1983, will apply to the Macau Special Administrative Region with effect from 20 December 1999. The Government of the People's Republic of China also wishes to make the following declaration:

The reservation made by the Government of the People's Republic of China to Article 9 of the Convention will also apply to the Macau Special Administrative Region.

The Government of the People's Republic of China will assume responsibility for the international rights and obligations arising from the application of the Convention to the Macau Special Administrative Region.

13 Notification of territorial application received on 30 January 1970 (Channel Islands, Isle of Man, Dominica, Grenada, St. Lucia, St.Vincent, Bahamas, Bermuda, British Virgin Islands, Falkland Islands and Dependencies, Fiji, Gibraltar, Hong Kong, Pitcairn, St. Helena and Dependencies, Seychelles, Turks and Caicos Islands) and 2 June 1970 (Kingdom of Tonga).

State	*Signatures*	*Ratifications, Accessions, Notifications of Succession or Continuity (C)*
Viet Nam[14]	–	9 June 1981 *Res.*
Yemen[15]	–	9 February 1987 *Res.*
Yugoslavia (Serbia and Montenegro)[16, 17]	–	12 March 2001 *Res.*
Zimbabwe	-	13 May 1991

[14] Accession on behalf of the Republic of Viet Nam on 11 August 1950. (For the text of objections to some of the reservations made upon the said accession, see publication, (ST/LEG/SER.D/13, p.91).

[15] The Yemen Arab Republic acceded to the Convention on 6 April 1989.

[16] The former Yugoslavia was an original Member of the United Nations, the Charter having been signed and ratified on its behalf on 26 June 1945, and 19 October 1945, respectively. The following Republics constituting the former Yugoslavia declared their independence on the dates indicated: Slovenia (25 June 1991), The former Yugoslav Republic of Macedonia (17 September 1991), Croatia (25 June 1991), and Bosnia and Herzegovina (6 March 1992). Yugoslavia came into being on 27 April 1992 following the promulgation of the constitution of the Federal Republic of Yugoslavia on that day. Yugoslavia nevertheless advised the Secretary-General on 27 April 1992 that it claimed to continue the international legal personality of the former Yugoslavia. Yugoslavia accordingly claimed to be a member of those international organizations of which the former Yugoslavia had been a member. It also claimed that all those treaty acts that had been performed by the former Yugoslavia were directly attributable to it, as being the same state (see document S/23877 and A/46/915). Bosnia and Herzegovina, Croatia, Slovenia and The former Yugoslav Republic of Macedonia, all of which had applied for and were admitted to membership in the United Nations, in accordance with Article 4 of the Charter (by resolutions 46/237 adopted on 22 May 1992, 46/238 adopted on 22 May 1992, 46/236 adopted on 22 May 1992, and 47/225 adopted on 8 April 1993 respectively), objected to this claim.

In its resolution 47/1 of 22 September 1992, the General Assembly, acting upon the recommendation of the Security Council in its resolution 777 (1992) of 19 September 1992, considered that Yugoslavia could not continue automatically the membership of the former Yugoslavia in the United Nations, and decided that it should accordingly apply for membership in the Organization. It also decided that Yugoslavia could not participate in the work of the General Assembly. The Legal Counsel took the view, however, that this resolution of the General Assembly neither terminated nor suspended the membership of the former Yugoslavia in the United Nations. At the same time, the Legal Counsel expressed the view that the admission of a new Yugoslavia to membership in the United Nations, in accordance with Article 4 of the Charter of the United Nations, would terminate the situation that had been created by General Assembly resolution 47/1 (see document A/47/485).

The General Assembly admitted Yugoslavia to membership by its resolution A/55/12 on 1 November 2000. At the same time, Yugoslavia renounced its claim to have continued the international legal personality of the former Yugoslavia. See objections to Yugoslavia's instrument of accession and its reservation by Bosnia-Herzegovina, Croatia and Sweden, pp. 857, 858, 862.

[17] The Socialist Federal Republic of Yugoslavia signed the present Convention on 11 December 1948 and ratified it on 29 August 1950. See also note 5.

DECLARATIONS AND RESERVATIONS[1]

ALBANIA (*reservation made on accession*)
As regards Article 9: The People's Republic of Albania does not consider as binding upon itself the provision of Article 9 which provides that disputes between the Contracting Parties with regard to the interpretation, application and implementation of the Convention shall be referred for examination to the International Court at the request of any party to the dispute. The People's Republic of Albania declares that, as regards the International Court's jurisdiction in respect of disputes concerning the interpretation, application and implementation of the Convention, the People's Republic of Albania will, as hitherto, maintain the position that in each particular case the agreement of all parties to the dispute is essential for the submission of any particular dispute to the International Court for decision.

As regards Article 12: The People's Republic of Albania declares that it is not in agreement with Article 12 of the Convention and considers that all the provisions of the Convention should extend to non-self-governing territories, including trust territories.

On 19 July 1999, the Government of Albania informed the Secretary-General that it had decided to withdraw its reservation regarding Article 9 made upon accession.

ALGERIA (*reservation made on accession*)
The Democratic and Popular Republic of Algeria does not consider itself bound by Article 9 of the Convention, which confers on the International Court of Justice jurisdiction in all disputes relating to the said Convention.

The Democratic and Popular Republic of Algeria declares that no provision of Article 6 of the said Convention shall be interpreted as depriving its tribunals of jurisdiction in cases of genocide or other acts enumerated in Article 3 which have been committed in its territory or as conferring such jurisdiction on foreign tribunals.

International tribunals may, as an exceptional measure, be recognized as having jurisdiction, in cases in which the Algerian Government has given its express approval.

The Democratic and Popular Republic of Algeria declares that it does not accept the terms of Article 12 of the Convention and considers that all the provisions of the said Convention should apply to non-self-governing territories, including trust territories.

ARGENTINA (*reservation made on accession*)
Ad Article 9: The Argentine Government reserves the right not to submit to the procedure laid down in this article any dispute relating directly or indirectly to the territories referred to in its reservation to Article 12.

Ad Article 12: If any other Contracting Party extends the application of the Convention to territories under the sovereignty of the Argentine Republic, this extension shall in no way affect the rights of the Republic.

BAHRAIN[2] (*reservation made on accession*)
With reference to article 9 of the Convention the Government of the State of Bahrain declares that, for the submission of any dispute in terms of this article to the jurisdiction of the International Court of Justice, the express consent of all the parties to the dispute is required in each case.

Moreover, the accession by the State of Bahrain to the said Convention shall in no way constitute recognition of Israel or be a cause for the establishment of any relations of any kind therewith.

---

1 Unless otherwise indicated, the declarations and reservations were made upon ratification, accession or succession. For objections by certain states to some of these reservations, see pp. 859–865.

2 See declaration of Israel, p. 843, note 3.

BANGLADESH (*declaration made on accession*)
Article 9: For the submission of any dispute in terms of this article to the jurisdiction of the International Court of Justice, the consent of all parties to the dispute will be required in each case."

BELARUS *see Byelorussian Soviet Socialist Republic*

BULGARIA (*reservation made on accession*)
As regards Article 9: The People's Republic of Bulgaria does not consider as binding upon itself the provisions of Article 9 which provides that disputes between the Contracting Parties with regard to the interpretation, application and implementation of the present Convention shall be referred for examination to the International Court at the request of any party to the dispute, and declares that, as regards the International Court's jurisdiction in respect of disputes concerning the interpretation, application and implementation of the Convention, the People's Republic of Bulgaria will, as hitherto, maintain the position that in each particular case the agreement of all parties to the dispute is essential for the submission of any particular dispute to the International Court for decision.

As regards Article 12: The People's Republic of Bulgaria declares that it is not in agreement with Article 12 of the Convention and considers that all the provisions of the Convention should extend to non-self-governing territories, including trust territories.

On 24 June 1992, the Government of Bulgaria notified the Secretary-General its decision towithdraw the reservation to Article 9 of the Convention, made upon accession.

BURMA (*reservation made on ratification*)
1. With reference to Article 6, the Union of Burma makes the reservation that nothing contained in the said Article shall be construed as depriving the Courts and tribunals of the Union of jurisdiction or as giving foreign Courts and tribunals jurisdiction over any cases of genocide or any of the other acts enumerated in Article 3 committed within the Union territory.
2. With reference to Article 8, the Union of Burma makes the reservation that the said Article shall not apply to the Union.

BYELORUSSIAN Soviet Socialist Republic (*reservation made on ratification*)
As regards Article 9: The Byelorussian SSR does not consider as binding upon itself the provisions of Article 9 which provides that disputes between the Contracting Parties with regard to the interpretation, application and implementation of the present Convention shall be referred for examination to the International Court at the request of any party to the dispute, and declares that, as regards the International Court's jurisdiction in respect of disputes concerning the interpretation, application and implementation of the Convention, the Byelorussian SSR will, as hitherto, maintain the position that in each particular case the agreement of all parties to the dispute is essential for the submission of any particular dispute to the International Court for decision.

As regards Article 12: The Byelorussian SSR declares that it is not in agreement with Article 12 of the Convention and considers that all the provisions of the Convention should extend to non-self-governing territories, including trust territories.

In communications received on 19 April 1989, the Government of the Byelorussian Soviet Socialist Republic notified the Secretary-General that it had decided to withdraw the reservation relating to Article 9.

CHINA
Declaration made on ratification (18 April 1983)
1. The ratification to the said Convention by the Taiwan local authorities on 19 July 1951 in the name of China is illegal and therefore null and void.

Reservation made on ratification

2. The People's Republic of China does not consider itself bound by article 9 of the said Convention.

CZECH REPUBLIC *see Czechoslovakia*

CZECHOSLOVAKIA (*reservation made on ratification*)
As regards Article 9: Czechoslovakia does not consider as binding upon itself the provisions of Article 9 which provides that disputes between the Contracting Parties with regard to the interpretation, application and implementation of the present Convention shall be referred for examination to the International Court at the request of any party to the dispute, and declares that, as regards the International Court's jurisdiction in respect of disputes concerning the interpretation, application and implementation of the Convention, Czechoslovakia will, as hitherto, maintain the position that in each particular case the agreement of all parties to the dispute is essential for the submission of any particular dispute to the International Court for decision.

As regards Article 12: Czechoslovakia declares that it is not in agreement with Article 12 of the Convention and considers that all the provisions of the Convention should extend to non-self-governing territories, including trust territories.

By a notification received on 26 April 1991, the Government of Czechoslovakia notified the Secretary-General of its decision to withdraw the reservation to Article 9, made upon signature and confirmed upon ratification.

FINLAND (*reservation made on accession*)
Subject to the provisions of Article 47, paragraph 2, of the Constitution Act, 1919, concerning the impeachment of the President of the Republic of Finland.

On 5 January 1998, the Government of Finland notified the Secretary-General that it had decided to withdraw its reservation made upon accession to the Convention.

[GERMAN DEMOCRATIC REPUBLIC (*reservation made on accession*)
As regards Article 9: The German Democratic Republic does not consider itself bound by the provisions of article 9 of the Convention, which provides that disputes between the Contracting Parties relating to the interpretation, application or fulfilment of the Convention are, at the request of any of the parties to the dispute, to be submitted to the International Court of Justice, and declares that, as regards the jurisdiction of the International Court of Justice in respect of disputes relating to the interpretation, application or fulfilment of the Convention, the German Democratic Republic takes the position that, in each individual case, the consent of all parties to the dispute is necessary for the submission of a given dispute to the International Court of Justice for decision.

As regards Article 12: The German Democratic Republic declares that it cannot accept the provisions of article 12 of the Convention and considers that the Convention should also extend to Non-Self-Governing Territories, including Trust Territories.

The German Democratic Republic deems it necessary to state that article 11 of the Convention deprives a number of States of the opportunity to become Parties to the Convention. As the Convention regulates matters affecting the interests of all States, it should be open to participation by all States whose policies are guided by the purposes and principles of the Charter of the United Nations.]

HUNGARY (*reservation made on accession*)
The Hungarian People's Republic reserves its rights with regard to the provisions of Article 9 of the Convention which grant wide jurisdiction to the International Court at The Hague, and with regard to the provisions of Article 12 which do not define the obligations of countries having colonies with regard to questions of colonial exploitation and to acts which might be described as genocide.

In a communication received on 8 December 1989, the Government of Hungary notified the Secretary-General that it had decided to withdraw the reservation relating to Article 9 made upon accession.

INDIA (*reservation made on ratification*)
With reference to Article 9 of the Convention, the Government of India declares that, for the submission of any dispute in terms of this Article to the jurisdiction of the International Court of Justice, the consent of all the parties to the dispute is required in each case.

MALAYSIA
Reservation
That with reference to article 9 of the Convention, before any dispute to which Malaysia is a party may be submitted to the jurisdiction of the International Court of Justice under this article, the specific consent of Malaysia is required in each case.

Understanding
That the pledge to grant extradition in accordance with a state's laws and treaties in force found in article 7 extends only to acts which are criminal under the law of both the requesting and the requested state.

MONGOLIA (*reservation made on accession*)
The Government of the Mongolian People's Republic deems it necessary to state that the Mongolian People's Republic does not consider itself bound by the provisions of Article 9 which stipulates that disputes between the Contracting Parties relating to the interpretation, application or implementation of the present Convention shall be submitted to the International Court of Justice at the request of any of the parties to the dispute and declares that the Mongolian People's Republic will maintain the position that in each particular case the consent of all contending parties is essential for the submission of any particular dispute to the International Court of Justice.

The Government of the Mongolian People's Republic declares that it is not in a position to agree with Article 12 of the Convention and considers that the provisions of the said article should be extended to non-self-governing territories, including trust territories.

The Government of the Mongolian People's Republic deems it appropriate to draw attention to the discriminatory character of Article 11 of the Convention, under the terms of which a number of States are precluded from acceding to the Convention and declares that the Convention deals with matters which affect the interests of all States and it should, therefore, be open for accession by all States.

In a communication received on 19 July 1990, the Government of Mongolia notified the Secretary-General of its decision to withdraw the reservation relating to Article 9 made upon accession.

MOROCCO (*reservation made on accession*)
With reference to Article 6, the Government of His Majesty the King considers that Moroccan courts and tribunals alone have jurisdiction with respect to acts of genocide committed within the territory of the Kingdom of Morocco.

The competence of international courts may be admitted exceptionally in cases with respect to which the Moroccan Government has given its specific agreement.

With reference to Article 9, the Moroccan Government states that no dispute relating to the interpretation, application or fulfilment of the present Convention can be brought before the International Court of Justice, without the prior agreement of the parties to the-dispute.

MYANMAR *see Burma*

PHILIPPINES (*reservation made on ratification*)
1. With reference to Article 4 of the Convention, the Philippine Government cannot sanction any situation which would subject its Head of State, who is not a ruler, to

conditions less favourable than those accorded other Heads of State, whether constitutionally responsible Rulers or not. The Philippine Government does not consider the said article, therefore, as overriding the existing immunities from judicial processes guaranteed certain public officials by the Constitution of the Philippines.

2. With reference to Article 7 of the Convention, the Philippine Government does not undertake to give effect to said article until the Congress of the Philippines has enacted the necessary legislation defining and punishing the crime of genocide, which legislation, under the Constitution of the Philippines, cannot have any retroactive effect.
3. With reference to Articles 6 and 9 of the Convention, the Philippine Government takes the position that nothing contained in said articles shall be construed as depriving Philippine courts of jurisdiction over all cases of genocide committed within Philippine territory save only in those cases where the Philippine Government consents to have the decision of the Philippine courts reviewed by either of the international tribunals referred to in said articles. With further reference to Article 9 of the Convention, the Philippine Government does not consider said article to extend the concept of State responsibility beyond that recognized by the generally accepted principles of international law.

POLAND (*reservation made on accession*)
As regards Article 9: Poland does not regard itself as bound by the provisions of this article since the agreement of all the parties to a dispute is a necessary condition in each specific case for submission to the International Court of Justice.

As regards Article 12: Poland does not accept the provisions of this article considering that the Convention should apply to non-self-governing territories, including trust territories.

On 16 October 1997, the Government of Poland notified the Secretary-General that it had decided to withdraw its reservation with regard to Article 9 of the Convention made upon accession.

PORTUGAL (*declaration*)
The Portuguese Republic declares that it will interpret article 7 of the [said Convention] as recognizing the obligation to grant extradition established therein in cases where such extradition is not prohibited by the Constitution and other domestic legislation of the Portuguese Republic.

ROMANIA (*reservation made on accession*)
As regards Article 9: The People's Republic of Romania does not consider itself bound by the provisions of Article 9 which provides that disputes between the Contracting Parties relating to the interpretation, application or fulfilment of the Convention shall be submitted to the International Court of Justice at the request of any of the parties to the dispute, and declares that as regards the jurisdiction of the Court in disputes relating to the interpretation, application or fulfilment of the Convention, the People's Republic of Romania will adhere to the view which it has held up to the present, that in each particular case the agreement of all the parties to a dispute is required before it can be referred to the International Court of Justice for settlement.

As regards Article 12: The People's Republic of Romania declares that it is not in agreement with Article 12 of the Convention, and considers that all the provisions of the Convention should apply to the non-self-governing territories, including the trust territories.

On 2 April 1997, the Government of Romania informed the Secretary-General that it had decided to withdraw its reservation with regard to Article 9 of the Convention.

RUSSIAN FEDERATION *see Union of Soviet Socialist Republics*

RWANDA (*reservation made on accession*)
The Rwandese Republic does not consider itself as bound by article 9 of the Convention.

SINGAPORE (*reservation*)
That with reference to article 9 of the Convention, before any dispute to which the Republic of Singapore is a party may be submitted to the jurisdiction of the International Court of Justice under this article, the specific consent of the Republic of Singapore is required in each case.

SLOVAKIA *see Czechoslovakia*

SPAIN (*reservation made on accession*)
With a reservation in respect of the whole of Article 9 (jurisdiction of the International Court of Justice).

UKRAINIAN SOVIET SOCIALIST REPUBLIC (*reservation made on ratification*)
As regards Article 9: The Ukrainian SSR does not consider as binding upon itself the provisions of Article 9 which provides that disputes between the Contracting Parties with regard to the interpretation, application and implementation of the present Convention shall be referred for examination to the International Court at the request of any party to the dispute, and declares that, as regards the International Court's jurisdiction in respect of disputes concerning the interpretation, application and implementation of the Convention, the Ukrainian SSR will, as hitherto, maintain the position that in each particular case the agreement of all parties to the dispute is essential for the submission of any particular dispute to the International Court for decision.

As regards Article 12: The Ukrainian SSR declares that it is not in agreement with Article 12 of the Convention and considers that all the provisions of the Convention should extend to non-self-governing territories, including trust territories.

In a communication received on 20 April 1989, the Governments of the Ukrainian Soviet Socialist Republic notified the Secretary-General that they had decided to withdraw the reservation relating to Article 9.

UNION OF SOVIET SOCIALIST REPUBLICS (*reservation made on ratification*)
As regards Article 9: The Soviet Union does not consider as binding upon itself the provisions of Article 9 which provides that disputes between the Contracting Parties with regard to the interpretation, application and implementation of the present Convention shall be referred for examination to the International Court at the request of any party to the dispute, and declares that, as regards the International Court's jurisdiction in respect of disputes concerning the interpretation, application and implementation of the Convention, the Soviet Union will, as hitherto, maintain the position that in each particular case the agreement of all parties to the dispute is essential for the submission of any particular dispute to the International Court for decision.

As regards Article 12: The Union of Soviet Socialist Republics declares that it is not in agreement with Article 12 of the Convention and considers that all the provisions of the Convention should extend to non-self-governing territories, including trust territories.

In a communication received on 8 March 1989, the Governments of the Union of Soviet Socialist Republics notified the Secretary-General that they had decided to withdraw the reservation relating to Article 9.

UNITED STATES OF AMERICA
Reservations
1. That with reference to article 9 of the Convention, before any dispute to which the United States is a party may be submitted to the jurisdiction of the International

Court of Justice under this article, the specific consent of the United States is required in each case.

2[3]. That nothing in the Convention requires or authorizes legislation or other action by the United States of America prohibited by the Constitution of the United States as interpreted by the United States.

Understandings

1. That the term "intent to destroy, in whole or in part, a national, ethnical, racial, or religious group as such" appearing in article 2 means the specific intent to destroy, in whole or in substantial part, a national, ethnical, racial or religious group as such by the acts specified in article 2.
2. That the term "mental harm" in article 2(b) means permanent impairment of mental faculties through drugs, torture or similar techniques.
3. That the pledge to grant extradition in accordance with a state's laws and treaties in force found in article 7 extends only to acts which are criminal under the laws of both the requesting and the requested state and nothing in article 6 affects the right of any state to bring to trial before its own tribunals any of its nationals for acts committed outside a state.
4. That acts in the course of armed conflicts committed without the specific intent required by article 2 are not sufficient to constitute genocide as defined by this Convention.
5. That with regard to the reference to an international penal tribunal in article 6 of the Convention, the United States declares that it reserves the right to effect its participation in any such tribunal only by a treaty entered into specifically for that purpose with the advice and consent of the Senate.

VENEZUELA (*reservation made on accession*)

With reference to Article 6, notice is given that any proceedings to which Venezuela may be a party before an international penal tribunal would be invalid without Venezuela's prior express acceptance of the jurisdiction of such international tribunal.

With reference to Article 7, notice is given that the laws in force in Venezuela do not permit the extradition of Venezuelan nationals.

With reference to Article 9, the reservation is made that the submission of a dispute to the International Court of Justice shall be regarded as valid only when it takes place with Venezuela's approval, signified by the express conclusion of a prior agreement in each case.

VIET NAM (*reservation made on accession*)

1. The Socialist Republic of Viet Nam does not consider itself bound by article 9 of the Convention which provides the jurisdiction of the International Court of Justice in solving disputes between the Contracting Parties relating to the interpretation, application or fulfilment of the Convention at the request of any of the parties to disputes. The Socialist Republic of Viet Nam is of the view that, regarding the jurisdiction of the International Court of Justice in solving disputes referred to in article 9 of the Convention, the consent of the parties to the disputes except the criminals is diametrically necessary for the submission of a given dispute to the International Court of Justice for decision.
2. The Socialist Republic of Viet Nam does not accept article 12 of the Convention and considers that all provisions of the Convention should also extend to non-self-Governing Territories, including Trust Territories.
3. The Socialist Republic of Viet Nam considers that article 11 is of a discriminatory nature, depriving a number of States of the opportunity to become parties to the Convention, and holds that the Convention should be open for accession by all States.

---

[3] For objections to this reservation by Finland, Germany, Greece, Ireland, Italy, Norway, Spain and Sweden, see pp. 859–862.

YEMEN, PEOPLE'S DEMOCRATIC REPUBLIC (*reservation made on accession*)
In acceding to the aforesaid Convention, the People's Democratic Republic of Yemen does not consider itself bound by the provisions of Article 9 of that Convention, which stipulates that disputes between the Contracting Parties relating to the implementation, application or fulfilment of the Convention shall be submitted to the International Court of Justice at the request of any of the parties to the dispute. In no circumstances may the said Court have competence without the express agreement of all parties to the dispute.

YUGOSLAVIA (*reservation*)
The Federal Republic of Yugoslavia does not consider itself bound by Article 9 of the Convention on the Prevention and Punishment of the Crime of Genocide and, therefore, before any dispute to which the Federal Republic of Yugoslavia is a party may be validly submitted to the jurisdiction of the International Court of Justice under this Article, the specific and explicit consent of the FRY is required in each case.

OBJECTIONS[1]

ARGENTINA[2] (*3 October 1983*)[3]
[The Government of Argentina makes a] formal objection to the [declaration] of territorial extension issued by the United Kingdom with regard to the Malvinas Islands (and dependencies), which that country is illegally occupying and refers to as the "Falkland Islands". The Argentine Republic rejects and considers null and void the [said declaration] of territorial extension.

AUSTRALIA
15 November 1950
The Australian Government does not accept any of the reservations contained in the instrument of accession of the People's Republic of Bulgaria, or in the instrument of ratification of the Republic of the Philippines.
Also, the Australian Government does not accept any of the reservations made at the time of signature of the Convention by the Byelorussian Soviet Socialist Republic, Czechoslovakia, the Ukrainian Soviet Socialist Republic and the Union of Soviet Socialist Republics.

19 January 1951
The Australian Government does not accept the reservations contained in the instruments of accession of the Governments of Poland and Romania.

BELGIUM
The Government of Belgium does not accept the reservations made by Bulgaria, Byelorussian Soviet Socialist Republic, Czechoslovakia, Poland, Romania, the Ukrainian Soviet Socialist Republic and the Union of Soviet Socialist Republics.

---

1 Unless otherwise indicated, the objections were communicated to the Secretary-General on ratification, accession or succession by the objecting state.

2 On 28 February 1985, the Secretary-General received from the Government of the United Kingdom of Great Britain and Northern Ireland the following declaration:
"The Government of the United Kingdom of Great Britain and Northern Ireland have no doubt as to their right, by notification to the Depositary under the relevant provisions of the above-mentioned Convention, to extend the application of the Convention in question to the Falkland Islands or to the Falkland Islands Dependencies, as the case may be.
For this reason alone, the Government of the United Kingdom are unable to regard the Argentine [communication under reference] as having any legal effect."

3 Dates indicating the date of communication received by the depositary.

BOSNIA-HERZEGOVINA (27 December 2001)
On 21 March 2001 the Secretary-General of the United Nations confirmed to the Permanent Representative of Yugoslavia to the United Nations the receipt of a 'Notification of Accession to the Convention on the Prevention and Punishment of the Crime of Genocide (1948)'. The note of the Secretary-General carries reference as LA41 TR/221/1 (4-1).

The Presidency of Bosnia and Herzegovina objects to the deposition of this instrument of accession.

On 29 June 2001, Bosnia and Herzegovina, the Republic of Croatia, the Republic of Macedonia, the Republic of Slovenia and the Federal Republic of Yugoslavia signed an "Agreement on Succession Issues" in which these States, among other things, declare that they are "in sovereign equality the five successor States to the former Socialist Federal Republic of Yugoslavia". A copy of the Agreement is enclosed. [Copy not reproduced herein.] For this reason, there can be no question of "accession", but rather there is an issue of succession. This, in itself, implies that the Federal Republic of Yugoslavia has effectively succeeded the former Socialist Federal Republic of Yugoslavia as of 27 April 1992 (the date of the proclamation of the FRY) as a Party to the Genocide Convention.

Apart from that, the Federal Republic of Yugoslavia upon its proclamation on 27 April 1992 declared – and communicated this to the Secretary-General – that it would "strictly abide by all the commitments that the Socialist Federal Republic of Yugoslavia assumed internationally" (UN Doc. A/46/915).

For these two reasons it is not possible for the FRY to effectively lay down a reservation with regards to part of the Genocide Convention (i.e. Article 9 of the Convention) several years after 27 April 1992, the day on which FRY became bound to the Genocide Convention in its entirety. Bosnia and Herzegovina refers to Articles 2(1)(d) and 19 of the 1969 Vienna Convention on the Law of Treaties, which explicitly states that a reservation may only be formulated "when signing, ratifying, accepting, approving or acceding to a treaty".

The Presidency of Bosnia and Herzegovina therefore deems the so-called "Notification of Accession to the Convention on the Prevention and Punishment of the Crime of Genocide (1948)" submitted by the Government of the Federal Republic of Yugoslavia to be null and void. Moreover, the International Court of Justice declared in its Judgement of 11 July 1996, "Yugoslavia was bound by the provisions of the Convention" at least at the date of the filing of the Application in the case introduced by Bosnia and Herzegovina on 20 March 1993 (ICJ Rep. 1996, p. 610, para.17). The Federal Republic of Yugoslavia continues to be bound under the same conditions, that is without any reservation.

BRAZIL
The Government of Brazil objects to the reservations made to the Convention by Bulgaria, the Byelorussian Soviet Socialist Republic, Czechoslovakia, the Philippines, Poland, Romania, the Ukrainian Soviet Socialist Republic and the Union of Soviet Socialist Republics. The Brazilian Government considers the said reservations as incompatible with the object and purpose of the Convention.

The position taken by the Government of Brazil is founded on the Advisory Opinion of the International Court of Justice of 28 May 1951,[4] and on the resolution adopted by the sixth session of the General Assembly on 12 January 1952, on reservations to multilateral conventions.[5]

The Brazilian Government reserves the right to draw any such legal consequences as it may deem fit from its formal objection to the above-mentioned reservations.

---

4 *International Court of Justice, Report 1951*, p. 15.

5 Resolution 598 (VI) of 12 January 1952; see *Official Records of the General Assembly, Sixth Session, Supplement No. 20* (A/2119), p. 84.

CHINA[6] (*15 November 1954*)
The Government of China ... objects to all the identical reservations made at the time of signature or ratification or accession to the Convention by Albania, Bulgaria, Burma, Byelorussian Soviet Socialist Republic, Czechoslovakia, Hungary, Poland, Romania, the Ukrainian Soviet Socialist Republic and the Union of Soviet Socialist Republics. The Chinese Government considers the above-mentioned reservations as incompatible with the object and purpose of the Convention and, therefore, by virtue of the Advisory Opinion of the International Court of Justice of 28 May 1951,[7] would not regard the above-mentioned States as being Parties to the Convention.[8]

CROATIA (*18 May 2001*)
The Government of the Republic of Croatia objects to the deposition of the instrument of accession of the Federal Republic of Yugoslavia to the Convention on the Prevention and Punishment of the Crime of Genocide, due to the fact that the Federal Republic of Yugoslavia is already bound by the Convention since its emergence as one of the five equal successor states to the former Socialist Federal Republic of Yugoslavia.

This fact was confirmed by the Federal Republic of Yugoslavia in its Declaration of 27 April 1992, as communicated to the Secretary-General (UN doc. A/46/915). Notwithstanding the political reasoning behind it, in its 1992 Declaration the Federal Republic of Yugoslavia stated that it "shall strictly abide by all the commitments that the former Socialist Federal Republic of Yugoslavia made internationally".

In this regard the Republic of Croatia notes in particular the decision of the International Court of Justice in its judgement of 11 July 1996 that the Federal Republic of Yugoslavia "was bound by provisions of the [Genocide] Convention on the date of the filing of [the Application by Bosnia and Herzegovina], namely on 20 March 1993" (ICJ Reports 1996, p. 595, at para. 17).

The Government of the Republic of Croatia further objects to the reservation made by the Federal Republic of Yugoslavia in respect of Article 9 of the Convention on the Prevention and Punishment of the Crime of Genocide, and considers it to be incompatible with the object and purpose of the Convention. The Government of the Republic of Croatia considers the Convention on the Prevention and Punishment of the Crime of Genocide to be fully in force and applicable between the Republic of Croatia and the Federal Republic of Yugoslavia, including Article 9.

The Government of the Republic of Croatia deems that neither the purported way of becoming a party to the Genocide Convention *ex nunc* by the Federal Republic of Yugoslavia, nor its purported reservation, have any legal effect regarding the jurisdiction of the International Court of Justice with respect to the pending proceedings initiated before the International Court of Justice by the Republic of Croatia against the Federal Republic of Yugoslavia pursuant to the Genocide Convention.

CUBA
The Government of Cuba does not accept the reservations made by Bulgaria, the Byelorussian Soviet Socialist Republic, Czechoslovakia, Poland, Romania, the Ukrainian Soviet Socialist Republic and the Union of Soviet Socialist Republics.

By a notification received by the Secretary-General on 29 January 1982, the Government of Cuba withdrew the declaration made on its behalf upon ratification of the said Convention with respect to the reservations to articles 9 and 12 by Bulgaria, the Byelorussian Soviet Socialist Republic, Czechoslovakia, Poland, Romania, the Ukrainian Soviet Socialist Republic and the Union of Soviet Socialist Republics.

---

6 See note 7 on p. 844 and declaration of the People's Republic of China, p. 850–851.

7 *International Court of Justice, Report 1951*, p. 15.

8 Communications received on 15 November 1954, 13 September 1955 and 25 July 1956, the last two in respect of the reservations by Albania and Burma, respectively.

DENMARK (*27 December 1989*)
With regard to reservation (2) made by the United States of America:
In the view of the Government of Denmark this reservation is subject to general principle of treaty interpretation according to which a party may not invoke the provisions of its internal law as justification for failure to perform a treaty.

ECUADOR
The Government of Ecuador is not in agreement with the reservations made to Articles 9 and 12 of the Convention by the Governments of Bulgaria, Byelorussian Soviet Socialist Republic, Czechoslovakia, the Ukrainian Soviet Socialist Republic and the Union of Soviet Socialist Republics and, therefore, they do not apply to Ecuador which accepted without any modifications the integral text of the Convention.[9]

The Government of Ecuador does not accept the reservations made by the Governments of Poland and Romania to Articles 9 and 12 of the Convention.[10]

ESTONIA
With regard to reservation (2) made by the United States of America:
The Estonian Government objects to this reservation on the grounds that it creates uncertainty, as to the extent of the obligations the Government of the United States of America is prepared to assume with regard to the Convention. According to article 27 of the Vienna Convention on the Law of Treaties, no party may invoke the provisions of its domestic law as justification for failure to perform a treaty.

FINLAND (*22 December 1989*)
With respect to reservation (2) made by the United States of America:
In the view of the Government of Finland this reservation is subject to the general principle of treaty interpretation according to which a party may not invoke the provisions of its internal law as justification for failure to perform a treaty.

GERMANY (*11 January 1990*)
On 11 January 1990, the Secretary-General received from the Government of the Federal Republic of Germany the following declaration:

The Government of the Federal Republic of Germany has taken note of the declarations made under the heading "Reservations" by the Government of the United States of America upon ratification of the Convention on the Prevention and Punishment of the Crime of Genocide adopted by the General Assembly of the United Nations on 9 December 1948. The Government of the Federal Republic of Germany interprets paragraph (2) of the said declaration as a reference to article 5 of the Convention and therefore as not in any way affecting the obligations of the United States of America as a state party to the Convention.

GREECE
We further declare that we have not accepted and do not accept any reservation which has already been made or which may hereafter be made by the countries signatory to this instrument or by countries which have acceded or may hereafter accede thereto.

26 January 1990
The Government of the Hellenic Republic cannot accept the first reservation entered by the United States of America upon ratifying the Agreement on the Prevention and Punishment of the Crime of Genocide, for it considers such a reservation to be incompatible with the Convention.

---

9 Communications received on 31 March 1950 and 21 August 1950, the latter with respect to the reservations made by the Government of Bulgaria.

10 Communication received on 9 January 1951.

With regard to reservation (2) made by the United States of America:
In the view of the Government of the Hellenic Republic this reservation is subject to general principle of treaty interpretation according to which a party may not invoke the provisions of its internal law as justification for failure to perform a treaty.

IRELAND (*22 December 1989*)
The Government of Ireland is unable to accept the second reservation made by the United States of America on the occasion of its ratification of the [said] Convention on the grounds that as a generally accepted rule of international law a party to an international agreement may not, by invoking the terms of its internal law, purport to override the provisions of the Agreement.

ITALY (*29 December 1989*)
The Government of the Republic of Italy objects to the second reservation entered by the United States of America. It creates uncertainty as to the extent of the obligations which the Government of the United States of America is prepared to assume with regard to the Convention.

MEXICO (*4 June 1990*)
The Government of Mexico believes that the reservation made by the United States Government to article 9 of the aforesaid Convention should be considered invalid because it is not in keeping with the object and purpose of the Convention, nor with the principle governing the interpretation of treaties whereby no State can invoke provisions of its domestic law as a reason for not complying with a treaty.

If the aforementioned reservation were applied, it would give rise to a situation of uncertainty as to the scope of the obligations which the United States Government would assume with respect to the Convention.

Mexico's objection to the reservation in question should not be interpreted as preventing the entry into force of the 1948 Convention between the [Mexican] Government and the United States Government.

NETHERLANDS
The Government of the Kingdom of the Netherlands declares that it considers the reservations made by Albania, Algeria, Bulgaria, the Byelorussian Soviet Socialist Republic, Czechoslovakia, Hungary, India, Morocco, Poland, Romania, the Ukrainian Soviet Socialist Republic and the Union of Soviet Socialist Republics in respect of Article 9 of the Convention on the Prevention and Punishment of the Crime of Genocide, opened for signature at Paris on 9 December 1948, to be incompatible with the object and purpose of the Convention. The Government of the Kingdom of the Netherlands therefore does not deem any State which has made or which will make such reservation a party to the Convention.

27 December 1989
With regard to the reservations made by the United States of America:
As concerns the first reservation, the Government of the Kingdom of the Netherlands recalls its declaration, made on 20 June 1966 on the occasion of the accession of the Kingdom of the Netherlands to the Convention [...] stating that in its opinion the reservations in respect of article 9 of the Convention, made at that time by a number of states, were incompatible with the object and purpose of the Convention, and that the Government of the Kingdom of the Netherlands did not consider states making such reservations parties to the Convention. Accordingly, the Government of the Kingdom of the Netherlands does not consider the United States of America a party to the Convention. Similarly, the Government of the Kingdom of the Netherlands does not consider parties to the Convention other states which have made such reservations, i.e., in addition to the states mentioned in the aforementioned declaration, the People's Republic of China, Democratic Yemen, the German Democratic Republic, the Mongo-

lian People's Republic, the Philippines, Rwanda, Spain, Venezuela, and Viet Nam, on the other hand, the Government of the Kingdom of the Netherlands does consider parties to the Convention those states that have since withdrawn their reservations, i.e. the Union of Soviet Socialist Republics, the Byelorussian Soviet Socialist Republic, and the Ukrainian Soviet Socialist Republic.

As the Convention may come into force between the Kingdom of the Netherlands and the United States of America as a result of the latter withdrawing its reservation in respect of article 9, the Government of the Kingdom of the Netherlands deems it useful to express the following position on the second reservation of the United States of America:

The Government of the Kingdom of the Netherlands objects to this reservation on the ground that it creates uncertainty as to the extent of the obligations the Government of the United States of America is prepared to assume with regard to the Convention. Moreover, any failure by the United States of America to act upon the obligations contained in the Convention on the ground that such action would be prohibited by the constitution of the United States would be contrary to the generally accepted rule of international law, as laid down in article 27 of the Vienna Convention on the law of treaties (Vienna, 23 May 1969).

23 February 1996
With regard to the reservations made by Malaysia and Singapore made upon accession:
The Government of the Kingdom of the Netherlands recalls its declaration made on 20 June 1966 on the occasion of the accession [to the said Convention].

Accordingly, the Government of the Netherlands declares that it considers the reservations made by Malaysia and Singapore in respect of article 9 of the Convention incompatible with the object and purpose of the Convention. The Government of the Kingdom of the Netherlands does not consider Malaysia and Singapore Parties to the Convention.

On the other hand, the Government of the Kingdom of the Netherlands does consider Parties to the Convention those States that have since withdrawn their reservations in respect of article 9 of the Convention, i.e. Hungary, Bulgaria and Mongolia.

NORWAY
10 April 1952
The Norwegian Government does not accept the reservations made to the Convention by the Government of the Philippines at the time of ratification.

22 December 1989
With regard to reservation (2) made by the United States of America:
In the view of the Government of Norway this reservation is subject to the general principle of treaty interpretation according to which a party may not invoke the provisions of its internal law as justification for failure to perform a treaty.

14 October 1996
... In [the view of the Government of Norway], reservations in respect of article 9 of the Convention are incompatible with the object and purpose of the said Convention. Accordingly, the Government of Norway does not accept the reservations entered by the Governments of Singapore and Malaysia to article 9 of the said Convention.

SPAIN (*29 December 1989*)
With regard to reservation (2) made by the United States of America:
Spain interprets the reservation entered by the United States of America to the Convention on the Prevention and Punishment of the Crime of Genocide adopted by the General Assembly of the United Nations on 9 December 1948 [...] to mean that legislation or other action by the United States of America will continue to be in accordance with the provisions of the Convention on the Prevention and Punishment of the Crime of Genocide.

SRI LANKA (*6 February 1951*)
The Government of Ceylon does not accept the reservations made by Romania to the Convention.

SWEDEN
22 December 1989
With regard to reservation (2) made by the United States of America:
The Government of Sweden is of the view that a State party to the Convention may not invoke the provisions of its national legislation, including the Constitution, to justify that it does not fulfil its obligations under the Convention and therefore objects to the reservation.

This objection does not constitute an obstacle to the entry into force of the Convention between Sweden and the United States of America.

2 April 2002
With regard to the reservation made by the Government of Yugoslavia upon accession:
The Government of Sweden has taken note of the Secretary-General's circular notification 164.2001.TREATIES-.1 of 15 March 2001, stating the intent of the Federal Republic of Yugoslavia to accede, with a reservation, to the 1948 Convention on the Prevention and Punishment of the Crime of Genocide. The Government of Sweden regards the Federal Republic of Yugoslavia as one successor state to the Socialist Federal Republic of Yugoslavia and, as such, a Party to the Convention from the date of the entering into force od the Convention for the Socialist Federal Republic of Yugoslavia. The Government of Sweden hereby communicates that it considers the said reservation as having been made too late, according to article 19 of the 1969 Vienna Convention on the Law of Treaties, and thus null and void.

UNITED KINGDOM OF GREAT BRITAIN AND NORTHERN IRELAND
The Government of the United Kingdom does not accept the reservations to Articles 4, 7, 8, 9 or 12 of the Convention made by Albania, Algeria, Argentina, Bulgaria, Burma, the Byelorussian Soviet Socialist Republic, Czechoslovakia, Hungary, India, Mongolia, Morocco, the Philippines, Poland, Romania, Spain, the Ukrainian Soviet Socialist Republic, the Union of Soviet Socialist Republics or Venezuela.

21 November 1975
The Government of the United Kingdom of Great Britain and Northern Ireland have consistently stated that they are unable to accept reservations in respect of article 9 of the said Convention; in their view this is not the kind of reservation which intending parties to the Convention have the right to make.

Accordingly, the Government of the United Kingdom do not accept the reservation entered by the Republic of Rwanda against article 9 of the Convention. They also wish to place on record that they take the same view of the similar reservation made by the German Democratic Republic as notified by the circular letter C.N.85.1973. TREATIES-2 of 25 April 1973.

26 August 1983
With regard to a declaration and reservation made by Viet Nam and China concerning Article 9:
The Government of the United Kingdom have consistently stated that they are unable to accept reservations to this article. Likewise, in conformity with the attitude adopted by them in previous cases, the Government of the United Kingdom do not accept the reservation entered by Viet Nam relating to article 12.

30 December 1987
With regard to a reservation made by Democratic Yemen concerning Article 9:
The Government of the United Kingdom of Great Britain and Northern Ireland have consistently stated that they are unable to accept reservations in respect of article 9 of

the said Convention; in their view this is not the kind of reservation which intending parties to the Convention have the right to make.

Accordingly the Government of the United Kingdom of Great Britain and Northern Ireland do not accept the reservation entered by the People's Democratic Republic of Yemen against article 9 of the Convention.

22 December 1989
The Government of the United Kingdom have consistently stated that they are unable to accept reservations to article 9. Accordingly, in conformity with the attitude adopted by them in previous cases, the Government of the United Kingdom do not accept the first reservation entered by the United States of America.

The Government of the United Kingdom object to the second reservation entered by the United States of America. It creates uncertainty as to the extent of the obligations which the Government of the United States of America is prepared to assume with regard to the Convention.

20 March 1996
With regard to reservations to article 9 made by Malaysia and Singapore upon accession:
The Government of the United Kingdom of Great Britain and Northern Ireland have consistently stated that they are unable to accept reservations to article 9. In their view, these are not the kind of reservations which intending parties to the Convention have the right to make.

Accordingly, the Government of the United Kingdom do not accept the reservations entered by the Government of Singapore and Malaysia to article 9 of the Convention.

VIET NAM, REPUBLIC OF
[Referring to the reservations to Articles 9 and 12 made on signature by the Byelorussian Soviet Socialist Republic, Czechoslovakia, the Ukrainian Soviet Socialist Republic and the Union of Soviet Socialist Republics, and on accession by Bulgaria, and to the reservations to Articles 4, 6, 7 and 9 of the Convention made on ratification by the Philippines, the Government of the Republic of Viet Nam informed the Secretary-General that it was the intent of the Government of Viet Nam in acceding to the Convention for the Prevention and Punishment of the Crime of Genocide, to accept only the text of that Convention as approved on 9 December 1948 in resolution 260 A (III) and voted by the General Assembly of the United Nations at its 179th plenary meeting, and not the reservations submitted by the above-mentioned States or by any other State at the time of signature by their representatives, or of deposit of their instruments of ratification or accession to the Convention.][11]

[11] Communication received on 3 November 1950. The Democratic Republic of Viet Nam and the Republic of South Viet Nam (the latter of which replaced the Republic of Viet Nam) united on 2 July 1976 to constitute the Socialist Republic of Viet Nam. The Socialist Republic of Viet Nam acceded to this Convention on 9 June 1981 with reservation (see p. 855) but without objections.

No. 62

HUMANITARIAN ASSISTANCE TO VICTIMS OF NATURAL DISASTERS AND SIMILAR EMERGENCY SITUATIONS

I. Resolution 43/131 adopted by the United Nations General Assembly, 8 December 1988

II. Resolution 45/100 adopted by the United Nations General Assembly, 14 December 1990

INTRODUCTORY NOTE: Following the Chernobyl accident, the Copenhagen Symposium convened by the International Academy of Human Rights in 1986 expressed the opinion that the right to humanitarian assistance, as well as the obligation of states to contribute to such assistance, needed to be recognized and expressed in an international document approved by all states members of the international community. An International Conference on Humanitarian Law and Morals, held in Paris in January 1987, considered "that the right to humanitarian assistance is a right of the human being which must be recognized for each individual or group of individuals threatened or victim of serious encroachments on their life and their physical and mental health". This right includes the right to solicit assistance and to benefit from it without discrimination. On the initiative of France, the United Nations General Assembly adopted three consecutive resolutions on humanitarian assistance: the following resolutions 43/131, on 8 December 1988, 45/100, on 14 December 1990, reproduced below, and the resolution 46/182, on 19 December 1991, which is reproduced in *No. 63*.

At the XXIth Ordinary Session the General Assembly of the Organization of American States, on 7 June 1991, at Santiago, Chile, adopted an Inter-American Convention to facilitate disaster assistance and to regulate international procedures for providing it (*OEA Documentos Oficiales*, OEA/Ser.A/49 (SEPF), Serie sobre tratados 74, 55 p.) It entered into force on 16 October 1996, but was ratified by only two states (Panama and Peru). It is applicable only when a state furnishes assistance in response to a request from another state.

AUTHENTIC TEXT: Arabic, Chinese, English, French, Russian and Spanish.

TEXT PUBLISHED IN:
I. Resolution 43/131: Resolutions and decisions adopted by the General Assembly during the forty-third session, Volume I, *September 20 - December 22, 1988,* General Assembly, Official Records, Forty-third session, Supplement No. 49 (A/43/49), New York, United Nations, 1989, p. 207 (Engl., also editions in Arabic, Chinese, French, Russian and Spanish); *Droit de conflits armés*, pp. 937–942 (French).
II. Resolution 45/100: Resolutions and decisions adopted by the General Assembly during the forty-fifth session, Vol. I, *September 18 – December 21, 1991*, General Assembly, Official Records, Forty-fifth session, Supplement No. 49 (A/45/49), New York, United Nations, 1991, pp. 183-184 (Engl.), also editions in Arabic, Chinese, French, Russian and Spanish); *Droit des conflits armés*, pp. 937–942 (French).

* * *

I. 43/131 Humanitarian assistance to victims of natural disasters and similar emergency situtations

The General Assembly,

Recalling *that one of the purposes of the United Nations is to achieve international co-operation in solving international problems of an economic, social, cultural or humanitarian character, and in promoting and encouraging respect for human rights and fundamental freedoms for all without distinction as to race, sex, language, or religion,*

Reaffirming *the sovereignty, territorial integrity and national unity of States, and recognizing that it is up to each State first and foremost to take care of the victims of natural disasters and similar emergency situations occurring on its territory,*

Deeply *concerned about the suffering of the victims of natural disasters and similar emergency situations, the loss in human lives, the destruction of property and the mass displacement of populations that result from them,*

Bearing in mind *that natural disasters and similar emergency situations have grave consequences for the economic and social plans of all countries concerned,*

Desiring *that the international community should respond speedily and effectively to appeals for emergency humanitarian assistance made in particular through the Secretary-General,*

Mindful *of the importance of humanitarian assistance for the victims of natural disasters and similar emergency situations,*

Recognizing *that the international community makes an important contribution to the sustenance and protection of such victims, whose health and life may be seriously endangered,*

Considering *that the abandonment of the victims of natural disasters and similar emergency situations without humanitarian assistance constitutes a threat to human life and an offence to human dignity,*

Concerned *about the difficulties that victims of natural disasters and similar emergency situations may experience in receiving humanitarian assistance,*

Convinced *that, in providing humanitarian assistance, in particular the supply of food, medicines or health care, for which access to victims is essential, rapid relief will avoid a tragic increase in their number,*

Aware *that alongside the action of Governments and intergovernmental organizations, the speed and efficiency of this assistance often depends on the help and aid of local and non-governmental organizations working with strictly humanitarian motives,*

Recalling *that, in the event of natural disasters and similar emergency situations, the principles of humanity, neutrality and impartiality must be given utmost consideration by all those involved in providing humanitarian assistance,*

1. Reaffirms *the importance of humanitarian assistance for the victims of natural disasters and similar emergency situations;*
2. Reaffirms *also the sovereignty of affected States and their primary role in the initiation, organization, co-ordination and implementation of humanitarian assistance within their respective territories;*
3. Stresses *the important contribution made in providing humanitarian assistance by intergovernmental and non-governmental organizations working with strictly humanitarian motives;*

4. Invites *all States in need of such assistance to facilitate the work of these organizations in implementing humanitarian assistance, in particular the supply of food, medicines and health care, for which access to victims is essential;*
5. Appeals, *therefore, to all States to give their support to these organizations working to provide humanitarian assistance, where needed, to the victims of natural disasters and similar emergency situations;*
6. Urges *States in proximity to areas of natural disasters and similar emergency situations, particularly in the case of regions that are difficult to reach, to participate closely with the affected countries in international efforts with a view to facilitating, to the extent possible, the transit of humanitarian assistance;*
7. Calls *upon all the intergovernmental, governmental and non-governmental organizations dealing with humanitarian assistance to co-operate as closely as possible with the Office of the United Nations Disaster Relief Co-ordinator or any other ad hoc mechanism set up by the Secretary-General in the co-ordination of aid;*
8. Requests *the Secretary-General to seek the views of Governments, intergovernmental, governmental and non-governmental organizations with regard to the possibility of enhancing the effectiveness of international mechanisms and increasing the speed of assistance in the best possible conditions for the victims of natural disasters and similar emergency situations, where needed, and to report his findings to the General Assembly at its forty-fifth session;*
9. Decides *to consider this question at its forty-fifth session.*

II. 45/100 Humanitarian assistance to victims of natural disasters and similar emergency situations

The General Assembly,

Recalling *its resolution 43/131 of 8 December 1988,*

Recalling *that one of the principles of the United Nations is to achieve international co-operation in solving international problems of an economic, social, cultural or humanitarian character and in promoting and encouraging respect for human rights and fundamental freedoms for all without distinction as to race, sex, language, or religion,*

Reaffirming *the sovereignty, territorial integrity and national unity of States, and recognizing that it is up to each State first and foremost to take care of the victims of natural disasters and similar emergency situations occurring on its territory,*

Deeply concerned *about the suffering of the victims of natural disasters and similar emergency situations, the loss in human lives, the destruction of property and the mass displacement of populations that results from them,*

Concerned *about the fate of persons who, following such displacement, are in an extremely precarious situation, particularly in a country other than that of which they are nationals,*

Considering *that the abandonment of the victims of natural disasters and similar emergency situations without humanitarian assistance constitutes a threat to human life and an offence to human dignity,*

Strongly desiring *that the international community should respond speedily and effectively to the needs for emergency humanitarian assistance expressed in particular through the Secretary-General,*

Concerned *about the difficulties and obstacles that victims of natural disasters and similar emergency situations may encounter in receiving humanitarian assistance,*

Convinced *that, in providing humanitarian assistance, in particular the supply of food, medicines or health care, for which access to victims is essential, rapid relief will avoid a tragic increase in the number of victims,*

Recalling, *in this regard, the Cairo Declaration adopted by the World Food Council at its fifteenth session, proposing, inter alia, an international agreement on the transport of emergency food aid,*

Aware *that alongside the action of Governments and intergovernmental organizations, the speed and efficiency of this assistance often depend on the help and aid of local and non-governmental organizations working in an impartial manner and with strictly humanitarian motives*

Reaffirming *the need for the intergovernmental, governmental and non-governmental organizations dealing with humanitarian assistance to co-operate as closely as possible with the Office of the United Nations Disaster Relief Co-ordinator or any ad hoc mechanism set up by the Secretary-General in the co-ordination of aid,*

Concerned *about the effectiveness of such assistance, which requires an accurate evaluation of needs, efficient preparation of actions and effective co-ordination in conducting them,*

Recalling *that, in the event of natural disasters and similar emergency situations, the principles of humanity, neutrality and impartiality must be given utmost consideration by all those involved in providing humanitarian assistance,*

1. Reaffirms *the cardinal importance of humanitarian assistance for the victims of natural disasters and similar emergency situations;*
2. Reaffirms *also the sovereignty of affected States and their primary role in the initiation, organization, co-ordination and implementation of humanitarian assistance within their respective territories;*
3. Stresses *the important contribution made in providing humanitarian assistance by intergovernmental and non-governmental organizations working impartially and with strictly humanitarian motives;*
4. Invites *all States whose populations are in need of such assistance to facilitate the work of these organizations in implementing humanitarian assistance, in particular the supply of food, medicines and health care, for which access to victims is essential;*
5. Appeals, *therefore, to all States to give their support to these organizations working to provide humanitarian assistance, where needed, to the victims of natural disasters and similar emergency situations;*
6. Notes *with satisfaction the report of the Secretary-General on the implementation of resolution 43/131 and the suggestions which he makes concerning means of facilitating humanitarian assistance operations, in particular the possibility of establishing, on a temporary basis, where needed, and by means of concerted action by affected Governments and the Governments and intergovernmental, governmental and non-governmental organizations concerned, relief corridors for the distribution of emergency medical and food aid;*

7. Urges *States in proximity to areas of natural disasters and similar emergency situations, particularly in the case of regions that are difficult to reach, to participate closely with the affected countries in international efforts with a view to facilitating, to the extent possible, the transit of humanitarian assistance;*
8. Requests *the Secretary-General to pursue, within existing resources,the necessary consultations with Governments and intergovernmental, governmental and non-governmental organizations with a view to determining means of facilitating the delivery of appropriate humanitarian assistance to the victims of natural disasters or similar emergency situations, including the establishment of relief corridors, on the basis of the report of the Secretary-General and on the terms set out in paragraph 6 of the present resolution, and to report thereon to the General Assembly at its forty-seventh session;*
9. Invites *the Secretary-General to study, within existing resources, the possibility of preparing, on the basis of information furnished by Governments and the relevant governmental and non-governmental international organizations and taking into account the work already done in this area by the United Nations, in particular by the Office of the United Nations Disaster Relief Co-ordinator, an indicative list of persons and bodies with expert knowledge of the delivery and management of emergency humanitarian assistance whom the United Nations could call upon, with the consent of the States concerned, to make an accurate and speedy assessment of the needs and a realistic determination of the best means of delivering the aid;*
10. Decides *to consider this question at its forty-seventh session.*

VOTE

I. Resolution 43/131 was adopted by the United Nations General Assembly on 8 December 1988 without vote (A/43/PV.75, p. 180)

II. Resolution 45/100 was adopted by the United Nations General Assembly on 14 December 1990 without vote (A/45/PV.68, p. 38)

No. 63

STRENGTHENING OF THE COORDINATION OF HUMANITARIAN EMERGENCY ASSISTANCE OF THE UNITED NATIONS

Resolution 46/182 adopted by the United Nations General Assembly, 19 December 1991

INTRODUCTORY NOTE: The adoption of Resolutions 43/131 and 45/100 (*No. 62*) provoked an intense diplomatic activity within the United Nations, as well as an in-depth discussion in the General Assembly. A special open-ended group prepared and presented a draft of this resolution. The resolution was adopted by consensus.

AUTHENTIC TEXT: Arabic, Chinese, English, French, Russian and Spanish.

TEXT PUBLISHED IN: *Resolutions and decisions adopted by the General Assembly during its forty-sixth session*, Vol. I, *September 17–December 20 1991*, General Assembly Official Records, Forty-sixth session, Supplement No. 49 (A/46/49), New York, United Nations, 1992, pp. 49–52 (Engl. – also editions in Arabic, Chinese, French, Russian, and Spanish); *Droit des conflits armés*, pp. 943–951 (French).

TABLE OF CONTENTS

* * *

The General Assembly,

Recalling its resolution 2816 (XXVI) of 14 December 1971 and its subsequent resolutions and decisions on humanitarian assistance, including its resolution 45/100 of 14 December 1990,

Recalling also its resolution 44/236 of 22 December 1989, the annex to which contains the International Framework of Action for the International Decade for Natural Disaster Reduction,

Deeply concerned about the suffering of the victims of disasters and emergency situations, the loss in human lives, the flow of refugees, the mass displacement of people and the material destruction,

Mindful of the need to strengthen further and make more effective the collective efforts of the international community, in particular the United Nations system, in providing humanitarian assistance,

Taking note with satisfaction of the report of the Secretary-General on the review of the capacity, experience and coordination arrangements in the United Nations system for humanitarian assistance,

1. *Adopts the text contained in the annex to the present resolution for the strengthening of the coordination of emergency humanitarian assistance of the United Nations system;*
2. *Requests the Secretary-General to report to the General Assembly at its forty-seventh session on the implementation of the present resolution.*

ANNEX

I. GUIDING PRINCIPLES

1. *Humanitarian assistance is of cardinal importance for the victims of natural disasters and other emergencies.*
2. *Humanitarian assistance must be provided in accordance with the principles of humanity, neutrality and impartiality.*
3. *The sovereignty, territorial integrity and national unity of States must be fully respected in accordance with the Charter of the United Nations. In this context, humanitarian assistance should be provided with the consent of the affected country and in principle on the basis of an appeal by the affected country.*
4. *Each State has the responsibility first and foremost to take care of the victims of natural disasters and other emergencies occurring on its territory*

   Hence, the affected State has the primary role in the initiation, organization, coordination, and implementation of humanitarian assistance within its territory.
5. *The magnitude and duration of many emergencies may be beyond the response capacity of many affected countries. International cooperation to address emergency situations and to strengthen the response capacity of affected countries is thus of great importance. Such cooperation should be provided in accordance with international law and national laws. Intergovernmental and non-governmental organizations working impartially and with strictly humanitarian motives should continue to make a significant contribution in supplementing national efforts.*
6. *States whose populations are in need of humanitarian assistance are called upon to facilitate the work of these organizations in implementing humanitarian assistance, in particular the supply of food, medicines, shelter and health care, for which access to victims is essential.*
7. *States in proximity to emergencies are urged to participate closely with the affected countries in international efforts, with a view to facilitating, to the extent possible, the transit of humanitarian assistance.*

8. *Special attention should be given to disaster prevention and preparedness by the Governments concerned, as well as by the international community.*
9. *There is a clear relationship between emergency, rehabilitation and development. In order to ensure a smooth transition from relief to rehabilitation and development, emergency assistance should be provided in ways that will be supportive of recovery and long-term development. Thus, emergency measures should be seen as a step towards long-term development.*
10. *Economic growth and sustainable development are essential for prevention of and preparedness against natural disasters and other emergencies. Many emergencies reflect the underlying crisis in development facing developing countries. Humanitarian assistance should therefore be accompanied by a renewal of commitment to economic growth and sustainable development of developing countries. In this context, adequate resources must be made available to address their development problems.*
11. *Contributions for humanitarian assistance should be provided in a way which is not to the detriment of resources made available for international cooperation for development.*
12. *The United Nations has a central and unique role to play in providing leadership and coordinating the efforts of the international community to support the affected countries. The United Nations should ensure the prompt and smooth delivery of relief assistance in full respect of the above-mentioned principles, bearing in mind also relevant General Assembly resolutions, including resolutions 2816 (XXVI) of 14 December 1971 and 45/100 of 14 December 1990. The United Nations system needs to be adapted and strengthened to meet present and future challenges in an effective and coherent manner. It should be provided with resources commensurate with future requirements. The inadequacy of such resources has been one of the major constraints in the effective response of the United Nations to emergencies.*

II. PREVENTION

13. *The international community should adequately assist developing countries in strengthening their capacity in disaster prevention and mitigation, both at the national and regional levels, for example, in establishing and enhancing integrated programmes in this regard.*
14. *In order to reduce the impact of disasters there should be increased awareness of the need for establishing disaster mitigation strategies, particularly in disaster-prone countries. There should be greater exchange and dissemination of existing and new technical information related to the assessment, prediction and mitigation of disasters. As called for in the International Decade for Natural Disaster Reduction, efforts should be intensified to develop measures for prevention and mitigation of natural disasters and similar emergencies through programmes of technical assistance and modalities for favourable access to, and transfer of, relevant technology.*
15. *The disaster management training programme recently initiated by the Office of the United Nations Disaster Relief Coordinator and the United Nations Development Programme should be strengthened and broadened.*
16. *Organizations of the United Nations system involved in the funding and the provision of assistance relevant to the prevention of emergencies should be provided with sufficient and readily available resources.*

17. *The international community is urged to provide the necessary support and resources to programmes and activities undertaken to further the goals and objectives of the Decade.*

III. PREPAREDNESS

18. *International relief assistance should supplement national efforts to improve the capacities of developing countries to mitigate the effects of natural disasters expeditiously and effectively and to cope efficiently with all emergencies. The United Nations should enhance its efforts to assist developing countries to strengthen their capacity to respond to disasters, at the national and regional levels, as appropriate.*

Early warning

19. *On the basis of existing mandates and drawing upon monitoring arrangements available within the system, the United Nations should intensify efforts, building upon the existing capacities of relevant organizations and entities of the United Nations, for the systematic pooling, analysis and dissemination of early-warning information on natural disasters and other emergencies. In this context, the United Nations should consider making use as appropriate of the early-warning capacities of Governments and intergovernmental and non-governmental organizations.*
20. *Early-warning information should be made available in an unrestricted and timely manner to all interested Governments and concerned authorities, in particular of affected or disaster-prone countries. The capacity of disaster-prone countries to receive, use and disseminate this information should be strengthened. In this connection, the international community is urged to assist these countries upon request with the establishment and enhancement of national early-warning systems.*

IV. STAND-BY CAPACITY

(a) Contingency funding arrangements

21. *Organizations and entities of the United Nations system should continue to respond to requests for emergency assistance within their respective mandates. Reserve and other contingency funding arrangements of these organizations and entities should be examined by their respective governing bodies to strengthen further their operational capacities for rapid and coordinated response to emergencies.*
22. *In addition, there is a need for a complementary central funding mechanism to ensure the provision of adequate resources for use in the initial phase of emergencies that require a system-wide response.*
23. *To that end, the Secretary-General should establish under his authority a central emergency revolving fund as a cash-flow mechanism to ensure the rapid and coordinated response of the organizations of the system.*
24. *This fund should be put into operation with an amount of 50 million United States dollars. The fund should be financed by voluntary contributions. Consultations among potential donors should be held to this end. To achieve this target, the Secretary-General should launch an appeal to potential donors and convene a meeting of those donors in the first quarter of 1992 to secure contributions to the fund on an assured, broad-based and additional basis.*

25. *Resources should be advanced to the operational organizations of the system on the understanding that they would reimburse the fund in the first instance from the voluntary contributions received in response to consolidated appeals.*
26. *The operation of the fund should be reviewed after two years.*

(b) Additional measures for rapid response

27. *The United Nations should, building upon the existing capacities of relevant organizations, establish a central register of all specialized personnel and teams of technical specialists, as well as relief supplies, equipment and services available within the United Nations system and from Governments and intergovernmental and non-governmental organizations, that can be called upon at short notice by the United Nations.*
28. *The United Nations should continue to make appropriate arrangements with interested Governments and intergovernmental and non-governmental organizations to enable it to have more expeditious access, when necessary, to their emergency relief capacities, including food reserves, emergency stockpiles and personnel, as well as logistic support. In the context of the annual report to the General Assembly mentioned in paragraph 35 (i) below, the Secretary-General is requested to report on progress in this regard.*
29. *Special emergency rules and procedures should be developed by the United Nations to enable all organizations to disburse quickly emergency funds, and to procure emergency supplies and equipment, as well as to recruit emergency staff.*
30. *Disaster-prone countries should develop special emergency procedures to expedite the rapid procurement and deployment of equipment and relief supplies.*

V. CONSOLIDATED APPEALS

31. *For emergencies requiring a coordinated response, the Secretary-General should ensure that an initial consolidated appeal covering all concerned organizations of the system, prepared in consultation with the affected State, is issued within the shortest possible time and in any event not longer than one week. In the case of prolonged emergencies, this initial appeal should be updated and elaborated within four weeks, as more information becomes available.*
32. *Potential donors should adopt necessary measures to increase and expedite their contributions, including setting aside, on a stand-by basis, financial and other resources that can be disbursed quickly to the United Nations system in response to the consolidated appeals of the Secretary-General.*

VI. COORDINATION, COOPERATION AND LEADERSHIP

(a) Leadership of the Secretary-General

33. *The leadership role of the Secretary-General is critical and must be strengthened to ensure better preparation for, as well as rapid and coherent response to, natural disasters and other emergencies. This should be achieved through coordinated support for prevention and preparedness measures and the optimal utilization of, inter alia, an inter-agency standing*

committee, consolidated appeals, a central emergency revolving fund and a register of stand-by capacities.

34. *To this end, and on the understanding that the requisite resources envisaged in paragraph 24 above would be provided, a high-level official (emergency relief coordinator) would be designated by the Secretary-General to work closely with and with direct access to him, in cooperation with the relevant organizations and entities of the system dealing with humanitarian assistance and in full respect of their mandates, without prejudice to any decisions to be taken by the General Assembly on the overall restructuring of the Secretariat of the United Nations. This high-level official should combine the functions at present carried out in the coordination of United Nations response by representatives of the Secretary-General for major and complex emergencies, as well as by the United Nations Disaster Relief Coordinator.*

35. *Under the aegis of the General Assembly and working under the direction of the Secretary-General, the high-level official would have the following responsibilities:*
    - *(a) Processing requests from affected Member States for emergency assistance requiring a coordinated response;*
    - *(b) Maintaining an overview of all emergencies through, inter alia, the systematic pooling and analysis of early-warning information as envisaged in paragraph 19 above, with a view to coordinating and facilitating the humanitarian assistance of the United Nations system to those emergencies that require a coordinated response;*
    - *(c) Organizing, in consultation with the Government of the affected country, a joint inter-agency needs-assessment mission and preparing a consolidated appeal to be issued by the Secretary-General, to be followed by periodic situation reports including information on all sources of external assistance;*
    - *(d) Actively facilitating, including through negotiation if needed, the access by the operational organizations to emergency areas for the rapid provision of emergency assistance by obtaining the consent of all parties concerned, through modalities such as the establishment of temporary relief corridors where needed, days and zones of tranquility and other forms;*
    - *(e) Managing, in consultation with the operational organizations concerned, the central emergency revolving fund and assisting in the mobilization of resources;*
    - *(f) Serving as a central focal point with Governments and intergovernmental and non-governmental organizations concerning United Nations emergency relief operations and, when appropriate and necessary, mobilizing their emergency relief capacities, including through consultations in his capacity as Chairman of the Inter-Agency Standing Committee;*
    - *(g) Providing consolidated information, including early warning on emergencies, to all interested Governments and concerned authorities, particularly affected and disaster-prone countries, drawing on the capacities of the organizations of the system and other available sources;*
    - *(h) Actively promoting, in close collaboration with concerned organizations, the smooth transition from relief to rehabilitation and reconstruction as relief operations under his aegis are phased out;*

(i) Preparing an annual report for the Secretary-General on the coordination of humanitarian emergency assistance, including information on the central emergency revolving fund, to be submitted to the General Assembly through the Economic and Social Council.

36. The high-level official should be supported by a secretariat based on a strengthened Office of the United Nations Disaster Relief Coordinator and the consolidation of existing offices that deal with complex emergencies. This secretariat could be supplemented by staff seconded from concerned organizations of the system. The high-level official should work closely with organizations and entities of the United Nations system, as well as the International Committee of the Red Cross, the League of Red Cross and Red Crescent Societies, the International Organization for Migration and relevant non-governmental organizations. At the country level, the high-level official would maintain close contact with and provide leadership to the resident coordinators on matters relating to humanitarian assistance.

37. The Secretary-General should ensure that arrangements between the high- level official and all relevant organizations are set in place, establishing responsibilities for prompt and coordinated action in the event of emergency.

(b) Inter-Agency Standing Committee

38. An Inter-Agency Standing Committee serviced by a strengthened Office of the United Nations Disaster Relief Coordinator should be established under the chairmanship of the high-level official with the participation of all operational organizations and with a standing invitation to the International Committee of the Red Cross, the League of Red Cross and Red Crescent Societies, and the International Organization for Migration. Relevant non-governmental organizations can be invited to participate on an ad hoc basis. The Committee should meet as soon as possible in response to emergencies.

(c) Country-level coordination

39. Within the overall framework described above and in support of the efforts of the affected countries, the resident coordinator should normally coordinate the humanitarian assistance of the United Nations system at the country level. He/She should facilitate the preparedness of the United Nations system and assist in a speedy transition from relief to development. He/She should promote the use of all locally or regionally available relief capacities. The resident coordinator should chair an emergency operations group of field representatives and experts from the system.

VII. CONTINUUM FROM RELIEF TO REHABILITATION AND DEVELOPMENT

40. Emergency assistance must be provided in ways that will be supportive of recovery and long-term development. Development assistance organizations of the United Nations system should be involved at an early stage and should collaborate closely with those responsible for emergency relief and recovery, within their existing mandates.

41. *International cooperation and support for rehabilitation and reconstruction should continue with sustained intensity after the initial relief stage. The rehabilitation phase should be used as an opportunity to restructure and improve facilities and services destroyed by emergencies in order to enable them to withstand the impact of future emergencies.*
42. *International cooperation should be accelerated for the development of developing countries, thereby contributing to reducing the occurrence and impact of future disasters and emergencies.*

VOTE

The resolution 46/182 was adopted by the United Nations General Assembly on 19 December 1991 by consensus (A/46/PV.78, p. 41).

No. 64

THE PROTECTION OF HUMAN RIGHTS AND THE PRINCIPLE OF NON-INTERVENTION IN INTERNAL AFFAIRS OF STATES

Resolution adopted by the Institute of International Law at its Santiago de Compostela session, on 13 September 1989

INTRODUCTORY NOTE: In several respects, the present resolution is of direct concern to the laws of armed conflicts. First, the "frequent gross violations of human rights" to which the resolution refers (see preamble, paragraph 4) often also constitute violations of the laws of armed conflict. Second, Article 1, paragraph 2, calls upon states to ensure the effective protection of human rights throughout the world in a similar way as Article 1, common to the Geneva Conventions of 1949, imposes a duty upon states to ensure respect for the Geneva Conventions. Activities to this end *vis-à-vis* other states cannot be considered an unlawful intervention in the internal affairs of these states (see also Article 5, paragraph 1). Finally, Article 5 directly touches humanitarian law by regulating the offer by a state, an international organization and the ICRC of food and medical supplies to a state in whose territory the life or health of the population is seriously threatened. The resolution was adopted by a vote of 32 in favour and 4 abstentions (*Annuaire de l'Institut de Droit international*, Vol. 63-II, 1990, pp. 338–345).

AUTHENTIC TEXT: French and English. The text below is reproduced from *Annuaire de l'Institut de droit international*, Vol. 63-II, 1990, pp. 338–345.

TEXT PUBLISHED IN: *Annuaire de l'Institut de droit international*, Vol. 63-II, 1990, pp. 338–345 (Engl., French); Institute of International Law, *Table of Adopted Resolutions (1957–1991)*, Paris, Pedone, 1992, pp. 206–213 (Engl., French); *Droit des conflits armés*, pp. 953–955 (French).

* * *

The Institute of International Law,

Recalling its Declarations of New York (1929) on "International Human Rights" and of Lausanne (1947) on "The Fundamental Human Rights as a Basis for Restoring International Law" as well as its Resolutions of Oslo (1932) and Aix-en-Provence (1954) on "The Determination of the 'Reserved Domain' and its Effects";

Considering,

That the protection of human rights as a guarantee of the physical and moral integrity and of the fundamental freedom of every person has been given expression in both the constitutional systems of States and in the international legal system, especially in the charters and constituent instruments of international organizations;

That the members of the United Nations have undertaken to ensure, in co-operation with the Organization, universal respect for and observance of human rights and fundamental freedoms, and that the General Assembly, recognizing that a common understanding of these rights and freedoms is of the highest importance for the full realization of this undertaking, has adopted and proclaimed the Universal Declaration of Human Rights on 10 December 1948;

That frequent gross violations of human rights, including those affecting ethnic, religious and linguistic minorities, cause legitimate and increasing outrage to public opinion and impel many States and international organizations to have recourse to various measures to ensure that human rights are respected;

That these reactions, as well as international doctrine and jurisprudence, bear witness that human rights, having been given international protection, are no longer matters essentially within the domestic jurisdiction of States;

That it is nonetheless important, in the interest of maintaining peace and friendly relations between sovereign States as well as in the interest of protecting human rights, to define more precisely the conditions and limitations imposed by international law on the measures that may be taken by States and international organizations in response to violations of human rights,

Adopts the following Resolution:

Article 1. Human rights are a direct expression of the dignity of the human person. The obligation of States to ensure their observance derives from the recognition of this dignity as proclaimed in the Charter of the United Nations and in the Universal Declaration of Human Rights.

This international obligation, as expressed by the International Court of Justice, is *erga omnes*; it is incumbent upon every State in relation to the international community as a whole, and every State has a legal interest in the protection of human rights. The obligation further implies a duty of solidarity among all States to ensure as rapidly as possible the effective protection of human rights throughout the world.

Art. 2. A State acting in breach of its obligations in the sphere of human rights cannot evade its international responsibility by claiming that such matters are essentially within its domestic jurisdiction.

Without prejudice to the functions and powers which the Charter attributes to the organs of the United Nations in case of violation of the obligations assumed by the members of the Organization, States, acting individually or collectively, are entitled to take diplomatic, economic and other measures towards any other State which has violated the obligation set forth in Article 1 provided such measures are permitted under international law and do not involve the use of armed force in violation of the Charter of the United Nations. These measures cannot be considered an unlawful intervention in the internal affairs of that State.

Violations justifying recourse to the measures referred to above shall be viewed in the light of their gravity and of all the relevant circumstances. Measures designed to ensure the collective protection of human rights are particularly justified when taken in response to especially grave violations of these rights, notably large-scale or systematic violations, as well as those infringing rights that cannot be derogated from in any circumstances.

Art. 3. Diplomatic representations as well as purely verbal expressions of concern or disapproval regarding any violations of human rights are lawful in all circumstances.

Art. 4. All measures, individual or collective, designed to ensure the protection of human rights shall meet the following conditions:

(1) except in case of extreme urgency, the State perpetrating the violation shall be formally requested to desist before the measures are taken;
(2) measures taken shall be proportionate to the gravity of the violation;
(3) measures taken shall be limited to the State perpetrating the violation;
(4) the States having recourse to measures shall take into account the interests of individuals and of third States, as well as the effect of such measures on the standard of living of the population concerned.

Art. 5. An offer by a State, a group of States, an international organization or an impartial humanitarian body such as the International Committee of the Red Cross, of food or medical supplies to another State in whose territory the life or health of the population is seriously threatened cannot be considered an unlawful intervention in the internal affairs of that State. However, such offers of assistance shall not, particularly by virtue of the means used to implement them, take a form suggestive of a threat of armed intervention or any other measure of intimidation; assistance shall be granted and distributed without discrimination.

States in whose territories these emergency situations exist should not arbitrarily reject such offers of humanitarian assistance.

Art. 6. The provisions of this Resolution apply without prejudice to the procedures prescribed in matters of human rights by the terms of or pursuant to the constitutive instruments and the conventions of the United Nations and of specialized agencies or regional organizations.

Art. 7. It is highly desirable to strengthen international methods and procedures, in particular methods and procedures of international organizations, intended to prevent, punish and eliminate violations of human rights.

No. 65

CONVENTION AGAINST TORTURE AND OTHER CRUEL, INHUMAN OR DEGRADING TREATMENT OR PUNISHMENT

Adopted by resolution 39/46 of the United Nations General Assembly, 10 December 1984

I. CONVENTION

II. AMENDMENTS TO ARTICLES 17(7) AND 18(5) OF THE CONVENTION

Adopted by the Conference of States Parties, 8 September 1992

III. OPTIONAL PROTOCOL TO THE CONVENTION AGAINST TORTURE AND OTHER CRUEL, INHUMAN OR DEGRADING TREATMENT OR PUNISHMENT

Adopted by resolution 57/199 of the United Nations General Assembly, 18 December 2002

INTRODUCTORY NOTE: Torture, cruel, inhuman and degrading treatment are prohibited by many national legislative acts and international instruments. The 1949 Geneva Conventions for the protection of victims of war (*Nos. 49–52*) and the Additional Protocols of 1977 (*Nos. 56–57*) prohibit torture and humiliating and degrading treatment. The international instruments of human rights, notably the Universal Declaration of Human Rights (1948) and the International Covenant on Civil and Political Rights (1966) stipulate that "no one shall be subjected to torture, or to cruel, inhuman or degrading treatment or punishment".

By resolution 3452 (XXX) of 9 December 1975, the General Assembly adopted the Declaration on the Protection of All Persons from Being Subjected to Torture and Other Cruel, Inhuman or Degrading Treatment or Punishment. On 8 December 1977, in resolution 32/62, it requested the United Nations Commission on Human Rights to draw up a draft convention in the light of the principles embodied in the Declaration. The Commission carried out the work of preparing the draft convention as a matter of highest priority at each of the annual sessions between 1979 and 1984. It entrusted this task to an open-ended working group. At its fortieth session, the Commission decided to transmit to the General Assembly the report of the working group containing the draft convention. The General Assembly adopted it by consensus, on 10 December 1984 (Resolution 39/46). The Convention was opened for signature at New York on 4 February 1985. It entered into force on 26 June 1987, after twenty states had ratified it.

On 9 January 1992, the Australian Government proposed amendments to Article 17(7) 18(5) of the Convention. In accordance with Article 29(1) of the Convention, the Secretary-General communicated the proposed amendments to the states parties with a request to notify him whether they favoured a conference of states parties for the purpose of considering and voting upon the proposal. As more than one third of the states favoured such a conference, the Secretary-General convened the conference. On 8 September 1992 the conference adopted the amendments. This decision was endorsed by the General Assembly in resolution 47/111 of 16 December 1992. In accordance with Article 29(1) the amendments were submitted to all the states parties for acceptance. An amendment enters into force when two-thirds of the states parties to the Convention have notified the Secretary-General that they have accepted it in accordance with their respective constitutional processes. On 30 October 2002 only 25 states of a total of 131 states parties to the Convention had accepted the amendments (see list on p. 944). The amendments have therefore not yet entered into force.

To ensure respect and implementation of the Convention, Costa Rica proposed the adoption of an optional protocol creating a mechanism of application. The United Nations Human Rights Commission included the Costa Rican proposal on the agenda, considering it also as an opportunity to "take note ... of the experience of the European Convention for the prevention of torture" (*No. 66*). By its resolution 1992/43 of 3 March 1992, the Commission created an open-ended Working Group given the task of elaborating a draft optional protocol to the Convention based on the draft proposed by Costa Rica (E/CN.4/1991/66). The working group presented its report to the Commission in 2002. The Commission adopted it on 20 April 2002, the Economic and Social Council on 24 July 2002 and the General Assembly on 18 December 2002.

It is worth mentioning that an Inter-American Convention to prevent and punish torture was signed at Cartagena de Indias, Columbia, on 9 December 1985, at the 15th regular session of the General Assembly of the Organization of American States (*OAS, Treaty Series*, No. 67).[1]

ENTRY INTO FORCE:
Convention: 26 June 1987.
The *Amendments* and the *Optional Protocol* have have not yet entered into force.

AUTHENTIC TEXT:
Convention: Arabic, Chinese, English, French, Russian and Spanish. The text below is reproduced from an original copy of the Convention which we acquired from the United Nations Treaty Section; see also *Resolutions and Decisions Adopted by the General Assembly During the Course of the Thirty-ninth Session, September 18 - December 18, 1984 and April 9-12, 1985* General Assembly Official Record: Thirty-ninth Session, Supplement No. 51 (A/39/51), New York, United Nations, 1985, pp. 206–211.
Amendments: the text of the amendments is reproduced from Doc. CAT/sp/1992/L.1
Optional Protocol: Resolution 57/199 of the United Nations General Assembly, Annex; *ILM*, Vol. 42, 2003, pp. 26–38 (Engl.); UN website: http://untreaty. un.org.

[1] The Convention entered into force on 28 February 1987. On 7 May 2000 the Convention was signed by 20 states and ratified by 16 states: Argentina, Brazil, Colombia, Costa Rica, Dominican Republic, Ecuador, El Salvador, Guatemala, Mexico, Panama, Paraguay, Peru, Surinam, Uruguay and Venezuela.

TEXT PUBLISHED IN:
Convention: Resolution of the United Nations General Assembly: A/RES/39/46; *Resolutions and Decisions Adopted by the General Assembly During the Course of the Thirty-ninth Session, September 18– December 18, 1984 and April 9-12, 1985*, General Assembly Official Records: Thirty-ninth Session, Supplement No. 51 (A/39/51), New York, United Nations, 1985, pp. 197–201 (Engl.– see also the editions in Arabic, Chinese, French, Russ. and Span.); *UNTS*, Vol. 1465, p. 85; *GBTS,* Misc. 12 (1985), Cmnd. 9593 (Engl.); 6 European Human Rights Reports, August 1984, Part 23, p. 259 (Engl.); *Human Rights – A Compilation of International Instrument,* Vol. I (First Part), New York, United Nations, 1993, pp. 293–307 (English); *Droits de l'Homme – Recueil d'instruments internationaux*, New York, United Nations, 1988, pp. 212–266 (French); *Derechos Humanos – Recopilacion de instrumentos internacionales*, Nueva York, Naciones Unidas, 1988, pp. 211–225 (Span.); *Derechos Humanos*, pp. 278–310 (Spanish); *Prava cheloveka – Sbornik mezhdunarodnykh dokumentov*, N'yu-York, OON, 1989, pp. 238–254 (Russ.); *ILM* , Vol. 23 (1984), pp. 1027–1037, Vol. 24 (1985), p. 535 (Engl.); *Vedomosit Verkovnogo Soveta SSSR*, No. 45 (2431), 1987, st. 747 (Russ.); Ministerstvo inostraanykh del, *SSSR i mezhdunarodnoe sotrudnichestvo v oblasti prav cheloveka.* Dokumentary i materialy. Moskva, Mezhdunarodnye otnosheniya, 1989, pp. 384–397 (Russ.); Information forms of the United Nations: *Mechanisms to fight against torture*, UNTS/HR(05)H8 No. 4 – Rights of Man – Information From No. 4, p. 32 (Arabic, Chin., Engl., French, Russ. and Span.); *The Committee against torture,* UNTS/HR(05)H8 No. 17 – Rights of Man – Information form No. 17, p. 40 (Arabic, Chin., Eng., French, Russ. and Span.); *Droit des conflits armés*, pp. 957–1004 (French); United Nations website: http://untreaty.un.org.
Amendments: Doc. CAT/sp/1992/L.1; *Official Records of the General Assembly of the United Nations, Forty-seventh Session*, Supplement No. 49 (A/47/49), p. 192; United Nations website: http://untreaty.un.org.
Optional Protocol: *ILM*, Vol. 42, 2003, pp. 26–38 (Engl.); UN website: http://untreaty. un.org.

* * *

I. CONVENTION AGAINST TORTURE AND OTHER CRUEL, INHUMAN OR DEGRADING TREATMENT OR PUNISHMENT

The States Parties to this Convention,

Considering that, in accordance with the principles proclaimed in the Charter of the United Nations, recognition of the equal and inalienable rights of all members of the human family is the foundation of freedom, justice and peace in the world,

Recognizing that those rights derive from the inherent dignity of the human person,

Considering the obligation of States under the Charter, in particular Article 55, to promote universal respect for, and observance of, human rights and fundamental freedoms,

Having regard to article 5 of the Universal Declaration of human Rights and article 7 of the International Covenant on Civil and Political Rights, both of which provide that no one shall be subjected to torture or to cruel, inhuman or degrading treatment or punishment,

Having regard also to the Declaration on the Protection of All Persons from Being Subjected to Torture and Other Cruel, Inhuman or Degrading Treatment or Punishment, adopted by the General Assembly on 9 December 1975,

Desiring to make more effective the struggle against torture and other cruel, inhuman or degrading treatment or punishment throughout the world,

Have agreed as follows:

PART I[1]

Article 1.[2]

1. For the purposes of this Convention, the term "torture" means any act by which severe pain or suffering, whether physical or mental, is intentionally inflicted on a person for such purposes as obtaining from him or a third person information or a confession, punishing him for an act he or a third person has committed or is suspected of having committed, or intimidating or coercing him or a third person, or for any reason based on discrimination of any kind, when such pain or suffering is inflicted by or at the instigation of or with the consent or acquiescence of a public official or other person acting in an official capacity. It does not include pain or suffering arising only from, inherent in or incidental to lawful sanctions.
2. This article is without prejudice to any international instrument or national legislation which does or may contain provisions of wider application.

Art. 2.

1.[3] Each State Party shall take effective legislative, administrative, judicial or other measures to prevent acts of torture in any territory under its jurisdiction.

---

[1] For declaration in respect of Articles 1–16 by the United States of America, see pp. 921–922.

[2] For declaration in respect of this article by Botswana, Luxembourg and the Netherlands, see pp. 914, 919.

[3] For declaration in respect of this paragraph by Cuba, see pp. 915–916.

2. No exceptional circumstances whatsoever, whether a state of war or a threat of war, internal political instability or any other public emergency, may be invoked as a justification of torture.
3. An order from a superior officer or a public authority may not be invoked as a justification of torture.

Art. 3.[4]

1. No State Party shall expel, return ("refouler") or extradite a person to another State where there are substantial grounds for believing that he would be in danger of being subjected to torture.
2. For the purpose of determining whether there are such grounds, the competent authorities shall take into account all relevant considerations including, where applicable, the existence in the State concerned of a consistent pattern of gross, flagrant or mass violations of human rights.

Art. 4.

1. Each State Party shall ensure that all acts of torture are offences under its criminal law. The same shall apply to an attempt to commit torture and to an act by any person which constitutes complicity or participation in torture.
2. Each State Party shall make these offences punishable by appropriate penalties which take into account their grave nature.

Art. 5.[5]

1. Each State Party shall take such measures as may be necessary to establish its jurisdiction over the offences referred to in article 4 in the following cases:
   (a) When the offences are committed in any territory under its jurisdiction or on board a ship or aircraft registered in that State;
   (b) When the alleged offender is a national of that State;
   (c) When the victim is a national of that State if that State considers it appropriate.
2. Each State Party shall likewise take such measures as may be necessary to establish its jurisdiction over such offences in cases where the alleged offender is present in any territory under its jurisdiction and it does not extradite him pursuant to article 8 to any of the States mentioned in paragraph 1 of this article.
3. This Convention does not exclude any criminal jurisdiction exercised in accordance with internal law.

Art. 6.

1. Upon being satisfied, after an examination of information available to it, that the circumstances so warrant, any State Party in whose territory a person alleged to have committed any offence referred to in article 4 is present shall take him into custody or take other legal measures to ensure his presence. The custody and other legal measures shall be as provided in

---

4 For reservation in respect of this article by Germany and understanding by the United States of America, see pp. 917, 922.

5 For declaration in respect of this article by Austria, see p. 914.

the law of that State but may be continued only for such time as is necessary to enable any criminal or extradition proceedings to be instituted.

2. Such State shall immediately make a preliminary inquiry into the facts.
3. Any person in custody pursuant to paragraph 1 of this article shall be assisted in communicating immediately with the nearest appropriate representative of the State of which he is a national, or, if he is a stateless person, with the representative of the State where he usually resides.
4. When a State, pursuant to this article, has taken a person into custody, it shall immediately notify the States referred to in article 5, paragraph 1, of the fact that such person is in custody and of the circumstances which warrant his detention. The State which makes the preliminary inquiry contemplated in paragraph 2 of this article shall promptly report its findings to the said States and shall indicate whether it intends to exercise jurisdiction.

Art. 7.

1. The State Party in the territory under whose jurisdiction a person alleged to have committed any offence referred to in article 4 is found shall in the cases contemplated in article 5, if it does not extradite him, submit the case to its competent authorities for the purpose of prosecution.
2. These authorities shall take their decision in the same manner as in the case of any ordinary offence of a serious nature under the law of that State. In the cases referred to in article 5, paragraph 2, the standards of evidence required for prosecution and conviction shall in no way be less stringent than those which apply in the cases referred to in article 5, paragraph 1.
3. Any person regarding whom proceedings are brought in connection with any of the offences referred to in article 4 shall be guaranteed fair treatment at all stages of the proceedings.

Art. 8.[6]

1. The offences referred to in article 4 shall be deemed to be included as extraditable offences in any extradition treaty existing between States Parties. States Parties undertake to include such offences as extraditable offences in every extradition treaty to be concluded between them.
2. If a State Party which makes extradition conditional on the existence of a treaty receives a request for extradition from another State Party with which it has no extradition treaty, it may consider this Convention as the legal basis for extradition in respect of such offences. Extradition shall be subject to the other conditions provided by the law of the requested State.
3. States Parties which do not make extradition conditional on the existence of a treaty shall recognize such offences as extraditable offences between themselves subject to the conditions provided by the law of the requested State.
4. Such offences shall be treated, for the purpose of extradition between States Parties, as if they had been committed not only in the place in which they occurred but also in the territories of the States required to establish their jurisdiction in accordance with article 5, paragraph 1.

Art. 9.

1. States Parties shall afford one another the greatest measure of assistance in connection with criminal proceedings brought in respect of any of the

[6] For declaration concerning extradition of nationals by Ecuador, see p. 916.

offences referred to in article 4, including the supply of all evidence at their disposal necessary for the proceedings.

2. States Parties shall carry out their obligations under paragraph 1 of this article in conformity with any treaties on mutual judicial assistance that may exist between them.

Art. 10.[7]

1. Each State Party shall ensure that education and information regarding the prohibition against torture are fully included in the training of law enforcement personnel, civil or military, medical personnel, public officials and other persons who may be involved in the custody, interrogation or treatment of any individual subjected to any form of arrest, detention or imprisonment.
2. Each State Party shall include this prohibition in the rules or instructions issued in regard to the duties and functions of any such persons.

Art. 11.[7] Each State Party shall keep under systematic review interrogation rules, instructions, methods and practices as well as arrangements for the custody and treatment of persons subjected to any form of arrest, detention or imprisonment in any territory under its jurisdiction, with a view to preventing any cases of torture.

Art. 12.[7] Each State Party shall ensure that its competent authorities proceed to a prompt and impartial investigation, wherever there is reasonable ground to believe that an act of torture has been committed in any territory under its jurisdiction.

Art. 13.[7] Each State Party shall ensure that any individual who alleges he has been subjected to torture in any territory under its jurisdiction has the right to complain to, and to have his case promptly and impartially examined by, its competent authorities. Steps shall be taken to ensure that the complainant and witnesses are protected against all ill-treatment or intimidation as a consequence of his complaint or any evidence given.

Art. 14.[8]

1. Each State Party shall ensure in its legal system that the victim of an act of torture obtains redress and has an enforceable right to fair and adequate compensation, including the means for as full rehabilitation as possible. In the event of the death of the victim as a result of an act of torture, his dependants shall be entitled to compensation.
2. Nothing in this article shall affect any right of the victim or other persons to compensation which may exist under national law.

Art. 15.[9] Each State Party shall ensure that any statement which is established to have been made as a result of torture shall not be invoked as evidence in any proceedings, except against a person accused of torture as evidence that the statement was made.

---

[7] For declaration in respect of these articles by the United States of America, see p. 922.

[8] For declaration in respect of this article by Bangladesh and the United States of America, see pp. 914, 922.

[9] For declaration in respect of this article by Austria and the United States of America, see pp. 914, 922.

Art. 16.[10]

1. Each State Party shall undertake to prevent in any territory under its jurisdiction other acts of cruel, inhuman or degrading treatment or punishment which do not amount to torture as defined in article 1, when such acts are committed by or at the instigation of or with the consent or acquiescence of a public official or other person acting in an official capacity. In particular, the obligations contained in articles 10, 11, 12 and 13 shall apply with the substitution for references to torture of references to other forms of cruel, inhuman or degrading treatment or punishment.
2. The provisions of this Convention are without prejudice to the provisions of any other international instrument or national law which prohibits cruel, inhuman or degrading treatment or punishment or which relates to extradition or expulsion.

PART II

Art. 17.

1. There shall be established a *Committee against Torture* (hereinafter referred to as the Committee) which shall carry out the functions hereinafter provided. The Committee shall consist of ten experts of high moral standing and recognized competence in the field of human rights, who shall serve in their personal capacity. The experts shall be elected by the States Parties, consideration being given to equitable geographical distribution and to the usefulness of the participation of some persons having legal experience.
2. The members of the Committee shall be elected by secret ballot from a list of persons nominated by States Parties. Each State Party may nominate one person from among its own nationals. States Parties shall bear in mind the usefulness of nominating persons who are also members of the Human Rights Committee established under the International Covenant on Civil and Political Rights and who are willing to serve on the Committee against Torture.
3. Elections of the members of the Committee shall be held at biennial meetings of States Parties convened by the Secretary-General of the United Nations. At those meetings, for which two thirds of the States Parties shall constitute a quorum, the persons elected to the Committee shall be those who obtain the largest number of votes and an absolute majority of the votes of the representatives of States Parties present and voting.
4. The initial election shall be held no later than six months after the date of the entry into force of this Convention. At least four months before the date of each election, the Secretary-General of the United Nations shall address a letter to the States Parties inviting them to submit their nominations within three months. The Secretary-General shall prepare a list in alphabetical order of all persons thus nominated, indicating the States Parties which have nominated them, and shall submit it to the States Parties.
5. The members of the Committee shall be elected for a term of four years. They shall be eligible for re-election if renominated. However, the term of five of the members elected at the first election shall expire at the end of

[10] For declarations in respect of this article by the United States of America, see pp. 921–922.

two years; immediately after the first election the names of these five members shall be chosen by lot by the chairman of the meeting referred to in paragraph 3 of this article.

6. If a member of the Committee dies or resigns or for any other cause can no longer perform his Committee duties, the State Party which nominated him shall appoint another expert from among its nationals to serve for the remainder of his term, subject to the approval of the majority of the States Parties. The approval shall be considered given unless half or more of the States Parties respond negatively within six weeks after having been informed by the Secretary-General of the United Nations of the proposed appointment.
7.[11] States Parties shall be responsible for the expenses of the members of the Committee while they are in performance of Committee duties.

Art. 18.

1. The Committee shall elect its officers for a term of two years. They may be re-elected.
2. The Committee shall establish its own rules of procedure, but these rules shall provide, inter alia, that:
   (a) Six members shall constitute a quorum;
   (b) Decisions of the Committee shall be made by a majority vote of the members present.
3. The Secretary-General of the United Nations shall provide the necessary staff and facilities for the effective performance of the functions of the Committee under this Convention.
4. The Secretary-General of the United Nations shall convene the initial meeting of the Committee. After its initial meeting, the Committee shall meet at such times as shall be provided in its rules of procedure.
5.[11] The States Parties shall be responsible for expenses incurred in connection with the holding of meetings of the States Parties and of the Committee, including reimbursement to the United Nations for any expenses, such as the cost of staff and facilities, incurred by the United Nations pursuant to paragraph 3 of this article.

Art. 19.

1. The States Parties shall submit to the Committee, through the Secretary-General of the United Nations, reports on the measures they have taken to give effect to their undertakings under this Convention, within one year after the entry into force of the Convention for the State Party concerned. Thereafter the States Parties shall submit supplementary reports every four years on any new measures taken and such other reports as the Committee may request.
2. The Secretary-General of the United Nations shall transmit the reports to all States Parties.
3. Each report shall be considered by the Committee which may make such general comments on the report as it may consider appropriate and shall forward these to the State Party concerned. That State Party may respond with any observations it chooses to the Committee.

---

11 [For declaration in respect of this paragraph by German Democratic Republic (withdrawn), see p. 917.]

4. The Committee may, at its discretion, decide to include any comments made by it in accordance with paragraph 3 of this article, together with the observations thereon received from the State Party concerned, in its annual report made in accordance with article 24. If so requested by the State Party concerned, the Committee may also include a copy of the report submitted under paragraph 1 of this article.

Art. 20.[12]

1.[13] If the Committee receives reliable information which appears to it to contain well-founded indications that torture is being systematically practised in the territory of a State Party, the Committee shall invite that State Party to co-operate in the examination of the information and to this end to submit observations with regard to the information concerned.
2. Taking into account any observations which may have been submitted by the State Party concerned, as well as any other relevant information available to it, the Committee may, if it decides that this is warranted, designate one or more of its members to make a confidential inquiry and to report to the Committee urgently.
3. If an inquiry is made in accordance with paragraph 2 of this article, the Committee shall seek the co-operation of the State Party concerned. In agreement with that State Party, such an inquiry may include a visit to its territory.
4. After examining the findings of its member or members submitted in accordance with paragraph 2 of this article, the Committee shall transmit these findings to the State Party concerned together with any comments or suggestions which seem appropriate in view of the situation.
5. All the proceedings of the Committee referred to in paragraphs 1 to 4 of this article shall be confidential, and at all stages of the proceedings the co-operation of the State Party shall be sought. After such proceedings have been completed with regard to an inquiry made in accordance with paragraph 2, the Committee may, after consultations with the State Party concerned, decide to include a summary account of the results of the proceedings in its annual report made in accordance with article 24.

Art. 21.[14]

1.[15] A State Party to this Convention may at any time declare under this article that it recognizes the competence of the Committee to receive and consider

---

[12] For declarations or reservations in respect of this article by Afghanistan, Bahrain (withdrawn), Belarus, Bulgaria, Chile, China, Cuba, Czech Republic (withdrawn), [German Democratic Republic (withdrawn)], Hungary (withdrawn), Indonesia, Kuwait, Morocco, Poland, Russian Federation, Slovakia (withdrawn), Tunisia, (made on signature and withdrawn at ratification), Ukraine and Zambia (withdrawn), see pp. 914–922.

[13] For reservation in respect of this paragraph by Morocco, see p. 919.

[14] For reservations in respect of this article by Qatar and Tunisia (made on signature and withdrawn at ratification), see pp. 919, 920.

[15] On 22 September 2002, the following states had made a declaration according to this paragraph: Algeria, Argentina, Australia, Austria, Azerbaijan, Belgium, Bulgaria, Cameroon, Canada, Costa Rica, Croatia, Cyprus, Czech Republic, Denmark, Ecuador, Finland, France, Germany, Ghana, Greece, Hungary, Iceland, Irekand, Italy, Japan, Liechtenstein, Luxembourg, Malta, Mexico, Monaco, Netherlands, New Zealand, Norway, Paraguay, Poland, Portugal, Russian Federation, Senegal, Seychelles, Slovakia, Slovenia, South Africa, Spain, Sweden, Switzerland, Togo, Tunisia, Turkey, Uganda, United Kingdom, United States of America, Uruguay, Venezuela, Yugoslavia (Serbia and Montenegro).

communications to the effect that a State Party claims that another State Party is not fulfilling its obligations under this Convention. Such communications may be received and considered according to the procedures laid down in this article only if submitted by a State Party which has made a declaration recognizing in regard to itself the competence of the Committee. No communication shall be dealt with by the Committee under this article if it concerns a State Party which has not made such a declaration. Communications received under this article shall be dealt with in accordance with the following procedure:

(a) If a State Party considers that another State Party is not giving effect to the provisions of this Convention, it may, by written communication, bring the matter to the attention of that State Party. Within three months after the receipt of the communication the receiving State shall afford the State which sent the communication an explanation or any other statement in writing clarifying the matter, which should include, to the extent possible and pertinent, reference to domestic procedures and remedies taken, pending or available in the matter;

(b) If the matter is not adjusted to the satisfaction of both States Parties concerned within six months after the receipt by the receiving State of the initial communication, either State shall have the right to refer the matter to the Committee, by notice given to the Committee and to the other State;

(c) The Committee shall deal with a matter referred to it under this article only after it has ascertained that all domestic remedies have been invoked and exhausted in the matter, in conformity with the generally recognized principles of international law. This shall not be the rule where the application of the remedies is unreasonably prolonged or is unlikely to bring effective relief to the person who is the victim of the violation of this Convention;

(d) The Committee shall hold closed meetings when examining communications under this article;

(e) Subject to the provisions of subparagraph (c), the Committee shall make available its good offices to the States Parties concerned with a view to a friendly solution of the matter on the basis of respect for the obligations provided for in this Convention. For this purpose, the Committee may, when appropriate, set up an ad hoc conciliation commission;

(f) In any matter referred to it under this article, the Committee may call upon the States Parties concerned, referred to in subparagraph (b), to supply any relevant information;

(g) The States Parties concerned, referred to in subparagraph (b), shall have the right to be represented when the matter is being considered by the Committee and to make submissions orally and/or in writing;

(h) The Committee shall, within twelve months after the date of receipt of notice under subparagraph (b), submit a report:

   (i) If a solution within the terms of subparagraph (e) is reached, the Committee shall confine its report to a brief statement of the facts and of the solution reached;

   (ii) If a solution within the terms of subparagraph (e) is not reached, the Committee shall confine its report to a brief statement of the facts; the written submissions and record of the oral submissions made by the States Parties concerned shall be attached to the report. In every matter, the report shall be communicated to the States Parties concerned.

2. The provisions of this article shall come into force when five States Parties to this Convention have made declarations under paragraph 1 of this article. Such declarations shall be deposited by the States Parties with the Secretary-General of the United Nations, who shall transmit copies thereof to the other States Parties. A declaration may be withdrawn at any time by notification to the Secretary-General. Such a withdrawal shall not prejudice the consideration of any matter which is the subject of a communication already transmitted under this article; no further communication by any State Party shall be received under this article after the notification of withdrawal of the declaration has been received by the Secretary-General, unless the State Party concerned has made a new declaration.

Art. 22.[16] [17]

1. A State Party to this Convention may at any time declare under this article that it recognizes the competence of the Committee to receive and consider communications from or on behalf of individuals subject to its jurisdiction who claim to be victims of a violation by a State Party of the provisions of the Convention. No communication shall be received by the Committee if it concerns a State Party which has not made such a declaration.
2. The Committee shall consider inadmissible any communication under this article which is anonymous or which it considers to be an abuse of the right of submission of such communications or to be incompatible with the provisions of this Convention.
3. Subject to the provisions of paragraph 2, the Committee shall bring any communications submitted to it under this article to the attention of the State Party to this Convention which has made a declaration under paragraph 1 and is alleged to be violating any provisions of the Convention. Within six months, the receiving State shall submit to the Committee written explanations or statements clarifying the matter and the remedy, if any, that may have been taken by that State.
4. The Committee shall consider communications received under this article in the light of all information made available to it by or on behalf of the individual and by the State Party concerned.
5. The Committee shall not consider any communications from an individual under this article unless it has ascertained that:
   (a) The same matter has not been, and is not being, examined under another procedure of international investigation or settlement;
   (b) The individual has exhausted all available domestic remedies; this shall not be the rule where the application of the remedies is unreasonably prolonged or is unlikely to bring effective relief to the person who is the victim of the violation of this Convention.
6. The Committee shall hold closed meetings when examining communications under this article.

[16] On 22 September 2002, the same states had made a declaration according to this article as those mentioned in note 15. Japan made the declaration according to article 21 only.

[17] For reservations in respect of this article and Article 21 by Qatar, see p. 919.

7. The Committee shall forward its views to the State Party concerned and to the individual.
8. The provisions of this article shall come into force when five States Parties to this Convention have made declarations under paragraph 1 of this article. Such declarations shall be deposited by the States Parties with the Secretary-General of the United Nations, who shall transmit copies thereof to the other States Parties. A declaration may be withdrawn at any time by notification to the Secretary-General. Such a withdrawal shall not prejudice the consideration of any matter which is the subject of a communication already transmitted under this article; no further communication by or on behalf of an individual shall be received under this article after the notification of withdrawal of the declaration has been received by the Secretary-General, unless the State Party has made a new declaration.

Art. 23. The members of the Committee and of the ad hoc conciliation commissions which may be appointed under article 21, paragraph 1 (e), shall be entitled to the facilities, privileges and immunities of experts on mission for the United Nations as laid down in the relevant sections of the Convention on the Privileges and Immunities of the United Nations.

Art. 24. The Committee shall submit an annual report on its activities under this Convention to the States Parties and to the General Assembly of the United Nations.

PART III

Art. 25.
1. This Convention is open for signature by all States.
2. This Convention is subject to ratification. Instruments of ratification shall be deposited with the Secretary-General of the United Nations.

Art. 26. This Convention is open to accession by all States. Accession shall be effected by the deposit of an instrument of accession with the Secretary-General of the United Nations.

Art. 27.
1. This Convention shall enter into force on the thirtieth day after the date of the deposit with the Secretary-General of the United Nations of the twentieth instrument of ratification or accession.
2. For each State ratifying this Convention or acceding to it after the deposit of the twentieth instrument of ratification or accession, the Convention shall enter into force on the thirtieth day after the date of the deposit of its own instrument of ratification or accession.

Art. 28.
1.[18] Each State may, at the time of signature or ratification of this Convention or accession thereto, declare that it does not recognize the competence of the Committee provided for in article 20.

---

[18] For declarations in respect of this article by Guatemala (withdrawn) and Israel, see pp. 917, 918.

2. Any State Party having made a reservation in accordance with paragraph 1 of this article may, at any time, withdraw this reservation by notification to the Secretary-General of the United Nations.

Art. 29.

1. Any State Party to this Convention may propose an amendment and file it with the Secretary-General of the United Nations. The Secretary-General shall thereupon communicate the proposed amendment to the States Parties with a request that they notify him whether they favour a Conference of States Parties for the purpose of considering and voting upon the proposal. In the event that within four months from the date of such communication at least one third of the States Parties favours such a conference, the Secretary-General shall convene the conference under the auspices of the United Nations. Any amendment adopted by a majority of the States Parties present and voting at the conference shall be submitted by the Secretary-General to all the States Parties for acceptance.
2. An amendment adopted in accordance with paragraph 1 of this article shall enter into force when two thirds of the States Parties to this Convention have notified the Secretary-General of the United Nations that they have accepted it in accordance with their respective constitutional processes.
3. When amendments enter into force, they shall be binding on those States Parties which have accepted them, other States Parties still being bound by the provisions of this Convention and any earlier amendments which they have accepted.

Art. 30.[19]

1.[20] Any dispute between two or more States Parties concerning the interpretation or application of this Convention which cannot be settled through negotiation shall, at the request of one of them, be submitted to arbitration. If within six months from the date of the request for arbitration the Parties are unable to agree on the organization of the arbitration, any one of those Parties may refer the dispute to the International Court of Justice by request in conformity with the Statute of the Court.

2. Each State may, at the time of signature or ratification of this Convention or accession thereto, declare that it does not consider itself bound by paragraph 1 of this article. The other States Parties shall not be bound by paragraph 1 of this article with respect to any State Party having made such a reservation.
3. Any State Party having made a reservation in accordance with paragraph 2 of this article may at any time withdraw this reservation by notification to the Secretary-General of the United Nations.

---

[19] For declarations in respect of this article by Cuba and Ghana, see pp. 916, 917.

[20] For reservations or declarations in respect of this paragraph by Afghanistan, Bahrain, Belarus (withdrawn), Bulgaria (withdrawn), Chile (withdrawn), China, Cuba, Czechoslovakia (withdrawn), France, [German Democratic Republic], Guatemala (withdrawn), Hungary (withdrawn), Indonesia, Israel, Kuwait, Monaco, Panama, Poland, Russian Federation (withdrawn), Slovakia (withdrawn), South Africa, Turkey, Ukraine and United States of America, see pp. 914–921.

Art. 31.

1. A State Party may denounce this Convention by written notification to the Secretary-General of the United Nations. Denunciation becomes effective one year after the date of receipt of the notification by the Secretary-General.
2. Such a denunciation shall not have the effect of releasing the State Party from its obligations under this Convention in regard to any act or omission which occurs prior to the date at which the denunciation becomes effective, nor shall denunciation prejudice in any way the continued consideration of any matter which is already under consideration by the Committee prior to the date at which the denunciation becomes effective.
3. Following the date at which the denunciation of a State Party becomes effective, the Committee shall not commence consideration of any new matter regarding that State.

Art. 32. The Secretary-General of the United Nations shall inform all States Members of the United Nations and all States which have signed this Convention or acceded to it of the following:

(a) Signatures, ratifications and accessions under article 25 and 26;
(b) The date of entry into force of this Convention under article 27 and the date of the entry into force of any amendments under article 29;
(c) Denunciations under article 31.

Art. 33.

1. This Convention, of which the Arabic, Chinese, English, French, Russian and Spanish texts are equally authentic, shall be deposited with the Secretary-General of the United Nations.
2. The Secretary-General of the United Nations shall transmit certified copies of this Convention to all States.

II. AMENDMENTS PROPOSED BY THE GOVERNMENT OF AUSTRALIA AND ADOPTED BY THE CONFERENCE OF STATES PARTIES TO THE CONVENTION ON 8 SEPTEMBER 1992, BUT NOT YET IN FORCE[1]

To delete article 17, paragraph 7, and article 18, paragraph 5,

And insert a new paragraph 4 of article 18 to read:

"The members of the Committee established under the present Convention shall receive emoluments from the United Nations resources on such terms and conditions as the General Assembly shall decide."

And as a result of inserting this provision, the existing paragraph 4 of article 18 should be renumbered as paragraph 5.

III. OPTIONAL PROTOCOL TO THE CONVENTION AGAINST TORTURE AND OTHER CRUEL, INHUMAN OR DEGRADING TREATMENT OR PUNISHMENT

PREAMBLE

The States Parties to the present Protocol,

Reaffirming that torture and other cruel, inhuman or degrading treatment or punishment are prohibited and constitute serious violations of human rights,

Convinced that further measures are necessary to achieve the purposes of the Convention against Torture and Other Cruel, Inhuman or Degrading Treatment or Punishment (hereinafter referred to as the Convention) and to strengthen the protection of persons deprived of their liberty from torture and other cruel, inhuman or degrading treatment or punishment,

Recalling that articles 2 and 16 of the Convention oblige each State Party to take effective measures to prevent acts of torture and other cruel, inhuman or degrading treatment or punishment in any territory under its jurisdiction,

Recognizing that States have the primary responsibility for implementing these articles, that strengthening the protection of people deprived of their liberty and the full respect for their human rights is a common responsibility shared by all, and that international implementing bodies complement and strengthen national measures,

Recalling that the effective prevention of torture and other cruel, inhuman or degrading treatment or punishment requires education and a combination of various legislative, administrative, judicial or other measures,

Recalling also that the World Conference on Human Rights firmly declared that efforts to eradicate torture should first and foremost be concentrated on prevention and called for the adoption of an optional protocol to the Convention which is intended to establish a preventive system of regular visits to places of detention,

Convinced that the protection of persons deprived of their liberty against torture and other cruel, inhuman or degrading treatment or punishment can be strengthened by non-judicial means of a preventive nature, based on regular visits to places of detention,

Have agreed as follows:

---

[1] For the state of acceptance of the Amendments, see p. 944.

PART I. GENERAL PRINCIPLES

Article 1. The objective of this Protocol is to establish a system of regular visits undertaken by independent international and national bodies to places where people are deprived of their liberty, in order to prevent torture and other cruel, inhuman or degrading treatment or punishment.

Art. 2.
1. A Subcommittee on Prevention of Torture and Other Cruel, Inhuman or Degrading Treatment or Punishment of the Committee against Torture (hereinafter referred to as the Subcommittee on Prevention) shall be established and shall carry out the functions laid down in the present Protocol.
2. The Subcommittee on Prevention shall carry out its work within the framework of the Charter of the United Nations and will be guided by the purposes and principles thereof, as well as the norms of the United Nations concerning the treatment of people deprived of their liberty.
3. Equally, the Subcommittee on Prevention shall be guided by the principles of confidentiality, impartiality, non-selectivity, universality and objectivity.
4. The Subcommittee on Prevention and the States Parties shall cooperate in the implementation of the present Protocol.

Art. 3. Each State Party shall set up, designate or maintain at the domestic level one or several visiting bodies for the prevention of torture and other cruel, inhuman or degrading treatment or punishment (hereinafter referred to as the national preventive mechanism).

Art. 4.
1. Each State Party shall allow visits, in accordance with the present Protocol, by the mechanisms referred to in articles 2 and 3 to any place under its jurisdiction and control where persons are or may be deprived of their liberty, either by virtue of an order given by a public authority or at its instigation or with its consent or acquiescence (hereinafter referred to as places of detention). These visits shall be undertaken with a view to strengthening, if necessary, the protection of these persons against torture and other cruel, inhuman or degrading treatment or punishment.
2. For the purposes of the present Protocol deprivation of liberty means any form of detention or imprisonment or the placement of a person in a public or private custodial setting, from which this person is not permitted to leave at will by order of any judicial, administrative or other authority.

PART II. SUBCOMMITTEE ON PREVENTION

Art. 5.
1. The Subcommittee on Prevention shall consist of ten members. After the fiftieth ratification or accession to the present Protocol, the number of the members of the Subcommittee on Prevention shall increase to twenty-five.
2. The members of the Subcommittee on Prevention shall be chosen from among persons of high moral character, having proven professional experience in the field of the administration of justice, in particular criminal law, prison or police administration, or in the various fields relevant to the treatment of persons deprived of their liberty.
3. In the composition of the Subcommittee on Prevention due consideration shall be given to the equitable geographic distribution and to the representation of different forms of civilization and legal systems of the States Parties.
4. In this composition consideration shall also be given to the balanced gender representation on the basis of the principles of equality and non-discrimination.

5. No two members of the Subcommittee on Prevention may be nationals of the same State.
6. The members of the Subcommittee on Prevention shall serve in their individual capacity, shall be independent and impartial and shall be available to serve the Subcommittee on Prevention efficiently.

Art. 6.
1. Each State Party may nominate, in accordance with paragraph 2, up to two candidates possessing the qualifications and meeting the requirements set out in article 5, and in doing so shall provide detailed information on the qualifications of the nominees.
2. (a) The nominees shall have the nationality of a State Party to the present Protocol;
   (b) At least one of the two candidates shall have the nationality of the nominating State Party;
   (c) No more than two nationals of a State Party shall be nominated;
   (d) Before a State Party nominates a national of another State Party, it shall seek and obtain the consent of that State Party.
3. At least five months before the date of the meeting of the States Parties during which the elections will be held, the Secretary-General of the United Nations shall address a letter to the States Parties inviting them to submit their nominations within three months. The Secretary-General shall submit a list, in alphabetical order, of all persons thus nominated, indicating the States Parties which have nominated them.

Art. 7.
1. The members of the Subcommittee on Prevention shall be elected in the following manner:
   (a) Primary consideration shall be given to the fulfilment of the requirements and criteria of article 5 of the present Protocol;
   (b) The initial election shall be held no later than six months after the entry into force of the present Protocol;
   (c) The States Parties shall elect the members of the Subcommittee by secret ballot;
   (d) Elections of the members of the Subcommittee on Prevention shall be held at biennial meetings of the States Parties convened by the Secretary-General of the United Nations. At those meetings, for which two thirds of the States Parties shall constitute a quorum, the persons elected to the Subcommittee on Prevention shall be those who obtain the largest number of votes and an absolute majority of the votes of the representatives of the States Parties present and voting.
2. If, during the election process, two nationals of a State Party have become eligible to serve as members of the Subcommittee on Prevention, the candidate receiving the higher number of votes shall serve as the member of the Subcommittee on Prevention. Where nationals have received the same number of votes, the following procedure applies:
   (a) Where only one has been nominated by the State Party of which he or she is a national, that national shall serve as the member of the Subcommittee on Prevention;
   (b) Where both candidates have been nominated by the State Party of which they are nationals, a separate vote by secret ballot shall be held to determine which national shall become member;
   (c) Where neither candidate has been nominated by the State Party of which he or she is a national, a separate vote by secret ballot shall be held to determine which candidate shall be the member.

Art. 8. If a member of the Subcommittee on Prevention dies or resigns, or for any cause can no longer perform his or her duties, the State Party which nominated the member shall nominate another eligible person possessing the qualifications and meeting the requirements set out in article 5, taking into account the need for a proper balance among the various fields of competence, to serve until the next meeting of the States Parties, subject to the approval of the majority of the States Parties. The approval shall be considered given unless half or more of the States Parties respond negatively within six weeks after having been informed by the Secretary-General of the United Nations of the proposed appointment.

Art. 9. The members of the Subcommittee on Prevention shall be elected for a term of four years. They shall be eligible for re-election once if renominated. The term of half the members elected at the first election shall expire at the end of two years; immediately after the first election the names of these members shall be chosen by lot by the Chairman of the meeting referred to in article 7, paragraph 1 (d).

Art. 10.

1. The Subcommittee on Prevention shall elect its officers for a term of two years. They may be re-elected.
2. The Subcommittee on Prevention shall establish its own rules of procedure. These rules shall provide, inter alia, that:
   (a) Half plus one members shall constitute a quorum;
   (b) Decisions of the Subcommittee on Prevention shall be made by a majority vote of the members present;
   (c) The Subcommittee on Prevention shall meet in camera.
3. The Secretary-General of the United Nations shall convene the initial meeting of the Subcommittee on Prevention. After its initial meeting, the Subcommittee shall meet at such times as shall be provided by its rules of procedure. The Subcommittee on Prevention and the Committee against Torture shall hold their sessions simultaneously at least once a year.

PART III. MANDATE OF THE SUBCOMMITTEE ON PREVENTION

Art. 11. The Subcommittee on Prevention shall:

(a) Visit the places referred to in article 4 and make recommendations to States Parties concerning the protection of persons deprived of their liberty from torture and other cruel, inhuman or degrading treatment or punishment;

(b) In regard to the national preventive mechanisms:

- (i) Advise and assist States Parties, when necessary, in their establishment;
- (ii) Maintain direct, if necessary confidential, contact with the national preventive mechanisms and offer them training and technical assistance with a view to strengthening their capacities;
- (iii) Advise and assist them in the evaluation of the needs and the means necessary to strengthen the protection of persons deprived of their liberty from torture and other cruel, inhuman or degrading treatment or punishment;
- (iv) Make recommendations and observations to the States Parties with a view to strengthening the capacity and the mandate of the national preventive mechanisms for the prevention of torture and other cruel, inhuman or degrading treatment or punishment;

(c) Cooperate, for the prevention of torture in general, with the relevant United Nations organs and mechanisms as well as with the international, regional and national institutions or organizations working toward the strengthening of the protection of persons from torture and other cruel, inhuman or degrading treatment or punishment.

Art. 12. In order to enable the Subcommittee on Prevention to comply with its mandate as laid out in article 11, the States Parties undertake:

(a) To receive the Subcommittee on Prevention in its territory and grant it access to the places of detention as defined in article 4 of the present Protocol;

(b) To provide all relevant information the Subcommittee on Prevention may request to evaluate the needs and measures that should be adopted in order to strengthen the protection of persons deprived of their liberty from torture and other cruel, inhuman or degrading treatment or punishment;
(c) To encourage and facilitate contacts between the Subcommittee on Prevention and the national preventive mechanisms;
(d) To examine the recommendations of the Subcommittee on Prevention and enter into dialogue with it on possible implementation measures.

Art. 13.
1. The Subcommittee on Prevention shall establish, at first by lot, a programme of regular visits to the States Parties in order to fulfil its mandate as established in article 11.
2. After consultations, the Subcommittee on Prevention shall notify its programme to the States Parties in order that they may, without delay, make the necessary practical arrangements for the visits to take place.
3. The visits shall be conducted by at least two members of the Subcommittee on Prevention. These members can be accompanied, if needed, by experts of demonstrated professional experience and knowledge in the fields covered by the present Protocol who shall be selected from a roster of experts prepared on the basis of proposals made by the States Parties, the Office of the United Nations High Commissioner for Human Rights and the United Nations Centre for International Crime Prevention. In preparing the roster, the States Parties concerned shall propose no more than five national experts. The State Party concerned may oppose the inclusion of a specific expert in the visit, whereupon the Subcommittee on Prevention shall propose another expert.
4. If the Subcommittee on Prevention considers it appropriate, it can propose a short follow-up visit after regular visit.

Art. 14.
1. In order to enable the Subcommittee on Prevention to fulfil its mandate, the States Parties to the present Protocol undertake to grant it:
   (a) Unrestricted access to all information concerning the number of persons deprived of their liberty in places of detention as defined in article 4, as well as the number of places and their location;
   (b) Unrestricted access to all information referring to the treatment of these persons as well as their conditions of detention;
   (c) Subject to paragraph 2, unrestricted access to all places of detention and their installations and facilities;
   (d) The opportunity to have private interviews with the persons deprived of their liberty without witnesses, either personally or with a translator if deemed necessary, as well as with any other person whom the Subcommittee on Prevention believes may supply relevant information;
   (e) The liberty to choose the places it wants to visit and the persons it wants to interview.
2. Objection to a visit to a particular place of detention can only be made on urgent and compelling grounds of national defence, public safety, natural disaster or serious disorder in the place to be visited which temporarily prevent the carrying out of such a visit. The existence of a declaration of a state of emergency as such shall not be invoked by a State Party as a reason to object to a visit.

Art. 15. No authority or official shall order, apply, permit or tolerate any sanction against any person or organization for having communicated to the Subcommittee on Prevention or to its delegates any information, whether true or false, and no such person or organization shall be otherwise prejudiced in any way.

Art. 16.
1. The Subcommittee on Prevention shall communicate its recommendations and observations confidentially to the State Party and, if relevant, to the national mechanism.
2. The Subcommittee on Prevention shall publish its report, together with any comments of the State Party concerned, whenever requested to do so by that State Party. If the State Party makes part of the report public, the Subcommittee on Prevention may publish the report in whole or in part. However, no personal data shall be published without the express consent of the person concerned.
3. The Subcommittee on Prevention shall present a public annual report on its activities to the Committee against Torture.
4. If the State Party refuses to cooperate with the Subcommittee on Prevention according to articles 12 and 14, or to take steps to improve the situation in the light of the recommendations of the Subcommittee on Prevention, the Committee against Torture may, at the request of the Subcommittee on Prevention, decide, by a majority of its members, after the State Party has had an opportunity to make its views known, to make a public statement on the matter or to publish the report of the Subcommittee on Prevention.

PART IV. NATIONAL PREVENTIVE MECHANISMS

Art. 17. Each State Party shall maintain, designate or establish, at the latest one year after the entry into force of the present Protocol or of its ratification or accession, one or several independent national preventive mechanisms for the prevention of torture at the domestic level. Mechanisms established by decentralized units may be designated as national preventive mechanisms for the purposes of the present Protocol, if they are in conformity with its provisions.

Art. 18.
1. The States Parties shall guarantee the functional independence of the national preventive mechanisms as well as the independence of their personnel.
2. The States Parties shall take the necessary measures in order for the experts of the national mechanism to have the required capabilities and professional knowledge. They shall strive for a gender balance and the adequate representation of ethnic and minority groups in the country.
3. The States Parties undertake to make available the necessary resources for the functioning of the national preventive mechanisms.
4. When establishing national preventive mechanisms, States Parties shall give due consideration to the Principles relating to the status and functioning of national institutions for the promotion and protection of human rights.

Art. 19. The national preventive mechanisms shall be granted at least the powers:
(a) To regularly examine the treatment of the persons deprived of their liberty in places of detention as defined in article 4, with a view to strengthening, if necessary, their protection from torture, cruel, inhuman or degrading treatment or punishment;
(b) To make recommendations to the relevant authorities with the aim of improving the treatment and the conditions of the persons deprived of their liberty and to prevent torture and cruel, inhuman or degrading treatment or punishment, taking into consideration the relevant norms of the United Nations;
(c) To submit proposals and observations concerning existing or draft legislation.

Art. 20. In order to enable the national preventive mechanisms to fulfil their mandate, the States Parties to the present Protocol undertake to grant them:

(a) Access to all information concerning the number of persons deprived of their liberty in places of detention as defined in article 4, as well as the number of places and their location;
(b) Access to all information referring to the treatment of these persons as well as their conditions of detention;
(c) Access to all places of detention and their installations and facilities;
(d) The opportunity to have private interviews with the persons deprived of their liberty without witnesses, either personally or with a translator if deemed necessary, as well as with any other person whom the national preventive mechanism believes may supply relevant information;
(e) The liberty to choose the places they want to visit and the persons they want to interview;
(f) The right to have contacts with the Subcommittee on Prevention, to send it information and to meet with it.

Art. 21.

1. No authority or official shall order, apply, permit or tolerate any sanction against any person or organization for having communicated to the national preventive mechanism any information, whether true or false, and no such person or organization shall be otherwise prejudiced in any way.
2. Confidential information collected by the national preventive mechanism shall be privileged. No personal data shall be published without the express consent of the person concerned.

Art. 22. The competent authorities of the State Party concerned shall examine the recommendations of the national preventive mechanism and enter into a dialogue with it on possible implementation measures.

Art. 23. The States Parties to the present Protocol undertake to publish and disseminate the annual reports of the national preventive mechanisms.

PART V. DECLARATION

Art. 24.

1. Upon ratification, States Parties can make a declaration postponing the implementation of their obligations either under Part III or under Part IV of the present Protocol.
2. This postponement shall be valid for a maximum of three years. After due representations made by the State Party and after consultation with the Subcommittee on Prevention, the Committee against Torture may extend this period for an additional two-year period.

PART VI. FINANCIAL PROVISIONS

Art. 25.

1. The expenditure incurred by the Subcommittee on Prevention in the implementation of the present Protocol shall be borne by the United Nations.
2. The Secretary-General of the United Nations shall provide the necessary staff and facilities for the effective performance of the functions of the Subcommittee on Prevention under the present Protocol.

Art. 26.

1. A Special Fund shall be set up in accordance with the relevant procedures of the General Assembly, to be administered in accordance with the financial regulations

and rules of the United Nations, to help finance the implementation of the recommendations made by the Subcommittee on Prevention to a State Party after a visit, as well as education programmes of the national preventive mechanisms.

2. The Special Fund may be financed through voluntary contributions made by Governments, intergovernmental and non-governmental organizations and other private or public entities.

PART VII. FINAL PROVISIONS

Art. 27.

1. The present Protocol is open for signature by any State which has signed the Convention.
2. The present Protocol is subject to ratification by any State which has ratified or acceded to the Convention. Instruments of ratification shall be deposited with the Secretary-General of the United Nations.
3. The present Protocol shall be open to accession by any State which has ratified or acceded to the Convention.
4. Accession shall be effected by the deposit of an instrument of accession with the Secretary-General of the United Nations.
5. The Secretary-General of the United Nations shall inform all States which have signed the present Protocol or acceded to it of the deposit of each instrument of ratification or accession.

Art. 28.

1. The present Protocol shall enter into force on the thirtieth day after the date of deposit with the Secretary-General of the United Nations of the twentieth instrument of ratification or accession.
2. For each State ratifying the present Protocol or acceding to it after the deposit with the Secretary-General of the United Nations of the twentieth instrument of ratification or accession, the present Protocol shall enter into force on the thirtieth day after the date of the deposit of its own instrument of ratification or accession.

Art. 29. The provisions of the present Protocol shall extend to all parts of federal States without any limitations or exceptions.

Art. 30. No reservations shall be made to the present Protocol.

Art. 31. The provisions of the present Protocol shall not affect the obligations of States Parties under any regional convention instituting a system of visits to places of detention. The Subcommittee on Prevention and the bodies established under such regional conventions are encouraged to consult and cooperate with a view to avoiding duplication and promoting effectively the objectives of the present Protocol.

Art. 32. The provisions of the present Protocol shall not affect the obligations of States Parties to the four Geneva Conventions of 12 August 1949 and the Additional Protocols thereto of 8 June 1977, or the opportunity available to any State Party to authorize the International Committee of the Red Cross to visit places of detention in situations not covered by international humanitarian law.

Art. 33.

1. Any State Party may denounce the present Protocol at any time by written notification addressed to the Secretary-General of the United Nations, who shall thereafter inform the other States Parties to the present Protocol and the Convention. Denunciation shall take effect one year after the date of receipt of the notification by the Secretary-General.

2. Such a denunciation shall not have the effect of releasing the State Party from its obligations under the present Protocol in regard to any act or situation which occurs prior to the date at which the denunciation becomes effective, or to the actions that the Subcommittee on Prevention has decided or may decide to adopt with respect to the State Party concerned, nor shall denunciation prejudice in any way the continued consideration of any matter which is already under consideration by the Subcommittee on Prevention prior to the date at which the denunciation becomes effective.
3. Following the date at which the denunciation of the State Party becomes effective, the Subcommittee on Prevention shall not commence consideration of any new matter regarding that State.

Art. 34.

1. Any State Party to the present Protocol may propose an amendment and file it with the Secretary-General of the United Nations. The Secretary-General shall thereupon communicate the proposed amendment to the States Parties to the present Protocol with a request that they notify him whether they favour a conference of States Parties for the purpose of considering and voting upon the proposal. In the event that within four months from the date of such communication at least one third of the States Parties favour such a conference, the Secretary-General shall convene the conference under the auspices of the United Nations. Any amendment adopted by a majority of two thirds of the States Parties present and voting at the conference shall be submitted by the Secretary-General of the United Nations to all States Parties for acceptance.
2. An amendment adopted in accordance with paragraph 1 of the present article shall come into force when it has been accepted by a two-thirds majority of the States Parties to the present Protocol in accordance with their respective constitutional process.
3. When amendments come into force, they shall be binding on those States Parties which have accepted them, other States Parties still being bound by the provisions of the present Protocol and any earlier amendment which they have accepted.

Art. 35. Members of the Subcommittee on Prevention and of the national preventive mechanisms shall be accorded such privileges and immunities as are necessary for the independent exercise of their functions. Members of the Subcommittee on Prevention shall be accorded the privileges and immunities specified in section 22 of the Convention on Privileges and Immunities of the United Nations of 13 February 1946, subject to the provisions of section 23 of that Convention.

Art. 36. When visiting a State Party the members of the Subcommittee on Prevention shall, without prejudice to the provisions and purposes of the present Protocol and such privileges and immunities as they may enjoy:

(a) Respect the laws and regulations of the visited State; and
(b) Refrain from any action or activity incompatible with the impartial and international nature of their duties.

Art. 37.

1. The present Protocol, of which the Arabic, Chinese, English, French, Russian and Spanish texts are equally authentic, shall be deposited with the Secretary-General of the United Nations.
2. The Secretary-General of the United Nations shall transmit certified copies of the present Protocol to all States.

SIGNATURES, RATIFICATIONS, ACCESSIONS AND NOTIFICATIONS OF SUCCESSION OR CONTINUITY TO THE CONVENTION[1]

State	*Signatures*	*Ratifications, Accessions, Notifications of Succession or Continuity (C)*
Afghanistan	4 February 1985	1 April 1987 *Res.*
Albania	–	11 May 1994
Algeria*	26 November 1985	12 September 1989
Andorra	–	5 August 2002
Antigua and Barbuda	–	19 July 1993
Argentina*	4 February 1985	24 September 1986
Armenia	–	13 September 1993
Australia*	10 December 1985	8 August 1989
Austria *	14 March 1985	29 July 1987 *Res.*
Azerbaijan*	–	16 August 1996
Bahrain	–	6 March 1998 *Res.*[2]
Bangladesh	–	5 October 1998 *Dec.*[3]
Belarus	19 December 1985	13 March 1987 *Res.*[4]
Belgium*	4 February 1985	25 June 1999
Belize	–	17 March 1986
Benin	–	12 March 1992
Bolivia	4 February 1985	12 April 1999
Bosnia and Herzegovina	–	1 September 1993 (C)
Botswana	* September 2000	8 September 2000 *Dec.*
Brazil	23 September 1985	28 September 1989
Bulgaria*	10 June 1986	16 December 1986[5]
Burkina Faso	–	4 January 1999
Burundi	–	18 February 1993
Cameroon*	–	19 December 1986
Cambodia	–	15 October 1992
Canada*	23 August 1985	24 June 1987
Cape Verde	–	4 June 1992
Chad	–	9 June 1995
Chile	23 September 1987	30 September 1988[6]
China[7]	12 December 1986 *Res.*	4 October 1988 *Res.*

[1] Based on the indications in *Multilateral Treaties Deposited with the Secretary-General, New York, United Nations*, (ST/LEG/SER.E) as available on http://untreaty.un.org, of 26 January 2003. One asterisk (*) indicates that the state made the declaration according to Articles 21 and 22 of the Convention. Two asterisks indicates that the state made the declaration according to Article 21 only.

[2] For partial withdrawal of the reservation, see p. 914.

[3] For the objection by France, see p. 935.

[4] For partial withdrawal of the reservation, see p. 914.

[5] For the withdrawn reservation, see p. 915.

[6] For the withdrawn reservation, see p. 915.

[7] On 10 June 1997, the Government of China and the United Kingdom of Great Britain and Northern Ireland notified the Secretary-General of the following:

"In accordance with the Declaration of the Government of the People's Republic of China and the United Kingdom of Great Britain and Northern Ireland on the question of Hong Kong signed on 19 December 1984, the People's Republic of China will resume the exercise of sovereignty over Hong Kong with effect from 1 July 1997. Hong Kong will, with effect from that date, become a Special Administrative Region of the People's Republic of China and will enjoy a high degree of autonomy, except in foreign and defence affairs which are the responsibility of the Central People's Government of the People's Republic of China.

The Convention, which the Government of the People's Republic of China ratified on 4 October 1988, will apply to Hong Kong Special Administrative Region with effect from 1

State	Signatures	Ratifications, Accessions, Notifications of Succession or Continuity (C)
Colombia	10 April 1985	8 December 1987
Comoros	22 September 2000	–
Costa Rica*	4 February 1985	11 November 1993
Côte d'Ivoire	–	18 December 1995
Croatia*	–	12 October 1992 (C)

cont.

July 1997. The Government of the People's Republic of China will assume responsibility for the international rights and obligations arising from the application of the Convention to Hong Kong Special Administrative Region. The reservation made by the Government of the People's Republic of China to article 20 and paragraph 1 of article 30 of the Convention will also apply to the Hong Kong Special Administrative Region.'

Subsequently, on 10 June 1997, the Government of the United Kingdom of Great Britain and Northern Ireland notified the Secretary-General of the following:

' In accordance with the Joint Declaration of the Government of the United Kingdom of Great Britain and Northern Ireland and the Government of the People's Republic of China on the Question of Hong Kong signed on 19 December 1984, the Government of the United Kingdom will restore Hong Kong to the People's Republic of China with effect from 1 July 1997. The government of the United Kingdom will continue to have international responsibility for Hong Kong until that date. Therefore, from that date the Government of the United Kingdom will cease to be responsible for the international rights and obligations arising from the application of the Convention to Hong Kong."

On 15 June 1999, the Government of Portugal notified the Secretary-General that the Convention would apply to Macau. Subsequently, the Secretary-General received the following communications:

China (19 October 1999)

In accordance with the Joint Declaration of the Government of the People's Republic of China and the Government of the Republic of Portugal on the Question of Macau (hereinafter referred to as the Joint Declaration), the Government of the People's Republic of China will resume the exercise of sovereignty over Macau with effect form 20 December 1999. Macau will, from that date, become a Special Administrative Region of the People's Republic of China and will enjoy a high degree of autonomy, except in foreign and defense affairs which are the responsibilities of the Central People's Government of the People's Republic of China.

In this connection, [the Government of the People's Republic of China informs the Secretary-General of the following:]

The Convention Against Torture and Other Cruel, Inhuman or Degrading Treatment of Punishment (hereinafter referred to as the "Convention"), to which the Government of the People's Republic of China deposited the instrument of ratification on 4 October 1988, will apply to the Macau Special Administrative Region with effect from 20 December 1999. The Government of the People's Republic of China also wishes to make the following declaration:

"The reservation made by the government of the People's Republic of China to Article 20 and paragraph 1 of Article 30 of the Convention will also apply to the Macau Special Administrative Region.

The Government of the People's Republic of China will assume responsibility for the international rights and obligations arising from the application of the Convention to the Macau Special Administrative Region."

Portugal (21 October 1999)

In accordance with the Joint Declaration of the Government of the Portuguese Republic and the Government of the People's Republic of China on the Question of Macau signed on 13 April 1987, the Portuguese Republic will continue to have international responsibility for Macau until 19 December 1999 and form that date onwards the People's Republic of China will resume the exercise of sovereignty over Macau with effect from 20 December 1999.

From 20 December 1999 onwards the Portuguese Republic will cease to be responsible for the international rights and obligations arising from the applciation of the Convention to Macau.

State	*Signatures*	*Ratifications, Accessions, Notifications of Succession or Continuity (C)*
Cuba	27 January 1986	17 May 1995 *Dec.*
Cyprus*	9 October 1985	18 July 1991
Czech Republic[8]	–	22 February 1993 (C)

[8] Czechoslovakia had signed and ratified the Convention on 8 September 1986 and 7 July 1988, respectively, with the following reservations:

' The Czechoslovak Socialist Republic does not consider itself bound, in accordance with Article 30, paragraph 2, by the provisions of Article 30, paragraph 1, of the Convention.

The Czechoslovak Socialist Republic does not recognize the competence of the Committee against Torture as defined by article 20 of the Convention."

Subsequently, on 26 April 1991, the Government of Czechoslovakia notified the Secretary-General of its decision to withdraw the reservation with respect to article 30 (See p.916). In a letter dated 16 February 1993, received by the Secretary-General on 22 February 1993 and accompanied by a list of multilateral treaties deposited with the Secretary-General, the Government of the Czech Republic notified that:

' In conformity with the valid principles of international law and to the extent defined by it, the Czech Republic, as a successor State to the Czech and Slovak Federal Republic, considers itself bound, as of 1 January 1993, i.e. the date of the dissolution of the Czech and Slovak Federal Republic, by multilateral international treaties to which the Czech and Slovak Federal Republic was a party on that date, including reservations and declarations to their provisions made earlier by the Czech and Slovak Federal Republic.

The Government of the Czech Republic have examined multilateral treaties the list of which is attached to this letter. [The Government of the Czech Republic] considers to be bound by these treaties as well as by all reservations and declarations to them by virtue of succession as of 1 January 1993.

The Czech Republic, in accordance with the well established principles of international law, recognizes signatures made by the Czech and Slovak Federal Republic in respect of all signed treaties as if they were made by itself.'

Subsequently, in a letter dated 19 May 1993 and also accompanied by a list of multilateral treaties deposited with the Secretary-General, received by the Secretary-General on 28 May 1993, the Government of the Slovak Republic notified that:

' In accordance with the relevant principles and rules of international law and to the extent defined by it, the Slovak Republic, as a successor State, born from the dissolution of the Czech and Slovak Federal Republic, considers itself bound, as of January 1, 1993, i.e., the date on which the Slovak Republic assumed responsibility for its international relations, by multilateral treaties to which the Czech and Slovak Federal Republic was a party as of 31 December 1992, including reservations and declarations made earlier by Czechoslovakia, as well as objections by Czechoslovakia to reservations formulated by other treaty-parties.

The Slovak Republic wishes further to maintain its status as a contracting State of the treaties to which Czechoslovakia was a contracting State and which were not yet in force at the date of the dissolution of the Czech and Slovak Federal Republic, as well as the status of a signatory State of the treaties which were previously signed but not ratified by Czechoslovakia as listed in the Annex to this letter.'

In view of the information above, entries in status lists pertaining to formalities (i.e. signatures, ratifications, accessions, declarations and reservations, etc.) effected by the former Czechoslovakia prior to dissolution, in respect of treaties to which the Czech Republic and/or Slovakia have succeeded, will be replaced by the name of 'Czech Republic' and/or 'Slovakia' with the corresponding date of deposit of the notification of succession. A footnote will indicate the date and type of formality effected by the former Czechoslovakia, the corresponding indicator being inserted next to 'Czech Republic' and 'Slovakia', as the case may be.

As regards treaties in respect of which formalities were effected by the former Czechoslovakia and not listed in the notification of succession by either the Czech Republic or Slovakia, a footnote indicating the date and type of formality effected by the former Czechoslovakia will be included in the status of the treaties concerned, the corresponding footnote indicator being inserted next to the heading 'Participant'.

On 17 March 1995 and 3 September 1996, respectively, the Governments of Slovakia and the Czech Republic notified the Secretary-General that they had decided to withdraw the

State	*Signatures*	*Ratifications, Accessions, Notifications of Succession or Continuity (C)*
Democratic Republic of the Congo	–	18 March 1996
Denmark*	4 February 1985	27 May 1987
Djibouti	–	5 November 2002
Dominican Republic	4 February 1985	–
Ecuador*	4 February 1985	30 March 1988 *Res.*
Egypt	–	25 June 1986
El Salvador	–	17 June 1996
Equatorial Guinea	–	8 October 2002. *Res.*
Estonia	–	21 October 1991
Ethiopia	–	14 March 1994
Finland*	4 February 1985	30 August 1989
France*	4 February 1985	18 February 1986 *Res.*
Gabon	21 January 1986	8 September 2000
Gambia	23 October 1985	–
Georgia	–	26 October 1994
Germany* [9] [10]	13 October 1986 *Res.*	1 October 1990 *Res.*
Ghana*	7 September 2000	7 September 2000 *Dec.*
Greece*	4 February 1985	6 October 1988
Guatemala	–	5 January 1990[11]
Guinea	30 May 1986	10 October 1989
Guinea-Bissau	12 September 2000	–
Guyana	25 January 1988	19 May 1988
Holy See	–	26 June 2002 *Dec.*
Honduras	–	5 December 1996
Hungary*	28 November 1986	15 April 1987[12]
Iceland*	4 February 1985	23 October 1996
India	14 October 1997	–
Indonesia	23 October 1985	28 October 1998 *Res.*
Ireland*	28 September 1992	11 April 2002
Israel	22 October 1986	3 October 1991 *Res.*
Italy*	4 February 1985	12 January 1989
Japan**	–	29 June 1999
Jordan	–	13 November 1991
Kazakhstan	–	26 August 1998
Kenya	–	21 February 1997
Kuwait	–	8 March 1996 *Res.*
Kyrgyzstan	–	5 September 1997
Latvia	–	14 April 1992
Lebanon	–	5 October 2000

cont.

reservation with respect to article 20 made by Czechoslovakia upon signature, and confirmed upon ratification (see pp. 918, 920).

9 The German Democratic Republic had signed and ratified the Convention on 7 April 1986 and 9 September 1987, respectively, with reservations and declaration. See pp. 916–917.
For the objections to these reservations by certain states, see p. 916. The German Democratic Republic also made the declarations according to the article 21 and 22 of the Convention, see p. 925.

10 In a letter accompanying the instrument of ratification, the Government of the Federal Republic of Germany declared that the Convention shall also apply to Berlin (West) with effect from the date on which it enters into force for the Federal Republic of Germany.

11 For the withdrawn reservation see p. 917.

12 For withdrawn reservation, see p. 918.

State	*Signatures*	*Ratifications, Accessions, Notifications of Succession or Continuity (C)*
Lesotho	–	12 November 2001
Libyan Arab Jamahiriya	–	16 May 1989
Liechtenstein*	27 June 1985	2 November 1990
Lithuania	–	1 February 1996
Luxembourg*	22 February 1985	29 September 1987 *Dec.*
Macedonia	–	12 December 1994 (C)
Madagascar	1 October 2001	–
Malawi	–	11 June 1996
Mali	–	26 February 1999
Malta*	–	13 September 1990
Mauritius	–	9 December 1992
Mexico*	18 March 1985	23 January 1986
Monaco*	–	6 December 1991 *Res.*
Mongolia	–	24 January 2002
Morocco	8 January 1986	21 June 1993 *Dec.*
Mozambique	–	14 September 1999
Namibia	–	28 November 1994
Nauru	12 November 2001	–
Nepal	–	14 May 1991
Netherlands[13]*	4 February 1985	21 December 1988 *Dec.*
New Zealand*	14 January 1986	10 December 1989 *Res.*
Nicaragua	15 April 1985	–
Niger	–	5 October 1998
Nigeria	28 July 1988	–
Norway*	4 February 1985	9 July 1986
Panama	22 February 1985	24 August 1987 *Res.*
Paraguay*	23 October 1989	12 March 1990
Peru*	29 May 1985	7 July 1988
Philippines	–	18 June 1986
Poland*	13 January 1986	26 July 1989 *Res.*
Portugal*[14]	4 February 1985	9 February 1989
Qatar	–	11 January 2000 *Res.*
Republic of Korea	–	9 January 1995
Republic of Moldova	–	28 November 1995
Romania	–	18 December 1990
Russian Federation*	10 December 1985	3 March 1987[15]
Saint Vincent and the Grenadines	–	1 August 2001
Sao Tome e Principe	6 September 2000	–

[13] For the Kingdom in Europe, the Netherlands Antilles and Aruba.

[14] 17 On 15 June 1999, the Government of Portugal informed the Secretary-General that the Convention would apply to Macao.

Subsequently, the Secretary-General received, on 21 October 1999, from the Government of Portugal, the following communication:

"In accordance with the Joint Declaration of the Government of the Portuguese Republic and the Government of the People's Republic of China on the Question of Macao signed on 13 April 1987, the Portuguese Republic will continue to have international responsibility for Macao until 19 December 1999 and from that date onwards the People's Republic of China will resume the exercise of sovereignty over Macao with effect from 20 December 1999.

From 20 December 1999 onwards the Portuguese Republic will cease to be responsible for the international rights and obligations arising from the application of the Convention to Macao."

[15] For partial withdrawal of the reservation, see p. 920.

State	Signatures	Ratifications, Accessions, Notifications of Succession or Continuity (C)
Saudi Arabia	–	23 September 1997 *Res.*
Senegal*	4 February 1985	21 August 1986
Seychelles*	–	5 May 1992
Sierra Leone	18 March 1985	–
Slovakia* [16]	–	28 May 1993 (C)
Slovenia*	–	16 July 1993 (C)
Somalia	–	24 January 1990
South Africa*	29 January 1993	10 December 1998 *Dec.*
Spain*	4 February 1985	21 October 1987
Sri Lanka	–	3 January 1994
Sudan	4 June 1986	–
Sweden*	4 February 1985	8 January 1986
Switzerland*	4 February 1985	2 December 1986
Tajikistan	–	11 January 1995
Togo*	25 March 1987 *Res.*	18 November 1987 *Res.*
Tunisia*	26 August 1987 *Res.*	23 September 1988[17]
Turkey*	25 January 1988	2 August 1988 *Res.*
Turkmenistan	–	25 June 1999
Uganda*	–	3 November 1986
Ukraine	27 February 1986 *Res.*	24 February 1987 *Res.*[18]
United Kingdom[19 20]**	15 March 1985 *Dec.*	8 December 1988 [21]
United States of America[22]**	18 April 1988 *Dec.*	21 October 1994 *Res.*[23]

16 See note 8 above.

17 Reservation withdrawn at ratification, see p. 920.

18 For partial withdrawal of the reservation, see p. 920.

19 See note 7 above.

20 For the United Kingdom of Great Britain and Northern Ireland, Anguilla, British Virgin Islands, Cayman Islands, Falkland Islands, Gibraltar, Monserrat, Pitcairn, Henderson, Ducie and Oeno Islands, Saint Helena, Saint Helena Dependencies, and Turks and Caicos Islands.

In this connection, on 14 April 1989, the Secretary-General received from the Government of Argentina an objection reaffirming Argentina's sovereignty over the Malvinas Islands, available on United Nations website http.//untreaty.un.org.

Subsequently, on 17 April 1991, the Secretary-General received from the Government of Argentina the following declaration:

"The Argentine Government rejects the extension of the application of the [said] Convention to the Malvinas Islands, effected by the United Kingdom of Great Britain and Northern Ireland on 8 December 1988, and reaffirms the rights of sovereignty of the Argentine Republic over those Islands, which are an integral part of its national territory.

The Argentine Republic recalls that the United Nations General Assembly has adopted resolutions 2065 (XX), 3160 (XXVIII), 31/49, 37/9, 38/12, 39/6, 40/21, 41/40, 42/19 and 43/25, in which it recognizes the existence of a sovereignty dispute and requests the Governments of the Argentine Republic and the United Kingdom of Great Britain and Northern Ireland to initiate negotiations with a view to finding the means to resolve peacefully and definitively the pending questions of sovereignty, in accordance with the Charter of the United Nations."

On 9 December 1992, the Government of the United Kingdom of Great Britain and Northern Ireland notified the Secretary-General that the Convention applies to the Bailiwick of Guernsey, the Bailiwick of Jersey, the Isle of Man, Bermuda and Hong Kong (see also note 2 above).

21 For declaration concerning the reservation made by German Democratic Republic, see p. 922.

22 On 3 June 1994, the Secretary-General received a communication from the Government of the United States of America requesting, in compliance with a condition set forth by the Senate of the United States of America, in giving advice and consent to the ratification of the Convention, and in contemplation of the deposit of an instrument of ratification of the Convention by the Government of the United States of America, that a notification should be

State	*Signatures*	*Ratifications, Accessions, Notifications of Succession or Continuity (C)*
Uruguay*	4 February 1985	24 October 1986
Uzbekistan	–	28 September 1995
Venezuela*	15 February 1985	29 July 1991
Yemen	–	5 November 1991
Yugoslavia* (Serbia and Montenegro)[24]	–	12 March 2001 (C)
Zambia	–	7 October 1998[25]

cont.
made to all present and prospective ratifying Parties to the Convention to the effect that: "nothing in this Convention requires or authorizes legislation, or other action, by the United States of America prohibited by the Constitution of the United States as interpreted by the United States".

23 Finland, Netherlands and Sweden made objections and Germany a declaration concerning the reservation made by the United States of America. See pp. 933, 935, 937–938, 941.

24 The former Yugoslavia, the Socialist Federal Republic of Yugoslavia signed the present Convention on 18 April 1989 and ratified it on 10 September 1991. See note 17 in the document *No. 61,* p. 848.

25 For the withdrawn reservation, see p. 922.

DECLARATIONS AND RESERVATIONS[1]

AFGHANISTAN (*reservation made upon ratification*)
While ratifying the above-mentioned Convention, the Democratic Republic of Afghanistan, invoking paragraph 1 of the article 28, of the Convention, does not recognize the authority of the committee as foreseen in the article 20 of the Convention.

Also according to paragraph 2 of the article 30, the Democratic Republic of Afghanistan, will not be bound to honour the provisions of paragraph 1 of the same article since according to that paragraph 1 the compulsory submission of disputes in connection with interpretation or the implementation of the provisions of this Convention by one of the parties concerned to the International Court of Justice is deemed possible. Concerning to this matter, it declares that the settlement of disputes between the States Parties, such disputes may be referred to arbitration or to the International Court of Justice with the consent of all the Parties concerned and not by one of the Parties.

AUSTRIA (*reservation made upon ratification*)
1. Austria will establish its jurisdiction in accordance with article 5 of the Convention irrespective of the laws applying to the place where the offence occurred, but in respect of paragraph 1 (c) only if prosecution by a State having jurisdiction under paragraph 1 (a) or paragraph 1 (b) is not to be expected.
2. Austria regards article 15 as the legal basis for the inadmissibility provided for therein of the use of statements which are established to have been made as a result of torture.

BAHRAIN (*reservations made on accession*)
1. The State of Bahrain does not recognize the competence of the Committee for which provision is made in article 20 of the Convention.
2. The State of Bahrain does not consider itself bound by paragraph 1 of article 30 of the Convention.

On 4 August 1998, the Government Bahrain withdrew the reservation to article 20 made upon accession.

BANGLADESH (*declaration made on accession*)[2]
The Government of the People's Republic of Bangladesh will apply article 14 para. 1 in consonance with the existing laws and legislation in the country.

BELARUS (*reservations made upon signature and confirmed upon ratification*)
The Byelorussian Soviet Socialist Republic does not recognize the competence of the Committee against Torture as defined by article 20 of the Convention.

[The Byelorussian Soviet Socialist Republic does not consider itself bound by the provisions of paragraph 1 of article 30 of the Convention.]
In communications received on 19 April 1989 the Governments of the Byelorussian Soviet Socialist Republic notified the Secretary-General that they had decided to withdraw the reservations concerning article 30(1) made upon ratification.

BOTSWANA (*reservation made upon signature and confirmed upon ratification*)[3]
The Government of the Republic of Botswana considers itself bound by Article 1 of the Convention to the extent that "torture" means the torture and inhuman or degrading

[1] Unless otherwise indicated, the declarations and reservations were made upon ratification, accession or succession.

[2] Finland, France, Spain and Sweden made objections against this declaration: see pp. 934, 935, 940, 941.

[3] The following states made objections against Botswana's reservation: Denmark, Norway and Sweden: see pp. 933, 939, 942.

punishment or other treatment prohibited by Section 7 of the Constitution of the Republic of Bostwana.

BULGARIA (*reservations made upon signature and confirmed upon* ratification)[4]
On 24 June 1992 and 25 June 1999, respectively, the Government of Bulgaria notified the Secretary-General of its decision to withdraw the reservations to article 30 (1) and 20, made upon signature and confirmed upon ratification.

CHILE
Upon signature

. . .

2. The Government of Chile does not consider itself bound by the provisions of article 30, paragraph 1, of the Convention.
3. The Government of Chile reserves the right to formulate, upon ratifying the Convention, any declarations or reservations it may deem necessary in the light of its domestic law.

Upon ratification[5]
The Government of Chile declares that in its relations with American States that are Parties to the Inter-American Convention to Prevent and Punish Torture, it will apply that Convention in cases where its provisions are incompatible with those of the present Convention.
In a communication received on 7 September 1990, the Government of Chile notified the Secretary-General that it had decided to withdraw the declaration made by virtue of article 28(1) upon signature and confirmed upon ratification by which the Government did not recognize the competence of the Committee against torture as defined by article 20 of the Convention. The Government of Chile further decided to withdraw the following reservations, made upon ratification, to article 2(3) and article 3, of the Convention:

[(a) [To] Article 2, paragraph 3, in so far as it modifies the principle of "obedience upon reiteration" contained in Chilean domestic law. The Government of Chile will apply the provisions of that international norm to subordinate personnel governed by the Code of Military Justice, provided that the order patently intended to lead to perpetration of the acts referred to in article 1 is not insisted on by the superior officer after being challenged by his subordinate.
(b) Article 3, by reason of the discretionary and subjective nature of the terms in which it is drafted.]

Further, in a communication received on 3 September 1999, the Government of Chile informed the Secretary-General that it withdrew the following reservation made upon ratification:
The Government of Chile will not consider itself bound by the provisions of article 30, paragraph 1 of the Convention.

CHINA (*reservations made upon signature and confirmed upon ratification*)

1. The Chinese Government does not recognize the competence of the Committee against Torture as provided for in article 20 of the Convention.
2. The Chinese Government does not consider itself bound by paragraph 1 of article 30 of the Convention.

CUBA (*declarations made upon ratification*)
The Government of the Republic of Cuba deplores the fact that even after the adoption of General Assembly resolution 1514 (XV) containing the Declaration on the granting

---

4 For the text of the reservations, see *UNTS* , Vol. 1465, p. 198.

5 The following states made objections against Chile's reservation: Austria, Australia, Bulgaria, Canada, Czechoslovakia, Denmark, Finland, France, Greece, Italy, Luxembourg, Norway, New Zealand, Netherlands, Portugal, Spain, Sweden, Switzerland, Turkey. For the text of the objections, see pp. 931–943.

of independence to colonial countries and peoples, a provision such as paragraph 1 of article 2 was included in the Convention against Torture and Other Cruel, Inhuman or Degrading Treatment or Punishment.

The Government of the Republic declares, in accordance with article 28 of the Convention, that the provisions of paragraphs 1, 2 and 3 of article 20 of the Convention will have to be invoked in strict compliance with the principle of the sovereignty of States and implemented with the prior consent of the States Parties.

In connection with the provisions of article 30 of the Convention, the Government of the Republic of Cuba is of the view that any dispute between Parties should be settled by negotiation through the diplomatic channel.

CZECHOSLOVAKIA (*reservations made on signature and confirmed on ratification*)
The Czechoslovak Socialist Republic does not consider itself bound, in accordance with Article 30, paragraph 2, by the provisions of Article 30, paragraph 1, of the Convention.

The Czechoslovak Socialist Republic does not recognize the competence of the Committee against Torture as defined by article 20 of the Convention.

Subsequently, on 26 April 1991, the Government of Czechoslovakia notified the Secretary-General of its decision to withdraw the reservation with respect to article 30.

On 17 March 1995 and 3 September 1996, respectively, the Governments of Slovakia and the Czech Republic notified the Secretary-General that they had decided to withdraw the reservation with respect to article 20 made by Czechoslovakia upon signature, and confirmed upon ratification.

CZECH REPUBLIC (*for reservations by Czechoslovakia, see above*)
On 17 March 1995 and 3 September 1996, respectively, the Governments of Slovakia and the Czech Republic notified the Secretary-General that they had decided to withdraw the reservation with respect to article 20 made by Czechoslovakia upon signature, and confirmed upon ratification.

ECUADOR (*reservation made on ratification*)
Ecuador declares that, in accordance with the provisions of article 42 of its Political Constitution, it will not permit extradition of its nationals.

EQUATORIAL GUINEA (*declaration and reservation made on accession*)
First: The Government of Equatorial Guinea hereby declares that, pursuant to article 28 of this Convention, it does not recognize the competence of the Committee provided for in article 20 of the Convention.
Second: With reference to the provisions of article 30, the Government of Equatorial Guinea does not consider itself bound by paragraph 1 thereof.

FRANCE (*reservation made on ratification*)
The Government of France declares in accordance with article 30, paragraph 2, of the Convention, that it shall not be bound by the provisions of paragraph 2 of [article 30].

[GERMAN DEMOCRATIC REPUBLIC[6]
The German Democratic Republic had signed and ratified the Convention on 7 April 1986 and 9 September 1987, respectively, with the following reservations and declaration:

[6] The following states made objections against the declarations made by the German Democratic Republic: Austria, Australia, Bulgaria, Canada, Denmark, Finland, France, Greece, Italy, Luxembourg, Norway, New Zealand, Netherlands, Portugal, Spain, Sweden and Switzerland. For the text of the objections, see pp. 933–944. The United Kingdom made a declaration in respect of the reservation made by the Government of German Democratic Republic, see p. 922.

Reservations made upon signature and ratification
The German Democratic Republic declares in accordance with article 28, paragraph 1 of the Convention that it does not recognize the competence of the Committee provided for in article 20.
The German Democratic Republic declares in accordance with article 30, paragraph 2 of the Convention that it does not consider itself bound by paragraph 1 of this article.

Declaration made on signature and ratification
The German Democratic Republic declares that it will bear its share only of those expenses in accordance with article 17, paragraph 7, and article 18, paragraph 5, of the Convention arising from activities under the competence of the Committee as recognized by the German Democratic Republic.

Subsequently, in a communication received on 13 September 1990, the Government of the German Democratic Republic notified the Secretary-General that it had decided to withdraw the reservations, made upon ratification, to articles 17(7), 18(5), 20 and 30(1) of the Convention.

Further, the Government of the German Democratic Republic made the declaration in respect of articles 21 and 22 of the Convention.]

GERMANY
Reservation made upon signature
The Government of the Federal Republic of Germany reserves the right to communicate, upon ratification, such reservations or declarations of interpretation as are deemed necessary especially with respect to the applicability of article 3.

Reservation made upon ratification
Article 3
This provision prohibits the transfer of a person directly to a State where this person is exposed to a concrete danger of being subjected to torture. In the opinion of the Federal Republic of Germany, article 3 as well as the other provisions of the Convention exclusively establish State obligations that are met by the Federal Republic of Germany in conformity with the provisions of its domestic law which is in accordance with the Convention.

Declaration made upon ratification
In a letter accompanying the instrument of ratification, the Government of the Federal Republic of Germany declared that the Convention shall also apply to Berlin (West) with effect from the date on which it enters into force for the Federal Republic of Germany.

GHANA (*declaration made on ratification*)
[The Government of Ghana declares] in accordance with Article 30(2) of the said Convention that the submission under Article 30(1) to arbitration or the International Court of Justice of disputes between the States Parties relating to the interpretation or application of the said Convention shall be by the consent of ALL the Parties concerned and not by one or more of the parties concerned.

GUATEMALA
In a communication received on 30 May 1990, the Government of Guatemala notified the Secretary-General that it has decided to withdraw the reservations made by virtue of the provisions of articles 28(1) and 30(2), made upon accession to the Convention.

HOLY SEE (*declaration made on accession*)
The Holy See considers the Convention against Torture and Other Cruel, Inhuman or Degrading Treatment or Punishment a valid and suitable instrument for fighting against acts that constitute a serious offence against the dignity of the human person. In recent

times the Catholic Church has consistently pronounced itself in favour of unconditional respect for life itself and unequivocally condemned "whatever violates the integrity of the human person, such as mutilation, torments inflicted on body or mind, attempts to coerce the will itself" (Second Vatican Council, Pastoral Constitution Gaudium et spes, 7 December 1965.).

The law of the Church (Code of Canon Law, 1981) and its catechism (Catechism of the Catholic Church, 1987) enumerate and clearly identify forms of behaviour that can harm the bodily or mental integrity of the individual, condemn their perpetrators and call for the abolition of such acts. On 14 January 1978, Pope Paul VI, in his last address to the diplomatic corps, after referring to the torture and mistreatment practised in various countries against individuals, concluded as follows: "How could the Church fail to take up a stern stand ... with regard to torture and to similar acts of violence inflicted on the human person?" Pope John Paul II, for his part, has not failed to affirm that "torture must be called by its proper name" (message for the celebration of the World Day of Peace, 1 January 1980). He has expressed his deep compassion for the victims of torture (World Congress on Pastoral Ministry for Human Rights, Rome, 4 July 1998), and in particular for tortured women (message to the Secretary-General of the United Nations, 1 March 1993). In this spirit the Holy See wishes to lend its moral support and collaboration to the international community, so as to contribute to the elimination of recourse to torture, which is inadmissable and inhuman.

The Holy See, in becoming a party to the Convention on behalf of the Vatican City State, undertakes to apply it insofar as it is compatible, in practice, with the peculiar nature of that State.

HUNGARY (*reservation made on ratification*)

The Hungarian People's Republic does not recognize the competence of the Committee against Torture as defined by article 20 of the Convention. The Hungarian People's Republic does not consider itself bound by the provisions of paragraph 1 of article 30 of the Convention.

In a communication received on 13 September 1989, the Government of Hungary notified the Secretary-General that it has decided to withdraw the reservations relating to articles 20 and 30(1) made upon ratification.

INDONESIA

Declaration made on ratification

The Government of the Republic of Indonesia declares that the provisions of paragraphs 1, 2, and 3 of article 20 of the Convention will have to be implemented in strict compliance with the principles of the sovereignty and territorial integrity of States.

Reservation made on ratification

The Government of the Republic of Indonesia does not consider itself bound by the provision of article 30, paragraph 1, and takes the position that disputes relating to the interpretation and application of the Convention which cannot be settled through the channel provided for in paragraph 1 of the said article, may be referred to the International Court of Justice only with the consent of all parties to the disputes.

ISRAEL (*reservations made on ratification*)

1. In accordance with article 28 of the Convention, the State of Israel hereby declares that it does not recognize the competence of the Committee provided for in article 20.
2. In accordance with paragraph 2 of article 30, the State of Israel hereby declares that it does not consider itself bound by paragraph 1 of that article.

KUWAIT (*reservation made on accession*)

With reservations as to Article 20 and the provision of paragraph 1 from Article 30 of the Convention.

LUXEMBOURG (*interpretative declaration made on ratification*)
Article 1
The Grand Duchy of Luxembourg hereby declares that the only 'lawful sanctions' that it recognizes within the meaning of article 1, paragraph 1, of the Convention are those which are accepted by both national law and international law.

MONACO (*reservation made on accession*)
In accordance with paragraph 2 of article 30 of the Convention, the Principality of Monaco declares that it does not consider itself bound by paragraph 1 of that article.

MOROCCO (*declaration made upon signature and confirmed upon ratification*)
The Government of the Kingdom of Morocco does not recognize the competence of the Committee provided for in article 20.

The Government of the Kingdom of Morocco does not consider itself bound by paragraph 1 of the same article.

NETHERLANDS (*interpretative declaration with respect to Article 1 made on ratification*)
It is the understanding of the Government of the Kingdom of the Netherlands that the term "lawful sanctions" in article 1, paragraph 1, must be understood as referring to those sanctions which are lawful not only under national law but also under international law.

NEW ZEALAND (*reservation made on ratification*)
The Government of New Zealand reserves the right to award compensation to torture victims referred to in article 14 of the Convention Against Torture only at the discretion of the Attorney-General of New Zealand.

PANAMA (*reservation made on ratification*)
The Republic of Panama declares in accordance with article 30, paragraph 2 of the Convention that it does not consider itself bound by the provisions of paragraph 1 of the said article.

POLAND (*reservation made upon signature*)
Under article 28, the Polish People's Republic does not consider itself bound by article 20 of the Convention.

Furthermore, the Polish People's Republic does not consider itself bound by article 30, paragraph 1, of the Convention.

QATAR[7] (*reservations made on accession*)
(a) Any interpretation of the provisions of the Convention that are incompatible with the precepts of Islamic law and the Islamic religion;
and
(b) The competence of the Committee as indicated in articles 21 and 22 of the Convention.

[RUSSIAN FEDERATION *see Union of Soviet Socialist Republics*]

SAUDI ARABIA (*reservations made on accession*)
The Kingdom of Saudi Arabia does not recognize the jurisdiction of the Committee as provided for in article 20 of this Convention.

The Kingdom of Saudi Arabia shall not be bound by the provisions of paragraph (1) of article 30 of this Convention.

---

7 The following states made objections against Qatar's reservation: Denmark, Italy, Portugal, United Kingdom; see pp. 932, 933, 936, 939, 943.

SLOVAKIA *for reservations by Czechoslovakia maintained by the Czech Republic and Slovak Republic on succession, see above.*
On 17 March 1995 and 3 September 1996, respectively, the Governments of Slovakia and the Czech Republic notified the Secretary-General that they had decided to withdraw the reservation with respect to article 20 made by Czechoslovakia upon signature, and confirmed upon ratification.

SOUTH AFRICA (*declaration made on ratification*)
[The Republic of South Africa declares that] it recognizes, for the purposes of article 30 of the Convention, the competence of the International Court of Justice to settle a dispute between two or more State Parties regarding the interpretation or application of the Convention, respectively.

TOGO (*reservation made upon signature*)
The Government of the Togolese Republic reserves the right to formulate, upon ratifying the Convention, any reservations or declarations which it might consider necessary.

TUNISIA (*reservation made upon signature*)
[The Government of Tunisia reserves the right to make at some later stage any reservation or declaration which it deems necessary, in particular with regard to articles 20 and 21 of the said Convention.]

Withdrawal of the reservation on ratification
[The Government of Tunisia] confirms that the reservations made at the time of signature of the Convention on Tunisia's behalf on 26 August 1987 have been completely withdrawn.]

TURKEY (*reservation made upon ratification*)
The Government of Turkey declares in accordance with article 30, paragraph 2, of the Convention, that it does not consider itself bound by the provisions of paragraph 1 of this article.

UKRAINE (*reservations made upon signature and confirmed upon ratification*)
The Ukrainian Soviet Socialist Republic does not recognize the competence of the Committee against Torture as defined by article 20 of the Convention.

[The Ukrainian Soviet Socialist Republic does not consider itself bound by the provisions of paragraph 1 of article 30 of the Convention.]

In communications received on 20 April 1989, the Government of the Ukrainian Soviet Socialist Republic notified the Secretary-General that it had decided to withdraw the reservations concerning article 30(1) made upon ratification.

[UNION OF SOVIET SOCIALIST REPUBLICS
The Union of Soviet Socialist Republics does not consider itself bound by the provisions of paragraph 1 of article 30 of the Convention.

The Union of Soviet Socialist Republics does not recognize the competence of the Committee against Torture as defined by article 20 of the Convention.

In communications received on 8 March 1989, the Government of the Union of Soviet Socialist Republics notified the Secretary-General that it had decided to withdraw the reservations concerning article 30 (1) made upon ratification.

On 1 October 1991, the Government of the Union of Soviet Socialist Republics notified the Secretary-General that it had decided to withdraw the reservation with regard to article 20 made upon signature and confirmed upon ratification.]

UNITED KINGDOM OF GREAT BRITAIN AND NORTHERN IRELAND (*declaration upon signature*)
The United Kingdom reserves the right to formulate, upon ratifying the Convention, any reservations or interpretative declarations which it might consider necessary.

In a letter accompanying its instrument of ratification, the Government of the United Kingdom of Great Britain and Northern Ireland declared in respect of the reservation and declaration made by the German Democratic Republic, the following:

The Government of the United Kingdom of Great Britain and Northern Ireland has taken note of the reservations formulated by the Government of the German Democratic Republic pursuant to article 28, paragraph 1, and article 30, paragraph 2, respectively, and the declaration made by the German Democratic Republic with reference to article 17, paragraph 7, and article 18, paragraph 5. It does not regard the said declaration as affecting in any way the obligations of the German Democratic Republic as a State Party to the Convention (including the obligations to meet its share of the expenses of the Committee on Torture as apportioned by the first meeting of the States Parties held on 26 November 1987 or any subsequent such meetings) and do not accordingly raise objections to it. It reserves the rights of the United Kingdom in their entirety in the event that the said declaration should at any future time be claimed to affect the obligations of the German Democratic Republic as aforesaid.

UNITED STATES OF AMERICA[8]
Declaration made upon signature
The Government of the United States of America reserves the right to communicate, upon ratification, such reservations, interpretive understandings, or declarations as are deemed necessary.

Reservation, understandings and declarations made upon ratification
I. The Senate's advice and consent is subject to the following reservations:
   1. That the United States considers itself bound by the obligation under article 16 to prevent 'cruel, inhuman or degrading treatment or punishment', only insofar as the term 'cruel, inhuman or degrading treatment or punishment' means the cruel, unusual and inhumane treatment or punishment prohibited by the Fifth, Eighth, and/or Fourteenth Amendments to the Constitution of the United States.
   2. That pursuant to article 30 (2) the United States declares that it does not consider itself bound by Article 30(1), but reserves the right specifically to agree to follow this or any other procedure for arbitration in a particular case.
II. The Senate's advice and consent is subject to the following understandings, which shall apply to the obligations of the United States under this Convention:
   1. (a) That with reference to article 1, the United States understands that, in order to constitute torture, an act must be specifically intended to inflict severe physical or mental pain or suffering and that mental pain or suffering refers to prolonged mental harm caused by or resulting from (1) the intentional infliction or threatened infliction of severe physical pain or suffering; (2) the administration or application, or threatened administration or application, of mind altering substances or other procedures calculated to disrupt profoundly the senses or the personality; (3) the threat of imminent death; or (4) the threat that another person will imminently be subjected to death, severe physical pain or suffering, or the administration or application of mind altering substances or other procedures calculated to disrupt profoundly the senses or personality.
   (b) That the United States understands that the definition of torture in article 1 is intended to apply only to acts directed against persons in the offender's custody or physical control.
   (c) That with reference to article 1 of the Convention, the United States understands that "sanctions" includes judicially-imposed sanctions and other enforcement actions authorized by United States law or by judicial interpretation of such law. Nonetheless, the United States understands that a State Party could not through its domestic sanctions defeat the object and purpose of the Convention to prohibit torture.
   (d) That with reference to article 1 of the Convention, the United States understands that the term "acquiescence" requires that the public official, prior to

[8] The following states made objections against reservations and understandings of the United States of America: Finland, Germany, Netherlands and Sweden. For the text of these objections see pp. 933, 935, 937–938, 941.

the activity constituting torture, have awareness of such activity and thereafter breach his legal responsibility to intervene to prevent such activity.

(e) That with reference to article 1 of the Convention, the Unites States understands that noncompliance with applicable legal procedural standards does not *per se* constitute torture.

2. That the United States understands the phrase, "where there are substantial grounds for believing that he would be in danger of being subjected to torture," as used in article 3 of the Convention, to mean "if it is more likely than not that he would be tortured."
3. That it is the understanding of the United States that article 14 requires a State Party to provide a private right of action for damages only for acts of torture committed in territory under the jurisdiction of that State Party.
4. That the United States understands that international law does not prohibit the death penalty, and does not consider this Convention to restrict or prohibit the United States from applying the death penalty consistent with the Fifth, Eighth and/or Fourteenth Amendments to the Constitution of the United States, including any constitutional period of confinement prior to the imposition of the death penalty.
5. That the United States understands that this Convention shall be implemented by the United States Government to the extent that it exercises legislative and judicial jurisdiction over the matters covered by the Convention and otherwise by the state and local governments. Accordingly, in implementing articles 10–14 and 16, the United States Government shall take measures appropriate to the Federal system to the end that the competent authorities of the constituent units of the United States of America may take appropriate measures for the fulfillment of the Convention.

III. The Senate's advice and consent is subject to the following declarations:

1. That the United States declares that the provisions of articles 1 through 16 of the Convention are not self-executing.

ZAMBIA (*reservation on Article 20 made on accessions*)
In a notification received on 19 February 1999, the Government of Zambia informed the Secretary-General that it had decided to withdraw its reservation to Article 20 of the Convention made upon accession.

DECLARATIONS RECOGNIZING THE COMPETENCE OF THE COMMITTEE AGAINST TORTURE UNDER ARTICLES 21 AND 22[1]

ALGERIA
Article 21
The Algerian Government declares, pursuant to article 21 of the Convention, that it recognizes the competence of the Committee Against Torture to receive and consider communications to the effect that a State Party claims that another State Party is not fulfilling its obligations under this Convention.

Article 22
The Algerian Government declares, pursuant to article 22 of the Convention, that it recognizes the competence of the Committee to receive and consider communications from or on behalf of individuals subject to its jurisdiction who claim to be victims of a violation by a State Party of the provisions of the Convention.

ARGENTINA
The Argentine Republic recognizes the competence of the Committee against Torture to receive and consider communications to the effect that a State Party claims that another State Party is not fulfilling its obligations under this Convention. It also recognizes the

[1] Unless otherwise indicated, the declarations were made upon ratification, accession or succession.

competence of the Committee to receive and consider communications from or on behalf of individuals subject to its jurisdiction who claim to be victims of a violation by a State Party of the provisions of the Convention.

AUSTRALIA (*28 January 1993*)
The Government of Australia hereby declares that it recognizes, for and on behalf of Australia, the competence of the Committee to receive and consider communications to the effect that a State Party claims that another State Party is not fulfilling its obligations under the aforesaid Convention; and

The Government of Australia hereby declares that it recognizes, for and on behalf of Australia, the competence of the Committee to receive and consider communications from or on behalf of individuals subject to Australia's jurisdiction who claim to be victims of a violation by a State Party of the provisions of the aforesaid Convention.

AUSTRIA
Austria recognizes the competence of the Committee against Torture to receive and consider communications to the effect that a State Party claims that another State Party is not fulfilling its obligations under this Convention.

Austria recognizes the competence of the Committee against Torture to receive and consider communications from or on behalf of individuals subject to Austrian jurisdiction who claim to be victims of a violation of the provisions of the Convention.

BELGIUM
In accordance with article 21, paragraph 1, of the Convention, Belgium declares that it recognizes the competence of the Committee against Torture to receive and consider communications to the effect that a State Party claims that another State Party is not fulfilling its obligations under the Convention.

In accordance with article 22, paragraph 1, of the Convention, Belgium declares that it recognizes the competence of the Committee against Torture to receive and consider communications from or on behalf of individuals subject to its jurisdiction who claim to be victims of a violation by a State Party of the provisions of the Convention.

BULGARIA (*12 May 1993*)
The Republic of Bulgaria declares that in accordance with article 21(2) of the Convention it recognizes the competence of the Committee against Torture to receive and consider communications to the effect that a State Party claims that another State Party is not fulfilling its obligations under this Convention.

The Republic of Bulgaria declares that in accordance with article 22(1) of the Convention it recognizes the competence of the Committee against Torture to receive and consider communications from or on behalf of individuals subject to its jurisdiction who claim to be victims of a violation by a State Party of the provisions of this Convention.

CAMEROON (*12 October 2000*)
[The Republic of Cameroon declares] that [it] recognizes the competence of the Committee against Torture to receive and consider communications from a State Party claiming that the Republic of Cameroon is not fulfilling its obligations under the Convention. However, such communications will not be receivable unless they refer to facts and situations subsequent to this declaration and emanate from a State Party which has made a similar declaration indicating its reciprocal acceptance of the competence of the Committee with regard to itself at least twelve (12) months before submitting the communication. [The Republic of Cameroon also declares] that it recognizes, in the case of situations and facts subsequent to this declaration, the competence of the Committee against Torture to receive and consider communications from or on behalf of individuals subject to its jurisdiction who claim to be victims of a violation by a State Party of the provisions of the Convention.

CANADA (*13 November 1989*)
The Government of Canada declares that it recognizes the competence of the Committee Against Torture, pursuant to article 21 of the said Convention, to receive and consider communications to the effect that a state party claims that another state party is not fulfilling its obligations under this Convention.

The Government of Canada also declares that it recognizes the competence of the Committee Against Torture, pursuant to article 22 of the said Convention, to receive and consider communications from or on behalf of individuals subject to its jurisdiction who claim to be victims of a violation by a state party of the provisions of the Convention.

CROATIA
[The] Republic of Croatia . . . accepts the competence of the Committee in accordance with articles 21 and 22 of the said Convention.

CYPRUS (*8 April 1993*)
The Republic of Cyprus recognizes the competence of the Committee established under article 17 of the Convention [...]:

I. to receive and consider communications to the effect that a State Party claims that another State Party is not fulfilling its obligations under the Convention (article 21), and
II. to receive and consider communications from or on behalf of individuals subject to its jurisdiction who claim to be victims of a violation by a State Party of the provisions of the Convention (Article 22).

CZECH REPUBLIC (*3 September 1996*)
The Czech Republic declares, in accordance with article 21, paragraph 1, of the Convention that it recognizes the competence of the Committee to receive and consider communications to the effect that a State Party claims that another State Party is not fulfilling its obligations under this Convention.

The Czech Republic declares, in accordance with article 22, paragraph 1, of the Convention, that it recognizes the competence of the Committee to receive and consider communications from or on behalf of individuals within its jurisdiction who claim to be victims of violation by a State Party of the provisions of the Convention.

DENMARK
The Government of Denmark [. . .] recognizes the competence of the Committee to receive and consider communications to the effect that the State Party claims that another State Party is not fulfilling its obligations under this Convention.

The Government of Denmark [. . .] recognizes the competence of the Committee to receive and consider communications from or on behalf of individuals subject to its jurisdiction who claim to be victims of a violation by a State Party of the provisions of the Convention.

ECUADOR (*6 September 1988*)
The Ecuadorian State, pursuant to article 21 of the International Convention Against Torture and Other Cruel, Inhuman or Degrading Treatment or Punishment, recognizes the competence of the Committee against Torture to receive and consider communications to the effect that a State Party claims that another State Party is not fulfilling its obligations under the Convention; it also recognizes in regard to itself the competence of the Committee, in accordance with article 21.

It further declares, in accordance with the provisions of article 22 of the Convention, that it recognizes the competence of the Committee to receive and consider communications from or on behalf of individuals subject to its jurisdiction who claim to be victims of a violation by a State Party of the provisions of the Convention.

FINLAND
Finland declares that it recognizes fully the competence of the Committee against Torture as specified in article 21, paragraph 1 and article 22, paragraph 1 of the Convention.

FRANCE (*23 June 1988*)
The Government of France declares [. . .] that it recognizes the competence of the Committee against Torture to receive and consider communications to the effect that a State Party claims that another State Party is not fulfilling its obligations under the Convention.

The Government of France declares [. . .] that it recognizes the competence of the Committee against Torture to receive and consider communications from or on behalf of individuals subject to its jurisdiction who claim to be victims of a violation by a State Party of the provisions of the Convention.

GERMAN DEMOCRATIC REPUBLIC
The German Democratic Republic declares in accordance with article 21, paragraph 1, that it recognizes the competence of the Committee to receive and consider communications to the effect that a State Party claims that another State Party is not fulfilling its obligations under this Convention.

The German Democratic Republic in accordance with article 22, paragraph 1, declares that it recognizes the competence of the Committee to receive and consider communications from or on behalf of individuals subject to its jurisdiction who claim to be victims of a violation by a State Party of the provisions of the Convention.

GERMANY (*19 October 2001*)
In accordance with article 21(1) of the Convention, the Federal Republic of Germany declares that it recognizes the competence of the Committee against Torture to receive and consider communications to the effect that a State Party claims that another State Party is not fulfilling its obligations under the Convention. In accordance with article 22(1) of the Convention, the Federal Republic of Germany declares that it recognizes the competence of the Committee against Torture to receive and consider communications from or on behalf of individuals subject to its jurisdiction who claim to be victims of a violation by the Federal Republic of Germany of the provisions of the Convention.

GHANA
The Government of the Republic of Ghana recognises the competence of the Committee Against Torture to consider complaints brought by or against the Republic in respect of another State Party which has made a Declaration recognising the competence of the Committee as well as individuals subject to the jurisdiction of the Republic who claim to be victims of any violations by the Republic of the provisions of the said Convention.

The Government of the Republic of Ghana interprets Article 21 and Article 22 as giving the said Committee the competence to receive and consider complaints in respect of matters occurring after the said Convention had entered into force for Ghana and shall not apply to decisions, acts, omissions or events relating to matters, events, omissions acts or developments occurring before Ghana becomes a party.

GREECE
Article 21
The Hellenic Republic declares, pursuant to article 21, paragraph 1, of the Convention, that it recognizes the competence of the Committee against Torture to receive and consider communications to the effect that a State Party claims that another State Party is not fulfilling its obligations under the Convention.

Article 22
The Hellenic Republic declares, pursuant to article 22, paragraph 1, of the Convention, that it recognizes the competence of the Committee against Torture to receive and consider communications from or on behalf of individuals subject to its jurisdiction who claims to be victims of a violation by a State Party of the provisions of the Convention.

HUNGARY
13 September 1989
[The Government of Hungary] recognizes the competence of the Committee against Torture provided for in articles 21 and 22 of the Convention.

ICELAND
23 October 1996
[The Government of Iceland declares], pursuant to article 21, paragraph 1, of the [said] Convention, that Iceland recognizes the competence of the Committee against Torture to receive and consider communications to the effect that a State Party claims that another State Party is not fulfilling its obligations under the Convention and, pursuant to article 22, paragraph 1, of the Convention, that Iceland recognizes the competence of the Committee against Torture to receive and consider communications from or on behalf of individuals subject to its jurisdiction who claim to be victims of a violation by a State Party of the provisions of the Convention.

ITALY
10 October 1989
Article 21: Italy hereby declares, in accordance with article 21, paragraph 1, of the Convention, that it recognizes the competence of the Committee against torture to receive and consider communications to the effect that a State Party claims that another State Party is not fulfilling its obligations under this Convention;

Article 22: Italy hereby declares, in accordance with article 22, paragraph 1, of the Convention, that it recognizes the competence of the Committee against torture to receive and consider communications from or on behalf of individuals subject to its jurisdiction who claim to be victims of violations by a State Party of the provisions of the Convention.

JAPAN
The Government of Japan declares under article 21 of the Convention that it recognizes the competence of the Committee against Torture to receive and consider communications to the effect that a State Party claims that another State Party is not fulfilling its obligations under this Convention.

LIECHTENSTEIN
The Principality of Liechtenstein recognizes, in accordance with article 21, paragraph 1, of the Convention, the competence of the Committee against Torture to receive and consider communications to the effect that a State Party claims that another State Party is not fulfilling its obligations under this Convention.

The Principality of Liechtenstein recognizes in accordance with article 22, paragraph 1, the competence of the Committee against Torture to receive and consider communications from or on behalf of individuals subject to its jurisdiction who claim to be victims of a violation by a State Party of the provisions of the Convention.

LUXEMBOURG
Article 21
The Grand Duchy of Luxembourg hereby declares [. . .] that it recognizes the competence of the Committee against Torture to receive and consider communications to the effect that a State Party claims that another State Party is not fulfilling its obligations under this Convention.

Article 22
The Grand Duchy of Luxembourg hereby declares [. . .] that it recognizes the competence of the Committee against Torture to receive and consider communications from or on behalf of individuals subject to its jurisdiction who claim to be victims of a violation by a State Party of the provisions of the Convention.

MALTA
The Government of Malta fully recognizes the competence of the Committee against Torture as specified in article 21, paragraph 1, and article 22, paragraph 1, of the Convention.

MONACO
In accordance with article 21, paragraph 1, of the Convention, the Principality of Monaco declares that it recognizes the competence of the Committee against Torture to receive and consider communications to the effect that a State Party claims that another State Party is not fulfilling its obligations under this Convention.

In accordance with article 22, paragraph 1, of the Convention, the Principality of Monaco declares, that it recognizes the competence of the Committee against Torture to receive and consider communications from or on behalf of individuals subject to its jurisdiction who claim to be victims of a violation by a State Party of the provisions of the Convention.

NETHERLANDS
With respect to Article 21:
The Government of the Kingdom of the Netherlands hereby declares that it recognizes the competence of the Committee against Torture under the conditions laid down in article 21, to receive and consider communications to the effect that another State Party claims that the Kingdom is not fulfilling its obligations under this Convention;

With respect to Article 22:
The Government of the Kingdom of the Netherlands hereby declares that it recognizes the competence of the Committee against Torture, under the conditions laid down in article 22, to receive and consider communications from or on behalf of individuals subject to its jurisdiction who claim to be victims of a violation by the Kingdom of the provisions of the Convention.

NEW ZEALAND
1. In accordance with article 21, paragraph 1, of the Convention, [the Government of New Zealand declares] that it recognises the competence of the Committee Against Torture to receive and consider communications to the effect that a State Party claims that another State Party is not fulfilling its obligations under the Convention; and
2. In Accordance with article 22, paragraph 1, of the Convention, [the Government of New Zealand] recognises the competence of the Committee Against Torture to receive and consider communications from or on behalf of individuals subject to its jurisdiction who claim to be victims of a violation by a State Party of the provisions of the Convention.

NORWAY
Norway recognizes the competence of the Committee to receive and consider communications to the effect that a State Party claims that another State Party is not fulfilling its obligations under this Convention.

Norway recognizes the competence of the Committee to receive and consider communications from or on behalf of individuals subject to its jurisdiction who claim to be victims of a violation by a State Party of the provisions of the Convention.

POLAND (*12 May 1993*)
The Government of the Republic of Poland, in accordance with articles 21 and 22 of the Convention, recognizes the competence of the Committee against Torture to receive and consider communications to the effect that a State Party claims that the Republic of Poland is not fulfilling its obligations under the Convention or communications from or on behalf of individuals subject to its jurisdiction who claim to be victims of a violation by the Republic of Poland of the provisions of the Convention.

PORTUGAL
Article 21
Portugal hereby declares, in accordance with article 21, paragraph 1, of the Convention, that it recognizes the competence of the Committee Against Torture to receive and consider communications to the effect that the State Party claims that another State Party is not fulfilling its obligations under this Convention.

Article 22
Portugal hereby declares, in accordance with article 22, paragraph 1 of the Convention, that it recognizes the competence of the Committee Against Torture to receive and consider communications from or on behalf of individuals subject to its jurisdiction who claim to be victims of violation by State Party of the provisions of the Convention.

RUSSIAN FEDERATION *see Union of Soviet Socialist Republics*

SENEGAL (*16 October 1996*)
The Government of the Republic of Senegal declares, in accordance with article 21, paragraph 1, of the Convention that it recognizes the competence of the Committee against Torture to receive and consider communications to the effect that a State Party claims that another State Party is not fulfilling its obligations under this Convention.

The Government of the Republic of Senegal declares, in accordance with article 22, paragraph 1, of the Convention that it recognizes the competence of the Committee against Torture to receive and consider communications from or on behalf of individuals subject to its jurisdiction who claim to be victims of a violation by a State Party of the provisions of the Convention.

SEYCHELLES (*6 August 2001*)
Article 22
The republic of Seychelles accepts without reservations the competence of the Committee Against Torture.

SLOVAKIA (*17 March 1995*)
The Slovak Republic, pursuant to article 21 of the [said Convention] recognizes the competence of the Committee against Torture to receive and consider communications to the effect that a State Party claims that another State Party is not fulfilling its obligations under this Convention.

The Slovak Republic further declares, pursuant to article 22 of the Convention, that it recognizes the competence of the Committee to receive and consider communications from individuals subject to its jurisdiction who claim to be victims of a violation by a State Party of the provisions of the Convention.

SLOVENIA
1. The Republic of Slovenia declares that it recognizes the competence of the Committee against Torture, pursuant to article 21 of the said Convention, to receive and consider communications to the effect that a State Party claims that another State Party is not fulfilling its obligations under this Convention.
2. The Republic of Slovenia also declares that it recognizes the competence of the Committee against Torture, pursuant to the competence of the Committee against Torture, pursuant to article 22 of the said Convention, to receive and consider communications from or on behalf of individuals subject to its jurisdiction who claim to be victims of a violation by a State Party of the provisions of the Convention.

SOUTH AFRICA
The Republic of South Africa declares that
(a) it recognises, for the purposes of article 21 of the Convention, the competence of the Committee Against Torture to receive and consider communications that a State Party claims that another State Party is not fulfilling its obligations under the Convention;

(b) it recognises, for the purposes of article 22 of the Convention, the competence of the Committee Against Torture to receive and consider communications from, or on behalf of individuals who claim to be victims of torture by a State Party.

SPAIN

Spain declares that, pursuant to article 21, paragraph 1, of the Convention, it recognizes the competence of the Committee to receive and consider communications to the effect that a State Party claims that the Spanish State is not fulfilling its obligations under this Convention. It is Spain's understanding that, pursuant to the above-mentioned article, such communications shall be accepted and processed only if they come from a State Party which has made a similar declaration.

Spain declares that, pursuant to article 22, paragraph l, of the Convention, it recognizes the competence of the Committee to receive and consider communications sent by, or on behalf of, persons subject to Spanish jurisdiction who claim to be victims of a violation by the Spanish State of the provisions of the Convention. Such communications must be consistent with the provisions of the above-mentioned article and, in particular, of its paragraph 5.

SWEDEN

Sweden recognizes the competence of the Committee to receive and consider communications to the effect that a State Party claims that another State Party is not fulfilling its obligations under this Convention.

Sweden recognizes the competence of the Committee to receive and consider communications from or on behalf of individuals subject to its jurisdiction who claim to be victims of a violation by a State Party of the provisions of the Convention.

SWITZERLAND

(a) Pursuant to the Federal Decree of 6 October 1986 on the approval of the Convention against Torture and Other Cruel, Inhuman or Degrading Treatment or Punishment, the Federal Council declares, in accordance with article 21, paragraph 1, of the Convention, that Switzerland recognizes the competence of the Committee against Torture to receive and consider communications to the effect that a State Party claims that Switzerland is not fulfilling its obligations under this Convention.

(b) Pursuant to the above-mentioned Federal Decree, the Federal Council declares, in accordance with article 22, paragraph 1, of the Convention, that Switzerland recognizes the competence of the Committee to receive and consider communications from or on behalf of individuals subject to its jurisdiction who claim to be victims of a violation by Switzerland of the provisions of the Convention.

TOGO

The Government of the Republic of Togo recognizes the competence of the Committee against Torture to receive and consider communications to the effect that a State Party claims that another State Party is not fulfilling its obligations under this Convention.

The Government of the Republic of Togo recognizes the competence of the Committee against Torture to receive and consider communications from or on behalf of individuals subject to its jurisdiction who claim to be victims of a violation by a State Party of the provisions of the Convention.

TUNISIA

[The Government of Tunisia] declares that it recognizes the competence of the Committee Against Torture provided for in article 17 of the Convention to receive communications pursuant to articles 21 and 22, thereby withdrawing any reservation made on Tunisia's behalf in this connection.

TURKEY

The Government of Turkey declares, pursuant to article 21, paragraph 1, of the Convention that it recognizes the competence of the Committee Against Torture to receive and consider communications to the effect that a State Party is not fulfilling its obligations under the Convention.

The Government of Turkey declares, pursuant to article 22, paragraph 1, of the Convention that it recognizes the competence of the Committee Against Torture to receive and consider communications from or on behalf of individuals subject to its jurisdiction who claim to be victims of a violation by a State Party of the provisions of the Convention.

[UNION OF SOVIET SOCIALIST REPUBLICS (*1 October 1991*)
The Union of Soviet Socialist Republics declares that, pursuant to article 21 of the Convention, it recognizes the competence of the Committee against Torture to receive and consider communications in respect of situations and events occurring after the adoption of the present declaration, to the effect that a State Party claims that another State Party is not fulfilling its obligations under the Convention.

The Union of Soviet Socialist Republics also declares that, pursuant to article 22 of the Convention, it recognizes the competence of the Committee to receive and consider communications in respect of situations or events occurring after the adoption of the present declaration, from or on behalf of individuals subject to its jurisdiction who claim to be victims of a violation by a State Party of the provisions of the Convention.]

UNITED KINGDOM OF GREAT BRITAIN AND NORTHERN IRELAND
The Government of the United Kingdom declares under article 21 of the said Convention that it recognizes the competence of the Committee Against Torture to receive and consider communications submitted by another State Party, provided that such other State Party has, not less than twelve months prior to the submission by it of a communication in regard to the United Kingdom, made a declaration under article 21 recognizing the competence of the Committee to receive and consider communications in regard to itself.

UNITED STATES OF AMERICA
The United States declares, pursuant to article 21, paragraph 1, of the Convention, that it recognizes the competence of the Committee against Torture to receive and consider communications to the effect that a State Party claims that another State Party is not fulfilling its obligations under the Convention. It is the understanding of the United States that, pursuant to the above-mentioned article, such communications shall be accepted and processed only if they come from a State Party which has made a similar declaration.

URUGUAY (*7 July 1988*)
The Government of Uruguay recognizes the competence of the Committee Against Torture to receive and consider communications referring to the said articles [21 and 22].

VENEZUELA (*26 April 1994*)
The Government of the Republic of Venezuela recognizes the competence of the Committee against Torture as provided for under articles 21 and 22 of the Convention.

YUGOSLAVIA
Yugoslavia recognizes, in compliance with article 21, paragraph 1 of the Convention, the competence of the Committee against Torture to receive and consider communications in which one State Party to the Convention claims that another State Party does not fulfil the obligations pursuant to the Convention;

Yugoslavia recognizes, in conformity with article 22, paragraph 1 of the Convention, the competence of the Committee against Torture to receive and consider communications from or on behalf of individuals subject to its jurisdiction who claim to be victims of a violation by a State Party of the provisions of the Convention.

OBJECTIONS[2]

AUSTRALIA

Objections of 8 August 1989 in respect of the declaration made by German Democratic Republic

The Government of Australia considers that this declaration is incompatible with the object and purpose of the Convention and, accordingly, hereby conveys Australia's objection to the declaration.

Objections of 7 November 1989 in respect of the declaration made by Chile

[The Government of Australia] has come to the conclusion that these reservations are incompatible with the object and purpose of the Convention and therefore are impermissible according to article 19 of the Vienna Convention on the Law of Treaties. The Government of Australia therefore objects to these reservations. This objection does not have the effect of preventing the Convention from entering into force between Australia and Chile, and the afore-mentioned reservations cannot alter or modify, in any respect, the obligations arising from the Convention.

AUSTRIA

Objections of 29 September 1988 in respect of the declaration made by German Democratic Republic

The Declaration [. . .] cannot alter or modify, in any respect, the obligations arising from that Convention for all States Parties thereto.

Objections of 9 November 1989 in respect of the declaration made by Chile

The reservations [. . .] are incompatible with the object and purpose of the Convention and are therefore impermissible under article 19 (c) of the Vienna Convention on the Law of Treaties. The Republic of Austria therefore objects against these reservations and states that they cannot alter or modify, in any respect, the obligations arising from the Convention for all States Parties thereto.

BULGARIA

Objections of 24 January 1990 in respect of the declaration made by Chile

The Government of the People's Republic of Bulgaria considers the reservations made by Chile with regard to art. 2, para. 3 and art. 3 of the Convention against torture and other forms of cruel, inhuman or degrading treatment or punishment of December 10, 1984 incompatible with the object and the purpose of the Convention.

The Government of the People's Republic of Bulgaria holds the view that each State is obliged to take all measures to prevent any acts of torture and other forms of cruel and inhuman treatment within its jurisdiction, including the unconditional qualification of such acts as crimes in its national criminal code. It is in this sense that art. 2, para. 3 of the Convention is formulated.

The provisions of art. 3 of the Convention are dictated by the necessity to grant the most effective protection to persons who risk to suffer torture or other inhuman treatment. For this reason these provisions should not be interpreted on the basis of subjective or any other circumstances, under which they were formulated.

In view of this the Government of the People's Republic of Bulgaria does not consider itself bound by the reservations.

CANADA

Objections of 5 October 1988 in respect of the declaration made by German Democratic Republic

The Government of Canada considers that this declaration is incompatible with the object and purpose of the Convention against Torture, and thus inadmissible under art-

---

2 Unless otherwise indicated, the objections were made upon ratification, accession or succession.

icle 19 (c) of the Vienna Convention on the Law of Treaties. Through its functions and its activities, the Committee against Torture plays an essential role in the execution of the obligations of States parties to the Convention against Torture. Any restriction whose effect is to hamper the activities of the Committee would thus be incompatible with the object and purpose of the Convention.

Objections of 23 October 1989 in respect of the declaration made by Chile
The reservations by Chile are incompatible with the object and purpose of the Convention Against Torture and thus inadmissible under article 19 (c) of the Vienna Convention on the Law of Treaties.

[CZECHOSLOVAKIA
Objections of 20 September 1989 in respect of the declaration made by Chile
The Czechoslovak Socialist Republic considers the reservations of the Government of Chile [. . .] as incompatible with the object and purpose of this Convention.

"The obligation of each State to prevent acts of torture in any territory under its jurisdiction is unexceptional. It is the obligation of each State to ensure that all acts of torture are offences under its criminal law. This obligation is confirmed, inter alia, in article 2, paragraph 3 of the Convention concerned.

The observance of provisions set up in article 3 of this Convention is necessitated by the need to ensure more effective protection for persons who might be in danger of being subjected to torture and this is obviously one of the principal purposes of the Convention.

Therefore, the Czechoslovak Socialist Republic does not recognize these reservations as valid.

DENMARK
Objections of 29 September 1988 in respect of the declaration made by German Democratic Republic
The Government of Denmark hereby enters its formal objection to [the declaration] which it considers to be a unilateral statement with the purpose of modifying the legal effect of certain provisions of the Convention against Torture, and Other Cruel, Inhuman or Degrading Treatment or Punishment in their application to the German Democratic Republic. It is the position of the Government of Denmark that the said declaration has no legal basis in the Convention or in international treaty law.

This objection is not an obstacle to the entry into force of the said Convention between Denmark and the German Democratic Republic.

Objections of 7 September 1989 in respect of the declaration made by Chile
The Danish Government considers the said reservations as being incompatible with the object and purpose of the Convention and therefore invalid.

This objection is not an obstacle to the entry into force of the said Convention between Denmark and Chile.

The Secretary-General of the United Nations received on 21 February 2001 the communication relating to the reservation made by Qatar upon accession:
The Government of Denmark has examined the contents of the reservation made by the Government of Qatar to the Convention against Torture and Other Cruel, Inhuman or Degrading Treatment or punishment regarding any interpretation of the provisions of the Convention that is incompatible with the precepts of Islamic law and the Islamic religion. The Government of Denmark considers that the reservation, which is of a general nature, is incompatible with the object and purpose of the Convention. it is the opinion of the Government of Denmark that no time limit applies to objections against reservations which are inadmissible under international law.

For the above-mentioned reasons, the Government of Denmark objects to this reservation made by the Government of Qatar. This objection does no preclude the entry into force of the Convention between Qatar and Denmark.

Objection of 4 October 2001 with regard to the reservation made by Botswana upon ratification:
The Government of Denmark has examined the contents of the reservation made by the Government of Botswana to the Convention against Torture and Other Cruel, Inhuman or Degrading Treatment or Punishment. The reservation refers to legislation in force in Botswana as to the definition of torture and thus to the scope of application of the Convention. In the absence of further clarification the Government of Denmark considers that the reservation raises doubts as to the commitment of Botswana to fullfil her objections under the Convention and is compatible with the object and purpose of the Convention.

For these reasons, the Government of Denmark objects to this reservation made by the Government of Botswana. This objection does not preclude the entry itno force of the Convention in its entirety between Botswana and Denmark without Botswana benefiting from the reservation.

FINLAND

Objections of 20 October 1989 in respect of the declaration made by the German Democratic Republic
The Government of Finland considers that any such declaration is without legal effect, and cannot in any manner diminish the obligation of a government to contribute to the costs of the Committee in conformity with the provisions of the Convention.

Objections of 20 October 1989 in respect of the declaration made by Chile
The Government of Finland considers the said reservations as being incompatible with the object and purpose of the Convention and therefore invalid.
This objection is not an obstacle to the entry into force of the said Convention between Finland and Chile.

Objection of 27 February 1996 with regard to the reservations, understandings and declarations made by the United States of America upon ratification
A reservation which consists of a general reference to national law without specifying its contents does not clearly define to the other Parties of the Convention the extent to which the reserving State commits itself to the Convention and therefore may cast doubts about the commitment of the reserving State to fulfil its obligations under the Convention. Such a reservation is also, in the view of the Government of the Finland, subject to the general principle to treaty interpretation according to which a party may not invoke the provisions of its internal law as justification for failure to perform a treaty.

The Government of Finland therefore objects to the reservation made by the United States to article 16 of the Convention [(cf. Reservation I.(1)]. In this connection the Government of Finland would also like to refer to its objection to the reservation entered by the United States with regard to article 7 of the International Covenant on Civil and Political Rights.[3] It is also the view of the Government of Finland that the understandings expressed by the United States do not release the United States as a Party to the Convention from the responsibility to fulfil the obligations undertaken therein.

13 December 1999 objection with regard to the declaration made by Bangladesh upon accession

The Government of Finland has examined the contents of the declaration made by the Government of Bangladesh to Article 14 paragraph 1 to the Convention Against Torture and Other Cruel, Inhuman or Degrading Treatment or Punishment and notes

---

3 For the text of the objection see under "Objections" in chapter IV.4 of the *Multilateral Treaties Deposited with the Secretary-General, New York, United Nations* (ST/LEG/SER.E) as available on *http://untreaty.un.org*.

that the declaration constitutes a reservation as it seems to modify the obligations of Bangladesh under the said article.

A reservation which consists of a general reference to national law without specifying its contents does not clearly define for the other Parties of the Convention the extent to which the reserving State commits itself to the Convention and therefore may raise doubts as to the commitment of the reserving state to fulfil its obligations under the Convention. Such a reservation is also, in the view of the Government of Finland, subject to the general principle of treaty interpretation according to which a party may not invoke the provisions of its domestic law as justification for a failure to perform its treaty obligations.

Therefore the Government of Finland objects to the aforesaid reservations to Article 14 paragraph 1 made by the Government of Bangladesh. The objection does not preclude the entry into force of the Convention between Bangladesh and Finland. The Convention will thus become operative between the two States without Bangladesh benefitting from these reservations.

Objections of 16 January 2001 with regard to the reservation made by Qatar upon accession

The Government of Finland has examined the context of the reservation made by the Government of Qatar regarding any interpretation incompatible with the precepts of Islamic law and the Islamic religion. The Government of Finland notes that a reservation which consists of a general reference to national law without specifying its contents does not clearly define for the other Parties to the Convention the extent ot which the reserving State commits itself to the Convention and may therefore raise doubts as to the commitment of the reserving State to fulfil its obligations under the Convention. Such a reservation, in the view of the Government of Finland, is subject to the general principle of treaty interpretation according to which a party may not invoke the provisions of its domestic law as justification for a failure to perform its treaty obligations.

The Government of Finland also notes that the reservation of Qatar, being of such a general nature, raises doubts as to the full commitment of Qatar to the object and prupose of the Convention and would like to recall that, according to the Vienna Convention on the Law of Treaties, a reservation incompatible with the object and purpose of the Convention shall not be permitted.

For the above-mentioned reasons the Government of Finland objects to the reservation made by the Government of Qatar. This objection does not preclude the entry into force of the Convention between Qatar and Finland. The Convention will tus become operative between the two States without Qatar benefitting from this reservation.

FRANCE

Objections of 23 June 1988 in respect of the declaration made by German Democratic Republic

France makes an objection to [the declaration] which it considers contrary with the object and purpose of the Convention.

The said objection is not an obstacle to the entry into force of the said Convention between France and the German Democratic Republic.

Objections of 20 September 1989 in respect of the declaration made by Chile

France considers that the reservations made by Chile are not valid as being incompatible with the object and purpose of the Convention.

Such objection is not an obstacle to the entry into force of the Convention between France and Chile.

With regard to the declaration made by Bangladesh upon accession
30 September 1999

The Government of France notes that the declaration made by Bangladesh in fact constitutes a reservation since it is aimed at precluding or modifying the legal effect of certain provisions of the treaty. A reservation which consists in a general reference to domestic law without specifying its contents does not clearly indicate to the other parties to what extent the State which issued the reservation commits itself when acceding to the Convention. The Government of France considers the reservation of Bangladesh incompatible with the objective and purpose of the treaty, in respect of which the provisions relating to the right of victims of acts of torture to obtain redress and compensation, which ensure the effectiveness and tangible realization of obligations under the Convention, are essential, and consequently lodges an objection to the reservation entered by Bangladesh regarding article 14, paragraph 1. This objection does not prevent the entry into force of the Convention between Bangladesh and France.

Objection of 24 January 2001 with regard to the reservation made by Qatar upon accession
The Government of the French Republic has carefully considered the reservation made by the Government of Qatar to the Convention Against Torture and Other Cruel, Inhuman or Degrading Treatment or Punishment of 10 October 1984, whereby it excludes any interpretation of the Convention which would be incompatible with the precepts of Islamic law and the Islamic religion. The reservation, which seeks ot give precedence to domestic law and practices over the Convention to an indeterminate extent, is comprehensive in scope. Its terms undermine the commitment of Qatar and make it impossible for the other States parties to assess the extent of that commitment. The Government of France therefore objects to the reservation made by Qatar.

GERMANY
Declaration of 26 February 1996 in respect of the reservation of the United States of America
On 26 February 1996, the Government of Germany notified the Secretary-General that with respect to the reservations under I (1) and understandings under II (2) and (3) made by the United States of America upon ratification "it is the understanding of the Government of the Federal Republic of Germany that [the said reservations and understandings] do not touch upon the obligations of the United States of America as State Party to the Convention.

23 January 2001 objections with regard to the reservation made by Qatar upon accession
The Government of the Federal Republic of Germany has examined the reservation to the Convention against Torture and Other Cruel, Inhuman or Degrading Treatment of Punishment made by the government of Qatar. The Government of the Federal Republic of Germany is of the view that the reservation with regard to compatibility of the rules of the Convention with the precepts of Islamic law and the Islamic religion raises doubts as to the commitment of Qatar to fulfil its obligations under the Convention. The Government of the Federal Republic of Germany considers this reservation to be incompatible with the object and purpose of the Convention. Therefore the Government of the Federal Republic of Germany objects to the aforesaid reservation made by the Government of Qatar to the Convention.

This objection does not preclude the entry into force of the Convention between Federal Republic of Germany and Qatar.

GREECE
Objections of 6 October 1988 in respect of the declaration made by German Democratic Republic
The Hellenic Republic raises an objection to [the declaration], which it considers to be in violation of article 19, paragraph (b), of the Vienna Convention on the Law of Treaties. The Convention against Torture expressly sets forth in article 28, paragraph 1, and article 30, paragraph 2, the reservations which may be made. The declaration of

the German Democratic Republic is not, however, in conformity with these specified reservations.

This objection does not preclude the entry into force of the said Convention as between the Hellenic Republic and the German Democratic Republic.

Objections of 13 October 1989 in respect of the declaration made by Chile
Greece does not accept the reservation since they are incompatible with the purpose and object of the Convention.

The above-mentioned objection is not an obstacle to the entry into force of the Convention between Greece and Chile.

ITALY

Objections of 12 January 1989 in respect of the declaration made by German Democratic Republic
The Convention authorizes only the reservations indicated in article 28(1) and 30(2). The reservation made by the German Democratic Republic is not therefore admissible under the terms of article 19(b) of the 1969 Vienna Convention on the Law of Treaties.

Objections of 14 August 1989 in respect of the declaration made by Chile
The Government of Italy considers that the reservations entered by Chile are not valid, as they are incompatible with the objection and purpose of the Convention. The present objection is in no way an obstacle to the entry into force of this Convention between Italy and Chile.

The Secretary-General of the United Nations received on 5 February 2001 the communication relating to the reservation made by Qatar upon accession:
The Government of the Italian Republic has examined the reservation to the Convention against torture and other cruel, inhuman or degrading treatment or punishment made by the Government of Qatar. The Government of the Italian Republic believes that the reservation concerning the compatibility of the rules of the Convention with the precepts of Islamic law and the Islamic Religion raises doubts as to the commitment of Qatar to fulfill its obligations under the Convention. The Government of the Italian Republic considers this reservation to e incompatible with the object and purpose of the Convention according to article 19 of the 1969 Vienna Convention on the Law of Treaties. This reservation does not fall within the rule of article 20, paragraph 5 and can be objected anytime.

Therefore, the Government of the Italian Republic objects to the aforesaid reservation made by the Government of Qatar to the Convention.

This objection does not preclude the entry into force of the Convention between Italy and Qatar.

LUXEMBOURG

Objections of 9 September 1988 in respect of the declaration made by German Democratic Republic
The Grand Duchy of Luxembourg objects to this declaration, which it deems to be a reservation the effect of which would be to inhibit activities of the Committee in a manner incompatible with the purpose and the goal of the Convention.

The present objection does not constitute an obstacle to the entry into force of the said Convention between the Grand Duchy of Luxembourg and the German Democratic Republic.

Objections of 12 September 1989 in respect of the declaration made by Chile
The Grand Duchy of Luxembourg objects to the reservations, which are incompatible with the intent and purpose of the Convention.

This objection does not represent an obstacle to the entry into force of the said Convention between the Grand Duchy of Luxembourg and Chile.

Objection of 6 April 2000 with regard to the reservation made by Qatar upon accession
The Government of the Grand Duchy of Luxembourg has examined the reservation made by the Government of the State of Qatar [to the Convention] regarding any interpretation incompatible with the precepts of Islamic law and the Islamic religion.

The Government of the Grand Duchy of Luxembourg considers that this reservation, by referring in a general way to both Islamic law and the Islamic religion without specifying their content, raises doubts among other States Parties about the degree to hich the State of Qatar is committed to the observance of the Convention. The Government of the Grand duchy of Luxembourg believes that the aforementioned reservation of the Government of the State of Qatar is incompatible with the objective and purpose of the Convention, because it refers to it as a whole and seriously limits or even excludes its application on a poorly defined basis, as in the case of the global reference to Islamic law.

Consequently, the Government of the Grand Duchy of Luxembourg objects to the aforementioned reservation made by the Government of the State of Qatar [to the Convention]. This objection does not prevent the netry into force of the Convention between the Grand Duchy of Luxembourg and the State of Qatar.

NETHERLANDS
Objections of 21 December 1989 in respect of the declaration made by German Democratic Republic
This declaration, clearly a reservation according to article 2, paragraph 1, under (d), of the Vienna Convention on the Law of Treaties, not only "purports to exclude or modify the legal effect" of articles 17, paragraph 7, and 18, paragraph 5, of the present Convention in their application to the German Democratic Republic itself, but it would also affect the obligations of the other States Parties which would have to pay additionally in order to ensure the proper functioning of the Committee Against Torture. For this reason the reservation is not acceptable to the Government of the Kingdom of the Netherlands.

Thus, the assessment of the financial contributions of the States Parties to be made under article 17, paragraph 7, and article 18, paragraph 5, must be drawn up in disregard of the declaration of the German Democratic Republic.

Objections of 7 November 1989 in respect of the declaration made by Chile
Since the purpose of the Convention is strengthening of the existing prohibition of torture and similar practices the reservation to article 2, paragraph 3, to the effect to an order from a superior officer or a public authority may – in some cases – be invoked as a justification or torture, must be rejected as contrary to the object and purpose of the Convention.

For similar reasons the reservation to article 3 must be regarded as incompatible with the object and purpose of the Convention.

These objections are not an obstacle to the entry into force of this Convention between the Kingdom of the Netherlands and Chile.

Objections of 26 February 1996 with regard to the reservations, understandings and declarations made by the United States of America upon ratification
The Government of the Netherlands considers the reservation made by the United States of America regarding the article 16 of [the Convention] to be incompatible with the object and purpose of the Convention, to which the obligation laid down in article 16 is essential. Moreover, it is not clear how the provisions of the Constitution of the United States of America relate to the obligations under the Convention. The Government of the Kingdom of the Netherlands therefore objects to the said reservation. This objection shall not preclude the entry into force of the Convention between the Kingdom of the Netherlands and the United States of America.

The Government of the Kingdom of the Netherlands considers the following understandings to have no impact on the obligations of the United States of America under the Convention:

II. 1a This understanding appears to restrict the scope of the definition of torture under article 1 of the Convention.

1d This understanding diminishes the continuous responsibility of public officials for behaviour of their subordinates.

The Government of the Kingdom of the Netherlands reserves its position with regard to the understandings II. 1b, 1c and 2 as the contents thereof are insufficiently clear."

Objections of 19 |January 2001 with regard to the reservation made by Qatar upon accession

The Government of the Kingdom of the Netherlands considers that the reservation concerning the national law of Qatar, which seeks to limit the responsibilities of the reserving State under the Convention by invoking national law, may raise doubts as to the commitment of this State to the object and purpose of the Convention and, moreover, contribute to undermining the basis of international treaty law.

It is in the common interest of States that treaties to which they have chosen to become party should be respected, as to object and purpose by all parties.

The Government of the Kingdom of the Netherlands therefore objects to the aforesaid reservation made by the Government of Qatar.

This objection shall not preclude the entry into force of the Convention between the Kingdom of the Netherlands and Qatar.

NEW ZEALAND

Objections of 10 December 1989 in respect of the declaration made by German Democratic Republic

The Government of New Zealand considers that this declaration is incompatible with the object and purpose of the Convention. This objection does not constitute an obstacle to the entry into force of the Convention between New Zealand and the German Democratic Republic.

Objections of 10 December 1989 in respect of the declaration made by Chile

The New Zealand Government considers the said reservations to be incompatible with the object and purpose of the Convention. This objection does not constitute and obstacle to the entry into force of the Convention between New Zealand and Chile.

NORWAY

Objections of 29 September 1988 in respect of the declaration made by German Democratic Republic

The Government of Norway cannot accept this declaration entered by the German Democratic Republic. The Government of Norway considers that any such declaration is without legal effect, and cannot in any manner diminish the obligation of a government to contribute to the costs of the Committee in conformity with the provisions of the Convention.

Objections of 28 September 1989 in respect of the declaration made by Chile

The Government of Norway considers the said reservations as being incompatible with the object and purpose of the Convention and therefore invalid.

This objection is not an obstacle to the entry into force of the said Convention between Norway and Chile.

Objections of 18 January 2001 with regard to the reservation made by Qatar upon accession

It is the Government of Norway's position that paragraph (a) of the reservation, due to its unlimited scope and undefined character, is contrary to the object and purpose of the Convention, and thus impermissible according to well established treaty law. The Government of Norway therefore objects to paragraph (a) of the reservation.

This objection does not preclude the entry into force in its entirety of the Convention between the Kingdom of Norway and Qatar. The Convention this becomes operative between Norway and Qatar without Qatar benefitting from the said reservation.

Objections of 4 October 2001 with regard to the reservation made by Botswana on ratification
The Government of Norway has examined the contents of the reservation made by the Government of the Republic of Botswana upon ratification of the Convention Against Torture and other Cruel, Inhuman or Degrading Treatment or Punishment.

The reservation's reference to the national Constitution without further description of its contents, exempts the other States Parties to the Convention form the possibility of assessing the effects of the reservation. In addition, as the reservation concerns one of the core provisions of the Convention, it is the position of the Government of Norway that the reservation is contrary to the object and purpose of the Convention. Norway therefore objects to the reservation made by the Government of Botswana.

This objection does not preclude the entry into force in its entirety of the Convention between the Kingdom of Norway and the Republic of Botswana. The Convention thus becomes operative between Norway and Botswana without Botswana benefiting from the said reservation.

PORTUGAL

Objections of 9 February 1989 in respect of the declaration made by German Democratic Republic
The Government of Portugal considers that this declaration is incompatible with the object and purpose of the present Convention. This objection does not constitute an obstacle to the entry into force of the Convention between Portugal and G.D.R.

Objections of 6 October 1989 in respect of the declaration made by Chile
The Government of Portugal considers such reservations to be incompatible with the object and purpose of this Convention and therefore invalid.

This objection does not constitute an obstacle to the entry into force of the Convention between Portugal and Chile.

The Secretary-General of the United Nations received on 20 July 2001 the communication relating to the reservation made by Qatar upon accession
The Government of the Portuguese Republic has examined the reservation made by the Government of Qatar to the Convention Against Torture and Other Cruel, Inhuman or Degrading Treatment of Punishment (New York, 10 December 1984), whereby it excludes any interpretation of the said Convention which would be incompatible with the precepts of Islamic law and the Islamic religion.

The Government of the Portuguese Republic is of the view that this reservation foes against the general principle of treaty interpretation according to which a State party to a treaty may not invoke the provisions of its internal law as justification for failure to perform according to the obligations set out by the said treaty, creating legitimate doubts on its commitment to the Convention and, moreover, contribute to undermine the basis of international law.

Furthermore, the said reservation is incompatible with the object and purpose of the Convention.

The Government of the Portuguese Republic wishes, therefore, to express disagreement with the reservation made by the Government of Qatar.

SPAIN

Objections of 6 October 1988 in respect of the declaration made by German Democratic Republic
The Government of the Kingdom of Spain feels that such a reservation is a violation of article 19, paragraph (b), of the Vienna Convention on the Law of Treaties of 23 May 1969, because the Convention against Torture and Other Cruel, Inhuman or Degrading Treatment or Punishment sets forth, in article 28, paragraph 1, and article 30, paragraph 2, the only reservations that may be made to the Convention, and the above-mentioned reservation of the German Democratic Republic does not conform to either of those reservations.

Objections of 26 September 1989 in respect of the declaration made by Chile
The aforementioned reservations are contrary to the purposes and aims of the Convention.

The present objection does not constitute an obstacle to the entry into force of the Convention between Spain and Chile.

Objections of 13 December 1999 with regard to the declaration to article 14(1) made by Bangladesh upon accession
The Government of the Kingdom of Spain considers that this declaration is actually a reservation, since its purpose is to exclude or modify the application of the legal effect of certain provisions of the Convention. Moreover, in referring in a general way to the domestic laws of Bangladesh, without specifying their content, the reservation raises doubts among the other States parties as to the extent to which the People's Republic of Bangladesh is committed to ratifying the Convention.

The Government of the Kingdom of Spain believes that the reservation lodged by the Government of the People's Republic of Bangladesh is incompatible with the objective and purpose of the Convention, for which the provisions concerning redress and compensation for victims of torture are essential factors in teh concrete fulfilment of the commitments made under the Convention.

The Government of the Kingdom of Spain therefore states an objection to the above-mentioned reservation lodged by the Government of the People's Republic of Bangladesh to the Convention against Torture and Other Cruel, Inhuman or Degrading Treatment or Punishment, concerning article 14, paragraph 1, of that Convention.

This objection does not affect the entry into force of the above-mentioned Convention between the Kingdom of Spain and the People's Republic of Bangladesh.

Objections of 14 March 2000 with regard to the reservation made by Qatar upon accession

The Government of the Kingdom of Spain has examined the reservation made by the Government of the State of Qatar to the Convention against Torture and Other Cruel, Inhuman or Degrading Treatment or Punishment on 11 January 2000, as to any interpretation of the Convention that is incompatible with the precepts of Islamic law and the Islamic religion.

The Government of the Kingdom of Spain considers that, by making a general reference to Islamic law and religion rather than to specific content, this reservation raises doubts among the other States parties as to the extent of the commitment of the State of Qatar to abide by the Convention.

The Government of the Kingdom of Spain considers the reservation made by the Government of the State of Qatar to be incompatible with the purpose and aim of the Convention, in that it relates to the entire Convention and seriously limits or even excludes its application on a basis which is not clearly defined, namely a general reference to Islamic law.

Accordingly, the Government of the Kingdom of Spain objects to the above-mentioned reservation made by the Government of the State of Qatar to the Convention against Torture and Other Cruel, Inhuman or Degrading Treatment or Punishment. This objection does not prevent the Convention's entry into force between the Government of Spain and the Government of the State of Qatar.

SWEDEN

Objections of 28 September 1988 in respect of the declaration made by German Democratic Republic
According to article 2, paragraph 1 (d) of the Vienna Convention on the Law of Treaties a unilateral statement, whereby a State e.g., when ratifying a treaty, purports to exclude the legal effect of certain provisions of the Treaty in their application, is regarded as a reservation. Thus, such unilateral statements are considered as reservations regardless of their name or phrase. The Government of Sweden has come to the conclusion that the declaration made by the German Democratic Republic is incompatible with the object and purpose of the Convention and therefore is invalid according to article 19(c)

of the Vienna Convention on the Law of Treaties. For this reason the Government of Sweden objects to this declaration.

Objections of 25 September 1989 in respect of the declaration made by Chile
These reservations are incompatible with the object and purpose of the Convention and therefore are impermissible according to article 19(c) of the Vienna Convention on the Law of Treaties. For this reason the Government of Sweden objects to these reservations. This objection does not have the effect of preventing the Convention from entering into force between Sweden and Chile, and the said reservations cannot alter or modify, in any respect, the obligations arising from the Convention.

Objection of 27 February 1996 with regard to the reservations, understandings and declarations made by the United States of America upon ratification
The Government of Sweden would like to refer to its objections to the reservations entered by the United States of America with regard to article 7 of the International Covenant on Civil and Political Rights.[6] The same reasons for objection apply to the now entered reservation with regard to article 16 reservation I (1) of [the Convention]. The Government of Sweden therefore objects to that reservation.

It is the view of the Government of Sweden that the understandings expressed by the United States of America do not relieve the United States of America as a party to the Convention from the responsibility to fulfil the obligations undertaken therein.

Objections of 14 December 1999 with regard to article 14(1) made by Bangladesh upon accession
Objections of 14 December 1999 with regard to the declaration to article 14(1) made by Bangladesh upon accession:

In this context the Government of Sweden would like to recall, under well-established international treaty law, the name assigned to a statement whereby the legal effect of certain provisions of a treaty is excluded or modified, does not determine its status as a reservation to the treaty. Thus, the Government of Sweden considers that the declaration made by the Government of Bangladesh, in the absence of further clarification, in substance constitutes a reservation to the Convention.

The Government of Sweden notes that the said declaration implies that the said article of the Convention is being made subject to a general reservation referring to the contents of existing laws and regulations in the country.

The Government of Sweden is of the view that this declaration raise doubts as to the commitment of Bangladesh to the object and purpose of the Convention and would recall that, according to well-established international law, a reservation incompatible with the object and purpose of a treaty shall not be permitted.

It is in the common interest of States that treaties to which they have chosen to become parties are respected, as to their object and purpose, by all parties and that States are prepared to undertake any legislative changes necessary to comply with their obligations under these treaties.

The Government of Sweden therefore objects to the aforesaid declaration made by the Government of Bangladesh to the Convention against Torture and other Cruel, Inhuman or Degrading Treatment or Punishment.

Objection of 27 April 2000 with regard to the reservations made by Qatar upon accession
The Government of Sweden has examined the reservations made by the Government of Qatar at the time of its accession to the [Convention], as to the competence of the committee and to any interpretation of the provisions of the Convention that is incompatible with the precepts of Islamic laws and the Islamic religion.

6 For the text of the objection see under "Objections" in chapter IV.4 of the *Multilateral Treaties Deposited with the Secretary-General, New York, United Nations* (ST/LEG/SER.E) as available on http://untreaty.un.org.

The Government of Sweden is of the view that as regards the latter, this general reservation, which does not clearly specify the provision of the Convention to which it applies and the extent of the derogation therefrom, raises doubts as to the commitment of Qatar to the object and purpose of the Convention.

It is in the common interest of States that treaties to which they have chosen to become parties are respected as to their object and purpose, and that States are prepared to undertake any legislation changes necessary to comply with their obligations under the treaties.

According to customary law as codified in the Vienna Convention on the Law of Treaties, a reservation incompatible with the object and purpose of the Convention shall not be permitted. The Government of Sweden therefore objects to the aforesaid general reservation by the Government of the State of Qatar to the [Convention].

This shall not preclude the entry into force of the Convention between the State of Qatar and the Kingdom of Sweden, without Qatar benefiting from the said reservation.

Objection of 2 October 2001 with regard to the reservation made by Botswana upon ratification

The Government of Sweden has examined the reservation made by Botswana upon ratification of the 1984 Convention Against Torture and other Cruel, Inhuman or Degrading Treatment or Punishment, regarding article 1 of the Convention. The Government of Sweden notes that the said article of the Convention is being made subject to a general reservation referring to the contents of existing legislation in Botswana. Article 1(2) of the Convention states that the definition of torture in article 1(1) is "without prejudice to any international instrument or national legislation which does or may contain provisions of wider application".

The Government of Sweden is of the view that this reservation, in the absence of further clarification, raises doubts as to the commitment of Botswana to the object and purpose of the Convention. The government of Sweden would like to recall that, according to customary international law as codified in the Vienna Convention on the Law of Treaties, a reservation incompatible with the object and purpose of a treaty shall not be permitted.

It is in te common interest of States that treaties to which they have chosen to become parties are respected as to their object and purpose, by all parties, and that States ar prepared to undertake any legislative changes necessary to comply with their obligations under the treaties.

The Government of Sweden therefore objects to the aforesaid reservation made by the Government of Botswana to the Convention Against Torture and other Cruel, Inhuman or Degrading Treatment or Punishment.

The objection shall not preclude the entry into force of the Convention between Botswana and Sweden. The Convention enters into force in its entirety bewteen the two States, without Botswana benefiting from its reservation.

SWITZERLAND

Objections of 7 October 1988 in respect of the declaration made by German Democratic Republic

That reservation is contrary to the purpose and aims of the Convention which are, through the Committee's activities, to encourage respect for a vitally important human right and to enhance the effectiveness of the struggle against torture the world over. This objection does not have the effect of preventing the Convention from entering into force between the Swiss Confederation and the German Democratic Republic.

Objections of 8 November 1989 in respect of the declaration made by Chile

These reservations are not compatible with the object and purpose of the Convention, which are to improve respect for human right of fundamental importance and to make more effective the struggle against torture throughout the world.

This objection does not have the effect of preventing the Convention from entering into force between the Swiss Confederation and the Republic of Chile.

TURKEY

Objections of 3 November 1989 in respect of the declaration made by Chile

The Government of Turkey considers such reservations to be incompatible with the object and purpose of this Convention and therefore invalid.

This objection does not constitute an obstacle to the entry into force of the Convention between Turkey and Chile.

UNITED KINGDOM OF GREAT BRITAIN AND NORTHERN IRELAND

Objections of 8 November 1989 in respect of the declaration made by Chile

The United Kingdom is unable to accept the reservation to article 2, paragraph 3, or the reservation to article 3.

In the same communication, the Government of the United Kingdom notified the Secretary-General of the following:

(a) The reservations to article 28, paragraph 1, and to article 30, paragraph 1, being reservations expressly permitted by the Convention, do not call for any observations by the United Kingdom.

(b) The United Kingdom takes note of the reservation referring to the Inter-American Convention to Prevent and Punish Torture, which cannot, however, affect the obligations of Chile in respect of the United Kingdom, as a non-Party to the said Convention.

The Secretary-General of the United Nations received on 29 November 2001 the communication relating to the reservation made by Qatar upon accession

The Government of the United Kingdom have examined the reservation made by the Government of Qatar on 11 January 2000 in respect of the Convention, which reads as follows:

... with reservation as to: (a) Any interpretation of the provisions of the Convention that is incompatible with the precepts of Islamic law and the Islamic religion."

The Government of the United Kingdom note that a reservation which consists of a general reference to national law without specifying its contents does not clearly define for the other States Parties to the Convention the extent to which the reserving State has accepted the obligations of the Convention. The Government of the United Kingdom therefore object to the reservation made by the Government of Qatar.

This objection shall not preclude the entry into force of the Convention between the United Kingdom of Greta Britain and Northern Ireland and Qatar.

ACCEPTANCE OF AMENDMENTS TO ARTICLES 17, PARAGRAPH 7 AND 18 PARAGRAPH 5 OF THE CONVENTION[5]

State	*Acceptance*
Australia	15 October 1993
Bulgaria	2 March 1995
Canada	8 February 1995
China	10 July 2002
Colombia	1 September 1999
Cyprus	22 February 1994
Denmark	3 September 1993
Ecuador	6 September 1995
Finland	5 February 1993
France	24 May 1994
Germany	8 October 1996
Iceland	23 October 1996
Liechtenstein	24 August 1994
Mexico	15 March 2002
Netherlands[6]	24 January 1995
New Zealand	8 October 1993
Norway	6 October 1993
Philippines	27 November 1996
Portugal	17 April 1998
Seychelles	23 July 1993
Spain	5 May 1999
Sweden	14 May 1993
Switzerland	10 December 1993
Ukraine	17 June 1994
United Kingdom	7 February 1994

[5] Based on indications in *Multilateral Treaties Deposited with the Secretary-General,* New York, United Nations (ST/LEG/SER.E) as avilable on http://untreaty.un.org.

[6] For the Kingdom in Europe, the Netherlands Antilles and Aruba.

No. 66

EUROPEAN CONVENTION FOR THE PREVENTION OF TORTURE AND INHUMAN OR DEGRADING TREATMENT OR PUNISHMENT (AS AMENDED BY PROTOCOLS I AND II OF 4 NOVEMBER 1993)

Opened for signature, Strasbourg, 26 November 1987

INTRODUCTORY NOTE: Most legal instruments prohibiting torture and inhuman or degrading treatment or punishment do not possess any mechanism of implementation ensuring the respect of the obligations they created. The adoption of the European Convention had its origin in the proposal of Jean-Jacques Gautier, Genevese banker, who proposed in 1976 a convention instituting a system of visits of places of detention by a group of independent experts. The proposal was taken up by Costa Rica which, in 1980, proposed to the UN Human Rights Commission to supplement the projected United Nations Convention (*No. 65*) with an optional protocol instituting such a system of visits. The draft of the optional protocol had been elaborated by the Swiss Committee against Torture and the International Commission of Jurists.

On the European level, the Parliamentary Assembly of the Council of Europe, in 1983, on the basis of a report of the French deputy Noel Berrier, adopted resolution 971 which included, in its annex, the draft of the present Convention based on the Costa Rica proposal to the United Nations. In 1986, after intergovernmental discussions, the Committee of Ministers charged a committee of experts to elaborate the text of a convention. It adopted the text on 26 June 1987 after having consulted the European Commission and the European Court of Human Rights. The Convention was opened for signature by the member States of the Council of Europe on 26 November 1987.

On 4 November 1993, the states members of Council of Europe signed two Protocols to the Convention. Protocol I has the purpose of allowing non-member states of the Council of Europe to accede to the Convention by invitation of the Committee of Ministers. Protocol II provides that the members of the European Committee for the prevention of torture and inhuman or degrading treatment and punishment may be re-elected twice and that half of the membership shall be renewed every two years. The texts of the Protocols are integrated into the text of the Convention.

ENTRY INTO FORCE: 1 February 1989. The amendments of 4 November 1993 entered into force on 1 March 2002.

AUTHENTIC TEXT: English, French. The text below is reproduced from the document of the Council of Europe H (87) 4, pp. 2–9.

TEXT PUBLISHED IN: *ETS* 126 (*Convention*), 151 (*Protocol I*), 152 (*Protocol II*; *GBTS,* 1988, Misc. 5 (1988), Cm. 339 (Engl.); *ILM*, Vol. 27, 1988, pp. 1152–1159 (Engl.); *Derechos humanos*, pp. 651–660 (Span.); *Droit des conflits armés*, pp. 1005–1021 (French). Council of Europe website: http://conventions.coe.int.

* * *

The member States of the Council of Europe, signatory hereto,

Having regard to the provisions of the Convention for the Protection of Human Rights and Fundamental Freedoms,

Recalling that, under Article 3 of the same Convention, "no one shall be subjected to torture or to inhuman or degrading treatment or punishment";

Noting that the machinery provided for in that Convention operates in relation to persons who allege that they are victims of violations of Article 3;

Convinced that the protection of persons deprived of their liberty against torture and inhuman or degrading treatment or punishment could be strengthened by non-judicial means of a preventive character based on visits,

Have agreed as follows:

Chapter I

Article 1. There shall be established a European Committee for the Prevention of Torture and Inhuman or Degrading Treatment or Punishment (hereinafter referred to as "the Committee"). The Committee shall, by means of visits, examine the treatment of persons deprived of their liberty with a view to strengthening, if necessary, the protection of such persons from torture and from inhuman or degrading treatment or punishment.

Art. 2. Each Party shall permit visits, in accordance with this Convention, to any place within its jurisdiction where persons are deprived of their liberty by a public authority.

Art. 3. In the application of this Convention, the Committee and the competent national authorities of the Party concerned shall co-operate with each other.

Chapter II

Art. 4.

1. The Committee shall consist of a number of members equal to that of the Parties.
2. The members of the Committee shall be chosen from among persons of high moral character, known for their competence in the field of human rights or having professional experience in the areas covered by this Convention.
3. No two members of the Committee may be nationals of the same State.
4. The members shall serve in their individual capacity, shall be independent and impartial, and shall be available to serve the Committee effectively.

Art. 5.

1. The members of the Committee shall be elected by the Committee of Ministers of the Council of Europe by an absolute majority of votes, from a list of names drawn up by the Bureau of the Consultative Assembly of the Council of Europe; each national delegation of the Parties in the Consultative Assembly shall put forward three candidates, of whom two at least shall be its nationals.

   Where a member is to be elected to the Committee in respect of a non-member State of the Council of Europe, the Bureau of the Consultative Assembly shall invite the Parliament of that State to put forward three candidates, of whom at least two shall by its nationals. The election by the Committee of Ministers shall take place after consultation with the Party concerned.[1]

2. The same procedure shall be followed in filling casual vacancies.
3. The members of the Committee shall be elected for a period of four years. They may be re-elected twice.[2] However, among the members elected at the first election, the terms of three members shall expire at the end of two years. The members whose terms are to expire at the end of the initial period of two years shall be chosen by lot by the Secretary General of the Council of Europe immediately after the first election has been completed.
4.[3] In order to ensure that, as far as possible, one half of the membership of the Committee shall be renewed every two years, the Committee of Ministers may decide, before proceeding to any subsequent election, that the term or terms of office of one or more members to be elected shall be for a period other than four years but not more than six and not less than two years.
5.[3] In cases where more than one term of office is involved and the Committee of Ministers applies the preceding paragraph, the allocation of the terms of office shall be effected by the drawing of lots by the Secretary General, immediately after the election.

Art. 6.

1. The Committee shall meet in camera. A quorum shall be equal to the majority of its members. The decisions of the Committee shall be taken by a majority of the members present, subject to the provisions of Article 10, paragraph 2.
2. The committee shall draw up its own rules of procedure.
3. The Secretariat of the Committee shall be provided by the Secretary General of the Council of Europe.

Chapter III

Art. 7.

1. The Committee shall organise visits to places referred to in Article 2. Apart from periodic visits, the Committee may organise such other visits as appear to it to be required in the circumstances.
2. As a general rule, the visits shall be carried out by at least two members of the Committee. The Committee may, if it considers it necessary, be assisted by experts and interpreters.

Art. 8.

1. The Committee shall notify the Government of the Party concerned of its intention to carry out a visit. After such notification, it may at any time visit any place referred to in Article 2.
2. A Party shall provide the Committee with the following facilities to carry out its task:

---

[1] Subparagraph added by Protocol I of 4 November 1993, in force since 1 March 2002.

[2] Second sentence of paragraph 2 as amended by Protocol II of 4 November 1993, in force since 1 March 2002.

[3] Paragraphs 4 and 5 added by Protocol II of 4 November 1993, in force since 1 March 2002.

(a) access to its territory and the right to travel without restriction;
(b) full information on the places where persons deprived of their liberty are being held;
(c) unlimited access to any place where persons are deprived of their liberty, including the right to move inside such places without restriction;
(d) other information available to the Party which is necessary for the Committee to carry out its task.

In seeking such information, the Committee shall have regard to applicable rules of national law and professional ethics.

3. The Committee may interview in private persons deprived of their liberty.
4. The Committee may communicate freely with any person whom it believes can supply relevant information.
5. If necessary, the Committee may immediately communicate observations to the competent authorities of the Party concerned.

Art. 9.

1. In exceptional circumstances, the competent authorities of the Party concerned may make representations to the Committee against a visit at the time or to the particular place proposed by the Committee. Such representations may only be made on grounds of national defence, public safety, serious disorder in places where persons are deprived of their liberty, the medical condition of a person or that an urgent interrogation relating to a serious crime is in progress.
2. Following such representations, the Committee and the Party shall immediately enter into consultations in order to clarify the situation and seek agreement on arrangements to enable the Committee to exercise its functions expeditiously. Such arrangements may include the transfer to another place of any person whom the Committee proposed to visit. Until the visit takes place, the Party shall provide information to the Committee about any person concerned.

Art. 10.

1. After each visit, the Committee shall draw up a report on the facts found during the visit, taking account of any observations which may have been submitted by the Party concerned. It shall transmit to the latter its report containing any recommendations it considers necessary. The Committee may consult with the Party with a view to suggesting, if necessary, improvements in the protection of persons deprived of their liberty.
2. If the Party fails to co-operate or refuses to improve the situation in the light of the Committee's recommendations, the Committee may decide, after the Party has had an opportunity to make known its views, by a majority of two-thirds of its members to make a public statement on the matter.

Art. 11.

1. The information gathered by the Committee in relation to a visit, its report and its consultations with the Party concerned shall be confidential.
2. The Committee shall publish its report, together with any comments of the Party concerned, whenever requested to do so by that Party.
3. However, no personal data shall be published without the express consent of the person concerned.

Art. 12.[4] Subject to the rules of confidentiality in Article 11, the Committee shall every year submit to the Committee of Ministers a general report on its activities which shall be transmitted to the Consultative Assembly and to any non-member State of the Council of Europe which is a party to the Convention, and made public.

Art. 13. The members of the Committee, experts and other persons assisting the Committee are required, during and after their terms of office, to maintain the confidentiality of the facts or information of which they have become aware during the discharge of their functions.

Art. 14.
1. The names of persons assisting the Committee shall be specified in the notification under Article 8, paragraph 1.
2. Experts shall act on the instructions and under the authority of the Committee. They shall have particular knowledge and experience in the areas covered by this Convention and shall be bound by the same duties of independence, impartiality and availability as the members of the Committee.
3. A Party may exceptionally declare that an expert or other person assisting the Committee may not be allowed to take part in a visit to a place within its jurisdiction.

Chapter IV

Art. 15. Each Party shall inform the Committee of the name and address of the authority competent to receive notifications to its Government, and of any liaison officer it may appoint.

Art. 16. The Committee, its members and experts referred to in Article 7, paragraph 2 shall enjoy the privileges and immunities set out in the Annex to this Convention.

Art. 17.
1. This Convention shall not prejudice the provisions of domestic law or any international agreement which provide greater protection for persons deprived of their liberty.
2. Nothing in this Convention shall be construed as limiting or derogating from the competence of the organs of the European Convention on Human Rights or from the obligations assumed by the Parties under that Convention.
3. The Committee shall not visit places which representatives or delegates of Protecting Powers or the International Committee of the Red Cross effectively visit on a regular basis by virtue of the Geneva Conventions of 12 August 1949 and the Additional Protocols of 8 June 1977 thereto.

Chapter V

Art. 18.
1. This Convention shall be open for signature by the member States of the Council of Europe. It is subject to ratification, acceptance or approval.

[4] Article 12 as amended by Protocol II of 4 November 1993, in force since 1 March 2002.

Instruments of ratification, acceptance or approval shall be deposited with the Secretary General of the Council of Europe.

2.[5] The Committee of Ministers of the Council of Europe may invite any non-member State of the Council or Europe to accede to the Convention.

Art. 19.

1. This Convention shall enter into force on the first day of the month following the expiration of a period of three months after the date on which seven member States of the Council of Europe have expressed their consent to be bound by the Convention in accordance with the provisions of Article 18.

2.[6] In respect of any State which subsequently expresses its consent to be bound by it, the Convention shall enter into force on the first day of the month following the expiration of a period of three months after the date of the deposit of the instrument of ratification, acceptance, approval or accession.

Art. 20.

1.[7] Any State may at the time of signature or when depositing its instrument of ratification, acceptance, approval or accession, specify the territory or territories to which this Convention shall apply.

2. Any State may at any later date, by a declaration addressed to the Secretary General of the Council of Europe, extend the application of this Convention to any other territory specified in the declaration. In respect of such territory the Convention shall enter into force on the first day of the month following the expiration of a period of three months after the date of receipt of such declaration by the Secretary General.

3. Any declaration made under the two preceding paragraphs may, in respect of any territory specified in such declaration, be withdrawn by a notification addressed to the Secretary General. The withdrawal shall become effective on the first day of the month following the expiration of a period of three months after the date of receipt of such notification by the Secretary General.

Art. 21. No reservation may be made in respect of the provisions of this Convention.

Art. 22.

1. Any Party may, at any time, denounce this Convention by means of a notification addressed to the Secretary General of the Council of Europe.
2. Such denunciation shall become effective on the first day of the month following the expiration of a period of twelve months after the date of receipt of the notification by the Secretary General.

Art. 23.[8] The Secretary General of the Council of Europe shall notify the member States and any non-member State of the Council of Europe party to the Convention of:

[5] Paragraph 2 added by Protocol I of 4 November 1993, in force since 1 March 2002.
[6] Paragraph 2 added by Protocol I of 4 November 1993, in force since 1 March 2002.
[7] Paragraph 1 as amended by Protocol I of 4 November 1993, in force since 1 March 2002.
[8] Article 23 as amended by Protocol I of 4 November 1993, in force since 1 March 2002.

(a) any signature;
(b) the deposit of any instrument of ratification, acceptance, approval or accession;
(c) any date of entry into force of this Convention in accordance with Articles 19 and 20;
(d) any other act, notification or communication relating to this Convention, except for action taken in pursuance of Articles 8 and 10.

In witness whereof, the undersigned, being duly authorised thereto, have signed this Convention.

Done at Strasbourg, the 26 November 1987, in English and French, both texts being equally authentic, in a single copy which shall be deposited in the archives of the Council of Europe. The Secretary General of the Council of Europe shall transmit certified copies to each member State of the Council of Europe.

ANNEX

Privileges and immunities (Article 16)

1. For the purpose of this annex, references to members of the Committee shall be deemed to include references to experts mentioned in Article 7, paragraph 2.
2. The members of the Committee shall, while exercising their functions and during journeys made in the exercise of their functions, enjoy the following privileges and immunities:
   (a) immunity from personal arrest or detention and from seizure of their personal baggage and, in respect of words spoken or written and all acts done by them in their official capacity, immunity from legal process of every kind;[9]
   (b) exemption from any restrictions on their freedom of movement on exit from and return to their country of residence, and entry into and exit from the country in which they exercise their functions, and from alien registration in the country which they are visiting or through which they are passing in the exercise of their functions.
3. In the course of journeys undertaken in the exercise of their functions, the members of the Committee shall, in the matter of customs and exchange control, be accorded:
   (a) by their own Government, the same facilities as those accorded to senior officials travelling abroad on temporary official duty;
   (b) by the Governments of other Parties, the same facilities as those accorded to representatives of foreign Governments on temporary official duty.
4. Documents and papers of the Committee, in so far as they relate to the business of the Committee, shall be inviolable. The official correspondence and other official communications of the Committee may not be held up or subjected to censorship.

[9] For declaration in respect of this provision by Italy, see p. 953.

5. In order to secure for the members of the Committee complete freedom of speech and complete independence in the discharge of their duties, the immunity from legal process in respect of words spoken or written and all acts done by them in discharging their duties shall continue to be accorded, notwithstanding that the persons concerned are no longer engaged in the discharge of such duties.
6. Privileges and immunities are accorded to the members of the Committee, not for the personal benefit of the individuals themselves but in order to safeguard the independent exercise of their functions. The Committee alone shall be competent to waive the immunity of its members; it has not only the right, but is under a duty, to waive the immunity of one of its members in any case where, in its opinion, the immunity would impede the course of justice, and where it can be waived without prejudice to the purpose for which the immunity is accorded.

SIGNATURES, RATIFICATIONS AND ACCESSIONS TO THE EUROPEAN CONVENTION[1]

State	*Signature*	*Ratification, Accession*
Albania	2 October 1996	2 October 1996
Andorra	10 September 1996	6 January 1997
Armenia	11 May 2001	18 June 2002
Austria	26 November 1987	6 January 1989
Azerbaijan	21 December 2001	15 April 2002
Belgium	26 November 1987	23 July 1991
Bosnia and Herzegovina	12 July 2002	12 July 2002
Bulgaria	30 September 1993	3 May 1994
Croatia	6 November 1996	11 October 1997
Cyprus	26 November 1987	3 April 1989
Czech Republic	23 December 1992[2]	7 September 1995
Denmark	26 November 1987	2 May 1989
Estonia	28 June 1996	6 November 1996
Finland	16 November 1989	20 December 1990
France	26 November 1987	9 January 1989
Georgia	16 February 2000	20 June 2000 *Dec.*
Germany	26 November 1987	21 February 1990
Greece	26 November 1987	2 August 1991
Hungary	9 February 1993	4 November 1993
Iceland	26 November 1987	19 June 1990
Ireland	14 March 1988	14 March 1988
Italy	26 November 1987	29 December 1988 *Dec.*
Latvia	11 September 1997	10 February 1998
Liechtenstein	26 November 1987	12 September 1991
Lithuania	14 September 1995	26 November 1998 *Dec.*
Luxembourg	26 November 1987	6 September 1988
Macedonia, the former Yugoslav Republic of	14 June 1996	6 June 1997
Malta	26 November 1987	7 March 1988

[1] Based on the communication received from the Council of Europe and the Council of Europe website: http://conventions.coe.int.

[2] Date of signature by Czech and Slovak Federal Republic.

State	*Signature*	*Ratification, Accession*
Moldova	2 May 1996	2 October 1997
Netherlands	26 November 1987	12 October 1988 *Dec.*
Norway	26 November 1987	21 April 1989
Poland	11 July 1994	10 October 1994
Portugal	26 November 1987	29 March 1990
Romania	4 November 1993	4 October 1994
Russia	28 February 1996	5 May 1998
San Marino	16 November 1989	31 January 1990
Slovakia	23 December 1992[3]	11 May 1994
Slovenia	4 November 1993	2 February 1994
Spain	26 November 1987	2 May 1989
Sweden	26 November 1987	21 June 1988
Switzerland	26 November 1987	7 October 1988
Turkey	11 January 1988	26 February 1988
Ukraine	2 May 1996	5 May 1997
United Kingdom	26 November 1987	24 June 1988

RESERVATIONS AND DECLARATIONS

AZERBAIJAN (*declaration made at the time of ratification*)
The Republic of Azerbaijan declares that it is unable to guarantee the application of the provisions of the Convention in the territories occupied by the Republic of Armenia until these territories are liberated from that occupation (the schematic map of the occupied territories of the Republic of Azerbaijan is enclosed).

GEORGIA (*declaration made at the time of ratification*)
Georgia declares that it will not be responsible for violations of the provisions of the Convention and the safety of the members of the European Committee for the Prevention of Torture and Inhuman or Degrading Treatment or Punishment on the territories of Abkhazia and the Tskhinval region until the territorial integrity of Georgia is restored and full and effective control over these territories is exercised by the legitimate authorities.

GERMANY (*declaration made at the time of ratification*)
In connection with the deposit today of the instrument of ratification to the Convention for the Prevention of Torture and Inhuman or Degrading Treatment or Punishment of 26 November 1987, I have the honour to declare on behalf of the Government of the Federal Republic of Germany that the said Convention shall apply to Land Berlin with effect from the date on which it enters into force for the Federal Republic of Germany.

ITALY (*declaration contained in a letter from the Permanent Representative of Italy, dated 30 January 1989*)
The Italian government declares that paragraph 2(a) of the Annex on Privileges and Immunities should not be interpreted as excluding any police or customs check of the luggage of the members of the Committee, provided the check is carried out in compliance with the rules on confidentiality set forth in Article 11 of the Convention.

Explanatory note
In its explanatory report to the Senate of the Republic, dated 4 July 1988, on the ratification of the Convention, the Italian Government had indicated that "at the time of

[3] Date of signature by Czech and Slovak Federal Republic.

deposit of the instrument of ratification, [the Government] shall make a declaration of interpretation of paragraph 2(a) of the Annex on Privileges and Immunities, under which the said paragraph 2(a) should not be interpreted as excluding any police or customs check of the luggage of the members of the Committee, provided the check is carried out in compliance with the rules of confidentiality set forth in Article 11 of the Convention.

Due to an omission, the declaration was not made to the Secretary General, depository of the treaty, upon deposit of the instrument of ratification on 29 December 1988.

The Government of Italy corrects today this clerical mistake by forwarding to the Secretary General the text of the above mentioned declaration, to take effect at the date of entry into force of the Convention in respect of Italy.

NETHERLANDS (*declaration contained in the instrument of acceptance*)
The Kingdom of the Netherlands accepts the said Convention with Annex for the Kingdom in Europe, the Netherlands Antilles and Aruba.

UNITED KINGDOM
Declaration at the time of ratification
The convention is ratified in respect of the United Kingdom of Great Britain and Northern Ireland, the Bailiwick of Jersey and the Isle of Man.

Declarations contained in letter of Permanent Representative of the United Kingdom dated 2 September 1988 and 7 November 1994
In accordance with Article 20(2) of the European Convention for the Prevention of Torture and Inhuman or Degrading Treatment of Punishment the Government of the United Kingdom extend the application of the Convention to Gibraltar.

In accordance with Article 20(2), the Government of the United Kingdom extend the application of the Convention to the Bailiwick of Guernsey.

No. 67

CONVENTION ON THE RIGHTS OF THE CHILD

Adopted by resolution 44/25 of the United Nations General Assembly, 20 November 1989

I. CONVENTION (ARTICLES 38 AND 39, RELATING TO ARMED CONFLICTS)

II. OPTIONAL PROTOCOL TO THE CONVENTION ON THE RIGHTS OF THE CHILD ON THE INVOLVEMENT OF CHILDREN IN ARMED CONFLICT

Adopted by resolution 54/263 of the United Nations General Assembly, 25 May 2000

INTRODUCTORY NOTE:

Convention: The physical and mental vulnerability and fragility of children require special protection and care. The necessity of this protection had already been expressed in the 1924 Geneva Declaration on the Rights of the Child, adopted by the League of Nations. In 1959, the United Nations General Assembly proclaimed the Declaration of the Rights of the Child (resolution 1386 (XIV) of 20 November 1959), containing ten principles aimed at the goal of assuring respect for the rights and liberties of children. In 1974, the Declaration on the Protection of Women and Children in Emergency and Armed Conflict was adopted (Resolution 3318 (XXIX), 14 December 1974 (*No. 35*).

On 21 December 1976, the United Nations General Assembly declared 1979 to be the International Year of the Child in commemoration of the Twentieth Anniversary of the Declaration of the Rights of the Child, proclaimed by it on 20 November 1959 (resolution 1386 (XIV)). In the course of the preparations for this commemoration the Polish government proposed that a draft Convention on the rights of the child be drawn up. The first draft was presented to the Commission on Human Rights in 1978 and was followed by an amended version on 5 October 1979. The Commission on Human Rights continued examination of this issue from its 35th (1979) to 42nd (1986) sessions. An open-ended working group was created in 1979. The group met each year for one week preceding the sessions of the Commission on Human Rights to accelerate drafting of the new Convention.

The Convention was adopted on 20 November 1989 by General Assembly Resolution 44/25. It puts forth all the fundamental rights of the child, whether civil, political, economic, social or cultural. Article 38 and, in part, Article 39, make provision for children in situations of armed conflict. They are the only ones reproduced below.

Article 43 provides for the creation of a Committee on the rights of the child, consisting of ten experts, to follow the progress made by States Parties in fulfilling the obligations undertaken by virtue of the Convention.

Optional Protocol: According to Article 38 of the Convention states have to ensure that children under 15 do not take a direct part in hostilities and have to refrain from recruiting those under 15 and give priority to the oldest among those under 18. This provision has been subject to considerable criticism, because all other provisions protect the child until it has reached the age of 18. A number of states have for several years sought to develop an Optional Protocol to the Convention that would raise the minimum age for participation in hostilities and for recruitment to 18 years. The United Nations Working group established to draft the Optional Protocol worked by consensus, which was not possible to reach because of the opposition tot he adoption of the 18-years minimum age. To overcome the stalemate, several NGOs started a campaign aimed at generating enough political pressure to have the Optional Protocol developed outside the United Nations Working Group. After several regional conferences, in January 2000, the United Nations Working Group finally met for substantive negotiations, reached the compromise with the states which were previously opposed to consensus and successfully concluded the drafting of an agreed text, which was adopted by the United Nations General Assembly in May 2000 and was open for signature and ratification.

ENTRY INTO FORCE:
Convention: 2 September 1990.
Optional Protocol: 12 February 2002.

AUTHENTIC TEXTS: Arabic, Chinese, English, French, Russian, Spanish. The text of Articles 38 and 39 below is reproduced from a copy of the original Convention which was transmitted to us from the Treaty Section of the United Nations. The text of the Optional Protocol is reproduced from General Assembly resolution A/RES/54/263.

TEXT PUBLISHED IN:
Convention: United Nations General Assembly Resolution 44725, Annex; *Resolutions and decisions adopted by the general Assembly during its forty-forth Session,* Vol. I, *September 19–December 29, 1989,* Official Records of the General Assembly, Forty-fourth Session, Supplement no. 49 (A/44/49), New York, United Nations, pp. 166–173 (Engl. – see also French, Chinese, Russian and Spanish editions); *UNTS*, Vol. 1577, p.3; *GBTS,* Cmnd. 4421 (English); *Human Rights – A Compilation of International Instruments,* Vol. I (First part), New York, United Nations, 1993, pp. 174–195 (Engl.); *ILM*, Vol. 28, November 1989, pp. 1448–1476 (Engl.); *Derechos Humanos*, pp. 311–340 (Span.); *Droit des conflits armés*, pp. 1023–1032 (French). UN website: http://untreaty.un.org; http://www.unicef.org/ crc/ crc.htm (Engl., French, Span.); ICRC website: www.icrc.org/ihl.nsf (Engl., French, Span.); University of Minnesota website: www.umn.edu/humanrts/ instree/ k2crc.htm (Arabic, Engl., French, Japanese, Russ., Span.). Other website: www. unicefusa.org/ infoactiv/ text.htm (Engl.); www.ngos.net/ childsrights/text.html (Engl.).
Optional Protocol: United Nations General Assembly resolution A/RES/ 54/263 (Arabic, Chinese, Engl., French, Russ. and Span.). *ILM*, Vol. 39, November 2000, pp. 1286–1290; UN website: http://untreaty.un.org; http:// www.unicef.org/crc/crc/htm (Engl., French, Span.); ICRC website: www.icrc. org/ihl.nsf (Engl., French, Span.).

* * *

I. CONVENTION ON THE RIGHTS OF THE CHILD (ARTICLES 38 AND 39 RELATING TO ARMED CONFLICTS)

Article 38.[1]

1. States Parties undertake to respect and to ensure respect for rules of international humanitarian law applicable to them in armed conflicts which are relevant to the child.
2.[2] States Parties shall take all feasible measures to ensure that persons who have not attained the age of fifteen years do not take a direct part in hostilities.
3.[3] States Parties shall refrain from recruiting any person who has not attained the age of fifteen years into their armed forces. In recruiting among those persons who have attained the age of fifteen years but who have not attained the age of eighteen years, States Parties shall endeavour to give priority to those who are oldest.
4. In accordance with their obligations under international humanitarian law to protect the civilian population in armed conflicts, States Parties shall take all feasible measures to ensure protection and care of children who are affected by an armed conflict.

Article 39.

States Parties shall take all appropriate measures to promote physical and psychological recovery and social reintegration of a child victim of: any form of neglect, exploitation, or abuse; torture or any other form of cruel, inhuman or degrading treatment or punishment; or armed conflicts. Such recovery and reintegration shall take place in an environment which fosters the health, self-respect and dignity of the child.

II. OPTIONAL PROTOCOL TO THE CONVENTION ON THE RIGHTS OF THE CHILD ON THE INVOLVEMENT OF CHILDREN IN ARMED CONFLICT

The States Parties to the present Protocol,

Encouraged by the overwhelming support for the Convention on the Rights of the Child, demonstrating the widespread commitment that exists to strive for the promotion and protection of the rights of the child,

Reaffirming that the rights of children require special protection, and calling for continuous improvement of the situation of children without distinction, as well as for their development and education in conditions of peace and security,

Disturbed by the harmful and widespread impact of armed conflict on children and the long-term consequences it has for durable peace, security and development,

---

[1] For reservations by Colombia, Netherlands and Poland and the declaration by Ecuador, in respect of this article, see pp. 969–970.

[2] For declarations by Andorra, Argentina, Austria, Germany, Spain and the reservations of Colombia and Uruguay in respect of this paragraph, see p. 969–970.

[3] For reservations by Colombia, Uruguay and declaration of Spain in respect of this paragraph, see pp. 969–970.

Condemning the targeting of children in situations of armed conflict and direct attacks on objects protected under international law, including places that generally have a significant presence of children, such as schools and hospitals,

Noting the adoption of the Rome Statute of the International Criminal Court, in particular, the inclusion therein as a war crime, of conscripting or enlisting children under the age of 15 years or using them to participate actively in hostilities in both international and non-international armed conflicts,

Considering therefore that to strengthen further the implementation of rights recognized in the Convention on the Rights of the Child there is a need to increase the protection of children from involvement in armed conflict,

Noting that article 1 of the Convention on the Rights of the Child specifies that, for the purposes of that Convention, a child means every human being below the age of 18 years unless, under the law applicable to the child, majority is attained earlier,

Convinced that an optional protocol to the Convention that raises the age of possible recruitment of persons into armed forces and their participation in hostilities will contribute effectively to the implementation of the principle that the best interests of the child are to be a primary consideration in all actions concerning children,

Noting that the twenty-sixth International Conference of the Red Cross and Red Crescent in December 1995 recommended, *inter alia*, that parties to conflict take every feasible step to ensure that children below the age of 18 years do not take part in hostilities,

Welcoming the unanimous adoption, in June 1999, of International Labour Organization Convention No. 182 on the Prohibition and Immediate Action for the Elimination of the Worst Forms of Child Labour, which prohibits, *inter alia*, forced or compulsory recruitment of children for use in armed conflict,

Condemning with the gravest concern the recruitment, training and use within and across national borders of children in hostilities by armed groups distinct from the armed forces of a State, and recognizing the responsibility of those who recruit, train and use children in this regard,

Recalling the obligation of each party to an armed conflict to abide by the provisions of international humanitarian law,

Stressing that the present Protocol is without prejudice to the purposes and principles contained in the Charter of the United Nations, including Article 51, and relevant norms of humanitarian law,

Bearing in mind that conditions of peace and security based on full respect of the purposes and principles contained in the Charter and observance of applicable human rights instruments are indispensable for the full protection of children, in particular during armed conflicts and foreign occupation,

Recognizing the special needs of those children who are particularly vulnerable to recruitment or use in hostilities contrary to the present Protocol owing to their economic or social status or gender,

Mindful of the necessity of taking into consideration the economic, social and political root causes of the involvement of children in armed conflicts,

Convinced of the need to strengthen international cooperation in the implementation of the present Protocol, as well as the physical and psychosocial rehabilitation and social reintegration of children who are victims of armed conflict,

Encouraging the participation of the community and, in particular, children and child victims in the dissemination of informational and educational programmes concerning the implementation of the Protocol,

Have agreed as follows:

Article 1. States Parties shall take all feasible measures to ensure that members of their armed forces who have not attained the age of 18 years do not take a direct part in hostilities.

Art. 2. States Parties shall ensure that persons who have not attained the age of 18 years are not compulsorily recruited into their armed forces.

Art. 3.

1. States Parties shall raise the minimum age for the voluntary recruitment of persons into their national armed forces from that set out in article 38, paragraph 3, of the Convention on the Rights of the Child, taking account of the principles contained in that article and recognizing that under the Convention persons under the age of 18 years are entitled to special protection.
2. Each State Party shall deposit a binding declaration upon ratification of or accession to the present Protocol that sets forth the minimum age at which it will permit voluntary recruitment into its national armed forces and a description of the safeguards it has adopted to ensure that such recruitment is not forced or coerced.
3. States Parties that permit voluntary recruitment into their national armed forces under the age of 18 years shall maintain safeguards to ensure, as a minimum, that:
   (a) Such recruitment is genuinely voluntary;
   (b) Such recruitment is carried out with the informed consent of the person's parents or legal guardians;
   (c) Such persons are fully informed of the duties involved in such military service;
   (d) Such persons provide reliable proof of age prior to acceptance into national military service.
4. Each State Party may strengthen its declaration at any time by notification to that effect addressed to the Secretary-General of the United Nations, who shall inform all States Parties. Such notification shall take effect on the date on which it is received by the Secretary-General.
5. The requirement to raise the age in paragraph 1 of the present article does not apply to schools operated by or under the control of the armed forces of the States Parties, in keeping with articles 28 and 29 of the Convention on the Rights of the Child.

Art. 4.

1. Armed groups that are distinct from the armed forces of a State should not, under any circumstances, recruit or use in hostilities persons under the age of 18 years.
2. States Parties shall take all feasible measures to prevent such recruitment and use, including the adoption of legal measures necessary to prohibit and criminalize such practices.
3. The application of the present article shall not affect the legal status of any party to an armed conflict.

Art. 5. Nothing in the present Protocol shall be construed as precluding provisions in the law of a State Party or in international instruments and international humanitarian law that are more conducive to the realization of the rights of the child.

Art. 6.

1. Each State Party shall take all necessary legal, administrative and other measures to ensure the effective implementation and enforcement of the provisions of the present Protocol within its jurisdiction.
2. States Parties undertake to make the principles and provisions of the present Protocol widely known and promoted by appropriate means, to adults and children alike.
3. States Parties shall take all feasible measures to ensure that persons within their jurisdiction recruited or used in hostilities contrary to the present Protocol are demobilized or otherwise released from service. States Parties shall, when necessary, accord to such persons all appropriate assistance for their physical and psychological recovery and their social reintegration.

Art. 7.

1. States Parties shall cooperate in the implementation of the present Protocol, including in the prevention of any activity contrary thereto and in the rehabilitation and social reintegration of persons who are victims of acts contrary thereto, including through technical cooperation and financial assistance. Such assistance and cooperation will be undertaken in consultation with the States Parties concerned and the relevant international organizations.
2. States Parties in a position to do so shall provide such assistance through existing multilateral, bilateral or other programmes or, *inter alia*, through a voluntary fund established in accordance with the rules of the General Assembly.

Art. 8.

1. Each State Party shall, within two years following the entry into force of the present Protocol for that State Party, submit a report to the Committee on the Rights of the Child providing comprehensive information on the measures it has taken to implement the provisions of the Protocol, including the measures taken to implement the provisions on participation and recruitment.
2. Following the submission of the comprehensive report, each State Party shall include in the reports it submits to the Committee on the Rights of the Child, in accordance with article 44 of the Convention, any further information with respect to the implementation of the Protocol. Other States Parties to the Protocol shall submit a report every five years.
3. The Committee on the Rights of the Child may request from States Parties further information relevant to the implementation of the present Protocol.

Art. 9.

1. The present Protocol is open for signature by any State that is a party to the Convention or has signed it.
2. The present Protocol is subject to ratification and is open to accession by any State. Instruments of ratification or accession shall be deposited with the Secretary-General of the United Nations.
3. The Secretary-General, in his capacity as depositary of the Convention and the Protocol, shall inform all States Parties to the Convention and all States

that have signed the Convention of each instrument of declaration pursuant to article 3.

Art. 10.

1. The present Protocol shall enter into force three months after the deposit of the tenth instrument of ratification or accession.
2. For each State ratifying the present Protocol or acceding to it after its entry into force, the Protocol shall enter into force one month after the date of the deposit of its own instrument of ratification or accession.

Art. 11.

1. Any State Party may denounce the present Protocol at any time by written notification to the Secretary-General of the United Nations, who shall thereafter inform the other States Parties to the Convention and all States that have signed the Convention. The denunciation shall take effect one year after the date of receipt of the notification by the Secretary-General. If, however, on the expiry of that year the denouncing State Party is engaged in armed conflict, the denunciation shall not take effect before the end of the armed conflict.
2. Such a denunciation shall not have the effect of releasing the State Party from its obligations under the present Protocol in regard to any act that occurs prior to the date on which the denunciation becomes effective. Nor shall such a denunciation prejudice in any way the continued consideration of any matter that is already under consideration by the Committee on the Rights of the Child prior to the date on which the denunciation becomes effective.

Art. 12.

1. Any State Party may propose an amendment and file it with the Secretary-General of the United Nations. The Secretary-General shall thereupon communicate the proposed amendment to States Parties with a request that they indicate whether they favour a conference of States Parties for the purpose of considering and voting upon the proposals. In the event that, within four months from the date of such communication, at least one third of the States Parties favour such a conference, the Secretary-General shall convene the conference under the auspices of the United Nations. Any amendment adopted by a majority of States Parties present and voting at the conference shall be submitted to the General Assembly of the United Nations for approval.
2. An amendment adopted in accordance with paragraph 1 of the present article shall enter into force when it has been approved by the General Assembly and accepted by a two-thirds majority of States Parties.
3. When an amendment enters into force, it shall be binding on those States Parties that have accepted it, other States Parties still being bound by the provisions of the present Protocol and any earlier amendments they have accepted.

Art. 13.

1. The present Protocol, of which the Arabic, Chinese, English, French, Russian and Spanish texts are equally authentic, shall be deposited in the archives of the United Nations.

2. The Secretary-General of the United Nations shall transmit certified copies of the present Protocol to all States Parties to the Convention and all States that have signed the Convention.

SIGNATURES, RATIFICATIONS, ACCESSIONS AND NOTIFICATIONS OF SUCCESSION OR CONTINUITY TO THE CONVENTION[1]

State	*Signatures*	*Ratifications, Accessions, Notifications of Succession or Continuity (C)*
Afghanistan	27 September 1990	28 March 1994
Albania	26 January 1990	27 February 1992
Algeria	26 January 1990	16 April 1993
Andorra	2 October 1995	2 January 1996 *Dec.*
Angola	14 February 1990	5 December 1990
Antigua and Barbuda	12 March 1991	5 October 1993
Argentina	29 June 1990 Dec.	4 December 1990 *Dec.*
Armenia	–	23 June 1993
Australia	22 August 1990	17 December 1990
Austria	26 January 1990	6 August 1992
Azerbaijan	–	13 August 1992
Bahamas	30 October 1990	20 February 1991
Bahrain	–	13 February 1992
Bangladesh	26 January 1990	3 August 1990
Barbados	19 April 1990	9 October 1990
Belarus	26 January 1990	1 October 1990
Belgium	26 January 1990	16 December 1991
Belize	2 March 1990	2 May 1990
Benin	25 April 1990	3 August 1990
Bhutan	4 June 1990 `	1 August 1990
Bolivia	8 March 1990	26 June 1990
Bosnia and Herzegovina	–	1 September 1993 (C)
Botswana	–	14 March 1995
Brazil	26 January 1990	24 September 1990
Brunei Darussalam	–	27 December 1995
Bulgaria	31 May 1990	3 June 1991
Burkina Faso	26 January 1990	31 August 1990
Burundi	8 May 1990	19 October 1990
Cambodia	–	15 October 1992
Cameroon	25 September 1990	11 January 1993
Canada	28 May 1990	13 December 1991
Cape Verde	–	4 June 1992
Central African Republic	30 July 1990	23 April 1992
Chad	30 September 1990	2 October 1990
Chile	26 January 1990	13 August 1990
China[2]	29 August 1990	2 March 1992

[1] Based on the indications in *Multilateral Treaties Deposited with the Secretary-General, New York, United Nations*, (ST/LEG/SER.E) as available on http://untreaty.un.org, of 31 December 2002. The indications "*Res.*" or "*Dec.*" refers only to reservations and declarations concerning Articles 38 and 39.

[2] On 10 June 1997, the Government of China and the United Kingdom of Great Britain and Northern Ireland notified the Secretary-General of the following:

In accordance with the Declaration of the Government of the People's Republic of China and the United Kingdom of Great Britain and Northern Ireland on the question of Hong Kong signed on 19 December 1984, the People's Republic of China will resume the exercise

State	*Signatures*	*Ratifications, Accessions, Notifications of Succession or Continuity (C)*
Colombia	26 January 1990 Res.	28 January 1991 Res.
Comoros	30 September 1990	22 June 1993
Congo	–	14 October 1993
Cook Islands	–	6 June 1997
Costa Rica	26 January 1990	21 August 1990
Côte d'Ivoire	26 January 1990	4 February 1991
Croatia	–	12 October 1992 (C)
Cuba	26 January 1990	21 August 1991
Cyprus	5 October 1990	7 February 1991
Czech Republic[3]	–	22 February 1993 (C)
Democratic People's Republic of Korea	23 August 1990	21 September 1990
Democratic Republic of the Congo	20 March 1990	27 September 1990
Denmark	26 January 1990	19 July 1991
Djibouti	30 September 1990	6 December 1990
Dominica	26 January 1990	13 March 1991
Dominican Republic	8 August 1990	11 June 1991
Ecuador	26 January 1990 *Dec.*	23 March 1990
Egypt	5 February 1990	6 July 1990
El Salvador	26 January 1990	10 July 1990
Equatorial Guinea	–	15 June 1992
Eritrea	20 December 1993	3 August 1994
Estonia	–	21 October 1991
Ethiopia	–	14 May 1991
Fiji	2 July 1993	13 August 1993
Finland	26 January 1990	20 June 1991
France	26 January 1990	7 August 1990
Gabon	26 January 1990	9 February 1994
Gambia	5 February 1990	8 August 1990
Georgia	–	2 June 1994
Germany[4]	26 January 1990	6 March 1992

cont.

of sovereignty over Hong Kong wiht effect from 1 July 1997. Hong Kong will, with effect from that date, become a Special Administrative Region of the People's Republic of China and will enjoy a high degree of autonomy, except in foreign and defence affairs which are the responsibility of the Central People's Government of the People's Republic of China.

The Convention, which the Government of the People's Republic of China ratified on 2 March 1992, will apply to the Hong Kong Special Administrative Region with effect from 1 July 1997. The Government of the People's Republic of China will assume responsibility for the international rights and obligations arising from the application of the Convention to Hong Kong Special Administrative Region.

In addition, the notification made by the Government of the People's Republic of China contained a declaration relating to the provisions of the Convention, but it does not refer to article 38 and 39.

3 Czechoslovakia had signed and ratified the Convention on 30 September 1990 and 7 January 1991, respectively, with a declaration in respect of Article 7(1).

In a letter dated 16 February 1993, received by the Secretary-General on 22 February 1993 and accompanied by a list of multilateral treaties deposited with the Secretary-General, the Government of the Czech Republic gave a notification with a text identical with that reproduced above at p. 909, note 8, paras 4–11 (from "in conformity with" until "the heading 'Participant'".

4 The German Democratic Republic had signed and ratified the Convention on 7 March 1990 and 2 October 1990, respectively.

State	*Signatures*	*Ratifications, Accessions, Notifications of Succession or Continuity (C)*
Ghana	29 January 1990	5 February 1990
Greece	26 January 1990	11 May 1993
Grenada	21 February 1990	5 November 1990
Guatemala	26 January 1990	6 June 1990
Guinea	–	13 July 1990
Guinea-Bissau	26 January 1990	20 August 1990
Guyana	30 September 1990	14 January 1991
Haiti	26 January 1990	8 June 1995
Holy See	20 April 1990	20 April 1990
Honduras	31 May 1990	10 August 1990
Hungary	14 March 1990	7 October 1991
Iceland	26 January 1990	28 October 1992
India	–	11 December 1992
Indonesia	26 January 1990	5 September 1990
Iran (Islamic Republic of)	5 September 1991	13 July 1994
Iraq	–	15 June 1994
Ireland	30 September 1990	28 September 1992
Israel	3 July 1990	3 October 1991
Italy	26 January 1990	5 September 1991
Jamaica	26 January 1990	14 May 1991
Japan	21 September 1990	22 April 1994
Jordan	29 August 1990	24 May 1991
Kazakhstan	16 February 1994	12 August 1994
Kenya	26 January 1990	30 July 1990
Kiribati	–	11 December 1995
Kuwait	7 June 1990	21 October 1991

---

cont.

In a communication dated 3 October 1990, the Federal Minister for Foreign Affairs of the Federal Republic of Germany notified the Secretary-General of the following:

"Through the accession of the German Democratic Republic to the Federal Republic of Germany with effect from 3 October 1990, the two German States have united to form one sovereign State, which as a single Member of the United Nations remains bound by the provisions of the Charter in accordance with the solemn declaration of 12 June 1973. As from the date of unification, the Federal Republic of Germany will act in the United Nations under the designation `Germany'."

Consequently, and in the light of articles 11 and 12 of the Treaty of 31 August 1990 (Unification Treaty) between the Federal Republic of Germany and the German Democratic Republic, entries in status lists pertaining to formalities (i.e. signatures, ratifications, accessions, declarations and reservations, etc.) effected by the Federal Republic of Germany will now appear under "Germany" and indicate the dates of such formalities.

As regards treaties in respect of which formalities had been effected by both the Federal Republic of Germany and the former German Democratic Republic prior to unification, the entry will similarly indicate in the corresponding table the type of formality effected by the Federal Republic of Germany and the date on which it took place, while the type of formality effected by the former German Democratic Republic and the date thereof will appear in a footnote.

Finally, as regards the treatment of treaties in respect of which formalities were effected by the former German Democratic Republic alone, article 12, para. 3 of the Unification Treaty contains the following provision: "Should the united Germany intend to accede to international organizations or other multilateral treaties of which the German Democratic Republic but not the Federal Republic of Germany is a member, agreement shall be reached with the respective contracting parties and with the European Communities where the latter's competence is affected". Accordingly, a footnote indicating the date and type of formality effected by the former German Democratic Republic will be included in the status of the treaties concerned, the corresponding footnote indicator being inserted next to the heading "Participant".

State	*Signatures*	*Ratifications, Accessions, Notifications of Succession or Continuity (C)*
Kyrgyzstan	–	7 October 1994
Lao People's Democratic Republic	–	8 May 1991
Latvia	–	14 April 1992
Lebanon	26 January 1990	14 May 1991
Lesotho	21 August 1990	10 March 1992
Liberia	26 April 1990	4 June 1993
Libyan Arab Jamahiriya	–	15 April 1993
Liechtenstein	30 September 1990	22 December 1995
Lithuania	–	31 January 1992
Luxembourg	21 March 1990	7 March 1994
Madagascar	9 April 1990	19 March 1991
Macedonia, the former Yugoslav Republic of[5]	–	2 December 1993 (C)
Malawi	–	2 January 1991
Malaysia	–	17 February 1995
Maldives	21 August 1990	11 February 1991
Mali	26 January 1990	20 September 1990
Malta	26 January 1990	30 September 1990
Marshall Islands	14 April 1993	4 October 1993
Mauritania	26 January 1990	16 May 1991
Mauritius	–	26 July 1990
Mexico	26 January 1990	21 September 1990
Micronesia (Federated States of)	–	5 May 1993
Monaco	–	21 June 1993
Mongolia	26 January 1990	5 July 1990
Morocco	26 January 1990	21 June 1993
Mozambique	30 September 1990	26 April 1994
Myanmar	–	15 July 1991
Namibia	26 September 1990	30 September 1990
Nauru	–	27 July 1994
Nepal	26 January 1990	14 September 1990
Netherlands[6]	26 January 1990	6 February 1995 *Dec.*
New Zealand[7]	1 October 1990	6 April 1993

5 On 12 April 1994, the Secretary-General received from the Government of Greece the following communication: "Succession of the former Yugoslave Republic of Macedonia to the Convention on the Rights of the Child, adopted by the General Assembly of the United Nations on 20 November 1989, does not imply its recognition on behalf of the Hellenic Republic."

6 For the Kingdom in Europe. Subsequently, on 17 December 1997, the Government of the Netherlands informed the Secretary-General that it had decided to accept the Convention on behalf of the Netherlands Antilles subject to the following reservations and declarations: Reservations in respect of Articles 26, 37 and 40 and declarations in respect of Articles 14, 22 and 38. We reproduce only the declaration concerning Article 38: "With regard to article 38 of the Convention, the Government of the Kingdom of the Netherlands declares that it is of the opinion that States should not be allowed to involve children directly or indirectly in hostilities and that the minimum age for the recruitment or incorporation of children in the armed forces should be above fifteen years.

In times of armed conflict, provisions shall prevail that are most conducive to guaranteeing the protection of children under international law, as referred to in article 41 of the Convention."

7 The instrument of ratification also specifies that "such ratification shall extend to Tokelau only upon notification to the Secretary-General of the United Nations of such extension".

State	*Signatures*	*Ratifications, Accessions, Notifications of Succession or Continuity (C)*
Nicaragua	6 February 1990	5 October 1990
Niger	26 January 1990	30 September 1990
Nigeria	26 January 1990	19 April 1991
Niue	–	20 December 1995
Norway	26 January 1990	8 January 1991
Oman	–	9 December 1996
Pakistan	20 September 1990	12 November 1990
Palau	–	4 August 1995
Panama	26 January 1990	12 December 1990
Papua New Guinea	30 September 1990	2 March 1993
Paraguay	4 April 1990	25 September 1990
Peru	26 January 1990	4 September 1990
Philippines	26 January 1990	21 August 1990
Poland	26 January 1990	7 June 1991 *Res.*
Portugal[8]	26 January 1990	21 September 1990
Qatar	8 December 1992	3 April 1995
Republic of Korea	25 September 1990	20 November 1991
Republic of Moldova	–	26 January 1993
Romania	26 January 1990	28 September 1990
Russian Federation	26 January 1990	16 August 1990
Rwanda	26 January 1990	24 January 1991
Saint Kitts and Nevis	26 January 1990	24 July 1990
Saint Lucia	30 September 1990	16 June 1993
Saint Vincent and the Grenadines	20 September 1993	26 October 1993
Samoa	30 September 1990	29 November 1994
San Marino	–	25 November 1991
Sao Tome and Principe	–	14 May 1991
Saudi Arabia	–	26 January 1996
Senegal	26 January 1990	31 July 1990
Seychelles	–	7 September 1990
Sierra Leone	13 February 1990	18 June 1990
Singapore	–	5 October 1995
Slovakia[9]	–	28 May 1993 (C)
Slovenia	–	6 July 1992 (C)
Solomon Islands	–	10 April 1995
South Africa	29 January 1993	16 June 1995
Spain	26 January 1990	6 December 1990 *Dec.*
Sri Lanka	26 January 1990	12 July 1991
Sudan	24 July 1990	3 August 1990
Suriname	26 January 1990	1 March 1993

[8] On 27 April 1999, the Government of Portugal informed the Secretary-General that the Convention would apply to Macau. Subsequently, the Secretary-General received, on 21 October 1999, from the Government of Portugal, the following communication: "In accordance with the Joint Declaration of the Government of the Portuguese Republic and the Government of the People's Republic of China on the Question of Macau signed on 13 April 1987, the Portuguese Republic will continue to have international responsibility for Macau until 19 December 1999 and from that date onwards the People's Republic of China will resume the exercise of sovereignty over Macau with effect from 20 December 1999.

From 20 December 1999 onwards the Portuguese Republic will cease to be responsible for the international rights and obligations arising from the application of the Convention to Macau."

[9] See note 3.

State	*Signatures*	*Ratifications, Accessions, Notifications of Succession or Continuity (C)*
Swaziland	22 August 1990	7 September 1995
Sweden	26 January 1990	29 June 1990
Switzerland	1 May 1991	24 February 1997
Syrian Arab Republic	18 September 1990	15 July 1993
Tajikistan	–	26 October 1993
Thailand	–	27 March 1992
Togo	26 January 1990	1 August 1990
Tonga	–	6 November 1995
Trinidad and Tobago	30 September 1990	5 December 1991
Tunisia	26 February 1990	30 January 1992
Turkey	14 September 1990	4 April 1995
Turkmenistan	–	20 September 1993
Tuvalu	–	22 September 1995
Uganda	17 August 1990	17 August 1990
Ukraine	21 February 1990	28 August 1991
United Arab Emirates	–	3 January 1997
United Kingdom[10] [11]	19 April 1990	16 December 1991

[10] See note 2.

[11] In a communication received on 7 September 1994, the Government of the United Kingdom of Great Britain and Northern Ireland indicated that the Convention will apply to the Isle of Man, Anguilla, Bermuda, British Virgin Islands, Cayman Islands, Falkland Islands, Hong Kong (see also note 2 in this chapter), Montserrat, Pitcairn, Henderson, Ducie and Oeno Islands, St. Helena, St. Helena Dependencies, South Georgia and the South Sandwich Islands, Turks and Caicos Islands.

In this regard, the Secretary-General received, on 3 April 1995, from the Government of Argentina the following communication: "The Government of Argentina rejects the extension of the application of the [said Convention] to the Malvinas Islands, South Georgia and the South Sandwich Islands, effected by the United Kingdom of Great Britain and Northern Ireland on 7 September 1994, and reaffirms its sovereignty over those islands, which are an integral part of its national territory."

Subsequently, on 17 January 1996, the Secretary-General received from the Government of the United Kingdom of Great Britain and Northern Ireland the following communication:.

"The Government of the United Kingdom has no doubt about the sovereignty of the United Kingdom over the Falkland Islands and over South Georgia and the South Sandwich Islands and its consequential right to extend the said Convention to these Territories. The United Kingdom Government rejects as unfounded the claims by the Government of Argentina and is unable to regard the Argentine objection as having any legal effect."

Subsequently, on 5 October 2000, the Secretary-General received form the Government of Argentina the following communication:

[The Argentine Republic] wishes to refer to the report submitted by the United Kingdom of Great Britain and Northern Ireland to the Committee on the rights of the Child, which contains an addendum entitled "Overseas Dependent Territories and Crown Dependencies of the United Kingdom of Great Britain and Northern Ireland" (CRC/C/41/Add.9).

In that connection, the Argentine Republic wishes to recall that by its note of 3 April 1995 it rejected the extension of the application of the Convention on the rights of the Child to the Malvinas Islands, South Georgia and the South Sandwich Islands, effected by the United Kingdom of Great Britain and Northern Ireland on 7 September 1994.

The Government of Argentina rejects the designation of the Malvinas Islands as Overseas Dependent Territories of the United Kingdom or any other similar designation.

Consequently, the Argentine Republic does not recognize the section concerning the Malvinas Islands contained in the report which the United Kingdom has submitted to the Committee on the rights of the Child (CRC/C/41/Add.9) or any other document or instrument having a similar tenor that may derive from this alleged territorial expansion.

The United Nations General Assembly has adopted resolutions 2065 (XX), 3160 (XXVIII), 31/49, 37/9, 38/12, 39/16, 40/21, 41/40, 42/19 and 43/25, in which it recognizes that a dispute exists concerning sovereignty over the Malvinas Islands and urges the Argentine

State	*Signatures*	*Ratifications, Accessions, Notifications of Succession or Continuity (C)*
United Republic of Tanzania	1 June 1990	10 June 1991
United States of America	16 February 1995	–
Uruguay	26 January 1990	20 November 1990
Uzbekistan	–	29 June 1994
Vanuatu	30 September 1990	7 July 1993
Venezuela	26 January 1990	13 September 1990
Viet Nam	26 January 1990	28 February 1990
Yemen[12]	13 February 1990	1 May 1991
Yugoslavia	–	12 March 2001[13]
Zambia	30 September 1990	6 December 1991
Zimbabwe	8 March 1990	11 September 1990

cont.

Republic and the United Kingdom of Great Britain and Northern Ireland to continue negotiations with a view to resolving the dispute peacefully and definitively as soon as possible, assisted by the good offices of the Secretary-General of the United Nations, who is to report to the General Assembly on the progress made.

The Argentine Republic reaffirms its rights of sovereignty over the Malvinas Islands, South Georgia and the South Sandwich Islands and the surrounding maritime spaces, which are an integral part of its national territory.

Further, on 20 December 2000, the Secretary-General received from the Government of the United Kingdom of Great Britain and Northern Ireland, the following communication:

The Government of the United Kingdom of Great Britain and Northern Ireland rejects as unfounded the claims made by the Argentine Republic in its communication to the depositary of 5 October 2000. The Government of the United Kingdom recalls that in its declaration received by the depositary on 16 January 1996 it rejected the objection by the Argentine Republic to the extension by the United Kingdom of the Convention on the rights of the Child to the Falkland Islands and to South Georgia and the South Sandwich Islands. The Government of the United Kingdom has no doubt about the sovereignty of the United Kingdom over the Falkland Islands and over South Georgia and the South Sandwich Islands and its consequential rights to apply the Convention with respect to those territories.

[12] The signature was affixed on behalf of the Yemen Arab Republic.

[13] The former Yugoslavia had signed the Convention on 26 January 1990 and ratified it on 3 January 1991.

DECLARATIONS AND RESERVATIONS CONCERNING THE ARTICLES 38 AND 39 OF THE CONVENTION

ANDORRA (*declarations*)
A. The Principality of Andorra deplores the fact that the [said Convention] does not prohibit the use of children in armed conflicts. It also disagrees with the provisions of article 38, paragraphs 2 and 3, concerning the participation and recruitment of children from the age of 15.
[….]

ARGENTINA (*declarations made upon signature and confirmed upon ratification*)
[…]
Concerning article 38 of the Convention, the Argentine Republic declares that it would have liked the Convention categorically to prohibit the use of children in armed conflicts, such a prohibition exists in its domestic law which, by virtue of article 41 of the Convention, it shall continue to apply in this regard.

AUSTRIA (*declarations*)
1. Austria will not make any use of the possibility provided for in article 38, paragraph 2, to determine an age limit of 15 years for taking part in hostilities as this rule is incompatible with article 3, paragraph 1, which determines that the best interests of the child shall be a primary consideration.
2. Austria declares, in accordance with its constitutional law, to apply article 38, paragraph 3, provided that only male Austrian citizens are subject to compulsory military service.

COLOMBIA
Reservation made upon signature
The Colombian Government considers that, while the minimum age of 15 years for taking part in armed conflicts, set forth in article 38 of the Convention, is the outcome of serious negotiations which reflect various legal, political and cultural systems in the world, it would have been preferable to fix that age at 18 years in accordance with the principles and norms prevailing in various regions and countries, Colombia among them, for which reason the Colombian Government, for the purpose of article 38 of the Convention, shall construe the age in question to be 18 years.

Reservation made upon ratification
The Government of Colombia, pursuant to article 2, paragraph 1 (d) of the Convention, declares that for the purposes of article 38, paragraphs 2 and 3, of the Convention, the age referred to in said paragraphs shall be understood to be 18 years, given the fact that, under Colombian law, the minimum age for recruitment into the armed forces of personnel called for military service is 18 years.

ECUADOR (*declaration made upon signature*)
While the minimum age set in article 38 was, in its view, too low, [the Government of Ecuador] did not wish to endanger the chances for the Convention's adoption by consensus and therefore would not propose any amendment to the text.

GERMANY (*declaration made upon ratification*)
The Government of the Federal Republic of Germany regrets the fact that under article 38 (2) of the Convention even fifteen-year-olds may take a part in hostilities as soldiers, because this age limit is incompatible with the considerartion of a child's best interest (article 3 (1) of the Convention). It declares that it will not make any use of the possibility afforded by the Convention of fixing this age limit at fifteen years.

NETHERLANDS (*Declarations made upon ratification)*
[...]
Article 38
With regard to article 38 of the Convention, the Government of the Kingdom of the Netherlands declares that it is of the opinion that States would not be allowed to involve children directly or indirectly in hostilities and that the minimum age for the recruitment or incorporation of children in the armed forces should be above fifteen years.

In times of armed conflict, provisions shall prevail that are most conducive to guaranteeing the protection of children under international law, as referred to in article 41 of the Convention.

POLAND (*reservations made on ratification*)
[...]
The law of the Republic of Poland shall determine the age from which call-up to military or similar service and participation in military operations are permissible. That age limit may not be lower than the age limit set out in article 38 of the Convention.

SPAIN (*declarations made upon ratification*)
[...]
2. Spain, wishing to make common cause with those States and humanitarian organizations which have manifested their disagreement with the contents of article 38, paragraphs 2 and 3, of the Convention, also wishes to express its disagreement with the age limit fixed therein and to declare that the said limit appears insufficient, by permitting the recruitment and participation in armed conflict of children having attained the age of fifteen years.

URUGUAY (*reservations made upon ratification*)
The Government of the Eastern Republic of Uruguay affirms, in regard to the provisions of article 38, paragraphs 2 and 3, that in accordance with Uruguayan law it would have been desirable for the lower age limit for taking a direct part in hostilities in the event of an armed conflict to be set at 18 years instead of 15 years as provided in the Convention.

Furthermore, the Government of Uruguay declares that, in the exercise of its sovereign will, it will not authorize any persons under its jurisdiction who have not attained the age of 18 years to take a direct part in hostilities and will not under any circumstances recruit persons who have not attained the age of 18 years.

SIGNATURES, RATIFICATIONS AND ACCESSIONS TO THE OPTIONAL PROTOCOL[1]

States	*Signature*	*Ratification, Accession*
Andorra	7 September 2000	30 April 2001 *Dec.*
Argentina	15 June 2000	10 September 2002 *Dec.*
Austria	6 September 2000	1 February 2002 *Dec.*
Azerbaijan	8 September 2000	3 July 2002 *Dec.*
Bangladesh	6 September 2000	6 September 2000 *Dec.*
Belgium [2]	6 September 2000 *Dec.*	6 May 2002 *Dec.*
Belize	6 September 2000	
Benin	22 February 2001	
Bosnia and Herzegovina	7 September 2000	
Brazil	6 September 2000	

[1] List established on the basis of indications in United Nations web site: http://untreaty.un.org of 27 September 2002.

[2] For the Kingdom of Belgium.

States	*Signature*	*Ratification, Accession*
Bulgaria	8 June 2001	12 February 2002 *Dec.*
Burkina Faso	16 November 2001	
Burundi	13 November 2001	
Cambodia	27 June 2000	
Cameroon	5 October 2001	
Canada	5 June 2000	7 July 2000 *Dec.*
Cape Verde	–	10 May 2002 *Dec.*
Chad	3 May 2002	
Chile	15 November 2001	
China	15 March 2001	
Colombia	6 September 2000	
Costa Rica	7 September 2000	
Croatia	8 May 2002	
Cuba	13 October 2000	
Czech Republic	6 September 2000	30 November 2001 *Dec.*
Democratic Republic of the Congo	8 September 2000	11 November 2001 *Dec.*
Denmark	7 September 2000	27 August 2002
Dominica	–	20 September 2002 *Dec.*
Dominican Republic	9 May 2002	
Ecuador	6 September 2000	
El Salvador	18 September 2000	18 April 2002 *Dec.*
Finland	7 September 2000	10 April 2002 *Dec.*
France	6 September 2000	
Gabon	8 September 2000	
Gambia	21 December 2000	
Germany	6 September 2000	
Greece	7 September 2000	
Guatemala	7 September 2000	9 May 2002 *Dec.*
Guinea-Bissau	8 September 2000	
Holy See	10 October 2000	24 October 2001 *Dec.*
Honduras	–	14 August 2002 *Dec.*
Hungary	11 March 2002	
Iceland	7 September 2000	1 October 2001 *Dec.*
Indonesia	24 September 2001	
Ireland	7 September 2000	18 November 2002
Israel	14 November 2001	
Italy	6 September 2000	9 May 2002 *Dec.*
Jamaica	8 September 2000	9 May 2002 *Dec.*
Japan	10 May 2002	
Jordan	6 September 2000	
Kazakhstan	6 September 2000	
Kenya	8 September 2000	28 January 2002 *Dec.*
Latvia	1 February 2002	
Lebanon	11 February 2002	
Lesotho	6 September 2000	
Liechtenstein	8 September 2000	
Lithuania	13 February 2002	
Luxembourg	8 September 2000	
Macedonia, the former Yugoslav Republic of	17 July 2001	5 August 2002 *Dec.*
Madagascar	7 September 2000	
Malawi	7 September 2000	
Maldives	10 May 2002	
Mali	8 September 2000	16 May 2002 *Dec.*
Malta	7 September 2000	9 May 2002 *Dec.*

States	*Signature*	*Ratification, Accession*
Mauritius	11 November 2001	
Mexico	7 September 2000	15 March 2002 *Dec.*
Micronesia (Federated States)	18 May 2002	
Monaco	26 June 2000	13 November 2001 *Dec.*
Mongolia	12 November 2001	
Morocco	8 September 2000	22 May 2002 *Dec.*
Namibia	8 September 2000	16 April 2002 *Dec.*
Nauru	8 September 2000	
Nepal	8 September 2000	
Netherlands	7 September 2000	
New Zealand[3]	7 September 2000	12 November 2001 *Dec.*
Nigeria	8 September 2000	
Norway	13 June 2000	
Pakistan	26 September 2001	
Panama	31 October 2000	8 August 2001 *Dec.*
Paraguay	13 September 2000	27 September 2002
Peru	1 November 2000	8 May 2002 *Dec.*
Philippines	8 September 2000	
Poland	13 February 2002	
Portugal	6 September 2000 *Dec.*	
Qatar	–	25 July 2002 *Dec.*
Republic of Korea	6 September 2000	
Republic of Moldova	8 February 2002	
Romania	6 September 2000	10 November 2001 *Dec.*
Russian Federation	15 February 2001	
Rwanda	–	23 April 2002 *Dec.*
San Marino	5 June 2000	
Senegal	8 September 2000	
Seychelles	23 January 2001	
Sierra Leone	8 September 2000	15 May 2002 *Dec.*
Singapore	7 September 2000	
Slovakia	30 November 2001	
Slovenia	8 September 2000	
South Africa	8 February 2002	
Spain	6 September 2000	8 March 2002 *Dec.*
Sri Lanka	21 August 2000	8 September 2000 *Dec.*
Sudan	9 May 2002	
Surinam	10 May 2002	
Sweden	8 June 2000	
Switzerland	7 September 2000	26 June 2002 *Dec.*
Tajikistan	–	5 August 2002 *Dec.*
Togo	15 November 2001	
Tunisia	22 April 2002	2 January 2003 *Dec.*
Turkey	8 September 2000	
Uganda	–	6 May 2002 *Dec.*
Ukraine	7 September 2000	
United Kingdom of Great Britain and Northern Ireland	7 September 2000	

[3] With the following territorial exclusion: consistent with the constitutional status of Tokelau and taking into account the commitment of the Government of New Zealand to the development of self-government for Tokelau through an act of self-determination under the Charter of the United Nations, this acceptance shall not extend to Tokelau unless and until a Declaration to this effect is lodged by the Government of New Zealand with the Depositary on the basis of appropriate consultation with that territory.

States	*Signature*	*Ratification, Accession*
United States of America	5 July 2000	23 December 2002 *Dec.*
Uruguay	7 September 2000	
Venezuela	7 September 2000	
Viet Nam	8 September 2000	20 December 2001 *Dec.*
Yugoslavia	8 October 2001	

DECLARATIONS AND RESERVATIONS CONCERNING THE OPTIONAL PROTOCOL

ANDORRA (*declaration made on ratification*)
With regard to article 3, paragraph 2, of the Protocol, the Principality of Andorra declares that it currently has no armed forces. The only specialized forces in the Principality are those of the Police and Customs, for which the minimum recruitment age is that specified in article 2 of the Optional Protocol. Moreover, the Principality wishes to reiterate in this declaration its disagreement with the content of article 2, in that that article permits the voluntary recruitment of children under the age of 18 years.

ARGENTINA (*declaration made on ratification*)
The Argentine Republic declares that the minimum age required for voluntary recruitment into the national Armed Forces is eighteen (18) years.

AUSTRIA (*declaration made on ratification*)
Under Austrian law the minimum age for the voluntary recruitment of Austrian citizens into the Austrian army (Bundesheer) is 17 years.

According to paragraph 15, in conjunction with paragraph 65 (c) of the Austrian National Defence Act 1990 (Wehrgesetz 1990), the explicit consent of parents or other legal guardians is required for the voluntary recruitment of a person between 17 and 18 years.

The provisions of the Austrian National Defence Act 1990, together with the subjective legal remedies guaranteed by the Austrian Federal Constitution, ensure that legal protection in the context of such a decision is afforded to volunteers under the age of 18. A further guarantee derives from the strict application of the principles of rule of law, good governance and effective legal protection.

AZERBAIJAN (*declaration made on ratification*)
Pursuant to Article 3 of the protocol, the Republic of Azerbaijan declares that in accordance with the Law of the Republic of Azerbaijan on the military service of 3 November 1992, the citizens of of the Republic of Azerbaijan and other persons, who are meeting the defined requirements of the military service, may voluntarily enter and be admitted in age of 17 the active miltary service of the cadets military school. The legislation of the Republic of Azerbaijan guarantees that this service shall not be forced or coerced, shall be realized on the basis of deliberative consent of the parents and the legal representatives of those persons, that those persons shall be provided with the full information of the duties regarding this service, and that the documents certifying their age shall be required before the admission to the service in the national armed forces.

BANGLADESH (*declaration made on ratification*)
"In accordance with Article 3 (2) of [the Optional Protocol], the Government of the People's Republic of Bangladesh declares that the minimum age at which it permits voluntary recruitment into its national Armed Forces is sixteen years for non-commissioned soldiers and seventeen years for commissioned officers, with informed consent of parents or legal guardian, without any exception.

The Government of the People's Republic of Bangladesh further provides hereunder a description of the safeguards it has adopted to ensure that such recruitment is not forced or coerced:

The process of recruitment in the national Armed Forces is initiated through advertisement in the national press and the media for officers and other ranks without exception.

The first induction of new recruits is conducted invariably in a public place such as a national park, school ground or a similar place. Public participation is welcomed in such programmes.

Before a recruit presents himself he has to submit a written declaration from his parents or legal guardians consenting to his recruitment. If the parent or legal guardian is illiterate the declaration is verified and counter signed by the Chairmain of the Union Parishad.

The recruit is required to present birth certificate, matriculation certificate and full school records.

All recruits whether officers or other ranks have to undergo rigorous medical examination including checks for puberty. A recruit found to be pre-pubescent is automatically rejected.

Officers and other ranks without exception are required to undergo two years of compulsory training. This ensures that they are not assigned to combat units before the age of 18. All officers and other ranks are carefully screened before being assigned to combat units. These tests include tests of psychological maturity including an understanding of the elements of international law of armed conflict inculcated at all levels.

The Government of the People's Republic of Bangladesh declares that stringent checks in accordance with the obligations assumed under the Optional Protocol will continue to be applied without exception.

BELGIUM[4] (*declarations made on ratification*)

1. In accordance with article 3, paragraph 2, and bearing in mind article 3, paragraph 5, the Government of the Kingdom of Belgium states that the minimum age for voluntary recruitment into the Belgian armed forces is not lower than 18 years.
2. The Government of the Kingdom of Belgium states that it is absolutely forbidden under Belgian law for any person under the age of 18 years to participate in times of war and in times of peace in any peacekeeping operation or in any kind of armed operational engagement. Moreover, non-governmental militias are prohibited, regardless of the age of the persons concerned.
3. The Government of the Kingdom of Belgium shall not act upon a request for judicial cooperation where doing so would lead to discrimination between governmental and non-governmental forces in violation of the principle of international humanitarian law of equality of parties to a conflict, including in the event of armed conflict of a non-international nature.

BULGARIA (*declaration made on ratification*)

The Republic of Bulgaria declares hereby that all men, Bulgarian citizens who have attained 18 years of age shall be subject to a compulsory military service.

Bulgarian citizens who have been sworn in and done their military service or have done two thirds of the mandatory term of their military service shall be admitted, voluntarily, to regular duty.

Persons who have not come of age shall be trained at military schools subject to the conclusion of a training agreement to be signed by them with the consent of their parents or guardians. Having come of age, the trainees shall sign a training agreement on a regular military duty.

[4] For the Kingdom of Belgium.

CANADA (*declaration made on ratification*)

1. The Canadian Armed Forces permit voluntary recruitment at the minimum age of 16 years.
2. The Canadian Armed Forces have adopted the following safeguards to ensure that recruitment of personnel under the age of 18 years is not forced or coerced:
   (a) all recruitment of personnel in the Canadian Forces is voluntary. Canada does not practice conscription or any form of forced or obligatory service. In this regard, recruitment campaigns of the Canadian Forces are informational in nature. If an individual wishes to enter the Canadian Forces, he or she fills in an application. If the Canadian Forces offer a particular position to the candidate, the latter is not obliged to accept the position;
   (b) recruitment of personnel under the age of 18 is done with the informed and written consent of the person's parents or legal guardians. Article 20, paragraph 3, of the National Defence Act states that 'a person under the age of eighteen years shall not be enrolled without the consent of one of the parents or the guardian of that person',
   (c) personnel under the age of 18 are fully informed of the duties involved in military service. The Canadian Forces provide, among other things, a series of informational brochures and films on the duties involved in military service to those who wish to enter the Canadian Forces; and
   (d) personnel under the age of 18 must provide reliable proof of age prior to acceptance into national military service. An applicant must provide a legally recognized document, that is an original or a certified copy of their birth certificate or baptismal certificate, to prove his or her age.

CAPE VERDE (*declaration made on accession*)

[The Republic of Cape Verde] declare[s] on behalf of the Cape Verdean Government, that the minimum age for special voluntary recruitment into the Cape Verdean armed forces is 17 years in accordance with article 31 of Legislative Decree No. 6/93 of 24 May 1993, published in official gazette No.18, series I.

Moreover, Decree-Law No. 37/96 of 30 September 1986, published in official gazette No. 32, series I, which governs the provisions contained in the above-mentioned Legislative Decree, states the following in its article 60:

Special recruitment shall apply to citizens, who of their own freely expressed will, decide to enter military service subject to meeting the following requirements:

(a) They must have attained the minimum age of 17 years;
(b) They must have the consent of their parents or legal guardians;
(c) They must be mentally and physically fit for military service.

Article 17 of Legislative Decree No. 6/93 and articles 29 and 63 of Decree-Law No. 37/96 provide that persons to be enrolled must be fully informed through appropriate documentation prepared by the high command of the armed forces about the duties involved in national military service.

Under article 28 of that Decree-Law, all volunteers shall provide, prior to enlistment and as reliable proof of identity, their national identity card or passport.

While article 8 of Legislative Decree No. 6/93 provides that in war time the minimum/maximum age for recruitment may be amended, the fact that Cape Verde is bound by the Convention on the Rights of the Child and is becoming a party to the Optional Protocol to the Convention on the Rights of the Child on the involvement of children in armed conflict, means that in no case shall the minimum age for recruitment be lower than 17 years. Indeed, article 12, paragraph 4, of the Constitution provides that the norms and principles of general international law and international treaty law duly approved or ratified shall take precedence, after their entry into force in the international and domestic legal system, over all domestic municipal legislative or normative acts under the Constitution.

CZECH REPUBLIC (*declaration made on ratification*)
Adopting this Protocol we declare in accordance with article 3 paragraph 2 of the Protocol that the minimum age at which voluntary recruitment into its national armed forces is permitted is 18 years. This age limit is prescribed by law.

DEMOCRATIC REPUBLIC OF THE CONGO (*declaration made on ratification*)
Pursuant to article 3, paragraph 2, of the Protocol, the Democratic Republic of the Congo undertakes to implement the principle of prohibiting the recruitment of children into the armed forces, in accordance with Decree-Law No. 066 of 9 June 2000 on the demobilization and rehabilitation of vulnerable groups on active service in the armed forces, and to take all feasible measures to ensure that persons who have not yet attained the age of 18 years are not recruited in any way into the Congolese armed forces or into any other public or private armed group throughout the territory of the Democratic Republic of the Congo.

DOMINICA (*declaration made on accession*)
... the minimum age at which voluntary recruitment will be permitted into the Police Force (in the absence of national and armed forces) is eighteen (18) years in accordance with the Police Act, Chapter 14:01, Section 5 (a);
... recruitment will be carried out only through a recognised registered body;
... the consent of recruits is voluntary and is witnessed to with a signed declaration;
... an orientation period is provided prior to recruitment with the option of voluntary withdrawal.

EL SALVADOR (*declaration made on ratification*)
[P]ursuant to article 3, paragraph 2 of the above-mentioned Protocol, the Government of the Republic of El Salvador declares that the minimum age for Salvadorans who wish to enlist voluntarily for military service is 16 years, in accordance with articles 2 and 6 of the Act on Military Service and Reserves of the Armed Forces of El Salvador. The following is a description of the safeguards that the relevant Salvadoran authorities have adopted to ensure that the military service provided is legally voluntary:

- The 16-year-old minor must submit a written request to the Recruitment and Reserves Office or its subsidiary offices, unequivocally stating a desire to provide military service;
- Submission of the original birth certificate or minor's card;
- Document certifying knowledge of and consent to the request to provide military service from the minor's parents, guardian or legal representative, all in accordance with the provisions of title II on parental authority, article 206 et seq. of the Family Code;
- Acceptance of the request shall be subject to the needs for military service.

FINLAND (*declaration made on ratification*)
The Government of Finland declares in accordance with Article 3, paragraph 2, of the Optional Protocol that the minimum age for any recruitment of persons into its national armed forces is 18 years. The minimum age applies equally to the military service of men and to the voluntary service of women.

GUATEMALA (*declaration made on ratification*)
Guatemala shall not permit the compulsory recruitment of persons under 18 years of age into its armed forces, and, in keeping with article 3, paragraph 4, of the Convention on the Rights of the Child on the involvement of children in armed conflict, the description of the safeguards it has adopted to ensure that such recruitment is not forced or coerced shall be submitted at a later date.

HOLY SEE (*declaration made on ratification*)
The Holy See, with regard to article 3, paragraph 2, of the Protocol, declares that, for what concerns the Vatican City State, the Regulations of the Pontifical Swiss Guard, approved in 1976, establish that the recruitment of its members is only voluntary and that the minimum age is set forth at 19 years.

HONDURAS (*declaration made on accession*)
I (a). Under the legislation of the State of Honduras, the minimum age for voluntary recruitment into the armed forces is 18 years, as part of the country's educational, social, humanist and democratic system.
II This Agreement shall be submitted to the Sovereign National Congress for consideration, for the purposes of article 205, number 30, of the Constitution of the Republic.

ICELAND (*declaration made on ratification*)
With regard to Article 3, paragraph 2, of the Optional Protocol to the Convention on the Rights of the Child on the Involvement of Children in Armed Conflict, the Republic of Iceland declares that it has no national armed forces, and hence, a minimum age for recruitment is not applicable in the case of the Republic of Iceland.

ITALY (*declaration made on ratification*)
The Government of the Italian Republic declares, in compliance with article 3:
- That Italian legislation on voluntary recruitment provides that a minimum age of 17 years shall be required with respect to requests for early recruitment for compulsory military service or voluntary recruitment (military duty on a short-term and yearly basis);
- That the legislation in force guarantees the application, at the time of voluntary recruitment, of the provisions of article 3, paragraph 3, of the Protocol, inter alia, as regards the requirement of the consent of the parent or guardian of the recruit.

JAMAICA (*declaration made on ratification*)
Pursuant to Article 3 (2) of the Optional Protocol to the Convention on the Rights of the Child on the involvement of Children in Armed Conflict, Jamaica hereby declares that:
1. The Jamaica Defence Force permits voluntary recruitment and enlistment at the minimum age of 18 years.
2. The Jamaica Defence Force has adopted the following safeguards, under the 1962 Defence (Regular Force Enlistment and Service Regulations) Act, to ensure that recruitment of personnel under the age of 18 is not forced or coerced;
   (a) All recruitment to the Jamaica Defence Force is voluntary. If an individual wishes to enter the Jamaica Defence Force, he or she completes the relevant application (Notice Paper) form in accordance with Section 5 of the Act;
   (b) The applicant is given the notice paper with the condition and warning that if he knowingly makes a false attestation, he is liable to be punished;
   (c) The recruiting officer shall satisfy himself that the person offering to enlist is, or as the case may be, is not, over the age of eighteen years;
   (d) The recruiting officer shall read or cause to be read to the person the questions set out in the attestation paper and shall ensure that the answers are duly recorded thereon;
   (e) Written parental consent is required for applicants who have attained the age of 17 1/2 years. Persons in this category are not permitted to graduate as trained soldiers from training institutions, until they have attained the age of eighteen (18) years.
3. Personnel must provide reliable proof of age prior to acceptance into national military service, in the form of a legally recognized document, that is, an original or a certified copy of their birth certificate.

If the Jamaica Defence Force offers a particular position to the candidate, he or she is not compelled to accept the position.

KENYA (*declaration made on ratification*)
The Government of the Republic of Kenya declares that the minimum age for the recruitment of persons into the armed forces is by law set at eighteen years. Recruitment is entirely and genuinely voluntary and is carried out with the full informed consent of the persons being recruited. There is no conscription in Kenya.

The Government of the Republic of Kenya reserves the right at any time by means of a notification addressed to the Secretary-General of the United Nations, to add, amend or strengthen the present declaration. Such notifications shall take effect from the date of their receipt by the Secretary General of the United Nations.

MALI (*declaration made on ratification*)
In accordance with article 3, paragraph 2, of the Optional Protocol to the Convention on the Rights of the Child on the Involvement of Children in Armed Conflict, the Government of the Republic of Mali declares that the minimum age for voluntary recruitment into the national armed forces is 18 years of age or older. No boy or girl under 18 years of age may be recruited or be allowed to be recruited, even on a voluntary basis, or be enrolled as a member of the national armed forces.

The Government of Mali is fully committed to this declaration and pledges to impose on anyone who violates such provision a penalty commensurate with the seriousness of the offence as provided for under its criminal law.

Children who are unlawfully recruited into the armed forces may, depending on their individual circumstances, receive support for their economic and social rehabilitation and reintegration.

MALTA (*declaration made on ratification*)
Under the Malta Armed Forces Act (Chapter 220 of the Laws of Malta), enacted in 1970, enlistment in the Armed Forces of Malta shall be made on a voluntary basis and no person under the age of seventeen years and six months may be so enlisted. A person under 18 years may not be enlisted unless consent to the enlistment is given in writing by the father of such person or, if such person is not subject to paternal authority, by the mother or by an other person in whose care the person offering to enlist may be. In any case, the term of engagement of a person enlisting under the age of 18 expires on reaching 18 years of age and enlistment has to be renewed. It is a mandatory condition for enlistment of potential recruits to produce a birth certificate from the national Civil Status Office to attest their age.

The Malta Armed Forces Act also provides that any person of whatever age offering to enlist in the regular force shall, before enlistment, be given a notice on the prescribed form stating the general conditions of engagement and the recruiting officer shall not enlist any person in the regular force unless satisfied that the potential recruit has been given such notice, understood its contents and wishes to be enlisted.

In practice the Armed Forces of Malta do not recruit and have not since 1970 recruited persons under the age of 18 years. The Government of Malta further declares that if in future recruitment of persons under 18 years were made such members of the armed forces will not take part in hostilities.

Regulations under the Malta Armed Forces Act provide for a Junior Leaders Scheme whereby persons under the age of seventeen and six months could be recruited for training but in a non-combatant position, but in effect no such recruitment has taken place since 1970.

MEXICO (*declaration made on ratification*)
In accordance with article 3, paragraph 2 of the Optional Protocol, the United Mexican States declares:

(i) That the minimum age for voluntary recruitment of its nationals into the armed forces is 18 years;

(ii) That article 24 of the Military Service Act provides that only volunteers will be accepted into the armed forces for active service until the figure set annually by the Ministry of Defence has been met and provided that the following conditions are fulfilled:

I. They must submit an application;

II. They must be Mexican nationals who are over 18 but not over 30, and must be under 40 in the case of personnel enlisted as specialists in the army;

Those over 16 and under 18 shall be accepted into signals units for training as technicians under contracts with the State not exceeding five years in duration. Moreover, under article 25 of the Military Service Act, only the following persons may be accepted for early enlistment in the armed forces:

I. Those who wish to leave the country at the time when they would be required by law to undertake military service if they are over 16 at the time of requesting enlistment;

II. Those who are obliged to request early enlistment because of their studies.

The maximum number of individuals who may be allowed to enlist early shall be set every year by the Ministry of Defence; and

Interpretative declaration

In ratifying the Optional Protocol to the Convention on the Rights of the Child on the involvement of children in armed conflict, adopted by the General Assembly of the United Nations on 25 May 2000, the Government of the United Mexican States considers that any responsibility deriving therefrom for non-governmental armed groups for the recruitment of children under 18 years or their use in hostilities lies solely with such groups and shall not be applicable to the Mexican State as such. The latter shall have a duty to apply at all times the principles governing international humanitarian law.

MONACO (*declaration made on ratification*)

The Principality of Monaco declares, in accordance with article 3, paragraph 2, of the Optional Protocol to the Convention on the Rights of the Child on the involvement of children in armed conflict, that it is bound by the Franco-Monaguesque Treaty of 17 July 1918 and that the French Republic thereby ensures the defence of the territorial integrity of the Principality of Monaco.

The only bodies having military status in the Principality are the Prince's Guard and the Fire Brigade. In accordance with the provisions of Sovereign Ordinance No. 8017 of 1 June 1984 relating to the Police Code, members of the Guard and the Fire Brigade must be at least 21 years of age.

MOROCCO (*declaration made on ratification*)

Pursuant to paragraph 2 of the article concerning the involvement of children in armed conflicts, the Kingdom of Morocco declares that the minimum age required by national law for voluntary recruitment in the armed forces is 18 years.

NAMIBIA (*declaration made on ratification*)

1. The Namibian Defence Force permit voluntary recruitment at the minimum age of 18 years.
2. The Namibian Defence Force have adopted the following safeguards to ensure that recruitment of personnel at the age between 18 and 25 years is not forced or coerced.
   (a) Advertisements on the availability of military career opportunities in the Namibian Defence Force are placed yearly in the local print and broadcast for the purposes of inviting interested young men and women to apply.
   (b) As a standpoint the candidate is not obliged to accept the position if the Namibian Defence Force offer a particular position.
   (c) Military career opportunities may emanate from Infantry, Engineering, Air wing, Maritime Wing, Communication and Medical Services. The potential recruits undergo instruction courses to give them an overview of what is expected of

them as future soldiers in respect of military career opportunities stated under paragraph 2 c). The recruits may select their career paths after training.

(d) To ensure the absence of any possible form of remote or direct coercion the Namibian Defence Force requires that

(i) the potential recruit should not have previous criminal records or convictions

(ii) the potential recruits be Namibian Citizens.

3. As a standpoint and policy Namibia Defence Force does not allow voluntary recruitment under the age of 18 years thus:

(i) as proof of age requires that the candidates show certified copies of legally recognised Namibian identity documents as well as birth certificates.

4. All recruitments of personnel in the Namibian Defence Force are voluntary. Namibia does not practice conscription or any form of forced obligatory service.

NEW ZEALAND (*declaration made on ratification*)

The Government of New Zealand declares that the minimum age at which New Zealand will permit voluntary recruitment into its national armed forces shall be 17 years. The Government of New Zealand further declares that the safeguards which it has adopted to ensure that such recruitment is not forced or coerced include the following:

(a) Defence Force recruitment procedures requiring that persons responsible for recruitment ensure that such recruitment is genuinely voluntary;

(b) legislative requirements that the consent of parent or guardian is obtained for enlistment where such consent is necessary under NZ law. The parent or guardian must also acknowledge that the person enlisting will be liable for active service after reaching the age of 18 years;

(c) a detailed and informative enlistment process, which ensures that all persons are fully informed of the duties involved in military service prior to taking an oath of allegiance; and

(d) a recruiting procedure, which requires enlistees to produce their birth certificate as reliable proof of age.

PANAMA (*declaration made on ratification*)

The Republic of Panama, in ratifying the Protocol, declares that it has no armed forces. The Republic of Panama has a civilian security force consisting of the National Police, the National Air Service, the National Maritime Service and the Institutional Protection Service. Their legal charters define the requirements for recruitment of personnel by such institutions and stipulate that recruits must have reached the age of majority, i.e. 18 years.

PARAGUAY (*declaration made on ratification*)

...on behalf of the Government of the Republic of Paraguay, that in accordance with the relevant national and international legal norms, it has been decided to establish the age sixteen (16) years as the minimum age for voluntary recruitment into the armed forces. Moreover, the measures adopted to permit voluntary recruitment will be in conformity with the principles laid down in article 3, paragraph 3 of the Optional Protocol.

PERU (*declaration made on ratification*)

In depositing the instrument of ratification of the Optional Protocol to the Convention on the Rights of the Child on the involvement of children in armed conflict, the Government of Peru declares that, in compliance with its article 3, paragraph 2, the minimum age for voluntary recruitment into the national armed forces, under national legislation, is 18 years.

PORTUGAL (*declaration made on signature*)

Concerning article 2 of the Protocol, the Portuguese Republic considering that it would have preferred the Protocol to exclude all types or recruitment of persons under the age of 18 years – whether this recruitment is voluntary or not, declares that it will apply its domestic legislation which prohibits the voluntary recruitment of persons under the age of 18 years and will deposit a binding declaration, in conformity with paragraph 2 of article 3 of the Protocol, setting forth 18 years as the minimum age for voluntary recruitment in Portugal.

QATAR (*declaration made on accession*)
The State of Qatar declares that recruitment to its armed forces and other regular forces is voluntary and is for those who have attained the age of 18 years and that it takes account of the safeguards set forth in paragraph 3 of the same article.

In making this declaration, the State of Qatar affirms that its national legislation makes no provision for any form of compulsory or coercive recruitment.

ROMANIA (*declaration made on ratification*)
According to the law, military service is compulsory for Romanian citizens, males, who reached the age of 20, except in case of war or upon request, during peacetime, when they may be recruited after the age of 18.

RWANDA (*declaration made on accession*)
Minimum age for voluntary recruitment:18 years.

Minimum age for entry into schools operated by or under the control of armed forces: Not applicable.

Status of pupils in these schools (are they part of the armed forces: Not applicable.

What reliable proof of age is required: birth certificate.

What do the armed forces comprise: Adult men and women.

SIERRA LEONE (*declaration made on ratification*)
1. The minimum age for voluntary recruitment into the Armed Forces is 18 years;
2. There is no compulsory, forced or coerced recruitment into the National Armed Forces;
3. Recruitment is exclusively on a voluntary basis.

SPAIN (*declaration made on ratification*)
For the purposes of the provisions of article 3 of the Protocol, Spain declares that the minimum age for voluntary recruitment into its armed forces is 18 years.

SRI LANKA (*declaration made on ratification*)
(a) there is no compulsory, forced or coerced recruitment into the national armed forces;
(b) recruitment is solely on a voluntary basis;
(c) the minimum age for voluntary recruitment into national armed forces is 18 years.

SWITZERLAND (*declaration made on ratification*)
The Swiss Government declares, in accordance with article 3, paragraph 2, of the Optional Protocol, that the minimum age for the recruitment of volunteers into its national armed forces is 18 years. That age is specified by the Swiss legal system.

TAJIKISTAN (*declaration made on accession*)
On behalf of the Republic of Tajikistan, the Ministry of Foreign Affairs has the honor to declare that, in accordance with [paragraph] 2 of article 3 of the Optional Protocol to the Convention on the Rights of a Child with respect to participation of children in military conflicts, the voluntary recruitment of those under age of 18 to the armed forces of the Republic of Tajikistan shall be prohibited.

TUNISIA (*declaration made on ratification*)
Under Tuisian law, the minimum age for voluntary recruitment of Tunisian citizens into the armed forces is 18 years.

In accordance with article 1 of Act No. 51-1989 of 14 March 1989 on military service, "all citizens aged 20 shall perform national service in person, except in the case of a medically certified impediment.

However, citizens may, at their request, and with the consent of their legal guardian, perform military service at the age of 18 years, subject to the approval of the Secretary General of the Ministry of Defence."

In accordance with article 27 of Act No. 51-1989 of 14 March 1989 on military service, "any citizen between the ages of 18 and 23 may be admitted into military schools subject to such conditions as may be determined by the Secretary General of the Ministry of Defence.

Young people who have not attained the age of majority must first get the consent of their legal guardian; in such case, the first year of service shall count towards the fulfilment of military service obligations and be considered as enlistment before call-up."

Articles 1 and 27 of the Act of 14 March 1989 provide legal safegaurds for citizens under the age of 18 years, since acceptance into national military service or recruitment into the armed forces is on a strictly voluntary basis.

UGANDA (*declaration made on accession*)

The Government of the Republic of Uganda declares that the minimum age for the recruitment of persons into the armed forces is by law set at eighteen (18) years. Recruitment is entirely and squarely voluntary and is carried out with the full informed consent of the persons being recruited. There is no conscription in Uganda.

The Government of the Republic of Uganda reserves the right at any time by means of a notification addressed to the Secretary-General of the United Nations, to add, amend or strengthen the present declaration. Such notifications shall take effect from the date of their receipt by the Secretary-General of the United Nations.

UNITED KINGDOM OF GREAT BRITAIN AND NORTHERN IRELAND (*declaration made on signature*)

The United Kingdom of Great Britain and Northern Ireland will take all feasible measures to ensure that members of its armed forces who have not attained the age of 18 years do not take a direct part in hostilities.

The United Kingdom understands that article 1 of the Optional Protocol would not exclude the deployment of members of its armed forces under the age of 18 to take a direct part in hostilities where:

(a) there is a genuine military need to deploy their unit or ship to an area in which hostilities are taking place; and
(b) by reason of the nature and urgency of the situation:
   (i) it is not practicable to withdraw such persons before deployment; or
   (ii) to do so would undermine the operational effectiveness of their ship or unit, and thereby put at risk the successful completion of the military mission and/or the safety of other personnel.

UNITED STATES OF AMERICA (*declaration made on ratification*)

(A) the minmum age at which the United States permits voluntary recruitment into the Armed Forces of the United States is 17 years of age;
(B) The United States has established safeguards to ensure that such recruitment is not forced or coerced, including a requirement in section 505 (a) of title 10 United States Code, that no person under 18 years of age may be originally enlisted in the Armed Forces of the United States without the written consent of the person's parent or guardian, if the parent or guardian is entitled to the person's custody and control;
(C) each person recruited into the Armed Forces of the United States receives a comprehensive briefing and must sign an enlistment contract that, taken together, specify the duties involved in military service; and
(D) all persons recruited into the Armed Forces of the United States must provide reliable proof of age before their entry into military service.

Understandings:

(1) NO ASSUMPTION OF OBLIGATIONS UNDER THE CONVENTION OF THE RIGHTS OF THE CHILD. - The United Staes understands that the United States assumes no obligations under the Convention on the Rights of the Child by becoming a party to the Protocol.

(2) IMPLEMENTATION OF OBLIGATION NOT TO PERMIT CHILDREN TO TAKE DIRECT PART IN HOSTILITIES. - The United States understands that, with respect to Article 1 of the Protocol -

(A) the term "feasible measures" means those measures that are practical or practically possible, taking into account all the circumstances ruling at the time, including humanitarian and military considerations;

(B) the phrase "direct part in hostilities" -

(i) means immediate and actual action on the battlefield likely to cause harm to the enemy because there is a direct causal relationship between the activity engaged in and the harm done to the enemy; and

(ii) does not mean indirect participation in hostilities, such as gathering and transmitting military information, transporting weapons, munitions, or other supplies, or forward deployment; and

(C) any decision by any military commander, military personnel, or other person responsible for planning, authorizing, or executing military action, including the assignment of military personnel, shall only be judged on the basis of all the relevant circumstances and on the basis of that person's assessment of the information reasonably available to the person at the time the person planned, authorized, or executed the action under review, and shall not be judged on the basis of information that come sto light after the action under review was taken.

(3) MINIMUM AGE FOR VOLUNTARY RECRUITMENT. - The United States understands that Article 3 of the Protocol obligates States Parties to the Protocol to raise the minimum age for voluntary recruitment into their national armed forces from the current international standard of 15 years of age.

(4) ARMED GROUPS. - The United States understands that the term 'armed groups' in Article 4 of the Protocol means nongovernmental armed groups such as rebel groups, dissident armed forces, and other insurgent groups.

(5) NO BASIS FOR JURISDICTION BY ANY INTERNATIONAL TRIBUNAL. - The United States understands that nothing in the Protocol establishes a basis for jurisdiction by any international tribunal, including the International Criminal Court.

VIET NAM (*declaration made on ratification*)

To defend the Homeland is the sacred duty and right of all citizens. Citizens have the obligation to fulfil military service and participate in building the all-people national defense.

Under the law of the Socialist Republic of Vietnam, only male citizens at the age of 18 and over shall be recruited in the military service. Those who are under the age of 18 shall not be directly involved in military battles unless there is an urgent need for safeguarding national independence, sovereignty, unity and territorial integrity.

Male citizens up to the age of 17 who wish to make a long-term service in the army may be admitted to military schools. Voluntary recruitment to military schools shall be ensured by measures which, inter alia, include:

- The Law on Military Duty and other regulations on the recruitment to military schools are widely disseminated through mass media;
- Those who wish to study at a military school shall, on the voluntary basis, file their application, participate in and pass competitive examinations; they shall submit their birth certificates provided by the local authority, their education records, secondary education diploma; they shall also undergo health check in order to ensure that they are physically qualified to study and serve the military.

No. 68

AFRICAN CHARTER ON THE RIGHTS AND WELFARE OF THE CHILD (ARTICLES RELATED TO ARMED CONFLICT)

Adopted by the Twenty-sixth Conference of the Heads of State and Government of the Organization of African Unity, Addis Ababa, Ethiopia, July 1990

INTRODUCTORY NOTE: The Assembly of Heads of State and Government of the Organization of African Unity, meeting for its sixth ordinary session at Monrovia (Liberia) from 17 to 20 July 1979, adopted the Declaration on the Rights and Welfare of Children in Africa (AHG/ST.4 (XVI) Rev. 1). In July, 1990, the Twenty-sixth Conference of the Heads of State and Government of the OAU adopted the African Charter on the Rights and Welfare of Child. This Charter contains provisions related to armed conflict, which are reproduced here: Article 1 (Obligations of State members), Article 2 (Definition of Child), Article 22 (Armed conflicts), Article 23 (Refugee Children), and Article 25 (Separation from Parents).

ENTRY INTO FORCE: 29 November 1999.

AUTHENTIC TEXT: English and French. The text below is reproduced from the Organization of African Unity document. CAB/LEG/TSG/Rev. 2.

PUBLICATION OF THE TEXT: Document of the Organization of African Unity. CAB/LEG/153/Rev.2 (English, French); *Droit des conflits armés*, pp. 1033–1036 (French).

* * *

PREAMBLE

...

Noting with concern that the situation of most African children remains critical due to the unique factors of their socioeconomic, cultural, traditional and developmental circumstances, natural disasters, armed conflicts, exploitation and hunger, and on account of the child's physical and mental immaturity he/she needs special safeguards and care,

Reaffirming adherence to the principles of the rights and welfare of the child contained in the declaration, conventions and other instruments of the Organization of African Unity and in the United Nations and in particular the United Nations Convention on the Rights of the Child; and the OAU Heads of State and Government's Declaration on the Rights and Welfare of the African Child:

Have agreed as follows:

PART 1. RIGHTS AND DUTIES

Chapter One: Rights and Welfare of the Child

Article I. Obligation of States Parties

1. The Member States of the Organization of African Unity Parties to the present Charter shall recognize the rights, freedoms and duties enshrined in this Charter and shall, undertake to take the necessary steps, in accordance with their Constitutional processes and with the provisions of the present Charter, to adopt such legislative or other measures as may be necessary to give effect to the provisions of this Charter.
2. Nothing in this Charter shall affect any provisions that are more conducive to the realization of the rights and welfare of the child contained in the law of a State Party or in any other international convention or agreement in force in that State.
3. Any custom, tradition, cultural or religious practice that is inconsistent with the rights, duties and obligations contained in the present Charter shall to the extent of such inconsistency be discouraged.

Art. II. Definition of a child

For the purposes of this Charter, a child means every human being below the age of 18 years.

Art. XXII. Armed conflicts

1. States Parties to this Charter shall undertake to respect and ensure respect for rules of international humanitarian law applicable in armed conflicts which affect the child.
2. States Parties to the present Charter shall take all necessary measures to ensure that no child shall take a direct part in hostilities and refrain in particular, from recruiting any child.
3. States Parties to the present Charter shall, in accordance with their obligations under international humanitarian law, protect the civilian population in armed conflicts and shall take all feasible measures to ensure the protection and care of children who are affected by armed conflicts. Such rules shall also apply to children in situation of internal armed conflicts, tension and strife.

Art. XXIII. Refugee children

1. States Parties to the present Charter shall take all appropriate measures to ensure that a child who is seeking refugee status or who is considered a refugee in accordance with applicable international or domestic law shall, whether unaccompanied or accompanied by parents, legal guardians or close relatives, receive appropriate protection and humanitarian assistance in the enjoyment of the rights set out in this Charter and other international human right and humanitarian instruments to which the States are parties.
2. States Parties shall undertake to cooperate with existing international organizations which protect and assist refugees in their efforts to protect and assist such a child and to trace the parents or other close relatives of an unaccompanied refugee child in order to obtain information necessary for reunification with the family.

3. Where no parents, legal guardians or close relatives can be found, the child shall be accorded the same protection as any other child permanently or temporarily deprived of his family environment for any reason.
4. .The provisions of this Article apply *mutatis mutandis* to internally displaced children whether through natural disaster, internal armed conflicts, civil strife, breakdown of economic and social rder or howsoever caused.

Art. XXV. Separation from parents

1. Any child who is permanently or temporarily deprived of his family environment for any reasons shall be entitled to special protection and assistance;
2. States Parties to the present Charter:
   (a) shall ensure that a child who is parentless, or who is temporarily or permanently deprived of his or her family environment, or who in his or her best interest cannot be brought up or allowed to remain in that environment shall be provided with alternative family care, which could include, among others, foster placement, or placement in suitable institutions for the care of children;
   (b) shall take all necessary measures to trace and re-unite children with parents or relatives where separation is caused by internal and external displacement arising from armed conflicts or natural disasters.
3. When considering alternative family care of the child and the best interests of the child, due regard shall be paid to the desirability of continuity in a child's up-bringing and to the child's ethnic, religious or linguistic background.

SIGNATURES, RATIFICATIONS AND ACCESSION[1]

State	*Signatures*	*Ratifications Accessions*[2]
Algeria	21 May 1999	–
Angola	–	7 October 1999
Benin	27 February 1992	30 May 1997
Botswana	10 July 2001	10 July 2001
Burkina Faso	27 February 1992	10 July 1992
Cameroon	16 September 1992	23 June 1999
Cape Verde	27 February 1992	1 September 1993
Chad	–	4 April 2000
Congo	28 February 1992	–
Djibouti	28 February 1992	–
Egypt	30 June 1999	22 May 2001 *Res.*
Eritrea	–	25 January 2000
Gabon	27 February 1992	–
Gambia	–	30 March 2001
Ghana	18 August 1997	21 January 2001
Guinea	22 May 1998	–

[1] Based on the communications received from the Organization of African Unity of 7 December 2001 and on African Union website news: www.africa-union.org.

[2] Indicates the date of deposit of the instruments of ratification or accession.

State	*Signatures*	*Ratifications Accession*
Kenya	–	10 August 2000
Lesotho	–	29 October 1999
Liberia	14 May 1992	–
Libya	9 June 1998	3 November 2000
Madagascar	27 February 1992	–
Malawi	13 July 1999	17 November 1999
Mali	28 February 1996	14 August 1998
Mauritius	7 November 1991	27 February 1992
Mozambique	–	22 December 1998
Namibia	13 July 1999	–
Niger	13 July 1996	5 March 1997
Nigeria	13 May 2001	–
Rwanda	2 October 1991	17 May 2001
Sahrahwi Arab Democratic Republic	23 October 1992	
Senegal	18 May 1992	30 October 1998
Seychelles	27 February 1992	27 February 1992
Sierra Leone	14 April 1992	18 June 2002
Somalia	1 June 1991	–
South Africa	10 October 1997	21 January 2000
Swaziland	29 June 1992	–
Tanzania	23 October 1998	–
Togo	27 February 1992	18 May 1998
Tunisia	16 June 1995	–
Uganda	26 February 1992	21 October 1994
Zambia	27 February 1992	–
Zimbabwe	28 February 1992	22 February 1995

RESERVATIONS

BOTSWANA (*reservation made upon signature*)
The Government of the Republic of Botswana does not consider itself bound by Article 2 of the Charter.

EGYPT (*reservation made upon accession*)
Reservation on Article 21, paragraph 2, Article 24, Article 30, lettre (e), Article 44 and Article 45, paragraph 1.

* * *

See also Nos. 33–36, 55–57, 95, 96

VII

PROTECTION OF CULTURAL PROPERTY

No. 69

TREATY ON THE PROTECTION OF ARTISTIC AND SCIENTIFIC INSTITUTIONS AND HISTORIC MONUMENTS (ROERICH PACT)

Signed at Washington, 15 April 1935

INTRODUCTORY NOTE: Provision was made for the special protection of cultural property in earlier treaties, particularly in Article 27 of the Hague Regulations of 1899 and 1907 (*Nos. 7 and 8*, Annexes) and Article 5 of the Hague Convention (IX) concerning Bombardment by Naval Forces in Time of War of 1907 (*No. 79*). Both treaties make it the duty of the inhabitants to indicate cultural property by distinctive signs. Further provisions were included in the Hague Rules of Air Warfare of 1922/23, especially in Articles 25 and 26 (*No. 26*).

Following a suggestion made in 1929 by Professor Nicholas Roerich of New York, the present treaty was prepared, at the request of the Roerich Museum in New York, by Mr. Georges Chklaver and was thereupon discussed by the International Museums Office of the League of Nations. Private conferences held at Bruges in 1931 and 1932 and at Washington in 1933 recommended its adoption by governments. In 1933, the Seventh International Conference of American States recommended the signature of the Roerich Pact. The treaty was then drawn up by the Governing Board of the Pan-American Union and signed on 15 April 1935.

In the relations between states bound by the Hague Convention for the Protection of Cultural Property in the Event of Armed Conflict of 1954 (*No. 71*) the latter Convention is supplementary to the Roerich Pact (see Article 36, paragraph 2, of the Convention of 1954, *No. 71*).

ENTRY INTO FORCE: 26 August 1935.

AUTHENTIC TEXTS: English, French, Portuguese, Spanish. The text below is reprinted from *LNTS*, Vol. 67, 1936, pp. 290–294, No. 3874.

TEXT PUBLISHED IN: OAS, Treaty Series, No. 33 (Engl., French, Portuguese, Span.); *LNTS*, Vol. 67, 1936, pp. 290–294, No. 3874 (Engl., French, Span., Portuguese); Martens, *NRGT*, 3ème série, Vol. XXXIII, pp. 650–657 (Engl., Span.); Hudson, Vol. VII, pp. 56-59, No. 408 (Engl., Span.); Deltenre, pp. 760-765 (Engl., French, German, Dutch); *BFSP*, Vol. 139, pp. 316–317 (Engl.); *US Statutes at Large*, Vol. 49, pp. 3267–3275 (Engl., French, Span., Portuguese); Malloy, Vol. IV, pp. 4815–4817 (Engl.,); *AJIL*, Vol. 30, 1936, Suppl. pp. 195–198 (Engl.); Bevans, Vol. III, pp. 254–256 (Engl.); *Droit des conflits armés*, pp. 1039–1042 (French); Jiri Toman, *The Protection of Cultural Property in the Event of Armed Conflict*, Aldershot, Dartmouth, 1996, pp. 399–401. Websites: www.roerich.org/Roerich_Pact.html (Engl.); www.sangha.net/roerich/ roerich-pact.html (Engl.); www.icrc.org/ihl.nsf (Engl., French, Span.).

* * *

The High Contracting Parties, animated by the purpose of giving conventional form to the postulates of the resolution approved on 16 December 1933, by all the States represented at the Seventh International Conference of American States, held at Montevideo, which recommended to "the Governments of America which have not yet done so that they sign the 'Roerich Pact', initiated by the 'Roerich Museum' in the United States, and which has as its object the universal adoption of a flag, already designed and generally known, in order thereby to preserve in any time of danger all nationally and privately owned immovable monuments which form the cultural treasure of peoples", have resolved to conclude a Treaty with that end in view and to the effect that the treasures of culture be respected and protected in time of war and in peace, have agreed upon the following Articles:

Article 1. The historic monuments, museums, scientific, artistic, educational and cultural institutions shall be considered as neutral and as such respected and protected by belligerents.

The same respect and protection shall be due to the personnel of the institutions mentioned above.

The same respect and protection shall be accorded to the historic monuments, museums, scientific, artistic, educational and cultural institutions in time of peace as well as in war.

Art. 2. The neutrality of, and protection and respect due to, the monuments and institutions mentioned in the preceding Article, shall be recognized in the entire expanse of territories subject to the sovereignty of each of the Signatory and Acceding States, without any discrimination as to the State allegiance of said monuments and institutions. The respective Governments agree to adopt the measures of internal legislation necessary to insure said protection and respect.

Art. 3. In order to identify the monuments and institutions mentioned in Article 1, use may be made of a distinctive flag (red circle with a triple red sphere in the circle on a white background) in accordance with the model attached to this Treaty.[1]

Art. 4. The Signatory Governments and those which accede to this Treaty shall send to the Pan American Union, at the time of signature or accession, or at any time thereafter, a list of the monuments and institutions for which they desire the protection agreed to in this Treaty.

The Pan American Union, when notifying the Governments of signatures or accessions, shall also send the list of monuments and institutions mentioned in this Article, and shall inform the other Governments of any changes in said list.

Art. 5. The monuments and institutions mentioned in Article 1 shall cease to enjoy the privileges recognized in the present Treaty in case they are made use of for military purposes.

Art. 6. The States which do not sign the present Treaty on the date it is opened for signature may sign or adhere to it at any time.

[1] See p. 994.

Art. 7. The instruments of accession, as well as those of ratification and denunciation of the present Treaty, shall be deposited with the Pan American Union, which shall communicate notice of the act of deposit to the other Signatory or Acceding States.

Art. 8. The present Treaty may be denounced at any time by any of the Signatory or Acceding States, and the denunciation shall go into effect three months after notice of it has been given to the other Signatory or Acceding States.

In witness whereof the undersigned Plenipotentiaries, after having deposited their full powers, found to be in due and proper form, sign this Treaty on behalf of their respective Governments, and affix thereto their seals, on the dates appearing opposite their signatures.

[Here follow signatures]

SIGNATURES, RATIFICATIONS[1]

State	*Signature*	*Ratification*[2]
Argentina	15 April 1935	–
Bolivia	15 April 1935	–
Brazil	15 April 1935	5 August 1936
Chile	15 April 1935	8 September 1936
Colombia	15 April 1935	20 February 1937
Costa Rica	15 April 1935	–
Cuba	15 April 1935	26 August 1935
Dominican Republic	15 April 1935	2 November 1936
Ecuador	15 April 1935	–
El Salvador	15 April 1935	1 May 1936
Guatemala	15 April 1935	16 September 1936
Haiti	15 April 1935	–
Honduras[3]	15 April 1935	–
Mexico	15 April 1935	2 October 1936
Nicaragua	15 April 1935	–
Panama	15 April 1935	–
Paraguay	15 April 1935	–
Peru	15 April 1935	–
United States of America	15 April 1935	13 July 1935
Uruguay	15 April 1935	–
Venezuela	15 April 1935	11 November 1936

RESERVATIONS

None

1 Based on *Inter-American Treaties and Conventions*, General Secretariat, Organization of American States, Washington DC, 1985, and on a communication received from the Organisation of American States, 3 December 2001. See also www.icrc.org/ihl.nsf.

2 Date of the deposit of instruments of ratification.

3 Ratified on 27 January 1936, but ratification not deposited.

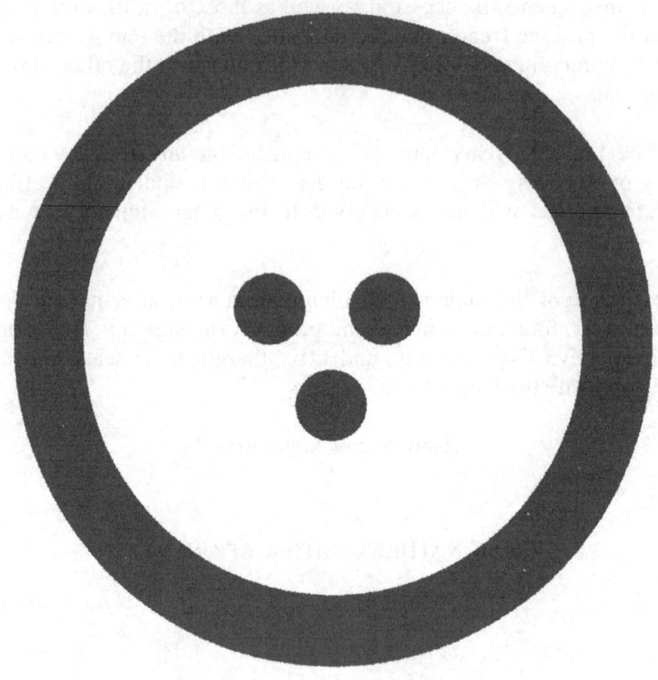

Emblem of the 1935 Roerich Pact for the Protection of Cultural Property

No. 70

FINAL ACT OF THE INTERGOVERNMENTAL CONFERENCE ON THE PROTECTION OF CULTURAL PROPERTY IN THE EVENT OF ARMED CONFLICT

Signed at The Hague, 14 May 1954

INTRODUCTORY NOTE: Following the signature of the Roerich Pact by the American States in 1935 (*No. 69*) attempts were undertaken to draft a more comprehensive convention for the protection of monuments and works of art in time of war. In 1939, a draft convention, elaborated under the auspices of the International Museums Office, was presented to governments by the Netherlands. On account of the outbreak of World War II no further steps could be taken. After the war, a new proposal was submitted to UNESCO by the Netherlands in 1948. The General Conference of UNESCO in 1951 decided to convene a committee of government experts to draft a convention. This committee met in 1952 and thereafter submitted its drafts to the General Conference. The revised drafts were then transmitted to governments for advice. The Intergovernmental Conference which adopted the Convention and the further acts (*Nos. 71–73*) took place at The Hague from 21 April to 14 May 1954 and 56 states were represented.

The Final Act has no force of law.

AUTHENTIC TEXTS: English, French, Russian, Spanish. The text below is reprinted from *Intergovernmental Conference on the Protection of Cultural Property in the Event of Armed Conflict*, The Hague 1954, Records, The Government of the Netherlands, 1961, pp. 1–80.

TEXT PUBLISHED IN: (indications are given for the Final Act as well as for the Convention and Regulations, for the Protocol and for the Resolutions) (*Nos. 44–47*): *Final Act of the Intergovernmental Conference on the Protection of Cultural Property in the Event of Armed Conflict*, UNESCO, The Hague 1954, *Final Act*, pp. 3–5, *Convention and Regulations*, pp. 7–67, *Protocol*, pp. 69–77, *Resolutions*, pp. 79–83 (Engl., French, Russian, Span.); *Intergovernmental Conference on the Protection of Cultural Property in the Event of Armed Conflict*, Records, The Government of the Netherlands, 1961, The Hague, 1954, *Final Act*, pp. 2–3, *Convention and Regulations*, pp. 5–65, *Protocol*, pp. 67–75, *Resolutions*, pp. 77–81 (Engl., French, Russian, Span.); *Conference intergouvernementale sur la protection des biens culturels en cas de conflit armé, Actes de la Conference convoquée par l'Organisation des Nations Unies pour l'éducation, la science et la culture, tenue à La Haye du 21 avril au 14 mai 1954*, publiés par le Gouvernement des Pays-Bas, La Haye, Staatsdrukkerij-en Uitgeverijbedrijf, 1961, *Conventions et Règlement d'exécution*, pp. 5–65, *Protocole*, pp. 67–75, *Résolution*, pp. 77–81 (Engl., French, Russ., Span.); *Les textes normatifs de l'Unesco*, Paris, Unesco, 1980, IV.A.3 (*Convention and Regulations, Protocol, Resolutions*), 34 p. (French); *Unesco's Standard Setting Instruments*, Paris, Unesco, 1980, IV.A.3 (*Convention and Regulations, Protocol, Resolutions*), 34 p. (Engl.); *Conventions and Recommendations of*

Unesco concerning the protection of the Cultural Heritage, Paris, Unesco, 1983, *Convention and Regulations*, pp. 13–43, *Protocol*, pp. 44–47, *Resolutions*, pp. 48–49 (Engl.); *Conventions et recommendations de l'Unesco relatives à la protection du patrimoine culturel*, Paris, Unesco, 1983, *Convention and Regulations*, pp. 15–44, *Protocol*, pp. 45–48, *Resolutions*, pp. 49–50 (French); *UNTS*, Vol. 249, *Final Act* (with attached *Resolutions*), pp. 216–239, *Convention and Regulations*, pp. 240–357, Protocol, pp. 358–386, (Engl., French, Russian, Span.); *International Red Cross Handbook*, 1983, *Convention and Regulations*, pp. 339–365, *Protocol*, pp. 366–368, *Resolutions*, p. 369 (Engl.); *Manuel de la Croix-Rouge internationale*, 1983, *Convention and Regulations*, pp. 351–377, *Protocol*, pp. 378–380, *Resolutions*, p. 381 (French); *Manual de la Cruz Roja internacional*, 1983, *Convention and Regulations*, pp. 343–369, *Protocol*, pp. 370–372, *Resolutions*, p. 373 (Span.); *Handbook of the International Movement*, 1994, *Convention and Regulations*, pp. 316–342; *Protocol*, pp. 343–345; *Resolutions*, p. 346 (Engl.); *Manuel du Mouvement international*, 1994, *Convention and Regulations*, pp. 328–354; *Protocol*, pp. 355–357; *Resolutions*, p. 358 (French); *Manual del Movimiento internacional*, 1994, *Convention and Regulations*, pp. 320–346; *Protocol*, pp. 347–349; *Resolutions*, p. 350 (Span.); Miscellaneous No. 6 (1956), Cmd. 9837, *Final Act*, *Resolutions*, p. 50 (Engl.); Roberts and Guelff, *Convention and Regulations*, pp. 371–395, *Protocol*, pp. 397–405 (Engl.); *Droit des conflits armés*, *Acte final*, pp. 1043–1045, *Convention et Règlement d'exécution*, pp. 1047–1081, *Protocol*, pp. 1083–1089, *Resolutions*, pp. 1091–1092 (French); Ronzitti, *Convention and Regulations*, pp. 545–578, *Protocol*, pp. 578–581 (Engl.); Jiri Toman, *La protection des biens culturels en cas de conflit armé, Commentaire de la Convention de La Haye du 14 mai 1954 pour la protection des biens culturels en cas de conflit armé ainsi que d'autres instruments de droit international relatifs à cette protection*, Paris, Editions UNESCO, 1994, *Convention et Règlement d'exécution*, pp. 445–472, *Protocole*, pp. 473–476, *Résolutions*, pp. 477–478 (French); Jiri Toman, *The Protection of Cultural Property in the Event of Armed Conflict. Commentary on the Convention for the Protection of Cultural Property in the Event of Armed Conflict and its Protocol, signed on 14 May 1954 in The Hague, and on other instruments of international law concerning such protection*, Aldershot, Dartmouth, 1996, *Convention and Regulations*, pp. 415–441, *Protocol*, pp. 443–446, *Resolutions*, pp. 447–448 (Engl.); *Vedomosti Verkhovnogo Soveta SSSR*, No. 3, 1957, *Convention, Regulations and Protocol*, pp. 67–91 (Russ.); *Sbornik dogovorov SSSR*, Vyp. 19, *Convention and Regulations*, pp. 114–142, *Protocol*, pp. 143–146 (Russ.); *Mezhdunarodnoe pravo*, Vol. III, *Convention, Regulations and Protocol*, pp. 113–140 (Russ. – extracts); Blatova, *Convention*, pp. 794–804 (Russ. – extracts); websites: www.unesco.org (Engl., French, Span.); www.icrc.org/ihl.nsf (Engl., French, Span.).

* * *

The Conference convened by the United Nations Educational, Scientific and Cultural Organization for the purpose of drawing up and adopting

a *Convention for the Protection of Cultural Property in the Event of Armed Conflict.*

b *Regulations for the Execution of the said Convention, and c Protocol to the Convention for the Protection of Cultural Property in the Event of Armed Conflict*

was held at the Hague, on the invitation of the Government of the Netherlands from 21 April to 14 May, 1954, and deliberated on the basis of drafts prepared by the United Nations Educational, Scientific and Cultural Organization.

The Conference established the following texts:

Convention of The Hague for the Protection of Cultural Property in the Event of Armed Conflict and Regulations for the execution of the said Convention;

Protocol for the Protection of Cultural Property in the Event of Armed Conflict.

This Convention, these Regulations and this Protocol, the texts of which were established in the English, French, Russian and Spanish languages, are attached to the present Act.

[Here follow signatures]

SIGNATURES

Andorra[1]
Australia
Belgium
Brazil
Byelorussian SSR
China
Cuba
Czechoslovakia
Ecuador
Egypt
El Salvador
France
Germany (Federal Republic)
Greece
Holy See
Hungary
India
Indonesia
Iraq
Iran
Ireland
Israel
Italy
Japan
Libya
Luxemburg
Monaco
Nicaragua
Norway
Netherlands
Peru
Philippines
Poland
Portugal
Romania
San Marino
Spain
Switzerland
Syria
Ukrainian SSR
USSR
United Kingdom
United States of America
Uruguay
Yugoslavia

[1] Signed for the Bishop of Urgel, Co-Prince of Andorra.

No. 71

CONVENTION FOR THE PROTECTION OF CULTURAL PROPERTY IN THE EVENT OF ARMED CONFLICT

Signed at The Hague, 14 May 1954

INTRODUCTORY NOTE: See note introducing the Final Act of the Inter-governmental Conference of 1954 (*No. 70*).

The Regulations for the execution of the present Convention (see pp. 1012–1019) constitute and integral part of this Convention.

ENTRY INTO FORCE: 7 August 1956.

AUTHENTIC TEXTS: See indications under *No. 70.*

TEXT PUBLISHED IN: See indications under *No. 70.*

TABLE OF CONTENTS

Articles

CONVENTION

REGULATIONS FOR THE EXECUTION OF THE CONVENTION FOR THE PROTECTION OF CULTURAL PROPERTY IN THE EVENT OF ARMED CONFLICT

* * *

The High Contracting Parties,

Recognizing that cultural property has suffered grave damage during recent armed conflicts and that, by reason of the developments in the technique of warfare, it is in increasing danger of destruction;

Being convinced that damage to cultural property belonging to any people whatsoever means damage to the cultural heritage of all mankind, since each people makes its contribution to the culture of the world;

Considering that the preservation of the cultural heritage is of great importance for all peoples of the world and that it is important that this heritage should receive international protection;

Guided by the principles concerning the protection of cultural property during armed conflict, as established in the Conventions of The Hague of 1899 and of 1907 and in the Washington Pact of 15 April, 1935;

Being of the opinion that such protection cannot be effective unless both national and international measures have been taken to organize it in time of peace;

Being determined to take all possible steps to protect cultural property;

Have agreed upon the following provisions:

Chapter I. General Provisions Regarding Protection

Article 1. Definition of cultural property

For the purposes of the present Convention, the term "cultural property" shall cover, irrespective of origin or ownership:

(a) movable or immovable property of great importance to the cultural heritage of every people, such as monuments of architecture, art or history, whether religious or secular; archaeological sites; groups of buildings which, as a whole, are of historical or artistic interest; works of art; manuscripts, books and other objects of artistic, historical or archaeological interest; as well as scientific collections and important collections of books or archives or of reproductions of the property defined above;

(b) buildings whose main and effective purpose is to preserve or exhibit the movable cultural property defined in sub-paragraph (a) such as museums, large libraries and depositories of archives, and refuges intended to shelter, in the event of armed conflict, the movable cultural property defined in sub-paragraph (a);

(c) centres containing a large amount of cultural property as defined in sub-paragraphs (a) and (b), to be known as "centres containing monuments".

Art. 2. Protection of cultural property

For the purposes of the present Convention, the protection of cultural property shall comprise the safeguarding of and respect for such property.

Art. 3. Safeguarding of cultural property

The High Contracting Parties undertake to prepare in time of peace for the safeguarding of cultural property situated within their own territory against the foreseeable effects of an armed conflict, by taking such measures as they consider appropriate.

Art. 4. Respect for cultural property

1. The High Contracting Parties undertake to respect cultural property situated within their own territory as well as within the territory of other High

Contracting Parties by refraining from any use of the property and its immediate surroundings or of the appliances in use for its protection for purposes which are likely to expose it to destruction or damage in the event of armed convict; and by refraining from any act of hostility directed against such property.

2. The obligations mentioned in paragraph 1 of the present Article may be waived only in cases where military necessity imperatively requires such a waiver.
3. The High Contracting Parties further undertake to prohibit, prevent and, if necessary, put a stop to any form of theft, pillage or misappropriation of, and any acts of vandalism directed against, cultural property. They shall refrain from requisitioning movable cultural property situated in the territory of another High Contracting Party.
4. They shall refrain from any act directed by way of reprisals against cultural property.
5. No High Contracting Party may evade the obligations incumbent upon it under the present Article, in respect of another High Contracting Party, by reason of the fact that the latter has not applied the measures of safeguard referred to in Article 3.

Art. 5. Occupation

1. Any High Contracting Party in occupation of the whole or part of the territory of another High Contracting Party shall as far as possible support the competent national authorities of the occupied country in safeguarding and preserving its cultural property.
2. Should it prove necessary to take measures to preserve cultural property situated in occupied territory and damaged by military operations, and should the competent national authorities be unable to take such measures, the Occupying Power shall, as far as possible, and in close co-operation with such authorities, take the most necessary measures of preservation.
3. Any High Contracting Party whose government is considered their legitimate government by members of a resistance movement, shall, if possible, draw their attention to the obligation to comply with those provisions of the Convention dealing with respect for cultural property.

Art. 6. Distinctive marking of cultural property

In accordance with the provisions of Article 16, cultural property may bear a distinctive emblem so as to facilitate its recognition.

Art. 7. Military measures

1. The High Contracting Parties undertake to introduce in time of peace into their military regulations or instructions such provisions as may ensure observance of the present Convention, and to foster in the members of their armed forces a spirit of respect for the culture and cultural property of all peoples.
2. The High Contracting Parties undertake to plan or establish in peacetime, within their armed forces, services or specialist personnel whose purpose will be to secure respect for cultural property and to co-operate with the civilian authorities responsible for safeguarding it.

Chapter II. Special Protection

Art. 8. Granting of special protection

1. There may be placed under special protection a limited number of refuges intended to shelter movable cultural property in the event of armed conflict, of centres containing monuments and other immovable cultural property of very great importance, provided that they:
   (a) are situated at an adequate distance from any large industrial centre or from any important military objective constituting a vulnerable point, such as, for example, an aerodrome, broadcasting station, establishment engaged upon work of national defense, a port or railway station of relative importance or a main line of communication;
   (b) are not used for military purposes.
2. A refuge for movable cultural property may also be placed under special protection, whatever its location, if it is so constructed that, in all probability, it will not be damaged by bombs.
3. A centre containing monuments shall be deemed to be used for military purposes whenever it is used for the movement of military personnel or material, even in transit. The same shall apply whenever activities directly connected with military operations, the stationing of military personnel, or the production of war material are carried on within the centre.
4. The guarding of cultural property mentioned in paragraph 1 above by armed custodians specially empowered to do so, or the presence, in the vicinity of such cultural property, of police forces normally responsible for the maintenance of public order shall not be deemed to be use for military purposes.
5. If any cultural property mentioned in paragraph 1 of the present Article is situated near an important military objective as defined in the said paragraph, it may nevertheless be placed under special protection if the High Contracting Party asking for that protection undertakes, in the event of armed conflict, to make no use of the objective and particularly, in the case of a port, railway station or aerodrome, to divert all traffic therefrom. In that event, such diversion shall be prepared in time of peace.
6. Special protection is granted to cultural property by its entry in the "International Register of Cultural Property under Special Protection". This entry shall only be made, in accordance with the provisions of the present Convention and under the conditions provided for in the Regulations for the execution of the Convention.

Art. 9. Immunity of cultural property under special protection

The High Contracting Parties undertake to ensure the immunity of cultural property under special protection by refraining, from the time of entry in the International Register, from any act of hostility directed against such property and, except for the cases provided for in paragraph 5 of Article 8, from any use of such property or its surroundings for military purposes.

Art. 10. Identification and control

During an armed conflict, cultural property under special protection shall be marked with the distinctive emblem described in Article 16, and shall be open to international control as provided for in the Regulations for the execution of the Convention.

Art. 11. Withdrawal of immunity

1. If one of the High Contracting Parties commits, in respect of any item of cultural property under special protection, a violation of the obligations under Article 9, the opposing Party shall, so long as this violation persists, be released from the obligation to ensure the immunity of the property concerned.

Nevertheless, whenever possible, the latter Party shall first request the cessation of such violation within a reasonable time.

2. Apart from the case provided for in paragraph 1 of the present Article, immunity shall be withdrawn from cultural property under special protection only in exceptional cases of unavoidable military necessity, and only for such time as that necessity continues. Such necessity can be established only by the officer commanding a force the equivalent of a division in size or larger. Whenever circumstances permit, the opposing Party shall be notified, a reasonable time in advance, of the decision to withdraw immunity.
3. The Party withdrawing immunity shall, as soon as possible, so inform the Commissioner-General for cultural property provided for in the Regulations for the execution of the Convention, in writing, stating the reasons.

Chapter III. Transport of Cultural Property

Art. 12. Transport under special protection

1. Transport exclusively engaged in the transfer of cultural property, whether within a territory or to another territory, may, at the request of the High Contracting Party concerned, take place under special protection in accordance with the conditions specified in the Regulations for the execution of the Convention.
2. Transport under special protection shall take place under the international supervision provided for in the aforesaid Regulations and shall display the distinctive emblem described in Article 16.
3. The High Contracting Parties shall refrain from any act of hostility directed against transport under special protection.

Art. 13. Transport in urgent cases

1. If a High Contracting Party considers that the safety of certain cultural property requires its transfer and that the matter is of such urgency that the procedure laid down in Article 12 cannot be followed, especially at the beginning of an armed conflict, the transport may display the distinctive emblem described in Article 16, provided that an application for immunity referred to in Article 12 has not already been made and refused. As far as possible, notification of transfer should be made to the opposing Parties. Nevertheless, transport conveying cultural property to the territory of another country may not display the distinctive emblem unless immunity has been expressly granted to it.
2. The High Contracting Parties shall take, so far as possible, the necessary precautions to avoid acts of hostility directed against the transport described in paragraph 1 of the present Article and displaying the distinctive emblem.

Art. 14. Immunity from seizure, capture and prize

1. Immunity from seizure, placing in prize, or capture shall be granted to:

(a) cultural property enjoying the protection provided for in Article 12 or that provided for in Article 13;
(b) the means of transport exclusively engaged in the transfer of such cultural property.

2. Nothing in the present Article shall limit the right of visit and search.

Chapter IV. Personnel

Art. 15. Personnel

As far as is consistent with the interests of security, personnel engaged in the protection of cultural property shall, in the interests of such property, be respected and, if they fall into the hands of the opposing Party, shall be allowed to continue to carry out their duties whenever the cultural property for which they are responsible has also fallen into the hands of the opposing Party.

Chapter V. The Distinctive Emblem

Art. 16. Emblem of the convention

1. The distinctive emblem of the Convention shall take the form of a shield, pointed below, per saltire blue and white (a shield consisting of a royal blue square, one of the angles of which forms the point of the shield, and of a royal-blue triangle above the square, the space on either side being taken up by a white triangle).
2. The emblem shall be used alone, or repeated three times in a triangular formation (one shield below), under the conditions provided for in Article 17.

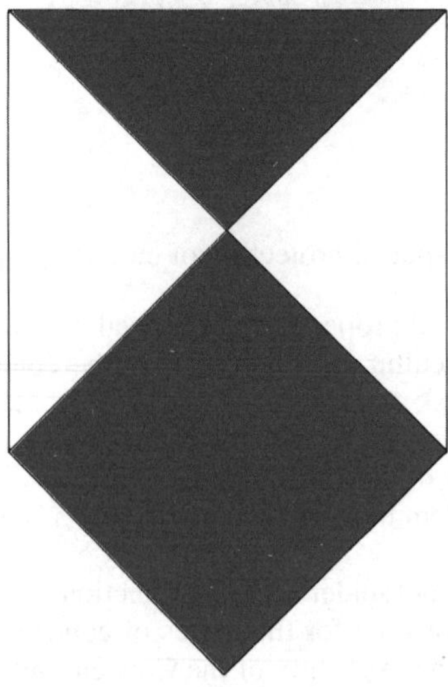

Fig. 1. Emblem for the protection of cultural property.

Art. 17. Use of the emblem

1. The distinctive emblem repeated three times may be used only as means of identification of:

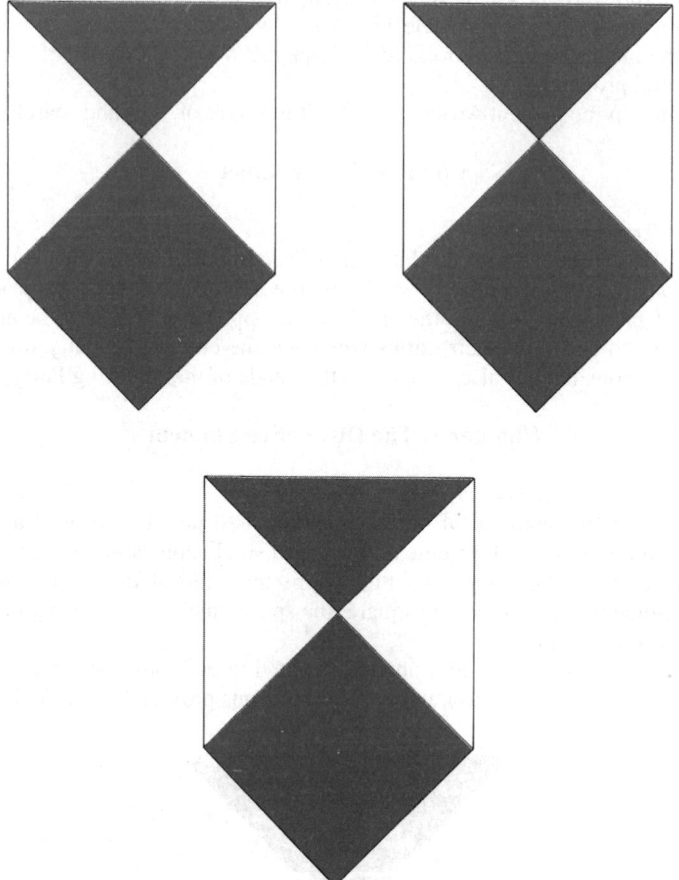

Fig. 2. Emblem for the special protection of cultural property.

(a) immovable cultural property under special protection;
(b) the transport of cultural property under the conditions provided for in Articles 12 and 13;
(c) improvised refuges, under the conditions provided for in the Regulations for the execution of the Convention.

2. The distinctive emblem may be used alone only as a means of identification of:
   (a) cultural property not under special protection;
   (b) the persons responsible for the duties of control in accordance with the Regulations for the execution of the Convention;
   (c) the personnel engaged in the protection of cultural property;
   (d) the identity cards mentioned in the Regulations for the execution of the Convention.
3. During an armed conflict, the use of the distinctive emblem in any other cases than those mentioned in the preceding paragraphs of the present Article, and the use for any purpose whatever of a sign resembling the distinctive emblem, shall be forbidden.

4. The distinctive emblem may not be placed on any immovable cultural property unless at the same time there is displayed an authorization duly dated and signed by the competent authority of the High Contracting Party.

Chapter VI. Scope of Application of the Convention

Art. 18. Application of the Convention

1. Apart from the provisions which shall take effect in time of peace, the present Convention shall apply in the event of declared war or of any other armed conflict which may arise between two or more of the High Contracting Parties, even if the state of war is not recognized by one or more of them.
2. The Convention shall also apply to all cases of partial or total occupation of the territory of a High Contracting Party, even if the said occupation meets with no armed resistance.
3. If one of the Powers in conflict is not a Party to the present Convention, the Powers which are Parties thereto shall nevertheless remain bound by it in their mutual relations. They shall furthermore be bound by the Convention, in relation to the said Power, if the latter has declared that it accepts the provisions thereof and so long as it applies them.

Art. 19. Conflicts not of an international character

1. In the event of an armed conflict not of an international character occurring within the territory of one of the High Contracting Parties, each party to the conflict shall be bound to apply, as a minimum, the provisions of the present Convention which relate to respect for cultural property.
2. The parties to the conflict shall endeavor to bring into force, by means of special agreements, all or part of the other provisions of the present Convention.
3. The United Nations Educational, Scientific and Cultural Organization may offer its services to the parties to the conflict.
4. The application of the preceding provisions shall not affect the legal status of the parties to the conflict.

Chapter VII. Execution of the Convention

Art. 20. Regulations for the execution of the Convention

The procedure by which the present Convention is to be applied is defined in the Regulations for its execution, which constitute an integral part thereof.

Art. 21. Protecting Powers

The present Convention and the Regulations for its execution shall be applied with the co-operation of the Protecting Powers responsible for safeguarding the interests of the Parties to the conflict.

Art. 22. Conciliation procedure

1. The Protecting Powers shall lend their good offices in all cases where they may deem it useful in the interests of cultural property, particularly if there is disagreement between the Parties to the conflict as to the application or interpretation of the provisions of the present Convention or the Regulations for its execution.
2. For this purpose, each of the Protecting Powers may, either at the invitation of one Party, of the Director-General of the United Nations Educational,

Scientific and Cultural Organization, or on its own initiative, propose to the Parties to the conflict a meeting of their representatives, and in particular of the authorities responsible for the protection of cultural property, if considered appropriate on suitably chosen neutral territory.

The Parties to the conflict shall be bound to give effect to the proposals for meeting made to them. The Protecting Powers shall propose for approval by the Parties to the conflict a person belonging to a neutral Power or a person presented by the Director-General of the United Nations Educational, Scientific and Cultural Organization, which person shall be invited to take part in such a meeting in the capacity of Chairman.

Art. 23. Assistance of UNESCO

1. The High Contracting Parties may call upon the United Nations Educational, Scientific and Cultural Organization for technical assistance in organizing the protection of their cultural property, or in connexion with any other problem arising out of the application of the present Convention or the Regulations for its execution. The Organization shall accord such assistance within the limits fixed by its programme and by its resources.
2. The Organization is authorized to make, on its own initiative, proposals on this matter to the High Contracting Parties.

Art. 24. Special agreements

1. The High Contracting Parties may conclude special agreements for all matters concerning which they deem it suitable to make separate provision.
2. No special agreement may be concluded which would diminish the protection afforded by this present Convention to cultural property and to the personnel engaged in its protection.

Art. 25. Dissemination of the Convention

The High Contracting Parties undertake, in time of peace as in time of armed conflict, to disseminate the text of the present Convention and the Regulations for its execution as widely as possible in their respective countries. They undertake, in particular, to include the study thereof in their programmes of military and, if possible, civilian training, so that its principles are made known to the whole population, especially the armed forces and personnel engaged in the protection of cultural property.

Art. 26. Translations, reports

1. The High Contracting Parties shall communicate to one another, through the Director-General of the United Nations Educational, Scientific and Cultural Organization, the official translations of the present Convention and of the Regulations for its execution.
2. Furthermore, at least once every four years, they shall forward to the Director-General a report giving whatever information they think suitable concerning any measures being taken, prepared or contemplated by their respective administrations in fulfillment of the present Convention and of the Regulations for its execution.

Art. 27. Meetings

1. The Director-General of the United Nations Educational, Scientific and Cultural Organization may, with the approval of the Executive Board, con-

vene meetings of representatives of the High Contracting Parties. He must convene such a meeting if at least one-fifth of the High Contracting Parties so request.

2. Without prejudice to any other functions which have been conferred on it by the present Convention or the Regulations for its execution, the purpose of the meeting will be to study problems concerning the application of the Convention and of the Regulations for its execution, and to formulate recommendations in respect thereof.
3. The meeting may further undertake a revision of the Convention or the Regulations for its execution if the majority of the High Contracting Parties are represented, and in accordance with the provisions of Article 39.

Art. 28. Sanctions

The High Contracting Parties undertake to take, within the framework of their ordinary criminal jurisdiction, all necessary steps to prosecute and impose penal or disciplinary sanctions upon those persons, of whatever nationality, who commit or order to be committed a breach of the present Convention.

Final Provisions

Art. 29. Language

1. The present Convention is drawn up in English, French, Russian and Spanish, the four texts being equally authoritative.
2. The United Nations Educational, Scientific and Cultural Organization shall arrange for translations of the Convention into the other official languages of its General Conference.

Art. 30. Signature

The present Convention shall bear the date of 14 May 1954 and, until the date of 31 December, 1954, shall remain open for signature by all States invited to the Conference which met at The Hague from 21 April, 1954 to 14 May, 1954.

Art. 31. Ratification

1. The present Convention shall be subject to ratification by signatory States in accordance with their respective constitutional procedures.
2. The instruments of ratification shall be deposited with the Director-General of the United Nations Educational, Scientific and Cultural Organization.

Art. 32. Accession

From the date of its entry into force, the present Convention shall be open for accession by all States mentioned in Article 30 which have not signed it, as well as any other State invited to accede by the Executive Board of the United Nations Educational, Scientific and Cultural Organization. Accession shall be effected by the deposit of an instrument of accession with the Director-General of the United Nations Educational, Scientific and Cultural Organization.

Art. 33. Entry into force

1. The present Convention shall enter into force three months after five instruments of ratification have been deposited.
2. Thereafter, it shall enter into force, for each High Contracting Party, three months after the deposit of its instrument of ratification or accession.

3. The situations referred to in Articles 18 and 19 shall give immediate effect to ratifications or accessions deposited by the Parties to the conflict either before or after the beginning of hostilities or occupation. In such cases the Director-General of the United Nations Educational, Scientific and Cultural Organization shall transmit the communications referred to in Article 38 by the speediest method.

Art. 34. Effective application

1. Each State Party to the Convention on the date of its entry into force shall take all necessary measures to ensure its effective application within a period of six months after such entry into force.
2. This period shall be six months from the date of deposit of the instruments of ratification or accession for any State which deposits its instrument of ratification or accession after the date of the entry into force of the Convention.

Art. 35. Territorial extension of the Convention

Any High Contracting Party may, at the time of ratification or accession, or at any time thereafter, declare by notification addressed to the Director-General of the United Nations Educational, Scientific and Cultural Organization, that the present Convention shall extend to all or any of the territories for whose international relations it is responsible. The said notification shall take effect three months after the date of its receipt.

Art. 36. Relation to previous Conventions

1. In the relations between Powers which are bound by the Conventions of The Hague concerning the Laws and Customs of War on Land (IV) and concerning Naval Bombardment in Time of War (IX), whether those of 29 July, 1899 or those of 18 October, 1907, and which are Parties to the present Convention, this last Convention shall be supplementary to the aforementioned Convention (IX) and to the Regulations annexed to the aforementioned Convention (IV) and shall substitute for the emblem described in Article 5 of the aforementioned Convention (IX) the emblem described in Article 16 of the present Convention, in cases in which the present Convention and the Regulations for its execution provide for the use of this distinctive emblem.
2. In the relations between Powers which are bound by the Washington Pact of 15 April 1935 for the Protection of Artistic and Scientific Institutions and of Historic Monuments (Roerich Pact) and which are Parties to the present Convention, the latter Convention shall be supplementary to the Roerich Pact and shall substitute for the distinguishing flag described in Article III of the Pact the emblem defined in Article 16 of the present Convention, in cases in which the present Convention and the Regulations for its execution provide for the use of this distinctive emblem.

Art. 37. Denunciation

1. Each High Contracting Party may denounce the present Convention, on its own behalf, or on behalf of any territory for whose international relations it is responsible.
2. The denunciation shall be notified by an instrument in writing, deposited with the Director-General of the United Nations Educational, Scientific and Cultural Organization.

3. The denunciation shall take effect one year after the receipt of the instrument of denunciation. However, if, on the expiry of this period, the denouncing Party is involved in an armed conflict, the denunciation shall not take effect until the end of hostilities, or until the operations of repatriating cultural property are completed, whichever is the later.

Art. 38. Notifications

The Director-General of the United Nations Educational, Scientific and Cultural Organization shall inform the States referred to in Articles 30 and 32, as well as the United Nations, of the deposit of all the instruments of ratification, accession or acceptance provided for in Articles 31, 32 and 39 and of the notifications and denunciations provided for respectively in Articles 35, 37 and 39.

Art. 39. Revision of the Convention and of the regulations for its execution

1. Any High Contracting Party may propose amendments to the present Convention or the Regulations for its execution. The text of any proposed amendment shall be communicated to the Director-General of the United Nations Educational, Scientific and Cultural Organization who shall transmit it to each High Contracting Party with the request that such Party reply within four months stating whether it:
   (a) desires that a Conference be convened to consider the proposed amendment;
   (b) favours the acceptance of the proposed amendment without a Conference; or
   (c) favours the rejection of the proposed amendment without a Conference.
2. The Director-General shall transmit the replies, received under paragraph 1 of the present Article, to all High Contracting Parties.
3. If all the High Contracting Parties which have, within the prescribed time-limit, stated their views to the Director-General of the United Nations Educational, Scientific and Cultural Organization, pursuant to paragraph 1 (b) of this Article, inform him that they favour acceptance of the amendment without a Conference, notification of their decision shall be made by the Director-General in accordance with Article 38. The amendment shall become effective for all the High Contracting Parties on the expiry of ninety days from the date of such notification.
4. The Director-General shall convene a Conference of the High Contracting Parties to consider the proposed amendment if requested to do so by more than one-third of the High Contracting Parties.
5. Amendments to the Convention or to the Regulations for its execution, dealt with under the provisions of the preceding paragraph, shall enter into force only after they have been unanimously adopted by the High Contracting Parties represented at the Conference and accepted by each of the High Contracting Parties.
6. Acceptance by the High Contracting Parties of amendments to the Convention or to the Regulations for its execution, which have been adopted by the Conference mentioned in paragraphs 4 and 5, shall be effected by the deposit of a formal instrument with the Director-General of the United Nations Educational, Scientific and Cultural Organization.
7. After the entry into force of amendments to the present Convention or to the Regulations for its execution, only the text of the Convention or of the

Regulations for its execution thus amended shall remain open for ratification or accession.

Art. 40. Registration
In accordance with Article 102 of the Charter of the United Nations, the present Convention shall be registered with the Secretariat of the United Nations at the request of the Director-General of the United Nations Educational, Scientific and Cultural Organization.

In faith whereof the undersigned, duly authorized, have signed the present Convention.

Done at The Hague, this fourteenth day of May, 1954, in a single copy which shall be deposited in the archives of the United Nations Educational, Scientific and Cultural Organization, and certified true copies of which shall be delivered to all the States referred to in Articles 30 and 32 as well as to the United Nations.

REGULATIONS FOR THE EXECUTION OF THE CONVENTION FOR THE PROTECTION OF CULTURAL PROPERTY IN THE EVENT OF ARMED CONFLICT

Chapter I. Control

Article 1. International list of persons
On the entry into force of the Convention, the Director-General of the United Nations Educational, Scientific and Cultural Organization shall compile an international list consisting of all persons nominated by the High Contracting Parties as qualified to carry out the functions of Commissioner-General for Cultural Property. On the initiative of the Director-General of the United Nations Educational, Scientific and Cultural Organization, this list shall be periodically revised on the basis of requests formulated by the High Contracting Parties.

Art. 2. Organization of control
As soon as any High Contracting Party is engaged in an armed conflict to which Article 18 of the Convention applies:
(a) It shall appoint a representative for cultural property situated in its territory; if it is in occupation of another territory, it shall appoint a special representative for cultural property situated in that territory;
(b) The Protecting Power acting for each of the Parties in conflict with such High Contracting Party shall appoint delegates accredited to the latter in conformity with Article 3 below;
(c) A Commissioner-General for Cultural Property shall be appointed to such High Contracting Party in accordance with Article 4.

Art. 3. Appointment of delegates of Protecting Powers
The Protecting Power shall appoint its delegates from among the members of its diplomatic or consular staff or, with the approval of the Party to which they will be accredited, from among other persons.

Art. 4.Appointment of a Commissioner-General

1. The Commissioner-General for Cultural Property shall be chosen from the international list of persons by joint agreement between the Party to which he will be accredited and the Protecting Powers acting on behalf of the opposing Parties.
2. Should the Parties fail to reach agreement within three weeks from the beginning of their discussions on this point, they shall request the President of the International Court of Justice to appoint the Commissioner-General, who shall not take up his duties until the Party to which he is accredited has approved his appointment.

Art. 5. Functions of delegates

The delegates of the Protecting Powers shall take note of violations of the Convention, investigate, with the approval of the Party to which they are accredited, the circumstances in which they have occurred, make representations locally to secure their cessation and, if necessary, notify the Commissioner-General of such violations. They shall keep him informed of their activities.

Art. 6. Functions of the Commissioner-General

1. The Commissioner-General for Cultural Property shall deal with all matters referred to him in connexion with the application of the Convention, in conjunction with the representative of the Party to which he is accredited and with the delegates concerned.
2. He shall have powers of decision and appointment in the cases specified in the present Regulations.
3. With the agreement of the Party to which he is accredited, he shall have the right or order an investigation or to conduct it himself.
4. He shall make any representations to the Parties to the conflict or to their Protecting Powers which he deems useful for the application of the Convention.
5. He shall draw up such reports as may be necessary on the application of the Convention and communicate them tot he Parties concerned and to their Protecting Powers. He shall send copies to the Director-General of the United Nations Educational, Scientific and Cultural Organization, who may make use only of their technical contents.
6. If there is no Protecting Power, the Commissioner-General shall exercise the functions of the Protecting Power as laid down in Articles 21 and 22 of the Convention.

Art. 7. Inspectors and experts

1. Whenever the Commissioner-General for Cultural Property considers it necessary, either at the request of the delegates concerned or after consultation with them, he shall propose, for the approval of the Party to which he is accredited, an inspector of cultural property to be charged with a specific mission. An inspector shall be responsible only to the Commissioner-General.
2. The Commissioner-General, delegates and inspectors may have recourse to the services of experts, who will also be proposed for the approval of the party mentioned in the preceding paragraph.

Art. 8. Discharged of the mission of control

The Commissioners-General for Cultural Property, delegates of the Protecting Powers, inspectors and experts shall in no case exceed their mandates. In particular, they shall take account of the security needs of the High Contracting Party to which they are accredited and shall in all circumstances act in accordance with the requirements of the military situation as communicated to them by that High Contracting Party.

Art. 9. Substitutes for Protecting Powers
If a Party to the conflict does not benefit or ceases to benefit from the activities of a Protecting Power, a neutral State may be asked to undertake those functions of a Protecting Power which concern the appointment of a Commissioner-General for Cultural Property in accordance with the procedure laid down in Article 4. The Commissioner-General thus appointed shall, if need be, entrust to inspectors the function of delegates of Protecting Powers as specified in the present Regulations.

Art. 10. Expenses
The remuneration and expenses of the Commissioner-General for Cultural Property, inspectors and experts shall be met by the Party to which they are accredited. Remuneration and expenses of delegates of the Protecting Powers shall be subject to agreement between those Powers and the states whose interests they are safeguarding.

Chapter II. Special Protection

Art. 11. Improvised refuges
1. If, during an armed conflict, any High Contracting Party is induced by unforeseen circumstances to set up an improvised refuge and desires that it should be placed under special protection, it shall communicate this fact forthwith to the Commissioner-General accredited to that Party.
2. If the Commissioner-General considers that such a measure is justified by the circumstances and by the importance of the cultural property sheltered in this improvised refuge, he may authorize the High Contracting Party to display on such refuge the distinctive emblem defined in Article 16 of the Convention. He shall communicate his decision without delay to the delegates of the Protecting Powers who are concerned, each of whom may, within a time-limit of 30 days, order the immediate withdrawal of the emblem.
3. As soon as such delegates have signified their agreement or if the time-limit of 30 days has passed without any of the delegates concerned having made an objection, and if, in the view of the Commissioner-General, the refuge fulfils the conditions laid down in Article 8 of the Convention, the Commissioner-General shall request the Director-General of the United Nations Educational Scientific and Cultural Organization to enter the refuge in the Register of Cultural Property under Special Protection.

Art. 12. International Register of Cultural Property under Special Protection
1. An "International Register of Cultural Property under Special Protection" shall be prepared.
2. The Director-General of the United Nations Educational, Scientific and Cultural Organization shall maintain the Register. He shall furnish copies to the Secretary-General of the United Nations and to the High Contracting Parties.

3. The Register shall be divided into sections, each in the name of a High Contracting Party. Each section shall be sub-divided into three paragraphs, headed: Refuges, Centres containing Monuments, Other Immovable Cultural Property. The Director-General shall determine what details each sections shall contain.

Art. 13. Requests for registration

1. Any High Contracting Party may submit to the Director-General of the United Nations Educational, Scientific and Cultural Organization an application for the entry in the Register of certain refuges, centres containing monuments or other immovable cultural property situated within its territory. Such application shall contain a description of the location of such property and shall certify that the property complies with the provisions of Article 8 of the Convention.
2. In the event of occupation, the Occupying Powers shall be competent to make such application.
3. The Director-General of the United Nations Educational, Scientific and Cultural Organization shall, without delay, send copies of applications for registration to each of the High Contracting Parties.

Art. 14. Objections

1. Any High Contracting Party may, by letter addressed to the Director-General of the United Nations Educational, Scientific and Cultural Organization, lodge an objection to the registration of cultural property. This letter must be received by him within four months of the day on which he sent a copy of the application for registration.
2. Such objection shall state the reasons giving rise to it, the only valid grounds being that:
   (a) the property is not cultural property;
   (b) the property does not comply with the conditions mentioned in Article 8 of the Convention.
3. The Director-General shall send a copy of the letter of objection to the High Contracting Parties without delay. He shall, if necessary, seek the advice of the International Committee on Monuments, Artistic and Historic Sites and Archaeological Excavations and also, if he thinks fit, of any other competent organization or person.
4. The Director-General, or the high Contracting Party requesting registration, may make whatever representations they deem necessary to the High Contracting Parties which lodged the objection, with a view to causing the objection to be withdrawn.
5. If a High Contracting Party which has made an application for registration in time of peace becomes involved in an armed conflict before entry has been made, the cultural property concerned shall at once be provisionally entered in the Register, by the Director-General, pending the confirmation, withdrawal or cancellation of any objection that may be, or may have been, made.
6. If, within a period of six months from the date of receipt of the letter of objection, the Director-General has not received from the High Contracting Party lodging the objection a communication stating that it has been withdrawn, the High Contracting Party applying for registration may request arbitration in accordance with the procedure in the following paragraph.

7. The request for arbitration shall not be made more than one year after the date of receipt by the Director-General of the latter of objection. Each of the two Parties to the dispute shall appoint an arbitrator. When more than one objection has been lodged against an application for registration, the High Contracting Parties which have lodged the objections shall, by common consent, appoint a single arbitrator. These two arbitrators shall select a chief arbitrator from the international list mentioned in Article 1 of the present Regulations. If such arbitrators cannot agree upon their choice, they shall ask the President of the International Court of Justice to appoint a chief arbitrator who need not necessarily be chosen form the international list. The arbitral tribunal thus constituted shall fix its own procedure. There shall be no appeal from its decision.
8. Each of the High Contracting Parties may declare, whenever a dispute to which it is a party arises, that it does not wish to apply the arbitration procedure provided for in the preceding paragraph. In such cases, the objection to an application for registration shall be submitted by the Director- General to the High Contracting Parties, The objection will be confirmed only if the High Contracting Parties so decide by a two-third majority of the High Contracting Parties voting. The vote shall be taken by correspondence, unless the Director-General of the United Nations Educational, Scientific and Cultural Organization deems it essential to convene a meeting under the powers conferred upon him by Article 27 of the Convention. If the Director-General decides to proceed with the vote by correspondence, he shall invite the High Contracting Parties to transmit their votes by sealed letter within six months from the day on which they were invited to do so.

Art. 15. Registration

1. The Director-General of the United Nations Educational, Scientific and Cultural Organization shall cause to be entered in the Register, under a serial number, each item of property for which an application for registration is made, provided that he has not received an objection within the time-limit prescribed in Paragraph 1 of Article 14.
2. If an objection has been lodged, and without prejudice to the provision of paragraph 5 of Article 14, the Director-General shall enter property in the Register only if the objection has been withdrawn or has failed to be confirmed following the procedures laid down in either paragraph 7 of paragraph 8 of Article 14.
3. Whenever paragraph 3 of Article 11 applies, the Director-General shall enter property in the Register if so requested by the Commissioner-General for Cultural Property.
4. The Director-General shall send without delay to the Secretary-General of the United Nations, to the High Contracting Parties, and, at the request of the Party applying for registration, to all other States referred to in Articles 30 and 32 of the Convention, a certified copy of each entry in the Register. Entries shall become effective thirty days after dispatch of such copies.

Art. 16. Cancellation

1. The Director-General of the United Nations Educational, Scientific and Cultural Organization shall cause the registration of any property to be cancelled:

(a) at the request of the High Contracting Party within whose territory the cultural property is situated;
(b) if the High Contracting Party which requested registration has denounced the Convention, and when that denunciation has taken effect;
(c) in the special case provided for in Article 14, paragraph 5, when an objection has been confirmed following the procedures mentioned either in paragraph 7 or in paragraph 8 of Article 14.

2. The Director-General shall send without delay, to the Secretary-General of the United Nations and to all States which received a copy of the entry in the Register, a certified copy of its cancellation. Cancellation shall take effect thirty days after the despatch of such copies.

Chapter III. Transport of Cultural Property

Art. 17. Procedure to obtain immunity

1. The request mentioned in paragraph 1 of Article 12 of the Convention shall be addressed to the Commissioner-General for Cultural Property. It shall mention the reasons on which it is based and specify the approximate number and the importance of the objects to be transferred, their present location, the location now envisaged, the means of transport to be used, the route to be followed, the date proposed for the transfer, and any other relevant information.
2. If the Commissioner-General, after taking such opinions as he deems fit, considers that such transfer is justified, he shall consult those delegates of the Protecting Powers who are concerned, on the measures proposed for carrying it out. Following such consultation, he shall notify the Parties to the conflict concerned of the transfer, including in such notification all useful information.
3. The Commissioner-General shall appoint one or more inspectors, who shall satisfy themselves that only the property stated in the request is to be transferred and that the transport is to be by the approved methods and bears the distinctive emblem. The inspector or inspectors shall accompany the property to its destination.

Art. 18. Transport abroad

Where the transfer under special protection is to the territory of another country, it shall be governed not only by Article 12 of the Convention and by Article 17 of the present Regulation, but by the following further provisions:

(a) while the cultural property remains on the territory of another State, that State shall be its depositary and shall extend to it as great a measure of care as that which it bestow upon its own cultural property of comparable importance;
(b) the depositary State shall return the property only on the cessation of the conflict; such return shall be effected within six months from the date on which it was requested;
(c) during the various transfer operations, and while it remains on the territory of another State, the cultural property shall be exempt from confiscation and may not be disposed of either by the depositor or the depositary. Nevertheless, when the safety of the property requires it, the depositary may, with the assent of the depositor, have the property transported to the territory of a third country, under the conditions laid down in the present article;

(d) the request for special protection shall indicate that the State to whose territory the property is to be transferred accepts the provisions of the present Article.

Art. 19. Occupied territory
Whenever a High Contracting Party occupying territory of another High Contracting Party transfers cultural property to a refuge situated elsewhere in that territory, without being able to follow the procedure provided for in Article 17 of the Regulation, the transfer in question shall not be regarded as misappropriation within the meaning of Article 4 of the Convention, provided that the Commissioner-General for Cultural Property certifies in writing, after having consulted the usual custodians, that such transfer was rendered necessary by circumstances.

Chapter IV. The Distinctive Emblem

Art. 20. Affixing the emblem
1. The placing of the distinctive emblem and its degree of visibility shall be left to the discretion of the competent authorities of each high Contracting Party. It may be displayed on flags or armlets; it may be painted on an object or represented in any other appropriate form.
2. However, without prejudice to any possible fuller markings, the emblem shall, in the event of armed conflict and in the cases mentioned in Article 12 and 13 of the Convention, be placed on the vehicles of transport so as to be clearly visible in daylight from the air as well as from the ground.
   The emblem shall be visible from the ground:
   (a) at regular intervals sufficient to indicate clearly the perimeter of a centre containing monuments under special protection;
   (b) at the entrance to other immovable cultural property under special protection.

Art. 21. Identification of persons
1. The persons mentioned in Article 17, paragraph 2(b) and (c) of the Convention may wear an armlet bearing the distinctive emblem issued and stamped by the competent authorities.
2. Such persons shall carry a special identity card bearing the distinctive emblem. This card shall mention at least the surname and first names, the date of birth, the title or rank, and the function of the holder. The card shall bear the photograph of the holder as well as his signature or fingerprints, or both. It shall bear the embossed stamp of the competent authorities.
3. Each High Contracting Party shall make out its own type of identity card, guided by the model annexed, by way of example, to the present Regulations. The High Contracting Parties shall transmit to each other a specimen of the model they are using. Identity cards shall be made out, if possible, at least in duplicate, one copy being kept by the issuing Power.
4. The said persons may not, without legitimate reason, be deprived of their identity card or the right to wear the armlet.

[Here follow signatures]

IDENTITY CARD

for personnel engaged in the protection of cultural property

Surname ....

First names ....

Date of Birth ....

Title or Rank ....

Function ....

is the bearer of this card under the terms of the Convention of The Hague, dated 14 May 1954, for the Protection of Cultural Property in the event of Armed Conflict.

Date of issue .... Number of Card ....

Photo of bearer

Signature of bearer or finger-prints or both

Embossed stamp of authority issuing card

Height	Eyes	Hair

Other distinguishing marks

....

....

....

....

....

....

....

SIGNATURES, RATIFICATIONS AND ACCESSIONS[1]

State	*Signature*	*Ratification, Accession Notifications of Succession or Continuity (C)*
Albania	–	20 December 1960
Andorra	14 May 1954[2]	–
Argentina	–	22 March 1989
Armenia	–	5 September 1993 (C)[3]
Australia	14 May 1954	19 September 1984
Austria	31 December 1954	25 March 1964
Azerbaijan	–	20 September 1993
Barbados	–	9 April 2002
Belarus	14 May 1954 *Res.*	7 May 1957
Belgium	14 May 1954	16 September 1960
Bosnia and Herzegovina	–	12 July 1993 (C)[4]
Botswana	–	3 January 2002
Brazil	31 December 1954	12 September 1958
Bulgaria	–	7 August 1956
Burkina Faso	–	18 December 1969
Cambodia	17 December 1954	4 April 1962
Cameroon	–	12 October 1961
Canada	–	11 December 1998
China, People's Republic	[14 May 1954][5]	5 January 2000
Colombia	–	18 June 1998

[1] List established on the basis of UNESCO website with the state as of 20 July 2001. Based also on the communications from UNESCO of 28 July 1986, 15 May 1995, 27 July 1999 and 29 November 2001 and on website www.unesco.org (15 October 2002).

[2] The Director-General of UNESCO received a communication from the Government of the French Republic, dated 5 August 1954, concerning the appending of the signature on the Convention in the name of the Bishop of Urgel, Co-Prince of Andorra. This communication was transmitted to the interested states. A communication from the Bishop of Urgel, dated 6 December 1954, was also transmitted to the interested states.

[3] Armenia lodged a notification of succession at the mentioned date, by which it stated that it was bound by the Convention and its Protocol which the USSR ratified on 4 January 1957.

[4] Bosnia and Herzegovina lodged a notification of succession at the mentioned date, by which it stated that it was bound by the Convention and its Protocol which Yugoslavia ratified on 13 February 1956.

[5] Signed on behalf of China by its representatives to the United Nations and Unesco at the time of signature. China is an original Member of the United Nations, the Charter having been signed and ratified in its name, on 26 and 28 September 1945, respectively, by the Government of the Republic of China, which continuously represented China in the United Nations until 25 October 1971.

China is likewise an original Member of Unesco, the Constitution having been signed and accepted in its name by the Government of the Republic of China which continuously represented China in Unesco until 29 October 1971.

On 25 October 1971, the General Assembly of the United Nations adopted Resolution 2758 (XXVI), which reads as follows:

"The General Assembly,

Recalling the principles of the Charter of the United Nations,

Considering that the restoration of the lawful rights of the lawful rights of the People's Republic of China is essential both for the protection of the Charter of the United nations and for the cause that the United nations must serve under the Charter,

Recognizing that the representative of the Government of the People's Republic of China are the only lawful representatives of China to the United Nations and that the People's Republic of China is one of the five members of the Security Council,

Decides to restore all its rights to the People's Republic of China and to recognize the representatives of its Government as the only legitimate representatives of China to the United

State	*Signature*	*Ratification, Accession Notifications of Succession or Continuity (C)*
Congo, Democratic Republic of	–	18 April 1961
Costa Rica	–	3 June 1998
Côte d'Ivoire	–	24 January 1980
Croatia	–	6 July 1992 (C)[6]
Cuba	14 May 1954	26 November 1957
Cyprus	–	9 September 1964[7]

cont.

Nations, and to expel forthwith the representatives of Chiang Kai-shek from the place which they unlawfully occupy at the United Nations and in all the organizations related to it."

The establishing of the Government of the People's Republic of China, occurring on 1 October 1949, was made known to the United Nations on 18 November 1949. Various proposals were formulated between that date and that of the adoption of the above-quoted resolution with a view to changing the representation of China at the United Nations, but these proposals were not adopted.

On 29 October 1971, the Executive Board of Unesco, at its 88th session, adopted the following decision (88 EX/Decision 9):

"The Executive Board,

1. *Taking into account* the resolution adopted by the United Nations General Assembly on 25 October 1971, whereby the representatives of the People's Republic of China were recognized as the only lawful representatives of China to the United Nations,
2. *Recalling* resolution 396 adopted by the United Nations General Assembly at its fifth regular session on 14 December 1950 recommending that 'the attitude adopted by the General Assembly' on the question of the representation of a Member State 'should be taken into account in other organs of the United Nations and in the Specialized Agencies'.
3. *Decides* that, from today onwards, the Government of the People's Republic of China is the only legitimate representative of China in Unesco and *invites* the Director-General to act accordingly."

On 29 September 1972 the Secretary-General of the United Nations received the following communication from the Minister of Foreign Affairs of the People's Republic of China (translation):

1. As concerns the multilateral treaties which the defunct Chinese Government signed, ratified or acceded to before the establishing of the Government of the People's Republic of China, my government will examine their terms before deciding, in the light of circumstances, whether they should or not be recognized.
2. As from 1 October 1949, day of the founding of the People's Republic of China, the Chiang Kai-shek clique has no right to represent China. Its signing and ratifying of any multilateral treaty, or its acceding to any multilateral treaty, by usurping the name of 'China', are all illegal and void. My government will study these multilateral treaties before deciding, in the light of circumstances, whether it is or not appropriate to accede to them."

On depositing the instrument of acceptance of the Agreement, the Government of Romania stated that it considered the above-mentioned signature as null and void, inasmuch as the only Government competent to assume obligations on behalf of China and to represent China at the international level is the Government of the People's Republic of China.

In a letter addressed to the Secretary-General in regard to the above-mentioned declaration, the Permanent Representative of the Republic of China to the United Nations stated: The Republic of China, a sovereign State and member of the United Nations, attended the Fifth Session of the General Conference of the United Nations Educational, Scientific and Cultural Organization, contributed to the formulation of the Agreement on the Importation of Educational, Scientific and Cultural Materials and duly signed the said Agreement on 22 November 1950 at the Interim Headquarters of the United Nations at Lake Success. Any statement relating to the said Agreement that is incompatible with or derogatory to the legitimate position of the Government of the Republic of China shall in no way affect the rights and obligations of the Republic of China as a signatory of the said Agreement."

6 This state lodged a notification of succession at the mentioned date, by which it stated that it was bound by the Convention and its Protocol which Yugoslavia ratified on 13 February 1956.

7 According to the information provided by UNESCO, this accession was made subject to approval. On 9 September 1964, the Director-General of UNESCO received a notification

State	*Signature*	*Ratification, Accession Notifications of Succession or Continuity (C)*
[Czechoslovakia	14 May 1954	6 December 1957]
Czech Republic	–	26 March 1993 (C)[8]
Denmark	18 October 1954	–
Dominican Republic	–	5 January 1960
Ecuador	14 May 1954	2 October 1956
Egypt	30 December 1954	17 August 1955[9]
El Salvador	14 May 1954	19 July 2001
Estonia	–	4 April 1995
Finland	–	16 September 1994
France	14 May 1954	7 June 1957
Gabon	–	4 December 1961
Georgia	–	4 November 1992 (C)[10]
[German Democratic Republic	–	16 January 1974][11]

cont.
from the Government of Cyprus informing him that the necessary constitutional formalities for the approval of the accession by the Cypriot Authorities had been completed. By reason of the then prevailing situation in Cyprus, the Convention took effect immediately for Cyprus as from the date of receipt of the said notification, in accordance with Article 33, paragraph 3, of the Convention.

8 The Czech Republic lodged a notification of succession at the mentioned date, by which it stated that it was bound by the Convention and its Protocol which Czechoslovakia ratified on 6 December 1957.

9 In conformity with the procedure set forth in the Convention and the Protocol, both agreements entered into force, for the first five states, three months after the deposit of an instrument of ratification by the fifth state, Mexico.

10 Georgia lodged a notification of succession at the mentioned date, by which it stated that it was bound by the Convention and its Protocol which the USSR ratified on 4 January 1957.

11 The German Democratic Republic deposited an instrument of accession to the Convention and its Protocol on 16 January 1974. The Federal Republic of Germany deposited an instrument of ratification of the Convention and its Protocol on 11 August 1967. Through the accession of the German Democratic Republic to the Basic Law of the Federal Republic of Germany, with effect from 3 October 1990, the two German states have united to form one sovereign state.

The Federal Republic of Germany deposited the instrument of ratification with notification declaring that the Convention and Protocol will also apply to the *Land* of Berlin with effect from the date on which the Convention and Protocol enter into force for the Federal Republic of Germany (see letter CL/1904 of 26 September 1967).

With reference to this notification the following States stated that they considered the above mentioned statement as having no legal effect since Berlin (West) has never been and is not a part of the Federal Republic of Germany: Union of Soviet Socialist Republics (16 October 1967), Ukranian Soviet Socialist Republic (23 October 1967), Byelorussian Soviet Socialist Republic (31 October 1967); Poland (27 December 1967); Romania (29 December 1967); Bulgaria (27 March 1969) (letters CL/1926 of 29 February 1968 and CL/2043 of 25 August 1969). In a further communication received on 4 April 1968, the Government of the Federal Republic of Germany informed the Director-General that the following supplementary phrase should be added to the above mentioned declaration: "account being taken of the rights and responsibilities of the Allied Authorities, in particular the powers retained by them with regard to the maintenance of the security of Berlin, and notably, those in the military field."

In regard to this communication the Union of Soviet Socialist Republics (15 July 1968), Ukranian Soviet Socialist Republic (23 July 1968), Byelorussian Soviet Socialist Republic (29 July 1968) reaffirmed, in substance their position previously adopted and the Federal Republic of Germany, United States of America, United Kingdom (5 September 1968) (letter CL/1984 of 25 November 1968) affirmed that they did not consider Berlin (West) as belong ing to the Federal Republic of Germany. This point of view was later on shared by France(10 September 1970) (letter CL/2112 of 6 November 1970) and reaffirmed by these states on several occasions. See *UNESCO's Standard-Setting Instruments IV.A.3,* Ratif. 4.

State	*Signature*	*Ratification, Accession Notifications of Succession or Continuity (C)*
Germany	14 May 1954 *Res.*	11 August 1967[12]
Ghana	–	25 July 1960
Greece	14 May 1954	9 February 1981
Guatemala	–	2 October 1985
Guinea	–	20 September 1960
Holy See	–	24 February 1958
Hungary	14 May 1954	17 May 1956
India	14 May 1954	16 June 1958
Indonesia	24 December 1954	10 January 1967
Iran	14 May 1954	22 June 1959
Iraq	14 May 1954	21 December 1967
Ireland	14 May 1954	–
Israel	14 May 1954	3 October 1957
Italy	14 May 1954	9 May 1958
Japan	6 September 1954	–
Jordan	22 December 1954	2 October 1957
Kazakhstan	–	14 March 1997 (C)[13]
Kuwait	–	6 June 1969
Kyrghyzstan	–	3 July 1995
Lebanon	25 May 1954	1 June 1960
Libyan Arab Jamahiriya	14 May 1954	19 November 1957
Liechtenstein	–	28 April 1960
Lithuania	–	27 July 1998
Luxembourg	14 May 1954	29 September 1961
Madagascar	–	3 November 1961
Malaysia	–	12 December 1960
Mali	–	18 May 1961
Mexico	29 December 1954	7 May 1956
Monaco	14 May 1954	10 December 1957
Mongolia	–	4 November 1964
Morocco	–	30 August 1968
Myanmar[14]	31 December 1954	10 February 1956
Netherlands	14 May 1954	14 October 1958
New Zealand	20 December 1954	–
Nicaragua	14 May 1954	25 November 1959
Niger	–	6 December 1976
Nigeria	–	5 June 1961
Norway	14 May 1954	19 September 1961 *Res.*
Oman	–	26 October 1977
Pakistan	–	27 March 1959
Panama	–	17 July 1962
Peru	–	21 July 1989
Philippines	14 May 1954	–

[12] On 12 January 1962, the Director-General of UNESCO received a communication from the Government of the Federal Republic of Germany whereby this Government declared that the Federal Republic of Germany, in accordance with Article 18, paragraph 3, of the Convention, accepted the provisions of the Convention and would apply them. This communication was transmitted to the interested states.

[13] Kazakhstan lodged a notification of succession at the mentioned date, by which it stated that it was bound by the Convention and its Protocol which the USSR ratified on 4 January 1957.

[14] In conformity with the procedure set forth in the Convention and the Protocol, both agreements entered into force, for the first five states, three months after the deposit of an instrument of ratification by the fifth state, Mexico.

State	*Signature*	*Ratification, Accession Notifications of Succession or Continuity (C)*
Poland	14 May 1954	6 August 1956
Republic of Moldova	–	9 December 1999
Portugal	14 May 1954	4 August 2000
Qatar	–	31 July 1973
Romania	14 May 1954	21 March 1958
Russian Federation[15]	14 May 1954 *Res.*	4 January 1957
Rwanda	–	28 December 2000
San Marino[16]	14 May 1954	9 February 1956
Saudi Arabia	–	20 January 1971
Senegal	–	17 June 1987
Slovakia	–	31 March 1993 (C)[17]
Slovenia	–	5 November 1992 (C)[18]
Spain	14 May 1954	7 July 1960
Sudan	–	23 July 1970[19]
Sweden	–	22 January 1985
Switzerland	–	15 May 1962
Syrian Arab Republic	14 May 1954	6 March 1958
Tajikistan	–	28 August 1992 (C)[20]
Tanzania, United Rep.	–	23 September 1971
Thailand	–	2 May 1958
The former Yugoslav Republic of Macedonia	–	30 April 1997 (C)[21]
Tunisia	–	28 January 1981
Turkey	–	15 December 1965
Ukraine	14 May 1954 *Res.*	6 February 1957
United Kingdom	30 December 1954	–
United States of America	14 May 1954	–
Uruguay	14 May 1954	24 September 1999
[USSR	14 May 1954 *Res.*	4 January 1957]
Uzbekistan	–	21 February 1996
Yemen[22]	–	6 February 1970

15 The instrument of ratification was deposited by the USSR on 4 January 1957. The Director-General has been informed that the Russian Federation would continue the participation of the USSR in Unesco conventions.

16 In conformity with the procedure set forth in the Convention and the Protocol, both agreements entered into force, for the first five states, three months after the deposit of an instrument of ratification by the fifth state, Mexico.

17 Slovakia lodged a notification of succession at the mentioned date, by which it stated that it was bound by the Convention and its Protocol which Czechoslovakia ratified on 6 December 1957.

18 Slovenia lodged a notification of succession at the mentioned date, by which it stated that it was bound by the Convention and its Protocol which Yugoslavia ratified on 13 February 1956.

19 See the declaration of Sudan on p. 1025.

20 Tajikistan lodged a notification of succession at the mentioned date, by which it stated that it was bound by the Convention and its Protocol which the USSR ratified on 4 January 1957.

21 Macedonia lodged a notification of sucsession at the mentioned date, by which it stated that it was bound by the Convention and its Protocol which Yugoslavia ratified on 13 Feburary 1956.

22 The People's Democratic Republic of Yemen deposited its instrument of accession on 6 February 1970. After the unification of the People's Democratic Republic of Yemen and the Yemen Arab Republic into a single sovereign state called "the Republic of Yemen", the Ministers of Foreign Affairs of the Yemen Arab Republic and the People's Democratic Republic of Yemeninformed the Secretary-General of the United Nation on 19 May 1990 that all treaties and agreements concluded between either the Yemen Arab Republic or the People's Democratic Republic of Yemen and other states and international organizations in accordance with international law which are in force on 22 May 1990, would remain in effect.

State	*Signature*	*Ratification, Accession Notifications of Succession or Continuity (C)*
Yugoslavia[23]	–	11 September 2001
Zimbabwe	–	9 June 1998

RESERVATIONS AND DECLARATIONS

BYELORUSSIAN SSR (*declaration made on signature*)
On signing the Convention and Regulations, the Representative of the Byelorussian Soviet Socialist Republic noted that various provisions included in the Convention and Regulations weakened these agreements with regard to the conservation and defense of cultural property in the event of armed conflict and that, for that reason, he could not express his satisfaction.

GERMANY, FEDERAL REPUBLIC OF (*declaration made on signature*)
As however ... ratification will take some time, owing to the federal character of the Federal Republic of Germany ... in accordance with Article 18(3) of the above-mentioned Convention ... the Federal Republic of Germany accepts and applies the provisions of the said Convention ... accordingly, under the above mentioned Article 18(3), all other Parties to the said Convention are thereby bound in relation to the Federal Republic of Germany" (see letter ODG/SJ/2/467 of 2 May 1962).

NORWAY (*reservation made at ratification of the Convention and Protocol*)
The return of the cultural property in accord with the provisions of Section I and II of the Protocol cannot be demanded after the end of a period of twenty years, starting from the date when the property concerned came into the possession of a holder in good faith.

Sixteen states made observations to the depositary about this reservation. In a note to the Depositary dated 3 October 1979 Norway withdrew the reservation.

SUDAN (*communication of 25 August 1972*)
In a communication dated 25 August 1972, *re* an application by the Khmer Republic for an entry in the International Register of Cultural Property under Special Protection, Sudan stated that it "considers that the Royal Government of the National Union of Cambodia, of Samdeck Norodom Sihanouk is the only Government empowered to represent the Kingdom of Cambodia" and therefore it "does not recognize the right of the Phnom-Penh regime to enter into international obligations on behalf of the Kingdom of Cambodia".

UKRAINIAN SSR (*declaration made on signature*)
On signing the Convention and the Regulations for its Execution, I believe it essential to state that a large number of provisions of the Convention and Regulations are unsatisfactory since they weaken the meaning of the agreements for the purpose of conserving and defending, cultural property in the event of armed conflict.

UNION OF SOVIET SOCIALIST REPUBLICS (*declaration made on signature*)
On signing the Convention for the conservation of Cultural Property in the event of Armed Conflict and the Regulations for its execution, the USSR delegation states that both the Convention and Regulations contain a large number of provisions which weaken its effectiveness for the preservation and defense of cultural property in the event of armed conflict and are, for that reason, unsatisfactory.

[23] The Federal Republic of Yugoslavia lodged a notification of succession at the mentioned date, by which it stated that it was bound by the Convention and its Protocol which the Socialist Federal Republic of Yugoslavia ratified on 13 February 1956.

No. 72

PROTOCOL FOR THE PROTECTION OF CULTURAL PROPERTY IN THE EVENT OF ARMED CONFLICT

Signed at The Hague, 14 May 1954

INTRODUCTORY NOTE: The purpose of the present Protocol is to prevent the exportation of cultural property and to provide for the restitution of illegally exported objects. In view of the difficulties of several governments in adopting provisions on the restitution of property (the original draft contained more far-reaching provisions) it was decided to separate them from the Convention (*No. 71*) and to adopt them in the form of a separate Protocol.

ENTRY INTO FORCE: 7 August 1956.

AUTHENTIC TEXTS: See indications under *No. 70.*

TEXT PUBLISHED IN: See indications under *No. 70.*

* * *

The High Contracting Parties are agreed as follows:

I

1. Each High Contracting Party undertakes to prevent the exportation, from a territory occupied by it during an armed conflict, of cultural property as defined in Article 1 of the Convention for the Protection of Cultural Property in the Event of Armed Conflict, signed at The Hague on 14 May, 1954.
2. Each High Contracting Party undertakes to take into its custody cultural property imported into its territory either directly or indirectly from any occupied territory. This shall either be effected automatically upon the importation of the property or, failing this, at the request of the authorities of that territory.
3. Each High Contracting Party undertakes to return, at the close of hostilities, to the competent authorities of the territory previously occupied, cultural property which is in its territory, if such property has been exported in contravention of the principle laid down in the first paragraph. Such property shall never be retained as war reparations.
4. The High Contracting Party whose obligation it was to prevent the exportation of cultural property from the territory occupied by it, shall pay an indemnity to the holders in good faith of any cultural property which has to be returned in accordance with the preceding paragraph.

II

5. Cultural property coming from the territory of a High Contracting Party and deposited by it in the territory of another High Contracting Party for the purpose of protecting such property against the dangers of an armed conflict, shall be returned by the latter, at the end of hostilities, to the competent authorities of the territory from which it came.

III

6. The present Protocol shall bear the date of 14 May, 1954 and, until the date of 31 December, 1954, shall remain open for signature by all States invited to the Conference which met at The Hague from 21 April, 1954 to 14 May, 1954.
7. (a) The present Protocol shall be subject to ratification by signatory States in accordance with their respective constitutional procedures.
   (b) The instruments of ratification shall be deposited with the Director-General of the United Nations Educational, Scientific and Cultural Organization.
8. From the date of its entry into force, the present Protocol shall be open for accession by all States mentioned in paragraph 6 which have not signed it as well as any other State invited to accede by the Executive Board of the United Nations Educational, Scientific and Cultural Organization. Accession shall be effected by the deposit of an instrument of accession with the Director-General of the United Nations Educational, Scientific and Cultural Organization.
9. The States referred to in paragraphs 6 and 8 may declare, at the time of signature, ratification or accession, that they will not be bound by the provisions of Section I or by those of Section II of the present Protocol.
10. (a) The present Protocol shall enter into force three months after five instruments of ratification have been deposited.
   (b) Thereafter, it shall enter into force, for each High Contracting Party, three months after the deposit of its instrument of ratification or accession.
   (c) The situations referred to in Articles 18 and 19 of the Convention for the Protection of Cultural Property in the Event of Armed Conflict, signed at The Hague on 14 May, 1954, shall give immediate effect to ratifications and accessions deposited by the Parties to the conflict either before or after the beginning of hostilities or occupation. In such cases, the Director-General of the United Nations Educational, Scientific and Cultural Organization shall transmit the communications referred to in paragraph 14 by the speediest method.
11. (a) Each State Party to the Protocol on the date of its entry into force shall take all necessary measures to ensure its effective application within a period of six months after such entry into force.
   (b) This period shall be six months from the date of deposit of the instruments of ratification or accession for any State which deposits its instrument of ratification or accession after the date of the entry into force of the Protocol.
12. Any High Contracting Party may, at the time of ratification or accession, or at any time thereafter, declare by notification addressed to the Director-

General of the United Nations Educational, Scientific and Cultural Organization, that the present Protocol shall extend to all or any of the territories for whose international relations it is responsible. The said notification shall take effect three months after the date of its receipt.

13. (a) Each High Contracting Party may denounce the present Protocol, on its own behalf, or on behalf of any territory for whose international relations it is responsible.
    (b) The denunciation shall be notified by an instrument in writing, deposited with the Director-General of the United Nations Educational, Scientific and Cultural Organization.
    (c) The denunciation shall take effect one year after receipt of the instrument of denunciation. However, if, on the expiry of this period, the denouncing Party is involved in an armed conflict, the denunciation shall not take effect until the end of hostilities, or until the operations of repatriating cultural property are completed, whichever is the later.
14. The Director-General of the United Nations Educational, Scientific and Cultural Organization shall inform the States referred to in paragraphs 6 and 8, as well as the United Nations, of the deposit of all the instruments of ratification, accession or acceptance provided for in paragraphs 7, 8 and 15 and the notifications and denunciations provided for respectively in paragraphs 12 and 13.
15. (a) The present Protocol may be revised if revision is requested by more than one-third of the High Contracting Parties.
    (b) The Director-General of the United Nations Educational, Scientific and Cultural Organization shall convene a Conference for this purpose.
    (c) Amendments to the present Protocol shall enter into force only after they have been unanimously adopted by the High Contracting Parties represented at the Conference and accepted by each of the High Contracting Parties.
    (d) Acceptance by the High Contracting Parties of amendments to the present Protocol, which have been adopted by the Conference mentioned in subparagraphs (b) and (c), shall be effected by the deposit of a formal instrument with the Director-General of the United Nations Educational, Scientific and Cultural Organization.
    (e) After the entry into force of amendments to the present Protocol, only the text of the said Protocol thus amended shall remain open for ratification or accession.

In accordance with Article 102 of the Charter of the United Nations, the present Protocol shall be registered with the Secretariat of the United Nations at the request of the Director-General of the United Nations Educational, Scientific and Cultural Organization.

In faith whereof the undersigned, duly authorized, have signed the present Protocol.

Done at The Hague, this fourteenth day of May, 1954, in English, French, Russian and Spanish, the four texts being equally authoritative, in a single copy which shall be deposited in the archives of the United Nations Educational, Scientific and Cultural Organization, and certified true copies of which shall be delivered to all the States referred to in paragraphs 6 and 8 as well as to the United Nations.

SIGNATURES, RATIFICATIONS AND ACCESSIONS[1]

State	*Signature*	*Ratification, Accession, Succession (C)*
Albania	–	20 December 1960
Armenia	–	5 September 1993 (C)[2]
Austria	31 December 1954	25 March 1964
Azerbaijan	–	20 September 1993
Belarus	14 May 1954.	7 May 1957
Belgium	14 May 1954	16 September 1960
Bosnia and Herzegovina	–	12 July 1993 (C)[3]
Brazil	31 December 1954	12 September 1958
Bulgaria	–	9 October 1958
Burkina Faso	–	4 February 1987
Cambodia	17 December 1954	4 April 1962
Cameroon	–	12 October 1961
China[4]	[14 May 1954]	5 January 2000
Colombia	–	18 June 1998
Congo, Democratic Republic of	–	18 April 1961
Costa Rica	–	3 June 1998
Croatia	–	6 July 1992 (C)[5]
Cuba	14 May 1954	26 November 1957
Cyprus	–	9 September 1964[6]
[Czechoslovakia	14 May 1954	6 December 1957]
Czech Republic	–	26 March 1993 (C)[7]
Denmark	18 October 1954	–
Ecuador	14 May 1954	8 February 1961
Egypt	30 December 1954	17 August 1955[8]
El Salvador	14 May 1954	–
Finland	–	16 September 1994
France	14 May 1954	7 June 1957
Gabon	–	4 December 1961

1 List established on the basis of Unesco website with the state as at 8 October 2002. Based also on the communications from Unesco of 28 July 1986, 15 May 1995 and 27 July 1999 and 29 November 2001.

2 Armenia lodged a notification of succession at the mentioned date, by which it stated that it was bound by the Convention and its Protocol which the USSR ratified on 4 January 1957.

3 Bosnia-Herzegovina lodged a notification of succession at the mentioned date, by which it stated that it was bound by the Convention and its Protocol which Yugoslavia ratified on 13 February 1956.

4 See note 5 concerning the representation of China on p. 1020.

5 Croatia lodged a notification of succession at the mentioned date, by which it stated that it was bound by the Convention and its Protocol which Yugoslavia ratified on 13 February 1956.

6 According to the information provided by Unesco, this accession was made subject to approval. On 9 September 1964, the Director-General of Unesco received a notification from the Government of Cyprus informing him that the necessary constitutional formalities for the approval of the accession by the Cypriot Authorities had been completed. By reason of the then prevailing situation in Cyprus, the Convention took effect immediately for Cyprus as from the date of receipt of the said notification, in accordance with Article 33, paragraph 3, of the Convention.

7 The Czech Republic lodged a notification of succession at the mentioned date, by which it stated that it was bound by the Convention and its Protocol which Czechoslovakia ratified on 6 December 1957.

8 In conformity with the procedure set forth in the Convention and the Protocol, both agreements entered into force, for the first five states, three months after the deposit of an instrument of ratification by the fifth state, Mexico.

State	*Signature*	*Ratification, Accession, Succession (C)*
Georgia	–	4 November 1992 (C)[9]
[German Democratic Republic)	–	16 January 1974]
Germany	14 May 1954	11 August 1967[10]
Ghana	-	25 July 1960
Greece	14 May 1954	9 February 1981
Guatemala	–	2 October 1985
Guinea	–	11 December 1961
Holy See	–	24 February 1958
Hungary	14 May 1954	16 August 1956
India	14 May 1954	16 June 1958
Indonesia	24 December 1954	26 July 1967
Iran	14 May 1954	22 June 1959
Iraq	14 May 1954	21 December 1967
Israel	14 May 1954	1 April 1958
Italy	14 May 1954	9 May 1958
Japan	6 September 1954	–
Jordan	22 December 1954	2 October 1957
Kazakhstan	–	14 March 1997 (C)[11]
Kuwait	–	11 February 1970
Lebanon	25 May 1954	1 June 1960
Libyan Arab Jamahiriya	14 May 1954	19 November 1957
Liechtenstein	–	28 April 1960
Lithuania	–	27 July 1998
Luxembourg	14 May 1954	29 September 1961
Macedonia, the former Yugoslav Republic of	–	30 April 1997 (C)[12]
Madagascar	–	3 November 1961
Malaysia	–	12 December 1960
Mali	–	18 May 1961
Mexico	29 December 1954	7 May 1956
Moldova	–	9 December 1999
Monaco	14 May 1954	10 December 1957
Morocco	–	30 August 1968
Myanmar[13]	31 December 1954	10 February 1956
Netherlands	14 May 1954	14 October 1958
Nicaragua	14 May 1954	25 November 1959
Niger	–	6 December 1976

[9] Georgia lodged a notification of succession at the mentioned date, by which it stated that it was bound by the Convention and its Protocol which the USSR ratified on 4 January 1957.

[10] The German Democratic Republic deposited an instrument of accession to the Convention and its Protocol on 16 January 1974. The Federal Republic of Germany deposited an instrument of ratification of the Convention and its Protocol on 11 August 1967. Through the accession of the German Democratic Republic to the Basic Law of the Federal Republic of Germany, with effect from 3 October 1990, the two German States have united to form one sovereign state. See also note 11 on p. 1022.

[11] Kazakhstan lodged a notification of succession at the mentioned date, by which it stated that it was bound by the Convention and its Protocol which the USSR ratified on 4 January 1957.

[12] Macedonia lodged a notification of succession at the mentioned date, by which it stated that it was bound by the Convention and its Protocol which Yugoslavia ratified on 13 February 1956.

[13] In conformity with the procedure set forth in the Convention and the Protocol, both agreements entered into force, for the first five states, three months after the deposit of an instrument of ratification by the fifth state, Mexico.

State	*Signature*	*Ratification, Accession, Succession (C)*
Nigeria	–	5 June 1961
Norway	14 May 1954	19 September 1961 *Res.*
Pakistan	–	27 March 1959
Panama	–	8 March 2001
Peru	–	21 July 1989
Philippines	14 May 1954	–
Poland	14 May 1954	6 August 1956
Portugal	14 May 1954	–
Romania	14 May 1954	21 March 1958
Russian Federation[14]	14 May 1954	4 January 1957
San Marino[15]	14 May 1954	9 February 1956
Senegal	–	17 June 1987
Slovakia	–	31 March 1993 (C)[16]
Slovenia	–	5 November 1992 (C)[17]
Spain	–	26 June 1992
Sweden	–	22 January 1985
Switzerland	–	15 May 1962
Syrian Arab Republic	14 May 1954	6 March 1958
Tajikistan	–	28 August 1992 (C)[18]
Thailand	–-	2 May 1958
Tunisia	–	28 January 1981
Turkey	–	15 December 1965
Ukraine	14 May 1954 .	6 February 1957
Uruguay	14 May 1954	24 September 1999
[USSR	14 May 1954	4 January 1957]
Yemen[19]	–	6 February 1970
Yugoslavia[20]	–	10 September 2001

[14] The instrument of ratification was deposited by the USSR on 4 January 1957. The Director-General has been informed that the Russian Federation would continue the participation of the USSR in UNESCO conventions.

[15] In conformity with the procedure set forth in the Convention and the Protocol, both agreements entered into force, for the first five states, three months after the deposit of an instrument of ratification by the fifth state, Mexico.

[16] Slovakia lodged a notification of succession at the mentioned date, by which it stated that it was bound by the Convention and its Protocol which Czechoslovakia ratified on 6 December 1957.

[17] Slovenia lodged a notification of succession at the mentioned date, by which it stated that it was bound by the Convention and its Protocol which Yugoslavia ratified on 13 February 1956.

[18] Tajikistan lodged a notification of succession at the mentioned date, by which it stated that it was bound by the Convention and its Protocol which the USSR ratified on 4 January 1957.

[19] The People's Democratic Republic of Yemen deposited its instrument of accession on 6 February 1970. After the unification of the People's Democratic Republic of Yemen and the Yemen Arab Republic into a single sovereign state called "the Republic of Yemen", the Ministers of Foreign Affairs of the Yemen Arab Republic and the People's Democratic Republic of Yemen informed the Secretary-General of the United Nation on 19 May 1990 that all treaties and agreements concluded between either the Yemen Arab Republic or the People's Democratic Republic of Yemen and other states and international organizations in accordance with international law which are in force on 22 May 1990, would remain in effect.

[20] The Federal Republic of Yugoslavia lodged a notification of succession at the mentioned date, by which it stated that it was bound by the Convention and its Protocol which the Socialist Federal Republic of Yugoslavia ratified on 13 February 1956.

RESERVATIONS

NORWAY (*reservation made at ratification of the Convention and Protocol*)
The return of the cultural property in accord with the provisions of Section I and II of the Protocol cannot be demanded after the end of a period of twenty years, starting from the date when the property concerned came into the possession of a holder in good faith.

Sixteen states made observations to the depositary about this reservation. In a note to the depositary dated 3 October 1979 Norway withdrew the reservation.

No. 73

RESOLUTIONS OF THE INTERGOVERNMENTAL CONFERENCE ON THE PROTECTION OF CULTURAL PROPERTY IN THE EVENT OF ARMED CONFLICT

The Hague, 14 May 1954

INTRODUCTORY NOTE: See the introductory note of the Final Act of the Intergovernmental Conference of 1954 (*No. 70*). These resolutions do not have the force of law.

AUTHENTIC TEXTS: See indications under *No. 70*.

TEXT PUBLISHED IN: See indications under *No. 70*.

* * *

Resolution I

The Conference expresses the hope that the competent organs of the United Nations should decide, in the event of military action being taken in implementation of the Charter, to ensure application of the provisions of the Convention by the armed forces taking part in such action.

Resolution II

The Conference expresses the hope that each of the High Contracting Parties, on acceding to the Convention, should set up, within the framework of its constitutional and administrative system, a national advisory committee consisting of a small number of distinguished persons: for example, senior officials of archaeological services, museums, etc., a representative of the military general staff, a representative of the Ministry of Foreign Affairs, a specialist in international law and two or three other members whose official duties or specialized knowledge are related to the fields covered by the Convention.

The Committee should be under the authority of the minister of State or senior official responsible for the national service chiefly concerned with the care of cultural property. Its chief functions would be:

(a) to advise the government concerning the measures required for the implementation of the Convention in its legislative, technical or military aspects, both in time of peace and during an armed conflict;

(b) to approach its government in the event of an armed conflict or when such a conflict appears imminent, with a view to ensuring that cultural property situated within its own territory or within that of other countries is known to, and respected and protected by the armed forces of the country, in accordance with the provisions of the Convention;

(c) to arrange, in agreement with its government, for liaison and co-operation with other similar national committees and with any competent international authority.

Resolution III

The Conference expresses the hope that the Director-General of the United Nations Educational, Scientific and Cultural Organization should convene, as soon as possible after the entry into force of the Convention for the Protection of Cultural Property in the Event of Armed Conflict, a meeting of the High Contracting Parties.

VOTE

Resolution I

The draft resolution CBC/DR/162 was unanimously approved by the Main Commission and adopted by the plenary session of the Conference without registration of the vote.[1]

Resolution II

The draft resolution CBC/DR/163 was adopted by the plenary session of the Conference by 25 votes and 15 abstentions.[2]

Resolution III

The draft resolution CBC/DR/151 was adopted by the plenary session of the Conference by 9 votes in favour, 3 against and 27 abstentions.[3]

1 Final Act of the Intergovernmental Conference on the Protection of Cultural Property in the Event of Armed Conflict, Unesco, The Hague, 1954, par. 2159.
2 *Idem*, para. 2160.
3 *Idem*, para. 2160.

No. 74

SECOND PROTOCOL TO THE HAGUE CONVENTION OF 1954 FOR THE PROTECTION OF CULTURAL PROPERTY IN THE EVENT OF ARMED CONFLICT

Adopted at The Hague, 26 March 1999

INTRODUCTORY NOTE: The 1954 Hague Convention was strongly influenced by the 1949 Geneva Conventions. Later developments of international humanitarian law and serious gaps in the implementation of the Hague Convention called for a review of the Convention. In 1994, a group of experts elaborated the so-called Lauswolt document, which was revised on the basis of governmental comments in 1997. A preliminary draft protocol prepared by the Netherlands in cooperation with the Unesco Secretariat was submitted to a diplomatic conference which adopted the present Protocol on 26 March 1999. The Protocol was open for signature at The Hague from 17 May until 31 December 1999. The most important improvements brought about by the Protocol are the clearer definition of military necessity, the new system of enhanced protection, the reinforcement of individual criminal responsibility and the extension of the application to non-international armed conflicts.

ENTRY INTO FORCE: Not yet in force.

AUTHENTIC TEXTS: Arabic, Chinese, English, French, Spanish, Russian.

TEXT PUBLISHED IN: Unesco Doc. HC/1999/7, *ILM*, Vol. 38, No. 4, July 1999, pp. 769–782 (Engl.); Roberts and Guelff, pp. 699–719 (Engl.); Website of Unesco: www.unesco.org. (Engl., French, Span.); Website of ICRC: www.icrc.org/ihl.nsf (Engl., French, Span.).

TABLE OF CONTENTS

* * *

The Parties,

Conscious of the need to improve the protection of cultural property in the event of armed conflict and to establish an enhanced system of protection for specifically designated cultural property;

Reaffirming the importance of the provisions of the Convention for the Protection of Cultural Property in the Event of Armed Conflict, done at the Hague on 14 May 1954, and emphasizing the necessity to supplement these provisions through measures to reinforce their implementation;

Desiring to provide the High Contracting Parties to the Convention with a means of being more closely involved in the protection of cultural property in the event of armed conflict by establishing appropriate procedures therefor;

Considering that the rules governing the protection of cultural property in the event of armed conflict should reflect developments in international law;

Affirming that the rules of customary international law will continue to govern questions not regulated by the provisions of this Protocol;

Have agreed as follows:

Chapter 1. Introduction

Article 1. Definitions

For the purposes of this Protocol:

(a) "Party" means a State Party to this Protocol;
(b) "cultural property" means cultural property as defined in Article 1 of the Convention;
(c) "Convention" means the Convention for the Protection of Cultural Property in the Event of Armed Conflict, done at The Hague on 14 May 1954;
(d) "High Contracting Party" means a State Party to the Convention;
(e) enhanced protection" means the system of enhanced protection established by Articles 10 and 11;
(f) "military objective" means an object which by its nature, location, purpose, or use makes an effective contribution to military action and whose total or partial destruction, capture or neutralisation, in the circumstances ruling at the time, offers a definite military advantage;
(g) "illicit" means under compulsion or otherwise in violation of the applicable rules of the domestic law of the occupied territory or of international law.
(h) "List" means the International List of Cultural Property under Enhanced Protection established in accordance with Article 27, sub-paragraph 1(b);
(i) "Director-General" means the Director-General of UNESCO;
(j) "UNESCO" means the United Nations Educational, Scientific and Cultural Organization;
(k) "First Protocol" means the Protocol for the Protection of Cultural Property in the Event of Armed Conflict done at The Hague on 14 May 1954;

Art. 2. Relation to the Convention

This Protocol supplements the Convention in relations between the Parties.

Art. 3. Scope of application

1. In addition to the provisions which shall apply in time of peace, this Protocol shall apply in situations referred to in Article 18 paragraphs 1 and 2 of the Convention and in Article 22 paragraph 1.
2. When one of the parties to an armed conflict is not bound by this Protocol, the Parties to this Protocol shall remain bound by it in their mutual relations. They shall furthermore be bound by this Protocol in relation to a State party to the conflict which is not bound by it, if the latter accepts the provisions of this Protocol and so long as it applies them.

Art. 4. Relationship between Chapter 3 and other provisions of the Convention and this Protocol

The application of the provisions of Chapter 3 of this Protocol is without prejudice to:

(a) the application of the provisions of Chapter I of the Convention and of Chapter 2 of this Protocol;
(b) the application of the provisions of Chapter II of the Convention save that, as between Parties to this Protocol or as between a Party and a State which accepts and applies this Protocol in accordance with Article 3 paragraph 2, where cultural prop-

erty has been granted both special protection and enhanced protection, only the provisions of enhanced protection shall apply.

Chapter 2. General provisions regarding protection

Art. 5. Safeguarding of cultural property
Preparatory measures taken in time of peace for the safeguarding of cultural property against the foreseeable effects of an armed conflict pursuant to Article 3 of the Convention shall include, as appropriate, the preparation of inventories, the planning of emergency measures for protection against fire or structural collapse, the preparation for the removal of movable cultural property or the provision for adequate in situ protection of such property, and the designation of competent authorities responsible for the safeguarding of cultural property.

Art. 6. Respect for cultural property
With the goal of ensuring respect for cultural property in accordance with Article 4 of the Convention:
(a) a waiver on the basis of imperative military necessity pursuant to Article 4 paragraph 2 of the Convention may only be invoked to direct an act of hostility against cultural property when and for as long as:
(i) that cultural property has, by its function, been made into a military objective; and
(ii) there is no feasible alternative available to obtain a similar military advantage to that offered by directing an act of hostility against that objective;
(b) a waiver on the basis of imperative military necessity pursuant to Article 4 paragraph 2 of the Convention may only be invoked to use cultural property for purposes which are likely to expose it to destruction or damage when and for as long as no choice is possible between such use of the cultural property and another feasible method for obtaining a similar military advantage;
(c) the decision to invoke imperative military necessity shall only be taken by an officer commanding a force the equivalent of a battalion in size or larger, or a force smaller in size where circumstances do not permit otherwise;
(d) in case of an attack based on a decision taken in accordance with sub-paragraph (a), an effective advance warning shall be given whenever circumstances permit.

Art. 7. Precautions in attack
Without prejudice to other precautions required by international humanitarian law in the conduct of military operations, each Party to the conflict shall:
(a) do everything feasible to verify that the objectives to be attacked are not cultural property protected under Article 4 of the Convention;
(b) take all feasible precautions in the choice of means and methods of attack with a view to avoiding, and in any event to minimizing, incidental damage to cultural property protected under Article 4 of the Convention;
(c) refrain from deciding to launch any attack which may be expected to cause incidental damage to cultural property protected under Article 4 of the Convention which would be excessive in relation to the concrete and direct military advantage anticipated; and
(d) cancel or suspend an attack if it becomes apparent:
(i) that the objective is cultural property protected under Article 4 of the Convention
(ii) that the attack may be expected to cause incidental damage to cultural property protected under Article 4 of the Convention which would be excessive in relation to the concrete and direct military advantage anticipated.

Art. 8. Precautions against the effects of hostilities
The Parties to the conflict shall, to the maximum extent feasible:

(a) remove movable cultural property from the vicinity of military objectives or provide for adequate in situ protection;
(b) avoid locating military objectives near cultural property.

Art. 9. Protection of cultural property in occupied territory

1. Without prejudice to the provisions of Articles 4 and 5 of the Convention, a Party in occupation of the whole or part of the territory of another Party shall prohibit and prevent in relation to the occupied territory:
   (a) any illicit export, other removal or transfer of ownership of cultural property;
   (b) any archaeological excavation, save where this is strictly required to safeguard, record or preserve cultural property;
   (c) any alteration to, or change of use of, cultural property which is intended to conceal or destroy cultural, historical or scientific evidence.
2.[1] Any archaeological excavation of, alteration to, or change of use of, cultural property in occupied territory shall, unless circumstances do not permit, be carried out in close co-operation with the competent national authorities of the occupied territory.

Chapter 3. Enhanced protection

Art. 10. Enhanced protection

Cultural property may be placed under enhanced protection provided that it meets the following three conditions:
(a) it is cultural heritage of the greatest importance for humanity;
(b) it is protected by adequate domestic legal and administrative measures recognising its exceptional cultural and historic value and ensuring the highest level of protection;
(c) it is not used for military purposes or to shield military sites and a declaration has been made by the Party which has control over the cultural property, confirming that it will not be so used.

Art. 11. The granting of enhanced protection

1. Each Party should submit to the Committee a list of cultural property for which it intends to request the granting of enhanced protection.
2. The Party which has jurisdiction or control over the cultural property may request that it be included in the List to be established in accordance with Article 27 subparagraph 1(b). This request shall include all necessary information related to the criteria mentioned in Article 10. The Committee may invite a Party to request that cultural property be included in the List.
3. Other Parties, the International Committee of the Blue Shield and other non-governmental organisations with relevant expertise may recommend specific cultural property to the Committee. In such cases, the Committee may decide to invite a Party to request inclusion of that cultural property in the List.
4. Neither the request for inclusion of cultural property situated in a territory, sovereignty or jurisdiction over which is claimed by more than one State, nor its inclusion, shall in any way prejudice the rights of the parties to the dispute.
5. Upon receipt of a request for inclusion in the List, the Committee shall inform all Parties of the request. Parties may submit representations regarding such a request to the Committee within sixty days. These representations shall be made only on the basis of the criteria mentioned in Article 10. They shall be specific and related to facts. The Committee shall consider the representations, providing the Party requesting inclusion with a reasonable opportunity to respond before taking the decision. When such representations are before the Committee, decisions for inclusion in the List shall be taken, notwithstanding Article 26, by a majority of four-fifths of its members present and voting.

[1] For the reservation in respect of this paragraph by Azerbaijan, see p. 1051.

6. In deciding upon a request, the Committee should ask the advice of governmental and non-governmental organisations, as well as of individual experts.
7. A decision to grant or deny enhanced protection may only be made on the basis of the criteria mentioned in Article 10.
8. In exceptional cases, when the Committee has concluded that the Party requesting inclusion of cultural property in the List cannot fulfil the criteria of Article 10 sub-paragraph (b), the Committee may decide to grant enhanced protection, provided that the requesting Party submits a request for international assistance under Article 32.
9. Upon the outbreak of hostilities, a Party to the conflict may request, on an emergency basis, enhanced protection of cultural property under its jurisdiction or control by communicating this request to the Committee. The Committee shall transmit this request immediately to all Parties to the conflict. In such cases the Committee will consider representations from the Parties concerned on an expedited basis. The decision to grant provisional enhanced protection shall be taken as soon as possible and, notwithstanding Article 26, by a majority of four-fifths of its members present and voting. Provisional enhanced protection may be granted by the Committee pending the outcome of the regular procedure for the granting of enhanced protection, provided that the provisions of Article 10 sub-paragraphs (a) and (c) are met.
10. Enhanced protection shall be granted to cultural property by the Committee from the moment of its entry in the List.
11. The Director-General shall, without delay, send to the Secretary-General of the United Nations and to all Parties notification of any decision of the Committee to include cultural property on the List.

Art. 12. Immunity of cultural property under enhanced protection

The Parties to a conflict shall ensure the immunity of cultural property under enhanced protection by refraining from making such property the object of attack from any use of the property or its immediate surroundings in support of military action.

Art. 13. Loss of enhanced protection

1. Cultural property under enhanced protection shall only lose such protection:
   (a) if such protection is suspended or cancelled in accordance with Article 14; or
   (b) if, and for as long as, the property has, by its use, become a military objective.
2. In the circumstances of sub-paragraph 1(b), such property may only be the object of attack if:
   (a) the attack is the only feasible means of terminating the use of the property referred to in sub-paragraph 1(b);
   (b) all feasible precautions are taken in the choice of means and methods of attack, with a view to terminating such use and avoiding, or in any event minimising, damage to the cultural property;
   (c) unless circumstances do not permit, due to requirements of immediate self-defence:
      (i) the attack is ordered at the highest operational level of command;
      (ii) effective advance warning is issued to the opposing forces requiring the termination of the use referred to in sub-paragraph 1(b); and
      (iii) reasonable time is given to the opposing forces to redress the situation.

Art.14. Suspension and cancellation of enhanced protection

1. Where cultural property no longer meets any one of the criteria in Article 10 of this Protocol, the Committee may suspend its enhanced protection status or cancel that status by removing that cultural property from the List.
2. In the case of a serious violation of Article 12 in relation to cultural property under enhanced protection arising from its use in support of military action, the Committee may suspend its enhanced protection status. Where such violations are continuous, the Committee may exceptionally cancel the enhanced protection status by removing the cultural property from the List.

3. The Director-General shall, without delay, send to the Secretary-General of the United Nations and to all Parties to this Protocol notification of any decision of the Committee to suspend or cancel the enhanced protection.
4. Before taking such a decision, the Committee shall afford an opportunity to the Parties to make their views known.

Chapter 4. Criminal responsibility and jurisdiction

Art. 15. Serious violations of this Protocol

1. Any person commits an offence within the meaning of this Protocol if that person intentionally and in violation of the Convention or this Protocol commits any of the following acts:
   (a) making cultural property under enhanced protection the object of attack;
   (b) using cultural property under enhanced protection or its immediate surroundings in support of military action;
   (c)[2] extensive destruction or appropriation of cultural property protected under the Convention and this Protocol;
   (d) making cultural property protected under the Convention and this Protocol the object of attack;
   (e) theft, pillage or misappropriation of, or acts of vandalism directed against cultural property protected under the Convention.
2. Each Party shall adopt such measures as may be necessary to establish as criminal offences under its domestic law the offences set forth in this Article and to make such offences punishable by appropriate penalties. When doing so, Parties shall comply with general principles of law and international law, including the rules extending individual criminal responsibility to persons other than those who directly commit the act.

Art. 16. Jurisdiction

1 Without prejudice to paragraph 2, each Party shall take the necessary legislative measures to establish its jurisdiction over offences set forth in Article 15 in the following cases:
   (a) when such an offence is committed in the territory of that State;
   (b) when the alleged offender is a national of that State;
   (c)[2] in the case of offences set forth in Article 15 sub-paragraphs (a) to (c), when the alleged offender is present in its territory.

2 With respect to the exercise of jurisdiction and without prejudice to Article 28 of the Convention:
   (a) this Protocol does not preclude the incurring of individual criminal responsibility or the exercise of jurisdiction under national and international law that may be applicable, or affect the exercise of jurisdiction under customary international law;
   (b) Except in so far as a State which is not Party to this Protocol may accept and apply its provisions in accordance with Article 3 paragraph 2, members of the armed forces and nationals of a State which is not Party to this Protocol, except for those nationals serving in the armed forces of a State which is a Party to this Protocol, do not incur individual criminal responsibility by virtue of this Protocol, nor does this Protocol impose an obligation to establish jurisdiction over such persons or to extradite them.

Art. 17. Prosecution

1. The Party in whose territory the alleged offender of an offence set forth in Article 15 sub-paragraphs 1 (a) to (c) is found to be present shall, if it does not extradite that person, submit, without exception whatsoever and without undue delay, the case to

[2] For interpretative declaration in respect of this paragraph by Austria, see p. 1051.

its competent authorities, for the purpose of prosecution, through proceedings in accordance with its domestic law or with, if applicable, the relevant rules of international law.

2. Without prejudice to, if applicable, the relevant rules of international law, any person regarding whom proceedings are being carried out in connection with the Convention or this Protocol shall be guaranteed fair treatment and a fair trial in accordance with domestic law and international law at all stages of the proceedings, and in no cases shall be provided guarantees less favorable to such person than those provided by international law.

Art. 18. Extradition

1. The offences set forth in Article 15 sub-paragraphs 1 (a) to (c) shall be deemed to be included as extraditable offences in any extradition treaty existing between any of the Parties before the entry into force of this Protocol. Parties undertake to include such offences in every extradition treaty to be subsequently concluded between them.
2. When a Party which makes extradition conditional on the existence of a treaty receives a request for extradition from another Party with which it has no extradition treaty, the requested Party may, at its option, consider the present Protocol as the legal basis for extradition in respect of offences as set forth in Article 15 sub-paragraphs 1 (a) to (c).
3. Parties which do not make extradition conditional on the existence of a treaty shall recognise the offences set forth in Article 15 sub-paragraphs 1 (a) to (c) as extraditable offences between them, subject to the conditions provided by the law of the requested Party.
4. If necessary, offences set forth in Article 15 sub-paragraphs 1 (a) to (c) shall be treated, for the purposes of extradition between Parties, as if they had been committed not only in the place in which they occurred but also in the territory of the Parties that have established jurisdiction in accordance with Article 16 paragraph 1.

Art. 19. Mutual legal assistance

1. Parties shall afford one another the greatest measure of assistance in connection with investigations or criminal or extradition proceedings brought in respect of the offences set forth in Article 15, including assistance in obtaining evidence at their disposal necessary for the proceedings.
2. Parties shall carry out their obligations under paragraph 1 in conformity with any treaties or other arrangements on mutual legal assistance that may exist between them. In the absence of such treaties or arrangements, Parties shall afford one another assistance in accordance with their domestic law.

Art. 20. Grounds for refusal

1. For the purpose of extradition, offences set forth in Article 15 sub-paragraphs 1 (a) to (c), and for the purpose of mutual legal assistance, offences set forth in Article 15 shall not be regarded as political offences or as offences connected with political offences or as offences inspired by political motives. Accordingly, a request for extradition or for mutual legal assistance based on such offences may not be refused on the sole ground that it concerns a political offence or an offence connected with a political offence or an offence inspired by political motives.
2. Nothing in this Protocol shall be interpreted as imposing an obligation to extradite or to afford mutual legal assistance if the requested Party has substantial grounds for believing that the request for extradition for offences set forth in Article 15 sub-paragraphs 1(a) to (c) or for mutual legal assistance with respect to offences set forth in Article 15 has been made for the purpose of prosecuting or punishing a person on account of that person's race, religion, nationality, ethnic origin or political opinion or that compliance with the request would cause prejudice to that person's position for any of these reasons.

Art. 21. Measures regarding other violations
Without prejudice to Article 28 of the Convention, each Party shall adopt such legislative, administrative or disciplinary measures as may be necessary to suppress the following acts when committed intentionally:
(a) any use of cultural property in violation of the Convention or this Protocol;
(b) any illicit export, other removal or transfer of ownership of cultural property from occupied territory in violation of the Convention or this Protocol.

Chapter 5. The protection of cultural property in armed conflicts not of an international character

Art. 22. Armed conflicts not of an international character
1. This Protocol shall apply in the event of an armed conflict not of an international character, occurring within the territory of one of the Parties.
2. This Protocol shall not apply to situations of internal disturbances and tensions, such as riots, isolated and sporadic acts of violence and other acts of a similar nature.
3. Nothing in this Protocol shall be invoked for the purpose of affecting the sovereignty of a State or the responsibility of the government, by all legitimate means, to maintain or re-establish law and order in the State or to defend the national unity and territorial integrity of the State.
4. Nothing in this Protocol shall prejudice the primary jurisdiction of a Party in whose territory an armed conflict not of an international character occurs over the violations set forth in Article 15.
5. Nothing in this Protocol shall be invoked as a justification for intervening, directly or indirectly, for any reason whatever, in the armed conflict or in the internal or external affairs of the Party in the territory in which that conflict occurs.
6. The application of this Protocol to the situation referred to in paragraph 1 shall not affect the legal status of the parties to the conflict.
7. UNESCO may offer its services to the parties to the conflict.

Chapter 6. Institutional issues

Art. 23. Meeting of the Parties
1. The Meeting of the Parties shall be convened at the same time as the General Conference of UNESCO, and in co-ordination with the Meeting of the High Contracting Parties, if such a meeting has been called by the Director-General.
2. The Meeting of the Parties shall adopt its Rules of Procedure.
3. The Meeting of the Parties shall have the following functions:
   (a) to elect the Members of the Committee, in accordance with Article 24 paragraph 1;
   (b) to endorse the Guidelines developed by the Committee in accordance with Article 27 sub-paragraph 1(a);
   (c) to provide guidelines for, and to supervise the use of the Fund by the Committee;
   (d) to consider the report submitted by the Committee in accordance with Article 27 sub-paragraph 1(d);
   (e) to discuss any problem related to the application of this Protocol, and to make recommendations, as appropriate.
4. At the request of at least one-fifth of the Parties, the Director-General shall convene an Extraordinary Meeting of the Parties.

Art. 24. Committee for the protection of cultural property in the event of armed conflict
1. The Committee for the Protection of Cultural Property in the Event of Armed Conflict is hereby established. It shall be composed of twelve Parties which shall be elected by the Meeting of the Parties.
2. The Committee shall meet once a year in ordinary session and in extra-ordinary sessions whenever it deems necessary.

3. In determining membership of the Committee, Parties shall seek to ensure an equitable representation of the different regions and cultures of the world.
4. Parties members of the Committee shall choose as their representatives persons qualified in the fields of cultural heritage, defence or international law, and they shall endeavour, in consultation with one another, to ensure that the Committee as a whole contains adequate expertise in all these fields.

Art. 25. Term of office

1. A Party shall be elected to the Committee for four years and shall be eligible for immediate re-election only once.
2. Notwithstanding the provisions of paragraph 1, the term of office of half of the members chosen at the time of the first election shall cease at the end of the first ordinary session of the Meeting of the Parties following that at which they were elected. These members shall be chosen by lot by the President of this Meeting after the first election.

Art. 26. Rules of procedure

1. The Committee shall adopt its Rules of Procedure.
2. A majority of the members shall constitute a quorum. Decisions of the Committee shall be taken by a majority of two-thirds of its members voting.
3. Members shall not participate in the voting on any decisions relating to cultural property affected by an armed conflict to which they are parties.

Art. 27. Functions

1. The Committee shall have the following functions:
   (a) to develop Guidelines for the implementation of this Protocol;
   (b) to grant, suspend or cancel enhanced protection for cultural property and to establish, maintain and promote the List of cultural property under enhanced protection;
   (c) to monitor and supervise the implementation of this Protocol and promote the identification of cultural property under enhanced protection;
   (d) to consider and comment on reports of the Parties, to seek clarifications as required, and prepare its own report on the implementation of this Protocol for the Meeting of the Parties;
   (e) to receive and consider requests for international assistance under Article 32;
   (f) to determine the use of the Fund;
   (g) to perform any other function which may be assigned to it by the Meeting of the Parties.
2. The functions of the Committee shall be performed in co-operation with the Director-General.
3. The Committee shall co-operate with international and national governmental and non-governmental organizations having objectives similar to those of the Convention, its First Protocol and this Protocol. To assist in the implementation of its functions, the Committee may invite to its meetings, in an advisory capacity, eminent professional organizations such as those which have formal relations with UNESCO, including the International Committee of the Blue Shield (ICBS) and its constituent bodies. Representatives of the International Centre for the Study of the Preservation and Restoration of Cultural Property (Rome Centre) (ICCROM) and of the International Committee of the Red Cross (ICRC) may also be invited to attend in an advisory capacity.

Art. 28. Secretariat

The Committee shall be assisted by the Secretariat of UNESCO which shall prepare the Committee's documentation and the agenda for its meetings and shall have the responsibility for the implementation of its decisions.

Art. 29. The Fund for the protection of cultural property in the event of armed conflict

1. A Fund is hereby established for the following purposes:
   (a) to provide financial or other assistance in support of preparatory or other measures to be taken in peacetime in accordance with, inter alia, Article 5, Article 10 sub-paragraph (b) and Article 30; and
   (b) to provide financial or other assistance in relation to emergency, provisional or other measures to be taken in order to protect cultural property during periods of armed conflict or of immediate recovery after the end of hostilities in accordance with, inter alia, Article 8 sub-paragraph (a).
2. The Fund shall constitute a trust fund, in conformity with the provisions of the financial regulations of UNESCO.
3. Disbursements from the Fund shall be used only for such purpose as the Committee shall decide in accordance with the guidelines as defined in Article 23 sub-paragraph 3(c). The Committee may accept contributions to be used only for a certain programme or project, provided that the Committee shall have decided on the implementation of such programme or project.
4. The resources of the Fund shall consist of:
   (a) voluntary contributions made by the Parties;
   (b) contributions, gifts or bequests made by:
      (i) other States;
      (ii) UNESCO or other organizations of the United Nations system;
      (iii) other intergovernmental or non-governmental organizations; and
      (iv) public or private bodies or individuals;
   (c) any interest accruing on the Fund;
   (d funds raised by collections and receipts from events organized for the benefit of the Fund; and
   (e) all other resources authorized by the guidelines applicable to the Fund.

Chapter 7. Dissemination of information and international assistance

Art. 30. Dissemination

1. The Parties shall endeavour by appropriate means, and in particular by educational and information programmes, to strengthen appreciation and respect for cultural property by their entire population.
2. The Parties shall disseminate this Protocol as widely as possible, both in time of peace and in time of armed conflict.
3. Any military or civilian authorities who, in time of armed conflict, assume responsibilities with respect to the application of this Protocol, shall be fully acquainted with the text thereof. To this end the Parties shall, as appropriate:
   (a) incorporate guidelines and instructions on the protection of cultural property in their military regulations;
   (b) develop and implement, in cooperation with UNESCO and relevant governmental and non-governmental organizations, peacetime training and educational programmes;
   (c) communicate to one another, through the Director-General, information on the laws, administrative provisions and measures taken under sub-paragraphs (a) and (b);
   (d) communicate to one another, as soon as possible, through the Director-General, the laws and administrative provisions which they may adopt to ensure the application of this Protocol.

Art. 31. International cooperation

In situations of serious violations of this Protocol, the Parties undertake to act, jointly through the Committee, or individually, in cooperation with UNESCO and the United Nations and in conformity with the Charter of the United Nations.

Art. 32. International assistance

1. Parties may request from the Committee international assistance for cultural property under enhanced protection as well as assistance with respect to the preparation, development or implementation of the laws, administrative provisions and measures referred to in Article 10.
2. A party to the conflict, which is not a Party to this Protocol but which accepts and applies provisions in accordance with Article 3, paragraph 2, may request appropriate international assistance from the Committee.
3. The Committee shall adopt rules for the submission of requests for international assistance and shall define the forms the international assistance may take.
4. Parties are encouraged to give technical assistance of all kinds, through the Committee, to those Parties or parties to the conflict who request it.

Art. 33. Assistance of UNESCO

1. A Party may call upon UNESCO for technical assistance in organizing the protection of its cultural property, such as preparatory action to safeguard cultural property, preventive and organizational measures for emergency situations and compilation of national inventories of cultural property, or in connection with any other problem arising out of the application of this Protocol. UNESCO shall accord such assistance within the limits fixed by its programme and by its resources.
2. Parties are encouraged to provide technical assistance at bilateral or multilateral level.
3. UNESCO is authorized to make, on its own initiative, proposals on these matters to the Parties.

Chapter 8. Execution of this Protocol

Art. 34. Protecting Powers

This Protocol shall be applied with the co-operation of the Protecting Powers responsible for safeguarding the interests of the Parties to the conflict.

Art. 35. Conciliation procedure

1. The Protecting Powers shall lend their good offices in all cases where they may deem it useful in the interests of cultural property, particularly if there is disagreement between the Parties to the conflict as to the application or interpretation of the provisions of this Protocol.
2. For this purpose, each of the Protecting Powers may, either at the invitation of one Party, of the Director-General, or on its own initiative, propose to the Parties to the conflict a meeting of their representatives, and in particular of the authorities responsible for the protection of cultural property, if considered appropriate, on the territory of a State not party to the conflict. The Parties to the conflict shall be bound to give effect to the proposals for meeting made to them. The Protecting Powers shall propose for approval by the Parties to the conflict a person belonging to a State not party to the conflict or a person presented by the Director-General, which person shall be invited to take part in such a meeting in the capacity of Chairman.

Art. 36 Conciliation in absence of Protecting Powers

1. In a conflict where no Protecting Powers are appointed the Director-General may lend good offices or act by any other form of conciliation or mediation, with a view to settling the disagreement.
2. At the invitation of one Party or of the Director-General, the Chairman of the Committee may propose to the Parties to the conflict a meeting of their representatives, and in particular of the authorities responsible for the protection of cultural property, if considered appropriate, on the territory of a State not party to the conflict.

Art. 37. Translations and reports

1. The Parties shall translate this Protocol into their official languages and shall communicate these official translations to the Director-General.
2. The Parties shall submit to the Committee, every four years, a report on the implementation of this Protocol.

Art. 38. State responsibility

No provision in this Protocol relating to individual criminal responsibility shall affect the responsibility of States under international law, including the duty to provide reparation.

Chapter 9. Final clauses

Art. 39. Languages

This Protocol is drawn up in Arabic, Chinese, English, French, Russian and Spanish, the six texts being equally authentic.

Art. 40. Signature

This Protocol shall bear the date of 26 May 1999. It shall be opened for signature by all High Contracting Parties at The Hague from 17 May 1999 until 31 December 1999.

Art. 41. Ratification, acceptance or approval

1. This Protocol shall be subject to ratification, acceptance or approval by High Contracting Parties which have signed this Protocol, in accordance with their respective constitutional procedures.
2. The instruments of ratification, acceptance or approval shall be deposited with the Director-General.

Art. 42. Accession

1. This Protocol shall be open for accession by other High Contracting Parties from 1 January 2000.
2. Accession shall be effected by the deposit of an instrument of accession with the Director-General.

Art. 43. Entry into force

1. This Protocol shall enter into force three months after twenty instruments of ratification, acceptance, approval or accession have been deposited.
2. Thereafter, it shall enter into force, for each Party, three months after the deposit of its instrument of ratification, acceptance, approval or accession.

Art. 44. Entry into force in situations of armed conflict

The situations referred to in Articles 18 and 19 of the Convention shall give immediate effect to ratifications, acceptances or approvals of or accessions to this Protocol deposited by the parties to the conflict either before or after the beginning of hostilities or occupation. In such cases the Director-General shall transmit the communications referred to in Article 46 by the speediest method.

Art. 45. Denunciation

1. Each Party may denounce this Protocol.
2. The denunciation shall be notified by an instrument in writing, deposited with the Director-General.
3. The denunciation shall take effect one year after the receipt of the instrument of denunciation. However, if, on the expiry of this period, the denouncing Party is involved in an armed conflict, the denunciation shall not take effect until the end of hostilities, or until the operations of repatriating cultural property are completed, whichever is the later.

Art. 46. Notifications
The Director-General shall inform all High Contracting Parties as well as the United Nations, of the deposit of all the instruments of ratification, acceptance, approval or accession provided for in Articles 41 and 42 and of denunciations provided for in Article 45.

Art. 47. Registration with the United Nations
In conformity with Article 102 of the Charter of the United Nations, this Protocol shall be registered with the Secretariat of the United Nations at the request of the Director-General.

In faith whereof the undersigned, duly authorized, have signed the present Protocol.

Done at The Hague, this twenty-sixth day of March 1999, in a single copy which shall be deposited in the archives of the UNESCO, and certified true copies of which shall be delivered to all the High Contracting Parties.

SIGNATURES, RATIFICATIONS AND ACCESSIONS[1]

State	*Signature*	*Ratification, Accession Notifications of Succession or Continuity (C)*
Albania	17 May 1999	
Argentina	–	7 January 2002
Armenia	22 October 1999	
Austria	17 May 1999	1 March 2002 *Dec.*
Azerbaijan	–	17 April 2001 *Res.*
Belarus	17 December 1999	13 December 2000
Belgium	17 May 1999 *Dec.*	
Bulgaria	15 September 1999	14 June 2000
Cambodia	17 May 1999	
Colombia	31 December 1999	–
Côte d'Ivoire	17 May 1999	–
Croatia	17 May 1999	–
Cyprus	19 August 1999	16 May 2001
Ecuador	29 December 1999	–
Egypt	29 December 1999	–
Estonia	17 May 1999	–
Finland	17 May 1999	–
Germany	17 May 1999	–
Ghana	17 May 1999	–
Greece	17 May 1999	–
Holy See	17 May 1999	–
Hungary	17 May 1999	–
Indonesia	17 May 1999	–
Italy	17 May 1999	–
Libyan Arab Jamahiriya	–	20 July 2001
Luxembourg	17 May 1999	–
Macedonia, the former Yugoslav Republic of	17 May 1999	–

[1] List established on the basis of the communications from UNESCO of 29 November 2001 and of UNESCO website of 8 October 2002.

State	*Signature*	*Ratification, Accession Notifications of Succession or Continuity (C)*
Madagascar	17 May 1999	–
Morocco	21 December 1999	–
Netherlands	17 May 1999	–
Nicaragua	–	1 June 2001
Nigeria	17 May 1999	–
Oman	30 June 1999	–
Pakistan	17 May 1999	–
Panama	–	8 March 2001
Peru	13 July 1999	–
Qatar	17 May 1999	4 September 2000
Romania	8 November 1999	–
Slovakia	22 December 1999	–
Spain	17 May 1999	6 July 2001
Sweden	17 May 1999	
Switzerland	17 May 1999	
Syrian Arab Republic	17 May 1999	
Yemen	17 May 1999	

RESERVATIONS AND DECLARATIONS

AUSTRIA (*interpretative declaration made on ratification*)
Concerning *Article 15 sub-paragraph 1 (c)*:
The Republic of Austria considers that the term "appropriation' refers to the offence of (grave) theft as set forth in §§127 and 128 sub-paragraph 1 (3) of the Austrian Criminal Code (österreiciisches Strafgesetzbuch – StGB).

Concerning *Article 16 sub-paragraph 1 (c)*:
The Republic of Austria considers with regard to the provision of Article 17 paragraph 1 that the obligation under Article 16 sub-paragraph 1 (c) to establish jurisdiction over the serious violations set forth in Article 15 sub-paragraphs (a) to (c) only applies to such cases where the alleged offender cannot be extradited (aut dedere aut judicare).

AZERBAIJAN (*reservation made on accession*)
The Republic of Azerbaijan declares that under the definition of "the competent national authorities of the occupied territory" mentioned in Article 9, paragraph 2 of the Second Protocol to the Hague Convention of 1954 for the Protection of Cultural Property in the Event of Armed conflict, it understands the central competent authority dealing with the issues on the protection of the cultural properties situated over the whole territory of the Party to the Protocol.

BELGIUM (*declaration made on signature*)[2]
This signature engages also the French Community, the German-speaking Community, the Walloon region and the Brussels Capital Region. This signature also engages the Flemish Region.

* * *

See also Nos. 7, 8, 26, 56–58, 79

[2] Original in French. Translation made by editors.

VIII

WARFARE AT SEA

No. 75

DECLARATION RESPECTING MARITIME LAW

Signed at Paris, 16 April 1856

INTRODUCTORY NOTE. On the conclusion of the Treaty of Paris on 30 March 1856 that ended the Crimean War (1853–1856), the plenipotentiaries assembled in Paris signed the present Declaration. It is the outcome of a *modus vivendi,* which was adopted between France and Great Britain in 1854 and was originally intended for the Crimean War only. Both powers recognized that they would not seize enemy goods on neutral vessels nor neutral goods on enemy vessels. All the belligerents furthermore proclaimed that they would not issue letters of marque. The Declaration of Paris confirmed these rules and added to them the principle that blockades, in order to be binding, must be effective.

Virtually all states acceded to the Declaration. The United States, which aimed at a complete exemption of private property from capture at sea, withheld its formal adherence, its amendment not having been accepted by all the powers. In 1861, at the beginning of the Civil War, the United States announced nevertheless that it would respect the principles of the Declaration for the duration of the hostilities. Equally, in 1898 during the war against Spain, it was affirmed that the policy of the government of the United States would be to abide by the provisions of the Declaration throughout the hostilities. The rules laid down in the Declaration were later considered as part of general international law and even the United States, which is not formally a party thereto, abides by its provisions.

ENTRY INTO FORCE: 16 April 1856.

AUTHENTIC TEXT: French. The English translation below is reprinted from *British State Papers 1856*, Vol. 61, pp. 155–158.

TEXT PUBLISHED IN: Martens, *NRGT,* 1ère série, Vol. XV, pp. 791–792 (French); *Fontes Historiae Juris Gentium*, Vol. III/1, pp. 549–551 (Engl., French, German); Deltenre, pp. 24–29 (Engl., French, German, Dutch); *BFSP*, Vol. 46, pp. 26–27 (French); *British State Papers, 1856*, Vol. 61, pp. 155–158; *CTS*, Vol. 115, 1856, pp. 1–3 (French); Edward Hertslet, *The Map of Europe by Treaty*, Vol. 11, London 1875, pp. 1282–1283 (Engl.); Higgins, pp. 1–2 (Engl., French); Wilson-Tucker, pp. IV–V (Engl.); *AJIL*, Vol. 1, 1907, Suppl., pp. 89–90 (Engl.); Moore, *Digest of International Law*, Vol. 7, pp. 561–562 (Engl.); Friedman, pp. 156–157 (Engl.); Roberts and Guelff, pp. 23–27 (Engl.); Ronzitti, pp. 61–65 (Engl., French); *Droit des conflits armés*, pp. 1095–1099 (French); de Clercq, pp. 91–93 (French); *Les deux Conférences de la Paix*, pp. 175–176 (French); Genet, p. 516 (French); Heffter-Taube, pp. 91–92 (Russ.); F. de Martens, *Recueil des Traités et conventions conclus par la Russie avec les Puissances étrangères*, Vol. XV, St. Petersburg, 1909, pp. 332–334 (French, Russ.); *Mezhdunarodnoepravo,* Vol. 111, pp. 140–141 (Russ.); Korovin, pp. 29–30 (Russ.); *Sbornik dogovorov Rossii s drugimi gosudarstvami* 1856–1917, Moscow, Gosudarstvennoe izdatelstvo politicheskoi literatury, 1952, pp. 42–43 (Russ.); Arellano, p. 350 (Span.); Briceño, pp. 228–229 (Span.); Ceppi, p. 325

(Span.); Olivart, Vol. IV, pp. 1–3 (Span.); ICRC website: www.org/ihl.nsf (Engl., French, Span.).

* * *

The Plenipotentiaries who signed the Treaty of Paris of the thirtieth of March, one thousand eight hundred and fifty-six, assembled in Conference,
Considering:

That maritime law, in time of war, has long been the subject of deplorable disputes;

That the uncertainty of the law and of the duties in such a matter, gives rise to differences of opinion between neutrals and belligerents which may occasion serious difficulties, and even conflicts;

That it is consequently advantageous to establish a uniform doctrine on so important a point;

That the Plenipotentiaries assembled in Congress at Paris cannot better respond to the intentions by which their Governments are animated, than by seeking to introduce into international relations fixed principles in this respect;
The above-mentioned Plenipotentiaries, being duly authorized, resolved to concert among themselves as to the means of attaining this object; and, having come to an agreement, have adopted the following solemn Declaration:

1. Privateering is, and remains, abolished;
2. The neutral flag covers enemy's goods, with the exception of contraband of war;
3. Neutral goods, with the exception of contraband of war, are not liable to capture under enemy's flag;
4. Blockades, in order to be binding, must be effective, that is to say, maintained by a force sufficient really to prevent access to the coast of the enemy.

The Governments of the undersigned Plenipotentiaries engage to bring the present Declaration to the knowledge of the States which have not taken part in the Congress of Paris, and to invite them to accede to it.

Convinced that the maxims which they now proclaim cannot but be received with gratitude by the whole world, the undersigned Plenipotentiaries doubt not that the efforts of their Governments to obtain the general adoption thereof, will be crowned with full success.

The present Declaration is not and shall not be binding, except between those Powers who have acceded, or shall accede, to it.

Done at Paris, the sixteenth of April, one thousand eight hundred and fifty-six.

[Here follow signatures]

SIGNATURES AND ACCESSIONS[1]

The Declaration was signed by seven powers, parties to the Treaty of Peace of Paris of 30 March 1856.

Signatory States	*Date of Signature*
Austria	16 April 1856
France	16 April 1856
Prussia	16 April 1856
Russia	16 April 1856
Sardinia	16 April 1856
Turkey	16 April 1856
United Kingdom	16 April 1856

Acceding States[2]	*Date of Accession*
Anhalt-Dessau-Coethen	17 June 1856
Argentina	1 October 1856
Baden	30 July 1856
Bavaria	4 July 1856
Belgium	6 June 1856
Brazil	18 March 1858
Bremen	11 June 1856
Brunswick	7 December 1857
Chile	13 August 1856
Denmark	25 June 1856
Ecuador	6 December 1856
Frankfort	17 June 1856
German Confederation	10 July 1856
Greece	20 June 1856
Guatemala	30 August 1856
Hamburg	27 June 1856
Hanover	31 May 1856
Haiti	17 September 1856
Hesse-Cassel	4 June 1856
Hesse-Darmstadt	15 June 1856
Japan	30 October 1886
Lubeck	20 June 1856
Mecklenburg-Schwerin	22 July 1856
Mecklenburg-Strelitz	25 August 1856
Mexico	13 February 1909
Modena	29 July 1856
Nassau	18 June 1856
Netherlands	7 June 1856
Oldenburg	9 June 1856
Parma	20 August 1856
Peru	23 November 1857
Portugal	28 July 1856
Roman States	2 June 1856

[1] Based on communications from the Ministry of Foreign Affairs of France of 10 May 1995 and of the Foreign and Commonwealth Office of the United Kingdom of 7 December 2001. See also ICRC website.

[2] France and Great Britain undertook to make known this Declaration to the states which had not participated in the Congress of Paris and to urge their accessions. The above-mentioned states have notified the Governments of France or Great Britain of their accession to the Declaration.

Acceding States[2]	*Date of Accession*
Saxe-Altenburg	9 June 1856
Saxe-Coburg-Gotha	22 June 1856
Saxe-Meiningen	30 June 1856
Saxe-Weimar	22 June 1856
Saxony	16 June 1856
The Two Sicilies	31 May 1856
Spain	18 January 1908
Sweden and Norway	13 June 1856
Switzerland	28 July 1856
Tuscany	5 June 1856
Uruguay	2 September 1856
Wurttemberg	25 June 1856

NOTES

BULGARIA
The communication from the Ministry of Foreign Affairs of France states that the Declaration is applicable to Bulgaria by virtue of Article 8 of the Treaty of Berlin of 13 July 1878.

UNITED STATES OF AMERICA
The communication from the Foreign and Commonwealth Office of Great Britain states: "The United States expressed readiness to accede to the Declaration provided it were added, with reference to privateering, that the private property of subjects or citizens of belligerent nations was exempt from capture at sea by the respective naval forces."

NEW GRANADA (COLOMBIA AND VENEZUELA)
New Granada acceded to the whole text of the Declaration. We have no information whether the legislative assembly ratified the Declaration or whether the formal instrument of accession was deposited.

URUGUAY
On 2 September 1856, the Government of Uruguay expressed its approval of the whole text of the Declaration indicating that it will obtain in the appropriate time the co-operation of the Legislative corpus in order that these resolutions become the invariable rule of the Republic. The information provided by the legislative power of the Oriental Republic of Uruguay permits to affirm that the Parliament never ratified the Declaration (letter of the Minister of Foreign Affairs of Uruguay addressed to the Henry Dunant Institute on 31 August 1992).

VENEZUELA
Venezuela acceded only to the point two, three and four of the Declaration. We have no information if the legislative assembly ratified the Declaration or if the formal instrument of accession was deposited with the French Government (communication from Foreign and Commonwealth Office of the United Kingdom of 9 June 1993).

DENUNCIATIONS

None

RESERVATIONS

None

No. 76

CONVENTION (VI) RELATING TO THE STATUS OF ENEMY MERCHANT SHIPS AT THE OUTBREAK OF HOSTILITIES

Signed at The Hague, 18 October 1907

INTRODUCTORY NOTE: No rule of international law existed before the adoption of the present Convention preventing belligerent states from confiscating enemy merchantmen in their harbour or on the high seas at the outbreak of a war. From the beginning of the Crimean War, in 1854, it became a usage followed by some countries that enemy vessels in the harbours of the belligerent should be granted a reasonable time to depart unmolested and that such vessels, if met at sea, should be permitted to continue their voyage. It was, however, not before the Second Hague Peace Conference that binding rules to this effect were adopted.

ENTRY INTO FORCE: 26 January 1910.

AUTHENTIC TEXT: French. The English translation below is reprinted from Scott, *Hague Conventions*, pp. 141–145. It reproduces the translation of the United States Department of State. The marginal titles added to the Convention have no official character.

TEXT PUBLISHED IN: *Conference internationale de la Paix, 1907*, pp. 644–646 (French); *Les deux Conférences de la Paix*, pp. 123–126 (French); Scott, *Hague Conventions*, pp. 141–145 (Engl.); Scott, *Les Conventions de La Haye*, pp. 141–145 (French); Scott, *Les Conférences de La Haye*, pp. 70–72 (French); Martens, *NRGT*, 3ème série, Vol. III, pp. 533–556 (French, German); Deltenre, pp. 296–304 (Engl., French, German, Dutch); *GBTS*, 1910, No. 10, Cd. 5031 (Engl., French); *BFSP*, Vol. 100, 1906–1907, pp. 365–377 (French); *CTS*, Vol. 205, pp. 305–318 (French); Wilson-Tucker, pp. LXXI–LXXIII (Engl.); *AJIL*, Vol. 2, 1908, Suppl., pp. 127–133 pp. 141–142 (Engl.); Friedman, pp. 332–337 (Engl.); Ronzitti, pp. 93–101 (Engl., French); *Droit des conflits armés*, pp. 1101–1107 (French); Korovin, p. 388 (Russ.); Arellano, p. 374 (Span. – extract); Briceño, pp. 218–219 (Span. – extract); *Revista de Derecho Internacional y politica exterior*, Cronica, Año III, 1907, pp. 87–88 (Span.); Bustamante, Vol. II, pp. 315–320 (Span.); Ceppi, pp. 358–359 (Span. – extract); ICRC website: www.org/ihl.nsf (Engl., French, Span.).

TABLE OF CONTENTS

* * *

[List of Contracting Parties]

Anxious to ensure the security of international commerce against the surprises of war, and wishing, in accordance with modern practice, to protect as far as possible operations undertaken in good faith and in process of being carried out before the outbreak of hostilities, have resolved to conclude a Convention to this effect, and have appointed the following persons as their Plenipotentiaries:

[Here follow the names of plenipotentiaries]

Who, after having deposited their full powers, found in good and due form, have agreed upon the following provisions:

Merchant ships in enemy ports

Article 1. When a merchant ship belonging to one of the belligerent Powers is at the commencement of hostilities in an enemy port, it is desirable that it should be allowed to depart freely, either immediately, or after a reasonable number of days of grace, and to proceed, after being furnished with a pass, direct to its port of destination or any other port indicated.

The same rule should apply in the case of a ship which has left its last port of departure before the commencement of the war and entered a port belonging to the enemy while still ignorant that hostilities had broken out.

No confiscation

Art. 2. A merchant ship unable, owing to circumstances of *force majeure*, to leave the enemy port within the period contemplated in the above article, or which was not allowed to leave, cannot be confiscated. The belligerent may only detain it, without payment of compensation, but subject to the obligation of restoring it after the war, or requisition it on payment of compensation.

Enemy merchant ships on high seas

Art. 3.[1] Enemy merchant ships which left their last port of departure before the commencement of the war, and are encountered on the high seas while still ignorant of the outbreak of hostilities cannot be confiscated. They are only liable to detention on the understanding that they shall be restored after the war

[1] For reservations in respect of Article 3 and Article 4, by Germany and Russia, see p. 1064.

without compensation, or to be requisitioned, or even destroyed, on payment of compensation, but in such cases provision must be made for the safety of the persons on board as well as the security of the ship's papers.

After touching at a port in their own country or at a neutral port, these ships are subject to the laws and customs of maritime war.

Art. 4. Enemy cargo on board the vessels referred to in Articles 1 and 2 is likewise liable to be detained and restored after the termination of the war without payment of compensation, or to be requisitioned on payment of compensation, with or without the ship. The same rule applies in the case of cargo on board the vessels referred to in Article 3.

Enemy cargo

Art. 5. The present Convention does not affect merchant ships whose build shows that they are intended for conversion into war-ships.

Merchant ships intended for conversion into warships

Art. 6. The provisions of the present Convention do not apply except between Contracting Powers, and then only if all the belligerents are Parties to the Convention.

Powers bound

Art. 7. The present Convention shall be ratified as soon as possible. The ratifications shall be deposited at The Hague. The first deposit of ratifications shall be recorded in a *procès-verbal* signed by the representatives of the Powers which take part therein and by the Netherlands Minister for Foreign Affairs.

Ratification

The subsequent deposits of ratifications shall be made by means of a written notification addressed to the Netherlands Government and accompanied by the instrument of ratification.

A duly certified copy of the *procès-verbal* relative to the first deposit of ratifications, of the notifications mentioned in the preceding paragraph, as well as of the instruments of ratification, shall be at once sent by the Netherlands Government, through the diplomatic channel, to the Powers invited to the Second Peace Conference, as well as to the other Powers which have adhered to the Convention. In the cases contemplated in the preceding paragraph, the said Government shall at the same time inform them of the date on which it received the notification.

Art. 8. Non-Signatory Powers may adhere to the present Convention.

Adhesion

The Power which desires to adhere notifies in writing its intention to the Netherlands Government, forwarding to it the act of adhesion, which shall be deposited in the archives of the said Government.

The said Government shall at once transmit to all the other Powers a duly certified copy of the notification as well as of the act of adhesion, stating the date on which it received the notification.

Entry into force

Art. 9. The present Convention shall come into force, in the case of the Powers which were a party to the first deposit of ratifications, sixty days after the date of the *procès-verbal* of that deposit, and, in the case of the Powers which ratify subsequently or which adhere, sixty days after the notification of their ratification or of their adhesion has been received by the Netherlands Government.

Denunciation

Art. 10. In the event of one of the Contracting Powers wishing to denounce the present Convention, the denunciation shall be notified in writing to the Netherlands Government, which shall at once communicate a certified copy of the notification to all the other Powers, informing them of the date on which it was received. The denunciation shall only have effect in regard to the notifying Power, and one year after the notification has reached the Netherlands Government.

Register of ratifications

Art. 11. A register kept by the Ministry of Foreign Affairs shall give the date of the deposit of ratifications made in virtue of Article 7, paragraphs 3 and 4, as well as the date on which the notifications of adhesion (Article 8, paragraph 2) or of denunciation (Article 10, paragraph 1) have been received. Each Contracting Power is entitled to have access to this register and to be supplied with certified extracts from it.

In faith whereof the Plenipotentiaries have appended to the present Convention their signatures.

Done at The Hague, 18 October 1907, in a single copy, which shall remain deposited in the archives of the Netherlands Government, and duly certified copies of which shall be sent through the diplomatic channel, to the Powers which have been invited to the Second Peace Conference.

[Here follow signatures]

SIGNATURES, RATIFICATIONS, ACCESSIONS[1]

State	*Signature*	*Ratification, Accession*
Argentina	18 October 1907	–
Austria-Hungary	18 October 1907	27 November 1909
Belarus	–	4 June 1962
Belgium	18 October 1907	8 August 1910
Bolivia	18 October 1907	–
Brazil	18 October 1907	5 January 1914
Bulgaria	18 October 1907	–
Chile	18 October 1907	–
China	–	10 May 1917

[1] Based on a communication received from the Ministry of Foreign Affairs of the Netherlands of 12 December 2001. See also ICRC website.

State	*Signature*	*Ratification, Accession*
Colombia	18 October 1907	–
Cuba	18 October 1907	22 February 1912
Denmark	18 October 1907	27 November 1909
Dominican Republic	18 October 1907	–
Ecuador	18 October 1907	–
El Salvador	18 October 1907	27 November 1909
Ethiopia	–	5 August 1935
Finland[2]	–	10 April 1922
France[3]	18 October 1907	7 October 1910
Germany[4]	18 October 1907 *Res.*	27 November 1909 *Res.*
Great Britain[5]	18 October 1907	27 November 1909
Greece	18 October 1907	–
Guatemala	18 October 1907	15 March 1911
Haiti	18 October 1907	2 February 1910
Italy	18 October 1907	–
Japan	18 October 1907	13 December 1911
Liberia	–	4 February 1914
Luxemburg	18 October 1907	5 September 1912
Mexico	18 October 1907	27 November 1909
Montenegro	18 October 1907	–
Netherlands	18 October 1907	27 November 1909
Nicaragua	–	16 December 1909
Norway	18 October 1907	19 September 1910
Panama	18 October 1907	11 September 1911
Paraguay	18 October 1907	–
Persia	18 October 1907	–
Peru	18 October 1907	–
Poland	–	31 May 1935
Portugal	18 October 1907	13 April 1911
Romania	18 October 1907	1 March 1912
Russia[6]	18 October 1907 *Res.*	27 November 1909 *Res.*

2 By letter dated 12 May 1980, the Netherlands Ministry of Foreign Affairs stated (a) Finland's accession on 30 December 1918 to this and other 1907 Hague Conventions and to the 1907 Hague Declaration was initially regarded as provisional, pending the final resolution of Finland's international status; (b) after consultation with the other contracting powers, the depository stated on 9 June 1922 that Finland's accession should be regarded as final and complete, and (c) the Conventions and the Declaration entered into force for Finland on 9 June 1922.

3 France denounced the Convention on 13 July 1939 (effective as from 13 July 1940).

4 By a letter received at the Ministry of Foreign Affairs of the Kingdom of the Netherlands on February 1959, the Government of the German Democratic Republic has informed the Ministry that it reapplies the Convention. This declaration is aimless and only of historical importance after the conclusion of the Treaty of 31 August 1990 (Unification Treaty) between the Federal Republic of Germany and German Democratic Republic. See note 3 of document No. 18, p. 170 and note 35 of documents Nos. 49–52 p. 640.

5 Great Britain denounced the Convention on 14 November 1925 (effective as from 14 November 1926).

6 By the note of the Foreign Ministry of the USSR of 7 March 1955: "The Government of the USSR recognises the Conventions and Declarations of The Hague from 1899 and 1907, which were ratified by Russia to the extent that the Conventions and Declarations do not contradict the United Nations Charter and if they are not amended or replaced by ulterior international agreements to which the USSR is a Party, such as the 1925 Geneva Protocol for the Prohibition of Use of Asphyxiating, Poisonous and Other Gases and of Bacteriological Methods of Warfare and the 1949 Geneva Conventions for the Protection of Victims of War" (*Izvestiya*, 9 March 1955).

In January 1992, the Ministry of Foreign Affairs of the Russian Federation informed the heads of diplomatic missions in Moscow, that the Russian Federation continues to be a party

State	*Signature*	*Ratification, Accession*
Serbia	18 October 1907	–
Siam	18 October 1907	12 March 1910
Spain	18 October 1907	18 March 1913
Sweden	18 October 1907	27 November 1909
Switzerland	18 October 1907	12 May 1910
Turkey	18 October 1907	–
Uruguay	18 October 1907	–
Venezuela	18 October 1907	–

RESERVATIONS

GERMANY (*reservation made on signature and maintained on ratification*)
Under reservation of Article 3 and of Article 4, paragraph 2.[7]

RUSSIA (*reservation made on signature and maintained on ratification*)
Under the reservations made as to Article 3 and Article 4, paragraph 2, of the present Convention, and recorded in the minutes of the seventh plenary session of 27 September 1907.[7]

---

cont.
to all conventions which are in force for the Soviet Union. The Ministry of Foreign Affairs of the Kingdom of the Netherlands considers therefore that the Russian Federation is bound by the conventions to which the Soviet Union was party (Communication of the Depository to the Henry Dunant Institute of 6 November 1992).

On 4 June 1962, the Byelorussian Soviet Socialist Republic made a declaration similar to that made by the USSR.

7 The German and Russian delegations considered that those provisions established an inequality between states in imposing financial burden on those powers which, lacking naval stations in different parts of the world, are not in a position to take vessels which they have seized into a port, but find themselves compelled to destroy them. *Deuxième Conférence Internationale de la Paix*. La Haye, 15 Juin-Octobre 1907, *Actes et documents*, Vol. I, p. 236, Vol. II, p. 918; *The Proceedings of the Hague Peace Conferences*, 1907, Vol. I, p. 231, Vol. III, pp. 907–908. Cf. also J.B. Scott (ed.), *The Hague Conventions and Declarations of 1899 and 1907*, New York, Oxford University Press, 3rd edn., 1918, p. 145, n. 2.

No. 77

CONVENTION (VII) RELATING TO THE CONVERSION OF MERCHANT SHIPS INTO WAR-SHIPS

Signed at The Hague, 18 October 1907

INTRODUCTORY NOTE: When during the Franco-German war of 1870 the King of Prussia, as President of the North German Confederation, ordered the creation of a volunteer navy by inviting the owners of private German vessels to make them part of the German navy, the question was raised whether this scheme violated the Declaration of Paris by which the signatories had engaged themselves not to employ privateers. While in the following decades the principle was generally admitted that merchant ships might be incorporated into the regular navy, several questions remained unresolved. The signatories of the present Convention, concluded at the Second Hague Peace Conference, although agreeing on the general principle, were unable to settle all the questions that gave rise to controversy. In particular, they could not agree on the question whether conversion might be performed in a harbour of the converting state only or also on the high seas (see preamble). Nor could they resolve the question of whether it was permissible to reconvert a vessel that had been converted into a warship during the war into a merchantman before the war ended.

ENTRY INTO FORCE: 26 January 1910.

AUTHENTIC TEXT: French. The English translation below is reprinted from Scott, *Hague Conventions*, pp. 146–150. It reproduces the translation of the United States Department of State. The marginal titles added to the Convention have no official character.

TEXT PUBLISHED IN: *Conférence internationale de la Paix, 1907*, pp. 647–649 (French); *Les deux Conférences de la Paix*, pp. 127–129 (French); Scott, *Hague Conventions*, pp. 146–150 (Engl.); Scott, *Les Conventions de La Haye*, pp. 146–150 (French); Scott, *Les Conférences de La Haye*, pp. 72–74 (French); Martens, *NRGT*, 3ème série, Vol. III, pp. 557–579 (French, German); Deltenre, pp. 306–313 (Engl., French, German, Dutch); *GBTS*, 1910, No. 11, Cd. 5115 (Engl., French); *BFSP*, Vol. 100, 1906–1907, pp. 377–389 (French); *CTS*, Vol. 205, pp. 319–331 (French); Wilson-Tucker, pp. LXXIII–LXXVIII (Engl.); *AJIL*, Vol. 8, 1908, Vol. 2, Suppl., pp. 133–138 (Engl., French); Friedman, pp. 338–341 (Engl.); Roberts and Guelff, pp. 95–101 (Engl.); Ronzitti, pp. 111–119 (Engl., French); *Droit des conflits armés*, pp. 1109–1114 (French); Genet, pp. 522–523 (French); *Mezhdunarodnoe pravo*, Vol. III, p. 143 (Russ.); Korovin, p. 388 (Russ.); *Revista de Derecho Internacional y politica exterior*, Cronica, Año III, 1907, pp. 88–89 (Span.); Arellano, p. 374 (Span. – extract); Briceño, pp. 219 (Span.– extracts); Bustamante, pp. 320– 324 (Span.); Ceppi, pp. 360–361 (Span. – extract); ICRC website: www.org/ihl.nsf (Engl., French, Span.).

TABLE OF CONTENTS

* * *

[List of Contracting Parties]

Whereas it is desirable, in view of the incorporation in time of war of merchant ships in the fighting fleet, to define the conditions subject to which this operation may be effected;

Whereas, however, the Contracting Powers have been unable to come to an agreement on the question whether the conversion of a merchant ship into a war-ship may take place upon the high seas, it is understood that the question of the place where such conversion is effected remains outside the scope of this agreement and is in no way affected by the following rules;

Being desirous of concluding a Convention to this effect, have appointed the following as their Plenipotentiaries:

[Here follow the names of Plenipotentiaries]

Who, after having deposited their full powers, found in good and due form, have agreed upon the following provisions:

State control

Article 1. A merchant ship converted into a war-ship cannot have the rights and duties accruing to such vessels unless it is placed under the direct authority, immediate control, and responsibility of the Power whose flag it flies.

Distinguishing marks

Art. 2. Merchant ships converted into war-ships must bear the external marks which distinguish the war-ships of their nationality.

Commander

Art. 3. The commander must be in the service of the State and duly commissioned by the competent authorities. His name must figure on the list of the officers of the fighting fleet.

Military discipline

Art. 4. The crew must be subject to military discipline.

Art. 5. Every merchant ship converted into a war-ship must observe in its operations the laws and customs of war.

Laws and customs of war

Art. 6. A belligerent who converts a merchant ship into a war-ship must, as soon as possible, announce such conversion in the list of war-ships.

State control

Art. 7. The provisions of the present Convention do not apply except between Contracting Powers, and then only if all the belligerents are Parties to the Convention.

Powers bound

Art. 8. The present Convention shall be ratified as soon as possible.

Ratification

The ratifications shall be deposited at The Hague.

The first deposit of ratifications shall be recorded in a *procès-verbal* signed by the representatives of the Powers who take part therein and by the Netherlands Minister for Foreign Affairs.

The subsequent deposits of ratifications shall be made by means of a written notification, addressed to the Netherlands Government and accompanied by the instrument of ratification.

A duly certified copy of the *procès-verbal* relative to the first deposit of ratifications, of the notifications mentioned in the preceding paragraph, as well as of the instruments of ratification, shall be at once sent by the Netherlands Government, through the diplomatic channel, to the Powers invited to the Second Peace Conference, as well as to the other Powers which have adhered to the Convention. In the cases contemplated in the preceding paragraph the said Government shall at the same time inform them of the date on which it received the notification.

Art. 9. Non-Signatory Powers may adhere to the present Convention.

Adhesion

The Power which desires to adhere notifies its intention in writing to the Netherlands Government, forwarding to it the act of adhesion, which shall be deposited in the archives of the said Government.

That Government shall at once transmit to all the other Powers a duly certified copy of the notification as well as of the act of adhesion, stating the date on which it received the notification.

Art. 10. The present Convention shall come into force, in the case of the Powers which were a party to the first deposit of ratifications, sixty days after the date of the *procès-verbal* of this deposit, and, in the case of the Powers which ratify subsequently or which adhere, sixty days after the notification of their ratification or of their adhesion has been received by the Netherlands Government.

Entry into force

Denunciation

Art. 11. In the event of one of the Contracting Powers wishing to denounce the present Convention, the denunciation shall be notified in writing to the Netherlands Government, which shall at once communicate a duly certified copy of the notification to all the other Powers, informing them of the date on which it was received.

The denunciation shall only have effect in regard to the notifying Power, and one year after the notification has reached the Netherlands Government.

Register of ratifications

Art. 12. A register kept by the Netherlands Ministry for foreign Affairs shall give the date of the deposit of ratifications made in virtue of Article 8, paragraphs 3 and 4, as well as the date on which the notifications of adhesion (Article 9, paragraph 2) or of denunciation (Article 11, paragraph 1) have been received.

Each Contracting Power is entitled to have access to this register and to be supplied with duly certified extracts from it.

In faith whereof the Plenipotentiaries have appended their signatures to the present Convention.

Done at The Hague, 18 October 1907, in a single copy, which shall remain deposited in the archives of the Netherlands Government, and duly certified copies of which shall be sent, through the diplomatic channel, to the Powers which have been invited to the Second Peace Conference.

[Here follow signatures]

SIGNATURES, RATIFICATIONS, ACCESSIONS[1]

State	*Signature*	*Ratification, Accession, Notification of Continuity* (C)
Argentina	18 October 1907	–
Austria-Hungary	18 October 1907	27 November 1909
Belarus	–	4 June 1962
Belgium	18 October 1907	8 August 1910
Bolivia	18 October 1907	–
Brazil	18 October 1907	5 January 1914
Bulgaria	18 October 1907	–
Chile	18 October 1907	–
China	–	10 May 1917
Colombia	18 October 1907	–
Cuba	18 October 1907	–
Denmark	18 October 1907	27 November 1909
Dominican Republic	–	–
Ecuador	18 October 1907	–
El Salvador	18 October 1907	27 November 1909

1 Based on a communication received from the Ministry of Foreign Affairs of the Netherlands of 12 December 2001. See also ICRC website.

State	*Signature*	*Ratification, Accession, Notification of Continuity* (C)
Ethiopia	–	5 August 1935
Fiji	–	2 April 1973 (C)
Finland[2]	–	10 April 1922
France	18 October 1907	7 October 1910
Germany[3]	18 October 1907	27 November 1909
Great Britain	18 October 1907	27 November 1909
Greece	18 October 1907	–
Guatemala	18 October 1907	15 March 1911
Haiti	18 October 1907	2 February 1910
Italy	18 October 1907	–
Japan	18 October 1907	13 December 1911
Liberia	–	4 February 1914
Luxemburg	18 October 1907	5 September 1912
Mexico	18 October 1907	27 November 1909
Montenegro	18 October 1907	–
Netherlands	18 October 1907	27 November 1909
Nicaragua	–	16 December 1909
Norway	18 October 1907	19 September 1910
Panama	18 October 1907	11 September 1911
Paraguay	18 October 1907	–
Persia	18 October 1907	–
Peru	18 October 1907	–
Poland	–	1 May 1935
Portugal	18 October 1907	13 April 1911
Romania	18 October 1907	1 March 1912
Russia[4]	18 October 1907	27 November 1909
Serbia	18 October 1907	–

[2] By letter dated 12 May 1980 the Netherlands Ministry of Foreign Affairs stated (a) Finland's accession on 30 December 1918 to this and other 1907 Hague Conventions and to the 1907 Hague Declaration was initially regarded as provisional, pending the final resolution of Finland's international status; (b) after consultation with the other contracting powers, the depositary stated on 9 June 1922 that Finland's accession should be regarded as final and complete; and (c) the Conventions and the Declaration entered into force for Finland on 9 June 1922.

[3] By a letter received at the Ministry of Foreign Affairs of the Kingdom of the Netherlands on 9 February 1959, the Government of the German Democratic Republic has informed the Ministry that it reapplies the Convention. This declaration is aimless and only of historical importance after the conclusion of the Treaty of 31 August 1990 (Unification Treaty) between the Federal Republic of Germany and German Democratic Republic. See note 3 of document *No. 18*, p. 170 and note 35 of documents *Nos. 49–52*, p. 640.

[4] By the note of the Foreign Ministry of the USSR of 7 March 1955 "The Government of the USSR recognises the Conventions and Declarations of The Hague from 1899 and 1907, which were ratified by Russia to the extent that the Conventions and Declarations do not contradict the United Nations Charter and if they are not amended or replaced by ulterior international agreements to which the USSR is a Party, such as the 1925 Geneva Protocol for the Prohibition of Use of Asphyxiating, Poisonous and Other Gases and of Bacteriological Methods of Warfare and the 1949 Geneva Conventions for the Protection of Victims of War" (*Izvestiya*, 9 March 1955).

In January 1992, the Ministry of Foreign Affairs of the Russian Federation informed the heads of diplomatic missions in Moscow, that the Russian Federation continues to be a party to all conventions which are in force for the Soviet Union. The Ministry of Foreign Affairs of the Kingdom of the Netherlands considers therefore that the Russian Federation is bound by the conventions to which the Soviet Union was party (Communication of the Depository to the Henry Dunant Institute of 6 November 1992).

On 4 June 1962, the Byelorussian Soviet Socialist Republic made a declaration similar to that made by the USSR.

State	*Signature*	*Ratification, Accession, Notification of Continuity* (C)
Siam	18 October 1907	12 March 1910
South Africa	–	10 March 1978 (C)
Spain	18 October 1907	18 March 1913
Sweden	18 October 1907	27 November 1909
Switzerland	18 October 1907	12 May 1910
Turkey	18 October 1907 *Res.*	–
Venezuela	18 October 1907	–

RESERVATION

TURKEY (*reservation made on signature*)
Under reservation of the declaration made at the eighth plenary session of the Conference of 9 October, 1907.

Extract from the procès-verbal
The Imperial Ottoman Government does not engage to recognize as vessels of war ships, which, being in its waters or on the high seas under a merchant flag, are converted on the opening of hostilities. *Deuxième conférence Internationale de la Paix.*, La Haye, 15 Juin-18 October 1907, *Actes et documents*, Vol. I, p. 277; *The Proceedings of the Hague Peace Conventions, 1907*, Vol. I, p. 271, see also J.B. Scott (ed.), *The Hague Conventions and Declarations of 1899 and 1907*, New York, Oxford University Press, 3rd edn., 1918, p. 150.

No. 78

CONVENTION (VIII) RELATIVE TO THE LAYING OF AUTOMATIC SUBMARINE CONTACT MINES

Signed at The Hague, 18 October 1907

INTRODUCTORY NOTE: Mines have been used in wars since the middle of the 19th century. Their extensive use in the Russo-Japanese War in 1904–1905 made an international regulation desirable both to protect neutral commerce and to uphold the principle of immunity of enemy merchantmen from attack without warning. Based on preparatory work by the Institute of International Law and the International Law Association, the present Convention was concluded at the Second Hague Peace Conference. The powers were unable to reach complete agreement on the matter. The result of the deliberations was a compromise. Only Articles 1 and 5 contain clear and unequivocal regulations. Article 2, which forbids the laying of contact mines off the coast and the ports of the enemy with the sole object of intercepting commercial shipping, is of limited value, for a belligerent has only to allege that mines were laid for a purpose other than merely intercepting commercial navigation.

ENTRY INTO FORCE: 26 January 1910.

AUTHENTIC TEXT: French. The English translation below is reprinted from Scott, *Hague Conventions*, pp. 151–156. It reproduces the translation of the United States Department of State. The marginal titles added to the Convention have no official character.

TEXT PUBLISHED IN: *Conférence internationale de la Paix, 1907*, pp. 650–653 (French); *Les deux Conférences de la Paix*, pp. 131–134 (French); Scott, *Hague Conventions*, pp. 151–156 (Engl.); Scott, *Les Conventions de La Haye*, pp. 151–156 (French); Scott, *Les Conférences de La Haye*, pp. 74–76 (French); Martens, *NRGT*, 3ème série, Vol. III, pp. 580–603 (French, German); Deltenre, pp. 314–324 (Engl., French, German, Dutch); *International Red Cross Handbook*, 1983, p. 333 (Engl. – extract); *Manuel de la Croix-Rouge internationale*, 1983, p. 345 (French – extract); *Manual de la Cruz Roja internacional*, 1983, p. 337 (Span. – extract); *Handbook of the International Movement*, 1994, p. 312 (Engl.); *Manuel du Mouvement international*, 1994, p. 324 (French); *Manual del Movimiento internacional*, 1994, p. 316 (Span.); *GBTS*, 1910, No. 12, Cd. 5116 (Engl., French); *BFSP*, Vol. 100, 1906–1907, pp. 389– 401 (French, German); Higgins, pp. 322–327 (Engl., French); *US Statutes at Large*, Vol. 36, pp. 2332–2350 (Engl., French); *CTS*, Vol. 205, pp. 331–344 (French); *AJIL*, Vol. 2, 1908, pp. 138-145 (Engl., French); Malloy, Vol. II, pp. 2304–2314 (Engl.); Bevans, Vol. I, pp. 669–680 (Engl.); Friedman, pp. 342– 347 (Engl.); Roberts and Guelff, pp. 103–110 (Engl.); Ronzitti, pp. 129–139 (Engl., French); *Droit des conflits armés*, pp. 1115–1122 (French); Genet, pp. 523–525 (French); *Mezhdunarodnoe pravo*, Vol. III, pp. 144–145 (Russ.); Korovin, p. 391 (Russ.); *Revista de Derecho Internacional y politica exterior*, Cronica, Año III, 1907, pp 89–91 (Span.); Arellano, pp. 375–376 (Span. – extract); Briceño, pp. 220–222 (Span. – extract); Bustamante, Vol. II, pp. 324– 330 (Span.); Ceppi, pp. 362–363 (Span. – extract); ICRC website: www.icrc. org/ihl.nsf (Engl., French, Span.).

TABLE OF CONTENTS

* * *

[List of Contracting Parties]

Inspired by the principle of the freedom of sea routes, the common highway of all nations;

Seeing that, although the existing position of affairs makes it impossible to forbid the employment of automatic submarine contact mines, it is nevertheless desirable to restrict and regulate their employment in order to mitigate the severity of war and to ensure, as far as possible, to peaceful navigation the security to which it is entitled, despite the existence of war;

Until such time as it is found possible to formulate rules on the subject which shall ensure to the interests involved all the guarantees desirable;

Have resolved to conclude a Convention for this purpose, and have appointed the following as their Plenipotentiaries:

[Here follow the names of Plenipotentiaries]

Who, after having deposited their full powers, found in good and due form, have agreed upon the following provisions:

Article 1. It is forbidden –

Prohibitions

1. To lay unanchored automatic contact mines, except when they are so constructed as to become harmless one hour at most after the person who laid them ceases to control them;[1]

[1] For reservation in respect of Article 1, paragraph 1, by the Dominican Republic and Siam, see pp. 1076–1077.

2. To lay anchored automatic contact mines which do not become harmless as soon as they have broken loose from their moorings;
3. To use torpedoes which do not become harmless when they have missed their mark.

Art. 2.[2] It is forbidden to lay automatic contact mines off the coast and ports of the enemy, with the sole object of intercepting commercial shipping.

Commercial shipping

Art. 3. When anchored automatic contact mines are employed, every possible precaution must be taken for the security of peaceful shipping.

Protection of peaceful shipping

The belligerents undertake to do their utmost to render these mines harmless within a limited time, and, should they cease to be under surveillance, to notify the danger zones as soon as military exigencies permit, by a notice addressed to ship owners, which must also be communicated to the Governments through the diplomatic channel.

Art. 4. Neutral Powers which lay automatic contact mines off their coasts must observe the same rules and take the same precautions as are imposed on belligerents.

Mines laid by neutral Powers

The neutral Power must inform ship owners, by a notice issued in advance, where automatic contact mines have been laid. This notice must be communicated at once to the Governments through the diplomatic channel.

Art. 5. At the close of the war, the Contracting Powers undertake to do their utmost to remove the mines which they have laid, each Power removing its own mines.

Removal at close of war

As regards anchored automatic contact mines laid by one of the belligerents off the coast of the other, their position must be notified to the other party by the Power which laid them, and each Power must proceed with the least possible delay to remove the mines in its own waters.

Art. 6.[3] The Contracting Powers which do not at present own perfected mines of the pattern contemplated in the present Convention, and which, consequently, could not at present carry out the rules laid down in Articles 1 and 3, undertake to convert the *matériel* of their mines as soon as possible, so as to bring it into conformity with the foregoing requirements.

Adoption of perfected mines

Art. 7. The provisions of the present Convention do not apply except between Contracting Powers, and then only if all the belligerents are parties to the Convention.

Powers bound

2 For reservation in respect of this article by France and Germany, see p. 1076.

3 For reservation in respect of this article by Turkey, see p. 1077.

Ratification

Art. 8. The present Convention shall be ratified as soon as possible.

The ratifications shall be deposited at The Hague.

The first deposit of ratifications shall be recorded in a *procès-verbal* signed by the representatives of the Powers which take part therein and by the Netherlands Minister for Foreign Affairs.

The subsequent deposits of ratifications shall be made by means of a written notification addressed to the Netherlands Government and accompanied by the instrument of ratification.

A duly certified copy of the *procès-verbal* relative to the first deposit of ratifications, of the notifications mentioned in the preceding paragraph, as well as of the instruments of ratification, shall be at once sent, by the Netherlands Government, through the diplomatic channel, to the Powers invited to the Second Peace Conference, as well as to the other Powers which have adhered to the Convention. In the cases contemplated in the preceding paragraph, the said Government shall inform them at the same time of the date on which it has received the notification.

Adhesion

Art. 9. Non-Signatory Powers may adhere to the present Convention.

The Power which desires to adhere notifies in writing its intention to the Netherlands Government, transmitting to it the act of adhesion, which shall be deposited in the archives of the said Government.

This Government shall at once transmit to all the other Powers a duly certified copy of the notification as well as of the act of adhesion, stating the date on which it received the notification.

Entry into force

Art. 10. The present Convention shall come into force, in the case of the Powers which were a party to the first deposit of ratifications, sixty days after the date of the *procès-verbal* of this deposit, and, in the case of the Powers which ratify subsequently or adhere, sixty days after the notification of their ratification or of their adhesion has been received by the Netherlands Government.

Duration and denunciation

Art. 11. The present Convention shall remain in force for seven years, dating from the sixtieth day after the date of the first deposit of ratifications.

Unless denounced, it shall continue in force after the expiration of this period.

The denunciation shall be notified in writing to the Netherlands Government, which shall at once communicate a duly certified copy of the notification to all the Powers, informing them of the date on which it was received.

The denunciation shall only have effect in regard to the notifying Power, and six months after the notification has reached the Netherlands Government.

Art. 12. The Contracting Powers undertake to reopen the question of the employment of automatic contact mines six months before the expiration of the period contemplated in the first paragraph of the preceding article, in the event of the question not having been already reopened and settled by the Third Peace Conference. Reopening question

If the Contracting Powers conclude a fresh Convention relative to the employment of mines, the present Convention shall cease to be applicable from the moment it comes into force.

Art. 13. A register kept by the Netherlands Ministry for foreign Affairs shall give the date of the deposit of ratifications made in virtue of Article 8, paragraphs 3 and 4, as well as the date on which the notifications of adhesion (Article 9, paragraph 2) or of denunciation (Article 11, paragraph 3) have been received. Register of ratification

Each Contracting Power is entitled to have access to this register and to be supplied with duly certified extracts from it.

In faith whereof the Plenipotentiaries have appended their signatures to the present Convention.

Done at The Hague, 18 October 1907, in a single copy, which shall remain deposited in the archives of the Netherlands Government, and duly certified copies of which shall be sent, through the diplomatic channel, to the Powers which have been invited to the Second Peace Conference.

[Here follow signatures]

SIGNATURES, RATIFICATIONS AND ACCESSIONS[1]

State	*Signature*	*Ratification, Accession, Notification of Continuity (C)*
Argentina	18 October 1907	–
Austria-Hungary	18 October 1907	27 November 1909
Belgium	18 October 1907	8 August 1910
Bolivia	18 October 1907	–
Brazil	18 October 1907	5 January 1914
Bulgaria	18 October 1907	–
Chile	18 October 1907	–
China	–	10 May 1917
Colombia	18 October 1907	–
Cuba	18 October 1907	–
Denmark	18 October 1907	27 November 1909
Dominican Republic	18 October 1907 *Res.*	–

[1] Based on a communication received from the Ministry of Foreign Affairs of the Netherlands of 12 December 2001. See also ICRC website.

State	*Signature*	*Ratification, Accession, Notification of Continuity (C)*
Ecuador	18 October 1907	–
El Salvador	18 October 1907	27 November 1909
Ethiopia	–	5 August 1935
Fiji	–	2 April 1973 (C)
Finland[2]	–	10 April 1922
France	18 October 1907 *Res.*	7 October 1910 *Res.*
Germany	18 October 1907 *Res.*	27 November 1909 *Res.*
Great Britain	18 October 1907 *Res.*	27 November 1909 *Res.*
Greece	18 October 1907	–
Guatemala	18 October 1907	15 March 1911
Haiti	18 October 1907	2 February 1910
Italy	18 October 1907	–
Japan	18 October 1907	13 December 1911
Liberia	–	4 February 1914
Luxemburg	18 October 1907	5 September 1912
Mexico	18 October 1907	27 November 1909
Netherlands	18 October 1907	27 November 1909
Nicaragua	–	16 December 1909
Norway	18 October 1907	19 September 1910
Panama	18 October 1907	11 September 1911
Paraguay	18 October 1907	–
Persia	18 October 1907	–
Peru	18 October 1907	–
Romania	18 October 1907	1 March 1912
Serbia	18 October 1907	–
Siam	18 October 1907 *Res.*	12 March 1910 *Res.*
South Africa	–	10 March 1978 (C)
Switzerland	18 October 1907	12 May 1910
Turkey	18 October 1907 *Res.*	–
United States of America	18 October 1907	27 November 1909
Uruguay	18 October 1907	–
Venezuela	18 October 1907	–

RESERVATIONS

DOMINICAN REPUBLIC (*reservation made on signature*)
With reservation as to the first paragraph of Article 1.

FRANCE (*reservation made on signature and maintained on ratification*)
Under the reservation of Article 2.[1]

GERMANY (*reservation made on signature and maintained on ratification*)
Under the reservation of Article 2.[1]

GREAT BRITAIN (*reservation made on signature and maintained on ratification*)
In affixing their signatures to the above Convention, the British Plenipotentiaries declare that the mere fact that this Convention does not prohibit a particular act or pro-

[2] By letter dated 12 May 1980 the Netherlands Ministry of Foreign Affairs stated (a) Finland's accession on 30 December 1918 to this and other 1907 Hague Conventions and to the 1907 Hague Declaration was initially regarded as provisional, pending the final resolution of Finland's international status; (b) after consultation with the other contracting powers, the depositary stated on 9 June 1922 that Finland's accession should be regarded as final and complete; and (c) the Conventions and the Declaration entered into force for Finland on 9 June 1922.

ceeding must not be held to debar His Britannic Majesty's Government from contesting its legitimacy.

SIAM (*reservation made on signature*)
Under reservation of Article 1, paragraph 1.

TURKEY (*reservation made on signature*)
Under reservation of the declarations recorded in the *procès-verbal* of the eighth plenary meeting of the Conference held on 9 October 1907.

Extract from the procès-verbal:

(a) The Imperial Ottoman delegation cannot at the present time undertake any engagement whatever for perfected systems which are not yet universally known.
(b) The Imperial Ottoman delegation believes that it should declare that, given the exceptional situation created by treaties in force on the straits of the Dardanelles and the Bosporus, straits which are an integral part of the territory, the Imperial Government could not in any way subscribe to any undertaking tending to limit the means of defense that it may deem necessary to employ for these straits in case of war or with the aim of causing its neutrality to be respected.
(c) The Imperial Ottoman delegation cannot at the present time take part in any engagement as regards the conversion mentioned in Article 6.[3]

[3] *Deuxième Conférence internationale de la Paix*, La Haye, 15 Juin-18 October 1907, Actes et documents, Vol. 1, p. 280. *The Proceedings of the Hague Peace Conferences*, J.B. Scott (ed.), Vol. 1, pp. 273–278, 283–285; *The Hague Conventions and Declarations of 1899 and 1907*, 3rd edn., New York, Oxford University Press, 1918, p. 156.

No. 79

CONVENTION (IX) CONCERNING BOMBARDMENT BY NAVAL FORCES IN TIME OF WAR

Signed at The Hague, 18 October 1907

INTRODUCTORY NOTE. Before the adoption of the present Convention there was controversy as to whether or not undefended ports, towns and buildings might be bombarded by naval forces. There was a difference of opinion as to whether the rule applicable in land warfare prohibiting bombardment of undefended towns (Article 25 of the Hague Regulations of 1899 and 1907, *Nos. 7 and 8*) was also applicable to the bombardment by naval forces. The Institute of International Law, in 1896, declared that the law relating to bombardment was the same in land and sea warfare. This view, however, was not accepted by the powers at the Second Hague Peace Conference. Although Article 1 of the present Convention confirms the principle that undefended ports and towns may not be bombarded, Article 2 allows bombardment by naval forces of military objectives in undefended towns. This new rule eventually became applicable to air warfare, too.

ENTRY INTO FORCE: 26 January 1910.

AUTHENTIC TEXT: French. The English translation below is reprinted from Scott, *Hague Conventions*, pp. 157–162. It reproduces the translation of the United States Department of State. The marginal titles added to the Convention have no official character.

TEXT PUBLISHED IN: *Conférence internationale de la Paix, 1907*, pp. 654–657 (French); *Les deux Conférences de la Paix*, pp. 135–138 (French); Scott, *Hague Conventions*, pp. 157–162 (Engl.); Scott, *Les Conventions de La Haye*, pp. 157–162 (French); Scott, *Les Conférences de La Haye*, pp. 77–79 (French); Martens, *NRGT*, 3ème série, Vol. III, pp. 604–629 (French, German); Deltenre, pp. 326–337 (Engl., French, German, Dutch); *International Red Cross Handbook*, 1983, pp. 336–337 (Engl. – extract); *Manuel de la Croix-Rouge internationale*, 1983, pp. 348–349 (French – extract); *Manual de la Cruz Roja internacional*, 1983, pp. 340–341 (Span. – extract); *Handbook of the International Movement 1994*, pp. 313–314 (Engl.); *Manuel du Mouvement international*, 1994, pp. 325–326 (French); *Manual del Movimiento internacional*, 1994, pp. 317–318 (Span.); *GBTS*, 1910, No. 13, CD. 5117 (Engl., French); *BFSP*, Vol. 100, 1906–1907, pp. 401–415 (French); *CTS*, Vol. 205, pp. 345–359 (French); Higgins, pp. 346–352 (Engl., French); *US Statutes at Large*, Vol. 36, pp. 2351–2370 (Engl., French); *AJIL*, Vol. 2, 1908, Suppl., pp. 146–153 (Engl.); Malloy, Vol. II, pp. 2314–2325 (Engl.); Bevans, Vol. I, pp. 681–693 (Engl.); Friedman, pp. 348–353 (Engl.); Roberts and Guelff, pp. 111–117, (Engl.); Ronzitti, pp. 149–160 (Engl., French); *Droit des conflits armés*, pp. 1123–1131 (French); Genet, pp. 525–527 (French); *Mezhdunarodnoe pravo*, Vol. III, pp. 145–147 (Russ.); Korovin, p. 389 (Russ.); *Revista de Derecho Internacional y politica exterior*, Cronica, Año III, 1907, pp. 91–93 (Span.); Arellano, pp. 376–377 (Span. – extract); Briceño, pp. 222–223 (Span. – extract);

Bustamante, pp. 330–335 (Span.); Ceppi, pp. 364–366 (Span. – extract); ICRC website: www.icrc.org/ihl.nsf (Engl., French, Span.).

TABLE OF CONTENTS

* * *

[List of Contracting Parties]

Animated by the desire to realize the wish expressed by the first Peace Conference respecting the bombardment by naval forces of undefended ports, towns, and villages;

Whereas it is expedient that bombardments by naval forces should be subject to rules of general application which would safeguard the rights of the inhabitants and assure the preservation of the more important buildings, by applying as far as Possible to this operation of war the principles of the Regulation of 1899 respecting the laws and customs of land war;

Actuated, accordingly, by the desire to serve the interests of humanity and to diminish the severity and disasters of war;

Have resolved to conclude a Convention to this effect, and have, for this purpose, appointed the following as their Plenipotentiaries:

[Here follow the names of Plenipotentiaries]

Who, after depositing their full powers, found in good and due form, have agreed upon the following provisions:

Chapter I. The Bombardment of Undefended Ports, Towns, Villages, Dwellings, or Buildings

Prohibition of bombardment

Article 1. The bombardment by naval forces of undefended ports, towns, villages, dwellings, or buildings is forbidden.

A place cannot be bombarded solely because automatic submarine contact mines are anchored off the harbour.[1]

Art. 2. Military works, military or naval establishments, depots of arms or war *matériel*, workshops or plant which could be utilized for the needs of the hostile fleet or army, and the ships of war in the harbour, are not, however, included in this prohibition. The commander of a naval force may destroy them with artillery, after a summons followed by a reasonable time of waiting, if all other means are impossible, and when the local authorities have not themselves destroyed them within the time fixed.

Military establishments

He incurs no responsibility for any unavoidable damage which may be caused by a bombardment under such circumstances.

If for military reasons immediate action is necessary, and no delay can be allowed the enemy, it is understood that the prohibition to bombard the undefended town holds good, as in the case given in paragraph 1, and that the commander shall take all due measures in order that the town may suffer as little harm as possible.

Art. 3.[2] After due notice has been given, the bombardment of undefended ports, towns, villages, dwellings, or buildings may be commenced, if the local authorities, after a formal summons has been made to them, decline to comply with requisitions for provisions or supplies necessary for the immediate use of the naval force before the place in question.

Bombardment on declining to furnish provisions

These requisitions shall be in proportion to the resources of the place. They shall only be demanded in the name of the commander of the said naval force, and they shall, as far as possible, be paid for in cash; if not, they shall be evidenced by receipts.

Art. 4. Undefended ports, towns, villages, dwellings, or buildings may not be bombarded on account of failure to pay money contributions.

Money contributions

Chapter II. General Provisions

Art. 5. In bombardments by naval forces all the necessary measures must be taken by the commander to spare as far as possible sacred edifices, buildings used for artistic, scientific, or charitable purposes, historic monuments, hospitals, and places where the sick or wounded are collected, on the understanding that they are not used at the same time for military purposes.

Buildings to be spared

It is the duty of the inhabitants to indicate such monuments, edifices, or places by visible signs, which shall consist of large,

[1] For reservations in respect of Article 1, paragraph 2, by France, Germany, Great Britain and Japan, see p. 1086.

[2] For reservations in respect of this article by Chile, see p. 1086.

stiff rectangular panels divided diagonally into two coloured triangular portions, the upper portion black, the lower portion white.[3]

Warning to authorities

Art. 6. If the military situation permits, the commander of the attacking naval force, before commencing the bombardment, must do his utmost to warn the authorities.

Pillage

Art. 7. A town or place, even when taken by storm, may not be pillaged.

Chapter III. Final Provisions

Powers bound

Art. 8. The provisions of the present Convention do not apply except between Contracting Powers, and then only if all the belligerents are parties to the Convention.

Ratification

Art. 9. The present Convention shall be ratified as soon as possible.

The ratifications shall be deposited at The Hague.

The first deposit of ratifications shall be recorded in a *procès-verbal* signed by the representatives of the Powers which take part therein and by the Netherlands Minister of Foreign Affairs.

The subsequent deposits of ratifications shall be made by means of a written notification addressed to the Netherlands Government and accompanied by the instrument of ratification. A duly certified copy of the *procès-verbal* relative to the first deposit of ratifications, of the notifications mentioned in the preceding paragraph, as well as of the instruments of ratification, shall be at once sent by the Netherlands Government, through the diplomatic channel, to the Powers invited to the Second Peace Conference, as well as to the other Powers which have adhered to the Convention. In the cases contemplated in the preceding paragraph, the said Government shall inform them at the same time of the date on which it received the notification.

Adhesion

Art. 10. Non-Signatory Powers may adhere to the present Convention.

The Power which desires to adhere shall notify its intention to the Netherlands Government, forwarding to it the act of adhesion, which shall be deposited in the archives of the said Government.

---

[3] In the relations between states which are bound by the Hague Convention for the Protection of Cultural Property in the Event of Armed Conflict of 14 May 1954 (*No. 71*), the latter Convention is supplementary to this Convention (see Article 36, paragraph 1, of the Convention of 1954). The emblem described above is to be replaced by the emblem described in Article 16 of the Convention of 1954.

This Government shall immediately forward to all the other Powers a duly certified copy of the notification, as well as of the act of adhesion, mentioning the date on which it received the notification.

Art. 11. The present Convention shall come into force, in the case of the Powers which were a party to the first deposit of ratifications, sixty days after the date of the "procès-verbal" of that deposit, and, in the case of the Powers which ratify subsequently or which adhere, sixty days after the notification of their ratification or of their adhesion has been received by the Netherlands Government.

Entry into force

Art. 12. In the event of one of the Contracting Powers wishing to denounce the present Convention, the denunciation shall be notified in writing to the Netherlands Government, which shall at once communicate a duly certified copy of the notification to all the other Powers informing them of the date on which it was received. The denunciation shall only have effect in regard to the notifying Power, and one year after the notification has reached the Netherlands Government.

Denunciation

Art. 13. A register kept by the Netherlands Minister for foreign Affairs shall give the date of the deposit of ratifications made in virtue of Article 9, paragraphs 3 and 4, as well as the date on which the notifications of adhesion (Article 10, paragraph 2) or of denunciation (Article 12, paragraph I) have been received.

Register of ratifications

Each Contracting Power is entitled to have access to this register and to be supplied with duly certified extracts from it.

In faith whereof the Plenipotentiaries have appended their signatures to the present Convention.

Done at The Hague, 18 October 1907, in a single copy, which shall remain deposited in the archives of the Netherlands Government, and duly certified copies of which shall be sent, through the diplomatic channel, to the Powers which have been invited to the Second Peace Conference.

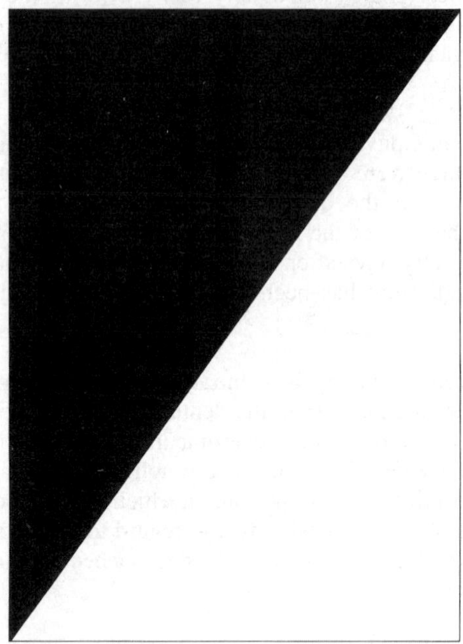

Emblem of buildings to be spared in case of naval bombardment

[Here follow signatures]

SIGNATURES, RATIFICATIONS AND ACCESSIONS[1]

State	*Signature*	*Ratification, Accession, Notification of Continuity (C)*
Argentina	18 October 1907	–
Austria-Hungary	18 October 1907	27 November 1909
Belarus	–	4 June 1962
Belgium	18 October 1907	8 August 1910
Bolivia	18 October 1907	27 November 1909
Brazil	18 October 1907	5 January 1914
Bulgaria	18 October 1907	–
Chile	18 October 1907 *Res.*	–
China	–	15 January 1910
Colombia	18 October 1907	–
Cuba	18 October 1907	22 February 1912
Denmark	18 October 1907	27 November 1909
Dominican Republic	18 October 1907	–
Ecuador	18 October 1907	–
El Salvador	18 October 1907	27 November 1909
Ethiopia	–	5 August 1935

[1] Based on a communication received from the Ministry of Foreign Affairs of the Netherlands of 12 December 2001. See also ICRC website.

State	*Signature*	*Ratification, Accession, Notification of Continuity (C)*
Fiji	–	2 April 1973 (C)
Finland	–	10 April 1922
France	18 October 1907 *Res.*	7 October 1910 *Res.*
Germany[2]	18 October 1907 *Res.*	27 November 1909 *Res.*
Great Britain	18 October 1907 *Res.*	27 November 1909 *Res.*
Greece	18 October 1907	–
Guatemala	18 October 1907	15 March 1911
Haiti	18 October 1907	2 February 1910
Italy	18 October 1907	–
Japan	18 October 1907 *Res.*	13 December 1911 *Res.*
Liberia	–	4 February 1914
Luxemburg	18 October 1907	5 September 1912
Mexico	18 October 1907	27 November 1909
Montenegro	18 October 1907	–
Netherlands	18 October 1907	27 November 1909
Nicaragua	–	16 December 1909
Norway	18 October 1907	19 September 1910
Panama	18 October 1907	11 September 1911
Paraguay	18 October 1907	–
Persia	18 October 1907	–
Peru	18 October 1907	–
Poland	–	31 May 1935
Portugal	18 October 1907	13 April 1911
Romania	18 October 1907	1 March 1912
Russia[3]	18 October 1907	27 November 1909
Serbia	18 October 1907	–
Siam	18 October 1907	12 March 1910
South Africa	–	10 March 1978 (C)
Spain	–	24 February 1913
Sweden	18 October 1907	27 November 1909
Switzerland	18 October 1907	12 May 1910

[2] By a letter received at the Ministry of Foreign Affairs of the Kingdom of the Netherlands on 9 February 1959, the Government of the German Democratic Republic has informed the Ministry that it reapplies the Convention. This declaration has lost its historical importance after the conclusion of the Treaty of 31 August 1990 (Unification Treaty) between the Federal Republic of Germany and German Democratic Republic. See note 3 of document *No. 18*, p. 170 and note 35 of documents *Nos. 49–52*, p. 640.

[3] By the note of the Foreign Ministry of the USSR of 7 March 1955: "The Government of the USSR recognises the Conventions and Declarations of The Hague from 1899 and 1907, which were ratified by Russia to the extent that the Conventions and Declarations do not contradict the United Nations Charter and if they are not amended or replaced by ulterior international agreements to which the USSR is a Party, such as the 1925 Geneva Protocol for the Prohibition of Use of Asphyxiating, Poisonous and Other Gases and of Bacteriological Methods of Warfare and the 1949 Geneva Conventions for the Protection of Victims of War" (*Izvestiya*, 9 March 1955).

In January 1992, the Ministry of Foreign Affairs of the Russian Federation informed the heads of diplomatic missions in Moscow, that the Russian Federation continues to be a party to all conventions which are in force for the Soviet Union. The Ministry of Foreign Affairs of the Kingdom of the Netherlands considers therefore that the Russian Federation is bound by the conventions to which the Soviet Union was party (communication of the Depository to the Henry Dunant Institute of 6 November 1992).

On 4 June 1962, the Byelorussian Soviet Socialist Republic made a declaration similar to that made by the USSR.

State	*Signature*	*Ratification, Accession, Notification of Continuity (C)*
Turkey	18 October 1907	–
United States of America	18 October 1907	27 November 1909
Uruguay	18 October 1907	–
Venezuela	18 October 1907	–

RESERVATIONS

CHILE (*reservation made on signature*)
Under the reservation of Article 3 made at the fourth plenary session of 17 August.

Extract from the procès-verbal:
The delegation of Chile makes reservation as to Article 3.[4]

FRANCE (*reservation made on signature and maintained on ratification*)
Under reservation of the second paragraph of Article 1.[4]

GERMANY (*reservation made on signature and maintained on ratification*)
Under reservation of Article 1, paragraph 2.[4]

GREAT BRITAIN (*reservation made on signature and maintained on ratification*)
Under reservation of the second paragraph of Article 1.[4]

JAPAN (*reservation made on signature and maintained on ratification*)
With reservation of paragraph 2 of Article 1.[4]

4 *Deuxième Conférence internationale de la Paix*, La Haye, 15 juin–18 octobre 1907, *Actes et documents*, Vol. I, p. 90; *The Proceedings of the Hague Peace Conferences*, Vol. I, p. 87.

No. 80

CONVENTION (XI) RELATIVE TO CERTAIN RESTRICTIONS WITH REGARD TO THE EXERCISE OF THE RIGHT OF CAPTURE IN NAVAL WAR

Signed at The Hague, 18 October 1907

INTRODUCTORY NOTE: Some of the restrictions on capture provided for in this Convention were previously applied by virtue of settled practice. This was the case particularly for coastal fishing boats and for vessels engaged in scientific discovery. The Convention extended the immunity to further cases. For military hospital ships, immunity from capture is provided for in Article 22 of Geneva Convention (II) of 1949 (*No. 50*).

ENTRY INTO FORCE: 26 January 1910.

AUTHENTIC TEXT: French. The English translation below is reprinted from Scott, *Hague Conventions*, pp. 182–187. It reproduces the translation of the United States Department of State. The marginal titles added to the Convention have no official character.

TEXT PUBLISHED IN: *Conférence internationale de la Paix 1907*, pp. 664–667 (French); *Les deux Conférences de la Paix*, pp. 147–150 (French); Scott, *Hague Conventions*, pp. 182–187 (Engl.); Scott, *Les Conventions de La Haye*, pp. 182–187 (French); Scott, *Les Conférences de La Haye*, pp. 84–86 (French); Martens, *NRGT*, 3ème série, Vol. III, pp. 663–687 (French, German); Deltenre, pp. 354–363 (Engl., French, Dutch); *GBTS*, 1910, No. 14, CD 5118 (Engl., French); *BFSP*, Vol. 100, 1906–1907, pp. 421–434 (French); *CTS*, Vol. 205, pp. 367–380 (French); Higgins, pp. 395–400 (Engl., French); Wilson-Tucker, pp. LXXVIII–LXXX (Engl.); *US Statutes at Large*, Vol. 36, pp. 2396–2414 (Engl., French); *AJIL*, Vol. 2, 1908, pp. 167–174 (Engl., French); Malloy, Vol. II, pp. 2341–2352 (Engl.); Bevans, Vol. I, pp. 711–722 (Engl.); Friedman, pp. 364–369 (Engl.); Roberts and Guelff, pp. 119–126 (Engl.); Ronzitti, pp. 173–182 (Engl., French); *Droit des conflits armés*, pp. 1133–1139 (French); Genet, pp. 533–534 (French); *Mezhdunarodnoe pravo*, Vol. III, pp. 147–149 (Russ.); Korovin, pp. 389–390 (Russ.); *Revista de Derecho Internacional y politica exterior*, Cronica, Año III, 1907, pp. 98–100 (Span.); Arellano, pp. 379–381 (Span. – extract); Bustamante, pp. 346–352 (Span.); Ceppi, pp. 374–376 (Span. – extract); ICRC website: www.icrc.org/ihl.nsf (Engl., French, Span.).

TABLE OF CONTENTS

* * *

Recognizing the necessity of more effectively ensuring than hitherto the equitable application of law to the international relations of maritime Powers in time of war;

Considering that, for this purpose, it is expedient, in giving up or, if necessary, in harmonizing for the common interest certain conflicting practices of long standing, to commence codifying in regulations of general application the guarantees due to peaceful commerce and legitimate business, as well as the conduct of hostilities by sea; that it is expedient to lay down in written mutual engagements the Principles which have hitherto remained in the uncertain domain of controversy or have been left to the discretion of Governments;

That, from henceforth, a certain number of rules may be made, without affecting the common law now in force with regard to the matters which that law has left unsettled;

Have appointed the following as their Plenipotentiaries:

[Here follow the names of Plenipotentiaries]

Who, after having deposited their full powers, found in good and due form, have agreed upon the following provisions:

Chapter I. Postal Correspondence

Inviolability of postal correspondence

Article 1. The postal correspondence of neutrals or belligerents, whatever its official or private character may be, found on the high seas on board a neutral or enemy ship, is inviolable. If the ship is detained, the correspondence is forwarded by the captor with the least possible delay.

The provisions of the preceding paragraph do not apply, in case of violation of blockade, to correspondence destined for or proceeding from a blockaded port.

Art. 2. The inviolability of postal correspondence does not exempt a neutral mail ship from the laws and customs of maritime war as to neutral merchant ships in general. The ship, however, may not be searched except when absolutely necessary, and then only with as much consideration and expedition as possible.

Neutral mail ships

Chapter II. The Exemption from Capture of Certain Vessels

Art. 3. Vessels used exclusively for fishing, along the coast or small boats employed in local trade are exempt from capture, as well as their appliances, rigging, tackle, and cargo.

Fishing vessels and boats of local trade

They cease to be exempt as soon as they take any part whatever in hostilities.

The Contracting Powers agree not to take advantage of the harmless character of the said vessels in order to use them for military purposes while preserving their peaceful appearance.

Art. 4. Vessels charged with religious, scientific, or philanthropic missions are likewise exempt from capture.

Religious, scientific vessels

Chapter III. Regulations Regarding the Crews of Enemy Merchant Ships Captured by a Belligerent

Art. 5. When an enemy merchant ship is captured by a belligerent, such of its crew as are nationals of a neutral State are not made prisoners of war.

Nationals of a neutral State

The same rule applies in the case of the captain and officers likewise nationals of a neutral State, if they promise formally in writing not to serve on an enemy ship while the war lasts.

Art. 6. The captain, officers, and members of the crew, when nationals of the enemy State, are not made prisoners of war, on condition that they make a formal promise in writing, not to undertake, while hostilities last, any service connected with the operations of the war.

Nationals of the enemy State

Art. 7. The names of the persons retaining their liberty under the conditions laid down in Article 5, paragraph 2, and in Article 6, are notified by the belligerent captor to the other belligerent. The latter is forbidden knowingly to employ the said persons.

Notification by captors

Art. 8. The provisions of the three preceding articles do not apply to ships taking part in the hostilities.

Ships not included

Chapter IV. Final Provisions

Art. 9. The provisions of the present Convention do not apply except between Contracting Powers, and then only if all the belligerents are parties to the Convention.

Powers bound

Ratification

Art. 10. The present Convention shall be ratified as soon as possible.

The ratifications shall be deposited at The Hague.

The first deposit of ratifications shall be recorded in a *procès-verbal* signed by the representatives of the Powers taking part therein and by the Netherlands Minister for Foreign Affairs.

Subsequent deposits of ratifications shall be made by means of a written notification, addressed to the Netherlands Government and accompanied by the instrument of ratification.

A duly certified copy of the *procès-verbal* relative to the first deposit of ratifications, of the notifications mentioned in the preceding paragraph, as well as of the instruments of ratification, shall be at once sent by the Netherlands Government, through the diplomatic channel, to the Powers invited to the Second Peace Conference, as well as to the other Powers which have adhered to the Convention. In the cases contemplated in the preceding paragraph, the said Government shall inform them at the same time of the date on which it received the notification.

Adhesion

Art. 11. Non-Signatory Powers may adhere to the present Convention.

The Power which desires to adhere notifies its intention in writing to the Netherlands Government, forwarding to it the act of adhesion, which shall be deposited in the archives of the said Government.

This Government shall at once transmit to all the other Powers a duly certified copy of the notification as well as of the act of adhesion, mentioning the date on which it received the notification.

Entry into force

Art. 12. The present Convention shall come into force in the case of the Powers which were a party to the first deposit of ratifications, sixty days after the *procès-verbal* of that deposit, and, in the case of the Powers which ratify subsequently or which adhere, sixty days after the notification of their ratification has been received by the Netherlands Government.

Denunciation

Art. 13. In the event of one of the Contracting Powers wishing to denounce the present Convention, the denunciation shall be notified in writing to the Netherlands Government, which shall at once communicate a duly certified copy of the notification to all the other Powers informing them of the date on which it was received.

The denunciation shall only have effect in regard to the notifying Power, and one year after the notification has reached the Netherlands Government.

Register of ratifications

Art. 14. A register kept by the Netherlands Ministry for Foreign Affairs shall give the date of the deposit of ratifications made in virtue of Article 10, paragraphs 3 and 4, as well as the date on which the notifications of adhesion (Article 11, paragraph 2) or of denunciation (Article 13, paragraph 1) have been received.

Each Contracting Power is entitled to have access to this register and to be supplied with duly certified extracts from it.

In faith whereof the Plenipotentiaries have appended their signatures to the present Convention.

Done at The Hague, 18 October 1907, in a single copy, which shall remain deposited in the archives of the Netherlands Government, and duly certified copies of which shall be sent, through the diplomatic channel, to the Powers invited to the Second Peace Conference.

[Here follow signatures]

SIGNATURES, RATIFICATIONS AND ACCESSIONS[1]

State	*Signature*	*Ratification, Accession, Notification of Continuity (C)*
Argentina	18 October 1907	–
Austria-Hungary	18 October 1907	27 November 1909
Belgium	18 October 1907	8 August 1910
Bolivia	18 October 1907	–
Brazil	18 October 1907	5 January 1914
Bulgaria	18 October 1907	–
Chile	18 October 1907	–
China	–	10 May 1917
Colombia	18 October 1907	–
Cuba	18 October 1907	–
Denmark	18 October 1907	27 November 1909
Dominican Republic	18 October 1907	–
Ecuador	18 October 1907	–
El Salvador	18 October 1907	27 November 1909
Ethiopia	–	5 August 1935
Fiji	–	2 April 1973 (C)
Finland[2]	–	10 April 1922
France	18 October 1907	7 October 1910
Germany	18 October 1907	27 November 1909
Great Britain	18 October 1907	27 November 1909
Greece	18 October 1907	–
Guatemala	18 October 1907	15 March 1911
Haiti	18 October 1907	2 February 1910
Italy	18 October 1907	–

1 Based on a communication received from the Ministry of Foreign Affairs of the Netherlands of 12 December 2001. See also ICRC website.

2 By letter dated 12 May 1980 the Netherlands Ministry of Foreign Affairs stated (a) Finland's accession on 30 December 1918 to this and other 1907 Hague Conventions and to the 1907 Hague Declaration was initially regarded as provisional, pending the final resolution of Finland's international status; (b) after consultation with other contracting powers, the depositary stated on 9 June 1922 that Finland's accession should be regarded as final and complete; and (c) the Conventions and Declaration entered into force for Finland on 9 June 1922.

State	*Signature*	*Ratification, Accession, Notification of Continuity (C)*
Japan	18 October 1907	13 December 1911
Liberia	–	4 February 1914
Luxemburg	18 October 1907	5 September 1912
Mexico	18 October 1907	27 November 1909
Netherlands	18 October 1907	27 November 1909
Nicaragua	–	16 December 1909
Norway	18 October 1907	19 September 1910
Panama	18 October 1907	11 September 1911
Paraguay	18 October 1907	–
Persia	18 October 1907	–
Peru	18 October 1907	–
Poland	–	2 June 1935
Portugal	18 October 1907	13 April 1911
Romania	18 October 1907	1 March 1912
Serbia	18 October 1907	–
Siam	18 October 1907	12 March 1910
South Africa	–	10 March 1978 (C)
Spain	18 October 1907	18 March 1913
Sweden	18 October 1907	27 November 1909
Switzerland	18 October 1907	12 May 1910
Turkey	18 October 1907	–
United States of America	18 October 1907	27 November 1909
Uruguay	18 October 1907	–
Venezuela	18 October 1907	–

RESERVATIONS

None

No. 81

CONVENTION (XII) RELATIVE TO THE CREATION OF AN INTERNATIONAL PRIZE COURT

Signed at The Hague, 18 October 1907

INTRODUCTORY NOTE: Proposals for the creation of an international prize court had been made since the 18th century. On several occasions international commissions or arbitration tribunals were instituted for prize cases on a bilateral basis. The International Prize Court provided for by the present Convention has never been established because the Convention failed to secure any ratifications. The Court would have served as a court of appeals against judgements of national prize courts. Neutral powers as well as neutral and enemy nationals would have been entitled to bring appeals. The debates at The Hague revealed that grave divergences existed with regard to the rules of prize law that the Court would have had to apply. In order to arrive at an agreement on these rules a Naval Conference met in London in 1908 and 1909 and produced the Declaration of London (*No. 83*). The fact that this Declaration was not ratified proved to be fatal to the proposal for an International Prize Court.

ENTRY INTO FORCE: Not in force.

AUTHENTIC TEXT: French. The English translation below is reprinted from Scott, *Hague Conventions*, pp. 188–203. It reproduces the translation of the United States Department of State. The marginal titles added to the Convention have no official character.

TEXT PUBLISHED IN: *Conférence internationale de la Paix, 1907*, pp. 668-679 (French); *Les deux Conférences de la Paix*, pp. 151–164 (French); Scott, *Hague Conventions*, pp. 188–203 (Engl.); Scott, *Les Conventions de la Haye*, pp. 188–203 (French); Scott, *Les Conférences de la Haye*, pp. 87–96 (French); Martens, *NRGT*, 3ème série, Vol. III, pp. 68–712 (French, German); Deltenre, pp. 364–397 (Engl., French, German, Dutch); *Fontes Historiae Juris Gentium*, Vol. III/1, pp. 621–625 (Engl., French, German); *Droits des conflits armés*, pp. 1141–1157 (French); *BFSP*, Vol. 100, 1906–1907, pp. 435–447 (French); *CTS*, Vol. 205, 1907, pp. 381–394 (French); Higgins, pp. 407–430 (Engl., French); *AJIL*, Vol. 2, 1908, pp. 174–202 (Engl., French); Friedman, pp. 370–384 (Engl.); Genet, pp. 535–546 (French); *Mezhdunarodnoe pravo*, Vol. III, pp. 149–151 (Russ.); Korovin, p. 390 (Russ.); *Revista de Derecho Internacional y politica exterior*, Cronicá, Año III, 1907, pp. 100–112 (Span.); Arellano, pp. 381–384 (Span. – extract); ICRC website: www.icrc.org/ihl.nsf (Engl., French, Span.).

TABLE OF CONTENTS

* * *

[List of Contracting Parties]

Animated by the desire to settle in an equitable manner the differences which sometimes arise in the course of a naval war in connection with the decisions of national prize courts;

Considering that, if these courts are to continue to exercise their functions in the manner determined by national legislation, it is desirable that in certain cases an appeal should be provided under conditions conciliating, as far as possible, the public and private interests involved in matters of prize;

Whereas, moreover, the institution of an International Court, whose jurisdiction and procedure would be carefully defined, has seemed to be the best method of attaining this object;

Convinced, finally, that in this manner the hardships consequent on naval war would be mitigated; that, in particular, good relations will be more easily maintained between belligerents and neutrals and peace better assured;

Desirous of concluding a Convention to this effect, have appointed the following as their Plenipotentiaries:

[Here follow the names of Plenipotentiaries]

Who, after depositing their full powers, found in good and due form, have agreed upon the following provisions:

PART I. GENERAL PROVISIONS

Determination of the validity of capture.

Article 1. The validity of the capture of a merchant ship or its cargo is decided before a prize court in accordance with the present Convention when neutral or enemy property is involved.

Jurisdiction in first instance

Art. 2. Jurisdiction in matters of prize is exercized in the first instance by the prize courts of the belligerent captor. The judgments of these courts are pronounced in public or are officially notified to parties concerned who are neutrals or enemies.

International Prize Court

Art. 3. The judgments of national prize courts may be brought before the International Prize Court –

1. When the judgment of the national prize courts affects the property of a neutral Power or individual;
2. When the judgment affects enemy property and relates to –
   (a) Cargo on board a neutral ship;
   (b) An enemy ship captured in the territorial waters of a neutral Power, when that Power has not made the capture the subject of a diplomatic claim;
   (c) A claim based upon the allegation that the seizure has been effected in violation, either of the provisions of a Convention in force between the belligerent Powers, or of an enactment issued by the belligerent captors.

The appeal against the judgment of the national court can be based on the ground that the judgment was wrong either in fact or in law.

Right to bring appeal

Art. 4. An appeal may be brought –

1. By a neutral Power, if the judgment of the national tribunals injuriously affects its property or the property of its nationals (Article 3, No. 1), or if the capture of an enemy vessel is alleged to have taken place in the territorial waters of that Power (Article 3, No. 2(b)).
2. By a neutral individual, if the judgment of the national court injuriously affects his property (Article 3, No. I), subject, however, to the reservation that the Power to which he belongs may forbid him to bring the case before the Court, or may itself undertake the proceedings in his place;
3. By an individual subject or citizen of an enemy Power, if the judgment of the national court injuriously affects his property in the cases referred to in Article 3, No. 2, except that mentioned in paragraph (b).

Successors in interest

Art. 5. An appeal may also be brought on the same conditions as in the preceding article, by persons belonging either to neutral States or to the enemy, deriving their rights from and entitled to represent an individual qualified to appeal, and who have taken part in the proceedings before the national court. Persons so entitled may appeal separately to the extent of their interest.

The same rule applies in the case of persons belonging either to neutral States or to the enemy who derive their rights from and are entitled to represent a neutral Power whose property was the subject of the decision.

Limitation upon jurisdiction of national courts

Art. 6. When, in accordance with the above Article 3, the International Court has jurisdiction, the national courts cannot deal with a case in more than two instances. The municipal law of the belligerent captor shall decide whether the case may be brought before the International Court after judgment has been given in first instance or only after an appeal.

If the national courts fail to give final judgment within two years from the date of capture, the case may be carried direct to the International Court.

Applicable Law

Art. 7.[1] If a question of law to be decided is covered by a treaty in force between the belligerent captor and a Power which is itself or whose subject or citizen is a party to the proceedings, the Court is governed by the provisions in the said treaty.

In the absence of such provisions, the Court shall apply the rules of international law. If no generally recognized rule exists, the Court shall give judgment in accordance with the general principles of justice and equity.

The above provisions apply equally to questions relating to the order and mode of proof.

If, in accordance with Article 3, No. 2(c), the ground of appeal is the violation of an enactment issued by the belligerent captor, the Court will enforce the enactment.

The Court may disregard failure to comply with the procedure laid down in the enactments of the belligerent captor, when it is of opinion that the of complying therewith are unjust and inequitable.

---

[1] The Naval Conference of London of 1908 and 1909 was convened in order to lay down the generally recognized rules of international law within the meaning of paragraph 2 of this article. See *No. 83*, preambles of the Final Act and of the Protocol.

Art. 8. If the Court pronounces the capture of the vessel or cargo to be valid, they shall be disposed of in accordance with the laws of the belligerent captor.[2]

Disposition of vessel and cargo

If it pronounces the capture to be null, the Court shall order restitution of the vessel or cargo, and shall fix, if there is occasion, the amount of the damages. If the vessel or cargo have been sold or destroyed, the Court shall determine the compensation to be given to the owner on this account.

If the national court pronounced the capture to be null, the Court can only be asked to decide as to the damages.

Art. 9. The Contracting Powers undertake to submit in good faith to the decisions of the International Prize Court and to carry them out with the least possible delay.

Carrying out of decisions

PART II. CONSTITUTION OF THE INTERNATIONAL PRIZE COURT

Art. 10. The International Prize Court is composed of judges and deputy judges, who will be appointed by the Contracting Powers, and must all be jurists of known proficiency in questions of international maritime law, and of the highest moral reputation.

Composition of Court

The appointment of these judges and deputy judges shall be made within six months after the ratification of the present Convention.

Art. 11. The judges and deputy judges are appointed for a period of six years, reckoned from the date on which the notification of their appointment is received by the Administrative Council established by the Convention for the pacific settlement of international disputes of the 29 July 1899. Their appointments can be renewed.

Term of service

Should one of the judges or deputy judges die or resign, the same procedure is followed for filling the vacancy as was followed for appointing him. In this case, the appointment is made for a fresh period of six years.

Vacancies

Art. 12. The judges of the International Prize Court are all equal in rank and have precedence according to the date on which the notification of their appointment was received (Article 11, paragraph 1), and if they sit by rota (Article 15, paragraph 2), according to the date on which they entered upon their duties. When the date is the same the senior in age takes precedence.

Rank of judges

The deputy judges when acting are assimilated to the judges. They rank, however, after them.

Art. 13. The judges enjoy diplomatic privileges and immunities in the performance of their duties and when outside their own country.

Privileges and immunities. Oath

Before taking their seat, the judges must swear, or make a solemn promise before the Administrative Council, to discharge their duties impartially and conscientiously.

Art. 14. The Court is composed of fifteen judges; nine judges constitute a quorum.

Number of judges

A judge who is absent or prevented from sitting is replaced by the deputy judge.

[2] See Article 2 of the Additional Protocol (*No. 82*).

Distribution of judges

Art. 15.[3] The judges appointed by the following Contracting Powers: Germany, the United States of America, Austria-Hungary, France, Great Britain, Italy, Japan, and Russia, are always summoned to sit.

The judges and deputy judges appointed by the other Contracting Powers sit by rota as shown in the table annexed to the present Convention; their duties may be performed successively by the same person. The same judge may be appointed by several of the said Powers.

Selection of judge by belligerent Power

Art. 16. If a belligerent Power has, according to the rota, no judge sitting in the Court, it may ask that the judge appointed by it should take part in the settlement of all cases arising from the war. Lots shall then be drawn as to which of the judges entitled to sit according to the rota shall withdraw. This arrangement does not affect the judge appointed by the other belligerent.

Disqualification of judges

Art. 17. No judge can sit who has been a party, in any way whatever, to the sentence pronounced by the national courts, or has taken part in the case as counsel or advocate for one of the parties.

No judge or deputy judge can, during his tenure of office, appear as agent or advocate before the International Prize Court nor act for one of the parties in any capacity whatever.

Assessors

Art. 18. The belligerent captor is entitled to appoint a naval officer of high rank to sit as assessor, but with no voice in the decision. A neutral Power, which is a party to the proceedings or whose subject or citizen is a party, has the same right of appointment; if as the result of this last provision more than one Power is concerned, they must agree among themselves, if necessary by lot, on the officer to be appointed.

Election of officers

Art. 19. The Court elects its president and vice-president by an absolute majority of the votes cast. After two ballots, the election is made by a bare majority, and, in case the votes are equal, by lot.

Compensation of judges

Art. 20. The judges on the International Prize Court are entitled to travelling allowances in accordance with the regulations in force in their own country, and in addition receive, while the Court is sitting or while they are carrying out duties conferred upon them by the Court, a sum of 100 Netherlands florins *per diem*.

These payments are included in the general expenses of the Court dealt with in Article 47, and are paid through the International Bureau established by the Convention of the 29 July 1899.

The judges may not receive from their own Government or from that of any other Power any remuneration in their capacity of members of the Court.

Seat of the Court

Art. 21. The seat of the International Prize Court is at The Hague and it cannot, except in the cases of *force majeure*, be transferred elsewhere without the consent of the belligerents.

Functions of Administrative Council

Art. 22. The Administrative Council fulfils, with regard to the International Prize Court, the same functions as to the Permanent Court of Arbitration, but only representatives of Contracting Powers will be members of it.

---

3 For reservation in respect of this article by Chile, Cuba, Ecuador, El Salvador, Guatemala, Haiti, Persia, Siam, Turkey and Uruguay, see p. 1105.

Art. 23. The International Bureau acts as registry to the International Prize Court and must place its offices and staff at the disposal of the Court. It has charge of the archives and carries out the administrative work.

International bureau acts as registry

The secretary general of the International Bureau acts as registrar. The necessary secretaries to assist the registrar, translators and shorthand writers are appointed and sworn in by the Court.

Art. 24. The Court determines which language it will itself use and what languages may be used before it.

Language used in proceedings

In every case the official language of the national courts which have had cognizance of the case may be used before the Court.

Art. 25. Powers which are concerned in a case may appoint special agents to act as intermediaries between themselves and the Court. They may also engage counsel or advocates to defend their rights and interests.

Agents and counsel

Art. 26. A private person concerned in a case will be represented before the Court by an attorney, who must be either an advocate qualified to plead before a court of appeal or a high court of one of the Contracting States, or a lawyer practising before a similar court, or lastly, a professor of law at one of the higher teaching centres of those countries.

Attorneys

Art. 27. For all notices to be served, in particular on the parties, witnesses, or experts, the Court may apply direct to the Government of the State on whose territory the service is to be carried out. The same rule applies in the case of steps being taken to procure evidence.

Notices and evidence

The requests for this purpose are to be executed so far as the means at the disposal of the Power applied to under its municipal law allow. They cannot be rejected unless the Power in question considers them calculated to impair its sovereign rights or its safety. If the request is complied with, the fees charged must only comprise the expenses actually incurred.

The Court is equally entitled to act through the Power on whose territory it sits.

Notices to be given to parties in the place where the Court sits may be served through the International Bureau.

PART III. PROCEDURE IN THE INTERNATIONAL PRIZE COURT

Art. 28.[4] An appeal to the International Prize Court is entered by means of a written declaration made in the national court which has already dealt with the case or addressed to the International Bureau; in the latter case the appeal can be entered by telegram.

Method and time of entering appeal

The period within which the appeal must be entered is fixed at 120 days, counting from the day the decision is delivered or notified (Article 2, paragraph 2).

Art. 29.[5] If the notice of appeal is entered in the national court, this Court, without considering the question whether the appeal was

Transmission of record to International Bureau

4 See Article 5 of the Additional Protocol (*No. 82*).

5 See Article 6 of the Additional Protocol (*No. 82*).

entered in due time, will transmit within seven days the record of the case to the International Bureau.

If the notice of the appeal is sent to the International Bureau, the Bureau will immediately inform the national court, when possible by telegraph. The latter will transmit the record as provided in the preceding paragraph.

When the appeal is brought by a neutral individual the International Bureau at once informs by telegraph the individual's Government, in order to enable it to enforce the rights it enjoys under Article 4, paragraph 2.

Appeal when national courts fail to give final judgment

Art. 30. In the case provided for in Article 6, paragraph 2, the notice of appeal can be addressed to the International Bureau only. It must be entered within thirty days of the expiration of the period of two years.

Belated appeal

Art. 31. If the appellant does not enter his appeal within the period laid down in Articles 28 or 30, it shall be rejected without discussion. Provided that he can show that he was prevented from so doing by *force majeure*, and that the appeal was entered within sixty days after the circumstances which prevented him entering it before had ceased to operate, the Court can, after hearing the respondent, grant relief from the effect of the above provision.

Respondent

Art. 32. If the appeal is entered in time, a certified copy of the notice of appeal is forthwith officially transmitted by the Court to the respondent.

Appeal of other parties

Art. 33. If, in addition to the parties who are before the Court, there are other parties concerned who are entitled to appeal, or if, in the case referred to in Article 29, paragraph 3, the Government who has received notice of an appeal has not announced its decision, the Court will await before dealing with the case the expiration of the period laid down in Articles 28 or 30.

Pleadings and arguments

Art. 34. The procedure before the International Court includes two distinct parts: the written pleadings and oral discussions.

The written pleadings consist of the deposit and exchange of cases, counter-cases, and, if necessary, of replies, of which the order is fixed by the Court, as also the periods within which they must be delivered. The Parties annex thereto all papers and documents of which they intend to make use.

A certified copy of every document produced by one Party must be communicated to the other Party through the medium of the Court.

Public sitting

Art. 35. After the close of the pleadings, a public sitting is held on a day fixed by the Court.

At this sitting the Parties state their view of the case both as to the law and as to the facts.

The Court may, at any stage of the proceedings, suspend speeches of counsel, either at the request of one of the Parties, or on their own initiative, in order that supplementary evidence may be obtained.

Supplementary evidence

Art. 36. The International Court may order the supplementary evidence to be taken either in the manner provided by Article 27, or before itself, or one or more of the members of the Court, provided that this can be done without resort to compulsion or the use of threats.

If steps are to be taken for the purpose of obtaining evidence by members of the Court outside the territory where it is sitting, the consent of the foreign Government must be obtained.

Art. 37. The Parties are summoned to take part in all stages of the proceedings and receive certified copies of the minutes.

Parties summoned for every stage of proceedings

Art. 38. The discussions are under the control of the president or vice-president, or, in case they are absent or cannot act, of the senior judge present. The judge appointed by a belligerent Party cannot preside.

Presidency

Art. 39. The discussions take place in public, subject to the right of a Government who is a Party to the case to demand that they be held in private.

Public Minutes

Minutes are taken of these discussions and signed by the president and registrar, and these minutes alone have an authentic character.

Art. 40. If a Party does not appear, despite the fact that it has been duly cited, or if a Party fails to comply with some step within the period fixed by the Court, the case proceeds without that Party, and the Court gives judgment in accordance with the material at its disposal.

Failure of party to appear

Art. 41. The Court official notifies to the Parties decrees or decisions made in their absence.

Notification of decrees or decisions

Art. 42. The Court takes into consideration in arriving at its decision all the facts, evidence, and oral statements.

Matters considered

Art. 43. The Court considers its decision in private and the proceedings are secret.

Manner of making decisions

All questions are decided by a majority of the judges present. If the number of judges is even and equally divided, the vote of the junior judge in the order of precedence laid down in Article 12, paragraph 1, is not counted.

Art. 44. The judgment of the Court must give the reasons on which it is based. It contains the names of the judges taking part in it, and also of the assessors, if any; if is signed by the president and registrar.

Reasons for judgment

Art. 45.[6] The sentence is pronounced in public sitting, the parties concerned being present or duly summoned to attend; the sentence is officially communicated to the parties.

Method of pronouncing sentence

When this communication has been made, the Court transmits to the national prize court the record of the case, together with copies of the various decisions arrived at and of the minutes of the proceedings.

Art. 46. Each party pays its own costs.

Payment of costs

The party against whom the Court decides bears, in addition, the costs of the trial, and also pays 1 per cent of the value of the subject-matter of the case as a contribution of the general expenses of the International Court. The amount of these payments is fixed in the judgment of the Court.

If the appeal is brought by an individual, he will furnish the International Bureau with security to an amount fixed by the Court,

6 See Article 7 of the Additional Protocol (*No. 82*).

for the purpose of guaranteeing eventual fulfilment of the two obligations mentioned in the preceding paragraph. The Court is entitled to postpone the opening of the proceedings until the security has been furnished.

General expenses of Court

Art. 47. The general expenses of the International Prize Court are borne by the Contracting Powers in proportion to their share in the composition of the Court as laid down in Article 15 and in the annexed table. The appointment of deputy judges does not involve any contribution.

The Administrative Council applies to the Powers for the funds requisite for the working of the Court.

Performance of duties when Court is not sitting

Art. 48. When the Court is not sitting, the duties conferred upon it by Article 32, Article 34, paragraphs 2 and 3, Article 35, paragraph 1, and Article 46, paragraph 3, are discharged by a delegation of three judges appointed by the Court. This delegation decides by a majority of votes.

Rules of procedure

Art. 49. The Court itself draws up its own rules of procedure, which must be communicated to the Contracting Powers.

It will meet to elaborate these rules within a year of the ratification of the present Convention.

Modifications in present Convention

Art. 50. The Court may propose modifications in the provisions of the present Convention concerning procedure. These proposals are communicated, through the medium of the Netherlands Government, to the Contracting Powers, which will consider together as to the measures to be taken.

PART IV. FINAL PROVISIONS

Applicability of Convention

Art. 51. The present Convention does not apply as of right except when the belligerent Powers are all parties to the Convention.

It is further fully understood that an appeal to the International Prize Court can only be brought by a Contracting Power or the subject or citizen of a Contracting Power.

In the cases mentioned in Article 5, the appeal is only admitted when both the owner and the person entitled to represent him are equally Contracting Powers or the subjects or citizens of Contracting Powers.

Ratifications

Art. 52. The present Convention shall be ratified and the ratifications shall be deposited at The Hague as soon as all the Powers mentioned in Article 15 and in the table annexed are in a position to do so.

The deposit of the ratifications shall take place, in any case, on the 30 June 1909, if the Powers which are ready to ratify furnish nine judges and nine deputy judges to the Court, qualified to validly constitute a Court. If not, the deposit shall be postponed until this condition is fulfilled.

A minute of the deposit of ratifications shall be drawn up, of which a certified copy shall be forwarded, through the diplomatic channel, to each of the Powers referred to in the first paragraph.

Signatures and adhesions

Art. 53. The Powers referred to in Article 15 and in the table annexed are entitled to sign the present Convention up to the deposit of the ratifications contemplated in paragraph 2 of the preceding article.

After this deposit, they can at any time adhere to it, purely and simply. A Power wishing to adhere, notifies its intention in writing to the Netherlands Government transmitting to it, at the same time, the act of adhesion, which shall be deposited in the archives of the said Government. The latter shall send, through the diplomatic channel, a certified copy of the notification and of the act of adhesion to all the Powers referred to in the preceding paragraph, informing them of the date on which it has received the notification.

Art. 54. The present Convention shall come into force six months from the deposit of the ratifications contemplated in Article 52, paragraphs 1 and 2. Entry into force

The adhesions shall take effect sixty days after notification of such adhesion has been received by the Netherlands Government, or as soon as possible on the expiration of the period contemplated in the preceding paragraph.

The International Court shall, however, have jurisdiction to deal with prize cases decided by the national courts at any time after the deposit of the ratifications or of the receipt of the notification of the adhesions. In such cases, the Period fixed in Article 28, paragraph 2, shall only be reckoned from the date when the Convention comes into force as regards a Power which has ratified or adhered.

Art. 55. The present Convention shall remain in force for twelve years from the time it comes into force, as determined by Article 54, paragraph 1, even in the case of Powers which adhere subsequently. Duration. Denunciation, Renewal

It shall be renewed tacitly from six years to six years unless denounced.

Denunciation must be notified in writing, at least one year before the expiration of each of the periods mentioned in the two preceding paragraphs, to the Netherlands Government, which will inform all the other Contracting Powers.

Denunciation shall only take effect in regard to the Power which has notified it. The Convention shall remain in force in the case of the other Contracting Powers, provided that their participation in the appointment of judges is sufficient to allow of the composition of the Court with nine judges and nine deputy judges.

Art. 56. In case the present Convention is not in operation as regards all the Powers referred to in Article 15 and the annexed table, the Administrative Council shall draw up a list on the lines of that article and table of the judges and deputy judges through whom the Contracting Powers will share in the composition of the Court. The times allotted by the said table to judges who are summoned to sit in rota will be redistributed between the different years of the six-year period in such a way that, as far as possible, the number of the judges of the Court in each year shall be the same. If the number of deputy judges is greater than that of the judges, the number of the latter can be completed by deputy judges chosen by lot among those Powers which do not nominate a judge. Selection of judges by Administrative Council

The list drawn up in this way by the Administrative Council shall be notified to the Contracting Powers. It shall be revised when the number of these Powers is modified as the result of adhesions or denunciations.

The change resulting from an adhesion is not made until I January after the date on which the adhesion takes effect, unless the adhering

Power is a belligerent Power, in which case it can ask to be at once represented in the Court, the provision of Article 16 being, moreover, applicable if necessary.

When the total number of judges is less than eleven, seven judges form a quorum.

Modification of Article 15

Art. 57. Two years before the expiration of each period referred to in paragraphs 1 and 2 of Article 55 any Contracting Power can demand a modification of the provisions of Article 15 and of the annexed table, relative to its participation in the composition of the Court. The demand shall be addressed to the Administrative Council, which will examine it and submit to all the Powers proposals as to the measures to be adopted. The Powers shall inform the Administrative Council of their decision with the least possible delay. The result shall be at once, and at least one year and thirty days before the expiration of the said period of two years, communicated to the Power which made the demand.

When necessary, the modifications adopted by the Powers shall come into force from the commencement of the fresh period.

In faith whereof the Plenipotentiaries have appended their signatures to the present Convention.

Done at The Hague, 18 October 1907, in a single copy, which shall remain deposited in the archives of the Netherlands Government, and duly certified copies of which shall be sent, through the diplomatic channel to the Powers designated in Article 15 and in the table annexed.

[Here follow signatures]

ANNEX TO ARTICLE 15

Distribution of Judges and Deputy Judges by Countries for Each Year of the Period of Six Years

JUDGES	DEPUTY JUDGES	JUDGES	DEPUTY JUDGES
First Year		*Second Year*	
1 Argentine	Paraguay	Argentine	Panama
2 Columbia	Bolivia	Spain	Spain
3 Spain	Spain	Greece	Romania
4 Greece	Romania	Norway	Sweden
5 Norway	Sweden	Netherlands	Belgium
6 Netherlands	Belgium	Turkey	Luxemburg
7 Turkey	Persia	Uruguay	Costa Rica
Third Year		*Fourth Year*	
1 Brazil	Dominican Rep.	Brazil	Guatemala
2 China	Turkey	China	Turkey
3 Spain	Portugal	Spain	Portugal
4 Netherlands	Switzerland	Peru	Honduras
5 Romania	Greece	Romania	Greece
6 Sweden	Denmark	Sweden	Denmark
7 Venezuela	Haiti	Switzerland	Netherlands

JUDGES	DEPUTY JUDGES	JUDGES	DEPUTY JUDGES
Fifth Year		*Sixth Year*	
1 Belgium	Netherlands	Belgium	Netherlands
2 Bulgaria	Montenegro	Chile	El Salvador
3 Chile	Nicaragua	Denmark	Norway
4 Denmark	Norway	Mexico	Ecuador
5 Mexico	Cuba	Portugal	Spain
6 Persia	China	Serbia	Bulgaria
7 Portugal	Spain	Siam	China

SIGNATURES[1]

The Convention was signed by the following states:

Argentina
Austro-Hungary
Belgium
Bolivia
Bulgaria
Chile *Res.*
Columbia
Cuba *Res.*
Denmark
Ecuador *Res.*
El Salvador *Res.*
France
Germany
Great Britain
Guatemala *Res.*
Haiti *Res.*
Italy
Japan
Mexico
Netherlands
Norway
Panama
Paraguay
Persia *Res.*
Peru
Portugal
Siam *Res.*
Spain
Sweden
Switzerland
Turkey *Res.*
United States of America
Uruguay *Res.*

RATIFICATIONS

None

ACCESSION

Nicaragua adhered to the Convention on 16 December 1909.

RESERVATIONS

Chile, Cuba, Ecuador, El Salvador, Guatemala, Haiti, Persia, Siam, Turkey and Uruguay signed the Convention with reservation of Article 15.

1 Based on a communication received from the Ministry of Foreign Affairs of the Netherlands of 12 December 2001. See also ICRC website.

No. 82

ADDITIONAL PROTOCOL TO THE CONVENTION RELATIVE TO THE ESTABLISHMENT OF AN INTERNATIONAL PRIZE COURT

Signed at The Hague, 19 September 1910

INTRODUCTORY NOTE: The Additional Protocol was adopted on the initiative of the United States. The Convention of 1907 seemed to be in conflict with the Constitution of the United States which vests the judicial power in the Supreme Court. The delegates assembled at the Naval Conference in London in 1908 and 1909 approved in principle the modifications submitted to them by the United States, but were not authorized to sign an additional protocol. See the wish expressed by the delegates in the Final Protocol of the Naval Conferenc, (*No. 83*). The Additional Protocol was signed at The Hague by thirteen powers and was later signed by all the remaining signatories of the original Convention.

ENTRY INTO FORCE: Not yet in force.

AUTHENTIC TEXT: French. The English translation below is reprinted from Scott, *Hague Conventions*, pp. 204–208. It reproduces the translation of the United States Department of State. The marginal titles added to the Protocol have no official character.

TEXT PUBLISHED IN: Martens, *NRGT*, 3ème série, Vol. VII, pp. 73–78 (French); *CTS*, Vol. 212, 1910–1911, pp. 173–177 (French); Scott, *Hague Conventions*, pp. 204–208 (Engl.); Deltenre, pp. 392–397 (Engl., French, German, Dutch); *BFSP*, Vol. 104, pp. 258–262 (French); *AJIL*, Vol. 5, Suppl., pp. 95–99 (Engl.); *RGDIP*, Vol. XVIII, 1911 – Documents; pp. 11–13 (French); Genet, pp. 564–565 (French); *Droit des conflits armés*, pp. 1159–1162 (French); ICRC website: www.icrc.org/ihl.nsf (Engl., French, Span.).

TABLE OF CONTENTS

* * *

[List of Contracting Parties]

Powers signatory to the Hague Convention dated 18 October 1907, for the establishment of an International Court of Prize,

Considering that for some of these Powers difficulties of a constitutional nature prevent the acceptance of the said Convention, in its present form,

Have deemed it expedient to agree upon an additional protocol taking into account these difficulties without jeopardizing any legitimate interest and have, to that end, appointed as their Plenipotentiaries, to wit:

[Here follow the names of plenipotentiaries]

Who, after depositing their full powers, found to be in good and due form, have agreed upon the following:

Rights of Powers signatory or adhering to Convention of October 18 1907

Article 1. The Powers signatory or adhering to the Hague Convention of 18 October 1907, relative to the establishment of an International Court of Prize, which are prevented by difficulties of a constitutional nature from accepting the said Convention in its present form, have the right to declare in the instrument of ratification or adherence that in prize cases, whereof their national courts have jurisdiction, recourse to the International Court of Prize can only be exercised against them in the form of an action in damages for the injury caused by the capture.

In case of an action for damages

Art. 2. In the case of recourse to the International Court of Prize, in the form of an action for damages, Article 8 of the Convention is not applicable; it is not for the Court to pass upon the validity or the nullity of the capture, nor to reverse or affirm the decision of the national tribunals.

If the capture is considered illegal, the Court determines the amount of damages to be allowed, if any, to the claimants.

Art. 3. The conditions to which recourse to the International Court of Prize is subject by the Convention are applicable to the action in damages.

Rules of procedure

Art. 4. Under reserve of the provisions hereinafter stated the rules of procedure established by the Convention for recourse to the International Court of Prize shall be observed in the action in damages.

In derogation of Article 28 of Convention

Art. 5. In derogation of Article 28, paragraph 1, of the Convention, the suit for damages can only be brought before the International Court of Prize by means of a written declaration addressed to the International Bureau of the Permanent Court of Arbitration; the case may even be brought before the Bureau by telegram.

In derogation of Article 29 of Convention

Art. 6. In derogation of Article 29 of the Convention the International Bureau shall notify directly, and if possible by telegram, the Government of the belligerent captor of the declaration of action brought before it.

The Government of the belligerent captor, without considering whether the prescribed periods of time have been observed, shall, within seven days of the receipt of the notification, transmit to the International Bureau the case, appending thereto a certified copy of the decision, if any, rendered by the national tribunal.

Art. 7. In derogation of Article 45, paragraph 2, of the Convention the Court rendering its decision and notifying it to the parties to the suit shall send directly to the Government of the belligerent captor the record of the case submitted to it, appending thereto a copy of the various intervening decisions as well as a copy of the minutes of the preliminary proceedings.

In derogation of Article 45 of the Convention

Art. 8. The present Additional Protocol shall be considered as forming an integral part of and shall be ratified at the same time as the Convention.

Ratification

If the declaration provided for in Article 1 herein above is made in the instrument of the ratification, a certified copy thereof shall be inserted in the *procès-verbal* of the deposit of ratifications referred to in Article 52, paragraph 3, of the Convention.

Art. 9. Adherence to the Convention is subordinated to adherence to the present Additional Protocol.

Adherence

In faith of which the Plenipotentiaries have affixed their signatures to the present Additional Protocol.

Done at The Hague, 19 September 1910, in a single copy, which shall remain deposited in the archives of the Government of the Netherlands and of which duly certified copies shall be forwarded through diplomatic channels to the Powers designated in Article 15 of the Convention relative to the establishment of an International Court of Prize of 18 October 1907, and in its appendix.

[Here follow signatures]

SIGNATURES[1]

The additional protocol was signed by the following states:

States	*Date of signing*
Argentina	19 September 1910
Austria-Hungry	19 September 1910
Belgium	17 December 1910

[1] Based on a communication received from the Ministry of Foreign Affairs of the Netherlands of 12 December 2001. See also ICRC website.

States	*Date of signing*
Bolivia	11 July 1911
Bulgaria	6 May 1911
Chile	19 September 1910
Columbia	5 January 1911
Cuba	10 March 1911
Denmark	19 September 1910
El Salvador	22 December 1910
Equador	3 June 1911
France	19 September 1910
Germany	19 September 1910
Great Britain	19 September 1910
Haiti	17 January 1911
Italy	9 January 1911
Japan	19 September 1910
Mexico	21 December 1910
Netherlands	19 September 1910
Norway	19 September 1910
Panama	30 December 1910
Paraguay	22 May 1911
Peru	26 January 1911
Persia	12 December 1910
Portugal	5 January 1911
Siam	30 December 1910
Spain	19 September 1910
Sweden	19 September 1910
Switzerland	11 January 1911
Turkey	27 January 1911
United States of America	19 September 1910
Uruguay	25 January 1911

RATIFICATIONS

None

ADHESIONS

None

RESERVATIONS

None

No. 83

NAVAL CONFERENCE OF LONDON

I. FINAL PROTOCOL

II. DECLARATION CONCERNING THE LAWS OF NAVAL WAR

Signed at London, 26 February 1909

INTRODUCTORY NOTE: The Hague Convention (XII) of 1907 relative to the creation of an International Prize Court (*No. 81*) provides in Article 7 that the Court shall apply the generally recognized rules of international law relative to prize. In view of the divergences which existed with regard to these rules, the British Government convened the main sea powers to a conference in order to lay down the rules mentioned above. Ten powers participated in the Conference. Most of the rules embodied in the present Declaration correspond to established practice and decisions of national prize courts. Due to its rejection by the British House of Lords, the Declaration was not ratified by any signatory. The rules laid down in the Protocol were, however, recognized by several belligerent states during World War I.

AUTHENTIC TEXT: French. The English translation below is reprinted from the *British Blue Book*, Misc. No. 4 (1909), Cd. 4554.

TEXT PUBLISHED IN: *Proceedings of the International Naval Conference, held in London, December 1908–February 1909. Presented to both Houses of Parliament by Command of His Majesty, March 1909. Miscellaneous. No. 5 (1909).* Cd. 4555, London, Printed for His Majesty's Stationery Office, by Harrison and Sons, St. Martin's Lane; *Conférence navale, Londres, 4 décembre 1908–26 février 1909. Actes et documents*, pp. 378–393 (French); Great Britain, *Parliamentary Papers*, Misc. No. 4 (1909), Cd. 4554 (Engl., French); *The Declaration of London February 26, 1909. A Collection of Official Papers and Documents Relating to the International Naval Conference held in London December, 1908 – February, 1909*. Edited by James Brown Scott, New York, Oxford University Press, 1919, pp. 112–129, 187–189 (Engl.); Norman Bentwitch, *The Declaration of London*, London 1911, pp. 131–157 (Engl., French); Deltenre, pp. 596–63 (German, Engl., French, Dutch); *Fontes Historiae Juris Gentium*, Vol. III/1, pp. 637–648 (German, Engl., French, extracts); *BFSP*, Vol. 104, 1911, pp. 242–255 (French); *CTS*, Vol. 208, 1908–1909, pp. 338–354 (French); Higgins, pp. 538–566 (Engl., French); Wilson-Tucker, pp. LXXXVI–C (Engl.); *AJIL*, Vol. 3, 1909, pp. 179–220 (Engl., French); Friedman, pp. 398–416 (Engl.); Ronzitti, pp. 223–256 (Engl., French); *Droit des conflits armés*, pp. 1163–1177 (French); Genet, pp. 551–569 (French); *Mezhdunarodnoe pravo*, Vol. III, pp. 151–161 (Russ.); Korovin, pp. 393–395 (Russ.); Briceno, pp. 229–242 (Span.); Ceppi, pp. 383–399 (Span. – extract); ICRC website: www,icrc.org/ihl.nsf (Engl., French, Span.).

TABLE OF CONTENTS

* * *

I. FINAL PROTOCOL

The London Naval Conference, called together by His Britannic Majesty's Government, assembled at the Foreign Office 4 December 1908, with the object of laying down the generally recognized principles of international law in accordance with Article 7 of the Convention signed at The Hague, 18 October 1907, for the establishment of an International Prize Court.

The Powers enumerated below took part in this Conference, at which they appointed as their representatives the following Delegates.

[Here follow the names of Plenipotentiaries]

In a series of meetings held from 4 December 1908 to 26 February 1909, the Conference has drawn up for signature by the Plenipotentiaries the Declaration concerning the laws of naval war, the text of which is annexed to the present Protocol.

Furthermore, the following wish has been recorded by the Delegates of those Powers which have signed or expressed the intention of signing the Convention of The Hague, 18 October 1907, for the establishment of an International Prize Court:

"The Delegates of the Powers represented at the Naval Conference which have signed or expressed the intention of signing the Convention of The Hague 18 October 1907, for the establishment of an International Prize Court, having regard to the difficulties of a constitutional nature which, in some States, stand in the way of the ratification of that Convention in its present form, agree to call the attention of their respective Governments to the advantage of concluding an arrangement under which such States would have the power, at the time of depositing their ratifications, to add thereto a reservation to the effect that resort to the International Prize Court in respect of decisions of their National Tribunals shall take the form of a direct claim for compensation, provided always that the effect of this reservation shall not be such as to impair the rights secured under the said Convention either to individuals or to their Governments, and that the terms of the reservation shall form the subject of a subsequent understanding between the Powers signatory of that Convention."

In faith whereof the Plenipotentiaries and the Delegates representing those Plenipotentiaries who have already left London have signed the present Protocol.

Done at London the twenty-sixth day of February, one thousand nine hundred and nine, in a single original, which shall be deposited in the archives of the British

Government and of which duly certified copies shall be sent through the diplomatic channel to the Powers represented at the Naval Conference.

[Here follow signatures]

SIGNATURES[1]

Austria-Hungary	Japan
France	Netherlands
Germany	Russia
Great Britain	Spain
Italy	United States of America

II. DECLARATION CONCERNING THE LAWS OF NAVAL WAR

[List of Contracting Parties]

Having regard to the terms in which the British Government invited various Powers to meet in conference in order to arrive at an agreement as to what are the generally recognized rules of international law within the meaning of Article 7 of the Convention of 18 October 1907, relative to the establishment of an International Prize Court;

Recognizing all the advantages which an agreement as to the said rules would, in the unfortunate event of a naval war, present, both as regards peaceful commerce, and as regards the belligerents and their diplomatic relations with neutral Governments;

Having regard to the divergence often found in the methods by which it is sought to apply in practice the general principles of international law;

Animated by the desire to ensure henceforward a greater measure of uniformity in this respect;

Hoping that a work so important to the common welfare will meet with general approval;

Have appointed as their Plenipotentiaries, that is to say:

[Here follow the names of plenipotentiaries]

Who, after having communicated their full powers, found to be in good and due form, have agreed to make the present Declaration:

Preliminary Provision

The Signatory Powers are agreed that the rules contained in the following Chapters correspond in substance with the generally recognized principles of international law.

Chapter I. Blockade in Time of War

Article 1. A blockade must not extend beyond the ports and coasts belonging to or occupied by the enemy.

---

[1] List of signatures was established according to the *Proceedings of the International Naval Conference, held in London, December 1908–February 1909. Presented to both Houses of Parliament by Command of His Majesty, March 1909, Miscellaneous No. 5 (1909),* Cd. 4555. London, Printed by His Majesty's Stationery Office, by Harrison and Sons, St Martin's Lane.

Art. 2. In accordance with the Declaration of Paris of 1856, a blockade, in order to be binding, must be effective – that is to say, it must be maintained by a force sufficient really to prevent access to the enemy coastline.

Art. 3. The question whether a blockade is effective is a question of fact.

Art. 4. A blockade is not regarded as raised if the blockading force is temporarily withdrawn on account of stress of weather.

Art. 5. A blockade must be applied impartially to the ships of all nations.

Art. 6. The commander of a blockading force may give permission to a warship to enter, and subsequently to leave, a blockaded port.

Art. 7. In circumstances of distress, acknowledged by an officer of the blockading force, a neutral vessel may enter a place under blockade and subsequently leave it, provided that she has neither discharged nor shipped any cargo there.

Art. 8. A blockade, in order to be binding, must be declared in accordance with Article 9, and notified in accordance with Articles 11 and 16.

Art. 9. A declaration of blockade is made either by the blockading Power or by the naval authorities acting in its name.

It specifies –

(1) The date when the blockade begins;
(2) the geographical limits of the coastline under blockade;
(3) the period within which neutral vessels may come out.

Art 10. If the operations of the blockading Power, or of the naval authorities acting in its name, do not tally with the particulars, which, in accordance with Article 9(1) and (2), must be inserted in the declaration of blockade, the declaration is void, and a new declaration is necessary in order to make the blockade operative.

Art. 11. A declaration of blockade is notified

(1) To neutral Powers, by the blockading Power, by means of a communication addressed to the Governments direct, or to their representatives accredited to it;
(2) To the local authorities, by the officer commanding the blockading force. The local authorities will, in turn, inform the foreign consular officers at the port or on the coastline under blockade as soon as possible.

Art. 12. The rules as to declaration and notification of blockade apply to cases where the limits of a blockade are extended, or where a blockade is re-established after having been raised.

Art. 13. The voluntary raising of a blockade, as also any restriction in the limits of a blockade, must be notified in the manner prescribed by Article 11.

Art. 14. The liability of a neutral vessel to capture for breach of blockade is contingent on her knowledge, actual or presumptive, of the blockade.

Art. 15. Failing proof to the contrary, knowledge of the blockade is presumed if the vessel left a neutral port subsequently to the notification of the blockade to the Power to which such port belongs, provided that such notification was made in sufficient time.

Art. 16. If a vessel approaching a blockaded port has no knowledge, actual or presumptive, of the blockade, the notification must be made to the vessel itself by an officer of one of the ships of the blockading force. This notification should be entered in the vessel's logbook, and must state the day and hour, and the geographical position of the vessel at the time.

If through the negligence of the officer commanding the blockading force no declaration of blockade has been notified to the local authorities, or, if in the declaration, as notified, no period has been mentioned within which neutral vessels may come out, a neutral vessel coming out of the blockaded port must be allowed to pass free.

Art. 17. Neutral vessels may not be captured for breach of blockade except within the area of operations of the warships detailed to render the blockade effective.

Art. 18. The blockading forces must not bar access to neutral ports or coasts.

Art. 19. Whatever may be the ulterior destination of a vessel or of her cargo, she cannot be captured for breach of blockade, if, at the moment, she is on her way to a non-blockaded port.

Art. 20. A vessel which has broken blockade outwards, or which has attempted to break blockade inwards, is liable to capture so long as she is pursued by a ship of the blockading force. If the pursuit is abandoned, or if the blockade is raised, her capture can no longer be effected.

Art. 21. A vessel found guilty of breach of blockade is liable to condemnation. The cargo is also condemned, unless it is proved that at the time of the shipment of the goods the shipper neither knew nor could have known of the intention to break the blockade.

Chapter II. Contraband of War

Art. 22. The following articles may, without notice,(1) be treated as contraband of war, under the name of absolute contraband:

(1) Arms of all kinds, including arms for sporting purposes, and their distinctive component parts.
(2) Projectiles, charges, and cartridges of all kinds, and their distinctive component parts.
(3) Powder and explosives specially prepared for use in war.
(4) Gun-mountings, limber boxes, limbers, military waggons, field forges, and their distinctive component parts.
(5) Clothing and equipment of a distinctively military character.
(6) All kinds of harness of a distinctively military character.
(7) Saddle, draught, and pack animals suitable for use in war.
(8) Articles of camp equipment, and their distinctive component parts.
(9) Armour plates.
(10) Warships, including boats, and their distinctive component parts of such a nature that they can only be used on a vessel of war.
(11) Implements and apparatus designed exclusively for the manufacture of munitions of war, for the manufacture or repair of arms, or war material for use on land or sea.

Art. 23. Articles exclusively used for war may be added to the list of absolute contraband by a declaration, which must be notified.

Such notification must be addressed to the Governments of other Powers, or to their representatives accredited to the Power making the declaration. A notification made after the outbreak of hostilities is addressed only to neutral Powers.

---

(1) In view of the difficulty of finding an exact equivalent in English for the expression "de plein droit", it has been decided to translate it by the words "without notice," which represent the meaning attached to it by the draftsman as appears from the General Report see p. 44 (*note in the original*).

Art. 24. The following articles, susceptible of use in war as well as for purposes of peace, may, without notice,[1] be treated as contraband of war, under the name of conditional contraband:

(1) Foodstuffs.
(2) Forage and grain, suitable for feeding animals.
(3) Clothing, fabrics for clothing, and boots and shoes, suitable for use in war.
(4) Gold and silver in coin or bullion; paper money.
(5) Vehicles of all kinds available for use in war, and their component parts.
(6) Vessels, craft, and boats of all kinds; floating docks, parts of docks and their component parts.
(7) Railway material, both fixed and rolling-stock, and material for telegraphs, wireless telegraphs, and telephones.
(8) Balloons and flying machines and their distinctive component parts, together with accessories and articles recognizable as intended for use in connection with balloons and flying machines.
(9) Fuel; lubricants.
(10) Powder and explosives not specially prepared for use in war.
(11) Barbed wire and implements for fixing and cutting the same.
(12) Horseshoes and shoeing materials.
(13) Harness and saddlery.
(14) Field glasses, telescopes, chronometers, and all kinds of nautical instruments.

Art. 25. Articles susceptive of use in war as well as for purposes of peace, other than those enumerated in Articles 22 and 24, may be added to the list of conditional contraband by a declaration, which must be notified in the manner provided for in the second paragraph of Article 23.

Art. 26. If a Power waives, so far as it is concerned, the right to treat as contraband of war an article comprised in any of the classes enumerated in Articles 22 and 24, such intention shall be announced by a declaration, which must be notified in the manner provided for in the second paragraph of Article 23.

Art. 27. Articles which are not susceptible of use in war may not be declared contraband of war.

Art. 28. The following may not be declared contraband of war:

(1) Raw cotton, wool, silk, jute, flax, hemp, and other raw materials of the textile industries, and yarns of the same.
(2) Oil seeds and nuts; copra.
(3) Rubber, resins, gums, and lacs; hops.
(4) Raw hides and horns, bones, and ivory.
(5) Natural and artificial manures, including nitrates and phosphates for agricultural purposes.
(6) Metallic ores.
(7) Earths, clays, lime, chalk, stone, including marble, bricks, slates, and tiles.
(8) Chinaware and glass.
(9) Paper and paper-making materials.
(10) Soap, paint and colours, including articles exclusively used in their manufacture, and varnish.
(11) Bleaching powder, soda ash, caustic soda, salt cake, ammonia, sulphate of ammonia, and sulphate of copper.
(12) Agricultural, mining, textile, and printing machinery.
(13) Precious and semi-precious stones, pearls, mother-of-pearl, and coral.
(14) Clocks and watches, other than chronometers.

---

(1) See note on previous page.

(15) Fashion and fancy goods.
(16) Feathers of all kinds, hairs, and bristles.
(17) Articles of household furniture and decoration; office furniture and requisites.

Art. 29. Likewise the following may not be treated as contraband of war:
(1) Articles serving exclusively to aid the sick and wounded. They can, however, in case of urgent military necessity and subject to the payment of compensation, be requisitioned, if their destination is that specified in Article 30.
(2) Articles intended for the use of the vessel in which they are found, as well as those intended for the use of her crew and passengers during the voyage.

Art. 30. Absolute contraband is liable to capture if it is shown to be destined to territory belonging to or occupied by the enemy, or to the armed forces of the enemy. It is immaterial whether the carriage of the goods is direct or entails transhipment or a subsequent transport by land.

Art. 31. Proof of the destination specified in Article 30 is complete in the following cases:
(1) When the goods are documented for discharge in an enemy port, or for delivery to the armed forces of the enemy.
(2) When the vessel is to call at enemy ports only, or when she is to touch at a enemy port or meet the armed forces of the enemy before reaching the neutral port for which the goods in question are documented.

Art. 32. Where a vessel is carrying absolute contraband, her papers are conclusive proof as to the voyage on which she is engaged, unless she is found clearly out of the course indicated by her papers, and unable to give adequate reasons to justify such deviation.

Art. 33. Conditional contraband is liable to capture if it is shown to be destined for the use of the armed forces or of a government department of the enemy State, unless in this latter case the circumstances show that the goods cannot in fact be used for the purposes of the war in progress. This latter exception does not apply to a consignment coming under Article 24 (4).

Art. 34. The destination referred to in Article 33 is presumed to exist if the goods are consigned to enemy authorities, or to a contractor established in the enemy country who, as a matter of common knowledge, supplies articles of this kind to the enemy. A similar presumption arises if the goods are consigned to a fortified place belonging to the enemy, or other place serving as a base for the armed forces of the enemy. No such presumption, however, arises in the case of a merchant vessel bound for one of these places if it is sought to prove that she herself is contraband.

In cases where the above presumptions do not arise, the destination is presumed to be innocent.

The presumptions set up by this Article may be rebutted.

Art. 35. Conditional contraband is not liable to capture, except when found on board a vessel bound for territory belonging to or occupied by the enemy, or for the armed forces of the enemy, and when it is not to be discharged in an intervening neutral port.
The ship's papers are conclusive proof both as to the voyage on which the vessel is engaged and as to the port of discharge of the goods, unless she is found clearly out of the course indicated by her papers, and unable to give adequate reasons to justify such deviation.

Art. 36. Notwithstanding the provisions of Article 35, conditional contraband, if shown to have the destination referred to in Article 33, is liable to capture in cases where the enemy country has no seaboard.

Art. 37. A vessel carrying goods liable to capture as absolute or conditional contraband may be captured on the high seas or in the territorial waters of the belligerents throughout the whole of her voyage, even if she is to touch at a port of call before reaching the hostile destination.

Art. 38. A vessel may not be captured on the ground that she has carried contraband on a previous occasion if such carriage is in point of fact at an end.

Art. 39. Contraband goods are liable to condemnation.

Art. 40. A vessel carrying contraband may be condemned if the contraband, reckoned either by value, weight, volume, or freight, forms more than half the cargo.

Art. 41. If a vessel carrying contraband is released, she may be condemned to pay the costs and expenses incurred by the captor in respect of the proceedings in the national prize court and the custody of the ship and cargo during the proceedings.

Art. 42. Goods which belong to the owner of the contraband and are on board the same vessel are liable to condemnation.

Art. 43. If a vessel is encountered at sea while unaware of the outbreak of hostilities or of the declaration of contraband which applies to her cargo, the contraband cannot be condemned except on payment of compensation; the vessel herself and the remainder of the cargo are not liable to condemnation or to the costs and expenses referred to in Article 41. The same rule applies if the master, after becoming aware of the outbreak of hostilities, or of the declaration of contraband, has had no opportunity of discharging the contraband.

A vessel is deemed to be aware of the existence of a state of war, or of a declaration of contraband, if she left a neutral port subsequently to the notification to the Power to which such port belongs of the outbreak of hostilities or of the declaration of contraband respectively, provided that such notification was made in sufficient time. A vessel is also deemed to be aware of the existence of a state of war if she left an enemy port after the outbreak of hostilities.

Art. 44. A vessel which has been stopped on the ground that she is carrying contraband, and which is not liable to condemnation on account of the proportion of contraband on board, may, when the circumstances permit, be allowed to continue her voyage if the master is willing to hand over the contraband to the belligerent warship.

The delivery of the contraband must be entered by the captor on the logbook of the vessel stopped, and the master must give the captor duly certified copies of all relevant papers.

The captor is at liberty to destroy the contraband that has been handed over to him under these conditions.

Chapter III. Unneutral Service

Art. 45. A neutral vessel will be condemned and will, in a general way, receive the same treatment as a neutral vessel liable to condemnation for carriage of contraband:

(1) If she is on a voyage especially undertaken with a view to the transport of individual passengers who are embodied in the armed forces of the enemy, or with a view to the transmission of intelligence in the interest of the enemy.

(2) If, to the knowledge of either the owner, the charterer, or the master, she is transporting a military detachment of the enemy, or one or more persons who, in the course of the voyage, directly assist the operations of the enemy.

In the cases specified under the above heads, goods belonging to the owner of the vessel are likewise liable to condemnation.

The provisions of the present Article do not apply if the vessel is encountered at sea while unaware of the outbreak of hostilities, or if the master, after becoming aware of the outbreak of hostilities, has had no opportunity of disembarking the passengers. The vessel is deemed to be aware of the existence of a state of war if she left an enemy port subsequently to the outbreak of hostilities, or a neutral port subsequently to the notification of the outbreak of hostilities to the Power to which such port belongs, provided that such notification was made in sufficient time.

Art. 46. A neutral vessel will be condemned and, in a general way, receive the same treatment as would be applicable to her if she were an enemy merchant vessel:
(1) if she takes a direct part in the hostilities;
(2) if she is under the orders or control of an agent placed on board by the enemy Government;
(3) if she is in the exclusive employment of the enemy Government;
(4) if she is exclusively engaged at the time either in the transport of enemy troops or in the transmission of intelligence in the interest of the enemy.
In the cases covered by the present Article, goods belonging to the owner of the vessel are likewise liable to condemnation.

Art. 47. Any individual embodied in the armed forces of the enemy who is found on board a neutral merchant vessel, may be made a prisoner of war, even though there be no ground for the capture of the vessel.

Chapter IV. Destruction of Neutral Prizes

Art. 48. A neutral vessel which has been captured may not be destroyed by the captor; she must be taken into such port as is proper for the determination there of all questions concerning the validity of the capture.

Art. 49. As an exception, a neutral vessel which has been captured by a belligerent warship, and which would be liable to condemnation, may be destroyed if the observance of Article 48 would involve danger to the safety of the warship or to the success of the operations in which she is engaged at the time.

Art. 50. Before the vessel is destroyed all persons on board must be placed in safety, and all the ship's papers and other documents which the parties interested consider relevant for the purpose of deciding on the validity of the capture must be taken on board the warship.

Art. 51. A captor who has destroyed a neutral vessel must, prior to any decision respecting the validity of the prize, establish that he only acted in the face of an exceptional necessity of the nature contemplated in Article 49. If he fails to do this, he must compensate the parties interested and no examination shall be made of the question whether the capture was valid or not.

Art. 52. If the capture of a neutral vessel is subsequently held to be invalid, though the act of destruction has been held to have been justifiable, the captor must pay compensation to the parties interested, in place of the restitution to which they would have been entitled.

Art. 53. If neutral goods not liable to condemnation have been destroyed with the vessel, the owner of such goods is entitled to compensation.

Art. 54. The captor has the right to demand the handing over, or to proceed himself to the destruction of, any goods liable to condemnation found on board a vessel not herself liable to condemnation, provided that the circumstances are such as would, under

Article 49, justify the destruction of a vessel herself liable to condemnation. The captor must enter the goods surrendered or destroyed in the logbook of the vessel stopped, and must obtain duly certified copies of all relevant papers. When the goods have been handed over or destroyed, and the formalities duly carried out, the master must be allowed to continue his voyage.

The provisions of Articles 51 and 52 respecting the obligations of a captor who has destroyed a neutral vessel are applicable.

Chapter V. Transfer to a Neutral Flag

Art. 55. The transfer of an enemy vessel to a neutral flag, effected before the outbreak of hostilities, is valid, unless it is proved that such transfer was made in order to evade the consequences to which an enemy vessel, as such, is exposed. There is, however, a presumption, if the bill of sale is not on board a vessel which has lost her belligerent nationality less than sixty days before the outbreak of hostilities, that the transfer is void. This presumption may be rebutted.

Where the transfer was effected more than thirty days before the outbreak of hostilities, there is an absolute presumption that it is valid if it is unconditional, complete, and in conformity with the laws of the countries concerned, and if its effect is such that neither the control of, nor the profits arising from the employment of the vessel remain in the same hands as before the transfer. If, however, the vessel lost her belligerent nationality less than sixty days before the outbreak of hostilities and if the bill of sale is not on board, the capture of the vessel gives no right to damages.

Art. 56. The transfer of an enemy vessel to a neutral flag, effected after the outbreak of hostilities, is void unless it is proved that such transfer was not made in order to evade the consequences to which an enemy vessel, as such, is exposed.

There, however, is an absolute presumption that a transfer is void –

(1) If the transfer has been made during a voyage or in a blockaded port.
(2) If a right to repurchase or recover the vessel is reserved to the vendor.
(3) If the requirements of the municipal law governing the right to fly the flag under which the vessel is sailing, have not been fulfilled.

Chapter VI. Enemy Character

Art. 57. Subject to the provisions respecting transfer to another flag, the neutral or enemy character of a vessel is determined by the flag which she is entitled to fly.

The case where a neutral vessel is engaged in a trade which is closed in time of peace, remains outside the scope of, and is in no wise affected by, this rule.

Art. 58. The neutral or enemy character of goods found on board an enemy vessel is determined by the neutral or enemy character of the owner.

Art. 59. In the absence of proof of the neutral character of goods found on board an enemy vessel, they are presumed to be enemy goods.

Art. 60. Enemy goods on board an enemy vessel retain their enemy character until they reach their destination, notwithstanding any transfer effected after the outbreak of hostilities while the goods are being forwarded.

If, however, prior to the capture, a former neutral owner exercises, on the bankruptcy of an existing enemy owner, a recognized legal right to recover the goods, they regain their neutral character.

Chapter VII. Convoy

Art. 61. Neutral vessels under national convoy are exempt from search. The commander of a convoy gives, in writing, at the request of the commander of a belligerent warship, all information as to the character of the vessels and their cargoes, which could be obtained by search.

Art. 62. If the commander of the belligerent warship has reason to suspect that the confidence of the commander of the convoy has been abused, he communicates his suspicions to him. In such a case it is for the commander of the convoy alone to investigate the matter. He must record the result of such investigation in a report, of which a copy is handed to the officer of the warship. If, in the opinion of the commander of the convoy, the facts shown in the report justify the capture of one or more vessels, the protection of the convoy must be withdrawn from such vessels.

Chapter VIII. Resistance to Search

Art. 63. Forcible resistance to the legitimate exercise of the right of stoppage, search, and capture, involves in all cases the condemnation of the vessel. The cargo is liable to the same treatment as the cargo of an enemy vessel. Goods belonging to the master or owner of the vessel are treated as enemy goods.

Chapter IX. Compensation

Art. 64. If the capture of a vessel or of goods is not upheld by the prize court, or if the prize is released without any judgement being given, the parties interested have the right to compensation, unless there were good reasons for capturing the vessel or goods.

Final Provisions

Art. 65. The provisions of the present Declaration must be treated as a whole, and cannot be separated.

Art. 66 The Signatory Powers undertake to insure the mutual observance of the rules contained in the present Declaration in any war in which all the belligerents are parties thereto. They will therefore issue the necessary instructions to their authorities and to their armed forces, and will take such measures as may be required in order to insure that it will be applied by their courts, and more particularly by their prize courts.

Art. 67. The present Declaration shall be ratified as soon as possible.

The ratifications shall be deposited in London.

The first deposit of ratifications shall be recorded in a Protocol signed by the representatives of the Powers taking part therein, and by His Britannic Majesty's Principal Secretary of State for Foreign Affairs.

The subsequent deposits of ratifications shall be made by means of a written notification addressed to the British Government, and accompanied by the instrument of ratification.

A duly certified copy of the Protocol relating to the first deposit of ratifications and of the notifications mentioned in the preceding paragraph as well as of the instruments of ratification which accompany them, shall be immediately sent by the British Government, through the diplomatic channel, to the Signatory Powers. The said Government shall, in the cases contemplated in the preceding paragraph, inform them at the same time of the date on which it received the notification.

Art. 68. The present Declaration shall take effect, in the case of the Powers which were parties to the first deposit of ratifications, sixty days after the date of the Protocol recording such deposit, and, in the case of the Powers which shall ratify subsequently, sixty days after the notification of their ratification shall have been received by the British Government.

Art. 69. In the event of one of the Signatory Powers wishing to denounce the present Declaration, such denunciation can only be made to take effect at the end of a period of twelve years, beginning sixty days after the first deposit of ratifications, and, after that time, at the end of successive periods of six years, of which the first will begin at the end of the period of twelve years.

Such denunciation must be notified in writing, at least one year in advance, to the British Government, which shall inform all the other Powers.

It will only operate in respect of the denouncing Power.

Art. 70. The Powers represented at the London Naval Conference attach particular importance to the general recognition of the rules which they have adopted, and therefore express the hope that the Powers which were not represented there will accede to the present Declaration. They request the British Government to invite them to do so.

A Power which desires to accede shall notify its intention in writing to the British Government, and transmit simultaneously the act of accession, which will be deposited in the archives of the said Government.

The said Government shall forthwith transmit to all the other Powers a duly certified copy of the notification, together with the act of accession, and communicate the date on which such notification was received. The accession takes effect sixty days after such date.

In respect of all matters concerning this Declaration, Acceding Powers shall be on the same footing as the Signatory Powers.

Art. 71. The present Declaration, which bears the date of 26 February 1909, may be signed in London up till 30 June 1909, by the Plenipotentiaries of the Powers represented at the Naval Conference.

In faith whereof the Plenipotentiaries have signed the present Declaration, and have thereto affixed their seals.

Done at London, the twenty-sixth day of February, one thousand nine hundred and nine, in a single original, which shall remain deposited in the archives of the British Government, and of which duly certified copies shall be sent through the diplomatic channel to the Powers represented at the Naval Conference.

[Here follow signatures]

SIGNATURES[2]

Austria-Hungary
France
Germany
Great Britain
Italy
Japan
Netherlands
Russia
Spain
United States of America

RATIFICATIONS

None

[2] List of signatures was established according to the *Proceedings of the International Naval Conference, held in London, December 1908–February 1909. Presented to both Houses of Parliament by Command of His Majesty, March 1909, Miscellaneous No. 5 (1909),* Cd. 4555. London, Printed by His Majesty's Stationery Office, by Harrison and Sons, St. Martin's Lane, and according to the communications of the Foreign and Commonwealth Office of the United Kingdom, of 7 December 2001.

No. 84

THE LAWS OF NAVAL WAR GOVERNING THE RELATIONS BETWEEN BELLIGERENTS

Manual adopted by the Institute of International Law (Oxford Manual of Naval War)

Adopted at Oxford, 9 August 1913

INTRODUCTORY NOTE: The Second International Peace Conference at The Hague expressed the wish "that the preparation of regulations relative to the laws and customs of naval war should figure in the programme of the next Conference". This wish induced the Institute of International Law to appoint a committee in 1910 "to search and choose the studies which may be of the most utility for the preparation of the Peace Conference and organize their discussion by the Institute". On the proposal of this committee it was decided to prepare regulations concerning the laws and customs of war at sea. A special committee, with Professor Fauchille as rapporteur, prepared a draft manual analogous to the *Oxford Manual on Land Warfare* of 1880 (*No. 3*). At its session in 1913, the Institute adopted the text below.

AUTHENTIC TEXT: French. The English translation below is reprinted from Scott, *Resolutions of the Institute of International Law*, pp. 174–201.

TEXT PUBLISHED IN: *Annuaire de l'Institut de Droit international*, Vol. 26 (1913), pp. 610–640; *Résolutions de l'Institut de Droit international 1873–1956*, pp. 231–258 (French); Scott, *Resolutions of the Institute of International Law*, pp. 174–201 (Engl.); Deltenre, pp. 667–715 (Engl., French, German, Dutch); *Revue de droit international et de législation comparée* (Bruxelles), Deuxième série, tome XV, 45e année, 1913, pp. 677–704 (French); *RGDIP*, tome XXI, 1914, pp. 87-103 (French); *Droit des conflits armés*, pp. 1179–1194 (French); Briceño, pp. 242–263 (Span.); ICRC website: www.icrc.org/ihl.nsf (Engl., French).

TABLE OF CONTENTS

* * *

Preamble

The Institute of International Law, at its Christiania session, declared itself in favour of firmly upholding its former Resolutions on the abolition of capture and of confiscation of enemy private property in naval warfare. But at the same time being aware that this principle is not yet accepted, and deeming that, for so long as it shall not be, regulation of the right of capture is indispensable, it entrusted a commission with the task of drawing up stipulations providing for either contingency. In pursuance of this latter action, the Institute, at its Oxford session on 9 August 1913, adopted the following Manual, based on the right of capture.[(1)]

Section I. On localities where hostilities may take place

Article 1. Rules peculiar to naval warfare are applicable only on the high seas and in the territorial waters of the belligerents, exclusive of those waters which, from the standpoint of navigation, ought not to be considered as maritime.

Section II. On the armed force of belligerent States

Art. 2. War-ships. Constituting part of the armed force of a belligerent State and, therefore, subject as such to the laws of naval warfare are:
(1) All ships belonging to the State which, under the direction of a military commander and manned by a military crew, carry legally the ensign and the pendant of the national navy.
(2) Ships converted by the State into war-ships in conformity with Articles 3–6.

Art. 3. Conversion of public and private vessels into war-ships. A vessel converted into a war-ship cannot have the rights and duties accruing to such vessels, unless it is placed under the direct authority, immediate control, and responsibility of the Power whose flag it flies.

Art. 4. Vessels converted into war-ships must bear the exterior marks which distinguish the war-ships of their nationality.

Art. 5. The commander must be in the service of the State and duly commissioned by the competent authorities; his name must appear on the list of officers of the fighting fleet.

Art. 6. The crew must be subject to the rules of military discipline.

---

(1) *Definitions:*
Capture is the act by which the commander of a war-ship substitutes his authority for that of the captain of the enemy ship, subject to the subsequent judgment of the prize court as to the ultimate fate of the ship and its cargo. '
Seizure, when applied to a ship, is the act by which a war-ship takes possession of the vessel detained, with or without the consent of the captain of the latter. Seizure differs from capture in that the ultimate fate of the vessel may not be involved as a result of its condemnation.
Applied to goods alone, seizure is the act by which the war-ship, with or without the consent of the captain of the vessel detained, takes possession of the goods and holds them or disposes of them subject to the subsequent judgment of the prize court.
Confiscation is the act by which the prize court renders valid the capture of a vessel or the seizure of its goods. The word *prize* is a general expression applying to a captured ship or to seized goods.
By *public ships* are meant all ships other than war-ships which, belonging to the State or to individuals, are set apart for public service and are under the orders of an officer duly commissioned by the State (*note in the original*).

Art. 7. Every vessel converted into a war-ship must observe in its operations the laws and customs of war.

Art. 8. The belligerent who converts a vessel into a war-ship must, as soon as possible, announce such conversion in the list of war-ships.

Art. 9. The conversion of a vessel into a war-ship may be accomplished by a belligerent only in its own waters, in those of an allied State also a belligerent, in those of the adversary, or, lastly, in those of a territory occupied by the troops of one of these States.

Art. 10. Conversion of war-ships into public or private vessels. A war-ship may not, while hostilities last, be converted into a public or a private vessel.

Art. 11. Belligerent personnel. Constituting part of the armed force of a belligerent State and, therefore, in so far as they carry on operations at sea, subject as such to the laws of naval warfare, are:
(1) The personnel of the ships mentioned in Article 2;
(2) The troops of the naval forces, active or reserve;
(3) The militarized personnel on the seacoasts;
(4) The regular forces, other than naval forces, or those regularly organized in conformity with Article 1 of the Hague Regulations of 18 October 1907, concerning the laws and customs of war on land.

Art. 12. Privateering, private vessels, public vessels not war-ships. Privateering is forbidden.

Apart from the conditions laid down in Articles 3 and following, neither public nor private vessels, nor their personnel, may commit acts of hostility against the enemy.

Both may, however, use force to defend themselves against the attack of an enemy vessel.

Art. 13. Population of unoccupied territory. The inhabitants of a territory which has not been occupied who, upon the approach of the enemy, spontaneously arm vessels to fight him, without having had time to convert them into war-ships in conformity with Articles 3 and following, shall be considered as belligerents, if they act openly and if they respect the laws and usages of war.

Section III. On means of injuring the enemy

Art. 14. Principle. The right of belligerents to adopt means of injuring the enemy is not unlimited.

Art. 15. Treacherous and barbarous methods. Ruses of war are considered permissible. Methods, however, which involve treachery are forbidden. Thus it is forbidden:
(1) To kill or wound treacherously individuals belonging to the opposite side;
(2) To make improper use of a flag of truce, to make use of false flags, uniforms, or insignia, of whatever kind, especially those of the enemy, as well as of the distinctive badges of the medical corps indicated in Articles 41 and 42.

Art. 16. In addition to the prohibitions which shall be established by special conventions, it is forbidden:
(1) To employ poison or poisoned weapons, or projectiles the sole object of which is the diffusion of asphyxiating or deleterious gases;
(2) To employ arms, projectiles, or materials calculated to cause unnecessary suffering. Entering especially into this category are explosive projectiles or those charged with fulminating or inflammable materials, less than 400 grammes in weight, and bullets which expand or flatten easily in the human body, such as bullets with a hard envelope which does not cover the core entirely or is pierced with incisions.

Art. 17. It is also forbidden:
(1) To kill or to wound an enemy who, having laid down his arms or having no longer means of defense, has surrendered at discretion;
(2) To sink a ship which has surrendered, before having taken off the crew;
(3) To declare that no quarter will be given.

Art. 18. Pillage and devastation are forbidden.
It is forbidden to destroy enemy property, except in the cases where such destruction is imperatively required by the necessities of war or authorized by provisions of the present regulations.

Art. 19. Torpedoes. It is forbidden to employ torpedoes which do not become harmless when they have missed their mark.

Art. 20. Submarine mines. It is forbidden to lay automatic contact mines, anchored or not, in the open sea.

Art. 21. Belligerents may lay mines in their territorial waters and in those of the enemy. But it is forbidden, even in territorial waters:
(1) To lay unanchored automatic contact mines unless they are so constructed as to become harmless one hour at most after the person who laid them ceases to control them;
(2) To lay anchored automatic contact mines which do not become harmless as soon as they have broken loose from their moorings.

Art. 22. A belligerent may not lay mines along the coast and harbours of his adversary except for naval and military ends. He is forbidden to lay them there in order to establish or to maintain a commercial blockade.

Art. 23. When automatic contact mines, anchored or unanchored, are employed, every precaution must be taken for the security of peaceful shipping. The belligerents must do their utmost to render these mines harmless within a limited time. Should the mines cease to be under surveillance, the belligerents shall notify the danger zones. as soon as military exigencies permit, by a notice addressed to ship-owners, which must also be communicated to the governments through the diplomatic channel.

Art. 24. At the close of the war, the belligerent States shall do their utmost to remove the mines that they have laid, each one its own.

As regards the anchored automatic contact mines laid by one of the belligerents off the coast of the other, their position must be notified to the other party by the State that has laid them, and each State must proceed, with the least possible delay, to remove the mines in its own waters.

Belligerent States upon whom rests the obligation of removing these mines after the war is over shall, with as little delay as possible, make known the fact that, so far as is possible, the mines have been removed.

Art. 25. Bombardment. The bombardment of undefended ports, towns, villages, dwellings, or buildings is forbidden.

A place cannot be bombarded solely because submarine automatic contact mines are anchored off its coast.

Art. 26. Military works, military or naval establishments, depots of arms or war *matériel*, workshops or plants which could be utilized for the needs of the hostile fleet or army, and the war-ships in the harbour, are not, however, included in this prohibition. The commander of a naval force may destroy them with artillery, after a summons followed by a reasonable time of waiting, if all other means are impossible, and when the local authorities have not themselves destroyed them within the time fixed.

He incurs no responsibility for any unavoidable damage which may be caused by a bombardment under such circumstances.

If for military reasons immediate action is necessary, and no delay can be allowed the enemy, it is understood that the prohibition to bombard the undefended town holds good, as in the case given in paragraph 1, and that the commander shall take all due measures in order that the town may suffer as little harm as possible.

Art. 27. The bombardment of undefended ports, towns, villages, dwellings, or buildings because of the non-payment of contributions of money, or the refusal to comply with requisitions for provisions or supplies is forbidden.

Art. 28. In bombardments all useless destruction is forbidden, and especially should all necessary measures be taken by the commander of the attacking force to spare, as far as possible, sacred edifices, buildings used for artistic, scientific, or charitable purposes, historic monuments, hospitals, and places where the sick or wounded are collected. on condition that they are not used at the same time for military purposes.

It is the duty of the inhabitants to indicate such monuments, edifices, or places by visible signs, which shall consist of large stiff rectangular panels divided diagonally into two coloured triangular portions, the upper portion black, the lower portion white.

Art. 29. If the military situation permits, the commander of the attacking naval force, before commencing the bombardment, must do his utmost to warn the authorities.

Art. 30. Blockade. Ports and coasts belonging to the enemy or occupied by him may be subjected to blockade according to the rules of international law.

Section IV. On the rights and duties of the belligerents with regard to enemy property

Art. 31. A. Ships and cargoes – War-ships. The armed forces of a State may attack the enemy's war-ships, to take possession of them or to destroy them, together with their equipment and supplies, whether these ships, at the beginning of the struggle, are in a harbour of the State, or are encountered at sea, in ignorance of hostilities; or by *force majeure* are either compelled to enter a port, or are cast on the shores of said State.

Art. 32. Public and private vessels – Stopping, visit, and search. All vessels other than those of the navy, whether they belong to the State or to individuals, may be summoned by a belligerent war-ship to stop, that a visit and search may be conducted on board them.

The belligerent war-ship, in ordering a vessel to stop, shall fire a charge of powder as a summons and, if that warning is not sufficient, shall fire a projectile across the bow of the vessel. Previously or at the same time, the war-ship shall hoist its flag, above which, at night, a signal light shall be placed. The vessel answers the signal by hoisting its own flag and by stopping at once; whereupon, the war-ship shall send to the stopped vessel a launch manned by an officer and a sufficient number of men, of whom only two or three shall accompany the officer on board the stopped vessel.

Visit consists in the first place in an examination of the ship's papers.

If the ship's papers are insufficient or not of a nature to allay suspicion, the officer conducting the visit has the right to proceed to a search of the vessel, for which purpose he must ask the cooperation of the captain.

Visit of post packets must, as Article 53 says, be conducted with all the consideration and all the expedition possible.

Vessels convoyed by a neutral war-ship are not subject to visit except in so far as permitted by the rules relating to convoys.

Art. 33. Principle of capture. Public and private vessels of enemy nationality are subject to capture, and enemy goods on board, public or private, are liable to seizure.

Art. 34. Capture and seizure are permitted even when the vessels or the goods have fallen into the power of the belligerent because of *force majeure* through shipwreck or by being compelled to put into port.

Art. 35. Vessels which possess no ship's papers, which have intentionally destroyed or hidden those that they had, or which offer false ones, are liable to seizure.

Art. 36. Extenuation of the principle of capture. When a public or private vessel belonging to one of the belligerent Powers is, at the commencement of hostilities, in an enemy port, it is allowed to depart freely, immediately or after a reasonable number of days of grace, and to proceed, after having been furnished with a passport, to its port of destination, or to any other port indicated.

The same rule should apply in the case of a ship which has left its last port of departure before the commencement of the war and entered an enemy port while still ignorant of hostilities.

Art. 37. The public or private vessel unable, owing to circumstances of *force majeure*, to leave the enemy port within the period contemplated in the preceding article, cannot be captured.

The belligerent may only detain it without payment of compensation but subject to the obligation of restoring it after the war, or requisition it on payment of compensation.

Art. 38. Enemy vessels, public or private, which left their last port of departure before the commencement of the war and which are encountered on the high seas while still ignorant of the outbreak of hostilities, cannot be captured. They are only liable to detention on the understanding that they shall be restored after the war without compensation, or requisitioned, or even destroyed, on payment of compensation, but in such case provision must be made for the safety of the passengers on board as well as for the security of the ship's papers.

But, where these vessels shall be encountered at sea before the expiration of a sufficient period to be granted by the belligerent, seizure is not permissible. Vessels thus encountered are free to proceed to their port of destination or to any other port indicated.

After touching at a port in their own country or at a neutral port, these vessels are subject to capture.

Art. 39. Enemy cargo found on board the ships detained under Articles 37 and 38 may likewise be held. It must be restored after the termination of the war without payment of indemnity, unless requisitioned on payment of compensation.

The same rule is applicable to goods which are contraband of war found on board the vessels mentioned in Articles 36, 37 and 38, even when these vessels are not subject to capture.

Art. 40. In all cases considered in Articles 36, 37 and 38, public or private ships whose build shows that they are intended for conversion into war-ships, may be seized or requisitioned upon payment of compensation. These vessels shall be restored after the war.

Goods found on board these ships shall be dealt with according to the rules in Article 39.

Art. 41. Exceptions to the principles in Articles 31 and 32 – Hospital ships. Military hospital ships, that is to say, ships constructed or assigned by States specially and solely with a view to assisting the wounded, sick and shipwrecked, the names of which have been communicated to the belligerent Powers at the commencement or during the course of hostilities, and in any case before they are employed, shall be respected, and cannot be captured while hostilities last.

Military hospital ships shall be distinguished by being painted white outside with a horizontal band of green about a metre and a half (five feet) in breadth.

The boats of the ships above mentioned, as also small craft which may be used for hospital work, shall be distinguished by similar painting.

All hospital ships shall make themselves known by hoisting, with their national flag the white flag with the red cross provided by the Geneva Convention.

The ships and boats above mentioned which wish to ensure by night the freedom from interference to which they are entitled, must, subject to the belligerent they are accompanying, take the measures necessary to render their special painting sufficiently plain.

The distinguishing signs referred to in this article can be used only outside with a horizontal band of green about a metre and a half (five feet) in breadth.

These ships cannot be used for any military purpose.

They must in no wise hamper the movements of the combatants.

During and after an engagement, they will act at their own risk and peril.

The belligerents shall have the right to control and search them; they can refuse to help them, order them off, make them take a certain course, and put a commissioner on board; they can even detain them, if important circumstances require it.

As far as possible, the belligerents shall enter in the log of the hospital ships the orders which they give them.

Hospital ships which, under the terms of this Article, are detained by the enemy, must haul down the national flag of the belligerent to whom they belong.

Art. 42. Hospital ships, equipped wholly or in part at the expense of private individuals or officially recognized relief societies, shall likewise be respected and exempt from capture, if the belligerent Power to whom they belong has given them an official commission and has notified their names to the hostile Power at the commencement of or during hostilities, and in any case before they are employed.

These ships must be provided with a certificate from competent authorities declaring that the vessels have been under their control while fitting out and on final departure.

The ships in question shall be distinguished by being painted white outside with a horizontal band of red about a metre and a half (five feet) in breadth.

They are subject to the regulations laid down for military hospital ships by Article 41.

Art. 43. In case of a fight on board a war-ship, the sick-wards and the *matériel* belonging to them shall be respected and spared as far as possible. Although remaining subject to the laws of war, they cannot be used for any purpose other than that for which they were originally intended, so long as they are required for the sick and wounded. The commander into whose power they have fallen may, however, apply them to other purposes, if the military situation requires it, after seeing that the sick and wounded on board are properly provided for.

Art. 44. Hospital ships and sick-wards of vessels are no longer entitled to protection if they are employed for the purpose of injuring the enemy. The fact that the staff of the said ships and sick-wards is armed for maintaining order and for defending the sick and wounded, and the presence of wireless telegraphy apparatus on board, are not sufficient reasons for withdrawing protection.

Art. 45. *Cartel ships*. Ships called cartel ships, which act as bearers of a flag of truce, may not be seized while fulfilling their mission, even if they belong to the navy.

A ship authorized by one of the belligerents to enter into a parley with the other and carrying a white flag is considered a cartel ship.

The commanding officer to whom a cartel ship is sent is not obliged to receive it under all circumstances. He can take all measures necessary to prevent the cartel ship from profiting by its mission to obtain information. In case it abuses its privileges, he has the right to hold the cartel ship temporarily.

A cartel ship loses its rights of inviolability if it is proved, positively and unexceptionably, that the commander has profited by the privileged position of his vessel to provoke or to commit a treacherous act.

Art. 46. Vessels charged with missions. Vessels charged with religious, scientific, or philanthropic missions are exempt from seizure.

Art. 47. Vessels used exclusively for fishing along the coast and for local trade. Vessels used exclusively for fishing along the coast, or for local trade, under which term are included those used exclusively for piloting or for light-house service, as well as the boats meant principally for the navigation of rivers, canals, and lakes, are exempt from seizure, together with their appliances, rigging, tackle and cargo.

It is forbidden to take advantage of the harmless character of said boats in order to use them for military purposes while preserving their peaceful appearance.

Art. 48. Vessels furnished with a safe-conduct or a licence. Enemy vessels provided with a safe-conduct or a licence are exempt from seizure.

Art. 49. Suspension of immunities. The exceptions considered in Articles 41, 42, 45, 46, 47 and 48 cease to be applicable if the vessels to which they refer participate in the hostilities in any manner whatsoever or commit other acts which are forbidden to neutrals as unneutral service.

The same suspension occurs if, summoned to stop to submit to search, they seek to escape by force or by flight.

Art. 50. Rights of the belligerent in the zone of operations. When a belligerent has not the right of seizing or of capturing enemy vessels, he may, even on the high seas, forbid them to enter the zone corresponding to the actual sphere of his operations.

He may also forbid them within this zone to perform certain acts calculated to interfere with his activities, especially certain acts of communication, such, for example, as the use of wireless telegraphy.

The simple infraction of these prohibitions will entail driving the vessel back, even by force, from the forbidden zone and the sequestration of the apparatus. The vessel, if it be proved that it has communicated with the enemy to furnish him with information concerning the conduct of hostilities, can be considered as having placed itself at the service of the enemy and, consequently, with its apparatus, shall be liable to capture.

Art. 51. Enemy character. The enemy or neutral character of a vessel is determined by the flag which it is entitled to fly.

The enemy or neutral character of goods found on board an enemy vessel is determined by the enemy or the neutral character of the owner.

Each State must declare, not later than the outbreak of hostilities, whether the enemy or neutral character of the owner of the goods is determined by his place of residence or his nationality.

Enemy goods found on board an enemy ship retain their enemy character until they reach their destination, notwithstanding any transfer effected after the outbreak of hostilities while the goods are being forwarded.

If, however, prior to the capture, a former neutral owner exercises, on the bankruptcy of an existing enemy owner, a recognized legal right to recover the goods, they regain their neutral character.

Art. 52. Transfer to a neutral flag. The transfer of an enemy vessel to a neutral flag, effected before the outbreak of hostilities, is valid, unless it is proved that such transfer was made in order to evade the consequences to which an enemy vessel as such is exposed. There is, however, a presumption, if the bill of sale is not on board a vessel which has lost its belligerent nationality less than sixty days before the outbreak of hostilities, that the transfer is void; this presumption may be rebutted.

Where the transfer was effected more than thirty days before the outbreak of hostilities, there is an absolute presumption that it is valid if it is unconditional, complete, and in conformity with the laws of the countries concerned, and if its effect is such that neither the control of, nor the profits arising from the employment of, the vessel remain in the same hands as before the transfer. If, however, the vessel lost her belligerent nationality less than sixty days before the outbreak of hostilities and if the bill of sale is not on board, the capture of the vessel gives no right to damages.

The transfer of an enemy vessel to a neutral flag effected after the outbreak of hostilities, is void unless it is proved that such transfer was not made in order to evade the consequences to which an enemy vessel, as such, is exposed.

There is, however, an absolute presumption that a transfer is void:

(1) if the transfer has been made during a voyage or in a blockaded port;
(2) if a right to repurchase or recover the vessel is reserved to the vendor;
(3) if the requirements of the municipal law governing the right to fly the flag under which the vessel is sailing, have not been fulfilled.

Art. 53. B. Postal correspondence. Postal correspondence, whatever its official or private character may be, found on the high seas on board an enemy ship, is inviolable, unless it is destined for or proceeding from a blockaded port.

The inviolability of postal correspondence does not exempt mail-boats from the laws and customs of maritime war as to ships in general. The ship, however, may not be searched except when absolutely necessary, and then only with as much consideration and expedition as possible.

If the ship on which the mail is sent be seized, the correspondence is forwarded by the captor with the least possible delay.

Art. 54. C. Submarine cables. In the conditions stated below, belligerent States are authorized to destroy or to seize only the submarine cables connecting their territories or two points in these territories, and the cables connecting the territory of one of the nations engaged in the war with a neutral territory.

The cable connecting the territories of the two belligerents or two points in the territory of one of the belligerents, may be seized or destroyed throughout its length, except in the waters of a neutral State.

A cable connecting a neutral territory with the territory of one of the belligerents may not, under any circumstances, be seized or destroyed in the waters under the power of a neutral territory. On the high seas, this cable may not be seized or destroyed unless there exists an effective blockade and within the limits of that blockade, on consideration of the restoration of the cable in the shortest time possible. This cable may be seized or destroyed on the territory of and in the waters belonging to the territory of the enemy for a distance of three marine miles from low tide. Seizure or destruction may never take place except in case of absolute necessity.

In applying the preceding rules no distinction is to be made between cables, according to whether they belong to the State or to individuals; nor is any regard to be paid to the nationality of their owners.

Submarine cables connecting belligerent territory with neutral territory, which have been seized or destroyed, shall be restored and compensation fixed when peace is made.

Section V. On the rights and duties of the belligerents with regard to individuals

Art. 55. A. Personnel of vessels –War-ships. When a war-ship is captured by the enemy, combatants and non-combatants forming part of the armed forces of the belligerents, arc to be treated as prisoners of war.

Art. 56. Public or private vessels. When an enemy ship, public or private, is seized by a belligerent, such of its crew as are nationals of a neutral State, are not made prisoners of war. The same rule applies in the case of the captain and officers likewise nationals of a neutral State, if they promise in writing not to take, during hostilities, any service connected with the operations of the war. The captain, officers and members of the crew, when nationals of the enemy State, are not made prisoners of war, on condition that they make a formal promise in writing not to undertake, while hostilities last, any service connected with the operations of the war.

Art. 57. The names of the persons retaining their liberty on condition of the promise provided for by the preceding article, are notified by the belligerent captor to the other belligerent. The latter is forbidden knowingly to employ the said persons.

Art. 58. All persons constituting part of the crew of a public or a private enemy ship are, in the absence of proof to the contrary, presumed to be of enemy nationality.

Art. 59. Members of the personnel of an enemy ship which, because of its special character, is itself exempt from seizure, cannot be held as enemies.

Art. 60. When a public or a private ship has directly or indirectly taken part in the hostilities, the enemy may retain as prisoners of war the whole personnel of the ship, without prejudice to the penalties he might otherwise incur.

Art. 61. Members of the personnel of a public or of a private vessel, who are personally guilty of an act of hostility towards the enemy, may be held by him as prisoners of war, without prejudice to the penalties he might otherwise incur.

Art. 62. B. Passengers. When individuals who follow a naval force without belonging to it, such as contractors, newspaper correspondents, etc., fall into the enemy's hands, and when the latter thinks it expedient to detain them, they may be detained only so long as military exigencies require. They are entitled to be treated as prisoners of war.

Art. 63. Passengers who, without forming part of the crew, are on board an enemy ship, may not be detained as prisoners of war, unless they have been guilty of a hostile act.

All passengers included in the armed force of the enemy may be made prisoners of war, even if the vessel is not subject to seizure.

Art. 64. C. *Religious, medical, and hospital personnel.* The religious, medical, and hospital staff of every vessel taken or seized is inviolable, and its members may not be made prisoners of war. On leaving the ship they take away with them the objects and surgical instruments which are their own private property.

This staff shall continue to discharge its duties while necessary, and can afterwards leave, when the commander in chief considers it possible.

The belligerents must guarantee to the said staff, when it has fallen into their hands, the same allowances and pay which are given to the staff of corresponding rank in their own navy.

The commissioner put by the belligerent on board the hospital ship of his adversary, in conformity with paragraph 10 of Article 41, enjoys the same protection as the medical staff.

The religious, medical, and hospital staffs lose their rights of inviolability, if they take part in hostilities, if, for example, they use their arms otherwise than for defense.

Art. 65. D. Parlementaires. The personnel of cartel ships is inviolable.

It loses its rights of inviolability if it is proved in a clear and incontestable manner that it has taken advantage of its privileged position to provoke or commit an act of treason.

Art. 66. E. Spies. A spy, even when taken in the act, may not be punished without first being tried.

Art. 67. A person can be considered a spy only when, acting clandestinely or on false pretenses, thus concealing his operations, he obtains or endeavours to obtain information in the zone of operations of a belligerent, with the intention of communicating it to the hostile party.

Hence, soldiers not wearing a disguise who have penetrated into the zone of operations of the hostile fleet for the purpose of obtaining information, may not be considered as spies but are to be treated as prisoners of war. Similarly, soldiers or civilians, carrying out their mission openly, entrusted with the delivery of dispatches, or engaged in transmitting and receiving dispatches by wireless telegraphy, are not to be considered as spies. To this class belong likewise persons sent in air-ships or in hydro-aeroplanes to act as scouts in the zone of operations of the enemy fleet or to maintain communications.

Art. 68. The spy who succeeds in escaping from the zone corresponding to the enemy's actual sphere of operations, or who has rejoined the armed force to which he belongs, if he later falls into the power of the enemy, incurs no responsibility for his previous acts.

Art. 69. F. Requisition of nationals of the enemy State – Guides, pilots, and hostages. A belligerent has no right to force persons who fall into his power, or nationals of the adverse party in general, to take part in the operations of the war directed against their own country, even when they were in his service before the beginning of the war, or to compel them to furnish information concerning their own State, its forces, its military position, or its means of defense.

He cannot force them to act as guides or as pilots.

He may, however, punish those who knowingly and voluntarily offer themselves in order to mislead him.

Compelling nationals of a belligerent to swear allegiance to the enemy Power is not permitted.

The taking of hostages is forbidden.

Art. 70. G. Prisoners of war. Prisoners of war are in the power of the hostile government, but not of the individuals or corps who capture them. They must be humanely treated. All their personal belongings, except arms, horses, military papers, and all objects in general which are specially adapted to a military end, remain their property.

Art. 71. Prisoners of war may be interned on a ship only in case of necessity and temporarily.

Art. 72. The government into whose hands prisoners of war have fallen is charged with their maintenance.

Art. 73. All prisoners of war, so long as they are on board a ship, shall be subject to the laws, regulations, and orders in force in the navy of the State in whose power they are.

Art. 74. Escaped prisoners who are retaken before succeeding in escaping from the enemy's actual sphere of action, or before being able to rejoin the armed force to which they belong, are liable to disciplinary punishment.

Prisoners who, after succeeding in escaping, are again taken prisoners, are not liable to any punishment on account of the previous flight.

Art. 75. Every prisoner of war is bound to give, if he is questioned on the subject, his true name and rank, and if he infringes this rule, he is liable to have the advantages given to prisoners of his class curtailed.

Art. 76. Prisoners of war may be set at liberty on parole if the laws of their country allow, and, in such cases, they are bound, on their personal honour, scrupulously to fulfil, both towards their own government and the government by whom they were made prisoners, the engagements they have contracted.

In such cases their own government is bound neither to require nor to accept from them any service incompatible with the parole given.

Art. 77. A prisoner of war cannot be compelled to accept his liberty on parole; similarly the hostile government is not obliged to accede to the request of the prisoner to be set at liberty on parole.

Art. 78. Prisoners of war liberated on parole and recaptured bearing arms against the government to whom they had pledged their honour, or against the allies of that government, forfeit their right to be treated as prisoners of war, and can be brought before the courts, unless, subsequent to their liberation, they have been included in an unconditional cartel of exchange.

Art. 79. Prisoners in naval warfare disembarked on land are subject to the rules laid down for prisoners in land warfare.

The same regulations should be applied, as far as possible, to prisoners of war interned on a vessel.

The preceding rules must, as far as it is possible to apply them, be followed toward prisoners of war from the moment they are captured, when they are on the ship which takes them to the place of their internment.

Art. 80. After the conclusion of peace, the repatriation of prisoners of war shall be carried out as quickly as possible.

Art. 81. H. Wounded, sick, shipwrecked and dead. Vessels used for hospital service shall afford relief and assistance to the wounded, sick and shipwrecked of the belligerents without distinction of nationality.

Art. 82. In case of the capture or seizure of an enemy vessel or a hospital ship that has failed in its duty, the sailors and soldiers on board, when sick or wounded, as well as other persons officially attached to fleets or armies, whatever their nationality, shall be respected and tended by their captors.

Art. 83. Any war-ship belonging to a belligerent may demand that sick, wounded or shipwrecked men on board military hospital ships, hospital ships belonging to relief societies or to private individuals, merchant ships, yachts, or boats, whatever the nationality of these vessels, should be handed over.

Art. 84. The shipwrecked, wounded, or sick of one of the belligerents who fall into the power of the other belligerent are prisoners of war. The captor must decide, according to circumstances, whether to keep them, send them to a port of his own country, to a neutral port, or even to an enemy port. In this last case, prisoners thus repatriated cannot serve again while the war lasts.

Art. 85. After every engagement, the two belligerents, so far as military interests permit, shall take steps to look for the shipwrecked and wounded, and to protect them, as well as the dead, from pillage and ill-treatment.

They shall see that the burial, whether by land or sea, or the cremation of the dead shall be preceded by a careful examination of the corpse.

Art. 86. Each belligerent shall send, as early as possible, to the authorities of their country, their navy, or their army the military marks or documents of identity found on the dead and the description of the sick and wounded picked up by him.

The belligerents shall keep each other informed as to internments and transfers as well as to admissions into hospitals and the deaths which have occurred among the sick and wounded in their hands. They shall collect, in order to have them forwarded to the persons concerned by the authorities of their own country, all the objects of personal use, valuables, letters, etc., which are found in the captured or seized ships, or which have been left by the sick or wounded who died in hospital.

Art. 87. In the case of operations of war between the land and sea forces of belligerents, the provisions of the present regulations on hospital assistance do not apply except between the forces actually on board ship.

Section VI. On the rights and duties of the belligerents in occupied territory

Art. 88. Occupation: extent and effects. Occupation of maritime territory, that is of gulfs, bays, roadsteads, ports, and territorial waters, exists only when there is at the same time an occupation of continental territory, by either a naval or a military force. The occupation, in that case, is subject to the laws and usages of war on land.

Section VII. On conventions between belligerents

Art. 89. General rules. The commander of any belligerent naval force may conclude agreements of a purely military character concerning the forces under his command. He may not, without authority from his government, conclude any agreement of a political character, such as a general armistice.

Art. 90. All agreements between belligerents must take into account the rules of military honour, and, once settled, must be scrupulously observed by the two parties.

Art. 91. Capitulation. After having concluded a capitulation the commander may neither damage nor destroy the ships, objects, or supplies in his possession, but must surrender them unless the right of so doing has been expressly reserved to him in the terms of the capitulation.

Art. 92. Armistice. An armistice suspends military operations.

Blockades established at the time of the armistice are not raised, unless by a special stipulation of the agreement.

The exercise of the right of visit continues to be permitted. The right of capture ceases except in cases where it exists with regard to neutral vessels.

Art. 93. An armistice may be general or partial. The first suspends the military operations of the belligerent States everywhere; the second, only between certain portions of the belligerent forces and within a fixed radius.

Art. 94. The agreement which proclaims an armistice must indicate precisely the moment it is to begin and the moment it is to end.

An armistice must be notified officially and in good time to the competent authorities as well as to the forces engaged.

Art. 95. Hostilities are suspended at the date fixed by the agreement, or, if no date has been set, immediately after the notification.

If the duration of the armistice has not been defined, the belligerent parties may resume operations at any time, provided always that the enemy is warned in good time.

Art. 96. The terms of a naval armistice shall settle, in cases where they permit the approach of enemy war-ships to certain points of the enemy's coast, the conditions of this approach and the communications of these ships either with the local authorities, or with the inhabitants.

Art. 97. Any serious violation of the armistice by one of the parties gives the other party the right of denouncing it, and even, in cases of urgency, of recommencing hostilities immediately.

Art. 98. A violation of the terms of the armistice by isolated individuals, acting on their own initiative, entitles the injured party only to demand the punishment of the offenders or, if necessary, compensation for the losses sustained.

Art. 99. Suspension of arms. A suspension of arms must, like an armistice, determine precisely the moment when hostilities are to be suspended and the moment when it ceases to be effective. If no time is set for resuming hostilities, the belligerent who intends to continue the struggle must warn the enemy of his intention in good time. The rupture of a suspension of arms by one of the belligerents or by isolated individuals entails the consequences stated in Articles 97 and 98.

Section VIII. On the formalities of seizure and on prize procedure

Art. 100. Formalities of seizure. When, after the search has been conducted, the vessel is considered subject to capture, the officer who seizes the ship must:
(1) Seal all the ship's papers after having inventoried them;
(2) Draw up a report of the seizure, as well as a short inventory of the vessel stating its condition;
(3) State the condition of the cargo which he has inventoried, then close the hatchways of the hold, the chests and the store-room and, as far as circumstances will permit, seal them;
(4) Draw up a list of the persons found on board;
(5) Put on board the seized vessel a crew sufficient to retain possession of it, maintain order upon it, and conduct it to such port as he may see fit.

If he thinks fit, the captain may, instead of sending a crew aboard a vessel, confine himself to escorting it.

Art. 101. Except for persons who may be considered prisoners of war or who are liable to punishment, a belligerent may not detain on a seized ship for more than a reasonable time, those necessary as witnesses in ascertaining the facts; but for insurmountable obstacles he must set them at liberty after the *procès-verbal* of their depositions has been drawn up.

If special circumstances require it, the captain, the officers, and a part of the crew of the captured ship may be taken on board the captor.

The captor shall attend to the maintenance of the persons detained, and shall always give them, as well as the crew, when they are set at liberty, means temporarily necessary for their further maintenance.

Art. 102. The seized ship must be taken to the nearest possible port belonging either to the captor State or to an allied belligerent Power, which offers safe refuge, and has means of easy communication with the prize court charged with deciding upon the capture.

During the voyage, the prize shall sail under the flag and the pendant carried by the war-ships of the State.

Art. 103. The seized ship and its cargo shall, as far as possible, be kept intact during the voyage to port.

If the cargo includes articles liable to deteriorate easily, the captor, so far as possible with the consent of the captain of the seized ship and in his presence, shall take the best measures toward the preservation of these articles.

Art. 104. Destruction of vessels and goods liable to confiscation. Belligerents are not permitted to destroy seized enemy ships, except in so far as they are subject to confiscation and because of exceptional necessity, that is, when the safety of the captor ship or the success of the war operations in which it is at that time engaged, demands it.

Before the vessel is destroyed all persons on board must be placed in safety, and all the ship's papers and other documents which the parties interested consider relevant for the purpose of deciding on the validity of the capture must be taken on board the warship. The same rule shall hold, as far as possible, for the goods.

A *procès-verbal* of the destruction of the captured ship and of the reasons which led to it must be drawn up.

Art. 105. The captor has the right to demand the handing over, or to proceed himself to the destruction of, any goods liable to condemnation found on board a vessel not herself liable to condemnation, provided that the circumstances are such as would, under the preceding article, justify the destruction of a vessel herself liable to condemnation. The captor must enter the goods surrendered or destroyed in the log-book of the vessel stopped, and must obtain duly certified copies of all relevant papers. When the goods have been handed over or destroyed, and the formalities duly carried out, the master must be allowed to continue his voyage.

Art. 106. Use of captured ships. If the captured ship or its cargo is necessary to the captor for immediate public use, he may use them thus. In this case, impartial persons shall make a careful estimate and inventory of the ship and its cargo, and this estimate shall be sent, together with the account of the capture, to the prize court.

Art. 107. Loss of prizes through the perils of the sea. If a prize is lost by the perils of the sea, the fact must be carefully ascertained. In that case no indemnity is due, either for the ship or for the cargo, provided that if the prize be subsequently annulled the captor is able to prove that the loss would have occurred even without capture.

Art. 108. Recapture. When a ship has been taken and retaken and is then captured from the recaptor, the last captor only has the right to it.

Art. 109. Prize procedure. The captured vessel and its cargo, once in the port of the captor or of an allied State, shall be turned over, with all necessary documents, to the competent authority.

Art. 110. The legality and the regularity of the capture of enemy vessels and of the seizure of goods must be established before a prize court.

Art. 111. All recaptures must likewise be judged by a prize court.

Art. 112. A belligerent State shall not obtain possession of the ship or goods that it has seized during the war until such time as, by final decree, the prize court shall have adjudged the confiscation of the said ship or said goods in its favour.

Art. 113. If the seizure of the ship or of the goods is not upheld by the prize court, or if the prize is released without any judgment being given, the parties interested have the right to compensation, unless there were good reasons for capturing the vessel or the goods.

Art. 114. In case of the destruction of a vessel, the captor shall be required to compensate the parties interested, unless he is able to justify the exceptional necessity of the destruction, or unless, the destruction having been justified, the capture is subsequently declared void.

The same rule is applicable to the case provided for in Article 105.

If goods not liable to confiscation have been destroyed, the owner of the goods has a right to an indemnity.

In the case of a captor's using the ship or the cargo after the seizure, he must, if his act is held to have been illegal, pay the interested parties an equitable indemnity, according to the documents drawn up at the time the vessel or goods were used.

Art. 115. Unlike non-military public ships and enemy private ships, belligerent war-ships taken by the adversary, as well as their *matériel*, become the property of the latter as soon as they fall into his possession, without the decision of a prize court being necessary.

Section IX. On the end of hostilities

Art. 116. Peace. Acts of hostility must cease upon the signing of the treaty of peace.

Notice of the end of the war shall be communicated by each government to the commander of its naval forces with as little delay as possible.

When hostile acts have been committed after the signing of the treaty of peace, the former status must, as far as possible, be restored.

When they have been committed after the official notification of the treaty of peace, they entail the payment of an indemnity and the punishment of the guilty.

Additional article

In conformity with Article 3 of the Hague Convention of 18 October 1907, concerning the laws and customs of war on land, the belligerent party which violates the provisions of the present regulations shall, if the case demands, be obliged to pay compensation; it shall be responsible for all acts committed by persons forming part of its armed naval forces.

No. 85

TREATY RELATING TO THE USE OF SUBMARINES AND NOXIOUS GASES IN WARFARE

Signed at Washington, 6 February 1922

INTRODUCTORY NOTE: The Washington Conference of 1922 on the Limitation of Armaments, in which five of the victorious Powers of World War I took part, adopted the present Treaty, which, due to the failure of France to ratify it, did not enter into force (see also note introducing *No. 12*)

ENTRY INTO IN FORCE: Not in force.

AUTHENTIC TEXTS: French, English. The text below is reprinted from *Conference on the Limitation of Armaments*, Washington, Government Printing Office, 1922.

TEXT PUBLISHED IN: *Conference on the Limitation of Armaments*, 12 November 1921–6 February 1922; *Conférence sur la limitation des Armements, 12 novembre 1921–6 février 1922*, Washington, Government Printing Office 1922, pp. 1605–1611 (Engl., French); Hudson, Vol. II, pp. 794–796 (Engl., French); Deltenre, pp. 454–459 (Engl., French, German, Dutch); *Fontes Historiae Juris Gentium*, Vol. III/2, pp. 1196–1199 (Engl., French, German); *GBTS*, 1924, No. 5, Cmd. 2036 (Engl.); *AJIL*, Vol. 16, 1922, Suppl., pp. 57–60 (Engl.); Malloy, Vol. III, pp. 3116–3119 (Engl.); Friedman, pp. 450–453 (Engl.); Ronzitti, pp. 343–346 (Engl.); *Droit des conflits armés*, pp. 1195–1197 (French); Genet, pp. 627–629 (French); Korovin, pp. 196–198 (Russ.); Ceppi, pp. 400–402 (Span. – extract); ICRC website: www.icrc.org/ihl.nsf (Engl., French).

* * *

The United States of America, The British Empire, France, Italy and Japan, hereinafter referred to as the Signatory Powers, desiring to make more effective the rules adopted by civilized nations for the protection of the lives of neutrals and noncombatants at sea in time of war, and to prevent the use in war of noxious gases and chemicals, have determined to conclude a treaty to this effect, and have appointed as their Plenipotentiaries:

[Here follow the names of plenipotentiaries]

Who, having communicated their full powers, found in good and due form, have agreed as follows:

Article 1. The Signatory Powers declare that among the rules adopted by civilized nations for the protection of the lives of neutrals and noncombatants at sea in time of war, the following are to be deemed an established part of international law:

(1) A merchant vessel must be ordered to submit to visit and search to determine its character before it can be seized.

A merchant vessel must not be attacked unless it refuses to submit to visit and search after warning, or to proceed as directed after seizure.

A merchant vessel must not be destroyed unless the crew and passengers have been first placed in safety.

(2) Belligerent submarines are not under any circumstances exempt from the universal rules above stated; and if a submarine cannot capture a merchant vessel in conformity with these rules the existing law of nations requires it to desist from attack and from seizure and to permit the merchant vessel to proceed unmolested.

Art. 2. The Signatory Powers invite all other civilized Powers to express their assent to the foregoing statement of established law so that there may be a clear public understanding throughout the world of the standards of conduct by which the public opinion of the world is to pass judgement upon future belligerents.

Art. 3. The Signatory Powers, desiring to ensure the enforcement of the humane rules of existing law declared by them with respect to attacks upon and the seizure and destruction of merchant ships, further declare that any person in the service of any Power who shall violate any of those rules, whether or not such a person is under orders of a governmental superior, shall be deemed to have violated the laws of war and shall be liable to trial and punishment as if for an act of piracy and may be brought to trial before the civil or military authorities of any Power within the jurisdiction of which he may be found.

Art. 4. The Signatory Powers recognize the practical impossibility of using submarines as commerce destroyers without violating, as they were violated in the recent war of 1914–1918, the requirements universally accepted by civilized nations for the protection of the lives of neutrals and noncombatants, and to the end that the prohibition of the use of submarines as commerce destroyers shall be universally accepted as a part of the law of nations, they now accept that prohibition as henceforth binding as between themselves and they invite all other nations to adhere thereto.

Art. 5. The use in war of asphyxiating, poisonous or other gases, and all analogous liquids, materials or devices, having been justly condemned by the general opinion of the civilized world and a prohibition of such use having been declared in treaties to which a majority of the civilized Powers are parties,

The Signatory Powers, to the end that this prohibition shall be universally accepted as a part of international law binding alike the conscience and practice of nations, declare their assent to such prohibition, agree to be bound thereby as between themselves and invite all other civilized nations to adhere thereto.

Art. 6. The present Treaty shall be ratified as soon as possible in accordance with the constitutional methods of the Signatory Powers and shall take effect on the deposit of all the ratifications, which shall take place at Washington.

The Government of the United States will transmit to all the Signatory Powers a certified copy of the *procès-verbal* of the deposit of ratifications.

The present Treaty, of which the French and English texts are both authentic, shall remain deposited in the archives of the Government of the United States, and duly certified copies thereof will be transmitted by that Government to each of the Signatory Powers.

Art. 7. The Government of the United States will further transmit to each of the non-Signatory Powers a duly certified copy of the present Treaty and invite its adherence thereto.

Any non-Signatory Power may adere to the present Treaty by communicating an instrument of adherence to the Government of the United States, which will thereupon transmit to each of the Signatory and Adhering Powers a certified copy of each instrument of adherence.

In faith whereof, the above named Plenipotentiaries have signed the present Treaty.

Done at the City of Washington, the sixth day of February, one thousand nine hundred and twenty-two.

[Here follow signatures]

SIGNATURES, RATIFICATIONS AND ACCESSIONS[1]

State	*Signature*	*Ratification, Accession*
Australia	6 February 1922	4 August 1922[2]
Canada	6 February 1922	4 August 1922
Ethiopia	—	7 October 1935[3]
France	6 February 1922	–
India	6 February 1922	4 August 1922[2]
Italy	6 February 1922	19 April 1923
Japan	6 February 1922	5 August 1922
New Zealand	6 February 1922	4 August 1922
South Africa	6 February 1922	4 August 1922[2]
United Kingdom	6 February 1922	4 August 1922
United States of America	6 February 1922	9 June 1923

RESERVATIONS

None

1 Based on a communication received from the United States Department of State of 23 June 1999.

2 Included in the ratification by the United Kingdom.

3 By a note of 7 October 1935, the Ethiopian Government notified the Government of the United States of America of its desire to accede to the Treaty. The depositary, the Government of the United States, stated to the Ethiopian Government that "inasmuch as the Treaty in question required ratification by all signatory Powers in order to give it effect, and as it was not so ratified by all signatories, it never became operative and is not now in force".

No. 86

TREATY FOR THE LIMITATION AND REDUCTION OF NAVAL ARMAMENTS (PART IV, ARTICLE 22, RELATING TO SUBMARINE WARFARE)

Signed at London, 22 April 1930

INTRODUCTORY NOTE: The powers which had signed the abortive Treaty of Washington of 1922 relating to the Use of Submarines and Noxious Gases in Warfare (*No. 85*), concluded the Treaty of London for the Limitation and Reduction of Naval Armaments of 22 April 1930. Article 22 deals with the use of submarines in warfare. It was laid down in the Treaty that this article – being declaratory of international law – should remain in force without limit of time (Article 23). Accordingly, when the Treaty of 1930 expired on 31 December 1936, Article 22 remained in force. However, in view of the last paragraph of Article 22, which states that the contracting parties invite all other powers to express their assent to the rules embodied in this Article, a *procès-verbal* was signed on 6 November 1936 (which incorporates *verbatim* the provisions of Article 22 of the Treaty of 1930 (see *No. 87*). A considerable number of states acceded to this *procès-verbal*.

ENTRY INTO FORCE: 31 December 1930.

AUTHENTIC TEXTS: English, French. The text below is reprinted from *LNTS*, Vol. 112, p. 88.

TEXT PUBLISHED IN: *LNTS*, Vol. 112, pp. 65–69, No. 2608 (Engl., French); Martens, *NRGT*, 3ème série, Vol. 23, pp. 645–680 (Engl., French); Hudson, Vol. V, pp. 394-422 (Engl., French); *Fontes Historiae Juris Gentium*, Vol. III/2, pp. 1023–1029 (Engl., French, German); *GBTS*, 1931, No. 1, Cmd. 3758 (Engl., French); *BFSP*, Vol. 132, pp. 603–619 (Engl.); *US Statutes at Large*, Vol. 46, pp. 2858–2885 (Engl., French); Malloy, Vol. IV, pp. 5268–5286 (Engl.); Bevans, Vol. II, pp. 1055–1075 (Engl.); *AJIL*, Vol. 25, 1931, Suppl., pp. 63–82 (Engl.); Hackworth, *Digest of International Law*, Vol. II, Washington 1941, p. 691 (Engl.); Ronzitti, pp. 347-348 (Engl.); *Droit des conflits armés*, pp. 1199–1202 French); ICRC website: www.icrc.org/ihl.nsf (Engl., French).

* * *

PART IV

Art. 22. The following are accepted as established rules of international law:

(1) In their action with regard to merchant ships, submarines must conform to the rules of international law to which surface vessels are subject.

(2) In particular, except in the case of persistent refusal to stop on being duly summoned, or of active resistance to visit or search, a warship, whether sur-

face vessel or submarine, may not sink or render incapable of navigation a merchant vessel without having first placed passengers, crew and ship's papers in a place of safety. For this purpose the ship's boats are not regarded as a place of safety unless the safety of the passengers and crew is assured, in the existing sea and weather conditions, by the proximity of land, or the presence of another vessel which is in a position to take them on board.

High Contracting Parties invite all other Powers to express their assent to the above rules.

SIGNATURES AND RATIFICATIONS[1]

State	*Signature*	*Ratification*
Australia	22 April 1930	27 October 1930
Canada	22 April 1930	27 October 1930
France	22 April 1930	6 November 1936[2]
India	22 April 1930	27 October 1930
Irish Free State	22 April 1930	31 December 1930
Italy	22 April 1930	6 November 1936
Japan	22 April 1930	27 October 1930
New Zealand	22 April 1930	27 October 1930
South Africa	22 April 1930	27 October 1930
United Kingdom *(including all parts of the British Empire not separate members of the League of Nations)*	22 April 1930	27 October 1930
United States of America	22 April 1930	27 October 1930

[1] Based on communications from the Foreign and Commonwealth Office of Great Britain of 7 December 2001.

[2] In respect of part IV only.

No. 87

PROCES-VERBAL RELATING TO THE RULES OF SUBMARINE WARFARE SET FORTH IN PART IV OF THE TREATY OF LONDON OF 22 APRIL 1930

Signed at London, 6 November 1936

INTRODUCTORY NOTE: See note introducing *No. 86*.

ENTRY INTO FORCE: 6 November 1936.

AUTHENTIC TEXTS: English, French. The text below is reprinted from *LNTS*, Vol. 173, p. 353.

TEXT PUBLISHED IN: *LNTS*, Vol. 173, 1936, pp. 353–357, No. 4025 (Engl., French); Martens, *NRGT*, 3ème série, Vol. 33, pp. 3–5 (Engl., French); Hudson, Vol. VII, pp. 490–492 (Engl., French); Deltenre, pp. 564–571 (Engl., French, German, Dutch); *GBTS*, Vol. 29, 1936. Cmd. 5302 (Engl., French); *BFSP*, Vol. 140, 1936, pp. 300–302 (Engl.); Bevans, Vol. III, pp. 298–299 (Engl.); *AJIL*, Vol. 31, 1937, pp. 137–139 (Engl.); Friedman, pp. 52–524 (Engl.); Roberts and Guelff, pp. 169–173 (Engl.); Ronzitti, pp. 349–352 (Engl.); *Droit des conflits armés*, pp. 1203–1205 (French); *Sobranie zakonov*, 1937, otdel vtoroj, No. 25, 170/1937 (Engl., French, Russ.); *Mezhdunarodnoe pravo*, Vol. III, pp. 161–162 (Russ.); ICRC website: www.icrc.org/ihl.nsf (Engl., French, Span.).

* * *

Whereas the Treaty for the Limitation and Reduction of Naval Armaments signed in London on 22 April 1930, has not been ratified by all the Signatories;

And whereas the said Treaty will cease to be in force after 31 December 1936, with the exception of Part IV thereof, which sets forth rules as to the action of submarines with regard to merchant ships as being established rules of international law, and remains in force without limit of time;

And whereas the last paragraph of Article 22 in the said Part IV states that the High Contracting Parties invite all other Powers to express their assent to the said rules;

And whereas the Governments of the French Republic and the Kingdom of Italy have confirmed their acceptance of the said rules resulting from the signature of the said Treaty;

And whereas all the Signatories of the said Treaty desire that as great a number of Powers as possible should accept the rules contained in the said Part IV as established rules of international law;

The undersigned, representatives of their respective Governments, bearing in mind the said Article 22 of the Treaty, hereby request the Government of the United Kingdom of Great Britain and Northern Ireland forthwith to communicate the said rules, as annexed thereto, to the Governments of all Powers which are not Signatories of the said Treaty, with an invitation to accede thereto definitely and without limit of time.

Rules

(1). In their action with regard to merchant ships, submarines must conform to the rules of international law to which surface vessels are subject.

(2). In particular, except in the case of persistent refusal to stop on being duly summoned, or of active resistance to visit or search, a warship, whether surface vessel or submarine, may not sink or render incapable of navigation a merchant vessel without having first placed passengers, crew and ship's papers in a place of safety. For this purpose the ship's boats are not regarded as a place of safety unless the safety of the passengers and crew is assured, in the existing sea and weather conditions, by the proximity of land, or the presence of another vessel which is in a position to take them on board.

Signed in London, the sixth day of November, nineteen hundred and thirty-six.

[Here follow signatures]

SIGNATURES AND ACCESSIONS[1]

Signatory states[2]	*Signature*
Australia	6 November 1936
Canada	6 November 1936
France	6 November 1936
India	6 November 1936
Irish Free State	6 November 1936
Italy	6 November 1936
Japan	6 November 1936
New Zealand	6 November 1936
South Africa	6 November 1936
United Kingdom	6 November 1936
United States of America	6 November 1936

Acceding states	*Accession or Notification of Continuity (C)*
Afghanistan	25 May 1937
Albania	3 March 1937
Austria	1 April 1937
Belgium	23 December 1936
Brazil	31 December 1937

[1] Based on communications from the Foreign and Commonwealth Office of Great Britain of 7 December 2001.

[2] The signatory states are bound by the ratification of the London Treaty of 1930 (*No. 86*).

Acceding states	*Accession or Notification of Continuity (C)*
Bulgaria	1 March 1937
Costa Rica	7 July 1937
Czechoslovakia	14 September 1937
Denmark	21 April 1937
Egypt	23 June 1937
El Salvador	24 November 1937
Estonia	26 June 1937
Fiji	6 March 1973 (C)
Finland	18 February 1937
Germany	23 November 1936
Greece	11 January 1937
Guatemala	8 September 1938
Haiti	23 January 1937
Holy See	16 March 1937
Hungary	8 December 1937
Iran	21 January 1939
Iraq	27 December 1937
Latvia	7 March 1938
Lithuania	27 January 1938
Mexico	3 January 1938
Nepal	27 January 1937
Netherlands[3]	30 September 1937
Norway	21 May 1937
Panama	26 February 1937
Peru	3 June 1937
Poland	21 July 1937
Saudi Arabia	11 June 1937
Siam	12 January 1938
Sweden	15 February 1937
Switzerland	22 May 1937
Tonga	7 July 1971 (C)
Turkey	7 July 1937
USSR	27 December 1936
Yugoslavia	19 April 1937

[3] In a note of 20 December 1985, the Government of the Netherlands informed the depositary that as from 1 January 1986 the present treaty as well as many other treaties will be applied separately to Netherlands Antilles and to Aruba. The island of Aruba which was a part of the Netherlands Antilles obtained internal autonomy as a separate country within the Kingdom of the Netherlands as of l January 1986.

No. 88

THE NYON ARRANGEMENT

I. THE NYON ARRANGEMENT

Signed at Nyon, on 14 September 1937

II. AGREEMENT SUPPLEMENTARY TO THE NYON ARRANGEMENT

Signed at Geneva, on 17 September 1937

INTRODUCTORY NOTE: During the Spanish Civil War, nine Powers agreed to take collective measures to suppress attacks by submarines against merchant vessels. The Agreement refers in its preamble to the provisions of the London Treaty of 1930, and the *Procès verbal* of 1936, concerning submarine warfare (*Nos. 86* and *87*). In the Supplementary Agreement of 17 September 1937, the same Powers made the principles of the first Agreement applicable to attacks by surface vessels and aircraft.

ENTRY INTO FORCE: 14 September 1937 (Supplementary Agreement on 17 September 1937).[1]

AUTHENTIC TEXTS: English and French. The text below is reprinted from *LNTS*, Vol. 181, No. 4184, pp. 136–140, and No. 4185, pp. 150–152.

TEXT PUBLISHED IN: *LNTS*, Vol. 181, No. 4184, pp. 137–152, and No. 1485, pp. 150–152 (Engl., French); Martens, *NRGT*, Vol. 34, 3rd Series, pp. 666–678 (Engl., French); Hudson, Vol. VII, pp. 831–841 (Engl., French); Deltenre, pp. 568–571 (Engl., French, German, Dutch); *GBTS*, No. 38, 1937, Cmd. 5568 (Engl., French); *BFSP*, Vol. 141, 1937, pp. 520–527 (Engl.); *AJIL*, Vol. 31, 1937, Suppl., pp. 179–182 (Engl.); Ronzitti, pp. 483–488 (Engl.); *Droit des conflits armés*, pp. 1207–1210 (Engl.); ICRC website: www.icrc.org/ihl.nsf (Engl., French).

* * *

I. THE NYON ARRANGEMENT

Whereas arising out of the Spanish conflict attacks have been repeatedly committed in the Mediterranean by submarines against merchant ships not belonging to either of the conflicting Spanish parties; and

Whereas these attacks are violations of the rules of international law referred to in Part IV of the Treaty of London of 22 April 1930, with regard to the sinking of merchant ships and constitute acts contrary to the most elementary dictates of humanity, which should be justly treated as acts of piracy; and

Whereas without in any way admitting the right of either party to the conflict in Spain to exercise belligerent rights or to interfere with merchant ships on the high

[1] Both instruments entered into force upon signature, without ratification.

seas even if the laws of warfare at sea are observed and without prejudice to the right of any participating Power to take such action as may be proper to protect its merchant shipping from any kind of interference on the high seas or to the possibility of further collective measures being agreed upon subsequently, it is necessary in the first place to agree upon certain special collective measures against piratical acts by submarines:

In view thereof the undersigned, being authorized to this effect by their respective Governments, have met in conference at Nyon between the 9 and the 14 September 1937, and have agreed upon the following provisions which shall enter immediately into force:

I. The participating Powers will instruct their naval forces to take the action indicated in paragraphs II and III below with a view to the protection of all merchant ships not belonging to either of the conflicting Spanish parties.

II. Any submarine which attacks such a ship in a manner contrary to the rules of international law referred to in the International Treaty for the Limitation and Reduction of Naval Armaments signed in London on 22 April 1930, and confirmed in the Protocol signed in London on 6 November 1936, shall be counter-attacked and, if possible, destroyed.

III. The instruction mentioned in the preceding paragraph shall extend to any submarine encountered in the vicinity of a position where a ship not belonging to either of the conflicting Spanish parties has recently been attacked in violation of the rules referred to in the preceding paragraph in circumstances which give valid grounds for the belief that the submarine was guilty of the attack.

IV. In order to facilitate the putting into force of the above arrangements in a practical manner, the participating Powers have agreed upon the following arrangements:

1. In the western Mediterranean and in the Malta Channel, with the exception of the Tyrrhenean Sea, which may form the subject of special arrangements, the British and French fleets will operate both on the high seas and in the territorial waters of the participating Powers, in accordance with the division of the area agreed upon between the two Governments.
2. In the eastern Mediterranean,
   (a) Each of the participating Powers will operate in its own territorial waters;
   (b) On the high seas, with the exception of the Adriatic Sea, the British and French fleets will operate up to the entrance to the Dardanelles, in those areas where there is reason to apprehend danger to shipping in accordance with the division of the area agreed upon between the two Governments. The other participating Governments possessing a sea border on the Mediterranean undertake, within the limit of their resources, to furnish these fleets any assistance that may be asked for; in particular, they will permit them to take action in their territorial waters and to use such of their ports as they shall indicate.
3. It is further understood that the limits of the zones referred to in sub-paragraphs I and 2 above, and their allocation shall be subject at any time to revision by the participating Powers in order to take account of any change in the situation.

V. The participating Powers agree that, in order to simplify the operation of the above-mentioned measures, they will for their part restrict the use of their submarines in the Mediterranean in the following manner:

(a) Except as stated in (b) and (c) below, no submarine will be sent to sea within the Mediterranean.

(b) Submarines may proceed on passage after notification to the other participating Powers, provided that they proceed on the surface and are accompanied by a surface ship.

(c) Each participating Power reserves for purposes of exercises certain areas defined in Annex I hereto[2] in which its submarines are exempt from the restrictions mentioned in (a) or (b).

---

[2] Annexes I and II, addendum to annexes and the charts are not reproduced in this collection. See *LNTS*, Vol. 181, No. 4184, pp. 142–152.

The participating Powers further undertake not to allow the presence in their respective territorial waters of any foreign submarines except in case of urgent distress, or where the conditions prescribed in sub-paragraph (b) above are fulfilled.

VI. The participating Powers also agree that, in order to simplify the problem involved in carrying out the measures above described, they may severally advise their merchant shipping to follow certain main routes in the Mediterranean agreed upon between them and defined in Annex II hereto.

VII. Nothing in the present agreement restricts the right of any participating Power to send its surface vessels to any part of the Mediterranean.

VIII. Nothing in the present agreement in any way prejudices existing international engagements which have been registered with the Secretariat of the League of Nations.

IX. If any of the participating Powers notifies its intention of withdrawing from the present arrangement, the notification will take effect after the expiry of thirty days and any of the other participating Powers may withdraw on the same date if it communicates its intention to this effect before that date.

Done at Nyon, this fourteenth day of September nineteen hundred and thirty-seven, in a single copy, in the English and French languages, both texts being equally authentic, and which will be deposited in the archives of the Secretariat of the League of Nations.

II. AGREEMENT SUPPLEMENTARY TO THE NYON ARRANGEMENT

Whereas under the arrangement signed at Nyon on 14 September 1937, whereby collective measures were agreed upon relating to piratical acts by submarines in the Mediterranean, the participating Powers reserved the possibility of taking further collective measures; and

Whereas it is now considered expedient that such measures should be taken against similar acts by surface vessels and aircraft;

In view thereof, the undersigned, being authorized to this effect by their respective Governments, have met in conference at Geneva on the seventeenth day of September and have agreed upon the following provisions which shall enter immediately into force:

I. The present Agreement is supplementary to the Nyon Arrangement and shall be regarded as an integral part thereof.

II. The present Agreement applies to any attack by a surface vessel or an aircraft upon any merchant vessel in the Mediterranean not belonging to either of the conflicting Spanish parties, when such attack is accompanied by a violation of the humanitarian principles embodied in the rules of international law with regard to warfare at sea, which are referred to in Part IV of the Treaty of London of 22 April 1930, and confirmed in the Protocol signed in London on 6 November 1936.

III. Any surface war vessel, engaged in the protection of merchant shipping in conformity with the Nyon Arrangement, which witnesses an attack of the kind referred to in the preceding paragraph shall:

(a) If the attack is committed by an aircraft, open fire on the aircraft;

(b) If the attack is committed by a surface vessel, intervene to resist it within the limits of its powers, summoning assistance if such is available and necessary.

In territorial waters each of the participating Powers concerned will give instructions as to the action to be taken by its own war vessels in the spirit of the present Agreement.

Done at Geneva, this seventeenth day of September 1937, in the English and French languages, both texts being equally authentic, in a single copy which will be deposited in the archives of the Secretariat of the League of Nations.

SIGNATURES[1]

Bulgaria
Egypt
France
Great Britain
Greece
Romania
Turkey
USSR
Yugoslavia

TITLES OF ANNEXES:

ANNEX I[2]
AREAS RESERVED FOR SUBMARINE EXERCISES

ANNEX II[2]
MAIN ROUTES WHICH EACH SIGNATORY POWER MAY ADVISE ITS MERCHANT SHIPS TO FOLLOW

CHARTS[2]

1 The Nyon Agreement and the Agreement supplementary to the Nyon Agreement were deposited in the archives of the League of Nations. The list of signatories was established according to the text published in *LNTS*, Vol. 181, No. 4184, pp. 136–140 and No. 4185, pp. 150–152. The indications were confirmed by the communication from the United Nations Treaty Section of 29 June 1999.

2 Annexes I and II, addendum to annexes and the charts are not reproduced in this collection. See *LNTS*, Vol. 181, No. 4184, pp. 142–152.

No. 89

SAN REMO MANUAL ON INTERNATIONAL LAW APPLICABLE TO ARMED CONFLICTS AT SEA

Prepared by international lawyers and naval experts convened by the International Institute of Humanitarian Law

Adopted in Livorno in June 1994

INTRODUCTORY NOTE: In its Resolution VII adopted on 31 October 1986, the XXVth International Conference of the Red Cross noted "that international humanitarian law relating to land warfare to a large extent has been reaffirmed and developed and that some areas of international humanitarian law relating to sea warfare are in need of reaffirmation and clarification on the basis of existing fundamental principles of international humanitarian law". The Conference appealed to governments to coordinate their efforts in appropriate fora in order to review the possibility of updating the relevant texts of international humanitarian law relating to sea warfare. It invited the ICRC to follow the question and to keep the Conference informed. In 1987, the International Institute of Humanitarian Law, organized an initial meeting of experts at San Remo in order to deliberate on this subject. This meeting was followed by others, and culminated in the adoption of the *Manual* reproduced below. The ICRC provided full support to this work. The origin and aim of the *Manual* are described in the introductory note at its beginning.

The rules of the *Manual* were completed by explanations that are not reproduced in the present Collection, but may be found in the San Remo Institute publication: *San Remo Manual on International Law Applicable to Armed Conflicts at Sea*, Cambridge, Cambridge University Press, 1995, pp. 57–246.

AUTHENTIC TEXT: English.

PUBLICATION OF THE TEXT: *San Remo Manual on International Law Applicable to Armed Conflicts at Sea*, Cambridge, Cambridge University Press, 1995, pp. 1–44 (with and explanation of the text), pp. 57–246 (English); *IRRC* 1995, pp. 595–637 (Engl.); *RICR* 1995, pp. 649–694 (French); *Droit des conflits armés,* pp. 1211–1244 (French); Roberts and Guelff, pp. 573–606 (Engl.); . ICRC website: www.icrc.org/ihl.nsf (Engl., French, Span.).

TABLE OF CONTENTS

* * *

INTRODUCTORY NOTE

The *San Remo Manual* was prepared during the period 1988–94 by a group of legal and naval experts participating in their personal capacity in a series of Round Tables convened by the International Institute of Humanitarian Law. The purpose of the *Manual* is to provide a contemporary restatement of international law applicable to armed conflicts at sea. The *Manual* includes a few provisions which might be considered progressive developments in the law but most of its provisions are considered to state the law which is currently applicable. The *Manual* is viewed by the participants of the Round Tables as being in many respects a modern equivalent to the *Oxford Manual on the Laws of Naval War Governing the Relations Between Belligerents* adopted by the Institute of International Law in 1913. A contemporary manual was considered necessary because of developments in the law since 1913 which for the most part have not been incorporated into recent treaty law, the Second Geneva Convention of 1949 being essentially limited to the protection of the wounded, sick and shipwrecked at sea. In particular, there has not been a development for the law of armed conflict at sea similar to that for the law of armed conflict on land with the conclusion of Protocol I of 1977 additional to the Geneva Conventions of 1949, Although some of the provisions of Additional Protocol I affect naval operations, in particular those supplementing the protection given to medical vessels and aircraft in the Second Geneva Convention of 1949, Part IV of the Protocol, which protects civilians against the effects of hostilities, is only applicable to naval operations which affect civilians and civilian objects on land.

A preliminary Round Table on International Humanitarian Law Applicable to Armed Conflicts at Sea, held in San Remo in 1987 and convened by the International Institute of Humanitarian Law, in co-operation with the Institute of International Law of the University of Pisa (Italy) and the University of Syracuse (USA), undertook an initial review of the law. The Madrid Round Table, convened by the International Institute of Humanitarian Law in 1988, developed a plan of action to draft a contemporary restatement of the law of armed conflict at sea. In conformity with its mandate to prepare developments in international humanitarian law, the International Committee of the Red Cross supported this project throughout. In order to implement the Madrid Plan of Action, the Institute held annual Round Tables which met in Bochum in 1989, in Toulon in 1990, in Bergen in 1991, in Ottawa in 1992, in Geneva in 1993 and finally in Livorno in 1994. Basing themselves on thorough reports made by rapporteurs between the meetings, comments thereto by participants and careful discussion during the meetings, these groups drafted the *Manual* which was adopted in Livorno in June 1994.

The related Explanation was prepared by a core group of experts who had also been the rapporteurs for the Round Tables. The *Manual* should be read together with this Explanation for a full understanding of the *Manual*'s provisions.

The authentic text of the *Manual* is English.

PART I. GENERAL PROVISIONS

Section I. Scope of Application of the Law

1. The parties to an armed conflict at sea are bound by the principles and rules of international humanitarian law from the moment armed force is used.
2. In cases not covered by this document or by international agreements, civilians and combatants remain under the protection and authority of the principles of international law derived from established custom, from the principles of humanity and from the dictates of the public conscience.

Section II. Armed Conflicts and the Law of Self-Defence

3. The exercise of the right of individual or collective self-defence recognized in Article 51 of the Charter of the United Nations is subject to the conditions and limitations laid down in the Charter, and arising from general international law, including in particular the principles of necessity and proportionality.
4. The principles of necessity and proportionality apply equally to armed conflict at sea and require that the conduct of hostilities by a State should not

exceed the degree and kind of force, not otherwise prohibited by the law of armed conflict, required to repel an armed attack against it and to restore its security.

5. How far a State is justified in its military actions against the enemy will depend upon the intensity and scale of the armed attack for which the enemy is responsible and the gravity of the threat posed.
6. The rules set out in this document and any other rules of international humanitarian law shall apply equally to all parties to the conflict. The equal application of these rules to all parties to the conflict shall not be affected by the international responsibility that may have been incurred by any of them for the outbreak of the conflict.

Section III. Armed Conflicts in which the Security Council has Taken Action

7. Notwithstanding any rule in this document or elsewhere on the law of neutrality, where the Security Council, acting in accordance with its powers under Chapter VII of the Charter of the United Nations, has identified one or more of the parties to an armed conflict as responsible for resorting to force in violation of international law, neutral States:
   (a) are bound not to lend assistance other than humanitarian assistance to that State; and
   (b) may lend assistance to any State which has been the victim of a breach of the peace or an act of aggression by that State.
8. Where, in the course of an international armed conflict, the Security Council has taken preventive or enforcement action involving the application of economic measures under Chapter VII of the Charter, Member States of the United Nations may not rely upon the law of neutrality to justify conduct which would be incompatible with their obligations under the Charter or under decisions of the Security Council.
9. Subject to paragraph 7, where the Security Council has taken a decision to use force, or to authorize the use of force by a particular State or States, the rules set out in this document and any other rules of international humanitarian law applicable to armed conflicts at sea shall apply to all parties to any such conflict which may ensue.

Section IV. Areas of Naval Warfare

10. Subject to other applicable rules of the law of armed conflict at sea contained in this document or elsewhere, hostile actions by naval forces may be conducted in, on or over:
    (a) the territorial sea and internal waters, the land territories, the exclusive economic zone and continental shelf and, where applicable, the archipelagic waters, of belligerent States;
    (b) the high seas; and
    (c) subject to paragraphs 34 and 35, the exclusive economic zone and the continental shelf of neutral States.
11. The parties to the conflict are encouraged to agree that no hostile actions will be conducted in marine areas containing:
    (a) rare or fragile ecosystems; or

(b) the habitat of depleted, threatened or endangered species or other forms of marine life.

12. In carrying out operations in areas where neutral States enjoy sovereign rights, jurisdiction, or other rights under general international law, belligerents shall have due regard for the legitimate rights and duties of those neutral States.

Section V. Definitions

13. For the purposes of this document:
   (a) "international humanitarian law" means international rules, established by treaties or custom, which limit the right of parties to a conflict to use the methods or means of warfare of their choice, or which protect States not party to the conflict or persons and objects that are, or may be, affected by the conflict;
   (b) "attack" means an act of violence, whether in offence or in defence;
   (c) "collateral" casualties or collateral damage means the loss of life of, or injury to, civilians or other protected persons, and damage to or the destruction of the natural environment or objects that are not in themselves military objectives;
   (d) "neutral" means any State not party to the conflict;
   (e) "hospital ships", coastal rescue craft and other medical transports means vessels that are protected under the Second Geneva Convention of 1949 and Additional Protocol I of 1977;
   (f) "medical aircraft" means an aircraft that is protected under the Geneva Conventions of 1949 and Additional Protocol I of 1977;
   (g) "warship" means a ship belonging to the armed forces of a State bearing the external marks distinguishing the character and nationality of such a ship, under the command of an officer duly commissioned by the government of that State and whose name appears in the appropriate service list or its equivalent, and manned by a crew which is under regular armed forces discipline;
   (h) "auxiliary vessel" means a vessel, other than a warship, that is owned by or under the exclusive control of the armed forces of a State and used for the time being on government non-commercial service;
   (i) "merchant vessel" means a vessel, other than a warship, an auxiliary vessel, or a State vessel such as a customs or police vessel, that is engaged in commercial or private service;
   (j) "military aircraft" means an aircraft operated by commissioned units of the armed forces of a State having the military marks of that State, commanded by a member of the armed forces and manned by a crew subject to regular armed forces discipline;
   (k) "auxiliary aircraft" means an aircraft, other than a military aircraft, that is owned by or under the exclusive control of the armed forces of a State and used for the time being on government non-commercial service;
   (l) "civil aircraft" means an aircraft other than a military, auxiliary, or State aircraft such as a customs or police aircraft, that is engaged in commercial or private service;
   (m) "civil airliner" means a civil aircraft that is clearly marked and engaged in carrying civilian passengers in scheduled or non-scheduled services along Air Traffic Service routes.

PART II. REGIONS OF OPERATIONS

Section I. Internal Waters, Territorial Sea and Archipelagic Waters

14. Neutral waters consist of the internal waters, territorial sea, and, where applicable, the archipelagic waters, of neutral States. Neutral airspace consists of the airspace over neutral waters and the land territory of neutral States.
15. Within and over neutral waters, including neutral waters comprising an international strait and waters in which the right of archipelagic sea lanes passage may be exercised, hostile actions by belligerent forces are forbidden. A neutral State must take such measures as are consistent with Section II of this Part, including the exercise of surveillance, as the means at its disposal allow, to prevent the violation of its neutrality by belligerent forces.
16. Hostile actions within the meaning of paragraph 15 include, inter alia:
    (a) attack on or capture of persons or objects located in, on or over neutral waters or territory;
    (b) use as a base of operations, including attack on or capture of persons or objects located outside neutral waters, if the attack or seizure is conducted by belligerent forces located in, on or over neutral waters;
    (c) laying of mines; or
    (d) visit, search, diversion or capture.
17. Belligerent forces may not use neutral waters as a sanctuary.
18. Belligerent military and auxiliary aircraft may not enter neutral airspace. Should they do so, the neutral State shall use the means at its disposal to require the aircraft to land within its territory and shall intern the aircraft and its crew for the duration of the armed conflict. Should the aircraft fail to follow the instructions to land, it may be attacked, subject to the special rules relating to medical aircraft as specified in paragraphs 181–183.
19. Subject to paragraphs 29 and 33, a neutral State may, on a non-discriminatory basis, condition, restrict or prohibit the entrance to or passage through its neutral waters by belligerent warships and auxiliary vessels.
20. Subject to the duty of impartiality, and to paragraphs 21 and 23–33, and under such regulations as it may establish, a neutral State may, without jeopardizing its neutrality, permit the following acts within its neutral waters:
    (a) passage through its territorial sea, and where applicable its archipelagic waters, by warships, auxiliary vessels and prizes of belligerent States; warships, auxiliary vessels and prizes may employ pilots of the neutral State during passage;
    (b) replenishment by a belligerent warship or auxiliary vessel of its food, water and fuel sufficient to reach a port in its own territory; and
    (c) repairs of belligerent warships or auxiliary vessels found necessary by the neutral State to make them seaworthy; such repairs may not restore or increase their fighting strength.
21. A belligerent warship or auxiliary vessel may not extend the duration of its passage through neutral waters, or its presence in those waters for replenishment or repair, for longer than 24 hours unless unavoidable on account of damage or the stress of weather. The foregoing rule does not apply in international straits and waters in which the right of archipelagic sea lanes passage is exercised.

22. Should a belligerent State be in violation of the regime of neutral waters, as set out in this document, the neutral State is under an obligation to take the measures necessary to terminate the violation. If the neutral State fails to terminate the violation of its neutral waters by a belligerent, the opposing belligerent must so notify the neutral State and give that neutral State a reasonable time to terminate the violation by the belligerent. If the violation of the neutrality of the State by the belligerent constitutes a serious and immediate threat to the security of the opposing belligerent and the violation is not terminated, then that belligerent may, in the absence of any feasible and timely alternative, use such force as is strictly necessary to respond to the threat posed by the violation.

Section II. International Straits and Archipelagic Sea Lanes

General rules

23. Belligerent warships and auxiliary vessels and military and auxiliary aircraft may exercise the rights of passage through, under or over neutral international straits and of archipelagic sea lanes passage provided by general international law.
24. The neutrality of a State bordering an international strait is not jeopardized by the transit passage of belligerent warships, auxiliary vessels, or military or auxiliary aircraft, nor by the innocent passage of belligerent warships or auxiliary vessels through that strait.
25. The neutrality of an archipelagic State is not jeopardized by the exercise of archipelagic sea lanes passage by belligerent warships, auxiliary vessels, or military or auxiliary aircraft.
26. Neutral warships, auxiliary vessels, and military and auxiliary aircraft may exercise the rights of passage provided by general international law through, under and over belligerent international straits and archipelagic waters. The neutral State should, as a precautionary measure, give timely notice of its exercise of the rights of passage to the belligerent State.

Transit passage and archipelagic sea lanes passage

27. The rights of transit passage and archipelagic sea lanes passage applicable to international straits and archipelagic waters in peacetime continue to apply in times of armed conflict. The laws and regulations of States bordering straits and archipelagic States relating to transit passage and archipelagic sea lanes passage adopted in accordance with general international law remain applicable.
28. Belligerent and neutral surface ships, submarines and aircraft have the rights of transit passage and archipelagic sea lanes passage through, under, and over all straits and archipelagic waters to which these rights generally apply.
29. Neutral States may not suspend, hamper, or otherwise impede the right of transit passage nor the right of archipelagic sea lanes passage.
30. A belligerent in transit passage through, under and over a neutral international strait, or in archipelagic sea lanes passage through, under and over neutral archipelagic waters, is required to proceed without delay, to refrain from the threat or use of force against the territorial integrity or political

independence of the neutral littoral or archipelagic State, or in any other manner inconsistent with the purposes of the Charter of the United Nations, and otherwise to refrain from any hostile actions or other activities not incident to their transit. Belligerents passing through, under and over neutral straits or waters in which the right of archipelagic sea lanes passage applies are permitted to take defensive measures consistent with their security, including launching and recovery of aircraft, screen formation steaming, and acoustic and electronic surveillance. Belligerents in transit or archipelagic sea lanes passage may not, however, conduct offensive operations against enemy forces, nor use such neutral waters as a place of sanctuary nor as a base of operations.

Innocent passage

31. In addition to the exercise of the rights of transit and archipelagic sea lanes passage, belligerent warships and auxiliary vessels may, subject to paragraphs 19 and 21, exercise the right of innocent passage through neutral international straits and archipelagic waters in accordance with general international law.
32. Neutral vessels may likewise exercise the right of innocent passage through belligerent international straits and archipelagic waters.
33. The right of non-suspendable innocent passage ascribed to certain international straits by international law may not be suspended in time of armed conflict.

Section III. Exclusive Economic Zone and Continental Shelf

34. If hostile actions are conducted within the exclusive economic zone or on the continental shelf of a neutral State, belligerent States shall, in addition to observing the other applicable rules of the law of armed conflict at sea, have due regard for the rights and duties of the coastal State, inter alia, for the exploration and exploitation of the economic resources of the exclusive economic zone and the continental shelf and the protection and preservation of the marine environment. They shall, in particular, have due regard for artificial islands, installations, structures and safety zones established by neutral States in the exclusive economic zone and on the continental shelf.
35. If a belligerent considers it necessary to lay mines in the exclusive economic zone or the continental shelf of a neutral State, the belligerent shall notify that State, and shall ensure, inter alia, that the size of the minefield and the type of mines used do not endanger artificial islands, installations and structures, nor interfere with access thereto, and shall avoid so far as practicable interference with the exploration or exploitation of the zone by the neutral State. Due regard shall also be given to the protection and preservation of the marine environment.

Section IV. High Seas and Sea-Bed beyond National Jurisdiction

36. Hostile actions on the high seas shall be conducted with due regard for the exercise by neutral States of rights of exploration and exploitation of the natural resources of the sea-bed, and ocean floor, and the subsoil thereof, beyond national jurisdiction.

37. Belligerents shall take care to avoid damage to cables and pipelines laid on the sea-bed which do not exclusively serve the belligerents.

PART III. BASIC RULES AND TARGET DISCRIMINATION

Section I. Basic Rules

38. In any armed conflict the right of the parties to the conflict to choose methods or means of warfare is not unlimited.
39. Parties to the conflict shall at all times distinguish between civilians or other protected persons and combatants and between civilian or exempt objects and military objectives.
40. In so far as objects are concerned, military objectives are limited to those objects which by their nature, location, purpose or use make an effective contribution to military action and whose total or partial destruction, capture or neutralization, in the circumstances ruling at the time, offers a definite military advantage.
41. Attacks shall be limited strictly to military objectives. Merchant vessels and civil aircraft are civilian objects unless they are military objectives in accordance with the principles and rules set forth in this document.
42. In addition to any specific prohibitions binding upon the parties to a conflict, it is forbidden to employ methods or means of warfare which:
    (a) are of a nature to cause superfluous injury or unnecessary suffering; or
    (b) are indiscriminate, in that:
        (i) they are not, or cannot be, directed against a specific military objective; or
        (ii) their effects cannot be limited as required by international law as reflected in this document.
43. It is prohibited to order that there shall be no survivors, to threaten an adversary therewith or to conduct hostilities on this basis.
44. Methods and means of warfare should be employed with due regard for the natural environment taking into account the relevant rules of international law. Damage to or destruction of the natural environment not justified by military necessity and carried out wantonly is prohibited.
45. Surface ships, submarines and aircraft are bound by the same principles and rules.

Section II. Precautions in Attack

46. With respect to attacks, the following precautions shall be taken:
    (a) those who plan, decide upon or execute an attack must take all feasible measures to gather information which will assist in determining whether or not objects which are not military objectives are present in an area of attack;
    (b) in the light of the information available to them, those who plan, decide upon or execute an attack shall do everything feasible to ensure that attacks are limited to military objectives;
    (c) they shall furthermore take all feasible precautions in the choice of methods and means in order to avoid or minimize collateral casualties or damage; and

(d) an attack shall not be launched if it may be expected to cause collateral casualties or damage which world be excessive in relation to the concrete and direct military advantage anticipated from the attack as a whole; an attack shall be cancelled or suspended as soon as it becomes apparent that the collateral casualties or damage would be excessive.

Section VI of this Part provides additional precautions regarding civil aircraft.

Section III. Enemy Vessels and Aircraft Exempt from Attack

Classes of vessels exempt from attack

47. The following classes of enemy vessels are exempt from attack:
   (a) hospital ships;
   (b) small craft used for coastal rescue operations and other medical transports;
   (c) vessels granted safe conduct by agreement between the belligerent parties including:
      (i) cartel vessels, e.g., vessels designated for and engaged in the transport of prisoners of war;
      (ii) vessels engaged in humanitarian missions, including vessels carrying supplies indispensable to the survival of the civilian population, and vessels engaged in relief actions and rescue operations;
   (d) vessels engaged in transporting cultural property under special protection;
   (e) passenger vessels when engaged only in carrying civilian passengers;
   (f) vessels charged with religious, non-military scientifc or philanthropic missions; vessels collecting scientific data of likely military applications are not protected;
   (g) small coastal fishing vessels and small boats engaged in local coastal trade, but they are subject to the regulations of a belligerent naval commander operating in the area and to inspection;
   (h) vessels designated or adapted exclusively for responding to pollution incidents in the marine environment;
   (i) vessels which have surrendered;
   (j) life rafts and life boats.

Conditions of exemption

48. Vessels listed in paragraph 47 are exempt from attack only if they:
   (a) are innocently employed in their normal role;
   (b) submit to identification and inspection when required; and
   (c) do not intentionally hamper the movement of combatants and obey orders to stop or move out of the way when required.

Loss of exemption

Hospital ships

49. The exemption from attack of a hospital ship may cease only by reason of a breach of a condition of exemption in paragraph 48 and, in such a case, only after due warning has been given naming in all appropriate cases a reason-

able time limit to discharge itself of the cause endangering its exemption, and after such warning has remained unheeded.

50. If after due warning a hospital ship persists in breaking a condition of its exemption, it renders itself liable to capture or other necessary measures to enforce compliance.

51. A hospital ship may only be attacked as a last resort if:
    (a) diversion or capture is not feasible;
    (b) no other method is available for exercising military control;
    (c) the circumstances of non-compliance are sufficiently grave that the hospital ship has become, or may be reasonably assumed to be, a military objective; and
    (d) the collateral casualties or damage will not be disproportionate to the military advantage gained or expected.

All other categories of vessels exempt from attack

52. If any other class of vessel exempt from attack breaches any of the conditions of its exemption in paragraph 48, it may be attacked only if:
    (a) diversion or capture is not feasible;
    (b) no other method is available for exercising military control;
    (c) the circumstances of non-compliance are sufficiently grave that the vessel has become, or may be reasonably assumed to be a military objective; and
    (d) the collateral casualties or damage will not be disproportionate to the military advantage gained or expected.

Classes of aircraft exempt from attack

53. The following classes of enemy aircraft are exempt from attack:
    (a) medical aircraft;
    (b) aircraft granted safe conduct by agreement between the parties to the conflicts; and
    (c) civil airliners.

Conditions of exemption for medical aircraft

54. Medical aircraft are exempt from attack only if they:
    (a) have been recognized as such;
    (b) are acting in compliance with an agreement as specified in paragraph 177;
    (c) fly in areas under the control of own or friendly forces; or
    (d) fly outside the area of armed conflict.

    In other instances, medical aircraft operate at their own risk.

Conditions of exemption for aircraft granted safe conduct

55. Aircraft granted safe conduct are exempt from attack only if they:
    (a) are innocently employed in their agreed role;
    (b) do not intentionally hamper the movements of combatants; and
    (c) comply with the details of the agreement, including availability for inspection.

Conditions of exemption for civil airliners

56. Civil airliners are exempt from attack only if they:
    (a) are innocently employed in their normal role; and
    (b) do not intentionally hamper the movements of combatants.

Loss of exemption

57. If aircraft exempt from attack breach any of the applicable conditions of their exemption as set forth in paragraphs 54–56, they may be attacked only if:
    (a) diversion for landing, visit and search, and possible capture, is not feasible;
    (b) no other method is available for exercising military control;
    (c) the circumstances of non-compliance are sufficiently grave that the aircraft has become, or may be reasonably assumed to be, a military objective; and
    (d) the collateral casualties or damage will not be disproportionate to the military advantage gained or anticipated.
58. In case of doubt whether a vessel or aircraft exempt from attack is being used to make an effective contribution to military action, it shall be presumed not to be so used.

Section IV. Other Enemy Vessels and Aircraft

Enemy merchant vessels

59. Enemy merchant vessels may only be attacked if they meet the definition of a military objective in paragraph 40.
60. The following activities may render enemy merchant vessels military objectives:
    (a) engaging in belligerent acts on behalf of the enemy, e.g., laying mines, minesweeping, cutting undersea cables and pipelines, engaging in visit and search of neutral merchant vessels or attacking other merchant vessels;
    (b) acting as an auxiliary to an enemy's armed forces, e.g., carrying troops or replenishing warships;
    (c) being incorporated into or assisting the enemy's intelligence gathering system, e.g., engaging in reconnaissance, early warning, surveillance, or command, control and communications missions;
    (d) sailing under convoy of enemy warships or military aircraft;
    (e) refusing an order to stop or actively resisting visit, search or capture;
    (f) being armed to an extent that they could inflict damage to a warship; this excludes light individual weapons for the defence of personnel, e.g., against pirates, and purely deflective systems such as chaff; or
    (g) otherwise making an effective contribution to military action, e.g., carrying military materials.
61. Any attacks on these vessels is subject to the basic rules set out in paragraphs 38–46.

Enemy civil aircraft

62. Enemy civil aircraft may only be attacked if they meet the definition of a military objective in paragraph 40.
63. The following activities may render enemy civil aircraft military objectives:
    (a) engaging in acts of war on behalf of the enemy, e.g., laying mines, minesweeping, laying or monitoring acoustic sensors, engaging in electronic warfare, intercepting or attacking other civil aircraft, or providing targeting information to enemy forces;
    (b) acting as an auxiliary aircraft to an enemy's armed forces, e.g., transporting troops or military cargo, or refuelling military aircraft;

(c) being incorporated into or assisting the enemy's intelligence-gathering system, e.g., engaging in reconnaissance, early warning, surveillance, or command, control and communications missions;

(d) flying under the protection of accompanying enemy warships or military aircraft; (e) refusing an order to identify itself, divert from its track, or proceed for visit and search to a belligerent airfield that is safe for the type of aircraft involved and reasonably accessible, or operating fire control equipment that could reasonably be construed to be part of an aircraft weapon system, or on being intercepted clearly manoeuvring to attack the intercepting belligerent military aircraft;

(f) being armed with air-to-air or air-to-surface weapons; or (g) otherwise making an effective contribution to military action.

64. Any attack on these aircraft is subject to the basic rules set out in paragraphs 38-46.

Enemy warships and military aircraft

65. Unless they are exempt from attack under paragraphs 47 or 53, enemy warships and military aircraft and enemy auxiliary vessels and aircraft are military objectives within the meaning of paragraph 40.
66. They may be attacked, subject to the basic rules in paragraphs 38–46.

Section V. Neutral Merchant Vessels and Civil Aircraft

Neutral merchant vessels

67. Merchant vessels flying the flag of neutral States may not be attacked unless they:
    (a) are believed on reasonable grounds to be carrying contraband or breaching a blockade, and after prior warning they intentionally and clearly refuse to stop, or intentionally and clearly resist visit, search or capture;
    (b) engage in belligerent acts on behalf of the enemy;
    (c) act as auxiliaries to the enemy's armed forces;
    (d) are incorporated into or assist the enemy's intelligence system;
    (e) sail under convoy of enemy warships or military aircraft; or
    (f) otherwise make an effective contribution to the enemy's military action, e.g., by carrying military materials, and it is not feasible for the attacking forces to first place passengers and crew in a place of safety. Unless circumstances do not permit, they are to be given a warning, so that they can re-route, off-load, or take other precautions.
68. Any attack on these vessels is subject to the basic rules in paragraphs 38–46.
69. The mere fact that a neutral merchant vessel is armed provides no grounds for attacking it.

Neutral civil aircraft

70. Civil aircraft bearing the marks of neutral States may not be attacked unless they:
    (a) are believed on reasonable grounds to be carrying contraband, and, after prior warning or interception, they intentionally and clearly refuse to divert from their destination, or intentionally and clearly refuse to pro-

ceed for visit and search to a belligerent airfield that is safe for the type of aircraft involved and reasonably accessible;
(b) engage in belligerent acts on behalf of the enemy;
(c) act as auxiliaries to the enemy's armed forces;
(d) are incorporated into or assist the enemy's intelligence system; or
(e) otherwise make an effective contribution to the enemy's military action, e.g., by carrying military materials, and, after prior warning or interception, they intentionally and clearly refuse to divert from their destination, or intentionally and clearly refuse to proceed for visit and search to a belligerent airfield that is safe for the type of aircraft involved and reasonably accessible.

71. Any attack on these aircraft is subject to the basic rules in paragraphs 38–46.

Section VI. Precautions Regarding Civil Aircraft

72. Civil aircraft should avoid areas of potentially hazardous military activity.
73. In the immediate vicinity of naval operations, civil aircraft shall comply with instructions from the belligerents regarding their heading and altitude.
74. Belligerent and neutral States concerned, and authorities providing air traffic services, should establish procedures whereby commanders of warships and military aircraft are aware on a continuous basis of designated routes assigned to or flight plans filed by civil aircraft in the area of military operations, including information on communication channels, identification modes and codes, destination, passengers and cargo.
75. Belligerent and neutral States should ensure that a Notice to Airmen (NOTAM) is issued providing information on military activities in areas potentially hazardous to civil aircraft, including activation of danger areas or temporary airspace restrictions. This NOTAM should include information on:
    (a) frequencies upon which the aircraft should maintain a continuous listening watch;
    (b) continuous operation of civil weather-avoidance radar and identification modes and codes;
    (c) altitude, course and speed restrictions;
    (d) procedures to respond to radio contact by the military forces and to establish two-way communications; and
    (e) possible action by the military forces if the NOTAM is not complied with and the civil aircraft is perceived by those military forces to be a threat.
76. Civil aircraft should file the required flight plan with the cognizant Air Traffic Service, complete with information as to registration, destination, passengers, cargo, emergency communication channels, identification modes and codes, updates en route and carry certificates as to registration, airworthiness, passengers and cargo. They should not deviate from a designated Air Traffic Service route or flight plan without Air Traffic Control clearance unless unforeseen conditions arise, e.g., safety or distress, in which case appropriate notification should be made immediately.
77. If a civil aircraft enters an area of potentially hazardous military activity, it should comply with relevant NOTAMs. Military forces should use all available means to identify and warn the civil aircraft, by using, inter alia, secondary surveillance radar modes and codes, communications, correlation with flight plan information, interception by military aircraft, and, when possible, contacting the appropriate Air Traffic Control facility.

PART IV. METHODS AND MEANS OF WARFARE AT SEA

Section I. Means of Warfare

Missiles and other projectiles

78. Missiles and projectiles, including those with over-the-horizon capabilities, shall be used in conformity with the principles of target discrimination as set out in paragraphs 38–46.

Torpedoes

79. It is prohibited to use torpedoes which do not sink or otherwise become harmless when they have completed their run.

Mines

80. Mines may only be used for legitimate military purposes including the denial of sea areas to the enemy.
81. Without prejudice to the rules set out in paragraph 82, the parties to the conflict shall not lay mines unless effective neutralization occurs when they have become detached or control over them is otherwise lost.
82. It is forbidden to use free-floating mines unless:
    (a) they are directed against a military objective; and
    (b) they become harmless within an hour after loss of control over them.
83. The laying of armed mines or the arming of pre-laid mines must be notified unless the mines can only detonate against vessels which are military objectives.
84. Belligerents shall record the locations where they have laid mines.
85. Mining operations in the internal waters, territorial sea or archipelagic waters of a belligerent State should provide, when the mining is first executed, for free exit of shipping of neutral States.
86. Mining of neutral waters by a belligerent is prohibited.
87. Mining shall not have the practical effect of preventing passage between neutral waters and international waters.
88. The minelaying States shall pay due regard to the legitimate uses of the high seas by, inter alia, providing safe alternative routes for shipping of neutral States.
89. Transit passage through international straits and passage through waters subject to the right of archipelagic sea lanes passage shall not be impeded unless safe and convenient alternative routes are provided.
90. After the cessation of active hostilities, parties to the conflict shall do their utmost to remove or render harmless the mines they have laid, each party removing its own mines. With regard to mines laid in the territorial seas of the enemy, each party shall notify their position and shall proceed with the least possible delay to remove the mines in its territorial sea or otherwise render the territorial sea safe for navigation.
91. In addition to their obligations under paragraph 90, parties to the conflict shall endeavour to reach agreement, both among themselves and, where appropriate, with other States and with international organizations, on the provision of information and technical and material assistance, including in appropriate circumstances joint operations, necessary to remove minefields or otherwise render them harmless.

92. Neutral States do not commit an act inconsistent with the laws of neutrality by clearing mines laid in violation of international law.

Section II. Methods of Warfare

Blockade

93. A blockade shall be declared and notified to all belligerents and neutral States.
94. The declaration shall specify the commencement, duration, location, and extent of the blockade and the period within which vessels of neutral States may leave the blockaded coastline.
95. A blockade must be effective. The question whether a blockade is effective is a question of fact.
96. The force maintaining the blockade may be stationed at a distance determined by military requirements.
97. A blockade may be enforced and maintained by a combination of legitimate methods and means of warfare provided this combination does not result in acts inconsistent with the rules set out in this document.
98. Merchant vessels believed on reasonable grounds to be breaching a blockade may be captured. Merchant vessels which, after prior warning, clearly resist capture may be attacked.
99. A blockade must not bar access to the ports and coasts of neutral States.
100. A blockade must be applied impartially to the vessels of all States.
101. The cessation, temporary lifting, re-establishment, extension or other alteration of a blockade must be declared and notified as in paragraphs 93 and 94.
102. The declaration or establishment of a blockade is prohibited if:
    (a) it has the sole purpose of starving the civilian population or denying it other objects essential for its survival; or
    (b) the damage to the civilian population is, or may be expected to be, excessive in relation to the concrete and direct military advantage anticipated from the blockade.
103. If the civilian population of the blockaded territory is inadequately provided with food and other objects essential for its survival, the blockading party must provide for free passage of such foodstuffs and other essential supplies, subject to:
    (a) the right to prescribe the technical arrangements, including search, under which such passage is permitted; and
    (b) the condition that the distribution of such supplies shall be made under the local supervision of a Protecting Power or a humanitarian organization which offers guarantees of impartiality, such as the International Committee of the Red Cross.
104. The blockading belligerent shall allow the passage of medical supplies for the civilian population or for the wounded and sick members of armed forces, subject to the right to prescribe technical arrangements, including search, under which such passage is permitted.

Zones

105. A belligerent cannot be absolved of its duties under international humanitarian law by establishing zones which might adversely affect the legitimate uses of defined areas of the sea.

106. Should a belligerent, as an exceptional measure, establish such a zone:
   (a) the same body of law applies both inside and outside the zone;
   (b) the extent, location and duration of the zone and the measures imposed shall not exceed what is strictly required by military necessity and the principles of proportionality;
   (c) due regard shall be given to the rights of neutral States to legitimate uses of the seas;
   (d) necessary safe passage through the zone for neutral vessels and aircraft shall be provided:
      (i) where the geographical extent of the zone significantly impedes free and safe access to the ports and coasts of a neutral State;
      (ii) in other cases where normal navigation routes are affected, except where military requirements do not permit; and
   (e) the commencement, duration, location and extent of the zone, as well as the restrictions imposed, shall be publicly declared and appropriately notified.

107. Compliance with the measures taken by one belligerent in the zone shall not be construed as an act harmful to the opposing belligerent.

108. Nothing in this Section should be deemed to derogate from the customary belligerent right to control neutral vessels and aircraft in the immediate vicinity of naval operations.

Section III. Deception, Ruses of War and Perfidy

109. Military and auxiliary aircraft are prohibited at all times from feigning exempt, civilian or neutral status.

110. Ruses of war are permitted. Warships and auxiliary vessels, however, are prohibited from launching an attack whilst flying a false flag, and at all times from actively simulating the status of:
   (a) hospital ships, small coastal rescue craft or medical transports;
   (b) vessels on humanitarian missions;
   (c) passenger vessels carrying civilian passengers;
   (d) vessels protected by the United Nations flag;
   (e) vessels guaranteed safe conduct by prior agreement between the parties, including cartel vessels;
   (f) vessels entitled to be identified by the emblem of the red cross or red crescent; or
   (g) vessels engaged in transporting cultural property under special protection.

111. Perfidy is prohibited. Acts inviting the confidence of an adversary to lead it to believe that it is entitled to, or is obliged to accord, protection under the rules of international law applicable in armed conflict, with intent to betray that confidence, constitute perfidy. Perfidious acts include the launching of an attack while feigning:
   (a) exempt, civilian, neutral or protected United Nations status;
   (b) surrender or distress by, e.g., sending a distress signal or by the crew taking to life rafts.

PART V. MEASURES SHORT OF ATTACK: INTERCEPTION, VISIT, SEARCH, DIVERSION AND CAPTURE

Section I. Determination of Enemy Character of Vessels and Aircraft

112. The fact that a merchant vessel is flying the flag of an enemy State or that a civil aircraft bears the marks of an enemy State is conclusive evidence of its enemy character.
113. The fact that a merchant vessel is flying the flag of a neutral State or a civil aircraft bears the marks of a neutral State is prima facie evidence of its neutral character.
114. If the commander of a warship suspects that a merchant vessel flying a neutral flag in fact has enemy character, the commander is entitled to exercise the right of visit and search, including the right of diversion for search under paragraph 121.
115. If the commander of a military aircraft suspects that a civil aircraft with neutral marks in fact has enemy character, the commander is entitled to exercise the right of interception and, if circumstances require, the right to divert for the purpose of visit and search.
116. If, after visit and search, there is reasonable ground for suspicion that the merchant vessel flying a neutral flag or a civil aircraft with neutral marks has enemy character, the vessel or aircraft may be captured as prize subject to adjudication.
117. Enemy character can be determined by registration, ownership, charter or other criteria.

Section II. Visit and Search of Merchant Vessels

Basic rules

118. In exercising their legal rights in an international armed conflict at sea, belligerent warships and military aircraft have a right to visit and search merchant vessels outside neutral waters where there are reasonable grounds for suspecting that they are subject to capture.
119. As an alternative to visit and search, a neutral merchant vessel may, with its consent, be diverted from its declared destination.

Merchant vessels under convoy of accompanying neutral warships

120. A neutral merchant vessel is exempt from the exercise of the right of visit and search if it meets the following conditions:
    (a) it is bound for a neutral port;
    (b) it is under the convoy of an accompanying neutral warship of the same nationality or a neutral warship of a State with which the flag State of the merchant vessel has concluded an agreement providing for such convoy;
    (c) the flag State of the neutral warship warrants that the neutral merchant vessel is not carrying contraband or otherwise engaged in activities inconsistent with its neutral status; and
    (d) the commander of the neutral warship provides, if requested by the commander of an intercepting belligerent warship or military aircraft,

all information as to the character of the merchant vessel and its cargo as could otherwise be obtained by visit and search.

Diversion for the purpose of visit and search

121. If visit and search at sea is impossible or unsafe, a belligerent warship or military aircraft may divert a merchant vessel to an appropriate area or port in order to exercise the right of visit and search.

Measures of supervision

122. In order to avoid the necessity of visit and search, belligerent States may establish reasonable measures for the inspection of cargo of neutral merchant vessels and certification that a vessel is not carrying contraband.
123. The fact that a neutral merchant vessel has submitted to such measures of supervision as the inspection of its cargo and grant of certificates of non-contraband cargo by one belligerent is not an act of unneutral service with regard to an opposing belligerent.
124. In order to obviate the necessity for visit and search, neutral States are encouraged to enforce reasonable control measures and certification procedures to ensure that their merchant vessels are not carrying contraband.

Section III. Interception, Visit and Search of Civil Aircraft

Basic rules

125. In exercising their legal rights in an international armed conflict at sea, belligerent military aircraft have a right to intercept civil aircraft outside neutral airspace where there are reasonable grounds for suspecting they are subject to capture. If, after interception, reasonable grounds for suspecting that a civil aircraft is subject to capture still exist, belligerent military aircraft have the right to order the civil aircraft to proceed for visit and search to a belligerent airfield that is safe for the type of aircraft involved and reasonably accessible.

If there is no belligerent airfield that is safe and reasonably accessible for visit and search, a civil aircraft may be diverted from its declared destination.
126. As an alternative to visit and search:
(a) an enemy civil aircraft may be diverted from its declared destination;
(b) a neutral civil aircraft may be diverted from its declared destination with its consent.

Civil aircraft under the operational control of an accompanying neutral military aircraft or warship

127. A neutral civil aircraft is exempt from the exercise of the right of visit and search if it meets the following conditions:
(a) it is bound for a neutral airfield;
(b) it is under the operational control of an accompanying:
(i) neutral military aircraft or warship of the same nationality; or

(ii) neutral military aircraft or warship of a State with which the flag State of the civil aircraft has concluded an agreement providing for such control;

(c) the flag State of the neutral military aircraft or warship warrants that the neutral civil aircraft is not carrying contraband or otherwise engaged in activities inconsistent with its neutral status; and

(d) the commander of the neutral military aircraft or warship provides, if requested by the commander of an intercepting belligerent military aircraft, all information as to the character of the civil aircraft and its cargo as could otherwise be obtained by visit and search.

Measures of interception and supervision

128. Belligerent States should promulgate and adhere to safe procedures for intercepting civil aircraft as issued by the competent international organization.

129. Civil aircraft should file the required flight plan with the cognizant Air Traffic Service, complete with information as to registration, destination, passengers, cargo, emergency communication channels, identification modes and codes, updates en route and carry certificates as to registration, airworthiness, passengers and cargo. They should not deviate from a designated Air Traffic Service route or flight plan without Air Traffic Control clearance unless unforeseen conditions arise, e.g., safety or distress, in which case appropriate notification should be made immediately.

130. Belligerents and neutrals concerned, and authorities providing air traffic services, should establish procedures whereby commanders of warships and military aircraft are continuously aware of designated routes assigned to and flight plans filed by civil aircraft in the area of military operations, including information on communication channels, identification modes and codes, destination, passengers and cargo.

131. In the immediate vicinity of naval operations, civil aircraft shall comply with instructions from the combatants regarding their heading and altitude.

132. In order to avoid the necessity of visit and search, belligerent States may establish reasonable measures for the inspection of the cargo of neutral civil aircraft and certification that an aircraft is not carrying contraband.

133. The fact that a neutral civil aircraft has submitted to such measures of supervision as the inspection of its cargo and grant of certificates of non-contraband cargo by one belligerent is not an act of unneutral service with regard to an opposing belligerent.

134. In order to obviate the necessity for visit and search, neutral States are encouraged to enforce reasonable control measures and certification procedures to ensure that their civil aircraft are not carrying contraband.

Section IV. Capture of Enemy Vessels and Goods

135. Subject to the provisions of paragraph 136, enemy vessels, whether merchant or otherwise, and goods on board such vessels may be captured outside neutral waters. Prior exercise of visit and search is not required.

136. The following vessels are exempt from capture:

(a) hospital ships and small craft used for coastal rescue operations;

(b) other medical transports, so long as they are needed for the wounded, sick and shipwrecked on board;
(c) vessels granted safe conduct by agreement between the belligerent parties including:
  (i) cartel vessels, e.g., vessels designated for and engaged in the transport of prisoners of war; and
  (ii) vessels engaged in humanitarian missions, including vessels carrying supplies indispensable to the survival of the civilian population, and vessels engaged in relief actions and rescue operations;
(d) vessels engaged in transporting cultural property under special protection;
(e) vessels charged with religious, non-military scientific or philanthropic missions; vessels collecting scientific data of likely military applications are not protected;
(f) small coastal fishing vessels and small boats engaged in local coastal trade, but they are subject to the regulations of a belligerent naval commander operating in the area and to inspection, and
(g) vessels designed or adapted exclusively for responding to pollution incidents in the marine environment when actually engaged in such activities.

137. Vessels listed in paragraph 136 are exempt from capture only if they:
(a) are innocently employed in their normal role;
(b) do not commit acts harmful to the enemy;
(c) immediately submit to identification and inspection when required; and
(d) do not intentionally hamper the movement of combatants and obey orders to stop or move out of the way when required.

138. Capture of a merchant vessel is exercised by taking such vessel as prize for adjudication. If military circumstances preclude taking such a vessel as prize at sea, it may be diverted to an appropriate area or port in order to complete capture. As an alternative to capture, an enemy merchant vessel may be diverted from its declared destination.

139. Subject to paragraph 140, a captured enemy merchant vessel may, as an exceptional measure, be destroyed when military circumstances preclude taking or sending such a vessel for adjudication as an enemy prize, only if the following criteria are met beforehand:
(a) the safety of passengers and crew is provided for; for this purpose, the ship's boats are not regarded as a place of safety unless the safety of the passengers and crew is assured in the prevailing sea and weather conditions by the proximity of land or the presence of another vessel which is in a position to take them on board;
(b) documents and papers relating to the prize are safeguarded; and
(c) if feasible, personal effects of the passengers and crew are saved.

140. The destruction of enemy passenger vessels carrying only civilian passengers is prohibited at sea. For the safety of the passengers, such vessels shall be diverted to an appropriate area or port in order to complete capture.

Section V. Capture of Enemy Civil Aircraft and Goods

141. Subject to the provisions of paragraph 142, enemy civil aircraft and goods on board such aircraft may be captured outside neutral airspace. Prior exercise of visit and search is not required.

142. The following aircraft are exempt from capture:
   (a) medical aircraft; and
   (b) aircraft granted safe conduct by agreement between the parties to the conflict.
143. Aircraft listed in paragraph 142 are exempt from capture only if they:
   (a) are innocently employed in their normal role;
   (b) do not commit acts harmful to the enemy;
   (c) immediately submit to interception and identification when required;
   (d) do not intentionally hamper the movement of combatants and obey orders to divert from their track when required; and
   (e) are not in breach of a prior agreement.
144. Capture is exercised by intercepting the enemy civil aircraft, ordering it to proceed to a belligerent airfield that is safe for the type of aircraft involved and reasonably accessible and, on landing, taking the aircraft as a prize for adjudication. As an alternative to capture, an enemy civil aircraft may be diverted from its declared destination.
145. If capture is exercised, the safety of passengers and crew and their personal effects must be provided for. The documents and papers relating to the prize must be safeguarded.

Section VI. Capture of Neutral Merchant Vessels and Goods

146. Neutral merchant vessels are subject to capture outside neutral waters if they are engaged in any of the activities referred to in paragraph 67 or if it is determined as a result of visit and search or by other means, that they:
   (a) are carrying contraband;
   (b) are on a voyage especially undertaken with a view to the transport of individual passengers who are embodied in the armed forces of the enemy;
   (c) are operating directly under enemy control, orders, charter, employment or direction;
   (d) present irregular or fraudulent documents, lack necessary documents, or destroy, deface or conceal documents;
   (e) are violating regulations established by a belligerent within the immediate area of naval operations; or
   (f) are breaching or attempting to breach a blockade.

   Capture of a neutral merchant vessel is exercised by taking such vessel as prize for adjudication.

147. Goods on board neutral merchant vessels are subject to capture only if they are contraband.
148. Contraband is defined as goods which are ultimately destined for territory under the control of the enemy and which may be susceptible for use in armed conflict.
149. In order to exercise the right of capture referred to in paragraphs 146(a) and 147, the belligerent must have published contraband lists. The precise nature of a belligerent's contraband list may vary according to the particular circumstances of the armed conflict. Contraband lists shall be reasonably specific.
150. Goods not on the belligerent's contraband list are "free goods", that is, not subject to capture. As a minimum, "free goods" shall include the following:
   (a) religious objects;

(b) articles intended exclusively for the treatment of the wounded and sick and for the prevention of disease;
(c) clothing, bedding, essential foodstuffs, and means of shelter for the civilian population in general, and women and children in particular, provided there is not serious reason to believe that such goods will be diverted to other purpose, or that a definite military advantage would accrue to the enemy by their substitution for enemy goods that would thereby become available for military purposes;
(d) items destined for prisoners of war, including individual parcels and collective relief shipments containing food, clothing, educational, cultural, and recreational articles;
(e) goods otherwise specifically exempted from capture by international treaty or by special arrangement between belligerents; and
(f) other goods not susceptible for use in armed conflict,

151. Subject to paragraph 152, a neutral vessel captured in accordance with paragraph 146 may, as an exceptional measure, be destroyed when military circumstances preclude taking or sending such a vessel for adjudication as an enemy prize, only if the following criteria are met beforehand:
(a) the safety of passengers and crew is provided for; for this purpose the ship's boats are not regarded as a place of safety unless the safety of the passengers and crew is assured in the prevailing sea and weather conditions, by the proximity of land, or the presence of another vessel which is in a position to take them on board;
(b) documents and papers relating to the captured vessel are safeguarded; and
(c) if feasible, personal effects of the passengers and crew are saved.

Every effort should be made to avoid destruction of a captured neutral vessel. Therefore, such destruction shall not be ordered without there being entire satisfaction that the captured vessel can neither be sent into a belligerent port, nor diverted, nor properly released. A vessel may not be destroyed under this paragraph for carrying contraband unless the contraband, reckoned either by value, weight, volume or freight, forms more than half the cargo. Destruction shall be subject to adjudication.

152. The destruction of captured neutral passenger vessels carrying civilian passengers is prohibited at sea. For the safety of the passengers, such vessels shall be diverted to an appropriate port in order to complete capture provided for in paragraph 146.

Section VII. Capture of Neutral Civil Aircraft and Goods

153. Neutral civil aircraft are subject to capture outside neutral airspace if they are engaged in any of the activities in paragraph 70 or if it is determined as a result of visit and search or by any other means, that they:
(a) are carrying contraband;
(b) are on a flight especially undertaken with a view to the transport of individual passengers who are embodied in the armed forces of the enemy;
(c) are operating directly under enemy control, orders, charter, employment or direction;
(d) present irregular or fraudulent documents, lack necessary documents, or destroy, deface or conceal documents;
(e) are violating regulations established by a belligerent within the immediate area of naval operations; or

(f) are engaged in a breach of blockade.

154. Goods on board neutral civil aircraft are subject to capture only if they are contraband.

155. The rules regarding contraband as prescribed in paragraphs 148–150 shall also apply to goods on board neutral civil aircraft.

156. Capture is exercised by intercepting the neutral civil aircraft, ordering it to proceed to a belligerent airfield that is safe for the type of aircraft involved and reasonably accessible and, on landing and after visit and search, taking it as prize for adjudication. If there is no belligerent airfield that is safe and reasonably accessible, a neutral civil aircraft may be diverted from its declared destination.

157. As an alternative to capture, a neutral civil aircraft may, with its consent, be diverted from its declared destination.

158. If capture is exercised, the safety of passengers and crew and their personal effects must be provided for. The documents and papers relating to the prize must be safeguarded.

PART VI. PROTECTED PERSONS, MEDICAL TRANSPORTS AND MEDICAL AIRCRAFT

General Rules

159. Except as provided for in paragraph 171, the provisions of this Part are not to be construed as in any way departing from the provisions of the Second Geneva Convention of 1949 and Additional Protocol I of 1977 which contain detailed rules for the treatment of the wounded, sick and shipwrecked and for medical transports.

160. The parties to the conflict may agree, for humanitarian purposes, to create a zone in a defined area of the sea in which only activities consistent with those humanitarian purposes are permitted.

Section I. Protected Persons

161. Persons on board vessels and aircraft having fallen into the power of a belligerent or neutral shall be respected and protected. While at sea and thereafter until determination of their status, they shall be subject to the jurisdiction of the State exercising power over them.

162. Members of the crews of hospital ships may not be captured during the time they are in the service of these vessels. Members of the crews of rescue craft may not be captured while engaging in rescue operations.

163. Persons on board other vessels or aircraft exempt from capture listed in paragraphs 136 and 142 may not be captured.

164. Religious and medical personnel assigned to the spiritual and medical care of the wounded, sick and shipwrecked shall not be considered prisoners of war. They may, however, be retained as long as their services for the medical or spiritual needs of prisoners of war are needed.

165. Nationals of an enemy State, other than those specified in paragraphs 162-164, are entitled to prisoner-of-war status and may be made prisoners of war if they are:

(a) members of the enemy's armed forces;

(b) persons accompanying the enemy's armed forces;
(c) crew members of auxiliary vessels or auxiliary aircraft;
(d) crew members of enemy merchant vessels or civil aircraft not exempt from capture, unless they benefit from more favourable treatment under other provisions of international law; or
(e) crew members of neutral merchant vessels or civil aircraft that have taken a direct part in the hostilities on the side of the enemy, or served as an auxiliary for the enemy.

166. Nationals of a neutral State:
(a) who are passengers on board enemy or neutral vessels or aircraft are to be released and may not be made prisoners of war unless they are members of the enemy's armed forces or have personally committed acts of hostility against the captor;
(b) who are members of the crew of enemy warships or auxiliary vessels or military aircraft or auxiliary aircraft are entitled to prisoner-of-war status and may be made prisoners of war;
(c) who are members of the crew of enemy or neutral merchant vessels or civil aircraft are to be released and may not be made prisoners of war unless the vessel or aircraft has committed an act covered by paragraphs 60, 63, 67 or 70, or the member of the crew has personally committed an act of hostility against the captor.

167. Civilian persons other than those specified in paragraphs 162–166 are to be treated in accordance with the Fourth Geneva Convention of 1949.

168. Persons having fallen into the power of a neutral State are to be treated in accordance with Hague Conventions V and Xlll of 1907 and the Second Geneva Convention of 1949.

Section II. Medical Transports

169. In order to provide maximum protection for hospital ships from the moment of the outbreak of hostilities, States may beforehand make general notification of the characteristics of their hospital ships as specified in Article 22 of the Second Geneva Convention of 1949. Such notification should include all available information on the means whereby the ship may be identified.

170. Hospital ships may be equipped with purely deflective means of defence, such as chaff and flares. The presence of such equipment should be notified.

171. In order to fulfil most effectively their humanitarian mission, hospital ships should be permitted to use cryptographic equipment. The equipment shall not be used in any circumstances to transmit intelligence data nor in any other way to acquire any military advantage.

172. Hospital ships, small craft used for coastal rescue operations and other medical transports are encouraged to implement the means of identification set out in Annex I of Additional Protocol I of 1977.

173. These means of identification are intended only to facilitate identification and do not, of themselves, confer protected status.

Section III. Medical Aircraft

174. Medical aircraft shall be protected and respected as specified in the provisions of this document.

175. Medical aircraft shall be clearly marked with the emblem of the red cross or red crescent, together with their national colours, on their lower, upper and lateral surfaces. Medical aircraft are encouraged to implement the other means of identification set out in Annex I of Additional Protocol I of 1977 at all times. Aircraft chartered by the International Committee of the Red Cross may use the same means of identification as medical aircraft. Temporary medical aircraft which cannot, either for lack of time or because of their characteristics, be marked with the distinctive emblem should use the most effective means of identification available.

176. Means of identification are intended only to facilitate identification and do not, of themselves, confer protected status.

177. Parties to the conflict are encouraged to notify medical flights and conclude agreements at all times, especially in areas where control by any party to the conflict is not clearly established. When such an agreement is concluded, it shall specify the altitudes, times and routes for safe operation and should include means of identification and communications.

178. Medical aircraft shall not be used to commit acts harmful to the enemy. They shall not carry any equipment intended for the collection or transmission of intelligence data. They shall not be armed, except for small arms for self-defence, and shall only carry medical personnel and equipment.

179. Other aircraft, military or civilian, belligerent or neutral, that are employed in the search for, rescue or transport of the wounded, sick and shipwrecked, operate at their own risk, unless pursuant to prior agreement between the parties to the conflict.

180. Medical aircraft flying over areas which are physically controlled by the opposing belligerent, or over areas the physical control of which is not clearly established, may be ordered to land to permit inspection. Medical aircraft shall obey any such order.

181. Belligerent medical aircraft shall not enter neutral airspace except by prior agreement. When within neutral airspace pursuant to agreement, medical aircraft shall comply with the terms of the agreement. The terms of the agreement may require the aircraft to land for inspection at a designated airport within the neutral State. Should the agreement so require, the inspection and follow-on action shall be conducted in accordance with paragraphs 182–183.

182. Should a medical aircraft, in the absence of an agreement or in deviation from the terms of an agreement, enter neutral airspace, either through navigational error or because of an emergency affecting the safety of the flight, it shall make every effort to give notice and to identify itself. Once the aircraft is recognized as a medical aircraft by the neutral State, it shall not be attacked but may be required to land for inspection. Once it has been inspected, and if it is determined in fact to be a medical aircraft, it shall be allowed to resume its flight.

183. If the inspection reveals that the aircraft is not a medical aircraft, it may be captured, and the occupants shall, unless agreed otherwise between the neutral State and the parties to the conflict, be detained in the neutral State where so required by the rules of international law applicable in armed conflict, in such a manner that they cannot again take part in the hostilities.

* * *

See also Nos. 40, 41, 43, 50, 113–115

IX

CIVIL WAR

No. 90

CONVENTION ON DUTIES AND RIGHTS OF STATES IN THE EVENT OF CIVIL STRIFE

Signed at Havana, 20 February 1928

INTRODUCTORY NOTE: The present Convention and the Protocol of 1957 (*No. 91*) were concluded between American states only. Their main objective is to prevent foreign states from supporting insurgents. Their provisions partly conform to generally recognized rules of international law, and partly go further and rest upon concepts and circumstances peculiar to American states. The question of the applicability of the law of armed conflicts is not dealt with in them.

The present Convention was adopted at the Sixth Pan-American Conference at Havana.

ENTRY INTO FORCE: 21 May 1929.

AUTHENTIC TEXTS: English, French, Portuguese, Spanish. The text below is reprinted from *LNTS*, Vol. 134, 1932, pp. 45–46.

TEXT PUBLISHED IN: *Sixth International Conference of American States, Final Act, Motions, Agreements, Resolutions and Conventions,* Habana, Imprenta y Papeleria de Rambala, Bouza y Ca., 1928, pp. 171–174 (Engl.); *Sixième Conférence Internationale Américaine, Acte Final, Motions, Décisions, Résolutions et Conventions*, Habana, Imprente y Papeleria de Rambala, Bouza y Ca., 1928, pp. 170–174 (French); *Sexta Conferencia Internacional Americana, Acta Final, Mociones, Acuerdos, Resolucinoes y Convenciones,* Habana, Imprenta y Papeleria de Rambala, Bouza y Ca., 1928, pp. 168–172 (Span.); *OAS, Série sur les Traités*, No. 7 (Engl., French, Portuguese, Span.); *LNTS*, Vol. 134, 1932, pp. 45–46, No. 3082 (Engl., French); *The International Conferences of American States 1889-1928*, New York, Oxford University Press, 1931, pp. 435–436 (Engl.); *Conferencias Internacionales Americanas 1889–1936*; Washington, Dotacion Carnegie para la Paz Internacional, 1938, pp. 388–389 (Span.); Hudson, Vol. IV, pp. 2416–2419 (Engl., French); *Droit des conflits armés*, pp. 1247–1250 (French); *BFSP*, Vol. 128, 1928, pp. 514–515 (Engl.); *US Statutes at Large*, Vol. 46, pp. 2749–2752 (Engl.); Malloy, Vol. IV, pp. 4725–4729 (Engl.); Bevans, Vol. II, pp. 694–697 (Engl.); *AJIL*, Vol. 22, 1928, Supplement, pp. 159–161 (Engl.).

* * *

The Governments of the Republics represented at the Sixth International Conference of American States, held in the city of Havana, Republic of Cuba, in the year 1928, desirous of reaching an agreement as to the duties and rights of States in the event of civil strife, have appointed the following Plenipotentiaries:

[Here follow the names of plenipotentiaries]

Who, after exchanging their respective full powers, which were found to be in good and due form, have agreed upon the following:

Article 1. The Contracting States bind themselves to observe the following rules with regard to civil strife in another one of them:

First: To use all means at their disposal to prevent the inhabitants of their territory, nationals or aliens, from participating in, gathering elements, crossing the boundary or sailing from their territory for the purpose of starting or promoting civil strife.

Second: To disarm and intern every rebel force crossing their boundaries, the expenses of internment to be borne by the State where public order may have been disturbed. The arms found in the hands of the rebels may be seized and withdrawn by the Government of the country granting asylum, to be returned, once the struggle has ended, to the State in civil strife.

Third: To forbid the traffic in arms and war material, except when intended for the Government, while the belligerency of the rebels has not been recognized, in which latter case the rules of neutrality shall be applied.

Fourth: To prevent that within their jurisdiction there be equipped, armed or adapted for warlike purposes any vessel intended to operate in favour of the rebellion.

Art. 2. The declaration of piracy against vessels which have risen in arms, emanating from a Government, is not binding upon the other States.

The State that may be injured by depredations originating from insurgent vessels is entitled to adopt the following punitive measures against them: Should the authors of the damages be warships, it may capture and return them to the Government of the State to which they belong, for their trial; should the damage originate with merchantmen, the injured State may capture and subject them to the appropriate penal laws.

The insurgent vessel, whether a warship or a merchantman, which flies the flag of a foreign country to shield its actions, may also be captured and tried by the State of said flag.

Art. 3. The insurgent vessel, whether a warship or a merchantman, equipped by the rebels, which arrives at a foreign country or seeks refuge therein, shall be delivered by the Government of the latter to the constituted Government of the State in civil strife, and the members of the crew shall be considered as political refugees.

Art. 4. The present Convention does not affect obligations previously undertaken by the Contracting Parties through international agreements.

Art. 5. After being signed, the present Convention shall be submitted to the ratification of the Signatory States. The Government of Cuba is charged with transmitting authentic certified copies to the Governments for the aforementioned purpose of ratification. The instrument of ratification shall be deposited in the archives of the Pan American Union in Washington, the Union to notify the signatory Governments of said deposit. Such notification shall be considered as an exchange of ratifications. This Convention shall remain open to the adherence of non-Signatory States.

In witness whereof the aforenamed Plenipotentiaries sign the present Convention in Spanish, English, French and Portuguese, in the city of Havana, the twentieth day of February 1928.

[Here follow signatures]

SIGNATURES AND RATIFICATIONS[1]

State	*Signature*[2]	*Ratification, Accession*
Argentina	20 February 1928	24 October 1957
Bolivia	20 February 1928	18 October 1950
Brazil	20 February 1928	29 August 1929
Chile	20 February 1928	–
Colombia	20 February 1928	30 September 1932
Costa Rica	20 February 1928	7 June 1933
Cuba	20 February 1928	18 July 1934
Dominican Republic	20 February 1928	8 April 1932
Ecuador	20 February 1928	4 September 1936
El Salvador	20 February 1928	9 January 1937
Guatemala	20 February 1928	–
Haiti	20 February 1928	9 March 1933
Honduras	20 February 1928	16 April 1945
Mexico	20 February 1928	6 February 1929
Nicaragua	20 February 1928	20 March 1930
Panama	20 February 1928	21 May 1929
Paraguay	20 February 1928	18 April 1950
Peru	20 February 1928	21 June 1945
United States of America	20 February 1928	21 May 1930 *Res.*
Uruguay	20 February 1928	16 September 1933
Venezuela	20 February 1928	–

RESERVATION

UNITED STATES OF AMERICA (*reservation made on ratification*)
Subject to the understanding that the provisions of Article 3 of the Convention shall not apply where a state of belligerency has been recognized.

[1] Based on a communication from the Organization of American States of 3 December 2001.
[2] The Convention was not signed separately, but the text incorporated in the Final Act of the Sixth International Conference of American States, the Spanish text of which was signed on behalf of the states represented at the Conference.

No. 91

PROTOCOL TO THE CONVENTION ON DUTIES AND RIGHTS OF STATES IN THE EVENT OF CIVIL STRIFE

Opened for signature at the Pan American Union on 1 May 1957

INTRODUCTORY NOTE: In 1950 the Council of the Organization of American States considered a report of the Investigating Committee previously appointed by that body to investigate the facts and antecedents of certain situations in which allegations concerning the fomenting of civil strife in the Caribbean area had been made. As a result of the Committee's recommendations, the Council approved a resolution calling for the strengthening of the Havana Convention of 1928. The study of the subject and drafting of a protocol extended over a period of several years. The final draft of the Protocol was approved by the Council on 20 February 1957, and the protocol was opened for signature by the American States, as from 1 May 1957.

ENTRY INTO FORCE: 9 December 1957.

AUTHENTIC TEXTS: English, French, Portuguese, Spanish. The text below is reprinted from the *Protocol to the Convention on Duties and Rights of States in the Event of Civil Strife*, Pan American Union, Washington 1959.

TEXT PUBLISHED IN: *UNTS*, Vol. 284, pp. 201–214 (Engl., French, Span., Portuguese); *Protocol to the Convention on Duties and Rights of States in the Event of Civil Strife*, Pan American Union, Washington 1959 (Engl., French, Span., Portuguese); *OAS*, *Treaty Series*, No. 7, 1959 (Engl., French, Portuguese, Span.); *Droit des conflits armés*, pp. 1251–1253 (French); OAS website: www oas/org/juridico/english/treaties (Engl.).

* * *

The High Contracting Parties, desirous of clarifying, supplementing, and strengthening the principles and rules stipulated in the Convention on Duties and Rights of States in the Event of Civil Strife, signed at Havana on 20 February 1928,

Have resolved, in order to carry out those purposes, to conclude the following Protocol:

Article 1. Each Contracting State shall, in areas subject to its jurisdiction:

(a) Keep under surveillance the traffic in arms and war material that it has reason to believe is intended for starting, promoting, or supporting civil strife in another American State;

(b) Suspend the exportation or importation of any shipment of arms and war material during the period of its investigation of the circumstances relating to the shipment, when it has reason to believe that such arms and war material may be intended for starting, promoting, or supporting civil strife in another American State; and

(c) Prohibit the exportation or importation of any shipment of arms and war material intended for starting, promoting, or supporting civil strife in another American State.

Art. 2. The provisions of Article 1 shall cease to be applicable for a Contracting State only when it has recognized the belligerency of the rebels, in which event the rules of neutrality shall be applied.

Art. 3. The term "traffic in arms and war material", which appears in the third paragraph of Article 1 of the Convention on Duties and Rights of States in the Event of Civil Strife as well as in this Protocol, includes land vehicles, vessels, and aircraft of all types, whether civil or military.

Art. 4. The provisions of the Convention on Duties and Rights of States in the Event of Civil Strife with respect to "vessels" are equally applicable to aircraft of all types, whether civil or military.

Art. 5. Each Contracting State shall, in areas subject to its jurisdiction and within the powers granted by its Constitution, use all appropriate means to prevent any person, national or alien, from deliberately participating in the preparation, organization, or carrying out of a military enterprise that has as its purpose the starting, promoting or supporting of civil strife in another Contracting State, whether or not the government of the latter has been recognized.

For the purposes of this Article, participation in the preparation, organization, or carrying out of a military enterprise includes, among other acts:

(a) The contribution, supply or provision of arms and war material;
(b) The equipment, training, collection, or transportation of members of a military expedition; or
(c) The provision or receipt of money, by any method, intended for the military enterprise.

Art. 6. The present Protocol does not affect obligations previously undertaken by the Contracting States through international agreements.

Art. 7. This Protocol shall remain open in the Pan American Union for signature by the American States, and shall be ratified in conformity with their respective constitutional procedures.

Art. 8. This Protocol may be ratified only by the States that have ratified or ratify the Convention on the Duties and Rights of States in the Event of Civil Strife. This Protocol shall enter into force between the States that ratify it, in the order in which they deposit their respective instruments of ratification.

Art. 9. The original instrument of this Protocol, the English, French, Portuguese, and Spanish texts of which are equally authentic, shall be deposited with the Pan American Union, which shall transmit certified copies thereof to the Governments for purposes of ratification. The instruments of ratification shall be deposited with the Pan American Union, which shall notify the Signatory States of such deposit. A certified copy of this Protocol shall be transmitted by the Pan American Union to the General Secretariat of the United Nations for registration.

Art. 10. This Protocol shall remain in force indefinitely between the Contracting States. It may be denounced by any of them upon one year's notice. Such denunciation shall be addressed to the Pan American Union, which shall notify the other Signatory States thereof.

Art. 11. Each Contracting State shall refrain from denouncing the Convention on Duties and Rights of States in the Event of Civil Strife while this Protocol remains in force for that State.

In witness whereof, the undersigned Plenipotentiaries, whose full powers have been presented and found to be in good and due form, sign this Protocol on the dates that appear opposite their respective signatures.

[Here follow signatures]

SIGNATURES, RATIFICATIONS[1]

State	*Signature*	*Ratification*
Argentina	8 August 1957	24 October 1957
Brazil	1 May 1957	–
Costa Rica	1 May 1957	24 June 1959
Cuba	19 July 1957	9 December 1957
Dominican Republic	17 September 1957	21 May 1958
El Salvador	27 March 1958	13 September 1960
Haiti	9 August 1957	31 January 1958
Honduras	18 December 1957	14 October 1960
Peru	18 June 1957	–
United States of America	15 July 1957	–

RESERVATIONS

None

[1] Based on a communication from the Organization of American States of 3 December 2001 and OAS website: www.oas.org/juridico/english.

No. 92

THE PRINCIPLE OF NON-INTERVENTION IN CIVIL WARS

Adopted by the Institute of International Law at its Wiesbaden Session on 14 August 1975

INTRODUCTORY NOTE: Like the Havana Convention of 1928 (*No. 90*) and its Protocol of 1957 (*No. 91*), the present Resolution primarily deals with the question of intervention in civil wars. Only Article 4 concerns international humanitarian law. It states that humanitarian aid to victims of a civil war is to be regarded as permissible. (See also the Resolutions of the Institute of International Law of 1989 (*No. 64*) and of 1999 (*No. 96*). The resolution was adopted by 16 votes to 6, with 16 abstentions. Several questions, especially the question of intervention on invitation, had remained controversial.

AUTHENTIC TEXT: French. The English text below is reprinted from *Annuaire de l'Institut de Droit international,* Vol. 56, 1975, pp. 545–549.

TEXT PUBLISHED IN: *Annuaire de l'Institut de Droit international,* Vol. 56, 1975, pp. 545–549 (French, Engl.); Institut de Droit international, *Tableau des Résolutions adoptées 1957–1991,* Paris, Pedone, 1992, pp. 120–125 (French, Engl.); *Droit des conflits armés,* pp. 1255–1257 (French).

TABLE OF CONTENTS

* * *

The Institute of International Law,

Noting the gravity of the phenomenon of civil wars and of the suffering which they cause;

Considering that any civil war may affect the interests of other States and may therefore result in an international conflict if no provision is made for very stringent obligations of non-intervention;

Considering in particular that the violation of the principle of non-intervention for the benefit of a party to a civil war often leads in practice to interference for the benefit of the opposite party;

Convinced therefore that it is necessary to specify the duties of other States in the event of civil war breaking out in the territory of a given State;

Reserving the study of issues arising from the danger of extermination of ethnic, religious or social groups or from other severe infringements of human rights during civil war,

Adopts the following Resolution:

Article 1. Concept of civil war

1. For the purposes of this Resolution, the term "civil war" shall apply to any armed conflict, not of an international character, which breaks out in the territory of a State and in which there is opposition between:
   (a) the established government and one or more insurgent movements whose aim is to overthrow the government or the political, economic or social order of the State, or to achieve secession or self-government for any part of that State, or
   (b) two or more groups which in the absence of any established government contend with one another for the control of the State.
2. Within the meaning of this Resolution, the term "civil war" shall not cover:
   (a) local disorders or riots;
   (b) armed conflicts between political enemies which are separated by an international demarcation line or which have existed *de facto* as States over a prolonged period of time, or conflicts between any such entity and a State;
   (c) conflicts arising from decolonization.

Art. 2. Prohibition from assistance

1. Third States shall refrain from giving assistance to parties to a civil war which is being fought in the territory of another State.
2. They shall in particular refrain from:
   (a) sending armed forces or military volunteers, instructors or technicians to any party to a civil war, or allowing them to be sent or to set out;
   (b) drawing up or training regular or irregular forces with a view to supporting any party to a civil war, or allowing them to be drawn up or trained;
   (c) supplying weapons or other war material to any party to a civil war, or allowing them to be supplied;
   (d) giving any party to a civil war any financial or economic aid likely to influence the outcome of that war, without prejudice to the exception provided for in Article 3 (b);
   (e) making their territories available to any party to a civil war or allowing them to be used by any such party, as bases of operations or of supplies, as places of refuge, for the passage of regular or irregular forces, or for the transit of war material. The last mentioned prohibition includes transmitting military information to any of the parties;
   (f) prematurely recognizing a provisional government which has no effective control over a substantial area of the territory of the State in question.
3. (a) Third States shall use all means to prevent inhabitants of their territories, whether natives or aliens, from raising contingents and collecting equipment, from crossing the border or from embarking from their territories with a view to fomenting or causing a civil war.
   (b) They shall disarm and intern any force of either of the parties to a civil war which crosses their borders, on the understanding that expenses resulting from internment will be charged to the State faced with the civil war. Weapons found with such forces shall be seized and retained by the third State and returned to the State faced with the civil war after the end of the latter.

Art. 3. Exceptions

Notwithstanding the provisions of Article 2, third States may:

(a) grant humanitarian aid in accordance with Article 4;
(b) continue to give any technical or economic aid which is not likely to have any substantial impact on the outcome of the civil war;

(c) give any assistance prescribed, authorized or recommended by the United Nations in accordance with its Charter and other rules of international law.

Art. 4. Humanitarian aid

1. The forwarding of relief or other forms of purely humanitarian aid for the benefit of victims of a civil war should be regarded as permissible.
2. In cases where the territory controlled by one party can be reached only by crossing the territory controlled by the other party or the territory of a third State, free passage over such territory should be granted to any relief consignment, at least insofar as is provided for in Article 23 of the Geneva Convention of 12 August 1949 on the Protection of Civilian Persons in Time of War.

Art. 5. Foreign intervention

Whenever it appears that intervention has taken place during a civil war in violation of the preceding provisions, third States may give assistance to the other party only in compliance with the Charter and any other relevant rule of international law, subject to any such measures as are prescribed, authorized or recommended by the United Nations.

No. 93

PROTOCOL ADDITIONAL TO THE GENEVA CONVENTIONS OF 12 AUGUST 1949, AND RELATING TO THE PROTECTION OF VICTIMS OF NON-INTERNATIONAL ARMED CONFLICTS

(PROTOCOL II)

Adopted at Geneva, 8 June 1977

Text reprinted under No. 57

No. 94

DECLARATION ON THE RULES OF INTERNATIONAL HUMANITARIAN LAW GOVERNING THE CONDUCT OF HOSTILITIES IN NON-INTERNATIONAL ARMED CONFLICTS

Adopted by the Council of the International Institute of Humanitarian Law at San Remo on 7 April 1990

INTRODUCTORY NOTE: Article 3 common to the four Geneva Conventions of 1949 (*Nos. 49–52*), and Protocol II of 1977 (*No. 57*), only marginally touch on the law governing the conduct of hostilities in non-international armed conflicts. The 14th Round Table of the San Remo Institute of Humanitarian Law, on 13–14 September 1989, examined the respective rules of international law. At the end of the session, the Round Table adopted conclusions and asked the Council to set them down in a more elaborate form. The Council, on 7 April 1990, approved conclusions and commentaries and adopted the Declaration reproduced below.

AUTHENTIC TEXTS: English, French. The text below is reproduced from *International Review of the Red Cross,* September-October 1990, No. 278, pp. 404–408.

TEXT PUBLISHED IN: *IRRC,* September-October 1990, No. 278, pp. 404–408 (Engl.); *RICR,* september–october 1990, No. 785, pp. 438–442 (French); *RICR* (Span.), septiembre–octubre de 1990, No. 101, pp. 434–438 (Span.); International Institute of Humanitarian Law, *Yearbook 1989–1990,* Milano, Giuffré Editore, 1992, pp. 441–445 (Engl.); *Droit des conflits armés,* pp. 1261–1264 (French).

TABLE OF CONTENTS

* * *

The Council of the International Institute of Humanitarian Law, meeting in Taormina on 7 April 1990,

basing itself on the work and the conclusions of the 14th Round Table on humanitarian law, organized by the International Institute of Humanitarian Law and held under its auspices at San Remo on 13 and 14 September 1989,

recalling that the topic of the 14th Round Table was "rules of international humanitarian law governing the conduct of hostilities in non-international armed conflicts",

noting that the 14th Round Table examined the application of certain rules to non-international armed conflicts independently of the existence of treaty rules expressly adopted for such conflicts,

noting that these rules comprise general rules governing the conduct of hostilities as well as those prohibiting or restricting the use of certain weapons,

bearing constantly in mind the principle of humanity which is at the foundation of all international humanitarian law as well as the Martens clause which provides that in cases not covered by the law in force human beings remain under the protection of the principle of humanity and the dictates of the public conscience,

taking into account the rules which inspired the first codification rules of international humanitarian law relating to the conduct of hostilities,

taking also into account the resolutions relative to the espect for human rights in armed conflicts adopted by the United Nations General Assembly,

considering that Article 3 common to the 1949 Geneva Conventions must be interpreted as affording protection to human beings against the effects of hostilities,

noting that international instruments on human rights also grant fundamental protection in armed conflicts,

basing itself on the shared conviction of States as set forth in legal instruments which have been taken into consideration,

identifies the following principles and norms as crystallized or as emergent rules of international law:

A. General Rules Governing the Conduct of Hostilities Applicable in Non-international Armed Conflicts

1. Distinction between combatants and civilians
The obligation to distinguish between combatants and civilians is a general rule applicable in non-international armed conflicts. It prohibits indiscriminate attacks.

2. Immunity of the civilian population
The prohibition of attacks against the civilian population as such or against individual civilians is a general rule applicable in non-international armed conflicts. Acts of violence intended primarily to spread terror among the civilian population are also prohibited.

3. Prohibition of superfluous injury or unnecessary suffering
The prohibition of superfluous injury or unnecessary suffering is a general rule applicable in non-international armed conflicts. It prohibits, in particular, the use of means of

warfare which uselessly aggravate the sufferings of disabled men or render their death inevitable.

4. Prohibition of perfidy
The prohibition to kill, injure or capture an adversary by resort to perfidy is a general rule applicable in non-international armed conflicts; in a non-international conflict, acts inviting the confidence of an adversary to lead him to believe that he is entitled to, or is obliged to accord, protection under the rules of international law applicable in non-international armed conflicts, with intent to betray that confidence, shall constitute perfidy.

5. Respect for and protection of medical and religious personnel and of medical units and transports
The obligation to respect and protect medical and religious personnel and medical units and transports in the conduct of military operations is a general rule applicable in non-international armed conflicts.

6. Prohibition of attacks on dwellings and other installations used only by the civilian population
The general rule prohibiting attacks against the civilian population implies, as a corollary, the prohibition of attacks on dwellings and other installations which are used only by the civilian population.

7. Protection of objects indispensable to the survival of the civilian population
The general rule prohibiting attacks against the civilian population implies, as a corollary, the prohibition to attack, destroy, remove or render useless objects indispensable to the survival of the civilian population.

8. Precautionary measures in attack
The general rule to distinguish between combatants and civilians and the prohibition of attacks against the civilian population as such or against individual civilians implies, in order to be effective, that all feasible precautions have to be taken to avoid injury, loss or damage to the civilian population.

B. Prohibitions and Restrictions on the Use of Certain Weapons in Non-international Armed Conflicts

1. Chemical and bacteriological weapons (1925 Protocol)
The customary rule prohibiting the use of chemical weapons, such as those containing asphyxiating or vesicant agents, and the use of bacteriological (biological) weapons is applicable in non-international armed conflicts.

2. Bullets which expand in the human body (such as dum-dum bullets)
The customary rule prohibiting the use of bullets which expand or flatten easily in the human body, such as dum-dum bullets, is applicable in non-international armed conflicts.

3. Poison
The customary rule prohibiting the use of poison as a means or method of warfare is applicable in non-international armed conflicts.

4. Mines, booby-traps and other devices
In application of the general rules listed in section A above, especially those on the distinction between combatants and civilians and on the immunity of the civilian population, mines, booby-traps and other devices within the meaning of Protocol II to the 1980 Convention on conventional weapons may not be directed against the civilian population as such or against individual civilians, nor used indiscriminately.

The prohibition of booby-traps listed in Article 6 of that Protocol extends to their use in non-international armed conflicts, in application of the general rules on the distinction between combatants and civilians, the immunity of the civilian population, the prohibition of superfluous injury or unnecessary suffering, and the prohibition of perfidy.

To ensure the protection of the civilian population referred to in the previous paragraphs, precaution must be taken to protect it from attacks in the form of mines, booby-traps and other devices.

5. Incendiary weapons

In application of the general rules listed in section A above, especially those on the distinction between combatants and civilians and on the immunity of the civilian population, incendiary weapons may not be directed against the civilian population as such, against individual civilians or civilian objects, nor used indiscriminately.

Furthermore, in the interest of promoting respect for international humanitarian law applicable in non-international armed conflicts, the Council of the International Institute of Humanitarian Law,

recalling the need to implement programmes aimed at disseminating and teaching international humanitarian law applicable in such circumstances,

taking note of the wishes expressed in this regard at the 14th Round Table,

makes the following recommendations:

1. The teaching of the rules of international humanitarian law on the conduct of hostilities given as part of military training should make no distinction based on the qualification (international or non-international) of the conflict.
2. The teaching of these rules of international humanitarian law should stress that they must be respected by all the parties involved in a non-international armed conflict.
3. The rules of international humanitarian law governing the conduct of hostilities should be disseminated not only in military circles but also among the civilian population, as in non-international armed conflicts the civilian population is often closely involved in hostilities.

No. 95

DECLARATION OF MINIMUM HUMANITARIAN STANDARDS

Adopted by an expert meeting convened by the Institute for Human Rights, Abo Akademi University, in Turku/Abo, Finland, on 30 November–2 December 1990

INTRODUCTORY NOTE: In situations of internal violence humanitarian principles and human rights are often violated. It is to be noted in this respect that conventions on humanitarian law do not apply in situations falling short of an armed conflict, and that provisions on human rights may be derogated from in time of public emergency unless derogation is expressly prohibited. It is therefore possible that neither humanitarian law nor human rights law is formally applicable. In order to reinforce the protection of persons in such situations, two experts drafted new texts. Theodor Meron proposed a draft declaration on internal strife (*IRRC* 1988, No. 262, pp. 66–76), Hans-Peter Gasser a code of conduct for internal disturbances and tensions (*IRRC* 1988, No. 262, pp. 38–58). Based on these drafts and other preparatory texts, an expert meeting, convened by the Abo Akademi University in Turku/Abo, Finland, adopted the Declaration reproduced below as a model to be taken into consideration by the United Nations and other international organizations. Its provisions are designed to be applied in all situations. The UN Subcommission on Prevention of Discrimination and Protection of Minorities, in 1994, decided to transmit the text of the Declaration to the Commission on Human Rights for further elaboration and eventual adoption. In 1995 and subsequent years, the Commission on Human Rights invited governments and interested organizations to provide comments on the Declaration, but no result has so far been achieved. In the United Nations, the topic has been given the title "Fundamental Standards of Humanity".

AUTHENTIC TEXT: English. The text below is reproduced from the UN document E/CN.4/Sub. 2/ 199/ 55 of 12 August 1991.

TEXT PUBLISHED IN: *IRRC,* May–June 1991, No. 282, pp. 330–336 (Engl.); *RICR,* mai–juin 1991, No. 789, pp. 350–356 (French); *RICR* (Span.), mayo–junio de 1991, No. 105, pp. 353–359 (Span.); UN Doc. E/CN.4/Sub.2/1991/55 (Arabic, Chinese, Engl., Russ. Span.); *Droit des conflits armés*, pp. 1265–1269 (French).

* * *

Recalling the reaffirmation by the Charter of the United Nations and the Universal Declaration of Human Rights of faith in the dignity and worth of the human person;

Considering that situations of internal violence, disturbances, tensions and public emergency continue to cause serious instability and great suffering in all parts of the world;

Concerned that in such situations human rights and humanitarian principles have often been violated;

Recognizing that the importance of respecting existing human rights and humanitarian norms;

Noting that international law relating to human rights and humanitarian norms applicable in armed conflicts do not adequately protect human beings in situations of internal violence, disturbances, tensions and public emergency;

Confirming that any derogation from obligation relating to human rights during a state of public emergency must remain strictly within the limits provided for by international law, that certain rights can never be derogated from and that humanitarian law does not admit of any derogation on grounds of public emergency;

Confirming further that measures derogating from such obligations must be taken in strict conformity with the procedural requirements laid down in those instruments, that the imposition of a state of emergency must be proclaimed officially, publicly, and in accordance with the provisions laid down by law, that measures derogating from such obligations will be limited to the extent strictly required by the exigencies of the situation, and that such measures must not discriminate on the grounds of race, color, sex, language, religion, social, national or ethnic origin;

Recognizing that in cases not covered by human rights and humanitarian instruments, all persons and groups remain under the protection of the principles of international law derived from established custom, from the principles of humanity and the dictates of public conscience;

Believing that it is important to reaffirm and develop principles governing behavior of all persons, groups and authorities in situations of internal violence, disturbances, tensions and public emergency;

Believing further in the need for the development and strict implementation of national legislation applicable to such situations, for strengthening co-operation necessary for more efficient implementation of national and international norms, including international mechanisms for monitoring, and for the dissemination and teaching of such norms;

Proclaim this Declaration of Minimum Humanitarian Standards

Article 1. This Declaration affirms minimum humanitarian standards which are applicable in all situations, including internal violence, disturbances, tensions, and public emergency, and which cannot be derogated from under any circumstances. These standards must be respected whether or not a state of emergency has been proclaimed.

Art. 2. These standards shall be respected by, and applied to all persons, groups and authorities, irrespective of their legal status and without any adverse discrimination.

Art. 3.

1. Everyone shall have the right to recognition everywhere as a person before the law. All persons, even if their liberty has been restricted, are entitled to respect for their person, honor and convictions, freedom of thought, conscience and religious practices. They shall, in all circumstances, be treated humanely, without any adverse distinction.
2. The following acts are, and shall remain, prohibited:

(a) violence to the life, health and physical or mental well-being of persons, in particular murder, torture, mutilation, rape, as well as cruel, inhuman, or degrading treatment or punishment, and other outrages upon personal dignity;
(b) collective punishments against persons and their property;
(c) the taking of hostages;
(d) practicing, permitting or tolerating the involuntary disappearance of individuals, including their abduction or unacknowledged detention;
(e) pillaging;

(f) deliberate deprivation of access to necessary food, drinking water and medicine;
(g) threats or incitement to commit any of the foregoing acts.

Art. 4.
1. All persons deprived of their liberty shall be held in recognized places of detention. Accurate information on their detention and whereabouts, including transfers, shall be made promptly available to their family members and counsel or other persons having a legitimate interest in the information.
2. All persons deprived of their liberty shall be allowed to communicate with the outside world including counsel in accordance with reasonable regulations promulgated by the competent authority.
3. The right to an effective remedy, including habeas corpus shall be guaranteed as a means to determine the whereabouts or the state of health of persons deprived of their liberty and for identifying the authority ordering or carrying out the deprivation of liberty. Everyone who is deprived of his or her liberty, by arrest or detention, shall be entitled to take proceedings by which the lawfulness of the detention shall be decided speedily by a court and his or her release ordered if the detention is not lawful.
4. All person deprived of their liberty shall be treated humanely, provided with adequate food and drinking water, decent accommodation and clothing, and be afforded safeguards as regards health, hygiene, and working and social conditions.

Art. 5.
1. Attacks against persons not taking part in acts of violence shall be prohibited in all circumstances.
2. Whenever the use of force is unavoidable, it shall be in proportion to the seriousness of the offense or the objective to be achieve.
3. Weapons or other material or methods prohibited in international armed conflicts must not be employed in any circumstances.

Art. 6. Acts, or threats, of violence, the primary purpose, or foreseeable effect of which is to spread terror among the population are prohibited.

Art. 7.
1. The displacement of the population or parts thereof shall not be ordered unless their safety or imperative security reasons so demand. Should such displacements have to be carried out, all possible measures shall be taken in order that the population may be transferred and received under satisfactory conditions of shelter, hygiene, health, safety, and nutrition. Persons or groups thus displaced shall be allowed to return to their homes as soon as the conditions which made their displacement imperative have ceased. Every effort shall be made to enable those displaced who wish to remain together to do so. Families whose members wish to remain together must be allowed to do so. The persons thus displaced shall be free to move around in the territory, subject only to the safety of the persons involved or reasons of imperative security.
2. No persons shall be compelled to leave their own territory.

Art. 8.
1. Every human being has the inherent right to life. This right shall be protected by law. No one shall be arbitrarily deprived of his or her life.
2. In addition to the guarantees of the inherent right to life, and the prohibition of genocide, in existing human rights and humanitarian instruments, the following provisions shall be respected as a minimum.
3. In countries which have not yet abolished the death penalty, sentences of death shall be carried out only for the most serious crimes. Sentences of death shall not be carried out on pregnant women, mothers of young children, or on children under eighteen years of age at the time of the commission of the offense.

4. No death sentence shall be carried out before the expiration of at least six months from the notification of the final judgment confirming such death sentence.

Art. 9. No sentence shall be passed and no penalty shall be executed on a person found guilty of an offense without previous judgment pronounced by a regularly constituted court affording all the judicial guarantees which are recognized as indispensable by the community of nations. In particular:
(a) the procedure shall provide for an accused to be informed, without delay, of the particulars of the offense alleged against him or her, shall provide for a trial within a reasonable time, and shall afford the accused before and during his or her trial all necessary rights and means of defense;
(b) no one shall be convicted of an offense except on the basis of individual penal responsibility;
(c) anyone charged with an offense is presumed innocent until proven guilty, according to law;
(d) anyone charged with an offense shall have the right to be tried in his or her presence;
(e) no one shall be compelled to testify against himself or herself, or to confess guilt;
(f) no one shall be liable to be tried or punished again for an offense for which he or she has already been finally convicted or acquitted, in accordance with the law and penal procedure;
(g) no one shall be held guilty of any criminal offense on account of any act or omission which did not constitute a criminal offense, under applicable law, at the time when it was committed.

Art. 10. Every child has the right to the measures of protection required by his or her condition as a minor and shall be provided with the care and aid the child requires. Children who have not yet attained the age of fifteen years shall not be recruited in or allowed to join the armed forces, or armed groups, or allowed to take part in acts of violence. All efforts shall be made not to allow persons below the age of eighteen to take parts in acts of violence.

Art. 11. If it is considered necessary, for imperative reasons of security, to subject any person to assigned residence, internment or administrative detention, such decisions shall be subject to a regular procedure prescribed by law affording all the judicial guarantees which are recognized as indispensable by the international community, including the right of appeal or to a periodical review.

Art. 12. In every circumstance, the wounded and sick, whether or not they have taken part in acts of violence, shall be protected and treated humanely, and shall receive, to the fullest extent practicable, and with the least possible delay, the medical care and attention required by their condition. There shall be no distinction among them on any grounds other than medical condition.

Art. 13. Every possible measure shall be taken, without delay, to search for, and collect, wounded, sick and missing persons, and to protect them against pillage and ill-treatment, to ensure their adequate care, and to search for the dead; prevent their being despoiled or mutilated, and to dispose of them with respect.

Art. 14.
1. Medical and religious personnel shall be respected and protected and shall be granted all available help for the performance of their duties. They shall not be compelled to carry out tasks which are not compatible with their humanitarian missions.
2. Under no circumstances shall any person be punished for having carried out medical activities compatible with the principles of medical ethics, regardless of the person benefitting therefrom.

Art. 15. In situations of internal violence, disturbances, tensions or public emergency, humanitarian organizations shall be granted all the facilities necessary to enable them to carry out their humanitarian activities.

Art. 16. In observing these standards, all efforts shall be made to protect the rights of groups, minorities and people, including their dignity and identity.

Art. 17. The observance of these standards shall not affect the legal status of any authorities, groups, or persons involved in situations of internal violence, disturbances, tensions or public emergency.

Art. 18.

1. Nothing in the present standards shall be interpreted as restricting or impairing the provisions of any international humanitarian or human rights instrument.
2. No restriction upon or derogation from any of the fundamental rights of human beings recgnized or existing in any country by virtue of law, treaties, regulations, custom, or principles of humanity shall be admitted on the pretext that the present standards do not recognize such rights or that they recognize them to a lesser extent.

No. 96

THE APPLICATION OF INTERNATIONAL HUMANITARIAN LAW AND FUNDAMENTAL HUMAN RIGHTS IN ARMED CONFLICTS IN WHICH NON-STATE ENTITIES ARE PARTIES

Resolution adopted by the Institute of International Law at its Berlin session on 25 August 1999

INTRODUCTORY NOTE: Concerned about the gross violations of international humanitarian law in many non-international armed conflicts of recent years, the Institute of International Law, in 1993, established a commission to deal with the respective problems. At its Berlin Session in 1999, the Institute adopted the present resolution by 33 votes in favor, none against and 1 abstention.

AUTHENTIC TEXT: French. The English text below is reprinted from *Annuaire de l'Institut de Droit international*, Vol. 68 - II, 1999, pp. 386–399.

TEXT PUBLISHED IN: *Annuaire de l'Institut de Droit international,* Vol. 68 - II, 1999, pp. 386–399 (Engl., French).

* * *

The Institute of International Law,

Recalling its Resolutions "*Droits et devoirs des Puissances étrangères, au cas de mouvement insurrectionel, envers les gouvernements établis et reconnus qui sont prises avec l'insurrection*" (Neuchâtel Session, 1900), "*The Principle of Non-Intervention in Civil Wars*" (Wiesbaden Session, 1975) and "*The Protection of Human Rights and the Principle of Non-Intervention in Internal Affairs of States*" (Santiago de Compostela Session, 1989);

Recalling further its Resolutions on the "*Conditions of Application of Humanitarian Rules of Armed Conflict to Hostilities in which United Nations Forces May Be Engaged*" (Zagreb Session, 1971) and on the "*Conditions of Application of Rules, Other than Humanitarian Rules, of Armed Conflict to Hostilities in which United Nations Forces May Be Engaged*" (Wiesbaden Session, 1977);

Considering that armed conflicts in which non-State entities are parties have become more and more numerous and increasingly motivated in particular by ethnic, religious or racial causes;

Noting that, as a consequence, the civilian population is increasingly affected by internal armed conflicts and ultimately bears the brunt of the resulting violence, causing great suffering death and privation;

Noting that armed conflicts in which non-State entities are parties do not only concern those States in which they take place, but also affect the interests of the international community as a whole;

Bearing in mind that, in the last fifty years, the principles of the United Nations Charter and of human rights law have had a substantial impact on the development and application of international humanitarian law;

Recalling the ruling of the International Court of Justice that the obligation laid down in Article 1 common to the Geneva Conventions "to respect" the Conventions and to "ensure respect" for them "in all circumstances" derives from the general principles of international humanitarian law, with the consequence that it has acquired the status of customary international law;

Emphasizing the ruling of the International Court of Justice that Article 3 common to the Geneva Conventions of 1949 reflects "elementary considerations of humanity" and that the fundamental rules of humanitarian law applicable in armed conflicts "are to be observed ... because they constitute intransgressible principles of international customary law";

Considering the ruling of the International Criminal Tribunal for the Former Yugoslavia whereby many principles and rules previously applicable only in international armed conflicts are now applicable in internal armed conflicts and serious violations of international humanitarian law committed within the context of the latter category of conflicts constitute war crimes;

Supporting the prosecution and punishment by national jurisdictions of those responsible for war crimes, crimes against humanity, genocide or other serious violations of international humanitarian law, as well as the establishment of international tribunals entrusted with this task;

Recognizing that, under Article 7 of the Rome Statute of the International Criminal Court, crimes against humanity can be committed by persons acting for States or non-State entities;

Noting that the actions undertaken by the Security Council under Chapter VII of the Charter in armed conflicts in which non-State entities were parties confirm that respect for international humanitarian law is an integral element of the security system of the World Organization;

Welcoming the United Nations Secretary General's regulation of 6 August 1999 on the Observance by United Nations Forces of international humanitarian law which reaffirms their obligation to comply strictly with humanitarian law, in particular as to the protection of the civilian population, and provides for the possibility of prosecuting members of the military personnel of such Forces in case of violations of humanitarian law, in particular in situations of internal armed conflicts;

Welcoming also the important role played by the International Committee of the Red Cross (ICRC) in recent conflicts to which non-State entities were parties in seeking to ensure humanitarian protection for all victims and in inviting parties to such conflicts to abide by elementary principles of humanity, notably to spare the civilian population the effects of violence and devastation;

Considering that it is desirable that international humanitarian law be reconsidered and adapted to new circumstances, so as to reinforce respect for this law and the protection of victims in armed conflict to which non-State entities are parties,

Adopts this Resolution:

I. For the purposes of this Resolution:

– the expression "armed conflicts in which non-State entities are parties" means internal armed conflicts between a government's armed forces and those of one or several non-State entities, or between several non-State entities; also included are internal armed conflicts in which peacekeeping forces intervene;
– the expression "non-State entities" means the parties to internal armed conflicts who oppose the government's armed forces or are fighting entities of a similar nature and who fulfill the conditions set forth in Article 3 common to the Geneva Conventions of 1949 on the Protection of Victims of War or in Article 1 of the 1977 Protocol Additional to the Geneva Conventions and relating to the Protection of Victims of Non-International Armed Conflicts (Protocol II).

II. All parties to armed conflicts in which non-State entities are parties, irrespective of their legal status, as well as the United Nations, and competent regional and other international organizations have the obligation to respect international humanitarian law as well as fundamental human rights. The application of such principles and rules does not affect the legal status of the parties to the conflict and is not dependent on their recognition as belligerents or insurgents.

III. Respect for international humanitarian law and fundamental human rights constitutes an integral part of international order for the maintenance and reestablishment of peace and security, in particular in armed conflicts in which non-State entities are parties.

IV. International law applicable to armed conflicts in which non-State entities are parties includes:

- Article 3 common to the Geneva conventions of 1949 as basic principles of international humanitarian law;
- Protocol II and all other conventions applicable to non-international armed conflicts;
- customary principles and rules of international humanitarian law on the conduct of hostilities and the protection of victims applicable to internal armed conflicts;
- the principles and rules of international law guaranteeing fundamental human rights;
- the principles and rules of international law applicable to internal armed conflicts, relating to war crimes, crimes against humanity, genocide and other international crimes;
- the principles of international law "derived form established custom, from the principles of humanity and from dictates of public conscience."

V. Every State and every non-State entity participating in an armed conflict are legally bound *vis-à-vis* each other as well as all other members of the international community to respect international humanitarian law in all circumstances, and any other State is legally entitled to demand respect fo this body of law. No State or non-State entity can escape its obligations by denying the existence of an armed conflict.

VI. In cases of serious violations of international humanitarian law or fundamental human rights, the United Nations and competent regional and other international organizations have the right to adopt appropriate measures in accordance with international law.

VII. Without prejudice to the functions and powers which the Charter attributes to the organs of the United Nations, in case of systematic and massive violations or humanitarian law or fundamental human rights, States, acting individually or collectively, are entitled to take diplomatic, economic and other measures towards any party to the armed conflict which has violated its obligations, provided such measures are permitted under international law.

VIII. Any serious violation of international humanitarian law in armed conflicts in which non-State entities are parties entails the individual responsibility of the persons involved, regardless of their status or official position, in accordance with international instruments that entrust the repression of these acts to national or international jurisdictions.

The competent authorities of a State on the territory of which is found a person against whom is alleged a serious violation of international humanitarian law committed in a non-international armed conflict are entitled to prosecute and try such a person before their courts; they are urged to do so.

IX. In order to achieve a better protection for the victims in armed conflicts in which non-State entities are parties and taking into account the experience of recent armed conflicts of a non-international character the following measures should be considered:

- the conclusion by the parties to such conflicts of special agreements, in accordance with Article 3 paragraph 2 common to the Geneva Conventions of 1949, on the application of all or part of the provision of the Conventions;
- the support of States, the United Nations, the ICRC as well as other international bodies of a humanitarian character for measures to verify and oversee the application of international humanitarian law in internal armed conflicts; furthermore, should

the State concerned claim that no internal armed conflict has broken out, the authorisation given to the United Nations or any other competent regional or international organisation to establish impartially whether international law is applicable;

- the application of Protocol II in all non-international armed conflicts, without waiting for its formal revision;
- the amendment of Protocol II, with a view to complementing its rules and in particular so as:
  (a) to establish an impartial and independent international body designed to investigate respect for international humanitarian law (*cf.* Article 90 of Protocol I);
  (b) to add a grave breaches provision addressing, in particular, issues of jurisdiction, extradition and surrender to an international criminal jurisdiction;.

X. To the extent that certain aspects of internal disturbances and tensions may not be covered by international humanitarian law, individuals remain under the protection of international law guaranteeing fundamental human rights. All parties are bound to respect fundamental human rights under the scrutiny of the international community.

XI. The Institute welcomes and encourages the progressive adaptation of the principles and rules relating to internal armed conflicts to the principles and rules applicable in international armed conflicts. Therefore it is desirable and necessary that States, the United Nations and competent regional and other international organizations, drawing special inspiration from the important work done by the ICRC in this field, draft and adopt a convention designed to regulate all armed conflicts and protect all victims, regardless of whether such conflicts are international, non-international or of a mixed character.

XII. All States and non-State entities must disseminate the principles and rules of humanitarian law and fundamental human rights which are applicable in internal armed conflicts.

* * *

See also Nos. 49–52, 57, 60, 61, 65–68, 71, 74, 109–111

X

APPLICATION OF THE LAW OF ARMED CONFLICTS TO HOSTILITIES IN WHICH UNITED NATIONS FORCES ARE ENGAGED

No. 97

CONDITIONS OF APPLICATION OF HUMANITARIAN RULES OF ARMED CONFLICT TO HOSTILITIES IN WHICH UNITED NATIONS FORCES MAY BE ENGAGED

Resolution adopted by the Institute of International Law at its session at Zagreb, 3 September 1971

INTRODUCTORY NOTE: No international treaty expressly provides for the application of the law of armed conflicts to hostilities in which United Nations Forces are engaged. However, from 1954 on, several resolutions, adopted by governmental and non-governmental bodies took up this question. The Hague Intergovernmental Conference on the Protection of Cultural Property of 1954, in Resolution I (*No. 70*) expressed the hope that the competent organs of the United Nations would decide, in the event of military action being taken in implementation of the Charter, to ensure the application of the provisions of the Hague Convention of 1954 by the armed forces taking part in such action. The Council of Delegates of the International Red Cross, at the Centenary Congress of the Red Cross in Geneva in 1963, adopted a resolution recommending, *inter alia*, that the United Nations be invited to adopt a solemn declaration accepting that the Geneva Conventions equally apply to their emergency forces as they apply to the forces of states parties to the said Conventions. The International Red Cross Conference in Vienna in 1965, in its resolution XXV, recommended, in particular, that appropriate agreements be concluded to ensure that armed forces placed at the disposal of the United Nations observe the provisions of the Geneva Conventions and are protected by them. The International Law Association, at its Helsinki Conference in 1966, took up the proposal that the United Nations should by declaration accept the provisions of the Geneva Conventions of 1949 and of the Hague Convention of 1954.

The Resolution of the Institute of International Law, reprinted below, was the first to set out more detailed rules for the problems involved. It was adopted by a vote of 42 in favour, none against and 1 abstention.

AUTHENTIC TEXT: French. The English translation below is reprinted from the *Annuaire de l'Institut de Droit international*, Vol. 54, II, 1971.

TEXT PUBLISHED IN: *Annuaire de l'Institut de Droit international*, Vol. 54, II, 1971, pp. 449–454 (French); pp. 465-170 (Engl.); Institut de Droit international, *Tableau des Résolutions adoptées, 1957–1991*, Paris, Pedone, 1992, pp. 86–93 (French, Engl.); *AJIL*, Vol. 66, 1972, pp. 465–468 (Engl.); *RGDIP*, tome 75, No. 4, octobre–décembre 1971, pp. 1257–1259 (French); *Droit des conflits armés*, pp. 1273–1276 (French).

* * *

The Institute of International Law,

Recalling its Resolution on "*Equality of application of the rules of the law of war to the parties to an armed conflict*" (Brussels Session, 1963);

Recalling its Resolutions on "*The distinction between military objectives and non-military objects in general and particularly the problems associated with weapons of mass destruction*" (Edinburgh Session, 1969);

Noting that the United Nations on various occasions made use of armed Forces and that such Forces, whatever their mission, might become involved in actual hostilities;

Considering that pending the elaboration of a comprehensive set of rules governing the status of United Nations Forces, it is necessary to determine the conditions under which the humanitarian rules of armed conflict apply to such Forces;

Reserving the study of the general problems of the effect which the outlawry of war and of the use of force may have upon the principle of non-discrimination in the application of the other rules relating to armed conflict;

Declaring, in addition, that the present Resolution is without prejudice to the solution which may be given to the problem connected with the competence of United Nations organs to create or to direct United Nations Forces;

Has adopted the following Articles:

Article 1. For the purposes of the present Articles, the term "United Nations Forces" shall apply to all armed units under the control of the United Nations.

Art. 2. The humanitarian rules of the law of armed conflict apply to the United Nations as of right and they must be complied with in every circumstance by United Nations Forces which are engaged in hostilities.

The rules referred to in the preceding paragraph include in particular

(a) the rules pertaining to the conduct of hostilities in general and especially those prohibiting the use or some uses of certain weapons, those concerning the means of injuring the other party, and those relating to the distinction between military and non-military objectives;

(b) the rules contained in the Geneva Conventions of 12 August 1949;

(c) the rules which aim at protecting civilian persons and property.

Art. 3.

A. If United Nations Forces are set up through individual recruitments, the United Nations shall issue regulations defining the rights and duties of the member of such Forces.

In the event of these Forces becoming involved in hostilities, these regulations shall name the international authorities which, in regard to the said Forces, shall be vested with the regulatory executive and judicial powers necessary to secure effective compliance with the humanitarian rules of armed conflict.

B. If United Nations Forces are composed of national contingents with regard to which the United Nations has not issued any regulations such as those mentioned in the preceding paragraph, effective compliance with the humanitarian rules of armed conflict must be secured through agreements concluded between the Organization and the several States which contribute contingents.

These agreements shall at least confer upon the United Nations the right to receive all information pertaining to, and the right to supervise at any time and at any place, the effective compliance with the humanitarian rules of armed conflict by each contingent.

Art. 4. In order to secure effective compliance with the humanitarian rules of armed conflict by United Nations Forces, it is necessary that the individuals who may be called upon to participate in such Forces receive adequate and previous instruction on the law of armed conflict in its entirety, and especially on the meaning and the scope of the Geneva Conventions of 12 August 1949.

It is desirable that the United Nations, as well as those of its specialized agencies which are concerned with furthering education and health, take all steps within their power in order to coordinate the measures which the States parties to the Geneva Conventions have been invited to take in this field by the International Conferences of the Red Cross.

Art. 5. In order to secure effective compliance with the humanitarian rules of armed conflict during hostilities in which United Nations Forces are engaged, it is necessary that the Organization should ensure that there are, within its Forces, health services composed of competent personnel in sufficient numbers and provided with means of action that are proportionate to the foreseeable needs.

If the direction of such services is entrusted to the States which have contributed contingents, the Organization shall take all measures in its power to coordinate the activities of these services.

Art. 6. In order to ensure effective compliance with the humanitarian rules of armed conflict during hostilities in which United Nations Forces could become involved, it is desirable, if there is no Protecting Power, that an impartial body be empowered to assume the duties entrusted to the Protecting Power by the Geneva Conventions of 12 August 1949.

The body referred to in the present Article as well as its members should enjoy all the facilities necessary to carry out their functions effectively.

Art. 7. Without prejudice to the individual or collective responsibility which derives from the very fact that the party opposing the United Nations Forces has committed aggression, that party shall make reparation for injuries caused in violation of the humanitarian rules of armed conflict. The United Nations is entitled to demand compliance with these rules for the benefit of its Forces and to claim damages for injuries suffered by its Forces in violation of these rules.

Art. 8. The United Nations is liable for damage which may be caused by its Forces in violation of the humanitarian rules of armed conflict, without prejudice to any possible recourse against the State whose contingent has caused the damage.

It is desirable that claims presented by persons thus injured be submitted to bodies composed of independent and impartial persons. Such bodies shall be designated or set up either by the regulations issued by the United Nations or by the agreements concluded by the Organization with the States which put contingents at its disposal and, possibly, with any other interested State.

It is equally desirable that if such bodies have been designated or set up by a binding decision of the United Nations, or if the jurisdiction of similar bodies has been accepted by the State of which the injured person is a national, no claims may be presented to the United Nations by that State unless the injured person has exhausted the remedy thus made available to it.

No. 98

CONDITIONS OF APPLICATION OF RULES, OTHER THAN HUMANITARIAN RULES, OF ARMED CONFLICT TO HOSTILITIES IN WHICH UNITED NATIONS FORCES MAY BE ENGAGED

Resolution adopted by the Institute of International Law at its session at Wiesbaden, 13 August 1975

INTRODUCTORY NOTE: The present resolution completes the resolution reprinted as *No. 97*. Whereas the former one deals with the application of humanitarian rules of armed conflict, the present one is concerned with the application of rules other than humanitarian rules. It was adopted by a vote of 24 in favour, 3 against and 9 abstentions.

AUTHENTIC TEXTS: French. The English translation below is reprinted from the *Annuaire de l'Institut de Droit international*, Vol. 56, 1975, p. 541.

TEXT PUBLISHED IN: *Annuaire de l'Institut de Droit international*, Vol. 56, 1975, pp. 540–544 (French and Engl.); Institut de Droit international, *Tableau des Résolutions adoptées 1957-1991*, Paris, Pedone, 1992, pp. 114–119 (Engl., French); *RGDIP*, tome 80, No. 4, octobre–décembre 1975, pp. 1244–1246 (French); *Droit des conflits armés*, pp. 1277–1278 (French).

* * *

The Institute of International Law,

Recalling its Resolution on "Equality of application of the rules of the law of war to parties to an armed conflict" (Brussels Session, 1963);

Recalling its Resolution on "The distinction between military objectives and non-military objects in general and particularly the problems associated with weapons of mass destruction" (Edinburgh Session, 1969);

Recalling its Resolution on the "Conditions of application of humanitarian rules of armed conflict to hostilities in which United Nations Forces may be engaged" (Zagreb Session, 1971);

Noting that the United Nations has made use of Armed Forces on various occasions and that such Forces, whatever their mission, might become involved in actual hostilities;

Considering that pending the elaboration of a comprehensive set of rules for United Nations Forces, it is necessary to determine the conditions under which the rules of armed conflict apply to such Forces;

Reserving the study of the problems of individual criminal responsibility;

Declaring, furthermore, that the present Resolution is without prejudice to the eventual solution of the problems concerning the competences respectively of organs of the United Nations in creating or directing United Nations Forces,

Adopts this Resolution:

Article 1. For the purposes of this Resolution, the term "United Nations Forces" shall apply to all armed units under the control of the United Nations.

Art. 2. Subject to the exceptions provided for in the following Articles, the rules of armed conflict shall apply to hostilities in which United Nations Forces are engaged, even if those rules are not specifically humanitarian in character.

Art. 3. Every State shall be entitled to give the United Nations Forces any assistance requested from it by the Organization.

The following Articles shall be without prejudice to the effects which an illegal use of armed Forces may have in general international law upon the principle of non-discrimination in the application of non-humanitarian rules of armed conflict.

Art. 4. Whenever United Nations Forces are engaged in hostilities, Member States of the Organization may not take advantage of the general rules of the law of neutrality in order to evade obligations laid upon them in pursuance of a decision of the Security Council acting in accordance with the Charter, nor may they depart from the rules of neutrality for the benefit of a party opposing the United Nations Forces.

Art. 5. No State shall be deprived of its status of neutrality, including permanent neutrality, for complying with the rules laid down in this Resolution, nor shall such compliance justify the application of reprisals or any other measures of coercion against that State.

Art. 6. The parties referred to in this Resolution shall be under the obligation to make reparation for any damage which they might cause in violation of the rules of armed conflict.

Recommendation I. It is desirable that the United Nations act upon Resolution I of the Intergovernmental Conference for the Protection of Cultural Property by enjoining their Forces to respect the Hague Convention of 14 May 1954 on the Protection of Cultural Property in the event of Armed Conflicts.

Recommendation II. It is desirable that the United Nations state in an appropriate form that it considers itself bound by the 1949 Geneva Convention in all operations to which its Forces might be parties.

No. 99

CONVENTION ON THE SAFETY OF UNITED NATIONS AND ASSOCIATED PERSONNEL

Adopted by Resolution 49/59 of the United Nations General Assembly on 9 December 1994

INTRODUCTORY NOTE: In the numerous operations undertaken by the United Nations in the early 1990s in states that had experienced a breakdown of law and order, UN personnel suffered casualties and mistreatment. This induced the General Assembly to establish, by resolution 48/37 of 9 December 1993, an *ad hoc* committee to elaborate a convention on the safety and security of UN and associated personnel. By resolution 49/59 of 9 December 1994, the General Assembly adopted the present Convention by consensus. Only few of its provisions are concerned with international humanitarian law. The question of the applicability of humanitarian law to UN personnel is not clearly regulated. Article 2(2) could give rise to the assumption that the law of armed conflicts applies only in case of a Security Council decision on an enforcement action, but Article 8 (at the end) and Article 20(a) lead to the conclusion that humanitarian law applies to UN personnel in all situations regulated by that law.

ENTRY INTO FORCE: 15 January 1999

AUTHENTIC TEXTS: Arabic, Chinese, English, French, Russian, Spanish.

TEXT PUBLISHED IN: Resolutions adopted by the General Assembly during its Forty-Ninth Session: resolution 49/59, *ILM*, 1995, pp. 484–493 (Engl.); *International Peacekeping* (Kluwer), Vol. 2, No. 5, 1995, pp. 123–125 (Engl.); Roberts and Guelff, pp. 623–638 (Engl.). UN web site: http://untreaty.un.org (Engl., French).

* * *

The States Parties to this Convention,

Deeply concerned over the growing number of deaths and injuries resulting from deliberate attacks against United Nations and associated personnel,

Bearing in mind that attacks against, or other mistreatment of, personnel who act on behalf of the United Nations are unjustifiable and unacceptable, by whomsoever committed,

Recognizing that United Nations operations are conducted in the common interest of the international community and in accordance with the principles and purposes of the Charter of the United Nations,

Acknowledging the important contribution that United Nations and associated personnel make in respect of United Nations efforts in the fields of preventive diplomacy, peacemaking, peace-keeping, peace-building and humanitarian and other operations,

Conscious of the existing arrangements for ensuring the safety of United Nations and associated personnel, including the steps taken by the principal organs of the United Nations, in this regard,

Recognizing none the less that existing measures of protection for United Nations and associated personnel are inadequate,

Acknowledging that the effectiveness and safety of United Nations operations are enhanced where such operations are conducted with the consent and cooperation of the host State,

Appealing to all States in which United Nations and associated personnel are deployed and to all others on whom such personnel may rely, to provide comprehensive support aimed at facilitating the conduct and fulfilling the mandate of United Nations operations,

Convinced that there is an urgent need to adopt appropriate and effective measures for the prevention of attacks committed against United Nations and associated personnel and for the punishment of those who have committed such attacks,

Have agreed as follows:

Article 1. Definitions

For the purposes of this Convention:

(a) "United Nations personnel" means:

(i) Persons engaged or deployed by the Secretary-General of the United Nations as members of the military, police or civilian components of a United Nations operation;

(ii) Other officials and experts on mission of the United Nations or its specialized agencies or the International Atomic Energy Agency who are present in an official capacity in the area where a United Nations operation is being conducted;

(b) "Associated personnel" means:

(i) Persons assigned by a Government or an intergovernmental organization with the agreement of the competent organ of the United Nations;

(ii) Persons engaged by the Secretary-General of the United Nations or by a specialized agency or by the International Atomic Energy Agency;

(iii) Persons deployed by a humanitarian non-governmental organization or agency under an agreement with the Secretary-General of the United Nations or with a specialized agency or with the International Atomic Energy Agency,

to carry out activities in support of the fulfilment of the mandate of a United Nations operation;

(c) "United Nations operation" means an operation established by the competent organ of the United Nations in accordance with the Charter of the United Nations and conducted under United Nations authority and control:

(i) Where the operation is for the purpose of maintaining or restoring international peace and security; or

(ii) Where the Security Council or the General Assembly has declared, for the purposes of this Convention, that there exists an exceptional risk to the safety of the personnel participating in the operation;

(d) "Host State" means a State in whose territory a United Nations operation is conducted;

(e) "Transit State" means a State, other than the host State, in whose territory United Nations and associated personnel or their equipment are in transit or temporarily present in connection with a United Nations operation.

Art. 2. Scope of application

1. This Convention applies in respect of United Nations and associated personnel and United Nations operations, as defined in article 1.
2.[1] This Convention shall not apply to a United Nations operation authorized by the Security Council as an enforcement action under Chapter VII of the Charter of the United Nations in which any of the personnel are engaged as combatants against organized armed forces and to which the law of international armed conflict applies.

Art. 3. Identification

1. The military and police components of a United Nations operation and their vehicles, vessels and aircraft shall bear distinctive identification. Other personnel, vehicles, vessels and aircraft involved in the United Nations operation shall be appropriately identified unless otherwise decided by the Secretary-General of the United Nations.
2. All United Nations and associated personnel shall carry appropriate identification documents.

Art. 4. Agreements on the status of the operation

The host State and the United Nations shall conclude as soon as possible an agreement on the status of the United Nations operation and all personnel engaged in the operation including, *inter alia*, provisions on privileges and immunities for military and police components of the operation.

Art. 5. Transit

A transit State shall facilitate the unimpeded transit of United Nations and associated personnel and their equipment to and from the host State.

Art. 6. Respect for laws and regulations

1. Without prejudice to such privileges and immunities as they may enjoy or to the requirements of their duties, United Nations and associated personnel shall:
   (a) Respect the laws and regulations of the host State and the transit State; and
   (b) Refrain from any action or activity incompatible with the impartial and international nature of their duties.
2. The Secretary-General of the United Nations shall take all appropriate measures to ensure the observance of these obligations.

Art. 7. Duty to ensure the safety and security of United Nations and associated personnel

1. United Nations and associated personnel, their equipment and premises shall not be made the object of attack or of any action that prevents them from discharging their mandate.
2. States Parties shall take all appropriate measures to ensure the safety and security of United Nations and associated personnel. In particular, States Parties shall take all appropriate steps to protect United Nations and associated personnel who are deployed in their territory from the crimes set out in article 9.

---

1 For reservation in respect of this paragraph by Costa Rica, see p. 1226.

3. States Parties shall cooperate with the United Nations and other States Parties, as appropriate, in the implementation of this Convention, particularly in any case where the host State is unable itself to take the required measures.

Art. 8. Duty to release or return United Nations and associated personnel captured or detained

Except as otherwise provided in an applicable status-of-forces agreement, if United Nations or associated personnel are captured or detained in the course of the performance of their duties and their identification has been established, they shall not be subjected to interrogation and they shall be promptly released and returned to United Nations or other appropriate authorities. Pending their release such personnel shall be treated in accordance with universally recognized standards of human rights and the principles and spirit of the Geneva Conventions of 1949.

Art. 9. Crimes against United Nations and associated personnel

1. The intentional commission of:
   (a) A murder, kidnapping or other attack upon the person or liberty of any United Nations or associated personnel;
   (b) A violent attack upon the official premises, the private accommodation or the means of transportation of any United Nations or associated personnel likely to endanger his or her person or liberty;
   (c)[2] A threat to commit any such attack with the objective of compelling a physical or juridical person to do or to refrain from doing any act;
   (d) An attempt to commit any such attack; and
   (e) An act constituting participation as an accomplice in any such attack, or in an attempt to commit such attack, or in organizing or ordering others to commit such attack, shall be made by each State Party a crime under its national law.
2. Each State Party shall make the crimes set out in paragraph 1 punishable by appropriate penalties which shall take into account their grave nature.

Art. 10. Establishment of jurisdiction

1. Each State Party shall take such measures as may be necessary to establish its jurisdiction over the crimes set out in article 9 in the following cases:
   (a) When the crime is committed in the territory of that State or on board a ship or aircraft registered in that State;
   (b) When the alleged offender is a national of that State.
2. A State Party may also establish its jurisdiction over any such crime when it is committed:
   (a) By a stateless person whose habitual residence is in that State; or
   (b) With respect to a national of that State; or
   (c) In an attempt to compel that State to do or to abstain from doing any act.
3. Any State Party which has established jurisdiction as mentioned in paragraph 2 shall notify the Secretary-General of the United Nations. If such State Party subsequently rescinds that jurisdiction, it shall notify the Secretary-General of the United Nations.
4. Each State Party shall take such measures as may be necessary to establish its jurisdiction over the crimes set out in article 9 in cases where the alleged

2 For interpretative declaration in respect of this paragraph by Belgium, see p. 1226.

offender is present in its territory and it does not extradite such person pursuant to article 15 to any of the States Parties which have established their jurisdiction in accordance with paragraph 1 or 2.

5. This Convention does not exclude any criminal jurisdiction exercised in accordance with national law.

Art. 11. Prevention of crimes against United Nations and associated personnel

States Parties shall cooperate in the prevention of the crimes set out in article 9, particularly by:

(a) Taking all practicable measures to prevent preparations in their respective territories for the commission of those crimes within or outside their territories; and

(b) Exchanging information in accordance with their national law and coordinating the taking of administrative and other measures as appropriate to prevent the commission of those crimes.

Art. 12. Communication of information

1. Under the conditions provided for in its national law, the State Party in whose territory a crime set out in article 9 has been committed shall, if it has reason to believe that an alleged offender has fled from its territory, communicate to the Secretary-General of the United Nations and, directly or through the Secretary-General, to the State or States concerned all the pertinent facts regarding the crime committed and all available information regarding the identity of the alleged offender.
2. Whenever a crime set out in article 9 has been committed, any State Party which has information concerning the victim and circumstances of the crime shall endeavour to transmit such information, under the conditions provided for in its national law, fully and promptly to the Secretary-General of the United Nations and the State or States concerned.

Art. 13. Measures to ensure prosecution or extradition

1. Where the circumstances so warrant, the State Party in whose territory the alleged offender is present shall take the appropriate measures under its national law to ensure that person's presence for the purpose of prosecution or extradition.
2. Measures taken in accordance with paragraph 1 shall be notified, in conformity with national law and without delay, to the Secretary-General of the United Nations and, either directly or through the Secretary-General, to:
   (a) The State where the crime was committed;
   (b) The State or States of which the alleged offender is a national or, if such person is a stateless person, in whose territory that person has his or her habitual residence;
   (c) The State or States of which the victim is a national; and
   (d) Other interested States.

Art. 14.[3] Prosecution of alleged offenders

The State Party in whose territory the alleged offender is present shall, if it does not extradite that person, submit, without exception whatsoever and without undue delay, the case to its competent authorities for the purpose of prosecu-

3 For declaration in respect of this article by the Netherlands, see p. 1227.

tion, through proceedings in accordance with the law of that State. Those authorities shall take their decision in the same manner as in the case of an ordinary offence of a grave nature under the law of that State.

Art. 15. Extradition of alleged offenders

1. To the extent that the crimes set out in article 9 are not extraditable offences in any extradition treaty existing between States Parties, they shall be deemed to be included as such therein. States Parties undertake to include those crimes as extraditable offences in every extradition treaty to be concluded between them.
2. If a State Party which makes extradition conditional on the existence of a treaty receives a request for extradition from another State Party with which it has no extradition treaty, it may at its option consider this Convention as the legal basis for extradition in respect of those crimes. Extradition shall be subject to the conditions provided in the law of the requested State.
3. States Parties which do not make extradition conditional on the existence of a treaty shall recognize those crimes as extraditable offences between themselves subject to the conditions provided in the law of the requested State.
4. Each of those crimes shall be treated, for the purposes of extradition between States Parties, as if it had been committed not only in the place in which it occurred but also in the territories of the States Parties which have established their jurisdiction in accordance with paragraph 1 or 2 of article 10.

Art. 16. Mutual assistance in criminal matters

1. States Parties shall afford one another the greatest measure of assistance in connection with criminal proceedings brought in respect of the crimes set out in article 9, including assistance in obtaining evidence at their disposal necessary for the proceedings. The law of the requested State shall apply in all cases.
2. The provisions of paragraph 1 shall not affect obligations concerning mutual assistance embodied in any other treaty

Art. 17. Fair treatment

1. Any person regarding whom investigations or proceedings are being carried out in connection with any of the crimes set out in article 9 shall be guaranteed fair treatment, a fair trial and full protection of his or her rights at all stages of the investigations or proceedings.
2. Any alleged offender shall be entitled:
   (a) To communicate without delay with the nearest appropriate representative of the State or States of which such person is a national or which is otherwise entitled to protect that person's rights or, if such person is a stateless person, of the State which, at that person's request, is willing to protect that person's rights; and
   (b) To be visited by a representative of that State or those States.

Art. 18. Notification of outcome of proceedings

The State Party where an alleged offender is prosecuted shall communicate the final outcome of the proceedings to the Secretary-General of the United Nations, who shall transmit the information to other States Parties.

Art. 19. Dissemination
The States Parties undertake to disseminate this Convention as widely as possible and, in particular, to include the study thereof, as well as relevant provisions of international humanitarian law, in their programmes of military instruction.

Art. 20. Savings clauses
Nothing in this Convention shall affect:
(a) The applicability of international humanitarian law and universally recognized standards of human rights as contained in international instruments in relation to the protection of United Nations operations and United Nations and associated personnel or the responsibility of such personnel to respect such law and standards;
(b) The rights and obligations of States, consistent with the Charter of the United Nations, regarding the consent to entry of persons into their territories;
(c) The obligation of United Nations and associated personnel to act in accordance with the terms of the mandate of a United Nations operation;
(d) The right of States which voluntarily contribute personnel to a United Nations operation to withdraw their personnel from participation in such operation; or
(e) The entitlement to appropriate compensation payable in the event of death, disability, injury or illness attributable to peace-keeping service by persons voluntarily contributed by States to United Nations operations.

Art. 21. Right of self-defence
Nothing in this Convention shall be construed so as to derogate from the right to act in self-defence.

Art. 22. Dispute settlement
1.[4] Any dispute between two or more States Parties concerning the interpretation or application of this Convention which is not settled by negotiation shall, at the request of one of them, be submitted to arbitration. If within six months from the date of the request for arbitration the parties are unable to agree on the organization of the arbitration, any one of those parties may refer the dispute to the International Court of Justice by application in conformity with the Statute of the Court.
2. Each State Party may at the time of signature, ratification, acceptance or approval of this Convention or accession thereto declare that it does not consider itself bound by all or part of paragraph 1. The other States Parties shall not be bound by paragraph 1 or the relevant part thereof with respect to any State Party which has made such a reservation.
3. Any State Party which has made a reservation in accordance with paragraph 2 may at any time withdraw that reservation by notification to the Secretary-General of the United Nations.

Art. 23. Review meetings
At the request of one or more States Parties, and if approved by a majority of States Parties, the Secretary-General of the United Nations shall convene a

[4] For reservations or declarations in respect of this paragraph by Lao People's Democratic Republic, Nepal, Slovakia and Tunisia, see pp. 1226-1227.

meeting of the States Parties to review the implementation of the Convention, and any problems encountered with regard to its application.

Art. 24. Signature
This Convention shall be open for signature by all States, until 31 December 1995, at United Nations Headquarters in New York.

Art. 25. Ratification, acceptance or approval
This Convention is subject to ratification, acceptance or approval. Instruments of ratification, acceptance or approval shall be deposited with the Secretary-General of the United Nations.

Art. 26. Accession
This Convention shall be open for accession by any State. The instruments of accession shall be deposited with the Secretary-General of the United Nations.

Art. 27. Entry into force
1. This Convention shall enter into force thirty days after twenty-two instruments of ratification, acceptance, approval or accession have been deposited with the Secretary-General of the United Nations.
2. For each State ratifying, accepting, approving or acceding to the Convention after the deposit of the twenty-second instrument of ratification, acceptance, approval or accession, the Convention shall enter into force on the thirtieth day after the deposit by such State of its instrument of ratification, acceptance, approval or accession.

Art. 28. Denunciation
1. A State Party may denounce this Convention by written notification to the Secretary-General of the United Nations.
2. Denunciation shall take effect one year following the date on which notification is received by the Secretary-General of the United Nations.

Art. 29. Authentic texts
The original of this Convention, of which the Arabic, Chinese, English, French, Russian and Spanish texts are equally authentic, shall be deposited with the Secretary-General of the United Nations, who shall send certified copies thereof to all States.

Done at New York on this ninth day of December one thousand nine hundred and ninety-four.

SIGNATURES, RATIFICATIONS, ACCESSIONS[1]

State	*Signatures*	*Ratifications, Accessions*
Albania	–	30 March 2001
Argentina	15 December 1994	6 January 1997
Australia	22 December 1995	4 December 2000
Austria	–	6 September 2000
Azerbaijan	–	3 August 2000
Bangladesh	21 December 1994	22 September 1999
Belarus	23 October 1995	29 November 2000
Belgium	21 December 1995	19 February 2002 *Dec.*
Bolivia	17 August 1995	–
Botswana	–	1 March 2000
Brazil	3 February 1995	6 September 2000
Brunei Darussalam	–	20 March 2002
Bulgaria	–	4 June 1998
Canada	15 December 1994	3 April 2002
Chile	–	27 August 1997
Costa Rica	–	17 October 2000 *Res.*
Côte d'Ivoire	–	13 March 2002
Croatia	–	27 March 2000
Czech Republic	27 December 1995	13 June 1997
Denmark	15 December 1994	11 April 1995
Ecuador	–	28 December 2000
Fiji	25 October 1995	1 April 1999
Finland	15 December 1994	5 January 2001
France	12 January 1995	5 June 2000
Germany	1 February 1995	22 April 1997 *Dec.*
Greece	–	3 August 2000
Guinea	–	7 September 2000
Haiti	19 December 1994	–
Honduras	17 May 1995	–
Hungary	–	13 July 1999
Iceland	–	10 May 2001
Italy	16 December 1994	5 April 1999
Jamaica	–	8 September 2000
Japan	6 June 1995	6 June 1995
Lao, People's Democratic Republic of	–	22 August 2002 *Res.*
Lesotho	–	6 September 2000
Libyan Arab Jamahiriya	–	22 September 2000
Liechtenstein	16 October 1995	11 December 2000
Lithuania	–	8 September 2000
Luxembourg	31 May 1995	30 July 2001
Macedonia, the former Yugoslav Republic of	–	6 March 2002
Malta	16 March 1995	–
Monaco	–	5 March 1999
Nauru	–	12 November 2001
Nepal	–	8 September 2000 *Dec.*
Netherlands	22 December 1995	7 February 2002 *Dec.*

[1] Based on the indications in *Multilateral Treaties Deposited with the Secretary-General, New York, United Nations*, (ST/LEG/SER.E) as available on http://untreaty.un.org of 19 October 2002.

State	*Signatures*	*Ratifications, Accessions*
New Zealand	15 December 1994	16 December 1998
Norway	15 December 1994	3 July 1995
Pakistan	8 March 1995	–
Panama	15 December 1994	4 April 1996
Philippines	27 February 1995	17 June 1997
Poland	17 March 1995	20 May 2000
Portugal	15 December 1994	14 October 1998
Republic of Korea	–	8 December 1997
Romania	27 September 1995	29 December 1997
Russian Federation	26 September 1995	25 June 2001
Samoa	16 January 1995	–
Senegal	21 February 1995	9 June 1999
Sierra Leone	13 February 1995	–
Singapore	–	26 March 1996
Slovakia	28 December 1995 *Dec.*	26 June 1996 *Dec.*
Spain	19 December 1994	13 January 1998
Sweden	15 December 1994	25 June 1996
Togo	22 December 1995	–
Tunisia	22 February 1995	12 September 2000 *Res.*
Turkmenistan	–	12 September 2000 *Dec.*
Ukraine	15 December 1994	17 August 1995
United Kingdom	19 December 1995	6 May 1998
United States of America	19 December 1994	–
Uruguay	17 November 1995	3 September 1999
Uzbekistan	–	3 July 1996

DECLARATIONS AND RESERVATIONS

BELGIUM (*interpretative declaration made upon ratification*)
The Belgian Government declares the following: article 9, paragraph 1 (c), only covers cases where the threat is credible.

COSTA RICA (*reservation made on accession*)
The Government of the Republic enters a reservation to article 2, paragraph 2, of the Convention, to the effect that limiting the scope of the application of the Convention is contrary to the pacifist thinking of our country and, accordingly, that, in the event of conflicts with the application of the Convention, Costa Rica will, where necessary, give precedence to humanitarian law.

GERMANY (*declaration made on accession*)
In accordance with German law, the authorities of the Federal Republic of Germany will communicate information on alleged offenders, victims and circumstances of the crime (personal data) directly to the states concerned and, in parallel with this, will inform the Secretary-General of the United Nations that such information has been communicated.

LAO PEOPLE'S DEMOCRATIC REPUBLIC (*reservation made on accession*)
In accordance with paragraph 2, Article 22 of the Convention on the Safety of United Nations and Associated Personnel, the Lao People's Democratic Republic does not consider itself bound by paragraph 1, article 22 of the present Convention. The Lao People's Democratic Republic declares that to refer dispute relating to interpretation and application of the present Convention to arbitration or International Court of Justice, the agreement of all parties concerned in the dispute is necessary.

NEPAL (*declaration made on accession*)
[The Government of Nepal] avails itself of the provisions of article 22, paragraph 2, and declares that it does not consider itself bound by the provisions of paragraph 1 of the said article under which any dispute between two or more States Parties concerning the interpretation or application of this Convention shall at the request of one of them, be submitted to arbitration or referred to the International Court of Justice, and states that in each individual case, prior consent of all parties to such a dispute is necessary for the submission of the dispute to arbitration or to the International Court of Justice.

NETHERLANDS (*declaration made upon ratification*)
The Kingdom of the Netherlands understands Article 14 of the Convention on the Safety of United Nations and Associated Personnel states that the competent national authorities must decide on a case submitted to them in accordance with national law and in the same manner as they would decide on ordinary offences of a grave nature. Consequently the Kingdom of the Netherlands understands this provision to include the right of its competent judicial authorities to decide not to prosecute a person alleged to have committed a crime as referred to in Article 9, paragraph 1, if, in the opinion of the competent judicial authorities, grave considerations of procedural law indicate that effective prosecution would be possible.

SLOVAKIA (*declaration made upon signature and confirmed upon ratification*)
If a dispute concerning the interpretation or application of the Convention is not settled by negotiation, the Slovak Republic prefers its submission to the International Court of Justice in accordance with article 22, paragraph 1 of the Convention. Therefore a dispute, to which the Slovak Republic might be a Party can be submitted to arbitration only with the explicit consent of the Slovak Republic.

TUNISIA (*reservation made upon ratification*)
The Tunisian Republic declares that it does not consider itself bound by the provisions of article 22, paragraph 1, of the Convention and that disputes concerning the interpretation or application of the Convention may be submitted to arbitration or to the International Court of Justice only with the prior consent of all the parties concerned.

No. 100

UN SECRETARY-GENERAL'S BULLETIN ON OBSERVANCE BY UNITED NATIONS FORCES OF INTERNATIONAL HUMANITARIAN LAW

Promulgated by the Secretary-General of the United Nations on 6 August 1999

INTRODUCTORY NOTE: Since the establishment of the first peacekeeping operations of the United Nations in the 1950s, the International Committee of the Red Cross has consistently drawn the Secretary-General's attention to the necessity of assuring the application of international humanitarian law by UN forces. In response to these requests, provisions on humanitarian law were inserted into regulations for UN forces and into agreements concluded with states furnishing contingents. These provisions generally state that the forces shall observe "the principles and spirit" of the international conventions applicable to the conduct of military personnel. When, in the early 1990's, UN forces became increasingly involved in situations occasioning the use of force, it was considered necessary to establish more precise rules. The ICRC, in 1994, organized a symposium on humanitarian action and peacekeeping operations which, in 1995, was followed by two meetings of experts. In the same year, the UN Special Committee on Peacekeeping Operations requested the Secretary-General to "complete the elaboration of a code of conduct for United Nations peacekeeping personnel, consistent with applicable international humanitarian law". At the end of the two expert meetings, organized by the ICRC, in 1995, the ICRC submitted to the UN Secretary-General a document recapitulating the essential rules of humanitarian law. After consultations on this text between the ICRC and the UN Secretariat, a revised text was submitted to the Secretary-General on 10 May 1996, entitled "Guidelines for UN forces regarding respect for international humanitarian law". The term "Guidelines" was later replaced by "Directives". The document was the subject of extensive deliberations within the UN and was again partly revised. On 6 August 1999, the Secretary-General issued the present Bulletin which entered into force on 12 August 1999, the day of the 50th anniversary of the Geneva Conventions of 1949 *(No. 49–52).* A Secretary-General's bulletin is an administrative issuance of the Secretary-General as the chief administrative officer of the UN, binding on UN personnel and, in the present case, on members of UN forces.

ENTRY INTO FORCE: 12 August 1999.

AUTHENTIC TEXTS: Arabic, Chinese, English, French, Russian, Spanish.

TEXT PUBLISHED IN: United Nations Document ST/SGB/1999/13 (Arabic, Chinese, Engl., French, Russ., Span.); *IRRC*, Vol. 81, 1999; No. 836, pp. 806–817 (Engl., French); *ILM,* Vol. 38, 1999, pp. 1656–1659 (Engl.); *International Peacekeeping* (Kluwer), Vol. 5, 1999, pp. 160–161 (Engl.); Roberts and Guelff, pp. 721–730 (Engl.).

* * *

The Secretary-General, for the purpose of setting out fundamental principles and rules of international humanitarian law applicable to United Nations forces conducting operations under United Nations command and control, promulgates the following:

Section 1. Field of application

1.1 The fundamental principles and rules of international humanitarian law set out in the present bulletin are applicable to United Nations forces when in situations of armed conflict that they are actively engaged therein as combatants, to the extent and for the duration of their engagement. They are accordingly applicable in enforcement actions, or in peacekeeping operations when the use of force is permitted in self-defence.

1.2 The promulgation of this bulletin does not affect the protected status of members of peacekeeping operations under the 1994 Convention on the Safety of United Nations and Associated Personnel or their status as non-combatants, as long as they are entitled to the protection given to civilians under the international law of armed conflict.

Section 2. Application of national law

The present provisions do not constitute an exhaustive list of principles and rules of international humanitarian law binding upon military personnel, and do not prejudice the application thereof, nor do they replace the national laws by which military personnel remain bound throughout the operation.

Section 3. Status-of-forces agreement

In the status-of-forces agreement concluded between the United Nations and a State in whose territory a United Nations force is deployed, the United Nations undertakes to ensure that the force shall conduct its operations with full respect for the principles and rules of the general conventions applicable to the conduct of military personnel. The United Nations also undertakes to ensure that members of the military personnel of the force are fully acquainted with the principles and rules of those international instruments. The obligation to respect the said principles and rules is applicable to United Nations forces even in the absence of a status-of-forces agreement.

Section 4. Violations of international humanitarian law

In case of violations of international humanitarian law, members of the military personnel of a United Nations force are subject to prosecution in their national courts.

Section 5. Protection of the civilian population

5.1 The United Nations force shall make a clear distinction at all times between civilians and combatants and between civilian objects and military objectives. Military operations shall be directed only against combatants and military objectives. Attacks on civilians or civilian objects are prohibited.

5.2 Civilians shall enjoy the protection afforded by this section, unless and for such time as they take a direct part in hostilities.

5.3 The United Nations force shall take all feasible precautions to avoid, and in any event to minimize, incidental loss of civilian life, injury to civilians or damage to civilian property.

5.4 In its area of operation, the United Nations force shall avoid, to the extent feasible, locating military objectives within or near densely populated areas, and take all necessary precautions to protect the civilian population, individual citizens and civilian objects against the dangers resulting from military operations. Military installations and equipment of peacekeeping operations, as such, shall not be considered military objectives.

5.5 The United Nations force is prohibited from launching operations of a nature likely to strike military objectives and civilians in an indiscriminate manner, as well as operations that may be expected to cause incidental loss of life among the civilian population or damage to civilian objects that would be excessive in relation to the concrete and direct military advantage anticipated.

5.6 The United Nations force shall not engage in reprisals against civilians or civilian objects.

Section 6. Means and methods of combat

6.1 The right of the United Nations force to choose methods and means of combat is not unlimited.

6.2 The United Nations force shall respect the rules prohibiting or restricting the use of certain weapons and methods of combat under the relevant instruments of international humanitarian law. These include, in particular, the prohibition on the use of asphyxiating, poisonous or other gases and biological methods of warfare; bullets which explode, expand or flatten easily in the human body; and certain explosive projectiles. The use of certain conventional weapons, such as non-detectable fragments, anti-personnel mines, booby traps and incendiary weapons, is prohibited.

6.3 The United Nations force is prohibited from employing methods of warfare which may cause superfluous injury or unnecessary suffering, or which are intended, or may be expected to cause, widespread, long-term and severe damage to the natural environment.

6.4 The United Nations force is prohibited from using weapons or methods of combat of a nature to cause unnecessary suffering.

6.5 It is forbidden to order that there shall be no survivors.

6.6 The United Nations force is prohibited from attacking monuments of art, architecture or history, archaeological sites, works of art, places of worship and museums and libraries which constitute the cultural or spiritual heritage of peoples. In its area of operation, the United Nations force shall not use such cultural property or their immediate surroundings for purposes which might expose them to destruction or damage. Theft, pillage, misappropriation and any act of vandalism directed against cultural property is strictly prohibited.

6.7 The United Nations force is prohibited from attacking, destroying, removing or rendering useless objects indispensable to the survival of the civilian population, such as foodstuff, crops, livestock and drinking-water installations and supplies.

6.8 The United Nations force shall not make installations containing dangerous forces, namely dams, dikes and nuclear electrical generating stations, the object of military operations if such operations may cause the release of dangerous forces and consequent severe losses among the civilian population.

6.9 The United Nations force shall not engage in reprisals against objects and installations protected under this section.

Section 7. Treatment of civilians and persons hors de combat

7.1 Persons not, or no longer, taking part in military operations, including civilians, members of armed forces who have laid down their weapons and persons placed *hors de combat* by reason of sickness, wounds or detention, shall, in all circumstances, be treated humanely and without any adverse distinction based on race, sex, religious convictions or any other ground. They shall be accorded full respect for their person, honour and religious and other convictions.

7.2 The following acts against any of the persons mentioned in section 7.1 are prohibited at any time and in any place: violence to life or physical integrity; murder as well as cruel treatment such as torture, mutilation or any form of corporal punishment; collective punishment; reprisals; the taking of hostages; rape; enforced prostitution; any form of sexual assault and humiliation and degrading treatment; enslavement; and pillage.

7.3 Women shall be especially protected against any attack, in particular against rape, enforced prostitution or any other form of indecent assault.

7.4 Children shall be the object of special respect and shall be protected against any form of indecent assault.

Section 8. Treatment of detained persons

The United Nations force shall treat with humanity and respect for their dignity detained members of the armed forces and other persons who no longer take part in military operations by reason of detention. Without prejudice to their legal status, they shall be treated in accordance with the relevant provisions of the Third Geneva Convention of 1949, as may be applicable to them *mutatis mutandis*. In particular:

(a) Their capture and detention shall be notified without delay to the party on which they depend and to the Central Tracing Agency of the International Committee of the Red Cross (ICRC), in particular in order to inform their families;

(b) They shall be held in secure and safe premises which provide all possible safeguards of hygiene and health, and shall not be detained in areas exposed to the dangers of the combat zone;

(c) They shall be entitled to receive food and clothing, hygiene and medical attention;

(d) They shall under no circumstances be subjected to any form of torture or ill-treatment;

(e) Women whose liberty has been restricted shall be held in quarters separated from men's quarters, and shall be under the immediate supervision of women;

(f) In cases where children who have not attained the age of sixteen years take a direct part in hostilities and are arrested, detained or interned by the United Nations force, they shall continue to benefit from special protection. In particular, they shall be held in quarters separate from the quarters of adults, except when accommodated with their families;

(g) ICRC's right to visit prisoners and detained persons shall be respected and guaranteed.

Section 9. Protection of the wounded, the sick, and medical and relief personnel

9.1 Members of the armed forces and other persons in the power of the United Nations force who are wounded or sick shall be respected and protected in all circumstances. They shall be treated humanely and receive the medical care and attention required by their condition, without adverse distinction. Only urgent medical reasons will authorize priority in the order of treatment to be administered.

9.2 Whenever circumstances permit, a suspension of fire shall be arranged, or other local arrangements made, to permit the search for and identification of the wounded, the sick and the dead left on the battlefield and allow for their collection, removal, exchange and transport.

9.3 The United Nations force shall not attack medical establishments or mobile medical units. These shall at all times be respected and protected, unless they are used, outside their humanitarian function, to attack or otherwise commit harmful acts against the United Nations force.

9.4 The United Nations force shall in all circumstances respect and protect medical personnel exclusively engaged in the search for, transport or treatment of the wounded or sick, as well as religious personnel.

9.5 The United Nations force shall respect and protect transports of wounded and sick or medical equipment in the same way as mobile medical units.

9.6 The United Nations force shall not engage in reprisals against the wounded, the sick or the personnel, establishments and equipment protected under this section.

9.7 The United Nations force shall in all circumstances respect the Red Cross and Red Crescent emblems. These emblems may not be employed except to indicate or to protect medical units and medical establishments, personnel and material. Any misuse of the Red Cross or Red Crescent emblems is prohibited.

9.8 The United Nations force shall respect the right of the families to know about the fate of their sick, wounded and deceased relatives. To this end, the force shall facilitate the work of the ICRC Central Tracing Agency.

9.9 The United Nations force shall facilitate the work of relief operations which are humanitarian and impartial in character and conducted without any adverse distinction, and shall respect personnel, vehicles and premises involved in such operations.

Section 10. Entry into force
The present bulletin shall enter into force on 12 August 1999.

XI

MERCENARIES

No. 101

CONVENTION FOR THE ELIMINATION OF MERCENARISM IN AFRICA

Adopted by the Assembly of the Heads of State and Government of the Organization of African Unity, at Libreville, 3 July 1977

INTRODUCTORY NOTE: Efforts to prohibit the use of mercenaries started in 1961, when Katanga was aided by mercenaries in its attempt to secede from the newly independent Congo (see Security Council Resolutions 161 A of 21 February 1961, and 169 of 24 November 1961). African governments became particularly active in combating the use of mercenaries, mercenaries being primarily employed against liberation movements and developing states. A committee of experts of the OAU, charged with drafting a convention on mercenaries, presented a report and a draft convention to the OAU's Council of Ministers in 1972. A further draft was prepared in 1976 by an international commission of enquiry that had attended judicial procedings in Luanda against thirteen mercenaries who had taken part in the civil war against the government of Angola. The Government of Angola presented this draft to the OAU Assembly of Heads of State and Government whereupon a committee of experts prepared the present Convention. The Convention was adopted on 3 July 1977, a few weeks after the adoption of Protocol I additional to the Geneva Conventions of 10 June 1977 (*No. 56*), whose Article 47 also deals with mercenaries. Article 47, however, seemed not to be sufficiently stringent for African states.

ENTRY INTO FORCE: 22 April 1985

AUTHENTIC TEXT: Arabic, English, French. The text below is reproduced in the Organization of African Unity, Doc. Cm/817 (XXXIX), Annex II, Rev. 1, pp. 1–7.

TEXT PUBLISHED IN: Document of the Organization of African Unity, Doc. CM/817 (XXXIX), Annex II, Rev. 1, pp. 1–7 (Arabic, English, French), *Droit des conflits armés*, pp. 1281–1287 (French); ICRC website: www.icrc.org/ihl.nsf (Engl., French).

TABLE OF CONTENTS

* * *

Preamble

We, the Heads of State and Government of the Member States of the Organization of African Unity;

Considering the grave threat which the activities of mercenaries present to the independence, sovereignty, security, territorial integrity and harmonious development of Member States of the Organization of African Unity;

Concerned with the threat which the activities of mercenaries pose to the legitimate exercise of the right of African People under colonial and racist domination to their independence and freedom;

Convinced that total solidarity and co-operation between Member States are indispensable for putting an end to the subversive activities of mercenaries in Africa;

Considering that the resolutions of the UN and the OAU, the statements of attitude and the practice of a great number of States are indicative of the development of new rules of international law making mercenarism an international crime;

Determined to take all necessary measures to eliminate from the African continent the scourge that mercenarism represents;

Have agreed as follows:

Article 1. Definition

1. A mercenary is any person who:
   (a) is specially recruited locally or abroad in order to fight in an armed conflicts;
   (b) does in fact take a direct part in the hostilities;
   (c) is motivated to take part in the hostilities essentially by the desire for private gain and in fact is promised by or on behalf of a party to the conflict material compensation;
   (d) is neither a national of a party to the conflict nor a resident of territory controlled by a party to the conflict;
   (e) is not a member of the armed forces of a party to the conflict; and
   (f) is not sent by a state other than a party to the conflict on official mission as a member of the armed forces of the said state.
2. The crime of mercenarism is committed by the individual, group or association, representative of a State or the State itself who with the aim of opposing by armed violence a process of self-determination stability or the territorial integrity of another State, practises any of the following acts:
   (a) Shelters, organises, finances, assists, equips, trains, promotes, supports or in any manner employs bands of mercenaries;
   (b) Enlists, enrols or tries to enrol in the said bands;
   (c) Allows the activities mentioned in paragraph (a) to be carried out in any territory under its jurisdiction or in any place under its control or affords

facilities for transit, transport or other operations of the above mentioned forces.

3. Any person, natural or juridical who commits the crime of mercenarism as defined in paragraph 1[1] of this Article commits an Offence considered as a crime against peace and security in Africa and shall be punished as such.

Art. 2. Aggravating circumstances
The fact of assuming command over or giving orders to mercenaries shall be considered as an aggravating circumstances.

Art. 3. Status of mercenaries
Mercenaries shall not enjoy the status of combatants and shall not be entitled to the prisoners of war status.

Art. 4. Scope of criminal responsibility
A mercenary is responsible both for the crime of mercenarism and all related offences, without prejudice to any other offences for which he may be prosecuted.

Art. 5. General responsibility of States and their representatives
1. When the representative of a State is accused by virtue of the provisions of Article 1 of this Convention for acts or omissions declared by the aforesaid article to be criminal, he shall be punished for such an act or omission.
2. When a State is accused by virtue of the provisions of Article 1 of this Convention for acts or omissions declared by the aforesaid article to be criminal, any other party to the present Convention may invoke the provisions of this Convention in its relations with the offending State and before any competent OAU or International Organisation tribunal or body.

Art. 6. Obligations of States
The contracting parties shall take all necessary measures to eradicate all mercenary activities in Africa.
To this end, each contracting State shall undertake to:
(a) Prevent its nationals or foreigners on its territory from engaging in any of the acts mentioned in Article 1 of this Convention;
(b) Prevent entry into or passage through its territory of any mercenary or any equipment destined for mercenary use;
(c) Prohibit on its territory any activities by persons or organisations who use mercenaries against any African State member of the Organization of African Unity or the people of Africa in their struggle for liberation;
(d) Communicate to the other Member States of the Organization of African Unity either directly or through the Secretariat of the OAU any information related to the activities of mercenaries as soon as it comes to its knowledge;
(e) Forbid on its territory the recruitment, training, financing and equipment of mercenaries and any other form of activities likely to promote mercenarism;
(f) Take all the necessary legislative and other measures to ensure the immediate entry into force of this Convention.

[1] It is the second paragraph of the first article of the African Convention, because the first paragraph deals with the definition of the mercenary and not with the definition of the crime of mercenarism.

Art. 7. Penalties
Each contracting State shall undertake to make the offence defined in Article 1 of this Convention punishable by severest penalties under its laws, including capital punishment.

Art. 8. Jurisdiction
Each contracting State shall undertake to take such measures as may be necessary to punish, in accordance with the provisions of Article 7, any person who commits an offence under Article 1 of this Convention and who is found on its territory if it does not extradite him to the State against which the offence has been committed.

Art. 9. Extradition
1. The crimes defined in Article 1 of this Convention, are not covered by national legislation excluding extradition for political offences.
2. A request for extradition shall not be refused unless the requested State undertakes to exercise jurisdiction over the offender in accordance with the provisions of Article 8.
3. Where a national is involved in the request for extradition, the requested State shall take proceedings against him for the offence committed if extradition is refused.
4. Where proceedings have been initiated in accordance with paragraphs 2 and 3 of this Article, the requested State shall inform the requesting State or any other State member of the OAU interested in the proceedings, of the result thereof.
5. A State shall be deemed interested in the proceedings within the meaning of paragraph 4 of this Article if the offence is linked in any way with its territory or is directed against its interests.

Art. 10. Mutual assistance
The contracting States shall afford one another the greatest measure of assistance in connection with the investigation and criminal proceedings brought in respect of the offence and other acts connected with the activities of the offender.

Art. 11. Judicial guarantee
Any person or group of persons on trial for the crime defined in Article 1 of this Convention shall be entitled to all the guarantees normally granted to any ordinary person by the State on whose territory he is being tried.

Art.12. Settlement of disputes
Any dispute regarding the interpretation and application of the provisions of this Convention shall be settled by the interested parties in accordance with the principle of the Charter of the Organization of African Unity and the Charter of the United Nations.

Art. 13. Signature, ratification and entry into force
1. This Convention shall be open for signature by the Members of the Organization of African Unity. It shall be ratified. The instruments of ratification shall be deposited with the Administrative Secretary-General of the Organization.

2. This Convention shall come into force 30 days after the date of the deposit of the seventeenth instrument of ratification.
3. As regard any signatory subsequently ratifying the Convention, it shall come into force 30 days after the date of the deposit of its instrument of ratification.

Art. 14. Accession

1. Any Member State of the Organization of African Unity may accede to this Convention.
2. Accession shall be deposit with the Administrative Secretary-General of the Organization of an instrument of accession, which shall take effect 30 days after the date of its deposit.

Art. 15. Notification and registration

1. The Administrative Secretary-General of the Organization of African Unity shall notify the Member States of the Organization of:
   (a) the deposit of any instrument of ratification or accession;
   (b) the date of entry into force of this Convention.
2. The Administrative Secretary-General of the Organization of African Unity shall transmit certified copies of the Convention to all Member States of the Organization.
3. The Administrative Secretary-General of the Organization of African Unity shall, as soon as this Convention comes into force, register it pursuant to Article 102 of the Charter of the United Nations.

In witness whereof, We, the Heads of States and Government of the Member States of the Organization of African Unity have appended our signatures to this Convention.

Done at Libreville, this 3rd day of July 1977 in the Arabic, English, and French languages, all texts being equally authoritative, in a single original copy which shall be deposited in the archives of the Organization of African Unity.

SIGNATURES, RATIFICATIONS AND ACCESSIONS[1]

State	*Signatures*	*Ratifications, Accessions*[2]
Algeria	21 July 1978	–
Angola	19 July 1979	–
Benin	16 July 1979	3 May 1982
Burkina Faso	5 March 1984	21 September 1984
Cameroon	19 July 1978	8 August 1987
Congo	–	9 September 1988
Congo, Dem. Rep. of	20 March 1979	13 July 1979
Egypt	31 March 1978	21 June 1978
Ethiopia	–	16 June 1982

[1] Based on the communication received from the Legal Counsel of the Organization of African Unity, of 3 December 2001.

[2] The table indicates the dates of deposit of the instruments of ratification or accession.

State	*Signatures*	*Ratifications, Accessions*[2]
Ghana	8 June 1978	21 August 1978
Guinea	10 February 1978	–
Lesotho	–	21 January 1983
Liberia	19 July 1985	9 June 1982
Mali	–	25 September 1978
Morocco	12 February 1980	–
Niger	8 November 1979	16 September 1980
Nigeria	10 February 1978	24 June 1986
Rwanda	13 March 1978	1 June 1979
Senegal	8 February 1978	8 January 1982
Seychelles	–	15 October 1979
Sudan	13 November 1978	16 August 1978
Tanzania	13 May 1979	22 March 1985
Togo	16 July 1978	5 May 1987
Tunisia	18 July 1985	4 June 1984
Zambia	14 April 1982	15 February 1983
Zimbabwe	–	14 February 1992

No. 102

INTERNATIONAL CONVENTION AGAINST THE RECRUITMENT, USE, FINANCING AND TRAINING OF MERCENARIES

Adopted by resolution 44/34 of the United Nations General Assembly on 4 December 1989

INTRODUCTORY NOTE. After repeated denunciations of the use of mercenaries by UN organs, and in view of the limited applicability of Article 47 of Protocol I Additional to the Geneva Conventions (*No. 56*), the General Assembly, in 1980, established an *ad hoc* committee to draft a convention against the recruitment, use, financing and training of mercenaries, composed of 35 states (Resolution 35/48 of 4 December 1980). Nine years later, the General Assembly, by consensus, adopted the present Convention.

ENTRY INTO FORCE: 20 October 2001.

AUTHENTIC TEXTS: Arabic, Chinese, English, French, Spanish, Russian. The text bellow is reproduced from an original copy received from the United Nations treaty section. See also: *Resolutions and decisions adopted by the General Assembly during its forty-,fourth session, 19 September – 29 December 1989,* General Assembly Official Records, Forty-fourth Session, Supplement No. 49 (A/44/49), pp. 306–308.

TEXT PUBLISHED IN: *Résolutions et décisions adoptées par l'Assemblée générale au cours de sa quarante-quatrième session, 19 septembre–29 décembre 1989, Assemblée générale Documents officiels: quarante-quatrième session*, Supplément No. 49 (A144149), New York, Nations Unies, 1990, pp. 322-324 (Arabic, Chinese, Engl., French, Span., Russ.); *Droit des conflits armés,* pp. 1289–1295 (French); *RGDIP,* 1990, pp. 561–568 (French); *ILM*, Vol. 29, 1990, pp. 89–97 (Engl.); E. Lawson, *Encyclopedia of Human Rights,* New York, Taylor & Francis Inc., 1991, pp. 924–925 (Engl., French); United Nations website: http://untreaty.un.org; ICRC website: www.icrc.org/ihl.nsf (Engl., French, Span.).

* * *

The States Parties to the present Convention,

Reaffirming the purposes and principles enshrined in the Charter of the United Nations and in the Declaration on Principles of International Law concerning Friendly Relations and Co-operation among States in accordance with the Charter of the United Nations,

Being aware of the recruitment, use, financing and training of mercenaries for activities which violate principles of international law, such as those of sovereign equality, political independence, territorial integrity of States and self-determination of peoples,

Affirming that the recruitment, use, financing and training of mercenaries should be considered as offences of grave concern to all States and that any person committing any of these-offences should be either prosecuted or extradited,

Convinced of the necessity to develop and enhance international co-operation among States for the prevention, prosecution and punishment of such offences,

Expressing concern at new unlawful international activities linking drug traffickers and mercenaries in the perpetration of violent actions which undermine the constitutional order of States,

Also convinced that the adoption of a convention against the recruitment, use, financing and training of mercenaries would contribute to the eradication of these nefarious activities and thereby to the observance of the purposes and principles enshrined in the Charter,

Cognizant that matters not regulated by such a convention continue to be governed by the rules and principles of international law,

Have agreed as follows:

Article 1.

For the purposes of the present Convention,

1. A mercenary is any person who:
   (a) Is specially recruited locally or abroad in order to fight in an armed conflict;
   (b) Is motivated to take part in the hostilities essentially by the desire for private gain and, in fact, is promised, by or on behalf of a party to the conflict, material compensation substantially in excess of that promised or paid to combatants of similar rank and functions in the armed forces of that party;
   (c) Is neither a national of a party to the conflict nor a resident of territory controlled by a party to the conflict;
   (d) Is not a member of the armed forces of a party to the conflict; and
   (e) Has not been sent by a State which is not a party to the conflict on official duty as a member of its armed forces.
2. A mercenary is also any person who, in any other situation:
   (a) Is specially recruited locally or abroad for the purpose of participating in a concerted act of violence aimed at:
      (i) Overthrowing a Government or otherwise undermining the constitutional order of a State; or
      (ii) Undermining the territorial integrity of a State;
   (b) Is motivated to take part therein essentially by the desire for significant private gain and is prompted by the promise or payment of material compensation;
   (c) Is neither a national nor a resident of the State against which such an act is directed;
   (d) Has not been sent by a State on official duty; and
   (e) Is not a member of the armed forces of the State on whose territory the act is undertaken.

Art. 2. Any person who recruits, uses, finances or trains mercenaries, as defined in article 1 of the present Convention, commits an offence for the purposes of the Convention.

Art. 3.
1. A mercenary, as defined in article 1 of the present Convention, who participates directly in hostilities or in a concerted act of violence, as the case may be, commits an offence for the purposes of the Convention.
2. Nothing in this article limits the scope of application of article 4 of the present Convention.

Art. 4. An offence is committed by any person who:
(a) Attempts to commit one of the offences set forth in the present Convention;
(b) Is the accomplice of a person who commits or attempts to commit any of the offences set forth in the present Convention.

Art. 5.
1. States Parties shall note recruit, use, finance or train mercenaries and shall prohibit such activities in accordance with the provisions of the present Convention.
2. States Parties shall not recruit, use, finance or train mercenaries for the purpose of opposing the legitimate exercise of the inalienable right of peoples to self-determination, as recognized by international law, and shall take, in conformity with international law, the appropriate measures to prevent the recruitment, use, financing or training of mercenaries for that purpose.
3. They shall make the offences set forth in the present Convention punishable by appropriate penalties which take into account the grave nature of those offences.

Art. 6.
States Parties shall co-operate in the prevention of the offences set forth in the present Convention, particularly by:
(a) Taking all practicable measures to prevent preparations in their respective territories for the commission of those offences within or outside their territories, including the prohibition of illegal activities of persons, groups and organizations that encourage, instigate, organize or engage in the perpetration of such offences;
(b) Co-ordinating the taking of administrative and other measures as appropriate to prevent the commission of those offences.

Art. 7.
States Parties shall co-operate in taking the necessary measures for the implementation of the present Convention.

Art. 8.
Any State Party having reason to believe that one of the offences set forth in the present Convention has been, is being or will be committed shall, in accordance with its national law, communicate the relevant information, as soon as it comes to its knowledge, directly or through the Secretary-General of the United Nations, to the States Parties affected.

Art. 9.
1. Each State Party shall take such measures as may be necessary to establish its jurisdiction over any of the offences set forth in the present Convention which are committed:

(a) In its territory or on board a ship or aircraft registered in that State;
(b) By any of its nationals or, if that State considers it appropriate, by those stateless persons who have their habitual residence in that territory.

2. Each State Party shall likewise take such measures as may be necessary to establish its jurisdiction over the offences set forth in articles 2, 3 and 4 of the present Convention in cases where the alleged offender is present in its territory and it does note extradite him to any of the States mentioned in paragraph 1 of this article.
3. The present Convention does not exclude any criminal jurisdiction exercised in accordance with national law.

Art. 10.

1. Upon being satisfied that the circumstances so warrant, any State Party in whose territory the alleged offender is present shall, in accordance with its laws, take him into custody or take such other measures to ensure his presence for such time as is necessary to enable any criminal or extradition proceedings to be instituted. The State Party shall immediately make a preliminary inquiry into the facts.
2. When a State Party, pursuant to this article, has taken a person into custody or has taken such other measures referred to in paragraph 1 of this article, it shall notify without delay either directly or through the Secretary-General of the United Nations:
   (a) The State Party where the offence was committed;
   (b) The State Party against which the offence has been directed or attempted;
   (c) The State Party of which the natural or juridical person against whom the offence has been directed or attempted is a national;
   (d) The State Party of which the alleged offender is a national or, if he is a stateless person, in whose territory he has his habitual residence;
   (e) Any other interested State Party which it considers it appropriate to notify.
3. Any person regarding whom the measures referred to in paragraph 1 of this article are being taken shall be entitled:
   (a) To communicate without delay with the nearest appropriate representative of the State of which he is a national or which is otherwise entitled to protect his rights or, if he is a stateless person, the State in whose territory he has his habitual residence;
   (b) To be visited by a representative of that State.
4. The provisions of paragraph 3 of this article shall be without prejudice to the right of any State Party having a claim to jurisdiction in accordance with article 9, paragraph 1(b), to invite the International Committee of the Red Cross to communicate with and visit the alleged offender.
5. The State which makes the preliminary inquiry contemplated in paragraph 1 of this article shall promptly report its findings to the States referred to in paragraph 2 of this article and indicate whether it intends to exercise jurisdiction.

Art. 11. Any person regarding whom proceedings are being carried out in connection with any of the offences set forth in the present Convention shall be guaranteed at all stages of the proceedings fair treatment and all the rights and guarantees provided for in the law of the State in question. Applicable norms of international law should be taken into account.

Art. 12. The State Party in whose territory the alleged offender is found shall, if it does not extradite him, be obliged, without exception whatsoever and whether or not the offence was committed in its territory, to submit the case to its competent authorities for the purpose of prosecution, through proceedings in accordance with the laws of that State. Those authorities shall take their decision in the same manner as in the case of any other offence of a grave nature under the law of that State.

Art. 13.
1. States Parties shall afford one another the greatest measure of assistance in connection with criminal proceedings brought in respect of the offences set forth in the present Convention, including the supply of all evidence at their disposal necessary for the proceedings. The law of the State whose assistance is requested shall apply in all cases.
2. The provisions of paragraph 1 of this article shall not affect obligations concerning mutual judicial assistance embodied in any other treaty.

Art. 14. The State Party where the alleged offender is prosecuted shall in accordance with its laws communicate the final outcome of the proceedings to the Secretary-General of the United Nations, who shall transmit the information to the other States concerned.

Art. 15.
1. The offences set forth in articles 2, 3 and 4 of the present Convention shall be deemed to be included as extraditable offences in any extradition treaty existing between States Parties. States Parties undertake to include such offences as extraditable offences in every extradition treaty to be concluded between them.
2. If a State Party which makes extradition conditional on the existence of a treaty receives a request for extradition from another State Party with which it has no extradition treaty, it may at its option consider the present Convention as the legal basis for extradition in respect of those offences. Extradition shall be subject to the other conditions provided by the law of the requested State.
3. States Parties which do not make extradition conditional on the existence of a treaty shall recognize those offences as extraditable offences between themselves, subject to the conditions provided by the law of the requested State.
4. The offences shall be treated, for the purpose of extradition between States Parties, as if they had been committed not only in the place in which they occurred but also in the territories of the State required to establish their jurisdiction in accordance with article 9 of the present Convention.

Art. 16. The present Convention shall be applied without prejudice to:
(a) The rules relating to the international responsibility of States;
(b) The law of armed conflict and international humanitarian law, including the provisions relating to the status of combatant or of prisoner of war.

Art. 17.

1.[1] Any dispute between two or more States Parties concerning the interpretation or application of the present Convention which is not settled by negotiation shall, at the request of one of them, be submitted to arbitration. If, within six months from the date of the request for arbitration, the parties are unable to agree on the organization of the arbitration, any one of those parties may refer the dispute to the International Court of Justice by a request in conformity with the Statute of the Court.
2. Each State may, at the time of signature or ratification of the present Convention or accession thereto, declare that it does not consider itself bound by paragraph 1 of this article. The other States Parties shall not be bound by paragraph 1 of this article with respect to any State party which has made such a reservation.
3. Any State Party which has made a reservation in accordance with paragraph 2 of this article may at any time withdraw that reservation by notification to the Secretary-General of the United Nations.

Art. 18.

1. The present Convention shall be open for signature by all States until 31 December 1990 at United Nations Headquarters in New York.
2. The present Convention shall be subject to ratification. The instruments of ratification shall be deposited with the Secretary-General of the United Nations.
3. The present Convention shall remain open for accession by any State. The instruments of accession shall be deposited with the Secretary-General of the United Nations.

Art. 19.

1. The present Convention shall enter into force on the thirtieth day following the date of deposit of the twenty-second instrument of ratification or accession with the Secretary-General of the United Nations.
2. For each State ratifying or acceding to the Convention after the deposit of the twenty-second instrument of ratification or accession, the Convention shall enter into force on the thirtieth day after deposit by such State of its instrument of ratification or accession.

Art. 20.

1. Any State Party may denounce the present Convention by written notification to the Secretary-General of the United Nations.
2. Denunciation shall take effect one year after the date on which the notification is received by the Secretary-General of the United Nations.

Art. 21. The original of the present Convention, of which the Arabic, Chinese, English, French, Russian and Spanish texts are equally authentic, shall be deposited with the Secretary-General of the United Nations, who shall send certified copies thereof to all States.

In witness whereof the undersigned, being duly authorized thereto by their respective Governments, have signed the present Convention.

[1] For reservation in respect of this paragraph by Saudi Arabia, see p. 1250.

SIGNATURES, RATIFICATIONS AND ACCESSIONS[1]

State	*Signatures*	*Ratifications, Accessions*
Angola	28 December 1990	–
Azerbaijan	–	4 December 1997
Barbados	–	10 July 1992
Belarus	13 December 1990	28 May 1997
Belgium	–	31 May 2002 *Res.*
Cameroon	21 December 1990	26 January 1996
Congo	20 June 1990	–
Costa Rica	–	20 September 2001
Croatia	–	27 March 2000
Cyprus	–	8 July 1993
Democratic Republic of the Congo	20 March 1990	–
Georgia	–	8 June 1995
Germany	20 December 1990	–
Italy	5 February 1990	21 August 1995
Libyan Arab Jamahiriya	–	22 September 2000
Maldives	17 July 1990	11 September 1991
Mali	–	12 April 2002
Mauritania	–	9 February 1998
Morocco	5 October 1990	–
Nigeria	4 April 1990	–
Poland	28 December 1990	–
Qatar	–	26 March 1999
Romania	17 December 1990	–
Saudi Arabia	–	14 April 1997 *Res.*
Senegal	–	9 June 1999
Seychelles	–	12 March 1990
Suriname	27 February 1990	10 August 1990
Togo	–	25 February 1991
Turkmenistan	–	18 September 1996
Ukraine	21 September 1990	13 September 1993
Uruguay	20 November 1990	14 July 1999
Uzbekistan	–	19 January 1998
Yugoslavia	12 March 2001[2]	–

DECLARATIONS AND RESERVATIONS

BELGIUM (*reservation made on accession*)
No provision of the present Convention should be interpreted as implying an obligation of mutual judicial assistance if the requested State party has reason to believe that the request for judicial assistance concerning certain offences has been submitted for the purposes of prosecuting or punishing a certain person on the grounds of ethnic origin, religion, nationality or political views, or if acceding to the request would prejudice the situation of that person on any of those grounds.

[1] Based on the communication received on 29 June 1999 from the United Nations Treaty Section and on the indications in *Multilateral Treaties Deposited with the Secretary-General, New York, United Nations* (ST/LEG/SER.E) as available on http://untreaty.un.org on 20 October 2002. See also ICRC website.

[2] The former Yugoslavia had signed the Convention on 12 December 1990.

No provision of the present Convention should be interpreted as implying an obligation of extradition if the requested State party has reason to believe that the request for extradition based on the offences set forth in the Convention has been submitted for the purposes of prosecuting or punishing a certain person on the grounds of ethnic origin, religion, nationality or political views, or if acceding to the request would prejudice the situation of that person on any of those grounds.

SAUDI ARABIA (*reservation made on accession*)
The Kingdom of Saudi Arabia does not consider itself bound by Article 17, paragraph 1, of the Convention.

* * *

See also No. 56

XII

WAR CRIMES

No. 103

AGREEMENT FOR THE PROSECUTION AND PUNISHMENT OF THE MAJOR WAR CRIMINALS OF THE EUROPEAN AXIS

Signed at London, 8 August 1945

INTRODUCTORY NOTE: In the course of World War II the Allied Governments issued several declarations concerning the punishment of war criminals. On 7 October 1942 it was announced that a United Nations War Crimes Commission would be set up for the investigation of war crimes. It was not, however, until 20 October 1943, that the actual establishment of the Commission took place. In the Moscow Declaration of 30 October 1943, the three main Allied Powers (United Kingdom, United States, USSR) issued a joint statement that the German war criminals should be judged and punished in the countries in which their crimes were committed, but that, "the major criminals, whose offences have no particular geographical localization", would be punished "by the joint decision of the Governments of the Allies". The Agreement reprinted below was drafted at a conference held in London from 26 June to 8 August 1945.

The International Military Tribunal for the Far East (Tokyo 1948) was established by a special proclamation of General MacArthur as the Supreme Commander in the Far East for the Allied Powers (not reproduced in the present volume).

ENTRY INTO FORCE: 8 August 1945.

AUTHENTIC TEXTS: English, French, Russian. The text below is reprinted from *UNTS*, Vol. 82, pp. 280–300.

TEXT PUBLISHED IN: *UNTS*, Vol. 82, pp. 280–311, No. 251 (Engl., French, Russ.); Hudson, Vol. IX, pp. 632–636 (Engl., French); *GBTS*, 1946, No. 27, Cmd. 6903 (Engl., French, Russ.); *US Statutes at Large*, Vol. 59, pp. 1544–1589 (Engl., French, Russ.); Bevans, Vol. III, pp. 1238–1247 (Engl.); *AJIL*, Vol. 39 1945, Suppl., pp. 257–264 (Engl.); Friedman, pp. 883–893 (Engl.); Benjamin B. Ferenz, *Defining International Aggression. The Search for World Peace. Documentary History and Analysis* Dobbs Ferry, Oceana Publications, 1975, pp. 406–414 (Engl.); Benjamin B. Ferenz, *An International Criminal Court: a step towards world peace. A Documentary History and Analysis* Dobbs Ferry, Oceana Publications, 1980, Vol. I, pp. 454–464 (Engl.); *Global War Crimes Tribunal collection*, J. Oppenheim, W. van der Wolf, Nijmegen, Global Law Association, 1997–1999, Vol. Ic, pp. 167–173 (Engl.); Henri Meyrowitz, *La repression par les tribunaux allemands des crimes contre l'humanité et de l'appartenance à une organisation criminelle en application de la loi No.10 du Conseil de Contrôle Allié*. Paris, LGDJ, 1960, pp. 476–487 (French); *Droit des conflits armés*, pp. 1299–1308 (French); *Sbornik dogovorov SSSR,* vyp. XI, 1955, pp. 165–172 (Russ. – extract); *Mezhdunarodnoe pravo,* Vol. III, pp. 393–403 (Russ. – extract); Blatova, pp. 825–831 (Russ. – extract). Web sites: ICRC: www.icrc.org/ihl.nsf; CD-ROM: International Humanitarian law, Version 5, 31 December 1998.

TABLE OF CONTENTS

* * *

Whereas the United Nations have from time to time made declarations of their intention that war criminals shall be brought to justice;

And whereas the Moscow Declaration of 30 October 1943, on German atrocities in Occupied Europe stated that those German officers and men and members of the Nazi Party who have been responsible for or have taken a consenting part in atrocities and crimes will be sent back to the countries in which their abominable deeds were done in order that they may be judged and punished according to the laws of these liberated countries and of the free Governments that will be created therein;

And whereas this Declaration was stated to be without prejudice to the case of major criminals whose offences have no particular geographical location and who will be punished by the joint decision of the Governments of the Allies;

Now therefore the Government of the United Kingdom of Great Britain and Northern Ireland, the Government of the United States of America, the Provisional Government of the French Republic and the Government of the Union of Soviet Socialist Republics (hereinafter called "the Signatories") acting in the interests of all the United Nations and by their representatives duly authorized thereto have concluded this Agreement.

Article 1. There shall be established after consultation with the Control Council for Germany an International Military Tribunal for the trial of war criminals whose offences have no particular geographical location whether they be accused individually or in their capacity as members of organizations or groups or in both capacities.

Art. 2. The constitution, jurisdiction and functions of the International Military Tribunal shall be those set out in the Charter annexed to this Agreement, which Charter shall form an integral part of this Agreement.

Art. 3. Each of the Signatories shall take the necessary steps to make available for the investigation of the charges and trial the major war criminals detained by them who are to be tried by the International Military Tribunal. The Signatories shall also use their best endeavours to make available for investigation of the charges against and the trial before the International Military Tribunal such of the major war criminals as are not in the territories of any of the Signatories.

Art. 4. Nothing in this Agreement shall prejudice the provisions established by the Moscow Declaration concerning the return of war criminals to the countries where they committed their crimes.

Art. 5. Any Government of the United Nations may adhere to this Agreement by notice given through the diplomatic channel to the Government of the United Kingdom, who shall inform the other signatory and adhering Governments of each such adherence.

Art. 6. Nothing in this Agreement shall prejudice the jurisdiction or the powers of any national or occupation court established or to be established in any Allied territory or in Germany for the trial of war criminals.

Art. 7. This Agreement shall come into force on the day of signature and shall remain in force for the period of one year and shall continue thereafter, subject to the right of any Signatory to give, through the diplomatic channel, one month's notice of intention to terminate it. Such termination shall not prejudice any proceedings already taken or any findings already made in pursuance of this Agreement.

In witness whereof the undersigned have signed the present Agreement.

Done in quadruplicate in London this eighth day of August 1945, each in English, French and Russian, and each text to have equal authenticity.

[Here follow signatures]

CHARTER OF THE INTERNATIONAL MILITARY TRIBUNAL

I. Constitution of the International Military Tribunal

Article 1. In pursuance of the Agreement signed on 8 August 1945, by the Government of the United Kingdom of Great Britain and Northern Ireland, the Government of the United States of America, the Provisional Government of the French Republic and the Government of the Union of Soviet Socialist Republics, there shall be established an International Military Tribunal (hereinafter called "the Tribunal") for the just and prompt trial and punishment of the major war criminals of the European Axis.

Art. 2. The Tribunal shall consist of four members, each with an alternate. One member and one alternate shall be appointed by each of the Signatories. The alternates shall, so far as they are able, be present at all sessions of the Tribunal. In case of illness of any member of the Tribunal or his incapacity for some other reason to fulfil his functions, his alternate shall take his place.

Art. 3. Neither the Tribunal, its members nor their alternates can be challenged by the prosecution, or by the Defendants or their Counsel. Each Signatory may replace its member of the Tribunal or his alternate for reasons of health or for other good reasons, except that no replacement may take place during a trial, other than by an alternate.

Art. 4.
(a) The presence of all four members of the Tribunal or the alternate for any absent member shall be necessary to constitute the quorum.
(b) The members of the Tribunal shall, before any trial begins, agree among themselves upon the selection from their number of a President, and the President shall hold office during that trial, or as may otherwise be agreed by a vote of not less than three members. The principle of rotation of presidency for successive trials is agreed. If, however, a session of the Tribunal takes place on the territory of one of the four Signatories, the representative of that Signatory on the Tribunal shall preside.
(c) Save as aforesaid the Tribunal shall take decisions by a majority vote and in case the votes are evenly divided, the vote of the President shall be decisive; provided always that convictions and sentences shall only be imposed by affirmative votes of at least three members of the Tribunal.

Art. 5. In case of need and depending on the numbers of the matters to be tried, other Tribunals may be set up; and the establishment, functions and procedure of each Tribunal shall be identical, and shall be governed by this Charter.

II. Jurisdiction and General Principles

Art. 6. The Tribunal established by the Agreement referred to in Article 1 hereof for the trial and punishment of the major war criminals of the European Axis countries shall have the power to try and punish persons who, acting in the interests of the European Axis countries, whether as individuals or as members of organizations, committed any of the following crimes.

The following acts, or any of them, are crimes coming within the jurisdiction of the Tribunal for which there shall be individual responsibility:
(a) *Crimes against peace*: namely, planning, preparation, initiation or waging of a war of aggression, or a war in violation of international treaties, agreements or assurances, or participation in a common plan or conspiracy for the accomplishment of any of the foregoing;
(b) *War crimes*: namely, violations of the laws or customs of war. Such violations shall include, but not be limited to, murder, ill-treatment or deportation to slave labour or for any other purpose of civilian population of or in occupied territory, murder or ill-treatment of prisoners of war or persons on the seas, killing of hostages, plunder of public or private property, wanton destruction of cities, towns or villages, or devastation not justified by military necessity;
(c) *Crimes against humanity*: namely, murder, extermination, enslavement, deportation, and other inhumane acts committed against any civilian population, before or during the war, or persecutions on political, racial or religious grounds in execution of or in connection with any crime within the jurisdiction of the Tribunal, whether or not in violation of the domestic law of the country where perpetrated.

Leaders, organizers, instigators and accomplices participating in the formulation or execution of a common plan or conspiracy to commit any of the foregoing crimes are responsible for all acts performed by any persons in execution of such plan.

Art. 7. The official position of defendants, whether as Heads of State or responsible officials in Government Departments, shall not be considered as freeing them from responsibility or mitigating punishment.

Art. 8. The fact that the Defendant acted pursuant to order of his Government or of a superior shall not free him from responsibility, but may be considered in mitigation of punishment if the Tribunal determines that justice so requires.

Art. 9. At the trial of any individual member of any group or organization the Tribunal may declare (in connection with any act of which the individual may be convicted) that the group or organization of which the individual was a member was a criminal organization.

After receipt of the Indictment the Tribunal shall give such notice as it thinks fit that the prosecution intends to ask the Tribunal to make such declaration and any member of the organization will be entitled to apply to the Tribunal for leave to be heard by the Tribunal upon the question of the criminal character of the organization. The Tribunal shall have power to allow or reject the application. If the application is allowed, the Tribunal may direct in what manner the applicants shall be represented and heard.

Art. 10. In cases where a group or organization is declared criminal by the Tribunal, the competent national authority of any Signatory shall have the right to bring individuals to trial for membership therein before national, military or occupation courts. In any such case the criminal nature of the group or organization is considered proved and shall not be questioned.

Art. 11. Any person convicted by the Tribunal may be charged before a national, military or occupation court, referred to in Article 10 of this Charter, with a crime other than of membership in a criminal group or organization and such court may, after convicting him, impose upon him punishment independent of and additional to the punishment imposed by the Tribunal for participation in the criminal activities of such group or organization.

Art. 12. The Tribunal shall have the right to take proceedings against a person charged with crimes set out in Article 6 of this Charter in his absence, if he has not been found or if the Tribunal, for any reason, finds it necessary, in the interests of justice, to conduct the hearing in his absence.

Art. 13. The Tribunal shall draw up rules for its procedure. These rules shall not be inconsistent with the provisions of this Charter.

III. Committee for the Investigation and Prosecution of Major War Criminals

Art. 14. Each Signatory shall appoint a Chief Prosecutor for the investigation of the charges against and the prosecution of major war criminals.

The Chief Prosecutors shall act as a committee for the following purposes:
(a) to agree upon a plan of the individual work of each of the Chief Prosecutors and his staff,
(b) to settle the final designation of major war criminals to be tried by the Tribunal,
(c) to approve the Indictment and the documents to be submitted therewith,
(d) to lodge the Indictment and the accompanying documents with the Tribunal,
(e) to draw up and recommend to the Tribunal for its approval draft rules of procedure, contemplated by Article 13 of this Charter. The Tribunal shall have power to accept, with or without amendments, or to reject, the rules so recommended.

The Committee shall act in all the above matters by a majority vote and shall appoint a Chairman as may be convenient and in accordance with the principle of rotation: provided that if there is an equal division of vote concerning the designation of a Defendant to be tried by the Tribunal, or the crimes with which he shall be charged, that proposal will be adopted which was made by the party which proposed that the particular Defendant be tried, or the particular charges be preferred against him.

Art. 15. The Chief Prosecutors shall individually, and acting in collaboration with one another, also undertake the following duties:
(a) investigation, collection and production before or at the Trial of all necessary evidence,
(b) the preparation of the Indictment for approval by the Committee in accordance with paragraph (c) of Article 14 hereof,
(c) the preliminary examination of all necessary witnesses and of the Defendants,
(d) to act as prosecutor at the Trial,
(e) to appoint representatives to carry out such duties as may be assigned to them,
(f) to undertake such other matters as may appear necessary to them for the purposes of the preparation for and conduct of the Trial.

It is understood that no witness or Defendant detained by any Signatory shall be taken out of the possession of that Signatory without its assent.

IV. Fair Trial for Defendants

Art. 16. In order to ensure fair trial for the Defendants, the following procedure shall be followed:
(a) The Indictment shall include full particulars specifying in detail the charges against the Defendants. A copy of the Indictment and of all the documents lodged with the Indictment, translated into a language which he understands, shall be furnished to the Defendant at a reasonable time before the Trial.
(b) During any preliminary examination or trial of a Defendant he shall have the right to give any explanation relevant to the charges made against him.
(c) A preliminary examination of a Defendant and his Trial shall be conducted in, or translated into, a language which the Defendant understands.
(d) A Defendant shall have the right to conduct his own defence before the Tribunal or to have the assistance of Counsel.

(e) A Defendant shall have the right through himself or through his Counsel to present evidence at the Trial in support of his defence, and to cross-examine any witness called by the Prosecution.

V. Powers of the Tribunal and Conduct of the Trial

Art. 17. The Tribunal shall have the power:
(a) to summon witnesses to the Trial and to require their attendance and testimony and to put questions to them,
(b) to interrogate any Defendant,
(c) to require the production of documents and other evidentiary material,
(d) to administer oaths to witnesses,
(e) to appoint officers for the carrying out of any task designated by the Tribunal including the power to have evidence taken on commission.

Art. 18. The Tribunal shall:
(a) confine the Trial strictly to an expeditious hearing of the issues raised by the charges,
(b) take strict measures to prevent any action which will cause unreasonable delay, and rule out irrelevant issues and statements of any kind whatsoever,
(c) deal summarily with any contumacy, imposing appropriate punishment, including exclusion of any Defendant or his Counsel from some or all further proceedings, but without prejudice to the determination of the charges.

Art. 19. The Tribunal shall not be bound by technical rules of evidence. It shall adopt and apply to the greatest possible extent expeditious and non-technical procedure, and shall admit any evidence which it deems to have probative value.

Art. 20. The Tribunal may require to be informed of the nature of any evidence before it is offered so that it may rule upon the relevance thereof.

Art. 21. The Tribunal shall not require proof of facts of common knowledge but shall take judicial notice thereof. It shall also take judicial notice of official governmental documents and reports of the United Nations, including the acts and documents of the committees set up in the various Allied countries for the investigation of war crimes, and the records and findings of military or other Tribunals of any of the United Nations.

Art. 22. The permanent seat of the Tribunal shall be in Berlin. The first meetings of the members of the Tribunal and of the Chief Prosecutors shall be held at Berlin in a place to be designated by the Control Council for Germany. The first trial shall be held at Nuremberg, and any subsequent trials shall be held at such places as the Tribunal may decide.

Art. 23. One or more of the Chief Prosecutors may take part in the prosecution at each Trial. The function of any Chief Prosecutor may be discharged by him personally, or by any person or persons authorized by him.

The function of Council for a Defendant may be discharged at the Defendant's request by any Counsel professionally qualified to conduct cases before the Courts of his own country, or by any other person who may be specially authorized thereto by the Tribunal.

Art. 24. The proceedings at the Trial shall take the following course:
(a) The Indictment shall be read in court.
(b) The Tribunal shall ask each Defendant whether he pleads "guilty" or "not guilty."
(c) The Prosecution shall make an opening statement.
(d) The Tribunal shall ask the Prosecution and the Defence what evidence (if any) they wish to submit to the Tribunal, and the Tribunal shall rule upon the admissibility of any such evidence.
(e) The witnesses for the Prosecution shall be examined and after that the witnesses for the Defence. Thereafter such rebutting evidence as may be held by the Tribunal to be admissible shall be called by either the Prosecution or the Defence.
(f) The Tribunal may put any question to any witness and to any Defendant, at any time.
(g) The Prosecution and the Defence shall interrogate and may cross-examine any witnesses and any Defendant who gives testimony.
(h) The Defence shall address the court.
(i) The Prosecution shall address the court.
(j) Each Defendant may make a statement to the Tribunal.
(k) The Tribunal shall deliver judgment and pronounce sentence.

Art. 25. All official documents shall be produced, and all court proceedings conducted, in English, French and Russian, and in the language of the Defendant. So much of the record and of the proceedings may also be translated into the language of any country in which the Tribunal is sitting, as the Tribunal considers desirable in the interests of justice and public opinion.

VI. Judgment and Sentence

Art. 26. The judgment of the Tribunal as to the guilt or the innocence of any Defendant shall give the reasons on which it is based, and shall be final and not subject to review.

Art. 27. The Tribunal shall have the right to impose upon a Defendant, on conviction, death or such other punishment as shall be determined by it to be just.

Art. 28. In addition to any punishment imposed by it, the Tribunal shall have the right to deprive the convicted person of any stolen property and order its delivery to the Control Council for Germany.

Art. 29. In case of guilt, sentences shall be carried out in accordance with the orders of the Control Council for Germany, which may at any time reduce or otherwise alter the sentences, but may not increase the severity thereof. If the Control Council for Germany, after any Defendant has been convicted and sentenced, discovers fresh evidence which, in its opinion, would found a fresh charge against him, the Council shall report accordingly to the Committee established under Article 14 hereof for such action as they may consider proper, having regard to the interests of justice.

VII. Expenses

Art. 30. The expenses of the Tribunal and of the Trials shall be charged by the Signatories against the funds allotted for maintenance of the Control Council for Germany.

SIGNATURES AND ACCESSIONS[1]

1. *Signatory Governments*	*Date of Signature*
France	8 August 1945
Union of Soviet Socialist Republics	8 August 1945
United Kingdom	8 August 1945
United States of America	8 August 1945

2. *Acceding Governments*	*Date of Accession*
Australia	5 October 1945
Belgium	5 October 1945
Czechoslovakia	26 September 1945
Denmark	10 September 1945
Ethiopia	9 October 1945
Greece	10 September 1945
Haiti	3 November 1945
Honduras	17 October 1945
India	22 December 1945
Luxembourg	1 November 1945
Netherlands	25 September 1945
New Zealand	19 November 1945
Norway	20 October 1945
Panama	17 October 1945
Paraguay	14 November 1945
Poland	25 September 1945
Uruguay	11 December 1945
Venezuela	17 November 1945
Yugoslavia	29 September 1945

RESERVATIONS

None

[1] Based on a communication from the Foreign and Commonwealth Office of Great Britain of 7 December 2001.

No. 104

AFFIRMATION OF THE PRINCIPLES OF INTERNATIONAL LAW RECOGNIZED BY THE CHARTER OF THE NUREMBERG TRIBUNAL

Resolution 95(I) of the United Nations General Assembly adopted on 11 December 1946

INTRODUCTORY NOTE: The present resolution was adopted by unanimous vote[1] of the General Assembly.

AUTHENTIC TEXTS: Chinese, English, French, Russian, Spanish. The text below is reprinted from *United Nations Resolutions adopted by the General Assembly during the Second part of its first session from 23 October to 15 December 1946*, Lake Success, New York, 1947, p. 188.

TEXT PUBLISHED IN: *United Nations Resolutions adopted by the General Assembly during the Second part of its first session from 23 October to 15 December 1946*, Lake Success, New York, 1947, p. 188 (Engl., French); *Yearbook of the United Nations*, 1946–1947, Lake Success, N.Y., United Nations, 1947, p. 254 (Engl.); Friedman, Vol. II, pp. 1027–1028 (Engl.); Benjamin B. Ferenz, *An International Criminal Court: a step towards world peace. A Documentary History and Analysis,* Dobbs Ferry, Oceana Publications, 1980, Vol. II, pp. 126–127 (Engl.); *Droit des conflits armés*, pp. 1309–1310 (French).

* * *

The General Assembly,

Recognizes *the obligation laid upon it by Article 13, paragraph 1, sub-paragraph (a), of the Charter, to initiate studies and make recommendations for the purpose of encouraging the progressive development of international law and its codification;*

Takes note *of the Agreement for the establishment of an International Military Tribunal for the prosecution and punishment of the major war criminals of the European Axis signed in London on 8 August 1945, and of the Charter annexed thereto, and of the fact that similar principles have been adopted in the Charter of the International Military Tribunal for the trial of the major war criminals in the Far East, proclaimed at Tokyo on 19 January 1946;*

Therefore,

Affirms *the principles of international law recognized by the Charter of the Nuremberg Tribunal and the judgment of the Tribunal;*

Directs *the Committee on the codification of international law established by the resolution of the General Assembly of 11 December 1946, to treat as a matter of primary importance plans for the formation, in the context of a general codification of offences against the peace and security of mankind, or of an International Criminal Code, of the principles recognized in the Charter of the Nuremberg Tribunal and in the judgment of the Tribunal.*

[1] A roll-call vote did not take place.

No. 105

PRINCIPLES OF INTERNATIONAL LAW RECOGNIZED IN THE CHARTER OF THE NUREMBERG TRIBUNAL AND IN THE JUDGMENT OF THE TRIBUNAL

Adopted by the International Law Commission of the United Nations, July 1950

INTRODUCTORY NOTE: Under General Assembly Resolution 177 (II), paragraph (a), the International Law Commission was directed to "formulate the principles of international law recognized in the Charter of the Nuremberg Tribunal and in the judgment of the Tribunal." In the course of the consideration of this subject the question arose as to whether or not the Commission should ascertain to what extent the principles contained in the Charter and judgment constituted principles of international law. The conclusion was that since the Nuremberg principles had been affirmed by the General Assembly, the task entrusted to the Commission was not to express any appreciation of these principles as principles of international law but merely to formulate them. The text below was adopted by the Commission at its second session. The Report of the Commission also contains commentaries on the principles (see *Yearbook of the International Law Commission*, 1950, Vol. II, pp. 374-378).

AUTHENTIC TEXT: English. The text below is reproduced from *Report of the International Law Commission Covering its Second Session, 5 June – 29 July 1950*, Document A/1316, pp. 11–14.

TEXT PUBLISHED IN: *Report of the International Law Commission Covering its Second Session, 5 June–29 July 1950*, Document A/1316, pp. 11–14 (Engl.); *Rapport de la Commission du droit international sur les travaux de sa deuxième session du 5 Juin au 29 Juillet 1950*, Document A/1316, pp. 12–16 (French); *Yearbook of the International Law Commission 1950*, Vol. II, pp. 374–380 (Engl.); *AJIL*, Vol. 44, 1950, Suppl., pp. 126–134 (Engl.); *Yearbook of the United Nations*, 1950, New York, United Nations, 1951, p. 852 (Engl.); Benjamin B. Ferenz, *An International Criminal Court: a step towards world peace. A Documentary History and Analysis*. Dobbs Ferry, Oceana Publications, 1980, Vol. II, pp. 235–239 (Engl.); *Droit des conflits armés*, pp. 1311–1313 (French).

* * *

Principle I

Any person who commits an act which constitutes a crime under international law is responsible therefor and liable to punishment.

Principle II

The fact that international law does not impose a penalty for an act which constitutes a crime under international law does not relieve the person who committed the act from responsibility under international law.

Principle III

The fact that a person who committed an act which constitutes a crime under international law acted as Head of State or responsible Government official does not relieve him from responsibility under international law.

Principle IV

The fact that a person acted pursuant to order of his Government or of a superior does not relieve him from responsibility under international law, provided a moral choice was in fact possible to him.

Principle V

Any person charged with a crime under international law has the right to a fair trial on the facts and law.

Principle VI

The crimes hereinafter set out are punishable as crimes under international law:

(a) Crimes against peace:
- (i) Planning, preparation, initiation or waging of a war of aggression or a war in violation of international treaties, agreements or assurances;
- (ii) Participation in a common plan or conspiracy for the accomplishment of any of the acts mentioned under (i).

(b) War crimes:
Violations of the laws or customs of war include, but are not limited to, murder, ill-treatment or deportation to slave-labour or for any other purpose of civilian population of or in occupied territory, murder or ill-treatment of prisoners of war, of persons on the seas, killing of hostages, plunder of public or private property, wanton destruction of cities, towns, or villages, or devastation not justified by military necessity.

(c) Crimes against humanity:
Murder, extermination, enslavement, deportation and other inhuman acts done against any civilian population, or persecutions on political, racial or religious grounds, when such acts are done or such persecutions are carried on in execution of or in connexion with any crime against peace or any war crime.

Principle VII

Complicity in the commission of a crime against peace, a war crime, or a crime against humanity as set forth in Principle VI is a crime under international law.

No. 106

CONVENTION ON THE NON-APPLICABILITY OF STATUTORY LIMITATIONS TO WAR CRIMES AND CRIMES AGAINST HUMANITY

Adopted by resolution 2391 (XXIII) of the United Nations General Assembly on 26 November 1968

INTRODUCTORY NOTE: The present Convention was occasioned by the fear, which grew in the mid-1960s, that German war criminals of World War II, who had not yet been apprehended, might escape prosecution because of the expiration of the periods of limitation applicable to their crimes. The Convention was prepared by the Human Rights Commission and thereafter adopted and opened for signature by the General Assembly of the United Nations. It will be noted that the definition of "crimes against humanity" was broadened compared with the definition contained in the Charter of the Nuremberg Tribunal.

ENTRY INTO FORCE: 11 November 1970.

AUTHENTIC TEXTS: Chinese, English, French, Russian, Spanish. The English text below is reprinted from *UNTS*, Vol. 754, 1970, No 10823, pp. 73–77.

TEXT PUBLISHED IN: *United Nations General Assembly Resolution 2391* (XXIII), Annex; see *Resolutions adopted by the General Assembly during its Twenty-third session, 24 September-21 December 1968.* General Assembly Official Records, Twenty-third session Supplement No. 18 (A/7218) New York, United Nations, 1969, pp. 40–41 (Engl.). See also Chinese, French, Russian and Spanish editions; *UNTS*, Vol. 754, 1970, No 10823, pp. 73–129 (Chinese, Engl., French, Russ. and Span.); *ILM*, Vol. VIII, No. 1, January 1969, pp. 68–72 (Engl.); Lillich, 380.1–380.5 (Engl.); Droit des conflits armés, pp. 1315–1325 (French); *Vedomosti Verkhovnogo Soveta SSSR,* No. 2, 1971, pp. 14–17 (Russ.); *Sovetsky ezhegodnik mezhdunarodnogo prava 1969, pp.* 468–470 (Russ.); Blatova, pp. 833–836 (Russ.); United Nations website: http://untreaty.un.org.

* * *

PREAMBLE

The States Parties to the present Convention,

Recalling resolutions of the General Assembly of the United Nations 3 (I) of 13 February 1946 and 170 (II) of 31 October 1947 on the extradition and punishment of war criminals, resolution 95 (I) of 11 December 1946 affirming the principles of international law recognized by the Charter of the International Military Tribunal, Nuremberg, and the judgment of the Tribunal, and resolutions 2184 (XXI) of 12 December 1966 and 2202 (XXI) of 16 December 1966 which expressly condemned as crimes against humanity the violation of the economic and political rights of the indigenous population on the one hand and the policies of apartheid on the other,

Recalling resolutions of the Economic and Social Council of the United Nations 1074 D (XXXIX) of 28 July 1965 and 1158 (XLI) of 5 August 1966 on the punishment of war criminals and of persons who have committed crimes against humanity,

Noting that none of the solemn declarations, instruments or conventions relating to the prosecution and punishment of war crimes and crimes against humanity made provision for a period of limitation,

Considering that war crimes and crimes against humanity are among the gravest crimes in international law,

Convinced that the effective punishment of war crimes and crimes against humanity is an important element in the prevention of such crimes, the protection of human rights and fundamental freedoms, the encouragement of confidence, the furtherance of co-operation among peoples and the promotion on international peace and security,

Noting that the application to war crimes and crimes against humanity of the rules of municipal law relating to the period of limitation for ordinary crimes is a matter of serious concern to world public opinion, since it prevents the prosecution and punishment of persons responsible for those crimes,

Recognizing that it is necessary and timely to affirm in international law, through this Convention, the principle that there is no period of limitation for war crimes and crimes against humanity, and to secure its universal application,

Have agreed as follows:

Article 1. No statutory limitation shall apply to the following crimes, irrespective of the date of their commission:

(a) War crimes as they are defined in the Charter of the International Military Tribunal, Nuremberg, of 8 August 1945 and confirmed by resolutions 3 (I) of 13 February 1946 and 95 (I) of 11 December 1946 of the General Assembly of the United Nations, particularly the "grave breaches" enumerated in the Geneva Convention of 12 August 1949 for the protection of war victims;

(b) Crimes against humanity whether committed in time of war or in time of peace as they are defined in the Charter of the International Military Tribunal, Nurernberg, of 8 August 1945 and confirmed by resolutions 3 (I) of 13 February 1946 and 95 ((I) of 11 December 1946 of the General Assembly of the United Nations, eviction by armed attack or occupation and inhuman acts resulting from the policy of apartheid, and the crime of genocide as defined in the 1948 Convention on the Prevention and Punishment of the Crime of Genocide, even if such acts do not constitute a violation of the domestic law of the country in which they were committed.

Art. 2. If any of the crimes mentioned in Article 1 is committed, the provisions of this Convention shall apply to representatives of the State authority and private individuals who, as principals or accomplices, participate in or who directly incite others to the commission of any of those crimes, or who conspire to commit them, irrespective of the degree of completion, and to representatives of the State authority who tolerate their commission.

Art. 3. The States Parties to the present Convention undertake to adopt all necessary domestic measures, legislative or otherwise, with a view to making possible the extradition, in accordance with international law, of the persons referred to in article 2 of this Convention.

Art. 4. The States Parties to the present Convention undertake to adopt, in accordance with their respective constitutional processes, any legislative or other measures necessary to ensure that statutory or other limitations shall not apply to the prosecution and punishment of the crimes referred to in articles 1 and 2 of this Convention and that, where they exist, such limitations shall be abolished.

Art. 5.[1] This Convention shall, until 31 December 1969, be open for signature by any State Member of the United Nations or member of any of its specialized agencies or of the International Atomic Energy Agency, by any State Party to the Statute of the International Court of Justice, and by any other State which has been invited by the General Assembly of the United Nations to become a Party to this Convention.

Art. 6. This Convention is subject to ratification. Instruments of ratification shall be deposited with the Secretary-General of the United Nations.

Art. 7.[1] This Convention shall be open to accession by any State referred to in article 5. Instruments of accession shall be deposited with the Secretary-General of the United Nations.

Art. 8.

1. This Convention shall enter into force on the ninetieth day after the date of the deposit with the Secretary-General of the United Nations of the tenth instrument of ratification or accession.
2. For each State ratifying this Convention or acceding to it after the deposit of the tenth instrument of ratification or accession, the Convention shall enter into force on the ninetieth day after the date of the deposit of its own instrument of ratification or accession.

Art. 9.

1. After the expiry of a period of ten years from the date on which this Convention enters into force, a request for the revision of the Convention may be made at any time by any Contracting Party by means of a notification in writing addressed to the Secretary-General of United Nations.
2. The General Assembly of the United Nations shall decide upon the steps, if any, to be taken in respect of such a request.

Art. 10.

1. This Convention shall be deposited with the Secretary-General of the United Nations.
2. The Secretary-General of the United Nations shall transmit certified copies of this Convention to all States referred to in Article 5.

[1] For declaration in respect of this article by Afghanistan, Albania, Bulgaria, Byelorussian SSR, Cuba, Czechoslovakia, German Democratic Republic, Guinea, Hungary, Lao People's Democratic Republic, Mongolia, Poland, Romania, Ukrainian SSR, USSR and Vietnam, see pp. 1273–1275.

3. The Secretary-General of the United Nations shall inform all States referred to in Article 5 of the following particulars:
   (a) Signatures of this Convention, and instruments of ratification and accession deposited under articles 5, 6 and 7;
   (b) The date of entry into force of this Convention in accordance with article 8;
   (c) Communications received under article 9.

Art. 11. This Convention, of which the Chinese, English, French, Russian and Spanish texts are equally authentic, shall bear the date of 26 November 1968.

In witness whereof the undersigned, being duly authorized for that purpose, have signed this Convention.

[Here follow signatures]

VOTE

Resolution 2391 (XXIII), embodying the Convention, was adopted by a vote of 58 in favour, 7 against and with *36* abstentions.

RECORDED VOTE

In favour: Algeria, Bulgaria, Burma, Byelorussian Soviet Socialist Republic, Central African Republic, Ceylon, Chad, Chile, China, Cuba, Cyprus, Czechoslovakia, Dahomey, Ethiopia, Gabon, Ghana, Guinea, Hungary, India, Indonesia, Iran, Iraq, Israel, Ivory Coast, Kenya, Kuwait, Lebanon, Liberia, Libya, Malaysia, Maldive Islands, Mauritania, Mexico, Mongolia, Morocco, Nepal, Niger, Nigeria, Pakistan, Philippines, Poland, Romania, Rwanda, Saudi Arabia, Senegal, Singapore, Southern Yemen, Sudan, Syria, Togo, Tunisia, Ukrainian Soviet Socialist Republic, Union of Soviet Socialist Republics; United Arab Republic, United Republic of Tanzania, Upper Volta, Yugoslavia, Zambia.

Against: Australia, El Salvador, Honduras, Portugal, South Africa, United Kingdom, United States of America.

Abstaining: Afghanistan, Argentina, Austria, Belgium, Bolivia, Brazil, Canada, Colombia, Costa Rica, Denmark, Ecuador, Finland, France, Greece, Guatemala, Guyana, Haiti, Iceland, Ireland, Italy, Jamaica, Japan, Laos, Luxemburg, Netherlands, New Zealand, Nicaragua, Norway, Panama, Peru, Spain, Sweden, Thailand, Turkey, Uruguay, Venezuela.

SIGNATURES, RATIFICATIONS AND ACCESSIONS[1]

State	*Signature*	*Ratification,* Accession, *Notifications of Succession or Continuity (C)*
Afghanistan	–	22 July 1983 *Dec.*
Albania	–	19 May 1971 *Dec.*
Armenia	–	23 June 1993
Azerbaijan	–	16 August 1996
Belarus	7 January 1969	8 May 1969 *Dec.*
Bolivia	–	6 October 1983
Bosnia and Herzegovina	–	1 September 1993 (C)
Bulgaria	21 January 1969	21 May 1969 *Dec.*
Cameroon	-	6 October 1972
Croatia	–	12 October 1992 (C)
Cuba	–	13 September 1972 *Dec.*
[Czechoslovakia[2]	21 May 1969	13 August 1970 *Dec.*]
Czech Republic[3]	–	22 February 1993 (C)
Estonia	–	21 October 1991
Gambia	–	29 December 1978
Georgia	–	31 March 1995
[Germany (Democratic Republic)[4]	–	27 March 1973 *Dec.]*

[1] Based on the indications in *Multilateral Treaties Deposited with the Secretary-General, New York, United Nations,* (ST/LEG/SER.E) as available on http://www.untreaty.un.org of 22 October 2002.

[2] Czechoslovakia had signed and ratified the Convention on 21 May 1969 and 13 August 1970, respectively, with a declaration. For the text of the declaration made upon signature, see p. 1273 and *UNTS*, Vol. 754, p. 124. Following the dissolution of the Czech and Slovak Federal Republic on 31 December 1992, at midnight, both the Czech Republic and the Slovak Republic informed the depositaries concerned that they considered themselves bound, as of 1 January 1993, by multilateral international treaties to which the Czech and Slovak Federal Republic was a party on that date, including reservations and declarations to their provisions made earlier by the Czech and Slovak Federal Republic.

[3] See note 2.

[4] The German Democratic Republic had acceded to the Convention on 27 March 1973 with declaration. For the text of the declaration, see p. 1273, and also *UNTS*, Vol. 862, p. 410.

In a communication dated 3 October 1990, the Federal Minister for Foreign Affairs of the Federal Republic of Germany notified the Secretary-General of the following:

"Through the accession of the German Democratic Republic to the Federal Republic of Germany with effect from 3 October 1990, the two German States have united to form one sovereign State… Consequently, and in the light of articles 11 and 12 of the Treaty of 31 August 1990 (Unification Treaty) between the Federal Republic of Germany and the German Democratic Republic, entries in status lists pertaining to formalities (i.e. signatures, ratifications, accessions, declarations and reservations, etc.) effected by the Federal Republic of Germany will now appear under 'Germany' and indicate the dates of such formalities.

As regards treaties in respect of which formalities had been effected by both the Federal Republic of Germany and the former German Democratic Republic prior to unification, the entry will similarly indicate in the corresponding table the type of formality effected by the Federal Republic of Germany and the date on which it took place, while the type of formality effected by the former German Democratic Republic and the date thereof will appear in a footnote. Finally, as regards the treatment of treaties in respect of which formalities were effected by the former German Democratic Republic alone, article 12, para. 3 of the Unification Treaty contains the following provision: 'Should the united Germany intend to accede to international organizations or other multilateral treaties of which the German Democratic Republic but not the Federal Republic of Germany is a member, agreement shall be reached with the respective contracting parties and with the European Communities where the latter's competence is affected".

State	*Signature*	*Ratification,* Accession, *Notifications of Succession or Continuity (C)*
Ghana	–	7 September 2000
Guinea	–	7 June 1971 *Dec.*
Hungary	25 March 1969	24 June 1969 *Dec.*
India	–	12 January 1971
Kenya	–	1 May 1972
Korea, Democratic People's Republic of	–	8 November 1984
Kuwait	–	7 March 1995
Lao People's Democratic Republic	–	28 December 1984 *Dec.*
Latvia		14 April 1992
Libyan Arab Jamahiriya		26 May 1989
Lithuania	–	1 February 1996
Macedonia, the former Yugoslav Republic of	–	18 January 1994 (C)
Mexico	3 July 1969	–
Moldova	–	26 January 1993
Mongolia	31 January 1969	21 May 1969 *Dec.*
Nicaragua	–	3 September 1986
Nigeria	–	1 December 1970
Philippines	–	15 May 1973
Poland	16 December 1968	14 February 1969 *Dec.*
Romania	17 April 1969	15 September 1969 *Dec.*
Russian Federation	6 January 1969	22 April 1969
Rwanda	–	16 April 1975
Saint Vincent and the Grenadines	–	9 November 1981
Slovakia[5]	–	28 May 1993 (C)
Slovenia	–	6 July 1992 (C)
Tunisia	–	15 June 1972
Ukraine	14 January 1969	19 June 1969 *Dec.*
[Union of Soviet Socialist Republics	6 January 1969	22 April 1969 *Dec.]*
Uruguay	–	21 September 2001
Viet Nam	–	6 May 1983 *Dec.*
Yemen[6]	–	9 February 1987
Yugoslavia[7]	–	21 March 2001

[5] See note 2, p. 1271.

[6] The formality was effected by Democratic Yemen. In a letter dated 19 May 1990, the Ministers of Foreign Affairs of the Yemen Arab Republic and the People's Democratic Republic of Yemen informed the Secretary-General of the following: "All treaties and agreements concluded between either the Yemen Arab Republic or the People's Democratic Republic of Yemen and other States and international organizations in accordance with international law which are in force on 22 May 1990 will remain in effect, and international relations existing on 22 May 1990 between the People's Democratic Republic of Yemen and the Yemen Arab Republic and other States will continue." As concerns the treaties concluded prior to their union by the Yemen Arab Republic or the People's Democratic Republic of Yemen, the Republic of Yemen (as now united) is accordingly to be considered as a party to those treaties as from the date when one of these states first became a party to those treaties.

[7] The former Yugoslavia, the Socialist Federal Rrepublic of Yugoslavia, signed the present Convention on 16 December 1968 and ratified it on 9 June 1970. See notes 16 and 17 in document *No. 61*, p. 848.

RESERVATIONS AND DECLARATIONS

AFGHANISTAN (*declaration made on accession*)
Since the provisions of articles 5 and 7 of the said Convention, according to which some States cannot become a party of the Convention, are not in conformity with the universal character of the Convention, the Presidium of the Revolutionary Council of the Democratic Republic of Afghanistan states that, on the basis of the principle of the sovereign equality of States, the Convention should remain open to all States.

ALBANIA (*declaration made on accession*)
The Government of the People's Republic of Albania states that the provisions of Articles 5 and 7 of the-Convention on the Non-Applicability of Statutory Limitations to War Crimes and Crimes against Humanity are unacceptable because, in preventing a number of States from becoming parties to the Convention, they are discriminatory in nature and thus violate the principle of the sovereign equality of States and are incompatible with the spirit and purposes of the Convention.

BELARUS (*declaration made on ratification*)
The Byelorussian Soviet Socialist Republic declares that the provisions of Articles 5 and 7 of the Convention on the Non-Applicability of Statutory Limitations to War Crimes and Crimes against Humanity, which prevent certain States from signing the Convention or acceding to it, are contrary to the principle of the sovereign equality of States.

BULGARIA (*declaration made on ratification*)
The People's Republic of Bulgaria deems it necessary at the same time to declare that the provisions of Articles 5 and 7 of the Convention on the Non-Applicability of Statutory Limitations to War Crimes and Crimes against Humanity, which prevent a number of States from signing the Convention or acceding to it, are contrary to the principle of the sovereign equality of States.

CUBA (*declaration made on accession*)
The Government of the Republic of Cuba declares that it regards the provisions of articles 5 and 7 of the Convention on the Non-Applicability of Statutory Limitations to War Crimes and Crimes against Humanity as discriminatory and contrary to the principle of the equality of States.

CZECH REPUBLIC[1] *see Czechoslovakia*

CZECHOSLOVAKIA (*declaration made on ratification*)[1]
The Czechoslovak Socialist Republic declares that the provisions of Articles 5 and 7 of the Convention on the Non-Applicability of Statutory Limitations to War Crimes and Crimes against Humanity, adopted by the General Assembly of the United Nations on 26 November 1968, are in contradiction with the principle that all States have the right to become parties to multilateral treaties governing matters of general interest.

[GERMAN DEMOCRATIC REPUBLIC (*declaration made on accession*)[2]
The German Democratic Republic deems it necessary to state that articles 5 and 7 of the Convention deprive a number of States of the opportunity to become Parties to the Convention. As the Convention regulates matters affecting the interests of all States, it should be open to participation by all States whose policies are guided by the purposes and principles of the Charter of the United Nations.]

---

[1] See note 2 on p. 1271.
[3] See note 4 on p. 1271.

GUINEA (*declaration made on accession*)
The Government of the Republic of Guinea considers that the dispositions of Articles 5 and 7 of the Convention on the Non-Applicability of Statutory Limitations to War Crimes and Crimes against Humanity, adopted by the General Assembly on 26 November 1968, make it impossible for a number of States to become parties to the Convention and are therefore of a discriminatory character which is contradictory to the object and aims of this Convention. The Government of the Republic of Guinea is of the opinion that, in accordance with the principle of sovereign equality of States, the Convention should be open to all States without any discrimination and limitation.

HUNGARY (*declaration made on ratification*)
The Government of the Hungarian People's Republic declares that the provisions contained in Articles 5 and 7 of the Convention on the Non-applicability of' Statutory Limitations to War Crimes and Crimes against Humanity adopted by the General Assembly of the United Nations on 26 November 1968, which deny the possibility to certain States to become signatories to the Convention are of discriminatory nature, violate the principles of sovereign equality of States and are more particularly incompatible with the objectives and purposes of the said Convention.

LAO PEOPLE'S DEMOCRATIC REPUBLIC (*declaration made on accession*)
The Lao People's Democratic Republic accedes to the above-mentioned Convention and undertakes to implement faithfully all its clauses, except for the provisions of articles 5 and 7 of the Convention on the Non-Applicability of Statutory Limitations to War Crimes and Crimes against Humanity adopted by the United Nations General Assembly on 26 November 1968, which contravene the principle of the sovereign equality of States. The Convention should be open to universal participation in accordance with the purposes and principles of the Charter of the United Nations.

MONGOLIA (*declaration made on ratification*)
The Mongolian People's Republic deems it necessary to state that the provisions of Articles 5 and 7 of the Convention on the Non-Applicability of Statutory Limitations to War Crimes and Crimes against Humanity have a discriminatory nature and seek to preclude certain States from participating in the Convention and declares that as the Convention deals with matters affecting the interests of all States it should be open to participation by all States without any discrimination or restriction.

POLAND (*declaration made on ratification*)
The Polish People's Republic considers that the dispositions of Articles 5 and 7 of the Convention on the Non-Applicability of Statutory Limitations to War Crimes and Crimes against Humanity, adopted by the General Assembly on 26 November 1968, make it impossible for a number of States to become parties to the Convention and are therefore of a discriminatory character which is contradictory to the object and aims of this Convention. The Polish People's Republic is of the opinion that, in accordance with the principle of sovereign equality of States, the Convention should be open to all States without any discrimination and limitation.

ROMANIA (*declaration made on ratification*)
The State Council of the Socialist Republic of Romania states that the provisions of Articles 5 and 7 of the Convention on the Non-Applicability of Statutory Limitations to War Crimes and Crimes against Humanity are not compatible with the principle that multilateral international treaties, the subject and purpose of which concern the international community as a whole, should be open for universal participation.

RUSSIAN FEDERATION *see Union of Soviet Socialist Republics*

SLOVAKIA[3] *see Czechoslovakia*

UKRAINE (*declaration made on ratification*)
The Ukrainian Soviet Republic declares that the provisions of articles 5 and 7 of the Convention on the Non-Applicability of Statutory Limitations to War Crimes and Crimes against Humanity, which prevent certain States from signing the Convention or acceding to it, are contrary to the principle of the sovereign equality of States.

[UNION OF SOVIET SOCIALIST REPUBLICS] *Declaration made on ratification*
The Union of Soviet Socialist Republics declares that the provisions of articles 5 and 7 of the Convention on the Non-Applicability of Statutory Limitations to War Crimes and Crimes against Humanity, which prevent certain States from signing the Convention or acceding to it, are contrary to the principle of the sovereign equality of States.

VIET NAM (*declaration made on accession*)
The Government of the Socialist Republic of Viet Nam deems it necessary to state in accordance with the principle of sovereign equality of States that the Convention should be open to all States without any discrimination and limitation.

---

3 See note 2 on p. 1271.

No. 107

PRINCIPLES OF INTERNATIONAL COOPERATION IN THE DETECTION, ARREST, EXTRADITION, AND PUNISHMENT OF PERSONS GUILTY OF WAR CRIMES AND CRIMES AGAINST HUMANITY

Resolution 3074 (XXVIII). Adopted by the United Nations General Assembly, 3 December 1973

INTRODUCTORY NOTE: In 1965, the United Nations Commission on Human Rights started its deliberations on the question of punishment of war criminals and of persons who had committed crimes against humanity. Its aim was to ensure that persons who had committed such crimes would be traced, apprehended and equitably punished by the competent country. These efforts first led to the Convention on the Non-Applicability of Statutory Limitations to War Crimes and Crimes Against Humanity, adopted by General Assembly resolution 2391 (XXIII) on 26 November 1968 (*No. 106*). In 1969, the Commission, on the basis of the General Assembly Resolutions that are cited in the Preamble of the present Resolution, resumed its work on the detection, arrest, extradition and punishment of persons responsible for war crimes and crimes against humanity. It drafted the present resolution, which was adopted on 3 December 1973 by 94 votes in favor, none against and 29 abstentions.

AUTHENTIC TEXT: Arabic, Chinese, English French, Russian, Spanish. The text of Resolution 3074 (XXVIII), reproduced below, is reprinted from: *Resolutions adopted by the General Assembly during its Twenty-eight session,* Vol. I, *September 18–December 18, 1973.* General Assembly, Official Records: Twenty-eighth session, Supplement No. 30 (A/9030), New York, United Nations, 1974, p. 78.

TEXT PUBLISHED IN: *Résolutions adoptées par l'Assemblée générale au cours de sa vingt-huitième session,* vol. I, *18 septembre–18 décembre 1973.* Assemblée générale, documents officiels, Vingt-huitième session, supplément No. 30 (A/9030), New York, Nations Unies, 1974 pp. 85–86 (French – see also Arabic, Chinese, English, Russian, and Spanish); *Human Rights – A Compilation of International Instruments*, Vol. I (Second Part), New York, United Nations, 1993, pp. 678–679 (English); *Droits de l'homme – Recueil d'instruments internationaux,* New York, Nations Unies, 1988, pp. 151–152 (French); *Derechos Humanos – Recopilacion de instrumentos internacionales*, Nueva York, Naciones Unidas, 1988, pp. 151–152 (Spanish); *Prava Cheloveka – Sbornik mezhdunarodnykh dokumentov,* N'yu York, OON, 1989, pp. 169–170 (Russian); *United Nations resolutions*, compiled and edited by Dusan J. Djonovich. Series I – Resolutions adopted by the General Assembly, Vol. XIV, 1927–1974, Dobbs Ferry, Oceana Publications, 1978, pp. 448–449 (Engl.); *Droit des conflits armés*, pp. 1327–1329 (French); Websites: www.unhchr.ch/html; University of Minnesota Human Rights Library: *www1.umn.edu/humanrts/instree/x5picoda.htm* (Engl.; French).

* * *

The General Assembly,

Recalling *its resolutions 2583 (XXIV) of 15 December 1969, 2712 (XXV) of 15 December 1970, 2840 (XXVI) of 18 December 1971 and 3020(XXVII) of 18 December 1972,*

Taking into account *the special need for international action in order to ensure the prosecution and punishment of persons guilty of war crimes and crimes against humanity,*

Having considered *the draft principles of international co-operation in the detection, arrest, extradition and punishment of persons guilty of war crimes and crimes against humanity,*

Declares *that the United Nations, in pursuance of the principles and purposes set forth in the Charter concerning the promotion of co-operation between peoples and the maintenance of international peace and security, proclaims the following principles of international co-operation in the detection, arrest, extradition and punishment of persons guilty of war crimes and crimes against humanity:*

1. *War crimes and crimes against humanity, wherever they are committed, shall be subject to investigation and the persons against whom there is evidence that they have committed such crimes shall be subject to tracing, arrest, trial and, if found guilty, to punishment.*
2. *Every State has the right to try its own nationals for war crimes against humanity.*
3. *States shall co-operate with each other on a bilateral and multilateral basis with a view to halting and preventing war crimes and crimes against humanity, and shall take the domestic and international measures necessary for that purpose.*
4. *States shall assist each other in detecting, arresting and bringing to trial persons suspected of having committed such crimes and, if they are found guilty, in punishing them.*
5. *Persons against whom there is evidence that they have committed war crimes and crimes against humanity shall be subject to trial and, if found guilty, to punishment, as a general rule in the countries in which they committed those crimes. In that connection, States shall co-operate on questions of extraditing such persons.*
6. *States shall co-operate with each other in the collection of information and evidence which would help to bring to trial the persons indicated in paragraph 5 above and shall exchange such information.*
7. *In accordance with article 1 of the Declaration on Territorial Asylum of 14 December 1967, States shall not grant asylum to any person with respect to whom there are serious reasons for considering that he has committed a crime against peace, a war crime or a crime against humanity.*
8. *States shall not take any legislative or other measures which may be prejudicial to the international obligations they have assumed in regard to the detection, arrest, extradition and punishment-of persons guilty of war crimes and crimes against humanity.*
9. *In co-operating with a view to the detection, arrest and extradition of persons against whom there is evidence that they have committed war crimes and crimes against humanity and, if found guilty, their punishment, States shall act in conformity with the provisions of the Charter of the United Nations and of the Declaration on Principles of International Law concern-*

ing Friendly Relations and Co-operation among States in accordance with the Charter of the United Nations.

VOTE

Resolution 3074 (XXVIII) was adopted by the General Assembly of the United Nations on 3 December 1973 by a vote of 94 in favour, 0 against and 29 abstentions.

RECORDED VOTE

In favour: Algeria, Australia, Austria, Barbade, Belgium, Bhutan, Burma, Botswana, Bulgaria, Burundi, Byelorussia (Soviet Socialist Republic of), Cambodia, Canada, Chad, Congo, Costa Rica, Cuba, Cyprus, Czechoslovakia, Dahomey, Denmark, Egypt, Ecuador, Equatorial Guinea, Ethiopia, Fiji, Finland, France, Gabon, Gambia, German Democratic Republic, Germany (Federal Republic of), Ghana, Greece. Guinea, Guyana, Haiti, Honduras, Hungary, India, Iran, Iraq, Ireland, Iceland, Israel, Italy, Ivory Coast, Jordan, Kenya, Laos, Lebanon, Lesotho, Libyan Arab Republic, Liberia, Luxembourg, Madagascar, Malaysia, Mali, Mauritania, Mexico, Mongolia, Morocco, Nepal, New Zealand, Nicaragua, Niger, Nigeria, Norway, Netherlands, Peru, Philippines, Poland Romania, Rwanda, Sierra Leone, Singapore, Somalia, Sri Lanka, Sudan, Syrian Arab Republic, Tanzania (United Republic of), Togo, Thailand, Tunisia, Uganda, Ukraine (Soviet Socialist Republic of), Upper Volta, Union of Soviet Socialist Republic, United Kingdom, United States of America, Upper Volta, Yemen, Yemen Democratic, Yugoslavia, Zambia.

Against: 0

Abstaining: Afghanistan, Argentina, Bahrain, Brazil, Cameroon, Central African Republic, Chile, Colombia, Dominican Republic, El Salvador, France, Greece, Guatemala, Indonesia, Japan, Kuwait, Malawi, Oman, Pakistan, Paraguay, Portugal, Qatar, Saudi Arabia, Spain, Sweden Turkey, United Arab Emirates, Uruguay, Venezuela, Zaire.

No. 108

EUROPEAN CONVENTION ON THE NON-APPLICABILITY OF STATUTORY LIMITATIONS TO CRIMES AGAINST HUMANITY AND WAR CRIMES

Opened for signature at Strasbourg, 25 January 1974

INTRODUCTORY NOTE: The attempts of the Council of Europe to adopt a convention on the non-applicability of statutory limitations to crimes against humanity preceded those of the United Nations. When the United Nations took up the question in 1965, the Council of Europe suspended its efforts. The UN Convention, however, which was adopted on 26 November 1968 (*No. 106*), seemed unacceptable to most members of the Council of Europe because of its broad definition of "crimes against humanity". The present Convention uses a narrower definition and, unlike the UN Convention, limits its applicability to cases for which the statutory limitation period has not expired at the time of the entry into force of it.

ENTRY INTO FORCE: Not yet in force.

AUTHENTIC TEXTS: English, French. The text reproduced below is reprinted from European Treaty Series – No. 82.

TEXT PUBLISHED IN: *European Treaty Series* – No. 82 (Engl., French); Council of Europe, *European Conventions and Agreements*, Vol. III, 1972–1974, Strasbourg, 1975, pp. 212–215 (Engl., French); *ILM*, Vol. XIII, No. 3, May 1974, pp. 540–543 (Engl.); *Droit des conflits armés*, pp. 1331–1334 (French). Websites: Council of Europe: http://conventions.coe.int, (Engl., French); ICRC: www.icrc.org/ihl.nsf (Engl., French, Span.).

* * *

The member States of the Council of Europe, signatory hereto,

Considering the necessity to safeguard human dignity in time of war and in time of peace;

Considering that crimes against humanity and the most serious violations of the laws and customs of war constitute a serious infraction of human dignity;

Concerned in consequence to ensure that the punishment of those crimes is not prevented by statutory limitations whether in relation to prosecution or to the enforcement of the punishment;

Considering the essential interest in promoting a common criminal policy in this field, the aim of the Council of Europe being to achieve a greater unity between its Members,

Have agreed as follows:

Article 1. Each Contracting State undertakes to adopt any necessary measures to secure that statutory limitation shall not apply to the prosecution of the following offences, or to the enforcement of the sentences imposed for such offences, in so far as they are punishable under its domestic law:

1. the crimes against humanity specified in the Convention on the Prevention and Punishment of the Crime of Genocide adopted on 9 December 1948 by the General Assembly of the United Nations;
2. (a) the violations specified in Article 50 of the 1949 Geneva Convention for the Amelioration of the Condition of the Wounded and Sick in Armed Forces in the Field, Article 51 of the 1949 Geneva Convention for the Amelioration of the Condition of Wounded, Sick and Shipwrecked Members of Armed Forces at Sea, Article 130 of the 1949 Geneva Convention relative to the Treatment of Prisoners of War and Article 147 of the 1949 Geneva Convention relative to the Protection of Civilian Persons in Time of War,
   (b) any comparable violations of the laws of war having effect at the time when this Convention enters into force and of customs of war existing at that time, which are not already provided for in the above-mentioned provisions of the Geneva Conventions, when the specific violation under consideration is of a particularly grave character by reason either of its factual and intentional elements or of the extent of its foreseeable consequences;
3. any other violation of a rule or custom of international law which may hereafter be established and which the Contracting State concerned considers according to a declaration under Article 6 as being of a comparable nature to those referred to in paragraph 1 or 2 of this article.

Art. 2.

1. The present Convention applies to offences committed after its entry into force in respect of the Contracting State concerned.
2. It applies also to offences committed before such entry into force in those cases where the statutory limitation period had not expired at that time.

Art. 3.

1. This Convention shall be open to signature by the member States of the Council of Europe. It shall be subject to ratification or acceptance. Instruments of ratification or acceptance shall be deposited with the Secretary General of the Council of Europe.
2. The Convention shall enter into force three months after the date of deposit of the third instrument of ratification or acceptance.
3. In respect of a signatory State ratifying or accepting subsequently, the Convention shall come into force three months after the date of the deposit of its instrument of ratification or acceptance.

Art. 4.

1. After the entry into force of this Convention, the Committee of Ministers of the Council of Europe may invite any non-member State to accede thereto, provided that the resolution containing such invitation receives the unanimous agreement of the Members of the Council who have ratified the convention.
2. Such accession shall be effected by depositing with the Secretary General of the Council of Europe an instrument of accession which shall take effect three months after the date of its deposit.

Art. 5.
1. Any State may, at the time of signature or when depositing its instrument of ratification, acceptance or accession, specify the territory or territories to which this Convention shall apply.
2. Any State may, when depositing its instrument of ratification, acceptance or accession or at any later date, by declaration addressed to the Secretary General of the Council of Europe, extend this Convention to any other territory or territories specified in the declaration and for whose international relations it is responsible or on whose behalf it is authorised to give undertakings.
3. Any declaration made in pursuance of the preceding paragraph may, in respect of any territory mentioned in such declaration, be withdrawn according to the procedure laid down in Article 7 of this Convention.

Art. 6.
1. Any Contracting State may, at any time, by declaration addressed to the Secretary General of the Council of Europe, extend this Convention to any violations provided for in Article 1, paragraph 3, of this Convention.
2. Any declaration made in pursuance of the preceding paragraph may be withdrawn according to the procedure laid down in Article 7 of this Convention.

Art. 7.
1. This Convention shall remain in force indefinitely.
2. Any Contracting State may, in so far as it is concerned, denounce this Convention by means of a notification addressed to the Secretary General of the Council of Europe.
3. Such denunciation shall take effect six months after the date of receipt by the Secretary General of such notification.

Art. 8. The Secretary General of the Council of Europe shall notify the member States of the Council and any State which has acceded to this Convention of:
(a) any signature;
(b) any deposit of an instrument of ratification, acceptance or accession;
(c) any date of entry into force of this Convention in accordance with Article 3 thereof;
(d) any declaration received in pursuance of the provisions of Article 5 or Article 6;
(e) any notification received in pursuance of the provisions of Article 7 and the date on which the denunciation takes effect.

In witness whereof the undersigned, being duly authorised thereto, have signed this Convention.

Done at Strasbourg, this 25th day of January 1974, in the English and French languages, both texts being equally authoritative, in a single copy which shall remain deposited in the archives of the Council of Europe. The Secretary General of the Council of Europe shall transmit certified copies to each of the signatory and acceding States.

SIGNATURES, RATIFICATIONS AND ACCESSIONS[1]

State	*Signature*	*Ratification/Accession*
Belgium	4 May 1984	–
France	25 January 1974	–
Netherlands	6 April 1979	25 November 1981 *Dec.*
Romania	20 November 1997	8 June 2000

DECLARATIONS

NETHERLANDS (*declaration contained in the instrument of acceptance*)
On the occasion of the deposit of the instrument of acceptance for the Kingdom of the Netherlands (the Kingdom of Europe) of the European Convention on the non-applicability of Statutory Limitation to Crimes against Humanity and War Crimes, I have the honour, on behalf of the Government of the Kingdom of the Netherlands and in accordance with Article 6, paragraph 1 of the Convention, to declare the following:

The offences specified in Article 85 of the Protocol Additional to the Geneva Conventions of 12 August 1949, and relating to the protection of victims of international armed conflicts (Protocol I) of 12 December 1977 are, for the purposes of Article 1, paragraph 3, to be regarded as violations of a nature comparable to those referred to in Article 1, paragraph 2 where these offences are particularly serious in view of the actual circumstances and measure of intent on the part of the perpetrator, and of the extent of the foreseeable consequences.

[1] Based on indications from The Council of Europe and on the Council of Europe website on 23 October 2002.

No. 109

STATUTE OF THE INTERNATIONAL TRIBUNAL FOR THE PROSECUTION OF PERSONS RESPONSIBLE FOR SERIOUS VIOLATIONS OF INTERNATIONAL HUMANITARIAN LAW COMMITTED IN THE TERRITORY OF THE FORMER YUGOSLAVIA SINCE 1991

Adopted by resolution 827 of the Security Council of 25 May 1993, amended by resolutions 1166 of 13 May 1998, 1329 of 5 December 2000, 1411 of 17 May 2002, and 1431 of 14 August 2002

INTRODUCTORY NOTE: Prior to the adoption of the present statute, the Security Council, in Resolution 764 (1992) of 3 July 1992 and in later resolutions, reaffirmed that all parties to the conflicts in the territory of the former Yugoslavia were bound to comply with the obligations under international humanitarian law, and that persons who commit or order the commission of grave breaches of the Geneva Conventions are individually responsible for such breaches. By Resolution 780 (1992) of 6 October 1992, the Security Council requested the Secretary-General to establish an impartial commission of experts to report on the evidence of grave breaches of the Geneva Conventions and other violations of international humanitarian law committed in the territory of the former Yugoslavia. After having considered the interim report of this commission, the Security Council, on 22 February 1993, adopted resolution 808 (1993) by which it decided to establish an International tribunal for the prosecution of persons responsible for serious violations of international humanitarian law committed in the territory of the former Yugoslavia since 1991. It requested that the Secretary-General submit to the Council a report on all aspects of the matter including specific proposals. On 8 May 1993, the Secretary-General presented his report (S/25704) to which the present Statute was annexed. By resolution 827 (1993) of 25 May 1993, the Security Council, acting under Chapter VII of the Charter, decided by unanimity to establish the Tribunal and to adopt the Statute annexed to the Secretary-General's report. The Statute was amended as indicated above.

ENTRY INTO FORCE: 25 May 1993.

AUTHENTIC TEXT: Arabic, Chinese, English, French, Russian, Spanish. The text below is reprinted from the English version of the United Nations Security Council document: S/RES/827 (1993), 25 May 1993, as amended by the resolutions indicated above.

TEXT PUBLISHED IN: UN doc.S/RES/827 (1993) of 25 May 1993, 2 p. (Engl., also Arabic, Chinese, French, Russian and Spanish versions); *ILM*, Vol. 32, 1993, pp. 1159–1205 (Engl.); *International Tribunal for the Prosecution of Persons Responsible for Serious Violations of International Humanitarian Law Committed in the Territory of the Former Yugoslavia since 1991*, Basic Documents, United Nations, 1995, Sales No. E/F.95.III.P.1, pp. 4-27 (Engl. French);

Global war crimes tribunal collection, J. Oppenheim, W. van der Wolf, Nijmegen, Global Law Association, 1997–1999, Vol. Ia, resolution 827 and Statute, pp. 172–173, 206–214 (Engl.); R. W. D. John Jones, *The Practice of the International Criminal Tribunal for the former Yugoslavia and Rwanda*, Irvington, Transnational, 1997, 355 p. (Engl.); *Droit des conflits armés*, pp. 1337–1350 (French); Roberts and Guelff, pp. 565–572 (extracts, Engl.). United Nations website: www.un.org/icty (Engl., French); ICRC website: www.icrc.org/ihl.nsf (Engl., French, Span,).

* * *

RESOLUTION 827 (1993)

Adopted by the Security Council at its 3217th meeting, on 25 May 1993

The Security Council,

Reaffirming *its resolution 713 (1991) of 25 September 1991 and all subsequent relevant resolutions,*

Having considered *the report of the Secretary-General (S/25704 and Add.1) pursuant to paragraph 2 of resolution 808 (1993),*

Expressing once again its grave alarm *at continuing reports of widespread and flagrant violations of international humanitarian law occurring within the territory of the former Yugoslavia, and especially in the Republic of Bosnia and Herzegovina, including reports of mass killings, massive, organized and systematic detention and rape of women, and the continuance of the practice of "ethnic cleansing", including for the acquisition and the holding of territory,*

Determining *that this situation continues to constitute a threat to international peace and security,*

Determined *to put an end to such crimes and to take effective measures to bring to justice the persons who are responsible for them,*

Convinced *that in the particular circumstances of the former Yugoslavia the establishment as an ad hoc measure by the Council of an international tribunal and the prosecution of persons responsible for serious violations of international humanitarian law would enable this aim to be achieved and would contribute to the restoration and maintenance of peace,*

Believing *that the establishment of an international tribunal and the prosecution of persons responsible for the above-mentioned violations of international humanitarian law will contribute to ensuring that such violations are halted and effectively redressed,*

Noting *in this regard the recommendation by the Co-Chairmen of the Steering Committee of the International Conference on the Former Yugoslavia for the establishment of such a tribunal (S/25221),*

Reaffirming *in this regard its decision in resolution 808 (1993) that an international tribunal shall be established for the prosecution of persons responsible for serious violations of international humanitarian law committed in the territory of the former Yugoslavia since 1991,*

Considering *that, pending the appointment of the Prosecutor of the International Tribunal, the Commission of Experts established pursuant to res-*

olution 780 (1992) should continue on an urgent basis the collection of information relating to evidence of grave breaches of the Geneva Conventions and other violations of international humanitarian law as proposed in its interim report (S/25274),

Acting *under Chapter VII of the Charter of the United Nations,*

1. Approves *the report of the Secretary-General;*
2. Decides *hereby to establish an international tribunal for the sole purpose of prosecuting persons responsible for serious violations of international humanitarian law committed in the territory of the former Yugoslavia between 1 January 1991 and a date to be determined by the Security Council upon the restoration of peace and to this end to adopt the Statute of the International Tribunal annexed to the above-mentioned report;*
3. Requests *the Secretary-General to submit to the judges of the International Tribunal, upon their election, any suggestions received from States for the rules of procedure and evidence called for in Article 15 of the Statute of the International Tribunal;*
4. Decides *that all States shall cooperate fully with the International Tribunal and its organs in accordance with the present resolution and the Statute of the International Tribunal and that consequently all States shall take any measures necessary under their domestic law to implement the provisions of the present resolution and the Statute, including the obligation of States to comply with requests for assistance or orders issued by a Trial Chamber under Article 29 of the Statute;*
5. Urges *States and intergovernmental and non-governmental organizations to contribute funds, equipment and services to the International Tribunal, including the offer of expert personnel;*
6. Decides *that the determination of the seat of the International Tribunal is subject to the conclusion of appropriate arrangements between the United Nations and the Netherlands acceptable to the Council, and that the International Tribunal may sit elsewhere when it considers it necessary for the efficient exercise of its functions;*
7. Decides also *that the work of the International Tribunal shall be carried out without prejudice to the right of the victims to seek, through appropriate means, compensation for damages incurred as a result of violations of international humanitarian law;*
8. Requests *the Secretary-General to implement urgently the present resolution and in particular to make practical arrangements for the effective functioning of the International Tribunal at the earliest time and to report periodically to the Council;*
9. Decides *to remain actively seized of the matter.*

ANNEX

to the Report of the Secretary-General of the United Nations S/25704 of 3 May 1993

STATUTE OF THE INTERNATIONAL TRIBUNAL

adopted by the Security Council of the United Nations on 25 May 1993, as amended on 13 May 1998, 5 December 2000, 17 May and 14 August 2002.

Having been established by the Security Council acting under Chapter VII of the Charter of the United Nations, the International Tribunal for the Prosecution of Persons Responsible for Serious Violations of International Humanitarian Law Committed in the Territory of the Former Yugoslavia since 1991 (hereinafter referred to as "the International Tribunal") shall function in accordance with the provisions of the present Statute.

Article 1. Competence of the International Tribunal
The International Tribunal shall have the power to prosecute persons responsible for serious violations of international humanitarian law committed in the territory of the former Yugoslavia since 1991 in accordance with the provisions of the present Statute.

Art. 2. Grave breaches of the Geneva Conventions of 1949
The International Tribunal shall have the power to prosecute persons committing or ordering to be committed grave breaches of the Geneva Conventions of 12 August 1949, namely the following acts against persons or property protected under the provisions of the relevant Geneva Convention:
(a) wilful killing;
(b) torture or inhuman treatment, including biological experiments;
(c) wilfully causing great suffering or serious injury to body or health;
(d) extensive destruction and appropriation of property, not justified by military necessity and carried out unlawfully and wantonly;
(e) compelling a prisoner of war or a civilian to serve in the forces of a hostile power;
(f) wilfully depriving a prisoner of war or a civilian of the rights of fair and regular trial;
(g) unlawful deportation or transfer or unlawful confinement of a civilian;
(h) taking civilians as hostages.

Art. 3. Violations of the laws or customs of war
The International Tribunal shall have the power to prosecute persons violating the laws or customs of war. Such violations shall include, but not be limited to:
(a) employment of poisonous weapons or other weapons calculated to cause unnecessary suffering;
(b) wanton destruction of cities, towns or villages, or devastation not justified by military necessity;
(c) attack, or bombardment, by whatever means, of undefended towns, villages, dwellings, or buildings;
(d) seizure of, destruction or wilful damage done to institutions dedicated to religion, charity and education, the arts and sciences, historic monuments and works of art and science;
(e) plunder of public or private property.

Art. 4. Genocide
1. The International Tribunal shall have the power to prosecute persons committing genocide as defined in paragraph 2 of this article or of committing any of the other acts enumerated in paragraph 3 of this article.
2. Genocide means any of the following acts committed with intent to destroy, in whole or in part, a national, ethnical, racial or religious group, as such:

(a) killing members of the group;
(b) causing serious bodily or mental harm to members of the group;
(c) deliberately inflicting on the group conditions of life calculated to bring about its physical destruction in whole or in part;
(d) imposing measures intended to prevent births within the group;
(e) forcibly transferring children of the group to another group.

3. The following acts shall be punishable:
(a) genocide;
(b) conspiracy to commit genocide;
(c) direct and public incitement to commit genocide;
(d) attempt to commit genocide;
(e) complicity in genocide.

Art. 5. Crimes against humanity
The International Tribunal shall have the power to prosecute persons responsible for the following crimes when committed in armed conflict, whether international or internal in character, and directed against any civilian population:
(a) murder;
(b) extermination;
(c) enslavement;
(d) deportation;
(e) mprisonment;
(f) torture;
(g) rape;
(h) persecutions on political, racial and religious grounds;
(i) other inhumane acts.

Art. 6. Personal jurisdiction
The International Tribunal shall have jurisdiction over natural persons pursuant to the provisions of the present Statute.

Art. 7. Individual criminal responsibility
1. A person who planned, instigated, ordered, committed or otherwise aided and abetted in the planning, preparation or execution of a crime referred to in articles 2 to 5 of the present Statute, shall be individually responsible for the crime.
2. The official position of any accused person, whether as Head of State or Government or as a responsible Government official, shall not relieve such person of criminal responsibility nor mitigate punishment.
3. The fact that any of the acts referred to in articles 2 to 5 of the present Statute was committed by a subordinate does not relieve his superior of criminal responsibility if he knew or had reason to know that the subordinate was about to commit such acts or had done so and the superior failed to take the necessary and reasonable measures to prevent such acts or to punish the perpetrators thereof.
4. The fact that an accused person acted pursuant to an order of a Government or of a superior shall not relieve him of criminal responsibility, but may be considered in mitigation of punishment if the International Tribunal determines that justice so requires.

Art. 8. Territorial and temporal jurisdiction
The territorial jurisdiction of the International Tribunal shall extend to the territory of the former Socialist Federal Republic of Yugoslavia, including its land surface, airspace and territorial waters. The temporal jurisdiction of the International Tribunal shall extend to a period beginning on 1 January 1991.

Art. 9. Concurrent jurisdiction
1. The International Tribunal and national courts shall have concurrent jurisdiction to prosecute persons for serious violations of international humanitarian law committed in the territory of the former Yugoslavia since 1 January 1991.

2. The International Tribunal shall have primacy over national courts. At any stage of the procedure, the International Tribunal may formally request national courts to defer to the competence of the International Tribunal in accordance with the present Statute and the Rules of Procedure and Evidence of the International Tribunal.

Art. 10. Non-bis-in-idem

1. No person shall be tried before a national court for acts constituting serious violations of international humanitarian law under the present Statute, for which he or she has already been tried by the International Tribunal.
2. A person who has been tried by a national court for acts constituting serious violations of international humanitarian law may be subsequently tried by the International Tribunal only if:
   (a) the act for which he or she was tried was characterized as an ordinary crime; or
   (b) the national court proceedings were not impartial or independent, were designed to shield the accused from international criminal responsibility, or the case was not diligently prosecuted.
3. In considering the penalty to be imposed on a person convicted of a crime under the present Statute, the International Tribunal shall take into account the extent to which any penalty imposed by a national court on the same person for the same act has already been served.

Art. 11. Organization of the International Tribunal

The International Tribunal shall consist of the following organs:

(a) The Chambers, comprising three Trial Chambers and an Appeals Chamber;
(b) The Prosecutor, and
(c) A Registry, servicing both the Chambers and the Prosecutor.

Art. 12. Composition of the Chambers

1. The Chambers shall be composed of sixteen permanent independent judges, no two of whom may be nationals of the same State, and a maximum at any one time of nine *ad litem* independent judges appointed in accordance with article 13*ter*, paragraph 2, of the Statute, no two of whom may be narionals of the same State.
2. Three permanent judges and a maximum at any one time of six *ad litem* judges shall be members of each Trial Chamber. Each Trial Chamber to which *ad litem* judges are assigned may be divided into sections of three judges each, composed of noth permanent and *ad litem* judges. A section of a Trial Chamber shall have the same powers and responsibilities as a Trial Chamber under the Statute and shall render judgement in accordance with the same rules.
3. Seven of the permanent judges shall be members of the Appeals Chamber. The Appeals Chamber shall, for each appeal, be composed of five of its members.
4. A person who for the purposes of membership of the Chambers of the Intermational Tribunal could be regarded as a national of more than one State shall be deemed to be a national of the State in which that person ordinarily exercises civil and political rights.

Art. 13. Qualifications of judges

1. The permanent and *ad litem* judges shall be persons of high moral character, impartiality and integrity who possess the qualifications required in their respective countries for appointment to the highest judicial offices. In the overall composition of the Chambers and sections of the Trial Chambers, due account shall be taken of the experience of the judges in criminal law, international law, including international humanitarian law and human rights law.

Art. 13bis. Election of permanent judges

1. Fourteen of the permanent judges of the International Tribunal shall be elected by the General Assembly from a list submitted by the Security Council, in the following manner:

(a) The Secretary-General shall invite nominations for judges of the International Tribunal from States Members of the United Nations and non-member States maintaining permanent observer missions at United Nations Headquarters;
(b) Within sixty days of the date of the invitation of the Secretary-General, each State may nominate up to two candidates meeting the qualifications set out in article 13 of the Statute, no two of whom shall be of the same nationality and neither of whom shall be of the same nationality as any judge who is a member of the Appeals Chamber and who was elected or appointed a permanent judge of the International Criminal Tribunal for the Prosecution of Persons Responsible for Genocide and Other Serious Violations of Intertnational Humanitarian Law Committed in the Territory of Rwanda and Rwandan Citizens Responsible for Genocide and Other Such Violations Committed in the Territory of Neighbouring States, between 1 January 1994 and 31 December 1994 (hereinafter referred to as "The International Tribunal for Rwanda") in accordance with article 12bis of the Statute of that Tribunal;
(c) The Secretary-General shall forward the nominations received to the Security Council. From the nominations received the Security Council shall establish a list of not less than twenty-eight and not more than forty-two candidates, taking due account of the adequate representation of the principal legal systems of the world;
(d) The President of the Security Council shall transmit the list of candidates to the President of the General Assembly. From that list the General Assembly shall elect fourteen permanent judges of the International Tribunal. The candidates who receive an absolute majority of the votes of the States Members of the United Nations and of the non-Member States maintaining permanent observer missions at United Nations Headquarters, shall be declared elected. Should two candidates of the same nationality obtain the required majority vote, the one who received the higher number of votes shall be considered elected.

2. In the event of a vacancy in the Chambers amongst the permanent judges elected or appointed in accordance with this article, after consultation with the Presidents of the Security Council and of the General Assembly, the Secretary-General shall appoint a person meeting the qualifications of article 13 of the Statute, for the remainder of the term of office concerned.
3. The permanent judges elected in accordance with this article shall be elected for a term of four years. The terms and conditions of service shall be those of the judges of the International Court of Justice. They shall be eligible for re-election.

Art. 13ter Election and appointment of ad litem *judges*

1. The *ad litem* judges of the International Tribunal shall be elected by the General Assembly from a list submitted by the Security Council, in the following manner:
   (a) The Secretary-General shall invite nominations for *ad litem* judges of the International Tribunal from States Members of the United Nations and non-member States maintaining permanent observer missions at United Nations Headquarters.
   (b) Within sixty days of the date of the invitation of the Secretary-General, each State may nominate up to four candidates meeting the qualifications set out in article 13 of the Statute, taking into account the importance of a fair representation of female and male candidates.
   (c) The Secretary-General shall forward the nominations received to the Security Council. From the nominations received the Security Council shall establish a list of not less than twenty-eight and not more than fifty-four candidates, taking due account of the adequate representation of the principal legal systems of the world and bearing in mind the importance of equitable geographical distribution.
   (d) The President of the Security Council shall transmit the list of candidates to the President of the General Assembly. From that list the General Assembly shall elect the twenty-seven *ad litem* judges of the International Tribunal. The candidates who receive an absolute majority of the votes of the States Members of the

United Nations and of the non-Member States maintaining permanent observer missions at United Nations Headquarters, shall be declared elected.
 (e) The *ad litem* judges shall be elected for a term of four years. They shall not be eligible for re-election.
2. During their term, *ad litem* judges will be appointed by the Secretary-General, upon request of the President of the International Tribunal, to serve in the Trial Chambers for one or more trials, for a cumulative period of up to, but not including, three years. When requesting the appointment of any particular *ad litem* judge, the President of the International Tribunal shall bear in mind the criteria set out in article 13 of the Statute regarding the composition of the Chambers and sections of the Trial Chambers, the considerations set out in paragraph 1 (b) and (c) above and the number of votes the *ad litem* judge received in the General Assembly.

Art 13quater. Status of ad litem *judges*
1. During the period in which they are appointed to serve in the International Tribunal, *ad litem* judges shall:
   (a) benefit from the same terms and conditions of service *mutatis mutandis* as the permanent judges of the International Tribunal;
   (b) enjoy, subject to paragraph 2 below, the same powers as the permanent judges of the International Tribunal;
   (c) enjoy the priveleges and immunities, exemptions and facilities of a judge of the International Tribunal.
2. During the period in which they are appointed to serve in the International Tribunal, *ad litem* judges shall not:
   (a) be eligible for election as, or to vote in the election of, the President of the Tribunal or the Presiding Judge of a Trial Chamber pursuant to article 14 of the Statute;
   (b) have power:
      (i) to adopt rules of procedure and evidence pursuant to article 15 of the Statute. They shall, however, be consulted before the adoption of those rules;
      (ii) to review an indictment pursuant to article 19 of the Statute;
      (iii) to consult with the President in relation to the assignment of judges pursuant to article 14 of the Statute or in relation to a pardon or commutation of sentence pursuant to article 28 of the Statute
      (iv) to adjudicate in pre-trial proceedings.

Art. 14. Officers and members of the Chambers
1. The permanent judges of the International Tribunal shall elect a President from amongst their number.
2. The President of the International Tribunal shall be a member of the Appeals Chamber and shall preside over its proceedings.
3. After consultation with the permanent judges of the International Tribunal, the President shall assign four of the permanent judges elected or appointed in accordance with Article 13bis of the Statute to the Appeals Chamber and nine to the Trial Chambers.
4. Two of the permanent judges of the International Tribunal for Rwanda elected or appointed in accordance with Article 12bis of the Statute of that Tribunal shall be assigned by the President of that Tribunal, in consultation with the President of the International Tribunal, to be members of the Appeals Chamber and permanent judges of the International Tribunal.
5. After consultation with the permanent judges of the International Tribunal, the President shall assign such *ad litem* judges as may from time to time be appointed to serve in the International Tribunal to the Trial Chambers.
6. A judge shall serve only in the Chamber to which he or she was assigned.
7. The permanent judges of each Trial Chamber shall elect a Presiding Judge from amongst their number, who shall oversee the work of the Trial Chamber as a whole.

Art. 15. Rules of procedure and evidence

The judges of the International Tribunal shall adopt rules of procedure and evidence for the conduct of the pre-trial phase of the proceedings, trials and appeals, the admission of evidence, the protection of victims and witnesses and other appropriate matters.

Art. 16. The Prosecutor

1. The Prosecutor shall be responsible for the investigation and prosecution of persons responsible for serious violations of international humanitarian law committed in the territory of the former Yugoslavia since 1 January 1991.
2. The Prosecutor shall act independently as a separate organ of the International Tribunal. He or she shall not seek or receive instructions from any Government or from any other source.
3. The Office of the Prosecutor shall be composed of a Prosecutor and such other qualified staff as may be required.
4. The Prosecutor shall be appointed by the Security Council on nomination by the Secretary-General. He or she shall be of high moral character and possess the highest level of competence and experience in the conduct of investigations and prosecutions of criminal cases. The Prosecutor shall serve for a four-year term and be eligible for reappointment. The terms and conditions of service of the Prosecutor shall be those of an Under-Secretary-General of the United Nations.
5. The staff of the Office of the Prosecutor shall be appointed by the Secretary-General on the recommendation of the Prosecutor.

Art. 17. The Registry

1. The Registry shall be responsible for the administration and servicing of the International Tribunal.
2. The Registry shall consist of a Registrar and such other staff as may be required.
3. The Registrar shall be appointed by the Secretary-General after consultation with the President of the International Tribunal. He or she shall serve for a four-year term and be eligible for reappointment. The terms and conditions of service of the Registrar shall be those of an Assistant Secretary-General of the United Nations.
4. The staff of the Registry shall be appointed by the Secretary-General on the recommendation of the Registrar.

Art. 18. Investigation and preparation of indictment

1. The Prosecutor shall initiate investigations *ex-officio* or on the basis of information obtained from any source, particularly from Governments, United Nations organs, intergovernmental and non-governmental organizations. The Prosecutor shall assess the information received or obtained and decide whether there is sufficient basis to proceed.
2. The Prosecutor shall have the power to question suspects, victims and witnesses, to collect evidence and to conduct on-site investigations. In carrying out these tasks, the Prosecutor may, as appropriate, seek the assistance of the State authorities concerned.
3. If questioned, the suspect shall be entitled to be assisted by counsel of his own choice, including the right to have legal assistance assigned to him without payment by him in any such case if he does not have sufficient means to pay for it, as well as to necessary translation into and from a language he speaks and understands.
4. Upon a determination that a prima facie case exists, the Prosecutor shall prepare an indictment containing a concise statement of the facts and the crime or crimes with which the accused is charged under the Statute. The indictment shall be transmitted to a judge of the Trial Chamber.

Art. 19. Review of the indictment

1. The judge of the Trial Chamber to whom the indictment has been transmitted shall review it. If satisfied that a *prima facie* case has been established by the Prosecutor, he shall confirm the indictment. If not so satisfied, the indictment shall be dismissed.

2. Upon confirmation of an indictment, the judge may, at the request of the Prosecutor, issue such orders and warrants for the arrest, detention, surrender or transfer of persons, and any other orders as may be required for the conduct of the trial.

Art. 20. Commencement and conduct of trial proceedings

1. The Trial Chambers shall ensure that a trial is fair and expeditious and that proceedings are conducted in accordance with the rules of procedure and evidence, with full respect for the rights of the accused and due regard for the protection of victims and witnesses.
2. A person against whom an indictment has been confirmed shall, pursuant to an order or an arrest warrant of the International Tribunal, be taken into custody, immediately informed of the charges against him and transferred to the International Tribunal.
3. The Trial Chamber shall read the indictment, satisfy itself that the rights of the accused are respected, confirm that the accused understands the indictment, and instruct the accused to enter a plea. The Trial Chamber shall then set the date for trial.
4. The hearings shall be public unless the Trial Chamber decides to close the proceedings in accordance with its rules of procedure and evidence.

Art. 21. Rights of the accused

1. All persons shall be equal before the International Tribunal.
2. In the determination of charges against him, the accused shall be entitled to a fair and public hearing, subject to article 22 of the Statute.
3. The accused shall be presumed innocent until proved guilty according to the provisions of the present Statute.
4. In the determination of any charge against the accused pursuant to the present Statute, the accused shall be entitled to the following minimum guarantees, in full equality:
   (a) to be informed promptly and in detail in a language which he understands of the nature and cause of the charge against him;
   (b) to have adequate time and facilities for the preparation of his defence and to communicate with counsel of his own choosing;
   (c) to be tried without undue delay;
   (d) to be tried in his presence, and to defend himself in person or through legal assistance of his own choosing; to be informed, if he does not have legal assistance, of this right; and to have legal assistance assigned to him, in any case where the interests of justice so require, and without payment by him in any such case if he does not have sufficient means to pay for it;
   (e) to examine, or have examined, the witnesses against him and to obtain the attendance and examination of witnesses on his behalf under the same conditions as witnesses against him;
   (f) to have the free assistance of an interpreter if he cannot understand or speak the language used in the International Tribunal;
   (g) not to be compelled to testify against himself or to confess guilt.

Art. 22. Protection of victims and witnesses

The International Tribunal shall provide in its rules of procedure and evidence for the protection of victims and witnesses. Such protection measures shall include, but shall not be limited to, the conduct of in camera proceedings and the protection of the victim's identity.

Art. 23. Judgement

1. The Trial Chambers shall pronounce judgements and impose sentences and penalties on persons convicted of serious violations of international humanitarian law.
2. The judgement shall be rendered by a majority of the judges of the Trial Chamber, and shall be delivered by the Trial Chamber in public. It shall be accompanied by a reasoned opinion in writing, to which separate or dissenting opinions may be appended.

Art. 24. Penalties

1. The penalty imposed by the Trial Chamber shall be limited to imprisonment. In determining the terms of imprisonment, the Trial Chambers shall have recourse to the general practice regarding prison sentences in the courts of the former Yugoslavia.
2. In imposing the sentences, the Trial Chambers should take into account such factors as the gravity of the offence and the individual circumstances of the convicted person.
3. In addition to imprisonment, the Trial Chambers may order the return of any property and proceeds acquired by criminal conduct, including by means of duress, to their rightful owners.

Art. 25. Appellate proceedings

1. The Appeals Chamber shall hear appeals from persons convicted by the Trial Chambers or from the Prosecutor on the following grounds:
   (a) an error on a question of law invalidating the decision; or
   (b) an error of fact which has occasioned a miscarriage of justice.
2. The Appeals Chamber may affirm, reverse or revise the decisions taken by the Trial Chambers.

Art. 26. Review proceedings

Where a new fact has been discovered which was not known at the time of the proceedings before the Trial Chambers or the Appeals Chamber and which could have been a decisive factor in reaching the decision, the convicted person or the Prosecutor may submit to the International Tribunal an application for review of the judgement.

Art. 27. Enforcement of sentences

Imprisonment shall be served in a State designated by the International Tribunal from a list of States which have indicated to the Security Council their willingness to accept convicted persons. Such imprisonment shall be in accordance with the applicable law of the State concerned, subject to the supervision of the International Tribunal.

Art. 28. Pardon or commutation of sentences

If, pursuant to the applicable law of the State in which the convicted person is imprisoned, he or she is eligible for pardon or commutation of sentence, the State concerned shall notify the International Tribunal accordingly. The President of the International Tribunal, in consultation with the judges, shall decide the matter on the basis of the interests of justice and the general principles of law.

Art. 29. Cooperation and judicial assistance

1. States shall cooperate with the International Tribunal in the investigation and prosecution of persons accused of committing serious violations of international humanitarian law.
2. States shall comply without undue delay with any request for assistance or an order issued by a Trial Chamber, including, but not limited to:
   (a) the identification and location of persons;
   (b) the taking of testimony and the production of evidence;
   (c) the service of documents;
   (d) the arrest or detention of persons;
   (e) the surrender or the transfer of the accused to the International Tribunal.

Art. 30. The status, privileges and immunities of the International Tribunal

1. The Convention on the Privileges and Immunities of the United Nations of 13 February 1946 shall apply to the International Tribunal, the judges, the Prosecutor and his staff, and the Registrar and his staff.
2. The judges, the Prosecutor and the Registrar shall enjoy the privileges and immunities, exemptions and facilities accorded to diplomatic envoys, in accordance with international law.

3. The staff of the Prosecutor and of the Registrar shall enjoy the privileges and immunities accorded to officials of the United Nations under articles V and VII of the Convention referred to in paragraph 1 of this article.
4. Other persons, including the accused, required at the seat of the International Tribunal shall be accorded such treatment as is necessary for the proper functioning of the International Tribunal.

Art. 31. Seat of the International Tribunal
The International Tribunal shall have its seat at The Hague.

Art. 32. Expenses of the International Tribunal
The expenses of the International Tribunal shall be borne by the regular budget of the United Nations in accordance with Article 17 of the Charter of the United Nations.

Art. 33. Working languages
The working languages of the International Tribunal shall be English and French.

Art. 34. Annual report
The President of the International Tribunal shall submit an annual report of the International Tribunal to the Security Council and to the General Assembly.

No. 110

STATUTE OF THE INTERNATIONAL CRIMINAL TRIBUNAL FOR THE PROSECUTION OF PERSONS RESPONSIBLE FOR GENOCIDE AND OTHER SERIOUS VIOLATIONS OF INTERNATIONAL HUMANITARIAN LAW COMMITTED IN THE TERRITORY OF RWANDA AND RWANDAN CITIZENS RESPONSIBLE FOR GENOCIDE AND OTHER SUCH VIOLATIONS COMMITTED IN THE TERRITORY OF NEIGHBOURING STATES, BETWEEN 1 JANUARY 1994 AND 31 DECEMBER 1994

Adopted by resolution 955 of the United Nations Security Council on 8 November 1994, amended by resolutions 1329 of 5 December 2000, 1411 of 17 May 2002, and 1431 of 14 August 2002

INTRODUCTORY NOTE: On 6 April 1994, the President of Rwanda and the President of Burundi were killed when their plane, near the airport of Kigali, was hit by a rocket. A systematic killing of Tutsis and Hutu moderates in Rwanda amounting to genocide began immediately afterwards. The Security Council, by Resolution 935 (1994) of 1 July 1994, established an impartial commission of experts with a view to providing it with the evidence of grave violations of international humanitarian law including acts of genocide. Based on the preliminary report of this commission, the Security Council, on 8 November 1994, acting under Chapter VII of the Charter, adopted the present resolution establishing the International Tribunal for Rwanda. The Statute of the Tribunal, annexed to the Resolution, is to a large extent identical to that of the Yugoslav Tribunal (*No. 109*). The conflict in Rwanda being of a non-international character, the competence of the Tribunal includes, apart from genocide and crimes against humanity, violations of Article 3 common to the Geneva Conventions (*Nos. 49–52*) and of Additional Protocol II (*No. 57*) (see Article 4 of the Statute).

AUTHENTIC TEXT: Arabic, Chinese, English, French, Russian, Spanish. The text is reproduced from UN doc.S/RES/955 (1994) of 8 November 1994. The Statute was amended as indicated above.

TEXT PUBLISHED IN: Document of the United Nations Security Council S/RES/955 (1994) of 8 November 1994 (English, also Arabic, Chinese, French, Spanish and Russian versions); *ILM*, Vol. 33, 1994, pp. 1698–1616 (Engl.); *RGDIP*, tome 98, 1995, pp. 1066–1080 (French); *Global war crimes tribunal collection*, J. Oppenheim, W. van der Wolf, Nijmegen, Global Law Association, 1997–1999, Vol. I (*Resolution and Statute*), pp. 175–182 (Engl.); R. W. D. John Jones, *The practice of the International Criminal Tribunal for the former Yugoslavia and Rwanda*, Irvington, Transnational Publishers, 1997, 355 p. (Engl.); V. Morris, M. P. Scharf, *The International Criminal Tribunal for Rwanda,*

Irvington, Transnational Publishers (*Resolution and Statute*), pp. 296–297, 3– 12 (Engl.); Roberts and Guelff (*extracts of Statute only*), pp. 615–621 (Engl.); *Rossiiski ezhegodnik mezhdunarodnogo prava 1995*, St. Petersburg, Rosia-Neva, 1996, pp. 217–229 (Statute only) (Russ.); ICTR website: www.ictr.org/. ICRC website: www.icrc.org/ihl.nsf

* * *

RESOLUTION 955 (1994)

The Security Council,

Reaffirming *all its previous resolutions on the situation in Rwanda,*

Having considered *the reports of the Secretary-General pursuant to paragraph 3 of resolution 935 (1994) of 1 July 1994 (S/1994/879 and S/1994/906), and having taken note of the reports of the Special Rapporteur for Rwanda of the United Nations Commission on Human Rights (S/1994/1157, annex I and annex II),*

Expressing appreciation *for the work of the Commission of Experts established pursuant to resolution 935 (1994), in particular its preliminary report on violations of international humanitarian law in Rwanda transmitted by the Secretary-General's letter of 1 October 1994 (S/1994/1125),*

Expressing *once again its grave concern at the reports indicating that genocide and other systematic, widespread and flagrant violations of international humanitarian law have been committed in Rwanda,*

Determining *that this situation continues to constitute a threat to international peace and security,*

Determined *to put an end to such crimes and to take effective measures to bring to justice the persons who are responsible for them,*

Convinced *that in the particular circumstances of Rwanda, the prosecution of persons responsible for serious violations of international humanitarian law would enable this aim to be achieved and would contribute to the process of national reconciliation and to the restoration and maintenance of peace,*

Believing *that the establishment of an international tribunal for the prosecution of persons responsible for genocide and the other above-mentioned violations of international humanitarian law will contribute to ensuring that such violations are halted and effectively redressed,*

Stressing *also the need for international cooperation to strengthen the courts and judicial system of Rwanda, having regard in particular to the necessity for those courts to deal with large numbers of suspects,*

Considering *that the Commission of Experts established pursuant to resolution 935 (1994) should continue on an urgent basis the collection of information relating to evidence of grave violations of international humanitarian law committed in the territory of Rwanda and should submit its final report to the Secretary-General by 30 November 1994,*

Acting *under Chapter VII of the Charter of the United Nations,*

1. Decides hereby, having received the request of the Government of Rwanda (S/1994/1115), to establish an international tribunal for the sole purpose of prosecuting persons responsible for genocide and other serious violations of international humanitarian law committed in the territory of Rwanda and Rwandan citizens responsible for genocide and other such violations committed in the territory of neighbouring States, between 1 January 1994 and 31 December 1994 and to this end to adopt the Statute of the International Criminal Tribunal for Rwanda annexed hereto;

2. *Decides that all States shall cooperate fully with the International Tribunal and its organs in accordance with the present resolution and the Statute of the International Tribunal and that consequently all States shall take any measures necessary under their domestic law to implement the provisions of the present resolution and the Statute, including the obligation of States to comply with requests for assistance or orders issued by a Trial Chamber under Article 28 of the Statute, and requests States to keep the Secretary-General informed of such measures;*
3. *Considers that the Government of Rwanda should be notified prior to the taking of decisions under articles 26 and 27 of the Statute;*
4. *Urges States and intergovernmental and non-governmental organizations to contribute funds, equipment and services to the International Tribunal, including the offer of expert personnel;*
5. *Requests the Secretary-General to implement this resolution urgently and in particular to make practical arrangements for the effective functioning of the International Tribunal, including recommendations to the Council as to possible locations for the seat of the International Tribunal at the earliest time and to report periodically to the Council;*
6. *Decides that the seat of the International Tribunal shall be determined by the Council having regard to considerations of justice and fairness as well as administrative efficiency, including access to witnesses, and economy, and subject to the conclusion of appropriate arrangements between the United Nations and the State of the seat, acceptable to the Council, having regard to the fact that the International Tribunal may meet away from its seat when it considers it necessary for the efficient exercise of its functions; and decides that an office will be established and proceedings will be conducted in Rwanda, where feasible and appropriate, subject to the conclusion of similar appropriate arrangements;*
7. *Decides to consider increasing the number of judges and Trial Chambers of the International Tribunal if it becomes necessary;*
8. *Decides to remain actively seized of the matter.*

ANNEX

Statute of the International Tribunal for Rwanda

Having been established by the Security Council acting under Chapter VII of the Charter of the United Nations, the International Criminal Tribunal for the Prosecution of Persons Responsible for Genocide and Other Serious Violations of International Humanitarian Law Committed in the Territory of Rwanda and Rwandan citizens responsible for genocide and other such violations committed in the territory of neighbouring States, between 1 January 1994 and 31 December 1994 (hereinafter referred to as "the International Tribunal for Rwanda") shall function in accordance with the provisions of the present Statute.

Art. 1. Competence of the International Tribunal for Rwanda
The International Tribunal for Rwanda shall have the power to prosecute persons responsible for serious violations of international humanitarian law committed in the territory of Rwanda and Rwandan citizens responsible for such violations committed in the territory of neighbouring States, between 1 January 1994 and 31 December 1994, in accordance with the provisions of the present Statute.

Art. 2. Genocide
1. The International Tribunal for Rwanda shall have the power to prosecute persons committing genocide as defined in paragraph 2 of this article or of committing any of the other acts enumerated in paragraph 3 of this article.
2. Genocide means any of the following acts committed with intent to destroy, in whole or in part, a national, ethnical, racial or religious group, as such:
   (a) Killing members of the group;
   (b) Causing serious bodily or mental harm to members of the group;
   (c) Deliberately inflicting on the group conditions of life calculated to bring about its physical destruction in whole or in part;
   (d) Imposing measures intended to prevent births within the group;
   (e) Forcibly transferring children of the group to another group.
3. The following acts shall be punishable:

(a) Genocide;
(b) Conspiracy to commit genocide;
(c) Direct and public incitement to commit genocide;
(d) Attempt to commit genocide;
(e) Complicity in genocide.

Art. 3. Crimes against humanity
The International Tribunal for Rwanda shall have the power to prosecute persons responsible for the following crimes when committed as part of a widespread or systematic attack against any civilian population on national, political, ethnic, racial or religious grounds:
(a) Murder;
(b) Extermination;
(c) Enslavement;
(d) Deportation;
(e) Imprisonment;
(f) Torture;
(g) Rape;
(h) Persecutions on political, racial and religious grounds;
(i) Other inhumane acts.

Art. 4. Violations of Article 3 common to the Geneva Conventions and of Additional Protocol II
The International Tribunal for Rwanda shall have the power to prosecute persons committing or ordering to be committed serious violations of Article 3 common to the Geneva Conventions of 12 August 1949 for the Protection of War Victims, and of Additional Protocol II thereto of 8 June 1977. These violations shall include, but shall not be limited to:
(a) Violence to life, health and physical or mental well-being of persons, in particular murder as well as cruel treatment such as torture, mutilation or any form of corporal punishment;
(b) Collective punishments;
(c) Taking of hostages;
(d) Acts of terrorism;
(e) Outrages upon personal dignity, in particular humiliating and degrading treatment, rape, enforced prostitution and any form of indecent assault;
(f) Pillage;

(g) The passing of sentences and the carrying out of executions without previous judgement pronounced by a regularly constituted court, affording all the judicial guarantees which are recognized as indispensable by civilized peoples;
(h) Threats to commit any of the foregoing acts.

Art. 5. Personal jurisdiction
The International Tribunal for Rwanda shall have jurisdiction over natural persons pursuant to the provisions of the present Statute.

Art. 6. Individual criminal responsibility
1. A person who planned, instigated, ordered, committed or otherwise aided and abetted in the planning, preparation or execution of a crime referred to in articles 2 to 4 of the present Statute, shall be individually responsible for the crime.
2. The official position of any accused person, whether as Head of State or Government or as a responsible Government official, shall not relieve such person of criminal responsibility nor mitigate punishment.
3. The fact that any of the acts referred to in articles 2 to 4 of the present Statute was committed by a subordinate does not relieve his or her superior of criminal responsibility if he or she knew or had reason to know that the subordinate was about to commit such acts or had done so and the superior failed to take the necessary and reasonable measures to prevent such acts or to punish the perpetrators thereof.
4. The fact that an accused person acted pursuant to an order of a Government or of a superior shall not relieve him or her of criminal responsibility, but may be considered in mitigation of punishment if the International Tribunal for Rwanda determines that justice so requires.

Art. 7. Territorial and temporal jurisdiction
The territorial jurisdiction of the International Tribunal for Rwanda shall extend to the territory of Rwanda including its land surface and airspace as well as to the territory of neighbouring States in respect of serious violations of international humanitarian law committed by Rwandan citizens.

The temporal jurisdiction of the International Tribunal for Rwanda shall extend to a period beginning on 1 January 1994 and ending on 31 December 1994.

Art. 8. Concurrent jurisdiction
1. The International Tribunal for Rwanda and national courts shall have concurrent jurisdiction to prosecute persons for serious violations of international humanitarian law committed in the territory of Rwanda and Rwandan citizens for such violations committed in the territory of neighbouring States, between 1 January 1994 and 31 December 1994.
2. The International Tribunal for Rwanda shall have primacy over the national courts of all States. At any stage of the procedure, the International Tribunal for Rwanda may formally request national courts to defer to its competence in accordance with the present Statute and the Rules of Procedure and Evidence of the International Tribunal for Rwanda.

Art. 9. Non bis in idem
1. No person shall be tried before a national court for acts constituting serious violations of international humanitarian law under the present Statute, for which he or she has already been tried by the International Tribunal for Rwanda.
2. A person who has been tried by a national court for acts constituting serious violations of international humanitarian law may be subsequently tried by the International Tribunal for Rwanda only if:
   (a) The act for which he or she was tried was characterized as an ordinary crime; or
   (b) The national court proceedings were not impartial or independent, were designed to shield the accused from international criminal responsibility, or the case was not diligently prosecuted.

3. In considering the penalty to be imposed on a person convicted of a crime under the present Statute, the International Tribunal for Rwanda shall take into account the extent to which any penalty imposed by a national court on the same person for the same act has already been served.

Art. 10. Organization of the International Tribunal for Rwanda
The International Tribunal for Rwanda shall consist of the following organs:
(a) The Chambers, comprising two Trial Chambers and an Appeals Chamber;
(b) The Prosecutor; and
(c) A Registry.

Art. 11. Composition of the Chambers
1. The Chambers shall be composed of sixteen permanent independent judges, no two of whom may be nationals of the same State, and a maximum at any one time of four ad litem independent judges appointed in accordance with article 12ter, paragraph 2, of the present Statute, no two of whom may be nationals of the same State.
2. Three permanent judges and a maximum at any one time of four *ad litem* judges shall be members of each Trial Chamber. Each Trial Chamber to which *ad litem* judges are assigned may be divided into sections of three judges each, composed of both permanent and *ad litem* judges. A section of a Trial Chamber shall have the same powers and responsibilities as a Trial Chamber under the present Statute and shall render judgement in accordance with the same rules.
3. Seven of the permanent judges shall be members of the Appeals Chamber. The Appeals Chamber shall, for each appeal, be composed of five of its members.
4. A person who for the purposes of membership of the Chambers of the International Tribunal for Rwanda could be regarded as a national of more than one State shall be deemed to be a national of the State in which that person ordinarily exercises civil and political rights.

Art. 12. Qualification and election of judges
1 The permanent and *ad litem* judges shall be persons of high moral character, impartiality and integrity who possess the qualifications required in their respective countries for appointment to the highest judicial offices. In the overall composition of the Chambers and sections of the Trial Chambers, due account shall be taken of the experience of the judges in criminal law, international law, including international humanitarian law and human rights law.

Art. 12bis. Election of permanent judges
1. Eleven of the permanent judges of the International Tribunal for Rwanda shall be elected by the General Assembly from a list submitted by the Security Council, in the following manner:
   (a) The Secretary-General shall invite nominations for permanent judges of the International Tribunal for Rwanda from States Members of the United Nations and non-member States maintaining permanent observer missions at United Nations Headquarters;
   (b) Within sixty days of the date of the invitation of the Secretary-General, each State may nominate up to two candidates meeting the qualifications set out in article 12 of the present Statute, no two of whom shall be of the same nationality and neither of whom shall be of the same nationality as any judge who is a member of the Appeals Chamber and who was elected or appointed a permanent judge of the International Tribunal for the Prosecution of Persons Responsible for Serious Violations of International Law Committed in the Territory of the Former Yugoslavia since 1991 (hereinafter referred to as "the International Tribunal for the Former Yugoslavia") in accordance with article 13 bis of the Statute of that Tribunal;
   (c) The Secretary-General shall forward nominations received to the Security Council. From the nominations received the Security Council shall establish a

list of not less than twenty two and not more than thirty three candidates, taking due account of the adequate representation on the International Tribunal for Rwanda of the principal legal systems of the world;

(d) The President of the Security Council shall transmit the list of candidates to the President of the General Assembly. From that list the General Assembly shall elect eleven permanent judges of the International Tribunal for Rwanda. The candidates who receive an absolute majority of the votes of the States Members of the United Nations and of the non-Member States maintaining permanent observer missions at United Nations Headquarters, shall be declared elected. Should two candidates of the same nationality obtain the required majority vote, the one who received the higher number of votes shall be considered elected.

2. In the event of a vacancy in the Chambers amongst the permanent judges elected or appointed in accordance with this article, after consultation with the Presidents of the Security Council and of the General Assembly the Secretary-General shall appoint a person meeting the qualifications of article 12 of the present Statute, for the remainder of the term of office concerned.
3. The permanent judges elected in accordance with this article shall be elected for a term of four years. The terms and conditions of service shall be those of the permanent judges of the International Tribunal for the Former Yugoslavia. They shall be eligible for re-election.

Article 12ter. Election and appointment of ad litem *judges*

1. The *ad litem* judges of the International Tribunal for Rwanda shall be elected by the General Assembly from a list submitted by the Security Council, in the following manner:
   (a) The Secretary-General shall invite nominations for *ad litem* judges of the International Tribunal for Rwanda from States Members of the United Nations and non-member States maintaining permanent observer missions at United Nations Headquarters.
   (b) Within sixty days of the date of the invitation of the Secretary-General, each State may nominate up to four candidates meeting the qualifications set out in article 12 of the present Statute, taking into account the importance of a fair representation of female and male candidates.
   (c) The Secretary-General shall forward the nominations received to the Security Council. From the nominations received the Security Council shall establish a list of not less than thirty-six candidates, taking due account of the adequate representation of the principal legal systems of the world and bearing in mind the importance of equitable geographical distribution.
   (d) The President of the Security Council shall transmit the list of candidates to the President of the General Assembly. From that list the General Assembly shall elect the eighteen *ad litem* judges of the International Tribunal for Rwanda. The candidates who receive an absolute majority of the votes of the States Members of the United Nations and of the non-Member States maintaining permanent observer missions at United Nations Headquarters, shall be declared elected.
   (e) The *ad litem* judges shall be elected for a term of four years. They shall not be eligible for re-election.
2. During their term, *ad litem* judges will be appointed by the Secretary-General, upon request of the President of the International Tribunal for Rwanda, to serve in the Trial Chambers for one or more trials, for a cumulative period of up to, but not including, three years. When requesting the appointment of any particular *ad litem* judge, the President of the International Tribunal for Rwanda shall bear in mind the criteria set out in article 12 of the present Statute regarding the composition of the Chambers and sections of the Trial Chambers, the considerations set out in paragraph 1 (b) and (c) above and the number of votes the *ad litem* judge received in the General Assembly.

Art 12quater. Status of ad litem *judges*

1. During the period in which they are appointed to serve in the International Tribunal for Rwanda, *ad litem* judges shall:
   (a) Benefit from the same terms and conditions of service *mutatis mutandis* as the permanent judges of the International Tribunal for Rwanda;
   (b) Enjoy, subject to paragraph 2 below, the same powers as the permanent judges of the International Tribunal for Rwanda;
   (c) Enjoy the priveleges and immunities, exemptions and facilities of a judge of the International Tribunal for Rwanda.
2. During the period in which they are appointed to serve in the International Tribunal for Rwanda, *ad litem* judges shall not:
   (a) Be eligible for election as, or to vote in the election of, the President of the International Tribunal for Rwanda or the Presiding Judge of a Trial Chamber pursuant to article 13 of the present Statute;
   (b) Have power:
      (i) To adopt rules of procedure and evidence pursuant to article 14 of the present Statute. They shall, however, be consulted before the adoption of those rules;
      (ii) To review an indictment pursuant to article 18 of the present Statute;
      (iii) To consult with the President of the International Tribunal for Rwanda in relation to the assignment of judges pursuant to article 13 of the present Statute or in relation to a pardon or commutation of sentence pursuant to article 27 of the present Statute;
      (iv) To adjudicate in pre-trial proceedings.

Art. 13. Officers and members of the Chambers

1. The permanent judges of the International Tribunal for Rwanda shall elect a President from amongst their number.
2. The President of the International Tribunal for Rwanda shall be a member of one of its Trial Chambers.
3. After consultation with the permanent judges of the International Tribunal for Rwanda, the President shall assign two of the permanent judges elected or appointed in accordance with Article 12bis of the present Statute to be members of the Appeals Chamber of the International Tribunal for the Former Yugoslavia and eight to the Trial Chambers of the International Tribunal for Rwanda.
4. The members of the Appeals Chamber of the International Tribunal for the Former Yugoslavia shall also serve as the members of the Appeals Chamber of the International Tribunal for Rwanda.
5. After consultation with the permanent judges of the International Tribunal for Rwanda, the President shall assign such *ad litem* judges as may from time to time be appointed to serve in the International Tribunal for Rwanda to the Trial Chambers.
6. A judge shall serve only in the Chamber to which he or she was assigned.
7. The permanent judges of each Trial Chamber shall elect a Presiding Judge from amongst their number, who shall oversee the work of that Trial Chamber as a whole.

Art. 14. Rules of procedure and evidence

The judges of the International Tribunal for Rwanda shall adopt, for the purpose of proceedings before the International Tribunal for Rwanda, the rules of procedure and evidence for the conduct of the pre-trial phase of the proceedings, trials and appeals, the admission of evidence, the protection of victims and witnesses and other appropriate matters of the International Tribunal for the Former Yugoslavia with such changes as they deem necessary.

Art. 15. The Prosecutor

1. The Prosecutor shall be responsible for the investigation and prosecution of persons responsible for serious violations of international humanitarian law committed in the territory of Rwanda and Rwandan citizens responsible for such violations commit-

ted in the territory of neighbouring States, between 1 January 1994 and 31 December 1994.

2. The Prosecutor shall act independently as a separate organ of the International Tribunal for Rwanda. He or she shall not seek or receive instructions from any Government or from any other source.
3. The Prosecutor of the International Tribunal for the Former Yugoslavia shall also serve as the Prosecutor of the International Tribunal for Rwanda. He or she shall have additional staff, including an additional Deputy Prosecutor, to assist with prosecutions before the International Tribunal for Rwanda. Such staff shall be appointed by the Secretary-General on the recommendation of the Prosecutor.

Art. 16. The Registry

1. The Registry shall be responsible for the administration and servicing of the International Tribunal for Rwanda.
2. The Registry shall consist of a Registrar and such other staff as may be required.
3. The Registrar shall be appointed by the Secretary-General after consultation with the President of the International Tribunal for Rwanda. He or she shall serve for a four-year term and be eligible for reappointment. The terms and conditions of service of the Registrar shall be those of an Assistant Secretary-General of the United Nations.
4. The staff of the Registry shall be appointed by the Secretary-General on the recommendation of the Registrar.

Art. 17. Investigation and preparation of indictment

1. The Prosecutor shall initiate investigations *ex-officio* or on the basis of information obtained from any source, particularly from Governments, United Nations organs, intergovernmental and non-governmental organizations. The Prosecutor shall assess the information received or obtained and decide whether there is sufficient basis to proceed.
2. The Prosecutor shall have the power to question suspects, victims and witnesses, to collect evidence and to conduct on-site investigations. In carrying out these tasks, the Prosecutor may, as appropriate, seek the assistance of the State authorities concerned.
3. If questioned, the suspect shall be entitled to be assisted by counsel of his or her own choice, including the right to have legal assistance assigned to the suspect without payment by him or her in any such case if he or she does not have sufficient means to pay for it, as well as to necessary translation into and from a language he or she speaks and understands.
4. Upon a determination that a *prima facie* case exists, the Prosecutor shall prepare an indictment containing a concise statement of the facts and the crime or crimes with which the accused is charged under the Statute. The indictment shall be transmitted to a judge of the Trial Chamber.

Art. 18. Review of the indictment

1. The judge of the Trial Chamber to whom the indictment has been transmitted shall review it. If satisfied that a *prima facie* case has been established by the Prosecutor, he or she shall confirm the indictment. If not so satisfied, the indictment shall be dismissed.
2. Upon confirmation of an indictment, the judge may, at the request of the Prosecutor, issue such orders and warrants for the arrest, detention, surrender or transfer of persons, and any other orders as may be required for the conduct of the trial.

Art. 19. Commencement and conduct of trial proceedings

1. The Trial Chambers shall ensure that a trial is fair and expeditious and that proceedings are conducted in accordance with the rules of procedure and evidence, with full respect for the rights of the accused and due regard for the protection of victims and witnesses.
2. A person against whom an indictment has been confirmed shall, pursuant to an order or an arrest warrant of the International Tribunal for Rwanda, be taken into custody,

immediately informed of the charges against him or her and transferred to the International Tribunal for Rwanda.

3. The Trial Chamber shall read the indictment, satisfy itself that the rights of the accused are respected, confirm that the accused understands the indictment, and instruct the accused to enter a plea. The Trial Chamber shall then set the date for trial.
4. The hearings shall be public unless the Trial Chamber decides to close the proceedings in accordance with its rules of procedure and evidence.

Art. 20. Rights of the accused

1. All persons shall be equal before the International Tribunal for Rwanda.
2. In the determination of charges against him or her, the accused shall be entitled to a fair and public hearing, subject to article 21 of the Statute.
3. The accused shall be presumed innocent until proved guilty according to the provisions of the present Statute.
4. In the determination of any charge against the accused pursuant to the present Statute, the accused shall be entitled to the following minimum guarantees, in full equality:
   (a) To be informed promptly and in detail in a language which he or she understands of the nature and cause of the charge against him or her;
   (b) To have adequate time and facilities for the preparation of his or her defence and to communicate with counsel of his or her own choosing;
   (c) To be tried without undue delay;
   (d) To be tried in his or her presence, and to defend himself or herself in person or through legal assistance of his or her own choosing; to be informed, if he or she does not have legal assistance, of this right; and to have legal assistance assigned to him or her, in any case where the interests of justice so require, and without payment by him or her in any such case if he or she does not have sufficient means to pay for it;
   (e) To examine, or have examined, the witnesses against him or her and to obtain the attendance and examination of witnesses on his or her behalf under the same conditions as witnesses against him or her;
   (f) To have the free assistance of an interpreter if he or she cannot understand or speak the language used in the International Tribunal for Rwanda;
   (g) Not to be compelled to testify against himself or herself or to confess guilt.

Art. 21. Protection of victims and witnesses

The International Tribunal for Rwanda shall provide in its rules of procedure and evidence for the protection of victims and witnesses. Such protection measures shall include, but shall not be limited to, the conduct of in camera proceedings and the protection of the victim's identity.

Art. 22. Judgement

1. The Trial Chambers shall pronounce judgements and impose sentences and penalties on persons convicted of serious violations of international humanitarian law.
2. The judgement shall be rendered by a majority of the judges of the Trial Chamber, and shall be delivered by the Trial Chamber in public. It shall be accompanied by a reasoned opinion in writing, to which separate or dissenting opinions may be appended.

Art. 23. Penalties

1. The penalty imposed by the Trial Chamber shall be limited to imprisonment. In determining the terms of imprisonment, the Trial Chambers shall have recourse to the general practice regarding prison sentences in the courts of Rwanda.
2. In imposing the sentences, the Trial Chambers should take into account such factors as the gravity of the offence and the individual circumstances of the convicted person.

3. In addition to imprisonment, the Trial Chambers may order the return of any property and proceeds acquired by criminal conduct, including by means of duress, to their rightful owners.

Art. 24. Appellate proceedings

1. The Appeals Chamber shall hear appeals from persons convicted by the Trial Chambers or from the Prosecutor on the following grounds:
   (a) An error on a question of law invalidating the decision; or
   (b) An error of fact which has occasioned a miscarriage of justice.
2. The Appeals Chamber may affirm, reverse or revise the decisions taken by the Trial Chambers.

Art. 25. Review proceedings

Where a new fact has been discovered which was not known at the time of the proceedings before the Trial Chambers or the Appeals Chamber and which could have been a decisive factor in reaching the decision, the convicted person or the Prosecutor may submit to the International Tribunal for Rwanda an application for review of the judgement.

Art. 26. Enforcement of sentences

Imprisonment shall be served in Rwanda or any of the States on a list of States which have indicated to the Security Council their willingness to accept convicted persons, as designated by the International Tribunal for Rwanda. Such imprisonment shall be in accordance with the applicable law of the State concerned, subject to the supervision of the International Tribunal for Rwanda.

Art. 27. Pardon or commutation of sentences

If, pursuant to the applicable law of the State in which the convicted person is imprisoned, he or she is eligible for pardon or commutation of sentence, the State concerned shall notify the International Tribunal for Rwanda accordingly. There shall only be pardon or commutation of sentence if the President of the International Tribunal for Rwanda, in consultation with the judges, so decides on the basis of the interests of justice and the general principles of law.

Art. 28. Cooperation and judicial assistance

1. States shall cooperate with the International Tribunal for Rwanda in the investigation and prosecution of persons accused of committing serious violations of international humanitarian law.
2. States shall comply without undue delay with any request for assistance or an order issued by a Trial Chamber, including, but not limited to:
   (a) The identification and location of persons;
   (b) The taking of testimony and the production of evidence;
   (c) The service of documents;
   (d) The arrest or detention of persons;
   (e) The surrender or the transfer of the accused to the International Tribunal for Rwanda.

Art. 29. The status, privileges and immunities of the International Tribunal for Rwanda

1. The Convention on the Privileges and Immunities of the United Nations of 13 February 1946 shall apply to the International Tribunal for Rwanda, the judges, the Prosecutor and his or her staff, and the Registrar and his or her staff.
2. The judges, the Prosecutor and the Registrar shall enjoy the privileges and immunities, exemptions and facilities accorded to diplomatic envoys, in accordance with international law.
3. The staff of the Prosecutor and of the Registrar shall enjoy the privileges and immunities accorded to officials of the United Nations under articles V and VII of the Convention referred to in paragraph 1 of this article.

4. Other persons, including the accused, required at the seat or meeting place of the International Tribunal for Rwanda shall be accorded such treatment as is necessary for the proper functioning of the International Tribunal for Rwanda.

Art. 30. Expenses of the International Tribunal for Rwanda
The expenses of the International Tribunal for Rwanda shall be expenses of the Organization in accordance with Article 17 of the Charter of the United Nations.

Art. 31. Working languages
The working languages of the International Tribunal shall be English and French.

Art. 32. Annual report
The President of the International Tribunal for Rwanda shall submit an annual report of the International Tribunal for Rwanda to the Security Council and to the General Assembly.

No. 111

I. ROME STATUTE OF THE INTERNATIONAL CRIMINAL COURT

Adopted by the United Nations Diplomatic Conference of Plenipotentiaries on the Establishment of an International Criminal Court on 17 July 1998

II. FINAL ACT OF THE UNITED NATIONS DIPLOMATIC CONFERENCE OF PLENIPOTENTIARIES ON THE ESTABLISHMENT OF AN INTERNATIONAL CRIMINAL COURT

Done at Rome on 17 July 1998

INTRODUCTORY NOTE: By resolution 260 (III) B of 9 December 1948 (adopted on the same day as the Genocide Convention (*No. 61*)), the UN General Assembly invited the International Law Commission "to study the desirability and possibility of establishing an international judicial organ for the trial of persons charged with genocide or other crimes over which jurisdiction will be conferred upon that organ by international conventions". By resolution 498 (V) of 12 December 1950, it established a committee on international criminal jurisdiction to prepare a draft statute for an international criminal court. The committee prepared such a draft which, in 1951, was transmitted to governments for observations. By resolution 688 (VII) of 20 December 1952, the General Assembly established a new committee on international criminal jurisdiction which, in 1954, submitted a revised draft. In 1954, the General Assembly decided to postpone further consideration of both the question of international criminal jurisdiction and of the draft code of offenses against the peace and security of mankind (elaborated by the International Law Commission on the request of the General Assembly) until the Special Committee on the question of defining aggression (established by resolution 895 (IX) of the General Assembly on 4 December 1954) had submitted its report (see resolutions 897 (IX) of 4 December 1954, 898 (IX) of 14 December 1954, and 1187 (XI I) of 11 December 1957). The Definition of Aggression, prepared by the Special Committee, was adopted by the General Assembly by resolution 3314 (XXIX) on 14 December 1974, but it was only in 1981 that the General Assembly invited the International Law Commission to resume its work on the draft code of offenses (resolution 36/106 of 10 December 1981), and in 1989 that it requested it to consider further the question of an international criminal court (resolutions 44/39 of 4 December 1989,45/41 of 28 November 1990, 46/54 of 9 December 1991). In 1992, the International Law Commission established a working group to draft a statute for an international criminal court, and, in 1994, it adopted a draft statute and recommended to the General Assembly to convene an international conference to study the draft statute and to conclude a convention on the establishment of an international criminal court. In the same year, the General Assembly established an *ad hoc* committee (from 1995 on called "preparatory committee") open to all states members of the United

Nations and specialized agencies, to review the major substantive and administrative issues arising out of the draft statute (resolutions 49/53 of 9 December 1954 and 50/46 of 11 December 1995). The preparatory committee completed its work in April 1998. The Diplomatic Conference on the Establishment of an International Criminal Court took place in Rome from 15 June to 17 July 1998. It adopted the Statute by a non-recorded vote of 120 in favour, 7 against and 21 abstentions. In accordance with its Article 125, the Statute was open for signature by all states in Rome at the Headquarters of the Food and Agriculture Organization of the United Nations on 17 July 1998. Thereafter, it remained open for signature in Rome at the Ministry of Foreign Affairs of Italy until 17 October 1998. After that date, the Statute remained open for signature in New York, at the United Nations Headquarters, until 31 December 2000.

ENTRY INTO FORCE: 1 July 2002.

AUTHENTIC TEXTS: Arabic, Chinese, French, English, Russian, Spanish. The text below is reprinted from the United Nations document A/CONF.183/9.[1]

TEXT PUBLISHED IN: UN Doc. A/CONF.183/9 (Arabic, Chinese, Engl., French, Russ., Span); *ILM,* 1998, pp. 1002-1069 (Engl.); *Die Friedenswarte* (Berlin), Vol. 73, 1998, pp. 348–414 (Engl.); Roberts and Guelff (extracts), pp. 667–697 (Engl.); Roy S.Lee, *The International Criminal Court: The Making of the Rome Statute*, Kluwer, 1999, pp. 479–571; United Nations Web site: http://www.un.org/law/icc/statute/romefra.htm (Statute); http://www.un.org/law/icc/statute/finalfra.htm (Final Act); ICRC Web site: http://www.icrc.org/ihl.nsf; University of Minnesota Human Rights Library: www1.umn.edu/humanrts/instree/Rome_Statute_ICC/Rome_ICC_toc.html.

TABLE OF CONTENTS

I. ROME STATUTE OF THE INTERNATIONAL CRIMINAL COURT

[1] Original text was corrected by the depositary notifications C.N. 577.1998.TREATIES-8 of 10 November 1998 and C.N.604.1999 TREATIES-18 of 12 July 1999 (*procés-verbaux* of rectification of the original text of the Statute (Arabic, Chinese, Engl., French, Russ., Span. authentic texts); C.N.1075.1999 TREATIES-28 of 30 November 1999 [*procés-verbal* of rectification of the original text of the Statute (French and Spanish authentic texts)]; C.N.266.2000.TREATIES-8 of 8 May 2000 [*procés-verbal* of rectification of the original text of the Statute (French and Spanish authentic texts)]; C.N.17.2001.TREATIES-1 of 17 January 2001 [*procés-verbal* of rectification of the original text of the Statute (authentic French, Russian and Spanish texts)]; C.N.765.2001.TREATIES-18 of 20 September 2001 (Proposals for corrections to the original text of the Statute (Spanish authentic text) and C.N.1439. 2001. Treaties-28 of 16 January 2002 (*procés-verbal).*

II. FINAL ACT OF THE UNITED NATIONS DIPLOMATIC CONFERENCE OF PLENIPOTENTIARIES ON THE ESTABLISHMENT OF AN INTERNATIONAL CRIMINAL COURT

* * *

I. ROME STATUTE OF THE INTERNATIONAL CRIMINAL COURT

[as corrected by the *procès-verbaux* of 10 November 1998 and 12 July 1999]

PREAMBLE

The States Parties to this Statute,

Conscious that all peoples are united by common bonds, their cultures pieced together in a shared heritage, and concerned that this delicate mosaic may be shattered at any time,

Mindful that during this century millions of children, women and men have been victims of unimaginable atrocities that deeply shock the conscience of humanity,

Recognizing that such grave crimes threaten the peace, security and well-being of the world,

Affirming that the most serious crimes of concern to the international community as a whole must not go unpunished and that their effective prosecution must be ensured by taking measures at the national level and by enhancing international cooperation,

Determined to put an end to impunity for the perpetrators of these crimes and thus to contribute to the prevention of such crimes,

Recalling that it is the duty of every State to exercise its criminal jurisdiction over those responsible for international crimes,

Reaffirming the Purposes and Principles of the Charter of the United Nations, and in particular that all States shall refrain from the threat or use of force against the territorial integrity or political independence of any State, or in any other manner inconsistent with the Purposes of the United Nations,

Emphasizing in this connection that nothing in this Statute shall be taken as authorizing any State Party to intervene in an armed conflict or in the internal affairs of any State,

Determined to these ends and for the sake of present and future generations, to establish an independent permanent International Criminal Court in relationship with the United Nations system, with jurisdiction over the most serious crimes of concern to the international community as a whole,

Emphasizing that the International Criminal Court established under this Statute shall be complementary to national criminal jurisdictions,

Resolved to guarantee lasting respect for and the enforcement of international justice,

Have agreed as follows

Part 1. Establishment of the Court

Article 1. The Court

An International Criminal Court ("the Court") is hereby established. It shall be a permanent institution and shall have the power to exercise its jurisdiction over persons for the most serious crimes of international concern, as referred to in this Statute, and shall be complementary to national criminal jurisdictions. The jurisdiction and functioning of the Court shall be governed by the provisions of this Statute.

Art. 2. Relationship of the Court with the United Nations
The Court shall be brought into relationship with the United Nations through an agreement to be approved by the Assembly of States Parties to this Statute and thereafter concluded by the President of the Court on its behalf.

Art. 3. Seat of the Court
1. The seat of the Court shall be established at The Hague in the Netherlands ("the host State").
2. The Court shall enter into a headquarters agreement with the host State, to be approved by the Assembly of States Parties and thereafter concluded by the President of the Court on its behalf.
3. The Court may sit elsewhere, whenever it considers it desirable, as provided in this Statute.

Art. 4 . Legal status and powers of the Court
1.[1] The Court shall have international legal personality. It shall also have such legal capacity as may be necessary for the exercise of its functions and the fulfilment of its purposes.
2. The Court may exercise its functions and powers, as provided in this Statute, on the territory of any State Party and, by special agreement, on the territory of any other State.

Part 2. Jurisdiction, Admissibility and Applicable Law

Art. 5. Crimes within the jurisdiction of the Court
1. The jurisdiction of the Court shall be limited to the most serious crimes of concern to the international community as a whole. The Court has jurisdiction in accordance with this Statute with respect to the following crimes:
   (a) The crime of genocide;
   (b) Crimes against humanity;
   (c) War crimes;
   (d) The crime of aggression.
2. The Court shall exercise jurisdiction over the crime of aggression once a provision is adopted in accordance with articles 121 and 123 defining the crime and setting out the conditions under which the Court shall exercise jurisdiction with respect to this crime. Such a provision shall be consistent with the relevant provisions of the Charter of the United Nations.

Art. 6. Genocide[2]
For the purpose of this Statute, "genocide" means any of the following acts committed with intent to destroy, in whole or in part, a national, ethnical, racial or religious group, as such:
(a) Killing members of the group;
(b) Causing serious bodily or mental harm to members of the group;
(c) Deliberately inflicting on the group conditions of life calculated to bring about its physical destruction in whole or in part;
(d) Imposing measures intended to prevent births within the group;
(e) Forcibly transferring children of the group to another group.

---

[1] For declaration in respect of this paragraph by Portugal, see p. 1392.
[2] For declaration in respect of this article by Australia, see p. 1385.

Art. 7. Crimes against humanity[3]

1. For the purpose of this Statute, "crime against humanity" means any of the following acts when committed as part of a widespread or systematic attack directed against any civilian population, with knowledge of the attack:
   (a) Murder;
   (b) Extermination;
   (c) Enslavement;
   (d) Deportation or forcible transfer of population;
   (e) Imprisonment or other severe deprivation of physical liberty in violation of fundamental rules of international law;
   (f) Torture;
   (g) Rape, sexual slavery, enforced prostitution, forced pregnancy, enforced sterilization, or any other form of sexual violence of comparable gravity;
   (h) Persecution against any identifiable group or collectivity on political, racial, national, ethnic, cultural, religious, gender as defined in paragraph 3, or other grounds that are universally recognized as impermissible under international law, in connection with any act referred to in this paragraph or any crime within the jurisdiction of the Court;
   (i) Enforced disappearance of persons;
   (j) The crime of apartheid;
   (k) Other inhumane acts of a similar character intentionally causing great suffering, or serious injury to body or to mental or physical health.
2. For the purpose of paragraph 1:
   (a) "Attack directed against any civilian population" means a course of conduct involving the multiple commission of acts referred to in paragraph 1 against any civilian population, pursuant to or in furtherance of a State or organizational policy to commit such attack;
   (b) "Extermination" includes the intentional infliction of conditions of life, *inter alia* the deprivation of access to food and medicine, calculated to bring about the destruction of part of a population;
   (c) "Enslavement" means the exercise of any or all of the powers attaching to the right of ownership over a person and includes the exercise of such power in the course of trafficking in persons, in particular women and children;
   (d) "Deportation or forcible transfer of population" means forced displacement of the persons concerned by expulsion or other coercive acts from the area in which they are lawfully present, without grounds permitted under international law;
   (e) "Torture" means the intentional infliction of severe pain or suffering, whether physical or mental, upon a person in the custody or under the control of the accused; except that torture shall not include pain or suffering arising only from, inherent in or incidental to, lawful sanctions;
   (f) "Forced pregnancy" means the unlawful confinement of a woman forcibly made pregnant, with the intent of affecting the ethnic composition of any population or carrying out other grave violations of international law. This definition shall not in any way be interpreted as affecting national laws relating to pregnancy;

---

[3] For declaration in respect of this article by Australia and Egypt, see pp. 1385 and 1388.

(g) "Persecution" means the intentional and severe deprivation of fundamental rights contrary to international law by reason of the identity of the group or collectivity;

(h) "The crime of apartheid" means inhumane acts of a character similar to those referred to in paragraph 1, committed in the context of an institutionalized regime of systematic oppression and domination by one racial group over any other racial group or groups and committed with the intention of maintaining that regime;

(i) "Enforced disappearance of persons" means the arrest, detention or abduction of persons by, or with the authorization, support or acquiescence of, a State or a political organization, followed by a refusal to acknowledge that deprivation of freedom or to give information on the fate or whereabouts of those persons, with the intention of removing them from the protection of the law for a prolonged period of time.

3. For the purpose of this Statute, it is understood that the term "gender" refers to the two sexes, male and female, within the context of society. The term "gender" does not indicate any meaning different from the above.

Art. 8. War crimes[4]

1. The Court shall have jurisdiction in respect of war crimes in particular when committed as part of a plan or policy or as part of a large-scale commission of such crimes.
2. For the purpose of this Statute, "war crimes" means:
   (a) Grave breaches of the Geneva Conventions of 12 August 1949, namely, any of the following acts against persons or property protected under the provisions of the relevant Geneva Convention:
      (i) Wilful killing;
      (ii) Torture or inhuman treatment, including biological experiments;
      (iii) Wilfully causing great suffering, or serious injury to body or health;
      (iv) Extensive destruction and appropriation of property, not justified by military necessity and carried out unlawfully and wantonly;
      (v) Compelling a prisoner of war or other protected person to serve in the forces of a hostile Power;
      (vi) Wilfully depriving a prisoner of war or other protected person of the rights of fair and regular trial;
      (vii) Unlawful deportation or transfer or unlawful confinement;
      (viii) Taking of hostages.
   (b)[5] Other serious violations of the laws and customs applicable in international armed conflict, within the established framework of international law, namely, any of the following acts:
      (i) Intentionally directing attacks against the civilian population as such or against individual civilians not taking direct part in hostilities;
      (ii) Intentionally directing attacks against civilian objects, that is, objects which are not military objectives;

---

4 For declaration in respect of this article by Australia, Colombia, Egypt, France, New Zealand, Sweden and United Kingdom, see pp. 1385–1393.

5 For declaration in respect of this paragraph by France and New Zealand, see pp. 1389–1391.

(iii) Intentionally directing attacks against personnel, installations, material, units or vehicles involved in a humanitarian assistance or peacekeeping mission in accordance with the Charter of the United Nations, as long as they are entitled to the protection given to civilians or civilian objects under the international law of armed conflict;

(iv) Intentionally launching an attack in the knowledge that such attack will cause incidental loss of life or injury to civilians or damage to civilian objects or widespread, long-term and severe damage to the natural environment which would be clearly excessive in relation to the concrete and direct overall military advantage anticipated;

(v) Attacking or bombarding, by whatever means, towns, villages, dwellings or buildings which are undefended and which are not military objectives;

(vi) Killing or wounding a combatant who, having laid down his arms or having no longer means of defence, has surrendered at discretion;

(vii) Making improper use of a flag of truce, of the flag or of the military insignia and uniform of the enemy or of the United Nations, as well as of the distinctive emblems of the Geneva Conventions, resulting in death or serious personal injury;

(viii) The transfer, directly or indirectly, by the Occupying Power of parts of its own civilian population into the territory it occupies, or the deportation or transfer of all or parts of the population of the occupied territory within or outside this territory;

(ix) Intentionally directing attacks against buildings dedicated to religion, education, art, science or charitable purposes, historic monuments, hospitals and places where the sick and wounded are collected, provided they are not military objectives;

(x) Subjecting persons who are in the power of an adverse party to physical mutilation or to medical or scientific experiments of any kind which are neither justified by the medical, dental or hospital treatment of the person concerned nor carried out in his or her interest, and which cause death to or seriously endanger the health of such person or persons;

(xi) Killing or wounding treacherously individuals belonging to the hostile nation or army;

(xii) Declaring that no quarter will be given;

(xiii) Destroying or seizing the enemy's property unless such destruction or seizure be imperatively demanded by the necessities of war;

(xiv) Declaring abolished, suspended or inadmissible in a court of law the rights and actions of the nationals of the hostile party;

(xv) Compelling the nationals of the hostile party to take part in the operations of war directed against their own country, even if they were in the belligerent's service before the commencement of the war;

(xvi) Pillaging a town or place, even when taken by assault;

(xvii) Employing poison or poisoned weapons;

(xviii) Employing asphyxiating, poisonous or other gases, and all analogous liquids, materials or devices;

(xix) Employing bullets which expand or flatten easily in the human body, such as bullets with a hard envelope which does not entirely cover the core or is pierced with incisions;

(xx) Employing weapons, projectiles and material and methods of warfare which are of a nature to cause superfluous injury or unnecessary suffering or which are inherently indiscriminate in violation of the international law of armed conflict, provided that such weapons, projectiles and material and methods of warfare are the subject of a comprehensive prohibition and are included in an annex to this Statute, by an amendment in accordance with the relevant provisions set forth in articles 121 and 123;

(xxi) Committing outrages upon personal dignity, in particular humiliating and degrading treatment;

(xxii) Committing rape, sexual slavery, enforced prostitution, forced pregnancy, as defined in article 7, paragraph 2 (f), enforced sterilization, or any other form of sexual violence also constituting a grave breach of the Geneva Conventions;

(xxiii) Utilizing the presence of a civilian or other protected person to render certain points, areas or military forces immune from military operations;

(xxiv) Intentionally directing attacks against buildings, material, medical units and transport, and personnel using the distinctive emblems of the Geneva Conventions in conformity with international law;

(xxv) Intentionally using starvation of civilians as a method of warfare by depriving them of objects indispensable to their survival, including wilfully impeding relief supplies as provided for under the Geneva Conventions;

(xxvi) Conscripting or enlisting children under the age of fifteen years into the national armed forces or using them to participate actively in hostilities.

(c)[6] In the case of an armed conflict not of an international character, serious violations of article 3 common to the four Geneva Conventions of 12 August 1949, namely, any of the following acts committed against persons taking no active part in the hostilities, including members of armed forces who have laid down their arms and those placed *hors de combat* by sickness, wounds, detention or any other cause:

(i) Violence to life and person, in particular murder of all kinds, mutilation, cruel treatment and torture;

(ii) Committing outrages upon personal dignity, in particular humiliating and degrading treatment;

(iii) Taking of hostages;

(iv) The passing of sentences and the carrying out of executions without previous judgement pronounced by a regularly constituted court, affording all judicial guarantees which are generally recognized as indispensable.

(d) Paragraph 2 (c) applies to armed conflicts not of an international character and thus does not apply to situations of internal disturbances and

6 For declaration in respect of this paragraph by France and New Zealand, see pp. 1389–1391.

tensions, such as riots, isolated and sporadic acts of violence or other acts of a similar nature.

(e)[7] Other serious violations of the laws and customs applicable in armed conflicts not of an international character, within the established framework of international law, namely, any of the following acts:

(i) Intentionally directing attacks against the civilian population as such or against individual civilians not taking direct part in hostilities;

(ii) Intentionally directing attacks against buildings, material, medical units and transport, and personnel using the distinctive emblems of the Geneva Conventions in conformity with international law;

(iii) Intentionally directing attacks against personnel, installations, material, units or vehicles involved in a humanitarian assistance or peacekeeping mission in accordance with the Charter of the United Nations, as long as they are entitled to the protection given to civilians or civilian objects under the international law of armed conflict;

(iv) Intentionally directing attacks against buildings dedicated to religion, education, art, science or charitable purposes, historic monuments, hospitals and places where the sick and wounded are collected, provided they are not military objectives;

(v) Pillaging a town or place, even when taken by assault;

(vi) Committing rape, sexual slavery, enforced prostitution, forced pregnancy, as defined in article 7, paragraph 2 (f), enforced sterilization, and any other form of sexual violence also constituting a serious violation of article 3 common to the four Geneva Conventions;

(vii) Conscripting or enlisting children under the age of fifteen years into armed forces or groups or using them to participate actively in hostilities;

(viii) Ordering the displacement of the civilian population for reasons related to the conflict, unless the security of the civilians involved or imperative military reasons so demand;

(ix) Killing or wounding treacherously a combatant adversary;

(x) Declaring that no quarter will be given;

(xi) Subjecting persons who are in the power of another party to the conflict to physical mutilation or to medical or scientific experiments of any kind which are neither justified by the medical, dental or hospital treatment of the person concerned nor carried out in his or her interest, and which cause death to or seriously endanger the health of such person or persons;

(xii) Destroying or seizing the property of an adversary unless such destruction or seizure be imperatively demanded by the necessities of the conflict;

(f) Paragraph 2(e) applies to armed conflicts not of an international character and thus does not apply to situations of internal disturbances and tensions, such as riots, isolated and sporadic acts of violence or other acts of a similar nature. It applies to armed conflicts that take place in the territory of a State when there is protracted armed conflict between governmental authorities and organized armed groups or between such groups.

---

7 For declaration in respect of this paragraph by United Kingdom, see p. 1393.

3. Nothing in paragraph 2(c) and (e) shall affect the responsibility of a Government to maintain or re-establish law and order in the State or to defend the unity and territorial integrity of the State, by all legitimate means.

Art. 9. Elements of Crimes

1. Elements of Crimes shall assist the Court in the interpretation and application of articles 6, 7 and 8. They shall be adopted by a two-thirds majority of the members of the Assembly of States Parties.
2. Amendments to the Elements of Crimes may be proposed by:
   (a) Any State Party;
   (b) The judges acting by an absolute majority;
   (c) The Prosecutor.
   Such amendments shall be adopted by a two-thirds majority of the members of the Assembly of States Parties.
3. The Elements of Crimes and amendments thereto shall be consistent with this Statute.

Art. 10. Nothing in this Part shall be interpreted as limiting or prejudicing in any way existing or developing rules of international law for purposes other than this Statute.

Art. 11.[8] *Jurisdiction* ratione temporis

1. The Court has jurisdiction only with respect to crimes committed after the entry into force of this Statute.
2. If a State becomes a Party to this Statute after its entry into force, the Court may exercise its jurisdiction only with respect to crimes committed after the entry into force of this Statute for that State, unless that State has made a declaration under article 12, paragraph 3.

Art. 12. Preconditions to the exercise of jurisdiction

1. A State which becomes a Party to this Statute thereby accepts the jurisdiction of the Court with respect to the crimes referred to in article 5.
2. In the case of article 13, paragraph (a) or (c), the Court may exercise its jurisdiction if one or more of the following States are Parties to this Statute or have accepted the jurisdiction of the Court in accordance with paragraph 3:
   (a) The State on the territory of which the conduct in question occurred or, if the crime was committed on board a vessel or aircraft, the State of registration of that vessel or aircraft;
   (b) The State of which the person accused of the crime is a national.
3. If the acceptance of a State which is not a Party to this Statute is required under paragraph 2, that State may, by declaration lodged with the Registrar, accept the exercise of jurisdiction by the Court with respect to the crime in question. The accepting State shall cooperate with the Court without any delay or exception in accordance with Part 9.

Art. 13. Exercise of jurisdiction

The Court may exercise its jurisdiction with respect to a crime referred to in article 5 in accordance with the provisions of this Statute if:

8 For declaration in respect of this article by Egypt, see p. 1388.

(a) A situation in which one or more of such crimes appears to have been committed is referred to the Prosecutor by a State Party in accordance with article 14;
(b) A situation in which one or more of such crimes appears to have been committed is referred to the Prosecutor by the Security Council acting under Chapter VII of the Charter of the United Nations; or
(c) The Prosecutor has initiated an investigation in respect of such a crime in accordance with article 15.

Art. 14. Referral of a situation by a State Party

1. A State Party may refer to the Prosecutor a situation in which one or more crimes within the jurisdiction of the Court appear to have been committed requesting the Prosecutor to investigate the situation for the purpose of determining whether one or more specific persons should be charged with the commission of such crimes.
2. As far as possible, a referral shall specify the relevant circumstances and be accompanied by such supporting documentation as is available to the State referring the situation.

Art. 15. Prosecutor

1. The Prosecutor may initiate investigations *proprio motu* on the basis of information on crimes within the jurisdiction of the Court.
2. The Prosecutor shall analyse the seriousness of the information received. For this purpose, he or she may seek additional information from States, organs of the United Nations, intergovernmental or non-governmental organizations, or other reliable sources that he or she deems appropriate, and may receive written or oral testimony at the seat of the Court.
3. If the Prosecutor concludes that there is a reasonable basis to proceed with an investigation, he or she shall submit to the Pre-Trial Chamber a request for authorization of an investigation, together with any supporting material collected. Victims may make representations to the Pre-Trial Chamber, in accordance with the Rules of Procedure and Evidence.
4. If the Pre-Trial Chamber, upon examination of the request and the supporting material, considers that there is a reasonable basis to proceed with an investigation, and that the case appears to fall within the jurisdiction of the Court, it shall authorize the commencement of the investigation, without prejudice to subsequent determinations by the Court with regard to the jurisdiction and admissibility of a case.
5. The refusal of the Pre-Trial Chamber to authorize the investigation shall not preclude the presentation of a subsequent request by the Prosecutor based on new facts or evidence regarding the same situation.
6. If, after the preliminary examination referred to in paragraphs 1 and 2, the Prosecutor concludes that the information provided does not constitute a reasonable basis for an investigation, he or she shall inform those who provided the information. This shall not preclude the Prosecutor from considering further information submitted to him or her regarding the same situation in the light of new facts or evidence.

Art. 16. Deferral of investigation or prosecution

No investigation or prosecution may be commenced or proceeded with under this Statute for a period of 12 months after the Security Council, in a resolution adopted under Chapter VII of the Charter of the United Nations, has requested the Court to that effect; that request may be renewed by the Council under the same conditions.

Art. 17. Issues of admissibility

1. Having regard to paragraph 10 of the Preamble and article 1, the Court shall determine that a case is inadmissible where:
   (a) The case is being investigated or prosecuted by a State which has jurisdiction over it, unless the State is unwilling or unable genuinely to carry out the investigation or prosecution;
   (b) The case has been investigated by a State which has jurisdiction over it and the State has decided not to prosecute the person concerned, unless the decision resulted from the unwillingness or inability of the State genuinely to prosecute;
   (c) The person concerned has already been tried for conduct which is the subject of the complaint, and a trial by the Court is not permitted under article 20, paragraph 3;
   (d) The case is not of sufficient gravity to justify further action by the Court.
2. In order to determine unwillingness in a particular case, the Court shall consider, having regard to the principles of due process recognized by international law, whether one or more of the following exist, as applicable:
   (a) The proceedings were or are being undertaken or the national decision was made for the purpose of shielding the person concerned from criminal responsibility for crimes within the jurisdiction of the Court referred to in article 5;
   (b) There has been an unjustified delay in the proceedings which in the circumstances is inconsistent with an intent to bring the person concerned to justice;
   (c) The proceedings were not or are not being conducted independently or impartially, and they were or are being conducted in a manner which, in the circumstances, is inconsistent with an intent to bring the person concerned to justice.

3.[9] In order to determine inability in a particular case, the Court shall consider whether, due to a total or substantial collapse or unavailability of its national judicial system, the State is unable to obtain the accused or the necessary evidence and testimony or otherwise unable to carry out its proceedings.

Art. 18. Preliminary rulings regarding admissibility

1. When a situation has been referred to the Court pursuant to article 13(a) and the Prosecutor has determined that there would be a reasonable basis to commence an investigation, or the Prosecutor initiates an investigation pursuant to articles 13(c) and 15, the Prosecutor shall notify all States Parties and those States which, taking into account the information available, would normally exercise jurisdiction over the crimes concerned. The Prosecutor may notify such States on a confidential basis and, where the Prosecutor believes it necessary to protect persons, prevent destruction of evidence or prevent the absconding of persons, may limit the scope of the information provided to States.

[9] For declaration in respect of this paragraph by Colombia, see p. 1387.

2. Within one month of receipt of that notification, a State may inform the Court that it is investigating or has investigated its nationals or others within its jurisdiction with respect to criminal acts which may constitute crimes referred to in article 5 and which relate to the information provided in the notification to States. At the request of that State, the Prosecutor shall defer to the State's investigation of those persons unless the Pre-Trial Chamber, on the application of the Prosecutor, decides to authorize the investigation.
3. The Prosecutor's deferral to a State's investigation shall be open to review by the Prosecutor six months after the date of deferral or at any time when there has been a significant change of circumstances based on the State's unwillingness or inability genuinely to carry out the investigation.
4. The State concerned or the Prosecutor may appeal to the Appeals Chamber against a ruling of the Pre-Trial Chamber, in accordance with article 82. The appeal may be heard on an expedited basis.
5. When the Prosecutor has deferred an investigation in accordance with paragraph 2, the Prosecutor may request that the State concerned periodically inform the Prosecutor of the progress of its investigations and any subsequent prosecutions. States Parties shall respond to such requests without undue delay.
6. Pending a ruling by the Pre-Trial Chamber, or at any time when the Prosecutor has deferred an investigation under this article, the Prosecutor may, on an exceptional basis, seek authority from the Pre-Trial Chamber to pursue necessary investigative steps for the purpose of preserving evidence where there is a unique opportunity to obtain important evidence or there is a significant risk that such evidence may not be subsequently available.
7. A State which has challenged a ruling of the Pre-Trial Chamber under this article may challenge the admissibility of a case under article 19 on the grounds of additional significant facts or significant change of circumstances.

Art. 19. Challenges to the jurisdiction of the Court or the admissibility of a case

1. The Court shall satisfy itself that it has jurisdiction in any case brought before it. The Court may, on its own motion, determine the admissibility of a case in accordance with article 17.
2. Challenges to the admissibility of a case on the grounds referred to in article 17 or challenges to the jurisdiction of the Court may be made by:
   (a) An accused or a person for whom a warrant of arrest or a summons to appear has been issued under article 58;
   (b) A State which has jurisdiction over a case, on the ground that it is investigating or prosecuting the case or has investigated or prosecuted; or
   (c) A State from which acceptance of jurisdiction is required under article 12.
3. The Prosecutor may seek a ruling from the Court regarding a question of jurisdiction or admissibility. In proceedings with respect to jurisdiction or admissibility, those who have referred the situation under article 13, as well as victims, may also submit observations to the Court.
4. The admissibility of a case or the jurisdiction of the Court may be challenged only once by any person or State referred to in paragraph 2. The challenge shall take place prior to or at the commencement of the trial. In exceptional circumstances, the Court may grant leave for a challenge to be

brought more than once or at a time later than the commencement of the trial. Challenges to the admissibility of a case, at the commencement of a trial, or subsequently with the leave of the Court, may be based only on article 17, paragraph 1 (c).

5. A State referred to in paragraph 2(b) and (c) shall make a challenge at the earliest opportunity.
6. Prior to the confirmation of the charges, challenges to the admissibility of a case or challenges to the jurisdiction of the Court shall be referred to the Pre-Trial Chamber. After confirmation of the charges, they shall be referred to the Trial Chamber. Decisions with respect to jurisdiction or admissibility may be appealed to the Appeals Chamber in accordance with article 82.
7. If a challenge is made by a State referred to in paragraph 2(b) or (c), the Prosecutor shall suspend the investigation until such time as the Court makes a determination in accordance with article 17.
8. Pending a ruling by the Court, the Prosecutor may seek authority from the Court:
   (a) To pursue necessary investigative steps of the kind referred to in article 18, paragraph 6;
   (b) To take a statement or testimony from a witness or complete the collection and examination of evidence which had begun prior to the making of the challenge; and
   (c) In cooperation with the relevant States, to prevent the absconding of persons in respect of whom the Prosecutor has already requested a warrant of arrest under article 58.
9. The making of a challenge shall not affect the validity of any act performed by the Prosecutor or any order or warrant issued by the Court prior to the making of the challenge.
10. If the Court has decided that a case is inadmissible under article 17, the Prosecutor may submit a request for a review of the decision when he or she is fully satisfied that new facts have arisen which negate the basis on which the case had previously been found inadmissible under article 17.
11. If the Prosecutor, having regard to the matters referred to in article 17, defers an investigation, the Prosecutor may request that the relevant State make available to the Prosecutor information on the proceedings. That information shall, at the request of the State concerned, be confidential. If the Prosecutor thereafter decides to proceed with an investigation, he or she shall notify the State to which deferral of the proceedings has taken place.

Art. 20. Ne bis in idem

1. Except as provided in this Statute, no person shall be tried before the Court with respect to conduct which formed the basis of crimes for which the person has been convicted or acquitted by the Court.
2. No person shall be tried by another court for a crime referred to in article 5 for which that person has already been convicted or acquitted by the Court.
3. No person who has been tried by another court for conduct also proscribed under article 6, 7 or 8 shall be tried by the Court with respect to the same conduct unless the proceedings in the other court:
   (a) Were for the purpose of shielding the person concerned from criminal responsibility for crimes within the jurisdiction of the Court; or

(b) Otherwise were not conducted independently or impartially in accordance with the norms of due process recognized by international law and were conducted in a manner which, in the circumstances, was inconsistent with an intent to bring the person concerned to justice.

Art. 21. Applicable law

1. The Court shall apply:
   (a) In the first place, this Statute, Elements of Crimes and its Rules of Procedure and Evidence;
   (b) In the second place, where appropriate, applicable treaties and the principles and rules of international law, including the established principles of the international law of armed conflict;
   (c) Failing that, general principles of law derived by the Court from national laws of legal systems of the world including, as appropriate, the national laws of States that would normally exercise jurisdiction over the crime, provided that those principles are not inconsistent with this Statute and with international law and internationally recognized norms and standards.
2. The Court may apply principles and rules of law as interpreted in its previous decisions.
3. The application and interpretation of law pursuant to this article must be consistent with internationally recognized human rights, and be without any adverse distinction founded on grounds such as gender as defined in article 7, paragraph 3, age, race, colour, language, religion or belief, political or other opinion, national, ethnic or social origin, wealth, birth or other status.

Part 3. General Principles of Criminal Law

Art. 22. Nullum crimen sine lege

1. A person shall not be criminally responsible under this Statute unless the conduct in question constitutes, at the time it takes place, a crime within the jurisdiction of the Court.
2. The definition of a crime shall be strictly construed and shall not be extended by analogy. In case of ambiguity, the definition shall be interpreted in favour of the person being investigated, prosecuted or convicted.
3. This article shall not affect the characterization of any conduct as criminal under international law independently of this Statute.

Art. 23. Nulla poena sine lege

A person convicted by the Court may be punished only in accordance with this Statute.

Art. 24.[10] *Non-retroactivity* ratione personae

1. No person shall be criminally responsible under this Statute for conduct prior to the entry into force of the Statute.
2. In the event of a change in the law applicable to a given case prior to a final judgement, the law more favourable to the person being investigated, prosecuted or convicted shall apply.

[10] For declaration in respect of this article by Egypt, see p. 1388.

Art. 25. Individual criminal responsibility

1. The Court shall have jurisdiction over natural persons pursuant to this Statute.
2. A person who commits a crime within the jurisdiction of the Court shall be individually responsible and liable for punishment in accordance with this Statute.
3. In accordance with this Statute, a person shall be criminally responsible and liable for punishment for a crime within the jurisdiction of the Court if that person:
   (a) Commits such a crime, whether as an individual, jointly with another or through another person, regardless of whether that other person is criminally responsible;
   (b) Orders, solicits or induces the commission of such a crime which in fact occurs or is attempted;
   (c) For the purpose of facilitating the commission of such a crime, aids, abets or otherwise assists in its commission or its attempted commission, including providing the means for its commission;
   (d) In any other way contributes to the commission or attempted commission of such a crime by a group of persons acting with a common purpose. Such contribution shall be intentional and shall either:
      (i) Be made with the aim of furthering the criminal activity or criminal purpose of the group, where such activity or purpose involves the commission of a crime within the jurisdiction of the Court; or
      (ii) Be made in the knowledge of the intention of the group to commit the crime;
   (e) In respect of the crime of genocide, directly and publicly incites others to commit genocide;
   (f) Attempts to commit such a crime by taking action that commences its execution by means of a substantial step, but the crime does not occur because of circumstances independent of the person's intentions. However, a person who abandons the effort to commit the crime or otherwise prevents the completion of the crime shall not be liable for punishment under this Statute for the attempt to commit that crime if that person completely and voluntarily gave up the criminal purpose.
4. No provision in this Statute relating to individual criminal responsibility shall affect the responsibility of States under international law.

Art. 26. Exclusion of jurisdiction over persons under eighteen

The Court shall have no jurisdiction over any person who was under the age of 18 at the time of the alleged commission of a crime.

Art. 27. Irrelevance of official capacity

1. This Statute shall apply equally to all persons without any distinction based on official capacity. In particular, official capacity as a Head of State or Government, a member of a Government or parliament, an elected representative or a government official shall in no case exempt a person from criminal responsibility under this Statute, nor shall it, in and of itself, constitute a ground for reduction of sentence.
2. Immunities or special procedural rules which may attach to the official capacity of a person, whether under national or international law, shall not bar the Court from exercising its jurisdiction over such a person.

Art. 28. Responsibility of commanders and other superiors
In addition to other grounds of criminal responsibility under this Statute for crimes within the jurisdiction of the Court:
(a) A military commander or person effectively acting as a military commander shall be criminally responsible for crimes within the jurisdiction of the Court committed by forces under his or her effective command and control, or effective authority and control as the case may be, as a result of his or her failure to exercise control properly over such forces, where:
 (i) That military commander or person either knew or, owing to the circumstances at the time, should have known that the forces were committing or about to commit such crimes; and
 (ii) That military commander or person failed to take all necessary and reasonable measures within his or her power to prevent or repress their commission or to submit the matter to the competent authorities for investigation and prosecution.
(b) With respect to superior and subordinate relationships not described in paragraph (a), a superior shall be criminally responsible for crimes within the jurisdiction of the Court committed by subordinates under his or her effective authority and control, as a result of his or her failure to exercise control properly over such subordinates, where:
 (i) The superior either knew, or consciously disregarded information which clearly indicated, that the subordinates were committing or about to commit such crimes;
 (ii) The crimes concerned activities that were within the effective responsibility and control of the superior; and
 (iii) The superior failed to take all necessary and reasonable measures within his or her power to prevent or repress their commission or to submit the matter to the competent authorities for investigation and prosecution.

Art. 29. Non-applicability of statute of limitations
The crimes within the jurisdiction of the Court shall not be subject to any statute of limitations.

Art. 30. Mental element
1. Unless otherwise provided, a person shall be criminally responsible and liable for punishment for a crime within the jurisdiction of the Court only if the material elements are committed with intent and knowledge.
2. For the purposes of this article, a person has intent where:
 (a) In relation to conduct, that person means to engage in the conduct;
 (b) In relation to a consequence, that person means to cause that consequence or is aware that it will occur in the ordinary course of events.
3. For the purposes of this article, "knowledge" means awareness that a circumstance exists or a consequence will occur in the ordinary course of events. "Know" and "knowingly" shall be construed accordingly.

Art. 31. Grounds for excluding criminal responsibility
1. In addition to other grounds for excluding criminal responsibility provided for in this Statute, a person shall not be criminally responsible if, at the time of that person's conduct:
 (a) The person suffers from a mental disease or defect that destroys that person's capacity to appreciate the unlawfulness or nature of his or her

conduct, or capacity to control his or her conduct to conform to the requirements of law;

(b) The person is in a state of intoxication that destroys that person's capacity to appreciate the unlawfulness or nature of his or her conduct, or capacity to control his or her conduct to conform to the requirements of law, unless the person has become voluntarily intoxicated under such circumstances that the person knew, or disregarded the risk, that, as a result of the intoxication, he or she was likely to engage in conduct constituting a crime within the jurisdiction of the Court;

(c)[11] The person acts reasonably to defend himself or herself or another person or, in the case of war crimes, property which is essential for the survival of the person or another person or property which is essential for accomplishing a military mission, against an imminent and unlawful use of force in a manner proportionate to the degree of danger to the person or the other person or property protected. The fact that the person was involved in a defensive operation conducted by forces shall not in itself constitute a ground for excluding criminal responsibility under this subparagraph;

(d) The conduct which is alleged to constitute a crime within the jurisdiction of the Court has been caused by duress resulting from a threat of imminent death or of continuing or imminent serious bodily harm against that person or another person, and the person acts necessarily and reasonably to avoid this threat, provided that the person does not intend to cause a greater harm than the one sought to be avoided. Such a threat may either be:

(i) Made by other persons; or

(ii) Constituted by other circumstances beyond that person's control.

2. The Court shall determine the applicability of the grounds for excluding criminal responsibility provided for in this Statute to the case before it.
3. At trial, the Court may consider a ground for excluding criminal responsibility other than those referred to in paragraph 1 where such a ground is derived from applicable law as set forth in article 21. The procedures relating to the consideration of such a ground shall be provided for in the Rules of Procedure and Evidence.

Art. 32. Mistake of fact or mistake of law

1. A mistake of fact shall be a ground for excluding criminal responsibility only if it negates the mental element required by the crime.
2. A mistake of law as to whether a particular type of conduct is a crime within the jurisdiction of the Court shall not be a ground for excluding criminal responsibility. A mistake of law may, however, be a ground for excluding criminal responsibility if it negates the mental element required by such a crime, or as provided for in article 33.

Art. 33. Superior orders and prescription of law

1. The fact that a crime within the jurisdiction of the Court has been committed by a person pursuant to an order of a Government or of a superior, whether military or civilian, shall not relieve that person of criminal responsibility unless:

[11] For declaration in respect of this paragraph by Belgium, see p. 1386.

(a) The person was under a legal obligation to obey orders of the Government or the superior in question;
(b) The person did not know that the order was unlawful; and
(c) The order was not manifestly unlawful.

2. For the purposes of this article, orders to commit genocide or crimes against humanity are manifestly unlawful.

Part 4. Composition and Administration of the Court

Art. 34. Organs of the Court

The Court shall be composed of the following organs:
(a) The Presidency;
(b) An Appeals Division, a Trial Division and a Pre-Trial Division;
(c) The Office of the Prosecutor;
(d) The Registry.

Art. 35. Service of judges

1. All judges shall be elected as full-time members of the Court and shall be available to serve on that basis from the commencement of their terms of office.
2. The judges composing the Presidency shall serve on a full-time basis as soon as they are elected.
3. The Presidency may, on the basis of the workload of the Court and in consultation with its members, decide from time to time to what extent the remaining judges shall be required to serve on a full-time basis. Any such arrangement shall be without prejudice to the provisions of article 40.
4. The financial arrangements for judges not required to serve on a full-time basis shall be made in accordance with article 49.

Art. 36. Qualifications, nomination and election of judges

1. Subject to the provisions of paragraph 2, there shall be 18 judges of the Court.
2. (a) The Presidency, acting on behalf of the Court, may propose an increase in the number of judges specified in paragraph 1, indicating the reasons why this is considered necessary and appropriate. The Registrar shall promptly circulate any such proposal to all States Parties.
   (b) Any such proposal shall then be considered at a meeting of the Assembly of States Parties to be convened in accordance with article 112. The proposal shall be considered adopted if approved at the meeting by a vote of two thirds of the members of the Assembly of States Parties and shall enter into force at such time as decided by the Assembly of States Parties.
   (c) (i) Once a proposal for an increase in the number of judges has been adopted under subparagraph (b), the election of the additional judges shall take place at the next session of the Assembly of States Parties in accordance with paragraphs 3 to 8, and article 37, paragraph 2;
   (ii) Once a proposal for an increase in the number of judges has been adopted and brought into effect under subparagraphs (b) and (c)(i), it shall be open to the Presidency at any time thereafter, if the workload of the Court justifies it, to propose a reduction in the number of judges, provided that the number of judges shall not be reduced

below that specified in paragraph 1. The proposal shall be dealt with in accordance with the procedure laid down in subparagraphs (a) and (b). In the event that the proposal is adopted, the number of judges shall be progressively decreased as the terms of office of serving judges expire, until the necessary number has been reached.

3. (a) The judges shall be chosen from among persons of high moral character, impartiality and integrity who possess the qualifications required in their respective States for appointment to the highest judicial offices.
   (b) Every candidate for election to the Court shall:
      (i) Have established competence in criminal law and procedure, and the necessary relevant experience, whether as judge, prosecutor, advocate or in other similar capacity, in criminal proceedings; or
      (ii) Have established competence in relevant areas of international law such as international humanitarian law and the law of human rights, and extensive experience in a professional legal capacity which is of relevance to the judicial work of the Court;
   (c) Every candidate for election to the Court shall have an excellent knowledge of and be fluent in at least one of the working languages of the Court.
4. (a) Nominations of candidates for election to the Court may be made by any State Party to this Statute, and shall be made either:
      (i) By the procedure for the nomination of candidates for appointment to the highest judicial offices in the State in question; or
      (ii) By the procedure provided for the nomination of candidates for the International Court of Justice in the Statute of that Court.

   Nominations shall be accompanied by a statement in the necessary detail specifying how the candidate fulfils the requirements of paragraph 3.
   (b) Each State Party may put forward one candidate for any given election who need not necessarily be a national of that State Party but shall in any case be a national of a State Party.
   (c) The Assembly of States Parties may decide to establish, if appropriate, an Advisory Committee on nominations. In that event, the Committee's composition and mandate shall be established by the Assembly of States Parties.
5. For the purposes of the election, there shall be two lists of candidates:

   List A containing the names of candidates with the qualifications specified in paragraph 3 (b) (i); and

   List B containing the names of candidates with the qualifications specified in paragraph 3 (b) (ii).

   A candidate with sufficient qualifications for both lists may choose on which list to appear. At the first election to the Court, at least nine judges shall be elected from list A and at least five judges from list B. Subsequent elections shall be so organized as to maintain the equivalent proportion on the Court of judges qualified on the two lists.
6. (a) The judges shall be elected by secret ballot at a meeting of the Assembly of States Parties convened for that purpose under article 112. Subject to paragraph 7, the persons elected to the Court shall be the 18 candidates who obtain the highest number of votes and a two-thirds majority of the States Parties present and voting.

(b) In the event that a sufficient number of judges is not elected on the first ballot, successive ballots shall be held in accordance with the procedures laid down in subparagraph (a) until the remaining places have been filled.

7. No two judges may be nationals of the same State. A person who, for the purposes of membership of the Court, could be regarded as a national of more than one State shall be deemed to be a national of the State in which that person ordinarily exercises civil and political rights.
8. (a) The States Parties shall, in the selection of judges, take into account the need, within the membership of the Court, for:
   (i) The representation of the principal legal systems of the world;
   (ii) Equitable geographical representation; and
   (iii) A fair representation of female and male judges.

   (b) States Parties shall also take into account the need to include judges with legal expertise on specific issues, including, but not limited to, violence against women or children.
9. (a) Subject to subparagraph (b), judges shall hold office for a term of nine years and, subject to subparagraph (c) and to article 37, paragraph 2, shall not be eligible for re-election.

   (b) At the first election, one third of the judges elected shall be selected by lot to serve for a term of three years; one third of the judges elected shall be selected by lot to serve for a term of six years; and the remainder shall serve for a term of nine years.

   (c) A judge who is selected to serve for a term of three years under subparagraph (b) shall be eligible for re-election for a full term.
10. Notwithstanding paragraph 9, a judge assigned to a Trial or Appeals Chamber in accordance with article 39 shall continue in office to complete any trial or appeal the hearing of which has already commenced before that Chamber.

Art. 37. Judicial vacancies

1. In the event of a vacancy, an election shall be held in accordance with article 36 to fill the vacancy.
2. A judge elected to fill a vacancy shall serve for the remainder of the predecessor's term and, if that period is three years or less, shall be eligible for re-election for a full term under article 36.

Art. 38. The Presidency

1. The President and the First and Second Vice-Presidents shall be elected by an absolute majority of the judges. They shall each serve for a term of three years or until the end of their respective terms of office as judges, whichever expires earlier. They shall be eligible for re-election once.
2. The First Vice-President shall act in place of the President in the event that the President is unavailable or disqualified. The Second Vice-President shall act in place of the President in the event that both the President and the First Vice-President are unavailable or disqualified.
3. The President, together with the First and Second Vice-Presidents, shall constitute the Presidency, which shall be responsible for:

   (a) The proper administration of the Court, with the exception of the Office of the Prosecutor; and

   (b) The other functions conferred upon it in accordance with this Statute.

4. In discharging its responsibility under paragraph 3(a), the Presidency shall coordinate with and seek the concurrence of the Prosecutor on all matters of mutual concern.

Art. 39. Chambers

1. As soon as possible after the election of the judges, the Court shall organize itself into the divisions specified in article 34, paragraph (b). The Appeals Division shall be composed of the President and four other judges, the Trial Division of not less than six judges and the Pre-Trial Division of not less than six judges. The assignment of judges to divisions shall be based on the nature of the functions to be performed by each division and the qualifications and experience of the judges elected to the Court, in such a way that each division shall contain an appropriate combination of expertise in criminal law and procedure and in international law. The Trial and Pre-Trial Divisions shall be composed predominantly of judges with criminal trial experience.
2. (a) The judicial functions of the Court shall be carried out in each division by Chambers.
   (b) (i) The Appeals Chamber shall be composed of all the judges of the Appeals Division;
   (ii) The functions of the Trial Chamber shall be carried out by three judges of the Trial Division;
   (iii) The functions of the Pre-Trial Chamber shall be carried out either by three judges of the Pre-Trial Division or by a single judge of that division in accordance with this Statute and the Rules of Procedure and Evidence;
   (c) Nothing in this paragraph shall preclude the simultaneous constitution of more than one Trial Chamber or Pre-Trial Chamber when the efficient management of the Court's workload so requires.
3. (a) Judges assigned to the Trial and Pre-Trial Divisions shall serve in those divisions for a period of three years, and thereafter until the completion of any case the hearing of which has already commenced in the division concerned.
   (b) Judges assigned to the Appeals Division shall serve in that division for their entire term of office.
4. Judges assigned to the Appeals Division shall serve only in that division. Nothing in this article shall, however, preclude the temporary attachment of judges from the Trial Division to the Pre-Trial Division or vice versa, if the Presidency considers that the efficient management of the Court's workload so requires, provided that under no circumstances shall a judge who has participated in the pre-trial phase of a case be eligible to sit on the Trial Chamber hearing that case.

Art. 40. Independence of the judges

1. The judges shall be independent in the performance of their functions.
2. Judges shall not engage in any activity which is likely to interfere with their judicial functions or to affect confidence in their independence.
3. Judges required to serve on a full-time basis at the seat of the Court shall not engage in any other occupation of a professional nature.
4. Any question regarding the application of paragraphs 2 and 3 shall be decided by an absolute majority of the judges. Where any such ques-

tion concerns an individual judge, that judge shall not take part in the decision.

Art. 41. Excusing and disqualification of judges

1. The Presidency may, at the request of a judge, excuse that judge from the exercise of a function under this Statute, in accordance with the Rules of Procedure and Evidence.
2. (a) A judge shall not participate in any case in which his or her impartiality might reasonably be doubted on any ground. A judge shall be disqualified from a case in accordance with this paragraph if, *inter alia*, that judge has previously been involved in any capacity in that case before the Court or in a related criminal case at the national level involving the person being investigated or prosecuted. A judge shall also be disqualified on such other grounds as may be provided for in the Rules of Procedure and Evidence.
   (b) The Prosecutor or the person being investigated or prosecuted may request the disqualification of a judge under this paragraph.
   (c) Any question as to the disqualification of a judge shall be decided by an absolute majority of the judges. The challenged judge shall be entitled to present his or her comments on the matter, but shall not take part in the decision.

Art. 42. The Office of the Prosecutor

1. The Office of the Prosecutor shall act independently as a separate organ of the Court. It shall be responsible for receiving referrals and any substantiated information on crimes within the jurisdiction of the Court, for examining them and for conducting investigations and prosecutions before the Court. A member of the Office shall not seek or act on instructions from any external source.
2. The Office shall be headed by the Prosecutor. The Prosecutor shall have full authority over the management and administration of the Office, including the staff, facilities and other resources thereof. The Prosecutor shall be assisted by one or more Deputy Prosecutors, who shall be entitled to carry out any of the acts required of the Prosecutor under this Statute. The Prosecutor and the Deputy Prosecutors shall be of different nationalities. They shall serve on a full-time basis.
3. The Prosecutor and the Deputy Prosecutors shall be persons of high moral character, be highly competent in and have extensive practical experience in the prosecution or trial of criminal cases. They shall have an excellent knowledge of and be fluent in at least one of the working languages of the Court.
4. The Prosecutor shall be elected by secret ballot by an absolute majority of the members of the Assembly of States Parties. The Deputy Prosecutors shall be elected in the same way from a list of candidates provided by the Prosecutor. The Prosecutor shall nominate three candidates for each position of Deputy Prosecutor to be filled. Unless a shorter term is decided upon at the time of their election, the Prosecutor and the Deputy Prosecutors shall hold office for a term of nine years and shall not be eligible for re-election.

5. Neither the Prosecutor nor a Deputy Prosecutor shall engage in any activity which is likely to interfere with his or her prosecutorial functions or to affect confidence in his or her independence. They shall not engage in any other occupation of a professional nature.
6. The Presidency may excuse the Prosecutor or a Deputy Prosecutor, at his or her request, from acting in a particular case.
7. Neither the Prosecutor nor a Deputy Prosecutor shall participate in any matter in which their impartiality might reasonably be doubted on any ground. They shall be disqualified from a case in accordance with this paragraph if, *inter alia*, they have previously been involved in any capacity in that case before the Court or in a related criminal case at the national level involving the person being investigated or prosecuted.
8. Any question as to the disqualification of the Prosecutor or a Deputy Prosecutor shall be decided by the Appeals Chamber.
   (a) The person being investigated or prosecuted may at any time request the disqualification of the Prosecutor or a Deputy Prosecutor on the grounds set out in this article;
   (b) The Prosecutor or the Deputy Prosecutor, as appropriate, shall be entitled to present his or her comments on the matter;
9. The Prosecutor shall appoint advisers with legal expertise on specific issues, including, but not limited to, sexual and gender violence and violence against children.

Art. 43. The Registry

1. The Registry shall be responsible for the non-judicial aspects of the administration and servicing of the Court, without prejudice to the functions and powers of the Prosecutor in accordance with article 42.
2. The Registry shall be headed by the Registrar, who shall be the principal administrative officer of the Court. The Registrar shall exercise his or her functions under the authority of the President of the Court.
3. The Registrar and the Deputy Registrar shall be persons of high moral character, be highly competent and have an excellent knowledge of and be fluent in at least one of the working languages of the Court.
4. The judges shall elect the Registrar by an absolute majority by secret ballot, taking into account any recommendation by the Assembly of States Parties. If the need arises and upon the recommendation of the Registrar, the judges shall elect, in the same manner, a Deputy Registrar.
5. The Registrar shall hold office for a term of five years, shall be eligible for re-election once and shall serve on a full-time basis. The Deputy Registrar shall hold office for a term of five years or such shorter term as may be decided upon by an absolute majority of the judges, and may be elected on the basis that the Deputy Registrar shall be called upon to serve as required.
6. The Registrar shall set up a Victims and Witnesses Unit within the Registry. This Unit shall provide, in consultation with the Office of the Prosecutor, protective measures and security arrangements, counselling and other appropriate assistance for witnesses, victims who appear before the Court, and others who are at risk on account of testimony given by such witnesses. The Unit shall include staff with expertise in trauma, including trauma related to crimes of sexual violence.

Art. 44. Staff

1. The Prosecutor and the Registrar shall appoint such qualified staff as may be required to their respective offices. In the case of the Prosecutor, this shall include the appointment of investigators.
2. In the employment of staff, the Prosecutor and the Registrar shall ensure the highest standards of efficiency, competency and integrity, and shall have regard, *mutatis mutandis*, to the criteria set forth in article 36, paragraph 8.
3. The Registrar, with the agreement of the Presidency and the Prosecutor, shall propose Staff Regulations which include the terms and conditions upon which the staff of the Court shall be appointed, remunerated and dismissed. The Staff Regulations shall be approved by the Assembly of States Parties.
4. The Court may, in exceptional circumstances, employ the expertise of gratis personnel offered by States Parties, intergovernmental organizations or non-governmental organizations to assist with the work of any of the organs of the Court. The Prosecutor may accept any such offer on behalf of the Office of the Prosecutor. Such gratis personnel shall be employed in accordance with guidelines to be established by the Assembly of States Parties.

Art. 45. Solemn undertaking

Before taking up their respective duties under this Statute, the judges, the Prosecutor, the Deputy Prosecutors, the Registrar and the Deputy Registrar shall each make a solemn undertaking in open court to exercise his or her respective functions impartially and conscientiously.

Art. 46. Removal from office

1. A judge, the Prosecutor, a Deputy Prosecutor, the Registrar or the Deputy Registrar shall be removed from office if a decision to this effect is made in accordance with paragraph 2, in cases where that person:
   (a) Is found to have committed serious misconduct or a serious breach of his or her duties under this Statute, as provided for in the Rules of Procedure and Evidence; or
   (b) Is unable to exercise the functions required by this Statute.
2. A decision as to the removal from office of a judge, the Prosecutor or a Deputy Prosecutor under paragraph 1 shall be made by the Assembly of States Parties, by secret ballot:
   (a) In the case of a judge, by a two-thirds majority of the States Parties upon a recommendation adopted by a two-thirds majority of the other judges;
   (b) In the case of the Prosecutor, by an absolute majority of the States Parties;
   (c) In the case of a Deputy Prosecutor, by an absolute majority of the States Parties upon the recommendation of the Prosecutor.
3. A decision as to the removal from office of the Registrar or Deputy Registrar shall be made by an absolute majority of the judges.
4. A judge, Prosecutor, Deputy Prosecutor, Registrar or Deputy Registrar whose conduct or ability to exercise the functions of the office as required by this Statute is challenged under this article shall have full opportunity to present and receive evidence and to make submissions in accordance with the Rules of Procedure and Evidence. The person in question shall not otherwise participate in the consideration of the matter.

Art. 47. Disciplinary measures

A judge, Prosecutor, Deputy Prosecutor, Registrar or Deputy Registrar who has committed misconduct of a less serious nature than that set out in article 46, paragraph 1, shall be subject to disciplinary measures, in accordance with the Rules of Procedure and Evidence.

Art. 48. Privileges and immunities

1. The Court shall enjoy in the territory of each State Party such privileges and immunities as are necessary for the fulfilment of its purposes.
2. The judges, the Prosecutor, the Deputy Prosecutors and the Registrar shall, when engaged on or with respect to the business of the Court, enjoy the same privileges and immunities as are accorded to heads of diplomatic missions and shall, after the expiry of their terms of office, continue to be accorded immunity from legal process of every kind in respect of words spoken or written and acts performed by them in their official capacity.
3. The Deputy Registrar, the staff of the Office of the Prosecutor and the staff of the Registry shall enjoy the privileges and immunities and facilities necessary for the performance of their functions, in accordance with the agreement on the privileges and immunities of the Court.
4. Counsel, experts, witnesses or any other person required to be present at the seat of the Court shall be accorded such treatment as is necessary for the proper functioning of the Court, in accordance with the agreement on the privileges and immunities of the Court.
5. The privileges and immunities of:
   (a) A judge or the Prosecutor may be waived by an absolute majority of the judges;
   (b) The Registrar may be waived by the Presidency;
   (c) The Deputy Prosecutors and staff of the Office of the Prosecutor may be waived by the Prosecutor;
   (d) The Deputy Registrar and staff of the Registry may be waived by the Registrar.

Art. 49. Salaries, allowances and expenses

The judges, the Prosecutor, the Deputy Prosecutors, the Registrar and the Deputy Registrar shall receive such salaries, allowances and expenses as may be decided upon by the Assembly of States Parties. These salaries and allowances shall not be reduced during their terms of office.

Art. 50. Official and working languages

1. The official languages of the Court shall be Arabic, Chinese, English, French, Russian and Spanish. The judgements of the Court, as well as other decisions resolving fundamental issues before the Court, shall be published in the official languages. The Presidency shall, in accordance with the criteria established by the Rules of Procedure and Evidence, determine which decisions may be considered as resolving fundamental issues for the purposes of this paragraph.
2. The working languages of the Court shall be English and French. The Rules of Procedure and Evidence shall determine the cases in which other official languages may be used as working languages.
3. At the request of any party to a proceeding or a State allowed to intervene in a proceeding, the Court shall authorize a language other than English or

French to be used by such a party or State, provided that the Court considers such authorization to be adequately justified.

Art. 51. Rules of Procedure and Evidence

1. The Rules of Procedure and Evidence shall enter into force upon adoption by a two-thirds majority of the members of the Assembly of States Parties.
2. Amendments to the Rules of Procedure and Evidence may be proposed by:
   (a) Any State Party;
   (b) The judges acting by an absolute majority; or
   (c) The Prosecutor.

Such amendments shall enter into force upon adoption by a two-thirds majority of the members of the Assembly of States Parties.

3. After the adoption of the Rules of Procedure and Evidence, in urgent cases where the Rules do not provide for a specific situation before the Court, the judges may, by a two-thirds majority, draw up provisional Rules to be applied until adopted, amended or rejected at the next ordinary or special session of the Assembly of States Parties.
4. The Rules of Procedure and Evidence, amendments thereto and any provisional Rule shall be consistent with this Statute. Amendments to the Rules of Procedure and Evidence as well as provisional Rules shall not be applied retroactively to the detriment of the person who is being investigated or prosecuted or who has been convicted.
5. In the event of conflict between the Statute and the Rules of Procedure and Evidence, the Statute shall prevail.

Art. 52. Regulations of the Court

1. The judges shall, in accordance with this Statute and the Rules of Procedure and Evidence, adopt, by an absolute majority, the Regulations of the Court necessary for its routine functioning.
2. The Prosecutor and the Registrar shall be consulted in the elaboration of the Regulations and any amendments thereto.
3. The Regulations and any amendments thereto shall take effect upon adoption unless otherwise decided by the judges. Immediately upon adoption, they shall be circulated to States Parties for comments. If within six months there are no objections from a majority of States Parties, they shall remain in force.

Part 5. Investigation and Prosecution

Art. 53. Initiation of an investigation

1. The Prosecutor shall, having evaluated the information made available to him or her, initiate an investigation unless he or she determines that there is no reasonable basis to proceed under this Statute. In deciding whether to initiate an investigation, the Prosecutor shall consider whether:
   (a) The information available to the Prosecutor provides a reasonable basis to believe that a crime within the jurisdiction of the Court has been or is being committed;
   (b) The case is or would be admissible under article 17; and
   (c) Taking into account the gravity of the crime and the interests of victims, there are nonetheless substantial reasons to believe that an investigation would not serve the interests of justice.

If the Prosecutor determines that there is no reasonable basis to proceed and his or her determination is based solely on subparagraph (c) above, he or she shall inform the Pre-Trial Chamber.

2. If, upon investigation, the Prosecutor concludes that there is not a sufficient basis for a prosecution because:
   (a) There is not a sufficient legal or factual basis to seek a warrant or summons under article 58;
   (b) The case is inadmissible under article 17; or
   (c) A prosecution is not in the interests of justice, taking into account all the circumstances, including the gravity of the crime, the interests of victims and the age or infirmity of the alleged perpetrator, and his or her role in the alleged crime;

   the Prosecutor shall inform the Pre-Trial Chamber and the State making a referral under article 14 or the Security Council in a case under article 13, paragraph (b), of his or her conclusion and the reasons for the conclusion.
3. (a) At the request of the State making a referral under article 14 or the Security Council under article 13, paragraph (b), the Pre-Trial Chamber may review a decision of the Prosecutor under paragraph 1 or 2 not to proceed and may request the Prosecutor to reconsider that decision.
   (b) In addition, the Pre-Trial Chamber may, on its own initiative, review a decision of the Prosecutor not to proceed if it is based solely on paragraph 1 (c) or 2 (c). In such a case, the decision of the Prosecutor shall be effective only if confirmed by the Pre-Trial Chamber.
4. The Prosecutor may, at any time, reconsider a decision whether to initiate an investigation or prosecution based on new facts or information.

Art. 54. Duties and powers of the Prosecutor with respect to investigations

1. The Prosecutor shall:
   (a) In order to establish the truth, extend the investigation to cover all facts and evidence relevant to an assessment of whether there is criminal responsibility under this Statute, and, in doing so, investigate incriminating and exonerating circumstances equally;
   (b) Take appropriate measures to ensure the effective investigation and prosecution of crimes within the jurisdiction of the Court, and in doing so, respect the interests and personal circumstances of victims and witnesses, including age, gender as defined in article 7, paragraph 3, and health, and take into account the nature of the crime, in particular where it involves sexual violence, gender violence or violence against children; and
   (c) Fully respect the rights of persons arising under this Statute.
2. The Prosecutor may conduct investigations on the territory of a State:
   (a) In accordance with the provisions of Part 9; or
   (b) As authorized by the Pre-Trial Chamber under article 57, paragraph 3 (d).
3. The Prosecutor may:
   (a) Collect and examine evidence;
   (b) Request the presence of and question persons being investigated, victims and witnesses;
   (c) Seek the cooperation of any State or intergovernmental organization or arrangement in accordance with its respective competence and/or mandate;

(d) Enter into such arrangements or agreements, not inconsistent with this Statute, as may be necessary to facilitate the cooperation of a State, intergovernmental organization or person;
(e) Agree not to disclose, at any stage of the proceedings, documents or information that the Prosecutor obtains on the condition of confidentiality and solely for the purpose of generating new evidence, unless the provider of the information consents; and
(f) Take necessary measures, or request that necessary measures be taken, to ensure the confidentiality of information, the protection of any person or the preservation of evidence.

Art. 55. Rights of persons during an investigation

1. In respect of an investigation under this Statute, a person:
   (a) Shall not be compelled to incriminate himself or herself or to confess guilt;
   (b) Shall not be subjected to any form of coercion, duress or threat, to torture or to any other form of cruel, inhuman or degrading treatment or punishment;
   (c) Shall, if questioned in a language other than a language the person fully understands and speaks, have, free of any cost, the assistance of a competent interpreter and such translations as are necessary to meet the requirements of fairness; and
   (d) Shall not be subjected to arbitrary arrest or detention, and shall not be deprived of his or her liberty except on such grounds and in accordance with such procedures as are established in this Statute.
2. Where there are grounds to believe that a person has committed a crime within the jurisdiction of the Court and that person is about to be questioned either by the Prosecutor, or by national authorities pursuant to a request made under Part 9, that person shall also have the following rights of which he or she shall be informed prior to being questioned:
   (a) To be informed, prior to being questioned, that there are grounds to believe that he or she has committed a crime within the jurisdiction of the Court;
   (b) To remain silent, without such silence being a consideration in the determination of guilt or innocence;
   (c) To have legal assistance of the person's choosing, or, if the person does not have legal assistance, to have legal assistance assigned to him or her, in any case where the interests of justice so require, and without payment by the person in any such case if the person does not have sufficient means to pay for it; and
   (d) To be questioned in the presence of counsel unless the person has voluntarily waived his or her right to counsel.

Art. 56. Role of the Pre-Trial Chamber in relation to a unique investigative opportunity

1. (a) Where the Prosecutor considers an investigation to present a unique opportunity to take testimony or a statement from a witness or to examine, collect or test evidence, which may not be available subsequently for the purposes of a trial, the Prosecutor shall so inform the Pre-Trial Chamber.

(b) In that case, the Pre-Trial Chamber may, upon request of the Prosecutor, take such measures as may be necessary to ensure the efficiency and integrity of the proceedings and, in particular, to protect the rights of the defence.

(c) Unless the Pre-Trial Chamber orders otherwise, the Prosecutor shall provide the relevant information to the person who has been arrested or appeared in response to a summons in connection with the investigation referred to in subparagraph (a), in order that he or she may be heard on the matter.

2. The measures referred to in paragraph 1 (b) may include:
   (a) Making recommendations or orders regarding procedures to be followed;
   (b) Directing that a record be made of the proceedings;
   (c) Appointing an expert to assist;
   (d) Authorizing counsel for a person who has been arrested, or appeared before the Court in response to a summons, to participate, or where there has not yet been such an arrest or appearance or counsel has not been designated, appointing another counsel to attend and represent the interests of the defence;
   (e) Naming one of its members or, if necessary, another available judge of the Pre-Trial or Trial Division to observe and make recommendations or orders regarding the collection and preservation of evidence and the questioning of persons;
   (f) Taking such other action as may be necessary to collect or preserve evidence.
3. (a) Where the Prosecutor has not sought measures pursuant to this article but the Pre-Trial Chamber considers that such measures are required to preserve evidence that it deems would be essential for the defence at trial, it shall consult with the Prosecutor as to whether there is good reason for the Prosecutor's failure to request the measures. If upon consultation, the Pre-Trial Chamber concludes that the Prosecutor's failure to request such measures is unjustified, the Pre-Trial Chamber may take such measures on its own initiative.
   (b) A decision of the Pre-Trial Chamber to act on its own initiative under this paragraph may be appealed by the Prosecutor. The appeal shall be heard on an expedited basis.
4. The admissibility of evidence preserved or collected for trial pursuant to this article, or the record thereof, shall be governed at trial by article 69, and given such weight as determined by the Trial Chamber.

Art. 57. Functions and powers of the Pre-Trial Chamber

1. Unless otherwise provided in this Statute, the Pre-Trial Chamber shall exercise its functions in accordance with the provisions of this article.
2. (a) Orders or rulings of the Pre-Trial Chamber issued under articles 15, 18, 19, 54, paragraph 2, 61, paragraph 7, and 72 must be concurred in by a majority of its judges.
   (b) In all other cases, a single judge of the Pre-Trial Chamber may exercise the functions provided for in this Statute, unless otherwise provided for in the Rules of Procedure and Evidence or by a majority of the Pre-Trial Chamber.

3. In addition to its other functions under this Statute, the Pre-Trial Chamber may:
   (a) At the request of the Prosecutor, issue such orders and warrants as may be required for the purposes of an investigation;
   (b) Upon the request of a person who has been arrested or has appeared pursuant to a summons under article 58, issue such orders, including measures such as those described in article 56, or seek such cooperation pursuant to Part 9 as may be necessary to assist the person in the preparation of his or her defence;
   (c) Where necessary, provide for the protection and privacy of victims and witnesses, the preservation of evidence, the protection of persons who have been arrested or appeared in response to a summons, and the protection of national security information;
   (d) Authorize the Prosecutor to take specific investigative steps within the territory of a State Party without having secured the cooperation of that State under Part 9 if, whenever possible having regard to the views of the State concerned, the Pre-Trial Chamber has determined in that case that the State is clearly unable to execute a request for cooperation due to the unavailability of any authority or any component of its judicial system competent to execute the request for cooperation under Part 9.
   (e) Where a warrant of arrest or a summons has been issued under article 58, and having due regard to the strength of the evidence and the rights of the parties concerned, as provided for in this Statute and the Rules of Procedure and Evidence, seek the cooperation of States pursuant to article 93, paragraph 1 (k), to take protective measures for the purpose of forfeiture, in particular for the ultimate benefit of victims.

Art. 58. Issuance by the Pre-Trial Chamber of a warrant of arrest or a summons to appear

1. At any time after the initiation of an investigation, the Pre-Trial Chamber shall, on the application of the Prosecutor, issue a warrant of arrest of a person if, having examined the application and the evidence or other information submitted by the Prosecutor, it is satisfied that:
   (a) There are reasonable grounds to believe that the person has committed a crime within the jurisdiction of the Court; and
   (b) The arrest of the person appears necessary:
      (i) To ensure the person's appearance at trial,
      (ii) To ensure that the person does not obstruct or endanger the investigation or the court proceedings, or
      (iii) Where applicable, to prevent the person from continuing with the commission of that crime or a related crime which is within the jurisdiction of the Court and which arises out of the same circumstances.
2. The application of the Prosecutor shall contain:
   (a) The name of the person and any other relevant identifying information;
   (b) A specific reference to the crimes within the jurisdiction of the Court which the person is alleged to have committed;
   (c) A concise statement of the facts which are alleged to constitute those crimes;

(d) A summary of the evidence and any other information which establish reasonable grounds to believe that the person committed those crimes; and
(e) The reason why the Prosecutor believes that the arrest of the person is necessary.

3. The warrant of arrest shall contain:
(a) The name of the person and any other relevant identifying information;
(b) A specific reference to the crimes within the jurisdiction of the Court for which the person's arrest is sought; and
(c) A concise statement of the facts which are alleged to constitute those crimes.
4. The warrant of arrest shall remain in effect until otherwise ordered by the Court.
5. On the basis of the warrant of arrest, the Court may request the provisional arrest or the arrest and surrender of the person under Part 9.
6. The Prosecutor may request the Pre-Trial Chamber to amend the warrant of arrest by modifying or adding to the crimes specified therein. The Pre-Trial Chamber shall so amend the warrant if it is satisfied that there are reasonable grounds to believe that the person committed the modified or additional crimes.
7. As an alternative to seeking a warrant of arrest, the Prosecutor may submit an application requesting that the Pre-Trial Chamber issue a summons for the person to appear. If the Pre-Trial Chamber is satisfied that there are reasonable grounds to believe that the person committed the crime alleged and that a summons is sufficient to ensure the person's appearance, it shall issue the summons, with or without conditions restricting liberty (other than detention) if provided for by national law, for the person to appear. The summons shall contain:
(a) The name of the person and any other relevant identifying information;
(b) The specified date on which the person is to appear;
(c) A specific reference to the crimes within the jurisdiction of the Court which the person is alleged to have committed; and
(d) A concise statement of the facts which are alleged to constitute the crime.

The summons shall be served on the person.

Art. 59. Arrest proceedings in the custodial State

1. A State Party which has received a request for provisional arrest or for arrest and surrender shall immediately take steps to arrest the person in question in accordance with its laws and the provisions of Part 9.
2. A person arrested shall be brought promptly before the competent judicial authority in the custodial State which shall determine, in accordance with the law of that State, that:
(a) The warrant applies to that person;
(b) The person has been arrested in accordance with the proper process; and
(c) The person's rights have been respected.
3. The person arrested shall have the right to apply to the competent authority in the custodial State for interim release pending surrender.
4. In reaching a decision on any such application, the competent authority in the custodial State shall consider whether, given the gravity of the alleged

crimes, there are urgent and exceptional circumstances to justify interim release and whether necessary safeguards exist to ensure that the custodial State can fulfil its duty to surrender the person to the Court. It shall not be open to the competent authority of the custodial State to consider whether the warrant of arrest was properly issued in accordance with article 58, paragraph 1 (a) and (b).

5. The Pre-Trial Chamber shall be notified of any request for interim release and shall make recommendations to the competent authority in the custodial State. The competent authority in the custodial State shall give full consideration to such recommendations, including any recommendations on measures to prevent the escape of the person, before rendering its decision.
6. If the person is granted interim release, the Pre-Trial Chamber may request periodic reports on the status of the interim release.
7. Once ordered to be surrendered by the custodial State, the person shall be delivered to the Court as soon as possible.

Art. 60. Initial proceedings before the Court

1. Upon the surrender of the person to the Court, or the person's appearance before the Court voluntarily or pursuant to a summons, the Pre-Trial Chamber shall satisfy itself that the person has been informed of the crimes which he or she is alleged to have committed, and of his or her rights under this Statute, including the right to apply for interim release pending trial.
2. A person subject to a warrant of arrest may apply for interim release pending trial. If the Pre-Trial Chamber is satisfied that the conditions set forth in article 58, paragraph 1, are met, the person shall continue to be detained. If it is not so satisfied, the Pre-Trial Chamber shall release the person, with or without conditions.
3. The Pre-Trial Chamber shall periodically review its ruling on the release or detention of the person, and may do so at any time on the request of the Prosecutor or the person. Upon such review, it may modify its ruling as to detention, release or conditions of release, if it is satisfied that changed circumstances so require.
4. The Pre-Trial Chamber shall ensure that a person is not detained for an unreasonable period prior to trial due to inexcusable delay by the Prosecutor. If such delay occurs, the Court shall consider releasing the person, with or without conditions.
5. If necessary, the Pre-Trial Chamber may issue a warrant of arrest to secure the presence of a person who has been released.

Art. 61. Confirmation of the charges before trial

1. Subject to the provisions of paragraph 2, within a reasonable time after the person's surrender or voluntary appearance before the Court, the Pre-Trial Chamber shall hold a hearing to confirm the charges on which the Prosecutor intends to seek trial. The hearing shall be held in the presence of the Prosecutor and the person charged, as well as his or her counsel.
2.[12] The Pre-Trial Chamber may, upon request of the Prosecutor or on its own motion, hold a hearing in the absence of the person charged to confirm the charges on which the Prosecutor intends to seek trial when the person has:
   (a) Waived his or her right to be present; or

[12] For declaration in respect of this paragraph by Colombia, see p. 1386.

(b) Fled or cannot be found and all reasonable steps have been taken to secure his or her appearance before the Court and to inform the person of the charges and that a hearing to confirm those charges will be held.

In that case, the person shall be represented by counsel where the Pre-Trial Chamber determines that it is in the interests of justice.

3. Within a reasonable time before the hearing, the person shall:
   (a) Be provided with a copy of the document containing the charges on which the Prosecutor intends to bring the person to trial; and
   (b) Be informed of the evidence on which the Prosecutor intends to rely at the hearing.

   The Pre-Trial Chamber may issue orders regarding the disclosure of information for the purposes of the hearing.
4. Before the hearing, the Prosecutor may continue the investigation and may amend or withdraw any charges. The person shall be given reasonable notice before the hearing of any amendment to or withdrawal of charges. In case of a withdrawal of charges, the Prosecutor shall notify the Pre-Trial Chamber of the reasons for the withdrawal.
5. At the hearing, the Prosecutor shall support each charge with sufficient evidence to establish substantial grounds to believe that the person committed the crime charged. The Prosecutor may rely on documentary or summary evidence and need not call the witnesses expected to testify at the trial.
6. At the hearing, the person may:
   (a) Object to the charges;
   (b) Challenge the evidence presented by the Prosecutor; and
   (c) Present evidence.
7. The Pre-Trial Chamber shall, on the basis of the hearing, determine whether there is sufficient evidence to establish substantial grounds to believe that the person committed each of the crimes charged. Based on its determination, the Pre-Trial Chamber shall:
   (a) Confirm those charges in relation to which it has determined that there is sufficient evidence, and commit the person to a Trial Chamber for trial on the charges as confirmed;
   (b) Decline to confirm those charges in relation to which it has determined that there is insufficient evidence;
   (c) Adjourn the hearing and request the Prosecutor to consider:
      (i) Providing further evidence or conducting further investigation with respect to a particular charge; or
      (ii) Amending a charge because the evidence submitted appears to establish a different crime within the jurisdiction of the Court.
8. Where the Pre-Trial Chamber declines to confirm a charge, the Prosecutor shall not be precluded from subsequently requesting its confirmation if the request is supported by additional evidence.
9. After the charges are confirmed and before the trial has begun, the Prosecutor may, with the permission of the Pre-Trial Chamber and after notice to the accused, amend the charges. If the Prosecutor seeks to add additional charges or to substitute more serious charges, a hearing under this article to confirm those charges must be held. After commencement of the trial, the Prosecutor may, with the permission of the Trial Chamber, withdraw the charges.
10. Any warrant previously issued shall cease to have effect with respect to any charges which have not been confirmed by the Pre-Trial Chamber or which have been withdrawn by the Prosecutor.

11. Once the charges have been confirmed in accordance with this article, the Presidency shall constitute a Trial Chamber which, subject to paragraph 9 and to article 64, paragraph 4, shall be responsible for the conduct of subsequent proceedings and may exercise any function of the Pre-Trial Chamber that is relevant and capable of application in those proceedings.

Part 6. The trial

Art. 62. Place of trial
Unless otherwise decided, the place of the trial shall be the seat of the Court.

Art. 63. Trial in the presence of the accused
1. The accused shall be present during the trial.
2. If the accused, being present before the Court, continues to disrupt the trial, the Trial Chamber may remove the accused and shall make provision for him or her to observe the trial and instruct counsel from outside the courtroom, through the use of communications technology, if required. Such measures shall be taken only in exceptional circumstances after other reasonable alternatives have proved inadequate, and only for such duration as is strictly required.

Art. 64. Functions and powers of the Trial Chamber
1. The functions and powers of the Trial Chamber set out in this article shall be exercised in accordance with this Statute and the Rules of Procedure and Evidence.
2. The Trial Chamber shall ensure that a trial is fair and expeditious and is conducted with full respect for the rights of the accused and due regard for the protection of victims and witnesses.
3. Upon assignment of a case for trial in accordance with this Statute, the Trial Chamber assigned to deal with the case shall:
   (a) Confer with the parties and adopt such procedures as are necessary to facilitate the fair and expeditious conduct of the proceedings;
   (b) Determine the language or languages to be used at trial; and
   (c) Subject to any other relevant provisions of this Statute, provide for disclosure of documents or information not previously disclosed, sufficiently in advance of the commencement of the trial to enable adequate preparation for trial.
4. The Trial Chamber may, if necessary for its effective and fair functioning, refer preliminary issues to the Pre-Trial Chamber or, if necessary, to another available judge of the Pre-Trial Division.
5. Upon notice to the parties, the Trial Chamber may, as appropriate, direct that there be joinder or severance in respect of charges against more than one accused.
6. In performing its functions prior to trial or during the course of a trial, the Trial Chamber may, as necessary:
   (a) Exercise any functions of the Pre-Trial Chamber referred to in article 61, paragraph 11;
   (b) Require the attendance and testimony of witnesses and production of documents and other evidence by obtaining, if necessary, the assistance of States as provided in this Statute;
   (c) Provide for the protection of confidential information;

(d) Order the production of evidence in addition to that already collected prior to the trial or presented during the trial by the parties;
(e) Provide for the protection of the accused, witnesses and victims; and
(f) Rule on any other relevant matters.

7. The trial shall be held in public. The Trial Chamber may, however, determine that special circumstances require that certain proceedings be in closed session for the purposes set forth in article 68, or to protect confidential or sensitive information to be given in evidence.
8. (a) At the commencement of the trial, the Trial Chamber shall have read to the accused the charges previously confirmed by the Pre-Trial Chamber. The Trial Chamber shall satisfy itself that the accused understands the nature of the charges. It shall afford him or her the opportunity to make an admission of guilt in accordance with article 65 or to plead not guilty.
(b) At the trial, the presiding judge may give directions for the conduct of proceedings, including to ensure that they are conducted in a fair and impartial manner. Subject to any directions of the presiding judge, the parties may submit evidence in accordance with the provisions of this Statute.
9. The Trial Chamber shall have, *inter alia*, the power on application of a party or on its own motion to:
(a) Rule on the admissibility or relevance of evidence; and
(b) Take all necessary steps to maintain order in the course of a hearing.
10. The Trial Chamber shall ensure that a complete record of the trial, which accurately reflects the proceedings, is made and that it is maintained and preserved by the Registrar.

Art. 65. Proceedings on an admission of guilt

1. Where the accused makes an admission of guilt pursuant to article 64, paragraph 8 (a), the Trial Chamber shall determine whether:
(a) The accused understands the nature and consequences of the admission of guilt;
(b) The admission is voluntarily made by the accused after sufficient consultation with defence counsel; and
(c) The admission of guilt is supported by the facts of the case that are contained in:
(i) The charges brought by the Prosecutor and admitted by the accused;
(ii) Any materials presented by the Prosecutor which supplement the charges and which the accused accepts; and
(iii) Any other evidence, such as the testimony of witnesses, presented by the Prosecutor or the accused.
2. Where the Trial Chamber is satisfied that the matters referred to in paragraph 1 are established, it shall consider the admission of guilt, together with any additional evidence presented, as establishing all the essential facts that are required to prove the crime to which the admission of guilt relates, and may convict the accused of that crime.
3. Where the Trial Chamber is not satisfied that the matters referred to in paragraph 1 are established, it shall consider the admission of guilt as not having been made, in which case it shall order that the trial be continued under the ordinary trial procedures provided by this Statute and may remit the case to another Trial Chamber.

4. Where the Trial Chamber is of the opinion that a more complete presentation of the facts of the case is required in the interests of justice, in particular the interests of the victims, the Trial Chamber may:
   (a) Request the Prosecutor to present additional evidence, including the testimony of witnesses; or
   (b) Order that the trial be continued under the ordinary trial procedures provided by this Statute, in which case it shall consider the admission of guilt as not having been made and may remit the case to another Trial Chamber.
5. Any discussions between the Prosecutor and the defence regarding modification of the charges, the admission of guilt or the penalty to be imposed shall not be binding on the Court.

Art. 66. Presumption of innocence

1. Everyone shall be presumed innocent until proved guilty before the Court in accordance with the applicable law.
2. The onus is on the Prosecutor to prove the guilt of the accused.
3. In order to convict the accused, the Court must be convinced of the guilt of the accused beyond reasonable doubt.

Art. 67. Rights of the accused

1. In the determination of any charge, the accused shall be entitled to a public hearing, having regard to the provisions of this Statute, to a fair hearing conducted impartially, and to the following minimum guarantees, in full equality:
   (a) To be informed promptly and in detail of the nature, cause and content of the charge, in a language which the accused fully understands and speaks;
   (b) To have adequate time and facilities for the preparation of the defence and to communicate freely with counsel of the accused's choosing in confidence;
   (c) To be tried without undue delay;
   (d)[13] Subject to article 63, paragraph 2, to be present at the trial, to conduct the defence in person or through legal assistance of the accused's choosing, to be informed, if the accused does not have legal assistance, of this right and to have legal assistance assigned by the Court in any case where the interests of justice so require, and without payment if the accused lacks sufficient means to pay for it;
   (e) To examine, or have examined, the witnesses against him or her and to obtain the attendance and examination of witnesses on his or her behalf under the same conditions as witnesses against him or her. The accused shall also be entitled to raise defences and to present other evidence admissible under this Statute;
   (f) To have, free of any cost, the assistance of a competent interpreter and such translations as are necessary to meet the requirements of fairness, if any of the proceedings of or documents presented to the Court are not in a language which the accused fully understands and speaks;
   (g) Not to be compelled to testify or to confess guilt and to remain silent, without such silence being a consideration in the determination of guilt or innocence;

[13] For declaration in respect of this paragraph by Colombia, see p. 1386.

(h) To make an unsworn oral or written statement in his or her defence; and
(i) Not to have imposed on him or her any reversal of the burden of proof or any onus of rebuttal.

2. In addition to any other disclosure provided for in this Statute, the Prosecutor shall, as soon as practicable, disclose to the defence evidence in the Prosecutor's possession or control which he or she believes shows or tends to show the innocence of the accused, or to mitigate the guilt of the accused, or which may affect the credibility of prosecution evidence. In case of doubt as to the application of this paragraph, the Court shall decide.

Art. 68. Protection of the victims and witnesses and their participation in the proceedings

1. The Court shall take appropriate measures to protect the safety, physical and psychological well-being, dignity and privacy of victims and witnesses. In so doing, the Court shall have regard to all relevant factors, including age, gender as defined in article 7, paragraph 3, and health, and the nature of the crime, in particular, but not limited to, where the crime involves sexual or gender violence or violence against children. The Prosecutor shall take such measures particularly during the investigation and prosecution of such crimes. These measures shall not be prejudicial to or inconsistent with the rights of the accused and a fair and impartial trial.
2. As an exception to the principle of public hearings provided for in article 67, the Chambers of the Court may, to protect victims and witnesses or an accused, conduct any part of the proceedings *in camera* or allow the presentation of evidence by electronic or other special means. In particular, such measures shall be implemented in the case of a victim of sexual violence or a child who is a victim or a witness, unless otherwise ordered by the Court, having regard to all the circumstances, particularly the views of the victim or witness.
3. Where the personal interests of the victims are affected, the Court shall permit their views and concerns to be presented and considered at stages of the proceedings determined to be appropriate by the Court and in a manner which is not prejudicial to or inconsistent with the rights of the accused and a fair and impartial trial. Such views and concerns may be presented by the legal representatives of the victims where the Court considers it appropriate, in accordance with the Rules of Procedure and Evidence.
4. The Victims and Witnesses Unit may advise the Prosecutor and the Court on appropriate protective measures, security arrangements, counselling and assistance as referred to in article 43, paragraph 6.
5. Where the disclosure of evidence or information pursuant to this Statute may lead to the grave endangerment of the security of a witness or his or her family, the Prosecutor may, for the purposes of any proceedings conducted prior to the commencement of the trial, withhold such evidence or information and instead submit a summary thereof. Such measures shall be exercised in a manner which is not prejudicial to or inconsistent with the rights of the accused and a fair and impartial trial.
6. A State may make an application for necessary measures to be taken in respect of the protection of its servants or agents and the protection of confidential or sensitive information.

Art. 69. Evidence

1. Before testifying, each witness shall, in accordance with the Rules of Procedure and Evidence, give an undertaking as to the truthfulness of the evidence to be given by that witness.
2. The testimony of a witness at trial shall be given in person, except to the extent provided by the measures set forth in article 68 or in the Rules of Procedure and Evidence. The Court may also permit the giving of *viva voce* (oral) or recorded testimony of a witness by means of video or audio technology, as well as the introduction of documents or written transcripts, subject to this Statute and in accordance with the Rules of Procedure and Evidence. These measures shall not be prejudicial to or inconsistent with the rights of the accused.
3. The parties may submit evidence relevant to the case, in accordance with article 64. The Court shall have the authority to request the submission of all evidence that it considers necessary for the determination of the truth.
4. The Court may rule on the relevance or admissibility of any evidence, taking into account, *inter alia*, the probative value of the evidence and any prejudice that such evidence may cause to a fair trial or to a fair evaluation of the testimony of a witness, in accordance with the Rules of Procedure and Evidence.
5. The Court shall respect and observe privileges on confidentiality as provided for in the Rules of Procedure and Evidence.
6. The Court shall not require proof of facts of common knowledge but may take judicial notice of them.
7. Evidence obtained by means of a violation of this Statute or internationally recognized human rights shall not be admissible if:
   (a) The violation casts substantial doubt on the reliability of the evidence; or
   (b) The admission of the evidence would be antithetical to and would seriously damage the integrity of the proceedings.
8. When deciding on the relevance or admissibility of evidence collected by a State, the Court shall not rule on the application of the State's national law.

Art. 70. Offences against the administration of justice

1. The Court shall have jurisdiction over the following offences against its administration of justice when committed intentionally:
   (a) Giving false testimony when under an obligation pursuant to article 69, paragraph 1, to tell the truth;
   (b) Presenting evidence that the party knows is false or forged;
   (c) Corruptly influencing a witness, obstructing or interfering with the attendance or testimony of a witness, retaliating against a witness for giving testimony or destroying, tampering with or interfering with the collection of evidence;
   (d) Impeding, intimidating or corruptly influencing an official of the Court for the purpose of forcing or persuading the official not to perform, or to perform improperly, his or her duties;
   (e) Retaliating against an official of the Court on account of duties performed by that or another official;
   (f) Soliciting or accepting a bribe as an official of the Court in connection with his or her official duties.

2. The principles and procedures governing the Court's exercise of jurisdiction over offences under this article shall be those provided for in the Rules of Procedure and Evidence. The conditions for providing international cooperation to the Court with respect to its proceedings under this article shall be governed by the domestic laws of the requested State.
3. In the event of conviction, the Court may impose a term of imprisonment not exceeding five years, or a fine in accordance with the Rules of Procedure and Evidence, or both.
4. (a) Each State Party shall extend its criminal laws penalizing offences against the integrity of its own investigative or judicial process to offences against the administration of justice referred to in this article, committed on its territory, or by one of its nationals;
   (b) Upon request by the Court, whenever it deems it proper, the State Party shall submit the case to its competent authorities for the purpose of prosecution. Those authorities shall treat such cases with diligence and devote sufficient resources to enable them to be conducted effectively.

Art. 71. Sanctions for misconduct before the Court

1. The Court may sanction persons present before it who commit misconduct, including disruption of its proceedings or deliberate refusal to comply with its directions, by administrative measures other than imprisonment, such as temporary or permanent removal from the courtroom, a fine or other similar measures provided for in the Rules of Procedure and Evidence.
2. The procedures governing the imposition of the measures set forth in paragraph 1 shall be those provided for in the Rules of Procedure and Evidence.

Art. 72. Protection of national security information

1. This article applies in any case where the disclosure of the information or documents of a State would, in the opinion of that State, prejudice its national security interests. Such cases include those falling within the scope of article 56, paragraphs 2 and 3, article 61, paragraph 3, article 64, paragraph 3, article 67, paragraph 2, article 68, paragraph 6, article 87, paragraph 6 and article 93, as well as cases arising at any other stage of the proceedings where such disclosure may be at issue.
2. This article shall also apply when a person who has been requested to give information or evidence has refused to do so or has referred the matter to the State on the ground that disclosure would prejudice the national security interests of a State and the State concerned confirms that it is of the opinion that disclosure would prejudice its national security interests.
3. Nothing in this article shall prejudice the requirements of confidentiality applicable under article 54, paragraph 3 (e) and (f), or the application of article 73.
4. If a State learns that information or documents of the State are being, or are likely to be, disclosed at any stage of the proceedings, and it is of the opinion that disclosure would prejudice its national security interests, that State shall have the right to intervene in order to obtain resolution of the issue in accordance with this article.
5. If, in the opinion of a State, disclosure of information would prejudice its national security interests, all reasonable steps will be taken by the State, acting in conjunction with the Prosecutor, the defence or the Pre-Trial

Chamber or Trial Chamber, as the case may be, to seek to resolve the matter by cooperative means. Such steps may include:

(a) Modification or clarification of the request;

(b) A determination by the Court regarding the relevance of the information or evidence sought, or a determination as to whether the evidence, though relevant, could be or has been obtained from a source other than the requested State;

(c) Obtaining the information or evidence from a different source or in a different form; or

(d) Agreement on conditions under which the assistance could be provided including, among other things, providing summaries or redactions, limitations on disclosure, use of in camera or ex parte proceedings, or other protective measures permissible under the Statute and the Rules of Procedure and Evidence.

6. Once all reasonable steps have been taken to resolve the matter through cooperative means, and if the State considers that there are no means or conditions under which the information or documents could be provided or disclosed without prejudice to its national security interests, it shall so notify the Prosecutor or the Court of the specific reasons for its decision, unless a specific description of the reasons would itself necessarily result in such prejudice to the State's national security interests.

7. Thereafter, if the Court determines that the evidence is relevant and necessary for the establishment of the guilt or innocence of the accused, the Court may undertake the following actions:

(a) Where disclosure of the information or document is sought pursuant to a request for cooperation under Part 9 or the circumstances described in paragraph 2, and the State has invoked the ground for refusal referred to in article 93, paragraph 4:

(i) The Court may, before making any conclusion referred to in subparagraph 7 (a) (ii), request further consultations for the purpose of considering the State's representations, which may include, as appropriate, hearings *in camera* and *ex parte*;

(ii) If the Court concludes that, by invoking the ground for refusal under article 93, paragraph 4, in the circumstances of the case, the requested State is not acting in accordance with its obligations under this Statute, the Court may refer the matter in accordance with article 87, paragraph 7, specifying the reasons for its conclusion; and

(iii) The Court may make such inference in the trial of the accused as to the existence or non-existence of a fact, as may be appropriate in the circumstances; or

(b) In all other circumstances:

(i) Order disclosure; or

(ii) To the extent it does not order disclosure, make such inference in the trial of the accused as to the existence or non-existence of a fact, as may be appropriate in the circumstances.

Art. 73. Third-party information or documents

If a State Party is requested by the Court to provide a document or information in its custody, possession or control, which was disclosed to it in confidence by a State, intergovernmental organization or international organization, it shall seek the consent of the originator to disclose that document or information. If the originator is a State Party, it shall either consent to disclosure of the information or document or undertake to resolve the issue of disclosure with the Court, subject to the provisions of article 72. If the originator is not a State Party and refuses to consent to disclosure, the requested State shall inform the Court that it is unable to provide the document or information because of a pre-existing obligation of confidentiality to the originator.

Art. 74. Requirements for the decision

1. All the judges of the Trial Chamber shall be present at each stage of the trial and throughout their deliberations. The Presidency may, on a case-by-case basis, designate, as available, one or more alternate judges to be present at each stage of the trial and to replace a member of the Trial Chamber if that member is unable to continue attending.
2. The Trial Chamber's decision shall be based on its evaluation of the evidence and the entire proceedings. The decision shall not exceed the facts and circumstances described in the charges and any amendments to the charges. The Court may base its decision only on evidence submitted and discussed before it at the trial.
3. The judges shall attempt to achieve unanimity in their decision, failing which the decision shall be taken by a majority of the judges.
4. The deliberations of the Trial Chamber shall remain secret.
5. The decision shall be in writing and shall contain a full and reasoned statement of the Trial Chamber's findings on the evidence and conclusions. The Trial Chamber shall issue one decision. When there is no unanimity, the Trial Chamber's decision shall contain the views of the majority and the minority. The decision or a summary thereof shall be delivered in open court.

Art. 75. Reparations to victims

1. The Court shall establish principles relating to reparations to, or in respect of, victims, including restitution, compensation and rehabilitation. On this basis, in its decision the Court may, either upon request or on its own motion in exceptional circumstances, determine the scope and extent of any damage, loss and injury to, or in respect of, victims and will state the principles on which it is acting.
2. The Court may make an order directly against a convicted person specifying appropriate reparations to, or in respect of, victims, including restitution, compensation and rehabilitation.

   Where appropriate, the Court may order that the award for reparations be made through the Trust Fund provided for in article 79.
3. Before making an order under this article, the Court may invite and shall take account of representations from or on behalf of the convicted person, victims, other interested persons or interested States.
4. In exercising its power under this article, the Court may, after a person is convicted of a crime within the jurisdiction of the Court, determine whether, in order to give effect to an order which it may make under this article, it is necessary to seek measures under article 93, paragraph 1.
5. A State Party shall give effect to a decision under this article as if the provisions of article 109 were applicable to this article.
6. Nothing in this article shall be interpreted as prejudicing the rights of victims under national or international law.

Art. 76. Sentencing

1. In the event of a conviction, the Trial Chamber shall consider the appropriate sentence to be imposed and shall take into account the evidence presented and submissions made during the trial that are relevant to the sentence.
2. Except where article 65 applies and before the completion of the trial, the Trial Chamber may on its own motion and shall, at the request of the Prosecutor or the accused, hold a further hearing to hear any additional evidence or submissions relevant to the sentence, in accordance with the Rules of Procedure and Evidence.
3. Where paragraph 2 applies, any representations under article 75 shall be heard during the further hearing referred to in paragraph 2 and, if necessary, during any additional hearing.
4. The sentence shall be pronounced in public and, wherever possible, in the presence of the accused.

Part 7. Penalties

Art. 77. Applicable penalties

1. Subject to article 110, the Court may impose one of the following penalties on a person convicted of a crime referred to in article 5 of this Statute:
   (a) Imprisonment for a specified number of years, which may not exceed a maximum of 30 years; or
   (b) A term of life imprisonment when justified by the extreme gravity of the crime and the individual circumstances of the convicted person.
2. In addition to imprisonment, the Court may order:
   (a) A fine under the criteria provided for in the Rules of Procedure and Evidence;
   (b) A forfeiture of proceeds, property and assets derived directly or indirectly from that crime, without prejudice to the rights of bona fide third parties.

Art. 78. Determination of the sentence

1. In determining the sentence, the Court shall, in accordance with the Rules of Procedure and Evidence, take into account such factors as the gravity of the crime and the individual circumstances of the convicted person.
2. In imposing a sentence of imprisonment, the Court shall deduct the time, if any, previously spent in detention in accordance with an order of the Court. The Court may deduct any time otherwise spent in detention in connection with conduct underlying the crime.
3. When a person has been convicted of more than one crime, the Court shall pronounce a sentence for each crime and a joint sentence specifying the total period of imprisonment. This period shall be no less than the highest individual sentence pronounced and shall not exceed 30 years imprisonment or a sentence of life imprisonment in conformity with article 77, paragraph 1 (b).

Art. 79. Trust Fund

1. A Trust Fund shall be established by decision of the Assembly of States Parties for the benefit of victims of crimes within the jurisdiction of the Court, and of the families of such victims.

2. The Court may order money and other property collected through fines or forfeiture to be transferred, by order of the Court, to the Trust Fund.
3. The Trust Fund shall be managed according to criteria to be determined by the Assembly of States Parties.

Art. 80. Non-prejudice to national application of penalties and national laws
Nothing in this Part affects the application by States of penalties prescribed by their national law, nor the law of States which do not provide for penalties prescribed in this Part.

Part 8. Appeal and revision

Art. 81. Appeal against decision of acquittal or conviction or against sentence
1. A decision under article 74 may be appealed in accordance with the Rules of Procedure and Evidence as follows:
   (a) The Prosecutor may make an appeal on any of the following grounds:
      (i) Procedural error,
      (ii) Error of fact, or
      (iii) Error of law;
   (b) The convicted person, or the Prosecutor on that person's behalf, may make an appeal on any of the following grounds:
      (i) Procedural error,
      (ii) Error of fact,
      (iii) Error of law, or
      (iv) Any other ground that affects the fairness or reliability of the proceedings or decision.
2. (a) A sentence may be appealed, in accordance with the Rules of Procedure and Evidence, by the Prosecutor or the convicted person on the ground of disproportion between the crime and the sentence;
   (b) If on an appeal against sentence the Court considers that there are grounds on which the conviction might be set aside, wholly or in part, it may invite the Prosecutor and the convicted person to submit grounds under article 81, paragraph 1 (a) or (b), and may render a decision on conviction in accordance with article 83;
   (c) The same procedure applies when the Court, on an appeal against conviction only, considers that there are grounds to reduce the sentence under paragraph 2 (a).
3. (a) Unless the Trial Chamber orders otherwise, a convicted person shall remain in custody pending an appeal;
   (b) When a convicted person's time in custody exceeds the sentence of imprisonment imposed, that person shall be released, except that if the Prosecutor is also appealing, the release may be subject to the conditions under subparagraph (c) below;
   (c) In case of an acquittal, the accused shall be released immediately, subject to the following:
      (i) Under exceptional circumstances, and having regard, *inter alia*, to the concrete risk of flight, the seriousness of the offence charged and the probability of success on appeal, the Trial Chamber, at the request of the Prosecutor, may maintain the detention of the person pending appeal;
      (ii) A decision by the Trial Chamber under subparagraph (c) (i) may be appealed in accordance with the Rules of Procedure and Evidence.

4. Subject to the provisions of paragraph 3 (a) and (b), execution of the decision or sentence shall be suspended during the period allowed for appeal and for the duration of the appeal proceedings.

Art. 82. Appeal against other decisions

1. Either party may appeal any of the following decisions in accordance with the Rules of Procedure and Evidence:
   (a) A decision with respect to jurisdiction or admissibility;
   (b) A decision granting or denying release of the person being investigated or prosecuted;
   (c) A decision of the Pre-Trial Chamber to act on its own initiative under article 56, paragraph 3;
   (d) A decision that involves an issue that would significantly affect the fair and expeditious conduct of the proceedings or the outcome of the trial, and for which, in the opinion of the Pre-Trial or Trial Chamber, an immediate resolution by the Appeals Chamber may materially advance the proceedings.
2. A decision of the Pre-Trial Chamber under article 57, paragraph 3 (d), may be appealed against by the State concerned or by the Prosecutor, with the leave of the Pre-Trial Chamber. The appeal shall be heard on an expedited basis.
3. An appeal shall not of itself have suspensive effect unless the Appeals Chamber so orders, upon request, in accordance with the Rules of Procedure and Evidence.
4. A legal representative of the victims, the convicted person or a bona fide owner of property adversely affected by an order under article 75 may appeal against the order for reparations, as provided in the Rules of Procedure and Evidence.

Art. 83. Proceedings on appeal

1. For the purposes of proceedings under article 81 and this article, the Appeals Chamber shall have all the powers of the Trial Chamber.
2. If the Appeals Chamber finds that the proceedings appealed from were unfair in a way that affected the reliability of the decision or sentence, or that the decision or sentence appealed from was materially affected by error of fact or law or procedural error, it may:
   (a) Reverse or amend the decision or sentence; or
   (b) Order a new trial before a different Trial Chamber.

For these purposes, the Appeals Chamber may remand a factual issue to the original Trial Chamber for it to determine the issue and to report back accordingly, or may itself call evidence to determine the issue. When the decision or sentence has been appealed only by the person convicted, or the Prosecutor on that person's behalf, it cannot be amended to his or her detriment.

3. If in an appeal against sentence the Appeals Chamber finds that the sentence is disproportionate to the crime, it may vary the sentence in accordance with Part 7.
4. The judgement of the Appeals Chamber shall be taken by a majority of the judges and shall be delivered in open court. The judgement shall state the reasons on which it is based. When there is no unanimity, the judgement of the Appeals Chamber shall contain the views of the majority and the

minority, but a judge may deliver a separate or dissenting opinion on a question of law.

5. The Appeals Chamber may deliver its judgement in the absence of the person acquitted or convicted.

Art. 84. Revision of conviction or sentence

1. The convicted person or, after death, spouses, children, parents or one person alive at the time of the accused's death who has been given express written instructions from the accused to bring such a claim, or the Prosecutor on the person's behalf, may apply to the Appeals Chamber to revise the final judgement of conviction or sentence on the grounds that:
   (a) New evidence has been discovered that:
      (i) Was not available at the time of trial, and such unavailability was not wholly or partially attributable to the party making application; and
      (ii) Is sufficiently important that had it been proved at trial it would have been likely to have resulted in a different verdict;
   (b) It has been newly discovered that decisive evidence, taken into account at trial and upon which the conviction depends, was false, forged or falsified;
   (c) One or more of the judges who participated in conviction or confirmation of the charges has committed, in that case, an act of serious misconduct or serious breach of duty of sufficient gravity to justify the removal of that judge or those judges from office under article 46.
2. The Appeals Chamber shall reject the application if it considers it to be unfounded. If it determines that the application is meritorious, it may, as appropriate:
   (a) Reconvene the original Trial Chamber;
   (b) Constitute a new Trial Chamber; or
   (c) Retain jurisdiction over the matter,

   with a view to, after hearing the parties in the manner set forth in the Rules of Procedure and Evidence, arriving at a determination on whether the judgement should be revised.

Art. 85. Compensation to an arrested or convicted person

1. Anyone who has been the victim of unlawful arrest or detention shall have an enforceable right to compensation.
2. When a person has by a final decision been convicted of a criminal offence, and when subsequently his or her conviction has been reversed on the ground that a new or newly discovered fact shows conclusively that there has been a miscarriage of justice, the person who has suffered punishment as a result of such conviction shall be compensated according to law, unless it is proved that the non-disclosure of the unknown fact in time is wholly or partly attributable to him or her.
3. In exceptional circumstances, where the Court finds conclusive facts showing that there has been a grave and manifest miscarriage of justice, it may in its discretion award compensation, according to the criteria provided in the Rules of Procedure and Evidence, to a person who has been released from detention following a final decision of acquittal or a termination of the proceedings for that reason.

Part 9. International Cooperation and Judicial Assistance

Art. 86. General obligation to cooperate
States Parties shall, in accordance with the provisions of this Statute, cooperate fully with the Court in its investigation and prosecution of crimes within the jurisdiction of the Court.

Article 87.[14] *Requests for cooperation: general provisions*
1. (a)[15] The Court shall have the authority to make requests to States Parties for cooperation. The requests shall be transmitted through the diplomatic channel or any other appropriate channel as may be designated by each State Party upon ratification, acceptance, approval or accession.
   Subsequent changes to the designation shall be made by each State Party in accordance with the Rules of Procedure and Evidence.
   (b) When appropriate, without prejudice to the provisions of subparagraph (a), requests may also be transmitted through the International Criminal Police Organization or any appropriate regional organization.
2.[16] Requests for cooperation and any documents supporting the request shall either be in or be accompanied by a translation into an official language of the requested State or one of the working languages of the Court, in accordance with the choice made by that State upon ratification, acceptance, approval or accession.
   Subsequent changes to this choice shall be made in accordance with the Rules of Procedure and Evidence.
3. The requested State shall keep confidential a request for cooperation and any documents supporting the request, except to the extent that the disclosure is necessary for execution of the request.
4. In relation to any request for assistance presented under this Part, the Court may take such measures, including measures related to the protection of information, as may be necessary to ensure the safety or physical or psychological well-being of any victims, potential witnesses and their families. The Court may request that any information that is made available under this Part shall be provided and handled in a manner that protects the safety and physical or psychological well-being of any victims, potential witnesses and their families.
5. (a) The Court may invite any State not party to this Statute to provide assistance under this Part on the basis of an ad hoc arrangement, an agreement with such State or any other appropriate basis.
   (b) Where a State not party to this Statute, which has entered into an ad hoc arrangement or an agreement with the Court, fails to cooperate with requests pursuant to any such arrangement or agreement, the Court may so inform the Assembly of States Parties or, where the Security Council referred the matter to the Court, the Security Council.

[14] For declaration in respect of this article by Hungary, see p. 1390.

[15] For declaration in respect of this paragraph by Andorra, Belgium, Belize, Colombia, Cyprus, Democratic Republic of Congo, Denmark, Egypt, Estonia, Gambia, Germany, Liechtenstein, Norway, Romania, Spain, Sweden and Switzerland, see pp. 1385–1393.

[16] For declaration in respect of this paragraph by Andorra, Argentina, Austria, Belgium, Brazil, Colombia, Cyprus, Denmark, Egypt, Estonia, Finland, France, Gambia, Germany, Latvia, Liechtenstein, Namibia, Norway, Poland, Portugal, Romania, Slovakia, Spain, Sweden, Switzerland, United Kingdom and Uruguay, see pp. 1385–1394.

6. The Court may ask any intergovernmental organization to provide information or documents. The Court may also ask for other forms of cooperation and assistance which may be agreed upon with such an organization and which are in accordance with its competence or mandate.
7. Where a State Party fails to comply with a request to cooperate by the Court contrary to the provisions of this Statute, thereby preventing the Court from exercising its functions and powers under this Statute, the Court may make a finding to that effect and refer the matter to the Assembly of States Parties or, where the Security Council referred the matter to the Court, to the Security Council.

Art. 88. Availability of procedures under national law
States Parties shall ensure that there are procedures available under their national law for all of the forms of cooperation which are specified under this Part.

Art. 89. Surrender of persons to the Court
1. The Court may transmit a request for the arrest and surrender of a person, together with the material supporting the request outlined in article 91, to any State on the territory of which that person may be found and shall request the cooperation of that State in the arrest and surrender of such a person. States Parties shall, in accordance with the provisions of this Part and the procedure under their national law, comply with requests for arrest and surrender.
2. Where the person sought for surrender brings a challenge before a national court on the basis of the principle of *ne bis in idem* as provided in article 20, the requested State shall immediately consult with the Court to determine if there has been a relevant ruling on admissibility. If the case is admissible, the requested State shall proceed with the execution of the request. If an admissibility ruling is pending, the requested State may postpone the execution of the request for surrender of the person until the Court makes a determination on admissibility.
3. (a) A State Party shall authorize, in accordance with its national procedural law, transportation through its territory of a person being surrendered to the Court by another State, except where transit through that State would impede or delay the surrender.
   (b) A request by the Court for transit shall be transmitted in accordance with article 87. The request for transit shall contain:
      (i) A description of the person being transported;
      (ii) A brief statement of the facts of the case and their legal characterization; and
      (iii) The warrant for arrest and surrender;
   (c) A person being transported shall be detained in custody during the period of transit;
   (d) No authorization is required if the person is transported by air and no landing is scheduled on the territory of the transit State;
   (e) If an unscheduled landing occurs on the territory of the transit State, that State may require a request for transit from the Court as provided for in subparagraph (b). The transit State shall detain the person being transported until the request for transit is received and the transit is effected, provided that detention for purposes of this subparagraph may not be

extended beyond 96 hours from the unscheduled landing unless the request is received within that time.

4. If the person sought is being proceeded against or is serving a sentence in the requested State for a crime different from that for which surrender to the Court is sought, the requested State, after making its decision to grant the request, shall consult with the Court.

Art. 90. Competing requests

1. A State Party which receives a request from the Court for the surrender of a person under article 89 shall, if it also receives a request from any other State for the extradition of the same person for the same conduct which forms the basis of the crime for which the Court seeks the person's surrender, notify the Court and the requesting State of that fact.
2. Where the requesting State is a State Party, the requested State shall give priority to the request from the Court if:
   (a) The Court has, pursuant to article 18 or 19, made a determination that the case in respect of which surrender is sought is admissible and that determination takes into account the investigation or prosecution conducted by the requesting State in respect of its request for extradition; or
   (b) The Court makes the determination described in subparagraph (a) pursuant to the requested State's notification under paragraph 1.
3. Where a determination under paragraph 2 (a) has not been made, the requested State may, at its discretion, pending the determination of the Court under paragraph 2 (b), proceed to deal with the request for extradition from the requesting State but shall not extradite the person until the Court has determined that the case is inadmissible. The Court's determination shall be made on an expedited basis.
4. If the requesting State is a State not Party to this Statute the requested State, if it is not under an international obligation to extradite the person to the requesting State, shall give priority to the request for surrender from the Court, if the Court has determined that the case is admissible.
5. Where a case under paragraph 4 has not been determined to be admissible by the Court, the requested State may, at its discretion, proceed to deal with the request for extradition from the requesting State.
6. In cases where paragraph 4 applies except that the requested State is under an existing international obligation to extradite the person to the requesting State not Party to this Statute, the requested State shall determine whether to surrender the person to the Court or extradite the person to the requesting State. In making its decision, the requested State shall consider all the relevant factors, including but not limited to:
   (a) The respective dates of the requests;
   (b) The interests of the requesting State including, where relevant, whether the crime was committed in its territory and the nationality of the victims and of the person sought; and
   (c) The possibility of subsequent surrender between the Court and the requesting State.
7. Where a State Party which receives a request from the Court for the surrender of a person also receives a request from any State for the extradition of the same person for conduct other than that which constitutes the crime for which the Court seeks the person's surrender:

(a) The requested State shall, if it is not under an existing international obligation to extradite the person to the requesting State, give priority to the request from the Court;

(b) The requested State shall, if it is under an existing international obligation to extradite the person to the requesting State, determine whether to surrender the person to the Court or to extradite the person to the requesting State. In making its decision, the requested State shall consider all the relevant factors, including but not limited to those set out in paragraph 6, but shall give special consideration to the relative nature and gravity of the conduct in question.

8. Where pursuant to a notification under this article, the Court has determined a case to be inadmissible, and subsequently extradition to the requesting State is refused, the requested State shall notify the Court of this decision.

Art. 91. Contents of request for arrest and surrender

1. A request for arrest and surrender shall be made in writing. In urgent cases, a request may be made by any medium capable of delivering a written record, provided that the request shall be confirmed through the channel provided for in article 87, paragraph 1 (a).
2. In the case of a request for the arrest and surrender of a person for whom a warrant of arrest has been issued by the Pre-Trial Chamber under article 58, the request shall contain or be supported by:
   (a) Information describing the person sought, sufficient to identify the person, and information as to that person's probable location;
   (b) A copy of the warrant of arrest; and
   (c) Such documents, statements or information as may be necessary to meet the requirements for the surrender process in the requested State, except that those requirements should not be more burdensome than those applicable to requests for extradition pursuant to treaties or arrangements between the requested State and other States and should, if possible, be less burdensome, taking into account the distinct nature of the Court.
3. In the case of a request for the arrest and surrender of a person already convicted, the request shall contain or be supported by:
   (a) A copy of any warrant of arrest for that person;
   (b) A copy of the judgement of conviction;
   (c) Information to demonstrate that the person sought is the one referred to in the judgement of conviction; and
   (d) If the person sought has been sentenced, a copy of the sentence imposed and, in the case of a sentence for imprisonment, a statement of any time already served and the time remaining to be served.
4. Upon the request of the Court, a State Party shall consult with the Court, either generally or with respect to a specific matter, regarding any requirements under its national law that may apply under paragraph 2 (c). During the consultations, the State Party shall advise the Court of the specific requirements of its national law.

Art. 92. Provisional arrest

1. In urgent cases, the Court may request the provisional arrest of the person sought, pending presentation of the request for surrender and the documents supporting the request as specified in article 91.

2. The request for provisional arrest shall be made by any medium capable of delivering a written record and shall contain:
   (a) Information describing the person sought, sufficient to identify the person, and information as to that person's probable location;
   (b) A concise statement of the crimes for which the person's arrest is sought and of the facts which are alleged to constitute those crimes, including, where possible, the date and location of the crime;
   (c) A statement of the existence of a warrant of arrest or a judgement of conviction against the person sought; and
   (d) A statement that a request for surrender of the person sought will follow.
3. A person who is provisionally arrested may be released from custody if the requested State has not received the request for surrender and the documents supporting the request as specified in article 91 within the time limits specified in the Rules of Procedure and Evidence. However, the person may consent to surrender before the expiration of this period if permitted by the law of the requested State. In such a case, the requested State shall proceed to surrender the person to the Court as soon as possible.
4. The fact that the person sought has been released from custody pursuant to paragraph 3 shall not prejudice the subsequent arrest and surrender of that person if the request for surrender and the documents supporting the request are delivered at a later date.

Art. 93. Other forms of cooperation

1. States Parties shall, in accordance with the provisions of this Part and under procedures of national law, comply with requests by the Court to provide the following assistance in relation to investigations or prosecutions:
   (a) The identification and whereabouts of persons or the location of items;
   (b) The taking of evidence, including testimony under oath, and the production of evidence, including expert opinions and reports necessary to the Court;
   (c) The questioning of any person being investigated or prosecuted;
   (d) The service of documents, including judicial documents;
   (e) Facilitating the voluntary appearance of persons as witnesses or experts before the Court;
   (f) The temporary transfer of persons as provided in paragraph 7;
   (g) The examination of places or sites, including the exhumation and examination of grave sites;
   (h) The execution of searches and seizures;
   (i) The provision of records and documents, including official records and documents;
   (j) The protection of victims and witnesses and the preservation of evidence;
   (k) The identification, tracing and freezing or seizure of proceeds, property and assets and instrumentalities of crimes for the purpose of eventual forfeiture, without prejudice to the rights of bona fide third parties; and
   (l) Any other type of assistance which is not prohibited by the law of the requested State, with a view to facilitating the investigation and prosecution of crimes within the jurisdiction of the Court.
2. The Court shall have the authority to provide an assurance to a witness or an expert appearing before the Court that he or she will not be prosecuted,

detained or subjected to any restriction of personal freedom by the Court in respect of any act or omission that preceded the departure of that person from the requested State.

3. Where execution of a particular measure of assistance detailed in a request presented under paragraph 1, is prohibited in the requested State on the basis of an existing fundamental legal principle of general application, the requested State shall promptly consult with the Court to try to resolve the matter. In the consultations, consideration should be given to whether the assistance can be rendered in another manner or subject to conditions. If after consultations the matter cannot be resolved, the Court shall modify the request as necessary.
4. In accordance with article 72, a State Party may deny a request for assistance, in whole or in part, only if the request concerns the production of any documents or disclosure of evidence which relates to its national security.
5. Before denying a request for assistance under paragraph 1 (l), the requested State shall consider whether the assistance can be provided subject to specified conditions, or whether the assistance can be provided at a later date or in an alternative manner, provided that if the Court or the Prosecutor accepts the assistance subject to conditions, the Court or the Prosecutor shall abide by them.
6. If a request for assistance is denied, the requested State Party shall promptly inform the Court or the Prosecutor of the reasons for such denial.
7. (a) The Court may request the temporary transfer of a person in custody for purposes of identification or for obtaining testimony or other assistance. The person may be transferred if the following conditions are fulfilled:
      (i) The person freely gives his or her informed consent to the transfer; and
      (ii) The requested State agrees to the transfer, subject to such conditions as that State and the Court may agree.
   (b) The person being transferred shall remain in custody. When the purposes of the transfer have been fulfilled, the Court shall return the person without delay to the requested State.
8. (a) The Court shall ensure the confidentiality of documents and information, except as required for the investigation and proceedings described in the request.
   (b) The requested State may, when necessary, transmit documents or information to the Prosecutor on a confidential basis. The Prosecutor may then use them solely for the purpose of generating new evidence.
   (c) The requested State may, on its own motion or at the request of the Prosecutor, subsequently consent to the disclosure of such documents or information. They may then be used as evidence pursuant to the provisions of Parts 5 and 6 and in accordance with the Rules of Procedure and Evidence.
9. (a) (i) In the event that a State Party receives competing requests, other than for surrender or extradition, from the Court and from another State pursuant to an international obligation, the State Party shall endeavour, in consultation with the Court and the other State, to meet both requests, if necessary by postponing or attaching conditions to one or the other request.
      (ii) Failing that, competing requests shall be resolved in accordance with the principles established in article 90.

(b) Where, however, the request from the Court concerns information, property or persons which are subject to the control of a third State or an international organization by virtue of an international agreement, the requested States shall so inform the Court and the Court shall direct its request to the third State or international organization.

10. (a) The Court may, upon request, cooperate with and provide assistance to a State Party conducting an investigation into or trial in respect of conduct which constitutes a crime within the jurisdiction of the Court or which constitutes a serious crime under the national law of the requesting State.

(b) (i) The assistance provided under subparagraph (a) shall include, *inter alia*:

a. The transmission of statements, documents or other types of evidence obtained in the course of an investigation or a trial conducted by the Court; and

b. The questioning of any person detained by order of the Court;

(ii) In the case of assistance under subparagraph (b) (i) a:

a. If the documents or other types of evidence have been obtained with the assistance of a State, such transmission shall require the consent of that State;

b. If the statements, documents or other types of evidence have been provided by a witness or expert, such transmission shall be subject to the provisions of article 68.

(c) The Court may, under the conditions set out in this paragraph, grant a request for assistance under this paragraph from a State which is not a Party to this Statute.

Art. 94. Postponement of execution of a request in respectof ongoing investigation or prosecution

1. If the immediate execution of a request would interfere with an ongoing investigation or prosecution of a case different from that to which the request relates, the requested State may postpone the execution of the request for a period of time agreed upon with the Court. However, the postponement shall be no longer than is necessary to complete the relevant investigation or prosecution in the requested State. Before making a decision to postpone, the requested State should consider whether the assistance may be immediately provided subject to certain conditions.
2. If a decision to postpone is taken pursuant to paragraph 1, the Prosecutor may, however, seek measures to preserve evidence, pursuant to article 93, paragraph 1 (j).

Art. 95. Postponement of execution of a request in respect of an admissibility challenge

Where there is an admissibility challenge under consideration by the Court pursuant to article 18 or 19, the requested State may postpone the execution of a request under this Part pending a determination by the Court, unless the Court has specifically ordered that the Prosecutor may pursue the collection of such evidence pursuant to article 18 or 19.

Art. 96. Contents of request for other forms of assistance under article 93

1. A request for other forms of assistance referred to in article 93 shall be made in writing. In urgent cases, a request may be made by any medium capable

of delivering a written record, provided that the request shall be confirmed through the channel provided for in article 87, paragraph 1 (a).

2. The request shall, as applicable, contain or be supported by the following:
   (a) A concise statement of the purpose of the request and the assistance sought, including the legal basis and the grounds for the request;
   (b) As much detailed information as possible about the location or identification of any person or place that must be found or identified in order for the assistance sought to be provided;
   (c) A concise statement of the essential facts underlying the request;
   (d) The reasons for and details of any procedure or requirement to be followed;
   (e) Such information as may be required under the law of the requested State in order to execute the request; and
   (f) Any other information relevant in order for the assistance sought to be provided.
3. Upon the request of the Court, a State Party shall consult with the Court, either generally or with respect to a specific matter, regarding any requirements under its national law that may apply under paragraph 2 (e). During the consultations, the State Party shall advise the Court of the specific requirements of its national law.
4. The provisions of this article shall, where applicable, also apply in respect of a request for assistance made to the Court.

Art. 97. Consultations

Where a State Party receives a request under this Part in relation to which it identifies problems which may impede or prevent the execution of the request, that State shall consult with the Court without delay in order to resolve the matter. Such problems may include, *inter alia*:

(a) Insufficient information to execute the request;

(b) In the case of a request for surrender, the fact that despite best efforts, the person sought cannot be located or that the investigation conducted has determined that the person in the requested State is clearly not the person named in the warrant; or

(c) The fact that execution of the request in its current form would require the requested State to breach a pre-existing treaty obligation undertaken with respect to another State.

Art. 98. Cooperation with respect to waiver of immunity and consent to surrender

1. The Court may not proceed with a request for surrender or assistance which would require the requested State to act inconsistently with its obligations under international law with respect to the State or diplomatic immunity of a person or property of a third State, unless the Court can first obtain the cooperation of that third State for the waiver of the immunity.
2. The Court may not proceed with a request for surrender which would require the requested State to act inconsistently with its obligations under international agreements pursuant to which the consent of a sending State is required to surrender a person of that State to the Court, unless the Court can first obtain the cooperation of the sending State for the giving of consent for the surrender.

Art. 99. Execution of requests under articles 93 and 96

1. Requests for assistance shall be executed in accordance with the relevant procedure under the law of the requested State and, unless prohibited by such law, in the manner specified in the request, including following any procedure outlined therein or permitting persons specified in the request to be present at and assist in the execution process.
2. In the case of an urgent request, the documents or evidence produced in response shall, at the request of the Court, be sent urgently.
3. Replies from the requested State shall be transmitted in their original language and form.
4. Without prejudice to other articles in this Part, where it is necessary for the successful execution of a request which can be executed without any compulsory measures, including specifically the interview of or taking evidence from a person on a voluntary basis, including doing so without the presence of the authorities of the requested State Party if it is essential for the request to be executed, and the examination without modification of a public site or other public place, the Prosecutor may execute such request directly on the territory of a State as follows:
   (a) When the State Party requested is a State on the territory of which the crime is alleged to have been committed, and there has been a determination of admissibility pursuant to article 18 or 19, the Prosecutor may directly execute such request following all possible consultations with the requested State Party;
   (b) In other cases, the Prosecutor may execute such request following consultations with the requested State Party and subject to any reasonable conditions or concerns raised by that State Party. Where the requested State Party identifies problems with the execution of a request pursuant to this subparagraph it shall, without delay, consult with the Court to resolve the matter.
5. Provisions allowing a person heard or examined by the Court under article 72 to invoke restrictions designed to prevent disclosure of confidential information connected with national security shall also apply to the execution of requests for assistance under this article.

Art. 100. Costs

1. The ordinary costs for execution of requests in the territory of the requested State shall be borne by that State, except for the following, which shall be borne by the Court:
   (a) Costs associated with the travel and security of witnesses and experts or the transfer under article 93 of persons in custody;
   (b) Costs of translation, interpretation and transcription;
   (c) Travel and subsistence costs of the judges, the Prosecutor, the Deputy Prosecutors, the Registrar, the Deputy Registrar and staff of any organ of the Court;
   (d) Costs of any expert opinion or report requested by the Court;
   (e) Costs associated with the transport of a person being surrendered to the Court by a custodial State; and
   (f) Following consultations, any extraordinary costs that may result from the execution of a request.

2. The provisions of paragraph 1 shall, as appropriate, apply to requests from States Parties to the Court. In that case, the Court shall bear the ordinary costs of execution.

Art. 101. Rule of speciality

1. A person surrendered to the Court under this Statute shall not be proceeded against, punished or detained for any conduct committed prior to surrender, other than the conduct or course of conduct which forms the basis of the crimes for which that person has been surrendered.
2. The Court may request a waiver of the requirements of paragraph 1 from the State which surrendered the person to the Court and, if necessary, the Court shall provide additional information in accordance with article 91. States Parties shall have the authority to provide a waiver to the Court and should endeavour to do so.

Art. 102. Use of terms

For the purposes of this Statute:

(a) "surrender" means the delivering up of a person by a State to the Court, pursuant to this Statute.

(b) "extradition" means the delivering up of a person by one State to another as provided by treaty, convention or national legislation.

Part 10. Enforcement

Art. 103. Role of States in enforcement of sentences of imprisonment

1. (a)[17] A sentence of imprisonment shall be served in a State designated by the Court from a list of States which have indicated to the Court their willingness to accept sentenced persons.
   (b)[18] At the time of declaring its willingness to accept sentenced persons, a State may attach conditions to its acceptance as agreed by the Court and in accordance with this Part.
   (c) A State designated in a particular case shall promptly inform the Court whether it accepts the Court's designation.
2. (a) The State of enforcement shall notify the Court of any circumstances, including the exercise of any conditions agreed under paragraph 1, which could materially affect the terms or extent of the imprisonment. The Court shall be given at least 45 days' notice of any such known or foreseeable circumstances. During this period, the State of enforcement shall take no action that might prejudice its obligations under article 110.
   (b) Where the Court cannot agree to the circumstances referred to in subparagraph (a), it shall notify the State of enforcement and proceed in accordance with article 104, paragraph 1.
3. In exercising its discretion to make a designation under paragraph 1, the Court shall take into account the following:

[17] For declaration in respect of this paragraph by Andorra, Liechtenstein, Spain and Switzerland, see pp. 1385–1393.

[18] For declaration in respect of this article by Slovakia and Spain, see pp. 1392–1393.

(a) The principle that States Parties should share the responsibility for enforcing sentences of imprisonment, in accordance with principles of equitable distribution, as provided in the Rules of Procedure and Evidence;
(b) The application of widely accepted international treaty standards governing the treatment of prisoners;
(c) The views of the sentenced person;
(d) The nationality of the sentenced person;
(e) Such other factors regarding the circumstances of the crime or the person sentenced, or the effective enforcement of the sentence, as may be appropriate in designating the State of enforcement.

4. If no State is designated under paragraph 1, the sentence of imprisonment shall be served in a prison facility made available by the host State, in accordance with the conditions set out in the headquarters agreement referred to in article 3, paragraph 2. In such a case, the costs arising out of the enforcement of a sentence of imprisonment shall be borne by the Court.

Art. 104. Change in designation of State of enforcement

1. The Court may, at any time, decide to transfer a sentenced person to a prison of another State.
2. A sentenced person may, at any time, apply to the Court to be transferred from the State of enforcement.

Art. 105. Enforcement of the sentence

1. Subject to conditions which a State may have specified in accordance with article 103, paragraph 1 (b), the sentence of imprisonment shall be binding on the States Parties, which shall in no case modify it.
2. The Court alone shall have the right to decide any application for appeal and revision. The State of enforcement shall not impede the making of any such application by a sentenced person.

Art. 106. Supervision of enforcement of sentences and conditions of imprisonment

1. The enforcement of a sentence of imprisonment shall be subject to the supervision of the Court and shall be consistent with widely accepted international treaty standards governing treatment of prisoners.
2. The conditions of imprisonment shall be governed by the law of the State of enforcement and shall be consistent with widely accepted international treaty standards governing treatment of prisoners; in no case shall such conditions be more or less favourable than those available to prisoners convicted of similar offences in the State of enforcement.
3. Communications between a sentenced person and the Court shall be unimpeded and confidential.

Art. 107. Transfer of the person upon completion of sentence

1. Following completion of the sentence, a person who is not a national of the State of enforcement may, in accordance with the law of the State of enforcement, be transferred to a State which is obliged to receive him or her, or to another State which agrees to receive him or her, taking into account any wishes of the person to be transferred to that State, unless the State of enforcement authorizes the person to remain in its territory.

2. If no State bears the costs arising out of transferring the person to another State pursuant to paragraph 1, such costs shall be borne by the Court.
3. Subject to the provisions of article 108, the State of enforcement may also, in accordance with its national law, extradite or otherwise surrender the person to a State which has requested the extradition or surrender of the person for purposes of trial or enforcement of a sentence.

Art. 108. Limitation on the prosecution or punishment of other offences

1. A sentenced person in the custody of the State of enforcement shall not be subject to prosecution or punishment or to extradition to a third State for any conduct engaged in prior to that person's delivery to the State of enforcement, unless such prosecution, punishment or extradition has been approved by the Court at the request of the State of enforcement.
2. The Court shall decide the matter after having heard the views of the sentenced person.
3. Paragraph 1 shall cease to apply if the sentenced person remains voluntarily for more than 30 days in the territory of the State of enforcement after having served the full sentence imposed by the Court, or returns to the territory of that State after having left it.

Art. 109. Enforcement of fines and forfeiture measures

1. States Parties shall give effect to fines or forfeitures ordered by the Court under Part 7, without prejudice to the rights of bona fide third parties, and in accordance with the procedure of their national law.
2. If a State Party is unable to give effect to an order for forfeiture, it shall take measures to recover the value of the proceeds, property or assets ordered by the Court to be forfeited, without prejudice to the rights of bona fide third parties.
3. Property, or the proceeds of the sale of real property or, where appropriate, the sale of other property, which is obtained by a State Party as a result of its enforcement of a judgement of the Court shall be transferred to the Court.

Art. 110. Review by the Court concerning reduction of sentence

1. The State of enforcement shall not release the person before expiry of the sentence pronounced by the Court.
2. The Court alone shall have the right to decide any reduction of sentence, and shall rule on the matter after having heard the person.
3. When the person has served two thirds of the sentence, or 25 years in the case of life imprisonment, the Court shall review the sentence to determine whether it should be reduced. Such a review shall not be conducted before that time.
4. In its review under paragraph 3, the Court may reduce the sentence if it finds that one or more of the following factors are present:
   (a) The early and continuing willingness of the person to cooperate with the Court in its investigations and prosecutions;
   (b) The voluntary assistance of the person in enabling the enforcement of the judgements and orders of the Court in other cases, and in particular providing assistance in locating assets subject to orders of fine, forfeiture or reparation which may be used for the benefit of victims; or
   (c) Other factors establishing a clear and significant change of circumstances sufficient to justify the reduction of sentence, as provided in the Rules of Procedure and Evidence.

5. If the Court determines in its initial review under paragraph 3 that it is not appropriate to reduce the sentence, it shall thereafter review the question of reduction of sentence at such intervals and applying such criteria as provided for in the Rules of Procedure and Evidence.

Art. 111. Escape
If a convicted person escapes from custody and flees the State of enforcement, that State may, after consultation with the Court, request the person's surrender from the State in which the person is located pursuant to existing bilateral or multilateral arrangements, or may request that the Court seek the person's surrender, in accordance with Part 9. It may direct that the person be delivered to the State in which he or she was serving the sentence or to another State designated by the Court.

Part 11. Assembly of States Parties

Art. 112. Assembly of States Parties
1. An Assembly of States Parties to this Statute is hereby established. Each State Party shall have one representative in the Assembly who may be accompanied by alternates and advisers. Other States which have signed this Statute or the Final Act may be observers in the Assembly.
2. The Assembly shall:
   (a) Consider and adopt, as appropriate, recommendations of the Preparatory Commission;
   (b) Provide management oversight to the Presidency, the Prosecutor and the Registrar regarding the administration of the Court;
   (c) Consider the reports and activities of the Bureau established under paragraph 3 and take appropriate action in regard thereto;
   (d) Consider and decide the budget for the Court;
   (e) Decide whether to alter, in accordance with article 36, the number of judges;
   (f) Consider pursuant to article 87, paragraphs 5 and 7, any question relating to non-cooperation;
   (g) Perform any other function consistent with this Statute or the Rules of Procedure and Evidence.
3. (a) The Assembly shall have a Bureau consisting of a President, two Vice-Presidents and 18 members elected by the Assembly for three-year terms.
   (b) The Bureau shall have a representative character, taking into account, in particular, equitable geographical distribution and the adequate representation of the principal legal systems of the world.
   (c) The Bureau shall meet as often as necessary, but at least once a year. It shall assist the Assembly in the discharge of its responsibilities.
4. The Assembly may establish such subsidiary bodies as may be necessary, including an independent oversight mechanism for inspection, evaluation and investigation of the Court, in order to enhance its efficiency and economy.
5. The President of the Court, the Prosecutor and the Registrar or their representatives may participate, as appropriate, in meetings of the Assembly and of the Bureau.
6. The Assembly shall meet at the seat of the Court or at the Headquarters of the United Nations once a year and, when circumstances so require, hold special sessions. Except as otherwise specified in this Statute, special ses-

sions shall be convened by the Bureau on its own initiative or at the request of one third of the States Parties.

7. Each State Party shall have one vote. Every effort shall be made to reach decisions by consensus in the Assembly and in the Bureau. If consensus cannot be reached, except as otherwise provided in the Statute:
   (a) Decisions on matters of substance must be approved by a two-thirds majority of those present and voting provided that an absolute majority of States Parties constitutes the quorum for voting;
   (b) Decisions on matters of procedure shall be taken by a simple majority of States Parties present and voting.
8. A State Party which is in arrears in the payment of its financial contributions towards the costs of the Court shall have no vote in the Assembly and in the Bureau if the amount of its arrears equals or exceeds the amount of the contributions due from it for the preceding two full years. The Assembly may, nevertheless, permit such a State Party to vote in the Assembly and in the Bureau if it is satisfied that the failure to pay is due to conditions beyond the control of the State Party.
9. The Assembly shall adopt its own rules of procedure.
10. The official and working languages of the Assembly shall be those of the General Assembly of the United Nations.

Part 12. Financing

Art. 113. Financial Regulations
Except as otherwise specifically provided, all financial matters related to the Court and the meetings of the Assembly of States Parties, including its Bureau and subsidiary bodies, shall be governed by this Statute and the Financial Regulations and Rules adopted by the Assembly of States Parties.

Art. 114. Payment of expenses
Expenses of the Court and the Assembly of States Parties, including its Bureau and subsidiary bodies, shall be paid from the funds of the Court.

Art. 115. Funds of the Court and of the Assembly of States Parties
The expenses of the Court and the Assembly of States Parties, including its Bureau and subsidiary bodies, as provided for in the budget decided by the Assembly of States Parties, shall be provided by the following sources:
(a) Assessed contributions made by States Parties;
(b) Funds provided by the United Nations, subject to the approval of the General Assembly, in particular in relation to the expenses incurred due to referrals by the Security Council.

Art. 116. Voluntary contributions
Without prejudice to article 115, the Court may receive and utilize, as additional funds, voluntary contributions from Governments, international organizations, individuals, corporations and other entities, in accordance with relevant criteria adopted by the Assembly of States Parties.

Art. 117. Assessment of contributions
The contributions of States Parties shall be assessed in accordance with an agreed scale of assessment, based on the scale adopted by the United Nations

for its regular budget and adjusted in accordance with the principles on which that scale is based.

Art. 118. Annual audit
The records, books and accounts of the Court, including its annual financial statements, shall be audited annually by an independent auditor.

Part 13. Final Clauses

Art. 119. Settlement of disputes
1. Any dispute concerning the judicial functions of the Court shall be settled by the decision of the Court.
2. Any other dispute between two or more States Parties relating to the interpretation or application of this Statute which is not settled through negotiations within three months of their commencement shall be referred to the Assembly of States Parties. The Assembly may itself seek to settle the dispute or may make recommendations on further means of settlement of the dispute, including referral to the International Court of Justice in conformity with the Statute of that Court.

Art. 120. Reservations
No reservations may be made to this Statute.

Art. 121. Amendments
1. After the expiry of seven years from the entry into force of this Statute, any State Party may propose amendments thereto. The text of any proposed amendment shall be submitted to the Secretary-General of the United Nations, who shall promptly circulate it to all States Parties.
2. No sooner than three months from the date of notification, the Assembly of States Parties, at its next meeting, shall, by a majority of those present and voting, decide whether to take up the proposal. The Assembly may deal with the proposal directly or convene a Review Conference if the issue involved so warrants.
3. The adoption of an amendment at a meeting of the Assembly of States Parties or at a Review Conference on which consensus cannot be reached shall require a two-thirds majority of States Parties.
4. Except as provided in paragraph 5, an amendment shall enter into force for all States Parties one year after instruments of ratification or acceptance have been deposited with the Secretary-General of the United Nations by seven-eighths of them.
5. Any amendment to articles 5, 6, 7 and 8 of this Statute shall enter into force for those States Parties which have accepted the amendment one year after the deposit of their instruments of ratification or acceptance. In respect of a State Party which has not accepted the amendment, the Court shall not exercise its jurisdiction regarding a crime covered by the amendment when committed by that State Party's nationals or on its territory.
6. If an amendment has been accepted by seven-eighths of States Parties in accordance with paragraph 4, any State Party which has not accepted the amendment may withdraw from this Statute with immediate effect, notwithstanding article 127, paragraph 1, but subject to article 127, paragraph 2, by giving notice no later than one year after the entry into force of such amendment.

7. The Secretary-General of the United Nations shall circulate to all States Parties any amendment adopted at a meeting of the Assembly of States Parties or at a Review Conference.

Art. 122. Amendments to provisions of an institutional nature

1. Amendments to provisions of this Statute which are of an exclusively institutional nature, namely, article 35, article 36, paragraphs 8 and 9, article 37, article 38, article 39, paragraphs 1 (first two sentences), 2 and 4, article 42, paragraphs 4 to 9, article 43, paragraphs 2 and 3, and articles 44, 46, 47 and 49, may be proposed at any time, notwithstanding article 121, paragraph 1, by any State Party. The text of any proposed amendment shall be submitted to the Secretary-General of the United Nations or such other person designated by the Assembly of States Parties who shall promptly circulate it to all States Parties and to others participating in the Assembly.
2. Amendments under this article on which consensus cannot be reached shall be adopted by the Assembly of States Parties or by a Review Conference, by a two-thirds majority of States Parties. Such amendments shall enter into force for all States Parties six months after their adoption by the Assembly or, as the case may be, by the Conference.

Art. 123. Review of the Statute

1. Seven years after the entry into force of this Statute the Secretary-General of the United Nations shall convene a Review Conference to consider any amendments to this Statute. Such review may include, but is not limited to, the list of crimes contained in article 5. The Conference shall be open to those participating in the Assembly of States Parties and on the same conditions.
2. At any time thereafter, at the request of a State Party and for the purposes set out in paragraph 1, the Secretary-General of the United Nations shall, upon approval by a majority of States Parties, convene a Review Conference.
3. The provisions of article 121, paragraphs 3 to 7, shall apply to the adoption and entry into force of any amendment to the Statute considered at a Review Conference.

Art. 124.[19] *Transitional Provision*

Notwithstanding article 12, paragraphs 1 and 2, a State, on becoming a party to this Statute, may declare that, for a period of seven years after the entry into force of this Statute for the State concerned, it does not accept the jurisdiction of the Court with respect to the category of crimes referred to in article 8 when a crime is alleged to have been committed by its nationals or on its territory. A declaration under this article may be withdrawn at any time. The provisions of this article shall be reviewed at the Review Conference convened in accordance with article 123, paragraph 1.

Art. 125. Signature, ratification, acceptance, approval or accession

1. This Statute shall be open for signature by all States in Rome, at the headquarters of the Food and Agriculture Organization of the United Nations, on 17 July 1998. Thereafter, it shall remain open for signature in Rome at the

[19] For declaration in respect of this article by Colombia and France, see pp.1387–1389.

Ministry of Foreign Affairs of Italy until 17 October 1998. After that date, the Statute shall remain open for signature in New York, at United Nations Headquarters, until 31 December 2000.

2. This Statute is subject to ratification, acceptance or approval by signatory States. Instruments of ratification, acceptance or approval shall be deposited with the Secretary-General of the United Nations.
3. This Statute shall be open to accession by all States. Instruments of accession shall be deposited with the Secretary-General of the United Nations.

Art. 126. Entry into force

1. This Statute shall enter into force on the first day of the month after the 60th day following the date of the deposit of the 60th instrument of ratification, acceptance, approval or accession with the Secretary-General of the United Nations.
2. For each State ratifying, accepting, approving or acceding to this Statute after the deposit of the 60th instrument of ratification, acceptance, approval or accession, the Statute shall enter into force on the first day of the month after the 60th day following the deposit by such State of its instrument of ratification, acceptance, approval or accession.

Art. 127. Withdrawal

1. A State Party may, by written notification addressed to the Secretary-General of the United Nations, withdraw from this Statute. The withdrawal shall take effect one year after the date of receipt of the notification, unless the notification specifies a later date.
2. A State shall not be discharged, by reason of its withdrawal, from the obligations arising from this Statute while it was a Party to the Statute, including any financial obligations which may have accrued. Its withdrawal shall not affect any cooperation with the Court in connection with criminal investigations and proceedings in relation to which the withdrawing State had a duty to cooperate and which were commenced prior to the date on which the withdrawal became effective, nor shall it prejudice in any way the continued consideration of any matter which was already under consideration by the Court prior to the date on which the withdrawal became effective.

Art. 128. Authentic texts

The original of this Statute, of which the Arabic, Chinese, English, French, Russian and Spanish texts are equally authentic, shall be deposited with the Secretary-General of the United Nations, who shall send certified copies thereof to all States.

IN WITNESS WHEREOF, the undersigned, being duly authorized thereto by their respective Governments, have signed this Statute.

DONE at Rome, this 17th day of July 1998.

II. FINAL ACT OF THE UNITED NATIONS DIPLOMATIC CONFERENCE OF PLENIPOTENTIARIES ON THE ESTABLISHMENT OF AN INTERNATIONAL CRIMINAL COURT

1. *The General Assembly of the United Nations, in its resolution 51/207of 17 December 1996, decided to hold a diplomatic conference of plenipotentiaries in 1998 with a view to finalizing and adopting a convention on the establishment of an international criminal court.*
2. *The General Assembly, in its resolution 52/160 of 15 December 1997, accepted with deep appreciation the generous offer of the Government of Italy to act as host to the conference and decided to hold the United Nations Diplomatic Conference of Plenipotentiaries on the Establishment of an International Criminal Court in Rome from 15 June to 17 July 1998.*
3. *Previously, the General Assembly, in its resolution 44/39 of 4 December 1989, had requested the International Law Commission to address the question of establishing an international criminal court; in resolutions 45/41 of 28 November 1990 and 46/54 of 9 December 1991, invited the Commission to consider further and analyse the issues concerning the question of an international criminal jurisdiction, including the question of establishing an international criminal court; and in resolutions 47/33 of 25 November 1992 and 48/31 of 9 December 1993, requested the Commission to elaborate the draft statute for such a court as a matter of priority.*
4. *The International Law Commission considered the question of establishing an international criminal court from its forty-second session, in 1990, to its forty-sixth session, in 1994. At the latter session, the Commission completed a draft statute for an international criminal court, which was submitted to the General Assembly.*
5. *The General Assembly, in its resolution 49/53 of 9 December 1994, decided to establish an ad hoc committee to review the major substantive and administrative issues arising out of the draft statute prepared by the International Law Commission and, in light of that review, to consider arrangements for the convening of an international conference of plenipotentiaries.*
6. *The Ad Hoc Committee on the Establishment of an International Criminal Court met from 3 to 13 April and from 14 to 25 August 1995, during which time the Committee reviewed the issues arising out of the draft statute prepared by the International Law Commission and considered arrangements for the convening of an international conference.*
7. *The General Assembly, in its resolution 50/46 of 11 December 1995, decided to establish a preparatory committee to discuss further the major substantive and administrative issues arising out of the draft statute prepared by the International Law Commission and, taking into account the different views expressed during the meetings, to draft texts with a view to preparing a widely acceptable consolidated text of a convention for an international criminal court as a next step towards consideration by a conference of plenipotentiaries.*
8. *The Preparatory Committee on the Establishment of an International Criminal Court met from 25 March to 12 April and from 12 to 30 August 1996, during which time the Committee discussed further the issues arising out of the draft statute and began preparing a widely acceptable consolidated text of a convention for an international criminal court.*

9. *The General Assembly, in its resolution 51/207 of 17 December 1996, decided that the Preparatory Committee would meet in 1997 and 1998 in order to complete the drafting of the text for submission to the Conference.*
10. *The Preparatory Committee met from 11 to 21 February, from 4 to 15 August and from 1 to 12 December 1997, during which time the Committee continued to prepare a widely acceptable consolidated text of a convention for an international criminal court.*
11. *The General Assembly, in its resolution 52/160 of 15 December 1997, requested the Preparatory Committee to continue its work in accordance with General Assembly resolution 51/207 and, at the end of its sessions, to transmit to the Conference the text of a draft convention on the establishment of an international criminal court prepared in accordance with its mandate.*
12. *The Preparatory Committee met from 16 March to 3 April 1998, during which time the Committee completed the preparation of the draft Convention on the Establishment of an International Criminal Court, which was transmitted to the Conference.*
13. *The Conference met at the headquarters of the Food and Agriculture Organization of the United Nations in Rome from 15 June to 17 July 1998.*
14. *The General Assembly, in its resolution 52/160, requested the Secretary-General to invite all States Members of the United Nations or members of specialized agencies or of the International Atomic Energy Agency to participate in the Conference. The delegations of 160 States participated in the Conference. The list of participating States is contained in annex II.*
15. *The General Assembly, in the same resolution, requested the Secretary-General to invite representatives of organizations and other entities that had received a standing invitation from the Assembly pursuant to its relevant resolutions to participate as observers in its sessions and work, on the understanding that such representatives would participate in that capacity, and to invite, as observers to the Conference, representatives of interested regional intergovernmental organizations and other interested international bodies, including the International Tribunals for the Former Yugoslavia and for Rwanda. The list of such organizations which were represented at the Conference by an observer is contained in annex III.*
16. *The Secretary-General, pursuant to the same resolution, invited non-governmental organizations accredited by the Preparatory Committee with due regard to the provisions of section VII of Economic and Social Council resolution 1996/31 of 25 July 1996, and in particular to the relevance of their activities to the work of the Conference, to participate in the Conference, along the lines followed in the Preparatory Committee and in accordance with the resolution, as well as the rules of procedure to be adopted by the Conference. The list of non-governmental organizations represented at the Conference by an observer is contained in annex IV.*
17. *The Conference elected Mr. Giovanni Conso (Italy) as President.*
18. *The Conference elected as Vice-Presidents the representatives of the following States: Algeria, Austria, Bangladesh, Burkina Faso, China, Chile, Colombia, Costa Rica, Egypt, France, Gabon, Germany, India, Iran (Islamic Republic of), Japan, Kenya, Latvia, Malawi, Nepal, Nigeria, Pakistan, Russian Federation, Samoa, Slovakia, Sweden, the former Yugoslav Republic of Macedonia, Trinidad and Tobago, United Kingdom of Great Britain and Northern Ireland, United Republic of Tanzania, United States of America and Uruguay.*

The following committees were set up by the Conference:

General Committee
Chairman: *The President of the Conference* Members: *The President and Vice-Presidents of the Conference, the Chairman of the Committee of the Whole and the Chairman of the Drafting Committee*

Committee of the Whole
Chairman: *Mr. Philippe Kirsch (Canada)* Vice-Chairmen: *Ms. Silvia Fernandez de Gurmendi (Argentina), Mr. Constantin Virgil Ivan (Romania) and Mr. Phakiso Mochochoko (Lesotho)* Rapporteur: *Mr.Yasumasa Nagamine (Japan)*

Drafting Committee
Chairman: *Mr. M. Cherif Bassiouni (Egypt)* Members: *Cameroon, China, Dominican Republic, France, Germany, Ghana, India, Jamaica, Lebanon, Mexico, Morocco, Philippines, Poland, Republic of-Korea, Russian Federation, Slovenia, South Africa, Spain, Sudan, Switzerland, Syrian Arab Republic, United Kingdom of Great Britain and Northern Ireland, United States of America and Venezuela.*

The Rapporteur of the Committee of the Whole participated ex officio *in the work of the Drafting Committee in accordance with rule 49 of the rules of procedure of the Conference.*

Credentials Committee
Chairman: *Ms. Hannelore Benjamin (Dominica)* Members: *Argentina, China, Côte d'Ivoire, Dominica, Nepal, Norway, Russian Federation, United States of America and Zambia.*

20. *The Secretary-General was represented by Mr. Hans Corell, Under-Secretary-General, the Legal Counsel. Mr. Roy S. Lee, Director of the Codification Division of the Office of Legal Affairs, acted as Executive Secretary of the Conference. The secretariat was further composed as follows: Mr. Manuel Rama-Montaldo, Secretary, Drafting Committee; Ms. Mahnoush H. Arsanjani, Secretary, Committee of the Whole; Mr. Mpazi Sinjela, Secretary, Credentials Committee; Assistant Secretaries of the Conference: Ms. Christiane Bourloyannis-Vrailas, Ms. Virginia Morris, Mr. Vladimir Rudnitsky, Mr. Renan Villacis.*
21. *The Conference had before it a draft Statute on the Establishment of an International Criminal Court transmitted by the Preparatory Committee in accordance with its mandate (A/CONF.183/2/Add.1).*
22. *The Conference assigned to the Committee of the Whole the consideration of the draft Convention on the Establishment of an International Criminal Court adopted by the Preparatory Committee. The Conference entrusted the Drafting Committee, without reopening substantive discussion on any matter, with coordinating and refining the drafting of all texts referred to it without altering their substance, formulating drafts and giving advice on drafting as requested by the Conference or by the Committee of the Whole and reporting to the Conference or to the Committee of the Whole as appropriate.*
23. *On the basis of the deliberations recorded in the records of the Conference (A/CONF.183/SR.1 to SR.9) and of the Committee of the Whole (A/CONF. 183/C.1/SR.1 to SR.42) and the reports of the Committee of the Whole (A/CONF.183/8) and of the Drafting Committee (A/CONF.183/C.1/L.64,*

L.65/Rev.1, L.66 and Add.1, L.67/Rev.1, L.68/Rev.2, L.82-L.88 and 91), the Conference drew up the Rome Statute of the International Criminal Court.

24. *The foregoing Statute, which is subject to ratification, acceptance or approval, was adopted by the Conference on 17 July 1998 and opened for signature on 17 July 1998, in accordance with its provisions, until 17 October 1998 at the Ministry of Foreign Affairs of Italy and, subsequently, until 31 December 2000, at United Nations Headquarters in New York. The same instrument was also opened for accession in accordance with its provisions.*
25. *After 17 October 1998, the closing date for signature at the Ministry of Foreign Affairs of Italy, the Statute will be deposited with the Secretary-General of the United Nations.*
26. *The Conference also adopted the following resolutions, which are annexed to the present Final Act:*

    Tribute to the International Law Commission

    Tribute to the participants at the Preparatory Committee on the Establishment of an International Criminal Court and its Chairman

    Tribute to the President of the Conference, to the Chairman of the Committee of the Whole and to the Chairman of the Drafting Committee

    Tribute to the People and the Government of Italy

    Resolution on treaty crimes

    Resolution on the Establishment of the Preparatory Commission for the International Criminal Court

IN WITNESS WHEREOF the representatives have signed this Final Act.

DONE at Rome this 17th day of July, one thousand nine hundred and ninety-eight, in a single copy in the Arabic, Chinese, English, French, Russian and Spanish languages, each text being equally authentic.

By unanimous decision of the Conference, the original of this Final Act shall be deposited in the archives of the Ministry of Foreign Affairs of Italy.

The President of the Conference:	*Giovanni Conso*
The Representative of the Secretary-General:	*Hans Corell*
The Executive Secretary of the Conference	*Roy S. Lee*

ANNEX I:

Resolutions adopted by the United Nations Diplomatic Conference of Plenipotentiaries on the Establishment of an International Criminal Court

A. Tribute to the International Law Commission
B. Tribute to the participants at the Preparatory Committee on the Establishment of an International Criminal Court and its Chairman
C. Tribute to the President of the Conference, to the Chairman of the Committee of the Whole and to the Chairman of the Drafting Committee

D. Tribute to the People and the Government of Italy

(The texts of the resolutions A to D omitted in this collection.)

E.

The United Nations Diplomatic Conference of Plenipotentiaries on the Establishment of an International Criminal Court,

Having adopted *the Statute of an International Criminal Court,*

Recognizing *that terrorist acts, by whomever and wherever perpetrated and whatever their forms, methods or motives, are serious crimes of concern to the international community,*

Recognizing *that the international trafficking of illicit drugs is a very serious crime, sometimes destabilizing the political and social and economic order in States,*

Deeply alarmed *at the persistence of these scourges, which pose serious threats to international peace and security,*

Regretting *that no generally acceptable definition of the crimes of terrorism and drug crimes could be agreed upon for the inclusion, within the jurisdiction of the Court,*

Affirming *that the Statute of the International Criminal Court provides for a review mechanism, which allows for an expansion in future of the jurisdiction of the Court,*

Recommends *that a Review Conference pursuant to article 111 of the Statute of the International Criminal Court consider the crimes of terrorism and drug crimes with a view to arriving at an acceptable definition and their inclusion in the list of crimes within the jurisdiction of the Court.*

F.

The United Nations Conference of Plenipotentiaries on the Establishment of an International Criminal Court,

Having adopted *the Statute of the International Criminal Court,*

Having decided t*o take all possible measures to ensure the coming into operation of the International Criminal Court without undue delay and to make the necessary arrangements for the commencement of its functions,*

Having decided *that a preparatory commission should be established for the fulfillment of these purposes,*

Decides *as follows:*

1. *There is hereby established the Preparatory Commission for the International Criminal Court. The Secretary-General of the United Nations shall convene the Commission as early as possible at a date to be decided by the General Assembly of the United Nations.*
2. *The Commission shall consist of representatives of States which have signed the Final Act of the United Nations Diplomatic Conference of Plenipotentiaries on the Establishment of an International Criminal Court and other States which have been invited to participate in the Conference.*
3. *The Commission shall elect its Chairman and other officers, adopt its rules of procedure and decide on its programme of work. These elections shall take place at the first meeting of the Commission.*
4. *The official and working languages of the Preparatory Commission shall be those of the General Assembly of the United Nations.*
5. *The Commission shall prepare proposals for practical arrangements for the establishment and coming into operation of the Court, including the draft texts of:*
   (a) Rules of Procedure and Evidence;
   (b) Elements of Crimes;
   (c) A relationship agreement between the Court and the United Nations;
   (d) Basic principles governing a headquarters agreement to be negotiated between the Court and the host country;
   (e) Financial regulations and rules;
   (f) An agreement on the privileges and immunities of the Court;
   (g) A budget for the first financial year;
   (h) The rules of procedure of the Assembly of States Parties.

6. *The draft texts of the Rules of Procedure and Evidence and of the Elements of Crimes shall be finalized before 30 June 2000.*
7. *The Commission shall prepare proposals for a provision on aggression, including the definition and Elements of Crimes of aggression and the conditions under which the International Criminal Court shall exercise its jurisdiction with regard to this crime. The Commission shall submit such proposals to the Assembly of States Parties at a Review Conference, with a view to arriving at an acceptable provision on the crime of aggression for inclusion in this Statute. The provisions relating to the crime of aggression shall enter into force for the States Parties in accordance with the relevant provisions of this Statute.*
8. *The Commission shall remain in existence until the* conclusion *of the first meeting of the Assembly of States Parties.*
9. *The Commission shall prepare a report on all matters within its mandate and submit it to the first meeting of the Assembly of States Parties.*
10. *The Commission shall meet at the Headquarters of the United Nations. The Secretary-General of the United Nations is requested to provide to the Commission such secretariat services as it may require, subject to the approval of the General Assembly of the United Nations.*
11. *The Secretary-General of the United Nations shall bring the present resolution to the attention of the General Assembly for any necessary action.*

ANNEX II

LIST OF STATES PARTICIPATING IN THE UNITED NATIONS DIPLOMATIC CONFERENCE OF PLENIPOTENTIARIES ON THE ESTABLISHMENT OF AN INTERNATIONAL CRIMINAL COURT

Afghanistan
Albania
Algeria
Andorra
Angola
Argentina
Armenia
Australia
Austria
Azerbaijan
Bahrain
Bangladesh
Barbados
Belarus
Belgium
Benin
Bolivia
Bosnia and Herzegovina
Iran (Islamic Republic of)
Botswana
Brazil
Brunei
Bulgaria
Burkina Faso
Burundi
Cameroon
Canada
Cape Verde
Central African Republic
Chad
Chile
China
Colombia
Comoros
Congo
Costa Rica
Côte d'Ivoire
Croatia
Cuba
Cyprus
Czech Republic
Darussalam
Democratic Republic of the Congo
Denmark
Djibouti
Dominica
Dominican Republic
Ecuador
Egypt
El Salvador
Eritrea
Estonia
Ethiopia
Finland
France
Gabon
Georgia
Germany
Ghana
Greece
Guatemala
Guinea
Guinea-Bissau
Haiti
Holy See
Honduras
Hungary
Iceland
India
Indonesia
Iraq
Ireland
Israel
Italy
Jamaica
Japan
Jordan
Kazakhstan
Kenya
Kuwait

Kyrgyzstan
Lao Peoples Democratic Republic
Latvia
Lebanon
Lesotho
Liberia
Libyan Arab Jamahiriya
Liechtenstein
Lithuania
Luxembourg
Madagascar
Malawi
Malaysia
Mali
Malta
Mauritania
Mauritius
Mexico
Monaco
Morocco
Mozambique
Namibia
Nepal
Netherlands
New Zealand
Nicaragua
Niger
Nigeria
Norway
Oman
Pakistan
Panama
Paraguay
Peru
Philippines
Poland
Portugal
Qatar
Republic of Korea
Republic of Moldova
Romania
Russian Federation
Rwanda
Samoa
San Marino
Sao Tome and Principe
Saudi Arabia
Senegal
Sierra Leone
Singapore
Slovakia
Slovenia
Solomon Islands
South Africa
Spain
Sri Lanka
Sudan
Swaziland
Sweden
Switzerland
Syrian Arab Republic
Tajikistan
Thailand
The former Yugoslav Republic of Macedonia
Togo
Trinidad and Tobago
Tunisia
Turkey
Uganda
Ukraine
United Arab Emirates
United Kingdom of Great Britain and Northern Ireland
United Republic of Tanzania
United States of America
Uruguay
Uzbekistan
Venezuela
Viet Nam
Yemen
Zambia
Zimbabwe

ANNEX III

LIST OF ORGANIZATIONS AND OTHER ENTITIES REPRESENTED AT THE CONFERENCE BY AN OBSERVER

(Not reproduced in this collection)

ANNEX IV

LIST OF NON-GOVERNMENTAL ORGANIZATIONS REPRESENTED AT THE CONFERENCE BY AN OBSERVER

(Not reproduced in this collection)

TABLE OF SIGNATURES, RATIFICATIONS AND ACCESSIONS[1]

State	*Signature*	*Ratification, Acceptance (A), Approval (AA), Accession (a)*
Albania	18 July 1998	–
Algeria	28 December 2000	–
Andorra	18 July 1998	30 April 2001 *Dec.*
Angola	7 October 1998	–
Antigua and Barbuda	23 October 1998	18 June 2001
Argentina	8 January 1999	8 February 2001 *Dec.*
Armenia	1 October 1999	–
Australia	9 December 1998	1 July 2002 *Dec.*
Austria	7 October 1998	28 December 2000 *Dec.*
Bahamas	29 December 2000	–
Bahrain	11 December 2000	–
Bangladesh	16 September 1999	–
Barbados	8 September 2000	–
Belgium	10 September 1998	28 June 2000 *Dec.*
Belize	5 April 2000	5 April 2000 *Dec.*
Benin	24 September 1999	22 January 2002
Bolivia	17 July 1998	27 June 2002
Bosnia and Herzegovina	17 July 2000	11 April 2002
Botswana	8 September 2000	8 September 2000
Brazil	7 February 2000	20 June 2002 *Dec.*
Bulgaria	11 February 1999	11 April 2002
Burkina Faso	30 November 1998	–
Burundi	13 January 1999	–
Cambodia	23 October 2000	–
Cameroon	17 July 1998	11 April 2002
Canada	18 December 1998	7 July 2000
Cape Verde	28 December 2000	–
Central African Republic	7 December 1999	3 October 2001
Chad	20 October 1999	–
Chile	11 September 1998	–
Colombia	10 December 1998	5 August 2002 *Dec.*
Comoros	22 September 2000	–
Congo (Brazzaville)	17 July 1998	–
Costa Rica	7 October 1998	7 June 2001
Cote d'Ivoire	30 November 1998	–
Croatia	12 October 1998	21 May 2001
Cyprus	15 October 1998	7 March 2002 *Dec.*
Czech Republic	13 April 1999	–
Democratic Republic of Congo	8 September 2000	11 April 2002 *Dec.*
Denmark[2]	25 September 1998	21 June 2001 *Dec.*
Djibouti	7 October 1998	–
Dominica	–	12 February 2001
Dominican Republic	8 September 2000	–
Ecuador	7 October 1998	5 February 2002
Egypt	26 December 2000 *Dec.*	–

[1] Status as at 4 November 2000 according to the *Multilateral Treaties Deposited with the Secretary-General, United Nations, New York* (ST/LEG/SER.E), as available on untreaty.un.org and United Nations website www.un.org/law/icc/statute/status.htm.

[2] With a territorial exclusion to the effect that "Until further notice, the Statute shall not apply to the Faroe Islands and Greenland".

State	*Signature*	*Ratification, Acceptance (A), Approval (AA), Accession (a)*
Eritrea	7 October 1998	–
Estonia	27 December 1999	30 January 2002 *Dec.*
Fiji	29 November 1999	29 November 1999
Finland	7 October 1998	29 December 2000 *Dec.*
France	18 July 1998	9 June 2000 *Dec.*
Gabon	22 December 1998	20 September 2000
Gambia	7 December 1998	28 June 2002 *Dec.*
Georgia	18 July 1998	–
Germany	10 December 1998	11 December 2000 *Dec.*
Ghana	18 July 1998	20 December 1999
Greece	18 July 1998	15 May 2002
Guinea	7 September 2000	–
Guinea-Bissau	12 September 2000	–
Guyana	28 December 2000	–
Haiti	26 February 1999	–
Honduras	7 October 1998	1 July 2002
Hungary	15 December 1998	30 November 2001 *Dec.*
Iceland	26 August 1998	25 May 2000
Iran (Islamic Republic of)	31 December 2000	–
Ireland	7 October 1998	11 April 2002
Israel[3]	31 December 2000	–
Italy	18 July 1998	26 July 1999
Jamaica	8 September 2000	–
Jordan	7 October 1998	11 April 2002 *Dec.*
Kenya	11 August 1999	–
Kuwait	8 September 2000	–
Kyrgyzstan	8 December 1998	–
Latvia	22 April 1999	28 June 2002 *Dec.*
Lesotho	30 November 1998	6 September 2000
Liberia	17 July 1998	–
Liechtenstein	18 July 1998	2 October 2001 *Dec.*
Lithuania	10 December 1998	–
Luxembourg	13 October 1998	8 September 2000
Madagascar	18 July 1998	–
Malawi	3 March 1999	19 September 2002
Mali	17 July 1998	16 August 2000
Malta	17 July 1998	–
Marshall Islands	6 September 2000	7 December 2000
Mauritius	11 November 1998	5 March 2002
Mexico	7 September 2000	–
Monaco	18 July 1998	–
Mongolia	29 December 2000	11 April 2002
Morocco	8 September 2000	–
Mozambique	28 December 2000	–
Namibia	27 October 1998	25 June 2002 *Dec.*
Nauru	13 December 2000	12 November 2001
Netherlands[4]	18 July 1998	17 July 2001 A

[3] On 28 August 2002, the Secretary-General received from the Government of Israel the following communication: "... in connection with the Rome Statute of the International Criminal Court adopted on 17 July 1998, [...] Israel does not intend to become a party to the treaty. Accordingly, Israel has no legal obligations arising from its signature on 31 December 2000. Israel requests that its intention not to become a party, as expressed in this letter, be reflected in the depositary's status lists relating to this treaty."

[4] For the Kingdom in Europe, the Netherlands Antilles and Aruba.

State	*Signature*	*Ratification, Acceptance (A), Approval (AA), Accession (a)*
New Zealand[5]	7 October 1998	7 September 2000 *Dec.*
Niger	17 July 1998	11 April 2002
Nigeria	1 June 2000	27 September 2001
Norway	28 August 1998	16 February 2000 *Dec.*
Oman	20 December 2000	–
Panama	18 July 1998	21 March 2002
Paraguay	7 October 1998	14 May 2001
Peru	7 December 2000	10 November 2001
Philippines	28 December 2000	–
Poland	9 April 1999	12 November 2001 *Dec.*
Portugal	7 October 1998	5 February 2002 *Dec.*
Republic of Korea	8 March 2000	–
Republic of Moldova	8 September 2000	–
Romania	7 July 1999	11 April 2002 *Dec.*
Russian Federation	13 September 2000	–
Saint Lucia	27 August 1999	–
Samoa	17 July 1998	16 September 2002
San Marino	18 July 1998	13 May 1999
Sao Tome and Principe	28 December 2000	–
Senegal	18 July 1998	2 February 1999
Seychelles	28 December 2000	–
Sierra Leone	17 October 1998	15 September 2000
Slovakia	23 December 1998	11 April 2002 *Dec.*
Slovenia	7 October 1998	31 December 2001
Solomon Islands	3 December 1998	–
South Africa	17 July 1998	27 November 2000
Spain	18 July 1998	24 October 2000 *Dec.*
Sudan	8 September 2000	–
Sweden	7 October 1998	28 June 2001 *Dec.*
Switzerland	18 July 1998	12 October 2001 *Dec.*
Syrian Arab Republic	29 November 2000	–
Tajikistan	30 November 1998	5 May 2000
Thailand	2 October 2000	–
The Former Yugoslav Republic of Macedonia	7 October 1998	6 March 2002
Timor-Leste	–	6 September 2002
Trinidad and Tobago	23 March 1999	6 April 1999
Uganda	17 March 1999	14 June 2002
Ukraine	20 January 2000	–
United Arab Emirates	27 November 2000	–
United Kingdom	30 November 1998	4 October 2001 *Dec.*
United Republic of Tanzania	29 December 2000	20 August 2002
United States of America[6]	31 December 2000	–

[5] With a declaration to the effect that "consistent with the constitutional status of Tokelau and taking into account its commitment to the development of self-government through an act of self-determination under the Charter of the United Nations, this ratification shall not extend to Tokelau unless and until a Declaration to this effect is lodged by the Government of New Zealand with the depositary on the basis of appropriate consultation with that territory."

[6] In acommunication received on 6 May 2002, the Government of the United States of America informed the Secretary-General of the following:

"This is to inform you, in connection with the Rome Statute of the International Criminal Court adopted on July 17, 1998, that the United States does not intend to become a party to

State	*Signature*	*Ratification, Acceptance (A), Approval (AA), Accession (a)*
Uruguay	19 December 2000	28 June 2002 *Dec.*
Uzbekistan	29 December 2000	–
Venezuela	14 October 1998	7 June 2000
Yemen	28 December 2000	–
Yugoslavia	19 December 2000	6 September 2001
Zambia	17 July 1998	–
Zimbabwe	17 July 1998	–

RESERVATIONS AND DECLARATIONS

ANDORRA (*declarations*)
With regard to article 87, paragraph 1, of the Rome Statute of the International Criminal Court, the Principality of Andorra declares that all requests for cooperation made by the Court under part IX of the Statute must be transmitted through the diplomatic channel. With regard to article 87, paragraph 2, of the Rome Statute of the International Criminal Court, the Principality of Andorra declares that all requests for cooperation and any supporting documents that it receives from the Court must, in accordance with article 50 of the Statute establishing Arabic, Chinese, English, French, Russian and Spanish as the official languages of the Court, be drafted in French or Spanish or accompanied, where necessary, by a translation into one of these languages.

With regard to article 103, paragraph 1 (a) and (b) of the Rome Statute of the International Criminal Court, the Principality of Andorra declares that it would, if necessary, be willing to accept persons of Andorran nationality sentenced by the Court, provided that the sentence imposed by the Court was enforced in accordance with Andorran legislation on the maximum duration of sentences.

ARGENTINA (*declaration*)
With regard to article 87, paragraph 2, of the Statute, the Argentine Republic hereby declares that requests for cooperation coming from the Court, and any accompanying documentation, shall be in Spanish or shall be accompanied by a translation into Spanish.

AUSTRALIA (*declaration*)
The Government of Australia, having considered the Statute, now hereby ratifies the same, for and on behalf of Australia, with the following declaration, the terms of which have full effect in Australian law, and which is not a reservation:

Australia notes that a case will be inadmissable before the International Criminal Court (the Court) where it is being investigated or prosecuted by a State. Australia reaffirms the primacy of its criminal jurisdiction in relation to crimes within the jurisdiction of the Court. To enable Australia to exercise its jurisdiction effectively, and fully adhering to its obligations under the Statute of the Court, no person will be surrendered to the Court by Australia until it has had the full opportunity to investigate or prosecute any alleged crimes. For this purpose, the procedure under Australian law implementing the Statute of the Court provides that no person can be surrendered to the Court unless the Australian Attorney-General issues a certificate allowing surrender. Australian law also provides that no person can be arrested pursuant to an arrest warrant issued by the Court without a certificate from the Attorney-General.

---

cont.
the treaty. Accordingly, the United States has no legal obligations arising from its signature on December 31, 2000. The United States requests that its intention not to become a party, as expressed in this letter, be reflected in the depositary's status lists relating to this treaty."

Australia further declares its understanding that the offences in Articles 6, 7 and 8 will be interpreted and applied in a way that accords with the way they are implemented in Australian domestic law.

AUSTRIA (*declaration*)
Pursuant to article 87, paragraph 2 of the Rome Statute the Republic of Austria declares that requests for cooperation and any documents supporting the request shall either be in or be accompanied by a translation into the German language.

BELGIUM
Declaration concerning article 31, paragraph 1 (c)
Pursuant to article 21, paragraph 1 (b) of the Statute and having regard to the rules of international humanitarian law which may not be derogated from, the Belgian Government considers that article 31, paragraph 1 (c), of the Statute can be applied and interpreted only in conformity with those rules.

Declaration concerning article 87, paragraph 1
With reference to article 87, paragraph 1, of the Statute, the Kingdom of Belgium declares that the Ministry of Justice is the authority competent to receive requests for cooperation.

Declaration concerning article 87, paragraph 2
With reference to article 87, paragraph 2, the Kingdom of Belgium declares that requests by the Court for cooperation and any documents supporting the request shall be in an official language of the Kingdom.

BELIZE (*declaration*)
Pursuant to Article 87 (1) (a) of the Statute of the International Criminal Court, Belize declares that all requests made to it in accordance with Chapter 9 be sent through diplomatic channels.

BRAZIL (*declaration*)
.... with regard to article 87, paragraph 2 of the said Statute, the official language of the Federative Republic of Brazil is Portuguese and that all requests for cooperation and any supporting documents that it receives from the Court must be drafted in Portuguese or accompanied by a translation into Portuguese.

COLOMBIA (*declarations*)
1. None of the provisions of the Rome Statute concerning the exercise of jurisdiction by the International Criminal Court prevent the Colombian State from granting amnesties, reprieves or judicial pardons for political crimes, provided that they are granted in conformity with the principles and norms of international law accepted by Colombia,

   Colombia declares that the provisions of the Statute must be applied and interpreted ina manner consistent with the provisions of international humanitarian law and, consequently, that nothing in the Statute affects the rights and obligations embodied in the norms of international humanitarian law, especially those set forth in article 3 common to the four Geneva Conventions and in Protocols I and II Additional thereto.

   Likewise, in the event that a Colombian national has to be investigated and prosecuted by the International Criminal Court, the Rome Statute must be interpreted and applied, where appropriate, in accordance with the principles and norms of international humanitarian law and international human rights law.
2. With respect to Articles 61(2)(b) and 67(1)(d), Colombia declares that it will always be in the interests of justice that Colombian nationals be fully guaranteed the right of defence, especially the right to be assisted by counsel during the phases of investigation and prosecution by the International Criminal Court.
3. Concerning article 3, Colombia declares that the use of the word 'otherwise' with respect to the determination of the State's ability to investigate or prosecute a case

refers to the obvious absence of objective conditions necessary to conduct the trial.

4. Bearing in mind that the scope of the Rome Statute is limited exclusively to the exercise of complementary jurisdiction by the International Criminal Court and to the cooperation of national authorities with it, Colombia declares that none of the provisions of the Rome statute alters the domestic law applied by the Colombian judicial authorities in exercise of their domestic jurisdiction within the territory of the Republic of Colombia.
5. Availing itself of the option provided in article 124 of the Statute and subject to the conditions established therein, the Government of Colombia declares that it does not accept the jurisdiction of the Court with respect to the category of crimes referred to in article 8 when a crime is alleged to have been committed by Colombian nationals or on Colombian territory.
6. In accordance with article 87(1)(a) and the first paragraph of article 87(2), the Government of Colombia declares that requests for cooperation or assistance shall be transmitted through the diplomatic channel and shall either be in or be accompanied by a translation into the Spanish language.

CYPRUS (*declaration*)

1. Pursuant to article 87 (1) of the Rome Statute of the International [Criminal] Court, the Republic of Cyprus declares that requests from the Court may also be transmitted directly to the Ministry of Justice and Public Order.
2. Pursuant to article 87 (2) of the Rome Statute of the International Criminal Court, the Republic of Cyprus declares that requests from the Court for cooperation and any documents supporting them shall be transmitted also in English, which is one of the working languages of the Court.

DEMOCRATIC REPUBLIC OF THE CONGO (*declaration*)

Pursuant to article 87, paragraph 1 (a) of the Rome Statute of the International Criminal Court, requests for cooperation issued by the Court shall be transmitted to the Government Procurator's Office of the Democratic Republic of the Congo.

For any request for cooperation within the meaning of article 87, paragraph 1 (a) of the Statute, French shall be the official language.

DENMARK (*declarations*)

Pursuant to article 87 (1) of the Statute, Denmark declares that requests from the Court shall be transmitted through the diplomatic channel or directly to the Ministry of Justice, which is the authority competent to receive such requests.

Pursuant to article 87 (2) of the Statute, Denmark declares that requests from the Court for cooperation and any documents supporting such requests shall be submitted either in Danish which is the official language of Denmark or in English, which is one of the working languages of the Court.

EGYPT (*declarations upon signature*)

1. Pursuant to article 87, paragraphs 1 and 2, the Arab Republic of Egypt declares that the Ministry of Justice shall be the party responsible for dealing with requests for cooperation with the Court. Such requests shall be transmitted through the diplomatic channel. Requests for cooperation and any documents supporting the request shall be in the Arabic language, being the official language of the State, and shall be accompanied by a translation into English being one of the working languages of the Court.
2. The Arab Republic of Egypt affirms the importance of the Statute being interpreted and applied in conformity with the general principles and fundamental rights which are universally recognized and accepted by the whole international community and with the principles, purposes and provisions of the Charter of the United Nations and the general principles and rules of international law and international humanitarian law. It further declares that it shall interpret and apply the references that appear in

the Statute of the Court to the two terms fundamental rights and international standards on the understanding that such references are to the fundamental rights and internationally recognized norms and standards which are accepted by the international community as a whole.

3. The Arab Republic of Egypt declares that its understanding of the conditions, measures and rules which appear in the introductory paragraph of article 7 of the Statute of the Court is that they shall apply to all the acts specified in that article.
4. The Arab Republic of Egypt declares that its understanding of article 8 of the Statute of the Court shall be as follows:
   (a) The provisions of the Statute with regard to the war crimes referred to in article 8 in general and article 8, paragraph 2 (b) in particular shall apply irrespective of the means by which they were perpetrated or the type of weapon used, including nuclear weapons, which are indiscriminate in nature and cause unnecessary damage, in contravention of international humanitarian law.
   (b) The military objectives referred to in article 8, paragraph 2 (b) of the Statute must be defined in the light of the principles, rules and provisions of international humanitarian law. Civilian objects must be defined and dealt with in accordance with the provisions of the Protocol Additional to the Geneva Conventions of 12 August 1949 (Protocol I) and, in particular, article 52 thereof. In case of doubt, the object shall be considered to be civilian.
   (c) The Arab Republic of Egypt affirms that the term "the concrete and direct overall military advantage anticipated" used in article 8, paragraph 2 (b) (iv), must be interpreted in the light of the relevant provisions of the Protocol Additional to the Geneva Conventions of 12 August 1949 (Protocol I). The term must also be interpreted as referring to the advantage anticipated by the perpetrator at the time when the crime was committed. No justification may be adduced for the nature of any crime which may cause incidental damage in violation of the law applicable in armed conflicts. The overall military advantage must not be used as a basis on which to justify the ultimate goal of the war or any other strategic goals. The advantage anticipated must be proportionate to the damage inflicted.
   (d) Article 8, paragraph 2 (b) (xvii) and (xviii) of the Statute shall be applicable to all types of emission which are indiscriminate in their effects and the weapons used to deliver them, including emissions resulting from the use of nuclear weapons.
5. The Arab Republic of Egypt declares that the principle of the non-retroactivity of the jurisdiction of the Court, pursuant to articles 11 and 24 of the Statute, shall not invalidate the well established principle that no war crime shall be barred from prosecution due to the statute of limitations and no war criminal shall escape justice or escape prosecution in other legal jurisdictions.

ESTONIA (*declaration*)
Pursuant to Article 87, paragraph 1 of the Statute the Republic of Estonia declares that the requests from the International Crminal Court shall be transmitted either through the diplomatic channels or directly to the Public Prosecutor's Office, which is the authority to receive such requests.

Pursuant to Article 87, paragraph 2 of the Statute the Republic of Estonia declares that requests from the International Crminal Court and any documents supporting such requests shall be submitted either in Estonian which is the official language of the Republic of Estonia or in English which is one of the working languages of the International Crminal Court.

FINLAND (*declarations*)
Pursuant to article 87 (1) (a) of the Statute, the Republic of Finland declares that requests for cooperation shall be transmitted either through the diplomatic channel or directly to the Ministry of Justice, which is the authority competent to receive such requests. The Court may also, if need be, enter into direct contact with other competent authorities of Finland. In matters relating to requests for surrender the Ministry of Justice is the only competent authority.

Pursuant to article 87 (2) of the Statute, the Republic of Finland declares that requests from the Court and any documents supporting such requests shall be submitted either in Finnish or Swedish, which are the official languages of Finland, or in English which is one of the working languages of the Court.

FRANCE
I. Interpretative declarations
1. The provisions of the Statute of the International Criminal Court do not preclude France from exercising its inherent right of self-defence in conformity with Article 51 of the Charter.
2. The provisions of article 8 of the Statute, in particular paragraph 2 (b) thereof, relate solely to conventional weapons and can neither regulate nor prohibit the possible use of nuclear weapons nor impair the other rules of international law applicable to other weapons necessary to the exercise by France of its inherent right of self-defence, unless nuclear weapons or the other weapons referred to herein become subject in the future to a comprehensive ban and are specified in an annex to the Statute by means of an amendment adopted in accordance with the provisions of articles 121 and 123.
3. The Government of the French Republic considers that the term 'armed conflict' in article 8, paragraphs 2 (b) and (c), in and of itself and in its context, refers to a situation of a kind which does not include the commission of ordinary crimes, including acts of terrorism, whether collective or isolated.
4. The situation referred to in article 8, paragraph 2 (b) (xxiii), of the Statute does not preclude France from directing attacks against objectives considered as military objectives under international humanitarian law.
5. The Government of the French Republic declares that the term "military advantage" in article 8, paragraph 2 (b) (iv), refers to the advantage anticipated from the attack as a whole and not from isolated or specific elements thereof.
6. The Government of the French Republic declares that a specific area may be considered a "military objective" as referred to in article 8, paragraph 2 (b) as a whole if, by reason of its situation, nature, use, location, total or partial destruction, capture or neutralization, taking into account the circumstances of the moment, it offers a decisive military advantage.

   The Government of the French Republic considers that the provisions of article 8, paragraph 2 (b) (ii) and (v), do not refer to possible collateral damage resulting from attacks directed against military objectives.
7. The Government of the French Republic declares that the risk of damage to the natural environment as a result of the use of methods and means of warfare, as envisaged in article 8, paragraph 2 (b) (iv), must be weighed objectively on the basis of the information available at the time of its assessment.

II. Declaration pursuant to article 87, paragraph 2
Pursuant to article 87, paragraph 2, of the Statute, the French Republic declares that requests for cooperation, and any documents supporting the request, addressed to it by the Court must be in the French language.

III. Declaration under article 124
Pursuant to article 124 of the Statute of the International Criminal Court, the French Republic declares that it does not accept the jurisdiction of the Court with respect to the category of crimes referred to in article 8 when a crime is alleged to have been committed by its nationals or on its territory.

GAMBIA (*declaration*)
Pursuant to article 87 (1) of the Statute the Republic of the Gambia declares that requests from the Court shall be transmitted through the diplomatic channel or directly to the Attorney-General's Chambers and the Department of State for Justice, which is the authority competent to receive such request.

Pursuant to article 87 (2) of the Statute the Republic of the Gambia declares that requests from the Court and any document supporting such requests shall be in English which is one of the working languages of the Court and the official language of the Republic of the Gambia.

GERMANY (*declarations*)
The Federal Republic of Germany declares, pursuant to article 87 (1) of the Rome Statute, that requests from the Court can also be transmitted directly to the Federal Ministry of Justice or an agency designated by the Federal Ministry of Justice in an individual case. Requests to the Court can be transmitted directly from the Federal Ministry of Justice or, with the Ministry's agreement, from another competent agency to the Court.

The Federal Republic of Germany further declares, pursuant to article 87 (2) of the Rome Statute, that requests for cooperation to Germany and any documents supporting the request must be accompanied by a translation into German.

HUNGARY (*declaration*)
The Government of the Republic of Hungary makes the following declaration in relation to Article 87 of the Statute of the International Criminal Court (Rome 17 July 1998):

Requests of the Court for cooperation shall be transmitted to the Government of the Republic of Hungary through diplomatic channel. These requests for cooperation and any documents supporting the request shall be made in English.

ISRAEL (*declaration upon signature*)
Being an active consistent supporter of the concept of an International Criminal Court, and its realization in the form of the Rome Statute, the Government of the State of Israel is proud to thus express its acknowledgement of the importance, and indeed indispensability, of an effective court for the enforcement of the rule of law and the prevention of impunity.

As one of the originators of the concept of an International Criminal Court, Israel, through its prominent lawyers and statesmen, has, since the early 1950's, actively participated in all stages of the formation of such a court. Its representatives, carrying in both heart and mind collective, and sometimes personal, memories of the holocaust – the greatest and most heinous crime to have been committed in the history of mankind – enthusiastically, with a sense of acute sincerity and seriousness, contributed to all stages of the preparation of the Statute. Responsibly, possessing the same sense of mission, they currently support the work of the ICC Preparatory Commission.

At the 1998 Rome Conference, Israel expressed its deep disappointment and regret at the insertion into the Statute of formulations tailored to meet the political agenda of certain states. Israel warned that such an unfortunate practice might reflect on the intent to abuse the Statute as a political tool. Today, in the same spirit, the Government of the State of Israel signs the Statute while rejecting any attempt to interpret provisions thereof in a politically motivated manner against Israel and its citizens. The Government of Israel hopes that Israel's expressions of concern of any such attempt would be recorded in history as a warning against the risk of politicization, that might undermine the objectives of what is intended to become a central impartial body, benefiting mankind as a whole.

Nevertheless, as a democratic society, Israel has been conducting ongoing political, public and academic debates concerning the ICC and its significance in the context of international law and the international community. The Court's essentiality – as a vital means of ensuring that criminals who commit genuinely heinous crimes will be duly brought to justice, while other potential offenders of the fundamental principles of humanity and the dictates of public conscience will be properly deterred – has never ceased to guide us. Israel's signature of the Rome Statute will, therefore, enable it to morally identify with this basic idea, underlying the establishment of the Court.

Today, [the Government of Israel is] honoured to express [its] sincere hopes that the Court, guided by the cardinal judicial principles of objectivity and universality, will indeed serve its noble and meritorious objectives.

JORDAN (*interpretative declaration*)
The Government of the Hashemite Kingdom of Jordan herby declares that nothing under its national law including the Constitution, is inconsistent with the Rome Statute of the International Criminal Court. As such, it interprets such national law as giving effect to the full application of the Rome Statute and the exercise of relevant jurisdiction thereunder.

LATVIA (*declaration*)
Pursuant to article 87, paragraph 2 of the Rome Statute of the International Criminal Court the Republic of Latvia declares that requests for cooperation and any documents supporting the request shall either be in or be accompanied by a translation into the Latvian language.

LIECHTENSTEIN
Declaration pursuant to article 87, paragraph 1 (a) of the Statute, concerning the central authority
Requests of the Court made pursuant to article 87, paragraph 1 (a) of the Statute, shall be transmitted to the central authority for cooperation with the International Criminal Court, namely the Ministry of Justice of the Government of the Principality of Liechtenstein.

Declaration pursuant to article 87, paragraph 1 (a) of the Statute, concerning direct service of document
Pursuant to article 87, paragraph 1 (a) of the Statute, the Court may serve in decisions and other records or documents upon recipients in the Principality of Liechtenstein directly by mail. A summons to appear before the Court as a witness or expert shall be accompanied by the Rule of Procedure and Evidence of the Court on self-incrimination; this Rule shall be given to the person concerned in a language that the person understands.

Declaration pursuant to article 87, paragraph 2 of the Statute, concerning the official language
The official language in the sense of article 87, paragraph 2 of the Statute is German. Requests and supporting documentation shall be submitted in the official language of the Principality of Liechtenstein, German, or translated into German.

Declaration pursuant to article 103, paragraph 1 of the Statute
Pursuant to article 103, paragraph 1 of the Statute, the Principality of Liechtenstein declares its willingness to accept persons sentenced to imprisonment by the Court, for purposes of execution of the sentence, if the persons are Liechtenstein citizens or if the person's usual residence is the Principality of Liechtenstein.

NAMIBIA (*declaration*)
.... with reference to Article 87 paragraph 2 of the Rome Statute of the International Criminal Court [the Republic of Namibia] declares that all requests for cooperation and any documents supporting the request, mustl either be in, or be accompanied by a translation into the English language.

NEW ZEALAND (*declaration*)
1. The Government of New Zealand notes that the majority of the war crimes specified in article 8 of the Rome Statute, in particular those in article 8 (2) (b) (i)-(v) and 8 (2) (e) (i)-(iv) (which relate to various kinds of attacks on civilian targets), make no reference to the type of the weapons employed to commit the particular crime. The Government of New Zealand recalls that the fundamental principle that underpins international humanitarian law is to mitigate and circumscribe the cruelty of war for humanitarian reasons and that, rather than being limited to weaponry of an earlier time, this branch of law has evolved, and continues to evolve, to meet contemporary circumstances. Accordingly, it is the view of the Government of New Zealand that it would be inconsistent with principles of international humanitarian law to purport to limit the scope of article 8, in particular article 8 (2) (b), to events that involve conventional weapons only.

2. The Government of New Zealand finds support for its view in the Advisory Opinion of the International Court of Justice on the Legality of the Threat or Use of Nuclear Weapons (1996) and draws attention to paragraph 86, in particular, where the Court stated that the conclusion that humanitarian law did not apply to such weapons "would be incompatible with the intrinsically humanitarian character of the legal principles in question which permeates the entire law of armed conflict and applies to all forms of warfare and to all kinds of weapons, those of the past, those of the present and those of the future."
3. The Government of New Zealand further notes that international humanitarian law applies equally to aggressor and defender states and its application in a particular context is not dependent on a determination of whether or not a state is acting in self-defence. In this respect it refers to paragraphs 40-42 of the Advisory Opinion in the Nuclear Weapons Case."

NORWAY (*declarations*)
1. With reference to Article 87, paragraph 1 (a), the Kingdom of Norway hereby declares that the Royal Ministry of Justice is designated as the channel for the transmission of requests from the Court.
2. With reference to Article 87, paragraph 2, the Kingdom of Norway hereby declares that requests from the Court and any documents supporting the request shall be submitted in English, which is one of the working languages of the Court.

POLAND (*declaration*)
In accordance with Article 87 paragraph 2 of the Statute the Republic of Poland declares that applications on cooperation submitted by the Court and documents added to them shall be made in the Polish language,

PORTUGAL (*declaration*)
The Portuguese Republic declares the intention to exercise its jurisdictional powers over every person found in the Portuguese territory, that is being prosecuted for the crimes set forth in article 5, paragraph 1 of the Rome Statute of the International Criminal Court, within the respect for the Portuguese criminal legislation, ...

With regard to article 87, paragraph 2 of the Rome Statute of the International Criminal Court, the Portuguese Republic declares that all requests for cooperation and any supporting documents that it receives from the Court must be drafted in Portuguese or accompanied by a translation into Portuguese.

ROMANIA (*declarations*)
1. With reference to article 87 paragraph 1 (a) of the Statute, the Ministry of Justice is the Romanian authority competent to receive the requets of the International Criminal Court, to send them immediately for resolution to the Romanian judicial competent bodies, and to communicate to the International Criminal Court the relevant documents.
2. With reference to article 87 paragraph 2 of the Statute, the requests of the International Criminal Court and the relevant documents shall be transmitted in the English language, or accompanied by official translations in this language.

SLOVAKIA (*declarations*)
Pursuant to Article 87, paragraph 2 of the Statute the Slovak Republic declares that requests from the Court for cooperation and any documents supporting such requests shall be submitted in English which is one of the working languages of the Court along with the translation into Slovak which is the official language of the Slovak Republic.
Pursuant to Article 103, paragraph 1 (b) of the Statute the Slovak Republic declares that it would accept, if necessary, persons sentenced by the Court, if the persons are citizens of the Slovak Republic or have a permanent residence in its territory, for the purposes of execution of the sentence of imprisonment and at the same time it will apply the principle of conversion of sentence imposed by the Court.

SPAIN

Declarations under article 87, paragraphs 1 and 2

In relation to article 87, paragraph 1, of the Statute, the Kingdom of Spain declares that, without prejudice to the fields of competence of the Ministry of Foreign Affairs, the Ministry of Justice shall be the competent authority to transmit requests for cooperation made by the Court or addressed to the Court.

In relation to article 87, paragraph 2, of the Statute, the Kingdom of Spain declares that requests for cooperation addressed to it by the Court and any supporting documents must be in Spanish or accompanied by a translation into Spanish.

Declaration under article 103, paragraph 1 (b)

Spain declares its willingness to accept at the appropriate time, persons sentenced by the International Criminal Court, provided that the duration of the sentence does not exceed the maximum stipulated for any crime under Spanish law.

SWEDEN (*declaration*)

In connection with the deposit of its instrument of ratification of the Rome Statute of the International Criminal Court and, with regard to the war crimes specified in Article 8 of the Statute which relate to the methods of warfare, the Government of the Kingdom of Sweden would like to recall the Advisory Opinion given by the International Court of Justice on 8 July 1996 on the Legality of the Threat or Use of Nuclear Weapons, and in particular paragraphs 85 to 87 thereof, in which the Court finds that there can be no doubt as to the applicability of humanitarian law to nuclear weapons.

With regard to Article 87, paragraph 1, of the Rome Statute of the International Criminal Court, the Kingdom of Sweden declares that all requests for cooperation made by the Court under part IX of the Statute must be transmitted through the Swedish Ministry of Justice.

With regard to Article 87, paragraph 2, of the Rome Statute of the International Criminal Court, the Kingdom of Sweden declares that all requests for cooperation and any supporting documents that it receives from the Court must be drafted in English or Swedish, or accompanied, where necessary, by a translation into one of these languages.

SWITZERLAND (*declaration*)

Requests for cooperation made by the Court under article 87, paragraph 1 (a), of the Statute shall be transmitted to the Central Office for Cooperation with the International Criminal Court of the Federal Bureau of Justice.

The official languages within the meaning of article 87, paragraph 2, of the Statute, shall be French, German and Italian.

The Court may serve notice of its decisions and other procedural steps or documents on the persons to whom such decisions or documents are addressed in Switzerland directly through the mail. Any summons to appear in Court as a witness or expert shall be accompanied by the provision of the Rules of Procedure and Evidence of the Court concerning self-incrimination; that provision shall be provided to the person concerned in a language which he or she is able to understand.

In accordance with article 103, paragraph 1, of the Statute, Switzerland declares that it is prepared to be responsible for enforcement of sentences of imprisonment handed down by the Court against Swiss nationals or persons habitually resident in Switzerland.

UNITED KINGDOM OF GREAT BRITAIN AND NORTHERN IRELAND (*declaration*)

The United Kingdom understands the term "the established framework of international law", used in article 8 (2) (b) and (e), to include customary international law as established by State practice and opinio iuris. In that context the United Kingdom confirms and draws to the attention of the Court its views as expressed, inter alia, in its statements made on ratification of relevant instruments of international law, including the Protocol Additional to the Geneva Conventions of 12th August 1949, and relating to the Protection of Victims of International Armed Conflicts (Protocol I) of 8th June 1997.

The United Kingdom declares, pursuant to article 87 (2) of the Statute, that requests for co-operation, and any documents supporting the request, must be in the English language.

URUGUAY (*interpretative declaration*)
As a State party to the Rome Statute, the Eastern Republic of Uruguay shall ensure its application to the full extent of the powers of the State insofar as it is competent in that respectand in strict accordance with the Constitutional provisions of the Republic.

Pursuant to the provisions of part 9 of the Statute entitled "International cooperation and judicial assistance", thr Executive shall within six months refer to the Legislature a bill establishing the procedures for ensuring the application of the Statute.

Declaration of 19 July 2002
... in accordance with article 87, paragraph 2, of the Statute of the International Criminal Court, the Government of the Eastern Republic of Uruguay wishes to inform the Secretary-General that requests for cooperation and any documents supporting such requests should be drawn up in Spanish or be accompanied by a translation into Spanish.

COMMUNICATIONS

UNITED STATES OF AMERICA (*communication of 5 November 1998 to the Secretary General*)
On 6 November 1998, the Secretary-General received from the Government of the United States of America the following communication dated 5 November 1998, relating to the proposed corrections to the Statute circulated on 25 September 1998
The United States wishes to note a number of concerns and objections regarding the procedure proposed for the correction of the six authentic texts and certified true copies:

First, the United States wishes to draw attention to the fact that, in addition to the corrections which the Secretary-General now proposes, other changes had already been made to the text which was actually adopted by the Conference, without any notice or procedure. The text before the Conference was contained in A/CONF.183/C.1/L.76 and Adds. 1-13. The text which was issued as a final document, A/CONF.183/9, is not the same text. Apparently, it was this latter text which was presented for signature on July 18, even though it differed in a number of respects from the text that was adopted only hours before. At least three of these changes are arguably substantive, including the changes made to Article 12, paragraph 2 (b), the change made to Article 93, paragraph 5, and the change made to Article 124. Of these three changes, the Secretary-General now proposes to "re-correct" only Article 124, so that it returns to the original text, but the other changes remain. The United States remains concerned, therefore, that the corrections process should have been based on the text that was actually adopted by the Conference.

Second, the United States notes that the Secretary-General's communication suggests that it is "established depository practice" that only signatory States or contracting States may object to a proposed correction. The United States does not seek to object to any of the proposed corrections, or to the additional corrections that were made earlier and without formal notice, although this should not be taken as an endorsement of the merits of any of the corrections proposed. The United States does note, however, that insofar as arguably substantive changes have been made to the original text without any notice or procedure, as noted above in relation to Articles 12 and 93, if any question of interpretation should subsequently arise it should be resolved consistent with A/CONF.183/C.1/L.76, the text that was actually adopted.

More fundamentally, however, as a matter of general principle and for future reference, the United States objects to any correction procedure, immediately following a diplomatic conference, whereby the views of the vast majority of the Conference participants on the text which they have only just adopted would not be taken into account. The United States does not agree that the course followed by the Secretary-General in July represents "established depository practice" for the type of circumstances presented here. To the extent that such a procedure has previously been established, it must necessarily rest on the assumption that the Conference itself had an adequate opportunity, in the first instance, to ensure the adoption of a technically correct text. Under the circumstances which have prevailed in some recent conferences, and which will likely recur, in which critical portions of the text are resolved at very late stages and there is no opportunity for the usual technical review by the Drafting Committee, the kind of corrections process which is contemplated here must be open to all.

In accordance with Article 77, paragraph 1 (e) of the 1969 Vienna Convention on the Law of Treaties, the United States requests that this note be communicated to all States which are entitled to become parties to the Convention.

* * *

See also Nos. 49–52 and 56

XIII

NEUTRALITY

No. 112

CONVENTION (V) RESPECTING THE RIGHTS AND DUTIES OF NEUTRAL POWERS AND PERSONS IN CASE OF WAR ON LAND

Signed at The Hague, 18 October 1907

INTRODUCTORY NOTE. The law of neutrality was mainly developed during the 19th century. The most important factors in its development were the two "Armed Neutralities" of 1780 and 1800 (treaties between neutral states, concluded on the initiative of Russia, to protect neutral rights in naval warfare, if necessary by armed force), the attitude of the United States towards neutrality, the permanent neutrality of Switzerland and Belgium and the Declaration of Paris of 1856 (*No. 75*). At the Second Hague Peace Conference the subject seemed to be ready for codification. In spite of being to a large extent declaratory of existing international law, the two Conventions on neutrality concluded at The Hague were not ratified by Great Britain, Italy and some other states. Apart from the two Conventions (*Nos. 112 and 113* of this volume) other Conventions concluded in 1907 are also important for the law of neutrality, particularly Convention (VII) relating to the Conversion of Merchant Ships into War-Ships (*No. 77*), Convention (XI) relative to Certain Restrictions with regard to the Exercise of the Right of Capture in Naval War (*No. 80*) and Convention (XII) relative to the Creation of an International Prize Court (*No. 81*). Furthermore, the unratified Declaration of London of 1909 contained the most important rules concerning neutrality in naval war (*No. 83*). As a consequence of the two World Wars, the prohibition of the resort to war and the systems of collective security established by the League of Nations and the United Nations, the traditional law of neutrality has lost much of its former importance.

ENTRY INTO FORCE: 26 January 1910.

AUTHENTIC TEXT: French. The English translation below is reprinted from Scott, *Hague Conventions*, pp. 133–140. It reproduces the translation of the United States Department of State.

The marginal titles added to the Convention have no official character.

TEXT PUBLISHED IN: *Conférence internationale de la Paix 1907*, pp. 638–643 (French); *Les deux Conférences de la Paix*, pp. 117–122 (French); Martens, *NRGT*, 3ème série, Vol. III, pp. 504–532 (French, German); Scott, *Hague Conventions*, pp. 133–140 (Engl.); Scott, *Les Conventions de La Haye*, pp. 133–140 (French); Scott, *Les Conférences de La Haye*, pp. 67–70 (French); Deltenre, pp. 282–295 (Engl., French, German, Dutch); *Fontes Historiae Juris Gentium*, Vol. III/1, pp. 615–620 (German, Engl. French – extract); *International Red Cross Handbook*, 1983, pp. 334–335 (Engl. – extract); *Manuel de la Croix-Rouge internationale*, 1983, pp. 346–347 (French – extract); *Manuel de la Cruz Roja internacional*, 1983, pp. 338–339 (Span. – extract); *Handbook of the International Movement 1994*, pp. 310–311 (Engl.– extract); *Manuel du Mouvement international 1994*, pp. 322–323 (French – extract); *Manual del Movimiento internacional 1994*, pp. 314–315 (Span.– extract); *BFSP*, Vol. 100, 1906–1907, pp. 359–364 (French); *CTS*, Vol. 205, pp. 299–304 (French); Higgins, pp. 281–289 (Engl., French); Wilson-Tucker, pp. LXVIII–LXXI (Engl.); *US Statutes at Large*, Vol. 36, pp. 2310–2331 (Engl., French); *AJIL*, Vol. 2, 1908, Suppl., pp. 117–127 (Engl., French); Malloy, Vol. II, pp. 2290–2303 (Engl.); Bevans, Vol. I, pp. 654–668 (Engl.); Friedman, pp. 324–331 (Engl.); Roberts and Guelff, pp. 85–94 (Engl.); *Droit des conflits armés*, pp. 1354–1363 (French); *Mezhdunarodnoe pravo*, Vol. III, pp. 266-270 (Russ.); ICRC website: www.icrc.org/ihl.nsf (Engl., French, Span.).

TABLE OF CONTENTS

* * *

[List of contracting parties]

With a view to laying down more clearly the rights and duties of neutral Powers in case of war on land and regulating the position of the belligerents who have taken refuge in neutral territory;

Being likewise desirous of defining the meaning of the term "neutral," pending the possibility of settling, in its entirety, the position of neutral individuals in their relations with the belligerents;

Have resolved to conclude a Convention to this effect, and have, in consequence, appointed the following as their plenipotentiaries:

[Here follow the names of Plenipotentiaries]

Who, after having deposited their full powers, found in good and due form, have agreed upon the following provisions:

Chapter I. The Rights and Duties of Neutral Powers

Article 1. The territory of neutral Powers is inviolable.

Inviolability of territory

Art. 2. Belligerents are forbidden to move troops or convoys of either munitions of war or supplies across the territory of a neutral Power.

Passage of troups or convoys

Art. 3. Belligerents are likewise forbidden to:
(a) Erect on the territory of a neutral Power a wireless telegraphy station or other apparatus for the purpose of communicating with belligerent forces on land or sea;
(b) Use any installation of this kind established by them before the war on the territory of a neutral Power for purely military purposes, and which has not been opened for the service of public messages.

Establishment of wireless telegraph stations

Art. 4. Corps of combatants cannot be formed nor recruiting agencies opened on the territory of a neutral Power to assist the belligerents.

Recruiting of combatants

Art. 5. A neutral Power must not allow any of the acts referred to in Articles 2 to 4 to occur on its territory. It is not called upon to punish acts in violation of its neutrality unless the said acts have been committed on its own territory.

Prevention by neutrals

Art. 6. The responsibility of a neutral Power is not engaged by the fact of persons crossing the frontier separately to offer their services to one of the belligerents.

Crossing frontier to enlist

Art. 7. A neutral Power is not called upon to prevent the export or transport, on behalf of one or other of the belligerents, of arms, munitions of war, or, in general, of anything which can be of use to an army or a fleet.

Shipment of arms

Art. 8. A neutral Power is not called upon to forbid or restrict the use on behalf of the belligerents of telegraph or telephone cables or of wireless telegraphy apparatus belonging to it or to companies or private individuals.

Use of telegraph

Art. 9. Every measure of restriction or prohibition taken by a neutral Power in regard to the matters referred to in Articles 7 and 8 must be impartially applied by it to both belligerents. A neutral Power must see to the same obligation being observed by companies or private individuals owning telegraph or telephone cables or wireless telegraphy apparatus.

Impartial treatment of belligerents

Art. 10. The fact of a neutral Power resisting, even by force, attempts to violate its neutrality cannot be regarded as a hostile act.

Resisting violation of neutrality

Chapter II. Belligerents Interned and Wounded Tended in Neutral Territory

Detention

Art. 11.[1] A neutral Power which receives on its territory troops belonging to the belligerent armies shall intern them, as far as possible, at a distance from the theatre of war.

It may keep them in camps and even confine them in fortresses or in places set apart for this purpose.

It shall decide whether officers can be left at liberty on giving their parole not to leave the neutral territory without permission.

Supplies to the interned

Art. 12.[1] In the absence of a special convention to the contrary, the neutral Power shall supply the interned with the food, clothing, and relief required by humanity.

At the conclusion of peace the expenses caused by the internment shall be made good.

Escaped prisoners of war

Art. 13. A neutral Power which receives escaped prisoners of war shall leave them at liberty. If it allows them to remain in its territory it may assign them a place of residence.

The same rule applies to prisoners of war brought by troops taking refuge in the territory of a neutral Power.

Care of sick and wounded

Art. 14.[1] A neutral Power may authorize the passage over its territory of the sick and wounded belonging to the belligerent armies, on condition that the trains bringing them shall carry neither personnel nor war material. In such a case, the neutral Power is bound to take whatever measures of safety and control are necessary for the purpose.

The sick or wounded brought under the these conditions into neutral territory by one of the belligerents, and belonging to the hostile party, must be guarded by the neutral Power so as to ensure their not taking part again in the military operations. The same duty shall devolve on the neutral State with regard to wounded or sick of the other army who may be committed to its care.

Application of Geneva Convention

Art. 15.[1] The Geneva Convention applies to sick and wounded interned in neutral territory.

Chapter III. Neutral Persons

Definition

Art. 16.[2] The nationals of a State which is not taking part in the war are considered as neutrals.

---

1 Articles 11, 12, 14 and 15 are identical in the original French with Articles 57, 58, 59 and 60 respectively of the 1899 Convention (II) respecting the laws and customs of war on land (*No. 7* above), except for the substitution of "Power" for "State".

2 For reservation in respect of Articles 16, 17 and 18 by Great Britain, see p. 1406.

Art. 17.[3] A neutral cannot avail himself of his neutrality

Acts prohibited

(a) If he commits hostile acts against a belligerent;

(b) If he commits acts in favor of a belligerent, particularly if he voluntarily enlists in the ranks of the armed force of one of the parties.

In such a case, the neutral shall not be more severly treated by the belligerent as against whom he has abandoned his neutrality than a national of the other belligerent State could be for the same act.

Art. 18.[3] The following acts shall not be considered as committed in favour of one belligerent in the sense of Article 17, letter (b):

Acts not prohibited

(a) Supplies furnished or loans made to one of the belligerents, provided that the person who furnishes the supplies or who makes the loans lives neither in the territory of the other party nor in the territory occupied by him, and that the supplies do not come from these territories;

(b) Services rendered in matters of police or civil administration.

Chapter IV. Railway Material

Art. 19.[4] Railway material coming from the territory of neutral Powers, whether it be the property of the said Powers or of companies or private persons, and recognizable as such, shall not be requisitioned or utilized by a belligerent except where and to the extent that it is absolutely necessary. It shall be sent back as soon possible to the country of origin.

Use by belligerents and neutrals

A neutral Power may likewise, in case of necessity, retain and utilize to an equal extent material coming from the territory of the belligerent Power.

Compensation shall be paid by one Party or the other in proportion to the material used, and to the period of usage.

Chapter V. Final Provisions

Art. 20. The provisions of the present Convention do not apply except between Contracting Powers and then only if all the belligerents are Parties to the Convention.

Powers bound

Art. 21. The present Convention shall be ratified as soon as possible.

Ratification

The ratifications shall be deposited at The Hague.

The first deposit of ratifications shall be recorded in a *procès-verbal* signed by the representatives of the Powers which take part therein and by the Netherlands Minister for Foreign Affairs.

The subsequent deposits of ratifications shall be made by means of a written notification, addressed to the Netherlands Government and accompanied by the instrument of ratification.

3 For reservation in respect of Articles 16, 17 and 18 by Great Britain, see p. 1406.

4 For reservation in respect of this article by Argentina, see p. 1406.

A duly certified copy of the *procès-verbal* relative to the first deposit of ratifications, of the notifications mentioned in the preceding paragraph, and of the instruments of ratification shall be immediately sent by the Netherlands Government, through the diplomatic channel, to the Powers invited to the Second Peace Conference as well as to the other Powers which have adhered to the Convention. In the cases contemplated in the preceding paragraph, the said Government shall at the same time inform them of the date on which it received the notification.

Adhesion

Art. 22. Non-Signatory Powers may adhere to the present Convention.

The Power which desires to adhere notifies its intention in writing to the Netherlands Government, forwarding to it the act of adhesion, which shall be deposited in the archives of the said Government.

This Government shall immediately forward to all the other Powers a duly certified copy of the notification as well as of the act of adhesion, mentioning the date on which it received the notification.

Entry into force

Art. 23. The present Convention shall come into force, in the case of the Powers which were a Party to the first deposit of ratifications, sixty days after the date of the *procès-verbal* of this deposit, and, in the case of the Powers which ratify subsequently or which adhere, sixty days after the notification of their ratification or of their adhesion has been received by the Netherlands Government.

Denunciation

Art. 24. In the event of one of the Contracting Powers wishing to denounce the present Convention, the denunciation shall be notified in writing to the Netherlands Government, which shall immediately communicate a duly certified copy of the notification to all the other Powers, informing them at the same time of the date on which it was received.

The denunciation shall only have effect in regard to the notifying Power, and one year after the notification has reached the Netherlands Government.

Register of ratification

Art. 25. A register kept by the Netherlands Ministry of Foreign Affairs shall give the date of the deposit of ratifications made in virtue of Article 21, paragraphs 3 and 4, as well as the date on which the notifications of adhesion (Article 22, paragraph 2) or of denunciation (Article 24, paragraph 1) have been received.

Each Contracting Power is entitled to have access to this register and to be supplied with duly certified extracts from it.

In faith whereof the Plenipotentiaries have appended their signatures to the present Convention.

Done at The Hague, 18 October 1907, in a single copy, which shall remain deposited in the archives of the Netherlands Government and duly certified copies of which shall be sent, through the diplomatic channel, to the Powers which have been invited to the Second Peace Conference.

[Here follow signatures]

SIGNATURES, RATIFICATIONS AND ACCESSIONS[1]

State	*Signature*	*Ratification, Accession*
Argentina	18 October 1907 *Res.*	–
Austria-Hungary	18 October 1907	27 November 1909
Belgium	18 October 1907	8 August 1910
Bolivia	18 October 1907	27 November 1909
Brazil	18 October 1907	5 January 1914
Bulgaria	18 October 1907	–
Chile	18 October 1907	–
China	–	15 January 1910
Colombia	18 October 1907	–
Cuba	18 October 1907	22 February 1912
Denmark	18 October 1907	27 November 1909
Dominican Republic	18 October 1907	–
Ecuador	18 October 1907	–
El Salvador	18 October 1907	27 November 1909
Ethiopia	–	5 August 1935
Finland	–	30 December 1918
France	18 October 1907	7 October 1910
Germany[2]	18 October 1907	27 November 1909
Great Britain	18 October 1907 *Res.*	–
Greece	18 October 1907	–
Guatemala	18 October 1907	15 March 1911
Haiti	18 October 1907	2 February 1910
Italy	18 October 1907	–
Japan	18 October 1907	13 December 1911
Liberia	–	4 February 1914
Luxemburg	18 October 1907	5 September 1912
Mexico	18 October 1907	27 November 1909
Montenegro	18 October 1907	–
Netherlands	18 October 1907	27 November 1909
Nicaragua	–	16 December 1909
Norway	18 October 1907	19 September 1910
Panama	18 October 1907	11 September 1911
Paraguay	18 October 1907	–

[1] Based on a communication received from the Ministry of Foreign Affairs of the Netherlands of 12 December 2001. See also ICRC website.

[2] By a letter received at the Ministry of Foreign Affairs of the Kingdom of the Netherlands on 9 February 1959, the Government of the German Democratic Republic has informed the Ministry that it reapplies the Convention. This declaration is aimless and only of historical importance after the conclusion of the Treaty of 31 August 1990 (Unification Treaty) between the Federal Republic of Germany and German Democratic Republic. See note 3 of Document *No. 18*, p. 170 and note 35 of Documents *Nos. 49–52*, p. 639.

State	*Signature*	*Ratification, Accession*
Persia	18 October 1907	–
Peru	18 October 1907	–
Poland	–	9 May 1925
Portugal	18 October 1907	13 April 1911
Romania	18 October 1907	1 March 1912
Russia[3]	18 October 1907	27 November 1909
Serbia	18 October 1907	–
Siam	18 October 1907	12 March 1910
Spain	18 October 1907	18 March 1913
Sweden	18 October 1907	27 November 1909
Switzerland	18 October 1907	12 May 1910
Turkey	18 October 1907	–
United States of America	18 October 1907	27 November 1909
Uruguay	18 October 1907	–
Venezuela	18 October 1907	–

RESERVATIONS

ARGENTINA (*reservation made on signature*)
The Argentine Republic makes reservation of Article 19.

GREAT BRITAIN (*reservation made on signature*)
Under reservation of Articles 16, 17 and 18.

3 By the note of the Foreign Ministry of the USSR of 7 March 1955 "The Government of the USSR recognizes the Conventions and Declarations of The Hague of 1899 and 1907, which were ratified by Russia, to the extent that the Conventions and Declarations do not contradict the United Nations Charter and if they are not amended or replaced by ulterior international agreements to which the USSR is a Party, such as the 1925 Geneva Protocol for the Prohibition of Use of Asphyxiating, Poisonous and Other Gases and of Bacteriological Methods of Warfare and the 1949 Geneva Conventions for the Protection of Victims of War" (*Izvestiya*, 9 March 1955).

In January 1992, the Ministry of Foreign Affairs of the Russian Federation informed the heads of diplomatic missions in Moscow, that the Russian Federation continues to be a party to all conventions which are in force for the Soviet Union. The Ministry of Foreign Affairs of the Kingdom of the Netherlands considers therefore that the Russian Federation is bound by the conventions to which the Soviet Union was party (Communication of the Depositary to the Henry Dunant Institute of 6 November 1992).

On 4 June 1962, the Byelorussian Soviet Socialist Republic made a declaration similar to the one made by the USSR.

No. 113

CONVENTION (XIII) CONCERNING THE RIGHTS AND DUTIES OF NEUTRAL POWERS IN NAVAL WAR

Signed at The Hague, 18 October 1907

INTRODUCTORY NOTE. See note introducing *No. 112*.

ENTRY INTO FORCE: 26 January 1910.

AUTHENTIC TEXT: French. The English translation below is reprinted from Scott, *Hague Conventions*, pp. 209-219. It reproduces the translation of the United States Department of State.

TEXT PUBLISHED IN: *Conférence internationale de la Paix 1907*, pp. 690–686 (French); *Les deux Conférences de la Paix*, pp. 165–172 (French); Martens, *NRGT*, 3ème série, Vol. III, pp. 713–744 (French, German); Scott, *Hague Conventions*, pp. 209-219 (Engl.); Scott, *Les Conventions de La Haye*, pp. 209–219 (French); Scott, *Les Conférences de La Haye*, pp. 96–101 (French); Deltenre, pp. 398–415 (Engl., French, German, Dutch); *Fontes Historiae Juris Gentium*, Vol. III/1, pp. 626–636 (German, Engl., French – extract); *BFSP*, Vol. 100, 1906–1907, pp. 448–454 (French); *CTS*, Vol. 205, pp. 395–402 (French); Higgins, pp. 445–456, (Engl., French); Wilson-Tucker, pp. LXXX–LXXXV (Engl.); *US Statutes at Large*, Vol. 36, pp. 2415–2438 (Engl., French); *AJIL*, Vol. 2, 1908, Suppl., pp. 202–216 (Engl., French); Malloy, Vol. II, pp. 2352–2366 (Engl.); Bevans, Vol. 1, pp. 723–738 (Engl.); Friedman, pp. 385–394 (Engl.); Roberts and Guelff, pp. 127–137; Ronzitti, pp. 193–210 (Engl., French); *Droit des conflits armés*, pp. 1365–1377 (French); Genet, pp. 546–551 (French); *Mezhdunarodnoe pravo*, Vol. III, pp. 270–275 (Russ.); Korovin, p. 390 (Russ.); *Revista de Derecho Internacional y politica exterior*, Cronica, Año III, 1907, pp. 112–116 (Span.); Arellano, pp. 385–386 (Span. – extract); Briceño, pp. 224– 228 (Span. – extract); Bustamante, Vol. 2, pp. 374–385 (Span.); Ceppi, pp. 377– 382 (Span. – extract); ICRC website: www.icrc.org/ihl.nsf (Engl., French, Span.).

TABLE OF CONTENTS

* * *

[List of contracting parties]

With a view to harmonizing the divergent views which, in the event of naval war, are still held on the relations between neutral Powers and belligerent Powers, and to anticipating the difficulties to which such divergence of views might give rise;

Seeing that, even if it is not possible at present to concert measures applicable to all circumstances which may in practice occur, it is nevertheless undeniably advantageous to frame, as far as possible, rules of general application to meet the case where war has unfortunately broken out;

Seeing that, in cases not covered by the present Convention, it is expedient to take into consideration the general principles of the law of nations;

Seeing that it is desirable that the Powers should issue detailed enactments to regulate the results of the attitude of neutrality when adopted by them;

Seeing that it is, for neutral Powers, an admitted duty to apply these rules impartially to several belligerents;

Seeing that, in this category of ideas, these rules should not, in principle, be altered in the course of the war, by a neutral Power, except in a case where experience has shown the necessity for such change for the protection of the rights of that Power;

Have agreed to observe the following common rules, which cannot however modify provisions laid down in existing general treaties, and have appointed as their Plenipotentiaries, namely:

[Here follow the names of Plenipotentiaries]

Who, after having deposited their full powers, found in good and due form, have agreed upon the following provisions:

Article 1. Belligerents are bound to respect the sovereign rights of neutral Powers and to abstain, in neutral territory or neutral waters, from any act which would, if knowingly permitted by any Power, constitute a violation of neutrality.

Respect of neutral territory

Art. 2. Any act of hostility, including capture and the exercise of the right of search, committed by belligerent war-ships in the territorial waters of a neutral Power, constitutes a violation of neutrality and is strictly forbidden.

Hostile acts in neutral waters

Art. 3. When a ship has been captured in the territorial waters of a neutral Power, this Power must employ, if the prize is still within its jurisdiction, the means at its disposal to release the prize with its officers and crew, and to intern the prize crew.

Ships captured in neutral waters

If the prize is not in the jurisdiction of the neutral Power, the captor Government, on the demand of that Power, must liberate the prize with its officers and crew.[1]

Art. 4. A prize court cannot be set up by a belligerent on neutral territory or on a vessel in neutral waters.

Prize courts

Art. 5. Belligerents are forbidden to use neutral ports and waters as a base of naval operations against their adversaries, and in particular to erect wireless telegraphy stations or any apparatus for the purpose of communicating with the belligerent forces on land or sea.

Use of neutral ports

Art. 6. The supply, in any manner, directly or indirectly, by a neutral Power to a belligerent Power, of war-ships, ammunition, or war material of any kind whatever, is forbidden.

War supplies to belligerents

Art. 7. A neutral Power is not bound to prevent the export or transit, for the use of either belligerent, of arms, ammunition, or, in general, of anything which could be of use to an army or fleet.

Export of war material

Art. 8. A neutral Government is bound to employ the means at its disposal to prevent the fitting out or arming of any vessel within its jurisdiction which it has reason to believe is intended to cruise, or engage in hostile operations, against a Power with which that Government is at peace. It is also bound to display the same vigilance to prevent the departure from its jurisdiction of any vessel intended to cruise, or engage in hostile operations, which had been adapted entirely or partly within the said jurisdiction for use in war.

Arming of vessels

Art. 9. A neutral Power must apply impartially to the two belligerents the conditions, restrictions, or prohibitions made by it

Impartiality

[1] For reservations in respect of the last clause of Article 3 by the United States of America, see p. 1416.

in regard to the admission into its ports, roadsteads, or territorial waters, of belligerent war-ships or of their prizes.

Nevertheless, a neutral Power may forbid a belligerent vessel which has failed to conform to the orders and regulations made by it, or which has violated neutrality, to enter its ports or roadsteads.

Passing through neutral waters

Art. 10.[2] The neutrality of a Power is not affected by the mere passage through its territorial waters of war-ships or prizes belonging to belligerents.

Pilots

Art. 11.[3] A neutral Power may allow belligerent war-ships to employ its licensed pilots.

Temporary stay in ports

Art. 12.[4] In the absence of special provisions to the contrary in the legislation of a neutral Power, belligerent war-ships are not permitted to remain in the ports, roadsteads, or territorial waters of the said Power for more than twenty-four hours, except in the cases covered by the present Convention.

Departure of warships on outbreak of hostilities

Art. 13.[5] If a Power which has been informed of the outbreak of hostilities learns that a belligerent war-ship is in one of its ports or roadsteads, or in its territorial waters, it must notify the said ship to depart within twenty-four hours or within the time prescribed by local regulations.

Prolongation of stay

Art. 14. A belligerent war-ship may not prolong its stay in a neutral port beyond the permissible time except on account of damage or stress of weather. It must depart as soon as the cause of the delay is at an end.

The regulations as to the question of the length of time which these vessels may remain in neutral ports, roadsteads, or waters, do not apply to war-ships devoted exclusively to religious, scientific, or philanthropic purposes.[6]

Maximum of war-ships allowed in ports

Art. 15. In the absence of special provisions to the contrary in the legislation of a neutral Power, the maximum number of warships belonging to a belligerent which may be in one of the ports or roadsteads of that Power simultaneously shall be three.

Departure of war-ships of both belligerents

Art. 16. When war-ships belonging to both belligerents are present simultaneously in a neutral port or roadstead, a period of not less than twenty-four hours must elapse between the

---

2 For reservations in respect of this article by Turkey, see p. 1416.

3 For reservations in respect of this article by Germany, see p. 1416.

4 For reservations in respect of this article by the Dominican Republic, Germany, Persia and Siam, see p. 1416.

5 For reservations in respect of this article by Germany, see p. 1416.

6 For reservation in respect of Article 14, paragraph 2 by China, see p. 1416.

departure of the ship belonging to one belligerent and the departure of the ship belonging to the other.

The order of departure is determined by the order of arrival, unless the ship which arrived first is so circumstanced that an extension of its stay is permissible.

A belligerent war-ship may not leave a neutral port or roadstead until twenty-four hours after the departure of a merchant ship flying the flag of its adversary.

Art. 17. In neutral ports and roadsteads belligerent war-ships may only carry out such repairs as are absolutely necessary to render them seaworthy, and may not add in any manner whatsoever to their fighting force. The local authorities of the neutral Power shall decide what repairs are necessary, and these must be carried out with the least possible delay. Repairs permitted

Art. 18. Belligerent war-ships may not make use of neutral ports, roadsteads, or territorial waters for replenishing or increasing their supplies of war material or their armament, or for completing their crews. Use of neutral ports

Art. 19.[7] Belligerent war-ships may only revictual in neutral ports or roadsteads to bring up their supplies to the peace standard. Similarly these vessels may only ship sufficient fuel to enable them to reach the nearest port in their own country. They may, on the other hand, fill up their bunkers built to carry fuel, when in neutral countries which have adopted this method of determining the amount of fuel to be supplied. Revictualizing

If, in accordance with the law of the neutral Power, the ships are not supplied with coal within twenty-four hours of their arrival, the permissible duration of their stay is extended by twenty-four hours.

Art. 20.[8] Belligerent war-ships which have shipped fuel in a port belonging to a neutral Power may not within the succeeding three months replenish their supply in a port of the same Power. Restriction on refueling

Art. 21.[9] A prize may only be brought into a neutral port on account of unseaworthiness, stress of weather, or want of fuel or provisions. Admission of prizes

It must leave as soon as the circumstances which justified its entry are at an end. If it does not, the neutral Power must order it to leave at once; should it fail to obey, the neutral Power must employ the means at its disposal to release it with its officers and crew and to intern the prize crew.

---

7 For reservations in respect of this article by China, Great Britain, Japan, Persia and Siam, see p. 1416.

8 For reservations in respect of this article by Germany, see p. 1416.

9 For reservations in respect of this article by Persia, see p. 1416.

Release of prizes

Art. 22. A neutral Power must, similarly, release a prize brought into one of its ports under circumstances other than those referred to in Article 21.

Sequestration of prizes

Art. 23.[10] A neutral Power may allow prizes to enter its ports and roadsteads, whether under convoy or not, when they are brought there to be sequestrated pending the decision of a Prize Court. It may have the prize taken to another of its ports.

If the prize is convoyed by a war-ship, the prize crew may go on board the convoying ship.

If the prize is not under convoy, the prize crew are left at liberty.

Detention of war-ships

Art. 24. If, notwithstanding the notification of the neutral Power, a belligerent ship of war does not leave a port where it is not entitled to remain, the neutral Power is entitled to take such measures as it considers necessary to render the ship incapable of taking the sea during the war, and the commanding officer of the ship must facilitate the execution of such measures.

When a belligerent ship is detained by a neutral Power, the officers and crew are likewise detained.

The officers and crew thus detained may be left in the ship or kept either on another vessel or on land, and may be subjected to the measures of restriction which it may appear necessary to impose upon them. A sufficient number of men for looking after the vessel must, however, be always left on board.

The officers may be left at liberty on giving their word not to quit the neutral territory without permission.

Surveillance by neutral Powers

Art. 25. A neutral Power is bound to exercise such surveillance as the means at its disposal allow to prevent any violation of the provisions of the above Articles occurring in its ports or roadsteads or in its waters.

Exercise of neutral rights

Art. 26. The exercise by a neutral Power of the rights laid down in the present Convention can under no circumstances be considered as an unfriendly act by one or other belligerent who has accepted the articles relating thereto.

Promulgation of laws

Art. 27.[11] The Contracting Powers shall communicate to each other in due course all laws, proclamations, and other enactments regulating in their respective countries the status of belligerent war-ships in their ports and waters, by means of a communication addressed to the Government of the Netherlands, and forwarded immediately by that Government to the other Contracting Powers.

[10] For reservations in respect of this article by Great Britain, Japan, Siam and the United States of America, see p. 1416.

[11] For reservation in respect of this article by China, see p. 1416.

Art. 28. The provisions of the present Convention do not apply except between Contracting Powers, and then only if all the belligerents are parties to the Convention. Powers bound

Art. 29. The present Convention shall be ratified as soon as possible. Ratification

The ratifications shall be deposited at The Hague.

The first deposit of ratifications shall be recorded in a *procès-verbal* signed by the representatives of the Powers which take part therein and by the Netherlands Minister for Foreign Affairs.

The subsequent deposits of ratifications shall be made by means of a written notification addressed to the Netherlands Government and accompanied by the instrument of ratification.

A duly certified copy of the *procès-verbal* relative to the first deposit of ratifications, of the ratifications mentioned in the preceding paragraph, as well as of the instruments of ratification, shall be at once sent by the Netherlands Government, through the diplomatic channel, to the Powers invited to the Second Peace Conference, as well as to the other Powers which have adhered to the Convention. In the cases contemplated in the preceding paragraph, the said Government shall inform them at the same time of the date on which it received the notification.

Art. 30. Non-Signatory Powers may adhere to the present Convention. Adhesion

The Power which desires to adhere notifies in writing its intention to the Netherlands Government, forwarding to it the act of adhesion, which shall be deposited in the archives of the said Government.

That Government shall at once transmit to all the other Powers a duly certified copy of the notification as well as of the act of adhesion, mentioning the date on which it received the notification.

Art. 31. The present Convention shall come into force in the case of the Powers which were a party to the first deposit of the ratifications, sixty days after the date of the *procès-verbal* of that deposit, and, in the case of the Powers who ratify subsequently or who adhere, sixty days after the notification of their ratification or of their decision has been received by the Netherlands Government. Entry into force

Art. 32. In the event of one of the Contracting Powers wishing to denounce the present Convention, the denunciation shall be notified in writing to the Netherlands Government, who shall at once communicate a duly certified copy of the notification to all the other Powers, informing them of the date on which it was received. Denunciation

The denunciation shall only have effect in regard to the notifying Power, and one year after the notification has been made to the Netherlands Government.

Register

Art. 33. A register kept by the Netherlands Ministry for Foreign Affairs shall give the date of the deposit of ratifications made by Article 29, paragraphs 3 and 4, as well as the date on which the notifications of adhesion (Article 30, paragraph 2) or of denunciation (Article 32, paragraph 1) have been received.

Each Contracting Power is entitled to have access to this register and to be supplied with duly certified extracts.

In faith whereof the Plenipotentiaries have appended their signatures to the present Convention.

Done at The Hague, 18 October 1907, in a single copy, which shall remain deposited in the archives of the Netherlands Government, and duly certified copies of which shall be sent, through the diplomatic channel, to the Powers which have been invited to the Second Peace Conference.

[Here follow signatures]

SIGNATURES, RATIFICATIONS AND ACCESSIONS[1]

State	*Signature*	*Ratification, Accession*
Argentina	18 October 1907	–
Austria-Hungary	18 October 1907	27 November 1909
Belgium	18 October 1907	8 August 1910
Bolivia	18 October 1907	–
Brazil	18 October 1907	5 January 1914
Bulgaria	18 October 1907	–
Chile	18 October 1907	–
China	–	15 January 1910 *Res.*
Colombia	18 October 1907	–
Denmark	18 October 1907	27 November 1909
Dominican Republic	18 October 1907 *Res.*	–
Ecuador	18 October 1907	–
El Salvador	18 October 1907	27 November 1909
Ethiopia	–	5 August 1935
Finland[2]	–	30 December 1918

[1] Based on a communication received from the Ministry of Foreign Affairs of the Netherlands of 12 December 2001.

[2] By a letter received at the Ministry of Foreign Affairs of the Kingdom of the Netherlands on 9 February 1959, the Government of the German Democratic Republic has informed the Ministry that it reapplies the Convention. This declaration is aimless and only of historical importance after the conclusion of the Treaty of 31 August 1990 (Unification Treaty) between the Federal Republic of Germany and German Democratic Republic. See note 3 of document *No. 18*, p. 170 and note 35 of documents *Nos. 49–52*, p. 639.

State	*Signature*	*Ratification, Accession*
France	18 October 1907	7 October 1910
Germany[3]	18 October 1907 *Res.*	27 November 1909 *Res.*
Great Britain	18 October 1907 *Res.*	–
Greece	18 October 1907	–
Guatemala	18 October 1907	15 March 1911
Haiti	18 October 1907	2 February 1910
Italy	18 October 1907	–
Japan	18 October 1907 *Res.*	13 December 1911 *Res.*
Liberia		4 February 1914
Luxemburg	18 October 1907	5 September 1912
Mexico	18 October 1907	27 November 1909
Montenegro	18 October 1907	–
Netherlands	18 October 1907	27 November 1909
Nicaragua	–	16 December 1909
Norway	18 October 1907	19 September 1910
Panama	18 October 1907	11 September 1911
Paraguay	18 October 1907	–
Persia	18 October 1907 *Res.*	–
Peru	18 October 1907	–
Portugal	18 October 1907	13 April 1911
Romania	18 October 1907	1 March 1912
Russia[3]	18 October 1907	27 November 1909
Serbia	18 October 1907	–
Siam	18 October 1907 *Res.*	12 March 1910 *Res.*
Sweden	18 October 1907	27 November 1909
Switzerland	18 October 1907	12 May 1910
Turkey	18 October 1907 *Res.*	–
United States of America	–	3 December 1909 *Res.*
Uruguay	18 October 1907	–
Venezuela	18 October 1907	–

[3] By the note of the Foreign Ministry of the USSR of 7 March 1955 "The Government of the USSR recognises the Conventions and Declarations of The Hague from 1899 and 1907, which were ratified by Russia to the extent that the Conventions and Declarations do not contradict the United Nations Charter and if they are not amended or replaced by ulterior international agreements to which the USSR is a Party, such as the 1925 Geneva Protocol for the Prohibition of Use of Asphyxiating, Poisonous and Other Gases and of Bacteriological Methods of Warfare and the 1949 Geneva Conventions for the Protection of Victims of War" (*Izvestiya*, 9 March 1955).

In January 1992, the Ministry of Foreign Affairs of the Russian Federation informed the heads of diplomatic missions in Moscow, that the Russian Federation continues to be a party to all conventions which are in force for the Soviet Union. The Ministry of Foreign Affairs of the Kingdom of the Netherlands considers therefore that the Russian Federation is bound by the conventions to which the Soviet Union was party (Communication of the Depository to the Henry Dunant Institute of 6 November 1992).

On 4 June 1962, the Byelorussian Soviet Socialist Republic made a declaration similar to one made by the USSR.

RESERVATIONS

CHINA (*reservation made on accession*)
Adhesion with reservation of paragraph 2 of Article 14, paragraph 3 of Article 19 and of Article 27.

DOMINICAN REPUBLIC (*reservation made on signature*)
With reservation regarding Article 12.

GERMANY (*reservation made on signature and maintained on ratification*)
Under reservation of Articles 11, 12, 13 and 20.

GREAT BRITAIN (*reservation made on signature*)
Under reservation of Articles 19 and 23.

JAPAN (*reservation made on signature and maintained on ratification*)
With reservation of Articles 19 and 23.

PERSIA (*reservation made on signature*)
Under reservation of Articles 12, 19 and 21.

SIAM (*reservation made on signature and maintained on ratification*)
Under reservation of Articles 12, 19 and 23.

TURKEY (*reservation made on signature*)
Under reservation of the declaration concerning Article 10 contained in the *procès-verbal* of the eighth plenary session of the Conference held on 9 October 1907.

Extract from the procès-verbal
The Ottoman delegation declares that the straits of the Dardanelles and the Bosporus cannot in any case be referred to by Article 10. The Imperial Government could undertake no engagement whatever tending to limit its undoubted rights over these straits (*Actes et documents*, Vol. 1, p. 285).

UNITED STATES OF AMERICA (*reservation made on accession*)
The act of adhesion contains the following reservation:
That the United States adheres to the said Convention, subject to the reservation and exclusion of its Article 23 and with the understanding that the last clause of Article 3 thereof implies the duty of a neutral Power to make the demand therein mentioned for the return of a ship captured within the neutral jurisdiction and no longer within that jurisdiction.

No. 114

CONVENTION ON MARITIME NEUTRALITY

Signed at Havana, 20 February 1928

INTRODUCTORY NOTE: The present Convention, which was adopted at the Sixth International Conference of American States at Havana in 1928, was based on a project drafted by the American Institute of International Law at its session in Havana in 1917. Many of its provisions reproduce substantially or literally the rules of the Hague Convention (XIII) of 1907 (*No. 113*). It contains, however, some innovations and additions to the latter Convention, some of which are based on the experiences of World War I.

ENTRY INTO FORCE: 12 January 1931.

AUTHENTIC TEXTS: English, French, Portuguese, Spanish. The text below is reprinted from *LNTS*, Vol. 135, pp. 187–217.

TEXT PUBLISHED IN: *Sixth International Conference of American States. Final Act, Motions, Agreements, Resolutions and Conventions*, Habana, Imprenta y Papeleria de Rambala, Bouza y Ca., 1928, pp. 157–166 (Engl.); *Sixième Conférence Internationale Américaine. Acte Final, Motions, Décisions, Résolutions et Conventions.* Habana, Imprenta y Papeleria de Rambala, Bouza y Ca., 1928, pp. 156–166 (French); *Sexta Conferencia Internacional Americana, Acta Final, Mociones, Acuerdos, Resoluciones y Convenciones*, Habana, Imprenta y Papeleria de Rambala, Bouza y Ca., 1928, pp. 154–164 (Span.); *LNTS*, Vol. 135, 1932, pp. 187–217, No. 3111 (Engl., French, Span., Portuguese); *OAS, Law and Treaty Series*, No. 34 (Engl., French, Portuguese, Span.);*The International Conferences of American States 1889–1928*, New York, Oxford University Press, 1931, pp. 428–433 (Engl.); *Conferencias Internacionales Americanas 1889–1936*, Washingtón, Dotacion Carnegie para la Paz Internacional, 1938, pp. 380–386 (Span.); Hudson, Vol. IV, pp. 2401– 2412 (Engl., French); *BFSP*, Vol. 130, 1929, pp. 386–392 (Engl.); *US Statutes at Large*, Vol. 47, pp. 1989–1996 (Engl.); Malloy, Vol. IV, pp. 4743–4750 (Engl.); Bevans, Vol. II, pp. 721–729 (Engl.); Friedman, pp. 457–466 (Engl.); Genet, pp. 639–645 (French); Ronzitti, pp. 769–778 (Engl.); *Droit des conflits armés*, pp. 1379–1387 (French); *AJIL*, Vol. 22, 1928, Suppl., pp. 151–157 (Engl.); *Revista de derecho internacional* (Habana), Ano VII, tome XIII, Enero-Junio de 1928, pp. 147–154 (Span.); ICRC website: www. icrc.org/ihl.nsf (Engl., French, Span.).

TABLE OF CONTENTS

* * *

The Governments of the Republics represented at the Sixth International Conference of America States, held in the City of Havana, Republic of Cuba, in the year 1928;

Desiring that, in case war breaks out-between two or more states the other states may, in the service of peace, offer their good offices or mediation to bring the conflict to an end, without such an action being considered as an unfriendly act;

Convinced that in case this aim cannot be attained, neutral states have equal interest in having their rights respected by the belligerents;

Considering that neutrality is the juridical situation of states which do not take part in the hostilities, and that it creates rights and imposes obligations of impartiality, which should be regulated;

Recognizing that international solidarity requires that the liberty of commerce should be always respected, avoiding as far as possible unnecessary burdens for the neutrals;

It being convenient, that as long as this object is not reached, to reduce those burdens as much as possible; and

In the hope that it will be possible to regulate the matter so that all interests concerned may have every desired guaranty;

Have resolved to formulate a convention to that effect and have appointed the following Plenipotentiaries:

[Here follow the names of plenipotentiaries]

Who, after having presented their credentials, which were found in good and correct form, have agreed upon the following provisions:

Section I. Freedom of Commerce in Time of War

Article 1. The following rules shall govern commerce of war:

1. Warships of the belligerents have the right to stop and visit on the high seas and in territorial waters that are not neutral any merchant ship with the object of ascertaining its character and nationality and of verifying whether it conveys cargo prohibited by international law or has committed any violation of blockade. If the merchant ship does not heed the signal to stop, it may be pursued by the warship and stopped by force; outside of such a case the ship cannot be attacked unless, after being hailed, it fails to observe the instructions given it.

   The ship shall not be rendered incapable of navigation before the crew and passengers have been placed in safety.
2. Belligerent submarines are subject to the foregoing rules. If the submarine cannot capture the ship while observing these rules, it shall not have the right to continue to attack or to destroy the ship.

Art. 2. Both the detention of the vessel and its crew for violation of neutrality shall be made in accordance with the procedure which best suits the state effecting it and at the expense of the transgressing ship. Said state, except in the case of grave fault on its part, is not responsible for damages which the vessel may suffer.

Section II. Duties and Rights of Belligerents

Art. 3. Belligerent states are obligated to refrain from performing acts of war in neutral waters or other acts which may constitute on the part of the state that tolerates them, a violation of neutrality.

Art. 4. Under the terms of the preceding article a belligerent state is forbidden:
(a) To make use of neutral waters as a base of naval operations against the enemy, or to renew or augment military supplies or the armament of its ships, or to complete the equipment of the latter;
(b) To install in neutral waters radio-telegraph stations or any other apparatus which may serve as a means of communication with its military forces, or to make use of installations of this kind it may have established before the war and which may not have been opened to the public.

Art. 5. Belligerent warships are forbidden to remain in the ports or waters of a neutral state more than twenty-four hours. This provision will be communicated to the ship as soon as it arrives in port or in the territorial waters, and if already there at the time of the declaration of war, as soon as the neutral state becomes aware of this declaration.

Vessels used exclusively for scientific, religious, or philanthropic purposes are exempted from the foregoing provisions.

A ship may extend its stay in port more than twenty-four hours in case of damage or bad conditions at sea, but must depart as soon as the cause of the delay has ceased.

When, according to the domestic law of the neutral state, the ship may not receive fuel until twenty-four hours after its arrival in port the period of its stay may be extended an equal length of time.

Art. 6. The ship which does not conform to the foregoing rules may be interned by order of the neutral government.

A ship shall be considered as interned from the moment it receives notice to that effect from the local neutral authority, even though a petition for reconsideration of the order has been interposed by the transgressing vessel, which shall remain under custody from the moment it receives the order.

Art. 7. In the absence of a special provision of the local legislation, the maximum number of ships of war of a belligerent which may be in a neutral port at the same time shall be three.

Art. 8. A ship of war may not depart from a neutral port within less than twenty-four hours after the departure of an enemy warship. The one entering first shall depart first, unless it is in such condition as to warrant extending its stay. In any case the ship which arrived later has the right to notify the other through the competent local authority that within twenty-four hours it will leave the port, the one first entering, however, having the right to depart within that time. If it leaves, the notifying ship must observe the interval which is above stipulated.

Art. 9. Damaged belligerent ships shall not be permitted to make repairs in neutral ports beyond those that are essential to the continuance of the voyage and which in no degree constitute an increase in its military strength.

Damages which are found to have been produced by the enemy's fire shall in no case be repaired.

The neutral state shall ascertain the nature of the repairs to be made and will see that they are made as rapidly as possible.

Art. 10. Belligerent warships may supply themselves with fuel and stores in neutral ports, under the conditions especially established by the local authority and in case there are no special provisions to that effect, they may supply themselves in the manner prescribed for provisioning in time of peace.

Art. 11. Warships which obtain fuel in a neutral port cannot renew their supply in the same state until a period of three months has elapsed.

Art. 12. Where the sojourn, supplying, and provisioning of belligerent ships in the ports and jurisdictional waters of neutrals are concerned, the provisions relative to ships of war shall apply equally:

1. To ordinary auxiliary ships;
2. To merchant ships transformed into warships, in accordance with Convention VII of The Hague of 1907.

   The neutral vessel shall be seized and in general subjected to the same treatment as enemy merchantmen:

(a) When taking a direct part in the hostilities.

(b) When at the orders or under direction of an agent placed on board by an enemy government;

(c) When entirely freight-loaded by an enemy government;

(d) When actually and exclusively destined for transporting enemy troops or for the transmission of information on behalf of the enemy.

   In the cases dealt with in this article, merchandise belonging to the owner of the vessel or ship shall also be liable to seizure.

3. To armed merchantmen.[1]

Art. 13. Auxiliary ships of belligerents, converted anew into merchantmen, shall be admitted as such in neutral ports subject to the following conditions:

1. That the transformed vessel has not violated the neutrality of the country where it arrives;
2. That the transformation has been made in the ports or jurisdictional waters of the country to which the vessel belongs, or in the ports of its allies;
3. That the transformation be genuine, namely, that the vessel show neither in its crew nor in its equipment that it can serve the armed fleet of its country as an auxiliary, as it did before.
4. That the government of the country to which the ship belongs communicate to the states the names of auxiliary craft which have lost such character in order to recover that of merchantmen; and
5. That the same government obligate itself that said ships shall not again be used as auxiliaries to the war fleet.

[1] For reservation in respect of this Article 12, section 3, by Cuba and the United States of America, see p. 1423.

Art. 14. The airships of belligerents shall not fly above the territorial waters of neutrals if it is not in conformity with the regulations of the latter.

Section III. Rights and Duties of Neutrals

Art. 15. Of the acts of assistance coming from the neutral states, and the acts of commerce on the part of individuals, only the first are contrary to neutrality.

Art. 16. The neutral state is forbidden:
(a) To deliver to the belligerent, directly or indirectly, or for any reason whatever, ships of war, munitions or any other war material;
(b) To grant it loans, or to open credits for it during the duration of war. Credits that a neutral state may give to facilitate the sale or exportation of its food products and raw materials are not included in this prohibition.

Art. 17. Prizes cannot be taken to a neutral port except in case of unseaworthiness, stress of weather, or want of fuel or provisions. When the cause has disappeared, the prizes must leave immediately; if none of the indicated conditions exist, the state shall suggest to them that they depart, and if not obeyed shall have recourse to the means at its disposal to disarm them with their officers and crew, or to intern the prize crew placed on board by the captor.

Art. 18. Outside of the cases provided for in Article 17, the neutral state must release the prizes which may have been brought into its territorial waters.

Art. 19. When a ship transporting merchandise is to be interned in a neutral state, cargo intended for said country shall be unloaded and that destined for others shall be transhipped.

Art. 20. The merchantman supplied with fuel or other stores in a neutral state which repeatedly delivers the whole or part of its supplies to a belligerent vessel, shall not again receive stores and fuel in the same state.

Art. 21. Should it be found that a merchantman flying a belligerent flag, by its preparations or other circumstances, can supply to warships of a state the stores which they need, the local authority may refuse it supplies or demand of the agent of the company a guaranty that the said ship will not aid or assist any belligerent vessel.

Art. 22. Neutral states are not obligated to prevent the export or transit at the expense of any one of the belligerents of arms, munitions and in general of anything which may be useful to their military forces.

Transit shall be permitted when, in the event of a war between two American nations, one of the belligerents is a mediterranean[2] country, having no other means of supplying itself, provided the vital interests of the country through which transit is requested do not suffer by the granting thereof.[3]

---

[2] Meaning landlocked.

[3] For reservation in respect of Article 22, paragraph 2, by Chile, see p. 1423.

Art. 23. Neutral states shall not oppose the voluntary departure of nationals of belligerent states even though they leave simultaneously in great numbers; but they may oppose the voluntary departure of their own nationals going to enlist in the armed forces.

Art. 24. The use by the belligerents of the means of communication of neutral states or which cross or touch their territory is subject to the measures dictated by the local authority.

Art. 25. If as the result of naval operations beyond the territorial waters of neutral states there should be dead or wounded on board belligerent vessels, said states may send hospital ships under the vigilance of the neutral government to the scene of the disaster. These ships shall enjoy complete immunity during the discharge of their mission.

Art. 26. Neutral states are bound to exert all the vigilance within their power in order to prevent in their ports or territorial waters any violation of the foregoing provisions.

Section IV. Fulfilment and Observance of the Laws of Neutrality

Art. 27. A belligerent shall indemnify the damage caused by its violation of the foregoing provisions. It shall likewise be responsible for the acts of persons who may belong to its armed forces.

Art. 28. The present Convention does not affect obligations previously undertaken by the Contracting Parties through international agreements.

Art. 29. After being signed, the present Convention shall be submitted to the ratification of the Signatory States. The Government of Cuba is charged with transmitting authentic certified copies to the governments for the aforementioned purpose of ratification. The instrument of ratification shall be deposited in the archives of the Pan American Union in Washington, the Union to notify the signatory governments of said deposit. Such notification shall be considered as an exchange of ratifications. This Convention shall remain open to the adherents of non-Signatory States.

In witness whereof, the aforenamed Plenipotentiaries sign the present Convention in Spanish, English, French and Portuguese, in the City of Havana, the twentieth day of February, 1928.

[Here follow signatures]

SIGNATURES, RATIFICATIONS[1]

State	*Signature*[2]	*Ratification*[3]
Argentina	20 February 1928	–
Bolivia	20 February 1928	9 March 1932
Brazil	20 February 1928	–
Chile	20 February 1928 *Res.*	–
Colombia	20 February 1928	17 January 1941
Costa Rica	20 February 1928	–
Cuba	20 February 1928 *Res.*	–
Dominican Republic	20 February 1928	4 January 1933
Ecuador	20 February 1928	4 September 1936
El Salvador	20 February 1928	–
Guatemala	20 February 1928	–
Haiti	20 February 1928	9 March 1933
Honduras	20 February 1928	–
Mexico	20 February 1928	–
Nicaragua	20 February 1928	12 January 1931
Panama	20 February 1928	21 May 1929
Paraguay	20 February 1928	–
Peru	20 February 1928	–
Uruguay	20 February 1928	–
United States of America	20 February 1928 *Res.*	22 March 1932 *Res.*
Venezuela	20 February 1928	–

RESERVATIONS

CHILE (*reservation made on signature*)
The Delegation of Chile signs the present Convention with a reservation concerning Article 22, paragraph 2.

CUBA (*reservation made on signature*)
The Delegation of the Republic of Cuba signs with a reservation in reference to Article 12, Section 3.

UNITED STATES OF AMERICA
Reservation made on signature
The Delegation of the United States of America signs the present Convention with a reservation concerning Article 12, Section 3.

Reservation made on ratification
... subject to a reservation regarding Article 12, Section 3, which the Government of the United States does not accept.

[1] Based on a communication from the Organization of American States of 7 December 2001. See also ICRC website.

[2] The convention was not signed separately, but the text was incorporated in the Final Act of the Sixth International Conference of American States, the Spanish text of which was signed on behalf of the States represented at the Conference

[3] Date of the deposit of instrument of ratification.

No. 115

HELSINKI PRINCIPLES ON THE LAW OF MARITIME NEUTRALITY

Adopted by the International Law Association at its Taipei Conference on 30 May 1998

INTRODUCTORY NOTE. In 1988 the International Law Association formed a Committee on Maritime Neutrality in response to issues arising out of the Iran-Iraq war of 1980-1988, in which neutral shipping had heavily suffered from attacks by belligerents. The Security Council, in several resolutions, had called upon the parties to the conflict to respect the right to free navigation and it condemned the attacks on neutral shipping (resolutions 540/1983, 552/1984, 582/1986, 598/1987). The present Principles restate and develop existing rules of maritime neutrality in armed conflicts in which the Security Council has not taken action. The first draft was submitted to the Buenos Aires Conference of the ILA in 1994. A revised draft of the Principles was adopted at the Helsinki Conference in 1996. The adoption of the Commentaries was postponed to the Taipei Conference in 1998 which adopted both the (slightly revised) Principles and the Commentaries to each Principle. The Commentaries are not reproduced below.

AUTHENTIC TEXT: English.

TEXT PUBLISHED IN: International Law Association, *Report of the 68th Conference, Taipei, 1998*, pp. 496–516 (the Commentaries are also reproduced therein).

TABLE OF CONTENTS

* * *

1. General provisions

1.1. Definition
For the purposes of the following Principles,
'neutral State' means any State which is not party to an international armed conflict;
'belligerent' means a State which is a party to that conflict;
'neutral waters' comprise the internal waters of a neutral State, its territorial sea, and, where applicable, its archipelagic waters within the meaning of Articles 9 and 50 of the United Nations Convention on the Law of the Sea of 1982 (hereinafter: UNCLOS);
prima facie 'neutral ships' are ships flying the flag of a neutral State.

1.2. The effect of the Charter of the United Nations
Nothing in the present Principles shall be construed as implying any limitation upon the powers of the Security Council under Chapters VII and VIII of the United Nations Charter. In particular, no State may rely upon the Principles stated herein in order to evade obligations laid upon it in pursuance of a binding decision of the Security Council. Nor shall the present Principles be construed as denying the inherent right of individual or collective self-defence recognized in Article 51 of the Charter.

1.3. General rule
The relations between a party to a conflict and the neutral State, are, as a matter of principle, governed by the law of peace. These relations may, however, be modified to the extent that there exist other principles or rules of international law to that effect, including those contained in the present Principles.

1.4. Inviolability of neutral territory
Belligerents must respect the inviolability of neutral territory.
In consequence, belligerents may not conduct hostilities in neutral territory and in neutral waters, except in individual or collective self-defence and subject to Principle 2.1.

In conducting hostilities elsewhere, belligerents must exercise due regard to prevent to the maximum extent possible collateral damage on neutral territory, neutral waters or the airspace over these areas.

2. Belligerent activities in neutral waters

2.1. Hostilities in neutral waters
If neutral waters are permitted or tolerated by the coastal State to be used for belligerent purposes, the other belligerent may take such action as is necessary and appropriate to terminate such use.

2.2. Twenty-four hours rule
The right of passage and sojourn of belligerent warships in neutral waters and ports is governed by the relevant provisions of The Hague Convention XIII of 1907, which reflect customary law. In particular, the duration of such passage and sojourn must not exceed 24 hours, except where the condition of the ship or the sea do not permit the ship to leave the neutral waters. The neutral State may establish different time limits, provided that the principle of impartiality is observed and the measure is given due publicity.

In case of a violation, the neutral State must take measures to terminate this violation.

2.3. Suspension of passage
The neutral State may suspend temporarily in specified areas of its territorial sea and archipelagic waters the innocent passage of foreign ships if such suspension is essential for the protection of its security, provided that the principle of impartiality is observed, and the suspension is duly published.

2.4. Special rights of passage
The 24 hour limitation does not apply to innocent passage through archipelagic waters, to transit passage through international straits or archipelagic sea lanes passage if the time ordinarily needed for this passage is more than 24 hours. In this case, the passage is subject to the relevant rules of international law. In particular, it must be continuous and expeditious.

3. Hostilities on the high seas

3.1. The Conduct of hostilities
In conducting hostilities on the high seas, the parties to the conflict must have due regard to the exercise of the freedoms of the high seas by neutral States.

In particular, neutral shipping and fishing activities may be limited pursuant to these Principles, but in no case completely excluded.

3.2. Areas of naval hostilities
Neutral ships should be aware of the risk and peril of operating in areas where active naval hostilities take place. Belligerents engaged in naval hostilities must, however, take reasonable precautions including appropriate warnings, if circumstances permit, to avoid damage to neutral ships.

3.3. Special zones
Subject to Principle 5.2.9 and without prejudice to the rights of commanders in the zone of immediate naval operations, the establishment by a belligerent of special zones does not confer upon that belligerent rights in relation to neutral shipping which it would not otherwise possess. In particular, the establishment of a special zone cannot confer upon a belligerent the right to attack neutral shipping merely on account of its presence in the zone.

However, a belligerent may, as an exceptional measure, declare zones where neutral shipping would be particularly exposed to risks caused by the hostilities. The extent, location and duration must be made public and may not go beyond what is required by military necessity, regard being paid to the principle of proportionality. Due regard shall also be given to the rights of all States to legitimate uses of the seas. Where such a zone significantly impedes free and safe access to the ports of a neutral State and the use of normal navigation routes, measures to facilitate safe passage shall be taken.

4. Sea areas subject to limited jurisdiction

Exclusive economic zone, fishery zones and continental shelf
When conducting hostilities, the belligerents shall have due regard for the neutral States' sovereign and jurisdictional rights over their exclusive economic zone, fishery zones or in sea areas above their continental shelf, for the preservation of the marine environment and for underwater cultural property in neutral States' territorial sea and contiguous zone. Belligerents shall, in particular, have due regard for artificial islands, installations, structures and safety zones established by neutral States in their exclusive economic zone and on their continental shelf.

5. Neutral ships and activities

5.1. Limitations on attacks

5.1.1. Neutral ships in belligerent ports
A neutral ship in a belligerent port enjoys the same protection against attacks as civilian objects in land warfare. Neutral ships exempt from attack, e.g. hospital ships, retain that exemption in belligerent ports. Neutral warships in belligerent ports retain their right of self-defence.

5.1.2. Protection against attacks
1. Subject to Principle 5.2, neutral ships enjoy freedom of navigation according to the law of the sea regardless of the existence of an armed conflict and even if they carry goods exported from a belligerent State to a neutral State.
2. Merchant ships flying the flag of a neutral State may not be attacked except as provided in paragraphs 3 and 4.
3. Merchant ships flying the flag of a neutral State may be attacked if they are believed on reasonable grounds to be carrying contraband or breaching a blockade, and after prior warning they intentionally and clearly refuse to stop, or intentionally and clearly resist visit, search, capture or diversion.
4. Merchant ships flying the flag of a neutral State may be attacked if they
   (a) engage in belligerent acts on behalf of the enemy;
   (b) act as auxiliaries to the enemy's armed forces;
   (c) are incorporated into or assist the enemy's intelligence system;
   (d) sail under convoy of enemy warships or military aircraft; or
   (e) otherwise make an effective contribution to the enemy's military action, e.g., by carrying military materials, and it is not feasible for the attacking forces to first place passengers and crew in a place of safety. Unless circumstances do not permit, they are to be given a warning, so that they can re-route, off-load, or take other precautions.
5. Merchant ships flying the flag of a neutral State and carrying only civilian passengers, e.g., liners, may not be attacked but must be diverted to an appropriate port to complete capture, unless they are incorporated into or assist the enemy's intelligence system.
6. Ships flying the flag of a neutral State and entitled to exemption from capture, e.g., hospital ships, may not be attacked if they are innocently employed in their normal role, do not commit acts harmful to the enemy, immediately submit to identifica-

tion and inspection when required, and do not intentionally hamper the movement of combatants and obey orders to stop or to move out of the way when required.

5.1.3. Precautions in attacks

In conducting attacks by whatever means, the armed forces of a party to the conflict must take all feasible precautions in order to avoid that

– the attack is directed against a neutral vessel or aircraft,

– lawful neutral activities on the high seas or in other sea areas where the neutral State possesses sovereign rights are unduly endangered.

5.2. Belligerent control over neutral shipping

5.2.1. Visit and search

As an exception to Principle 5.1.2. paragraph 1 and in accordance with Principle 1.3 (2nd sentence), belligerent warships have a right to visit and search vis-à-vis neutral commercial ships in order to ascertain the character and destination of their cargo. If a ship tries to evade this control or offers resistance, measures of coercion necessary to exercise this right are permissible. This includes the right to divert a ship where visit and search at the place where the ship is encountered are not practical.

5.2.2. Seizure and condemnation

Cargo constituting contraband and a ship carrying such cargo may be seized by a belligerent, brought before a prize court and condemned. Confiscation without a prize court decision is prohibited.

5.2.3. Contraband

Contraband are goods ultimately destined to the enemy of a belligerent which are designed for the use of war fighting and other goods useful for the war effort of the enemy.

5.2.4. Enemy destination

In cases of doubt concerning the enemy destination of goods or their use for enemy military purposes, the burden of proof lies with the captor State. Fuel or other material which could be used for energy production purposes destined for a belligerent constitutes contraband, unless a non-military destination is clearly established.

5.2.5. Exports

Goods with a neutral destination coming from a belligerent port do not constitute contraband.

5.2.6. Navicert

In order to simplify control procedures in respect of neutral shipping, a party to the conflict may issue an inspection document (navicert) to a neutral ship in the port of loading. This navicert constitutes proof that the ship in question is not carrying contraband if controlled by the party having issued the document. The navicert is not binding on the other party, but the fact that a ship carries a navicert issued by another party may not be used to the ship's disadvantage.

5.2.7. Public ships not subject to visit and search

A neutral warship or other governmental ship operated for non-commercial purposes is not subject to the right of visit and search or the rights described in Principle 5.2.10.

5.2.8. Immunity of convoys

The same rule stated in Principle 5.2.7 applies to a convoy of merchant ships flying a neutral flag and accompanied by one or more neutral warships. The commander of the convoy, or the neutral State whose flag the convoying warships fly, has the responsibility to certify that no contraband is carried in the convoy. The neutral flag State has to take all reasonable steps to ensure that the certificate is correct.

5.2.9. Transit
Neutral ships, whether commercial or warships, enjoy the right of transit passage through international straits, the right of archipelagic sea lanes passage through archipelagic waters and the right of innocent passage through the territorial sea or archipelagic waters of belligerents, regardless of the existence of an armed conflict. A coastal State may, however, subject such rights to reasonable defence requirements. The belligerent may not close international straits and archipelagic sea lanes.

5.2.10. Blockade
Blockade, i.e. the interdiction of all or certain maritime traffic coming from or going to a port or coast of a belligerent, is a legitimate method of naval warfare. In order to be valid, the blockade must be declared, notified to belligerent and neutral States, effective and applied impartially to ships of all States. A blockade may not bar access to neutral ports or coasts. Neutral vessels believed on reasonable and probable grounds to be breaching a blockade may be stopped and captured. If they, after prior warning, clearly resist capture, they may be attacked.

5.3. Relief
A blockade may not be used to prevent the passage of relief consignments which has to be free according to the applicable rules of international humanitarian law, in particular those contained in Articles 23, 59 and 61 of the Fourth Geneva Convention or Articles 69 and 70 of Protocol I Additional to the Geneva Conventions.

6. The protection of neutral shipping and other neutral activities

6.1. Right of convoy
The right of neutrals to convoy is recognized. Consequently, neutral States have the right to accompany commercial ships flying their own or another neutral State's flag by their warships. The exercise of a right of innocent passage, transit passage or archipelagic sealanes passage by such convoys does not constitute a forbidden use of force.

6.2. Mines
Neutral warships have the right to remove mines laid by a belligerent in violation of applicable rules of international law, in particular if they illegally hamper neutral shipping, on the high seas, in an exclusive economic zone (including its own) or in waters above the continental shelf. They may not do so within the territorial sea of a belligerent State, except to the extent necessary for the exercise of the right of transit passage or archipelagic sea lanes passage.

7. Land-locked States
Land-locked States
If a port in one belligerent State is used for the purposes of transit to and from a neutral landlocked State under any applicable international agreement or arrangement, the other belligerents shall not prevent ships carrying goods destined for, or exported by, the neutral landlocked State from leaving or entering the port. Nor shall the belligerent State through whose port such goods transit take measures to interfere with their passage other than in accordance with Article 125 of the UNCLOS.

* * *

See also Nos. 6, 26, 75, 81-84, 89 and 98

INDEX

Page numbers are given in italic, document numbers in bold and article numbers in medium point